China

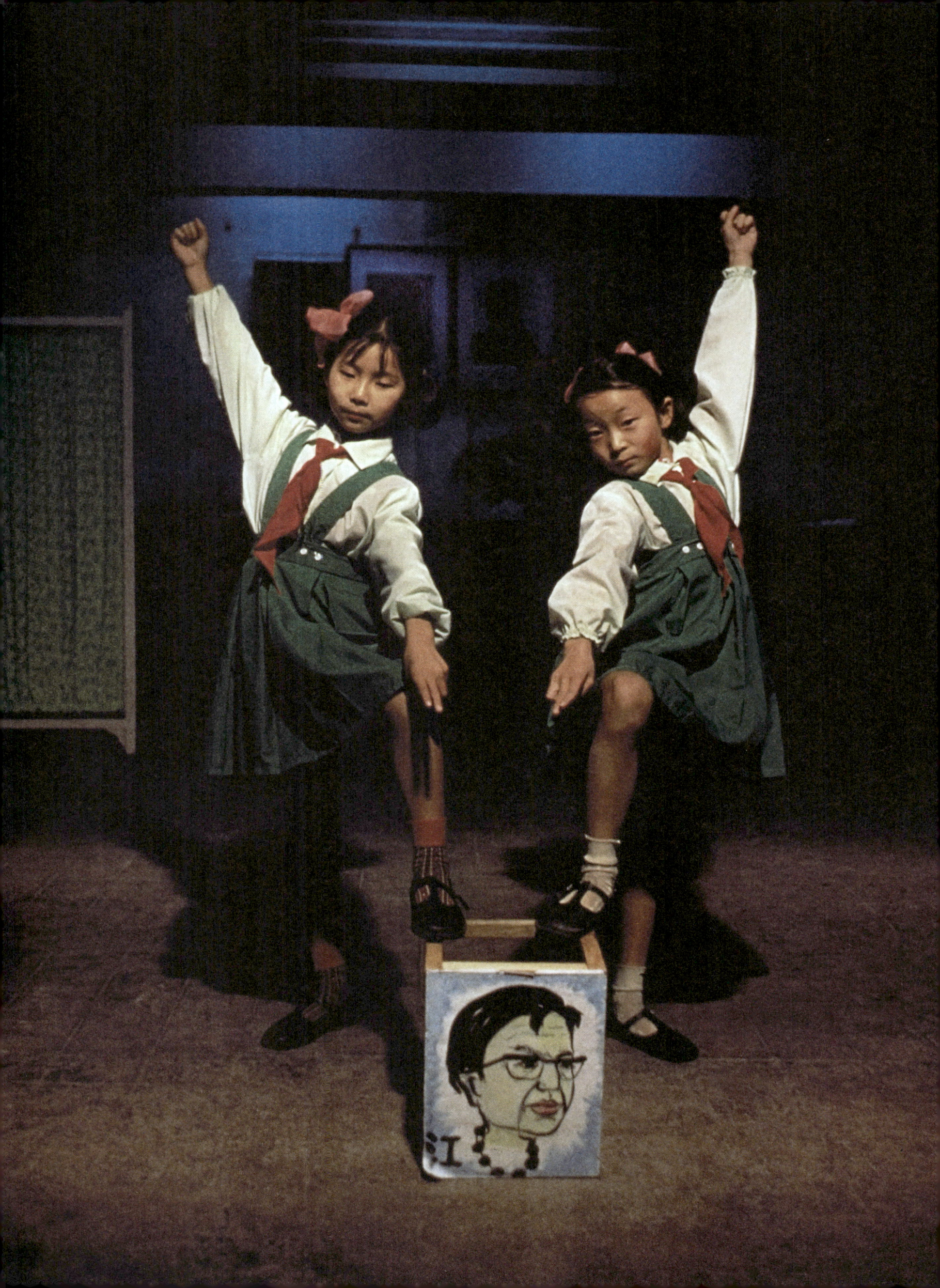

Liu Heung Shing (Ed.)

Directed and produced by Benedikt Taschen

China

Portrait of a Country • Porträt eines Landes • Portrait d'un pays
by 88 Chinese Photographers

TASCHEN

HONG KONG KÖLN LONDON LOS ANGELES MADRID PARIS TOKYO

Contents/Inhalt/Sommaire

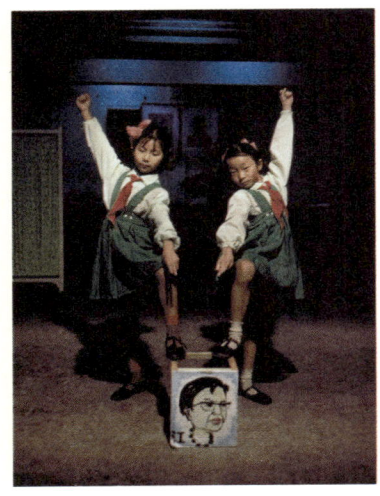 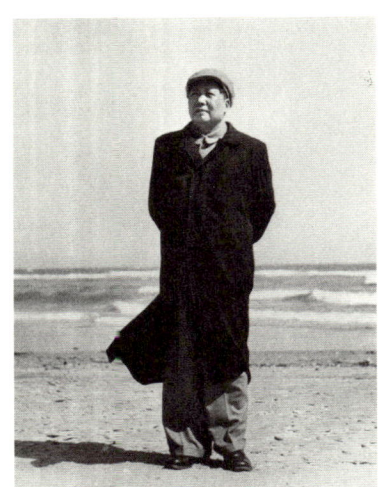 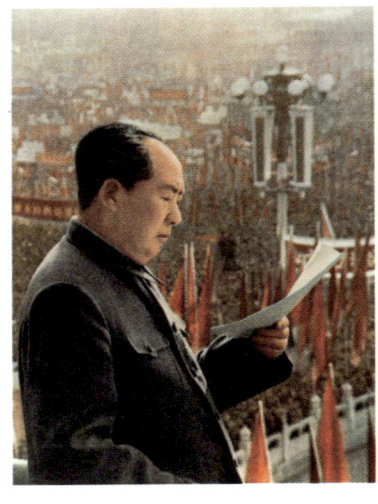 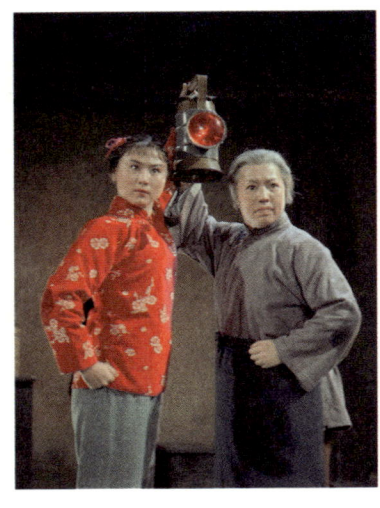

#1 #2 #3

p. 2
Liu Heung Shing, 1977

Two young schoolchildren in Shanghai
performing a skit denouncing Jiang Qing,
after the arrest of the Gang of Four, 1977.
The Gang of Four, of which Jiang Qing was
allegedly "the leader," represented the ultra
leftist ideologues in the Chinese Communist
Party.

Zwei Schulkinder führen nach der Verhaftung
der Viererbande 1977 in einer Schule in
Shanghai einen Sketch zur Verurteilung von
Jiang Qing auf. Die unter „Führung" von
Jiang Qing agierende so genannte Viererbande
verkörperte in der KP Chinas die ultralinke
Position.

Deux jeunes écoliers d'une école de Shanghai
jouent une scénette de dénonciation de Jiang
Qing après l'arrestation de la Bande des
quatre en 1977. Cette faction dont Jiang
Qing était le « leader » supposé regroupait
des idéologues de l'ultra-gauche du Parti
communiste.

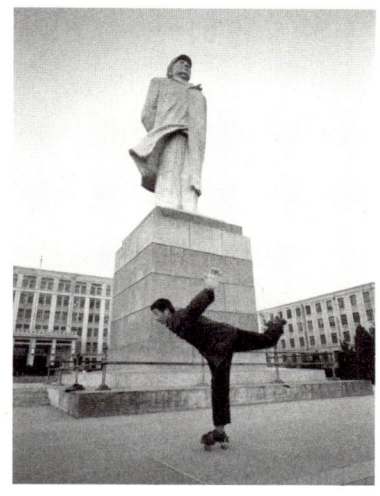

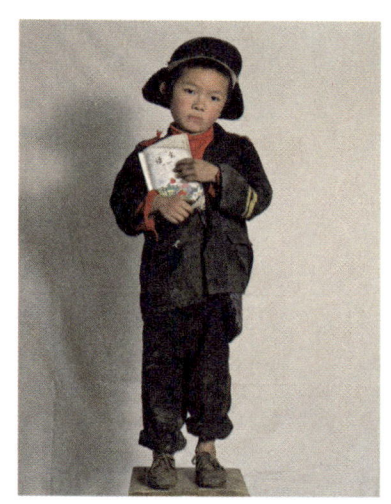

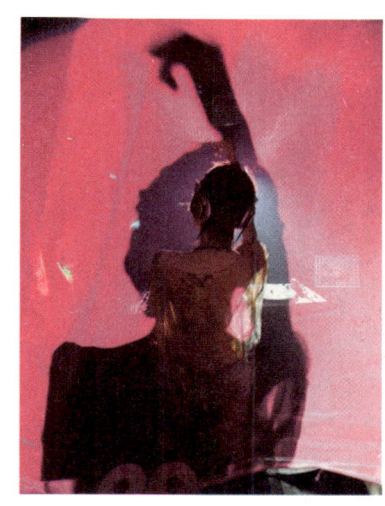

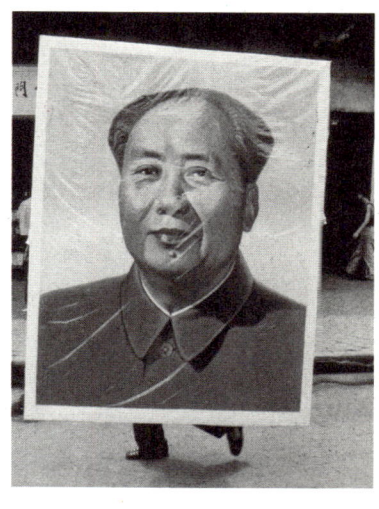

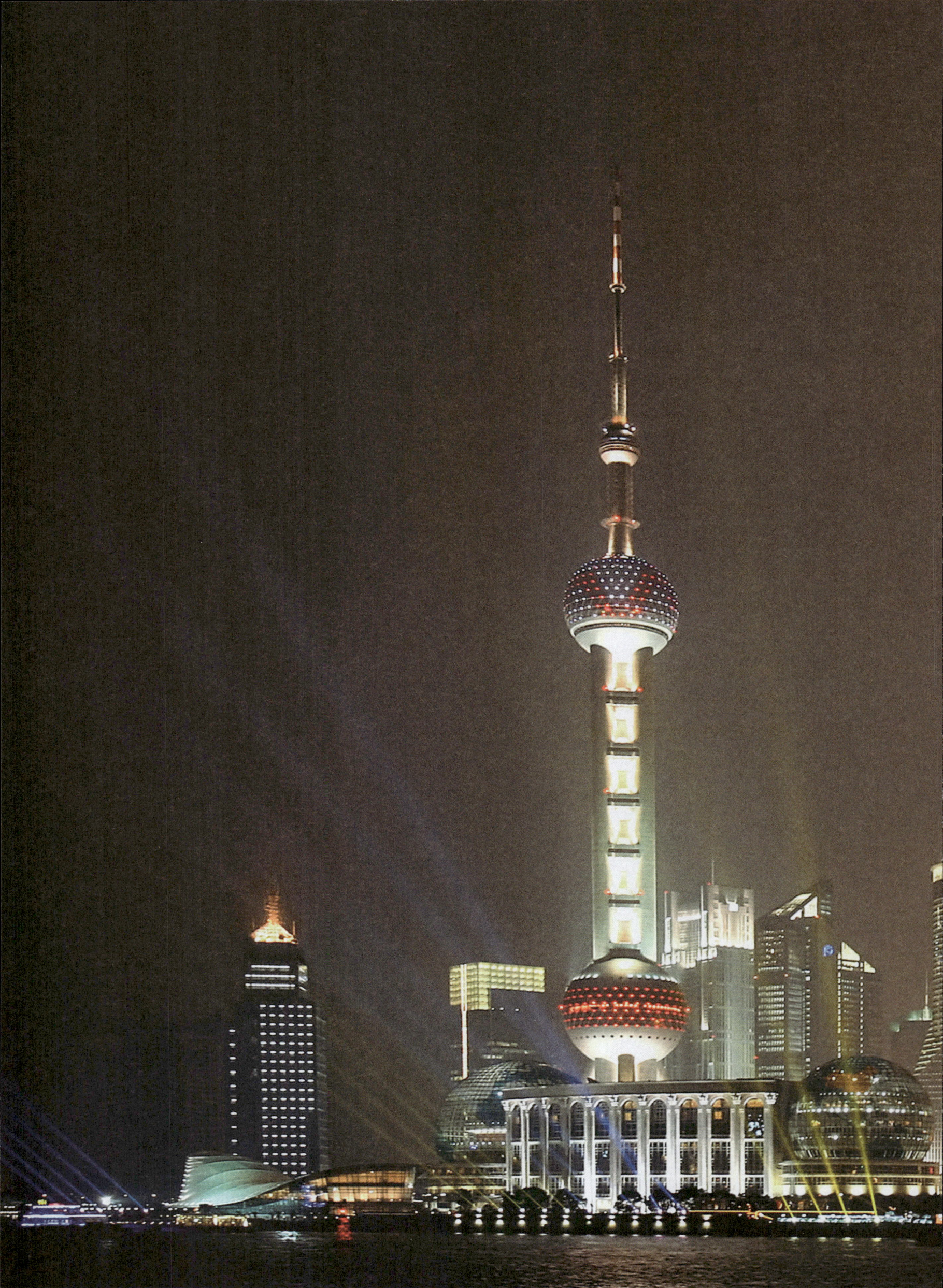

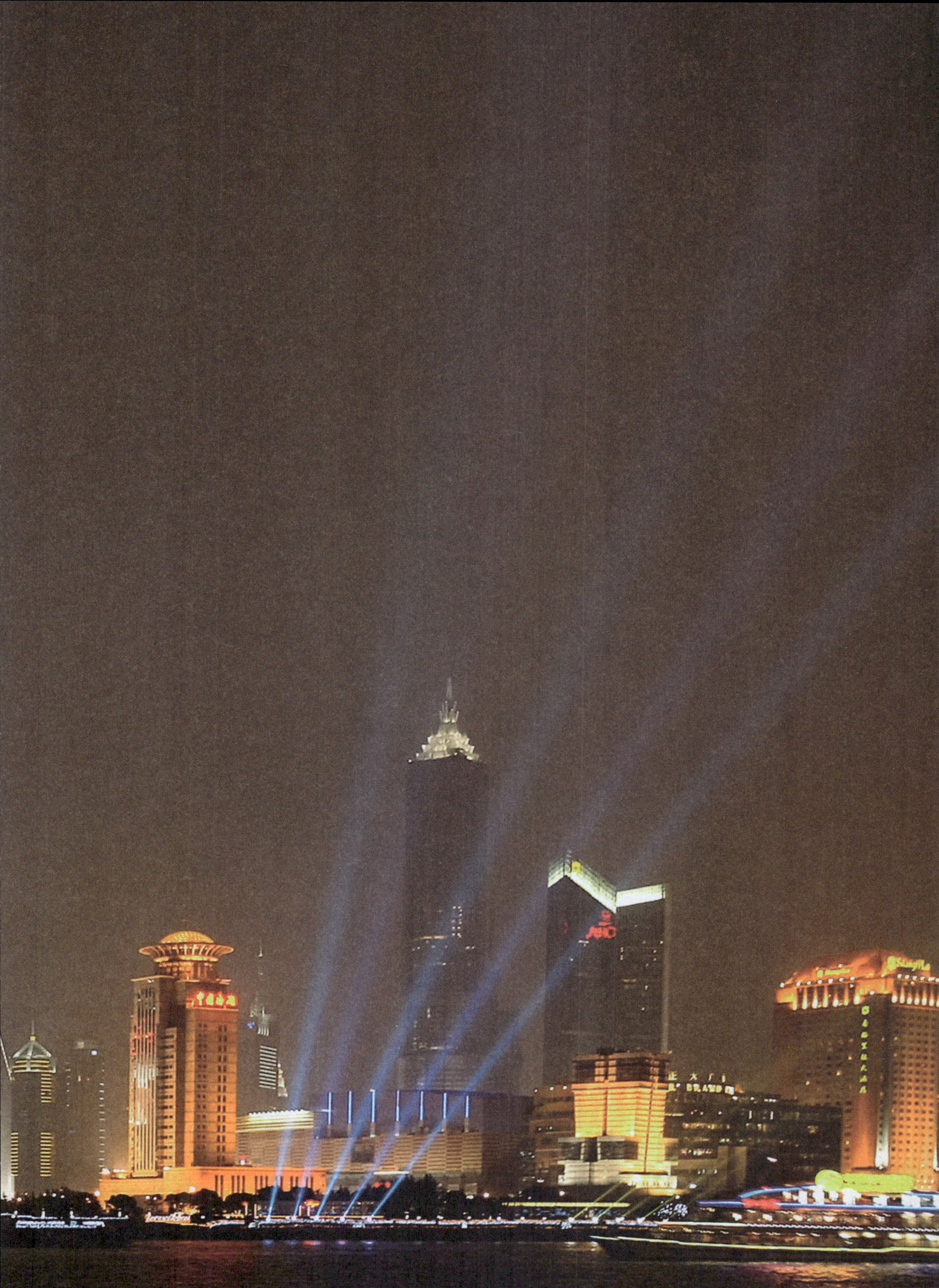

Editor's Note

By Liu Heung Shing

pp. 6/7

China Photo Agency, early 2000s

"Shanghai is devoured by urban envy and ambition. It fondly imagines itself as the world's next Wall Street. Since the early '90s, new infrastructure has hit Shanghai like a tsunami. There are three new subway lines, three new freeways, a new elevated highway that soars above the town at absurd and terrifying heights; there are four new bridges, a multilane traffic tunnel, and a fabulous French-designed new airport on the way." Bruce Sterling
View from the riverbanks of the Bund in Shanghai. Across the river, the burgeoning new metropolis of Pudong glitters in the dark. Pudong has been developed in less than ten years: a decade ago, the far side of the Bund at night was simply dark.

„Shanghai wird verzehrt von urbanen Ambitionen. Es sieht sich gern als die nächste Wall Street der Welt. Seit den frühen 1990er-Jahren ist die neue Infrastruktur über Shanghai hereingebrochen wie ein Tsunami. Es gibt drei neue Untergrundbahnen, drei neue Stadtautobahnen und eine neue hochgelegte Schnellstraße, die sich in absurder und erschreckender Höhe über der Stadt erhebt, vier neue Brücken, einen mehrspurigen Verkehrstunnel und einen fabelhaften neuen Flughafen, der von einem Franzosen konzipiert wurde und sich im Bau befindet."
Bruce Sterling
Blick über die Uferpromenade Bund in Shanghai. Am gegenüberliegenden Ufer glitzert die neue aufstrebende Metropole Pudong in der Dunkelheit. Pudong entstand in weniger als zehn Jahren; zuvor lag das andere Flussufer nachts im Dunkeln.

« Shanghai est dévorée par l'envie et l'ambition urbaines. Elle aime à s'imaginer en prochain Wall Street. Depuis le début des années 1990, de nouvelles infrastructures se sont abattues sur elle à la manière d'un tsunami. On trouve trois nouvelles lignes de métro, trois nouvelles autoroutes, dont une surélevée qui a surgi au-dessus de la ville à des hauteurs absurdes et terrifiantes, quatre nouveaux ponts, un tunnel à plusieurs voies et un fabuleux aéroport en cours de réalisation, conçu par un Français. »
Bruce Sterling
Vue sur le Bund à Shanghai. De l'autre côté de la rivière, s'élève la nouvelle métropole de Pudong qui scintille dans la nuit. Pudong s'est développée en moins de dix ans. Une décennie plus tôt, seule l'obscurité régnait à cette extrémité du Bund.

"When a Chinese describes an event, he places it within a dynasty. And of the fourteen imperial dynasties, ten have each lasted longer than the entire history of the United States."

HENRY KISSINGER (1923–), politician and Nobel Prize laureate, 2001

The First Frame

As the last remaining tourists left the Forbidden City, a diminutive Manchu, wearing a pair of large spectacles, guided me gently towards the Meridian Gate. The gatekeepers, who collect the entrance tickets, and whose job it is to close the gate, beamed and waved us in. As dusk crept through the Forbidden City, Pu Jie—the "diminutive Manchu"—and I walked towards the inner Gate of Heavenly Peace. "I was once scolded by my brother for wearing a gown with yellow trimming," Pu Jie confided as he led me towards a grand crimson-colored imperial walkway. "Here," he gestured, "my brother and I learned how to ride bicycles…" Then, pointing in another direction, he identified the pavilion in which, together with his brother again, he studied English with his famous Scottish tutor, Reginald Fleming Johnston.

In my long personal engagement with the People's Republic of China, this remains a memorable moment: a rare opportunity to photograph the man who might one day have succeeded his own brother, Pu Yi, the last Manchu emperor of the Qing dynasty, and within the earthly domain of the sons of heaven that was once, for a fleeting moment, their family home.

An Unsettled Childhood

I was born in Hong Kong at the dawn of the People's Republic, which was then still under British rule. This was not the place in which I passed my formative years. That was to be China, for my parents sent me back to the mainland in the early 1950s, not much more than a mere toddler, whose first hours of "play" were devoted to participating in the Destroy Four Pests Campaign aimed at ridding the country of enemies of the food chain. Initially, the four pests were defined as being rats, sparrows, mosquitoes, and flies. Later, it was realized that sparrows ate worms and, therefore, were not pests. As a consequence, the sparrow was replaced by the flea. The *People's Daily* reported that on April 19, 1958, three million Beijing residents had spent the entire day catching 83,249 sparrows. At the time of this national folly, it was suggested that four sparrows would consume 16 ounces of grain, which was equal to one person's daily food ration. This was a major part of my primary school education. I regularly turned in my homework—matchboxes brimming with mosquitoes and flies that I killed with vigorous diligence, though I only caught a couple of sparrows—but no matter how much effort I expended, the grade I was awarded for "political behavior" was rarely higher than a "C." The Destroy Four Pests Campaign turned out to be a way to turn people's attention away from severe food shortages.

My classmates, predominantly the progeny of ranking officers in the People's Liberation Army, regarded me as the offspring of the "Black Five Elements" (defined as landlords, wealthy peasants, counterrevolutionaries, bad elements, and rightists). I took part in the hysteria of the Great Leap Forward, and witnessed the debilitating effects of the widespread malnutrition that resulted: not merely amongst the *pinnong* (the poorest of the nation's people) but amongst our neighbors, my grandmother's neighbors, who had occupied the courtyard house that had once been the family home when property across the country was nationalized in 1954. Our home also included the house my grandmother gifted to my mother as a dowry for her marriage to my father. I have vivid memories of standing in line for hours to purchase my ration of 20 grams of pork fat when, on a rare occasion, the community was permitted to slaughter a pig. When I played with the neighboring children, I could see that they all had swollen arms and legs from a lack of basic nutrition.

In 1960, as the situation grew worse in the wake of the miserable failure of the Great Leap Forward, my father arranged for me to return to Hong Kong. China was in the throes of a three-year famine (1960–62) in which 30 million people reportedly died of hunger.[1]

Back in Hong Kong, I studied English and learned the local Cantonese dialect and, during the summer breaks, my father taught me how to translate Associated Press (AP) and Reuters English wire stories into Chinese. As the foreign editor of international news at *Ta Kung Pao*, a Beijing-supported daily newspaper, he would come home venting his frustrations, such as when Beijing censored the story that the American astronauts had landed on the moon!

Time away from Asia: The Start of a New Life

In 1970, I left Hong Kong to study in the United States, choosing to major in political science at Hunter College in New York. In the final year of my studies, I took a course in photography with famed *Life* magazine photographer Gjon Mili. This one semester was to shape the rest of my life: upon graduation, I followed Mili and took an internship at *Life* magazine. This put me in the right place, at the right time, for following the normalization of Sino-American diplomatic relations in 1979. Then I was given an assignment in China, which made me the first Chinese foreign correspondent to be sent to Beijing by *Time* magazine, and later joined the Associated Press.

My work as a photojournalist for the AP resulted in many relocations: China, the Unites States, India, South Korea, and the former Soviet Union. As I moved from country to country, my childhood experience in the People's Republic continued to loom large. I found myself comparing the poverty of India with that of China; the pragmatism of Chinese Communism with the political idealism of Russian Communism under Mikhail Gorbachev; and latterly (after moving back to Beijing in 1997), how overseas Chinese businessmen compared with the emergent generation of red capitalists in China. As a photojournalist, I would compare notes about Chinese politics with my fellow American reporters, all the while alert to the fact that China was not on the reporting agenda of American newspapers. It seemed that many of my Western colleagues ended their own tours in China saddened and disappointed. Perhaps it was the accumulated experience of the difficulties in daily reporting that they encountered, and the fact that China defies Western generalization. Former British ambassador to China, Sir Percy Craddock, commented in his memoirs: "China-watching is an acquired taste, much of it bitter."

Slow Boat to China

My introduction to China as a professional photojournalist began with a jolt. Shortly after reading news of the earthquake that devastated the Chinese city of Tangshan in 1976—with tremors also felt in Beijing, 450 kilometers northwest of Tangshan—I was in Europe, photographing the Portuguese communist candidates on the campaign trail in Lisbon. Following this, in the wake of Franco's death, I headed to Spain to photograph the socialist candidate Felipe Gonzalez, who was leading student rallies aimed at pulling Spain out of the Franco era. In Paris next, planning to photograph French Prime Minister Raymond Barre, I left the Hotel Matignon one morning to be confronted by a full-page photograph of Chairman Mao on the cover of that day's *Le Figaro*. Realizing Mao had died, I called my agent in New York, Robert Pledge, who got me an assignment to photograph Mao's funeral for *Time* magazine. However, I arrived in Guangzhou only to be refused permission to travel to Beijing, and had to make do with photographing people in mourning in Guangzhou. The faces I saw on the banks of the Pearl river suggested more of a sense of relief than of grief. Little did I know that I had embarked upon my journey to photograph China after Mao: first for *Time* magazine, 1979–81, and again in 1981–83, when I joined the Associated Press. In 1978, one of my reporting jobs was a daily bicycle ride to the bus depot in west Beijing that was later dubbed China's "Democracy Wall." It was here that prominent dissidents regularly posted hand-written posters—*dazibao*, which means "big-character posters"—on the wall urging China to open up and modernize and at the same time to introduce more democratic reforms.

Since 1976, a number of photography books about the People's Republic have been published by both foreign and domestic publishers. The paradoxes of China do not seem obvious in these books. China has been an elusive subject for editors in New York, London, or Paris. Editors well versed in the language of photography nevertheless encountered a "Chinese wall" when dealing with official institutions in China, and with its myriad socialist doctrines: notable efforts have been made to gain access to the negatives in some of the major photographic archives, such as the State-owned Xinhua News Agency, *China Pictorial, Nationalities Pictorial, People's Liberation Army Pictorial*, and the private archives of certain key photographers. Until now few have succeeded.

For thousands of years, the Chinese aesthetic was molded by Taoist principles of man in harmony with nature: an aesthetic that was honed in particular in brush paintings of landscapes. Photography was introduced to China in the 19th century by European explorers. When Chinese photographers took up a camera, it was landscape and portrait photography that interested them foremost, and which have evolved as the main subjects explored through a lens. The young woman photographer Hou Bo, who was Mao's official photographer from 1949 to 1961, created just such a frame, capturing Mao standing beneath willow trees on the banks of the West lake in Hangzhou (photo on page 13). Mao stands with his hands clasped behind his back, lost in silent contemplation: the pose of a great poet as invoked in so many Chinese ink paintings. Without doubt a large percentage of the nation's photographers regard landscape photography as the most worthy pursuit. Since the majority of Chinese photographers saw the world in terms of lofty landscapes, one must conclude that for many of them daily life appeared too trivial a subject for their cameras.

The Open Door

When China began to open up to the outside world in the early 1980s, the works of Western photographers were slowly introduced as the importation of books, catalogues, and monographs was once again permitted. When Chinese photographers looked at the images of China that had been taken by Western photographers, such as Henri Cartier-Bresson and Marc Riboud, they were astounded and at the same time fascinated by the highly stylized, undeniably charming images of daily life they represented. Perhaps it was also a result of sustained indoctrination that ultimately discouraged Chinese photographers from finding beauty in their immediate drab surroundings.

In the introduction for the photographic book *Face of China 1860–1912*, British historian Nigel Cameron wrote of Western photographers and travelers: "The scene on which the cameras of professionals and amateurs directed their brass-bound lenses in mid-century China was a sorry one indeed. It was a China in the dotage of a long life; a China in the confusion and turmoil of the recent past and the actual present, shaped by defeat at the hands of the West and by unrest within."

China has no doubt evolved from that period and its aftermath, in which the Communists fought the Japanese, and were mired in a civil war with the Nationalist Kuomintang.

In 1942, at the Yan'an Forum on Arts and Literature, Mao "explained" how all forms of art and literature should be placed in the service of the Chinese Communist Party, as its most handy propaganda tools. Seven years later, when Mao took power, proclaiming the establishment of the People's Republic, the directives of his "propaganda" policy were carried out with meticulous attention to detail. With hindsight, the uses to which photography was put, and the crude manipulation to which it was subject, especially documentary photography, suited the Chinese rather well: it is ironic that the official censors would encourage only the coverage of social achievements under the Chinese Communist Party. This is compounded by the ingrained attitude expressed in the Chinese proverb *jia chou bu ke wai yang* which means "scandal and ugliness in the family should not be broadcast outside the home."

New Visions of China

In 1972, following Nixon's visit to China, the Italian filmmaker Michelangelo Antonioni caused a national stir in China with a sympathetic filming of ordinary Chinese people in an incisive black-and-white documentary. This was the first "modern" documentary to show the daily life of the people: since the Cultural Revolution was launched the only filmed or stage entertainment that had been created about China were eight revolutionary operas produced by Mao's wife, Jiang Qing. Thus, the absolute honesty of Antonioni's approach was viewed in stark contrast to the exaggerated revolutionary zeal and idealism of Jiang Qing's propaganda plays. In the late 1970s and early 1980s, the "Antonioni Incident" was used by propaganda officials to censor foreign journalists in their reportage of China. However, when China began to open up under Deng Xiaoping's policy of reform, the same propaganda officials blamed the excessive nature of this censorial policy and control of the media on the "pernicious influence of the Gang of Four." Unknown in the West, most Chinese photographers fared less well under the restrictions placed upon them by the official censors than did foreign journalists. Against these harsh realities and the innate preference for landscape and portrait photography, it is therefore reassuring for me to discover the existence of images that document events in China since 1949—few of which have been published, either at home or abroad.

Returning to Beijing in 1997 and witnessing the dramatic nature of the change, I was keen to undertake a comprehensive photographic tour of the New China; my personal path has crossed with China for 25 years in different crucial periods. I realize there was a visceral impulse in me to edit this book and to use my own contextual understanding of the Chinese people to discover works that may have been buried by Chinese editors fearful of straying too far from the official Party line. Completing this project has been an assignment of discovery as well as self-discovery. Meeting photographers of different generations in different provinces and cities, finding dusty negatives in shoe boxes under their beds, and sharing their personal stories and photographs took almost four years. A number of the photographers I met divulged their personal tribulations and fear of releasing their photographs. I had to reassure them by meeting them in their homes, which entailed traveling to different parts of the country. Regrettably, a few of the elder photographers who were in their eighties, such as Zhou Jiandong and Lü Xiangyou, passed away before this book could be published. I was also privileged to hear the stories of photographers who shared with me the notes that Premier Zhou Enlai wrote in releasing the photo of the first Chinese hydrogen bomb test, and recalled that Mao had acted as photo editor in deciding which photographs of the historic handshake in 1972 between Nixon and Zhou were to be released to the press. Photographer Du Xiuxian, who took the famed photograph of the handshake, was, in 1966, accused by his colleagues at the New China News Agency of spying on Premier Zhou Enlai; he found the false charges incredulous but was nevertheless exiled in 1969 to the northwestern Xinjiang province bordering on the Soviet Union.

When the armed skirmishes on the Sino-Soviet border broke out in 1969, one of 70 Chinese killed at the border was his fellow documentary photographer. Fortunately Du escaped a similar fate when he was recalled back to Beijing-just two days before the border incident—by Premier Zhou to accompany the latter to North Korea. He was grateful to Zhou for ending the desolate exile in Xinjiang province. Another bizarre charge leveled at Du was that he photographed President Liu Shaoqi's glamorous wife, Wang Guangmei, wearing a traditional Chinese *qipao* during a state visit to Indonesia. The elegant dress was considered bourgeois and decadent. Liu, who restored the Chinese economy after the disastrous Great Leap Forward in 1958, was later purged by Mao during the Cultural Revolution. Liu was exiled from Beijing, and banished to Kaifeng in Henan province, where he died tragically. Meanwhile, in 1973, the same photographer, Du, photographed Jiang Qing wearing a dress of her own design. Du was later denounced again for photographing Chairman Hua Guofeng together with the cohorts of the Gang of Four as the nation mourned Mao's death in 1976. The years have left Du, 82 years old in 2007, hard of hearing, but thankfully perhaps, for he heard more than his fair share of criticism in his prime.

→
Hou Bo, 1954

Mao standing by the West lake in   *Mao am Westsee in Hangzhou, in der*   *Mao devant le Lac de l'Ouest à Hangzhou,*
Hangzhou city, Zhejiang province.   *Provinz Zhejiang.*   *province du Zhejiang.*

Photography Today

The last two chapters of this book reveal how the work of the current generation of photographers has evolved. Today, Chinese photographers are more open to new ideas, and materially better equipped to explore China. (Many early Chinese photographers of the 1950s and 1960s used 35 mm cinematic film in their still cameras. The imported 35 mm film was scarce and more expensive.) Their works, many of which reflect the prevailing influences of social documentary photography, represent a steady parting of ways with the prism through which their elder colleagues see China. I believe the journeys taken by this generation of photographers will increasingly open up new paths, and at a pace that will continue to accelerate in tandem with the explosive energy of today's China. Photographers like Lü Nan have spent years photographing China's underground Catholic communities—those who accept only the authority of the Vatican—in the remote province of Yunnan, as well as peasants in Tibet, following the best documentary tradition of W. Eugene Smith. Although Chinese photographers, like their counterparts in the West, have increasingly joined the digital culture of pixels, and employed techniques that are increasingly unmoored from corporeal reality,[2] myriad cultures and a large landmass of China still remain unexplored. As modern photographer Lisette Model once said, "Photography is the easiest art, which perhaps makes it the hardest."

It has been a daunting experience to sift through images of China taken by the many fine photographers I met during the four years that this book was in preparation. Henri Cartier-Bresson is quoted as saying: "Shooting a photograph is recognizing an event—it is a matter of putting your brain, your eye, and your heart in the same line of sight.

Today everyone talks about photography. I spent fifty years taking pictures, but how many of my frames can you look at for more than three seconds? Maybe 50? 100? That's about all."[3]

It is by looking at the images presented in this book that we are able to catch a glimpse of the myriad changes that China has undergone over the last six decades. To paraphrase British critic Herbert Read (who was speaking of art), these photographs are essentially a manifestation of the "human spirit," of modern-day Chinese people; "and though the censors may use them or abuse them for their own ends, they can neither manufacture them, nor control them, nor ultimately deny them."

In the early 20th century, photographer and publisher Alfred Stieglitz championed the notion that painting must be "anti-photographic." In the debate about the role of photography, Stieglitz sided with Marius de Zayas, who wrote in *Camera Work* in 1913: "Photography is not Art, it is not even an art. Art is the expression of the conception of an idea. Photography is the plastic verification of fact. Art has taught us to feel the emotions of the artist, but photography, because it presents reality to us in a heightened state of awareness, allows us to realize our own emotions about the scene presented."[4] Far from condemning photography, de Zayas celebrated it as a way of finally penetrating the objectivity of forms. In this way, he believed, forms expressed their own spirit, revealed in their own essence.

I owe a profound debt of gratitude to all of the photographers who contributed to this book and welcomed me into their homes and studios, letting me pore over hundreds of thousands of negatives and prints. They put their trust in me and shared their insights. This book pays tribute to Chinese photographers, for their perseverance and love of their country.

1. See Jasper Becker, *The Chinese*, Oxford University Press 2000, p. 24. According to the *Cambridge History of China*, the estimated number of deaths (primarily due to famine) during the Great Leap Forward was between 16 and 27 million people with over 10 million dying in 1960 alone (p. 370).
2. Peter Plagens, "Is Photography Dead?," *Newsweek*, Dec. 10, 2007.
3. Interview with *The New York Times*, 1994, quoted again by Alan Riding, *The New York Times*, May 29, 2003.
4. Sarah Greenough, *Alfred Stieglitz: Photographs & Writings*, National Gallery of Art, Washington, D.C., Bullfinch Press & Little, Brown, New York, 1998.

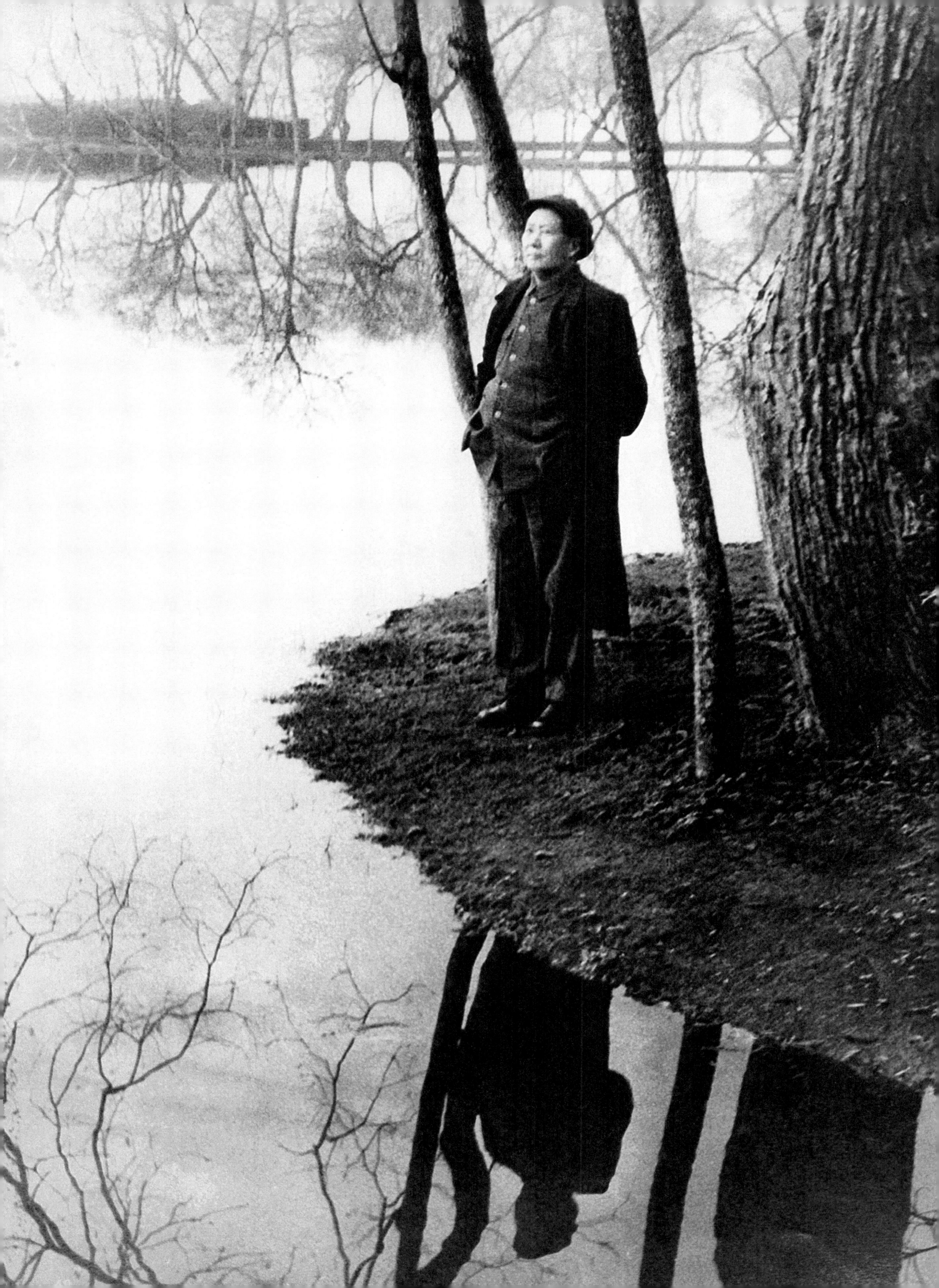

Vorwort des Herausgebers

Von Liu Heung Shing

„Wenn ein Chinese ein Ereignis beschreibt, ordnet er es einer Dynastie zu. Und von vierzehn kaiserlichen Dynastien, haben zehn jeweils länger gedauert, als die gesamte Geschichte der Vereinigten Staaten."

HENRY KISSINGER (1923–), Politiker und Nobelpreisträger, 2001

Das erste Bild

Als die letzten verbliebenen Touristen die Verbotene Stadt verließen, lotste mich ein winziger Mandschu mit einer großen Brille auf der Nase sanft zum Mittagstor. Die Torwächter, die die Eintrittskarten einsammelten und deren Aufgabe es war, das Tor zu schließen, strahlten und winkten uns herein. Während sich die Dämmerung über die Verbotene Stadt senkte, liefen Pu Jie, der kleine Mandschu, und ich auf das innere Tor des Himmlischen Friedens zu. „Mein Bruder tadelte mich einmal, weil ich einen Mantel mit gelbem Besatz trug", gestand er mir, während er mich zu einem beeindruckenden karmesinroten kaiserlichen Gehweg führte. „Hier", zeigte er, „lernten mein Bruder und ich Fahrrad fahren…". Dann wies er in eine andere Richtung auf einen Pavillon, in dem er, wiederum mit seinem Bruder, bei dem berühmten schottischen Privatlehrer Reginald Fleming Johnston Englisch gelernt hatte.

In meiner langen persönlichen Beschäftigung mit der Volksrepublik China bleibt dies eine denkwürdige Begegnung: Die wahrhaft seltene Gelegenheit, den Mann zu fotografieren, der eines Tages vielleicht die Nachfolge seines Bruders, Pu Yi, des letzten Mandschu-Herrschers der Qing-Dynastie, angetreten hätte und dies im irdischen Reich der Söhne des Himmels, das einst Sitz seiner Familie war.

Eine unbeständige Kindheit

Ich wurde bei Gründung der Volksrepublik im damals noch britischen Hongkong geboren. Meine prägenden Jahre verbrachte ich aber in China. Als Kleinkind bestand mein erstes „spielerisches" Tun in der Teilnahme an der Kampagne gegen die vier Plagen, die das Land von den die Nahrungsmittel bedrohenden Schädlingen befreien sollte. Anfangs wurden Ratten, Spatzen, Stechmücken und Fliegen als Schädlinge bezeichnet. Später erkannte man, dass Spatzen Würmer fressen und deshalb keine „Schädlinge" sind. In der Folge ersetzte man die Spatzen durch Flöhe. Am 19. April 1958 berichtete die *Volkszeitung*, dass drei Millionen Einwohner Pekings den ganzen Tag damit verbracht hatten, 83.249 Spatzen zu fangen. Zu Zeiten dieser nationalen Narretei hieß es, vier Spatzen fräßen 453 Gramm Getreide, was der Tagesration eines Menschen entspräche. Dies war ein bedeutender Teil meiner Grundschulbildung. Ich lieferte regelmäßig meine Hausarbeit ab – Streichholzschachteln, bis zum Rand gefüllt mit Moskitos und Fliegen, die ich mit tatkräftiger Emsigkeit getötet hatte. Aber ganz gleich, wie sehr ich mich bemühte, die Note, die ich für „politisches" Betragen bekam, war selten besser als eine „Drei". Die Kampagne gegen die vier Plagen sollte die Menschen von dem bedrohlichen Mangel an Nahrungsmitteln ablenken.

Meine Mitschüler, größtenteils der Nachwuchs hochrangiger Offiziere der Volksbefreiungsarmee, betrachteten mich als Abkömmling der Fünf Schwarzen Elemente (Grundbesitzer, reiche Bauern, Konterrevolutionäre, üble Elemente und Rechtsgerichtete). Ich nahm teil an der Hysterie des Großen Sprungs nach vorn und erlebte die daraus folgenden, lähmenden Auswirkungen der weit verbreiteten Mangelernährung: nicht nur bei den *Pinnong* (den Ärmsten der Bevölkerung), sondern auch bei unseren Nachbarn, den Nachbarn meiner Großmutter, die das Hofhaus bewohnt hatten, das einst Sitz der Familie war, bis 1954 im ganzen Land das Eigentum verstaatlicht wurde. Ich erinnere mich lebhaft daran, dass ich bei einer der seltenen Gelegenheiten, als es der Gemeinschaft gestattet war, ein Schwein zu schlachten, für den Erwerb meiner 20-Gramm-Ration Schweineschmalz stundenlang anstehen musste. Wenn ich mit den Nachbarskindern spielte, war mir bewusst, dass sie alle aufgrund von Mangelernährung geschwollene Arme und Beine hatten.

Als sich 1960 nach dem kläglichen Scheitern des Großen Sprungs nach vorn die Lage verschlechterte, organisierte mein Vater meine Rückkehr nach Hongkong. China befand sich mitten in einer drei Jahre währenden Hungersnot (1960–1962), bei der Berichten zufolge 30 Millionen Menschen starben.[1]

Zurück in Hongkong lernte ich Englisch und den lokalen kantonesischen Dialekt. Während der Sommerferien lehrte mich mein Vater, wie man englische Telegrafennachrichten von Associated Press und Reuters ins Chinesische übersetzte. Als Redakteur internationaler Nachrichten bei der *Ta Kung Pao*, einer von Peking unterstützten Tageszeitung, kam er häufig nach Hause und ließ seiner Frustration freien Lauf, wenn Peking beispielsweise die Meldung von der Mondlandung amerikanischer Astronauten zensierte!

Auszeit von Asien: Beginn eines neuen Lebens

1970 verließ ich Hongkong, um in den USA am Hunter College in New York ein Studium der Politikwissenschaft aufzunehmen. In meinem letzten Studienjahr belegte ich einen Kurs in Fotografie bei dem bekannten Fotografen Gjon Mili von der Zeitschrift *Life*. Dieses eine Semester sollte den Rest meines Lebens bestimmen: Nach dem Studienabschluss folgte ich Mili und absolvierte ein Praktikum bei der Zeitschrift *Life*. Dadurch war ich zur richtigen Zeit am richtigen Ort, denn nach der Annäherung zwischen China und den Vereinigten Staaten erhielt ich einen Auftrag in China, der mich zum ersten chinesischen Auslandskorrespondenten machte. Ich wurde im Auftrag der Zeitschrift *Time* nach Peking geschickt und schloss mich später Associated Press (AP) an.

Meine Arbeit als Fotojournalist für AP hatte zahlreiche Standortwechsel zur Folge: China, die Vereinigten Staaten, Indien, Südkorea und die frühere Sowjetunion. Während ich von einem Land ins nächste zog, ließen mich die Erfahrungen meiner frühen Kindheit in der Volksrepublik nicht los. Ich ertappte mich dabei, wie ich die Armut in Indien mit der in China verglich, den Pragmatismus des chinesischen Kommunismus mit dem politischen Idealismus des russischen Kommunismus unter Michail Gorbatschow und neuerdings (nachdem ich 1997 nach Peking zurückgekehrt war), wie sich chinesische Geschäftsleute im Ausland zur aufkommenden Generation roter Kapitalisten in China verhalten. Unterdessen war ich mir stets der Tatsache bewusst, dass China nicht zur redaktionellen Ausrichtung amerikanischer Zeitungen passte. Es schien, als beendeten viele meiner westlichen Kollegen ihre Zeit in China traurig und enttäuscht; vielleicht waren es die zahllosen Schwierigkeiten, denen sie bei der täglichen Arbeit begegneten, und die Tatsache, dass sich China westlicher Verallgemeinerung widersetzt. Der frühere britische Botschafter in China, Sir Percy Craddock, bemerkt in seinen Memoiren: „China zu beobachten ist Geschmackssache, ein Gutteil davon schmeckt bitter.“

Bummelzug nach China

Meine Einführung in China als professioneller Fotojournalist begann mit einem Schock. Kurz nachdem ich die Nachricht über ein Erdbeben gelesen hatte, das 1976 die chinesische Stadt Tangshan verwüstete – mit Erdstößen, die auch im 450 Kilometer nordwestlich von Tangshan gelegenen Peking noch zu spüren waren –, befand ich mich in Europa und fotografierte die Kandidaten der portugiesischen Kommunisten beim Wahlkampf in Lissabon. Unmittelbar danach, in den Nachwehen von Francos Tod, fuhr ich nach Spanien, um den sozialistischen Kandidaten Felipe Gonzalez zu fotografieren, der Studentenkundgebungen anführte, die Spanien aus der Franco-Ära befreien sollten. Anschließend in Paris, wo ich den französischen Premierminister Raymond Barre ablichten wollte, verließ ich eines Morgens das Hôtel Matignon und sah mich einem ganzseitigen Foto des Vorsitzenden Mao auf dem Titel von *Le Figaro* gegenüber. Nachdem ich begriffen hatte, dass Mao gestorben war, rief ich Robert Pledge, meinen Agenten in New York, an, der mir den Auftrag verschaffte, für *Time Magazine* Maos Beerdigung zu fotografieren. Ich landete jedoch in Guangzhou, wo man mir die Weiterreise nach Peking verweigerte. Ich musste mich damit begnügen, trauernde Menschen in Guangzhou zu fotografieren. Die Gesichter, die ich an den Ufern des Perlflusses sah, ließen allerdings eher auf ein Gefühl der Erleichterung als der Trauer schließen. Ich hatte damit angefangen, China in der Zeit nach Mao zu fotografieren; zuerst 1979 bis 1981 für *Time Magazine* und erneut 1981–1983, nachdem ich mich AP angeschlossen hatte. 1978 bestand eine meiner Aufgaben darin, täglich mit dem Fahrrad zum Busbahnhof im Westen von Peking zu fahren, der später Chinas „Mauer der Demokratie“ genannt wurde. Hier brachten prominente Dissidenten regelmäßig handgeschriebene „dazibao“, Wandzeitungen, an, auf denen sie China auf-

forderten, sich zu öffnen und zu modernisieren und gleichzeitig demokratische Reformen einzuführen.

Seit 1976 ist sowohl in ausländischen wie einheimischen Verlagen eine Reihe von Fotobüchern über die Volksrepublik erschienen. Die chinesischen Widersprüchlichkeiten werden in diesen Büchern nicht deutlich. China ist für Verlage in New York, London oder Paris ein schwer fassbares Gebiet. Selbst Verleger, die sich auf dem Gebiet der Fotografie gut auskannten, stießen beim Umgang mit offiziellen Einrichtungen in China und mit den zahllosen sozialistischen Doktrinen auf eine „Chinesische Mauer“. Es gab beachtliche Bemühungen Zugang zu einigen der wichtigsten Quellen für Fotomaterial zu erhalten wie der staatseigenen Nachrichtenagentur Xinhua (Neues China), *China Pictorial, Nationalities Pictorial, PLA Pictorial* sowie den Privatarchiven einiger bedeutender Fotografen. Bisher waren nur wenige erfolgreich.

Jahrtausendelang waren daoistische Prinzipien, die den Menschen im Einklang mit der Natur sehen, bestimmend für die chinesische Kunst, eine Kunst, für die besonders die Landschaftsmalerei charakteristisch ist. Die Fotografie gelangte im 19. Jahrhundert durch europäische Reisende nach China. Wenn chinesische Fotografen eine Kamera zur Hand nahmen, waren sie in erster Linie an Landschafts- und Porträtfotografie interessiert. Die junge Fotografin Hou Bo, die von 1949 bis 1961 Mao als „Leibfotografin“ diente, schuf ein dementsprechendes Bild, als sie Mao unter Weiden stehend am Ufer des Westsees in Hangzhou ablichtete (vgl. Abb. S. 13). Mao steht in Gedanken versunken da mit hinter dem Rücken gefalteten Händen: in der Pose des großen Poeten, wie man sie aus vielen chinesischen Tuschezeichnungen kennt. Zweifellos hält ein Gutteil der chinesischen Fotografen die Landschaftsfotografie für die verdienstvollste Betätigung. So liegt der Schluss nahe, dass vielen von ihnen der Alltag als allzu triviales Sujet für ihre Kameras erschien.

Die offene Tür

Als China zu Beginn der 1980er-Jahre begann, sich der Außenwelt zu öffnen, fanden die Arbeiten westlicher Fotografen langsam Verbreitung, da die Einfuhr von Büchern, Katalogen und Monografien wieder erlaubt war. Als sich chinesische Fotografen die Bilder anschauten, die westliche Fotografen wie Henri Cartier-Bresson und Marc Riboud in China aufgenommen hatten, waren sie gleichzeitig erstaunt und fasziniert von den hoch stilisierten, fraglos reizvollen Bildern des Alltags, die sie sahen. Vielleicht war es auch das Ergebnis anhaltender Indoktrination, das chinesische Fotografen letztlich daran hinderte, in ihrer augenblicklichen tristen Umgebung Schönheit zu entdecken.

In seiner Einführung zu dem Fotobuch *Face of China 1860–1912* schrieb der britische Historiker Nigel Cameron über westliche Fotografen und Reisende: „Die Szenerie, auf die Profis und Amateure ihre messing-gefassten Linsen im China der Jahrhundertmitte richteten, war in der Tat beklagenswert. Es war ein an Altersschwäche krankendes Land; ein China im heillosen Durcheinander und Aufruhr der jüngsten Vergangenheit und der konkreten Gegenwart, gezeichnet von Niederlagen durch den Westen und Unruhen im Inneren." China hat sich zweifellos von dieser Zeit und ihren Folgen erholt, in der die Kommunisten gegen die Japaner kämpften und gleichzeitig in einen Bürgerkrieg mit der nationalistischen Kuomintang verwickelt waren.

1942 „erklärte" Mao beim Forum zu Kunst und Literatur in Yan'an, wie sämtliche Spielarten von Kunst und Literatur als nützliche Propagandawerkzeuge in den Dienst der Kommunistischen Partei Chinas gestellt werden sollten. Als Mao sieben Jahre später die Macht ergriff und die Gründung der Volksrepublik verkündete, wurden die Direktiven seiner „Propagandapolitik" mit akribischer Genauigkeit umgesetzt. Im Nachhinein betrachtet kamen die Zwecke, für die Fotografie benutzt wurde, und die Manipulation, der insbesondere die Dokumentarfotografie ausgesetzt war, den Chinesen recht gut zupass: Es mutet ironisch an, dass die staatlichen Zensoren nur Berichte über soziale Leistungen unter der Kommunistischen Partei Chinas absegneten. Verschlimmert wurde dies durch die tief sitzende Empfindlichkeit, die in dem chinesischen Sprichwort „jia chou bu ke wai yang" zum Ausdruck kommt: Skandale und Unstimmigkeiten in der Familie sollten nicht außerhalb des Hauses verbreitet werden.

Neue Ansichten von China

Nach Nixons Besuch in China im Jahr 1972 erregte der italienische Regisseur Michelangelo Antonioni landesweit Aufsehen mit einem prägnanten schwarz-weißen Dokumentarfilm über ganz gewöhnliche Chinesen. Dies war die erste „moderne" Darstellung, die den Alltag der Menschen zeigte. Seit Beginn der Kulturrevolution waren die einzigen unterhaltenden Film- oder Bühnenprojekte, die sich mit China befassten, acht von Maos Frau Jiang Qing produzierte Revolutionsopern. Entsprechend stand die absolute Ehrlichkeit von Antonionis Ansatz in scharfem Kontrast zum übertriebenen revolutionären Eifer und Idealismus von Jiang Qings Propagandastücken. In den späten 1970er- und frühen 1980er-Jahren nutzten Propagandafunktionäre den „Antonioni-Vorfall" dazu, ausländische Journalisten bei ihren Berichten über China zu zensieren. Als sich China jedoch unter Deng Xiaopings Reformpolitik zu öffnen begann, wiesen dieselben Funktionäre die Schuld für die exzessiv betriebene Zensur und die Kontrolle der Medien dem „schädlichen Einfluss der Viererbande" zu. Ohne Kenntnis des Westens waren die meisten chinesischen Fotografen von den staatlichen Beschränkungen stärker betroffen als die ausländischen Journalisten. Eingedenk dieser krassen Realität und der traditionellen

Bevorzugung von Landschafts- und Porträtfotografie war es für mich beruhigend, von der Existenz von Bildern zu erfahren, die die Ereignisse in China seit 1949 dokumentieren und die im In- und Ausland kaum je zu sehen waren.

Nachdem ich 1997 nach Peking zurückgekehrt war und Zeuge der dramatischen Veränderungen wurde, wollte ich unbedingt eine umfassende Fotoreise durch das neue China unternehmen. Mein persönlicher Weg führte mich in 25 Jahren immer wieder zu unterschiedlichen, jeweils entscheidenden Zeiten nach China. Ich verspürte instinktiv das Bedürfnis, dieses Buch zu veröffentlichen und mein naturgegebenes Verständnis der chinesischen Menschen zu nutzen, um Arbeiten zu entdecken, die von chinesischen Verlegern aus Angst, zu weit von der offiziellen Linie der Partei abzuweichen, zurückgehalten wurden. Bei der Arbeit an diesem Projekt ging es ebenso um Erkenntnis wie um Selbsterkenntnis. Fast vier Jahre vergingen damit, Fotografen unterschiedlichen Alters in verschiedenen Provinzen und Städten zu treffen, Schuhkartons voller verstaubter Negative durchzublättern und ihre persönlichen Geschichten und Bilder kennenzulernen. Einige Fotografen berichteten von persönlichen Repressionen und hatten Angst, ihre Fotos freizugeben. Ich musste sie beruhigen, indem ich zu ihnen in die verschiedenen Landesteile reiste und sie zu Hause aufsuchte. Leider starben einige der älteren unter ihnen, die wie Zhou Jiandong und Lü Xiangyou schon jenseits der 80 waren, noch vor Erscheinen dieses Buches. Ich hatte das Glück, die Berichte der Fotografen zu hören, die mir Kommentare zeigten, die Premierminister Zhou Enlai bei der Freigabe des Fotos vom ersten chinesischen Test einer Wasserstoffbombe geschrieben hatte. Außerdem erfuhr ich, dass Mao darüber zu entscheiden hatte, welche Aufnahmen des historischen Händedrucks von Nixon und Zhou im Jahr 1972 an die Presse gingen. Der Fotograf Du Xiuxian, der damals jenes berühmte Foto aufnahm, war 1966 von seinen Kollegen bei der New China News Agency des Ausspähens von Premier Zhou Enlai beschuldigt worden. Dem Fotografen erschienen die falschen Anschuldigungen absurd, dennoch wurde er 1969 in die an die Sowjetunion grenzende Provinz Xinjiang verbannt.

Als 1969 die gewaltsamen Grenzstreitigkeiten zwischen China und der Sowjetunion ausbrachen, befand sich unter den 70 an der Grenze getöteten Chinesen ein als Dokumentarfotograf tätiger Kollege Dus. Zum Glück blieb Du ein ähnliches Schicksal erspart, nur zwei Tage vor dem Grenzzwischenfall hatte Premier Zhou Enlai ihn nach Peking zurückbeordert, weil er diesen nach Nordkorea begleiten sollte. Für das Ende des trostlosen Exils war er Zhou dankbar. Bei einer weiteren bizarren Anschuldigung gegen Du ging es um ein Foto, das er von Staatspräsident Liu Shaoqis Gattin Wang Guangmei in einem traditionellen chinesischen Kleid (qipao) aufgenommen hatte, das sie bei einem Staatsbesuch in In-

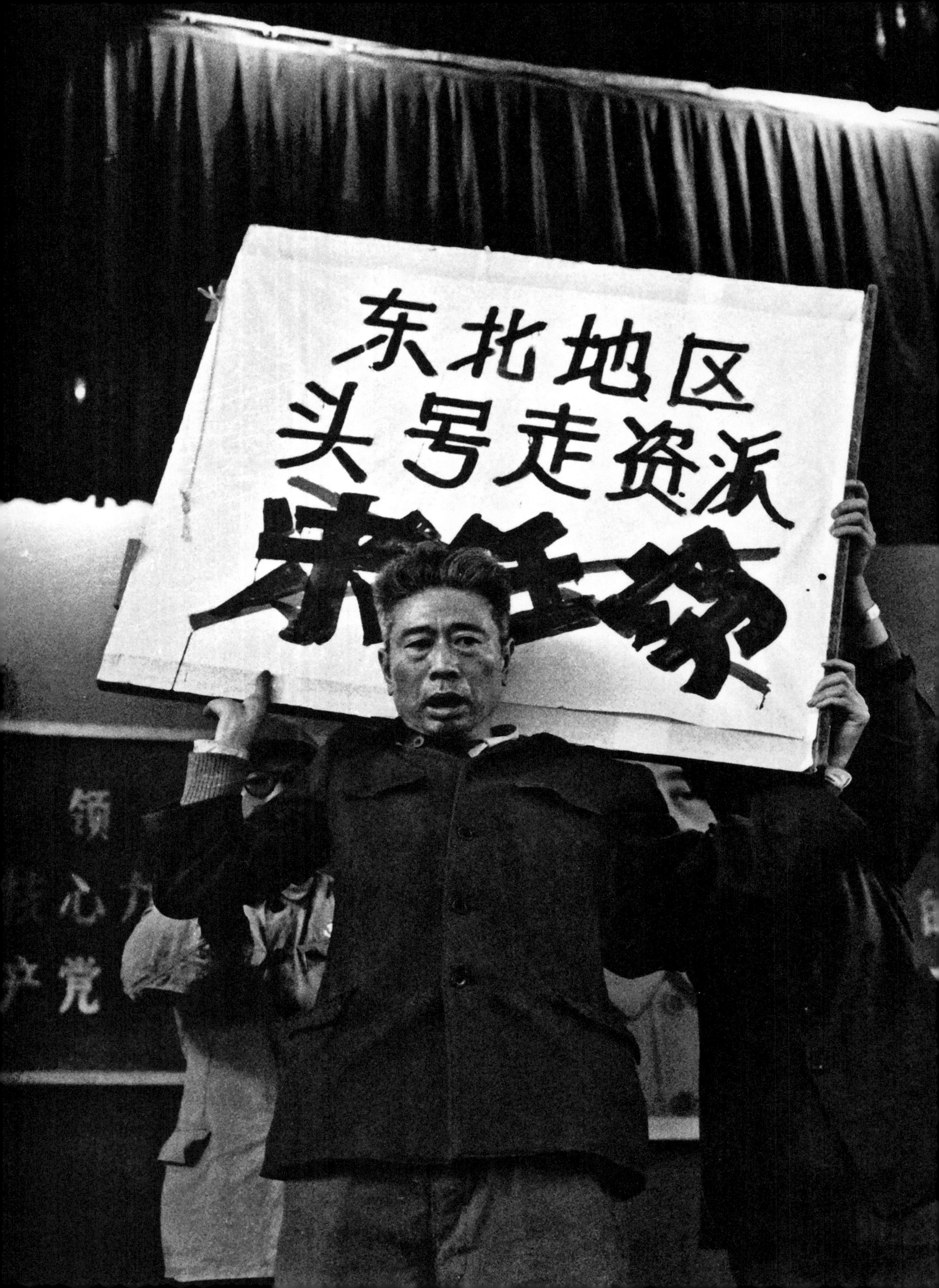
东北地区
头号走资派

←
Jiang Shaowu, 1966

Song Renjun, a senior official in Liaoning province in northeastern China, is publicly humiliated by having to hold a billboard denouncing himself at a rally in the provincial capital of Shenyang. The billboard says "The biggest capitalist of the Northeast."

Song Renjun, leitender Funktionär in der Provinz Liaoning im Nordosten Chinas, wird bei einer Demonstration in der Provinzhauptstadt Shenyang öffentlich gedemütigt, indem man ihn zwingt, ein Plakat zu tragen, auf dem er sich selbst bezichtigt, „der größte Kapitalist des Nordostens" zu sein.

Song Renjun, haut fonctionnaire de la province de Liaoning , dans le nord-est de la Chine, fut poursuivi et dut porter un panneau sur lequel il se dénonçait lui-même lors d'une manifestation de masse dans la ville de Shenyang : « Le plus grand capitaliste du Nord-est. »

donesien trug. Die elegante Robe hielt man für bourgeois und dekadent. Liu, der die chinesische Wirtschaft nach dem verhängnisvollen Großen Sprung nach vorn von 1958 wieder in Schwung gebracht hatte, wurde später von Mao während der Kulturrevolution aus der Partei ausgeschlossen. Liu wurde aus Peking exiliert und nach Kaifeng in der Provinz Henan verbannt, wo er tragisch starb. Unterdessen hatte derselbe Du Maos Ehefrau Jiang Qing in einem von ihr selbst entworfenen Kleid fotografiert. Später wurde Du erneut öffentlich verurteilt, weil er den Vorsitzenden Hua Guofeng zusammen mit der Viererbande fotografiert hatte, während die Nation 1976 Maos Tod betrauerte. Der inzwischen über 82-jährige Du ist eingedenk der reichlichen Kritik, die er Zeit seines Lebens zu hören bekam, mit seiner Schwerhörigkeit vielleicht ganz zufrieden.

Fotografie heute

Die beiden letzten Kapitel dieses Buchs offenbaren, wie sich das Schaffen der heutigen Fotografengeneration entwickelt. Chinesische Fotografen sind heute offener für neue Ideen und für die Erkundung des Landes mit besserem Material ausgerüstet. (In den 1950er- und 1960er-Jahren verwendeten viele chinesische Fotografen in ihren Kameras 35-Millimeter-Kinofilmmaterial. Importierte Kleinbildfilme waren rar und teuer.) Ihre Arbeiten, von denen viele den herrschenden Einfluss der sozialen Dokumentarfotografie widerspiegeln, künden von einer stetigen Ablösung von der Perspektive, aus der ihre älteren Kollegen China sahen. Ich glaube, dass die von dieser Generation von Fotografen gemachten Fortschritte zunehmend neue Wege ebnen werden, und zwar in einem Tempo, das sich, gemeinsam mit der Explosivkraft des heutigen China, weiter beschleunigen wird. Der Fotograf Lü Nan fotografierte in der abgelegenen Provinz Yunnan jahrelang im Untergrund lebende katholische Gemeinden, die nur die Autorität des Vatikans anerkennen, ebenso wie Bauern in Tibet in der besten Dokumentartradition eines W. Eugene Smith. Aber während sich Chinas Fotografen, ebenso wie ihre westlichen Kollegen, zunehmend der digitalen Kultur der Pixel bedienen und mit Techniken arbeiten, die sich immer mehr von der dinglichen Realität lösen[2], bleiben zahllose gesellschaftliche und kulturelle Phänomene und große Landesteile Chinas unerforscht. Wie die moderne Fotografin Lisette Model einmal sagte, ist „Fotografie die einfachste Kunst, was sie vielleicht zur schwersten macht".

Es ist eine einschüchternde Erfahrung, Bilder von China zu sichten, aufgenommen von so vielen guten Fotografen, die ich während der vierjährigen Vorbereitungszeit für dieses Buch kennenlernte. Von Henri Cartier-Bresson wird der Ausspruch zitiert: „Ein Foto machen heißt, ein Ereignis wahrnehmen – es geht darum, Hirn, Augen und Herz in eine Blickrichtung zu bringen. Heute redet jeder von Fotografie. Ich habe 50 Jahre lang Fotos gemacht, aber wie viele meiner Bilder kann man länger als drei Sekunden anschauen? Vielleicht 50? 100? Das wär's dann."[3]

Beim Betrachten der in diesem Buch zusammengetragenen Bilder können wir die tiefgreifenden Veränderungen erkennen, die China in den letzten sechs Jahrzehnten erlebt hat. In freier Wiedergabe der Worte des britischen Kritikers Herbert Read, der von Kunst sprach, stellen diese Fotografien letztlich eine Manifestation des „menschlichen Geistes" der heutigen Chinesen dar; „und obwohl die Zensoren sie für ihre eigenen Zwecke verwenden oder missbrauchen könnten, können sie sie weder verfälschen noch kontrollieren oder letztlich verleugnen."

Zu Beginn des 20. Jahrhunderts verfocht der Fotograf und Publizist Alfred Stieglitz die Vorstellung, Malerei müsse „antifotografisch" sein. In der Debatte über die Rolle der Fotografie ergriff er die Partei von Marius de Zayas, der 1913 in der Zeitschrift *Camera Work* schrieb: „Fotografie ist keine Kunst, sie ist noch nicht einmal eine Fertigkeit. Kunst ist der Ausdruck des Entwurfs einer Idee. Fotografie ist die plastische Verifizierung einer Tatsache. Kunst hat uns gelehrt, die Emotionen des Künstlers zu fühlen, während die Fotografie, weil sie uns die Realität in einem Zustand erhöhter Aufmerksamkeit präsentiert, es uns gestattet, unsere eigenen Emotionen angesichts der gezeigten Szene zu erkennen."[4] Zayas, dem es fern lag, die Fotografie zu verdammen, pries sie als einen Weg, schließlich die Objektivität der Form zu durchdringen. Auf diese Weise, so glaubte er, gäben Formen ihrem eigenen Geist Ausdruck, offenbarten ihr eigenes Wesen.

Ich bin jedem einzelnen der beteiligten Fotografen, die mich in ihren Häusern und Büros willkommen hießen, wo ich Hunderttausende von Negativen und Abzügen sichten durfte, zu tiefer Dankbarkeit verpflichtet. Sie schenkten mir ihr Vertrauen und ließen mich an ihren Erfahrungen teilhaben. Ich hoffe, dieses Buch wird den chinesischen Fotografen für ihre Beharrlichkeit und für die Liebe zu ihrem Land zur Ehre gereichen.

1. Vgl. *The Chinese*, Jasper Becker, Oxford University Press 2000, S. 24. Der *Cambridge History of China* zufolge lag die geschätzte Zahl der Toten (überwiegend Verhungerten) während des Großen Sprungs nach vorn zwischen 16 und 27 Millionen Menschen, wobei allein 1960 zehn Millionen starben (S. 370).
2. Peter Plagens, „Is Photography Dead?", *Newsweek*, 10. Dezember 2007.
3. Interview mit der *New York Times*, 1994, erneut zitiert von Alan Riding, *New York Times*, 29. Mai 2003.
4. Sarah Greenough, *Alfred Stieglitz, Photographs & Writings*, National Gallery of Art, Washington D.C. 1998.

Note de l'éditeur

Par Liu Heung Shing

« Lorsqu'un Chinois décrit un événement, il le place dans le cadre d'une dynastie. Sur les quatorze dynasties impériales, dix ont duré plus longtemps que toute l'histoire des États-Unis. »

HENRY KISSINGER (1923–), politicien et laureate du Prix Nobel, 2001

Première image

Alors que les derniers touristes quittaient la Citée interdite, un minuscule Mandchou arborant une énorme paire de lunettes me guida gentiment vers la Porte du Méridien. Les gardiens, qui prennent les billets d'entrée et qui étaient chargés de fermer le portail, nous sourirent et nous firent signe d'entrer. Alors que la nuit tombait sur la Cité, Pu Jie – le tout petit Mandchou – et moi nous dirigeâmes vers la porte intérieure du Palais de la Paix céleste. « Mon frère se moqua de moi un jour parce que je portais une robe à parements jaunes, » me dit-il en me conduisant vers une magnifique allée impériale de couleur écarlate. « Ici, » ajouta-t-il en faisant un geste de la main, « mon frère et moi avons appris à rouler à bicyclette… » Puis, montrant du doigt une autre direction, il expliqua que c'était le pavillon où, toujours en compagnie de son frère, il avait étudié l'anglais avec leur fameux tuteur écossais, Reginald Fleming Johnston.

Je me souviens particulièrement à cet instant de ma longue relation avec la République populaire chinoise, car c'était une rare chance de pouvoir photographier l'homme qui aurait pu succéder à son frère, Pu Yi, dernier empereur de la dynastie Qing, à l'intérieur même du palais terrestre des Fils du Ciel qui avait été le siège de leur famille.

Une enfance troublée

Je suis né aux débuts de la République populaire à Hong Kong, alors que la ville se trouvait encore sous administration britannique. Ce n'est pas là cependant que je fus élevé car mes parents me renvoyèrent en Chine au début des années 1950, alors que j'étais encore presque bébé. Mes premiers « jeux » furent de participer à la campagne « Détruire les quatre fléaux » qui devait éradiquer le pays des menaces pesant sur la chaîne alimentaire. Au départ, les quatre fléaux étaient les rats, les moineaux, les moustiques et les mouches. Plus tard, on comprit que les moineaux se nourrissaient de vers et n'étaient donc pas un « fléau » et ils furent remplacés par les puces. *Le Quotidien du Peuple* rapporta le 19 avril 1958 que trois millions de Pékinois avaient passé une journée entière à attraper 83 249 moineaux. À l'apogée de cette folie, on considérait que quatre moineaux consommaient 454 grammes de graines, c'est-à-dire l'équivalent de la ration quotidienne d'un être humain. Tout ceci faisait partie des éléments importants de mon éducation primaire. Je rapportais régulièrement mes « devoirs » faits à la maison : des boîtes d'allumettes débordantes de moustiques et de mouches que j'avais massacrés avec vigueur et diligence ; mais quels que soient mes efforts, je n'obtins jamais qu'un C pour mon « comportement politique ». Cette campagne des Quatre fléaux était en fait une manière indirecte de détourner l'attention des gens de sévères crises d'approvisionnement.

Mes camarades de classe, essentiellement la progéniture d'officiers de haut rang de l'armée populaire de libération, me considéraient comme un rejeton des « Cinq anti », c'est-à-dire les propriétaires, les paysans riches, les contre-révolutionnaires, les mauvais éléments et les gens de droite. Je pris part à l'hystérie du Grand bond en avant et fut témoin des effets débilitants de la malnutrition qu'il entraîna, non seulement parmi les *pinnong* (les plus pauvres des pauvres), mais chez nos voisins, ceux de ma grand-mère, qui occupaient la maison à cour, notre ancienne résidence familiale jusqu'à ce que les propriétés privées soient nationalisées en 1954. Celle-ci incluait également la maison de ma grand-mère, offerte en dot lors du mariage de ma mère à mon père. J'ai encore le souvenir très vivant d'avoir fait la queue pendant des heures pour acheter ma ration de vingt grammes de graisse lorsque, à de rares occasions, le quartier recevait l'autorisation de tuer un porc. Quand je jouais avec les enfants du voisinage, j'étais conscient que tous avaient les bras et les jambes enflés du fait de la malnutrition.

En 1960, alors que la situation se détériorait de plus en plus après le pitoyable échec du Grand bond en avant, mon père réussit à me faire revenir à Hong Kong. La Chine était plongée dans les affres d'une famine qui dura trois années (1960–1962) au cours desquelles 30 millions de personnes seraient mortes de faim[1].

De retour à Hong Kong, j'étudiai l'anglais et appris le dialecte cantonais local tandis que pendant les vacances d'été, mon père m'apprenait à traduire les câbles de l'Associated Press (AP) et de Reuters en chinois. Rédacteur responsable des pages internationales du *Ta Kung Pao*, un quotidien soutenu par Pékin, il rentrait souvent à la maison en donnant libre cours à ses frustrations lorsque, par exemple, les autorités pékinoises censuraient un article sur l'alunissage des astronautes américains.

Départ de l'Asie, débuts de ma nouvelle vie

En 1970, je quittai Hong Kong pour aller étudier aux États-Unis et m'orientai vers la préparation d'un diplôme de sciences politiques à Hunter College à New York. Pendant la dernière année de mes études, je suivis un cours de photographie donné par le célèbre photographe de *Life Magazine*, Gjon Mili. Ce seul semestre allait transformer ma vie. Une fois diplômé, je suivis Mill et devins stagiaire à *Life*. J'étais au bon endroit et au bon moment pour suivre la normalisation des relations diplomatiques américano-chinoises en 1979 et fus envoyé en Chine, ce qui fit de moi le premier correspondant étranger chinois à être nommé à Pékin par *Time Magazine* avant que je ne rejoigne par la suite l'agence Associated Press.

Mon travail de photojournaliste pour AP entraîna de nombreux déménagements en Chine, aux États-Unis, en Inde, en Corée du Sud et dans l'ancienne Union soviétique. En me déplaçant d'un pays à l'autre, je pus comparer la pauvreté de l'Inde et celle de la Chine, le pragmatisme du communisme chinois et l'idéalisme politique de la phase finale du communisme soviétique sous Mikhail Gorbatchev et plus tard (après être revenu à Pékin en 1997) comment se comportaient les hommes d'affaires de la diaspora chinoise et la génération émergente des nouveaux capitalistes rouges. Photojournaliste, je comparais mes notes sur la politique chinoise à celles de mes camarades reporters, chaque fois conscient que la réalité chinoise cadrait mal avec les projets de reportage des journaux américains. Beaucoup de mes collègues occidentaux terminaient leurs séjours en Chine tristes et déçus, ce qui s'expliquait peut-être par l'accumulation des difficultés rencontrées dans leur travail quotidien mais aussi par la résistance de la Chine aux généralisations occidentales. Ancien ambassadeur britannique en Chine, Sir Percy Craddock écrivit ainsi dans ses mémoires : « Observer la Chine est un goût acquis, pour une bonne part amer. »

Lent retour en Chine

Mon introduction à la Chine nouvelle en tant que photojournaliste professionnel débuta par un séisme. Peu après avoir lu l'annonce du tremblement de terre qui avait dévasté la ville chinoise de Tangshan en 1976, et dont les secousses se firent sentir jusqu'à Pékin, à 450 km de là, je me trouvais en Europe pour photographier les candidats communistes d'une campagne électorale au Portugal. Immédiatement après, et à la suite de la mort de Franco, je partis pour l'Espagne photographier le candidat socialiste Felipe Gonzalez, qui tenait de grandes réunions d'étudiants pour sortir le pays de l'ère franquiste. Peu après, me trouvant à Paris pour photographier le premier ministre français Raymond Barre, en quittant un matin l'hôtel Matignon, je tombai sur le portrait en pleine page du président Mao en couverture du *Figaro*. Comprenant que Mao était mort, j'appelai mon agent à New York, Robert Pledge, qui m'obtint la mission de photographier les funérailles pour *Time Magazine*. Une fois à Guangzhou, je me vis refuser le droit de continuer vers Pékin et dû me contenter de prendre sur place des photos de gens en deuil. Les visages que je saisis au bord de la Rivière des Perles suggéraient davantage le soulagement que la peine. Je n'avais pas vraiment compris que je commençais ainsi à photographier la Chine d'après Mao, ce que je fis d'abord pour *Time Magazine* (1978–81) puis, pour AP (1981–83). En 1978, l'un de mes reportages portait sur un tour quotidien en vélo au mur du dépôt des bus des quartiers ouest de Pékin, qui fut par la suite surnommé le Mur de la démocratie chinoise. C'est là que des dissidents importants placardaient régulièrement des affichettes rédigées à la main, les *dazibao* (« affiche en gros caractères ») pour inciter la Chine à s'ouvrir, à se moderniser et à introduire des réformes démocratiques.

Depuis 1976, un certain nombre de livres sur la République populaire ont été publiés aussi bien par des éditeurs chinois qu'étrangers. Les

paradoxes de ce pays n'y semblent pas vraiment évidents. La Chine a toujours été un sujet difficile à cerner pour les éditeurs de New York, Londres ou Paris. Certains, bien que familiers du langage photographique, se sont néanmoins heurtés à une « muraille de Chine » lors de leurs contacts avec les institutions officielles et la myriade de doctrines socialistes. Beaucoup d'efforts ont été dépensés pour avoir accès aux négatifs de certaines sources incontournables comme l'agence de presse Xinhua, *China Pictorial, Nationalities Pictorial, PLA Pictorial* et les archives privées de certains grands photographes. Jusqu'à maintenant, peu de démarches ont été couronnées de succès.

Pendant des milliers d'années, l'esthétique chinoise a été modelée par les principes taoïstes d'harmonie de l'homme et de la nature, d'où l'abondance de peintures de paysages qui la caractérise. La photographie a été introduite en Chine au XIX siècle par les Européens. Lorsque les premiers praticiens locaux commencèrent à maîtriser les appareils de prise de vue, ils s'intéressèrent essentiellement au paysage et au portrait, qui devinrent leurs principaux sujets. Hou Bo, photographe officielle de Mao de 1949 à 1961, créa ce type de cadrage où l'on voit Mao debout entre des saules sur les bords du lac de l'Ouest à Hangzhou (photo p.13). Mao s'y tient dressé, perdu dans un silence contemplatif, les mains croisées derrière le dos. C'est la pose du grand poète qu'évoquent tant de peintures chinoises à l'encre. Sans aucun doute, une vaste proportion des photographes chinois considèrent la photographie de paysage comme l'objet le plus valorisant de leur travail. Comme la majorité d'entre eux voyait encore le monde en termes de paysages vaporeux, on peut en conclure que, pour la plupart, la vie quotidienne paraissait un sujet trop trivial.

Les portes s'ouvrent

Lorsque la Chine commença à s'ouvrir au monde extérieur au début des années 1980, les œuvres des photographes occidentaux apparurent peu à peu grâce à l'importation de nouveau autorisée de livres, de catalogues et de monographies. Les photographes chinois furent étonnés et fascinés par le charme stylisé et incontestable de ces images de la vie quotidienne prises par des Occidentaux comme Henri Cartier-Bresson et Marc Riboud. L'endoctrinement permanent avait fini par les décourager de découvrir un peu de beauté dans leur sinistre environnement immédiat.

Dans l'introduction du livre de photos *Face of China 1860–1912*, l'historien britannique Nigel Cameron écrivait au sujet des voyageurs et des photographes occidentaux : « Dans la Chine du milieu du siècle, les scènes vers lesquelles les amateurs et les professionnels dirigeaient leurs objectifs à monture de cuivre était en effet bien tristes. C'était une Chine en phase finale de sa longue existence, prisonnière de la confusion et l'agitation d'un récent passé et d'un présent marqué par la défaite, les troubles intérieurs et la mainmise de l'Occident. »

La Chine a bien entendu évolué depuis cette période et ses suites, qui virent les Communistes combattre les Japonais et s'enfoncer dans la guerre civile avec le Kuomintang.

En 1942, lors du Forum sur les arts et la littérature de Yan'an, Mao expliqua comment toutes les formes d'art et de littérature, instruments de propagande des plus pratiques, devaient être mises au service du Parti communiste. Sept ans plus tard, lorsqu'il s'empara du pouvoir et proclama la République populaire, ses directives de « propagande » furent mises en œuvre avec un soin méticuleux. Rétrospectivement, l'usage qui fut fait de la photographie et les manipulations brutales auxquelles elle fut soumise, en particulier pour celle de documentation, étaient assez bien adaptés aux Chinois. Les censeurs encourageaient uniquement la couverture des réussites sociales du Parti communiste ce qui, non sans ironie, pouvait correspondre à la sensibilité qu'exprimait le vieux proverbe chinois « *jia chou bu ke wai yang* » : scandale et laideur dans la famille ne doivent pas sortir de la maison.

Nouvelles visions de la Chine

En 1972, à la suite de la visite du président Nixon en Chine, le cinéaste italien Michelangelo Antonioni provoqua un vif émoi pour avoir filmé avec sympathie des Chinois ordinaires dans un documentaire incisif en noir et blanc, premier film « moderne » à montrer la vie quotidienne du peuple. Depuis la Révolution culturelle, les seuls films ou spectacles créés sur la Chine consistaient en huit opéras révolutionnaires produits par l'épouse de Mao, Jiang Qing. L'honnêteté absolue du regard d'Antonioni contrastait fortement avec le zèle révolutionnaire exagéré et l'idéalisme des morceaux de propagande de celle-ci. À la fin des années 1970 et au début des années 1980, « l'incident Antonioni » fut utilisé par les propagandistes officiels pour censurer les journalistes étrangers souhaitant travailler en Chine. Lorsque le pays commença à s'ouvrir grâce à la politique de réformes de Deng Xiaoping, les mêmes n'en blâmèrent pas moins les excès de cette politique de censure et de contrôle des médias dont ils rejetèrent la faute sur « la pernicieuse influence de la Bande des quatre. » Inconnus en Occident, la plupart des photographes chinois étaient moins à l'aise devant les restrictions imposées que les journalistes étrangers. Malgré ces dures réalités et la préférence naturelle ambiante pour la photographie de portraits et de paysage, j'ai découvert avec plaisir l'existence d'images documentant les événements survenus en Chine depuis 1949, dont la plupart n'avaient été que rarement utilisées ou publiées aussi bien en République populaire qu'ailleurs.

De retour à Pékin en 1997, constatant le caractère spectaculaire des changements survenus, j'ai eu envie d'entreprendre un tour photographique complet de la nouvelle Chine. Mes pas avaient croisé ceux de la Chine pendant 25 ans lors de plusieurs périodes cruciales et je comprends maintenant que je ressentais alors le besoin viscéral de réaliser ce livre et de profiter de ma compréhension du peuple chinois pour faire connaître des œuvres qui avaient pu être écartées par les éditeurs chinois par crainte de s'éloigner de la ligne du Parti. Mener à bien ce projet a été une tâche d'explorateur mais aussi de découverte de moi-même. Il m'a fallu presque quatre années pour aller à la rencontre de photographes de différentes générations, pour retrouver des enveloppes de négatifs couvertes de poussière rangées dans des boîtes à chaussures sous leur lit et partager avec eux les histoires de leur vie. Un certain nombre de ces photographes m'ont expliqué leurs tribulations et leur crainte de montrer leurs photos. Je devais les rassurer et pour cela me rendre chez eux aux quatre coins du pays. Malheureusement, certains d'entre eux, comme Zhou Jiandong et Lü Xiangyou, avaient plus de quatre-vingts ans et disparurent avant que ce livre ne puisse être publié. J'ai eu par ailleurs le privilège d'entendre les récits de photographes qui me montrèrent les notes que le premier ministre Zhou Enlai rédigea pour autoriser la publication de photos des essais de la première bombe à hydrogène chinoise, ou de constater que Mao avait lui-même choisi les photographies de la poignée de main historique de 1972 entre Nixon et Zhou pouvant être remises à la presse. Le photographe Du Xiuxian, auteur de cette fameuse photo, fut accusé en 1968 par ses collègues de la Nouvelle agence de presse Chine nouvelle d'espionner le premier ministre. On ne pouvait croire à ces fausses accusations, mais il fut néanmoins exilé dans la province du Xinjiang, à la frontière avec l'Union soviétique, en 1969.

Lorsque des incidents armés se produisirent sur cette frontière la même année, l'un des 70 Chinois tués fut un de ses confrères, un photographe documentaire. Heureusement, Du échappa à ce sort et fut rappelé à Pékin juste deux jours avant cet incident par le premier ministre Zhou qui lui demanda de l'accompagner en Corée du Nord, ce dont il lui fut reconnaissant. D'autres charges curieuses retenues contre lui furent d'avoir photographié Wang Guangmei, la très belle épouse du président Liu Shaoqi qui portait un costume traditionnel *qipao* lors d'une visite d'État en Indonésie. Ce vêtement élégant fut jugé bourgeois et décadent. Liu, qui avait restauré l'économie après le désastre politique du Grand bond en 1958, fut par la suite éliminé par Mao pendant la révolution culturelle. Il fut exilé de Pékin à Kaifeng dans la province du Hénan, où il connut une mort tragique. Puis en 1973, le même photographe, Du, fut de nouveau dénoncé pour avoir photographié le président Hua Guofeng avec les séides de la Bande des quatre lors des funérailles de Mao en 1976.

→

Li Zhensheng, 1968

Model PLA soldier Wang Guoxiang appears at a three-week conference on Mao Zedong Thought and its application. The audience was full of admiration for the 170 Mao badges he wore. It is estimated that from 1966 to 1976, approximately 4.5 billion badges were produced, and 1.2 billion copies of Quotations from Chairman Mao Zedong *were printed: more than the total number of China's inhabitants.*

Der Modellsoldat der Volksbefreiungsarmee, Wang Guoxiang, bei einer dreiwöchigen Konferenz zum Erlernen und Anwenden der Gedanken von Mao Zedong. Die Zuhörerschaft hegte große Bewunderung für die 170 Mao-Abzeichen, die er trug. Zwischen 1966 und 1976 wurden schätzungsweise 4,5 Milliarden Abzeichen hergestellt und 1,2 Milliarden Exemplare der Worte des Vorsitzenden Mao Zedong *gedruckt, eine Zahl, die die der damaligen Gesamtbevölkerung Chinas übersteigt.*

Le soldat-modèle Wang Guoxiang participa à une conférence de trois semaines sur l'apprentissage et l'application de la pensée de Mao. Le public était empli d'admiration pour les 170 badges de Mao qu'il arborait. De 1966 à 1976, on estime qu'environ 4,5 milliards de badges furent fabriqués et 1,2 milliards d'exemplaires des Citations du Président Mao *imprimées, plus que le total des Chinois.*

Âgé de 82 ans en 2007, Du est aujourd'hui pratiquement sourd, fatigué sans doute d'avoir entendu tant de critiques.

La photographie aujourd'hui

Les deux derniers chapitres de ce livre montrent l'évolution de la génération des photographes actuels. Aujourd'hui, ceux-ci sont plus ouverts aux idées nouvelles et mieux équipés sur le plan du matériel. Beaucoup de leurs prédécesseurs des années 1950 et 1960 utilisaient des films de cinéma dans leurs appareils, car la pellicule photo 35 mm était rare et plus coûteuse. Leurs travaux, dont beaucoup témoignent de l'influence prédominante du documentaire social, montre une Chine très différente de celle de leurs anciens collègues. Je pense que les itinéraires suivis par cette génération ouvriront de plus en plus de voies nouvelles, et ce, à un rythme qui devrait encore s'accélérer au vu de l'explosion d'énergie que connaît actuellement le pays. Des photographes comme Lü Nan, qui a passé des années à photographier les communautés catholiques chinoises clandestines – celles qui n'acceptent que l'autorité du Vatican – dans la province éloignée du Yunnan où les paysans du Tibet suivent une tradition documentaire dans l'esprit de W. Eugene Smith. Mais alors que les praticiens chinois, comme leurs confrères occidentaux, adoptent toujours davantage des techniques numériques de plus en plus éloignées de la réalité matérielle[2], des myriades de sujets sociaux et une grande partie du territoire chinois restent inexplorés. Comme la photographe Lisette Model le dit un jour : « La photographie est l'art le plus facile, ce qui en fait peut-être le plus difficile des arts. »

C'est une expérience intimidante que de feuilleter les images de la Chine prises par tant de photographes de talent rencontrés pendant les quatre années qu'a duré la préparation de cet ouvrage. Henri Cartier-Bresson aurait dit : « Prendre une photographie, c'est reconnaître un événement, c'est une façon de mettre votre cerveau, votre œil et votre cœur dans le même axe de vision. Aujourd'hui, tout le monde parle de photographie. J'ai passé cinquante ans à prendre des images, mais combien d'entre elles pouvez-vous regarder plus de trois secondes ? Peut-être 50 ? 100 ? C'est à peu près tout. »[3]

C'est en regardant ces images réunies sous forme de livre que nous pouvons prendre conscience des changements massifs qu'a connus la Chine au cours des six dernières décennies. Pour paraphraser le critique britannique Herbert Read (qui parlait de l'art), elles sont une manifestation de « l'esprit humain » du peuple chinois d'aujourd'hui, « et même si les censeurs peuvent les utiliser, ou abuser d'elles pour leurs propres fins, il ne peuvent ni les fabriquer, ni les contrôler ni, au final, les réfuter. »

Au début du XXᵉ siècle, le photographe et éditeur Alfred Stieglitz défendait l'idée que la peinture devait être « anti-photographique. » Dans le débat sur le rôle de la photographie, il rejoignait Marius de Zayas qui écrivait dans *Camera Work* en 1913 : « La photographie n'est pas de l'art, elle n'est même pas un art. L'art est l'expression de la conception d'une idée. La photographie est la vérification plastique du fait. L'art nous a appris à ressentir les émotions de l'artiste, mais la photographie, parce qu'elle nous soumet la réalité dans un état de conscience renforcé, nous permet de comprendre nos propres émotions par rapport à la scène présentée. » Loin de condamner la photographie, de Zayas la célébrait comme une façon de se rapprocher de l'objectivité des formes. De cette façon, il pensait que les formes exprimaient leur propre esprit, se révélaient dans leur propre essence.[4]

Ma plus profonde gratitude va à chacun des photographes qui m'ont reçu et m'ont laissé plonger dans des centaines de milliers de négatifs et de tirages. Ils ont partagé avec moi leur confiance et leur vision. J'espère que ce livre sera un hommage aux photographes chinois, la reconnaissance de leur persévérance et de l'amour qu'ils portent à leur pays.

1. Voir Jasper Becker, *The Chinese*, Oxford University Press, 2000 (p. 24). Selon la *Cambridge History of China*, le nombre estimé de morts (essentiellement dues à la famine) pendant le Grand bond en avant aurait été de 16 à 27 millions de personnes, dont plus de 10 millions pour la seule année 1960 (p. 370).
2. Peter Plagens, « Is Photography Dead ? », *Newsweek*, 10 décembre 2007.
3. Entretien paru dans *The New York Times* en 1994, cité par Alan Riding, *The New York Times* du 29 mai 2003.
4. Sarah Grenough, *Alfred Stieglitz, Photographs & Writings*, National Gallery of Art, Washington, Bullfinch Press & Little, Brown, New York, 1998.

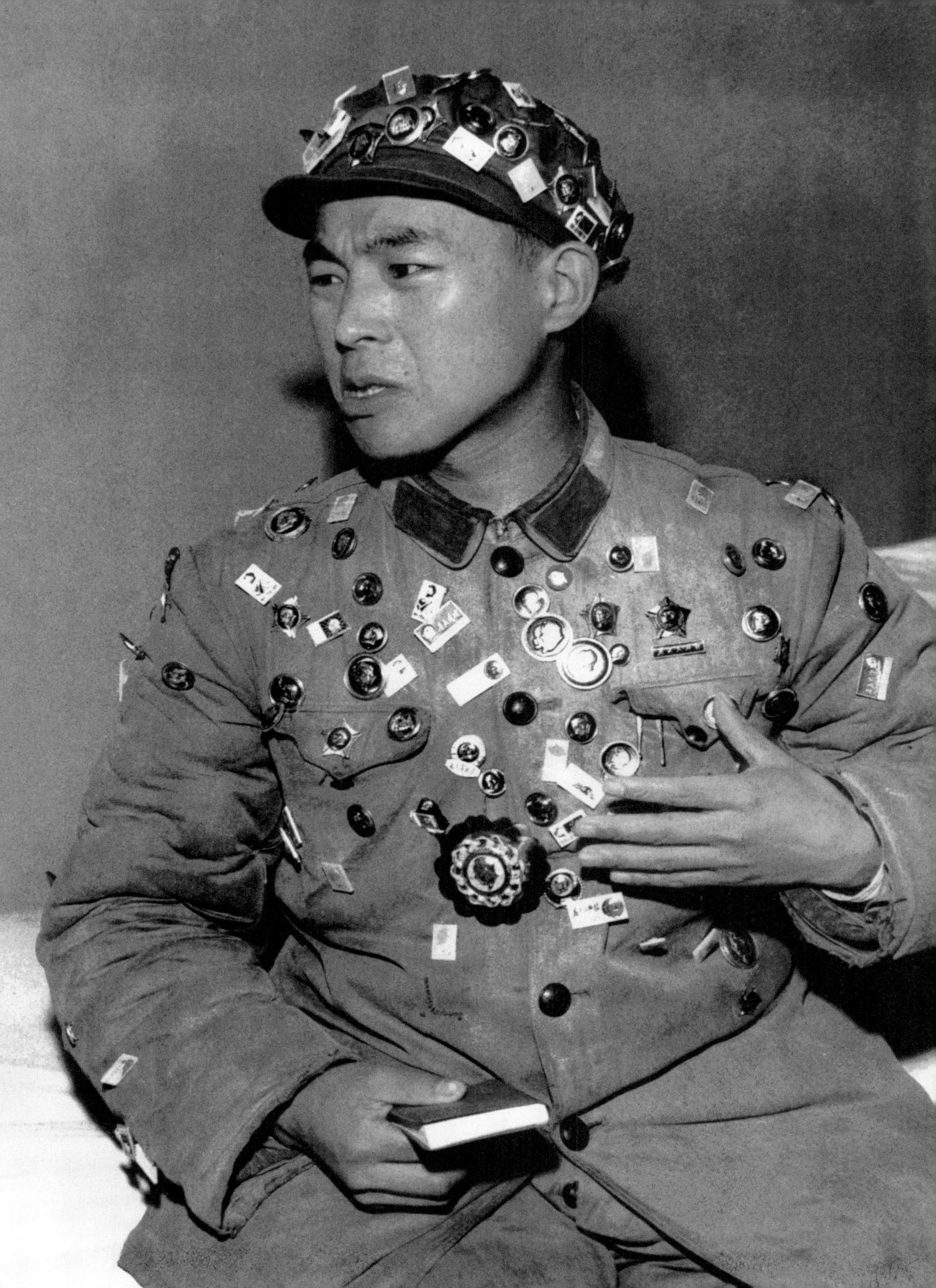

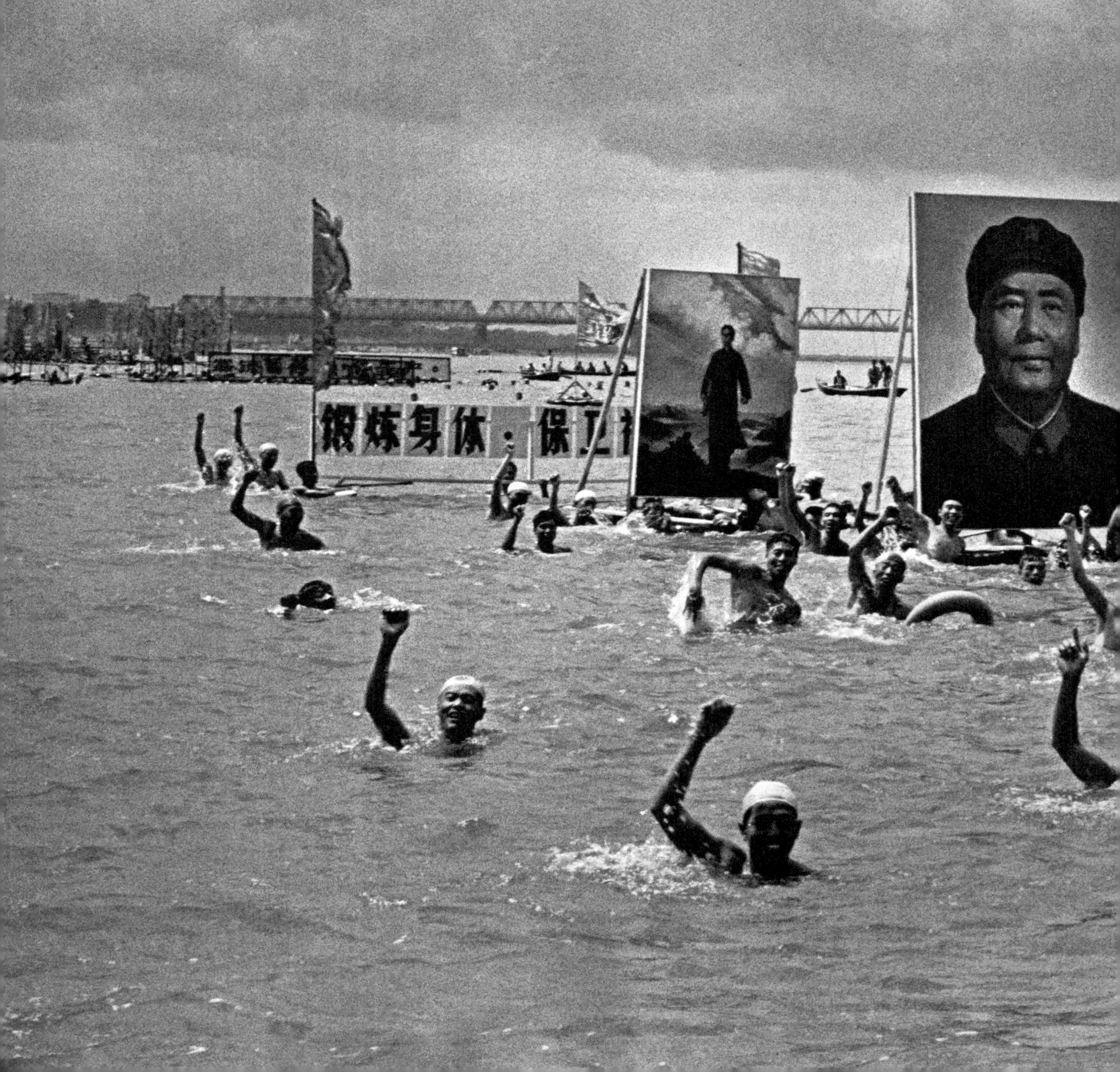

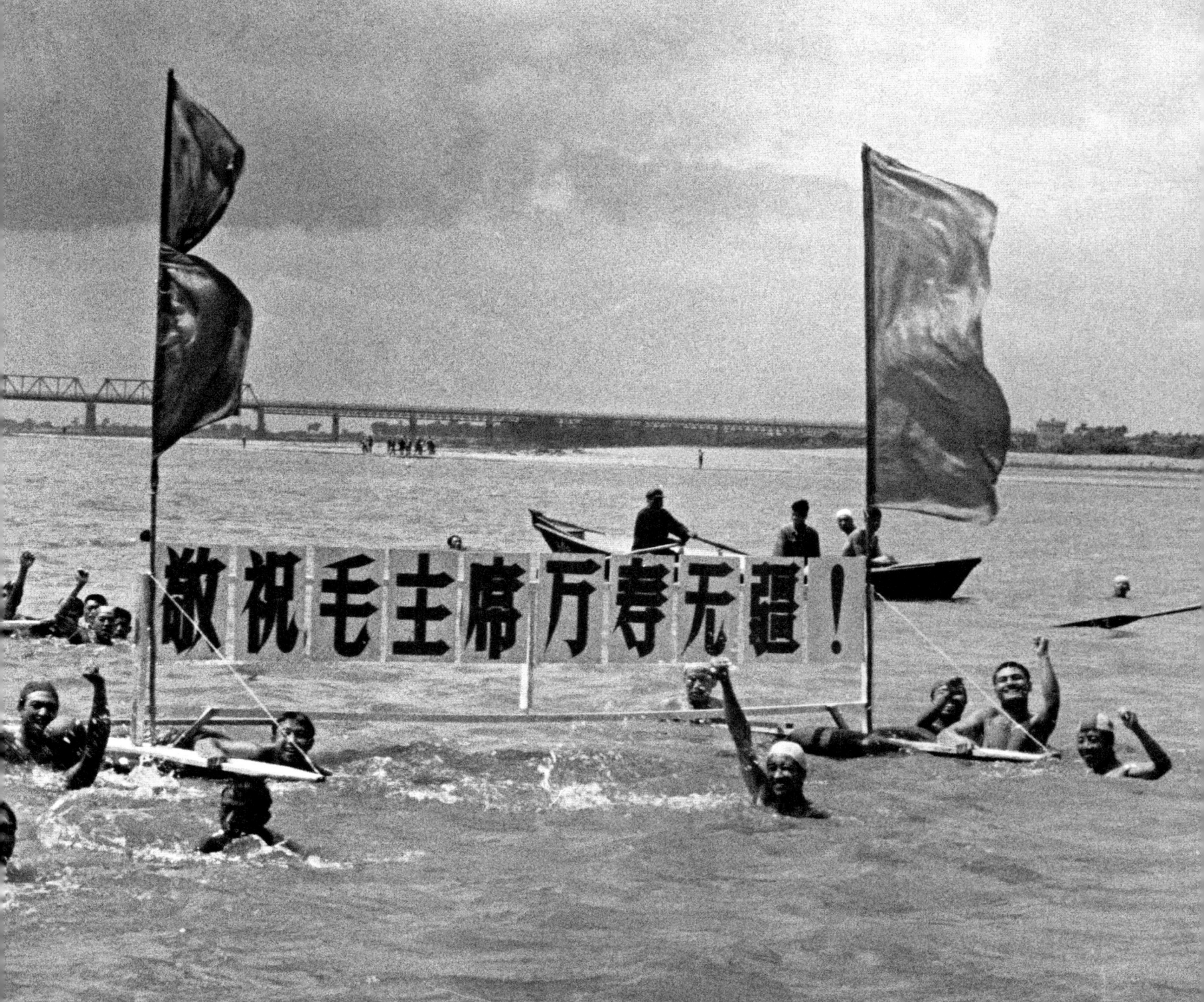

Historical Context

China 1949–today

By James Kynge

pp. 26/27
Li Zhensheng, 1968

Chinese swimmers in the Songhua river, Harbin, salute with fists, flags, banners bearing Mao's portrait, and others proclaiming "Long live Chairman Mao" as they commemorate the second anniversary of their leader's 1966 swim in the Yangtze river.
"In the Cultural Revolution, politics was put in command. The discourses of politics, of class struggle, social advancement, progress and state command dominated everything. People let politics seep deep into their hearts, but there, of course, it nearly broke them." Kerry Brown

Chinesische Schwimmer im Fluss Songhua in Harbin grüßen mit erhobenen Fäusten, Flaggen und Mao-Porträts und rufen „Lang lebe der Vorsitzende Mao", während sie an den zweiten Jahrestag von Maos Bad im Jangtse 1966 erinnern.
„Während der Kulturrevolution übernahm die Politik das Kommando. Die Gespräche über Politik, Klassenkampf, gesellschaftlichen Aufstieg, Fortschritt und Staatsgewalt beherrschten alles. Die Menschen ließen die Politik tief in ihre Herzen eindringen, aber dort hat sie sie natürlich beinahe zerbrochen." Kerry Brown

Dans le fleuve Songhua, à Harbin, des nageurs saluent le poing levé. Ils portent des drapeaux et des bannières à l'effigie de Mao ou proclamant « Longue vie au Président Mao » pour commémorer le second anniversaire du bain de celui-ci dans le Yang-Tsé en 1966.
« Pendant la Révolution culturelle, la politique était aux commandes. Les discours sur la politique, la lutte des classes, le progrès social, le contrôle de l'État dominait tout. Les gens laissèrent la politique s'insinuer dans leurs cœur ce qui, bien sûr, faillit les détruire. » Kerry Brown

"O words, they are but poor receipts for that which time hath stole away,
The antique pulpit trees and the play."

So wrote John Clare, the 17th-century British poet, to describe the familiar frustration that writers feel when words are the only tools available to render the panoply of history in all its subtle shades. No matter how skillfully words are deployed on the page, the result is sometimes a pale reflection of the way things were, a mere outline of people and events shorn of their animating emotions. Photographs, on the other hand, have the power to fill the spaces. Not only do they document the details of the day—such as the clothes that people wore, the way that buildings looked, and the lie of the land—they also, crucially, supply the sensations of the age. They do this through their unique capacity to suggest, infer, and hint at what cannot be seen. In this, they possess a transcendent quality, transporting the observer beyond form to meaning, rather in the same way that Zhuangzi, the 4th-century BC Chinese philosopher, described the distillation of thought.

"The fish trap exists because of the fish; once you've caught the fish, you can forget the trap. The rabbit snare exists because of the rabbit; once you've got the rabbit, you can forget the snare. Words exist because of meaning; once you've got the meaning, you can forget the words. Where can I find a man who has forgotten words so I can have a word with him?"

This book of photographs, compiled and edited by Pulitzer-prize winning photographer Liu Heung Shing, traces the history of China from 1948—the year before the People's Republic was proclaimed—until 2008, the year in which China was to take its place among the great powers of the world and host the Olympic Games in Beijing. The span of 60 years covered by the book falls well within the biblical definition of a lifetime and yet the transformations that it portrays are so fundamental and far-reaching that it feels as if time has been compressed. For thousands of years, China had been a country of villages and market towns connected by tracks that turned to mud in the winter and dust in the summer; a nation in which the dialect spoken in one valley was often unintelligible in the next; an economy that, in spite of a glittering record in technological innovation, was largely powered by muscle well into the 20th century. Yet in the space of time encompassed by the pages of this book, China's millennial mold has been smashed, discarded, and replaced by new realities, many of which are still evolving. Since the revolution, China has undergone—or is undergoing—several economic, political, social, spiritual, and cultural transformations all at the same time. It is turning from a rural into an urban country as hundreds of millions of farmers migrate to cities and towns, often to jobs on factory production lines, but sometimes to shiny new office blocks. The shift from agrarian to industrial is accompanied by an ascent up the technology ladder. No longer propelled merely by muscle, China currently builds three new power stations every week and in a single year installs enough generating capacity to satisfy all the electricity needs of a country such as the UK. Geographically, too, things are changing. For the first time in its long history, development and economic prosperity is radiating inland from the east and south coastal areas as a vast network of new highways connect formerly remote regions to the rest of the country and, by extension, to the world. Politically, things have rotated almost 360 degrees. After spending the first 30 years since the revolution installing a Communist dictatorship, nationalizing all private property, and keeping the population regimented within a pyramid of bureaucratic control, Beijing has devoted the last three decades to unpicking the stitches of time. Private property is now burgeoning, as are private companies and stockmarkets. Where once people dressed in regulation blue or green, and consumer choices were limited, the rise of individualism has created a market for a dizzying array of material variety. Virtually the only area of society that has remained singular is the Communist Party and its attitude toward keeping power; customers at Starbucks in Beijing may choose between lattes, espressos, cappuccinos, mochas, and frappucinos, but such liberty at the point of sale has yet to spread to the ballot box.

There can be no more immediate—or enjoyable—way of accessing this tumultuous history and understanding China's multiple transformations than through this excellent book. The photographs in it are displayed in chronological order, so that they chart the highs and lows of the national experience before arriving at the present day. This arrangement allows the reader to grasp not only how far China has come during the period of economic reform since late 1978, but also to glimpse the specters that haunt the collective memory from the two decades before that. The book starts with iconic images of the Chinese Communist Party's Long March to power. There can have been few flights in the history of warfare more epic than that of the Party's retreat from its shattered bases in southern China to Yan'an, a dusty town on northern China's Loess plateau. Although only about 10,000 of an original 100,000 marchers reached the sanctuary of Yan'an, the 6,000-mile (9,600-km) march became one of the Party's defining myths and its veterans were to populate the senior councils of state up until the late 1990s. Pursued most of the way by Chiang Kai-shek's Kuomintang troops and often under attack from local warlord armies, the Communist's First Front Army was led by Mao Zedong through nine provinces and, in spite of the crude exaggerations of later propaganda, performed many heroic acts along the way, fording

→
Du Xiuxian, 1973

Marshal Ye Jianying holds court on the beach at a seaside resort in Hainan province. Ye played a key role in arresting the Gang of Four, which effectively ended the chaos of the Cultural Revolution.

Marschall Ye Jianying hält Hof am Strand eines Seebades in der Provinz Hainan. Ye spielte eine entscheidende Rolle bei der Verhaftung der Viererbande, mit der das Chaos der Kulturrevolution faktisch endete.

Le maréchal Ye Jianying tient sa cour sur la plage d'une station balnéaire de la province du Hénan. Il joua un rôle essentiel dans l'arrestation de la Bande des quatre, opération qui mit effectivement fin au chaos de la Révolution culturelle.

rivers, traversing mountain ranges, and trekking across bleak plateaus (photo on page 114/115). The shared experience of the Long March conferred much of the sense of cohesion and pride that were essential to the Communists' eventual victory over Chiang. On October 1, 1949, the "New China" of the People's Republic was founded (photo on page 119) amid genuine enthusiasm and hope for peace and the reconstruction of a country that had been torn apart by almost continuous warfare since 1911.

China Stands Up

The character of the revolution had been prefigured by formative experiences, such as the Long March, and the rural nature of the Party's main constituency. Unlike in the Soviet Union, where the revolution was fomented first and foremost by the urban proletariat, in China it was the peasant farmer who was the main subject of the revolution and its main agent. In many parts of the country, peasants led lives mired in poverty, indebtedness, natural calamities, cruelty, superstition, and suppression at the hands of local landlords. As Chairman Mao said, such peasants were "poor and blank," and therefore beautiful—revolutionary things could be written upon them. In the first few years of reconstruction, progress and success were surprisingly swift. One of the first key areas was in land reform. Overpopulation, a shortage of land, and regular natural disasters had made life tough for the overwhelming majority of Chinese for centuries. Thus, almost every change of power in Chinese history, dynastic or revolutionary, had been accompanied by re-allocations of land among those who tilled it and a rebalancing of the tax burden. The strains caused by the Korean War in the early years of Communist rule injected urgency into the land reform process. Class labels were assigned to different segments of the rural population and peasants were encouraged to hold "speak-bitterness" sessions to recall past oppression at the hands of the landlords (photos on pages 120, 121, 122/123). These landlords—the sustainers of a rural tradition that dated back to ancient times—were then virtually wiped out. An estimated two million were either executed or killed in the space of a few months, and those that were allowed to survive were assigned to till small, marginal plots of land. The ultimate aim of land reform, however, was not class struggle but to create the conditions for an efficient agricultural sector that was capable of producing a surplus of food that was needed for industrialization. Thus the Party wasted no time in moving toward what it regarded as the essential precursor to agricultural efficiency—collectivization. The rationale was that peasant farmers, once freed from the yoke of their oppressors, would work hard on plots of land they collectively tilled. But in the event, the incentives to work harder and produce surpluses proved insufficient and by the mid-1950s Mao was growing impatient because the agricultural surpluses that he badly wanted to see failed to materialize.

Thus, in 1958, the Chairman devised a solution that was to become the most enduring symbol of his belief that sheer force of will can overcome all obstacles. The Great Leap Forward brought the "People's Communes" into the countryside as the collectives were merged and life in them was reorganized along strict, virtually military lines. Wages were replaced with a work points system and people were forced to eat in communal dining rooms. Money, in some communes, was done away with altogether. Peasant farmers may have known, in their hearts, at the outset that their inhospitable land could not be coaxed into bumper yields merely by a few new techniques such as close planting, new seed strains, deep ploughing, and a few new tools, but these farmers were powerless to resist. The Great Leap did not account for rational objections or detailed analysis. It was more romantic than that. It was about overcoming what farmers, experts, scientists, and intellectuals said were insurmountable obstacles through human persistence. It aimed not only to transform man but also nature.

Impatient to get the country's industrialization program going, Mao decided not to wait for the hoped-for grain surpluses that the communes were expected to bring forth. Millions of farmers were exhorted to construct dams, irrigation schemes, and other public works. Farmers joined urban residents in building "backyard furnaces" all over the country and fed them with bicycles, cooking woks, and farm utensils—anything they could find that could be melted down (photos on pages 134, 135 and 136/137). Another obsession of the age was the extermination of pests; campaigns of extraordinary intensity against rats, mice, sparrows, and other vermin were waged across the nation, diverting labour from productive pursuits.

These policies, coupled with uncontrolled population growth—also exhorted by Mao—proved catastrophic for China. Yet it took a long time for the leaders in Beijing to form an accurate picture of how bad things really were. On the one hand, Mao had instituted such a climate of fear among the upper echelons of the Communist Party that nobody wanted to be the first to report bad news and, on the other, the purge of intellectuals and specialists during the "one hundred flowers campaign" of the mid-1950s had left the government virtually incapable of collecting and assessing statistics reliably. These deficiencies prepared the ground for a tragic parody of totalitarianism. Famine swept the country, hitting the poorest regions such as Tibet, Qinghai, Gansu, Henan, and Anhui the hardest. Harvests failed or fell short of targets almost everywhere as farmers engaged in futile attempts to make low-grade steel in mud furnaces, hunted down vermin, threw themselves into massive civil-works projects, or attended an endless series of political rallies eulogizing Mao's leadership and the wisdom of the commune system. But as millions of people starved, the reports that found their way to Mao were overwhelm-

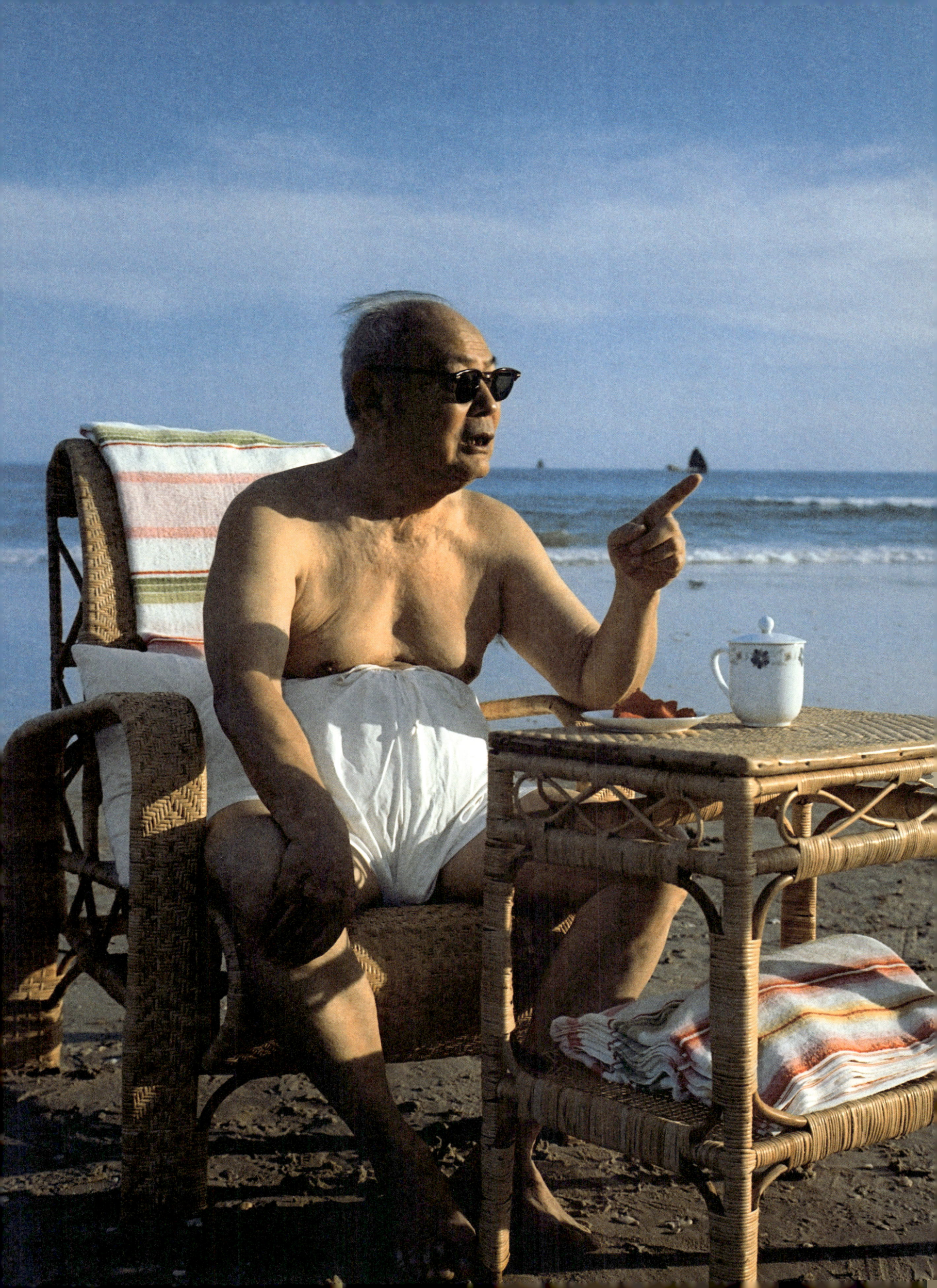

ingly positive. Absurdity became a propaganda staple; photographs were contrived to show crops growing so densely that they could support a person standing on top of the ears of grain.

A Bitter Harvest

Only one leader, Peng Dehuai, the Minister of Defence and a Long March veteran, had the courage to suggest that something was amiss with Mao's utopian vision and with the newly created communes. Even though Peng did not criticize Mao directly, but expressed his misgivings in a private letter to him during the Lushan conference in 1959, the Chairman's revenge was swift and uncompromising. Peng was disgraced and the fragile cohesion at the top of the Party among former comrades-in-arms was shattered, throwing China into a cycle of violence and persecution that lasted almost 20 years. The first campaign to be launched was against "rightist opportunists" and those who attempted to "split the Party"—code for people such as Peng who found fault with the communes and other aspects of Maoist policy. This made accurate reporting on the Great Leap's disasters even more perilous as critics could be arrested, shot, or shipped off to labour camps. By 1961, however, the leadership could no longer remain impervious to the calamity that had befallen China. It became clear that if the Party did not change its course, the new Communist regime could collapse. An estimated 30 million people had died in one of the worst man-made famines in history. Slowly and unevenly, the communes were scaled back, especially in areas where starvation was particularly widespread, such as in the central province of Anhui. Mao, however, remained defiant, refusing to recognize that the communes—his main contribution to the reconstruction of China since the 1949 revolution—had been an utter failure. This defiance in the face of his own grim record was to cloud Mao's actions and judgement henceforth, accentuating the suspicion he reserved for potential rivals and sharpening his sensitivity to criticism. Thus, when the Soviet Union's leader, Nikita Khrushchev, expressed his reservations over China's communes, Mao could not contain his fury, and relations between the two Communist giants began to crumble. In 1960, Moscow suddenly withdrew the industrial experts and advisors who were essential to several large-scale industrialization projects (photo on page 132/133).

One of the projects left in limbo was Beijing's plans to use Soviet technology to build an atomic bomb. Although Mao had dismissed the countries that had atomic weapons as "paper tigers" in the early 1950s, Beijing's quest to acquire nuclear-weapons technology was one of the most important projects in China's modernization program. In 1957, the golden year of Sino-Soviet relations, Moscow promised to help Beijing build the bomb. Visiting Moscow, Mao praised Soviet technology and said that the launch of the *Sputniks I* and *II*, as well as an intercontinental ballistic missile, showed that "The East wind is prevailing over the the West wind." But a few months later, another remark from Mao caused Khrushchev to wonder whether the plan to transfer nuclear technology to China was a risk better not taken. Mao urged socialist countries not to fear a nuclear war with the United States because even if "half of mankind died, the other half would remain while imperialism would be razed to the ground and the whole world would become socialist." But even after the Soviet's withdrawal of assistance, China persisted with its nuclear program and, in 1964, helped by Qian Xuesen, an American-trained nuclear physicist, China exploded a nuclear device for the first time. Three years later, at the height of the Cultural Revolution, China exploded its first hydrogen bomb.

The Great Proletarian Cultural Revolution (1966–76) had its origins in the failure of the Great Leap Forward and suspicion that infiltrated the top ranks of the Communist Party following the purge of Peng Dehuai. Millions of Chinese suffered or were killed as the nation was engulfed by cruelty and oppression on a horrific scale. Until this day, the events of the decade that ended with Mao's death in 1976 constitute a scar in the national psyche, and academic study of the period is forbidden. Mao was responsible for launching the Cultural Revolution in order to outmaneuver Liu Shaoqi, who had been president since 1959, Deng Xiaoping, and other leaders who appeared to believe that it was more important for China to be stronger and more prosperous rather than merely more "Red." This was anathema to Mao. To him, the revolution was going into reverse. He saw the bourgeoisie making a comeback while bureaucracy, hierarchy, and foreign influence proliferated. But above these transgressions, it was criticism of the Chairman himself that really irked, and it was no accident that the first target of Mao and his allies was a play, "The Dismissal of Hai Rui" by Wu Han. Wu had used the example of a virtuous official in the Ming dynasty who justly criticized the emperor to praise Peng Dehuai for having stood up to Mao over the Great Leap. Next on the list of targets were Peng Zhen, the reformist mayor of Beijing, Liu Shaoqi, and Deng. Of the three, Liu (photo on page 139), who was once regarded as Mao's successor, suffered the harshest treatment, being labeled a "traitor, renegade, and scab" before being tortured and eventually dying in prison in 1969. Deng escaped physical torment, but was banished to the countryside, where he tended pigs and repaired tractors while waiting for the political winds to change.

A Decade of Chaos

Although the Cultural Revolution got underway following Mao's celebrated swim in the Yangtze river in the summer of 1966 (photo on

"Looking back to the early 1960s, I revisit one of modern China's most bizarre periods, an era of unprecedented fanaticism. On one hand, those years saw the country in the grips of economic stagnation and individual deprivation. The people struggled to keep death from their door; on the other hand, it was a time of intense political passions, when starving citizens tightened their belts and followed the Party in its Communist experiment. We may have been famished, but we considered ourselves to be the luckiest people in the world. Two-thirds of the world's people, we believed, were living in dire misery, and it was our sacred duty to rescue them from the sea of suffering in which they were drowning."

MO YAN (1955–), author, 2003

page 142/143, showing a similar scene of Mao's first swim in 1956), it did not reach its violent crescendo until 1967 and 1968, when rival troops of Red Guards, all professing a purer loyalty to Mao, fought against each other as well as the perceived class enemies, traitors, and foreign sympathizers in their midst. In the central city of Wuhan, there were clashes on a scale reminiscent of a civil war and in the southern province of Guangxi, groups with artillery destroyed buildings, killing thousands. Most schools and universities were shut down, teachers humiliated, and many physical manifestations of Chinese culture and that of minority nationalities, including most of the monasteries in Tibet, were reduced to rubble. The chaos provided a perfect platform for the ascendancy of opportunists and thugs, symbolized by the Gang of Four, led by Jiang Qing, Mao's wife. But by 1969, the Chairman had begun to feel that the violence had gone on long enough. He retreated from radicalism and demobilized the Red Guards, sending many of them into the countryside to learn more bucolic pursuits from the peasants. Back in Beijing, the beneficiaries of the Cultural Revolution, especially Lin Biao, by then Mao's designated successor and the compiler of the Little Red Book, appeared to be consolidating their positions at the pinnacle of Chinese power. But the truth, in fact, was otherwise. As with many of the men who hoped to succeed him, Lin was in the process of a fall from grace. Seen in a rare unposed photograph with Premier Zhou Enlai, on page 182, as they decide upon the wording of a statement, the suspicion that would become Lin's undoing can already be seen glowing in Mao's eyes. Whatever was lurking between Mao and Lin then would come to a head by September 1971, when Lin and his allies allegedly attempted to assassinate the Chairman. They were killed in a plane crash in Mongolia while allegedly trying to flee to the Soviet Union.

At the end of the Cultural Revolution, the country was utterly exhausted and at its lowest ebb economically for hundreds of years (with the possible exception of during the Great Leap, when statistics were unreliable). Per capita income in 1976 was much lower than it had been 150 years earlier in the Qing dynasty or during the glory days of the Ming. When Mao died in 1976, a few months after his loyal Premier Zhou succumbed at last to cancer, neither man could have had the faintest inkling of the extraordinary renaissance that awaited China in the last two decades of the 20th century. It must have seemed to Zhou, in particular, that all the effort of the Long March, the Revolution, and the years since had achieved little. When finally the official verdict on the Cultural Revolution was published in 1981, it was bleak. It had been "responsible for the most severe setback and the heaviest losses suffered by the Party and the people since the founding of the People's Republic," the verdict said. Mao had made "gross mistakes," but these were more than offset by his contributions.

Then, the Era of Deng

Before the next era of reform and an opening up could be launched, several key issues needed attention. The radical Gang of Four had to be neutralized and Hua Guofeng, the ineffectual loyalist who Mao appointed as his successor, had to be persuaded to step aside for a man who was to steer China's destiny: Deng Xiaoping. Deng, who by the end of 1978 had obviously assumed the reins of power, was to do more than any other 20th-century leader to push China towards its long-held goals of wealth and power, enabling hundreds of millions of people to raise themselves out of poverty. In December 1978, it all began at the Third Plenum of the Eleventh Central Committee, which committed the Party to a program of fundamental economic modernization, reform, and engagement with the outside world that violated almost every tenet of the Cultural Revolution. But it also became clear early on, with the suppression of the "Democracy Wall" movement in Beijing, that Deng had no intention of allowing the zeal for reform to spread from economics to politics. At first Deng used the demonstrations and the big character posters that were pasted onto a wall at Xidan to help outmaneuver his political rivals, and then cracked down on the movement mercilessly. Wei Jingsheng, an electrician at Beijing zoo who was a leader of the movement, was to spend all but a few months of the next 18 years behind bars. This intolerance for political freedom would be seen again in 1989, when the People's Liberation Army, backed by tanks, crushed pro-democracy protests in central Beijing, killing hundreds, perhaps thousands of unarmed citizens. Nevertheless, for much of the 1980s, politicians in the West felt that Deng, a bridge-playing soccer fan who loved to eat croissants, was a man they could deal with, perhaps even a kindred spirit. Shortly after taking power, Deng started planning a visit to the United States, picking up where Richard Nixon had left off during this ground-breaking trip to China in 1972 (photos on pages 230 and 232/233). During his U.S. visit in 1979, he cut a very different figure from the austere, nationalistic Mao or the type of stodgy Soviet leader that Americans had become accustomed to; Deng donned a Stetsen for photographers and seemed keen to engage ordinary Americans in conversation. The positive impression he made was an important part of China's changing image in the minds of Westerners, an image that until the Tiananmen massacre in 1989 had as much to do with pandas, ping pong, and investment opportunities as with Mao suits and Communism.

Deng secured the appointment of his two key protégés, Hu Yaobang and Zhao Ziyang, and set about charting a course out of the economic crisis that China was in. Agriculture was decollectivized and households were encouraged to contract land. Farmers produced a fixed amount for the State and then were free to dispose of the surplus as they

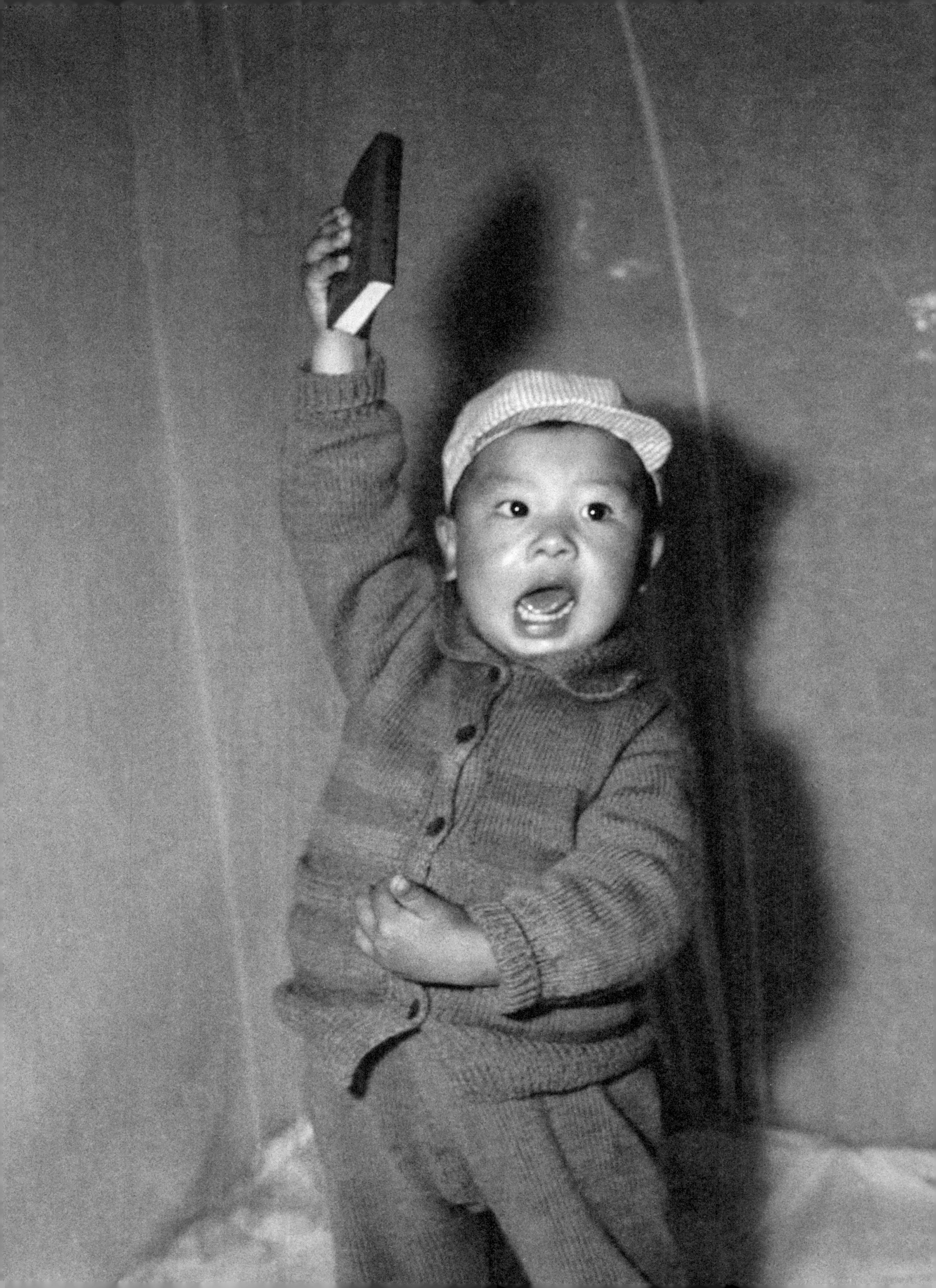

←

Xiao Zhuang, 1970

A child in Nanjing holds up a copy of Quotations from Chairman Mao Zedong, *shouting "Long live Chairman Mao."*

Ein Kind in Nanjing hält ein Exemplar der Worte des Vorsitzenden Mao *hoch und ruft „Lang lebe der Vorsitzende Mao".*

Un enfant de Nankin brandit un exemplaire des Citations du Président Mao *et crie « Longue vie au Président Mao. »*

wished. Control over industry was decentralized and factory managers delegated decision-making power. Foreign trade and investment was encouraged and joint ventures set up. Special Economic Zones, enclaves where capitalist reforms could be piloted without fear of contaminating the rest of the country, were established as China pursued a vision of "socialism with Chinese characteristics" in which some people were allowed to get rich before others. But as the country came alive, so did undesirable trends such as inflation, official corruption, pornography, and other forms of "spiritual pollution," which spawned considerable criticism. Even more serious, in Deng's eyes at least, was a tendency toward "bourgeois liberalism"—Party-speak for Western-style democracy—among certain sections of society. Both Hu and Zhao, who were seen as anointed successors, fell foul of their relatively relaxed attitude toward democracy. Hu was sacked in 1987 for not taking a hard enough line against a series of student protests, and Zhao was dismissed in 1989 for failing to support the use of military force against protestors. The Tiananmen massacre was to become the darkest hour in Deng's tenure, but did not prove to be his last important act. In 1992, at 87 years old and hard of hearing, he traveled to southern China to inject energy into economic reforms that had lost impetus in the aftermath of Tiananmen. The trip, which became known as the "southern tour," laid the foundations for the economic boom that swept China in the 1990s and sidelined a coterie of political conservatives who might—but for Deng—have succeeded in turning back the clock.

As the 1990s progressed, the boom unleashed by the "southern tour" grew into an event of global significance. The inflow of foreign investment into factories along the southern and eastern seaboards turned China into the "workshop of the world." Soon, the products on sale in supermarkets in Europe and the U.S. began to be sourced increasingly from smokestack zones in the Pearl river delta north of Hong Kong or from the 15 cities that cluster around Shanghai. China's trade surplus with the developed world started to balloon, while its factories bought so large a volume of commodities and components from its Asian neighbours that the U.S. looked to Beijing as a stabilizing influence during the Asian financial crisis at the end of the decade. At home, however, the gains were not evenly spread. The beneficiaries of the reform era were an emerging wealthy or middle class whose members, by the early years of the 21st century, were beginning to lead conspicuously consumer-oriented lifestyles, snapping up luxury goods, sending their children to study in exclusive private schools overseas or ivy league U.S. universities, and spending their holidays in villas on South-East Asian paradise islands. Much of the rest of the country, however, was left hardly affected by the coastal economic boom, leading lives that differed little from the 1980s. The yawning gulf between rich and poor, wider in China than in almost any other large nation, had become not only an embarrassment for a government that once professed egalitarian ideals but also a potentially incendiary social issue.

One Final Lap to the Olympics

Successive governments have sought to tackle this problem; Jiang Zemin sought to kick-start the development of inland and western areas of the country with a campaign called the "Big Development of the West" in the early 21st century. His successor, Hu Jintao, cultivated a more personal approach, spending time with farming families, coal miners, and other disadvantaged groups to promote his signature policy of "putting people first." Neither leader, though, could come up with an effective way of stopping or reversing the chronic environmental degradation that China's economic take-off has visited upon the country. As Beijing prepared to hold the Olympic Games in August 2008—and to showcase its achievements over the past 60 years of Communist Party rule—the biggest question hanging over the games' organizers, participants, and potential spectators was whether the thick plume of pollution that often hangs over the capital could be cleared away in time for the "greatest show on earth."

Historischer Hintergrund

China 1949–heute

Von James Kynge

„O Worte, sie sind nur unzureichende Behälter für das, was die Zeit gestohlen hat, uralte Bäume, Kanzeln gleich, und das Spiel."

Dies schrieb John Clare, ein britischer Poet des 17. Jahrhunderts, um die wohlbekannte Ernüchterung auszudrücken, die Autoren empfinden, wenn ihnen zur Schilderung des ganzen Prunks der Geschichte in all ihren subtilen Schattierungen einzig Worte zur Verfügung stehen. Gleichgültig, wie raffiniert die Worte zu Papier gebracht werden, ist das Ergebnis doch bisweilen nur ein blasser Abglanz des Gewesenen, ein bloßer Umriss der Menschen und Ereignisse, die ihrer lebendigen Emotionen beraubt sind. Fotografien andererseits sind mächtig genug, um die Lücken zu füllen. Sie dokumentieren nicht nur die Einzelheiten des Alltags – wie die Kleidung der Menschen, das Aussehen der Gebäude, die Lage der Dinge –, sondern sie vermitteln auch die Empfindungen der Zeit. Dies geschieht durch ihre einzigartige Fähigkeit, Unsichtbares zu suggerieren, es transparent zu machen und darauf anzuspielen. Fotos ist damit eine transzendente Natur eigen, die den Betrachter über die Form hinaus zur Bedeutung führt, fast auf die gleiche Weise, in der Zhuangzi, ein chinesischer Philosoph des 4. Jahrhunderts, das Extrahieren von Gedanken beschrieb:

„Es gibt die Fischreuse wegen der Fische; sobald man den Fisch gefangen hat, kann man die Reuse vergessen. Es gibt die Kaninchenschlinge wegen der Kaninchen; sobald man das Kaninchen hat, kann man die Schlinge vergessen. Es gibt Worte wegen der Bedeutung; sobald man die Bedeutung hat, kann man die Worte vergessen. Wo kann ich einen Mann finden, der Worte vergessen hat, so dass ich mit ihm Worte wechseln kann?"

Dieser Fotoband, zusammengetragen und herausgegeben von dem mit dem Pulitzerpreis ausgezeichneten Fotografen Liu Heung Shing, verfolgt die Geschichte Chinas von 1948 – dem Jahr vor der Ausrufung der Volksrepublik China – bis 2008, dem Jahr, in dem China seinen Platz unter den großen Nationen der Welt einnehmen und die Olympischen Spiele in Peking ausrichten wird. Der hier umfasste Zeitraum von 60 Jahren entspricht der biblischen Definition eines Lebensalters, und doch sind die darin geschilderten Veränderungen derart grundlegend und weitreichend, dass es scheint, als sei die Zeit verdichtet. Seit Tausenden von Jahren war China ein Land der Dörfer und Marktflecken, verbunden durch Wege, die im Winter zu Schlamm, im Sommer zu Staub wurden; eine Nation, in der der Dialekt eines Dorfes im Nachbardorf häufig nicht verstanden wurde; ein Wirtschaftssystem, das ungeachtet hervorragender Leistungen auf dem Gebiet technischer Innovationen bis weit ins 20. Jahrhundert hinein überwiegend von Muskelkraft angetrieben wurde. Und doch wurde in dem Zeitraum, den die Seiten dieses Buches umschreiben,

Chinas 1000-jährige Tradition zerschlagen, verworfen und durch neue Realitäten ersetzt, von denen viele noch im Begriff sind, sich herauszubilden. Seit der Revolution hat China gleichzeitig mehrere ökonomische, politische, soziale, geistige und kulturelle Umbrüche erlebt, oder es erlebt sie noch. Während Hunderte Millionen von Bauern in die Städte übersiedeln, häufig an die Fließbänder der Fabriken, aber zuweilen auch in spiegelnde neue Bürogebäude, verwandelt sich China von einem ländlich strukturierten in ein städtisch geprägtes Land. Die Verschiebung von der Agrar- zur Industriegesellschaft wird begleitet von einem technologischen Aufstieg. Das heute nicht mehr nur von Muskelkraft bewegte China erbaut derzeit wöchentlich drei neue Kraftwerke, und in einem einzigen Jahr entstehen ausreichend Elektrizitätswerke, um den Bedarf eines Landes wie Großbritannien zu decken. Auch in geografischer Hinsicht ändert sich die Situation. Dank eines riesigen neuen Straßennetzes, das ehemals abgelegene Gebiete mit dem Rest des Landes und gleichzeitig mit der Welt verbindet, verbreiten sich zum ersten Mal in Chinas langer Geschichte Entwicklung und wirtschaftlicher Wohlstand von den Küstenregionen im Osten und Süden auch ins Landesinnere. In politischer Hinsicht hat sich die Lage um fast 360 Grad gedreht. Nachdem man die ersten 30 Jahre nach der Revolution damit zubrachte, durch Verstaatlichung sämtlichen Privateigentums und Reglementierung der Bevölkerung in einem hierarchisch angelegten bürokratischen Kontrollsystem eine kommunistische Diktatur zu errichten, arbeitete Peking in den letzten drei Dekaden daran, diese Maßnahmen wieder aufzuheben. Privateigentum ebenso wie Privatfirmen und Aktienmärkte sind jetzt im Begriff sich zu entfalten. Wo sich die Menschen einst in vorgeschriebenes Blau oder Grün kleideten und die Wahlmöglichkeiten der Konsumenten begrenzt waren, ließ die zunehmende Individualisierung einen Markt mit einem schwindelerregenden Angebot materieller Vielfalt entstehen. Das im Grunde einzige Segment der Gesellschaft, das sich treu geblieben ist, ist die Kommunistische Partei und ihre Einstellung zum Machterhalt; Kunden bei Starbucks in Peking mögen zwischen Latte macchiato, Espresso, Cappuccino und Frappucino wählen können, an den Wahlurnen sind derartige Freiheiten bislang noch nicht angekommen.

Dieses Buch will den Leser dabei unterstützen, sich Chinas turbulenter Geschichte zu nähern und die vielen Wandlungen des Landes zu verstehen. Die chronologische Ordnung der Fotografien bildet die Höhepunkte und Tiefen der nationalen Entwicklung ab, ehe sie in der Gegenwart ankommen. So kann der Leser begreifen, wie weit China durch die Periode wirtschaftlicher Neuorientierung seit Ende 1978 gekommen ist, sie lässt ihn darüber hinaus auch einen kurzen Blick auf die Schreckgespenster aus den beiden vorangegangenen Jahrzehnten werfen, die das kollektive Gedächtnis belasten. Das Buch beginnt mit zutiefst symbolischen Bildern vom Langen Marsch der Kommunistischen Partei Chinas an die Macht. Es gibt in der Militärgeschichte wohl nur wenige so heroische Rückzüge, wie den der Partei von ihren zerstörten südchinesischen Standorten nach Yan'an, einem staubigen Ort auf dem nordchinesischen Lößplateau. Obgleich nur etwa 10.000 der ursprünglich 100.000 Marschierenden die Zuflucht Yan'an erreichten, wurde der 9600 Kilometer lange Marsch zu einem der Gründungsmythen der Partei, und seine Veteranen gehörten bis in die späten 1990er-Jahre hinein den obersten Staatsräten an. Fast ständig von den Kuomintang-Truppen Chiang Kai-sheks verfolgt und häufig Angriffen lokaler Kriegsherren ausgesetzt, wurde die Kommunistische Erste Frontarmee von Mao Zedong durch neun Provinzen geführt und vollbrachte unterwegs viele heroische Taten, durchwatete Flüsse, überquerte Gebirgszüge und zog über kahle Hochebenen (vgl. Abb. S. 114/115) – Ereignisse, die von der Propaganda später übertrieben dargestellt wurden. Die gemeinsame Erfahrung des Langen Marsches trug einen Gutteil zum Zusammengehörigkeitsgefühl und Stolz bei, die maßgeblich waren für den Sieg der Kommunisten über Chiang Kai-shek. Am 1. Oktober 1949 wurde mit wirklicher Begeisterung und Hoffnung auf Frieden und den Wiederaufbau eines seit 1911 durch nahezu ständige kriegerische Auseinandersetzung zerrissenen Landes das „neue" China der Volksrepublik gegründet (vgl. Abb. S. 119).

China erhebt sich

Der Charakter der Revolution hatte sich durch prägende Erfahrungen wie den Langen Marsch und die bäuerliche Herkunft der Hauptanhängerschaft der Partei angekündigt. Anders als in der Sowjetunion, wo die Revolution in erster Linie vom städtischen Proletariat getragen worden war, galt in China der Kleinbauer als hauptsächlicher Nutznießer der Revolution und als ihr wichtigster Akteur. In vielen Teilen des Landes fristeten die Bauern ein Leben in tiefster Armut, bedrängt durch Verschuldung, Naturkatastrophen, Aberglauben, Grausamkeit und Unterdrückung vonseiten lokaler Grundbesitzer. Wie der Vorsitzende Mao sagte, waren solche Bauern „arm und unbeschrieben", und deshalb boten sie eine jungfräuliche Leinwand, auf die man wunderbare revolutionäre Bilder malen konnte. In den Anfangsjahren des Wiederaufbaus kamen Fortschritt und Erfolg überraschend schnell. Als einer der ersten Bereiche wurde die Landreform in Angriff genommen. Seit Jahrhunderten hatten Überbevölkerung, Landknappheit und regelmäßige Naturkatastrophen der überwältigenden Mehrheit der Chinesen ein hartes Leben beschert. Folglich war nahezu jeder Machtwechsel in der chinesischen Geschichte, gleich ob dynastisch oder revolutionär, begleitet von einer Umverteilung des Landes an jene, die es bearbeiteten, und von einem Ausgleich der Steuerlast. Die in den frühen Jahren der kommunistischen Herrschaft vom

Koreakrieg ausgelösten Spannungen machten eine Landreform vordringlich. Den verschiedenen Schichten der Landbevölkerung wurden Klassenbezeichnungen zugeteilt und die Bauern angehalten, Sitzungen abzuhalten, in denen offen Anklage gegen die Vergangenheit erhoben wurde, um an die frühere Unterdrückung seitens der Grundbesitzer zu erinnern (vgl. Abb. S. 120, 121 und S. 122/123). Diese Schicht der Grundbesitzer – von alters her Träger der ländlichen Tradition – wurde in der Folge so gut wie ausgelöscht. Geschätzte zwei Millionen Menschen wurden innerhalb weniger Monate umgebracht. Denjenigen, die überlebten, wurde ein Stückchen Land mit wenig ertragreichem Boden zugewiesen, das sie zu bestellen hatten. Das eigentliche Ziel der Landreform war jedoch nicht der Klassenkampf, vielmehr sollte sie die Bedingungen für eine leistungsstarke Landwirtschaft schaffen, die in der Lage war, den für die Industrialisierung nötigen Mehrertrag an Nahrungsmitteln zu produzieren. Entsprechend nahm die Partei die aus ihrer Sicht unvermeidliche Vorstufe landwirtschaftlicher Effizienz, die Kollektivierung, in Angriff. Dahinter stand die Überlegung, dass die vom Joch der Unterdrückung befreiten Bauern auf den von ihnen gemeinsam bestellten Ländereien hart arbeiten würden. Schließlich erwiesen sich jedoch die Anreize, härter zu arbeiten und Mehrertrag zu erwirtschaften, als unzureichend, und um die Mitte der 1950er-Jahre verlor Mao angesichts des ausbleibenden Mehrertrags, den er so dringend benötigte, die Geduld.

Also ersann der Große Vorsitzende 1958 eine Lösung, die zum bleibenden Symbol seiner Überzeugung werden sollte, dass reine Willenskraft alle Hindernisse überwinden kann. Der Große Sprung nach vorn brachte die „Volkskommunen" aufs Land, während man die Kollektive vereinigte und das Leben in ihnen gemäß strenger, praktisch militärischer Richtlinien neu geregelt wurde. An die Stelle von Löhnen trat ein Punktesystem, und die Menschen wurden gezwungen, in Gemeinschaftskantinen zu essen. In einigen Kommunen wurde das Geld gänzlich abgeschafft. Die Kleinbauern haben im Innersten wahrscheinlich von Anfang an gewusst, dass es nicht möglich ist, ihrem unwirtlichen Land nur durch einige neue Techniken wie enge Aussaat, andere Saatgutstämme, tiefes Pflügen und einzelne neue Werkzeuge großartige Erträge abzuringen, aber diese Bauern waren zu Widerstand nicht in der Lage. Der Große Sprung berücksichtigte keine rationalen Einwände oder detaillierte Analysen. Das Bestreben war weit romantischer. Es ging darum, durch menschliche Beharrlichkeit zu bewältigen, was Bauern, Experten, Wissenschaftler und Intellektuelle für unüberwindliche Hindernisse hielten. Das Ziel war, nicht nur den Menschen, sondern auch die Natur umzukrempeln.

Mao, der darüber hinaus das Programm zur Industrialisierung des Landes voranbringen wollte, beschloss, nicht auf die von den Volkskommunen erhofften Getreideüberschüsse zu warten. Millionen von Bauern

„Wenn ich an die frühen 1960er-Jahre zurückdenke, gerate ich in eine der bizarrsten Perioden des modernen China, eine Zeit des beispiellosen Fanatismus. Einerseits befand sich das Land in jener Zeit im Würgegriff wirtschaftlicher Stagnation und individueller Entbehrungen. Die Menschen kämpften ums Überleben; andererseits war es eine Zeit glühender politischer Erregung, als hungernde Bürger ihre Gürtel enger schnallten und der Partei bei ihren kommunistischen Experimenten folgten. Wir mögen gehungert haben, aber wir hielten uns für die glücklichsten Menschen der Erde. Zwei Drittel der Weltbevölkerung, glaubten wir, lebten in äußerstem Elend und es war unsere heilige Pflicht, sie aus diesem Meer des Leidens zu erretten, in dem sie zu ertrinken drohten."

MO YAN (1955–), Autor, 2003

wurden angetrieben, Dämme, Bewässerungsanlagen und andere öffentliche Projekte zu bauen. Bauern standen Stadtbewohnern im ganzen Land beim Bau von „Hinterhof-Hochöfen" zur Seite, die sie mit Fahrrädern, Woks, landwirtschaftlichem Gerät, mit Allem, was sich einschmelzen ließ, befüllten (vgl. Abb. S. 134, 135 und 136/137). Ein weiteres dringendes Anliegen der Zeit war die Vernichtung von Schädlingen; man zog landesweit mit außerordentlicher Vehemenz gegen Ratten, Mäuse, Spatzen und anderes Ungeziefer zu Felde und hielt damit Arbeitskräfte von produktiven Aktivitäten ab.

Diese Strategien, gepaart mit dem ebenfalls von Mao geforderten ungebremsten Bevölkerungswachstum, erwiesen sich für China als verheerend. Dennoch brauchte die Führungsriege in Peking lange, um sich ein realistisches Bild von der desaströsen Lage zu verschaffen. Zum einen hatte Mao in den höheren Kadern der Kommunistischen Partei für eine derart angsterfüllte Atmosphäre gesorgt, dass niemand der Überbringer schlechter Nachrichten sein wollte, zum anderen hatten die Säuberungsaktionen gegen Intellektuelle und Funktionäre Mitte der 1950er-Jahre, während der Hundert-Blumen-Bewegung, die Regierung faktisch der Möglichkeit beraubt, sich verlässliches statistisches Material zu beschaffen. Diese Mängel bereiteten den Boden für eine tragische Parodie von Totalitarismus. Das Land wurde von einer Hungersnot heimgesucht, die die ärmsten Provinzen wie Tibet, Qinghai, Gansu, Henan und Anhui am härtesten traf. Es gab Missernten oder solche, die nahezu flächendeckend die angestrebten Quoten verfehlten, während die Bauern sinnlose Versuche unternahmen, in Lehmöfen minderwertigen Stahl zu kochen, Ungeziefer zur Strecke brachten, sich in gewaltige öffentliche Bauprojekte stürzten oder einem endlosen Turnus politischer Kundgebungen beiwohnten, in denen Maos Führung und die Weisheit des Systems der Volkskommunen gepriesen wurden. Während Millionen von Menschen hungerten, verkündeten die Berichte, die Mao erreichten, ausnahmslos Positives. Absurdität wurde zur Grundlage der Propaganda; auf manipulierten Fotos stand das Getreide so dicht, dass es einen auf den Ähren stehenden Menschen tragen konnte.

Eine bittere Ernte

Nur ein führender Politiker, Peng Dehuai, Verteidigungsminister und Veteran des Langen Marsches, hatte den Mut, darauf hinzuweisen, dass etwas an Maos utopischer Vision und den neu geschaffenen Volkskommunen nicht stimmte. Wenngleich Peng Mao nicht direkt kritisierte, sondern seine Befürchtungen in einem privaten Brief während der Konferenz von Lushan 1959 äußerte, war die Vergeltung des Vorsitzenden schnell und kompromisslos. Peng fiel in Ungnade, der brüchige Zusammenhalt unter den ehemaligen Kampfgenossen an der Parteispitze

zerbrach und stürzte China in einen Kreislauf aus Gewalt und Verfolgung, der fast 20 Jahre andauern sollte. Der erste Feldzug wandte sich gegen „rechtsgerichtete Opportunisten" und jene, die versuchten, „die Partei zu spalten" – das war die Bezeichnung für Personen wie Peng, die etwas an den Volkskommunen und anderen Aspekten der Politik Maos auszusetzen hatten. Danach wurde es noch gefährlicher, wahrheitsgemäß über die katastrophalen Folgen des Großen Sprungs zu berichten, da Kritiker festgenommen, erschossen oder in Arbeitslagern interniert wurden. 1961 konnte die Führung schließlich gegenüber dem Fiasko, das China ereilt hatte, nicht länger die Augen verschließen. Sollte die Partei ihren Kurs nicht ändern, so war klar, dass das neue kommunistische Regime stürzen würde. Schätzungsweise 30 Millionen Chinesen waren in einer der schlimmsten, von Menschen verursachten Hungersnöte der Geschichte umgekommen. Langsam und unsystematisch wurden die Volkskommunen eingeschränkt, insbesondere in Gegenden, wo die Hungersnot am größten war, wie in der zentralen Provinz Anhui. Gleichwohl blieb Mao unbelehrbar und weigerte sich anzuerkennen, dass die Volkskommunen – sein Hauptbeitrag zum Wiederaufbau Chinas nach der Revolution von 1949 – sich als völliger Fehlschlag erwiesen hatten. Dieser trotzige Widerstand sollte fortan einen Schatten auf Maos Taten und sein Urteil werfen. Er wurde potenziellen Rivalen gegenüber immer misstrauischer, und seine Unfähigkeit, Kritik zu ertragen, nahm zu. In der Folge konnte Mao seinen Zorn kaum beherrschen, als der sowjetische Präsident Nikita Chruschtschow seine Vorbehalte gegenüber Chinas Volkskommunen zum Ausdruck brachte, und die Beziehungen zwischen den beiden kommunistischen Riesenreichen begannen sich stetig zu verschlechtern. 1960 zog Moskau ohne Vorankündigung die Experten und Berater ab, die für mehrere große Industrialisierungsprojekte von entscheidender Bedeutung waren (vgl. Abb. S. 132/133).

Eines der unerledigten Projekte betraf Pekings Pläne, die sowjetische Technologie zum Bau einer Atombombe zu nutzen. Obgleich Mao zu Anfang der 50er-Jahre die über Atomwaffen verfügenden Länder als „Papiertiger" abgetan hatte, war das Streben nach dem Besitz nuklearer Waffen eines der wichtigsten Vorhaben in Chinas Modernisierungsprogramm. 1957, im goldenen Jahr der chinesisch-sowjetischen Beziehungen, hatte Moskau versprochen, Peking beim Bau der Bombe zu helfen. Anlässlich eines Besuchs in Moskau rühmte Mao die sowjetische Technologie und sagte, der Start der Sputniks I und II sowie die Interkontinentalraketen zeigten, dass „der Ostwind dem Westwind überlegen ist". Einige Monate später ließ eine weitere Bemerkung Maos Chruschtschow jedoch an der Richtigkeit des Plans, Nukleartechnik an China weiterzugeben, zweifeln. Mao empfahl den sozialistischen Ländern, den Nuklearkrieg mit den Vereinigten Staaten nicht zu fürchten, denn selbst

→

Tang Desheng, 1970

Once every few hundred years, the Grand Canal of China undergoes reconstruction, here in 1970. China sent more than a million Chinese intellectuals and workers to repair the Grand Canal. It took three years and the mobilization of people from 13 neighboring counties of Jiangsu province.

Chinas Großer Kanal wurde im Abstand von mehreren hundert Jahren saniert, so auch 1970. Zu diesem Zweck wurden über eine Million chinesischer Intellektueller und Arbeiter zur Reparatur abgeordnet. Sie dauerte drei Jahre und mobilisierte die Bevölkerung aus 13 benachbarten Kreisen der Provinz Jiangsu.

Régulièrement au cours de l'histoire, le Grand canal de Chine doit subir des travaux de reconstruction. En 1970, la Chine envoya plus d'un million d'intellectuels et d'ouvriers pour le réparer. Le chantier dura trois ans et mobilisa la population du 13 cantons avoisinants.

wenn „die Hälfte der Menschheit umkäme, bliebe die andere Hälfte erhalten, während der Imperialismus ausgelöscht und die ganze Welt sozialistisch würde". Selbst nach dem Entzug der sowjetischen Unterstützung hielt China an seinem Nuklearprogramm fest, und es gelang ihm 1964 mithilfe von Qian Xuesen, einem in den Vereinigten Staaten ausgebildeten Physiker, die erste Atombombe zu zünden. Drei Jahre später, auf dem Höhepunkt der Kulturrevolution, zündete China seine erste Wasserstoffbombe.

Zwei Umstände waren ursächlich für die Große Proletarische Kulturrevolution (1966–1976): Zum einen war der Große Sprung nach vorn gescheitert, zum anderen waren die obersten Kader der Kommunistischen Partei nach dem Sturz von Peng Dehuai voller Misstrauen. Millionen von Chinesen litten oder wurden getötet, als die Nation in einem Meer von Grausamkeit und Unterdrückung versank. Die Ereignisse dieses Jahrzehnts, das mit Maos Tod 1976 endete, hinterließen in der Psyche der Nation eine noch heute schmerzende Narbe, und wissenschaftliche Untersuchungen dieser Zeit sind verboten. Mao hatte die Kulturrevolution vorangetrieben, um Liu Shaoqi, Präsident seit 1959, Deng Xiaoping und andere Führer auszubooten, die anscheinend glaubten, es sei für China wichtiger, stärker und wohlhabender zu werden, als nur einfach kommunistischer. Diese Vorstellung war Mao ein Gräuel. Aus seiner Sicht hatte die Revolution den Rückwärtsgang eingelegt. Die Ausbreitung von Bürokratie, Hierarchie und der Einfluss des Auslandes kündeten für ihn die Rückkehr der Bourgeoisie an. Schwerer noch als diese Fehlentwicklungen traf allerdings die Kritik am Vorsitzenden selbst, und es war kein Zufall, dass sich Mao und seine Verbündeten als erste Zielscheibe das Theaterstück „Die Entlassung von Hai Rui" von Wu Han aussuchten. Wu hatte den Fall eines integren Beamten der Ming-Dynastie, der zu Recht den Kaiser provozierte, dazu benutzt, Peng Dehuai zu unterstützen, weil dieser Mao wegen des Großen Sprungs kritisiert hatte. Die nächsten Angriffsziele waren Peng Zhen, der reformerische Bürgermeister von Peking, Liu Shaoqi und Deng. Von den Dreien erfuhr Liu (Abb. S. 139), der einst als Maos Nachfolger galt, die härteste Behandlung; man schimpfte ihn „Verräter, Abtrünniger und Halunke", ehe er gefoltert wurde und schließlich 1969 im Gefängnis starb. Deng entging körperlicher Peinigung, wurde allerdings aufs Land verbannt, wo er Schweine hütete und Traktoren reparierte und darauf wartete, dass sich der politische Wind drehte.

Ein chaotisches Jahrzehnt

Obgleich die Kulturrevolution nach Maos berühmtem Bad im Jangtse im Sommer 1966 begann (vgl. Abb. S. 142/143, die eine ähnliche Szene zeigt: Maos erstes Bad im Jahr 1955), erreichte sie ihren gewalttäti-

gen Höhepunkt erst 1967 und 1968, als rivalisierende Truppen der Roten Garden, die ihre jeweils größere Loyalität zu Mao beteuerten, gegeneinander und gegen diejenigen in ihrer Mitte kämpften, die sie für Klassenfeinde, Verräter und Sympathisanten des Auslands hielten. In der zentral gelegenen Stadt Wuhan ereigneten sich Zusammenstöße im Ausmaß von Bürgerkriegen, und in der südlichen Provinz Guangxi zerstörten mit Artillerie bewaffnete Gruppen Gebäude und töteten Tausende. Die meisten Schulen und Universitäten wurden geschlossen, Lehrer gedemütigt und zahlreiche Zeugnisse der chinesischen Kultur und von Minderheiten, darunter die meisten tibetischen Klöster, in Schutt und Asche gelegt. Das herrschende Chaos bot eine ausgezeichnete Plattform für den Aufstieg von Opportunisten und Schlägern, personifiziert in der von Maos Frau Jiang Qing geführten Viererbande. 1969 begann der Vorsitzende gleichwohl zu ahnen, dass die Gewalt lang genug geherrscht hatte. Er wandte sich vom Radikalismus ab und löste die Roten Garden auf, von denen er viele aufs Land schickte, wo sie von den Bauern eine bukolischere Lebensweise erlernen sollten. In Peking festigten die Nutznießer der Kulturrevolution, insbesondere Lin Biao, unterdessen designierter Nachfolger Maos und Herausgeber der Mao-Bibel, anscheinend ihre Positionen an der Spitze der chinesischen Staatsmacht. In Wahrheit verhielt es sich jedoch anders. Wie viele von Maos potenziellen Nachfolgern stand auch Lin kurz davor, in Ungnade zu fallen. Auf einem der seltenen ungestellten Fotos auf Seite 182, auf dem er mit Premier Zhou Enlai den Wortlaut einer Erklärung festlegt, lauert der Argwohn, der Lins Ruin bedeuten sollte, bereits in Maos Blick. Was auch immer sich zwischen Mao und Lin zusammenbraute, sollte sich im September 1971 entladen, als Lin und seine Verbündeten angeblich versuchten, den Vorsitzenden zu ermorden. Sie kamen zu Tode, als das Flugzeug, mit dem sie wahrscheinlich in die Sowjetunion fliehen wollten, über der Mongolei abstürzte.

Am Ende der Kulturrevolution war das Land völlig entkräftet und wirtschaftlich an einem seit Jahrhunderten nicht unterschrittenen Tiefpunkt angelangt (möglicherweise mit Ausnahme der Zeit des Großen Sprungs nach vorn, als es keine verlässlichen Statistiken gab). Das Pro-Kopf-Einkommen lag 1976 weit unter dem vor 150 Jahren in der Qing-Dynastie oder während der ruhmreichen Zeiten der Ming. Als Mao 1976 starb, wenige Monate nachdem sein loyaler Premierminister Zhou schließlich einem Krebsleiden erlag, konnten beide nicht die leiseste Ahnung von der außerordentlichen Renaissance haben, die China in den beiden letzten Jahrzehnten des 20. Jahrhunderts erwartete. Insbesondere Zhou musste glauben, all die Mühen des Langen Marsches, der Revolution und der Jahre seither hätten zu nichts geführt. Als schließlich 1981 die offizielle Beurteilung der Kulturrevolution veröffentlicht wurde, fiel sie düster aus. Dort hieß es, die Kulturrevolution sei „für den schlimmsten Rückschlag

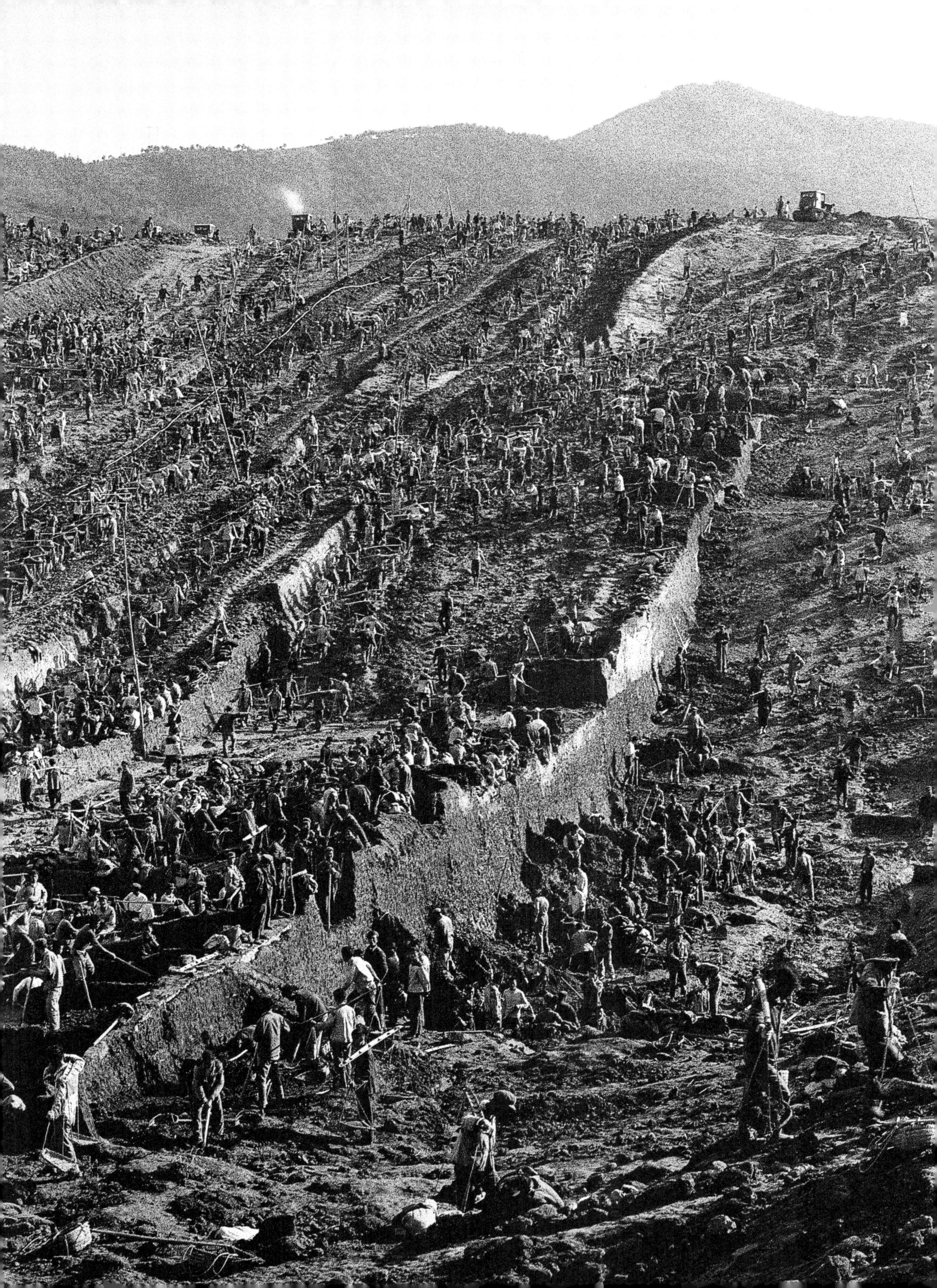

und die schwersten Verluste verantwortlich, die die Partei und das Volk seit Gründung der Volksrepublik erleiden mussten". Mao habe „schwere Fehler" begangen, die jedoch durch seine Verdienste mehr als ausgeglichen würden.

Schließlich die Ära Deng

Ehe jedoch die nächste Ära der Reform und Öffnung beginnen konnte, mussten einige Schlüsselfragen beantwortet werden. Die radikale Viererbande musste kaltgestellt und Hua Guofeng, der untaugliche Loyalist, den Mao zum Nachfolger bestimmt hatte, zum Rücktritt zugunsten eines Mannes überredet werden, dessen Name für China schicksalhaft werden sollte: Deng Xiaoping. Deng, der Ende 1978 offenkundig die Zügel der Macht übernommen hatte, sollte mehr als jeder andere Führer des 20. Jahrhunderts dafür tun, dass China dem lang ersehnten Reichtum und der Macht näher kam, wodurch Abermillionen von Menschen die Chance erhielten, sich aus ihrer Armut zu befreien. Alles begann im Dezember 1978 mit dem dritten Plenum des 11. Zentralkomitees, das die Partei auf ein Programm grundlegender ökonomischer Modernisierung, der Reform und des Kontakts mit der übrigen Welt verpflichtete, das schier jedes Gebot der Kulturrevolution brach. Mit dem Verbot der Mauer-der-Demokratie-Bewegung in Peking wurde jedoch auch früh klar, dass Deng nicht beabsichtigte, den Reformeifer von der Ökonomie auf die Politik übergreifen zu lassen. Anfangs nutzte Deng die Demonstrationen und Wandzeitungen in Xidan, um seine politischen Gegner auszubooten. Sodann griff er jedoch gnadenlos gegen die Bewegung durch. Wei Jingsheng, ein Elektriker im Zoo von Peking, war ein Anführer der Bewegung und sollte bis auf wenige Monate die nächsten 18 Jahre hinter Gittern verbringen. Dass man nicht gewillt war, politische Freiheiten zu dulden, zeigte sich erneut 1989, als die von Panzern unterstützte Volksbefreiungsarmee prodemokratische Proteste im Zentrum von Peking niederschlug und dabei Hunderte, wenn nicht Tausende unbewaffneter Zivilisten tötete. Gleichwohl glaubten westliche Politiker in den 80er-Jahren häufig, Deng, ein Bridge spielender Fußballanhänger mit einer Vorliebe für Croissants, sei ein Mann, mit dem auszukommen wäre, vielleicht sogar ein Gleichgesinnter. Kurz nachdem er die Macht übernommen hatte, begann Deng einen Besuch in den Vereinigten Staaten zu planen, um dort anzuknüpfen, wo Richard Nixon bei seinem wegweisenden Besuch in China 1972 aufgehört hatte (vgl. Abb. S. 230 und 232/233). Während seines USA-Besuchs 1979 hinterließ er einen ganz anderen Eindruck als der sittenstrenge, nationalistische Mao oder der Typ des schwerfälligen Sowjetführers, den man in Amerika gewöhnt war. Deng setzte für die Fotografen einen Stetson auf und schien lebhaft an Gesprächen mit einfachen Amerikanern interessiert. Der positive Eindruck, den er hinterließ, trug viel zum sich ändernden China-Bild im Westen bei, ein Image, das bis zum Massaker vom Tiananmen-Platz 1989 ebenso viel mit Pandabären, Ping-Pong und Investmentchancen zu tun hatte wie mit Mao-Anzügen und Kommunismus.

Deng sorgte für die Einsetzung zweier seiner wichtigsten Protegés, Hu Yaobang und Zhao Ziyang, und machte sich daran, einen Weg aus der Wirtschaftskrise zu planen, in der sich China befand. Die Landwirtschaft wurde entkollektiviert, Familien beim Erwerb von Land unterstützt. Die Bauern produzierten einen festgelegten Anteil für den Staat und konnten über den Mehrertrag frei verfügen. Die Überwachung der Industrie wurde dezentralisiert und den Verwaltern von Fabriken Entscheidungsfreiheit zugestanden. Auslandshandel und Investment wurden gefördert und Joint Ventures eingerichtet. Man gründete Sonderwirtschaftszonen als Enklaven, in denen kapitalistische Projekte getestet werden konnten, ohne das Risiko einzugehen, dass das übrige Land infiziert würde. China verfolgte unterdessen die Vision eines „Sozialismus mit chinesischen Merkmalen", in dem es einigen erlaubt war, vor den anderen reich zu werden. Während jedoch das Land zum Leben erwachte, stießen solch unerwünschte Entwicklungen wie Inflation, Bestechlichkeit, Pornografie und andere Formen „geistiger Verschmutzung" auf erhebliche Kritik. Zumindest in Dengs Augen noch schwerwiegender war eine Tendenz zum „bourgeoisen Liberalismus" – im Sprachgebrauch der Partei eine Demokratie westlichen Stils – in bestimmten Teilen der Gesellschaft. Hu und Zhao, die als ausersehene Nachfolger galten, gerieten beide in Konflikt mit ihrer eher lockeren Einstellung zur Demokratie. Hu musste 1987 zurücktreten, weil er gegen eine Reihe von Studentenprotesten nicht energisch genug vorgegangen war, und Zhao wurde 1989 abgesetzt, weil er sich nicht für den Einsatz des Militärs gegen die Protestierenden ausgesprochen hatte. Das Massaker auf dem Tiananmen-Platz sollte zwar zur dunkelsten Stunde in Dengs Regierungszeit werden, sich aber nicht als seine letzte bedeutende Tat erweisen. 1992 reiste er – 87 Jahre alt und schwerhörig – in den Süden Chinas, um Wirtschaftsreformen, die unter dem Eindruck von Tiananmen an Schwung verloren hatten, mit neuer Energie zu erfüllen. Die Tour, die als „Reise in den Süden" bekannt wurde, legte den Grundstein für den Wirtschaftsboom, den China in den 1990er-Jahren erlebte, und setzte eine Clique politisch Konservativer außer Gefecht, denen es ohne Deng vielleicht gelungen wäre, die Uhr zurückzustellen.

Im Lauf der 90er-Jahre entwickelte sich der von der „Reise in den Süden" ausgelöste Boom zu einem Ereignis von globaler Bedeutung. Der Zustrom ausländischen Kapitals in die Fabriken entlang der Süd- und Ostküste verwandelte China in die „Werkstätte der Welt". Bald stammten die auf den Hypermärkten Europas und der USA angebotenen Produkte zunehmend aus den Industriegebieten im Perlflussdelta nördlich von Hongkong oder aus den 15 Städten rund um Shanghai. Chinas Handelsüberschuss mit den Industrienationen schnellte in die Höhe, während seine Fabriken bei den asiatischen Nachbarn eine solche Menge an Waren und Bauteilen aufkauften, dass die USA während der Finanzkrise am Ende des Jahrzehnts auf Peking als stabilisierenden Faktor setzten. Zu Hause wurden die Gewinne indessen nicht gleichmäßig verteilt. Nutznießer der Reformära war eine aufkommende wohlhabende Schicht oder Mittelklasse, die in den Anfangsjahren des 21. Jahrhunderts begann, ihr Leben als neureiche Konsumenten zu gestalten, indem sie Luxusgüter aufkaufte, ihre Kinder auf exklusive Privatschulen in Übersee oder renommierte Ostküsten-Universitäten in den USA schickte und ihre Urlaube in Villen auf südostasiatischen Trauminseln verbrachte. Der Rest des Landes verspürte indessen zumeist kaum etwas vom Wirtschaftsboom der Küstenregionen, sondern verharrte weitgehend auf dem Stand der 1980er-Jahre. Die gähnende Kluft zwischen Reich und Arm, tiefer als in nahezu jedem anderen großen Land, war nicht nur blamabel für eine Regierung, die einst egalitäre Ideale vertreten hatte, sondern bedeutete auch potenzielle soziale Sprengkraft.

Die letzte Runde vor den Olympischen Spielen

Verschiedene Regierungen waren seither bemüht, dieses Problem anzugehen. Jiang Zemin versuchte in den Anfangsjahren des 21. Jahrhunderts, der Entwicklung westlicher und zentraler Gebiete mit einer Große Entwicklung des Westens genannten Kampagne Auftrieb zu verschaffen. Sein Nachfolger, Hu Jintao, legte Wert auf einen persönlicheren Ansatz und besuchte Familien von Bauern, Grubenarbeitern und andere benachteiligte Gruppen, um für sein Motto „Zuerst die Menschen" zu werben. Keiner von beiden fand allerdings eine wirksame Methode, mit der die chronische Umweltzerstörung aufzuhalten oder umzukehren war, die Chinas wirtschaftlicher Aufschwung dem Land gebracht hat. Während sich Peking vorbereitet, im August 2008 die Olympischen Spiele auszurichten und seine Errungenschaften der letzten 60 Jahre unter Herrschaft der Kommunistischen Partei vorzuzeigen, ist die größte Unwägbarkeit, die über den Organisatoren, Teilnehmern und potenziellen Besuchern der Spiele hängt, ob es gelingen wird, die häufig über der Hauptstadt sichtbare dicke Wolke schadstoffgeschwängerter Luft rechtzeitig vor der *Greatest Show on Earth* zu vertreiben.

Le contexte historique

Chine 1949–aujourd'hui

Par James Kynge

« Ô mots, qui ne sont que de pauvres reçus de ce que le temps a volé,
Les arbres antiques, dressés tels des chaires, et les jeux. »

Ainsi s'exprimait John Clare, poète britannique du XIXᵉ siècle, pour décrire cette frustration à laquelle sont confrontés les écrivains lorsque les mots sont les seuls outils disponibles pour reproduire le tableau de l'histoire dans toutes ses subtiles nuances. Quelle que soit la subtilité des termes déployés sur la page, le résultat n'est souvent que le pâle reflet de ce qu'ont été les choses, que de simples silhouettes d'hommes et d'événements, dénuées des émotions qui les ont animés. Les photographies, elles, ont le pouvoir de combler les vides. Non seulement elles rapportent les détails du quotidien – tels les vêtements que les gens portaient, le style des bâtiments et les conditions du moment –, mais elles permettent surtout de mieux appréhender les sensations de l'époque. Elles le font grâce à leur capacité unique à suggérer, inférer et faire allusion à ce qui ne peut être vu. En cela, elles possèdent une qualité transcendantale qui déplace le spectateur de la forme vers le sens, un peu à la façon dont Zhuangzi, philosophe chinois du IVᵉ siècle av. J.-C. décrivait le processus de distillation de la pensée :

« Le piège à poisson existe parce que le poisson existe : une fois que vous avez attrapé le poisson, vous pouvez oublier le piège. Le collet à lapin existe parce que le lapin existe : une fois que vous avez le lapin, vous pouvez oublier le collet. Les mots existent à cause du sens : une fois que vous avez le sens, vous pouvez oublier les mots. Où trouver un homme qui a oublié les mots pour que je puisse lui parler ? »

Ce livre de photographies réunies et assemblées par le photographe Liu Heung Shing, titulaire du prix Pulitzer, retrace l'histoire de la Chine entre 1948, juste avant la proclamation de la République populaire, et 2008, qui vit la Chine reprendre sa place dans le concert des grandes puissances mondiales et accueillir les Jeux olympiques à Pékin. Si les 60 années couvertes par cet ouvrage correspondent à la durée biblique d'une vie, les transformations qu'il retrace sont si fondamentales et si profondes que l'on a l'impression que plus de mille ans y ont été compressés. La Chine était un pays de villages et de bourgs de marché reliés par des routes transformées en bourbier l'hiver et en poussière l'été. On parlait des langues différentes d'une vallée à l'autre et l'économie, en dépit d'un brillant passé d'innovations technologiques, s'appuyait encore en grande partie sur l'énergie animale et humaine jusque tard au XXᵉ siècle. Au cours de la période que retracent ces pages, le moule millénaire chinois a été brisé, démonté et remplacé par de nouvelles réalités dont beaucoup sont encore en pleine évolution. Depuis sa révolution, la Chine a connu et connaît encore de nombreuses transformations économiques, politiques sociales et culturelles. Elle passe de la ruralité à l'urbanité et des centaines de millions de ses paysans émigrent vers les villes, souvent pour aller travailler à la chaîne en usine mais aussi parfois dans de superbes tours de bureaux. Cette évolution d'une société agraire à une société industrielle s'est accompagnée d'une rapide progression technologique. Après avoir abandonné l'énergie musculaire, le pays construit actuellement trois nouvelles centrales électriques par semaine et, en seule année, peut installer des capacités de production d'électricité qui suffiraient aux besoins d'un pays comme le Royaume-Uni. Sur le plan géographique, les choses changent également. Pour la première fois au cours de sa longue histoire, le développement et la prospérité économiques gagnent l'intérieur à partir des zones côtières orientales et méridionales tandis qu'un vaste réseau de routes nouvelles relie au reste du pays et, par extension, au monde des régions jadis éloignées. Sur le plan politique, les choses ont connu un revirement presque complet. Après 30 années tout d'abord consacrées à la mise en place d'une dictature communiste, à la nationalisation de la propriété privée et à l'embrigadement de la population soumise à un contrôle bureaucratique de type pyramidal, Pékin a consacré ces trois dernières décennies à défaire ce qui avait été construit. La propriété et les entreprises privées comme les marchés boursiers sont aujourd'hui en plein essor. Alors que les gens s'habillaient encore naguère de bleu ou de vert réglementaires et que le choix des consommateurs était très limité, la montée de l'individualisme a ouvert les magasins à une fabuleuse variété de produits. La seule sphère, ou presque, de la société à ne pas avoir été touchée est le Parti communiste, qui tient à conserver le pouvoir. Les clients des cafés Starbuck pékinois peuvent choisir entre latte, espressos, cappuccinos, mokas et frapuccinos, mais leur liberté s'arrête aux portes du bureau de vote.

Il ne peut y avoir de façon plus directe – et plus passionnante – d'accéder aux réalités de cette histoire tumultueuse et de comprendre les multiples transformations vécues par la Chine que de feuilleter ce remarquable ouvrage. Les photographies sont classées par ordre chronologique et décrivent les hauts et les bas de la construction de cette nation nouvelle, de sa naissance à nos jours. Ce choix permet au lecteur non seulement de percevoir à quel point elle a changé depuis les réformes économiques de la fin de 1978, mais aussi de comprendre les spectres qui hantent encore la mémoire collective des deux décennies précédentes. Le livre s'ouvre sur une image iconique, celle de la Longue marche du Parti communiste vers le pouvoir. Peu de moments de l'histoire des guerres sont aussi épiques que la retraite de ce parti chassé de ses bases de Chine du Sud vers Yan'an, une ville poussiéreuse située dans le nord de l'immense plateau de loess qui constitue la Chine. Bien que seuls 10 000 marcheurs sur les

100 000 du départ aient finalement rejoint ce sanctuaire, ces 9 600 km sont devenus l'un des mythes fondateurs du Parti et ses vétérans peuplèrent les différentes assemblées de l'État jusqu'à la fin des années 1990. Poursuivie sur la plus grande partie du chemin par les troupes du Kuomintang de Tchang Kaï-chek et souvent en butte aux attaques de seigneurs de guerre locaux, la Première armée communiste conduite par Mao Zedong traversa neuf provinces et, quelles que soient les exagérations grossières de la propagande ultérieure, accomplit de nombreux actes héroïques, traversant à gué des fleuves, franchissant des chaînes de montagnes et parcourant des plateaux dénudés (photo p. 114/115). Cette expérience partagée de la Longue marche explique pour une bonne part le sentiment de cohésion et de fierté qui joua un rôle essentiel dans la victoire finale des communistes sur Tchang. Le 1er octobre 1949, la « Chine nouvelle » de la République populaire prenait naissance (photo p. 119) au milieu d'un enthousiasme authentique et de l'espoir de paix et de reconstruction d'un pays déchiré par un état de guerre quasi permanent depuis 1911.

Quand la Chine se redresse

Le caractère de la Révolution avait été préfiguré par des aventures formatives, comme la Longue marche, mais était aussi marqué par la nature rurale de la base principale du Parti. À la différence de l'Union soviétique, où elle était née avant tout du prolétariat urbain, c'est le paysan qui en Chine fut son principal sujet et agent. Dans de nombreuses régions, les campagnes vivaient soumises sans le moindre espoir à la pauvreté, aux dettes, aux calamités naturelles, à la cruauté des mœurs, aux superstitions et à la répression des seigneurs locaux. Comme le disait Mao, ces paysans étaient « pauvres et comme une page blanche » sur laquelle de magnifiques envolées révolutionnaires pouvaient être écrites. Au début de la reconstruction, les progrès et les succès furent étonnamment rapides. L'un des premiers grands projets fut la réforme agraire. Depuis des siècles, la surpopulation, le manque de terres fertiles et la fréquence des désastres naturels rendaient l'existence très difficile pour l'immense majorité des Chinois. Chaque changement de pouvoir ou presque, qu'il soit dynastique ou révolutionnaire, s'était accompagné de l'allocation de terres à ceux qui les travaillaient et d'un rééquilibrage de la répartition des impôts. Les efforts nécessités par la guerre de Corée pendant les premières années du communisme accrurent l'urgence de la réforme agraire. Des étiquettes de classe furent affectées aux différents segments de la population rurale et les paysans furent encouragés à confesser en public leurs « mauvaises pensées » pour rappeler l'oppression passée des seigneurs (photos p. 120, 121 et 122/123). Ceux-ci – piliers d'une tradition rurale qui remontait à des temps très anciens – furent pratiquement éliminés. On estime à 2 millions le nombre de personnes ainsi exécutées ou tuées en l'espace de quelques mois, et ceux qui furent autorisés à survivre se virent allouer de petites parcelles sur des terres peu fertiles. Le but ultime de la réforme n'était cependant pas la lutte des classes mais la création des conditions d'un secteur agricole efficace capable de fournir des excédents de production nécessaires au développement industriel. Le Parti ne perdit pas de temps pour mettre en place ce qu'il considérait comme un pas essentiel vers l'amélioration de l'efficacité agricole : la collectivisation. Il croyait que les paysans, une fois libérés du joug de leurs oppresseurs, travailleraient plus dur sur les terres qu'ils posséderaient collectivement. Mais en réalité, les incitations à travailler plus et à produire davantage se révélèrent insuffisantes et, vers le milieu des années 1950, Mao se montrait de plus en plus impatient devant l'insuffisance de la production agricole.

C'est ainsi qu'en 1958, il imagina une solution qui allait devenir le symbole le plus marquant de sa conviction que la force et la volonté pouvaient surmonter tous les obstacles. Le Grand bond en avant conduisit à l'instauration de communes populaires dans les campagnes. Toutes les organisations collectives fusionnèrent dans ce type de structure où la vie fut réorganisée selon des principes stricts, pratiquement militaires. Les salaires furent remplacés par un système de points de travail et les gens forcés de se restaurer dans des salles à manger collectives. L'argent fut même supprimé dans certaines communes. Les paysans savaient sans doute au fond d'eux-mêmes que leurs pauvres terres ne pouvaient produire les récoltes miraculeuses attendues par la simple application de quelques techniques comme la plantation rapprochée, de nouvelles semences hybrides, le labour profond et quelques rares nouveaux outils, mais ils n'avaient aucun moyen de résister. Le Grand bond ne prenait en compte ni les objections rationnelles ni les analyses approfondies. Sa motivation était plus romantique. Il s'agissait de dépasser ce que les fermiers, les experts, les scientifiques et les intellectuels considéraient comme des obstacles insurmontables par l'effort humain et constant. Le but n'était pas seulement de transformer l'homme, mais aussi la nature.

Tout aussi impatient de lancer son programme d'industrialisation, Mao décida de ne pas attendre les excédents agricoles espérés des communes. Des millions de paysans furent exhortés à construire des barrages, des réseaux d'irrigation et à participer à des travaux publics. Des citadins se joignirent à eux pour édifier des hauts fourneaux ruraux dans tous le pays, alimentés en bicyclettes, woks et ustensiles agricoles et tout ce que l'on pouvait trouver et fondre (photos p. 134, 135 et 136/137). L'extermination des fléaux naturels fut également une des obsessions de cette période. Des campagnes d'une intensité extraordinaire contre les rats, les souris, les moineaux et vermines diverses furent lancées dans tout le pays, détournant les travailleurs de tâches plus productives.

« Lorsque je repense au début des années 1960, je vois l'une des périodes les plus bizarres de la Chine moderne, une ère de fanatisme sans précédent. D'un côté, ces années virent le pays englué dans la stagnation économique et les privations et le peuple se battre pour éviter de mourir. D'un autre côté, ce fut une période de passions politiques intenses, où les citoyens affamés serrèrent leur ceinture et suivirent le Parti dans ses expérimentations du communisme. Nous étions peut-être affamés, mais nous nous considérions comme le peuple le plus heureux de la terre. Les deux tiers du monde, croyions-nous, vivaient dans une misère pire et il allait de notre devoir sacré de les sauver de cet océan de souffrance dans lequel ils se noyaient. »

MO YAN (1955–), écrivain, 2003

Ces politiques, couplées à une croissance de la population non contrôlée également encouragée par Mao, se révélèrent catastrophiques. Beaucoup de temps s'écoula néanmoins avant que les responsables pékinois ne se fassent une idée précise de la gravité de la situation. D'une part, Mao avait institué un tel climat de peur aux échelons supérieurs du Parti que personne ne voulait être le premier à apporter de mauvaises nouvelles et de l'autre, la purge des intellectuels et des spécialistes lors de la « Campagne des Cent Fleurs » au milieu des années 1950 avait laissé le gouvernement pratiquement dépourvu de toute possibilité de rassembler et d'analyser de façon sûre des statistiques. Ces déficiences profondes allaient constituer la toile de fond tragique d'un nouveau totalitarisme. La famine ravagea le pays et frappa particulièrement les régions les plus pauvres comme le Tibet, le Qinghai, le Gansu, le Hénan et l'Anhui. Les récoltes s'effondrèrent et n'atteignirent presque nulle part les objectifs fixés : les paysans passaient leur temps à tenter de fabriquer de l'acier de mauvaise qualité dans des hauts fourneaux de boue séchée, à éradiquer divers fléaux, à travailler pour d'énormes projets de travaux publics ou assister à des cycles d'interminables réunions politiques à la gloire du leadership de Mao et de la sagesse du nouveau système communal. Alors que des millions de personnes mouraient de faim, les seuls rapports qui arrivaient au Président étaient positifs. L'absurdité devint une des caractéristiques de la propagande. Des photographes furent ainsi contraints à montrer des champs de blé si densément plantés qu'une personne pouvait se tenir debout sur les épis serrés.

Amère moisson

Un seul responsable, Peng Dehuai, ministre de la Défense et vétéran de la Longue marche eut le courage de suggérer que tout n'allait pas pour le mieux dans la vision utopique de Mao et le système de ces nouvelles communes. Bien qu'il n'ait pas directement critiqué le Président mais ait exprimé ses doutes dans une lettre personnelle qu'il lui fit parvenir pendant la conférence de Lushan en 1959, la réaction de Mao fut rapide et sans pitié. Peng fut disgracié, ce qui ébranla la fragile cohésion entre les anciens camarades d'armes au sommet du parti et jeta la Chine dans un cycle de violences et de persécutions qui dura près de vingt années. La première campagne lancée fut contre les « opportunistes droitiers » et ceux qui tentaient de « diviser le Parti », langage codé pour désigner les responsables qui, comme Peng, voyaient des défauts dans les communes et d'autres aspects de la politique maoïste. Les rapports sur l'efficacité du Grand bond en avant devinrent encore plus irréalistes, puisque toute critique pouvait valoir à son auteur d'être arrêté, fusillé ou expédié en camp de travail. En 1961 cependant, les hautes sphères du Parti ne pouvaient plus rester hermétiquement fermées aux calamités dont le pays était victime. Il devint enfin clair que si le Parti ne changeait pas de politique, le régime communiste pouvait s'effondrer. On estime à 30 millions le nombre de morts survenus au cours de cette famine qui fut l'une des pires jamais provoquées par l'Homme. Lentement et dans le désordre, le nombre de communes fut réduit, en particulier dans les régions où la famine était fortement présente comme dans la province centrale d'Anhui. Cependant Mao restait méfiant et refusait de reconnaître que les communes – sa principale contribution à la reconstruction chinoise depuis la révolution de 1949 – n'étaient qu'un échec supplémentaire. À partir de ce moment, le refus d'admettre ses torts allait peser sur ses actions et ses jugements, accentuer sa suspicion envers ses rivaux potentiels et aiguiser sa sensibilité à toute critique. Ainsi, lorsque le leader de l'Union soviétique, Nikita Khrouchtchev exprima des réserves sur la commune chinoise, Mao ne put contenir sa colère et les relations entre les deux géants communistes commencèrent à se détériorer. En 1960, Moscou rappela brusquement ses experts et ses conseillers industriels qui jouaient un rôle essentiel dans les énormes projets d'industrialisation (photos p. 132/133).

L'un des projets de coopération restés dans les limbes était celui d'un transfert du savoir soviétique dans la fabrication de la bombe atomique. Bien que Mao ait qualifié les pays qui possédaient ces armes de « tigres de papier » au début des années 1950, les efforts pour acquérir ces technologies militaires constituaient l'un des plus importants projets du programme de modernisation de la Chine. En 1957, période dorée des relations sino-soviétiques, Moscou promit d'aider Pékin à obtenir la bombe. Visitant Moscou, Mao complimenta la technologie soviétique et déclara que le lancement des Spoutniks I et II et de nouveaux missiles balistiques intercontinentaux montrait que « le vent d'Est l'emporte sur le vent d'Ouest. » Mais quelques mois plus tard, une autre déclaration du Président chinois sur le transfert de la technologie nucléaire à la Chine incita Khrouchtchev à se demander si ce n'était pas un risque qu'il valait mieux éviter. Mao incitait les pays socialistes à ne pas craindre un conflit nucléaire avec les États-Unis car « même si la moitié de l'humanité mourait, l'autre demeurerait. L'impérialisme serait ainsi éliminé de la surface de la terre et le monde entier pourrait devenir socialiste. » Mais même après le retrait de l'assistance soviétique, la Chine poursuivit son programme nucléaire et, en 1964, grâce à Qian Xuesen, physicien nucléaire formé en Amérique, elle fit exploser sa première bombe A. Trois ans plus tard, à l'apogée de la Révolution culturelle, elle possédait la bombe à hydrogène.

Les origines de la « Grande révolution culturelle prolétarienne » (1966–1976) s'expliquent à la fois par l'échec du Grand bond en avant et par les réserves et les doutes qui se développaient graduellement parmi les hauts responsables du Parti communiste après l'élimination de Peng

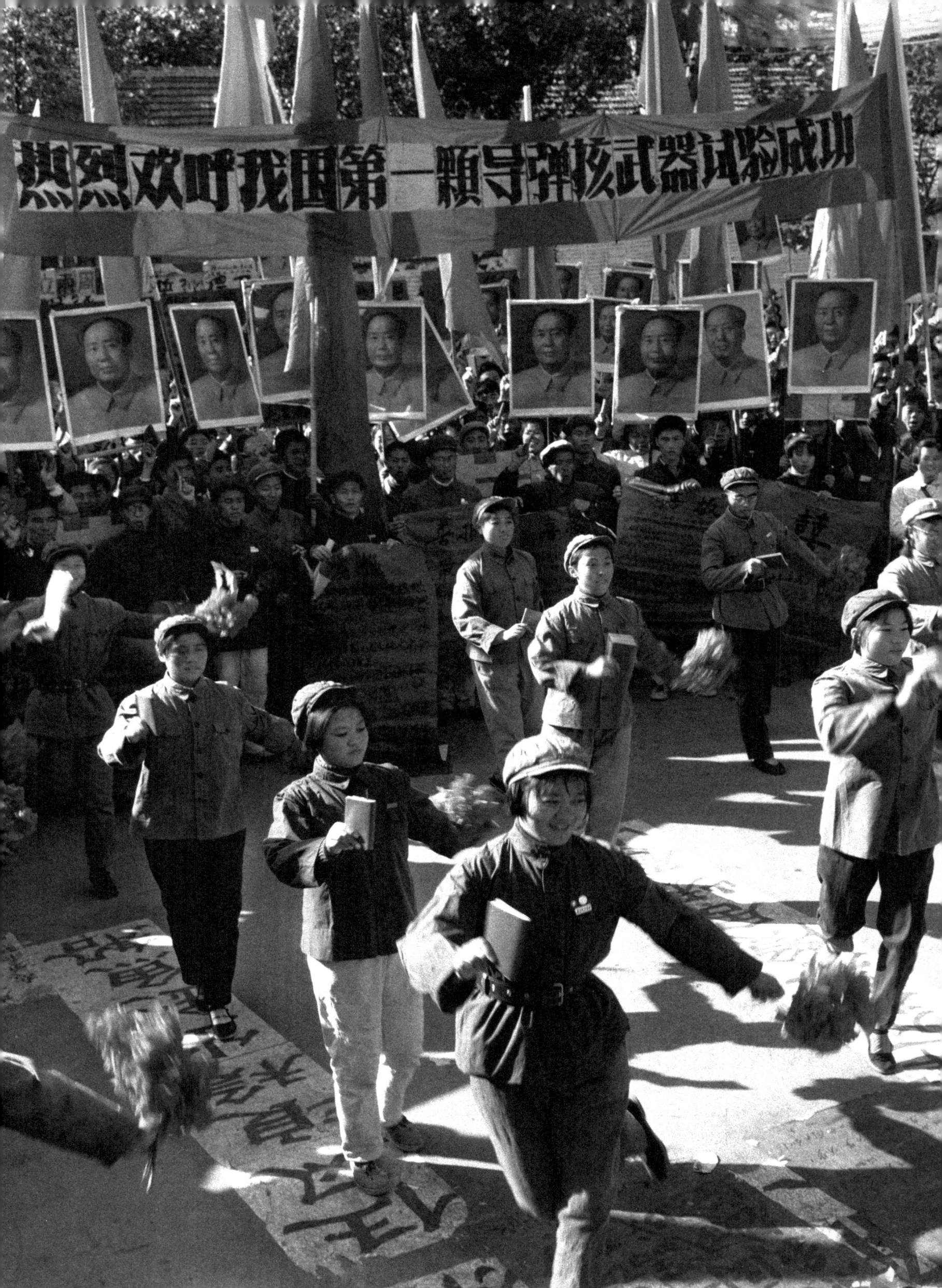

←

Xiao Zhuang, 1967

Workers in Nanjing celebrating another successful testing of a nuclear warhead.

Arbeiter in Nanjing bejubeln einen weiteren erfolgreichen Atomwaffentest.

Des travailleurs de Nankin célèbrent un nouvel essai nucléaire réussi.

Dehuai. Des millions de Chinois souffrèrent ou furent tués à mesure que la nation s'engouffrait dans un abîme de cruauté et d'oppression proprement terrifiant. Jusqu'à aujourd'hui, les événements de la décennie qui s'acheva par la mort de Mao en 1976 restent une blessure dans la psyché nationale et la recherche universitaire sur cette période est toujours interdite. Mao avait lancé la Révolution culturelle pour éliminer Liu Shaoqi, président depuis 1959, Deng Xiaoping et quelques autres responsables qui semblaient croire qu'il était plus important pour le pays d'être plus puissant et plus prospère que d'être plus « rouge ». Mao ne pouvait l'accepter. Pour lui, la révolution était en train de faire machine arrière. À ses yeux, la prolifération de la bureaucratie, la reconstitution de hiérarchies et la montée en puissance d'influences étrangères annonçaient le retour de la bourgeoisie. Mais au-delà de ces transgressions, c'étaient les critiques adressées au Président lui-même qu'il ne pouvait accepter et ce n'est pas par hasard que la première cible de Mao et de ses alliés fut une pièce de théâtre, *La destitution de Hai Rui* de Wu Han. Wu avait pris l'exemple d'un vertueux haut fonctionnaire de la dynastie Ming qui critiquait à juste titre l'empereur pour rendre hommage à l'interpellation lancée à Mao par Peng Dehuai lors du Grand bond. Les autres cibles furent Peng Zhen, maire réformateur de Pékin, Liu Shaoqi et Deng. Des trois, c'est Liu (photo p. 139), un temps considéré comme successeur possible de Mao, qui subit le traitement le plus brutal. Il fut qualifié de « traître, renégat et canaille » avant d'être torturé et finalement de mourir en prison en 1969. Deng échappa aux mauvais traitements physiques, mais fut exilé à la campagne où il s'occupait de porcs et réparait des tracteurs en attendant un changement d'orientation des grands vents politiques.

Une décennie de chaos

Bien que la Révolution culturelle ait déjà été en marche lorsque Mao prit son célèbre bain dans le Yang-Tsé à l'été 1966 (photo p. 142/143), elle n'atteignit des sommets de violence qu'en 1967 et 1968, lorsque des troupes rivales des Gardes rouges, chacune protestant de sa loyauté envers le Président, s'affrontèrent tout en poursuivant les ennemis de classe, les traîtres et les sympathisants de l'étranger. Dans la principale ville du Wuhan, se déroulèrent des combats rappelant ceux de la Guerre civile et dans la province méridionale du Guangxi, des groupes armés de canons détruisirent des bâtiments et firent des milliers de victimes. La plupart des écoles et des universités furent fermées, les enseignants humiliés et de nombreux témoignages matériels de la culture chinoise et des minorités nationales, dont ceux de la plupart des monastères du Tibet, furent détruits. Ce chaos constituait une plate-forme idéale pour divers opportunistes et bandits, symbolisés par la « Bande des quatre » conduite par Jiang Qing, l'épouse de Mao. Mais en 1969, le président

commençait à réaliser que la violence avait assez duré. Il mit de côté son radicalisme et démobilisa les Gardes rouges, dont beaucoup furent envoyés dans les campagnes pour recevoir une formation concrète auprès des paysans. De retour à Pékin, les bénéficiaires de la Révolution culturelle, en particulier Lin Biao, alors successeur désigné de Mao et qui avait compilé le fameux Petit livre rouge, semblaient avoir consolidé leurs positions au pinacle de l'appareil d'État. La vérité était tout autre. Comme beaucoup de ceux qui espèrent succéder à un grand personnage, Lin n'était pas loin de la disgrâce.

Comme on le voit dans une rare photographie instantanée où il figure en compagnie du Premier ministre Zhou Enlai en train de mettre au point avec lui la rédaction d'une déclaration, la suspicion qui allait entraîner la chute de Lin est déjà perceptible dans le regard de Mao. Quoi qu'il se fut tramé entre les deux hommes, cette situation prit fin en septembre 1971 avec l'accusation portée contre Lin et ses alliés d'avoir tenté d'assassiner le Président. Ils trouvèrent la mort dans un accident d'avion en Mongolie, apparemment en fuite vers l'Union soviétique.

À la fin de la Révolution culturelle, le pays était totalement épuisé et à son plus bas niveau économique depuis des centaines d'années, à l'exception peut-être de la période du Grand bond, dont les statistiques ne sont pas fiables. En 1976, le revenu par tête était nettement plus bas que 150 ans plus tôt sous la dynastie Qing ou pendant la glorieuse période des Ming. À la mort de Mao en 1976, peu après que son loyal premier ministre Zhou eut succombé à un cancer, personne n'avait la moindre intuition de l'extraordinaire renaissance qu'allait connaître la Chine pendant les deux dernières décennies du XXᵉ siècle. Lorsqu'enfin un triste bilan officiel de la Révolution culturelle fut publié en 1981, il dut sembler à Zhou, en particulier, que tous les efforts de la Longue marche, de la Révolution et des années qui suivirent n'avaient pas mené à grand-chose. Elle avait été responsable « de la plupart des sévères reculs et des plus lourdes pertes subies par le Parti et le peuple depuis la fondation de la République populaire ». Mao avait commis de « graves erreurs », mais celles-ci étaient plus que compensées par ses contributions.

Enfin, l'ère de Deng

Avant de lancer une nouvelle ère de réformes et d'ouverture, divers problèmes essentiels devaient être réglés. La Bande des quatre devait être neutralisée et Hua Guofeng, faible mais loyaliste, que Mao avait nommé pour lui succéder, devait être persuadé de s'écarter pour laisser place à un homme dont le nom était gravé dans le destin de la Chine : Deng Xiaoping. À la fin de 1978, celui-ci, un des grands chefs d'État du XXᵉ siècle, prenait enfin en main les rênes du pouvoir et allait faire plus que beaucoup d'autres pour faire résolument progresser son pays vers ses objectifs de prospérité et de puissance et permettre à des centaines de millions d'hommes d'échapper à la pauvreté. Tout commença lors du troisième plénum du XIe Comité central où le Parti s'engagea sur un programme fondamental de modernisation économique, de réformes et d'ouverture au monde extérieur qui violait pratiquement tous les principes de la Révolution culturelle. Mais il fut très vite évident, avec la répression du mouvement du Mur de la démocratie à Pékin, que Deng n'avait pas la moindre intention de permettre au zèle réformateur de s'étendre à la politique. Tout d'abord, il utilisa les manifestations et les affiches en gros caractères placardées sur un mur à Xidan pour éliminer ses rivaux politiques, puis réprima le mouvement sans pitié. Wei Jingsheng, un électricien du zoo de Pékin et un des leaders du mouvement, passera près de 18 ans derrières les barreaux. L'intolérance envers les libertés politiques allait se manifester de nouveau en 1989 lorsque l'armée populaire, soutenue par des tanks, écrasa des manifestations pour la démocratie dans le centre de la capitale, tuant des centaines, peut-être des milliers de citoyens non armés. Néanmoins, pendant la plus grande partie des années 1980, les politiciens occidentaux pensèrent que Deng, amateur de bridge et de football qui aimait les croissants, étaient un homme avec lequel on pouvait discuter et même un esprit avec lequel on pouvait avoir des affinités. Peu après sa prise du pouvoir, il planifia une visite aux États-Unis pour reprendre les relations où Richard Nixon les avait laissées lors de son célèbre voyage en Chine de 1972 (photos p. 230 et 232/233). Pendant cette visite qui se déroula en 1979, Deng donna une image très différente de celle des austères responsables nationalistes à la soviétique auxquels Washington s'était habituée et il sembla prendre goût à discuter avec des Américains ordinaires. L'impression positive qu'il donna constitua un important élément de la nouvelle image que la Chine donna d'elle-même aux Occidentaux, image qui, jusqu'au massacre de Tien'anmen en 1989, devait autant aux pandas, au ping-pong et aux opportunités d'investissement qu'aux costumes Mao et au communisme.

Deng fit nommer à de hautes fonctions ses deux principaux protégés, Hu Yaobang et Zhao Ziyang, et s'engagea résolument dans une politique nouvelle pour sortir la Chine de la crise économique. L'agriculture fut décollectivisée et les ménages encouragés à louer des terres. Les paysans produisaient pour l'État une quantité fixée et étaient libres de disposer du surplus à leur convenance. Le contrôle de l'industrie fut décentralisé et les directeurs d'usine se virent accorder des pouvoirs de décision. Le commerce international et les investissements étrangers furent encouragés et des entreprises montées en participation. Des zones économiques spéciales, enclaves où les réformes capitalistes pouvaient être mises en œuvre sans craindre de contaminer le reste du pays, furent créées alors que la Chine poursuivait ses ambitions de « socialisme à caractère

chinois » dans lequel certains pouvaient devenir riches avant les autres. Mais avec le réveil du pays, des phénomènes indésirables comme l'inflation, la corruption des responsables, la pornographie et autres formes de « pollution de l'esprit » se développèrent et entraînèrent de nombreuses critiques. Plus grave encore, du moins aux yeux de Deng, se dessinait dans certains secteurs de la société une tendance au « libéralisme bourgeois » – jargon du parti pour désigner la démocratie occidentale. Hu et Zhao, ses successeurs désignés, furent victimes de leur attitude relativement libérale envers la démocratie. Hu fut destitué en 1987 pour avoir réagi trop mollement à une série de manifestations étudiantes et Zhao dut démissionné en 1989 pour ne pas avoir utilisé la force armée contre des protestataires en 1989. Le massacre de Tien'anmen, une des heures les plus sombres du régime de Deng, ne fut cependant pas sa dernière décision d'importance. En 1992, âgé de 87 ans et pratiquement sourd, il parcourut le sud de la Chine pour réinsuffler de l'énergie dans les réformes économiques qui avaient perdu de leur dynamisme à la suite des événements de Tien'anmen. Ce voyage appelé « la tournée du sud » posa les bases du boom économique qui propulsa la Chine dans les années 1990 et écarta toute une coterie de conservateurs qui, sans Deng, aurait pu vouloir remettre les pendules à l'heure communiste.

Dans les années 1990, l'expansion économique relancée par cette tournée se transforma en phénomène aux répercussions internationales. L'afflux d'investissements étrangers sur les côtes méridionales et orientales fit de la Chine « le plus grand atelier du monde ». Bientôt, d'innombrables produits venus des zones industrielles polluées du delta de la Rivière des Perles au nord de Hong Kong ou des 15 villes qui entourent Shanghai, alimentèrent les hypermarchés européens et américains. L'excédent commercial chinois vis-à-vis du monde développé commença à enfler et l'industrie acheta de si énormes quantités de matières premières et de composants auprès des pays voisins asiatiques que les États-Unis virent en Pékin un élément de stabilisation lors de la crise financière asiatique de la fin de la décennie. Dans le pays, cependant, ces gains ne se répartirent pas également. Les bénéficiaires des réformes étaient les classes supérieures ou moyennes émergentes qui, au début du XXIe siècle, alimentèrent des bataillons de consommateurs effrénés, avides de produits de luxe, envoyant leurs enfants étudier dans des écoles privées à l'étranger et dans les grandes universités américaines, et passant leurs vacances sur les îles paradisiaques de l'Asie du Sud-Est. La plus grande partie du reste du pays n'était que peu concernée par la réussite économique des régions côtières, et la vie n'y était guère différente de celle des années 1980. L'écart béant entre les riches et les pauvres, plus large encore en Chine que dans les autres grands pays, était non seulement gênant pour un gouvernement professant des idéaux égalitaires, mais aussi un problème social explosif.

Dernière ligne droite avant les Jeux olympiques

Les récents gouvernements successifs ont tenté de le régler. Jiang Zemin a cherché à accélérer le développement des régions ouest et centrales du pays au moyen d'une campagne intitulée « Le grand développement de l'Ouest » au début du XXIᵉ siècle. Son successeur, Hu Jintao, qui a cultivé une approche plus personnelle, a été vu dans des familles paysannes, chez des mineurs et autres groupes désavantagés pour promouvoir sa politique du « peuple d'abord ». Aucun n'a cependant trouvé une façon efficace d'arrêter ou d'inverser la dégradation environnementale chronique qui accompagne le décollage économique du pays. Alors que Pékin se prépare à organiser les Jeux olympiques en août 2008 et à montrer au monde les réussites des 60 dernières années dues au Parti communiste, le plus grave problème qui menace les organisateurs, les participants et les spectateurs potentiels des Jeux était de savoir si l'épais matelas de pollution suspendu au-dessus de la capitale allait pouvoir être écarté à temps pour « the greatest show on earth. »

pp. 52/53
Jiang Shaowu, 1967

Hundreds of "big-character posters" and banners pasted over the walls of a building in Shenyang, Liaoning province, as different factions of Red Guards seek to demonstrate their loyalty to Mao over others. In the summer of 1967, factional fighting broke out across the country between rival groups of Red Guards. Mass armed battles took place, creating enormous civil unrest. Mao ultimately ordered Lin Biao to use the army to return society to order, but the attempt to unify the various factions failed. One such battle, in Wuhan, left 250 dead and 1,500 wounded.
"Back in the days of big-character posters, people's imaginations were driven to their fullest extremities, and every literary technique you can think of was put to use—outright fictions, exaggerations, metaphors, and satire—you name it. That was the first literature I ever encountered, and out on the streets, as the big-character posters were pasted up thicker and thicker, I began to love literature." Yu Hua

Hunderte von Wandzeitungen werden an die Wände eines Gebäudes in Shenyang, Provinz Liaoning, geklebt, als verschiedene Splittergruppen der Roten Garden sich gegenseitig in ihren Loyalitätsbekundungen an Mao zu übertreffen suchen. Im Sommer 1967 brachen überall im Land Kämpfe zwischen rivalisierenden Gruppen der Roten Garden aus. Es gab zahllose bewaffnete Auseinandersetzungen, die enorme Unruhen in der Zivilbevölkerung auslösten. Mao befahl schließlich Lin Biao, die Ordnung mithilfe der Streitkräfte wiederherzustellen, aber der Versuch, die verschiedenen Gruppen zu vereinen, scheiterte. Bei einem solchen Kampf in Wuhan gab es 250 Tote und 1500 Verletzte.
„Damals, in den Tagen der Wandzeitungen, wurde die Vorstellungskraft der Menschen bis zum Äußersten getrieben, und jede erdenkliche literarische Technik wurde angewendet – totale Fiktion, Übertreibungen, Metaphern und Satire –, was auch immer. Das war die erste Art von Literatur, die ich kennenlernte, und draußen auf den Straßen, wo die Plakate mit den großen Schriftzeichen immer dicker übereinander klebten, entdeckte ich meine Liebe zur Literatur." Yu Hua

Des centaines de bannières en « grands caractères » et d'affiches sont collées sur les murs d'un bâtiment à Shenyang, province du Liaoning, par diverses factions de Gardes rouges qui cherchent à témoigner de leur plus grande loyauté envers Mao. Pendant l'été 1967, des combats se déroulèrent, dans le pays entre des groupes de gardes rivaux. Des batailles de masse se déroulèrent provoquant une grande instabilité sociale. Mao finit par ordonner à Lin Biao de faire appel à l'armée pour remettre la société en ordre, mais les tentatives d'unifier les diverses factions échouèrent. Une bataille dans le Wuhan fit 250 morts et 1500 blessés.
« Du temps des affiches en grands caractères, l'imagination des gens était portée à toutes les extrémités et toutes les techniques d'écriture imaginables étaient utilisées : fiction, exagérations, métaphores et satyre, tout y passait. C'était la première forme de littérature que j'avais jamais connue et là, dans les rues, au fur et à mesure que ces affichettes étaient collées les unes sur les autres, je commençai à aimer la littérature. » Yu Hua

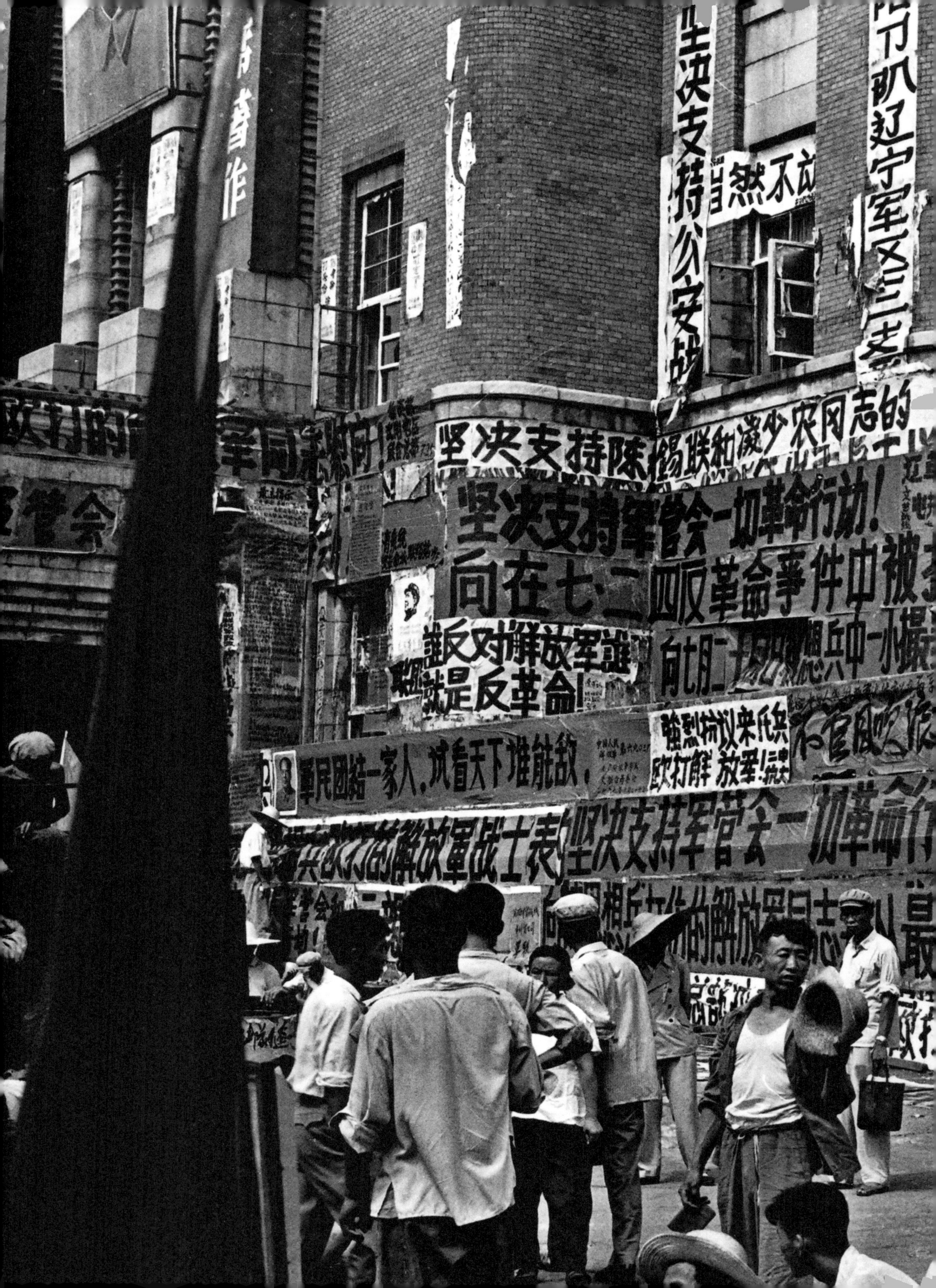

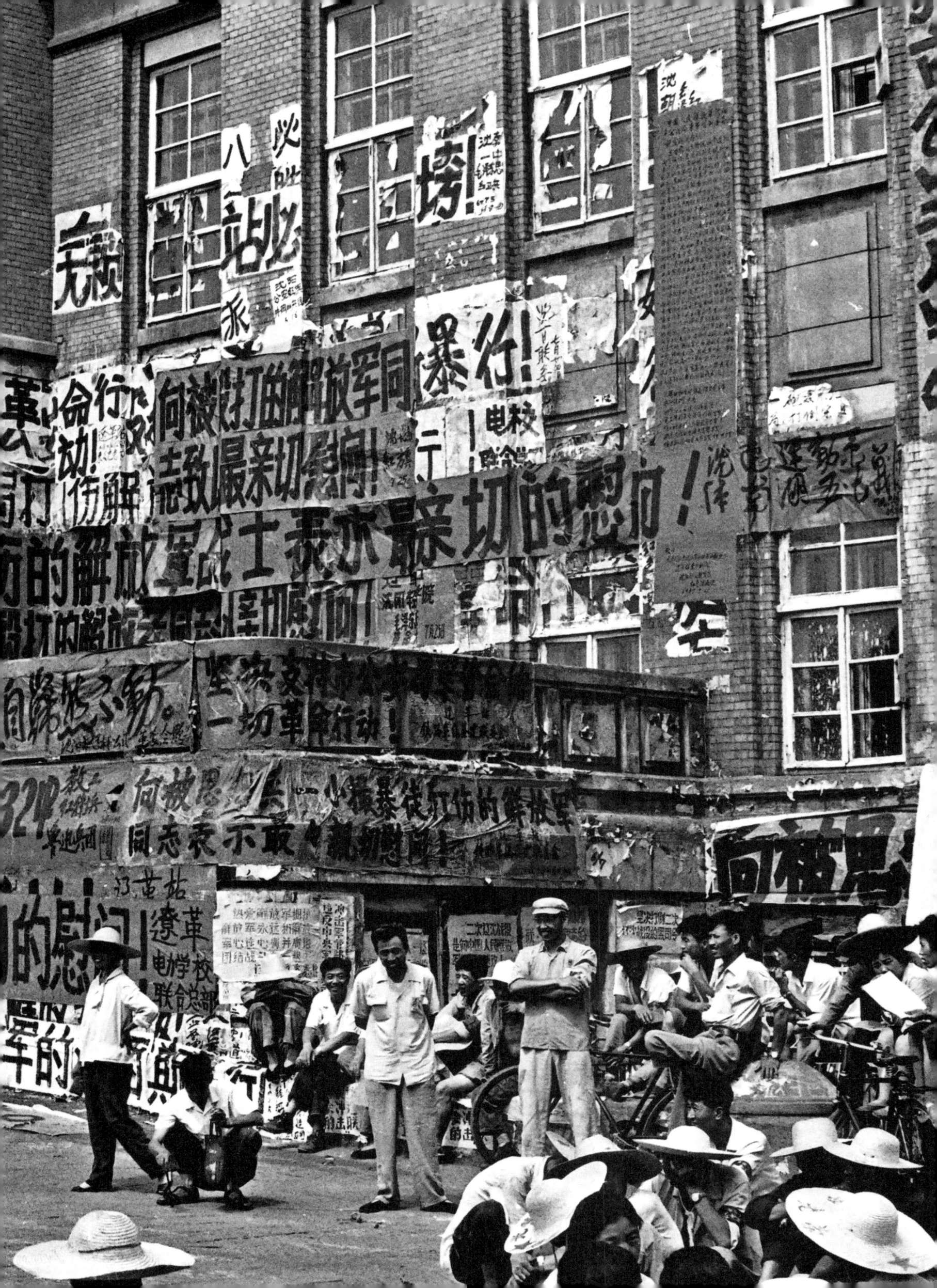

Picture This!

By Karen Smith

"Because each photograph is only a fragment, its moral and emotional weight depends on where it is inserted." [1]

A Vision of Truth

The arrival of photography in China in the 19th century provided the first "factual" visual records of the nation, its people, and its curious customs to the outside world: fragments of China that went out to speak for the whole culture. The 20th century did not produce much more of a cohesive picture: not in the half century prior to the founding of "New China," in 1949, as the Great Qing fell, and the country was consumed by civil strife, or simple survival. With the People's Republic established, and with the "door" effectively closed through the long Cold War years, the photographic picture became even more fragmented. Foreign journalists reported the impact of Mao Zedong's regime and his policies, the nature of their reports inalienably colored by their political sympathies. On the Chinese side, the vast majority of images released abroad, as in China, were officially authorized: fragments designed to illustrate the success of Mao's policies, and his revolutionary socialist vision. That they were largely disconnected from the Chinese reality was not immediately obvious. They belonged to a picture so big that it was impossible to grasp in one go. This described the stilted progress of the Communists' modernization program for social and economic advancement, but being foremost a man-made image (created by the propaganda bureau), it was hard to know which fragment was real. For a foreign audience, it was almost impossible to gauge the moral or emotional weight of the photographs they saw.

The situation changed little in the 1980s. Politically, China was already beginning to change, incrementally, but not yet enough to merit the type of international cultural exchange that has gathered momentum since the early 2000s. So many pieces of this complex jigsaw puzzle had to fall into place before the moment finally arrived, and it was possible, to gather all the fragments together, to insert them in their rightful place in a moment, and to present a balanced picture of China as seen by Chinese photographers.

China + Photography = ?

We don't immediately associate China with photography, although in the last 150 years it has enjoyed some currency as a photographic "subject," primarily for European and American photographers. Adventurers, travelers, "imperialist invaders," anthropologists, and even political sympathizers all tended to see China as an exotic, oriental Muse. Their images were largely responsible for revealing China to the outside world in pictures not words. In the history of photography, the West early on assumed a monopoly on ways of seeing, or of observing life, and of the rules defining what a photograph ought to be, or to contain. But this alone was not the reason that there was little Chinese-made photography available to a Western audience before 1949: it had yet to become a widespread phenomenon. Then, after 1949, photography was largely used as propaganda, and subject to all prevailing artistic constraints. As a result, "Chinese photography" is not a widely recognized genre. Chinese photographers are not credited with innovations in the photographic language, or with universal iconic images, even of China. Prior to a resurgence of energy within photography circles that came as recently as the mid-1990s, few members of those circles would have disputed this. How many Chinese photographers are household names? All too few, even in China, although a number of images here have an iconic status, such as portraits of Mao and the leaders of his era taken by Hou Bo. [2]

Most of the photographers that can be named today were not known prior to the very recent explosion of interest in the photographs taken by members of contemporary art circles. This comes primarily from European and American museum curators, gallery owners, and collectors. These so-called avant-garde artists turned to photography as recently as the mid-1990s, using the camera as a tool, the photographic frame as a canvas, and adopting an entirely postmodern irreverence towards the traditional values and practices accorded the medium. For them, the photograph is a distant relative of Cartier-Bresson's closely observed "decisive moment," or the menacing social melodrama captured by Sebastião Salgado, or the studied portraiture of Annie Leibovitz. One or two of the "pure" photographers acknowledge August Sander, Richard Avedon, or Diane Arbus. Later generations also name Nan Goldin and Robert Frank amongst their idols, most preferring Andreas Gursky and Yasumasa Morimura. But this is a relatively recent development. Compared with other forms of visual expression, photography has had less time to develop in China, or to close the gap between its experience and Western practice. This, however, is not a weakness.

China as Seen by the Chinese

This is a book that presents a unique portrait of China through a careful selection of photographs, all taken by photographers from the Chinese mainland. The photographers span several generations, and their careers traverse the succession of decades that begins with the founding of New China in 1949, and runs through to today. A significant number of the photographs chosen to reflect this history here are published for the first time, not necessarily because they were hidden before, but because only a limited number of people had reason to be aware of their existence. Of those that were, almost none would conceive of doing anything with them. Photography was late in being accepted as an independent art form, and lacked critical debate. Politically nuanced images might create problems for the photographers if taken out of context. There was no market for the works that might have made it worth the transgression. That is, until around 2005, when a feverish auction scene emerged in China. Prior to this time, few people had easy access to the images.

China, Portrait of a Country looks back on the major events that have shaped this momentous period, re-running that history frame by frame, in more or less chronological order, tracking the path from then to now. Across the passage of time, the nature of these frames reveals how shifts in the political framework have exerted their influence upon the moral and emotional weight of the images. Each photograph evokes a page in New China's history. Some cover the same page from a different perspective, and many present their subject with greater force today than was foreseen in the original moment. Others, because of the knowledge we acquire with hindsight, are imbued with an ambiguity that went undetected at the time.

Images Speaking Thousands of Words

Photographs are multifaceted; all are cogs in a massive memory machine that documents socio-cultural history. A few, courtesy of the vision of an individual photographer, become iconic because they challenge the facts of history, as well as socio-cultural attitudes and prejudices. These ultimately provide future generations with an informed visual legacy from the past. Whilst it is not always necessary to have an intimate knowledge of the broader aspects of a particular national framework to engage with a photograph, and China is a very particular framework indeed, a grasp of history does map out the context for the images: especially those photographs that were created in line with the dictates of propaganda and the prevailing political ideology. Dictatorships, totalitarian or Communist states, even democracies, might read the same in theory, but are very different in practice. The differences are always due to the local cultural nuances. From this standpoint, the details found in so many images in this book are fascinating, for they speak directly of the reality behind all the constructs of propaganda: of the distinctive Chinese cultural nuances. Beneath the surface of idealized goals and social mechanisms that underpin the Communist agenda, lie ingrained local philosophical and aesthetic sensibilities that no amount of politics could eradicate. The details help piece together the story that Mao's guidelines for artistic expression were designed to conceal within official pictures; often because that version of events is excluded from the public, or official, face of history, and did not match the claims made by the

ideology. An example would be the transition from the highly politicized era of Mao's regime, from 1949 to 1976, to the relative openness of Deng Xiaoping's leadership, which is reflected visually in the photographs as a shift away from the unified image of the people that was so necessary to national propaganda. In its stead, one discerns a resurgence of humanism, of gentle pleasures and new dreams, which had previously been denied—such as love, glimpsed in public parks by Liu Heung Shing in 1980 (page 290), or women having their hair permed in 1980 (page 296): in short, a return to an ordinary, humdrum existence for the average mainland citizen.

The social aspects of moments frozen in the independent visions of photographers from the early 1980s onwards remain political. Their choice of subject matter reveals a renewed interest in the diversity of the local population, which had been played down in the first decades of the People's Republic, or reduced to politicized pastiche. This diversity is primarily ethnic, and therefore cultural, as well as topographical. China's population is not the homogeneous entity that is conjured by the single name ascribed to the vast landmass. The ethnic diversity represented by the 56 minority peoples that are generally referred to as "Chinese," and the regional variations in climate and geographical features, mean that, outside the major cities, personal experience and a sense of New China is more atypical than uniform. The people will always be pragmatic over and above the political trend to which they are required to subscribe, because poverty forced a preoccupation with basic survival. Here, the enormous impact of New China's socio-political and ideological characteristics becomes clear. In broadly generalized terms, since 1949, the majority of Chinese people has been exposed to the same political ideology, been put through the same uniform education system (even if the levels of that education remain hugely uneven), and is aware of the nation's historical progress and program of modernization (although again, this process has taken quite a different turn in major cities from that in provincial towns, and from that in the vast rural areas). In short, every Chinese national over the age of 35—excepting the smallest minorities in the farthest-flung and poorest regions—has been primed with a similar knowledge and power of reasoning.[3]

New China's ideological and cultural characteristics thus form the parameters within which its history is mapped. A close look at the photographs of all eras shows how prominent these are.

All this played an enormous part in shaping the photography that resulted. It also shaped the people's general understanding, and appreciation, of the way reality appears as both the subject and object of a photographic frame, even as the people understood on some level that, in terms of its immediate socio-political framework, the photograph was foremost a visual tool. The State deployed a large number of photographers at the front line of socialist reforms and restructuring, which Mao implemented from the early 1950s. The photographs they created were disposed at the spearhead of propaganda campaigns, becoming the visual embodiment of the campaign message and goals, and pictures that spoke a thousand words. By their very nature, such assignments centered on positive visions of "reality," which would be further enhanced, or even altered, in the darkroom or the printing process, when deemed necessary. This is evidenced in the striking discrepancies between various versions of a great number of photographs published in official media in the first several decades of New China. Here, figures disappear and reappear, transmuted as if by magic in and out of the photographic frame, against backdrops that were regularly weeded of politically incorrect bodies and unsightly blemishes. Besides the most obvious example of Mao, most leaders received a rejuvenating makeover; their features were smoothed, their gestures, and those of the people around them, refined. This is one area of photography in New China for which local technicians clearly possessed remarkable and inventive creative aptitude.[4]

Secondly, between the late 1970s and the early 1980s, small groups of amateur photographers across the country clubbed together for moral support, and to embark upon a collective attempt to break free of the official aesthetic. This movement began quite by chance in Beijing in the wake of Zhou Enlai's death in April 1976, and although it had political origins, its members quickly developed very different (artistic) aspirations. Initially, the movement was prompted by an impulse to defy the authoritarian control projected by the Gang of Four after Mao's death, but was soon replaced by a new desire to embrace the mood of optimism sparked by Deng Xiaoping's economic reform policies, announced in 1978.

The Official Birth of Photographic Endeavor

Even before New China was founded, in 1949, a modest number of photographers were at work recording the advances made by Communist guerrilla forces in winning the people to their cause. At the end of the Long March in October 1936, they arrived in Yan'an, which Mao Zedong made his base until the final journey to Beijing began in 1946. The majority of these early photographers hailed from intellectual circles in Shanghai; an educated elite, born into financially comfortable familial circumstances. Such circumstances fostered a fascination with photography, as well as providing the means to acquire a modern camera. Many of these young intellectuals had followed the May Fourth (1919) movement —the need to modernize, to industrialize, and to become a self-sufficient nation free of foreign influence and control. In its wake, these passions were translated into a sympathetic attitude towards the philosophical ideals of Marxism, which in theory promised to eradicate the servitude and inequalities of the feudalist system, and transform China into a modern nation.[5] The camera was but one example of the practical mechanics of Western science that they believed could serve local socio-cultural needs. It also satisfied an appetite for creative expression.

In the early 1930s, independent photojournalists in Europe, and particularly America, had transformed news reporting, particularly the visual side, to which the popularity of *Life* magazine, launched in 1936,[6] attests. Dramatic photographs of world events were made possible by the invention of compact Leica and Ermanox cameras, produced around 1929. They were as lightweight and portable as could be imagined at the time.

In pre-1949 China, the communicative power of the photograph had yet to register amongst the general population by such direct means. A photograph was a portrait—be it of a group, family, or individual—and there was much suspicion that the camera stole something from the sitter. The founding of New China in 1949 changed this because, against the myriad regional dialects and ethnic languages (many of which did not have the vocabulary to articulate socialist ideas), photographs spoke a universally understandable language.[7] The great volume of monumental tableaux, either oil paintings or sculptures that were encouraged by the new regime, as directed by the propaganda bureau in the style of Social Realism, fed the people's hearts and minds with exhilarating visions of the socialist Utopia to come. The visual allure of iconic works depicting acts of heroism and faith is little diminished by the passage of time. But, at the end of the day, they were still artworks, designed and produced by artists who used their creative skills to construct a reality rather than capture one as a photograph could do. The power of the photograph soon asserted its worth. Only a photograph could capture the changing reality, and actual events, as experienced by real people feverishly struggling to build a new society. Photography upheld a truth with which artistic constructs could not compete—at least not intellectually. Thus, the photograph acquired a critical importance in communicating the urgent need to embrace and follow Mao's ideological vision for China, and in affirming the nation's progress, especially in its darkest hours. Ironically, it would take almost 50 years for the work of Chinese photographers to gain recognition on its own merit—either as historic documentation, reportage, or a personal endeavor—in China or abroad. Yet, from the early 1950s to the end of Mao's regime, it was undoubtedly one of the most powerful tools the Communists had at their fingertips.

Serving the People

Mao had a vision of the role that the arts—visual, literary, and performing—would play in fostering the ideals of the age. He first outlined

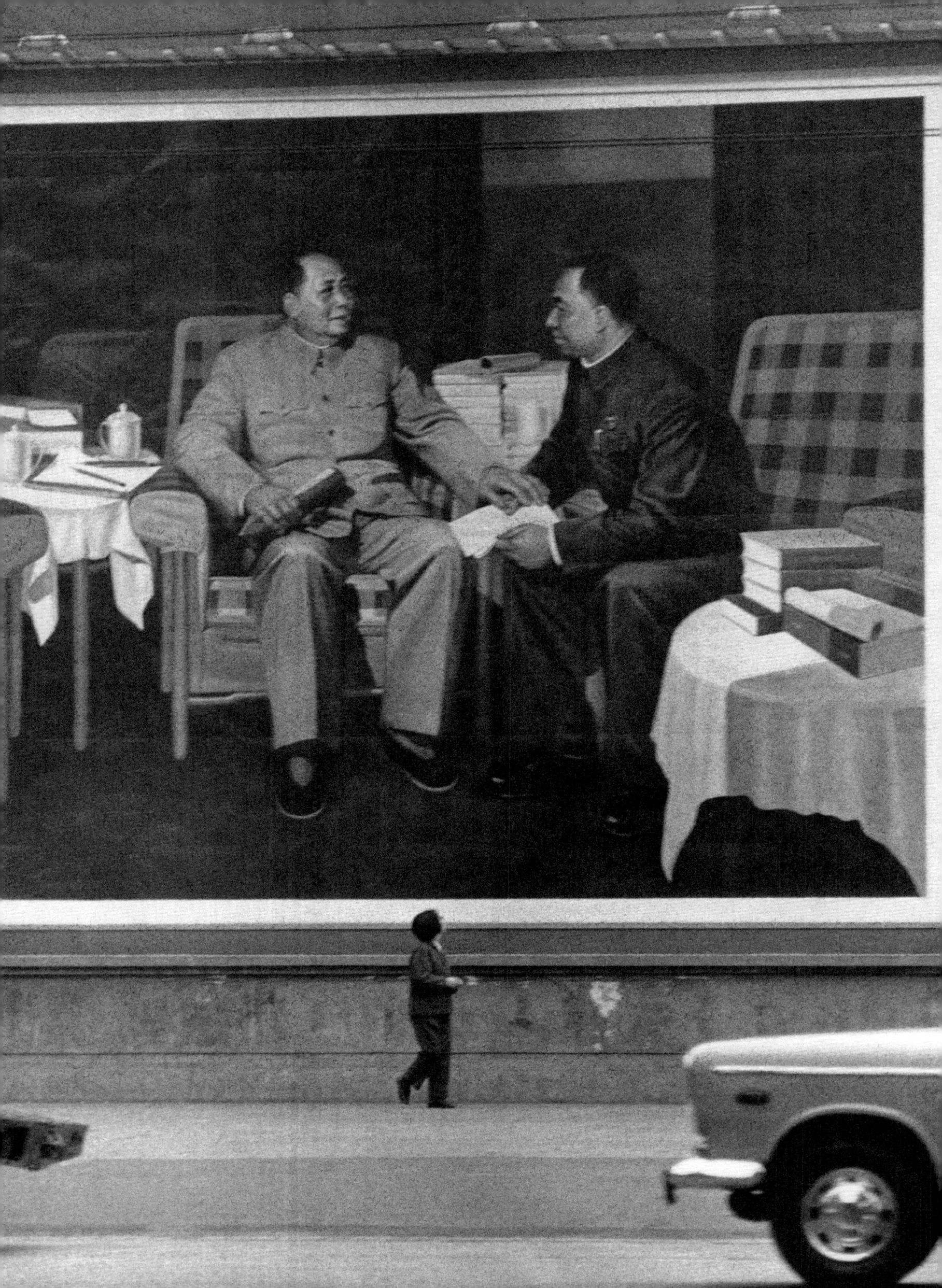

←
Liu Heung Shing, 1977

A huge propaganda boarding dwarfs a passing pedestrian on Shanghai's famous Bund. The painting depicts Chairman Mao, seated on the left, delivering the immortalized line to his chosen successor, Hua Guofeng: "With you in charge, I am at ease." Hua was sidelined as soon as Deng Xiaoping consolidated his power in 1978.

Das riesige Propagandaplakat lässt den Passanten auf Shanghais berühmter Uferpromenade Bund winzig erscheinen. Das Bild zeigt links den Vorsitzenden Mao, wie er seinem designierten Nachfolger Hua Guofeng den unvergesslichen Satz mit auf den Weg gibt: „Wenn Du die Verantwortung übernimmst, bin ich beruhigt." Sobald Deng Xiaoping seine Macht 1978 gefestigt hatte, wurde Hua entmachtet.

Un énorme panneau de propagande semble menacer un passant sur le célèbre Bund de Shanghai. Elle montre le Président Mao, assis à gauche, adressant ses fameuses paroles à son successeur désigné, Hua Guofeng : « Avec toi aux affaires, je suis tranquille ». Hua fut écarté dès que Deng Xiaoping consolida son pouvoir en 1977.

his thoughts in Yan'an in 1942,[8] and these would continue to be the basis of artistic expression for the ensuing decades: an approach to artistic expression in all forms of art that would "serve the people." Socialist Realism, anointed by Mao as the style du jour, had proven efficacy in the Soviet Union. Drawing upon ingrained cultural preferences across China, Mao's adaptation catered brilliantly to local tastes. The New China version of Socialist Realism deployed ink, brush, rice paper, mineral colors, for Chinese painting and New Year's pictures, and even used paper-cuts. Then there was the greatest art form of all, the calligraphic text. Similar to Socialist Realism, photography was a Western import. Unlike Socialist Realism, it was a mechanical tool and not a politically constructed artistic style. Of all the media brought to bear on New China's creative expression, photography alone lacked an independent aesthetic value. There had hardly been time for one to evolve. The camera was merely a tool, and a convenient means to an end. By the time New China was founded, the photographic experiments being carried out in Shanghai were overtaken by the task of building socialism, to which everyone initially wanted to contribute. Deciding the camera was merely a tool, the Party began appointing reliable people to take pictures. Those assigned to operate a camera were required to release the shutter at the appropriate moment from the best possible angle. No invocation of "mood" (other than "ideologically positive") was required, nor of lighting (other than "bright," meaning devoid of negative shadows), nor were attempts at clever, artistic composition (other than clarity of composition and focus, and that again would eliminate any possible ambiguity) considered appropriate.

We can see from the photographs of this period that a good many of those who took them, and who might never have come to choose photography under any other circumstances, had both aptitude and astute insight into the situation at any given moment. These images are then extraordinary records of history; fragment by fragment, they combine to form a well-rounded picture. Even at the height of political control over the masses, truth still "outs." The photographs belonging to the era of propaganda (1950s–1970s) in particular offer a stirring evocation of the times. At the risk of stating the obvious, propaganda art exerts a powerful resonance because, like any successful advertising campaign, it plays with visual common denominators that appeal directly to a general public, being both easy to understand and memorable. The camera deployed the directives of propaganda to great effect. Black and white, which was the only practicable film choice in the early years of New China, except for the few circumstances in which color was sanctioned, naturally enhanced the drama and the emotional charge in people's expressions. It also focused the viewers' attention

upon the action and the message. Yet in spite of the ideological constraints, looking back at these frames with fresh eyes today, we find in the artistry and sensitivity brought to framing so many of the photographs that the individuals who created them possessed enormous natural talent.

Picturing a New Society

The founding of New China ended "more than a century of humiliating defeat, unequal treaties, and foreign occupations,"[9] which was an unmitigated cause for celebration. In the wake of civil strife as the Nationalists limped on, and warlords engaged in their own battles, most people simply struggled to survive. As the Communist guerillas won increasing support, China was finally liberated. Photographs from 1949 (page 127) show exhausted soldiers of the People's Liberation Army (PLA) asleep on the streets, for they were forbidden to enter the homes of the communities they had liberated. Captivated by the new moral and egalitarian period of socialism, the people championed the cause, fired up by the opportunity to shake off the yoke of feudalism and bondage. Apart from freeing the people from veritable slavery, it seemed that the Communists would also give China back its dignity. Most Chinese people entered the 1950s believing themselves to be on the cusp of a glorious new era that would dispose of "evil" landlords (a process already begun in an active program of land reform), and put pay to the corruptive practices of the Nationalists, whose republic bore all the characteristics of yet another imperial dynasty. Mao served the people a taste of freedom, and they willingly embraced the exuberance of his propaganda. Not only did it advocate change for the better, Mao made it a promise. Indeed, many of the policies were thoroughly commendable. Ordinary people were to be educated: illiteracy was to be stamped out. Hunger was to be eradicated as poverty was eased. People would be trained for new jobs in industry that would make China a force to be reckoned with. Mao went as far as to proclaim "What the West has, China will also have" as part of a mass modernization program that would see China overtake Britain, and stride onwards to catch up with America in a matter of years. This was the impetus behind the disastrous Great Leap Forward that took place in 1958. In this context, photographs excelled in their ability to foster the spirit of optimism upon the largely illiterate rural communities and the urban poor. By highlighting feats of heroism and castigating acts of selfishness, photographs further inculcated the masses with a social duty to the community and responsibility to contribute to the communal good. Photographic images thus served as true evidence of achievements; benchmarks against which progress and change could be measured.

Half the Sky

One group that had reason to support Mao was the female segment of the population, who Mao released from centuries of subjugation under a social hierarchy aligned with Confucian doctrines, which effectively rendered women voiceless, without practicable rights. Mao declared women equal. Following his public proclamation that they "held up half the sky," women were entitled to a position in the work force alongside men: a right that was extolled in the 1950s as communes replaced existing social structures and communities, and women demonstrated that they were just as capable as men. This was celebrated in photography, too, at times by women photographers. But one should not imagine a feminist mentality at work. A small number of women had enjoyed an active presence in Yan'an. Here, female refugees from areas ravaged by civil strife, and the invading Japanese army, were offered the new equality of Communist ideology and given a basic education unimaginable in their former lives. One example is Hou Bo, who would serve as Mao's personal photographer from 1949 until 1961. Another is Xiao Zhuang, who joined a guerrilla force in Zhejiang in 1949, and was assigned the task of taking photographs for a local newspaper in 1950. As was the practice at the time, her basic training was acquired on the job. Two years later, in 1952, she was a fully-fledged photographer working for the *Xinhua Daily News*.[10] Whilst her background and political outlook stood her in good stead, Xiao's allegiance to the cause apparently never overrode her personal engagement with the subjects she photographed. It would be wrong to suggest that she ever departed from the Party line, yet her images exude a rare degree of empathy and understanding that go beyond a simple illustration of local politics. On occasion, one even finds a hint of the dilemma that confronts many photojournalists in the face of war, as witnesses to human conflict, for it is their job to record not to intervene, even when witnessing the atrocious behavior displayed during mass rallies, when all manner of humiliation was inflicted upon the victims of the moment.

From the 1950s to the 1970s, Xiao produced powerful documentary images, in simple, striking compositions. These range from crowds at mass rallies and the groundswell of support for Mao, to myriad expressions of the people's devotion to the Chairman—exuberant in its enthusiasm, violent in its extremes—and to his campaigns and the challenge of realizing the goals these set. These photographs also hint at the complex nature of the emotions all this political activity engendered. These emotions shifted from one moment to the next as the political winds changed direction in response to internal power struggles. Many of Xiao's pictures of mass rallies were taken from extraordinary vantage points that capture the massive scale of the gatherings, and the claustrophobic, menacing aura of their unfolding (pages 200/201 and 209). By these subtle means, she ensured that the photographs would capture the mood, and the mechanisms by which internal discord would alter the course of history. They plot the route by which society sunk into a darker reality in the 1970s: New China's most traumatic and confused moment. Whilst the significance of many details of the situations and events captured might be lost upon future generations, Xiao's finely tuned eye for composition and her intuitive sense of what she was witnessing, make her photographs an enlightening vision of those "irrational times."[11]

Similar to Xiao Zhuang, Hou Bo came to the role of photographer because of her ideologically reliable countenance, above and beyond any aptitude she possessed for photography. She had not so much as held a camera before being assigned to her career. In her 12 years at Mao's side, and as part of his entourage, she was present at pivotal moments in history and, having been counted as a member of his household, was present in all aspects of his daily life. The photographs she captured in private moments behind the scenes as the man relaxed, apparently at ease with the camera, stand in stark contrast to the austere authority of the official portraits of Mao, which are familiar around the world. She gives us man not god. Can one attribute her choice of frames to a feminine capacity for compassion? Perhaps: contemporaneous photographs taken by male photographers generally eschew obvious psychological inferences or any margin of ambiguity.

Male photographers were always going to outnumber the women in this period. Yet, the most enduring bodies of work belong to a modest group of individuals. Pre-eminent amongst this group are Jiang Shaowu, Wang Shilong, Meng Zhaorui, and Lü Xiangyou. Their photographs emphasize the lofty ambitions of Maoist ideology in uncompromising and unambiguous observations of the impact of his policies and campaigns.

Liaoning Daily News photographer Jiang Shaowu began his career in 1947. His photographs unapologetically present public humiliations that were staged before thunderous crowds in the feverishly ideological period of chaos from the mid-1960s to Mao's death in 1976. These have none of the alarming circus-style spectacle of comparable images taken by Li Zhensheng. They pretend nothing, and are strangely unambiguous about the incidents they document. They record the process of a nation, a people striving towards communal goals amidst the violent forfeiture of the privileges enjoyed by the elite for the greater benefit of all. With hindsight, such photographs as the blind man interpreting the *Quotations from Mao Zedong* (page 195) or the crocodile tears of a group of young men who are mourning Mao's passing in 1976 (pages 262/263), convey a compelling sense of the fallacy of so many of Mao's policies.

"It is my opinion that the international situation has now reached a new turning point. There are two winds in the world today, the East Wind and the West Wind There is a Chinese saying, 'Either the East Wind prevails over the West Wind or the West Wind prevails over the East Wind.' I believe it is characteristic of the situation today that the East Wind is prevailing over the West Wind."

MAO ZEDONG (1893–1976), first Chairman of the People's Republic of China, 1957

In common with the majority of photographers of the day, Henan native Wang Shilong enlisted in the military in 1948, whereupon he, too, was set to work taking photographs for his local propaganda bureau. Injury curtailed his activities as a military correspondent in Tibet, where he served alongside the PLA, but it did not prevent him from traveling far and wide across Henan and the neighboring provinces to photograph social advances in the newly formed People's Communes. His photographs are imbued with a particularly heavy, velvety depth of tone. Fixing his gaze across the vast terrain of the People's Communes, the re-organization of agricultural land on a scale hitherto unknown in China (pages 166/167 and 247) is invoked in an extraordinarily range of silvery grays, including every imaginable shade from black to white. Similarly, his photographs of mass activities as hundreds, thousands of people joined forces to complete a monumental feat of human endeavor through sheer persistence of will. Indeed, some photographs appear as illustrations of parables that Mao employed. The most famous one is the "foolish old man who moved the mountain."[12] Wang gives us communities moving mountains, altering the course of rivers, and maximizing crop yields from the land. He never lost sight of the moment, not of the day to day hardship of human existence in this era, nor of the inimitable quirks of human nature that could not be erased. In spite of all discouragement of any concern with one's personal appearance, he gives us the image of a young rural couple leaving a tailor's establishment, located in a cave, in a far-flung valley, lost in their momentary appreciation of a newly made garment.

The soldier Meng Zhaorui worked for the army magazine, *PLA Pictorial*. The special access that this afforded him to Mao and to events of national importance enabled him to capture China's first successful explosion of a hydrogen bomb in 1967. He was present at many of Mao Zedong's public appearances, and on Tiananmen Square for his meetings with the Red Guards (pages 180/181). In 1966, he snapped a portentous frame of Mao in his private quarters, seated in an armchair and gazing across the room in a most disquieting manner at Zhou Enlai and Lin Biao, as they pore over the draft of a document, quite oblivious to his expression. The image appears portentous because, by 1971, the then defense minister, Lin Biao, would be dead—killed in a plane crash en route to the Soviet Union following an unsuccessful *coup d'etat*, or so it was claimed. This fascinating frame is photography at its best: the undertone of Mao's expression attests to the complex nature of the political struggle that precipitated the height of the Cultural Revolution (1966–76) (page 182).

Picturing Utopia

During the first three decades of New China, photography was the province of the propaganda bureau. It is curious then that the "truth"

it recorded is an unabashed visual testimony to the harrowing process of social struggle, resulting in images that are shockingly frank, today appearing surprisingly impartial. They are fragments that combine to give a factual account of the passionate convictions that transformed the nation. Having crossed the threshold of a new millennium, this period of history is now firmly in the past. China has moved on. The photographs thus help us to appreciate the extraordinary hurdles that China has overcome. Importantly, they also provide a context for the complex mindset of Chinese society then and today.

The cushion of optimism upon which New China sashayed forward encouraged the slew of positive images produced during the 1950s. That reality underwent a dramatic shift between 1955 and 1965. The first hint of a dark side to Mao's policies came in 1957 with the launch of the anti-rightists' campaign. "Rightists" actually constituted a tiny percentage of the population, but the efficient machinery of the propaganda ministry meant that the anti-rightist campaigns had an enormous, and far-reaching, impact: it led by example. The disturbing dark force of these policies was temporarily eclipsed in 1958 as Mao called for the establishment of People's Communes (page 148). Events took a turn for the worst in 1959, precipitated by the Great Leap Forward (also launched in 1958), as the harvests failed and a harsh winter followed. By spring 1960, famine had broken out across the country. It continued until 1962, with more than 30 million people dying of starvation. Today, it is hard to imagine being immersed in such a climate. We wonder how people could ignore the discrepancies between the idealized visions spun out by the propaganda machine, and the reality before their eyes, as record yields were reported in swift succession, and yet most communes could not feed their own people. One effective countermeasure at this time that worked in the government's favor was the limited opportunities for ordinary people to travel. This kept communities isolated and incommunicado. The effective stasis of the rural populace allowed communities to believe that "over there," somewhere else in another part of the country, things were already better, and that patience would see them, too, prevail. Susan Sontag defines the persuasive truth of a photograph in simple terms: "Something we hear about, but doubt, seems proven when we're shown a photograph."[13] With all the visual proof provided by the propaganda ministry in a multitude of photographs, what was there to doubt?

The situation did not improve in the 1960s. Famine had eased by 1963, but in urban centers where political struggle was at its most intense, people found themselves embroiled in the tumult of the Cultural Revolution. This was reflected in a corresponding change in the visual format of photographs dating from this time. They became increasingly formulaic, stylized, more optimistic in expression, and frequently doctored.

→
Liu Heung Shing, 1980

A Sichuanese peasant eats a bowl of rice on his lunch break. Above him, behind a row of tattered shoes, is a portrait of Mao. Next to the portrait is a calligraphic inscription that reads "Listen to Chairman Hua." Hua was Mao's successor, who was sidelined by Deng Xiaoping after 1978, and ousted from power in 1981.

Ein Bauer aus Sichuan isst in seiner Mittagspause eine Schüssel Reis. Über ihm hängt hinter einer Reihe abgetragener Schuhe ein Porträt Maos. Seitlich davon befindet sich eine kalligrafische Inschrift mit der Bedeutung „Hört auf den Vorsitzenden Hua". Hua war Maos Nachfolger, wurde aber nach 1978 von Deng Xiaoping außer Gefecht gesetzt und 1981 entmachtet.

Un paysan du Sichuan mange un bol de riz pour son déjeuner. Derrière lui, au-dessus de vieilles chaussures, un portrait de Mao accompagné d'une inscription calligraphique disant « Écoutez le Président Hua », successeur de Mao, écarté par Deng Xiaoping après 1978 et chassé du pouvoir en 1981.

The Cultural Revolution was Mao's attempt to reaffirm his position and reassert his dogma, whereby all creative expression was subject to an absolute ideological paradigm. One suspects that at least a few photographers were aware of the construct they were instrumental in fabricating. None attempted to confront the contradictions directly, but one could hardly expect otherwise. We do have examples that suggest this awareness, such as the expression on Mao's face that Meng Zhaorui captured in 1966. The best-known body of this type of work was created by Li Zhensheng, and was published under the title *Red Colour News Soldier* in 2003.[14] Like other "news soldiers," Li Zhensheng's task was to "record the joys and triumphs of Mao's China." He alone would later claim to have interpreted this as an opportunity to create a scrupulous, candid indictment of history.

The Mao era was an extraordinary time to be a photographer, plunged in the midst of a socio-political theater that provided "…moments that became history almost instantaneously."[15] The images chosen to represent the 1950s, 1960s, and 1970s here are arguably the most powerful and memorable in China's modern history, and undeniably due to their political-ideological content. They speak to us of the surging, tumultuous forces of change that characterized the period, and illustrate the vicissitudes of the political mood in a relentless series of mass campaigns. Photographs transport us to another time and place, to share the experience of communities and individuals during a socially debilitating struggle between opposing—and desperate—political factions. John Szarkowski once wrote: "During photography's first century, it was generally understood that what photography did best was to describe things… The highest virtues of such photographs were clarity of statement and density of information."[16] If we accept this satement, can we not claim these photographs, clearly overflowing with information, to be both the "best," and of the highest virtue?

The Dawning of a New Era

The 1980s got off to a protracted start. In the wake of Mao's death, it took Deng Xiaoping two years to consolidate his power, and three more to get the Gang of Four behind bars.[17] Their widely publicized trial was a landmark event in China after Mao, a process of normalization systematically documented by Liu Heung Shing between 1979 and 1983. In 1978, Deng Xiaoping announced his utterly modernist Reform Policy. It proved to be tremendously important, as was the re-opening of universities (from 1978) and schools (1980) that had been closed since the mid-1970s. The enthusiastic devotion to academics is illustrated in Liu Heung Shing's photograph of students studying at night on Tiananmen Square, which in the early 1980s was the only place bright enough to read by in the evening (pages 288/289). It was a time of conflicting emotions: Deng's policies were reversing so many of Mao's ideals. At the turn of the decade, Deng gave instructions to reduce the number of Mao's omnipresent portraits in public spaces[18]—yet, a recurring cycle of "Mao crazes" spread through society during the 1980s, and even in 1993, the centenary of Mao's birth.

As a consequence of economic advances, a new phase of artistic expression in all its forms was on the horizon, from literature to poetry, visual art to music. Photographers felt no less of a need to look beyond the parameters of a politically sanctioned reflection of reality. In an attempt to draw upon broader social issues and human existence as a means of developing their own practice towards more profound ends, there was a flourish of experimentation, which had its roots in the April Photo Society and the flowering of amateur photography in the late 1970s. This force was unleashed immediately after the death of the Chinese premier Zhou Enlai in April 1976, when the Gang of Four forbade a public mourning of the "people's premier." Professional and amateur photographers who happened to be on Tiananmen Square as mourners began to gather prior to the order to disburse captured the event as it unfolded. They were still there when the police were ordered to clear the area later that day, and had produced a surprising volume of negatives in the brief hours afforded them, of which an even more surprising number survived the search-and-destroy operation that was launched in the days that followed. These images were ultimately compiled in a volume titled *People's Mourning*, released in 1979. Along with the first major photographic exhibition, which opened in Beijing at the end of 1978,[19] photography was given a new, independent lease on life.

In the 1980s, the opportunities for mounting exhibitions of any kind were limited. Until around 2005, photography did not enjoy a significant following in China, outside its own circles. An example that illustrates the widely differing fortunes of art and photography in China is a comparison between the importance attached to two exhibitions, both of which took place in Beijing around 1979. Each was organized by a fledgling group of non-official, largely amateur practitioners. One, the Stars Painting Group (usually referred to simply as the "Stars"), which held an unofficial exhibition on the perimeter of the China National Gallery in the center of Beijing. When the exhibition was closed down it became news, and even more so when the Stars dared to protest the confiscation of their works, and were successful in securing their return. Liu Heung Shing's 1979 photograph shows a triumphant Ma Desheng on the steps of the City Hall surrounded by an attentive crowd of supporters and passersby (page 272), and fellow group member Wang Keping parading a banner that demanded "freedom of expression" (page 273). Second, the

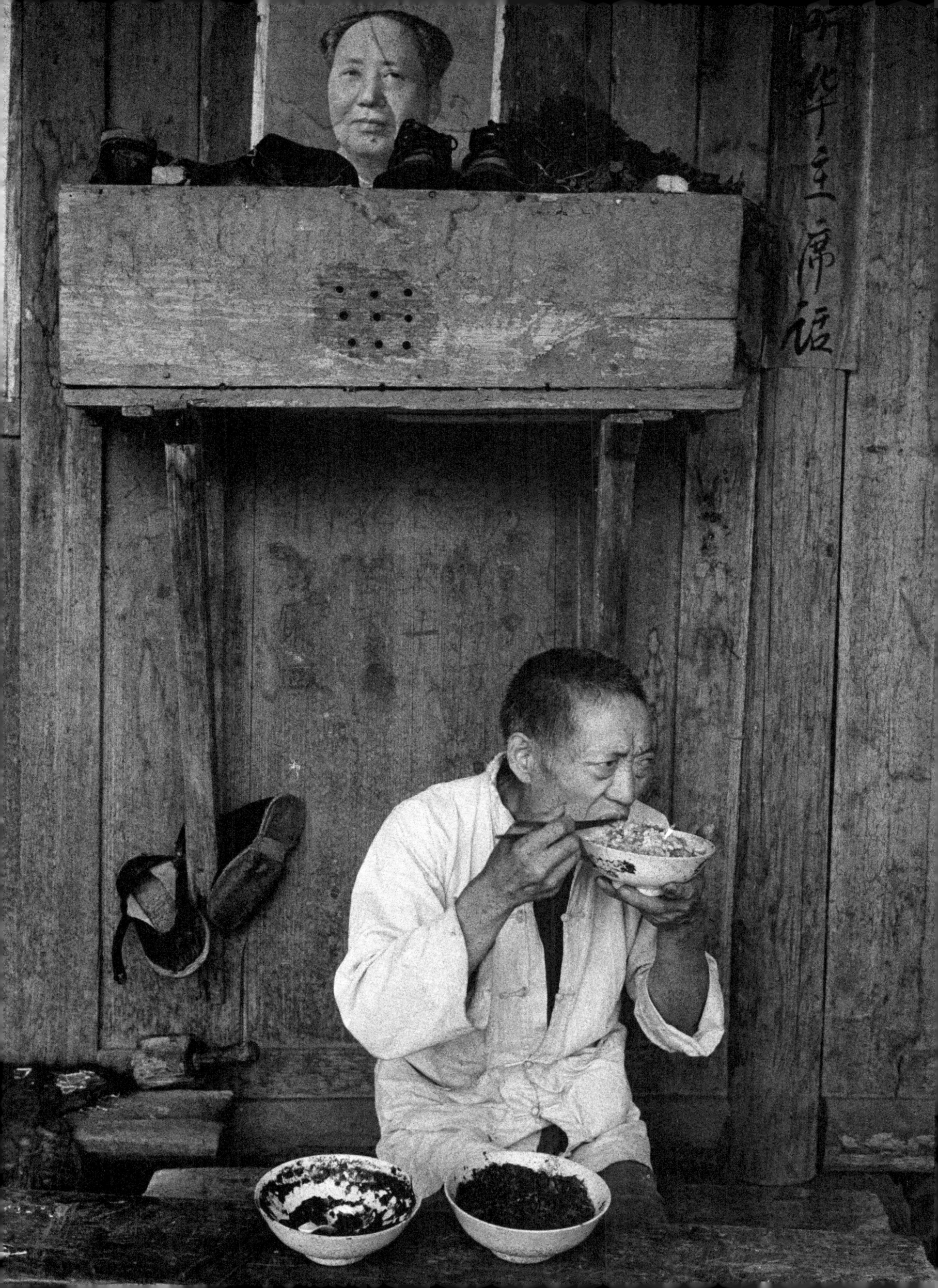

April Photo Society, a group of photographers who named this collective in honor of the event that brought them together, and whose exhibition, *Nature, Society, and Man,* which opened, appropriately, in April 1979, ran smoothly and did not make the headlines. Both this show, and two subsequent ones, held in 1980 and 1981, attracted respectable crowds, but neither enjoyed the legendary status of the Stars' art exhibitions.

It is curious considering that the modus operandi of the two groups was largely the same, as were their aspirations and influences. Similar to the "misty poets" and the metaphysical writers of the age, China's photographers clearly preferred their comment veiled. Characteristic images from the 1980s took landscape as their subject, frequently presented as a dream-like vista, filled with inferences of nature symbolism found in the ink painting tradition. The disparity between the official, authorized images produced by veteran Xinhua News photographer Lü Houmin, and the *National Geographic*-style celebration of the natural world that he made his focus in the 1980s, illustrates the paradigm shifts that were taking place in photographic practice during this decade. This was the era of "art for art's sake," but ironically, the April Photo Society's Achilles' heel would prove to be the very "salon style" aesthetic that had initially brought its members together. It encouraged a focus on beauty and an ethereal spirituality above all other considerations. Having said that, the photographs produced by members of the April Photo Society represented a dramatic departure from established conventions. In the 1970s, as "professional" photographers, each had created superb, iconic images. However, they did not hesitate to abandon the real world in favor of "art" aesthetics at the first opportunity. Former editor of *Creative Camera* magazine Bill Jay once commented: "Camera clubs … are primarily concerned with the production of pretty images, and not with revealing the truth about the picture's content."[20] Ultimately, this is what the salon mentality reduced their work to.

Back to Nature

The images produced by Chinese photographers in the 1980s are nothing if not sincere. The efforts they expended were tenacious, too, to which the vast compendium of images in *Humanism in China*[21] attests. Even here the volume of images from the 1980s is disproportionately small as compared with that of other decades. The photographs from the 1980s really are "fragments,"[22] and offer few hints as to their place in the bigger picture, or where they ought to be inserted.

By the late 1980s, a new generation was on the rise, one that knew little about what life was like under Mao, and that had grown up in the era of opening up, reform, and rapid modernization. This generation was also abreast of Western influences, and had an unprecedented amount of information at its fingertips. Members of this generation intuitively rejected the April Photo Society's primary aesthetics: the sentimental aspects of its humanist concerns. A good example is the Topic Group, formed in the early 1990s by young professional photographers, which included Liu Zheng *(The Workers' Daily)*, Jin Yongquan *(China Youth Daily)*, and Yuan Dongping *(China Nationalities Pictorial)*. Their goal was to bring photography back to issues, and to put content back into photographs. In the late 1980s, Yuan Dongping and Lü Nan created a documentary series of photographs of patients in a typical mental hospital. Like the images that preceded them during the height of the Cultural Revolution, these are characterized by an unflinching gaze, and an almost Victorian fascination with human oddities. Other visual explorations of specific social issues followed, produced by small groups of forward-looking individuals. In the 1990s, many issues continued to be sensitive topics for photographers, with significant restrictions upon what could be published. Their attempt to implement a discourse was clearly ahead of its time, and for that reason struggled to gain a broader momentum or exposure. This was largely due to the lack of a platform—a lack that has since been filled to some extent by the Internet, which, since the early 2000s, has become the main arena for tackling and debating contentious moral issues—or the kind of independent exhibition spaces that proliferate in the major cities today.

In spite of the momentary setback engendered by the June Fourth incident, the reform program continued to lead China towards new levels of openness and, by the 1990s, a younger generation of photographers had begun to buck the prevailing trends with a ready embrace of reality. Taking their cue from pioneering social commentators such as Diane Arbus, August Sander, and Richard Avendon, and the occasional reverential nod to the atmospherics of Eugène Atget, this new breed of internationally minded and highly ambitious photographers found a comparable array of surreal beings and settings to use as props in mounting their own attempts at an allegory of modern life in China. A good example of this is Liu Zheng's series *The Chinese*, created between 1994 and 1999—a timeframe that overlaps with his career as a photojournalist with *Workers' Daily*, 1991 to 1997. *The Chinese* is a group of arresting frames clearly oriented towards the sensibility of those Western photographers mentioned above, and features actors, singers, nuns, performers, bizarre personalities, and abnormal physical bodies (page 336), which inevitably have a morbid appeal.

Art + Photography = ?

The 1990s saw a momentous proliferation of photography practice across China. Standards of living were rising at a significant rate.

Urban centers had taken on a distinct air of modernity. The media was expanding to accommodate a range of lifestyle publications with lavish photographic illustrations. This was the decade in which contemporary art laid firm foundations upon which to build, and because it was relatively easy to be an artist, as a single independent unit that didn't need too much equipment or space, it was the visual arts—and to a lesser extent literary ones—that led the aesthetic discourse of the day. The nascent art world in China had begun to attract the attention of Western curators and art lovers. On a subconscious level, the new generation of photographers was increasingly encouraged to align its practices with the nation's contemporary artists, if for no other reason than this would provide opportunities for exchange, critical appraisal, and the exhibition of works, which were lacking within photography circles.

Until the late 1990s, it was hard to study photography in China. Photographers had to acquire their skills on the job, or as part of a course in journalism. For this reason, courses were confined to technical colleges with departments in journalism. Practical sessions tended to concentrate on camera mechanics and technical applications. Since photography was not considered a medium of fine art, aesthetics were not deemed necessary. Until the early 2000s, photography was deemed an applied art; thereafter it began to be considered a fine art. One of the prime movers in this arena was Rong Rong, who, in 1996, joined forces with Liu Zheng to produce the influential *New Photo* magazine. Frustrated by the content and constraints of official magazines such as *China Photography*, they perceived the need for a magazine that made no distinction between the work of an artist, a photojournalist, or a "pure" photographer. For professional photographers, meanwhile, the only choice lay in magazines like *China Photography*, which was published by the Photographers' Association. All such official magazines were traditional and conservative in content, placing emphasis upon the technical aspects of photography, and the mechanics of achieving certain visual effects, whilst avoiding the psychological/deeper sociological implications of the photograph. Their magazine took its lead from a free photography broadsheet, *Photo Reportage*, produced by Liu Heung Shing in 1995, and was distributed free of charge within photography circles, and employed a similar format and focus on the power of the photographic image.

As the 1990s unfolded, a preference for investigative photography emerged. Photographers identified a subject that interested them and pursued it as their own. Jiang Jian portrayed ordinary people from small communities in rural areas or small towns. Wu Jialin looked at life in the provinces, in mountain regions, and outlying towns, and Yang Yankang traveled the length and breadth of the country seeking out religious communities in rural areas (page 318). Wang Fuchun traveled around the country to witness the mass migration of workers from region to region in search of work on the nation's vast network of trains (page 322). Zeng Nian produced an extraordinary series of wide-format panoramas of the progress of the Three Gorges project and the impact this had upon the impoverished communities in the immediate vicinity (pages 324/325 and 326/327). Xie Hailong trained his lens on the plight of children in the remotest regions, who were united in a common desire to go to school (page 316 and 317). Xiao Quan, meanwhile, demonstrated a perceptive grasp of his generation in a comprehensive series of portraits of artists, curators, art critics, filmmakers, actors, writers, and poets, who were catapulting creative expression in New China into a whole new sphere. A selection was published in 1994 under the title *My Generation*,[23] which undoubtedly echoes The Who song of the same name: a reference that surely indicates similar, if subtle, aspirations on the part of the photographer to be a similar voice of a generation. These individuals represented a new generation of dedicated and talented photographers with a very particular sensitivity to the prevailing social phenomena of the times.

In the year 1996, photography found itself commandeered by the contemporary-art scene. For artists, used to constructing images to illustrate an idea, photography provided a way to survey the socio-political, economic, and cultural environment in a direct and contemporary way with little personal intervention, yet was rife with implications and inferences. Few attempts to use a camera were about the traditional values of the medium of photography per se. For artists, the concept was everything. Wang Jinsong demonstrated this better than most via a series of multiple portraits. Small details, such as the style or quality of children's shoes, speak volumes of the change in economic fortunes sweeping across the country demonstrated in Wang Jinsong's iconic work *Standard Family*. This features a family portrait of 200 one-child families: the children are all students of the same school, yet the images of their parents reveal them to be from very different backgrounds, and all walks of life (pages 328/329).

By 1998, the art world had become obsessed with photography. Xing Danwen's portrait of painter Zeng Fanzhi (now one of China's most sought-after artists, then just starting out on his career) and Wang Jin—during a performance work—shows how the photograph was shifting roles from "documentary record" to "artwork." Many photographic artworks reflected the increasing sense of ephemerality of the moment as the world moved towards a new millennium. At the same time, the camera was responsible for a range of dramatic, shocking, and seductive images. But whilst art brought color back to photography, demonstrating that it could be used to specific effect and did not detract from the drama, its own form of drama, centered on a particularly outlandish brand of imagination, soon began to seem jaded. In a prophetic statement, Ansel Adams described the dangers of art photography as "brilliant images of fuzzy concepts."[24] However, the contemporary-art scene did remind professional photographers of the potential of the medium, which encouraged a period of restrengthening and ultimately of advances.

This can be seen in the rich variety of photographic styles and approaches that are in evidence by 2000. The subject of these images ranges from contemporary life to social phenomenon: queues of girls looking for work (page 384), devastating floods in southern cities (pages 96/97), crowds at funfairs, octogenarian day-traders (page 390), children forced to sell flowers on the streets (page 315), SARS victims, stylish new dwellings of the burgeoning middle classes in Shanghai (pages 372, 373, 374 and 375), and the life of coal workers, corruption, and wealth. All these frames speak volumes about the issues of the times, the new arenas, as well as the new challenges being faced. One example that does this particularly well is Zhou Yue's documentation of the explosion of youth culture in the Chinese capital, and the inevitable air of nihilism that permeates that seam of newly freed spirits—almost entirely one-child progeny—who are beholden to no one, and indulge themselves at every turn. For these children and teenagers, China really is the land of opportunity (pages 338 and 339). These pictures form a striking contrast to Liu Heung Shing's haunting portrait of a young boy from the officially quoted poorest place in China (page 312). Shocking, seductive, highlighting the shift in social values in the face of modern distractions, these photographs speak of aspects of life that are not readily acknowledged or accepted, but whose existence is undeniable.

The Ultimate Picture

Compiling a photographic overview of a social, cultural, or political history always presents a challenge. The selected images are necessarily plucked from the context of their original time and place. Once inserted into an abridged version of history, the "moral and emotional weight" of each image is imbued with new significance and emphasis. Presented as part of a chronological sequence, individual frames become responsible for communicating moments, events, reality, political winds, economic shifts, the social atmosphere, and the human response at any given time. The dynamics of a frame are further altered by the contrast and comparison encouraged by juxtapositions that make photographs speak to each other across space and time. Time throws successive veils over the complexities of individual moments and the facts as experienced by those who were present, whilst subtle details that might have seemed irrelevant at the time are seen in a new light. Even though the intricacies of the events portrayed may not be readily apparent to later generations looking at the photographs that have survived, we understand that these images present an extraordinary visual record of China's momentous, tumultuous, and triumphant odyssey from Third-World population locked in agrarian peonage, via a state without leverage in international politics, to an economic powerhouse, home to a thriving modern society driven by the greatest manufacturing base the world has ever seen, and with a booming voice in global politics and trade that commands the attention of all.

To command attention and to stand the test of time, photography has to do more than just document facts. Photographs are part of a nation's collective memory, reference points for the communal space we inhabit as communities, as a people. They represent the external world, and its human subjects, which can be directed by a photographer, but that somehow, through the passage of time or distance from the original moment and environs, always exude their own truth. At times we need help in identifying the details of a historic narrative in any given photograph, and enough circumstantial information to enable us to read them and arrive at our own conclusions. *China, Portrait of a Country* brings together a

1. Susan Sontag, *On Photography*, Picador, New York, 1977, pp. 105–6.
2. Hou Bo was Mao's personal photographer from 1949 to 1961. Her career and work is described on page 409.
3. The same can be said of those under 35, the only difference being that their education is less political—or is it just as political but less ideological?—and is subject to the forces of economic reform, which has them versed in China with socialist characteristics that are distinctly capitalist in their embrace of consumerism. Also the information channels are different: the Internet for example.
4. An astounding range of examples can be found in Zhang Dali, *A Second History*, Walsh Gallery, Chicago, 2006.
5. Especially post-May 1919 the May Fourth Movement, which railed against the inequalities of the Versailles Treaty, which placed territorial divisions and external rights of governance over these territories in China.
6. By the mid-1940s, *Life* enjoyed a weekly circulation of over ten million copies.
7. This ultimately encouraged Mao to launch a campaign to enforce a common tongue—*putonghua*—which literally means "standard language." It was a process aided, in the 1950s, by the simplification of classical Chinese characters.
8. The "Talks on Literature and Art at Yan'an" in 1942 formed the basis of all art produced during the Mao era. All creative expression was subject to the theory he outlined here.
9. *China: Fifty Years Inside the People's Republic*, introduction by Rae Yang, exh. cat., Aperture, New York, 1999, p. 14.
10. *Xinhua Daily News*, established in Wuhan in 1938, banned by the Nationalists in 1947 and relaunched in April 1949, became the first public newspaper published in the People's Republic.
11. This is a reference to the title of Xiao Zhuang's collected works, *The Irrational Times*, published by Zhonghua Publishing House, China, 2004.
12. *Yu gong yi shan*.
13. See note 1, p. 6.
14. Li Zhensheng, *Red Colour News Soldier*, Phaidon Press, London, 2003.

pp. 68/69
Yu Haibo, 2005

In Shenzhen, on the border of Hong Kong, workers at a painting factory are trained to make copies of masterpieces by artists such as van Gogh, intended for export.
"If something is 'made in China', it has no chance, but if it is 'created in China', then who's to say it won't succeed?" Zhang Ruimin

In Shenzhen an der Grenze zu Hongkong werden Arbeiter in einer Gemäldefabrik darin ausgebildet, für den Export Meisterwerke von Künstlern wie van Gogh zu reproduzieren. „Wenn etwas ‚made in China' ist, hat es keine Chance, wenn es aber ‚created in China' ist, wer will dann sagen, dass es keinen Erfolg hat?" Zhang Ruimin

À Shenzhen, à la frontière avec Hong Kong, des travailleurs d'une usine de peinture s'entraînent à reproduire pour l'exportation des chefs-d'œuvre d'artistes comme van Gogh. « Si une chose est 'made in China' elle n'a aucune chance, mais si elle est 'créée en Chine', qui peut dire qu'elle ne réussira pas ? » Zhang Ruimin

multitude of fragments produced through the sequential decades of New China, carefully selected to construct a clear picture and yet preserve the full moral and emotional weight of each photograph. Ansel Adams once claimed that "Not everybody trusts paintings but people believe photographs." That fact at least ensures that these photographs will open a new discussion about how China has come to be where it is today.

15. See note 9.

16. John Szarkowski, "Photography and the Mass Media," *Creative Camera*, 1967, p. 30.

17. In Chinese history, the Gang of Four were the chief members of a radical faction that played a key role in orchestrating the Cultural Revolution, and tried to seize power following the death of Mao Zedong in 1976.

18. This was the subject of Liu Heung Shing's book *China after Mao*, Penguin, 1982, which extensively documents this phenomenon through images of everyday life. *China after Mao* was widely circulated in photography circles on the mainland after its publication, and remained highly influential throughout the 1990s.

19. *A Premier for the People: A People for the Premier*, December 26, 1978–February 4, 1979, put on public display an enormous photographic documentation of the "April Fifth Movement," as events surrounding the mourning of Zhou Enlai were termed, and thus was less about photography and more about a propaganda exercise of the new regime in an attempt to restore the people's faith in its policies and leadership.

20. Bill Jay, "In Praise of the Snapshot," *Creative Camera* (September 1971).

21. Exhibition titled "Humanism in China–A Contemporary Record of Photography," organized by the Guangdong Museum of Art, and later shown at Shanghai Art Museum, and National Art Museum of China, Beijing, in 2005–6. Tour abroad began in May 2006 to March 2008, at five museums across Germany, beginning with the Museum für Moderne Kunst, Frankfurt.

22. See note 1.

23. Published by Cinema Press Publishing House, China, 1994

24. The full quotation reads: "There's nothing worse than a brilliant image of a fuzzy concept."

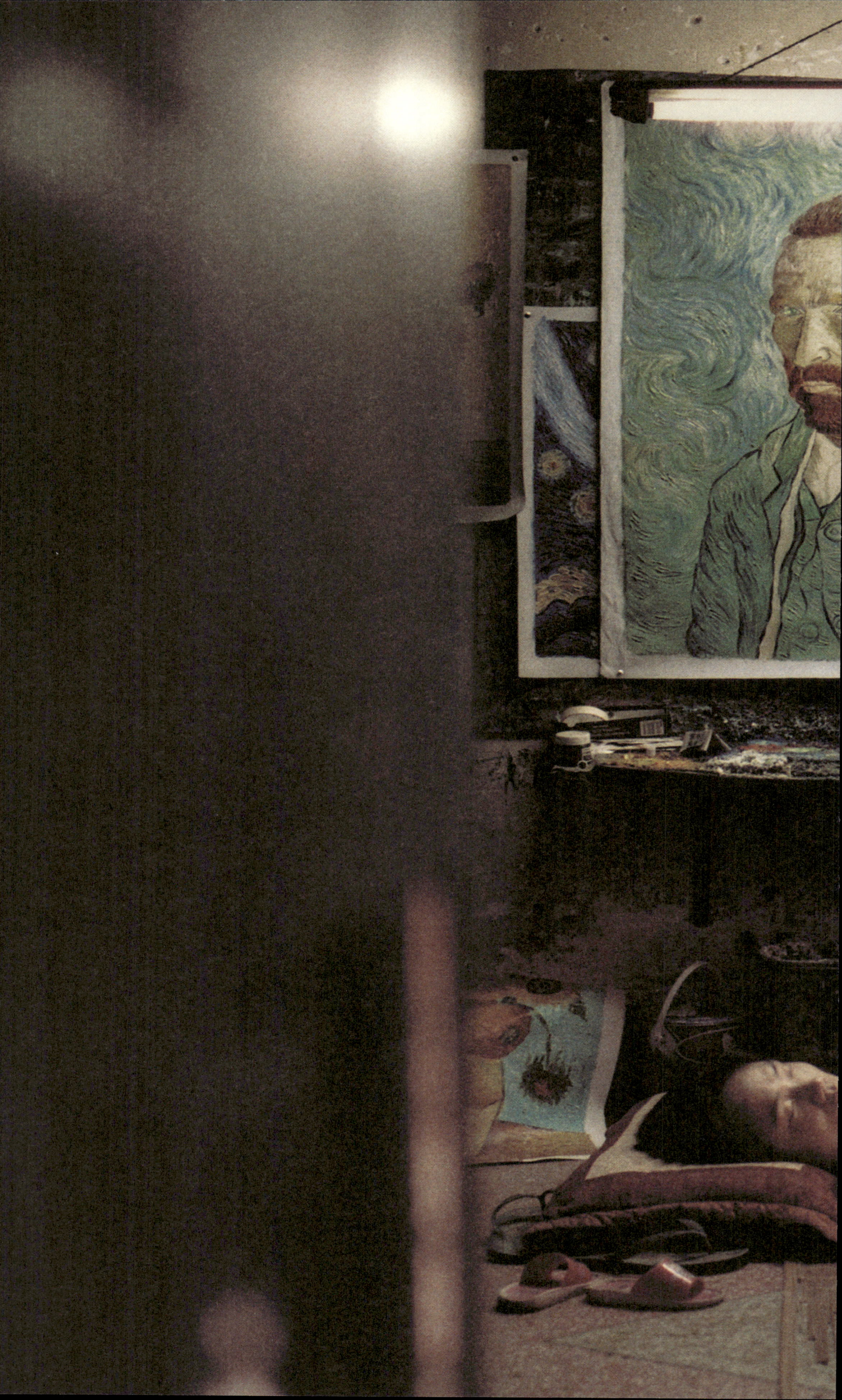

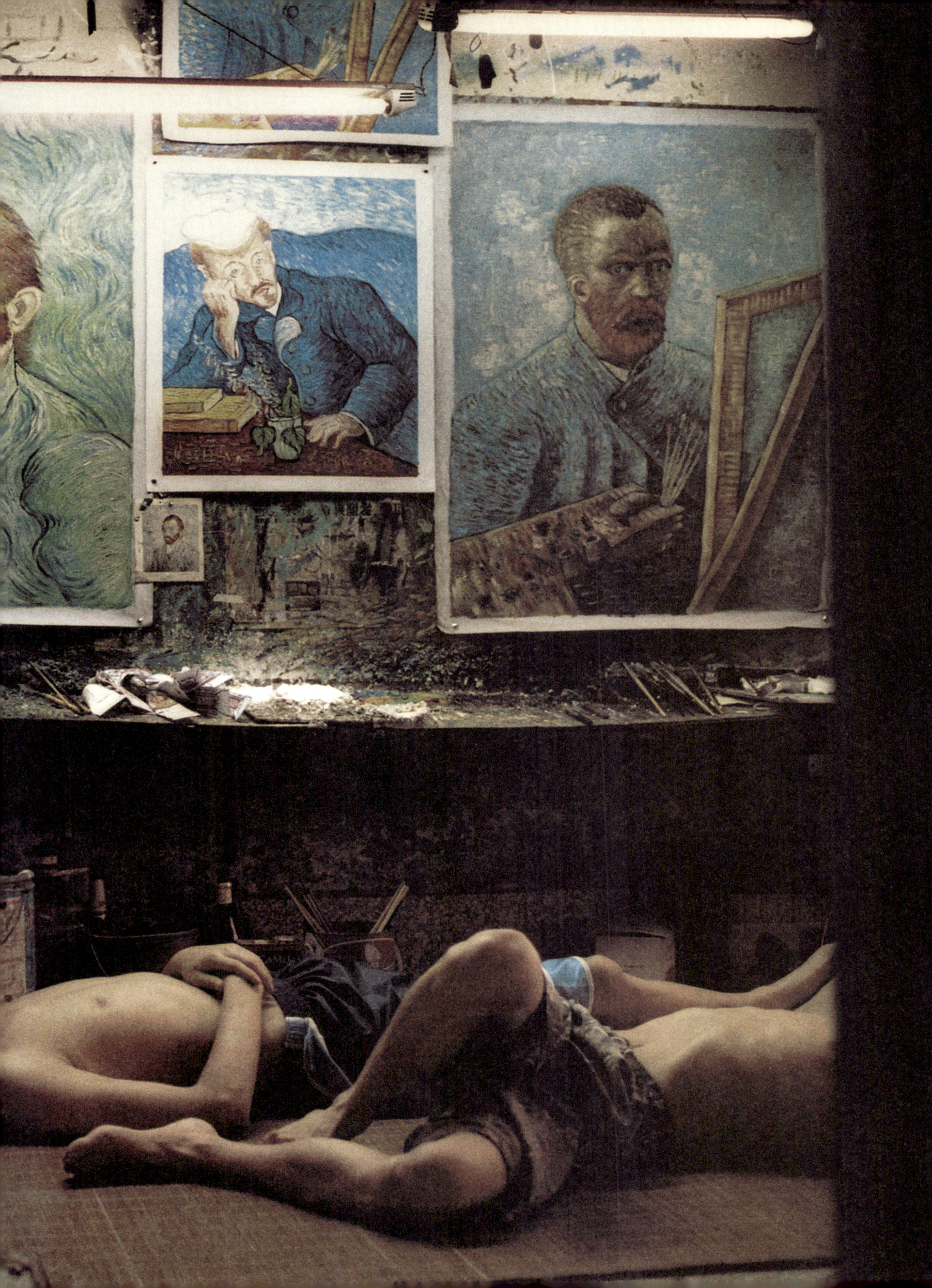

Mach dir ein Bild!

Von Karen Smith

„Weil jede Fotografie nur ein Fragment ist, hängt ihr moralisches und emotionales Gewicht davon ab, wo sie eingefügt wird."[1]

Eine Vision der Wahrheit

Als im 19. Jahrhundert die Fotografie in China Einzug hielt, lernte die übrige Welt die ersten „sachlichen" visuellen Zeugnisse der Nation, ihrer Menschen und seltsamen Bräuchen kennen: Fragmente von China, die für die gesamte Kultur standen. Auch das 20. Jahrhundert brachte kaum ein zusammenhängenderes Bild hervor: nicht in dem halben Jahrhundert vor der Gründung des neuen China im Jahr 1949, als die Qing-Dynastie stürzte und das Land seine gesamte Energie im Bürgerkrieg oder schlicht für den Kampf ums Überleben verbrauchte. Nachdem die Volksrepublik gegründet und durch lange Jahre des Kalten Krieges die Tür faktisch verschlossen war, wurde das von der Fotografie vermittelte Bild nur noch fragmentarischer. Ausländische Journalisten berichteten über die Auswirkungen von Maos Zedongs Regime und seiner Politik, wobei ihre Berichte zwangsläufig von ihren politischen Sympathien gefärbt waren.

Auf Seiten Chinas war die überwiegende Mehrzahl der für das Ausland freigegebenen Bilder, ebenso wie in China selbst, amtlich zensiert: Fragmente, die den Erfolg von Maos Politik und seiner revolutionären sozialistischen Vision veranschaulichen sollten. Die Tatsache, dass sie von der chinesischen Realität weit entfernt waren, fiel nicht sofort ins Auge. Das Bild, von dem die Fotos ein Teil waren, war zu groß, um es auf einmal zu erfassen. Auf ihm war der stotternde Fortschritt des kommunistischen Modernisierungsprogramms für sozialen und ökonomischen Aufstieg beschrieben. Da es sich jedoch in erster Linie um ein von Menschen geschaffenes Bild handelte (hergestellt vom Amt für Propaganda), war schwer zu entscheiden, welches Fragment der Realität entsprach. Für ein ausländisches Publikum war es nahezu unmöglich, die moralische oder emotionale Bedeutung der Fotografien einzuschätzen, die es zu sehen bekam.

In den 1980er-Jahren hatte sich die Situation nur wenig verändert. In politischer Hinsicht war China bereits dabei, sich schrittweise zu verändern, jedoch nicht ausreichend, um die Form von internationalem Kulturaustausch zuzulassen, die seit Beginn des neuen Jahrtausends an Schwung gewinnt. So viele Teile dieses komplizierten Puzzles mussten sich zusammenfügen, ehe der Zeitpunkt schließlich gekommen war, an dem es möglich und eine dringende Aufgabe war, all die Teilstücke zu sammeln und sie unverzüglich an die richtige Stelle zu setzen, um ein abgerundetes Bild Chinas aus der Sicht chinesischer Fotografen zu präsentieren.

China + Fotografie = ?

Wir bringen China nicht unmittelbar mit Fotografie in Verbindung, wenngleich sich das Land in den vergangenen 150 Jahren, speziell bei europäischen und amerikanischen Fotografen, als „Objekt" ihrer Aufnahmen einiger Beliebtheit erfreute. Abenteurer, Reisende, „imperialistische Invasoren", Anthropologen, ja selbst politische Sympathisanten neigten sämtlich dazu, China als exotische, ostasiatische Muse zu betrachten. Es waren hauptsächlich ihre Fotos, die China der Außenwelt in Bildern, nicht Worten, nahe brachten. In der Geschichte der Fotografie monopolisierte der Westen früh die Art und Weise, wie das Leben zu sehen oder zu verstehen war und was eine Fotografie sein oder enthalten sollte. Dies war jedoch nicht der einzige Grund, weshalb vor 1949 der westlichen Öffentlichkeit nur wenige in China entstandene Fotografien bekannt waren: Sie mussten erst zu einem weit verbreiteten Phänomen werden. Nach 1949 war Fotografie dann weitgehend gleichbedeutend mit Propaganda und sämtlichen geltenden Beschränkungen der Kunst unterworfen. „Chinesische Fotografie" galt folglich nicht als anerkanntes Genre. Chinesischen Fotografen wurden weder stilistische Neuerungen zugeschrieben noch universelle, ikonenhafte Bilder zugetraut, nicht einmal von China. Dieser Einschätzung würden wohl selbst die Angehörigen der Mitte der 1990er-Jahre wiedererstandenen fotografischen Zirkel nicht widersprechen. Wie viele chinesische Fotografen sind ein Begriff? Selbst in China nur allzu wenige, wenngleich eine Reihe von Bildern, wie die von Hou Bo[2] aufgenommenen Porträts von Mao und den Führern seiner Zeit, den Status von Ikonen haben.

Die meisten der heute namhaften Fotografen waren unbekannt, ehe in jüngster Zeit das Interesse an Fotos von Angehörigen der zeitgenössischen Kunstszene explosionsartig zunahm. Zu verdanken ist dies in erster Linie dem Einfluss europäischer und amerikanischer Museumskuratoren, Galeristen und Sammler. Diese so genannten Avantgardekünstler hatten sich erst Mitte der 1990er-Jahre der Fotografie zugewandt; sie nahmen die Kamera als Werkzeug, das Bild als Leinwand und machten sich eine gänzlich postmoderne Respektlosigkeit gegenüber den traditionellen Werten und Gewohnheiten des Mediums zu eigen. Für sie ist das Foto ein entfernter Verwandter des genau beobachteten „entscheidenden Moments" eines Cartier-Bresson oder des von Sebastião Salgado eingefangenen drohenden sozialen Melodrams oder der kunstvollen Porträtfotografie einer Annie Leibovitz. Einer oder zwei der „reinen" Fotografen erkennen August Sander, Richard Avedon und Diane Arbus an. Spätere Generationen zählen auch Nan Goldin und Robert Frank zu ihren Idolen, die meisten bevorzugen Andreas Gursky und Yasumasa Morimura. Hierbei handelt es sich jedoch um eine Entwicklung der jüngsten Zeit. Verglichen mit anderen Formen visuellen Ausdrucks hatte die Fotografie in

China weniger Zeit, sich zu entwickeln oder die Lücke zwischen ihrer Erfahrung und der westlichen Praxis zu schließen. Dies bedeutet jedoch keine Schwäche.

China, wie es die Chinesen sehen

Dank der sorgfältigen Auswahl von Fotografien, sämtlich Werke von Fotografen, die auf dem chinesischen Festland zu Hause sind, liegt hier ein einzigartiges Porträt Chinas vor. Das Alter der Fotografen überspannt mehrere Generationen, und ihre Laufbahnen durchziehen eine Abfolge von Jahrzehnten, die mit der Gründung der Volksrepublik China 1949 beginnt und bis heute reicht. Ein beachtlicher Teil der zur Illustration dieser Geschichte ausgewählten Fotografen wird hier zum ersten Mal veröffentlicht, nicht weil sie zuvor zwangsläufig geheim waren, sondern weil nur eine begrenzte Zahl von Menschen einen Grund hatte, von ihrer Existenz zu wissen. Von den Wissenden dachte nahezu keiner daran, etwas mit ihnen anzufangen. Da die Fotografie erst spät als eigenständige Kunstform anerkannt wurde, fehlte ihr der kritische Diskurs. Aus dem Zusammenhang gerissene Bilder mit politischen Untertönen hätten den Fotografen Schwierigkeiten bereiten können. Es gab keinen Markt für die Aufnahmen, der einen Regelverstoß gelohnt hätte. Dies galt bis etwa 2005, als in China eine fieberhafte Auktionstätigkeit einsetzte. Zuvor, das heißt bis heute, hatten nur wenige Personen Zugang zu diesem Bildmaterial.

China, Portrait eines Landes schaut zurück auf die wichtigen Ereignisse, die diese bedeutende Zeit prägten, indem es diese Geschichte Bild für Bild in weitgehend chronologischer Reihenfolge ablaufen lässt und den Weg von damals bis heute verfolgt. Über die Zeit hinweg offenbaren diese Bilder, wie Verschiebungen im politischen System ihr moralisches und emotionales Gewicht beeinflusst haben. Jede Fotografie ruft eine Seite der Geschichte des neuen China wach. Einige Fotos behandeln dasselbe Thema aus verschiedenen Perspektiven, und viele stellen ihr Anliegen heute mit größerer Intensität vor, als man ursprünglich ahnen konnte. Andere sind aufgrund unseres im Nachhinein erworbenen Wissens von einer Mehrdeutigkeit geprägt, die in ihrer Entstehungszeit unentdeckt blieb.

Bilder sprechen Tausende von Worten

Die Macht eines Fotos ist vielfältig. Die Bilder sind Rädchen in einer gewaltigen Speichermaschine, die die soziokulturelle Geschichte dokumentiert. Einige wenige werden dank des Weitblicks eines einzelnen Fotografen zu Ikonen, weil sie die historischen Tatsachen, ebenso wie soziokulturelle Einstellungen und Vorurteile, infrage stellen. Sie verschaffen künftigen Generationen ein sachkundiges visuelles Vermächtnis der Vergangenheit. Obwohl es nicht immer notwendig ist, über intime Kenntnisse der wesentlichen Aspekte eines bestimmten nationalen Systems zu

verfügen, um sich mit einem Foto zu beschäftigen – und China ist in der Tat ein ganz besonderes System –, legt historisches Wissen doch den Kontext der Bilder fest. Dies gilt insbesondere für jene Fotografien, die in Einklang mit der Propaganda und der politischen Ideologie entstanden. Diktaturen, totalitäre oder kommunistische Staaten, sogar Demokratien mögen sich in der Theorie gleichen, sind in der Praxis allerdings höchst verschieden. Die Unterschiede sind stets lokalen kulturellen Nuancen geschuldet. So gesehen sind die Details, die sich in zahlreichen Bildern dieses Buches finden, faszinierend, denn sie künden unmittelbar von der hinter den propagandistischen Konstrukten versteckten Realität: von den spezifisch chinesischen kulturellen Nuancen. Unter der Oberfläche idealisierter Zielsetzungen und sozialer Mechanismen, die die kommunistische Agenda untermauern, finden sich spezifische lokale philosophische und ästhetische Sichtweisen, die keine Politik auslöschen konnte. Mithilfe der Details lässt sich das Geschehen rekonstruieren, das Maos Richtlinien für künstlerischen Ausdruck in offiziellen Bildern verschleiern sollten; häufig, weil diese Version der Ereignisse von der Öffentlichkeit oder der offiziellen Geschichtsschreibung ausgeschlossen ist oder nicht zu den von der Ideologie erhobenen Ansprüchen passt. Beispielsweise spiegelt sich der zeitliche Übergang von der in hohem Maße politisierten Ära von Maos Regime zwischen 1949 und 1976 zum vergleichsweise offenen Führungsstil Deng Xiaopings in den Fotografien, die sich wegbewegen von dem für die nationale Propaganda so nötigen Einheitsbild der Menschen. An dessen Stelle erkennt man das Wiedererwachen von Humanismus, von sanften Freuden und ganz neuen, zuvor verdrängten Träumen, wie die von Liu Heung Shing 1979 und 1980 in öffentlichen Parks entdeckte Liebe (Abb. S. 290), oder die Frauen, die 1981 ihr Haar dauerwellen lassen (Abb. S. 296), kurz, die Rückkehr zu einem alltäglichen, gleichförmigen Dasein für den durchschnittlichen Bewohner des Festlandes, von dem anfänglich die meisten begeistert waren.

Die sozialen Aspekte von Momenten, die von den frühen 1980er-Jahren an in der unabhängigen Sichtweise von Fotografen festgehalten wurden, bleiben politisch. Die Themenwahl offenbart ein erneutes Interesse an der Vielfalt der einheimischen Bevölkerung, die in den Anfangsdekaden der Volksrepublik bagatellisiert oder auf ein politisiertes Pasticcio reduziert wurde. Diese Vielfalt ist in erster Linie ethnischer Art und daher ebenso sehr kulturell wie topografisch. Die Bevölkerung Chinas ist nicht die homogene Einheit, die heraufbeschworen wird, wenn diese riesige Landmasse mit einem einzigen Namen belegt wird. Die ethnische Vielfalt, die sich aus 56 Minoritäten zusammensetzt, die man im Allgemeinen als „Chinesen" bezeichnet, sowie die regionalen klimatischen und geografischen Unterschiede bedeuten, dass außerhalb der großen Städte die persönliche Erfahrung und Empfindung des neuen China eher heterogen als uniform ist. Jenseits des politischen Trends, dem sie zustimmen müssen, werden die Menschen immer pragmatisch bleiben, weil sie sich aus Armut vorrangig mit dem nackten Überleben beschäftigen müssen. An diesem Punkt wird der enorme Einfluss der soziopolitischen und ideologischen Merkmale des neuen China deutlich. Sehr allgemein gesprochen ist die Mehrheit der Chinesen seit 1949 derselben politischen Ideologie, einem uniformen Ausbildungssystem (wenn auch die Qualitätsstandards dieser Ausbildung nach wie vor enorm unterschiedlich sind) und dem allgemeinen Bewusstsein vom historischen Fortschritt und dem Modernisierungsprogramm des Landes ausgesetzt (obgleich dieses in den großen Städten einen anderen Verlauf nahm als in den Provinzstädten und auf dem Lande). Kurz, jeder Einwohner Chinas, der älter als 35 Jahre ist (ausgenommen die kleinsten Minoritäten in den abgelegensten und ärmsten Regionen), wurde mit ähnlichem Wissen und Urteilsvermögen ausgerüstet.[3] Die ideologischen und kulturellen Merkmale des neuen China bilden somit einen Parameter, innerhalb dessen seine Geschichte festgelegt ist. Eine genaue Betrachtung sämtlicher Fotografien aller Epochen belegt, wie markant diese sind.

All dies spielte eine große Rolle bei der Ausformung des Charakters der sich daraus ergebenden Fotografie. Es prägte darüber hinaus das allgemeine Verständnis der Menschen und ihre kritische Würdigung der Art, wie die Realität sowohl als Subjekt wie auch als Objekt eines Fotos erscheint, selbst wenn ihnen irgendwie klar war, dass hinsichtlich ihres unmittelbaren soziopolitischen Umfelds das Foto in erster Linie als visuelles Werkzeug diente. Der Staat schickte zahlreiche Fotografen an die Frontlinien der sozialistischen Reformen und Umstrukturierungen, die Mao seit Anfang der 1950er-Jahre durchführte. Die Fotos, die sie schufen, waren die Speerspitze der Propagandafeldzüge, wo sie zu visuellen Vertretern der Kampfbotschaft und der Ziele wurden und zu Bildern, die tausend Worte sprachen. Es lag in der Natur der Sache, dass sich derartige Aufträge auf die positiven Aspekte der „Realität" konzentrierten, die, falls es nötig schien, in der Dunkelkammer oder bei der Reproduktion noch weiter nachgebessert oder sogar verfälscht wurden. Dies ist anhand der auffallenden Unstimmigkeiten zwischen verschiedenen Fassungen bestimmter Fotografien nachweisbar, die in den Anfangsdekaden der Volksrepublik in öffentlichen Medien publiziert wurden. Hier erscheinen und verschwinden Personen wie durch Magie, vor Hintergründen, die regelmäßig von politisch unkorrekten Individuen und unansehnlichen Makeln gesäubert wurden. Weit über den augenscheinlichsten Fall Maos hinaus erhielten die meisten Führungskader eine verjüngende Behandlung, bei der ihre Gesichtszüge geglättet und ihre Gebärden und die der Menschen in ihrem Umkreis kultiviert wurden. Auf diesem Gebiet der Fotografie verfügten die heimischen Techniker offenkundig über bemerkenswertes kreatives Geschick.[4]

Außerdem schlossen sich zwischen dem Ende der 1970er- und dem Anfang der 1980er-Jahre überall im Land kleine Gruppen von Amateurfotografen zusammen, um sich moralisch zu unterstützen und den gemeinsamen Versuch zu unternehmen, sich von der offiziellen Ästhetik loszusagen. Diese Bewegung begann eher zufällig in Peking nach dem Tod Zhou Enlais im April 1976, und obgleich sie politisch motiviert war, entwickelten ihre Mitglieder rasch höchst unterschiedliche künstlerische Ansätze. Ursprünglich war dies von dem Impuls motiviert, sich nach Maos Tod der autoritären Kontrolle durch die Viererbande zu widersetzen, wurde jedoch bald ersetzt von dem neuen Wunsch, sich der optimistischen Stimmung anzuschließen, die Deng Xiaopings 1978 verkündete Politik der Wirtschaftsreform hervorgerufen hatte.

Der offizielle Beginn des Unternehmens Fotografie

Noch ehe die Volksrepublik 1949 gegründet wurde, hielt eine kleine Zahl von Fotografen die Fortschritte der kommunistischen Guerilla bei ihrer Überzeugungsarbeit im Bild fest. Am Ende des Langen Marsches im Oktober 1936 traf die Truppe in Yan'an ein, das Mao Zedong zu seinem Standort machte, bis 1946 der endgültige Marsch nach Peking begann. Die Mehrheit dieser frühen Fotografen kam aus intellektuellen Kreisen in Shanghai, eine gebildete Elite, die wohlhabenden, gesellschaftlich privilegierten Familien entstammte. Diese Verhältnisse beförderten das Faszinosum Fotografie und lieferten die Mittel zum Erwerb einer modernen Kamera. Viele dieser jungen Intellektuellen hatten sich der Bewegung des 4. Mai (1919) angeschlossen und begrüßten deren Theorien – die Notwendigkeit zu modernisieren, zu industrialisieren und eine unabhängige Nation zu werden, frei von ausländischer Beeinflussung und Kontrolle. In der Folgezeit wandelten sich diese Überzeugungen zu einer wohlwollenden Haltung gegenüber den philosophischen Idealen des Marxismus, die in der Theorie versprachen, Knechtschaft und Ungleichheiten des feudalen Systems auszumerzen und China in eine moderne Nation umzuwandeln.[5] Die Kamera war nur ein Beispiel für die praktischen Errungenschaften der westlichen Wissenschaft, von der junge Fotografen glaubten, man könne sie heimischen soziokulturellen Erfordernissen dienstbar machen. Darüber hinaus befriedigte sie den Hunger nach kreativen Ausdrucksmöglichkeiten.

In den frühen 1930er-Jahren hatten unabhängige Fotojournalisten in Europa und besonders in Amerika die Berichterstattung, insbesondere ihren visuellen Anteil, verändert, was die Beliebtheit der 1936 gegründeten Zeitschrift *Life* belegt.[6] Dramatische Fotos von internationalen Ereignissen wurden möglich durch die Entwicklung von Kompaktkameras wie Leica und Ermanox, die um 1929 hergestellt wurden. Sie waren für diese Zeit überraschend leicht und problemlos zu transportieren.

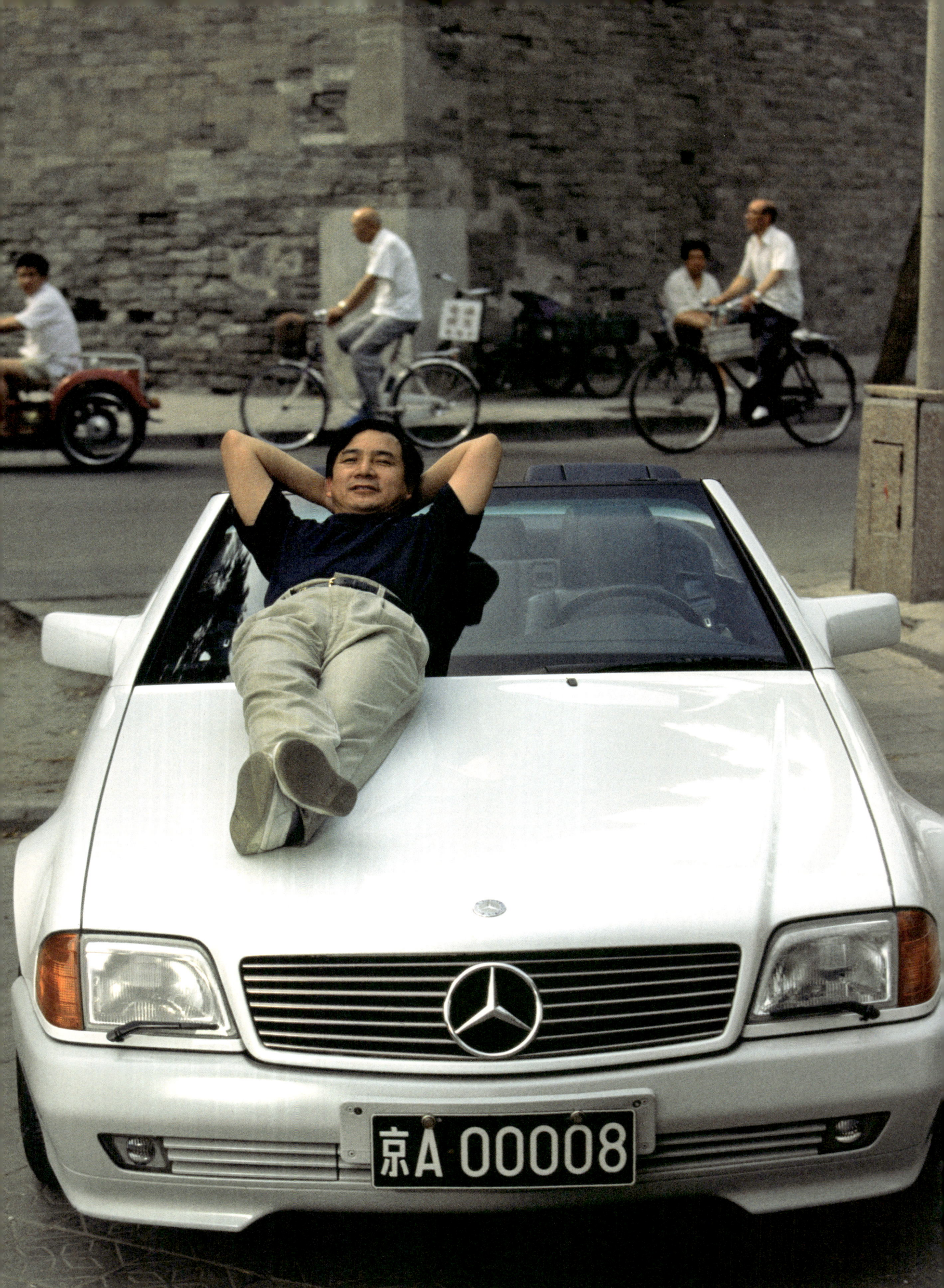

←
Liu Heung Shing, 1996

China's first millionaire, Li Xiaohua, a former Red Guard sent to the countryside during the Cultural Revolution, lies on the hood of his new Mercedes-Benz. Li made his fortune in trading when China began its economic reforms in 1980.

Chinas erster Millionär, Li Xiaohua, ein ehemaliger Rotgardist, der während der Kulturrevolution aufs Land verschickt wurde, liegt auf seinem neuen Mercedes-Benz. Li machte sein Vermögen im Handel, als 1980 die Wirtschaftsreformen in China begannen.

Le premier millionaire chinois, Li Xiaohua, ancien Garde rouge envoyé à la campagne pendant la Révolution culturelle, couché sur sa nouvelle Mercedes. Il fit fortune dans le commerce quand la Chine entama ses réformes économiques en 1980.

Vor 1949 musste sich in China die kommunikative Kraft des Fotos in der breiten Bevölkerung erst noch herumsprechen. Eine Fotografie zeigte das Porträt einer Gruppe, einer Familie oder eines Einzelnen, und es wurde viel darüber spekuliert, was die Kamera dem Modell stahl. Mit der Gründung der Volkrepublik 1949 änderte sich dies, denn im Gegensatz zu den unzähligen regionalen Dialekten und Volkssprachen (von denen es vielen an den Worten zum Artikulieren sozialistischer Ideen mangelte) waren Fotos universell verständlich.[7] Die große Zahl monumentaler Darstellungen, entweder als Ölgemälde oder Skulpturen, die auf Anweisung des Propagandabüros im Stil des Sozialistischen Realismus entstanden, füllte die Herzen und Köpfe der Menschen mit anregenden Visionen vom künftigen sozialistischen Utopia. Die visuelle Faszination ikonenhafter Werke, auf denen heroische Verdienste oder Taten dargestellt sind, verringerte sich im Lauf der Zeit kaum. Letzten Endes handelte es sich jedoch um Kunstwerke, von Künstlern entworfen und angefertigt, die ihre kreativen Fähigkeiten dazu verwandten, eine Realität zu *konstruieren*, anstatt sie *einzufangen*, wie ein Foto das konnte. Die Macht des Fotos erklärte bald seinen Wert. Einzig eine Fotografie konnte die sich verändernde Realität und tatsächliche Geschehnisse einfangen, wie sie wirkliche Menschen erlebten, die fieberhaft für den Aufbau einer neuen Gesellschaft kämpften. Die Fotografie bekräftigte die Wahrhaftigkeit einer Sache, bei der künstlerische Produkte nicht mithalten konnten, zumindest nicht verstandesmäßig. Somit erlangte das Foto entscheidende Bedeutung, wenn es darum ging zu vermitteln, dass es Maos ideologischer Vision für China unbedingt zu folgen galt, und den Fortschritt der Nation, besonders in ihren dunkelsten Zeiten, zu betonen. Ironischerweise sollte es fast 50 Jahre dauern, bis die Arbeit chinesischer Fotografen allein aufgrund ihrer Qualität, entweder als historische Dokumentation oder als persönliche Leistung, in China oder im Ausland anerkannt wurde. Gleichwohl war die Fotografie seit dem Beginn der 1950er-Jahre bis zum Ende von Maos Herrschaft zweifellos eines der wirkungsvollsten Werkzeuge, über das die Kommunisten verfügten.

Im Dienst der Menschen

Mao hatte eine genaue Vorstellung von der Rolle, die die Künste – gleichgültig ob bildend, literarisch oder darstellend – bei der Entfaltung der Ideale des Zeitalters spielen sollten. Zum ersten Mal umriss er sie 1942 in Yan'an[8], und die Auffassung, dass sämtliche Sparten der Kunst „dem Volk dienen" sollten, blieb während der folgenden Jahrzehnte die Grundlage künstlerischen Ausdrucks. Der von Mao als überzeugender Stil erkorene Sozialistische Realismus hatte sich in der Sowjetunion als tauglich erwiesen. Maos Variante, die auf in ganz China verwurzelten kulturellen Vorlieben gründete, entsprach hervorragend dem heimischen Geschmack.

Die in der Volksrepublik verbreitete Spielart des Sozialistischen Realismus verwendete Tusche, Pinsel, Reispapier und Mineralfarben für Malerei und Neujahrsbilder und sogar Papierschnitte. Und dann war da noch die größte aller Künste, die Kalligrafie. Ähnlich dem Sozialistischen Realismus war auch die Fotografie ein westlicher Import. Im Gegensatz zum Sozialistischen Realismus handelte es sich bei ihr jedoch um ein mechanisches Werkzeug, nicht um eine politisch entwickelte Kunstrichtung. Unter allen Medien, die zum künstlerischen Ausdruck der Volksrepublik beitrugen, mangelte es nur der Fotografie an eigenständigem ästhetischem Wert. Es hatte kaum Zeit für ihre Entfaltung gegeben. Die Kamera war bloß ein Werkzeug, ein praktisches Mittel zum Zweck. Bei der Gründung der Volksrepublik wurden die damals in Shanghai durchgeführten fotografischen Experimente eingeholt von der Aufgabe, den Sozialismus aufzubauen, zu der anfangs jeder einen Beitrag leisten wollte. Nachdem man beschlossen hatte, die Kamera als Werkzeug zu betrachten, begann die Partei, zuverlässige Leute mit dem Aufnehmen von Bildern zu beauftragen. Die Auserwählten mussten den Auslöser im passenden Moment vom bestmöglichen Blickwinkel aus betätigen. Keine Anmutung von „Stimmung" (über „ideologisch positiv" hinaus) war erforderlich, ebenso wenig wie Beleuchtung (nur hell, d.h. ohne negative Schatten) oder das Bemühen um geschickte, künstlerische Gestaltung (nur die eindeutige Haltung und einen klaren Fokus, was wiederum jegliche Mehrdeutigkeit eliminierte, hielt man für angemessen).

Man merkt den Fotografien dieser Zeit an, dass ein beträchtlicher Teil derer, die sie aufnahmen und die vielleicht unter anderen Umständen niemals zum Fotografieren gekommen wären, über Begabung und einen scharfsinnigen Einblick in die Situation verfügten. Diese Bilder sind deshalb außerordentliche historische Dokumente; Fragment für Fragment ergänzen sie sich zu einem vollständigen Bild. Selbst auf dem Höhepunkt der politischen Kontrolle über die Massen kommt die Wahrheit doch zum Vorschein. Insbesondere die in der Ära der Propaganda (1950er- bis 1970er-Jahre) entstandenen Fotos bieten eine bewegende, vielschichtige Darstellung der Zeit. Auf die Gefahr hin, nichts Neues zu sagen: Propagandakunst hat eine große Resonanz, weil sie, wie jede erfolgreiche Werbekampagne, mit visuellen Stereotypen spielt, die die Öffentlichkeit unmittelbar ansprechen, weil sie sowohl leicht verständlich als auch einprägsam sind. Die Kamera setzte die Weisungen der Propaganda äußerst wirkungsvoll um. In den Anfangsjahren der Volksrepublik stand, abgesehen von besonderen Umständen, in denen Farbe zugelassen war, nur Schwarzweißfilm zur Verfügung, der Dramatik und seelische Bewegung in den Gesichtern der Menschen naturgemäß steigerte. Wenn wir diese Bilder heute unvoreingenommen betrachten, entdecken wir ungeachtet der ideologischen Einschränkungen in so vielen der Fotos große Kunstfertigkeit und Sensibilität, dass die damaligen Fotografen sich wohl durch eine enorme natürliche Begabung ausgezeichnet haben müssen.

Abbild einer neuen Gesellschaft

Mit der Gründung der Volksrepublik endete „mehr als ein Jahrhundert demütigender Niederlagen, ungerechter Verträge und ausländischer Besatzung"[9], was Anlass zu grenzenlosem Jubel gab. In der Folge der Auseinandersetzungen, während die Nationalisten sich weiterschleppten und Kriegsherren ihre eigenen Schlachten ausfochten, kämpften die meisten Menschen schlicht ums Überleben. Als die kommunistische Guerilla zunehmend an Rückhalt gewann, wurde China schließlich befreit. 1949 entstandene Fotos zeigen erschöpfte Soldaten der Volksbefreiungsarmee schlafend auf den Straßen, weil es ihnen verboten war, die Häuser in den von ihnen befreiten Orten zu betreten (Abb. S. 127). Fasziniert von der neuen Moral und der egalitären Stimmung des Sozialismus, erwiesen sich die Menschen als williges Gefolge der Sache, angespornt von der Chance, sich vom Joch des Feudalismus und der Sklaverei zu befreien. Abgesehen davon, dass sie die Chinesen wirklich aus der Sklaverei befreiten, schien es, als gäben die Kommunisten dem Land auch seine Würde zurück. Die Mehrheit der Chinesen begann die 1950er-Jahre in dem Glauben, sie befänden sich an der Schwelle zu einer glorreichen neuen Ära, die aufräumen würde mit „bösen" Grundbesitzern (ein Prozess, der mit einem energischen Landreformprogramm bereits begonnen hatte) und mit den korrupten Praktiken der Nationalisten, deren Regime alle Merkmale einer weiteren imperialen Dynastie aufwies. Mao bediente die Menschen mit dem Vorgeschmack der Freiheit, und sie machten sich bereitwillig seine überschwängliche Propaganda zu eigen. Diese befürwortete Verbesserungen nicht nur, sondern Mao versprach sie ihnen regelrecht. In der Tat waren viele der Grundsätze äußerst lobenswert. Einfache Leute sollten Bildung erhalten, Analphabetentum ausgemerzt werden. Mit dem Schwinden der Armut sollte auch der Hunger verschwinden. Die Menschen würden für neue Arbeitsplätze in der Industrie ausgebildet und China zu einer bedeutenden Nation machen, mit der man rechnen müsste. Mao ging so weit zu verkünden „Was der Westen hat, wird China auch haben", dank eines umfassenden Modernisierungsprogramms, durch das China Großbritannien überholen und mit Amerika in wenigen Jahren gleichziehen würde. Dies war der Impetus hinter dem verhängnisvollen Großen Sprung nach vorn von 1958. In diesem Zusammenhang spielten Fotos eine wichtige Rolle, weil sie in den überwiegend von Analphabeten bewohnten Landgemeinden und der mittellosen Stadtbevölkerung die optimistische Stimmung wachhalten konnten. Indem sie heroische Großtaten herausstrichen und selbstsüchtiges Tun geißelten, schärften sie den Massen außerdem ihre soziale Verpflichtung

gegenüber der Gemeinschaft und ihre Verantwortung für das Gemeinwohl ein. Fotos dienten somit als wahrer Nachweis von Leistungen, als Bezugspunkte, an denen sich Fortschritt und Veränderung messen ließen.

Die Hälfte des Himmels

Eine Gruppe, die allen Grund hatte, Mao zu unterstützen, war der weibliche Teil der Bevölkerung, den Mao aus Jahrhunderten der Unterwerfung unter eine an konfuzianischen Grundsätzen ausgerichtete soziale Hierarchie befreite, die Frauen eine stumme, rechtlose Stellung zuwies. Mao erklärte die Frauen für gleichberechtigt. Nach seiner öffentlichen Proklamation, wonach sie „die Hälfte des Himmels" trügen, standen Frauen Arbeitsplätze an der Seite von Männern zu. Dieses Recht wurde in den 1950er-Jahren gerühmt, als man bestehende Sozialstrukturen und Gemeinschaften durch Volkskommunen ersetzte und Frauen bewiesen, dass sie ebenso leistungsfähig waren wie Männer. Auch in der Fotografie fand dies seinen Niederschlag, zuweilen durch Fotografinnen. Gleichwohl sollte man nicht glauben, dass hier ein feministischer Geist am Werke war. Einigen wenigen Frauen war in Yan'an eine aktive Rolle vergönnt gewesen. Hier erlebten weibliche Flüchtlinge aus Gebieten, die vom Bürgerkrieg und der einfallenden japanischen Armee verwüstet waren, die neue Gleichberechtigung der kommunistischen Ideologie und erhielten eine in ihrem früheren Dasein unvorstellbare Grundausbildung. Ein Beispiel hierfür ist Hou Bo, die von 1949 bis 1961 als Maos persönliche Fotografin wirken sollte. Ein weiteres ist Xiao Zhuang, die sich 1949 in Zhejiang einer Guerillatruppe anschloss und 1950 den Auftrag erhielt, für eine Lokalzeitung zu fotografieren. Wie damals üblich, erwarb sie ihre Grundkenntnisse bei der Arbeit. Zwei Jahre später, 1952, war sie eine erfahrene Fotografin im Dienst der *Xinhua News Daily*.[10] Wenngleich ihr ihre Herkunft und ihre politische Einstellung zustatten kamen, hatte ihre Loyalität zum Kommunismus offenkundig nie Vorrang vor ihrer persönlichen Beziehung zu den von ihr Fotografierten. Es wäre falsch zu vermuten, sie sei bewusst von der Parteilinie abgewichen, aber aus ihren Bildern spricht ein sonst unbekanntes Maß an Empathie und Mitgefühl, das über die schlichte Bebilderung von Lokalpolitik hinausgeht. Bisweilen entdeckt man sogar Spuren der Zwangslage, in der sich viele Fotojournalisten als Zeugen von Kampfhandlungen befinden, denn ihre Aufgabe ist es zu berichten, nicht einzugreifen, selbst wenn sie Zeuge schrecklicher Verbrechen werden.

Während der 1950er- bis zu den 1970er-Jahren gelangen Xiao Zhuang eindrucksvolle dokumentarische Bilder in einfachen, überzeugenden Kompositionen. Darunter finden sich Menschen bei Massenzusam-

*„Meiner Meinung nach hat die internationale Lage einen Wendepunkt erreicht.
Es gibt heute auf der Welt zwei Windrichtungen, den Ostwind und den Westwind.
Ein chinesisches Sprichwort sagt, entweder siegt der Ostwind über den Westwind,
oder der Westwind über den Ostwind. Ich denke für die heutige Situation ist es
bezeichnend, dass der Ostwind über den Westwind herrscht."*

MAO ZEDONG (1893–1976), erster Vorsitzender der Volksrepublik China, 1957

menkünften und die anschwellende Zustimmung für Mao bis hin zu den zahllosen Ausdrucksformen der Hingabe der Menschen an den Vorsitzenden – überschäumend in ihrer Begeisterung, gewalttätig im Übermaß – und seine Kampagnen und die Herausforderung, die dort gesetzten Ziele zu erreichen. Diese Fotos streifen auch den komplexen Charakter der von diesen politischen Aktivitäten ausgelösten Emotionen. Diese veränderten sich von einer Aktion zur nächsten, während der auf interne Machtkämpfe reagierende politische Wind die Richtung wechselte. Viele von Xiao Zhuangs Aufnahmen bei Massenveranstaltungen sind aus extremen Blickwinkeln aufgenommen, die die riesige Menschenmenge und die klaustrophobische, bedrohliche Atmosphäre bei ihrer Entstehung einfangen (Abb. S. 200/201 und 209). Durch diese subtilen Mittel konnten die Fotografien die Stimmungen und die Mechanismen festhalten, durch die interne Zwietracht den Lauf der Geschichte ändern sollte. Sie protokollieren den Weg, auf dem die Gesellschaft in den 1970er-Jahren in eine noch dunklere Epoche versank, die traumatischste und verworrenste Periode der Volksrepublik. Während die Bedeutung vieler Details von Situationen und Ereignissen künftigen Generationen unverständlich bleiben wird, machen Xiao Zhuangs geschultes Auge und ihr intuitives Gespür für das, was sie sah, ihre Fotografien zu einem erhellenden Blick auf jene „irrationalen" Zeiten.[11]

Ähnlich wie Xiao Zhuang kam auch Hou Bo nicht aufgrund irgendeiner besonderen Begabung zur Fotografie, sondern wegen ihrer ideologischen Zuverlässigkeit. Ehe sie ihren Posten zugewiesen bekam, hatte sie kaum je eine Kamera in der Hand gehabt. In den zwölf Jahren an Maos Seite und als Teil seines Gefolges war sie in entscheidenden historischen Augenblicken anwesend, und da sie als Mitglied seines Haushalts galt, waren ihr sämtliche Aspekte seines Alltags vertraut. Die Fotos, die sie in privaten Momenten hinter den Kulissen schoss, wenn sich der Politiker augenscheinlich gelöst vor der Kamera entspannte, stehen in deutlichem Kontrast zur asketischen Strenge der weltweit bekannten offiziellen Mao-Porträts. Sie zeigen uns den Menschen, nicht den Gott. Ist die Auswahl der Sujets einer weiblichen Fähigkeit zur Empathie zuzuschreiben? Vielleicht, denn gleichzeitig von männlichen Fotografen aufgenommene Bilder vermeiden in der Regel offensichtliche psychologische Andeutungen oder Mehrdeutigkeit.

In dieser Zeit sollten Fotografinnen immer eine Minderheit bleiben. Die einprägsamsten Werkreihen sind einer kleinen Gruppe von Einzelpersönlichkeiten zuzuschreiben. Herausragend sind hier Jiang Shaowu, Wang Shilong, Meng Zhaorui und Lü Xiangyou. Ihre Fotografien unterstreichen die hochgesteckten Ziele von Maos Ideologie, indem sie die Wirkung seiner Grundsätze und Aktionen kompromisslos und unzweideutig observieren.

Jiang Shaowu, Fotograf der *Liaoning Daily*, begann seine Laufbahn 1947. Seine Fotos dokumentieren ungerührt öffentliche Demütigungen und Selbstkritiken, die vor tobenden Menschenmengen in der fieberhaft-ideologischen Periode des Chaos von Mitte der 1960er-Jahre bis zu Maos Tod 1976 inszeniert wurden. Sie haben nichts von den erschreckend zirkusartigen Spektakeln vergleichbarer Aufnahmen von Li Zhensheng. Sie täuschen nichts vor und stehen den von ihnen festgehaltenen Vorfällen seltsam klar und unmissverständlich gegenüber. Sie verzeichnen den Werdegang einer Nation, eines Volkes, das gemeinsame Ziele anstrebt, inmitten des gewaltsamen Verlusts der Privilegien, derer sich die Elite erfreute. Rückblickend beweisen Fotos wie das eines Blinden, der die *Worte des Vorsitzenden Mao Zedong* auslegt (Abb. S. 195), oder das der Krokodilstränen einer Gruppe junger Männer, die 1976 Maos Ableben betrauern (Abb. S. 262/263), ein instinktives Gespür für die Falschheit so vieler von Maos Grundsätzen.

Wie die meisten Fotografen jener Zeit trat der in Henan geborene Wang Shilong 1948 in die Armee ein, wo er damit beauftragt wurde, für sein örtliches Propagandabüro zu fotografieren. Eine Verletzung beendete seine Tätigkeit als militärischer Korrespondent in Tibet, wo er in der Volksbefreiungsarmee diente. Dies hielt ihn allerdings nicht davon ab, Henan und die Nachbarprovinzen zu bereisen, um den sozialen Fortschritt in den neu gebildeten Volkskommunen zu fotografieren. Seine Bilder zeichnen sich durch einen besonderen, tonwertreichen Grundton aus. Seine Fotos des riesigen Terrains der Volkskommunen und der Neuverteilung des Ackerlandes beeindrucken durch ihre außerordentliche Skala silbergrauer Nuancen in jeder vorstellbaren Abstufung zwischen Schwarz und Weiß in einer bisher in China unbekannten Qualität (Abb. S. 166/167 und S. 247). Ähnlich sind seine Bilder von Massenveranstaltungen, bei denen sich Hunderte, ja Tausende von Menschen zusammentaten, um durch schiere Willenskraft eine gewaltige Großtat zu vollbringen. Tatsächlich wirken einige Fotos wie Illustrationen zu den Parabeln, die Mao verwendete. Die berühmteste ist die vom „Törichten alten Mann", der den Berg bewegte.[12] Wang Shilong zeigt uns Gemeinschaften, die Berge bewegen, den Verlauf von Flüssen verändern und dem Boden den größtmöglichen Ertrag abringen. Er verlor dennoch nie das Detail aus dem Auge, die täglichen Mühen des menschlichen Daseins in dieser Zeit oder die unverbesserlichen Schrullen der menschlichen Natur, die sich nicht abstellen ließen. Obgleich die Sorge um die äußere Erscheinung als unerheblich galt, zeigt er uns das Bild eines jungen bäuerlichen Paares in einem abgelegenen Tal, das eine in einer Höhle untergebrachte Schneiderwerkstatt verlässt, versunken in die Freude an einem neuen Kleidungsstück.

Der Soldat Meng Zhaorui arbeitete für die Armeezeitschrift *PLA Pictorial*. Wegen seiner besonderen Nähe zu Mao und zu Ereignissen von nationaler Bedeutung, die ihm diese Position verschaffte, war er zur Stelle, um Chinas erste erfolgreiche Zündung einer Wasserstoffbombe im Jahr 1967 einzufangen (Abb. S. 192/193). Er war bei vielen von Mao Zedongs öffentlichen Auftritten sowie bei seinen Treffen mit den Rotgardisten auf dem Tiananmen-Platz zugegen (Abb. S. 180/181). 1966 gelang ihm ein schicksalträchtiges Bild Maos, der in seinen Privaträumen in einem Sessel sitzend unheilvolle Blicke auf Zhou Enlai und Lin Biao wirft, die nichts ahnend in den Entwurf eines Dokuments vertieft sind. Das Bild erscheint prophetisch, denn 1971 ist der damalige Verteidigungsminister Lin Biao tot, umgekommen bei einem Flugzeugabsturz auf dem Weg in die Sowjetunion, wie es hieß, nach einem misslungenen Staatsstreich. Dieses faszinierende Bild ist beste Fotografie: Der Hintersinn von Maos Gesichtsausdruck zeugt von der Komplexität des politischen Ringens, das seinen Höhepunkt in der Kulturrevolution fand (1966–1976). (Abb. S. 182)

Utopia darstellen

Während der ersten drei Jahrzehnte der Volksrepublik fiel die Fotografie in den Aufgabenbereich des Propagandabüros. Es ist deshalb eigenartig, dass sich die von ihr festgehaltene „Wahrheit" als unerschrockenes visuelles Zeugnis vom quälenden Prozess des sozialen Kampfes präsentiert und Aufnahmen zeitigte, die unerhört freimütig sind, heute allerdings überraschend unbefangen erscheinen. Sie sind Fragmente, die sich zu einer auf Tatsachen beruhenden Darstellung der leidenschaftlichen Überzeugungen zusammenfügen, die die Nation veränderten. Jetzt, da ein neues Jahrtausend begonnen hat, gehört dieser Abschnitt der Geschichte endgültig der Vergangenheit an. China hat sich weiterentwickelt. Dank der Fotografien können wir die hohen Hürden, die das Land überwunden hat, richtig einschätzen. Darüber hinaus bilden sie den Kontext für die komplexe Denkungsart der damaligen und heutigen Gesellschaft Chinas.

Der das neue China beflügelnde Optimismus begünstigte die Flut positiver Bilder, die während der 1950er-Jahre entstanden. Diese Realität sollte sich zwischen 1955 und 1965 dramatisch verändern. Das erste Anzeichen für eine dunkle Seite an Maos Politik machte sich 1957 mit dem Beginn der Kampagne gegen Rechtsgerichtete bemerkbar. „Rechtsgerichtete" stellten tatsächlich einen verschwindend geringen Anteil der Bevölkerung dar, aber die gut funktionierende Maschinerie des Propagandaministeriums bewirkte, dass die Aktionen gegen solche Personen gewaltige, weitreichende Auswirkungen hatten: Das Beispiel machte Schule. Die dunkle Seite dieser politischen Linie verblasste 1958 vorübergehend, als Mao die Bildung von Volkskommunen befahl (Abb. S. 148). Ausgelöst durch den ebenfalls 1958 initiierten Großen Sprung nach vorn verschlechterte sich die Lage 1959 dramatisch, als Missernten und ein harter Winter eintraten. Im Frühjahr 1960 herrschte im ganzen Land eine Hungersnot, die bis 1962 anhielt und bei der mehr als 30 Millionen Menschen umkamen. Wir können uns heute nicht mehr vorstellen, von einer solchen Abfolge der Ereignisse überrollt zu werden. Wir fragen uns, wie die Menschen die Widersprüche zwischen den vom Propagandaministerium entworfenen idealisierten Visionen und der Realität übersehen konnten, wenn in rascher Folge von Rekorderträgen berichtet wurde, während die meisten Kommunen ihre Arbeiter nicht ernähren konnten. Ein wirksames Gegenmittel jener Zeit, das zugunsten der Regierung arbeitete, war die für gewöhnliche Menschen begrenzte Gelegenheit zu Reisen. Dadurch blieben die Kommunen isoliert und konnten sich nicht austauschen. Durch dieses abgeschirmte Dasein der Landbevölkerung konnten Kommunen in dem Glauben leben, dass sich „da drüben", in einem anderen Teil des Landes, die Lage bereits gebessert habe und dass mit Geduld auch sie sich durchsetzen würden. Susan Sontag beschreibt die Überzeugungskraft einer Fotografie in einfachen Worten: „Manches, von dem wir hören, es aber bezweifeln, scheint bewiesen, wenn man uns eine Fotografie zeigt."[13] Angesichts all der visuellen Belege, die das Propagandaministerium in Form einer Vielzahl von Fotografien vorlegte, was gab es da zu zweifeln?

In den 1960er-Jahren verbesserte sich die Lage nicht. Bis 1963 hatte sich die Hungersnot abgeschwächt, aber in den städtischen Ballungsräumen, wo die politischen Auseinandersetzungen am heftigsten tobten, wurden die Menschen in die Wirren der Kulturrevolution verwickelt. Dies findet seinen Niederschlag im veränderten Erscheinungsbild der Fotografien jener Zeit. Sie wurden zunehmend formelhaft, konventionell, optimistischer im Ausdruck und häufig retuschiert. Die notwendige Folge der Kulturrevolution, mit der Mao versuchte, seine Position erneut zu stärken und seine Lehre durchzusetzen, bestand darin, dass sämtliche kreativen Ausdrucksformen einem absoluten ideologischen Dogma unterworfen wurden. Man kann vermuten, dass zumindest einige Fotografen sich des geistigen Konstrukts bewusst waren, zu dessen Entstehung sie entscheidend beitrugen. Keiner von ihnen versuchte, die Widersprüche direkt zu benennen, aber das war auch kaum zu erwarten. Es gibt Beispiele, die auf eine solche Kenntnis schließen lassen, wie der Gesichtsausdruck Maos, den Meng Zhaorui 1966 einfing. Die bekannteste Werkreihe dieser Art wurde von Li Zhensheng geschaffen und 2003 unter dem Titel *Red Colour News Soldier* publiziert.[14] Ähnlich wie bei allen anderen „Nachrichtensoldaten" bestand Li Zhenshengs Aufgabe darin, „die Freuden und Triumphe von Maos China festzuhalten". Er behauptete später, dies als Gelegenheit verstanden zu haben, eine gewissenhafte, freimütige Anklage der Geschichte vorzulegen.

Der soziopolitische Schauplatz der Mao-Ära war für einen Fotografen eine ganz außerordentliche Zeit, die „Momente bot, die nahezu augenblicklich historisch wurden".[15] Bei den Bildern, die in diesem Buch die 1950er-, 1960er- und 1970er-Jahre repräsentieren, dürfte es sich um die ausdrucksvollste und einprägsamste Serie in der modernen Geschichte Chinas handeln, was zweifellos ihrem politisch-ideologischen Gehalt zuzuschreiben ist. Sie dokumentieren die zeittypisch aufwallenden, fanatischen Mächte des Wandels und veranschaulichen die wechselhafte politische Stimmung im unbarmherzigen Zyklus der Massenkampagnen. Nur Fotografien bringen uns vor Ort und lassen uns teilhaben an den den Repressionen, denen Gemeinschaften und Einzelne während des Ringens zwischen gegnerischen – und verzweifelten – politischen Gruppierungen ausgesetzt waren. Wenn man also John Szarkowskis Erklärung gelten lässt, dass man „während der ersten 100 Jahre der Fotografie allgemein davon ausging, Fotos könnten Dinge am besten wiedergeben… Die wichtigsten Vorzüge dieser Fotografien waren eine klare Aussage und kompakte Information"[16], könnte man dann nicht zu Recht diese voller Informationen steckenden Fotografien als die besten und vorzüglichsten einstufen?

Der Anbruch einer neuen Zeit

Die 1980er-Jahre begannen mit einem verschleppten Start. Nach Maos Tod brauchte Deng Xiaoping fast zwei Jahre, bis er seine Macht gefestigt hatte, und drei weitere, um die Viererbande hinter Gitter zu bringen.[17] Der von großem öffentlichem Interesse begleitete Prozess war in China nach Maos Tod ein herausragendes Ereignis, ein von Liu Heung Shing zwischen 1979 und 1983 systematisch dokumentierter Normalisierungsprozess. 1978 verkündete Deng Xiaoping seine absolut moderne Reformpolitik. Sie erwies sich als ungeheuer wichtig, ebenso wie die Wiedereröffnung der Universitäten (ab 1978) und Schulen (1980), die seit Mitte der 1970er-Jahre geschlossen waren. Die begeisterte Hingabe ans Lernen veranschaulicht Liu Heung Shings Foto von Studenten, die nachts auf dem Tiananmen-Platz lernen, dem einzigen Ort, an dem es in den 1980er-Jahren genug Licht zum Lesen gab (Abb. S. 288/289). Es war eine Zeit widersprüchlicher Emotionen: Dengs Grundsätze verkehrten häufig Maos Ideale in ihr Gegenteil. Am Ende des Jahrzehnts gab Deng Anweisungen, die Überfülle von Mao-Porträts im öffentlichen Raum zu verringern.[18] Ungeachtet dessen kamen in den 1980er-Jahren, ja selbst 1993 zu Maos 100. Geburtstag, in der Gesellschaft immer wieder Phasen der Mao-Begeisterung auf.

Als Folge des wirtschaftlichen Fortschritts begann eine neue Phase künstlerischen Ausdrucks in all seine Formen, von Literatur und Dichtung, bildender Kunst bis hin zur Musik. Auch Fotografen hatten das Bedürfnis, die Grenzen eines politisch sanktionierten Abbilds der Realität zu überschreiten. In dem Bemühen, sich umfassenderen gesellschaft-

lichen Fragen sowie der menschlichen Existenz zu widmen, um die eigene Arbeit hin zu profunderen Zielen weiterzuentwickeln, gab es eine Welle von Experimenten Einzelner, die ihren Ursprung in der April Photo Society und der Blüte der Amateurfotografie in den späten 1970er-Jahren hatten. Unmittelbar nach dem Tod von Ministerpräsident Zhou Enlai im April 1976, als die Viererbande die öffentliche Trauer um den „Premier des Volkes" verbot, wurde diese Bewegung spontan geboren. Berufs- und Amateurfotografen, die sich zufällig auf dem Tiananmen-Platz befanden, als die Trauernden sich zu versammeln begannen, noch ehe das Trauerverbot ergangen war, hielten das Geschehen fest. Sie befanden sich noch vor Ort, als die Polizei später den Befehl erhielt, den Platz zu räumen. Angesichts der kurzen Zeit hatten sie eine überraschend große Zahl von Bildern aufgenommen, von denen eine noch erstaunlichere Anzahl die in den folgenden Tagen angeordnete Such- und Vernichtungsaktion überstand. Diese Bilder erschienen schließlich 1979 in einem Band mit dem Titel *People's Mourning* (Trauer des Volkes). Zusammen mit der ersten bedeutenden Fotoausstellung, die Ende 1978 in Peking eröffnet wurde[19], erweckte dieses Buch die Fotografie zu neuem, eigenständigem Leben.

In den 1980er-Jahren waren die Gelegenheiten zu Ausstellungen jeglicher Art begrenzt. Bis etwa 2005 hatte die Fotografie außerhalb ihrer eigenen Zirkel in China keine bedeutende Anhängerschaft. Ein Beispiel, das die höchst unterschiedlichen Geschicke von bildender Kunst und Fotografie in China veranschaulicht, ist ein Vergleich der Bedeutung, die zwei um 1979 in Peking stattfindenden Ausstellungen beigemessen wurde. Beide wurden jeweils von einer neuen Gruppe organisiert, der keine offiziellen, sondern überwiegend als Amateure tätige Mitglieder angehörten. Eine, die Stars Painting Group (üblicherweise einfach als Stars bezeichnet), veranstaltete eine inoffizielle Ausstellung neben der chinesischen Nationalgalerie im Zentrum von Peking. Als die Ausstellung geschlossen wurde, machte dies Schlagzeilen, umso mehr als es die Künstler wagten, gegen die Beschlagnahmung ihrer Werke zu protestieren, und es ihnen gelang, sie zurückzubekommen. Liu Heung Shings Fotografie von 1979 zeigt einen triumphierenden Ma Desheng auf den Rathausstufen, umringt von einer aufmerksamen Menge aus Anhängern und Passanten (Abb. S. 272), sowie Wang Keping, auch er Mitglied der Gruppe, der eine Fahne mit der Aufschrift „Freiheit der Meinungsäußerung" schwenkt (Abb. S. 273). Die andere Ausstellung war die der April Photo Society, einer Gruppe von Fotografen, die ihre Gemeinschaft nach dem Ereignis benannt hatten, das sie zusammengebracht hatte. Ihre Ausstellung *Natur, Gesellschaft und Mensch*, die passenderweise im April 1979 eröffnet wurde, verlief ohne Störungen und kam nicht in die Nachrichten. Sowohl diese Ausstellung als auch zwei weitere in den Jahren 1980 und 1981 waren gut

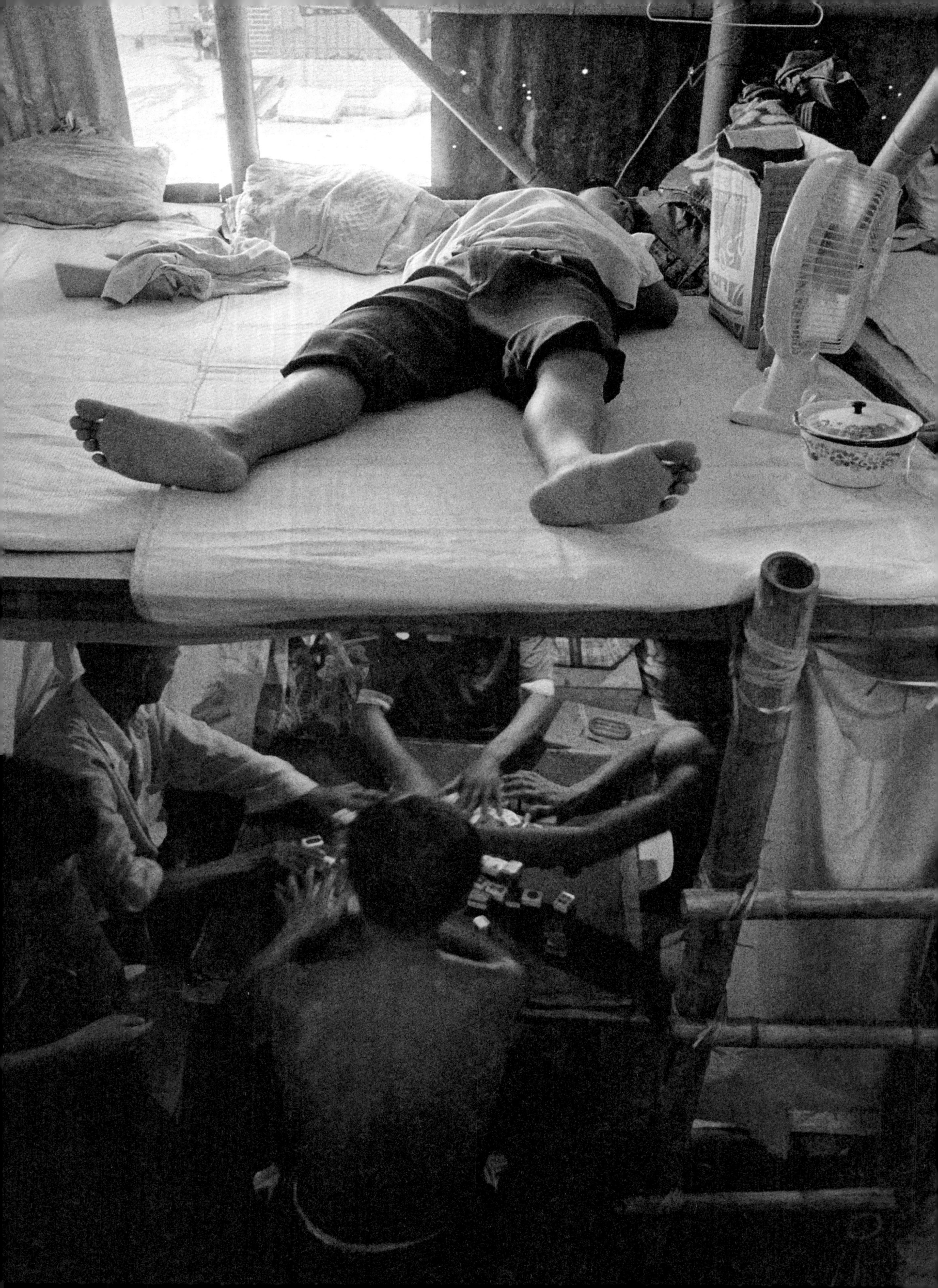

←
Yang Yankang, 1997

Migrant workers in Shenzhen. Cramped conditions mean that workers rotate the available bunk space, sleeping in shifts. Since shift work is required, it makes for an equitable use of space, if less than perfect rest for the workers.

Wanderarbeiter in Shenzhen. Beengte Verhältnisse bewirken, dass die Arbeiter die vorhandenen Schlafkojen turnusmäßig nutzen und in Schichten schlafen. Da auch in Schichten gearbeitet werden muss, wird der Raum perfekt, wenn auch für den Einzelnen kaum ruhegerecht genutzt.

Des travailleurs migrants à Shenzhen. Les dortoirs étaient si insuffisants que les travailleurs dormaient à tour de rôle. C'était appliquer au sommeil le principe du travail en équipe, solution plus qu'imparfaite pour les ouvriers.

besucht, erreichten jedoch nicht den legendären Status der Kunstausstellungen der Stars.

Dies ist ungewöhnlich, wenn man bedenkt, dass die Vorgehensweise der beiden Gruppen, ebenso wie ihre Ziele und ihr Einfluss weitgehend gleich waren. Wie die Verklärten Poeten und die metaphysischen Autoren der Zeit zogen Chinas Fotografen es vor, ihre Kommentare zu verschleiern. Typische Bilder aus den 1980er-Jahren hatten Landschaft zum Gegenstand, häufig in Form traumartiger Ansichten, voller Verweise auf Natursymbolik, bekannt aus der traditionellen Tuschemalerei. Der Unterschied zwischen den offiziellen, autorisierten Bildern Lü Houmins, des altgedienten Pressefotografen von Xinhua, und der weihevollen Naturfotografie nach Art von *National Geographic*, auf die er sich in den 80er-Jahren spezialisierte, verdeutlicht die paradigmatischen Verschiebungen, die sich in diesem Jahrzehnt in der Fotografie vollzogen. Dies war die Zeit des L'art pour l'art, aber ironischerweise sollte sich eben diese Salonästhetik, die die Mitglieder der April Photo Society ursprünglich zusammenbrachte, als ihre Achillesferse erweisen. Vor allen anderen Erwägungen förderte sie die Konzentration auf Schönheit und eine ätherische Spiritualität. Vor diesem Hintergrund bedeuten die von Angehörigen der April Photo Society geschaffenen Bilder eine dramatische Abkehr von bestehenden Konventionen. In den 1970er-Jahren hatten sie alle als Berufsfotografen großartige, ikonenhafte Bilder geschaffen. Gleichwohl zögerten sie nicht, bei der ersten Gelegenheit die Realität zugunsten künstlerischer Ästhetik aufzugeben. Dazu Bill Jay, ehemaliger Herausgeber der Zeitschrift *Creative Camera*: „Fotoklubs ... sind in erster Linie mit der Herstellung hübscher Bilder befasst, und nicht damit, die Wahrheit über den Bildinhalt zu offenbaren."[20] Letztendlich war es genau das, worauf die Salonmentalität ihre Arbeit reduzierte.

Zurück zur Natur

Die in den 1980er-Jahren in China entstandenen Fotografien zeichnen sich durch ihre Ehrlichkeit aus, wovon die riesige Sammlung von Bildern in *Humanism in China* zeugt.[21] Selbst hier ist der Anteil der Bilder aus den 1980er-Jahren verglichen mit dem anderer Jahrzehnte unverhältnismäßig klein. Bei den Aufnahmen aus diesen Jahren handelt es sich tatsächlich um „Fragmente"[22], die über ihren Standort im größeren Rahmen oder darüber, wo sie einzufügen wären, wenig verraten.

Am Ende dieses Jahrzehnts war eine neue Generation herangewachsen. Eine, die wenig über das Leben unter Mao wusste und die in einer Zeit der Öffnung, Reform und raschen Modernisierung groß geworden war. Sie hatte darüber hinaus Zugang zu westlichen Einflüssen und verfügte über eine beispiellose Flut von Informationen. Angehörige dieser Generation lehnten intuitiv die vordergründige Ästhetik der April Photo

Society und die gefühlvollen Anteile ihrer humanistischen Anliegen ab. Ein gutes Beispiel ist die Anfang der 1990er-Jahre von jungen Berufsfotografen gegründete Topic Group, der auch Liu Zheng *(Worker's Daily)*, Jin Yongquan *(China Youth Daily)* und Yuan Dongping *(China Nationalities Pictorial)* angehörten. Sie sahen ihr Ziel darin, mit ihrer Fotografie bestimmte Themen aufzugreifen und sie wieder mit Inhalt zu füllen. Ende der 1980er-Jahre schufen Yuan Dongping und Lü Nan eine Serie von dokumentarischen Fotografien, die Patienten in einer typischen Nervenheilanstalt zeigen. Wie die Bilder, die ihnen in der Hochzeit der Kulturrevolution vorausgingen, kennzeichnen sie ein unbestechlicher Blick und ein fast viktorianisches Interesse an menschlichen Sonderlingen.

In der Folge unterzogen kleine Gruppen vorausdenkender Einzelner weitere soziale Fragen einer visuellen Sondierung. Auch in den 1990er-Jahren blieben viele Bereiche für Fotografen heikles Terrain, und die Veröffentlichung entsprechender Fotos war nur beschränkt möglich. Mit dem Versuch, einen Diskurs anzuregen, waren sie ihrer Zeit deutlich voraus, und sie kämpften deshalb darum, voranzukommen oder Beachtung zu finden. Der Grund dafür war in erster Linie das Fehlen einer Plattform, wie sie heute das Internet darstellt, das seit der Jahrtausendwende zum wichtigsten Schauplatz für die Diskussion umstrittener moralischer Themen wurde. Außerdem fehlte es an freien Ausstellungsräumen, wie sie heute in Großstädten vermehrt zu finden sind.

Trotz eines zeitweisen Rückschlags, ausgelöst durch den „Zwischenfall vom 4. Juni", führte das Reformprogramm in China weiterhin zu neuer Offenheit. Zu Beginn der 1990er-Jahre widersetzte sich eine jüngere Generation von Fotografen den vorherrschenden Trends und nahm sich bereitwillig der Realität an. Dem Beispiel bahnbrechender Kommentatoren sozialer Missstände wie Diane Arbus, August Sander und Richard Avedon folgend und mit einer gelegentlichen ehrfurchtsvollen Reverenz an die atmosphärischen Stimmungen Eugène Atgets, präsentierte diese neue Spezies international gesinnter und äußerst ehrgeiziger Fotografen ein vergleichbares Aufgebot surrealer Geschöpfe und Schauplätze, die sie als Versatzstücke bei der Inszenierung ihrer eigenen Allegorie des Lebens im modernen China verwendeten. Ein gutes Beispiel hierfür ist Liu Zhengs Serie *The Chinese*, die zwischen 1994 und 1999 entstand, in einem Zeitraum, der sich teilweise mit seiner Tätigkeit als Bildjournalist bei *Workers' Daily* von 1991 bis 1997 deckt. Bei *The Chinese* handelt es sich um eine Sammlung fesselnder Aufnahmen, eindeutig orientiert an der Sicht der oben erwähnten westlichen Fotografen: Schauspieler, Sänger, Nonnen, Künstler, bizarre Persönlichkeiten und abnorme Körper (Abb. S. 336), die eine bewusst morbide Anmutung haben.

Kunst + Fotografie = ?

Die 1990er-Jahre erlebten eine rapide Ausbreitung von Fotostudios in ganz China. Der Lebensstandard stieg beachtlich schnell. Urbane Zentren hatten ein ausgeprägt modernes Aussehen angenommen. Die Medien erhielten Zuwachs durch eine Reihe von Lifestyle-Publikationen mit prächtigen Hochglanzfotos. In diesem Jahrzehnt legte die zeitgenössische Kunst tragfähige Fundamente, auf denen sich bauen ließ, und da es verhältnismäßig einfach war, ein unabhängiger Künstler zu sein, der nicht allzu viel Gerät oder Raum brauchte, war es die bildende Kunst, und in geringerem Maß auch die Literatur, die den aktuellen ästhetischen Diskurs anführte. Die erwachende Kunstszene in China hatte begonnen, die Aufmerksamkeit westlicher Kuratoren und Kunstinteressierter zu erregen. Unbewusst wurde die neue Generation von Fotografen zunehmend darin bestärkt, ihre Tätigkeit an der der zeitgenössischen Künstler des Landes auszurichten, und sei es nur, weil diese Szene Möglichkeiten zum Austausch, zur kritischen Würdigung und zum Ausstellen von Arbeiten bot, die es in rein fotografischen Kreisen nicht gab.

Während der 1990er-Jahre war es nicht einfach, das Fotografieren zu erlernen. Echte Fotografen lernten es immer noch bei der Arbeit oder als Teil eines Journalismuslehrgangs. Deshalb waren diese Kurse auf technische Hochschulen mit Abteilungen für Journalismus beschränkt. Der praktische Unterricht konzentrierte sich in erster Linie auf die Mechanik der Kamera und technische Funktionen. Ästhetische Fragen hielt man für überflüssig, da die Fotografie nicht als künstlerische Ausdrucksform galt. Erst seit den Anfangsjahren des neuen Jahrtausends, seit dem Einzug der Fotografie in die Welt der schönen Künste, hält man sie nicht mehr für Kunsthandwerk. Eine der treibenden Kräfte in dieser Szene war Rong Rong, der sich 1996 mit Liu Zheng zusammentat, um die maßgebliche Zeitschrift *New Photo* zu publizieren. Frustriert von dem Inhalt und den Beschränkungen offizieller Zeitschriften wie *China Photography*, erkannten sie den Bedarf nach einem Forum, das zwischen dem Werk eines Künstlers, eines Bildjournalisten oder eines „reinen" Fotografen keinen Unterschied macht. Unterdessen bestand die einzige Arbeitsmöglichkeit für Berufsfotografen in Zeitschriften wie *China Photography*, die von der Genossenschaft der Fotografen herausgegeben wurde. Der Inhalt all dieser offiziellen Magazine war traditionell und konservativ mit einem Schwerpunkt auf der Technik. Die Erörterung ästhetischer Fragen oder dessen, was eine Fotografie vermitteln kann, wurde bewusst vermieden. *China Photography* orientierte sich an der 1995 von Liu Heung Shing produzierten kostenlosen Fotozeitung *Photo Reportage* und wurde in Fotografenkreisen ebenfalls kostenlos verteilt; sie hatte ein ähnliches Format und widmete sich der Wirkung des fotografischen Bildes.

Im Lauf der 1990er-Jahre gewann der investigative Umgang mit Fotografie zunehmend an Bedeutung. Die Fotografen entdeckten eine für sie interessante Thematik und verfolgten sie eigenständig. Jiang Jian porträtierte einfache Menschen aus kleinen Landgemeinden oder ländlichen Kleinstädten. Wu Jialin widmete sich dem Leben in den Provinzen, in Bergregionen und abgelegenen Städten. Zeng Li reiste durch das ganze Land auf der Suche nach den Überresten der chinesischen Schwerindustrie, deren Anlagen zum Teil noch in Gebrauch, überwiegend aber stillgelegt sind. Yang Yankang wählte religiös geprägte Gemeinden in den ländlichen Gebieten (Abb. S. 318); Wang Fuchun bereiste das Land und verfolgte die rasch zunehmende Massenwanderung von Menschen, die auf der Suche nach Arbeit die Regionen mithilfe des feinmaschigen chinesischen Eisenbahnnetzes durchkämmen (Abb. S. 322); Zeng Nian schuf eine ungewöhnliche Folge großformatiger Panoramaansichten vom Fortschreiten des Drei-Schluchten-Projekts und von seinen Auswirkungen auf die verarmten Gemeinden in der unmittelbaren Umgebung (Abb. S. 324/325 und S. 326/327); Xie Hailong schließlich richtete seine Linse auf die Misere der Kinder in den abgelegensten Regionen, die der Wunsch eint, eine Schule zu besuchen (Abb. S. 316 und S. 317). Unterdessen bewies Xiao Quan das scharfsichtige Verständnis seiner Generation mit einer Folge von Porträts von Künstlern, Kuratoren, Kunstkritikern, Filmemachern, Schauspielern, Autoren und Poeten, die dem kreativen Schaffen im neuen China ganz neue Sphären erschlossen. 1994 erschien eine Auswahl unter dem Titel *My Generation*[23], zweifellos in Anlehnung an den gleichnamigen Song von The Who, ein Bezug, der gewiss erfüllt war von ähnlichen, wenngleich subtilen Ambitionen des Fotografen, ebenfalls einer Generation Ausdruck zu verleihen. Diese Personen verkörperten eine neue Generation engagierter und begabter Fotografen mit ausgeprägtem Verständnis für die vorherrschenden sozialen Gegebenheiten der Zeit.

Im Jahr 1996 sah sich die Fotografie von der zeitgenössischen Kunstszene mit Beschlag belegt. Für Künstler, die gewohnt sind, zur Veranschaulichung eines Gedankens Bilder zu malen, bot die Fotografie einen Weg, das sozio-politische, ökonomische und kulturelle Umfeld in einer Weise festzuhalten, die wenig persönliches Eingreifen erforderte und doch das endgültige Werk mit Andeutungen und Schlussfolgerungen bereicherte. Nur wenige Versuche in Sachen Fotografie hatten mit den traditionellen Werten des Mediums an sich zu tun. Für Künstler war allein die Idee von Bedeutung. Besser als den meisten anderen gelang es Wang Jinsong, dies in Form einer Reihe von Porträts zu demonstrieren. Details wie Stil oder Qualität von Kinderschuhen sprechen Bände hinsichtlich des wirtschaftlichen Wandels, der das Land erfasst hatte. Dies wird auch in Wang Jinsongs ikonischem Werk *Standard Family* deutlich. Es enthält Familienporträts von 200 Ein-Kind-Familien: Die Kinder besuchen alle dieselbe Schule, während das Aussehen ihrer Eltern auf eine Herkunft aus den unterschiedlichsten Gesellschaftsschichten schließen lässt (Abb. S. 328/329).

In den letzten Jahren des 20. Jahrhunderts war die Kunstszene vernarrt in die Fotografie. Xing Danwens Porträt des Malers Zeng Fanzhi (heute einer der gesuchtesten Künstler Chinas, damals am Beginn seiner Laufbahn stehend) und von Wang Jin während einer Performance zeigt, wie sich die Rolle des Fotos von der „dokumentarischen Aufzeichnung" zum wirklichen „Kunstwerk" verändert. Ein Gutteil der Fotokunst passte zu dem wachsenden Gefühl der Vergänglichkeit des Augenblicks, während sich die Welt auf ein neues Jahrtausend zu bewegte. Gleichzeitig zeichnete die Kamera für eine Reihe dramatischer, schockierender und verführerischer Bilder verantwortlich. Während jedoch die Kunst der Fotografie die Farbe zurückgab, indem sie bewies, dass sie für bestimmte Wirkungen eingesetzt werden konnte, ohne von der Dramatik abzulenken, erschien ihre eigene Dramatik, die sich um eine besonders bizarre Spielart der Fantasie drehte, bald schal und reizlos. Ansel Adams charakterisierte die Gefahren künstlerischer Fotografie als „brillante Bilder von unklaren Ideen"[24]. Gleichwohl erinnerte die zeitgenössische Kunstszene die Berufsfotografen an das Potenzial des Mediums, was eine Periode der erneuten Stärkung und letztendlich des Fortschritts einläutete.

Sichtbar wird dies an der um 2000 erkennbaren ideenreichen Vielfalt der fotografischen Stile und Auffassungen. Diese Bilder decken die ganze Skala zeitgenössischen Lebens und sozialer Motive ab: angefangen bei Mädchen auf Arbeitssuche (Abb. S. 384), verheerenden Überschwemmungen in den Städten des Südens (Abb. S. 96/97), Menschenmengen auf Jahrmärkten, 80-jährigen Straßenhändlern (Abb. S. 390), zum Blumenverkauf auf der Straße genötigten Kindern (Abb. S. 315), SARS, eleganten neuen Wohnstätten der aufblühenden Mittelklasse in Shanghai (Abb. S. 372, 373, 374 und 375) bis zum Leben der Grubenarbeiter, Korruption und Reichtum. All diese Aufnahmen sagen unendlich viel über die Themen der Zeit, über die neuen Schauplätze und ebenso über die sich neuerdings stellenden Herausforderungen. Ein besonders gutes Beispiel hierfür ist Zhou Yues Dokumentation über die explodierende Jugendkultur in der chinesischen Hauptstadt und den zwangsläufig nihilistischen Geist, der diese Schicht neuerlich befreiter Seelen durchdringt – nahezu sämtlich Einzelkinder, niemandem verpflichtet und unglaublich verwöhnt. Für diese Kinder und Teenager ist China wahrhaftig das Land der Möglichkeiten (Abb. S. 338 und 339); neben Liu Heung Shings erschreckendem Porträt eines kleinen Jungen aus dem offiziell ärmsten Ort Chinas ergibt sich ein bestürzender Kontrast (Abb. S. 312). Diese Fotos schockieren und verführen zugleich und unterstreichen die Verschiebung sozialer Werte, die sich angesichts moderner Zerstreuungen ergibt. Sie erzählen von Aspekten des Lebens, die nicht gern zur Kenntnis genommen oder akzeptiert werden, deren Wahrheit jedoch unleugbar ist.

Das ultimative Bild

Die Aufgabe, einen fotografischen Überblick einer sozialen, kulturellen oder politischen Geschichte zusammenzustellen, bedeutet immer eine Herausforderung. Zwangsläufig wurden die ausgewählten Bilder dem ursprünglichen zeitlichen und inhaltlichen Zusammenhang entnommen. Sobald man sie in eine verkürzte Version der Geschichte einfügt, erhält der „moralische und emotionale Gehalt" jeder Abbildung eine neue Bedeutung und Wertigkeit. Werden sie als Teil einer chronologischen Abfolge präsentiert, sind einzelne Bilder verantwortlich für die Vermittlung von Augenblicken, Ereignissen, Realität, politischen Strömungen, ökonomischen Veränderungen, der herrschenden Stimmung sowie der Reaktion der Menschen zu jeder beliebigen Zeit. Auch Gegensätzlichkeit und Vergleichbarkeit nebeneinander stehender Fotos, die so über Raum und Zeit hinweg in Beziehung gesetzt sind, können die Wirkung eines Bildes verändern. Die Zeit verschleiert die Vielschichtigkeit einzelner Momente und die Tatsachen, wie sie Zeitzeugen erlebten, während vormals als unwichtig geltende, subtile Details in neuem Licht erscheinen. Selbst wenn die Feinheiten der dargestellten Ereignisse späteren Generationen unverständlich bleiben, wissen wir, dass diese Fotos ein einzigartiges bildliches Dokument zu Chinas bedeutsamer, bewegter und siegreicher Odyssee darstellen; einer Odyssee, von einer in bäuerlicher Leibeigenschaft gehaltenen Bevölkerung, von einem Staat ohne Einfluss in der internationalen Politik, zu einer führenden Wirtschaftsmacht, belebt von einer gut funktionierenden, modernen Gesellschaft, angetrieben von einer bis dato nicht gekannten industriellen Produktion und ausgestattet mit einer vernehmlichen Stimme in Weltpolitik und Handel, die überall Beachtung findet.

Um Aufmerksamkeit zu rechtfertigen und sich zu bewähren, muss die Fotografie mehr tun, als nur Tatsachen festzuhalten. Fotografien sind Teil des kollektiven Gedächtnisses einer Nation, Bezugspunkte für den Raum, den wir gemeinschaftlich als ein Volk bewohnen. Sie repräsentieren die Außenwelt und ihre menschlichen Bewohner, die vom Fotografen manipuliert werden können, die aber irgendwie dennoch durch das Verstreichen der Zeit oder durch die Distanz zum ursprünglichen Augenblick und Umfeld stets ihre eigene Wahrheit mitteilen. Bisweilen benötigen wir alle Hilfe, um auf irgendeinem Foto Details einer historischen Darstellung wahrzunehmen. Versorgt mit genügend Informationen, können wir sie lesen und ohne Hilfe unsere eigenen Schlüsse ziehen. Aus der Vielzahl der visuellen Eindrücke, die im Laufe der Jahrzehnte von der Volksrepublik entstanden, wurde das von *China, Porträt eines Landes* präsentierte Bild

→
Lu Guang, 2008

Pedestrians walk past the new headquarters of Central Chinese Television (CCTV) in downtown Beijing. The modern architecture was designed by the Dutch architect Rem Koolhaas.

Passanten gehen an der neuen Zentrale von Central Chinese Television (CCTV) im Zentrum Pekings vorbei. Die hypermoderne Architektur ist ein Entwurf des niederländischen Architekten Rem Koolhaas.

Des passants devant le nouveau siège de la Centrale de télévision chinoise (CCTV), au cœur de Pékin. Cet édifice moderne a été conçu par l'architecte néerlandais, Rem Koolhaas.

sorgfältig zusammengestellt, um das vollständige moralische und emotionale Gewicht jeder Fotografie zu bewahren. Ansel Adams behauptete, dass „nicht jeder Gemälden vertraut, aber die Menschen Fotografien glauben". Zumindest dieser Umstand gewährleistet, dass diese Bilder eine neue Diskussion darüber eröffnen, wie China dahin kam, wo es heute ist.

1. Susan Sontag, *On Photography*, Picador, New York, 1977, S. 105–106.
2. Hou Bo war von 1949 bis 1961 als Maos persönliche Fotografin tätig. Zu ihrer Laufbahn und ihrem Werk s. S. 409.
3. Das Gleiche gilt für die unter 35-Jährigen, wobei deren Ausbildung ideologisch, aber weniger politisch war – oder ist sie ebenso politisch, aber weniger ideologisch? – und den Kräften der Wirtschaftsreform unterworfen, wodurch sie sich in China mit sozialistischen Besonderheiten auskennen, die durch die Akzeptanz des Konsumdenkens eindeutig kapitalistisch geprägt sind. Auch unterscheiden sich die Informationswege, zum Beispiel das Internet.
4. Eine erstaunliche Fülle von Beispielen findet sich in Zhang Dalis Buch *A Second History*, Walsh Gallery, Chicago, 2006.
5. Insbesondere nach dem Mai 1919 polemisierte die Bewegung des 4. Mai gegen die Ungerechtigkeiten des Versailler Vertrags, der territoriale Teilungen und externe Regierungsrechte über diese Gebiete in China verhängte.
6. Mitte der 1940er-Jahre hatte *Life* eine wöchentliche Auflage von über zehn Millionen Exemplaren erreicht.
7. Dies bestärkte Mao letztendlich darin, eine Kampagne zu starten, mit der eine gemeinsame Sprache – *putonghua,* wörtlich Standardsprache – durchgesetzt werden sollte. Dieser Prozess wurde im Lauf der 1950er-Jahre durch die Vereinfachung der klassischen chinesischen Schriftzeichen unterstützt.
8. Die *Gespräche über Literatur und Kunst in Yan'an* von 1942 bildeten bis zum Ende von Maos Regime die Grundlage sämtlichen Kunstschaffens. Jeglicher kreative Ausdruck unterlag der von ihm hier umrissenen Theorie.
9. *China: Fifty Years inside the People's Republic*, Katalog zur gleichnamigen Ausstellung, Einführung von Rae Wang, Aperture, New York, 1999, S. 14.
10. Die 1938 in Wuhan gegründete *Xinhua Daily News* wurde 1947 von den Nationalisten verboten und im April 1949 wieder belebt und damit zur ersten allgemeinen Zeitung der Volksrepublik.
11. Dies bezieht sich auf den Titel von Xiao Zhuangs gesammelten Werken, *The Irrational Times*, China, 2004.
12. *Yu gong yi shan.*
13. Susan Sontag, *On Photography*, Picador, New York, 1977, S. 6.
14. Li Zhensheng, *Red Colour News Soldier*, London, 2003.
15. *China: Fifty Years Inside the People's Republic*, Katalog zur gleichnahmigen Ausstellung, Einführung von Rae Yang, Aperture, New York, 1999, S. 14.
16. John Szarkowski, „Photography and the Mass Media", *Creative Camera*, 1967, S. 30.
17. Der Viererbande gehörten die wichtigsten Mitglieder einer radikalen Splittergruppe an, die bei der Lenkung der Kulturrevolution eine Schlüsselrolle spielten und nach dem Tod Mao Zedongs 1976 versuchten, die Macht zu ergreifen.
18. Dies war Gegenstand von Liu Heung Shings Buch *China after Mao*, das 1982 erschien und dieses Phänomen mit Bildern des Alltags ausführlich dokumentierte. Nach seinem Erscheinen war *China after Mao* in Fotografenkreisen in der Volksrepublik China weit verbreitet und blieb auch während der 1990er-Jahre höchst einflussreich.
19. *A Premier for the People, A People for the Premier*, 26. Dezember 1978 bis 4. Februar 1979 zeigte öffentlich eine riesige Fotodokumentation der „Bewegung 5. April", wie die Ereignisse um die Trauer um Zhou Enlai genannt wurden. Entsprechend ging es weniger um Fotografie als um eine Propagandaübung für das neue Regime, in dem Bemühen, das Vertrauen der Menschen in seine Politik und Führung wiederherzustellen.
20. Bill Jay, „In Praise of the Snapshot", *Creative Camera*, September 1971, England.
21. Die Ausstellung mit dem Titel *Humanism in China. A Contemporary Record of Photography*, wurde organisiert vom Kunstmuseum in Guangdong und war anschließend 2005 bis 2006 im Kunstmuseum Shanghai sowie im National Art Museum of China in Peking zu sehen. Im Mai 2006 wurde sie im Museum für Moderne Kunst, Frankfurt am Main, gezeigt und anschließend bis März 2008 in fünf weiteren Museen in Deutschland.
22. Susan Sontag, *On Photography*, Picador, New York, 1977, S. 105–106.
23. Erschienen bei Cinema Press, China 1994.
24. Das ganze Zitat lautet: „Nichts ist schlimmer als das scharfe Bild einer unklaren Idee."

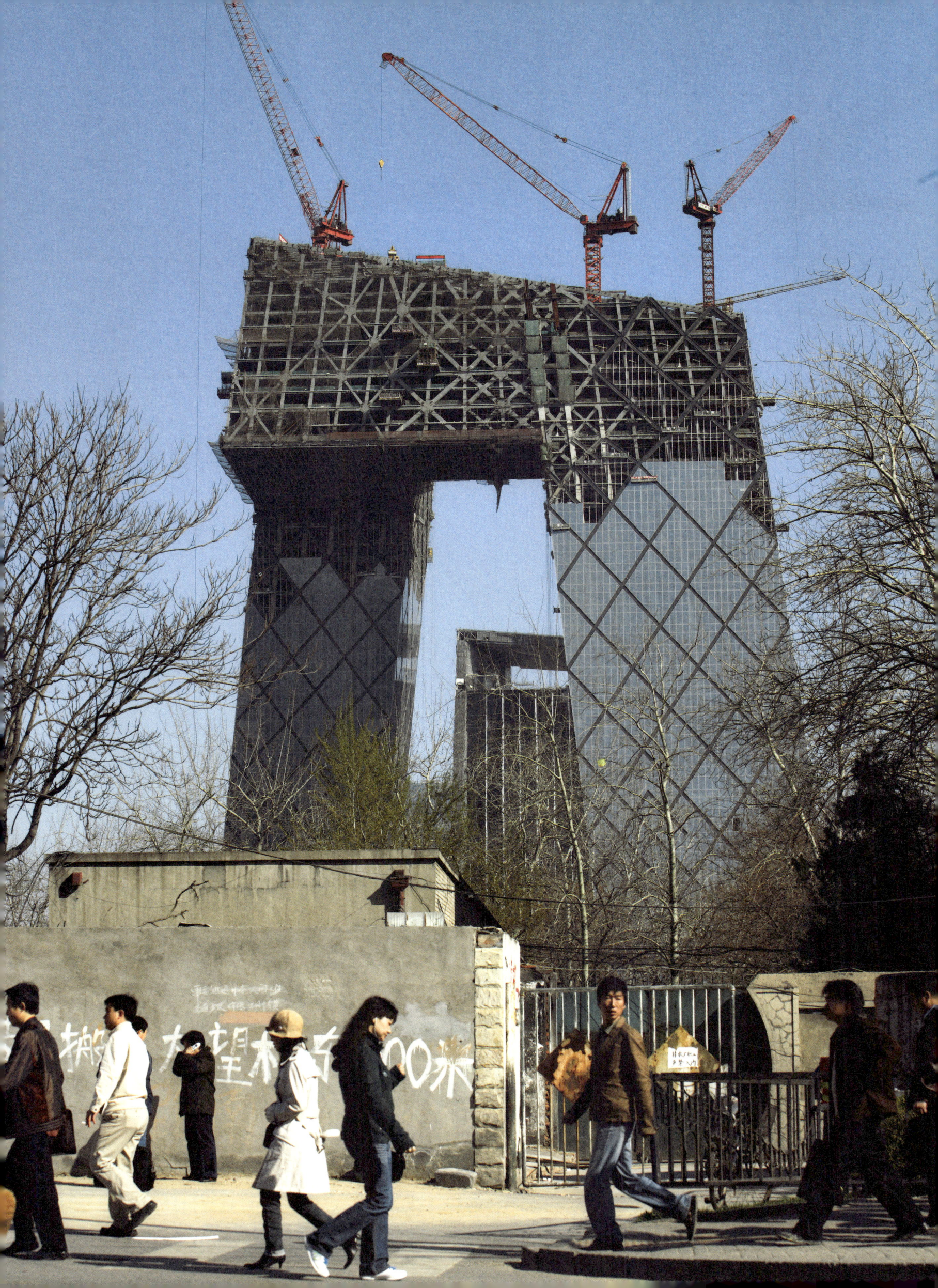

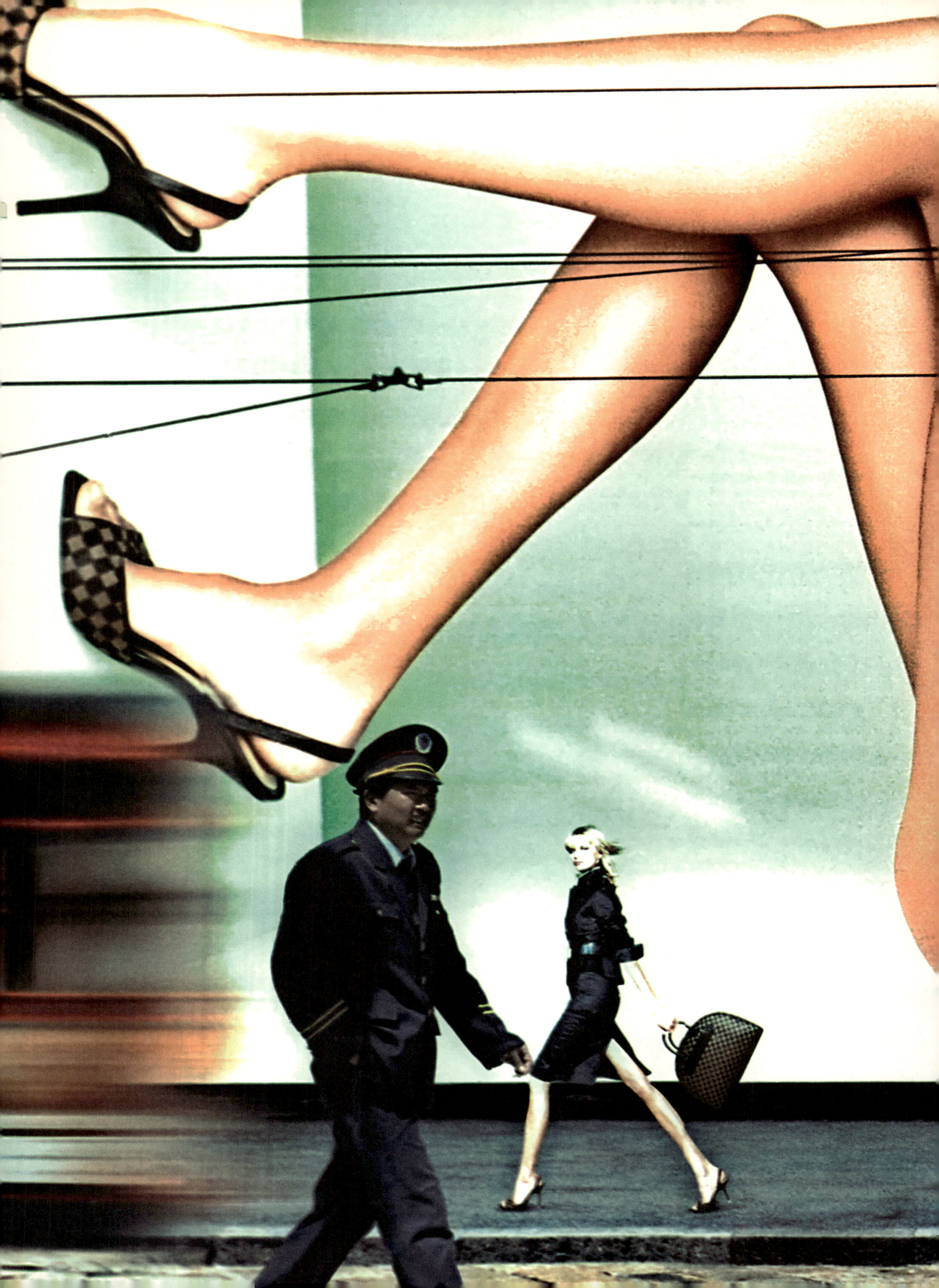

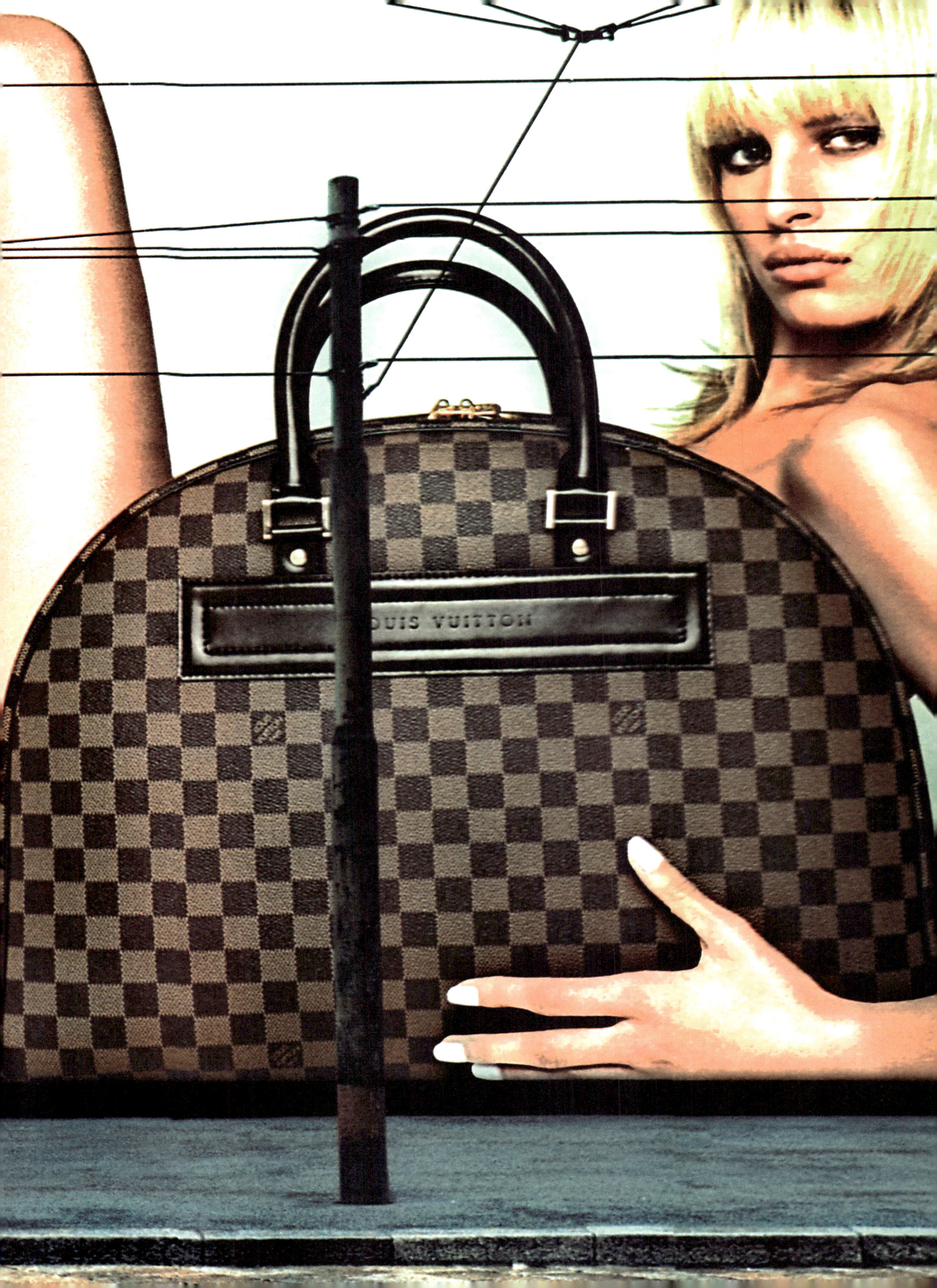

Prenez ça !

Par Karen Smith

pp. 86/87
Yong He, 2002

A giant billboard toting the signature handbag of French luxury brand Louis Vuitton advertises the opening of a flagship store for China on Shanghai's own Champs-Élysées, Nanjing West Road, something to which this pedestrian is apparently oblivious. Consumers of luxury products make up just 0.5 percent of the population in China, but the annual sales volume for luxury goods is estimated at close to US $ 3 billion per annum.

"In the final analysis materialism will triumph over religion, because Marxism-Leninism-Mao Zedong thought is true and scientific." Gandunjiazuo

Eine riesige Plakatwand mit einer Handtasche der französischen Luxusmarke Louis Vuitton wirbt für die Eröffnung eines Flagship-Stores in China an Shanghais „Champs-Élysées", der Nanjing West Road, ein Ereignis, für das der gemeine Passant offenbar keinen Blick hat. Konsumenten von Luxusgütern machen genau 0,5 % der chinesischen Bevölkerung aus, aber das jährliche Absatzvolumen für Luxusgüter wird auf fast 3 Milliarden US-Dollar geschätzt.

„In der Endabrechnung wird der Materialismus über die Religion triumphieren, weil der Marxismus-Leninismus und das Denken Mao Zedongs wahr und wissenschaftlich ist." Gandunjiazuo

Une affiche géante montrant un célèbre sac Louis Vuitton annonce l'ouverture d'un grand magasin de la marque sur les Champs-Élysées de Shanghai, Nankin West Road, événement qui ne semble pas troubler le piéton ordinaire. Les produits de consommation de luxe touchent seulement 0,5 % de la population chinoise mais leur volume de ventes annuel est estimé à près de 3 milliards de US $.

« En dernière analyse, le matérialisme triomphera de la religion, parce que la pensée marxiste-léniniste de Mao Zedong est vraie et scientifique. » Gandunjiazuo

« Parce que chaque photographie n'est qu'un fragment, son poids moral et émotionnel dépend de son contexte. »[1]

Une vision de la vérité

L'arrivée de la photographie en Chine au XIXe siècle permit de révéler au monde extérieur les premiers documents visuels « factuels » sur cette nation, ses peuples et ses curieuses coutumes. Ces fragments d'information avaient pour lourde charge d'exprimer l'ensemble d'une culture. Le XXe siècle n'a guère produit d'image beaucoup plus cohérente de ce pays, et certainement pas au cours du demi-siècle précédant la fondation de la Chine nouvelle en 1949. La dynastie Qing abolie, le pays se consuma dans des guerres civiles ou de simples préoccupations de survie. Après l'établissement de la République populaire et une fois les portes sur l'extérieur hermétiquement closes pendant toute la Guerre froide, l'image photographique de la Chine se fragmenta encore davantage. Si des journalistes étrangers pouvaient parler de l'impact du régime et de la politique de Mao Zedong, leurs sympathies coloraient indéniablement la nature de leurs articles.

Côté chinois, la très grande majorité des images diffusées à l'extérieur ou localement devait recevoir une autorisation officielle car ces fragments étaient censés illustrer les réussites de la politique de Mao et de sa vision socialiste révolutionnaire. Qu'ils aient été en grande partie déconnectés de la réalité n'était pas immédiatement perceptible. Ils appartenaient à un tableau si vaste que l'on ne pouvait l'appréhender d'un seul regard. Ils décrivaient les avancées magnifiées d'un programme communiste de modernisation supposée produire le progrès économique et social, mais comme il s'agissait essentiellement d'images fabriquées (créées par un bureau de propagande), il était difficile de savoir ce qui représentait vraiment la réalité. Pour un public étranger, il était quasi impossible d'évaluer le poids moral ou émotionnel de ces photographies.

La situation ne se modifia guère pendant les années 1980. Politiquement, la Chine commençait déjà à changer peu à peu, mais insuffisamment pour participer à des échanges culturels internationaux qui ne se développèrent qu'à partir du début des années 2000. De très nombreuses pièces de ce puzzle complexe allaient devoir trouver leur place avant que n'arrive enfin le moment où il devenait possible et urgent de réunir ces fragments pour les insérer à leur place précise, pour présenter une image complète de la Chine vue par les photographes chinois.

Chine + Photographie = ?

Nous n'associons pas immédiatement les mots Chine et photographie bien que ce pays ait été un « sujet » photographique assez apprécié au cours des 150 dernières années, en particulier par les photographes européens et américains. Aventuriers, voyageurs, « envahisseurs impérialistes », anthropologues et même sympathisants politiques, tous tendaient à voir dans cet immense pays une sorte de muse orientale. Leur production fut largement responsable de la révélation de la Chine au monde extérieur à travers des images et non des mots.

Dans l'histoire de la photographie, l'Occident avait acquis le monopole de la façon de voir, d'observer et de définir les principes de ce que devait être ou contenir une photo, mais ce n'est pas là l'unique raison qui explique qu'il n'y ait pas eu beaucoup de photographies d'origine chinoise accessibles au public occidental avant 1949. Ce mode de représentation n'était pas encore assez largement répandu. Après 1949, il devint en grande partie un outil de propagande soumis à toutes sortes de contraintes artistiques. Du coup, la « photographie chinoise » ne faisait pas partie des catégories reconnues. Ses acteurs n'ont pas été crédités d'innovation dans le domaine du langage visuel ni d'images de valeur iconique universelle, même dans leur pays. Avant que ne se dessine une énergie nouvelle au sein des cercles professionnels – pas avant le milieu des années 1990 –, peu de praticiens pouvaient nier cet état de fait. Combien de photographes chinois sont célèbres ? Trop peu, même en Chine, bien qu'un certain nombre d'images aient accédé au statut d'icône, comme les portraits de Mao et des dirigeants de cette période pris par Hou Bo[2].

La plupart des photographes qui peuvent être cités aujourd'hui étaient inconnus avant la très récente explosion de l'intérêt pour le travail photographique d'artistes contemporains, phénomène essentiellement né, il faut le noter, chez les conservateurs de musées, galeristes et collectionneurs européens et américains. Cette avant-garde, qui s'était tournée vers la photographie au milieu des années 1990, n'utilise l'appareil photo que comme un outil, le cadre photographique comme une toile et manifestait une irrévérence très post-moderne envers les valeurs et pratiques traditionnelles liées au médium. Pour eux, la photographie n'est qu'un parent lointain de « l'instant décisif » de Cartier-Bresson, des drames sociaux vus par Sebastião Salgado ou encore des portraits étudiés d'Annie Leibovitz. Un ou deux photographes « purs » reconnaissent cependant l'influence d'August Sander, de Richard Avedon ou de Diane Arbus. Les générations plus jeunes nomment également parmi leurs idoles Nan Goldin et Robert Frank, la plupart préférant Andreas Gursky et Yasumasa Morimura, mais ces développements restent récents. Si on la compare avec d'autres formes d'expression visuelle, la photographie chinoise a disposé de peu de temps pour se développer ou rattraper le retard entre ses propres expériences et la pratique occidentale. Ceci ne doit pas pour autant être analysé comme une faiblesse.

La Chine vue par les Chinois

Cet ouvrage offre un portrait unique de la Chine à travers une sélection soignée de photographies créées par des photographes de Chine continentale. Plusieurs générations d'entre eux sont représentées et leurs carrières couvrent plusieurs décennies, de la fondation de la Chine nouvelle en 1949 jusqu'à aujourd'hui. Un nombre significatif de ces images reflète cette histoire. Elles sont publiées ici pour la première fois, non forcément pour avoir été cachées, mais parce que seul un nombre limité de personnes était consciente de leur existence et, parmi elles, presque aucune ne pouvait imaginer en faire quoi que ce soit. La photographie, tardivement acceptée en tant que forme d'art indépendante, n'était pas l'objet d'un débat critique. Les images à contenu politique pouvaient créer des problèmes à leurs auteurs si elles étaient sorties de leur contexte. Il n'existait pas de marché pour des œuvres dont la transgression valait ce risque. Telle était la situation jusqu'au milieu des années 2000, avant que ne se développe un système de ventes aux enchères en Chine. Auparavant, peu de gens avaient accès à ces images. Les temps ont changé.

China, Portrait d'un pays revient sur les événements majeurs de cette période agitée et nous fait parcourir l'histoire chinoise image par image, dans un ordre plus ou moins chronologique. Au-delà du passage du temps, la nature de ces représentations révèle à quel point l'évolution du contexte politique a exercé une influence sur leur poids moral et émotionnel. Chaque photographie évoque une page de l'histoire de la Chine nouvelle. Certaines en donnent des perspectives différentes et beaucoup reproduisent leur sujet avec une force qui nous semble plus grande aujourd'hui que celle qu'elle avait au moment de la prise de vue. D'autres, parce que nous bénéficions de connaissances rétrospectives, sont teintées d'une ambiguïté qui n'était sans doute pas détectée à l'époque.

Une image vaut mille mots

La puissance d'une photographie est à multiples facettes, lesquelles sont autant de rouages d'une énorme machine mémorielle à documenter l'histoire socioculturelle. Quelques-unes, grâce à la vision personnelle de tel ou tel photographe, sont devenues des icônes parce qu'elles ont symbolisé le fait historique, les attitudes ou les préjugés socioculturels. Elles offrent aux générations futures un patrimoine visuel d'informations sur le passé. Bien qu'il ne soit pas toujours nécessaire de posséder une connaissance intime des aspects les plus larges d'un contexte national particulier pour apprécier une photographie (et à cet égard, le contexte chinois est très particulier), une certaine connaissance de l'histoire permet d'appréhender le contexte, en particulier celui des photographies qui obéissaient aux diktats de la propagande et de l'idéologie politiques. Les dictatures, totalitaires ou communistes, et même les démocraties, peuvent se présenter de la même façon en théorie, mais elles se révèlent très différentes dans la pratique. Il existe toujours des différences explicables par des caractéristiques locales. De ce point de vue, les détails que l'on observe dans de très nombreuses images de ce livre fascinent, car ils parlent directement de la réalité cachée derrière les constructions de la propagande et de différences culturelles clairement chinoises. Au-delà de l'apparence des idéaux et des mécanismes sociaux communistes, se révèlent des sensibilités locales, philosophiques et esthétiques, qu'aucune politique ne saurait éradiquer. Les détails aident à reconstituer l'histoire, celle que les directives de Mao sur l'expression artistique étaient chargées de masquer dans le tableau officiel, souvent parce que telle version des événements était exclue de l'histoire publique – ou officielle – et ne correspondait pas aux ambitions idéologiques. Par exemple, la transition entre l'ère maoïste extraordinairement politisée de 1949 à 1976 et l'ouverture relative du régime de Deng Xiaoping se reflète visuellement en photographie sous la forme d'une prise de recul par rapport à l'image d'unité du peuple chinois, si essentielle jusqu'ici à la propagande nationale. À sa place, on discerne une résurgence de l'humanisme, des plaisirs quotidiens, de rêves nouveaux et de sentiments préalablement déniés, telles ces scènes d'amour saisies dans les images prises dans des jardins publics par Liu Heung Shing en 1980 (photo p. 290) ou la photo d'une femme chez le coiffeur en 1981 (photo p. 296), en bref un retour à l'existence ordinaire du citoyen moyen à laquelle, initialement, la plupart aspirait.

Les aspects sociaux de ces évolutions captées par le regard personnel des photographes à partir des années 1980 restent politisés. Le choix du sujet témoigne d'un intérêt renouvelé pour la diversité de la population, qui avait été mise en sourdine pendant les premières décennies de la république ou réduite à des pastiches politiques. Cette diversité est essentiellement ethnique, donc culturelle et topographique. La population de la Chine n'est pas l'entité homogène que laisse entendre la dénomination de ces immenses territoires par un terme géographique unique. La diversité ethnique est faite de 56 peuples minoritaires qualifiés généralement de « Chinois ». Les variations régionales climatiques et géographiques signifient qu'en dehors des très grandes villes, l'expérience personnelle et le sentiment d'appartenir à la Chine nouvelle étaient plus atypiques qu'uniformes. Le peuple se plaçait au-dessus des injonctions politiques auxquelles il lui était demandé d'obéir car sa préoccupation principale était de survivre à son état de terrible pauvreté. Néanmoins, l'impact énorme de l'idéologie et des transformations sociopolitiques de la Chine maoïste était évident. Depuis 1949, la majorité du peuple chinois a généralement été exposée à une idéologie politique identique, à un processus d'éducation uniforme (même si les niveaux de celle-ci sont restés incroyablement inégaux) et à la prise de conscience commune d'une avancée historique collective et des programmes de modernisation bien que, là encore, ce processus ait pris un tour assez différent entre les très grands centres urbains, les villes de province et plus encore les campagnes. En bref, tout citoyen chinois âgé de plus de 35 ans, à l'exception de quelques petites minorités dans les régions les plus pauvres et les plus éloignées, s'est vu inculquer des connaissances et des modes de pensée similaires[3].

Les caractéristiques idéologiques et culturelles de la Chine nouvelle forment ainsi un ensemble de paramètres à l'intérieur duquel a pu se développer une histoire. L'analyse approfondie des photographies de ces époques montre à quel point son rôle a été dominant.

Ce contexte a joué un rôle prépondérant dans la nature de la mise en forme de la photographie chinoise. Il a également contribué à la compréhension et l'appréciation du monde par le peuple, la réalité étant à la fois le sujet et l'objet de l'image, même si on comprenait à un certain niveau que, dans le contexte sociopolitique du moment, la photographie était d'abord un outil. L'État envoya un grand nombre de photographes sur le front des réformes et des restructurations lancées à partir des années 1950. Leur production, plus parlante que des textes, servait dans les campagnes de propagande à matérialiser visuellement les messages et les objectifs. Par leur nature même, ces œuvres de commande donnaient des visions positives de la « réalité » non sans avoir été améliorées voire modifiées si nécessaire dans l'obscurité de la chambre noire. C'est particulièrement notable dans les écarts frappants entre diverses versions d'un grand nombre de photos publiées par les médias officiels pendant les premières décennies de la Chine nouvelle. Des personnages disparaissent ou réapparaissent, transmués comme par magie hors ou dans le cadre photographique, sur des fonds régulièrement épurés de toute présence politiquement incorrecte. En dehors de l'exemple le plus célèbre de Mao, la plupart des dirigeants sont rajeunis, leurs traits adoucis, leurs gestes et ceux des gens qui les entourent rendus plus élégants. C'est un aspect du travail créatif photographique pour lequel les techniciens locaux possédaient à l'évidence une aptitude remarquable.[4]

Par la suite, de la fin des années 1970 au début des années 1980, de petits groupes de photographes amateurs formèrent des clubs dans tout le pays pour se soutenir moralement et tenter de se libérer de l'esthétique officielle. Ce mouvement débuta presque par hasard à Pékin après la mort de Zhou Enlai en avril 1976 et malgré ses origines politiques, ses membres développèrent rapidement des aspirations (artistiques) très diverses. Il s'agissait au départ de défier le contrôle autoritaire de la Bande des quatre après la mort de Mao, mais bientôt apparut le désir nouveau de participer à l'atmosphère plus optimiste issue de la politique de réformes économiques, lancée par Deng Xiaoping en 1978.

Naissance officielle de l'outil photographique

Même avant la fondation de la Chine nouvelle en 1949, un petit nombre de photographes travaillaient sur le thème de la progression des forces de la guérilla communiste afin de gagner le peuple à leur cause. À l'issue de la Longue marche (octobre 1936), ces troupes arrivèrent à Yan'an, dont Mao fit sa base, avant de les lancer sur Pékin à partir de 1946. La majorité de ces photographes des débuts provenaient des cercles intellectuels de Shanghai. Élite bien éduquée, originaire de familles socialement privilégiées, ils étaient fascinés par la photographie et avaient les moyens financiers d'acheter des appareils modernes. Beaucoup de ces jeunes intellectuels avaient participé au Mouvement du 4 mai (1919) et étaient acquis à ses théories et au besoin de moderniser et d'industrialiser la Chine qu'ils espéraient devenir une nation indépendante libérée de l'influence et de la domination étrangères. Dans la foulée, ces prises de position passionnées évoluèrent en une attitude favorable à l'idéal philosophique du marxisme qui voulait également éradiquer la servitude et les inégalités d'un système encore féodal et faire de la Chine une nation moderne[5]. L'appareil photo n'était qu'un des exemples dont les applications pratiques de la science occidentale pouvaient servir aux besoins socioculturels du pays. Il permettait par ailleurs à ces jeunes gens de mettre en pratique leurs aspirations créatives.

Au début des années 1930, des photojournalistes indépendants européens, et surtout américains, avaient su faire évoluer leur métier, particulièrement dans ses aspects visuels, ce dont attestait le succès populaire d'un magazine comme *Life*, lancé en 1936[6]. On pouvait maintenant prendre des photographies spectaculaires d'événements survenus dans le monde, grâce, à partir de 1929, à l'apparition des appareils compacts Leica et Ermanox, aussi légers et portables que possible pour l'époque.

Dans la Chine d'avant 1949, la puissance de communication de la photographie n'était pas encore vraiment comprise du grand public. Une photo était d'abord un portrait individuel, familial ou de groupe et l'on craignait sérieusement que l'objectif ne subtilise quelque chose du modèle. La fondation de la nouvelle nation modifia complètement cette donne car, face à des myriades de dialectes régionaux et de langues ethniques (dont beaucoup ne possédaient même pas le vocabulaire nécessaire à la présentation des idées socialistes), la photographie parlait un langage compréhensible par tous.[7] L'importante quantité de sculptures ou de tableaux monumentaux, dont la réalisation était encouragée par le nouveau régime et orientée par le bureau de la propagande vers le style réaliste socialiste, était censée nourrir les cœurs et les esprits et célébrer l'utopie socialiste, en devenir. L'impact visuel de ces œuvres à caractère iconique, qui décrivaient des actes d'héroïsme et de foi, n'a guère diminué avec le temps. Néanmoins, elles restaient du domaine de l'art, conçues et produites par de bons

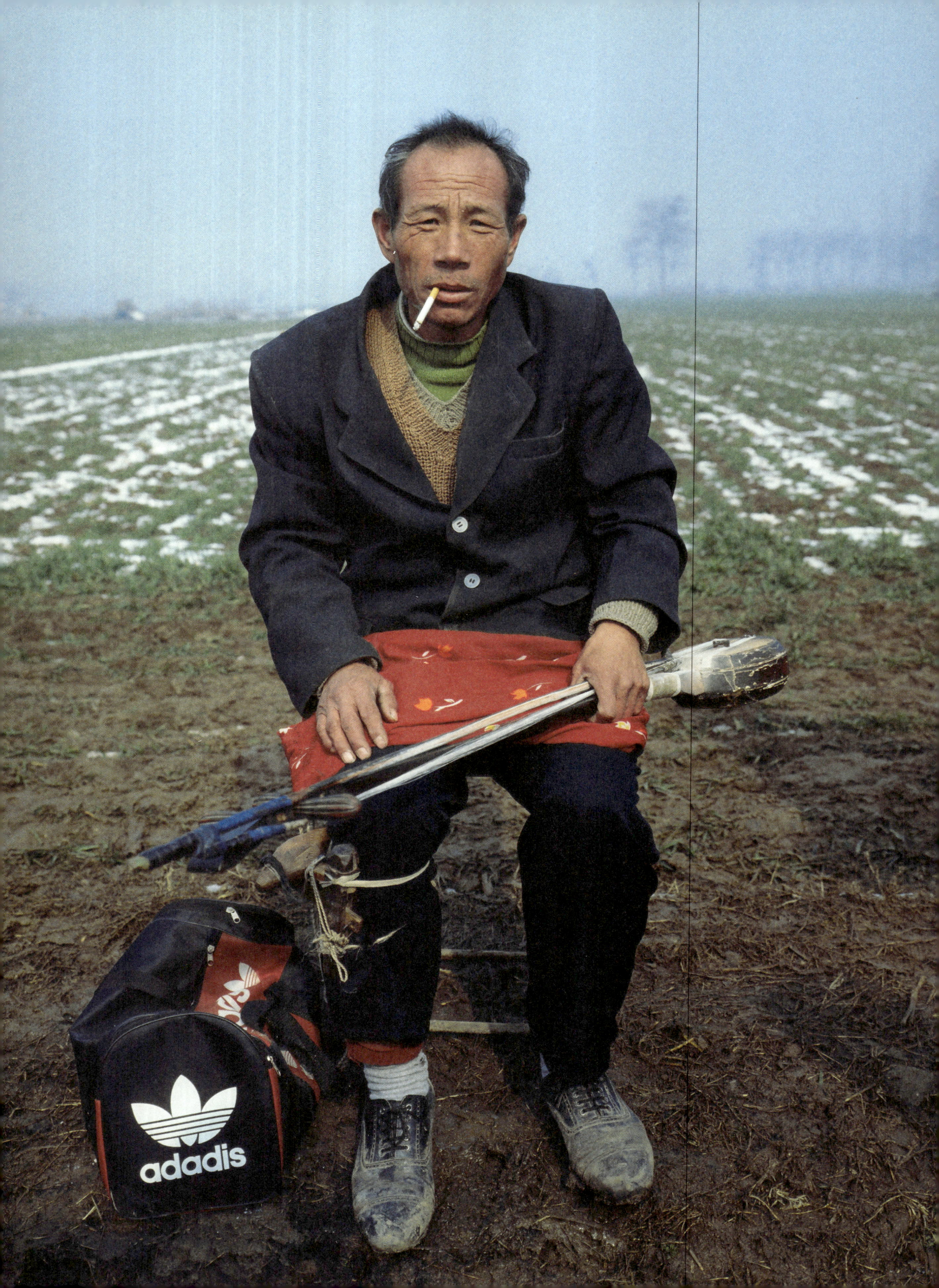

←
Jiang Jian, 2003

Fake brands are rampant in China, and attract large numbers of consumers. Foreign brands have frequently complained about trademark violation. After becoming a member of the World Trade Organization, China implemented a program to crack down on fake products. To many local people with limited means, like peasant Xu Nibei, sitting in a field with his fake "Adadis" bag, these products are an attractive option.

Gefälschte Markenartikel sind in China allgegenwärtig und locken Konsumenten in großer Zahl an. Ausländische Firmen beklagen häufig Verstöße gegen das Markenschutzgesetz. Nach seiner Aufnahme in die Welthandelsorganisation führte China ein Programm ein, mit dem energisch gegen gefälschte Produkte vorgegangen werden soll. Für viele Einheimische, wie den Bauern Xu Nibei, der mit seiner gefälschten „Adadis"-Tasche auf seinem Acker sitzt, stellen diese Produkte ein willkommenes Angebot für einen schmalen Geldbeutel dar.

Les contrefaçons de marque sont omniprésentes en Chine et attirent de très nombreux consommateurs. Les marques étrangères se plaignent fréquemment de ces violations du droit commercial et, à la suite de son entrée à l'OMC, la Chine a développé un programme pour mettre fin à cette industrie du faux. Pour de nombreux chinois aux moyens limités, comme le paysan Xu Nibei, assis dans un champ au côté d'un faux sac « Adadis », ces produits offrent l'avantage d'un prix réduit.

artistes qui mettaient leur talent créatif au service de la construction d'une réalité plutôt qu'à sa capture, ce que pouvait faire une photographie. Les pouvoirs de celle-ci lui conférèrent bientôt une valeur nouvelle. Elle seule pouvait capter une réalité changeante et des événements bien réels, vécus par des individus concrets plongés dans la fièvre du combat pour la construction d'une société nouvelle. Elle conférait au sujet une vérité à laquelle les artefacts artistiques ne pouvaient prétendre, et certainement pas sur le plan intellectuel. Elle acquit ainsi une importance essentielle pour communiquer l'urgence de rejoindre la vision idéologique maoïste et l'affirmation des progrès nationaux, en particulier aux heures les plus sombres. Ironiquement, 50 années furent nécessaires pour que le travail des photographes professionnels chinois – expression personnelle, œuvre documentaire ou reportage – soit reconnu en Chine et à l'étranger pour ses propres mérites. Néanmoins, du début des années 1950 à la fin du régime de Mao, il fut incontestablement l'un des plus puissants outils de communication mis à la disposition des communistes.

Servir le peuple

Mao avait une conception précise du rôle que les arts – arts visuels, littérature, spectacles – devaient jouer dans la défense des idéaux politiques. Il expliqua pour la première fois à Yan'an en 1942[8] ses idées dans ce domaine, qui allaient constituer la base de toute expression artistique pour les décennies à venir : l'art sous toutes ses formes d'expression devait être « au service du peuple ». Le réalisme socialiste, style à suivre selon Mao, ne s'était-il pas montré efficace en Union soviétique ? Appuyée sur des références culturelles historiques chinoises, l'adaptation maoïste s'adapta brillamment au goût local. La version « Chine nouvelle » utilisait l'encre, le pinceau, le papier de riz, les couleurs naturelles et même les papiers découpés. Le plus raffiné de tous les arts, la calligraphie, fut également appelé à la rescousse. Comme le réalisme socialiste, la photographie était importée d'Occident, mais à la différence de la peinture, elle restait un outil mécanique et non un style artistique. Parmi tous les médias au service de l'expression créative, elle seule manquait de valeurs esthétiques propres et n'avait eu le temps d'évoluer localement. L'appareil photo n'était guère qu'un outil pratique, à utiliser pour atteindre un but. Au moment de la fondation de la République populaire, les expérimentations photographiques menées à Shanghai furent rapidement dépassées par les nécessités de la construction du socialisme, tâche à laquelle tout le monde voulait contribuer au départ. Décidant, à son tour, que l'appareil photo n'était qu'un outil, le Parti commença par nommer des photographes de confiance. Ils étaient chargés d'actionner l'appareil à l'endroit et au moment requis, sous le meilleur angle possible. On ne parlait ni « d'atmosphère » (si ce n'est « idéologiquement positive ») ni d'éclairage (si

ce n'est « éclatant », c'est-à-dire sans ombres négatives), ni de recherche de compositions réfléchies ou artistiques (si ce n'est la clarté des attitudes et la précision du point qui, là encore, devait éliminer toute possibilité d'ambiguïté).

Nous pouvons voir d'après les photographies de cette période qu'un grand nombre de leurs auteurs, qui n'auraient peut-être jamais choisi la photographie en d'autres circonstances, possédaient à la fois une aptitude certaine et une bonne vision des situations instantanées. Ces images sont ainsi d'extraordinaires témoignages historiques. Fragment par fragment, elles constituent un tableau complet. Même à l'apogée du contrôle politique sur les masses, la vérité arrive encore à poindre. Les photographies de la grande période de la propagande (des années 1950 aux années 1970) en particulier restent une évocation émouvante de cette époque. Au risque de mettre le doigt sur une évidence, l'art de la propagande trouve de puissantes résonances car, comme toute campagne de publicité réussie, il joue sur des dénominateurs visuels communs qui parlent directement au grand public parce qu'ils sont à la fois faciles à comprendre et mémorisables. L'appareil illustre les directives avec beaucoup d'efficacité. Le noir et blanc qui, à de rares exceptions près, était le seul choix de film possible au début, en dehors de circonstances spéciales pour lesquelles la couleur était préférée, mettait naturellement en scène le drame et la charge émotive des expressions des personnages. Il concentrait également l'attention du spectateur sur l'action et le message. Cependant, malgré toutes ces contraintes idéologiques, ces images vues avec un regard contemporain expriment parfois un sens artistique et une sensibilité qui témoignent du grand talent de leurs créateurs.

Le portrait d'une nouvelle société

La création de la Chine nouvelle avait mis fin à « plus d'un siècle de défaites humiliantes, de traités inégaux et d'occupation étrangère »[9] qui représentaient autant de causes à célébrer. Tout au long de la guerre civile avec les nationalistes et les seigneurs de la guerre qui se battaient pour eux-mêmes, la plupart des gens devait simplement lutter pour survivre. Grâce au soutien populaire croissant, les guérillas communistes finirent par gagner. Les photographies de 1949 (photo p. 127) montrent des soldats de l'Armée de libération du peuple épuisés et endormis dans des rues car ils n'avaient pas le droit de pénétrer dans les maisons des villages conquis. Épris des nouveaux principes moraux et égalitaires du socialisme, le peuple était disposé à rejoindre la cause, et s'enflammait pour cette chance de se débarrasser du joug féodal. Il apparaissait aussi que les communistes allaient redonner au pays sa dignité. Au début des années 1950, la plupart des Chinois croyait être à l'aube d'une ère nouvelle et glorieuse qui éliminerait les seigneurs « diaboliques » (processus qui avait déjà débuté par la réforme agraire) et mettrait fin à la corruption des nationalistes, dont la république prenait toutes les caractéristiques d'une nouvelle dynastie impériale. Mao apportait au peuple le goût de la liberté et l'on s'enthousiasma pour sa propagande exubérante. Le nouveau leader expliquait le besoin de changement pour améliorer les choses, et le promettait. Concrètement, beaucoup des mesures politiques prévues étaient absolument nécessaires. Le peuple devait être éduqué et l'analphabétisme éradiqué. La faim devait disparaître et le fardeau de la pauvreté allégé. Les Chinois seraient formés aux nouveaux emplois industriels qui permettraient au pays de devenir une grande puissance. Mao alla jusqu'à proclamer : « Ce que l'Occident a, la Chine l'aura ! » Un programme massif de modernisation verrait bientôt la Chine dépasser le Royaume-Uni et rivaliser avec les États-Unis un peu plus tard. Telle était la volonté sous-jacente au désastreux Grand bond en avant de 1958. Dans ce contexte, les photographies excellaient à promouvoir un esprit d'optimisme dans les communautés rurales en grande partie analphabètes et parmi les foules urbaines misérables. En magnifiant les hauts faits d'héroïsme et en fustigeant les attitudes égoïstes, elles inculquaient aux masses le sens du devoir social et de leur responsabilité dans la participation au bien commun. Les images photographiques faisaient ainsi office de preuves et de références à l'aune desquelles les progrès et le changement pouvaient être mesurés.

La moitié du ciel

Un groupe social particulièrement motivé dans son soutien à Mao était celui des femmes, qu'il voulait libérer de siècles de domination masculine et des effets d'une hiérarchie sociale d'origine confucéenne ôtant aux femmes toute voix et tout droit concret. Mao les déclara égales aux hommes. Après qu'il ait proclamé qu'elles « soutenaient la moitié du ciel », elles purent accéder aux mêmes emplois que les hommes, droit qui fut exalté dans les années 1950 lorsque les communes remplacèrent les structures sociales et les communautés existantes et que la main d'œuvre féminine s'y montra aussi compétente que la main d'œuvre masculine. Cette avancée fut également célébrée par des femmes photographes, mais il ne faudrait pas pour autant imaginer l'existence d'une mentalité féministe. Un petit nombre de femmes avait déjà exercé une présence active à Yan'an. Les réfugiées de régions ravagées par la guerre civile et l'invasion japonaise étaient traitées selon les critères de la nouvelle égalité communiste et reçurent une éducation inimaginable dans l'ancien système. Un bon exemple en est le cas de Hou Bo, photographe personnelle du Président de 1949 à 1961, un autre celui de Xiao Zhuang qui rejoignit un groupe de guérilla dans le Zhejiang en 1949 et fut chargée de prendre des photos pour un journal local en 1950. Selon la pratique de l'époque, elle se forma sur le tas. Deux ans plus tard, en 1952, elle était déjà pleine-

ment opérationnelle et travaillait pour le quotidien *Xinhua*[10]. Même si son origine de « classe » et ses positions politiques lui permirent de conserver sa place, il semble que son allégeance à la cause communiste ne l'empêcha jamais de manifester un intérêt personnel pour les sujets qu'elle photographiait. Il serait erroné de suggérer qu'elle s'éloignait parfois de la ligne du parti, mais ses images témoignent d'un rare degré d'empathie et de compréhension qui va au-delà d'une illustration facile de causes politiques. À certaines occasions, on trouve même dans son travail des traces du dilemme auxquels sont confrontés de nombreux photojournalistes de guerre, témoins d'un conflit humain. Leur tâche est d'enregistrer et non d'intervenir, même s'ils sont témoins de comportements atroces lors de ces manifestations de masse où les pires humiliations étaient infligées aux victimes du moment.

Tout au long des années 1950 et jusqu'aux années 1970, Xiao Zhuang réalisa de solides images documentaires à la composition simple et frappante. Elles représentent aussi bien des foules prises lors de manifestations de masse de soutien à Mao, que de multiples expressions de la dévotion du peuple envers son Président – de l'enthousiasme exubérant aux extrémités les plus violentes –, la mise en œuvre des campagnes d'action ou l'illustration des nouveaux défis. Elles sont de bons indicateurs de la nature complexe des émotions engendrées par ces activités politiques, qui évoluaient d'une campagne d'action à l'autre selon l'orientation politique du moment et les luttes internes du Parti. Beaucoup de ces photos de grandes manifestations publiques ont été prises depuis des points de vue privilégiés pour rendre compte de leur énorme échelle mais aussi de l'atmosphère menaçante et fermée qui émane de leur déroulement (photos p. 200/201 et 209). Par des moyens subtils, elles préservent le rendu des ambiances et montrent les mécanismes par lesquels certains conflits allaient modifier le cours de l'histoire. Elles balisent le chemin qui voit la société chinoise plonger vers la période sombre des années 1970, moment le plus confus et le plus traumatisant de l'histoire de la Chine nouvelle. Si la signification de nombreux détails de situations et d'événements reproduits se perd peut-être pour les nouvelles générations, le sens subtil de la composition et de l'intuition dont elles témoignent fait de ces photographies de Xiao Zhuang un témoignage éclairant sur ces temps troublés et « irrationnels ».[11]

De manière similaire à Xiao Zhuang, Hou Bo devint photographe davantage parce qu'on avait confiance en ses convictions idéologiques que pour son aptitude. Elle avait à peine tenu un appareil photo avant de s'engager dans cette carrière. Au cours des 12 années vécues auprès de Mao et dans son entourage rapproché, elle fut témoin de moments historiques essentiels mais aussi de la vie privée du dirigeant. Ses prises de vue faites dans un cadre intime, loin du public, montrent un homme détendu, apparemment à l'aise face à l'appareil, en contraste marqué avec l'image de froide autorité donnée par les portraits officiels si répandus. Elles représentent un homme et non pas un dieu. Peut-on attribuer ce choix photographique à la capacité féminine de compassion de leur auteure ? C'est possible, car les photos prises au même moment par des hommes passent généralement à côté des aspects psychologiques du personnage et ne laissent aucune place à l'ambiguïté.

Dans le milieu de la photographie chinoise de l'époque, les hommes ont toujours été en nombre supérieur à celui des femmes. Ceci étant, les œuvres les plus intéressantes n'ont été le fait que d'un très petit groupe d'individus auquel appartenaient en particulier Jiang Shaowu, Wang Shilong, Meng Zhaorui et Lü Xiangyou. Leurs photographies mettent en scène les grandes ambitions de l'idéologie maoïste, sans négliger pour autant certaines observations claires sur l'impact de sa politique et de ses campagnes d'action.

Photographe pour le quotidien *Liaoning*, Jiang Shaowu a débuté en 1947. Ses photographies montrent des scènes publiques d'humiliation et d'autocritique devant des foules en colère, au cours de la période fiévreuse et chaotique qui va du milieu des années 1960 à la mort de Mao en 1976. Ces images n'ont rien du spectacle de cirque inquiétant d'un Li Zhensheng. Elles ne prétendent rien, et sont étrangement dénuées d'ambiguïté sur les incidents qu'elles reproduisent. Elles enregistrent simplement le processus de la naissance d'une nation, d'un peuple luttant pour des objectifs communs au bénéfice de tous, en réaction à la violence imposée par les privilèges d'une élite. Rétrospectivement, ces photographies, comme celle d'un aveugle interprétant les *Citations de Mao Zedong* (photo p. 195) ou les larmes de crocodile d'un groupe de jeunes gens pleurant sa disparition en 1976 (photo p. 262/263), illustrent étrangement les erreurs de tant d'entreprises politiques de Mao.

Comme beaucoup de photographes de l'époque, Wang Shilong, né dans le Hénan, s'engagea dans l'armée en 1948, où il fut chargé de prendre des photographies pour le bureau de la propagande local. Une blessure lui interdit de poursuivre ses activités de correspondant de guerre au Tibet, mais ne l'empêcha pas de sillonner le Hénan et les provinces voisines pour des reportages sur les progrès des nouvelles communes. Ses photographies d'aspect velouté se distinguent par une profondeur particulière. Observant la commune ou le réaménagement des terres agricoles à une échelle jusque-là inconnue en Chine (photos p. 166/167 et 247), il s'exprime à travers une extraordinaire gamme de gris argentés et toutes les nuances du noir et du blanc. De même, ses photos d'activités de masse qui mobilisaient les efforts de centaines et de milliers d'hommes et de femmes, célèbrent une aventure humaine monumentale mue par la seule force de la volonté. Certaines semblent illustrer des paraboles

de Mao dont la plus célèbre est celle du « Vieux fou qui déplaça une montagne ».[12] Wang Shilong nous montre des groupes d'hommes et de femmes déplaçant des montagnes, changeant le cours des rivières et multipliant les récoltes. Il ne perd jamais de vue l'instant, ni la dureté de l'existence quotidienne, ni les spécificités humaines qui échappent à toute censure. Si tout effort d'apparence personnelle était officiellement découragé, il nous montre cependant l'image d'un jeune couple de paysans quittant une échoppe de tailleur dans une cave, perdus dans le plaisir de la contemplation d'un nouveau vêtement.

Le soldat Meng Zhaorui travaillait pour le magazine de l'armée, *L'Illustré de l'ALP*, ce qui lui assurait un accès particulier à Mao et aux événements d'importance nationale. Il put ainsi photographier l'explosion réussie de la première bombe à hydrogène chinoise en 1967. Il était présent lors de nombreuses apparitions publiques de Mao et en particulier sur la place Tien'anmen pour sa rencontre avec les Gardes rouges (photo p. 180/181). En 1966, il prit une image prémonitoire du Président dans ses appartements privés, assis dans un fauteuil et regardant de façon très perturbante, sans prendre garde à son expression, Zhou Enlai et Lin Biao à l'autre bout de la pièce, qui rédigeaient un projet de document. L'image paraît prémonitoire car, en 1971, le ministre de la défense Lin Biao disparut, tué dans un accident d'avion lors de sa fuite en Union soviétique après une tentative de coup d'État, du moins selon la version officielle. Cette image fascinante est un sommet de l'art de la photographie : l'expression de Mao atteste de la nature complexe des combats politiques déclenchés par sa Révolution culturelle (1966–1976) (photo p. 182).

Le portrait d'une utopie

Durant les trois premières décennies de la Chine nouvelle, la photographie relevait du ministère de la propagande. Il est donc curieux que cette « vérité » présentée comme un témoignage visuel brut du processus douloureux des luttes sociales se soit traduite par des images qui semblent franches au point de choquer et de paraître même aujourd'hui étonnamment impartiales. Ce sont des fragments qui s'assemblent pour offrir une illustration factuelle des engagements passionnés qui ont transformé le pays. Cette période de l'histoire appartient maintenant au passé. La Chine a avancé. Les photographies nous aident à apprécier les extraordinaires difficultés qu'elle a traversées et décrivent le contexte de l'état complexe de la société chinoise, d'alors et d'aujourd'hui.

Au cours des années 1950, le nuage d'optimisme sur lequel la Chine nouvelle progressait encouragea la production d'une masse d'images « positives ». La représentation de la réalité connut une évolution spectaculaire entre 1955 et 1965. Les premières indications des côtés sombres de la politique de Mao apparurent vers 1957, à l'occasion du

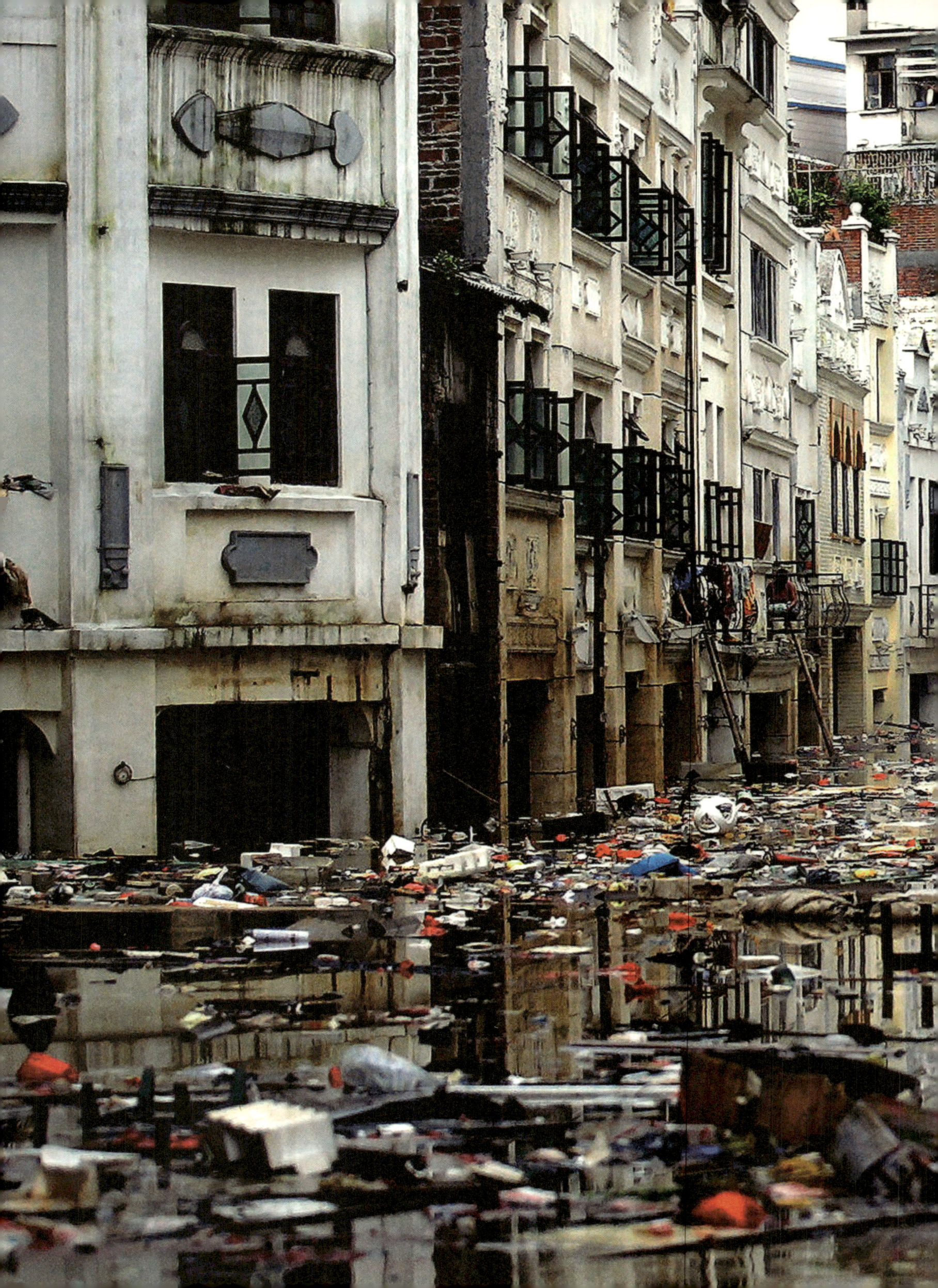

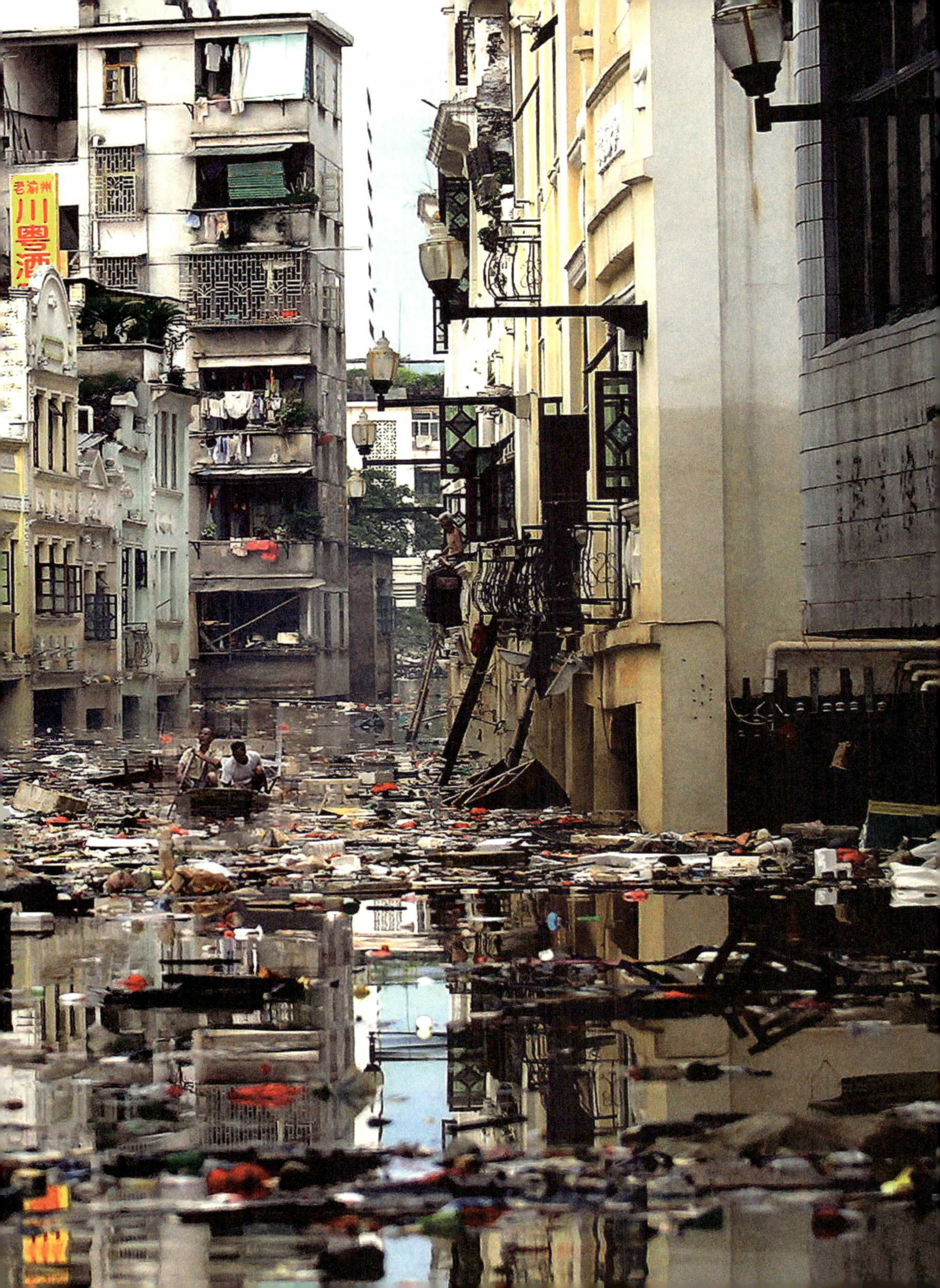

pp. 96/97
Shi Xunfeng, 2005

The aftermath of a flood in the city of Wuzhou, Guangxi province. Floods strike communities across China every year, affecting the lives and livelihoods of tens of millions of people.

Die Folgen einer Überschwemmung in der Stadt Wuzhou, Provinz Guangxi. Jedes Jahr werden Ortschaften in ganz China von Überschwemmungen heimgesucht, die Leben und Existenzgrundlage von Abermillionen Menschen bedrohen.

Après une inondation dans la ville de Wuzhou, province du Guangxi. Les inondations frappent de nombreuses villes chaque année, affectant la vie et les conditions d'existence de dizaines de millions de personnes.

lancement de la campagne contre la droite. Les « droitistes » constituaient en fait un assez faible pourcentage de la population mais la mécanique efficace du ministère de la propagande voulait que l'exemple de ces campagnes anti-droitistes aient un impact énorme. Cet aspect inquiétant fut temporairement éclipsé en 1958 par la mise en place des communes (photo p. 148). Les événements prirent un tour dramatique en 1959, précipités par le Grand bond en avant, également lancé en 1958. Aux mauvaises récoltes succéda un hiver très rude. La famine se répandit dans le pays au printemps 1960 et dura jusqu'en 1962, entraînant la mort de plus de 30 millions de personnes. Nous n'avons aucune idée aujourd'hui de l'atmosphère qui régnait alors. Comment les Chinois pouvaient-ils ignorer les écarts flagrants entre les visions idéales imposées par la machine de la propagande et la réalité de leur vécu ? On annonçait une succession de récoltes record et pourtant la majorité des communes ne pouvait nourrir leurs propres habitants. Une mesure allant dans le sens des intérêts du gouvernement fut de limiter les déplacements des gens ordinaires. L'isolement efficace de la population rurale permettait ainsi aux diverses communautés de croire que « là-bas », dans une autre partie du pays, les choses allaient déjà mieux et, qu'avec un peu de patience, tout s'arrangerait pour eux également. Susan Sontag définit la force de la vérité d'une photographie en ces termes simples : « Une chose dont nous avons entendu parler, mais dont nous doutons, semble prouvée lorsque nous la voyons en photographie. »[13] Face à toutes les preuves visuelles apportées par le ministère de la propagande par le biais de cette multitude d'images, qui pouvait encore douter ?

La situation ne s'améliora pas dans les années 1960. La famine avait régressé en 1963, mais dans les centres urbains pris dans des luttes politiques intenses, le peuple était précipité dans les errements de la Révolution culturelle. Ceci se refléta dans la modification du style des images prises à cette époque. Elles devinrent de plus en plus stéréotypées, stylisées, d'une expression plus optimiste et même plus soignée. Comme la Révolution culturelle était une tentative de Mao de réaffirmer son pouvoir et ses dogmes, toute expression créative devait nécessairement être soumise à son paradigme idéologique absolu. On imagine cependant que quelques photographes étaient conscients de la construction artificielle à laquelle ils participaient. Aucun n'essaya d'affronter directement ces contradictions, mais que pouvait-on attendre d'autre ? Nous possédons quelques exemples suggérant cette prise de conscience, comme l'expression du visage de Mao captée par Meng Zhaorui en 1966. Les photos les plus connues allant dans ce sens, signées Li Zhensheng, furent publiées en 2003 dans un ouvrage intitulé *Red-Color News Soldier*.[14] Comme pour tous les autres « soldats de l'information », la tâche de Li Zhensheng était « d'enregistrer les joies et les triomphes de la Chine de Mao. » Plus

tard, il affirma y avoir vu une opportunité d'écrire un scrupuleux plaidoyer objectif pour l'histoire.

L'ère maoïste fut une période extraordinaire pour les photographes projetés sur la scène du grand théâtre sociopolitique chinois. Ils vivaient « … des moments qui appartenaient presque instantanément à l'histoire. »[15] Les images choisies pour représenter les années 1950, 1960 et 1970 comptent sans doute parmi les plus fortes et les plus mémorables de l'histoire moderne de la Chine par leur contenu politique et idéologique. Elles parlent des forces tumultueuses du changement en cours et illustrent les vicissitudes de l'atmosphère politique tout au long du cycle ininterrompu des campagnes de masse. Elles nous transportent au cœur de l'événement, nous permettent de partager l'impact des mesures vécues par les communautés et les individus au cours de luttes entre factions politiques opposées et souvent désespérées. Elles constituent une excellente illustration du constat de John Szarkowski selon lequel : « Au cours du premier siècle de l'histoire de la photographie, on admettait généralement que la description des choses était ce qu'elle savait faire le mieux … Les plus hautes vertus des photographies étaient la clarté de la représentation et la densité de l'information. »[16]

L'aube d'une ère nouvelle

Les années 1980 démarrèrent lentement. Deux années furent nécessaires à Deng Xiaoping après la mort de Mao pour consolider son pouvoir et trois de plus pour mettre la Bande des quatre derrière les barreaux.[17] Leur procès très publicisé fut un des grands événements de l'après-Mao, le signe du processus de normalisation en cours, systématiquement documenté par Liu Heung Shing de 1979 à 1983. En 1978, Deng annonça sa grande politique de réformes. Il rouvrit les universités (à partir de 1978) et les écoles (1980) fermées depuis le milieu des années 1970. Le nouvel enthousiasme pour les études est illustré par Liu Heung Shing dans une photo de jeunes gens étudiant la nuit sur la place de Tian'anmen, seul lieu public assez éclairé au début des années 1980 pour lire la nuit (photo p. 288/289). Ce fut une période d'émotions contradictoires car Deng bousculait de multiples idéaux maoïstes. À la fin de la décennie, il donna des instructions pour réduire l'énorme volume de portraits de Mao dans les lieux publics[18], mais un nouveau cycle de « folie de Mao » se répandit au cours des années 1980 et même en 1993 au moment du centenaire de sa naissance.

Conséquence des progrès économiques, une nouvelle phase de l'expression artistique se profila, de la littérature à la poésie et des arts visuels à la musique. Les photographes eux aussi ressentaient le besoin de regarder au-delà des contraintes imposées par une reproduction politique de la réalité. Cette tentative de s'appuyer davantage sur les vrais enjeux sociaux et sur la vie quotidienne pour aboutir à des expressions plus authentiques déboucha sur une multiplication d'expérimentations individuelles autour de la Société photographique d'Avril et de l'essor de la photographie dans les campagnes de la fin des années 1970. Ce groupe se forma spontanément dès la mort du Premier ministre Zhou Enlai en avril 1976, quand la Bande des quatre décida d'interdire le deuil public du « Premier du peuple ». Les photographes professionnels et amateurs, qui se trouvaient place Tian'anmen lorsque les manifestants commencèrent à se réunir avant que ne soit donné l'ordre d'évacuer, purent saisir l'événement au fur et à mesure de son déroulement. Ils étaient toujours là lorsque la police intervint pour disperser la foule et produisirent une quantité étonnante de négatifs dont un nombre tout aussi surprenant survécut aux recherches et aux opérations de destruction menées les jours suivants. Ces images finirent par être réunies dans un ouvrage intitulé *Le Deuil du peuple* publié en 1979. Si l'on y ajoute la première grande exposition de photographies qui se tint à Pékin fin 1978,[19] la photographie prenait enfin une orientation nouvelle et plus indépendante.

Dans les années 1980, les opportunités de monter une exposition quelle qu'elle soit, étaient limitées. Jusqu'au milieu des années 2000, la photographie ne touchait aucun public significatif en Chine en dehors des cercles professionnels. La comparaison de l'importance accordée à deux expositions qui se déroulèrent à Pékin vers 1979 illustre le sort très différent fait à l'art et à la photographie. Chacune avait été organisée par un nouveau groupe composé en grande partie d'amateurs. Le premier, le « Groupe de peinture des étoiles » (généralement appelé les « Stars »), organisa une exposition non officielle dans le périmètre de la Galerie nationale de Chine au centre de la capitale. Elle fut fermée par les autorités, ce qui en fit un événement, encore plus remarqué lorsque les Stars osèrent protester contre la confiscation de leurs œuvres et réussirent à se les faire restituer. Une photographie de 1979 par Liu Heung Shing montre un Ma Desheng triomphant sur les marches de l'hôtel de ville, entouré d'une foule de supporters attentifs et de passants (photo p. 272), tandis qu'un membre du groupe, Wang Keping, brandit une bannière réclamant la « liberté d'expression » (photo p. 273). L'exposition de photos organisée par la Société photographique d'Avril, ainsi nommée en souvenir de l'événement qui avait réuni ses membres, organisa une exposition sur le thème « Nature, Société et Homme » qui ouvrit en avril 1979, se déroula assez bien et ne fit pas les titres des journaux. Cette manifestation et deux autres qui se déroulèrent en 1980 et 1981 attirèrent des foules importantes, mais sans bénéficier du statut vite légendaire de celle des Stars.

Il est intéressant de noter que le *modus operandi*, les inspirations et les influences de ces deux groupes étaient en grande partie les mêmes. Comme les « poètes brumeux » et les écrivains métaphysiques de cette période, les photographes chinois préféraient les commentaires voilés. Le paysage – vision rêveuse, pleine d'inférences de symbolisme de la nature inspirées de la tradition de la peinture à l'encre – faisait partie des thèmes favoris des années 1980. La disparité entre les images officielles autorisées produites par le photographe vétéran du journal *Xinhua*, Lū Houmin et la célébration dans le style de *National Geographic Magazine* du monde naturel auquel il s'intéressa principalement dans les années 1980, montre l'évolution de la situation du milieu photographique au cours de cette décennie. C'est la période de « l'art pour l'art », mais ironiquement, le tendon d'Achille de cette Société d'Avril allait être cette esthétique « de salon » qui avait réuni ses membres à l'origine et qui plaçait la beauté et une spiritualité éthérées au-dessus de toute autre considération. Ceci étant, les photographies des membres de ce groupe représentaient une évolution spectaculaire par rapport aux conventions établies. Dans les années 1970, ces « professionnels », qui avaient créé de superbes images à forte valeur iconique, n'hésitèrent pas à abandonner à la première occasion le monde du réel en faveur d'une esthétique « artistique ». L'ancien rédacteur en chef du magazine *Creative Camera*, Bill Jay, écrivit un jour que « Les clubs de photographes … s'intéressent essentiellement à la production de jolies images et non à la vérité de leur contenu. »[20] C'est sans doute ce à quoi l'esthétique « de salon » cantonnait l'œuvre de ces photographes chinois.

Retour à la nature

Les images produites dans les années 1980 étaient certainement sincères. Leur auteurs déployèrent de grands efforts, ce dont atteste l'important ensemble de photos réunies dans *Humanisme en Chine*.[21] Mais le volume d'images réalisé dans les années 1980 est faible par rapport à celui des autres décennies. Elles restent vraiment des « fragments »[22], difficiles à replacer dans le cadre d'une image plus ample de la Chine.

La fin des années 1980 vit l'apparition d'une nouvelle génération qui ne savait pas grand-chose des réalités de l'existence sous Mao et avait grandi dans une période d'ouverture et de réforme et de modernisation accélérée. Sensible aux influences occidentales, elle disposait d'une quantité d'information jusque-là inconnue dans le pays. Ses membres rejetaient intuitivement l'esthétique de la Société photographique d'Avril et les aspects sentimentaux de ses préoccupations humanistes. Un bon exemple en est le groupe Topic, formé au début des années 1990 par de jeunes photographes professionnels dont Liu Zheng (*Quotidien des travailleurs*), Jin Yongquan (*Quotidien de la jeunesse chinoise*) et Yuan Dongping (*Magazine des nationalités chinoises*). Leur but était de réorienter la photographie vers les grands enjeux et de retrouver du contenu. À la fin des années 1980, Yuan Dongping et Lü Nan réalisèrent ainsi une série de photos documentaires sur les patients d'un asile d'aliénés. Comme les images

→
Zhang Peng, 2007

In the trend towards art photography that gathered momentum in the early 2000s, incongruity is all the rage: a child is dressed in the ornate costume of a Beijing opera performer and wearing an oversized head- piece. Youth, tradition, luxury, wealth, and decadence are all common subjects of conceptual photographs.

In der künstlerischen Fotografie nach 2000 gibt es einen Trend zur Widersprüchlichkeit: Unter einem überdimensionierten Kopf- schmuck trägt ein Kind das reich verzierte Kostüm einer Darstellerin der Pekingoper. Jugend, Tradition, Luxus, Reichtum und Dekadenz sind häufig Themen der konzep- tuellen Fotografien.

Dans les nouvelles tendances de la photo- graphie artistique qui se sont développées à partir du début des années 2000, l'incon- gruité fait rage : Cette enfant est habillée en costume surchargé d'actrice de l'Opéra de Pékin. La jeunesse, la tradition, le luxe, la richesse et la décadence sont des thèmes courants des photographes conceptuels.

prises à l'apogée de la révolution culturelle, elles se caractérisent par un regard impassible et une fascination quasi victorienne pour les étrangetés humaines. D'autres enquêtes visuelles sur les problématiques sociales suivirent, produites par de petits groupes aux idées avancées. Dans les années 1990, ils couvrirent de nombreux sujets sensibles, non sans rencon- trer des restrictions significatives sur ce qu'ils pouvaient publier. Leur ten- tative de mise en place d'un discours structuré était à l'évidence en avance sur leur temps et ils durent se battre pour se faire reconnaître ou exposer. Ils ne disposaient pas alors de la plate-forme qu'est devenue Internet qui, depuis le début des années 2000 et avec les espaces d'exposition qui ont proliféré dans les grandes villes, est devenu la principale arène de débats et de confrontations sur les problèmes moraux et sociétaux.

Malgré le retard momentané provoqué par les événements du 4 juillet, le programme de réformes se poursuivit et, vers les années 1990, une génération de photographes plus jeunes commença à rejoindre la tendance à plus de réalisme. S'inspirant de pionniers de la photographie à préoccupations sociales comme Diane Arbus, August Sander ou Richard Avedon, et non sans quelques hommages aux atmosphères d'Eugène Atget, cette nouvelle race de photographes très ambitieux et tournés vers le monde extérieur recherchа de la même façon des contextes et des personnages étranges à utiliser pour composer une allégorie de la vie chinoise contemporaine. Un bon exemple en est la série « Les Chinois » de Liu Zheng, créée entre 1994 et 1999 (il était parallèlement photo- journaliste pour le *Quotidien des travailleurs* de 1991 à 1997). Elle est clairement inspirée de la sensibilité des photographes occidentaux cités plus haut et représente des acteurs, des religieuses, des personnalités bizarres et des corps anormaux (photo p. 336), non sans une certaine séduction morbide.

Art + photographie = ?

Les années 1990 virent la prolifération momentanée de la pratique photographique en Chine. Les conditions de vie s'amélioraient visiblement, les centres urbains rejoignaient la modernité, les médias se développaient et l'on trouvait maintenant une certaine diversité de publications sur les styles de vie, illustrées de belles photographies. L'art contemporain com- mença à se faire sérieusement reconnaître et, comme il était relativement aisé d'être artiste indépendant sans grands besoins d'espace ou d'équipe- ment, les arts visuels, à un moindre degré que la littérature, dominaient le discours artistique du moment. Ce monde naissant commençait à attirer l'attention des conservateurs de musée et des milieux de l'art occidentaux. À un niveau subconscient, la nouvelle génération de photo- graphes était de plus en plus encouragée à aligner sa pratique sur celle des artistes contemporains chinois, ne serait-ce que parce que cet uni-

vers offrait des opportunités d'échange, d'évaluation critique et d'expo- sition des œuvres qui manquaient aux cercles purement photogra- phiques.

Tout au long de ces années, il fut toujours aussi difficile d'étudier la photographie. Les photographes « purs » apprenaient encore leur métier sur le tas ou dans le cadre de cours de journalisme. Les enseignements étaient donc réservés aux collèges spécialisés disposant d'un département de journalisme. Les cours pratiques se concentraient sur les aspects tech- niques et les applications pratiques de l'appareil photo. Il faudra attendre le début des années 2000, et l'entrée de la photo dans le monde de l'art, pour qu'elle ne soit plus seulement considérée comme un art appliqué. L'un des premiers à se faire connaître dans ce domaine fut Rong Rong qui, en 1996, s'associa à Liu Zheng pour réaliser l'influent magazine *Nouvelle photo*. Frustrés par le contenu et les contraintes des magazines officiels comme *Photographie chinoise*, ils avaient ressenti le besoin d'un journal qui ne fasse pas de distinctions entre l'œuvre d'un artiste, le photojourna- lisme ou un photographe « pur ». Les professionnels cependant n'avaient guère comme choix que *Photographie chinoise*, publié par l'Association des photographes. Les journaux officiels de ce type offraient un contenu traditionnel conservateur et mettaient l'accent sur la technique en évitant délibérément tout débat sur l'esthétique ou le sens. *Nouvelle photo* s'in- spirait d'un petit journal, *Photo reportage,* produit par Liu Heung Shing en 1995 et diffusé dans les cercles photographiques. Il reprit le même format et s'intéressa essentiellement à la puissance de l'image photographique.

Les années 1990 furent marquées par une préférence pour la photo d'investigation. Des photographes identifiaient un sujet qui les intéressait et en faisaient une œuvre. Jiang Jian s'intéressa ainsi au portrait de Chinois ordinaires des communes rurales ou des petites villes. Wu Jialin docu- menta la vie dans les provinces, les régions montagneuses et les villes éloignées, et Zeng Li sillonna le pays en long et en large pour répertorier les sites, certains encore en fonction, mais souvent abandonnés, de l'industrie lourde chinoise. Yang Yankang choisit les communautés reli- gieuses des zones rurales (photo p. 318), Wang Fuchun voyagea dans tout le pays en train pour observer les migrations de travailleurs à la recherche d'un emploi (photo p. 322). Zeng Nian produisit une extraordinaire série de panoramiques sur la progression du chantier du barrage des Trois Gorges et de son impact sur les communautés appauvries de ses environs immédiats (photos p. 324/325 et 326/327), et Xie Hailong s'intéressa à la situation d'enfants de régions très excentrées réunis par le désir d'aller à l'école (photos p. 316 et 317). Xiao Quang, dans le même temps, montrait une perception aiguë de sa génération dans une vaste série de portraits d'artistes, de conservateurs, de critiques d'art, de réalisateurs de films, d'acteurs, d'écrivains et de poètes qui faisaient entrer l'expression créative

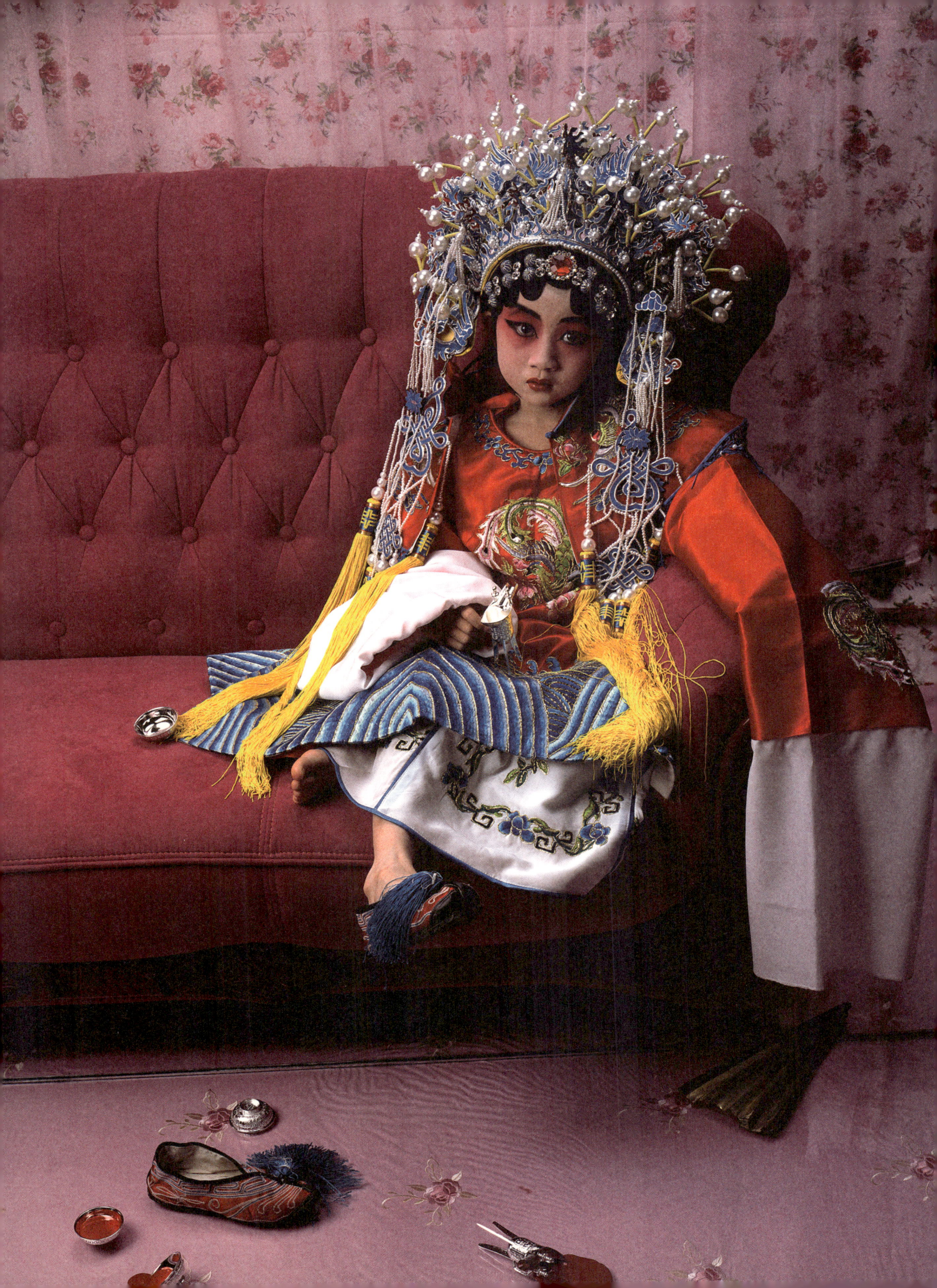

de la Chine nouvelle dans une sphère qui Lui était entièrement nouvelle. Une sélection en fut publiée en 1994 sous le titre de *Ma génération*[23], qui fait sans doute écho à la chanson éponyme du groupe The Who, référence qui exprimait certainement l'aspiration de ce photographe à être lui aussi la voix d'une génération. Ces individualités symbolisaient une nouvelle vague de photographes de talent, doués d'une sensibilité très particulière aux phénomènes sociaux majeurs de leur temps.

En 1996, la photographie fut réquisitionnée par le monde de l'art. Pour des artistes habitués à construire des images afin d'illustrer une idée, elle était le moyen idéal d'aborder l'environnement sociopolitique économique et culturel de façon directe et dans un esprit contemporain qui ne demandait pas de lourde intervention personnelle mais restait néanmoins chargé d'implications et d'inférences diverses. Peu s'intéressaient vraiment aux qualités traditionnelles du médium en tant que tel. Pour eux, tout était dans le concept. Wang Jinsong en fut un des meilleurs démonstrateurs dans sa série sur les personnes, comprenant de nombreux portraits. De petits détails comme le style ou la qualité des chaussures des enfants en disent beaucoup sur les changements survenus dans la situation économique du pays, élément qui se retrouve dans l'œuvre iconique de Wang Jinsong *Famille standard*. Ce travail porte sur des portraits de 200 familles avec un seul enfant, tous élèves d'une même école, même si l'image de leurs parents suggère qu'ils sont d'origines très variées (photos p. 328/329).

En 1998, le monde de l'art était de plus en plus intéressé par la photographie. Le portrait par Xing Danwen du peintre Zeng Fanzhi (aujourd'hui l'un des artistes chinois les plus recherchés, mais dont la carrière débutait alors) et de Wang Jin pendant une de ses performances, montre comment la photo passait du statut d'un « enregistrement documentaire » à celui d'une véritable œuvre d'art. À la proximité du changement de millénaire, de nombreuses œuvres artistiques photographiques exprimaient le sentiment grandissant d'ouverture. Dans le même temps, l'appareil permettait de multiples images spectaculaires, choquantes ou séduisantes. Par ailleurs, si l'art avait redécouvert la couleur, démontrant qu'elle pouvait servir à des effets spécifiques qui ne distrayaient pas de la forme dramatique spécifique à la photo, une certaine forme de fantaisie baroque sembla vite dépassée. Dans une remarque prophétique, Ansel Adams décrivait ainsi les dangers de la photographie d'art : « ces images brillantes de concepts flous. »[24] Néanmoins, le monde de l'art contemporain rappelait aux photographes professionnels le potentiel de leur médium, ce qui encourageait à son renforcement et finalement ses progrès.

Ceci s'observe dans la riche variété de styles et d'approches qui se diffusèrent vers l'an 2000. Ces images couvrent tous les aspects de la vie contemporaine et des phénomènes sociaux : files de jeunes filles cherchant du travail (photo p. 384), inondations dévastatrices dans les villes du Sud (photo p. 96/97), foules dans des fêtes foraines, petits marchands ambulants octogénaires (photo p. 390), enfants forcés à vendre des fleurs dans les rues (photo p. 315), grippe aviaire, nouveaux logements des classes moyennes à Shanghai (photos p. 372, 373, 374 et 375), vie des mineurs de charbon, corruption et richesse, etc. Toutes ces photos en disent énormément sur les problèmes de l'époque, les nouvelles sphères d'activité et les nouveaux défis. Un exemple particulièrement brillant est le travail de Zhou Yue sur l'explosion de la culture jeune à Pékin et l'atmosphère de nihilisme qui s'insinue dans l'esprit d'une progéniture presque entièrement composée d'enfants uniques, qui ne sont redevables de rien à personne et se permettent tout. Pour eux, la Chine est réellement devenue le pays de toutes les opportunités (photos p. 338 et 339), ce qui contraste et choque quand on regarde le portrait frappant, réalisé par Liu Heung Shing, d'un jeune garçon de la région officiellement la plus pauvre de Chine (photo p. 312). Choquantes, séduisantes, mettant en

1. Susan Sontag, *On Photography*, Picador, New York, 1977, p. 105–106
2. Hou Bo fut la photographe personnelle de Mao de 1949 à 1961. Sa carrière et son œuvre sont décrites page 409.
3. On pourrait dire de même de ceux qui sont âgés de moins de 35 ans, la seule différence étant leur éducation qui reste idéologique mais moins politique – ou aussi politique mais moins idéologique ? – et soumise à l'influence de la réforme économique qui l'a incluse dans la spécificité d'une Chine à caractéristiques socialistes, mais clairement capitaliste dans son approche de la consommation. Les canaux d'information sont différents (Internet par exemple).
4. Une étonnante variété d'exemples se trouve dans le livre de Zhang Dali, *A Second History*, publié par Walsh Gallery, Chicago, 2006.
5. Après mai 1919, le Mouvement du 4 mai lutte contre les Traités inégaux de Versailles qui instauraient des divisions territoriales et donnaient des droits à des puissances européennes sur des territoires chinois.
6. Vers le milieu des années 1940, *Life Magazine* était diffusé chaque semaine à plus de 10 millions d'exemplaires.
7. Ce fut l'encouragement ultime donné à Mao pour lancer une campagne de mise en place d'une langue commune, le *putonghua*, signifiant littéralement : langue standard.
8. Les « Conversations sur la littérature et l'art » de 1942 furent à la base de la production de tous les arts créatifs pendant la période de Mao. Toute expression créative devait être soumise à la théorie développée par ces textes.
9. *China : Fifty Years Inside the People's Republic*, catalogue de l'exposition éponyme, introduction par Rae Yang, Aperture, New York, 1999, p. 14
10. Le quotidien *Xinhua Daily News*, fondé à Wuhan en 1938, interdit par les Nationalistes en 1947 et relancé en avril 1949, fut le premier journal grand public créé en République populaire.
11. Référence au titre des œuvres complètes de Xiao Zhuang, *The Irrational Times*, publiées par les Éditions Zhonghua, Chine, 2004.
12. *Yu gong yi shan*
13. Susan Sontag, *On Photography*, Picador, New York, 1977, p. 105–106
14. Li Zhensheng, *Red Coulour News Soldier*, Londres, 2003
15. *China : Fifty Years Inside the People's Republic*, catalogue de l'exposition éponyme, introduction par Rae Yang, Aperture, New York, 1999, p. 14
16. John Szarkowski, 1967, « Photography and the Mass Media », *Creative Camera*, p. 30
17. En histoire chinoise, il s'agit des principaux membres de factions radicales qui jouèrent

pp. 104/105
Zhou Chao, 2007

Hundreds of devoted parents camping out on the floor of a school gymnasium, while their children take their high-school exams. With the one-child policy still in force, modern parents are obsessive about their child's education. Year-end high-school and university entrance examinations are deemed to be supremely important: so much so that the State grants time off for parents taking a child to their exams, and traffic priority. There are currently 40 million school children across China, with a further 14 million students attending the nation's universities.

Hunderte hingebungsvoller Eltern lagern auf dem Boden einer Schulturnhalle, während ihr Kind die Zugangsprüfung für die Oberschule ablegt. Die noch immer geltende Ein-Kind-Politik veranlasst moderne Eltern, sich zwanghaft mit der Schulbildung ihres Kindes zu beschäftigen. Prüfungen am Jahresende oder für die Zulassung zu Oberschule und Universität werden für außerordentlich wichtig gehalten, und zwar so sehr, dass der Staat den Eltern frei gibt, um ihr Kind zu den Prüfungen zu begleiten und ihnen im Verkehr Vorfahrt einräumt. Es gibt zurzeit in China 40 Millionen Schüler und weitere 14 Millionen Studenten an den Universitäten des Landes.

Des centaines de parents campent dans un gymnase scolaire pendant que leur enfant passe un examen. La politique de l'enfant unique étant toujours en vigueur, les parents modernes sont obsédés par la réussite scolaire de leur rejeton. Tout au long de l'année se déroulent des examens d'entrée au collège ou à l'université, qui sont suprêmement importants. Les parents ont droit à un congé et à une priorité de circulation pour accompagner leur enfant. Les écoles chinoises comptent actuellement 40 millions d'élèves et les universités 14 millions d'étudiants.

scène l'évolution des valeurs sociales face aux distractions modernes, ces photographies nous parlent d'aspects de la vie qui ne sont encore ni vraiment acceptés ni reconnus, même si leur vérité est indéniable.

Une dernière image

Réunir des photographies pour composer le survol d'une histoire sociale, culturelle ou politique est toujours un défi. Les images sélectionnées sont nécessairement sorties du contexte de leur époque et de leur lieu d'origine. Insérées dans une version abrégée de l'histoire, leur « poids moral et émotionnel » se charge de sens et d'accents nouveaux. Présentées comme les éléments d'une séquence chronologique, elles doivent communiquer des instants, des événements, des réalités, des changements politiques, des évolutions économiques, une atmosphère sociale et des réactions humaines à un instant donné. Par ailleurs, la dynamique d'une image risque d'être modifiée par les contrastes et les comparaisons favorisées par les juxtapositions qui ouvrent des dialogues entre les photos par-delà l'espace et le temps. Celui-ci jette des voiles successifs sur la complexité de chaque moment pris séparément et sur les faits vécus par les individus, tandis que des détails subtils qui ont pu sembler négligeables jadis apparaissent sous un jour nouveau. Même si les intrications des événements représentés peuvent devenir incompréhensibles pour les générations ultérieures de spectateurs, nous comprenons que ces images constituent un extraordinaire document visuel sur la tumultueuse et triomphale odyssée d'un peuple du tiers-monde resté longtemps enchaîné dans un système féodal agraire. Ce sujet d'un État sans présence internationale se retrouve aujourd'hui citoyen d'une grande nation devenue le foyer d'une société moderne, le plus grand centre d'industries manufacturières de l'histoire, une puissance commerciale sans équivalent, une voix qui s'affirme à l'échelle du monde.

Pour attirer l'attention et résister à l'épreuve du temps, la photographie doit accomplir davantage qu'un simple travail de documentation. Les images appartiennent à la mémoire collective d'une nation. Elles sont des points de référence dans l'espace commun que nous habitons en tant que peuple ou communauté. Elles représentent le monde extérieur et ces sujets humains qui ont été observés par un photographe mais qui, d'une certaine façon, quel que soit le temps passé et l'éloignement du moment et de son environnement, expriment toujours leur propre vérité. Parfois, nous avons besoin d'aide pour comprendre les détails d'une narration historique photographique et nous ne pouvons les lire et en faire notre propre interprétation que si nous recevons suffisamment d'informations circonstancielles. De la multitude de fragments photographiques produite au cours de ces premières décennies de la Chine nouvelle, l'image qui ressort a été soigneusement éditée pour préserver la plénitude du poids moral et émotionnel de chacun d'entre eux. Ansel Adams disait : « Tout le monde ne fait pas confiance à la peinture, mais les gens croient aux photographies. » Nous pouvons cependant être certains que ces photographies ouvriront un nouveau débat sur la manière dont la Chine est arrivée là où elle se trouve aujourd'hui.

un rôle-clé dans l'animation de la Révolution culturelle et tentèrent de s'emparer du pouvoir à la mort de Mao en 1976.

18. Ce thème était le sujet du livre de Liu Heung Shing, *China After Mao*, publié initialement par Penguin en 1982, qui contient une documentation complète sur ce phénomène à travers des images tirées de la vie quotidienne. *China After Mao* fut largement diffusé dans les cercles photographiques chinois et resta très influent tout au long des années 1990.

19. *A Premier for the People. A People for the Premier*, 26 décembre 1978-4 février 1979 rendit publique une énorme documentation photographique sur le « Mouvement du 5 avril » (nom donné aux événements survenus lors des funérailles de Zhou Enlai.) Il s'agissait moins d'une œuvre photographique que d'un exercice de propagande pour le nouveau régime et d'une tentative de restaurer la fidélité des Chinois dans sa politique et sa direction.

20. Bill Jay, « In Praise of the Snapshot », *Creative Camera*, septembre 1971, Grande-Bretagne.

21. Exposition intitulée « Humanisme in China – A Contemporary Record of Photography », organisée par le Musée d'art de Guangdong et également présentée au Musée d'art de Shanghai et au Musée national d'art de Chine à Pékin en 2005/2006. Elle voyagea à l'étranger de mai 2006 à mars 2008 dans cinq musées allemands dont le premier fut le Musée d'art moderne de Francfort.

22. Susan Sontag, *On Photography*, Picador, New York, 1977, p. 105–106

23. Publié par Cinema Press, Chine, 1994

24. La citation complète dit : « Il n'y a rien de pire qu'une brillante image pour un concept flou. »

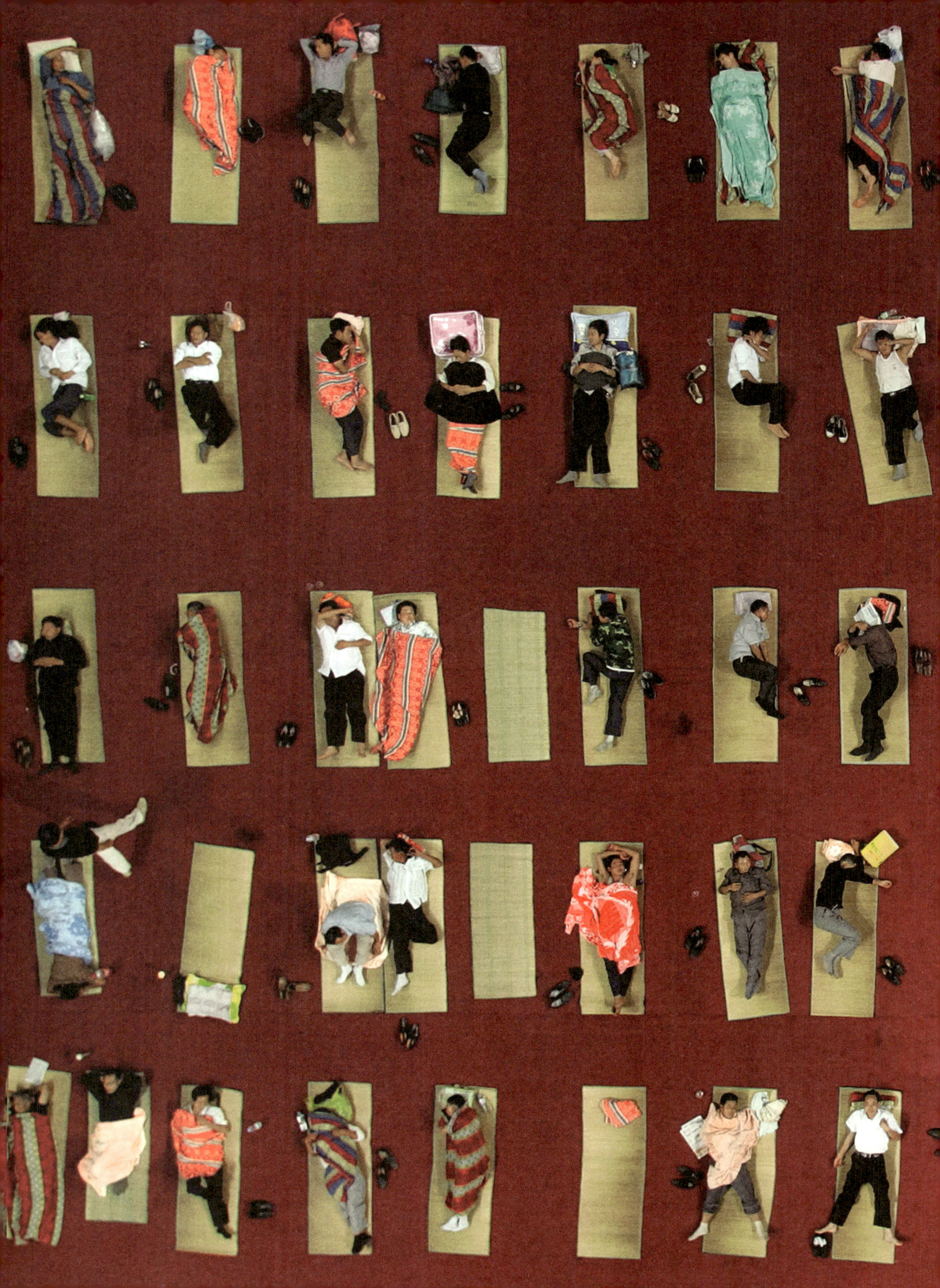

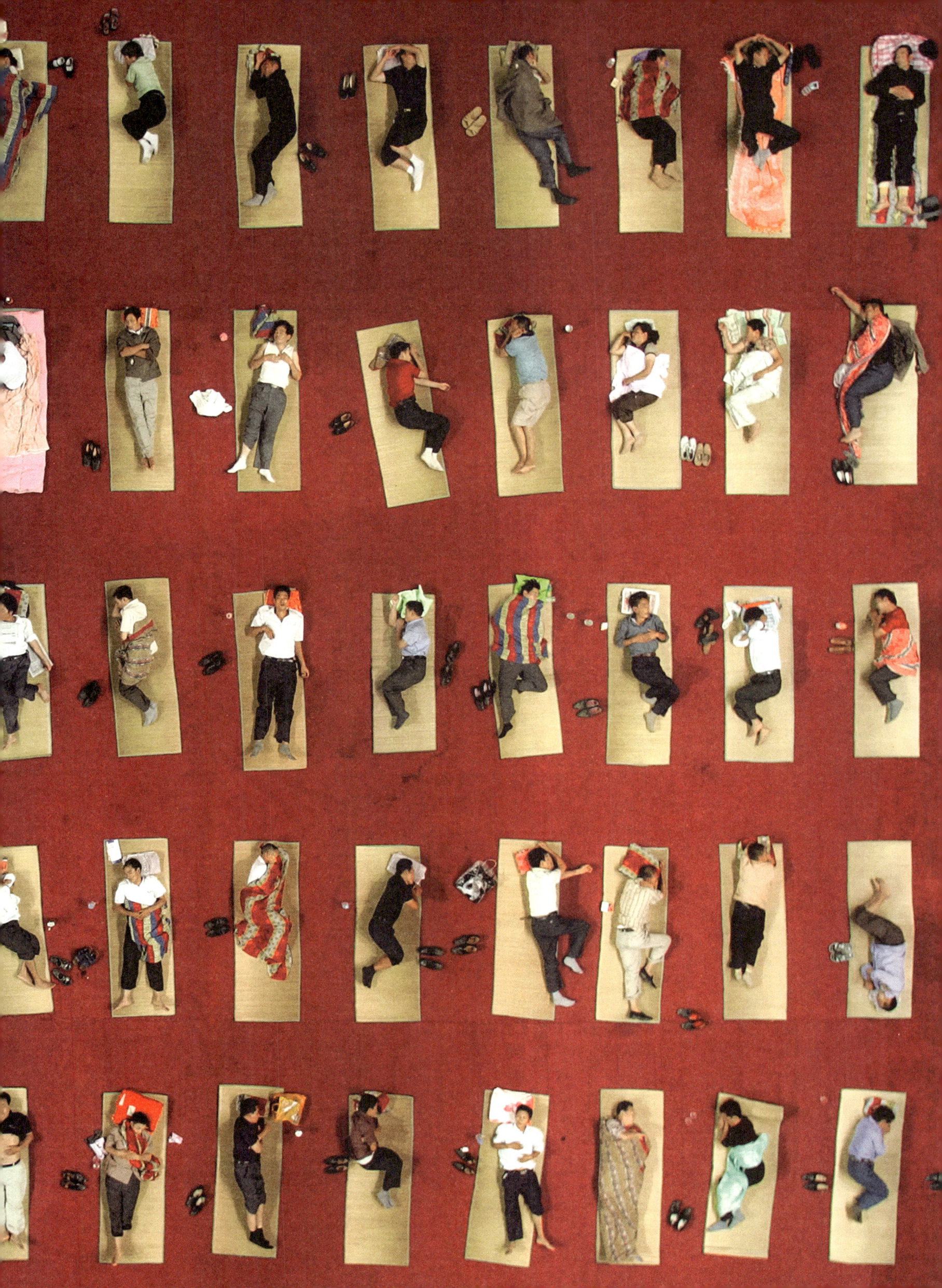

#1

1949–1959
The Birth of Modern China

*"Let a hundred flowers bloom,
let a hundred schools of thought contend."*

**Slogan used at the start of the Hundred Flowers
Campaign for open criticism of the communist government
that began in late 1956**

*Following the fall of the Qing dynasty in 1911, Sun Yat-sen founded
the Republic of China, only to be mired down in a continual power struggle amongst local warlords. The Chinese were humiliated by the Treaty of
Versailles, which redistributed foreign powers' extraterritorial concessions in
China. The Chinese Communist Party was founded in 1921 to right the
wrongs of Chinese society. After a series of debacles, such as the Long March,
the Chinese Communists at last fought the Japaneses, triumphing over the
better-equipped Kuomintang forces.*

Mao Zedong prolonged his entry into Beijing for nearly a year,
camping in Xibaibo in Hebei province as he waited for the final outcome
of the Communists' struggle to wrest the capital from the Kuomintang.
With the assistance of a Kuomintang general, who had been won over to
the Communist side, Beijing was captured with not a single shot fired.
Mao selected the moment to enter the capital carefully: one that was
fittingly auspicious in his mind. A short while later, on October 1, 1949,
Chairman Mao led his comrades-in-arms on Tiananmen Square, where
he made the famous proclamation "The Chinese people have stood up."
With those words, the People's Republic of China was founded.

Having triumphed over the Kuomintang, which, vanquished now,
had fled to Taiwan, a new era began to dawn. The people believed
Mao would put an end to the corruption and warlording that had
undermined the Kuomintang regime. Part of the reason for this were
social freedoms promised under the banner of Communist equality:
progressive and liberal-minded Chinese women, who had joined Mao's
guerilla task force in Yan'an, now worked to emancipate the female
portion of the population, whom Mao himself had described as "holding
up half the sky."

From 1951 to October of 1952, political campaigns attempted
to tackle other social problems: first the Three Antis (anti-corruption,
anti-squandering, anti-bureaucracy), then the Five Antis (anti-corruption,
anti-tax evasion, anti-embezzlement of State funds, anti-pilfering of
State property, and anti-collecting of State economic statistics). The
entire nation was thus motivated to help build a new China.

The Chairman Begins to Rule

Soon after the new government was established, Mao acted
swiftly in purging those who remained loyal to the old regimes, and
simultaneously carried out nationwide rural reforms. Land in China,
including property in the cities, was to be taken from the landlords and
given to the peasants.

Mao also sought to test the loyalties of the educated classes,
for which he launched a treacherous political campaign whose motto
was "Let a hundred flowers bloom, let a hundred schools of thought
contend." When the intellectuals spoke up, offering their contributions
on possible ways to move the young People's Republic forward, Mao
quickly launched a counter-campaign to stamp out what he now proclaimed to be dissent. This was the "Anti-Rightists" campaign, which saw
millions of educated people banished to the countryside, to "learn from
the peasants" and "correct" their "mistaken ideas."

A Grand Vision Masks a Monstrous Blind Spot

As a revolutionary, Mao was a bold strategist: when he became
suspicious of the activities of U.S. forces in Korea, and thought that the
war might expand to China, he ordered the Chinese voluntary army to
enter the war under the guise of supporting the North Koreans. His
son was amongst those who fought and died there, but the Chinese army
did succeed in holding the U.S.-led U.N. forces to the 38th parallel of
the Korean peninsula. This encouraged Mao to bolster the economy
of the People's Republic and especially to increase the industrial output.
He decided China could catch up with Great Britain in a matter of years,
and then take on America. Having launched the People's Communes in
1958, he was able to mobilize the masses for the Great Leap Forward.

By the end of the 1950s, the new Republic's halo was beginning
to lose its sheen. Mao's three major political initiatives were largely to
blame: the Anti-Rightist Campaign, the People's Communes, and the
Great Leap Forward—all subsequently condemned as policies of the
Leftists within the CCP—had sent the fledgling People's Republic down
the road to economic and social disaster.

#1

1949–1959
Die Geburt des neuen China

*„Lasst hundert Blumen blühen,
lasst hundert Schulen miteinander wetteifern."*

**Parole, mit der Ende 1956 die Hundert-Blumen-Bewegung
zur freien Kritik an der kommunistischen Regierung
eröffnet wurde**

Nach dem Sturz der Qing-Dynastie im Jahr 1911 gründete Sun Yat-sen die Republik China, nur um sogleich mit regionalen Militärmachthabern (Warlords) um die Macht zu ringen. Die Chinesen sahen sich durch den Versailler Vertrag gedemütigt, in dem die Ansprüche des Auslands auf chinesisches Territorium neu verteilt wurden. Die Kommunistische Partei Chinas wurde 1921 gegründet, um das Unrecht an der chinesischen Gesellschaft wieder gutzumachen. Nach einer Reihe von Fehlschlägen wie dem Langen Marsch bekämpften die chinesischen Kommunisten schließlich die japanischen Invasoren und siegten über die besser ausgerüsteten Truppen der Kuomintang.

Mao Zedong verzögerte seinen Einzug nach Peking um fast ein Jahr, während er in Xibaibo in der Provinz Hebei zurückblieb und den Ausgang des Kampfs abwartete, in dem die Kommunisten die Hauptstadt aus der Gewalt der Kuomintang befreien wollten. Mithilfe eines Generals der Kuomintang, der auf die Seite der Kommunisten übergelaufen war, konnte Peking kampflos eingenommen werden. Auch dann wählte Mao den Zeitpunkt seines Einzugs in die Hauptstadt noch sorgfältig aus; er sollte für sein Dafürhalten angemessen vom Glück begünstigt sein. Kurze Zeit später, am 1. Oktober 1949, versammelte der Vorsitzende Mao seine Waffengefährten auf dem Tiananmen-Platz, wo er mit der berühmten Proklamation „Das chinesische Volk hat sich erhoben" die Volksrepublik China gründete.

Nach dem Sieg über die Kuomintang, die nach Taiwan flohen, begann eine neue Ära voller Hoffnung. Die Menschen glaubten, Mao werde mit der Korruption und der Herrschaft der Warlords, die das Regime der Kuomintang zersetzt hatten, ein Ende machen. Ein Teil der Hoffnungen waren die den Menschen unter dem Banner der kommunistischen Gleichheit versprochenen sozialen Freiheiten. Fortschrittliche und liberale chinesische Frauen, die sich Maos Guerillatruppe in Yan'an angeschlossen hatten, arbeiteten jetzt daran, den weiblichen Teil der Massen zu emanzipieren, von dem Mao selbst gesagt hatte, er „halte die Hälfte des Himmels". Von 1951 bis Oktober 1952 sollten weitere politische Kampagnen dazu beitragen, der gesellschaftlichen Probleme Herr zu werden: Zunächst die drei Antis (Anti-Korruption, Anti-Verschwendung, Anti-Bürokratismus), dann die fünf Antis (Anti-Korruption, Anti-Steuerhinterziehung, Anti-Veruntreuung von Staatseigentum, Anti-Betrug und Anti-Verrat von Staatsgeheimnissen). Damit war die gesamte Nation motiviert, beim Bau eines neuen China mitzuhelfen.

Der Beginn der Herrschaft des Vorsitzenden

Kurz nach Etablierung der neuen Regierung trennte sich Mao rasch von den Weggefährten, die den alten Systemen weiterhin die Treue hielten, und führte gleichzeitig eine landesweite Agrarreform durch. Das Land, zu dem auch städtische Liegenschaften gehörten, sollte in China von den Grundbesitzern an die Bauern umverteilt werden.

Mao war darüber hinaus bestrebt, die Loyalität der gebildeten Klassen zu prüfen, für die er die trügerische politische Kampagne mit dem Namen „Lasst hundert Blumen blühen, lasst hundert Schulen miteinander wetteifern" lancierte. Als sich die Intellektuellen zu Wort meldeten, um zum Fortschritt der jungen Volksrepublik beizutragen, stieß Mao rasch eine Gegenkampagne an, die von ihm für abweichlerisch gehaltene Meinungen ausmerzen sollte. Dies war die Kampagne gegen Rechts, in deren Folge Millionen von Gebildeten aufs Land verschickt wurden, um dort „von den Bauern zu lernen" und ihre „irrigen Vorstellungen zu korrigieren".

Eine großartige Vision verschleiert einen gewaltigen wunden Punkt

Als Revolutionär war Mao ein kühner Stratege: Als die Aktivitäten der amerikanischen Streitkräfte in Korea bei ihm die Befürchtung aufkommen ließen, der Krieg könne sich auf China ausdehnen, befahl er Einheiten der chinesischen Streitkräfte, unter dem Vorwand, Nordkorea zu unterstützen, in den Krieg einzugreifen. Sein Sohn gehörte zu denen, die dort kämpften und starben, aber es gelang den chinesischen Truppen, die von den USA angeführten UN-Soldaten am 38. Breitengrad auf der koreanischen Halbinsel zurückzudrängen. Dies bestärkte Mao darin, sich um eine erhöhte wirtschaftliche, insbesondere industrielle Produktion zu bemühen. Er glaubte, China könne innerhalb weniger Jahre zu Großbritannien aufschließen und es dann mit Amerika aufnehmen. Mithilfe der 1958 von ihm gegründeten Volkskommunen konnte er die Massen zum Großen Sprung nach vorn mobilisieren.

Ende der 1950er-Jahre begann die positive Aura, mit der die junge Volksrepublik das Jahrzehnt begonnen hatte, sich zu verlieren. Verantwortlich dafür waren in erster Linie die von Mao angestoßenen drei großen politischen Kampagnen: gegen Rechtsabweichler, für Volkskommunen und der „Große Sprung nach vorn" – allesamt später als taktische Winkelzüge der Linken innerhalb der Kommunistischen Partei Chinas (KPCh) entlarvt –, die die Volksrepublik an den Rand einer steilen Abwärtsspirale wirtschaftlicher und sozialer Katastrophen führten.

#1

1949–1959
La naissance de la Chine moderne

« Que cent fleurs s'épanouissent,
que cent écoles de pensée rivalisent. »

Slogan utilisé au départ de la Campagne des cent fleurs
lancée fin 1956 pour susciter la critique du gouvernement

Après la chute de la dynastie Qing en 1911, Sun Yat-sen fonda la République de Chine qui sombra bientôt dans les luttes pour le pouvoir des seigneurs de guerre. Les Chinois furent humiliés par le Traité de Versailles qui redistribua les concessions étrangères extraterritoriales. Le parti communiste chinois fut fondé en 1921 pour remédier aux maux de la société chinoise. Après une série de débâcles, comme la Longue marche, les communistes combattirent l'invasion japonaise et triomphèrent des forces du Kuomintang pourtant mieux équipées.

Cantonné à Xibaibo dans la province de Hebei, Mao Zedong retarda son entrée dans Pékin de près d'un an en attendant l'issue des combats menés par les communistes pour libérer la capitale du Kuomintang. Avec l'assistance d'un général de Tchang Kaï-chek passé au communisme, la ville fut prise sans un seul coup de feu. Mao choisit néanmoins son moment pour faire une entrée prudente, ce qui lui semblait préférable et de meilleur augure. Peu après, le 1er octobre 1949, le Président Mao rassembla ses camarades d'arme sur la place Tian'anmen et leur adressa sa célèbre proclamation : « Le peuple chinois s'est levé. » La République populaire de Chine était ainsi fondée.

Le triomphe sur le Kuomintang, qui prit la fuite pour Taïwan, ouvrait une ère nouvelle et riche d'espoirs : le peuple croyait que Mao allait mettre fin à la corruption et aux entreprises des seigneurs de la guerre qui avaient miné le régime antérieur. De cette espérance faisaient partie les libertés promises par l'égalitarisme communiste. Par exemple, les Chinoises progressistes d'esprit libertaire qui avaient rejoint les forces de Mao à Yan'an œuvraient maintenant à l'émancipation des femmes du peuple dont Mao lui-même avait déclaré qu'elles « soutenaient la moitié du ciel. »

De 1951 à octobre 1952, des campagnes politiques tentèrent de régler d'autres types de problèmes sociaux. D'abord la campagne des Trois anti (anti-corruption, anti-gaspillage, anti-bureaucratie), puis celles des Cinq anti (anti-corruption, anti-évasion fiscale, anti-vol des biens de l'État, anti-pillage des matériaux d'État, anti-collecte de statistiques économiques étatiques). Ainsi, la nation était motivée pour aider à la construction d'une Chine nouvelle.

Les débuts du règne du Président

Peu après la mise en place du nouveau gouvernement, Mao s'empressa de se débarrasser des fidèles des anciens régimes et dans le même temps lança des réformes rurales nationales. La terre devait être prise aux propriétaires terriens et redistribuée aux paysans. La réforme concernait aussi la propriété urbaine. Mao chercha également à tester la loyauté des classes éduquées vers lesquelles il lança une campagne politique-piège appelée « Que cent fleurs s'épanouissent, que cent écoles de pensée rivalisent ». Lorsque les intellectuels prirent la parole pour contribuer à l'avancement de la jeune république, Mao précipita une contre-campagne pour dénoncer ce qu'il proclamait maintenant être de la dissidence. Ce fut la campagne « anti-droitière » qui vit des millions de personnes éduquées envoyées dans les campagnes pour « apprendre auprès des paysans » et « corriger leurs idées fausses ».

Une vision grandiose, un aveuglement monstrueux

Révolutionnaire, Mao était un stratège audacieux. Lorsqu'il commença à s'inquiéter des avancées des forces américaines en Corée et vit que la guerre risquait de gagner la Chine, il ordonna à une armée de volontaires chinois d'entrer dans le conflit sous prétexte de soutenir les Coréens du Nord. Son fils, qui faisait partie de ces combattants, y trouva la mort mais l'armée chinoise réussit à contenir les forces onusiennes dirigées par les Américains sur le 38e parallèle. Ceci encouragea Mao à faire redémarrer l'économie de son pays et en particulier la production industrielle. Il décida que la Chine pouvait égaler la Grande-Bretagne en quelques années puis dépasser les États-Unis. Après avoir lancé la réforme des communes populaires en 1958, il était maintenant en mesure de mobiliser les masses pour le Grand bond en avant.

À la fin des années 1950, l'aura positive dont jouissait la nouvelle république au début de la décennie commençait à pâlir. Les trois grandes initiatives de Mao en étaient en grande partie responsables : la campagne anti-droitière, les communes populaires et le Grand bond en avant – toutes condamnées par la suite comme des politiques gauchistes par le Parti communiste de Chine – faisaient entrer la nouvelle Chine dans une spirale infernale de désastres économiques et sociaux.

*"Let the domestic and foreign reactionaries tremble before us!
Let them say we are no good at this and no good at that. By our
own indomitable efforts we the Chinese people will unswervingly
reach our goal."*

*„Lasst die einheimischen und ausländischen Reaktionäre vor
uns zittern! Sollen sie sagen, wir seien hierin nicht gut und darin
nicht gut. Dank unserer unbändigen Anstrengungen werden wir,
das chinesische Volk, unser Ziel unbeirrbar erreichen."*

*« Que tremblent devant nous les réactionnaires d'ici et de l'étranger !
Laissons-les dire que nous ne savons pas faire ceci ou cela. Par
nos efforts sans relâche, nous, le peuple chinois, nous atteindrons
notre but. »*

Mao Zedong (1993–1976), first Chairman of the People's Republic of China, 1949

→
Hou Bo, 1954

In a famous pose that became the de facto model for the monumental statues of Mao erected across the country during his reign, Mao strikes a pensive pose on the beach at Beidaihe, a seaside resort to the east of Beijing, which remains the summer retreat of senior Party leaders.

Mao steht in Gedanken versunken am Strand von Beidaihe, einem östlich von Peking gelegenen Seebad, das hochrangigen Parteifunktionären noch immer als sommerlicher Erholungsort dient. Diese berühmte Pose wurde zum Modell für die monumentalen Mao-Statuen, die während seiner Regierungszeit überall im Land aufgestellt wurden.

Dans une pose fameuse qui fut le modèle de tant de statues monumentales érigées dans le pays au cours de son règne, Mao se tient, solidement ancré, sur la plage de Beidaihe, une station balnéaire à l'est de Pékin qui est toujours une des retraites estivales des hauts responsables du Parti.

pp. 114/115
Xu Xiaobing, 1943

Soldiers in Mao's Red Army cross the harsh desert of Shaanxi province. The need to retreat from the Kuomintang forced the Communists to embark on the Long March (1935–36). Eventually, the surviving forces regrouped in Yan'an, where they remained until 1947. There the numbers swelled owing to the new recruits from the surrounding areas.

Soldaten von Maos Roter Armee durchqueren ein unwirtliches Wüstengebiet in der Provinz Shaanxi. Die Notwendigkeit, sich vor den Truppen der Kuomintang zurückzuziehen, zwang die Kommunisten zum Langen Marsch (1935–1936). Schließlich sammelten sich die verbliebenen Truppen in Yan'an, wo sie ausharrten, bis sich ihnen 1947 neue Rekruten aus den umliegenden Gebieten anschlossen.

Des soldats de l'Armée rouge de Mao traversent un désert de la province du Shaanxi. La retraite devant les forces du Kuomintang forcèrent les communistes à entreprendre la Longue marche (1935–36). Leurs dernières forces se regroupèrent à Yan'an où elles demeurèrent jusqu'en 1947, leur nombre s'accroissant de nouvelles recrues venues des régions avoisinantes.

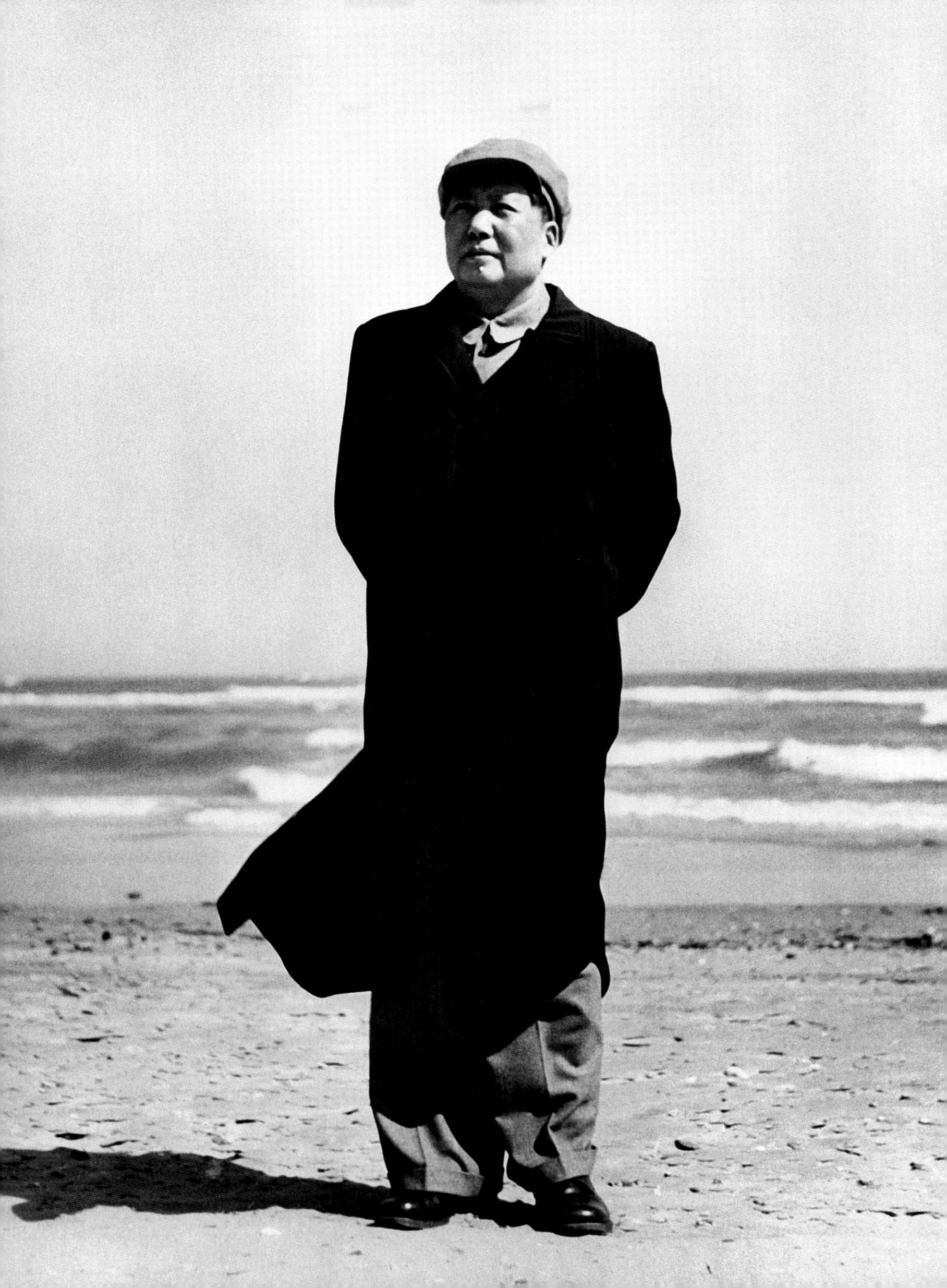

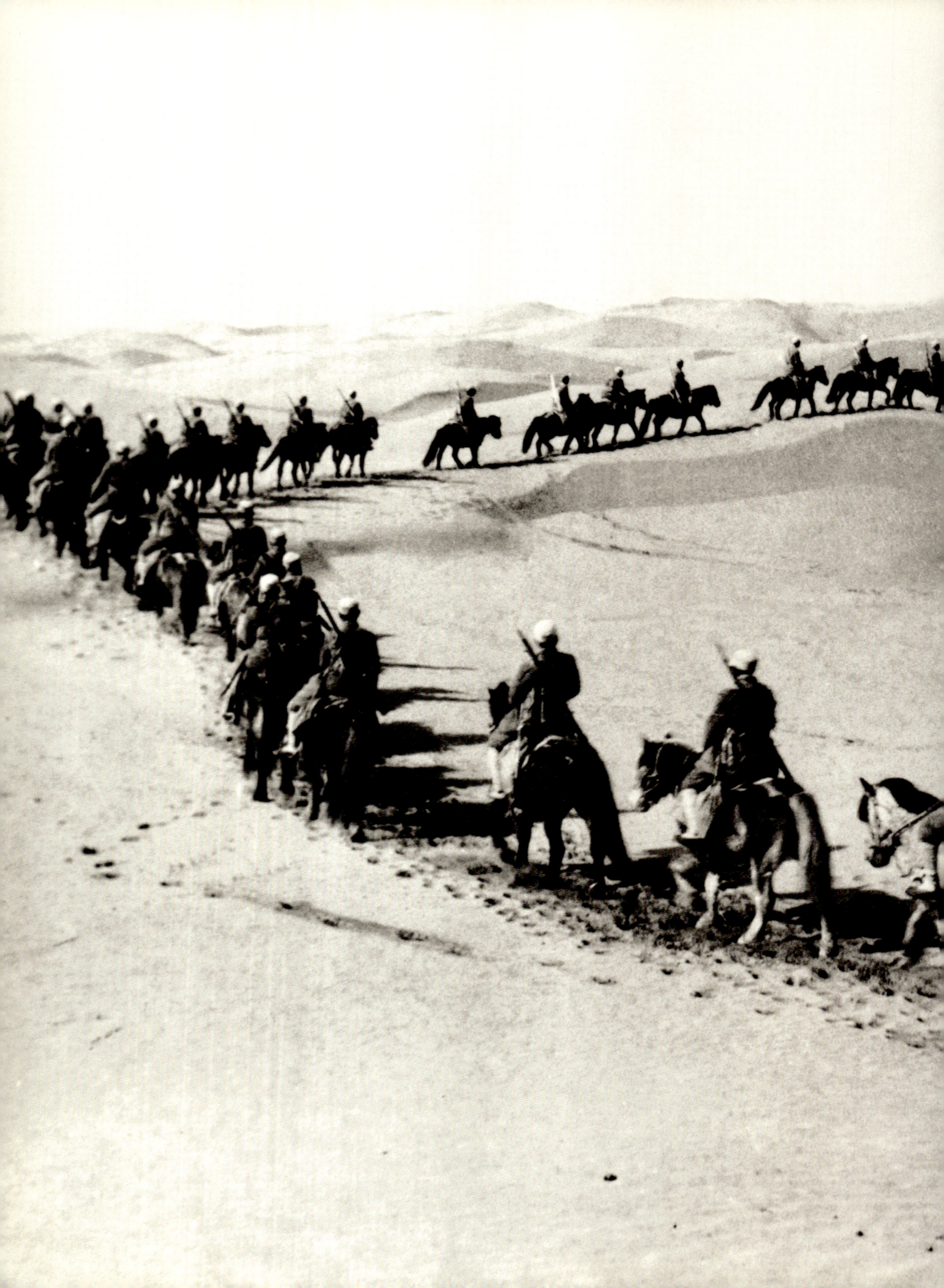

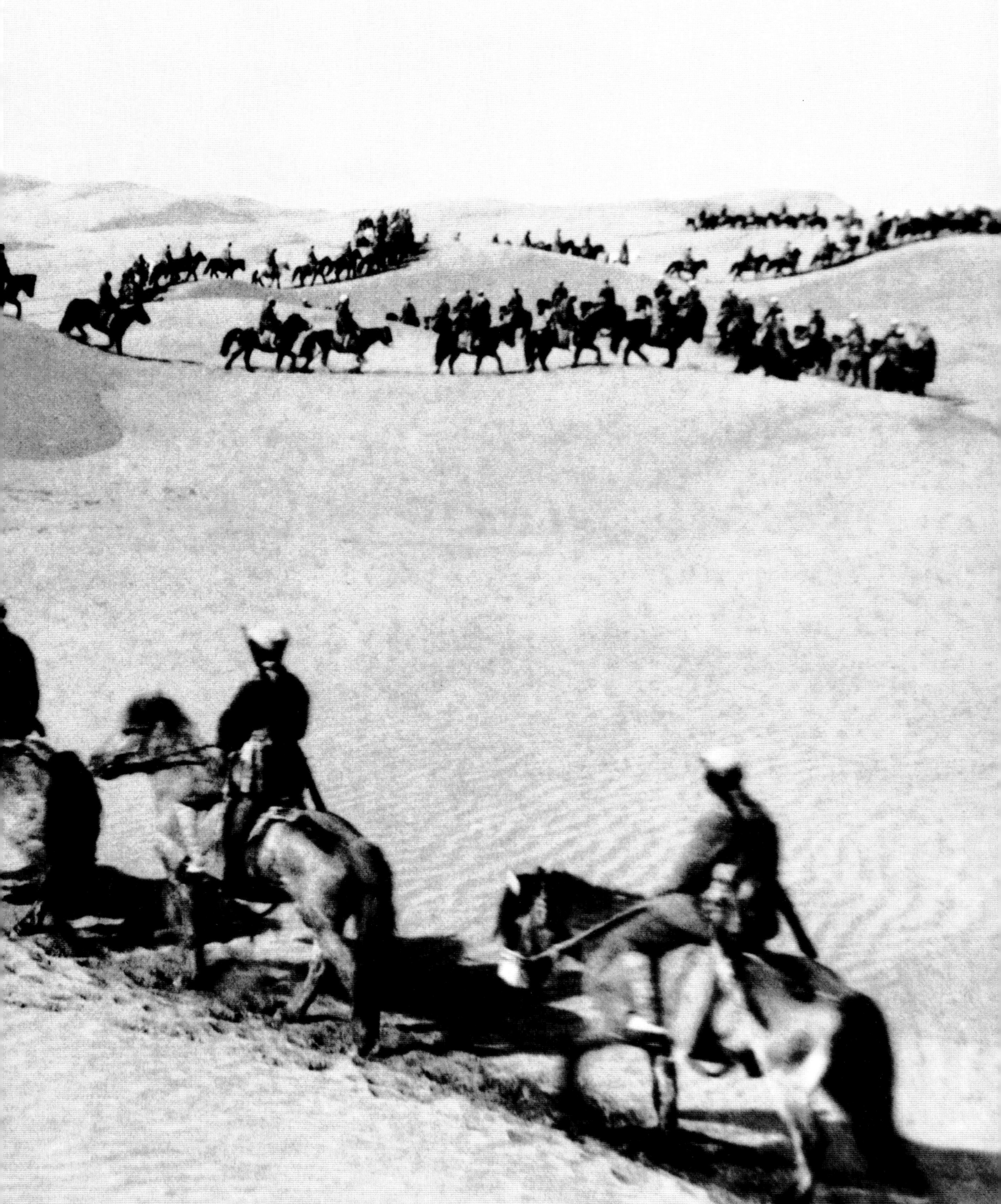

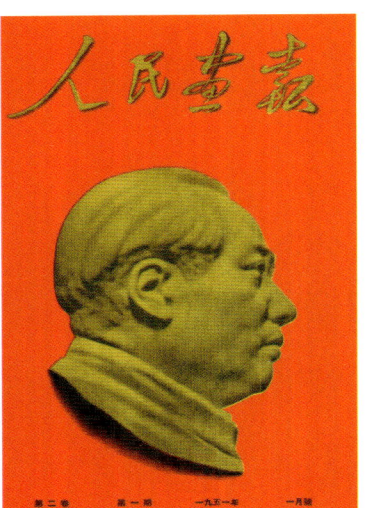

China Pictorial, January 1951

Mao's profile in plaster

←
China Pictorial

Launched in July, 1950, China Pictorial is the country's oldest illustrated magazine, having been published continuously for 58 years. The banner text used to mark the magazine's distinctive identity was a piece of calligraphy penned personally by Mao. Serving as the visual propaganda arm of the Chinese government, China Pictorial nevertheless tracked the tumultuous history of New China with its own brand of socialism with Chinese characteristics.

Bei der im Juli 1950 gegründeten Zeitschrift China Pictorial *handelt es sich um die älteste, seit 58 Jahren ununterbrochen erscheinende chinesische Illustrierte. Der Titelschriftzug, der der Zeitschrift seine graphische Identität gibt, wurde als kalligraphisches Element von Mao persönlich geschrieben. Ungeachtet ihrer Funktion als propagandistischer Arm der chinesischen Regierung verfolgt* China Pictorial *die bewegte Geschichte des Neuen China mit ihrer eigenen Spielart des Sozialismus mit chinesischen Merkmalen.*

Lancé en juillet 1950, China Pictorial *(L'illustré de la Chine) est le plus ancien magazine illustré chinois, publié sans interruption depuis 58 ans. Le texte en bannière qui donne au magazine son identité graphique est un élément calligraphique dû à Mao lui-même. Bras de la propagande visuelle du gouvernement chinois,* China Pictorial, *retrace néanmoins l'histoire tumultueuse de la Chine nouvelle qui suit sa propre voie socialiste à caractéristiques chinoises.*

↓
Hou Bo, 1949

Mao sits with his son, Mao Anying, in the Fragrant hills to the west of Beijing. A few years later, in 1952, this, his only, son would be killed fighting in the war between China-supported North Korea and the U.S.-backed south.

Mao sitzt mit seinem Sohn, Mao Anying, in den Fragrant Hills, westlich von Peking. Wenige Jahre später, 1952, kommt Maos einziger Sohn bei Kämpfen im Krieg zwischen dem auf Seiten Nordkoreas involvierten China und dem von den USA unterstützten Süden ums Leben.

Mao et son fils Mao Anying, dans les Fragrant Hills, à l'ouest de Pékin. Quelques années plus tard, en 1952, le fils unique du Grand timonier fut tué pendant la guerre de Corée, où la Chine soutenait la Corée communiste.

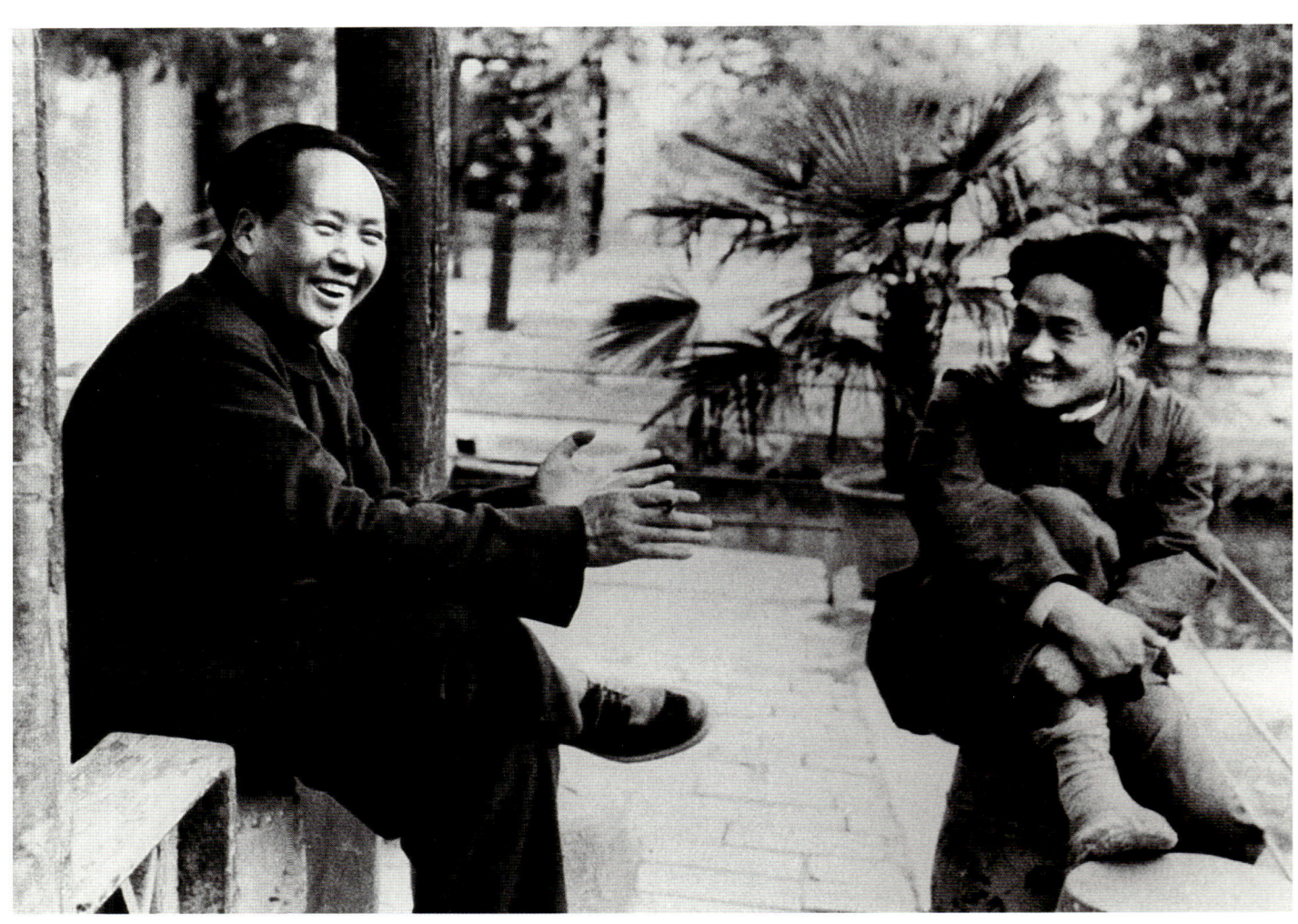

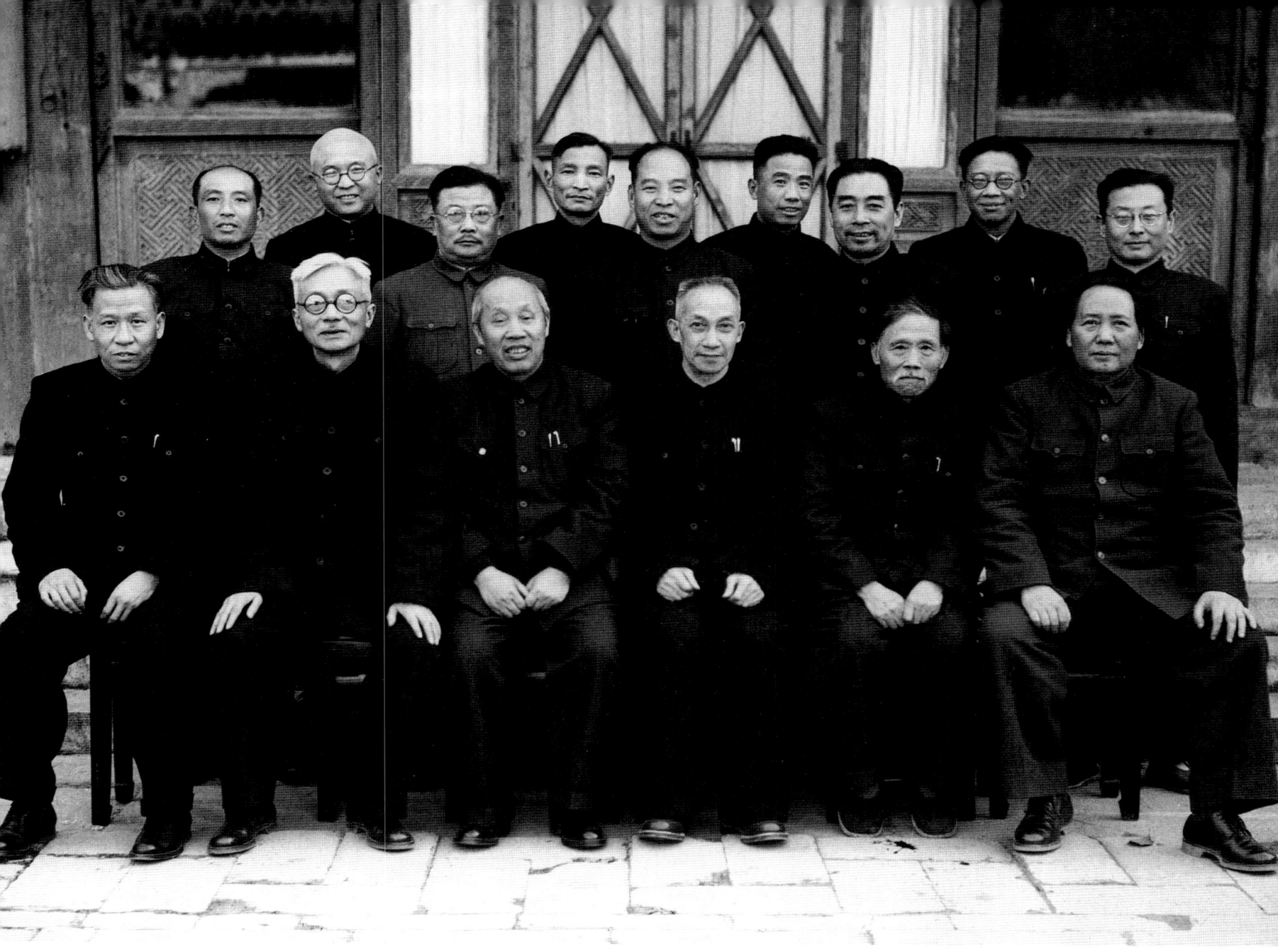

↑

Hou Bo, 1949

Mao poses with delegates of the first Chinese People's Political Consultative Conference. Front row, left to right: Liu Shaoqi, Lin Boqu, Dong Biwu, Wu Yuzhang, Xu Deli, Mao. Back row: An Ziwen, Liu Lantao, Li Kenong, Chen Yun, Peng Zhen, Xin Xiping, Zhou Enlai, Lu Dingyi and Qi Yanmin.

Mao lässt sich mit Delegierten der ersten Politischen Konsultativkonferenz des chinesischen Volkes ablichten. Erste Reihe von links nach rechts: Liu Shaoqi, Lin Boqu, Dong Biwu, Wu Yuzhang, Xu Deli, Mao. Hintere Reihe: An Ziwen, Liu Lantao, Li Kenong, Chen Yun, Peng Zhen, Xin Xiping, Zhou Enlai, Lu Dingyi und Qi Yanmin.

Mao pose avec des délégués à la Première conférence politique consultative du peuple chinois. De gauche à droite : Liu Shaoqi, Lin Boqu, Dong Biwu, Wu Yuzhang, Xu Deli, Mao. Second rang : An Ziwen, Liu Lantao, Li Kenong, Chen Yun, Peng Zhen, Xin Xiping, Zhou Enlai, Lu Dingyi et Qi Yanmin.

"China's 600 million people have two remarkable peculiarities: they are, first of all, poor, and, second, blank. That may seem like a bad thing, but it is really a good thing. Poor people want change, want to do things, want revolution. A clean sheet of paper has no blotches, and so the newest and most beautiful words can be written on it; the newest and most beautiful pictures can be painted on it."

„Chinas 600 Millionen Einwohner zeichnen sich durch zwei bemerkenswerte Besonderheiten aus: Zum einen sind sie arm, zum zweiten unbeschrieben. Das mag nachteilig erscheinen, aber es ist in Wirklichkeit ein Vorteil. Arme Menschen wollen Veränderung, wollen etwas tun, wollen Revolution. Ein weißes Stück Papier hat keine Flecken, und deshalb können die neuesten und schönsten Worte darauf geschrieben werden; die neuesten und schönsten Bilder können darauf gemalt werden."

« Les 600 millions de Chinois présentent deux particularités remarquables. D'abord et avant tout, ils sont pauvres, ensuite, ce sont des pages vierges. On pourrait penser que c'est une mauvaise chose, mais c'est au contraire une très bonne chose. Les pauvres veulent le changement, veulent agir, veulent la révolution. Une feuille de papier blanc n'a pas de taches, et l'on peut y écrire les mots les plus beaux et les plus neufs, on peut y peindre les images les plus belles et les plus neuves. »

MAO ZEDONG (1893–1976), first Chairman of the People's Republic of China, 1958

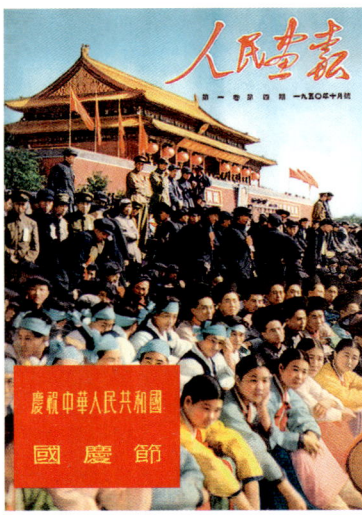

China Pictorial, October 1950

*First anniversary issue with the crowds
at the founding ceremony*

"Hope can be neither affirmed nor denied. Hope is like a path in
the countryside: originally there is no path—yet, if people walk on the same
spot frequently, a path emerges."

„Hoffnung kann weder erfüllt noch enttäuscht werden. Hoffnung
ist wie ein Pfad in der Landschaft: Ursprünglich gab es da keinen Pfad –
aber wenn Leute immer an der gleichen Stelle laufen, entsteht ein Weg."

« L'espoir ne peut être ni affirmé ni dénié. L'espoir est comme un
chemin de campagne. Au début, il n'y avait pas de chemin et comme
les gens passaient toujours au même endroit, une voie s'est dessinée. »

**LU XUN (Zhou Shuren, 1881–1936), short-story writer, essayist, poet,
the "father of modern Chinese literature"**

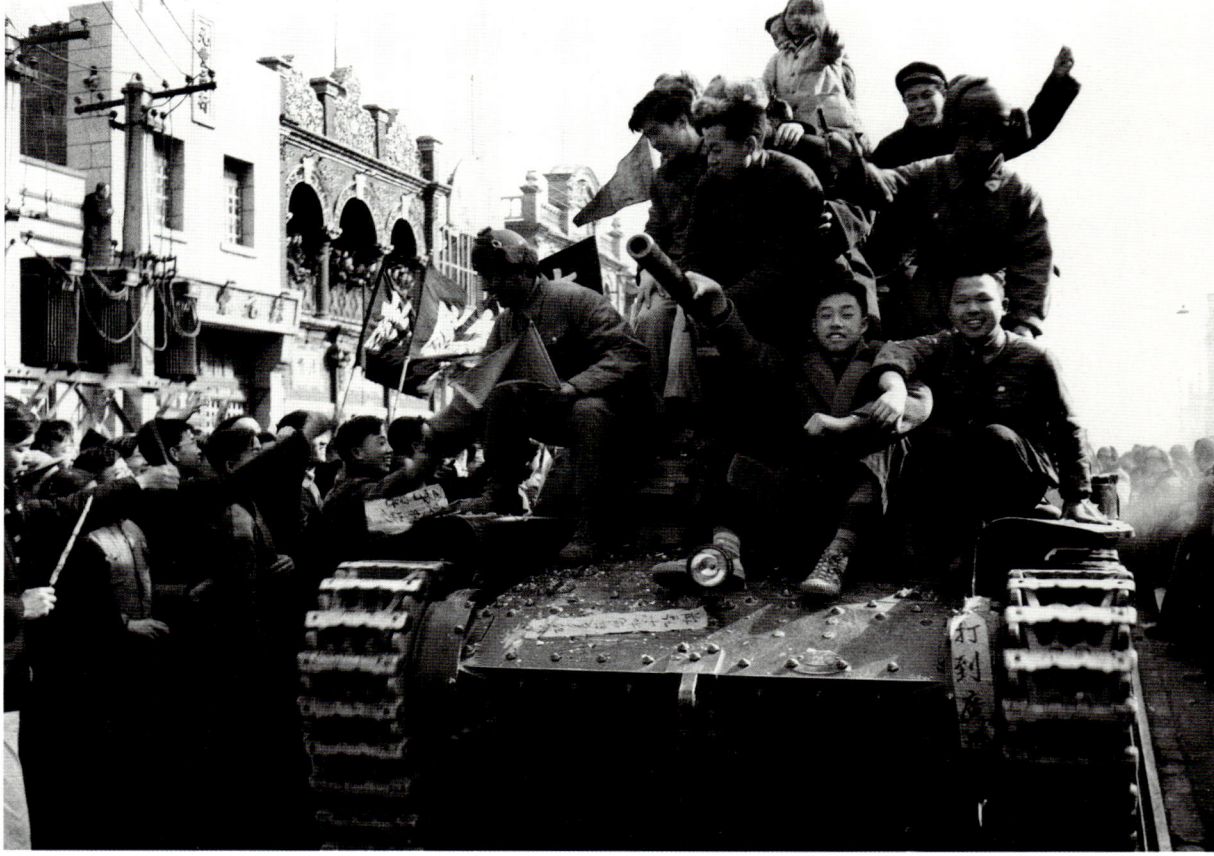

←
Meng Zhaorui, 1949

*Students and residents welcome troops of the
People's Liberation Army (PLA) as they enter
the capital in February 1949. With the com-
plicity of a rival Kuomintang general who
defected to the Communist side, not a single
shot was fired in liberating Beijing. The
People's Republic of China was formally
established a few months later, on October 1.*

*Bei ihrem Einzug in die Hauptstadt im
Februar 1949 werden die Truppen der
Volksbefreiungsarmee von Studenten und
Einwohnern begrüßt. Durch die Hilfe eines
abtrünnigen Generals der Kuomintang
fiel bei der Befreiung Pekings nicht ein einziger Schuss. Wenige Monate später, am
1. Oktober 1949, wurde die Volksrepublik
China offiziell gegründet.*

*Des étudiants et des habitants accueillent
les troupes de l'Armée populaire de libération
(APL) à leur entrée dans la capitale en février
1949. Grâce à la complicité d'un général
du Kuomintang, la ville fut prise sans un
seul coup de feu. La République populaire
de Chine fut formellement fondée quelques
mois plus tard, le 1ᵉʳ octobre.*

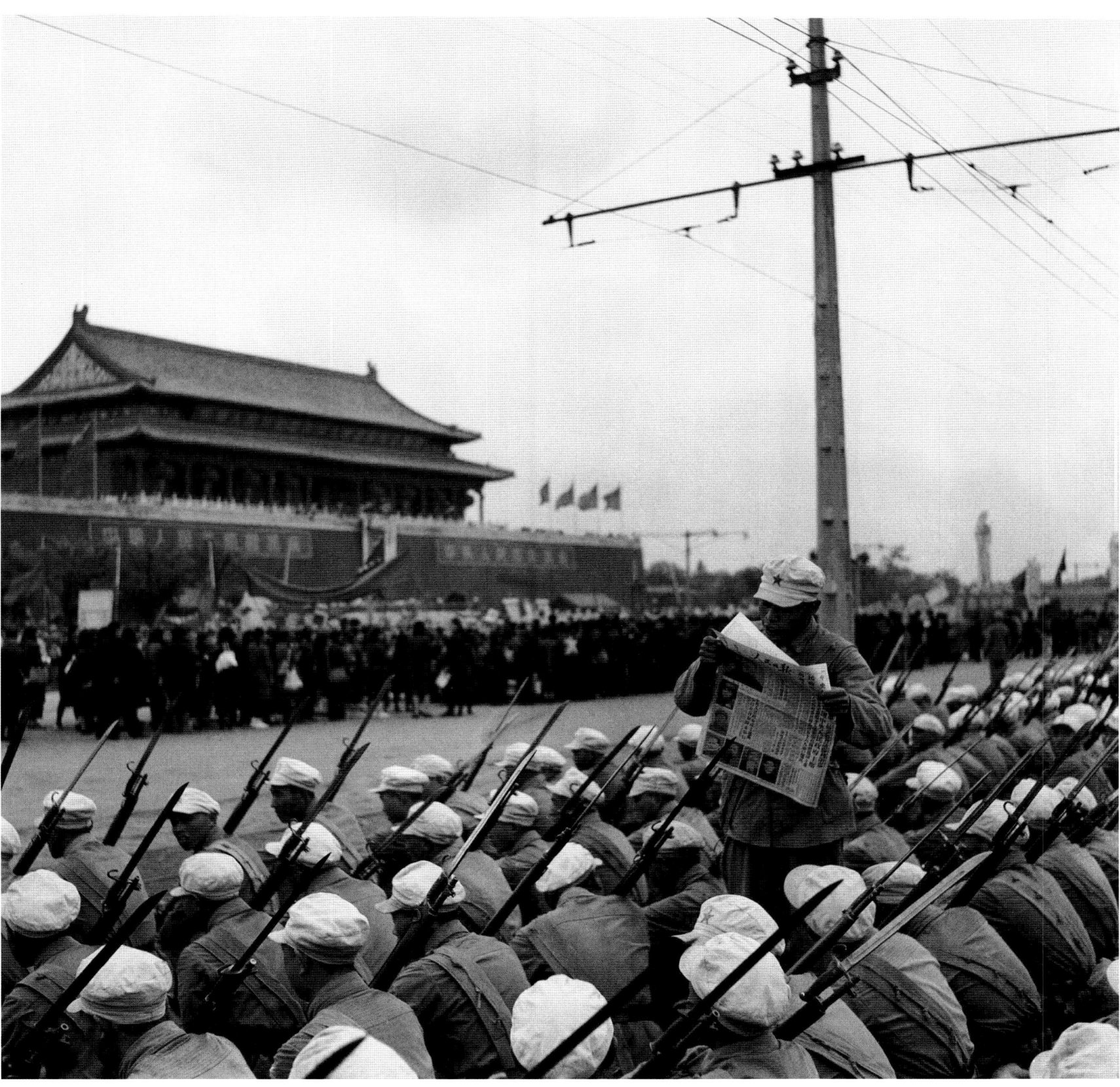

↑
Meng Zhaorui, 1949

On October 1, 1949, 300,000 soldiers from the People's Liberation Army gather on Tiananmen Square to await the declaration of the People's Republic. A platoon officer reads aloud that day's People's Daily headline announcing the founding of the People's Republic of China by Chairman Mao Zedong.

Am 1. Oktober 1949 versammeln sich 300.000 Soldaten der Volksbefreiungsarmee in Erwartung der Proklamation der Volksrepublik auf dem Tiananmen-Platz. Der Zugführer verliest die Schlagzeile der aktuellen Ausgabe von People's Daily, die die Gründung der Volksrepublik China unter Führung Mao Zedongs verkündet.

1ᵉʳ octobre 1949 : 300 000 soldats de l'APL se réunissent sur la place de Tian'anmen pour entendre la déclaration de création de la République populaire. Un officier lit à haute voix le titre du Quotidien du peuple annonçant la fondation de la République populaire de Chine présidée par Mao Zedong.

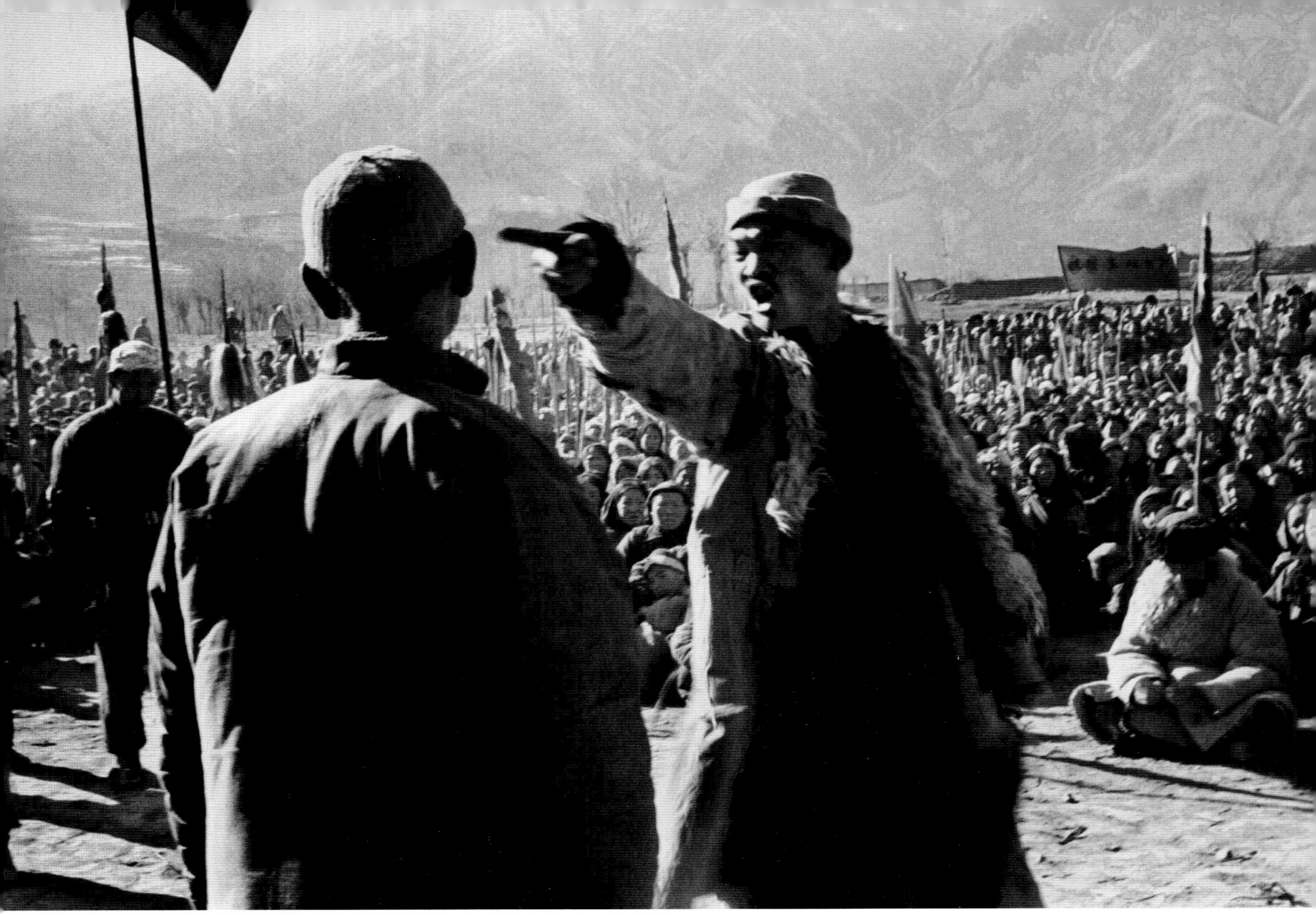

↓

Anon.
(image provided by Xiao Zhuang, 1950)

In 1950, the Chinese Communist Party launched a campaign to suppress counter-revolutionaries, which lasted until 1951. Here, a man accused of spying for the Kuomintang is taken for sentencing before a court in Nanjing. Some years later, in 1960, in an interview with American journalist Edgar Snow, Premier Zhou Enlai said that between 1934 and 1954, 830,000 "enemies of the people" (landlords, Kuomintang troops who did not flee, and spies) were killed. Other sources cited as many as five million executions of counterrevolutionaries during the land-reform period and the "Three Antis" and "Five Antis" political campaigns between 1949 and 1952.

Die KPCh startete 1950 eine Kampagne zur Unterdrückung von Konterrevolutionären, die bis 1951 andauerte. Hier steht ein Mann, der der Spionage für die Kuomintang beschuldigt wird, zur Verurteilung vor einem Volksgericht in Nanjing. Einige Jahre später erklärt Premierminister Zhou Enlai in einem Interview mit dem amerikanischen Journalisten Edgar Snow, dass zwischen 1934 und 1954 830.000 „Feinde des Volkes" (Grundbesitzer, nicht geflohene Kuomintang-Kämpfer und Spione) getötet wurden. Andere Quellen sprechen von bis zu fünf Millionen Hinrichtungen von Konterrevolutionären während der Landreform und der politischen Kampagnen Drei Antis und Fünf Antis zwischen 1949 und 1952.

En 1950, le Parti communiste lança une campagne d'élimination des contre-révolutionnaires qui dura jusqu'en 1951. Ici, un homme accusé d'espionnage pour le Kuomintang est jugé par un tribunal populaire de Nankin. Quelques années plus tard, dans un entretien avec le journaliste américain Edgar Snow en 1960, le premier ministre Zhou Enlai reconnut qu'entre 1934 et 1954, 830 000 « ennemis du peuple » (propriétaires terriens, troupes du Kuomintang qui n'avaient pas fui et espions) avaient été exécutés. D'autres sources citent cinq millions d'exécutions.

↑

Ru Suichu, 1951

A peasant points a finger at a landlord in a mass rally in Qinghai province. With the founding of the People's Republic in 1949, land reform was carried out nationwide, with the exception of Tibet.

Bei einer Massenversammlung in der Provinz Qinghai zeigt ein Bauer mit dem Finger auf einen Grundbesitzer. Nach der Gründung der Volksrepublik im Jahr 1949 wurde die Landreform mit Ausnahme von Tibet im ganzen Land durchgeführt.

Un paysan pointe le doigt vers un propriétaire terrien dans un rassemblement de masse dans la province du Qinghai. Après la fondation de la République en 1949, la réforme agraire fut imposée dans tout le pays, à l'exception du Tibet.

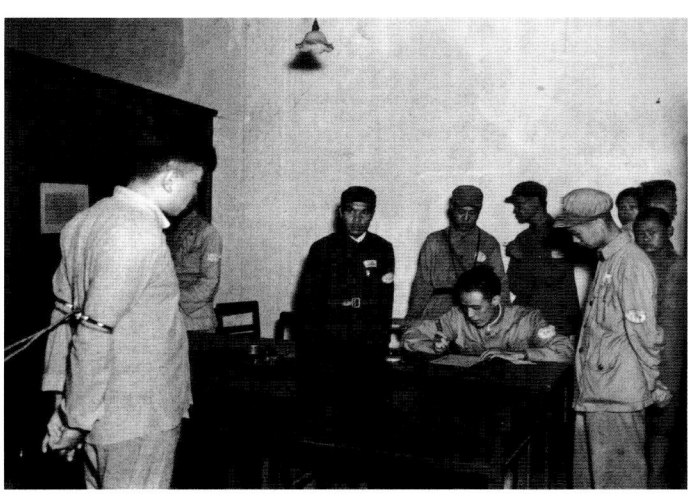

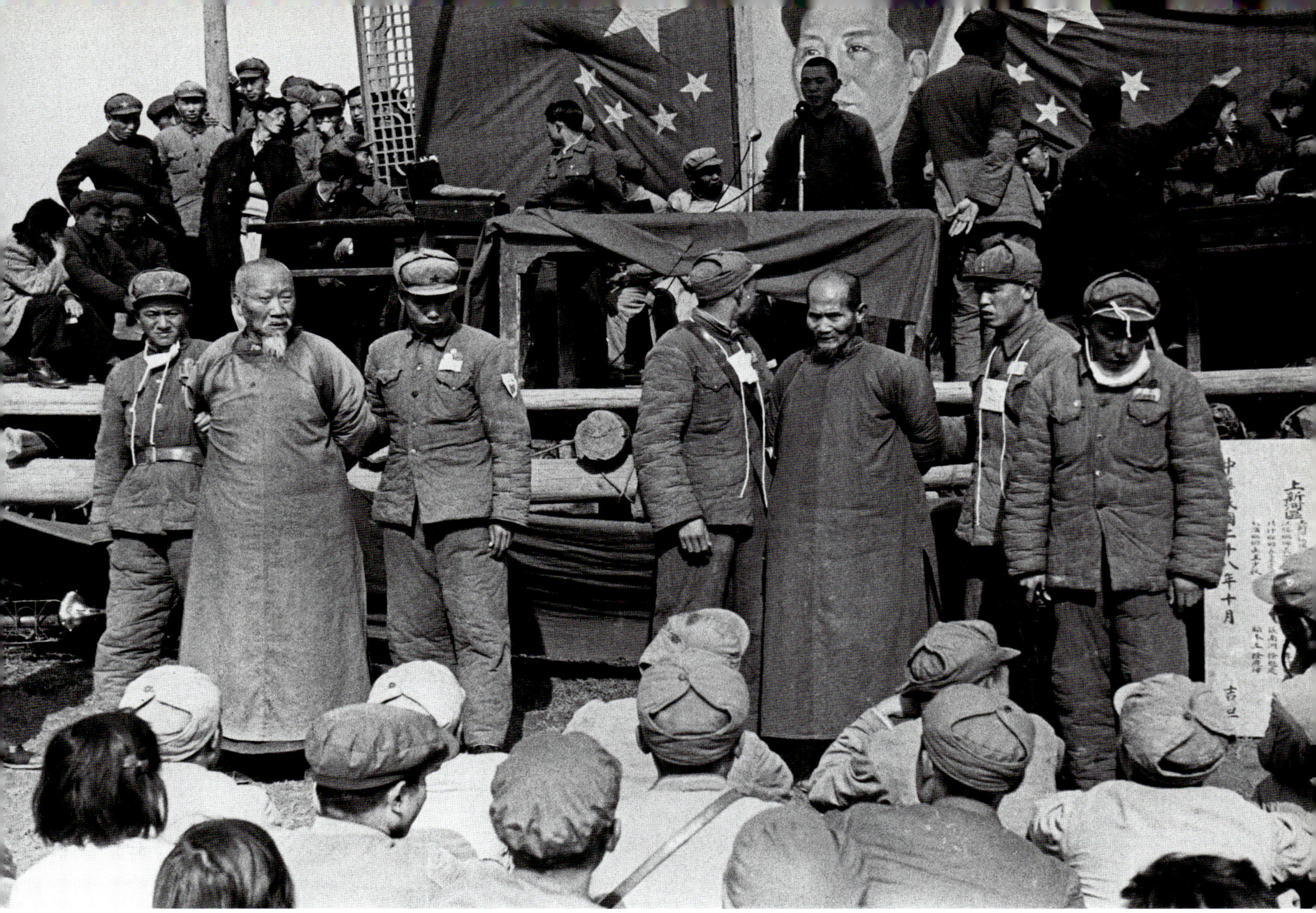

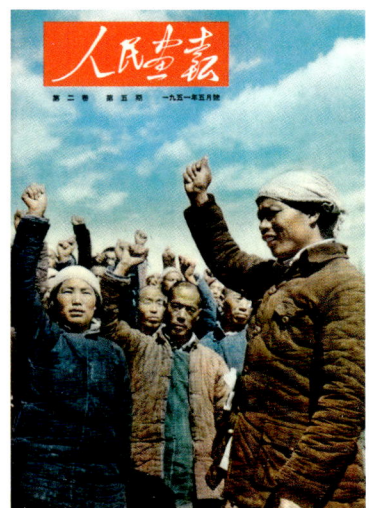

China Pictorial, May 1951

*Chinese peasants at a rally promoting
land reform*

↑ *and pp. 122/123*
Anon., 1952

*In 1950, a land-reform campaign was launch-
ed nationwide, and continued until the end
of 1952. "Reform" meant seizing land from
those who owned it, and redistributing it
amongst the poor. Community meetings
were held to denounce the landlord's exploitation of the peasants. Here, landlords
in Jiangsu province are brought before
the people and denounced for exploiting
the peasants on their land. Many landlords
were sentenced to death.*

*1950 wurde eine landesweite Kampagne zur
Landreform angestoßen und bis Ende 1952
weitergeführt. „Reform" bedeutete, Land
seinen Besitzern wegzunehmen und es an
arme Bauern zu verteilen. In den Gemeinden
hielt man Versammlungen ab, auf denen
die Ausbeutung der Bauern durch die Grundbesitzer angeprangert wurde. Hier werden
Grundbesitzer in der Provinz Jiangsu vor das
Volk gestellt und der Ausbeutung der Bauern
auf ihrem Land angeklagt. Viele Grundbesitzer wurden von den Volksgerichten zum
Tod verurteilt und hingerichtet.*

*En 1950, une campagne de réforme agraire
fut lancée dans tout le pays et se poursuivit
jusqu'à la fin de 1952. «Réforme» signifiait
saisir la terre de ceux qui la possédaient et
la redistribuer aux paysans pauvres. Des
réunions furent organisées pour dénoncer
l'exploitation des paysans par les propriétaires
terriens. Ici, des propriétaires de la province
du Jiangsu sont présentés aux gens et dénoncés pour leur exploitation. De nombreux
propriétaires furent exécutés au nom des
tribunaux populaires.*

*"Chinese are intuitively always active first in sizing up
the person next to them."*

*„Chinesen sind intuitiv immer damit beschäftigt,
als Erstes die Person unmittelbar neben sich abzuschätzen."*

*« Intuitivement, les Chinois commencent toujours par évaluer
la personne qui est à côté d'eux. »*

LIANG SUMIN (1893–1988), philosopher and author

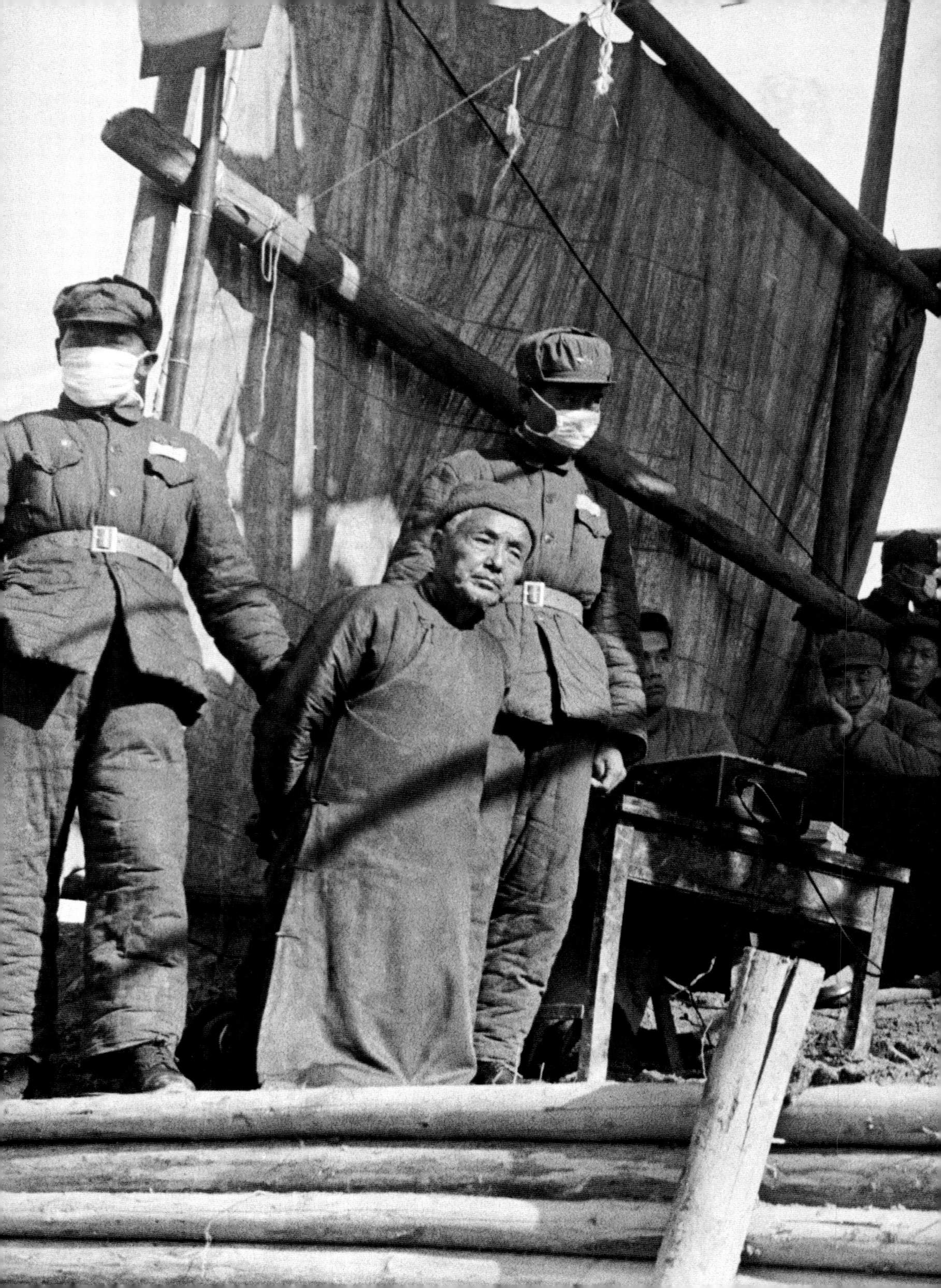

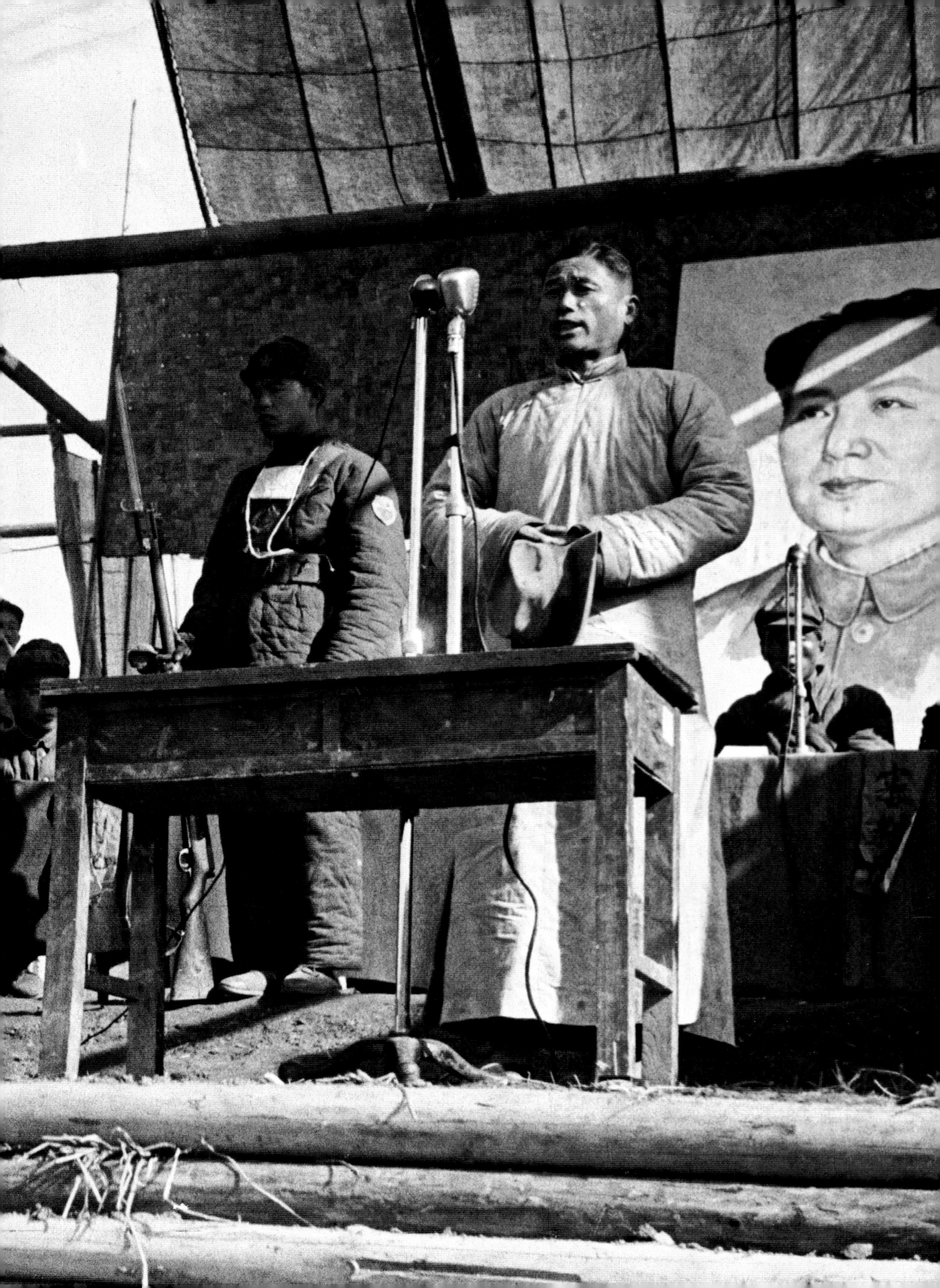

"The vase says: I'm worth a thousand hammers.
The hammer says: I've smashed a hundred vases.
The artisan says: I've made a thousand hammers.
The master says: I've killed a hundred artisans.
The hammer says: I've bludgeoned one master to death.
The vase says: I now contain that master's ashes."

„Die Vase sagt: Ich bin tausend Hämmer wert.
Der Hammer sagt: Ich habe hundert Vasen zertrümmert.
Der Handwerker sagt: Ich habe tausend Hämmer gemacht.
Der Meister sagt: Ich habe hundert Handwerker getötet.
Der Hammer sagt: Ich habe einen Meister zu Tode geprügelt.
Die Vase sagt: Ich berge jetzt die Asche des Meisters."

« Le vase dit : je vaux des milliers de marteaux.
Le marteau dit : j'ai brisé des centaines de vases.
L'artisan dit : j'ai fabriqué des milliers de marteaux.
Le maître dit : j'ai tué des milliers d'artisans.
Le marteau dit : j'ai frappé à mort un maître.
Le vase dit : je contiens maintenant les cendres de ce maître. »

GU CHENG (1956–1993), modern poet, essayist, and novelist

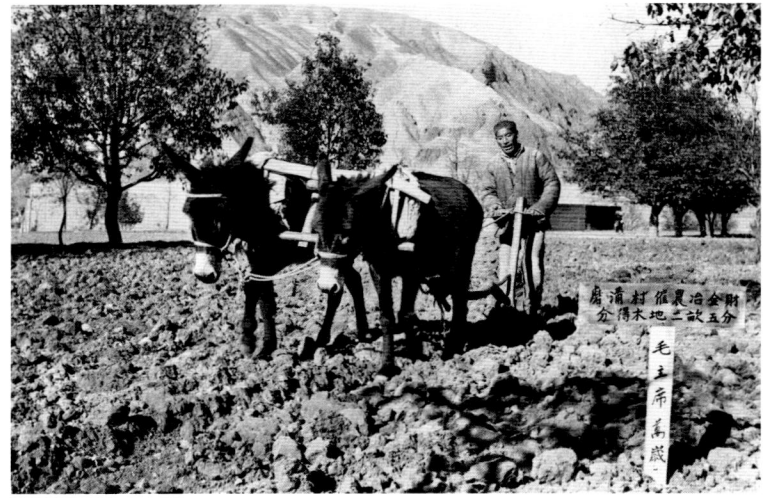

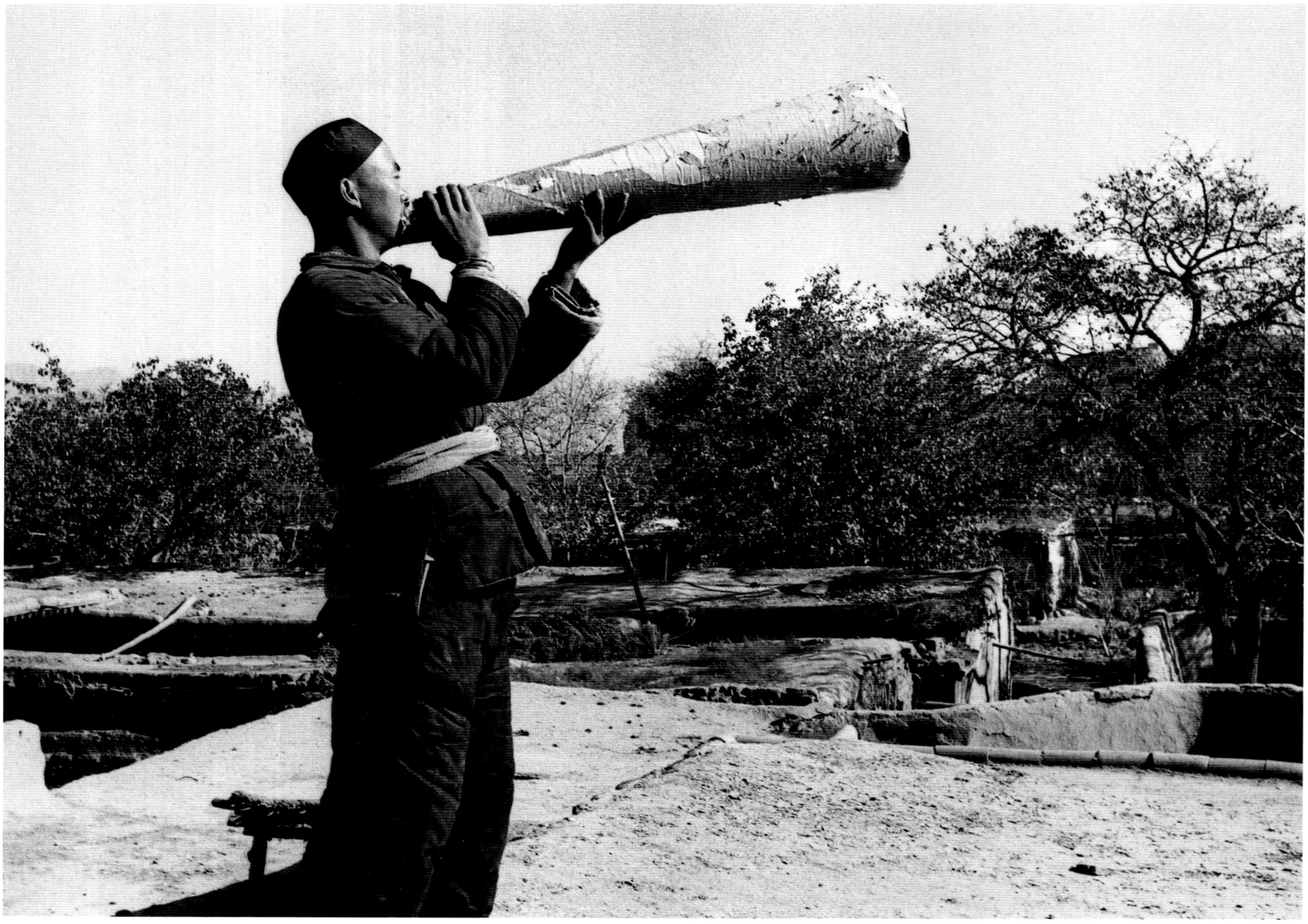

←

Ru Suichu, 1951

Photographer Ru Suichu was assigned by the northwestern CCP publicity department to document the process of land reform in Minghe county, northwestern Qinghai province. The sign on the right says, "Long live Chairman Mao."

Der Fotograf Ru Suichu erhielt von der Abteilung für Öffentlichkeitsarbeit der KPCh des Nordwestens den Auftrag, den Prozess der Landreform im Kreis Minghe, in der nordwestlichen Provinz Qinghai, zu dokumentieren. Auf dem Schild heißt es: „Lang lebe der Vorsitzende Mao".

Le photographe Ru Suichu avait été chargé par le département de propagande du Parti communiste chinois (PCC) du Nord-Ouest de photographier le processus de la réforme agraire dans le canton de Minghe au nord-ouest de la province du Qinghai. À droite, un panneau vertical proclame «Longue vie au Président Mao ».

↙

Ru Suichu, 1951

A peasant in Qinghai province uses a handmade megaphone to urge other peasants to take part in the land reforms. Launched in 1950, land reforms were a nationwide campaign in which the State confiscated the property of the landlords, and redistributed it amongst the poor.

Ein Bauer in der Provinz Qinghai benutzt ein selbstgefertigtes Megafon, um andere Bauern zur Teilnahme an der Landreform aufzufordern. Bei der 1950 gestarteten Landreform handelte es sich um eine landesweite Kampagne, bei der der Staat Land und Eigentum von Grundbesitzern konfiszierte und an die Bauern umverteilte.

Un paysan de la province du Qinghai utilise un porte-voix de fabrication personnelle pour inciter d'autres paysans à participer à la réforme agraire. Lancée en 1950, elle fut l'objet d'une campagne nationale qui vit l'État confisquer les terres et les biens des propriétaires terriens et les redistribuer aux paysans.

↓

Ru Suichu, 1951

A former landlord's possessions are confiscated by peasants, and put on public display in Qinghai province.

In der Provinz Qinghai wird das von Bauern konfiszierte Eigentum eines Grundbesitzers öffentlich zur Schau gestellt.

Les biens d'un ancien propriétaire de la province du Qinghai sont confisqués par les paysans et exposés en public.

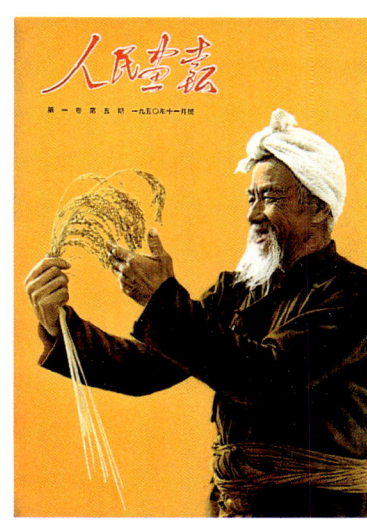

China Pictorial, November 1950
Better harvests made possible by land reform

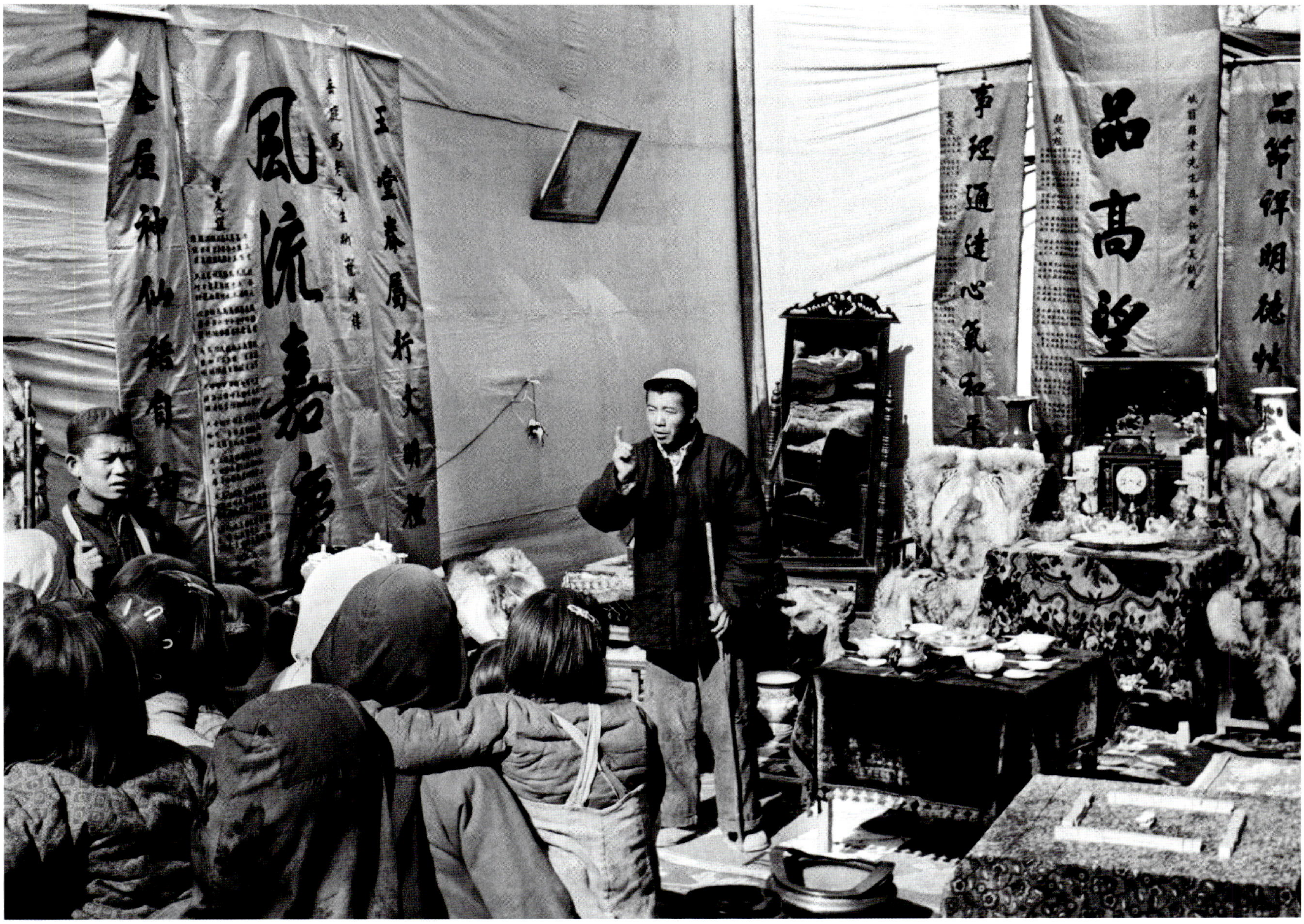

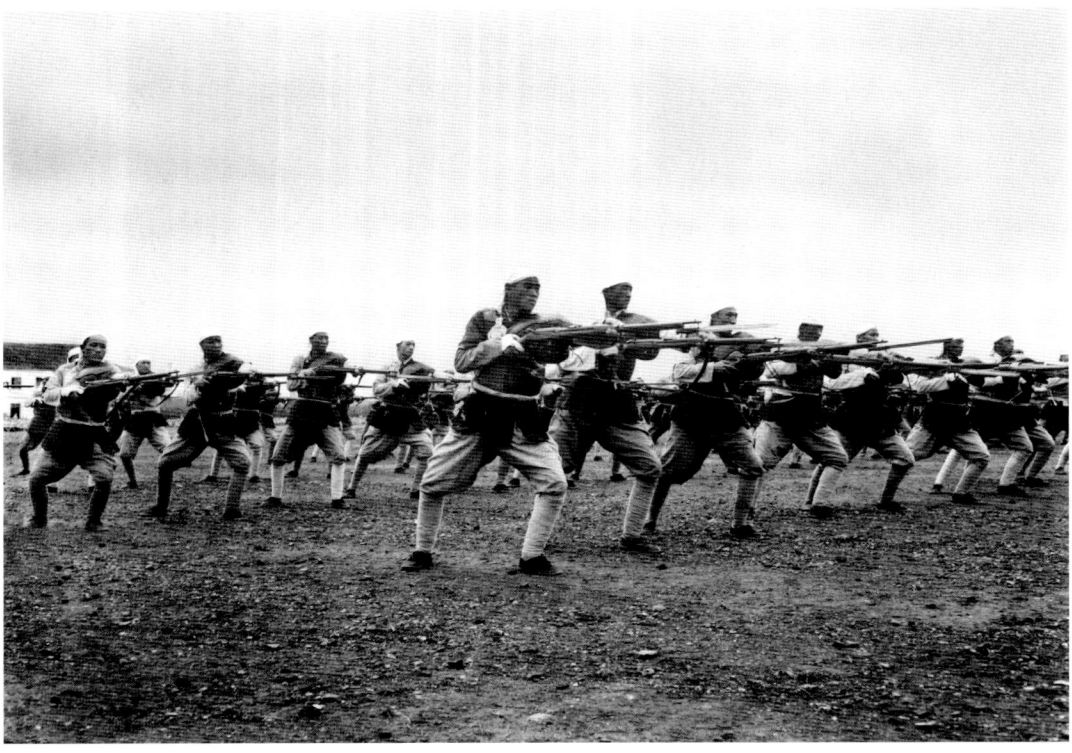

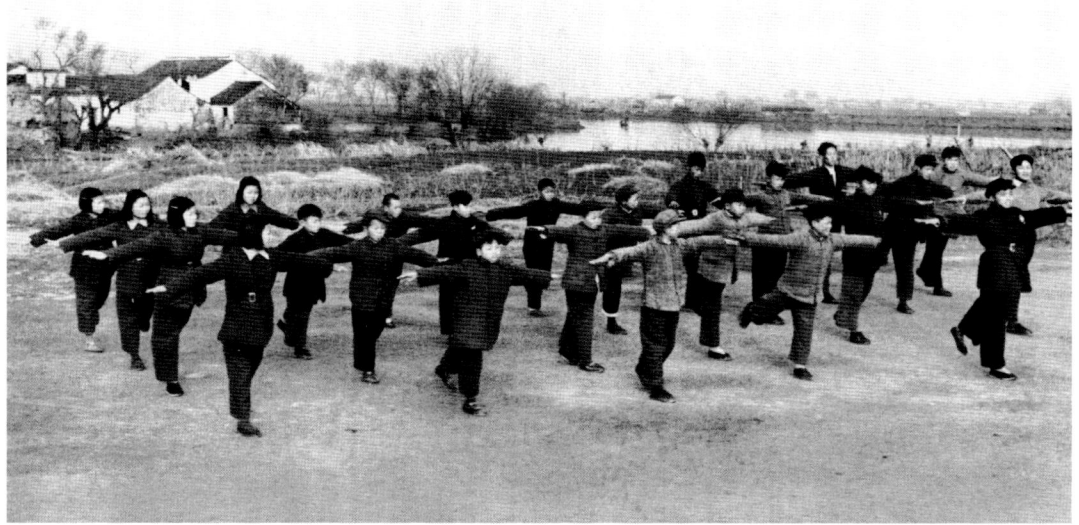

"Many people still find it hard to believe that the Chinese are really Communists and that Mao Zedong for all his dramatic efforts, can possibly change the character of a unique and historically great people."

„Vielen Leuten fällt es immer noch schwer zu glauben, dass die Chinesen wirklich Kommunisten sind und dass es Mao Zedong mit all seiner spektakulären Anstrengungen gelingen könnte, den Charakter eines so einzigartigen, historisch großen Volkes zu ändern."

« Beaucoup ont encore du mal à croire que les Chinois sont réellement communistes et que Mao Zedong, quels que soient ses spectaculaires efforts, puisse vraiment changer le caractère de ce peuple unique à la si grande histoire. »

LUCIAN W. PYE (1921–), Professor of Political Science, Massachussetts Institute of Technology, 1972

↑↑
Anon. (provided by Xiao Zhuang)

With their bayonets raised, PLA solidiers take part in a martial-arts competition in Nanjing in 1951.

Soldaten der Volksbefreiungsarmee nehmen 1951 mit aufgepflanzten Bajonetten an einem Wettbewerb asiatischer Kampfsportarten in Nanjing teil.

Des soldats de l'APL chargent, baïonnette au canon, lors d'un concours d'arts martiaux à Nankin en 1951.

↑
Xiao Zhuang, 1953

High-school students take morning exercise in a school yard in Nanjing.

Oberschüler bei der Morgengymnastik auf einem Schulhof in Nanjing.

Les élèves d'un lycée de Nankin pratiquent la gymnastique matinale dans une cour.

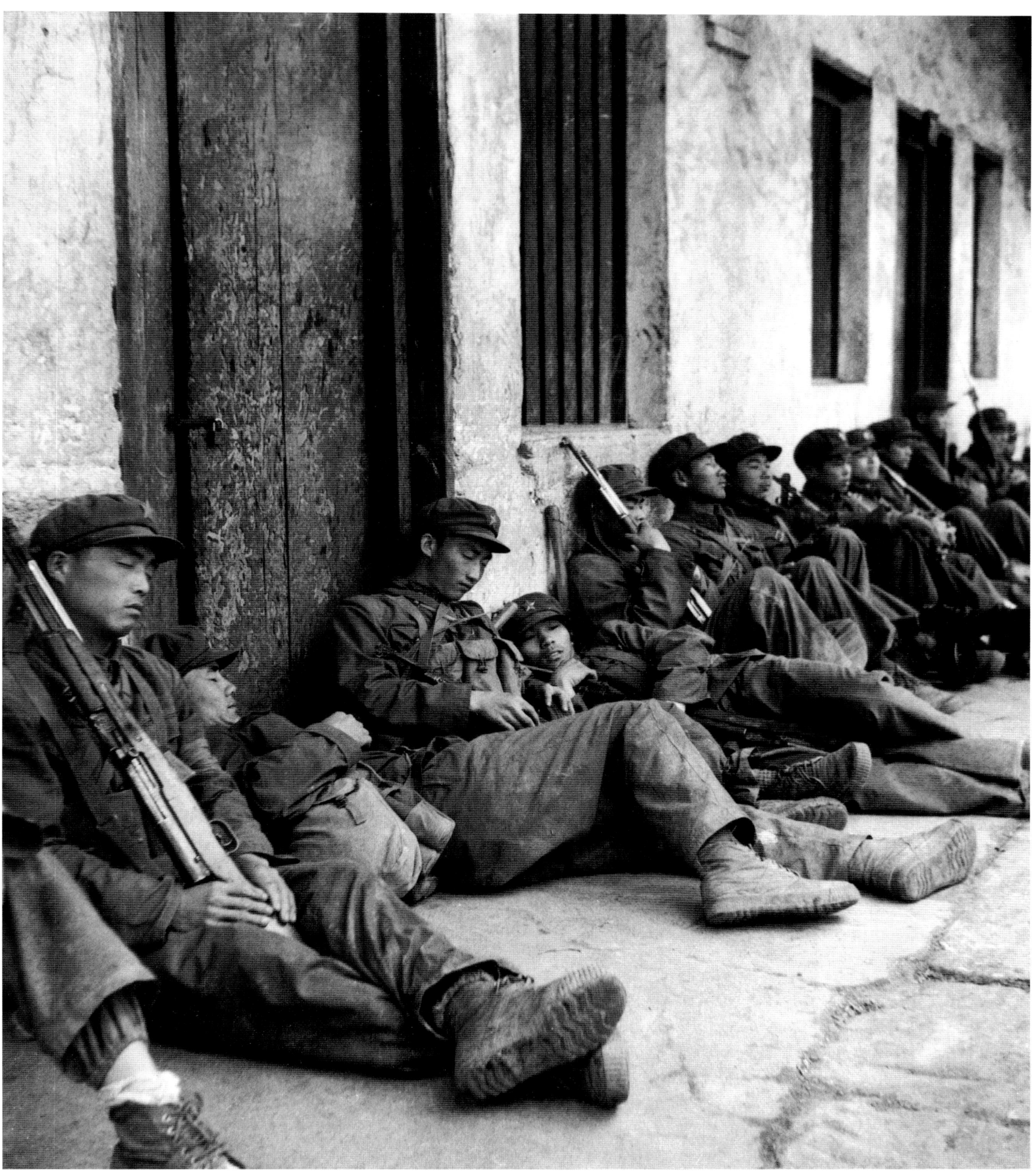

↑
Wang Shilong, 1954

Soldiers of the Chinese army repose, exhausted, on a street in Henan province, following a series of military drills. The PLA had a standing order that forbade soldiers to enter private homes.

Nach dem militärischen Drill ruhen sich erschöpfte Soldaten der chinesischen Armee an einer Straße in der Provinz Henan aus. Die Volksbefreiungsarmee hatte einen Dauerbefehl, der es den Soldaten verbot, Privathäuser zu betreten.

Des soldats de l'armée chinoise épuisés se reposent dans une rue (province du Hénan), après une série d'exercices. L'APL n'avait pas le droit d'entrer dans les maisons privées.

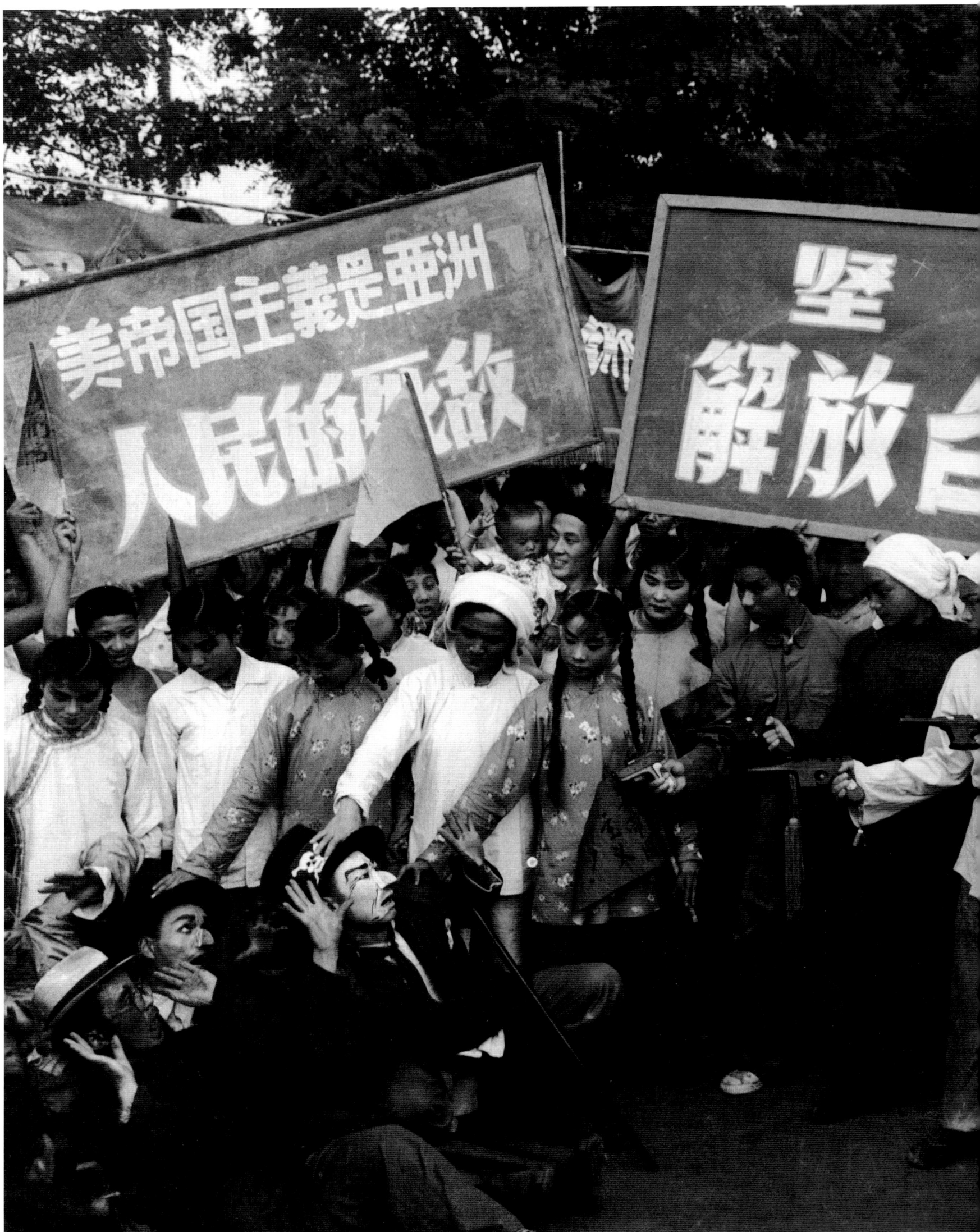

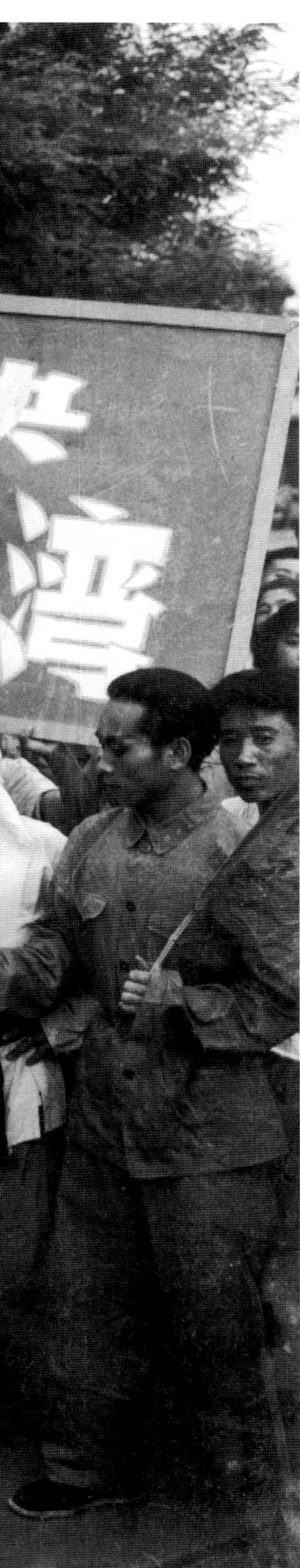

"The Chinese people have already stored up enough anger—the result of being trampled underfoot by the powerful. But they don't turn against the powerful; rather, they take out their anger on the weak. The most immediate example would be the way that soldiers and bandits don't fight one another, but both oppress the unarmed, common people."

„Das chinesische Volk hat schon genug Zorn aufgestaut – das Resultat der Tatsache, dass die Mächtigen auf ihm herumtrampeln. Aber sie wenden sich nicht gegen die Mächtigen; stattdessen lassen sie ihre Wut an den Schwachen aus. Die naheliegendste Möglichkeit wäre, dass Soldaten und Banditen sich nicht bekämpfen, sondern gemeinsam die unbewaffneten einfachen Leute unterdrücken."

« Les Chinois ont accumulé tant de colère pour avoir été piétinés par les puissants ! Mais ils ne se retournent pas contre ces puissants, et déchaînent plutôt leur colère contre les faibles. L'exemple le plus direct en est la façon dont les soldats et les bandits ne se battent pas les uns contre les autres, mais oppressent le petit peuple désarmé. »

LU XUN (Zhou Shuren, 1881–1936), short-story writer, essayist, poet, the "father of modern Chinese literature"

↓
Xiao Zhuang, 1951

Local residents in Jiangsu province stage a protest against the U.S. during the Korean War as China fights U.S. forces on Korean soil. At the head of the rally, protesters wear mock U.S., Japanese, and South Korean army uniforms.

Bewohner in der Provinz Jiangsu veranstalten während des Koreakriegs, als China auf koreanischem Boden gegen US-Truppen kämpfte, einen Protestmarsch gegen die USA. An der Spitze des Zugs tragen Protestierende Pseudouniformen der amerikanischen, japanischen und südkoreanischen Truppen.

Des habitants d'une ville de la province du Jiangsu participent à une manifestation contre les États-Unis pendant la guerre de Corée, alors que les forces chinoises affrontent les troupes américaines. En tête de la manifestation, des protestataires portent de faux uniformes américains, japonais et sud-coréens.

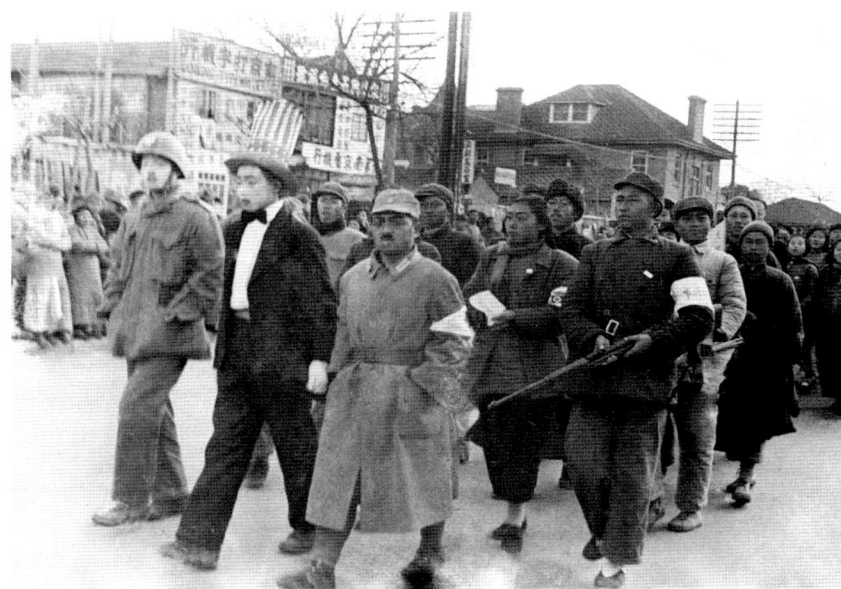

←
Wang Shilong, 1954

Street theater in Zhengzhou, Henan province: Chinese residents perform propaganda skits denouncing U.S. interference in Korea, and simultaneously pledge to "Liberate Taiwan." China fought U.S. forces in Korea in 1951, and won—in spite of the fact that Soviet leader Joseph Stalin reneged on his promise to provide air cover for the Chinese troops in North Korea. Mao feared a U.S. retaliation that would bring the war to the Chinese mainland.

Straßentheater in Zhengzhou, Provinz Henan. Chinesische Studenten führen Propagandasketche auf, die das Vorgehen der USA in Korea verurteilen und gleichzeitig dazu aufrufen, „Taiwan zu befreien". 1951 kämpfte China gegen die amerikanischen Truppen in Korea und siegte – obwohl der soujetische Führer Stalin sein Versprechen, die chinesischen Truppen in Korea aus der Luft zu unterstützen, nicht einlöste. Mao fürchtete Vergeltungsmaßnahmen der USA, die den Krieg auf das chinesische Festland tragen würden.

Théâtre de rue à Zhengzhou, province du Hénan : les habitants jouent des pièces de propagande dénonçant l'intervention américaine en Corée et simultanément réclament de « Libérer Taïwan. » La Chine combattit victorieusement les Américains en Corée en 1951 bien que Staline soit revenu sur sa promesse d'assurer une couverture aérienne aux troupes chinoises. Mao craignait des représailles américaines en Chine même.

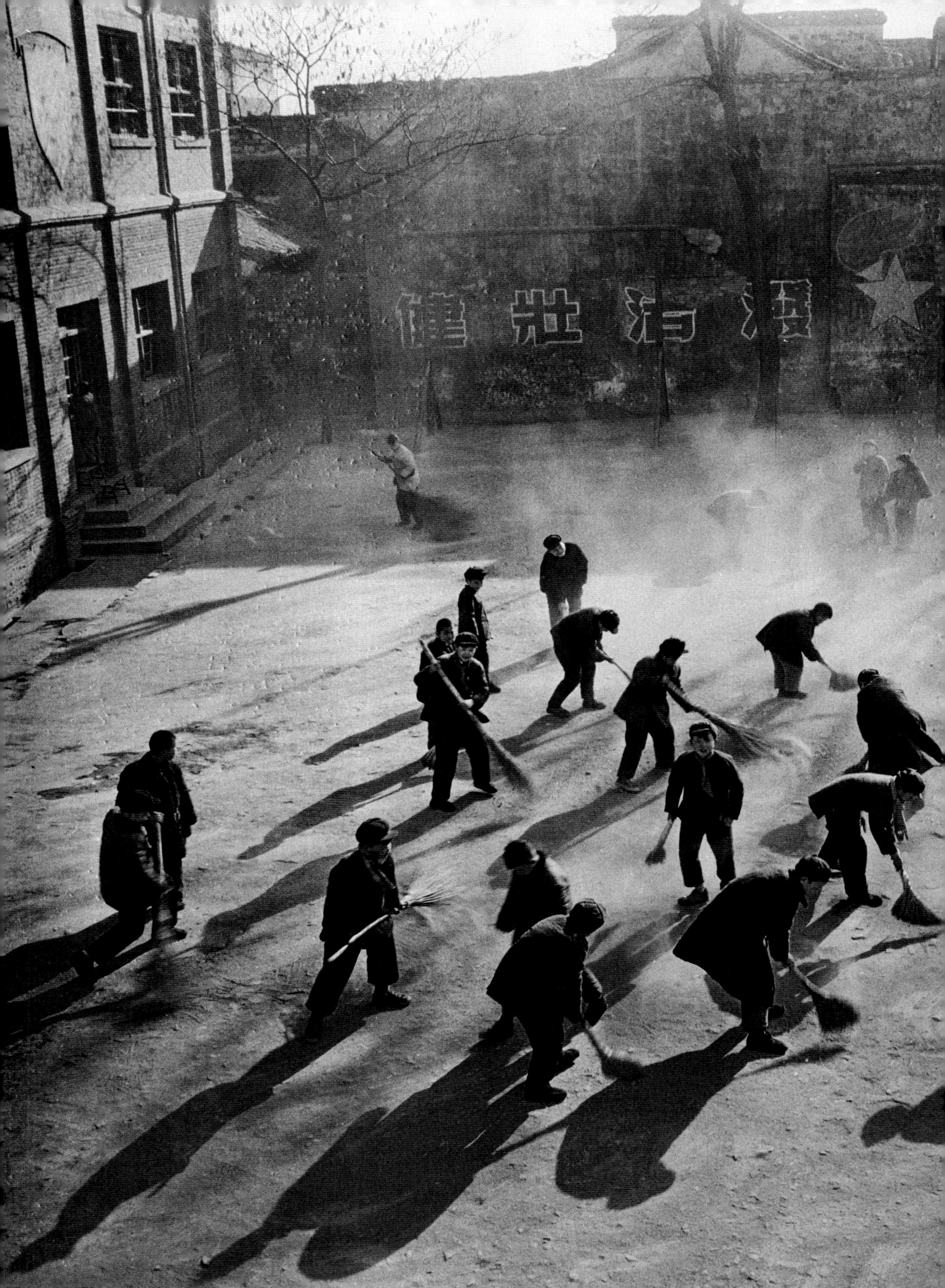

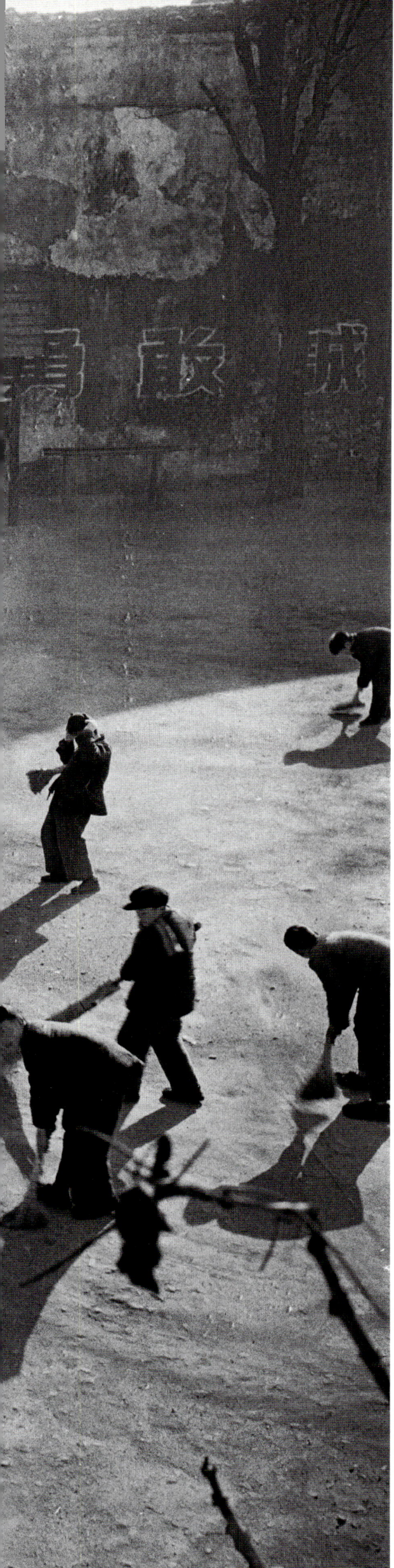

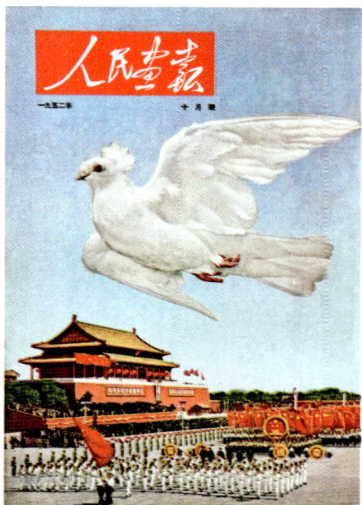

China Pictorial, October 1952

Photo montage of a peaceful dove flying over the Tiananmen square, Beijing

←
Xiao Zhuang, 1954

Students sweep the yard of their school in Nanjing.

Schüler kehren den Hof ihrer Schule in Nanjing.

Des élèves balaient la cour de leur école à Nankin.

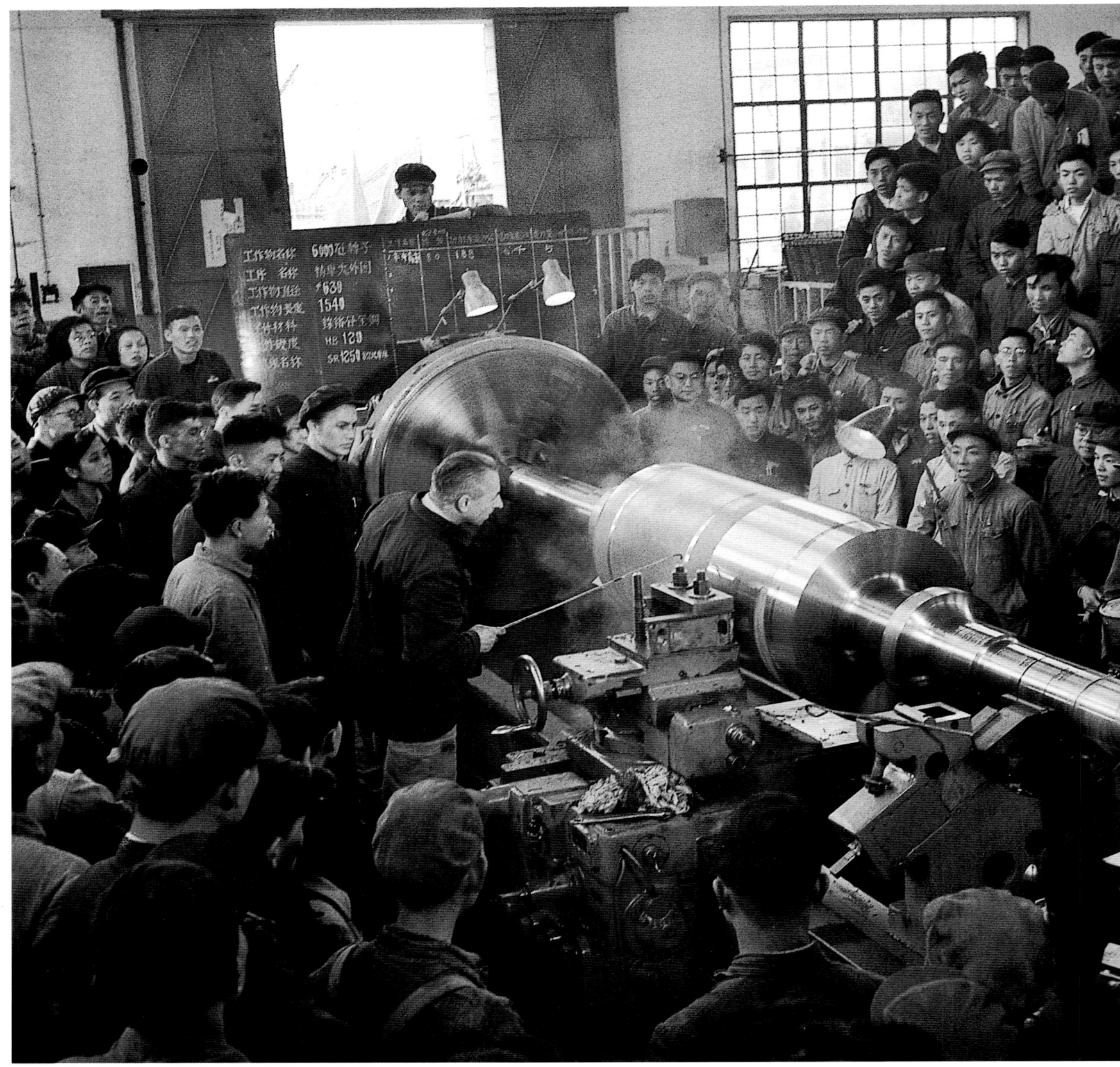

↑

Zuo Jiazhong, 1955

When the Chinese Communist Party assumed power, its relationship with the West was tense. Its natural ally was the Soviet Union, which provided China with industrial technology and support. During the first five-year plan (1953–57), the Soviet Union assisted China in achieving 154 industrial projects. Here, industrial workers in Shanghai listen to a Soviet expert at a machinery factory. Bilateral relations cooled right down in the summer of 1960, precipitated by Mao's break with Stalin's policies. Ultimately, when Mao voiced criticism of the Soviets' "revisionism," and its technical experts in China, as interfering with China's domestic affairs in 1963, the USSR withdrew its experts, along with precious blueprints for factories and industrial production lines. Decades later, a number of factory projects remained unfinished and inoperable.

Als die KPCh die Macht ergriff, waren ihre Beziehungen zum Westen angespannt. Ihr natürlicher Verbündeter war die Sowjetunion, die China mit Industrietechnik und Know-how versorgte. Während des ersten Fünfjahresplans (1953–1957) half die Sowjetunion China bei der Ausführung von 154 Industrieprojekten. Hier lauschen Industriearbeiter in einer Maschinenfabrik in Shanghai einem sowjetischen Experten. Die bilateralen Beziehungen kühlten im Sommer 1960 stark ab, beschleunigt von Maos Bruch mit Stalins Politik. Als Mao schließlich Kritik am sowjetischen „Revisionismus" übte und 1963 die sowjetischen Techniker beschuldigte, sich in chinesische Angelegenheiten einzumischen, zog die UdSSR ihre Experten samt den wertvollen Blaupausen für Fabriken und Produktionsanlagen ab. Noch Jahrzehnte später war eine Reihe von Fabriken unfertig und nicht funktionsfähig.

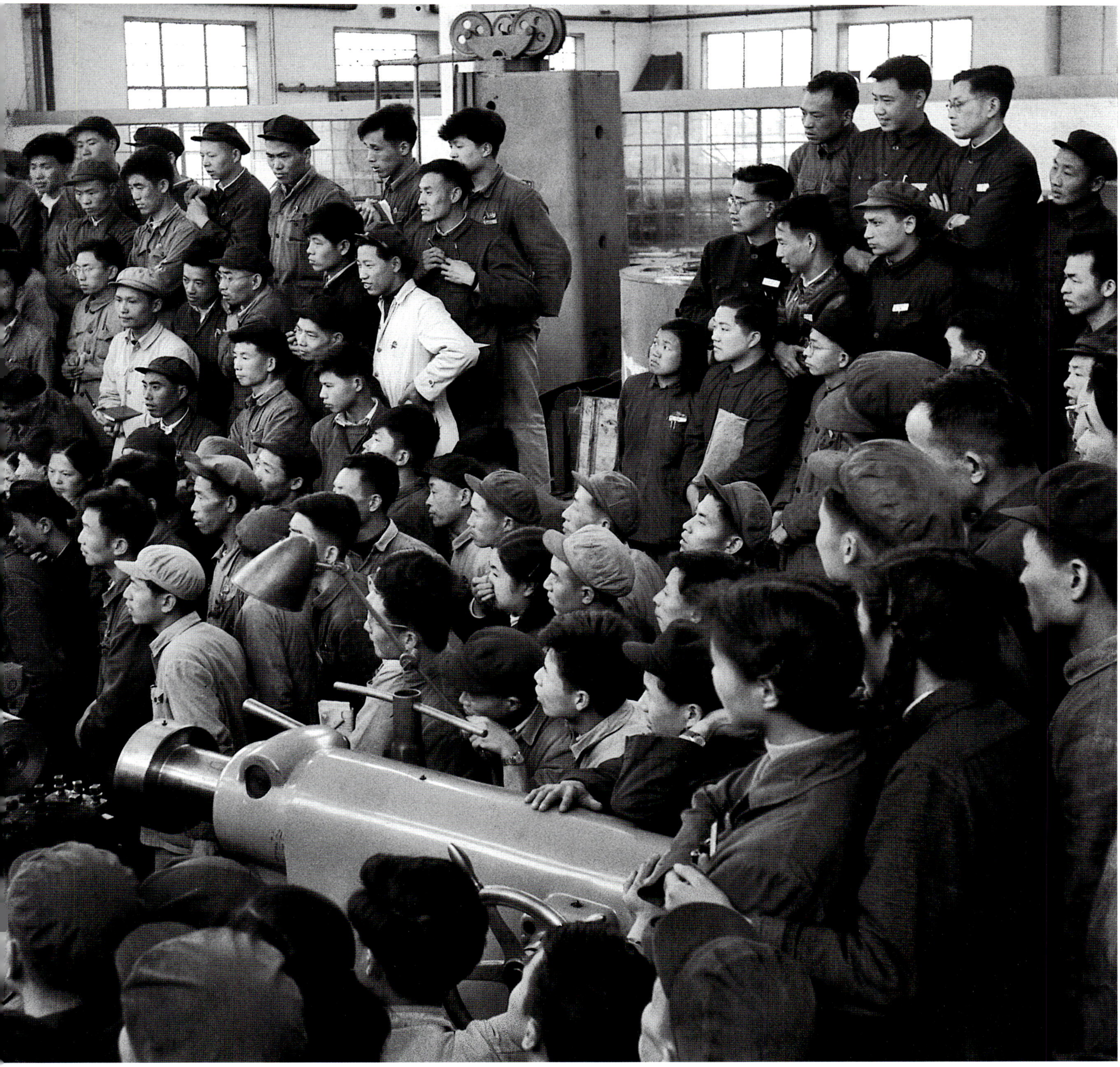

Les relations du Parti communiste chinois avec l'Occident étaient tendues lorsqu'il prit le pouvoir. Son allié naturel était l'Union soviétiques qui lui apportait ses technologies et son soutien. Pendant le premier plan quinquennal (1953–57), l'URSS aida la Chine à réaliser 154 projets industriels. Ici, des ouvriers de Shanghai écoutent un expert soviétique dans une fabrique de machines-outils. Les relations bilatérales se rafraîchirent à l'été 1960, lorsque Mao rompit avec la politique de Staline. Finalement, lorsque Mao émit des critiques contre le « révisionnisme » soviétique et ses experts techniciens qui interféraient avec les intérêts chinois en 1963, l'URSS retira ses experts emportant avec eux les plans des usines et des chaînes de production. Des décennies plus tard, un certain nombre de projets industriels restaient encore inachevés et inutilisables.

→

China Pictorial, January 1959

Chinese scientists at work in a laboratory

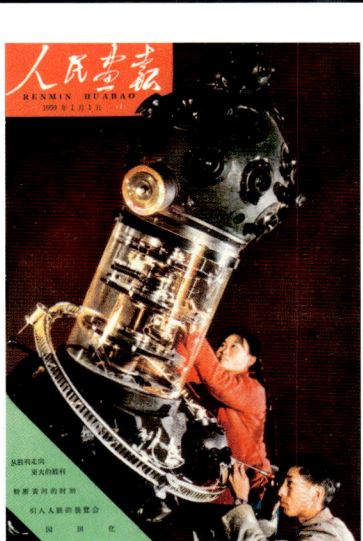

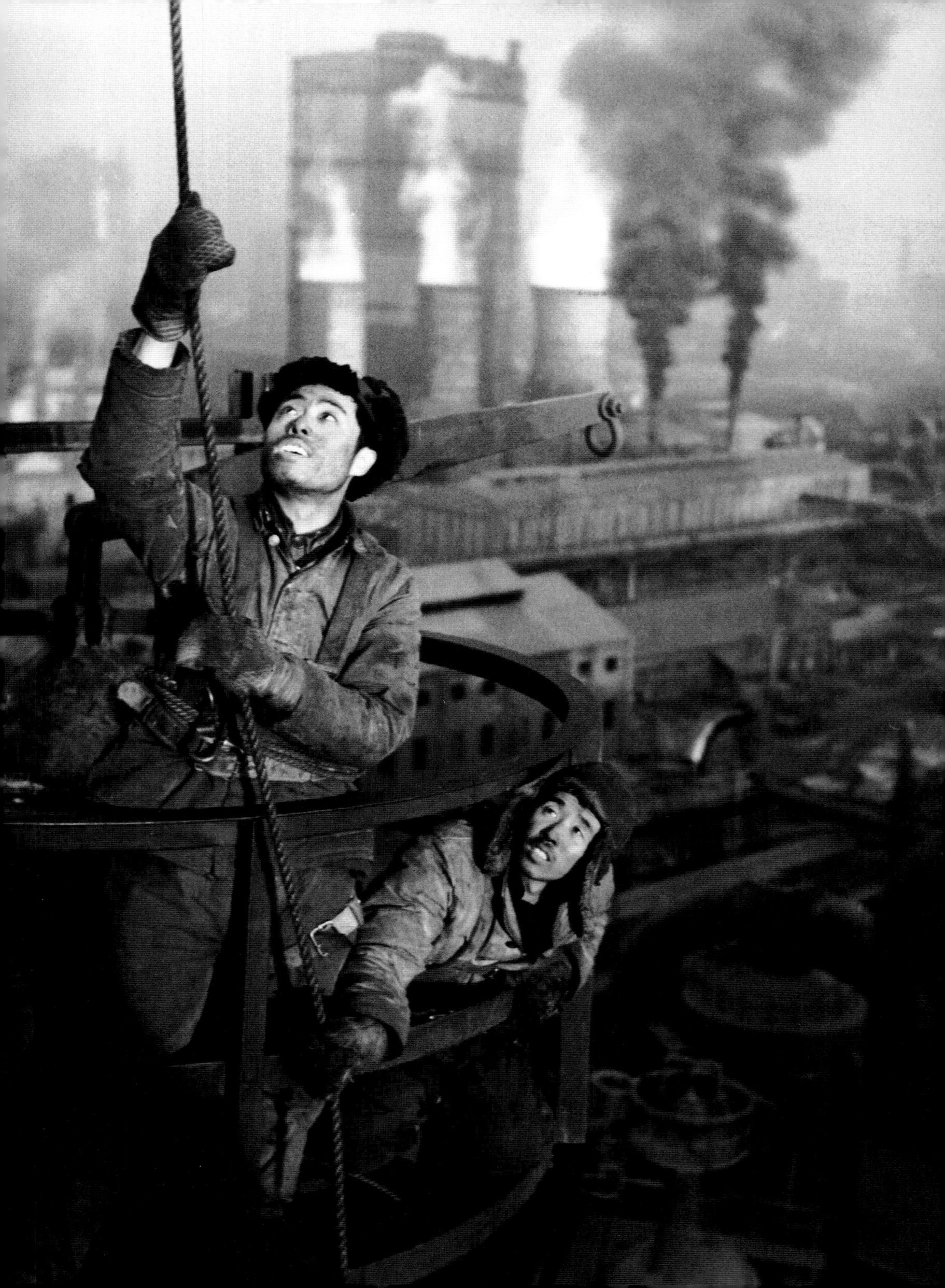

←
Cai Shangxiong, 1954

Workers at the Anshan Steel Refinery in Liaoning province. Liaoning is one of three provinces that make up China's northeast region, which, with the assistance of the Soviet Union, and several facilities left behind by the invading Japanese army, was the nation's industrial base until the early 1990s.

Arbeiter in der Stahlhütte von Anshan, Provinz Liaoning. Liaoning ist eine der drei Provinzen, die den Nordosten Chinas bilden, ein Gebiet, das bis Anfang der 1990er-Jahre dank der Sowjetunion und mehrerer von der japanischen Besatzungsmacht zurückgelassener Einrichtungen die industrielle Kernregion Chinas darstellte.

Ouvriers de l'aciérie d'Anshan dans la province du Liaoning. Cette région du nord-est fut l'une des trois provinces, qui, grâce à l'assistance soviétique et plusieurs installations laissées par les Japonais, constituèrent le principal foyer industriel chinois jusqu'au début des années 1990.

pp. 136/137
Wang Shilong, 1958

Workers in Henan province labor at a row of homemade furnaces, attempting to make steel from scrap metal. To comply with Mao's vision of "overtaking the level of steel production in Great Britain in 15 years," anything metal, from galvanized iron roofs, nails, bolts, hinges, barbed wire, locks to even small tractors, were thrown into the makeshift smelters.

Arbeiter in der Provinz Henan mühen sich vor einer Reihe von provisorischen Schmelzöfen, wo sie versuchen, aus Metallresten Stahl zu kochen. In dem Versuch, Maos Vision zu entsprechen, derzufolge man „den Stand der Stahlproduktion in Großbritannien in 15 Jahren übertreffen werde", landete alles Metallene, angefangen bei verzinkten Eisendächern, Nägeln, Riegeln, Scharnieren, Stacheldraht und Schlössern, bis hin zu kleinen Traktoren in den behelfsmäßigen Öfen.

Des ouvriers du Hénan travaillent sur une ligne de hauts fourneaux ruraux pour transformer en acier des métaux de récupération. Pour mettre en œuvre la vision de Mao – dépasser le niveau de la production d'acier de la Grande-Bretagne en 15 ans –, tous les métaux possibles, toitures galvanisées, clous, boulons, charnières, fil de fer barbelé et même petits tracteurs étaient fondus dans ces fours de fortune.

"The Chinese, then, would point up through the drizzle to where a factory was coughing up smoke at the end of a muddy lane; where bent-over people were dragging wooden carts loaded with pig iron. And they would say, 'This was once all prostitutes and bad elements and gambling and bright lights and dance halls.' You were supposed to be glad this sinful frivolity was gone, and fascinated by the factories, but I just sighed."

„Die Chinesen deuteten dann durch den Nieselregen auf die Stelle, wo am Ende eines schlammigen Weges eine Fabrik Rauch ausspuckte; wo gebückte Menschen mit Roheisen beladene Holzkarren zerrten und sagten: ,Da waren früher Prostituierte und üble Typen und Glücksspiel und helle Lichter und Tanzsäle.' Man erwartete von uns, froh darüber zu sein, dass diese sündige Frivolität verschwunden war und fasziniert von den Fabriken, aber ich seufzte nur."

« Les Chinois pointaient du doigt à travers la bruine vers une usine qui crachait de la fumée à l'extrémité d'une allée boueuse, où des gens courbés en deux tiraient sur des chariots de bois chargés de fonte. Ils ajoutaient : 'Jadis, il n'y avait là que des prostituées, de mauvais éléments, des lumières et des dancings.' Nous étions supposés montrer que nous étions heureux d'apprendre que cette coupable frivolité avait disparu et être fascinés par les usines, mais je me contentai de soupirer. »

PAUL THEROUX (1941–), travel writer and novelist, 1989

→
Xiao Zhuang, 1958

The large-scale production of iron and steel was part of the Great Leap Forward. All sectors of the national economy gave way to steel production and people from all walks of life were mobilized to contribute: here the people of Yangzhou, Jiangsu province, work at producing steel. Peasants nationwide reportedly abandoned the collective farms to put their energy into making steel. With the fields left untended, by the summer of 1959, insufficient grain was harvested to sustain the people through the winter of 1960. The man-made famine that resulted caused the death of upwards of 30 million people. At the end of 1958, it was announced that just over 11 million tons of steel and 13.6 million tons of pig iron had been produced, surpassing the goal of 10.7 million tons. In reality, only eight million tons of steel were up to the required standard; the rest was unusable.

Die umfangreiche Produktion von Eisen und Stahl war Teil des Großen Sprungs nach vorn. An die Spitze sämtlicher nationaler Wirtschaftszweige trat die Produktion von Stahl, und Menschen aus allen Schichten der Gesellschaft wurden aufgerufen, ihren Teil beizutragen: Hier sind zwei Männer in Yangzhou, Provinz Jiangsu, mit der Herstellung von Stahl beschäftigt. Aus dem ganzen Land wird von Bauern berichtet, die ihre Kommunen verlassen, um ihre Kräfte für die Stahlproduktion einzusetzen. Wegen der brachliegenden Felder fiel im Sommer 1959 die Getreideernte zu gering aus, um die Bevölkerung über den Winter 1960 zu ernähren. Die daraus folgende, von Menschen verursachte Hungersnot führte zum Tod von über 30 Millionen Chinesen. Ende 1958 wurde verkündet, dass über 11 Millionen Tonnen Stahl und 13,6 Millionen Tonnen Rohstahl produziert wurden und damit die Zielvorgabe von 10,7 Millionen Tonnen übertroffen wurde. In Wahrheit entsprachen nur acht Millionen Tonnen der erforderlichen Qualität, der Rest war unbrauchbar.

La production de fer et d'acier à grande échelle est un des objectifs du Grand bond. Elle a la priorité sur tous les autres secteurs de l'économie nationale et des Chinois de toutes origines professionnelles sont mobilisés pour y contribuer, comme ces habitants de Yangzhou, province du Jiangsu. Partout, des paysans abandonnent les fermes collectives pour fabriquer de l'acier. Les champs sont délaissés et, à l'été 1959, les récoltes de céréales sont insuffisantes pour alimenter la population pendant l'hiver. Cette famine organisée provoque la mort de plus de 30 millions de personnes. Fin 1958, on annonça que la production d'acier avait dépassé 11 millions de tonnes, celle de fonte de fer de 13,6 millions, soit plus que l'objectif de 10,7 millions. En réalité, seuls 8 millions de tonnes étaient utilisables.

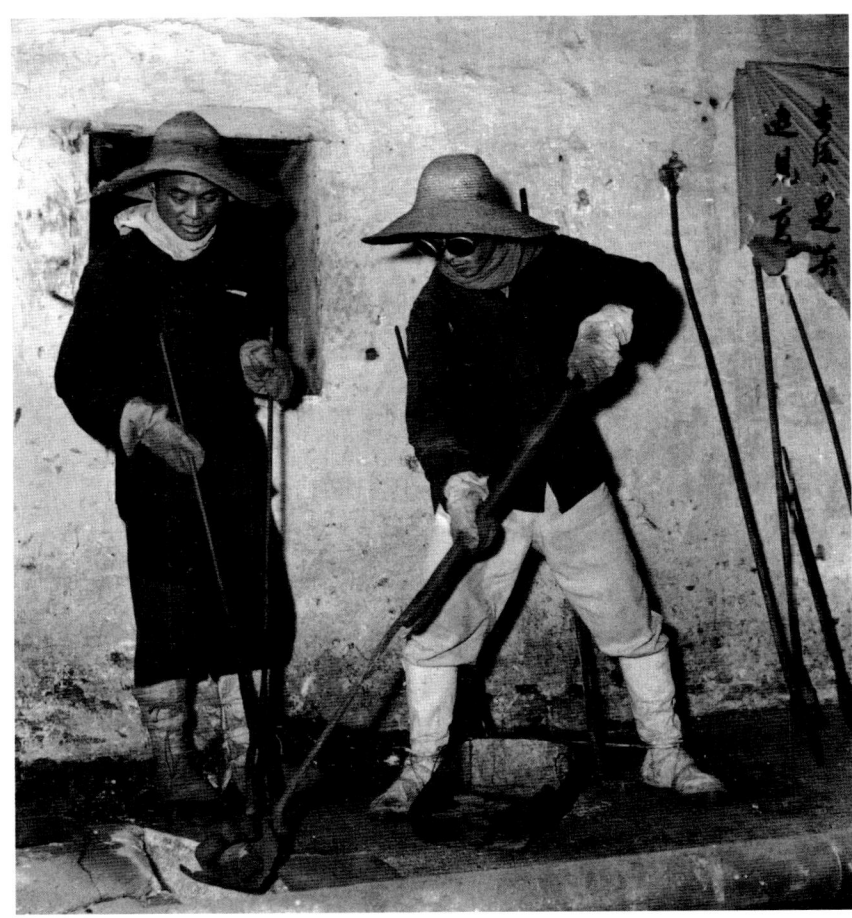

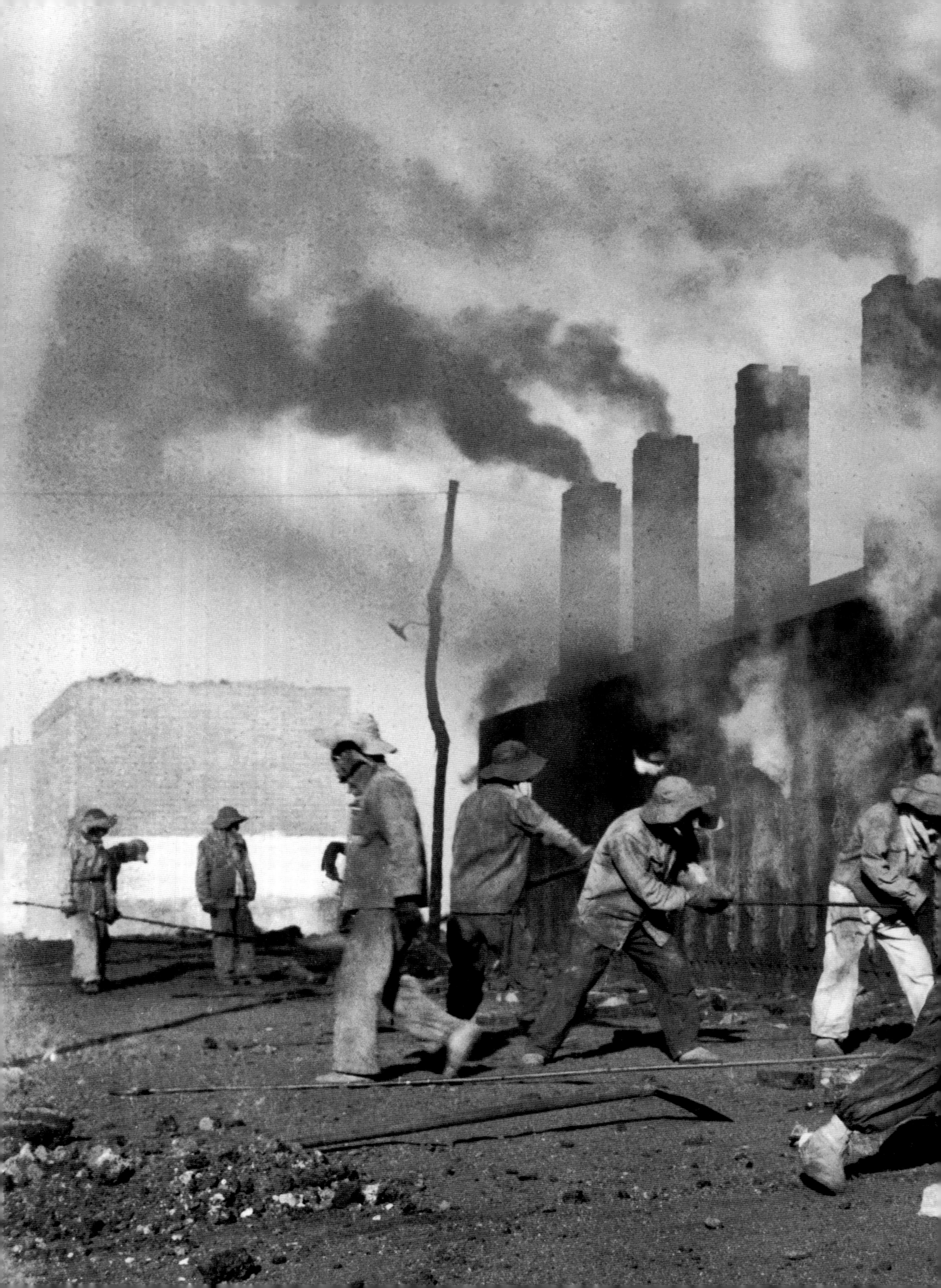

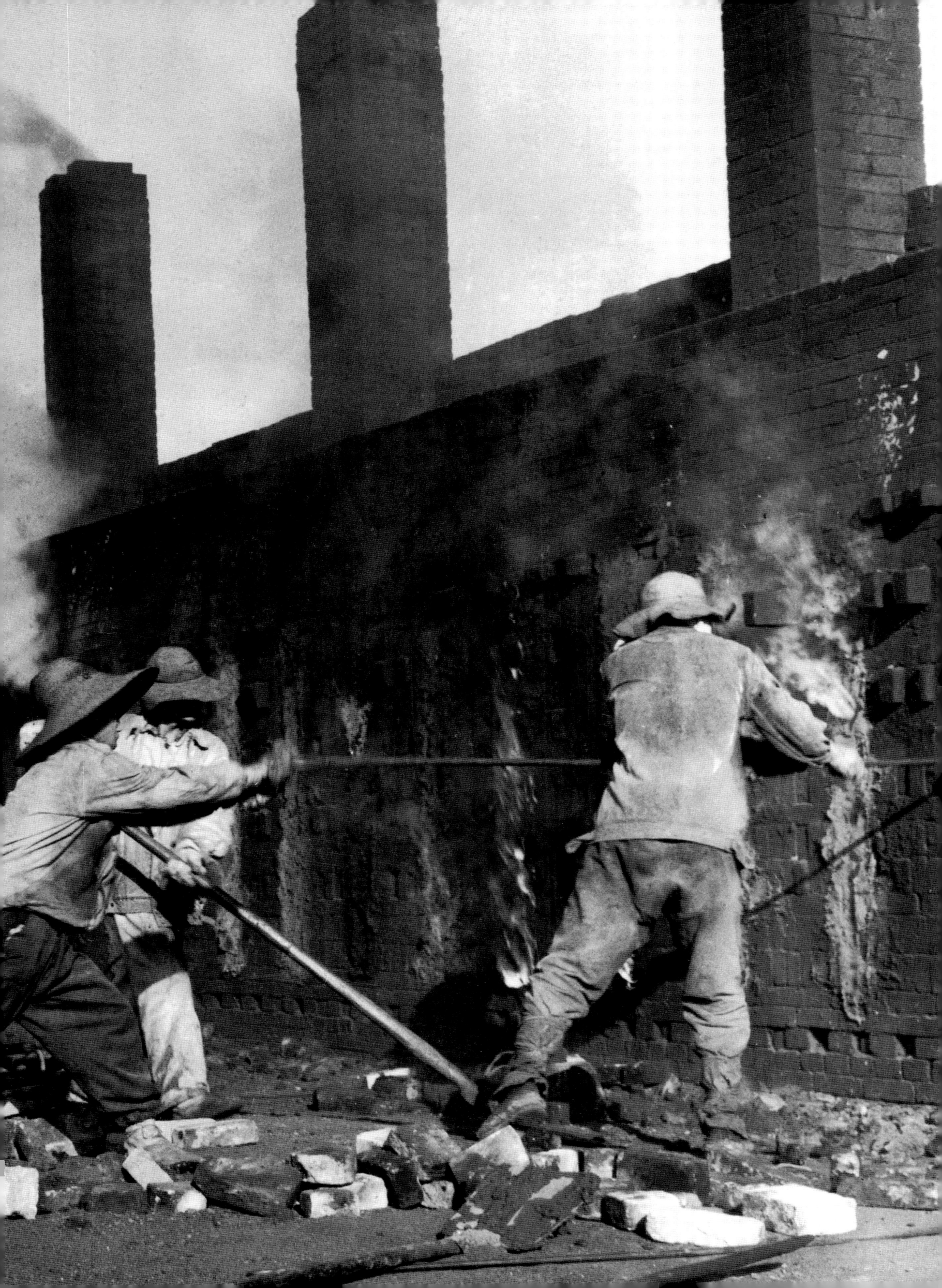

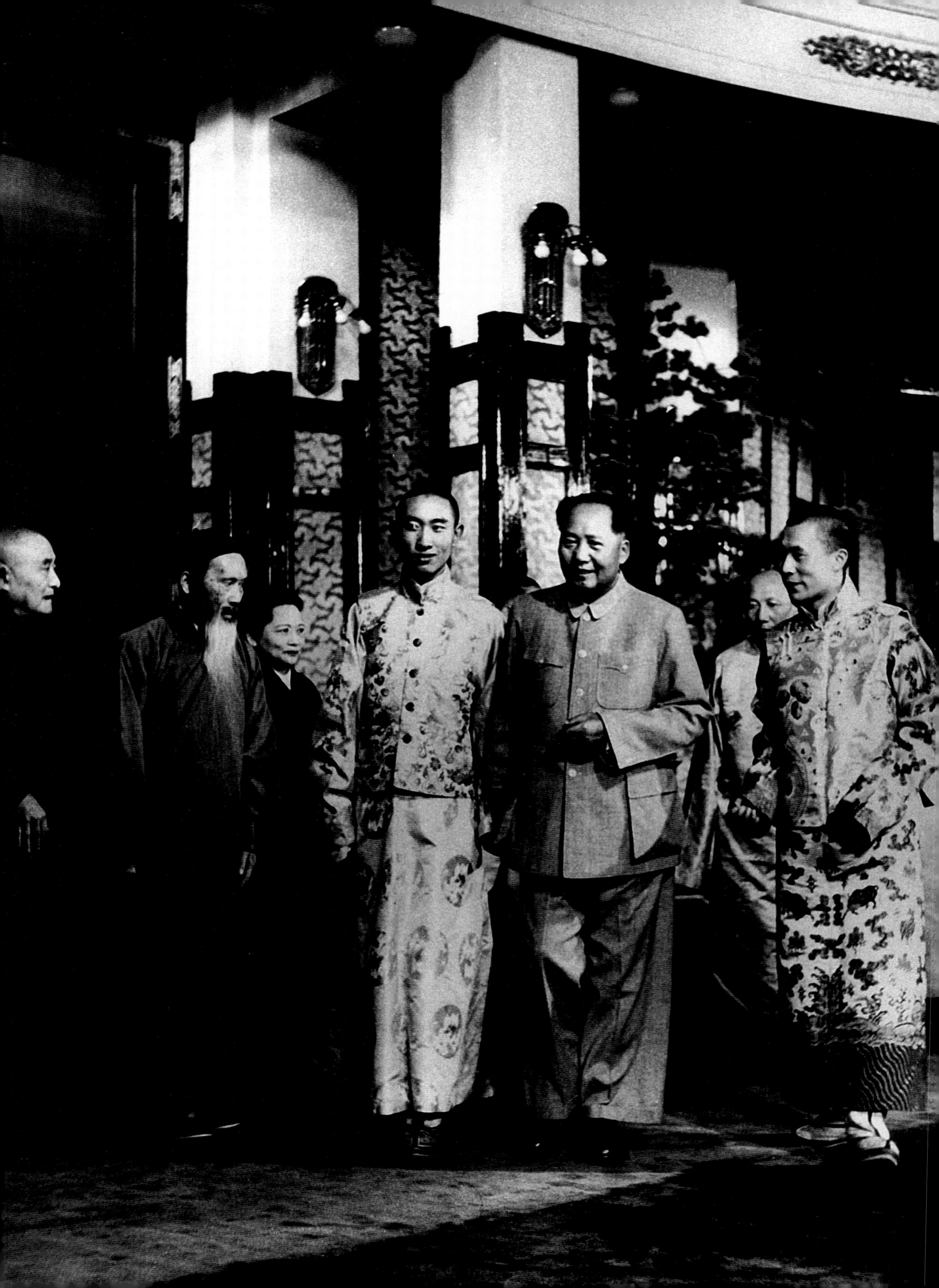

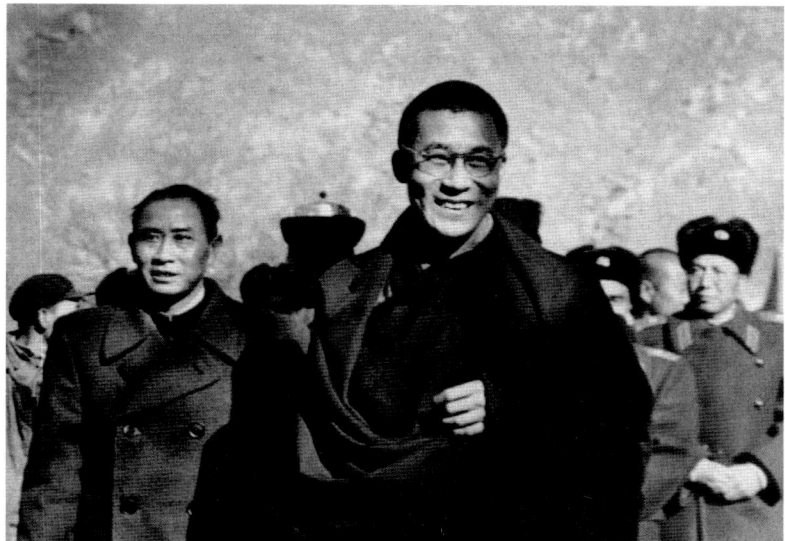

←
Yuan Kezhong, 1954

The Tibetan spiritual leader, the Dalai Lama, appears in public with the Chengdu military region political commissar (including jurisdiction over Tibet) Wang Jingwu (left) in Tibet, five years before fleeing to India with a number of his followers after a failed armed uprising against Chinese rule. The Dalai Lama remains in India to this day, and is a figure of controversy for Chinese leaders.

Der Dalai Lama, geistiger Führer der Tibeter, tritt in Tibet öffentlich mit Wang Jingwu (links vom Dalai Lama) auf, dem politischen Kommissar der Militärregion Chengdu, dem auch die Gerichtsbarkeit für Tibet untersteht. Fünf Jahre später flieht der Dalai Lama nach einem gescheiterten bewaffneten Aufstand gegen die chinesische Herrschaft mit einer Reihe von Anhängern nach Indien, wo der für die chinesische Führung unbequeme Tibeter bis heute lebt.

Le chef spirituel tibétain, le Dalaï-Lama, photographié en public avec le commissaire politique de la region militaire de Chengdu (qui avait juridiction sur le Tibet), Wang Jingwu (à gauche du Dalaï-Lama), au Tibet, cinq ans avant qu'il ne fuie en Inde avec quelques fidèles après un soulèvement armé manqué contre le pouvoir chinois. Le Dalaï-Lama vit encore en Inde et est devenu une figure de controverses pour le pouvoir chinois.

←
Hou Bo, 1954

Chairman Mao receives the Dalai Lama and the Panchen Lama, the two highest-ranking Tibetan spiritual leaders, in the Mao residence at Zhongnanhai, Beijing, as delegates of the first session of the First National People's Congress.

Der Vorsitzende Mao empfängt den Dalai Lama und den Panchen Lama, die beiden höchsten geistlichen Führer Tibets, die zur ersten Sitzung des Ersten Nationalen Volkskongresses als Delegierte geladen sind, in seiner Residenz in Zhongnanhai, Peking.

Le Président Mao reçoit le Dalaï-Lama et le Panchen-Lama, les chefs spirituels tibétains, dans sa résidence de Zhongnanhai, à Pékin. Tous deux étaient conviés comme délégués à la première session du Premier congrès national du peuple.

"There are no ancient laws in China under which the empire is governed in perpetuum… Whoever succeeds in getting possession of the throne, regardless of his ancestry, makes new laws according to his own way of thinking. His successors on the throne are obliged to enforce the laws which he promulgated as founder of the dynasty, and these laws cannot be changed without good reason…"

„Es gibt keine alten Gesetze in China, nach denen das Reich immerwährend regiert wird…Wer auch immer den Thron besteigt, wird ungeachtet seiner Vorfahren in Einklang mit seiner eigenen Denkungsart neue Gesetze erlassen. Seine Nachfolger auf dem Thron sind verpflichtet, die Gesetze anzuwenden, die er als Gründer der Dynastie verkündete, und diese Gesetze können nicht ohne schwerwiegende Gründe geändert werden…"

« En Chine, il n'existe pas de lois anciennes qui déterminent le gouvernement de la chose publique pour l'éternité… Celui qui réussit à prendre possession du trône édicte de nouvelles lois selon sa manière de penser. Ses successeurs sur le trône sont obligés d'appliquer les lois qu'il a promulguées en fondant la dynastie, et ces lois ne peuvent être changées sans une bonne raison… »

MATTEO RICCI (1552–1610), Jesuit missionary who spent most of his adult life in China

→
Anon. (photo provided by Liu Tingting)

Liu Shaoqi, president of the Chinese People's Republic (1959–68), with his daughter Liu Tingting, and his wife Wang Guangmei, in a photograph taken in 1956. Following three years of famine (1960–62), together with several other leaders, Liu Shaoqi initiated a series of measures to stabilize the economy. The initiative saw him accused of harboring "capitalist" inclinations and in 1968, Liu was formally expelled from the CCP. Weakened by physical abuse and denied medical treatment, he died in prison in 1969. He was posthumously rehabilitated in 1980.
"There is no such thing as a perfect leader either in the past or present, in China or elsewhere. If there is one, he is only pretending, like a pig inserting scallions into its nose in an effort to look like an elephant." Liu Shaoqi

Liu Shaoqi, Präsident der Volksrepublik China (1959–1968), mit seiner Tochter Liu Tingting und seiner Frau Wang Guangmei auf einem Foto von 1956. Nach drei Jahren Hungersnot (1960–1962) leitete Liu Shaoqi zusammen mit mehreren anderen Führern eine Reihe von Maßnahmen zur Stabilisierung der Wirtschaft in die Wege. Die Initiative brachte ihm eine Anklage wegen „kapitalistischer Tendenzen" ein, und 1968 wurde Liu offiziell aus der KPCh ausgeschlossen. Von körperlichen Misshandlungen und verweigerter medizinischer Behandlung geschwächt, starb Liu 1969 im Gefängnis. 1980 wurde er posthum rehabilitiert.
„Den perfekten Führer gibt es nicht, weder in der Vergangenheit noch in der Gegenwart, weder in China noch anderswo. Wenn es ihn gäbe, würde er sich nur verstellen, wie ein Schwein, dass sich Schalotten in den Rüssel steckt, um wie ein Elefant auszusehen." Liu Shaoqi

Liu Shaoqi, président de la république populaire de Chine (1959–1968) accompagné de sa fille Liu Tingting et de son épouse Wang Guangmei, en 1956. Après trois années de famine (1960–1962), Liu Shaoqi et d'autres responsables initièrent des mesures pour stabiliser l'économie. Son initiative lui valut d'être accusé de tendances « capitalistes » et, en 1968, il fut chassé du parti. Affaibli par des mauvais traitement et l'absence de soins, il mourut en prison en 1969. Il a été réhabilité en 1980.
« Le leader parfait n'existe pas, que ce soit dans le passé ou le présent, en Chine ou ailleurs. S'il y en avait un, il ne ferait que le prétendre, tel un cochon qui se met des échalottes dans les narines pour avoir l'air d'un éléphant. » Liu Shaoqi

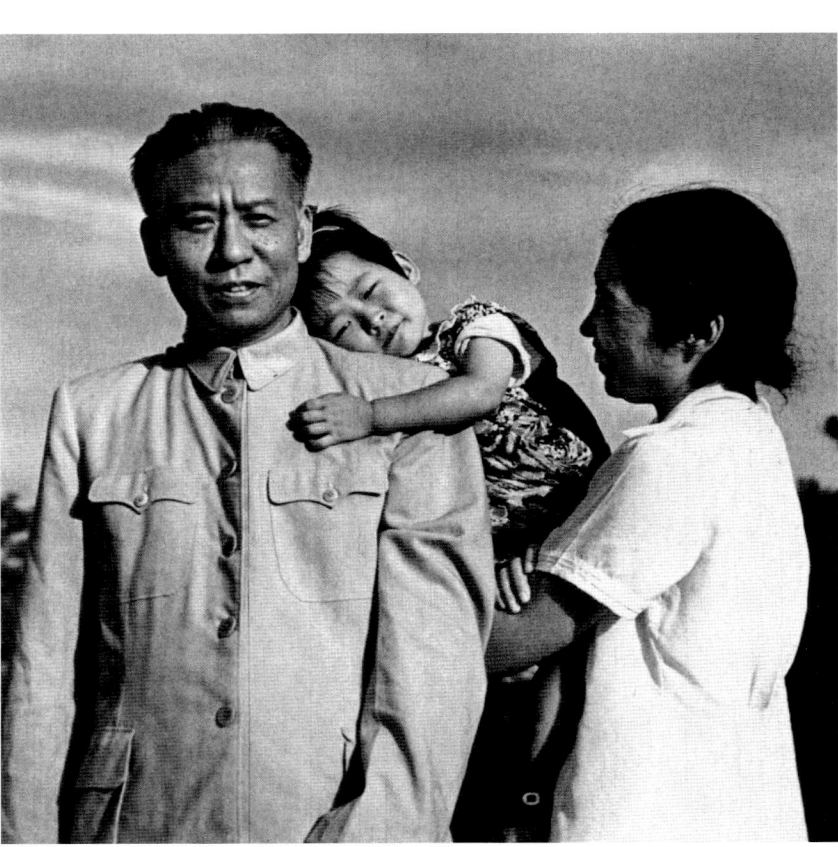

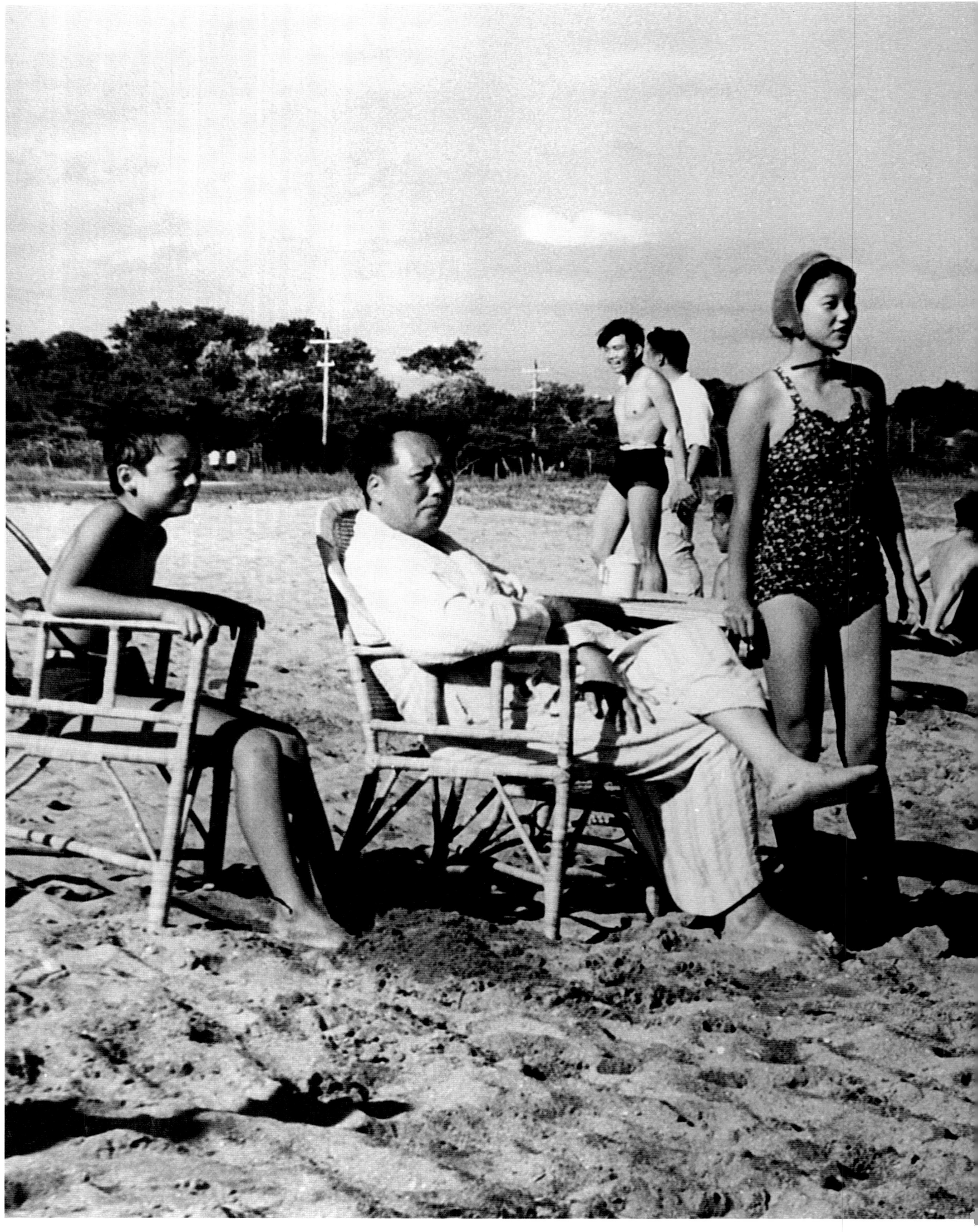

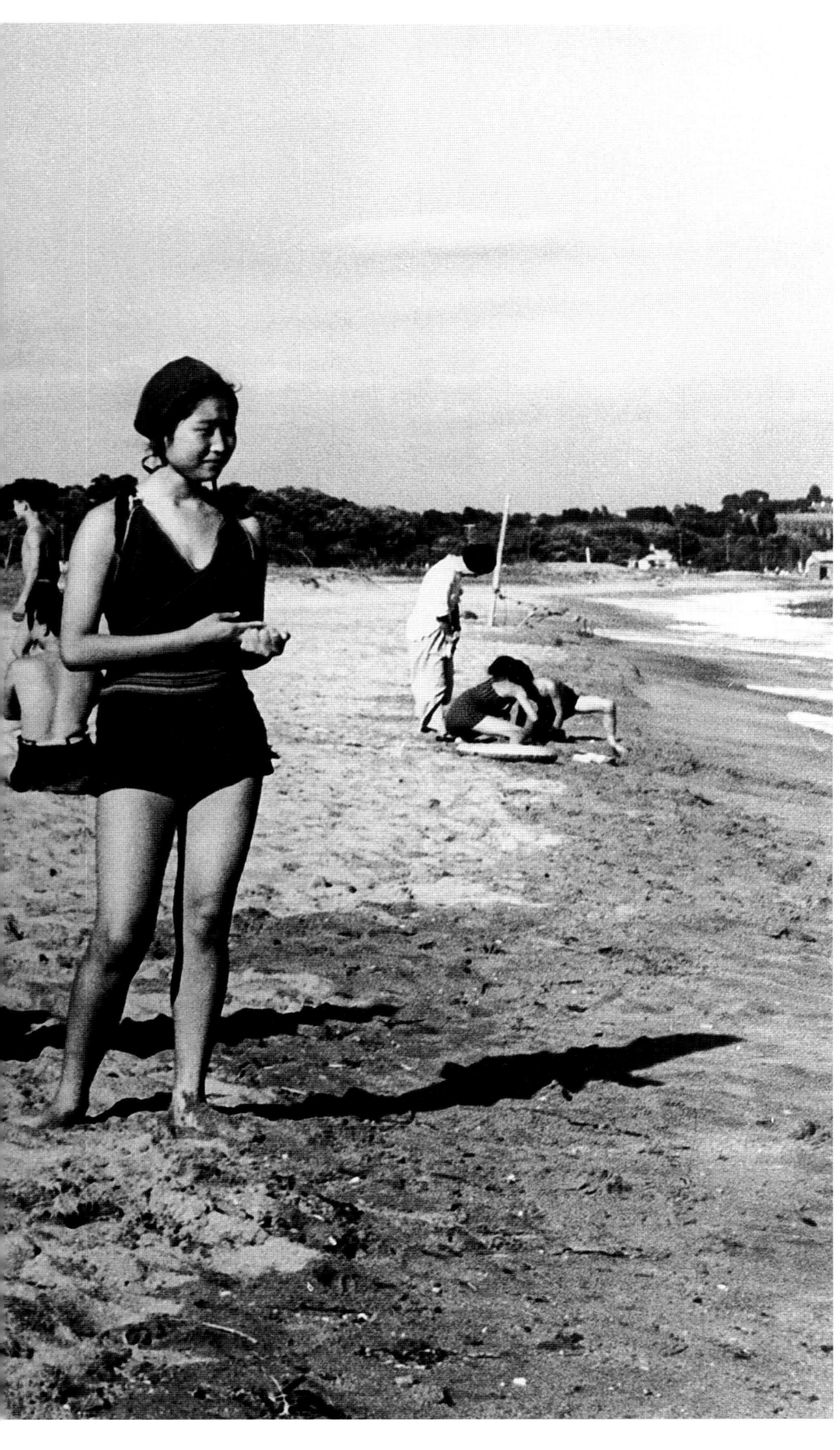

←
Hou Bo, 1954

Mao relaxes on the beach at Beidaihe together with his daughter in the company of other leaders' children.

Mao entspannt sich am Strand von Beidaihe mit seiner Tochter und in Begleitung der Kinder anderer führender Politiker.

Mao se détend sur la plage de Beidaihe en compagnie de sa fille et d'enfants de responsables du Parti.

pp. 142/143
Hou Bo, 1956

Mao swimming in the Yangtze river at Wuhan, June 1956.

Mao schwimmt im Jangtse bei Wuhan, Juni 1956.

Mao nagant dans le Yang-Tsé à Wuhan, juin 1956.

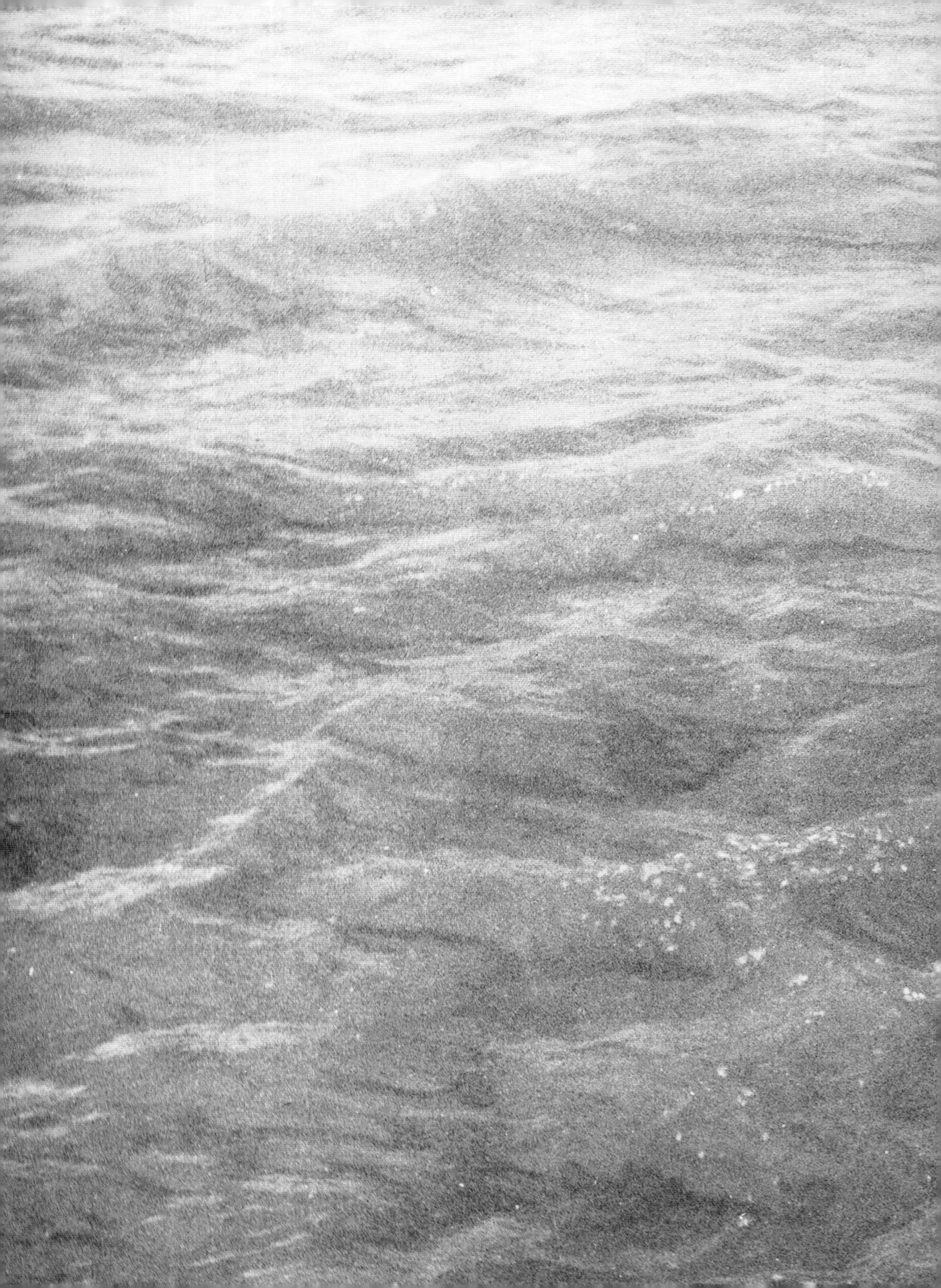

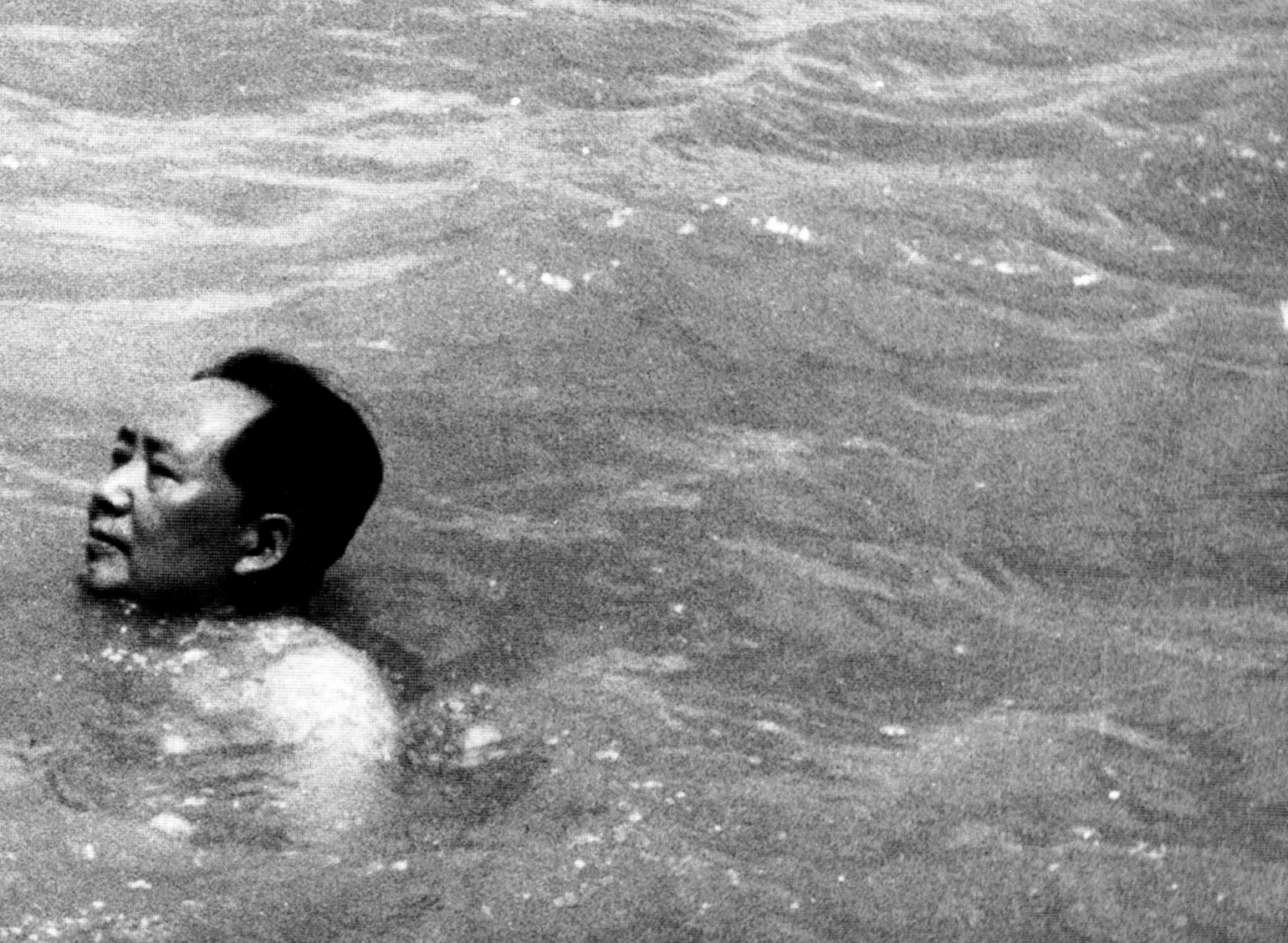

"Therefore, in the government of the Sage:
He empties their minds and fills their bellies;
Weakens their wills and strengthens their bones.
He constantly causes the people to be without knowledge and without desires.
And he makes those with knowledge not dare to act."

„Darum, unter der Herrschaft des Weisen:
Er leert ihre Köpfe und füllt ihre Bäuche;
Schwächt ihren Willen und stärkt ihre Knochen.
Er lässt die Menschen immerfort ohne Wissen und Wünsche sein.
Und er nimmt den Wissenden den Mut zu handeln."

« Il en va ainsi, dans le gouvernement du Sage :
Il vide leur esprit et remplit leurs ventres
Affaiblit leurs volontés et renforce leur cuir.
Toujours, il fait en sorte que les gens restent sans connaissances et sans désirs.
Et que ceux qui ont la connaissance n'osent pas agir. »

**LAOZI (c. 6th century BC), legendary author of
the Tao Te Ching and progenitor of the Taoist faith**

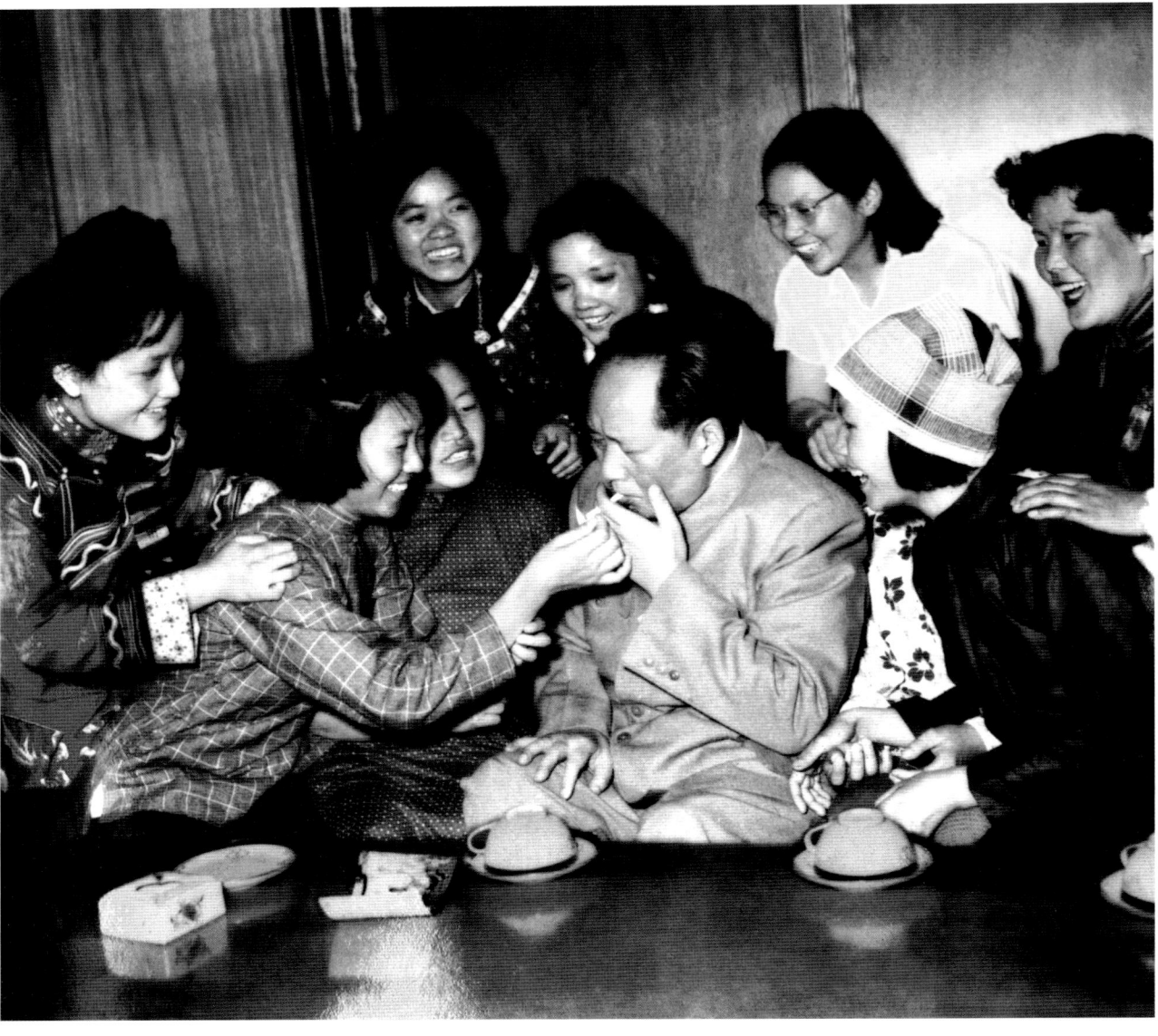

→
Hou Bo, 1956

On May 31, 1956, Mao Zedong, aged 63, took his first swim in the Yangtze river. Fresh from the swim, draped in a bathrobe and with mud covering his feet, he takes a moment with peasants from a bankside village. Mao swam in the Yangtze on 18 separate occasions. Today, on May 1 each year, swimmers compete to cross the treacherous waters of the great river in the Wuhan River Challenge.

Am 31. Mai 1956 nahm Mao Zedong im Alter von 63 Jahren sein erstes Bad im Jangtse. Frisch aus dem Wasser gestiegen, in einen Bademantel gehüllt und mit Schlamm an den Füßen, nimmt er sich Zeit für die Bauern aus einem am Ufer gelegenen Dorf. Mao schwamm bei 18 verschiedenen Gelegenheiten im Jangtse. Heutzutage wetteifern am 1. Mai jeden Jahres Schwimmer beim Wettbewerb von Wuhan darum, die tückischen Fluten des großen Flusses zu durchqueren.

Le 31 mai 1956, Mao Zedong, alors âgé de 63 ans, se baigne pour la première fois dans le Yang-Tsé. Juste après son bain, enveloppé dans un peignoir, les pieds encore couverts de boue, il passe un moment avec des paysans d'un village riverain. Mao nagea dans le fleuve à 18 reprises. Aujourd'hui, à chaque 1er mai, des nageurs font la course pour traverser les eaux tumultueuses du grand fleuve lors du Challenge du Wuhan.

↑
Hong Ke, 1957

Young women model workers light Mao's cigarette. To receive the title model worker was a coveted honor in Mao's time. It was bestowed on those believed to have made a special contribution to society, in particular, the quality of "self-sacrifice" to further political ideology. The practice began on a nationwide scale in 1950. From that time onwards, the State used model workers to inspire the masses to hard work, patriotism, and fervent belief in the Communist cause.

Junge Modellarbeiterinnen geben Mao Feuer. Der Titel eines Modellarbeiters gehörte zu Maos Zeiten zu den begehrten Auszeichnungen. Er wurde denjenigen verliehen, von denen man glaubte, sie hätten für die Gesellschaft einen besonderen Beitrag geleistet, insbesondere den der „Selbstaufopferung" im Dienst der politischen Ideologie. Landesweit nahm diese Praxis 1950 ihren Anfang. Von da an nutzte der Staat Modellarbeiter dazu, die Massen zu harter Arbeit, Patriotismus und inbrünstigem Glauben an die kommunistische Sache anzuspornen.

De jeunes ouvrières-modèles allument la cigarette de Mao. Recevoir le titre d'ouvrier modèle était un honneur convoité à l'époque. Il était accordé à ceux ou celles qui avaient apporté une contribution particulière à la société, en particulier fait preuve d'esprit de sacrifice. La pratique se développa à l'échelon national en 1950. L'État se servit d'eux pour inciter les masses à travailler davantage, faire preuve de patriotisme et croire en la cause communiste.

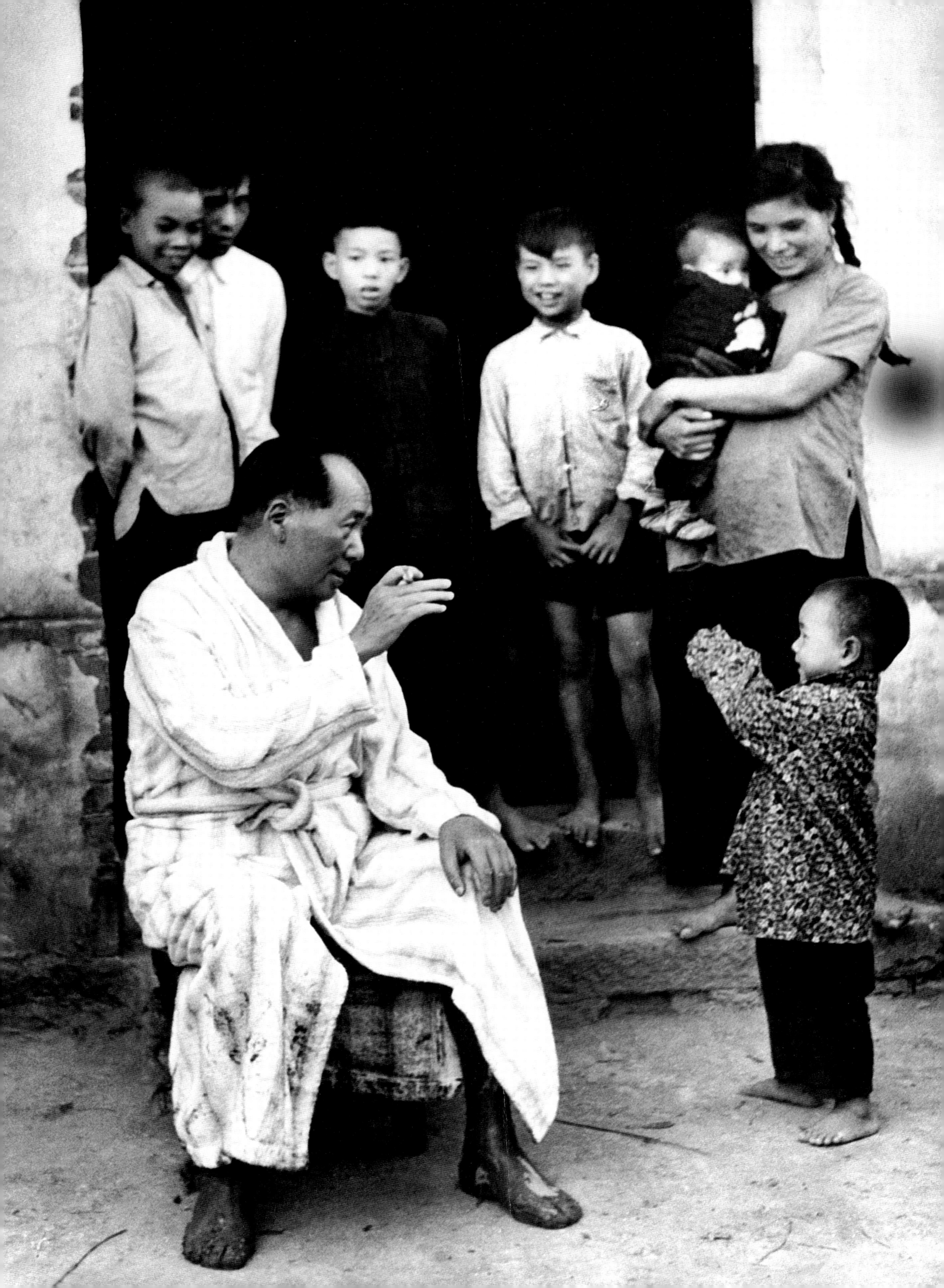

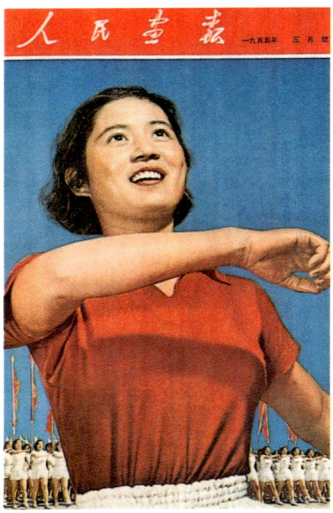

China Pictorial, March 1955

Chinese woman athlet attending a national sports competition

→
Anon., 1959
(image provided by *China Pictorial*)

Workers in a Tianjin textile factory following the daily exercise regime.

Arbeiter in einer Textilfabrik in Tianjin beim täglichen Trainingsprogramm.

Ouvriers dans une fabrique de textiles de Tianjin pratiquant leurs exercices de gymnastique quotidiens.

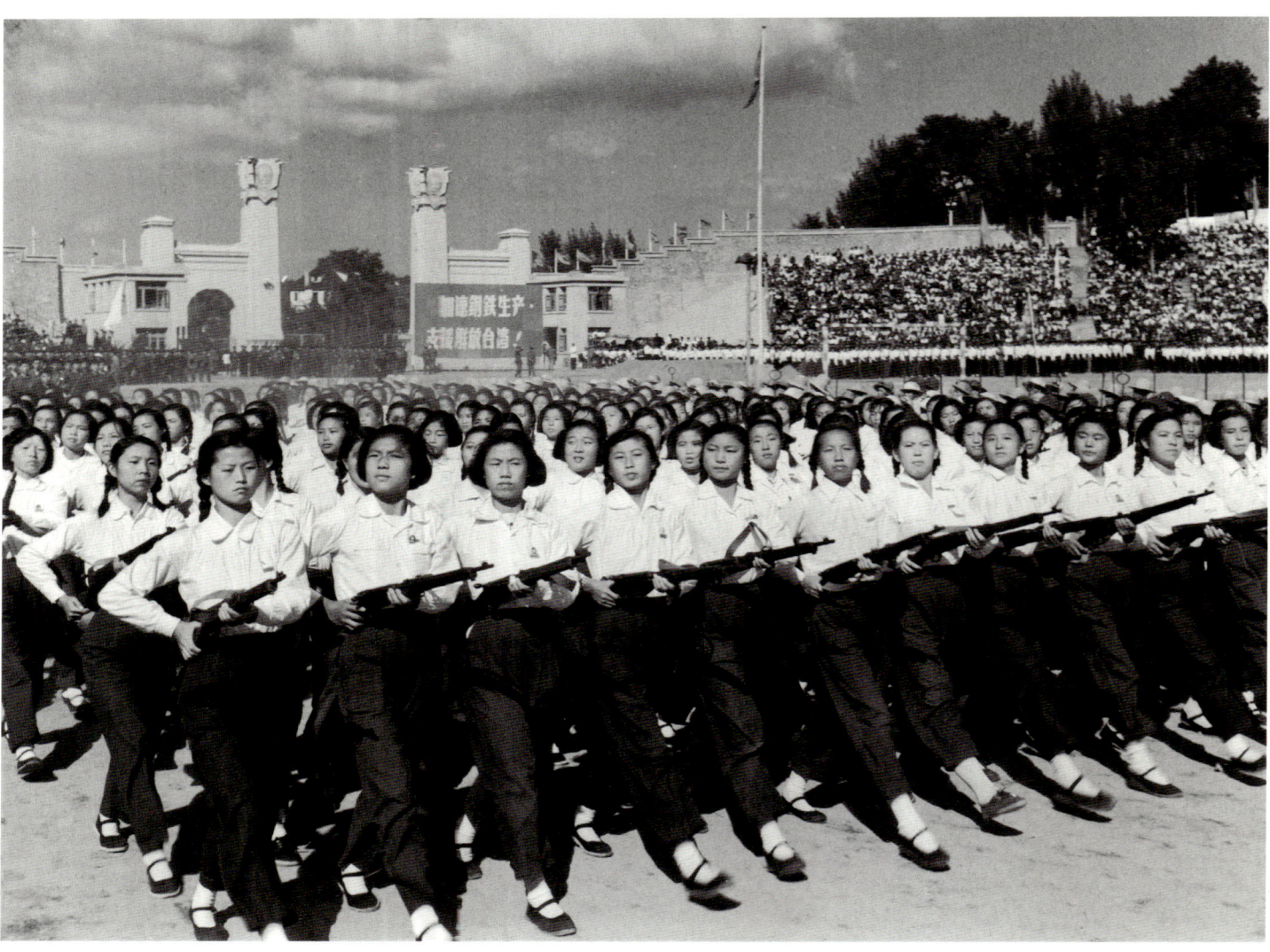

↑
Xiao Zhuang, 1958

Women militia on parade in Nanjing as part of a rally celebrating the founding of the provincial committee for Jiangsu province. The rally aimed at mobilizing the masses for the Great Leap Forward, which got fully underway in 1959. This required all individuals to consign any scrap of metal they possessed to homemade furnaces in order to boost steel production, and carry through the goals Mao set for steel production in 1958–59.

Weibliche Milizen bei einer Parade in Nanjing als Teil einer Kundgebung zur Feier der Gründung des Provinzialkomitees der Provinz Jiangsu. Die Kundgebung sollte die Massen für den Großen Sprung nach vorn mobilisieren, der 1959 seinen Höhepunkt erreichte. Alle Bürger waren verpflichtet, jedes Stückchen Metall in ihrem Besitz selbstgebauten Lehmhochöfen zu übereignen, um die Stahlproduktion zu steigern und die von Mao für 1958/59 vorgegebenen Quoten zu erreichen.

Des milices féminines paradent à Nankin lors d'un rassemblement célébrant la fondation du Comité de la province du Jiangsu. Cette manifestation avait pour but de mobiliser les masses pour la campagne du Grand bond en avant, qui avait pris toute son ampleur en 1959. Chacun devait récupérer tous les morceaux de métal qu'il possédait et les livrer aux hauts-fourneaux rustiques pour accroître la production d'acier et remplir les objectifs fixés par Mao pour 1958–59.

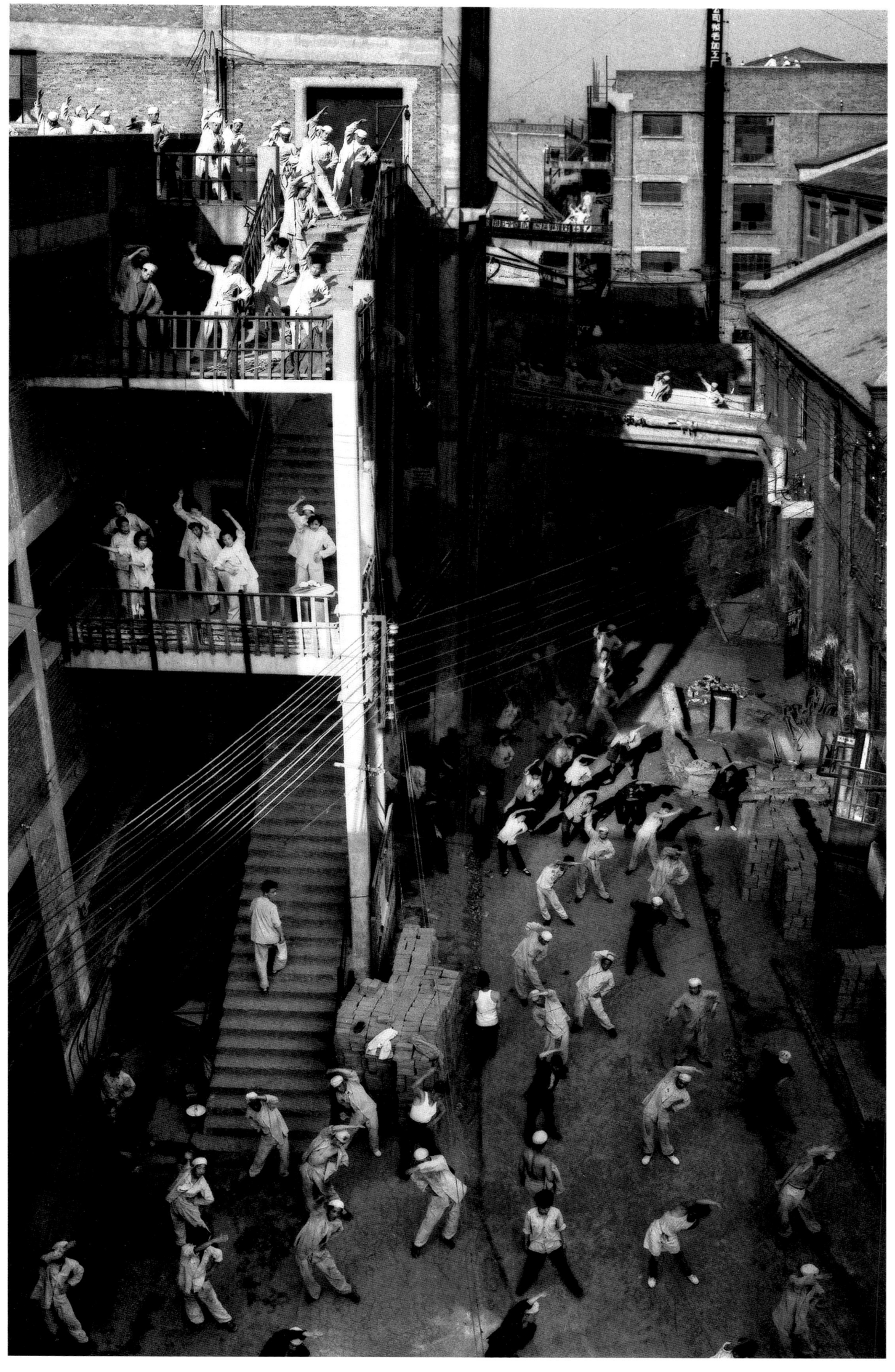

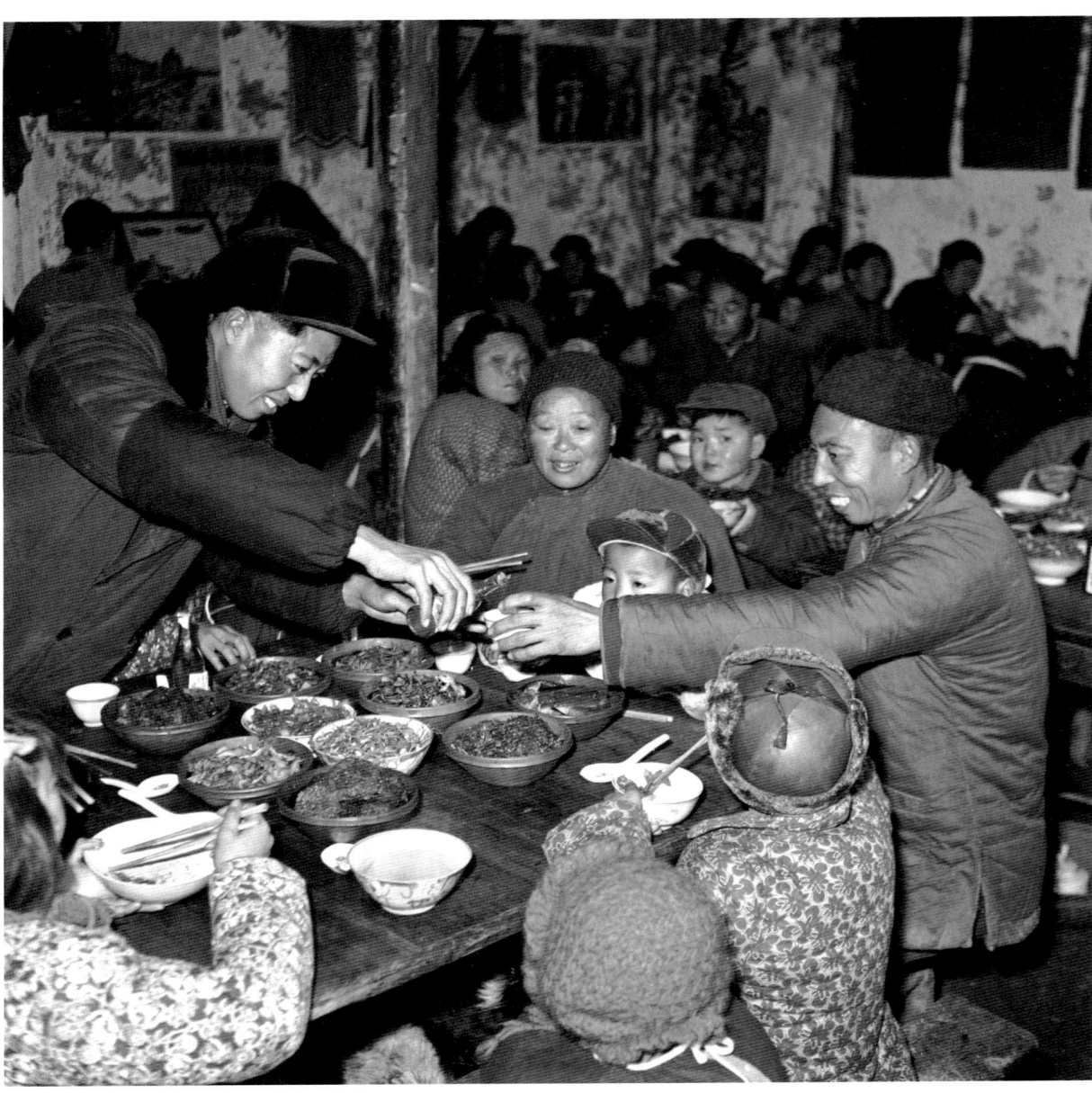

"The ruler's fate depends upon the people,
while the people's fates depend upon a full belly."

„Das Schicksal des Herrschers hängt vom Volk ab, während
das Schicksal des Volkes von einem vollen Bauch abhängt."

« Le destin du souverain dépend du peuple, tandis
que celui du peuple dépend de son ventre plein. »

**SIMA QIAN (c. 145–86 BC), court scribe and father of Chinese
historiography, c. 91 BC**

↑
Xiao Zhuang, 1959

*Peasants in the Yangziji commune outside
Nanjing enjoying a traditional Lunar New
Year's Eve dinner. As the Great Leap Forward intensified, the official media reported
on the happy lives of the people, with no
hint of the famine that was waiting to strike.*

*Bauern in der Kommune Yangziji bei Nanjing
erfreuen sich an einem traditionellen Essen
anlässlich des chinesichen Neujahrsfestes.
Während der Große Sprung nach vorn ins
Stolpern geriet, berichteten die staatlichen
Medien vom glücklichen Leben der Menschen,
ohne die sich abzeichnende Hungersnot zu
erwähnen.*

*Des paysans de la commune de Yangziji près
de Nankin participent à un diner traditionnel
pour fêter la nouvelle année lunaire. Pendant
l'intensification du Grand bond en avant,
les médias officiels montraient l'existence
heureuse des gens, sans donner la moindre
information sur la famine qui approchait.*

↓
Xiao Ye, 1959

The last emperor of the Qing dynasty, Aisin Gioro Pu Yi, sits on a kang bed, sewing his own shoes in a reform camp for political prisoners in the northeast of China. Pu Yi had placed his allegiance with the invading Japanese army, which invested him as the "puppet" emperor of Manchuria (Dongbei or the northeast of China). When the puppet regime fell at the end of the Second World War and when Japan surrendered to the U.S.-led Allied Forces, Pu Yi was detained as a war criminal, first in a Soviet prison before being extradited to China in 1950. He was arrested in 1951, released in 1959, and died in 1967, spending the final period of his life as a gardener at the Beijing Botanical Gardens, although he took part in the Political Consultative Conference.

Aisin Gioro Pu Yi, der letzte Kaiser der Qing-Dynastie, sitzt auf einem Kang-Bett und näht seine eigenen Schuhe in einem Reformlager für politische Gefangene im Nordosten Chinas. Pu Yi hatte den japanischen Invasionstruppen Loyalität gelobt, die ihn als Marionettenkaiser der Mandschurei einsetzten (Dongbei oder der Nordosten Chinas). Als Japan sich am Ende des Zweiten Weltkriegs den alliierten Truppen unter Führung der USA ergab, stürzte das Marionettenregime, und Pu Yi wurde als Kriegsverbrecher inhaftiert, zunächst in einem sowjetischen Gefängnis, ehe er 1950 an China ausgeliefert wurde. 1951 wurde er erneut festgenommen und 1959 entlassen. Die Jahre vor seinem Tod 1967 verbrachte er als Gärtner im Botanischen Garten von Peking, obgleich man ihn zum Mitglied in der Politischen Konsultativkonferenz gemacht hatte.

Le dernier empereur de la dynastie Qing, Aisin Gioro Pu Yi, assis sur un lit kang, coud ses propres souliers dans un camp de rééducation de prisonniers politiques du nord-est de la Chine. Pu Yi avait fait allégeance à l'armée japonaise qui en fit un empereur « pantin » de Mandchourie (Dongbei ou nord-est de la Chine). Lorsque ce régime de paille s'effondra à la fin de la Seconde guerre mondiale et que le Japon se rendit aux forces américaines, Pu Yi fut emprisonné comme criminel de guerre dans une prison soviétique avant d'être extradé vers la Chine en 1950. Il fut arrêté en 1951, relâché en 1959 et mourut en 1967. À la fin de sa vie, il était jardinier et travaillait pour les Jardins botaniques de Pékin, bien qu'il ait été fait membre de la Conférence politique consultative.

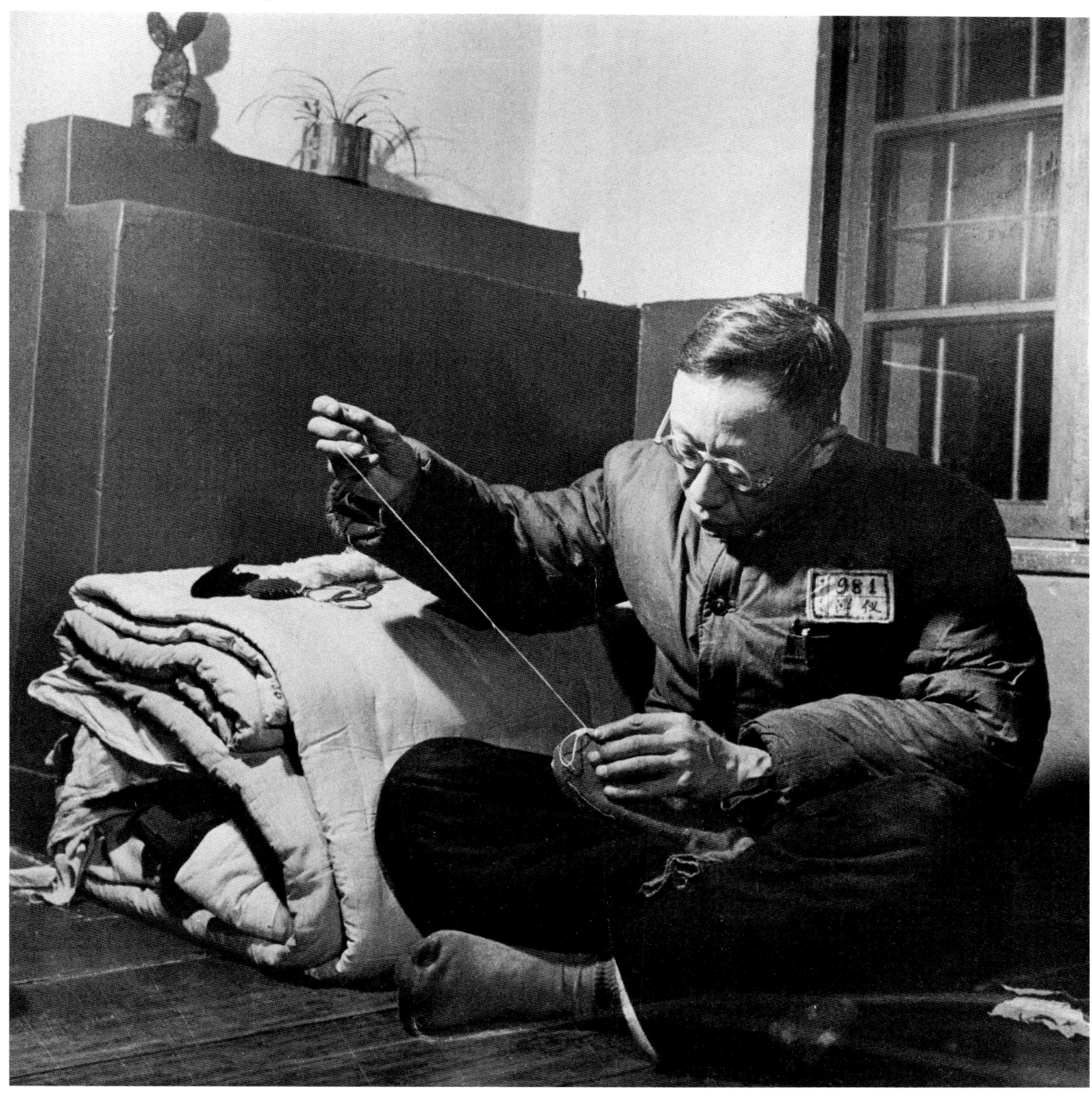

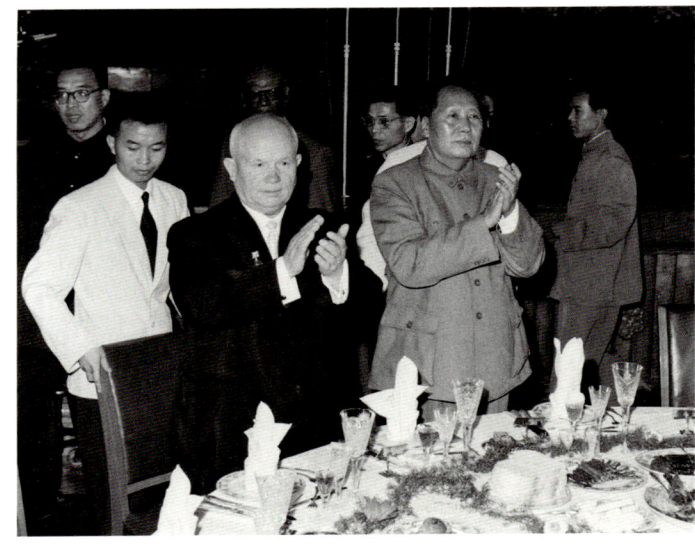

*"China and the USSR's situation is different.
Putting us in the same box won't work."*

*„Die Lage Chinas und die der UdSSR sind verschieden.
Uns in denselben Topf zu werfen, wird nicht funktionieren."*

*« La situation de la Chine et celle de l'URSS sont différentes.
Nous mettre dans le même sac ne marche pas. »*

**ZHAO QIZHENG (1940–), member of China People's Political
Consultative Congress, former vice mayor of Shanghai, 1989**

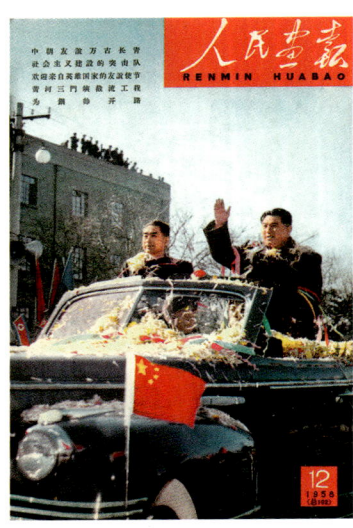

China Pictorial, February 1958

*Chinese Premier Zhou Enlai with visiting
North Korean strongman Kim Jong Il*

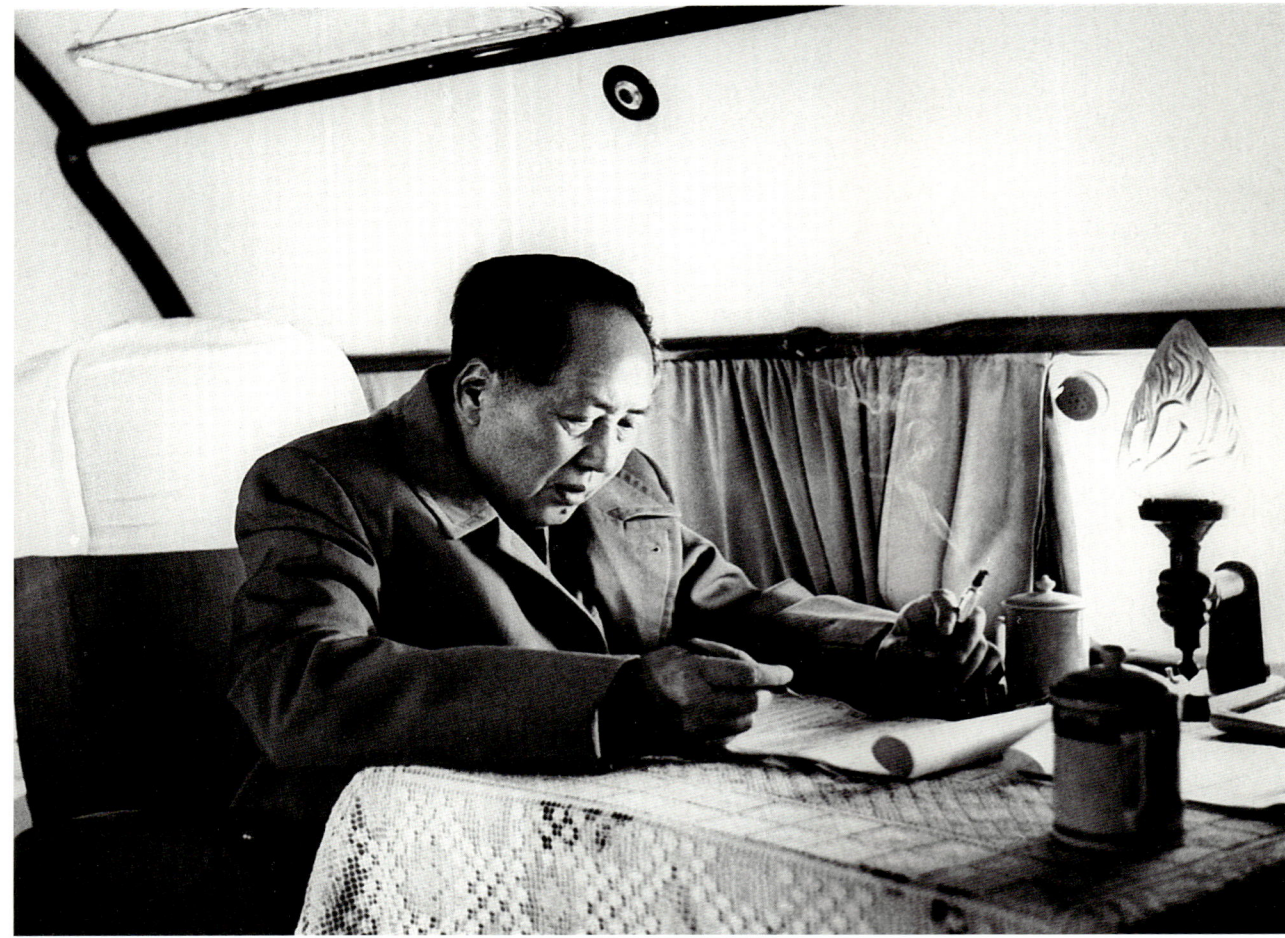

←
Hou Bo, 1957

*Mao works aboard a Soviet TU 104 aircraft
sent by the Soviets, correcting a draft of the
speech he would deliver in Moscow to mark
the 40th anniversary of USSR.*

*Mao arbeitet an Bord einer von der Sowjet-
union geschickten TU 104 an der Korrektur
des Entwurfs einer Rede, die er zum 40.
Jahrestag der UdSSR in Moskau halten wird.*

*Mao travaillant à bord d'un avion TU 104
envoyé par les Soviétiques. Il corrige le projet
d'un discours qu'il prononcera à Moscou
pour le quarantième anniversaire de l'URSS.*

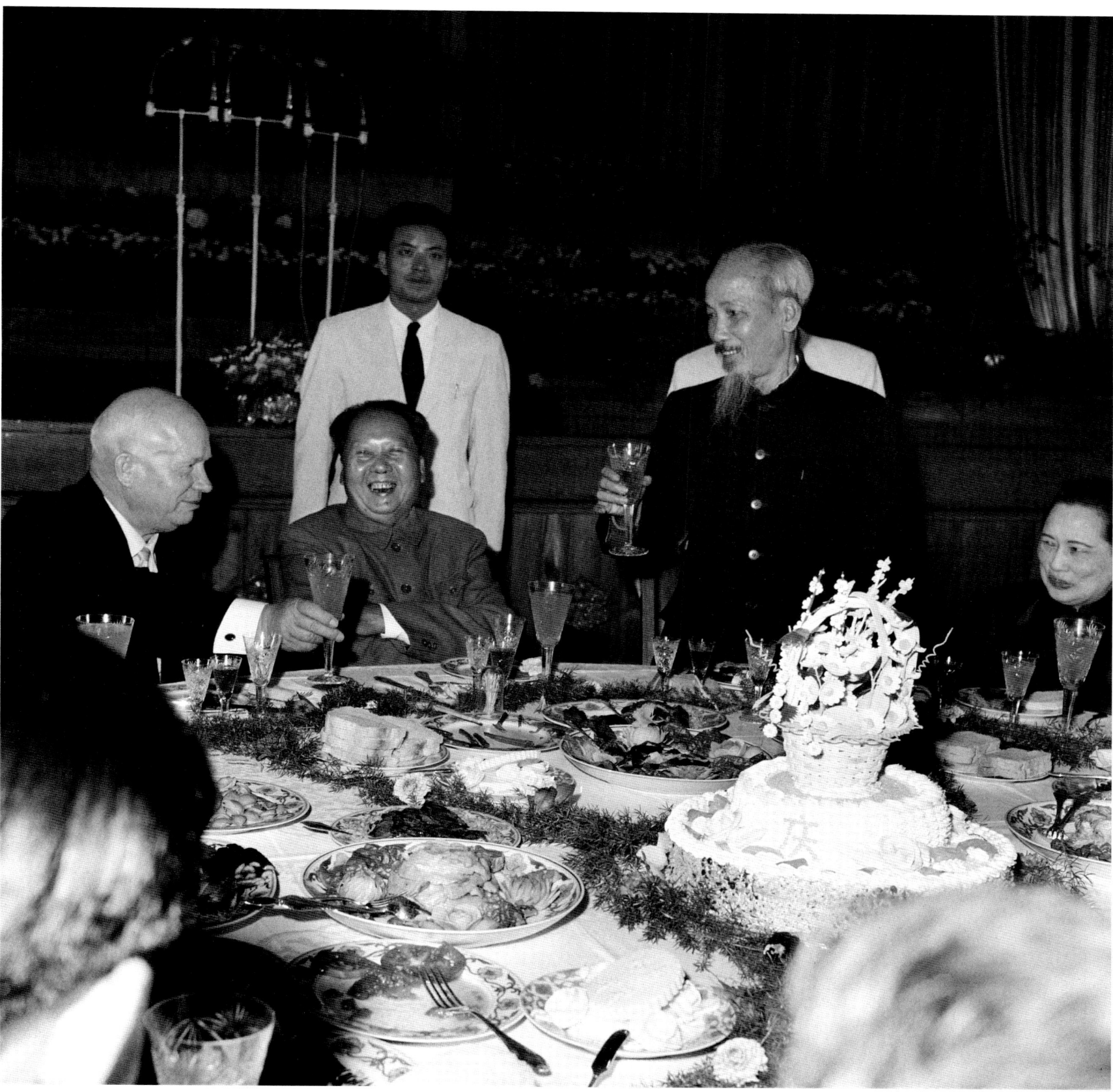

↖↑
Du Xiuxian, 1959

Soviet leader Nikita Khrushchev, Chairman Mao and the vietnamese President Ho Chi Minh in the Great Hall of People at the tenth anniversary celebrations of the founding of the People's Republic. This was to be the last meeting of the Sino-Soviet leaders before the relations deteriorated into armed border clashes.

Der sowjetische Führer Nikita Chruschtschow, der Vorsitzende Mao und der vietnamesische Präsident Ho Chi Minh in der Großen Halle des Volkes bei der Feier zum zehnten Jahrestag der Gründung der Volksrepublik China. Dies war das letzte Zusammentreffen der Führer der beiden Länder, ehe die Beziehungen auf das Niveau bewaffneter Grenzstreitigkeiten absanken.

Le dirigeant soviétique Nikita Khrouchtchev, le Président Mao et le président vietnamien Hô Chi Minh dans la grande salle du peuple lors de la célébration du 10ème anniversaire de la fondation de la République populaire de Chine. Ce fut la dernière rencontre des responsables soviétiques et chinois avant que leurs relations ne se détériorent et virent aux conflits frontaliers.

→
Hou Bo, 1958

Mao in a cornfield in Henan province: a man, a hat, a radiant beam of optimism that became the embodiment of all that New China's production brigades were claimed to be achieving. Meanwhile, the Great Leap Forward and communization of agricultural production this image re-enforced would end in appalling failure.

Mao in einem Getreidefeld in der Provinz Henan. Ein Mann, ein Hut, ein strahlend-optimistisches Lächeln: die Verkörperung all dessen, was die Produktionsbrigaden des neuen China vorgeblich leisteten. Unterdessen erwiesen sich der Große Sprung nach vorn und die von diesem Bild bestärkte Verlagerung der landwirtschaftlichen Produktion in Volkskommunen als fürchterliche Fehlschläge.

Mao dans un champ de blé, province du Hénan : un homme, un chapeau, un air optimiste radieux qui incarnaient ces objectifs que les brigades de production de la nouvelle Chine étaient censées remplir. Le Grand bond en avant et la communisation de la production agricole que cette image soutenait allaient s'achever par un terrible échec.

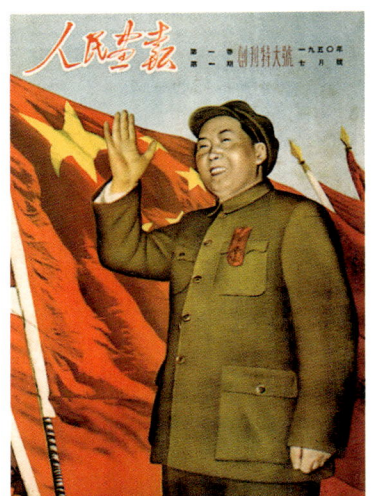

China Pictorial, July 1950

Photo montage of Mao and the Chinese national flag

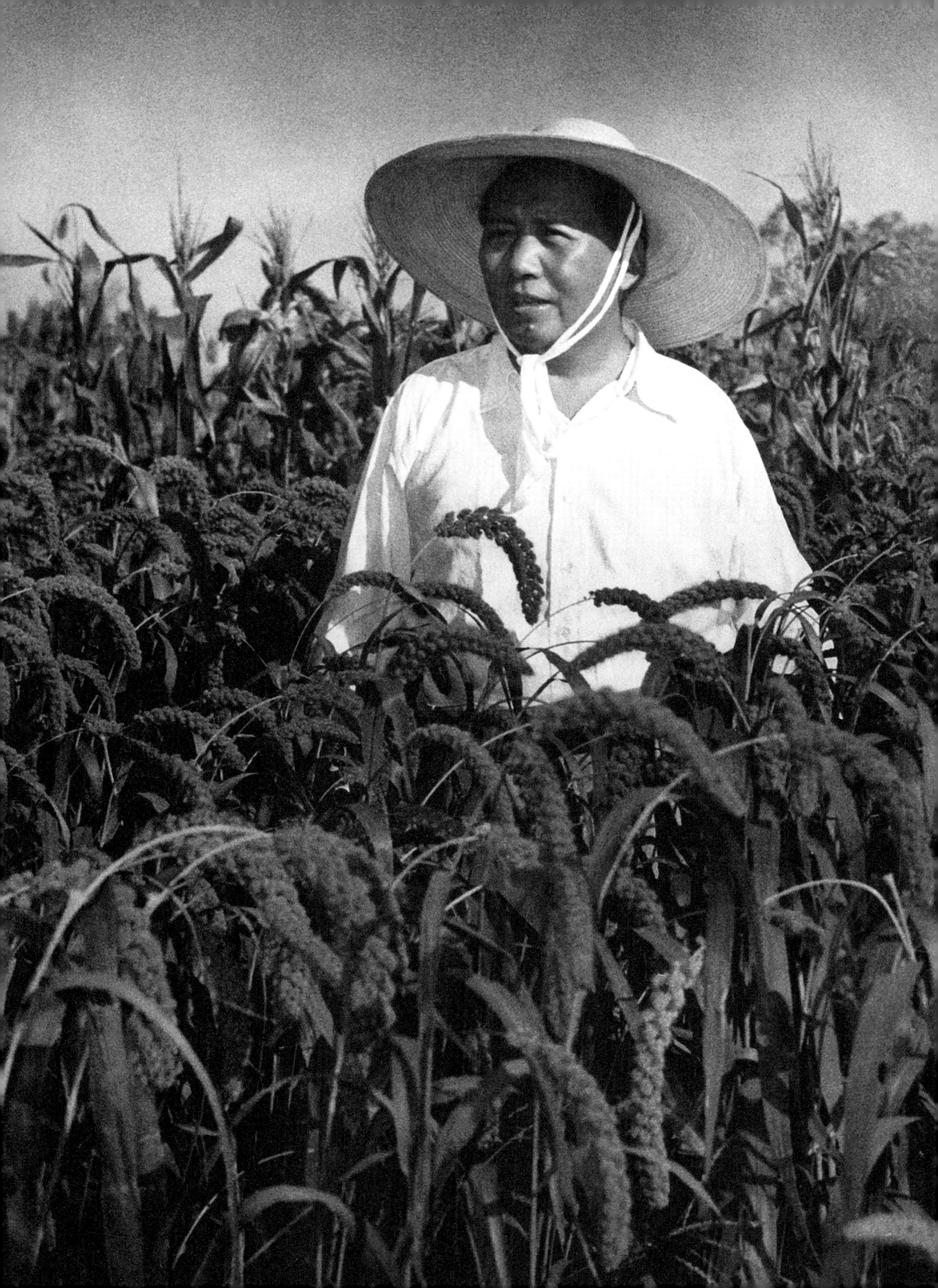

#2

1960–1969
Great Leap Backward

Faced with the widespread calamities resulting from unsound agricultural policies and the threat of competition from the Soviet Union, Mao pulled off a short-lived political retreat only to come back and purge his moderate colleagues by launching the holocaust called the Great Proletarian Cultural Revolution.

As the peace movement in America and Europe turned the Sixties into the decade of love, in China, it would be the most chaotic, and brutal, in living memory. When Mao ordered the people to focus on the Great Leap Forward, he opened the door for a nationwide famine that struck far and wide in 1960, worsening in 1961, and leaving an estimated 30 million people dead of starvation before it eased toward the end of 1962. This prompted the leadership to sideline Mao for almost five years, as Liu Shaoqi and Deng Xiaoping attempted to stabilize the economy and get the People's Republic back on track. This situation would incite its own backlash, and lead to countless further deaths.

China's Youth Kickstarts the Revolution

Although he appeared to accept the shift in power, Mao could not sit by idly and relinquish his position to others. In the ensuing political power play, Mao maneuvered the downfall of the pragmatists within the CCP, namely Liu and Deng. He furthermore paved the way for Marshal Lin Biao to seize control over the People's Liberation Army, and nurture a nationwide personality cult of Mao himself. All the behind-the-scenes activities culminated in 1966 in the launch of the Great Proletarian Cultural Revolution. The secret weapon Mao now unleashed was China's youth as millions were mobilized, with his blessing, to attack "corrupt" administrative power in the person of anyone deemed to uphold old, non-progressive ways, wherever they saw it. As Red Guards rampaged in the name of their loyalty to Chairman Mao, millions of people struggling, deprived of their possessions and freedoms, and many left injured or dead.

China's isolation from the international community in the 1960s was confounded by the ideological split from its socialist brother, the USSR, which as a result, pulled out all technical support and engineers. The relationship deteriorated further as the two sides contended borders between the two nations, which ended in several military skirmishes. The situation was complicated by the U.S. invasion of Vietnam, with China also drawn in on the side of the North Vietnamese cause.

In view of the impending military conflict with the Soviet Union, Mao ordered the people to dig tunnels and trenches everywhere, and move key industries to remote areas of China. These defensive moves further depleted China's scant resources. As the Sixties came to an end, with the exception of the late Qing dynasty period, China had never before been so fragile, and vulnerable.

"The chaos caused was on a grand scale, and I take responsibility. Comrades, you must all analyze your own responsibility. If you have to fart, fart. You will feel much better for it."

MAO ZEDONG (1893–1976), first Chairman of the People's Republic of China, 1959

#2

1960–1969
Der Große Sprung zurück

Angesichts der als Folge der falschen Agrarpolitik nahezu überall herrschenden Not und der Bedrohung und Rivalität seitens der Sowjetunion inszenierte Mao einen kurzzeitigen Rückzug, nur um wiederzukommen und den Holocaust der „Großen Proletarischen Kulturrevolution" anzuzetteln, in deren Verlauf er sich seiner gemäßigteren Mitstreiter entledigte.

Während die 1960er-Jahre durch die Friedensbewegung in Amerika und Europa zum Jahrzehnt der Liebe wurden, sollten sie in China zur chaotischsten und grausamsten Dekade seiner Geschichte werden. Als Mao den Menschen befahl, sich auf den „Großen Sprung nach vorn" zu konzentrieren, hatte das eine landesweite Hungersnot zur Folge, die 1960 wütete, sich im Verlauf des Jahres 1961 noch verschlimmerte und bei ihrem Ausklingen Ende 1962 geschätzte 30 Millionen Hungertote zurückließ. Dies veranlasste die politische Führung, Mao nahezu fünf Jahre lang kaltzustellen, während Liu Shaoqi und Deng Xiaoping versuchten, die Wirtschaft zu stabilisieren und die Volksrepublik wieder auf einen geordneten Kurs zu bringen. Dieser Beschluss sollte jedoch heftige Gegenreaktionen auslösen und zu zahllosen weiteren Opfern unter der Bevölkerung führen.

Chinas Jugend gibt der Revolution neuen Auftrieb

Obgleich Mao mit der neuen Machtverteilung einverstanden schien, konnte er nicht tatenlos zusehen und seine Position anderen überlassen. In dem sich anschließenden Machtpoker fädelte er den Sturz von Liu und Deng, den Pragmatikern in der KP Chinas, ein. Außerdem ebnete er Marschall Lin Biao den Weg an die Spitze der Volksbefreiungsarmee,

der anschließend den landesweiten Personenkult um Mao initiierte. All diese im Verborgenen ablaufenden Aktivitäten gipfelten 1966 im Ausbruch der „Großen Proletarischen Kulturrevolution". Die Geheimwaffe, die Mao jetzt zum Einsatz brachte, war das Millionenheer von Chinas Jugend, das mit seinem Segen gegen „korrupte" Verwaltungsbeamte vorging, und zwar in Person eines jeden, der alte, nicht progressive Methoden verfolgte. Als die Roten Garden im Namen ihrer Treue zum Vorsitzenden Mao losschlugen, wurden Millionen von Menschen für schuldig erklärt, ihrer Besitztümer und Freiheit beraubt und viele blieben verwundet oder tot auf der Strecke.

Chinas Isolation von der internationalen Gemeinschaft verstärkte sich noch durch den ideologischen Bruch mit dem sozialistischen Bruderland Sowjetunion, das in der Folge sämtliche technische Unterstützung und seine Ingenieure abzog. Die Beziehung verschlechterte sich weiter, als beide Seiten den Grenzverlauf zwischen ihren Ländern infrage stellten; mehrere militärische Auseinandersetzungen waren die Folge. Durch die Invasion der Vereinigten Staaten in Vietnam wurde die Lage noch komplizierter, da auch China aufseiten Nordvietnams in den Konflikt verwickelt war.

Angesichts eines drohenden Krieges mit der Sowjetunion befahl Mao, überall Tunnel und Schützengräben auszuheben und die Schlüsselindustrien in entlegene Gebiete Chinas zu verlegen. Diese Maßnahmen trugen zusätzlich dazu bei, Chinas ohnehin knappe Ressourcen zu verringern. Abgesehen von der Zeit der späten Qing-Dynastie war China niemals so instabil und verwundbar gewesen wie am Ende der 1960er-Jahre.

„Das angerichtete Chaos ist riesengroß, und ich übernehme die Verantwortung. Genossen, ihr müsst alle eure eigene Verantwortung überdenken. Wenn ihr furzen müsst, furzt. Danach wird es euch besser gehen."

MAO ZEDONG (1893–1976), erster Vorsitzender der Volksrepublik China, 1959

#2

1960–1969
Le Grand bond
en arrière

Confronté aux catastrophes provoquées par sa politique agricole aventureuse et à la menace ainsi qu'à la concurrence de l'Union soviétique, Mao se retira pour une brève retraite, avant de revenir en force et de purger le système des responsables modérés en lançant ce véritable holocauste que fut la Grande révolution culturelle prolétarienne.

Si les mouvements en faveur de la paix en Amérique et en Europe firent des années 1960 « la décennie de l'amour », la Chine connut alors la période la plus chaotique et la plus brutale de son histoire. Lorsque Mao ordonna au peuple de se préparer au Grand bond en avant, il déclencha une famine qui ravagea le pays en 1960, et s'aggrava en 1961, faisant selon les estimations 30 millions de morts, avant de se résorber fin 1962. La situation aboutit à la mise à l'écart de Mao pendant près de cinq années, tandis que Liu Shaoqi et Deng Xiaoping s'efforcèrent de stabiliser l'économie et de remettre la république sur ses rails. Cette période connut ses à-coups et ses contrecoups et provoqua des morts innombrables.

La jeunesse chinoise lance sa révolution

Bien qu'il ait semblé d'accord avec l'évolution de la répartition des pouvoirs, Mao ne pouvait rester inactif et abandonner ses positions. Dans le jeu politique complexe qui s'ensuivit, il manœuvra pour faire tomber les pragmatiques du parti, en particulier Liu et Deng. Il prépara la voie à une prise du pouvoir par l'Armée populaire de libération, dirigée par le maréchal Lin Biao, et encouragea dans tout le pays le culte de sa personnalité. Ce déploiement d'activités d'abord discret culmina avec le lancement de la Grande révolution culturelle prolétarienne en 1966. L'arme secrète de Mao était de mobiliser des millions de jeunes gens, pour attaquer avec son appui le pouvoir administratif « corrompu » en la personne de tous ceux soupçonnés de pratiquer des méthodes anciennes, non progressistes. Les Gardes rouges furent lâchés et, au nom de leur loyauté au Président Mao, s'en prirent à des millions de personnes privées de leurs biens et de leur liberté, beaucoup étant blessés ou tués.

L'isolement de la Chine sur la scène internationale dans les années 1960 fut renforcé par sa rupture idéologique avec son frère d'armes socialiste, l'URSS, qui retira la totalité de ses experts et ingénieurs. Les relations se détériorèrent encore davantage à l'occasion de contestations de frontière qui provoquèrent plusieurs escarmouches et lors de l'invasion américaine du Vietnam, la Chine défendant la cause du Nord-Vietnam.

Sensible à la menace d'un conflit avec l'Union soviétique, Mao ordonna à son peuple de creuser des tunnels et des tranchées dans tout le pays et de déplacer les industries essentielles vers les régions les plus éloignées. Ces mesures défensives pesèrent encore plus sur les faibles ressources chinoises. Vers la fin des années 1960 et à l'exception des derniers temps de la dynastie Qing, jamais la Chine n'avait été aussi fragile et vulnérable.

« Le chaos a été à grande échelle et j'en prends la responsabilité. Camarades, vous devez tous analyser votre propre responsabilité. Si vous devez péter, pétez. Vous vous sentirez beaucoup mieux après. »

MAO ZEDONG (1893–1976), premier président de la République populaire de Chine, 1959

"After the bad start of the Great Leap mass mobilization in 1957, in a secret speech to party leaders in December, Mao said, 'Half the Chinese population unquestionably will die … If you don't lose your jobs, I at least should lose mine.'"

„Nach dem schlechten Start der Massenmobilisierung zum Großen Sprung im Jahre 1957 sagte Mao im Dezember in einer geheimen Ansprache zu den Parteiführern: ‚Fraglos wird die Hälfte der chinesischen Bevölkerung sterben … Wenn Ihr schon Eure Posten nicht verliert, dann sollte zumindest ich meinen verlieren.'"

« Après le mauvais départ de la mobilisation des masses pour le Grand bond en avant en 1957, Mao déclara dans un discours secret aux responsables du parti en décembre : 'La moitié de la population chinoise va sans aucun doute mourir … Si vous ne perdez pas vos postes, moi je vais au moins perdre le mien.' »

JONATHAN SPENCE & ANNPING CHIN (1936–) and (1950–), Professors of History, Yale University, 1996

pp. 162/163
Wei Dezhong, 1960

Following the launch of the People's Commune movement, by 1959, 99 per cent of the 120 million-strong rural population belonged to the collective system. Here, Henan peasants thresh wheat by hand.

Nachdem die Bewegung der Volkskommunen begonnen hatte, gehörten 1959 99 Prozent der 120 Millionen Menschen zählenden Landbevölkerung zum kollektiven System. Hier dreschen Bauern in der Provinz Henan Weizen von Hand.

En 1959, à la suite de la mise en place des communes populaires, 99 % des 120 millions de Chinois ruraux relèvent désormais d'un système collectif. Ici, des paysans du Hénan battent du blé manuellement.

→
Du Xiuxian, 1965

Mao was reading a document before addressing a rally in Tienanmen Square to denounce the U.S. role in Vietnam.

Mao studiert ein Dokument, bevor er sich an die Menge auf dem Tiananmen-Platz wendet, um die Aktivitäten der USA in Vietnam zu geißeln.

Mao en train de lire un document avant d'assister, sur la place Tian'anmen, à un rassemblement destiné à dénoncer le rôle des États-Unis au Vietnam.

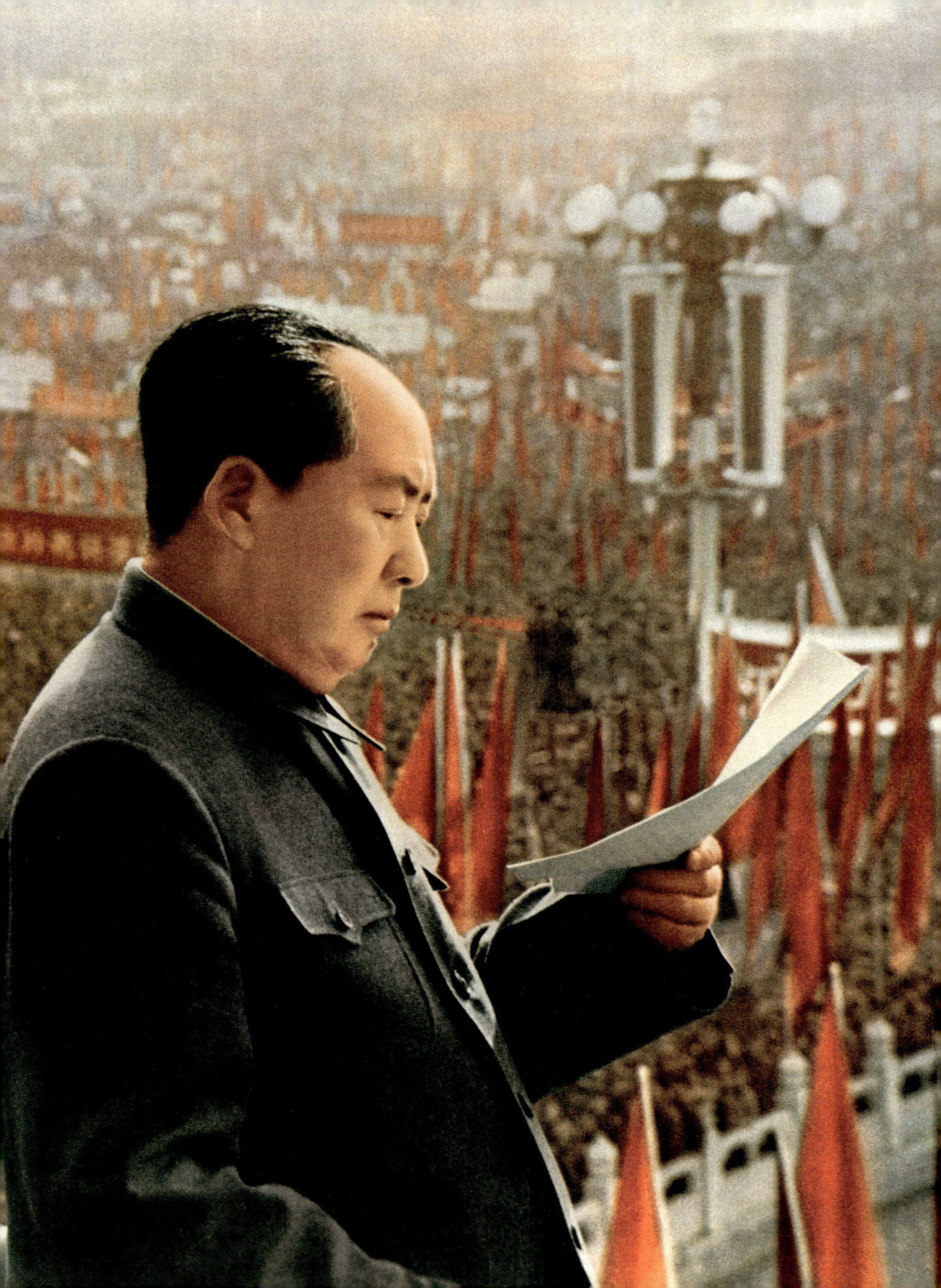

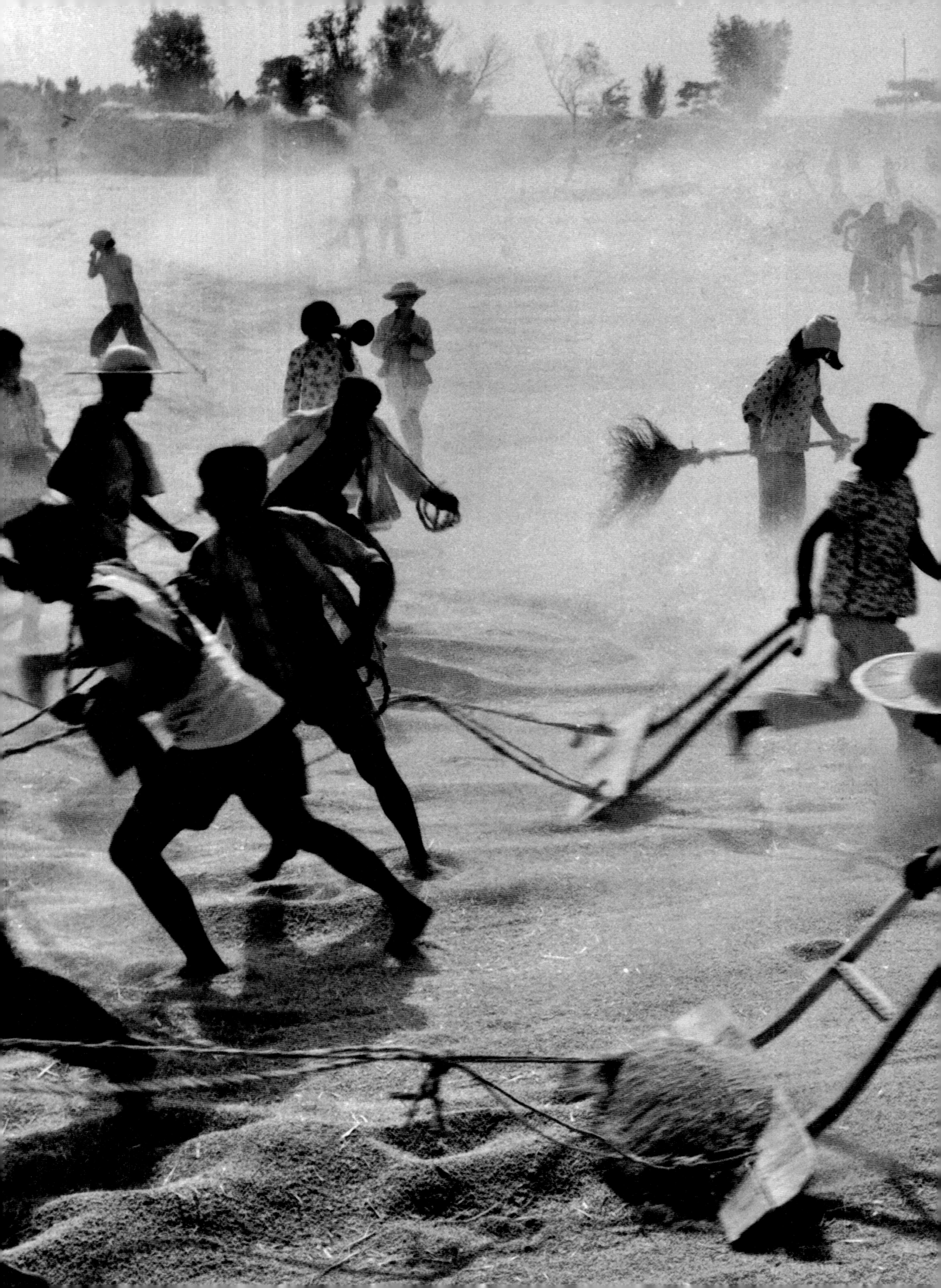

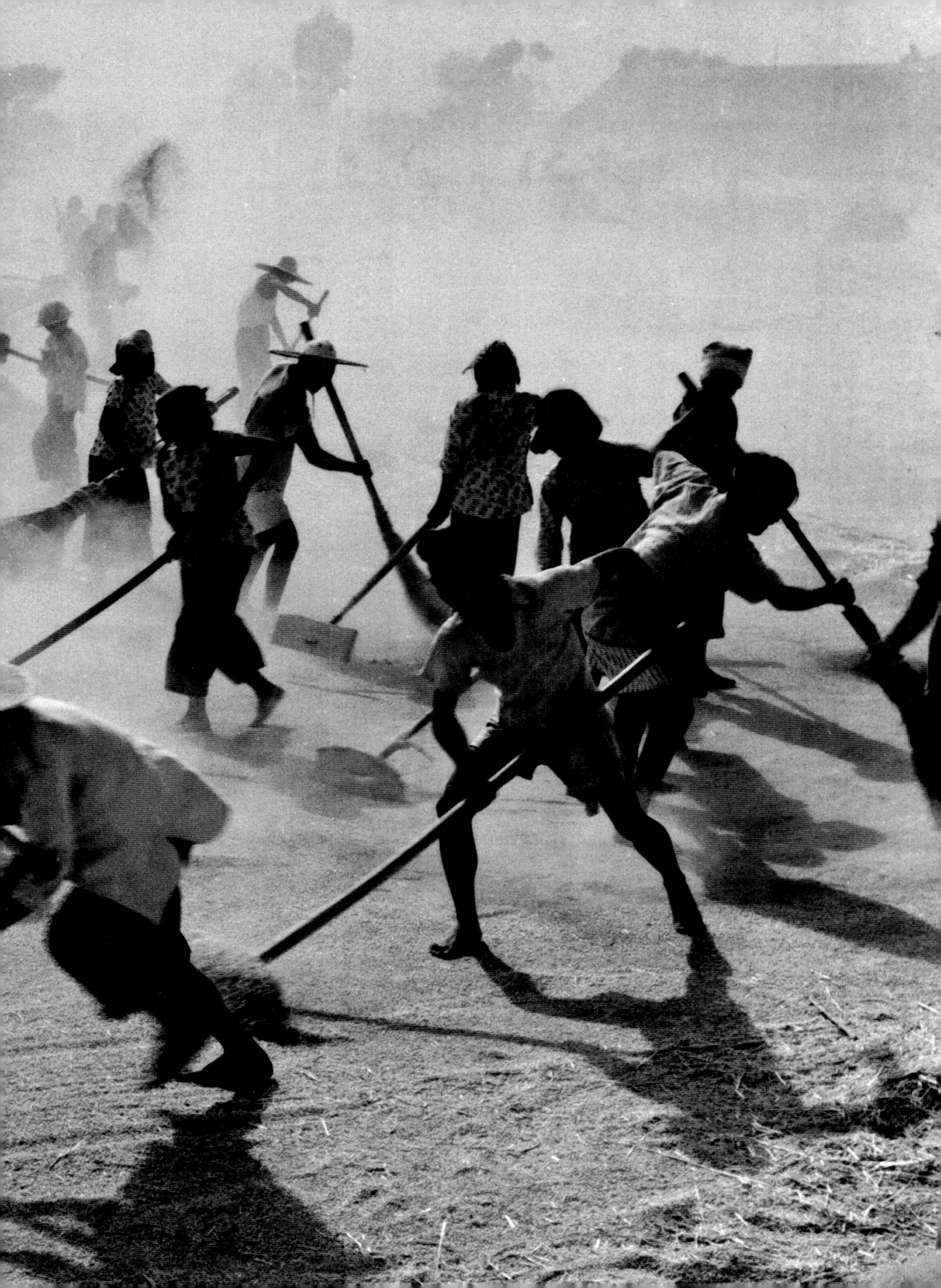

164

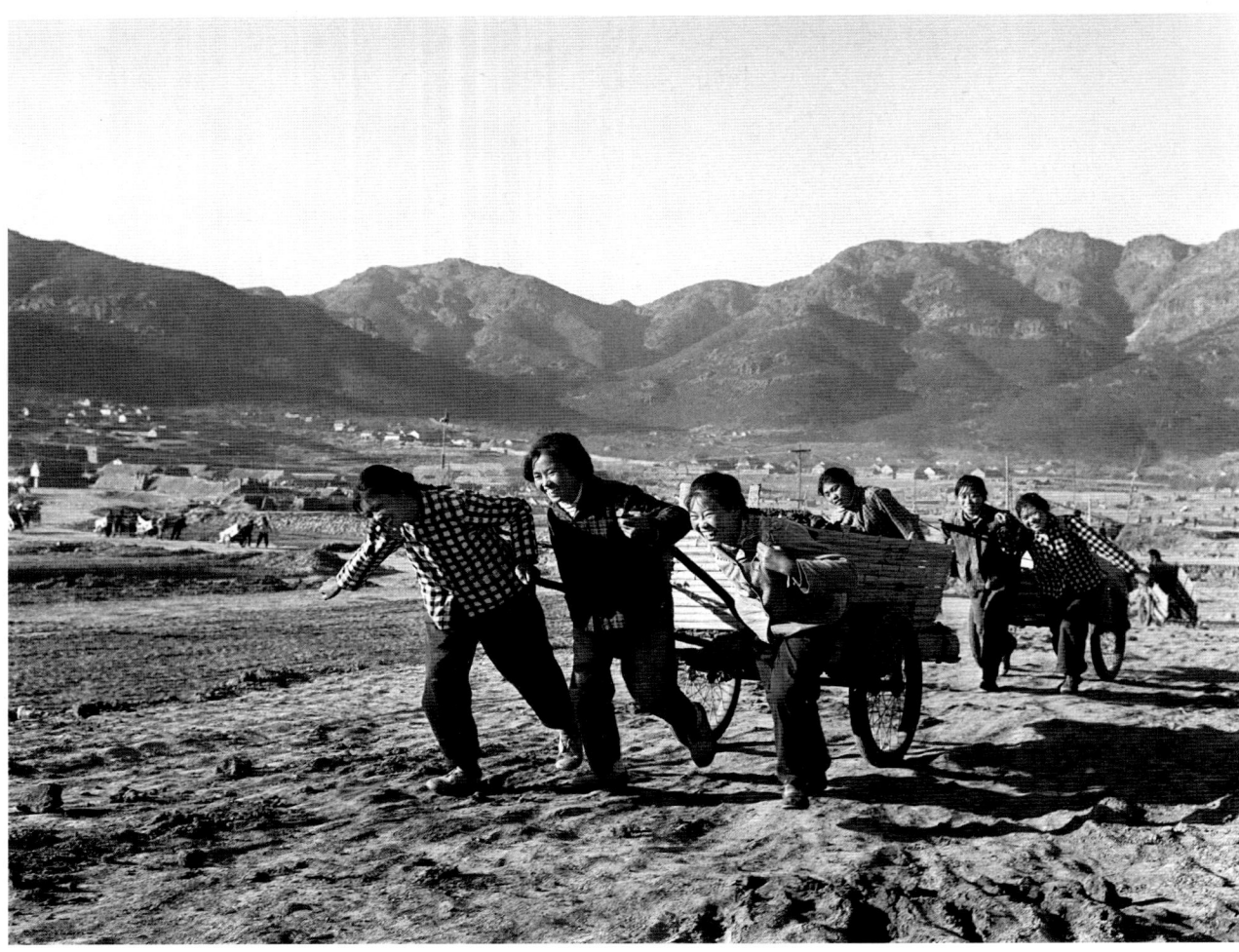

→
Li Zhensheng, 1964

A snow-covered village in the northeastern part of Heilongjiang province, where winter temperatures are known to plummet to almost −40 degrees Celsius.

Ein schneebedecktes Dorf im nordöstlichen Teil der Provinz Heilongjiang, wo die Temperaturen im Winter auf fast −40 Grad Celsius fallen können.

Un village enneigé dans la région du nord-est de la province du Heilongjiang, où les températures hivernales peuvent chuter à presque −40° C.

↑
Xiao Zhuang, 1962

In 1968, Mao urged educated urban young adults to volunteer to go to the countryside to receive "reeducation" from workers and peasants to help them achieve a "revolutionary world outlook." Prior to this, between 1956 and 1966, more than one million city dwellers had gone to the countryside to "build a new socialist countryside"—seen here near Yuntai mountain, Jiangsu province. Following Mao's appeal, between 1968 and 1975, 17 million young people were relocated: just over 10 per cent of the urban population. In principle, the program called for lifelong resettlement in the rural areas. After the Cultural Revolution, most were able to return to the cities. Some resigned themselves to their fate and decided to remain.

1968 forderte Mao gebildete städtische Jugendliche auf, aufs Land zu gehen und sich dort einer „Umschulung" durch Arbeiter und Bauern zu unterziehen, die ihnen helfen würde, eine „revolutionäre Weltsicht" zu erlangen. Zuvor waren zwischen 1956 und 1966 mehr als eine Million Stadtbewohner aufs Land gezogen, um dort den Sozialismus neu aufzubauen, wie hier beim Berg Yuntai in der Provinz Jiangsu zu sehen ist. Maos Appell folgend, wurden zwischen 1968 und 1975 17 Millionen junge Menschen umgesiedelt, etwas mehr als 10 Prozent der Stadtbevölkerung. Prinzipiell verlangte das Programm eine lebenslange Ansiedlung in den ländlichen Gebieten. Nach der Kulturrevolution war es den meisten möglich, in die Städte zurückzukehren. Einige ergaben sich in ihr Schicksal und blieben.

En 1968, Mao pressa les jeunes citadins éduqués d'aller dans les campagnes pour bénéficier d'une « rééducation » par les ouvriers et les paysans qui les aideraient à atteindre « à une conscience révolutionnaire du monde ». Auparavant, entre 1956 et 1966, plus d'un million d'habitants des villes étaient déjà partis dans les provinces pour « construire une nouvelle campagne socialiste », comme on le voit ici près de la montagne de Yuntai, province du Jiangsu. À la suite de l'appel de Mao, 17 millions de jeunes gens furent transférés dans les campagnes entre 1968 et 1975, soit 10 % de la population urbaine. En principe, ce programme visait une relocalisation dans les zones rurales. Après la Révolution culturelle, la plupart put retourner dans les villes. Certains se résignèrent à rester.

↓
Xiao Zhuang, 1963

Peasants at the Yinyang commune in Qidong county, Jiangsu province, listen to a broadcast on a homemade radio.

Bauern der Kommune Yinyang im Kreis Qidong in der Provinz Jiangsu lauschen einer Sendung in einem selbst gebastelten Radio.

Des paysans de la commune de Yinyang dans le canton de Qidong, province du Jiangsu, écoutent une émission sur une radio bricolée à la maison.

pp. 166/167
Wang Shilong, 1965

Peasants plant huge slogans in the fields promoting the spirit of the "Old man who moved the Mountain." Others read: "Long Live the Communist Party of China" and "Waste and corruption are serious crimes."

Bauern stellen auf den Feldern riesige Spruchbänder auf, die an den Geist vom „alten Mann, der den Berg bewegte" erinnern. Auf anderen steht: „Lang lebe die Kommunistische Partei Chinas" und „Verschwendung und Korruption sind schwere Verbrechen".

Des paysans mettent en place dans les champs des slogans en lettres énormes pour promouvoir l'esprit du « Vieil homme qui déplaça la montagne ». D'autres proclament « Longue vie au parti communiste de Chine » et « Le gaspillage et la corruption sont de grands crimes. »

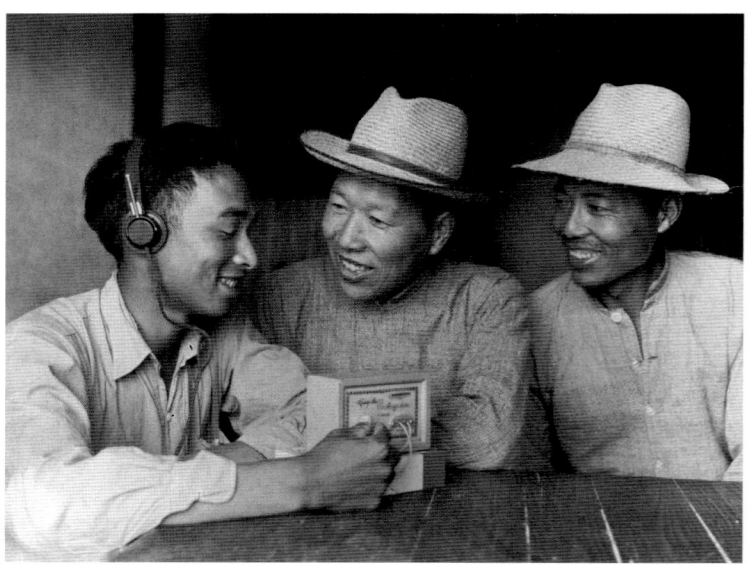

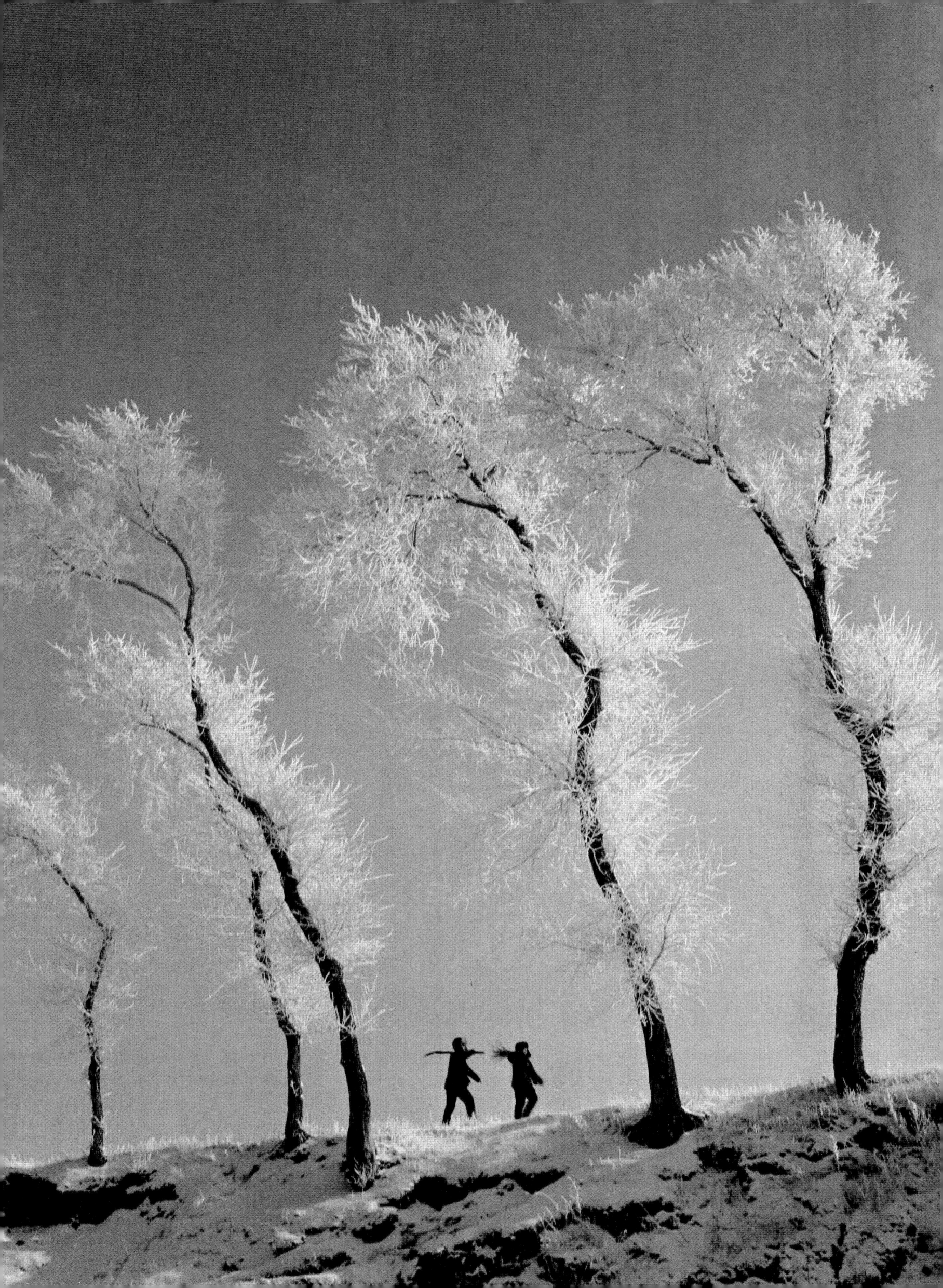

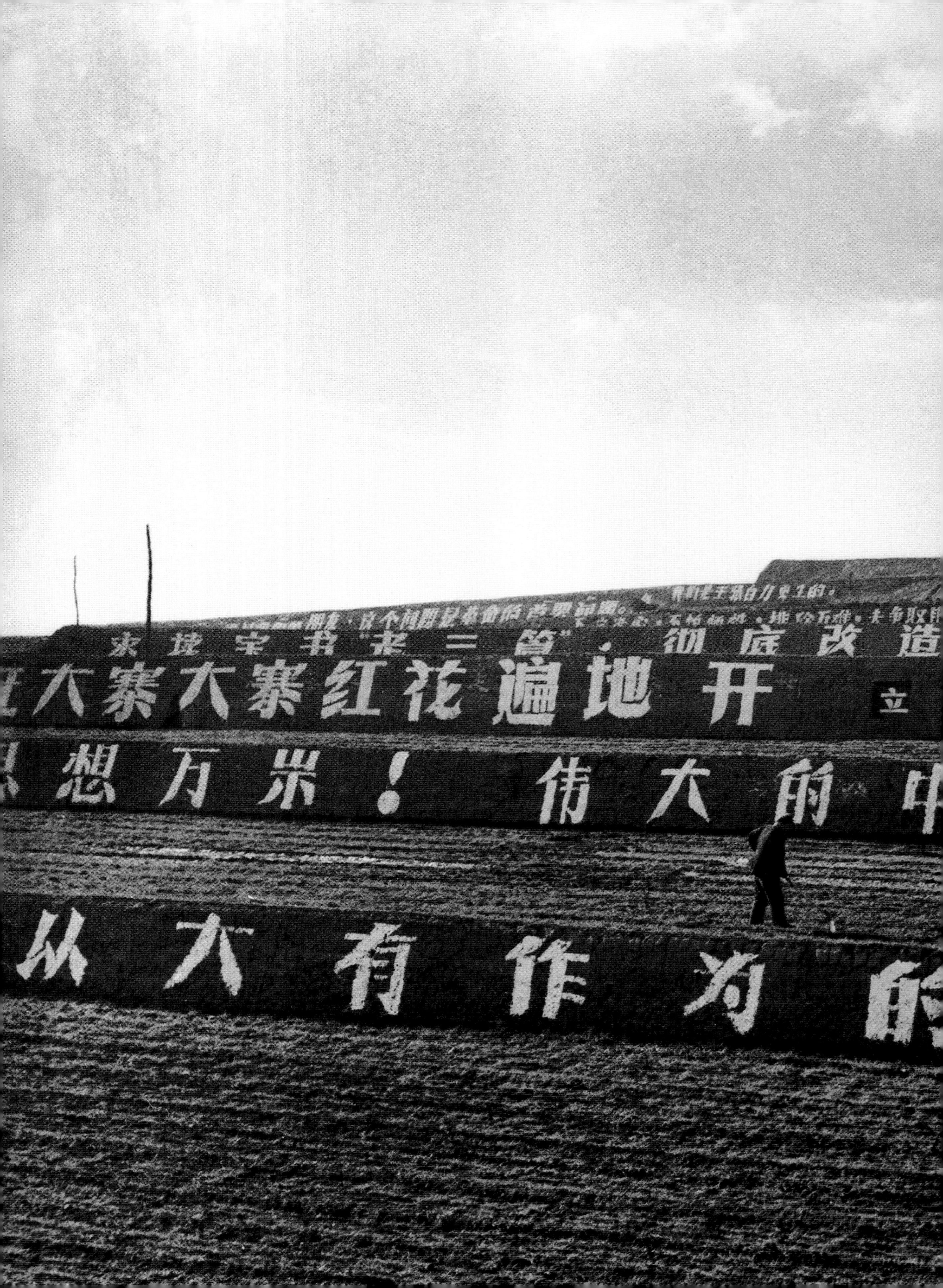
彻底改造
大寨大寨红花遍地开
立
想万岁！
伟大的
大有作为的

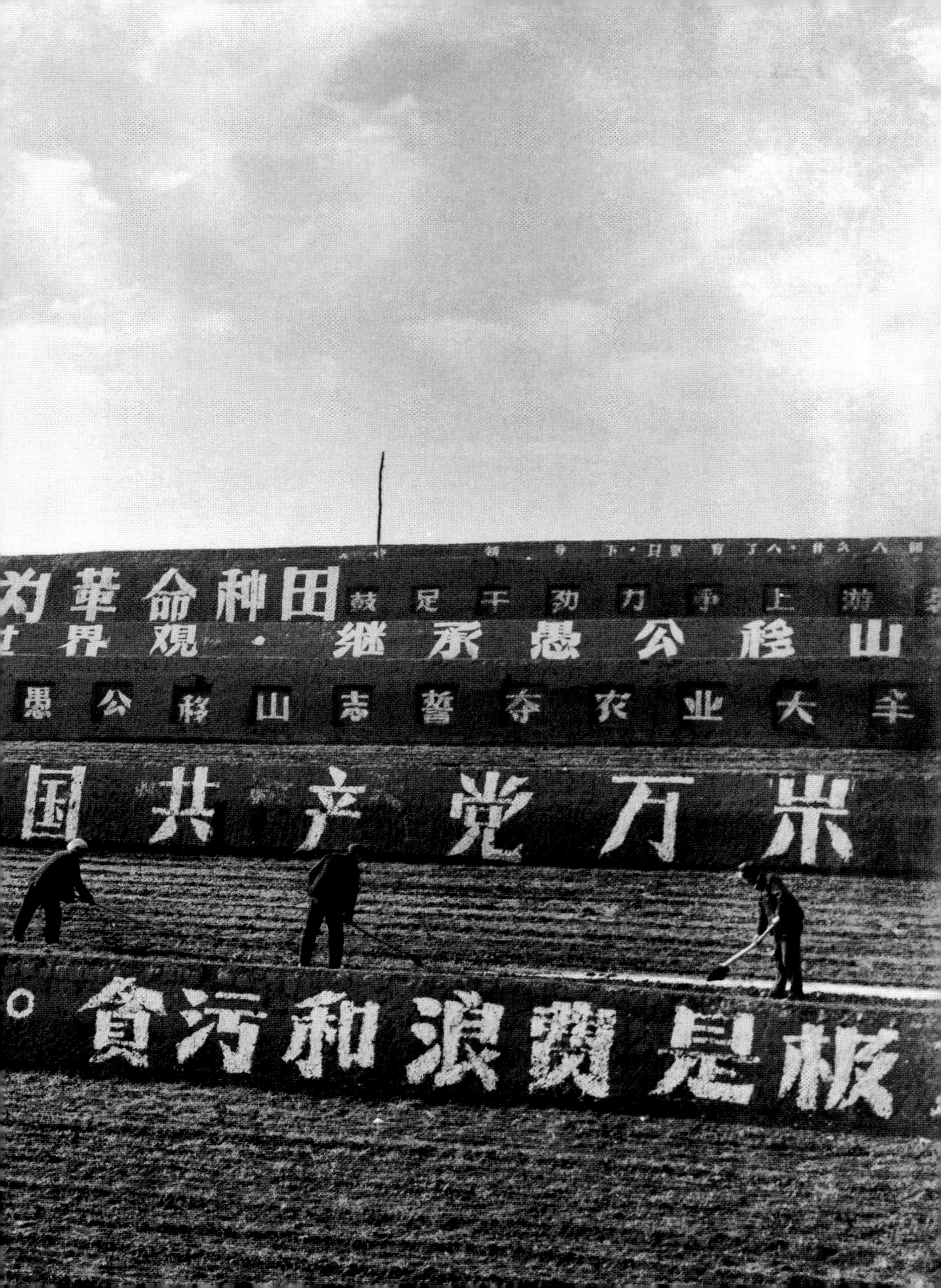
为革命种田
鼓足干劲力争上游
界观 · 继承愚公移山
愚公移山志誓夺农业大丰
国共产党万岁
貪污和浪费是极

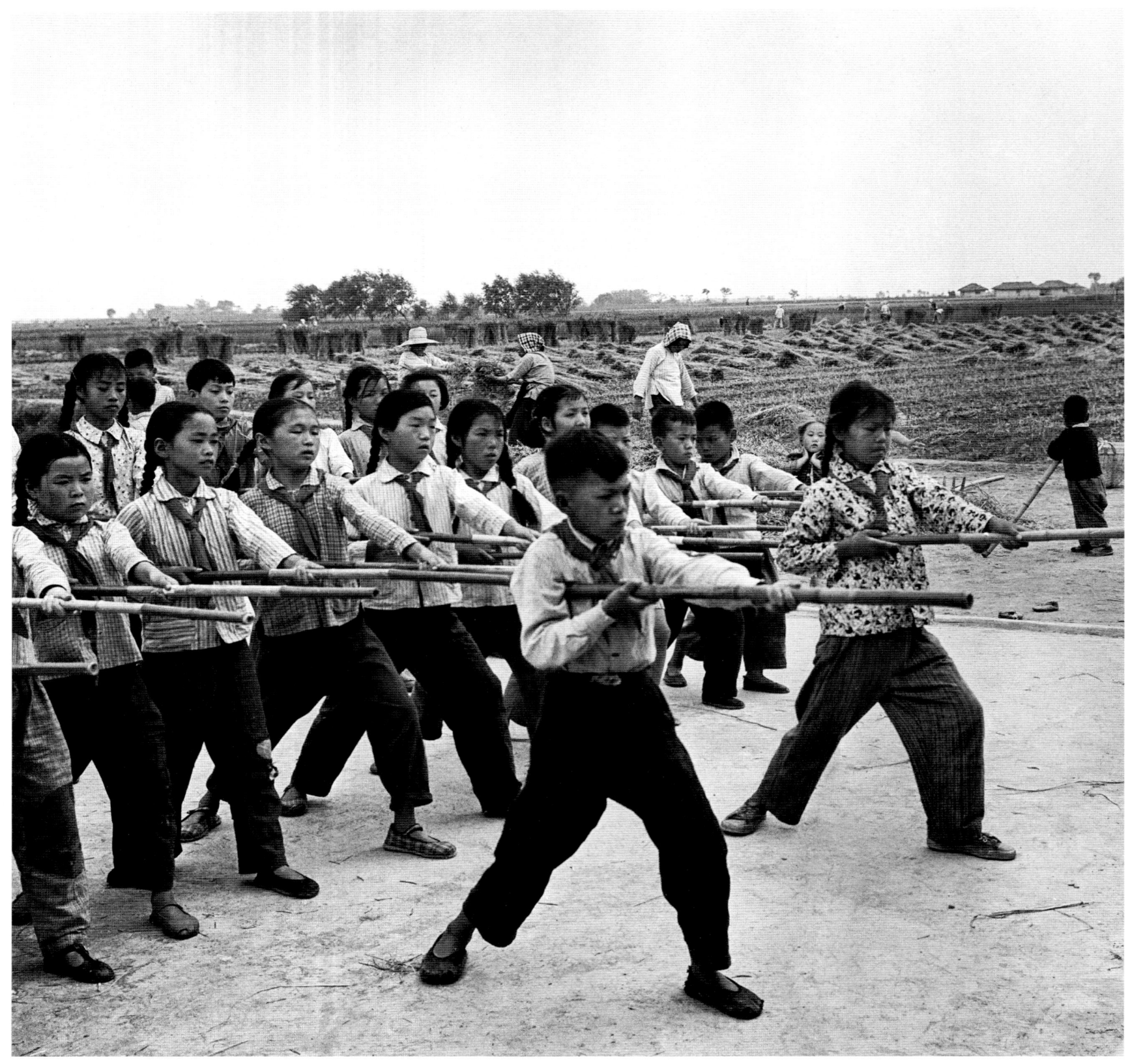

↑
Xiao Zhuang, 1965

In the early 1960s, China faced a number of enemies: a rumored counterattack by Kuomintang forces in Taiwan; as well as U.S. forces entrenched in southern Vietnam, fighting the Chinese-backed Vietnamese army in the north, and the Soviets, as China complained about the latter's interference in domestic policies. This resulted in the Soviets' angry withdrawal of technical support and expertise. As tension increased, across China, militia forces were organized and given military training: even elementary and middle-school children. Mao even ordered the entire nation to dig deep trenches in preparation for a potential war.

Zu Beginn der 1960er-Jahre sah sich China mit mehreren Gegnern konfrontiert: dem Gerücht eines bevorstehenden Gegenangriffs der Kuomintang-Truppen aus Taiwan sowie den in Südvietnam verschanzten US-Streitkräften, die gegen die von den Chinesen unterstützte Armee Nordvietnams kämpften, und den Sowjets, die von China der Einmischung in seine inneren Angelegenheiten beschuldigt wurden. Dies führte zum verärgerten Abzug von technischer Unterstützung und fachmännischem Können der Sowjets. Während sich die Spannung verschärfte, wurden überall in China Milizen aufgestellt und militärisch ausgebildet, sogar mit Kindern aus Grund- und Mittelschulen. Mao befahl außerdem der gesamten Nation, in Vorbereitung auf einen möglichen Krieg tiefe Schützengräben auszuheben.

Au début des années 1960, la Chine doit faire face à plusieurs ennemis : des rumeurs de contre-attaque des forces du Kuomintang à Taïwan, des armées américaines embourbées au Sud-Vietnam qui combattent les armées nord-vietnamiennes soutenues par la Chine, mais aussi les Soviétiques puisque Mao se plaint de leurs interférences dans sa politique intérieure. L'URSS, fâchée, retire ses experts et son soutien technique. La tension croit en Chine et des milices sont organisées et reçoivent une formation militaire. Même les enfants des écoles sont concernés. Mao demande de creuser des tranchées en préparation d'un conflit.

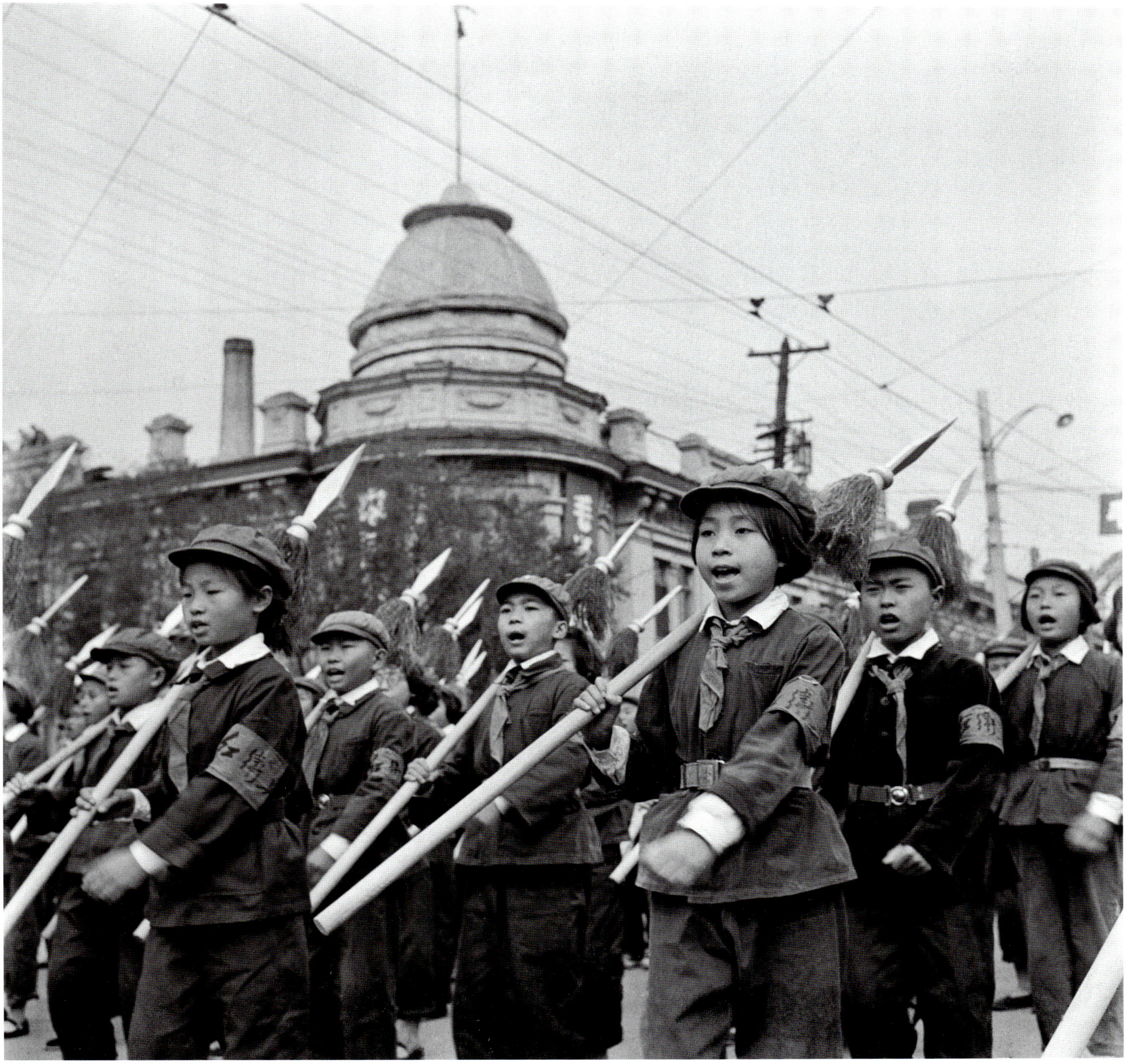

↑
Li Zhensheng, 1966

Schoolchildren shouldering wooden bayonets take part in the National Day parade in Harbin, Heilongjiang province. The building in the background was built by members of the thousand-strong community of Russians who fled to China after the Bolshevik Revolution in 1917.

Eine Gruppe von Schulkindern mit geschulterten Holzbajonetten beteiligt sich an der Parade zum Nationaltag in Harbin in der Provinz Heilongjiang. Das Gebäude im Hintergrund wurde von Angehörigen einer 1000-köpfigen russischen Gemeinde erbaut, die nach der bolschewistischen Revolution 1917 nach China geflohen waren.

Un groupe d'enfants des écoles, armes de bois à l'épaule, participe à la parade de la Fête nationale à Harbin, province d'Heilongjiang. Le bâtiment à coupole au second plan a été édifié par la communauté des milliers de Russes qui avaient fui leur pays après la révolution de 1917.

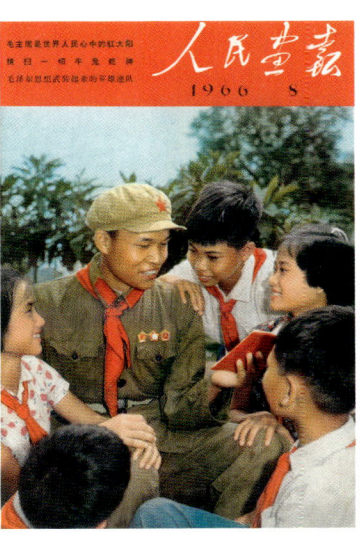

China Pictorial, August 1966

PLA soldier surrounded by young pioneers

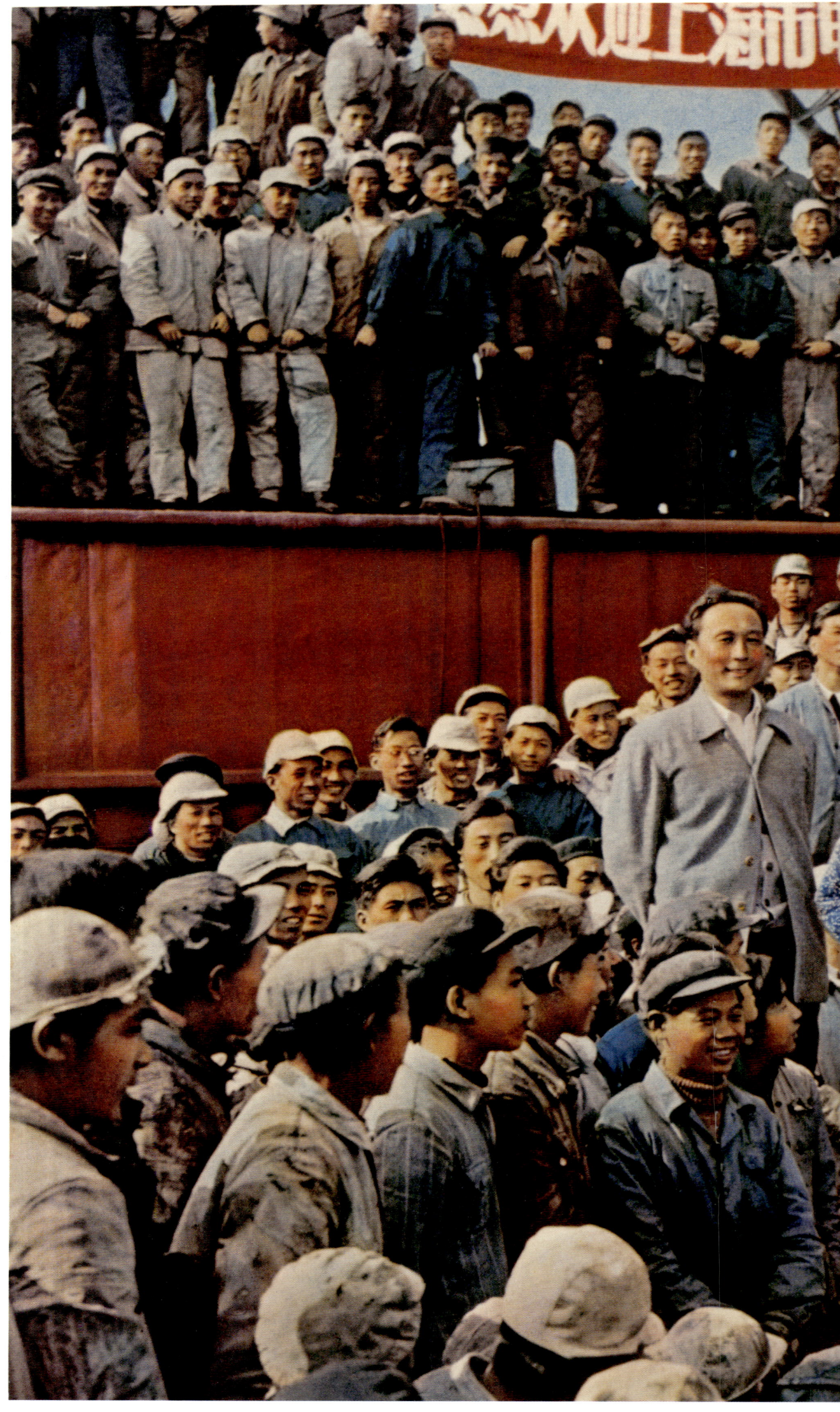

→
Yin Fukan, 1960

As efforts continued to build New China, the Chinese Communist Party called on actors and writers to "go deep into the life of workers, peasants, and soldiers," and spread the socialist message. Here, Chinese actors, including male star Zhao Dan (second from the right), sing for the workers of the Shanghai shipbuilding factory.

Im Zuge der fortgesetzten Bemühungen um den Aufbau des neuen China rief die Kommunistische Partei Schauspieler und Autoren dazu auf, „tief in das Leben von Arbeitern, Bauern und Soldaten einzudringen" und die sozialistische Botschaft zu verbreiten. Hier singen chinesische Schauspieler, darunter der Star Zhao Dan (Zweiter von rechts), für die Arbeiter der Shanghaier Schiffswerft.

Dans le cadre des efforts de construction de la Chine nouvelle, le Parti communiste demanda aux acteurs et aux écrivains « de s'intégrer en profondeur dans la vie des travailleurs, des paysans et des soldats », et de diffuser le message socialiste. Ici, des acteurs chinois, dont la vedette Zhao Dan (second à droite), chantent pour les ouvriers d'un chantier naval de Shanghai.

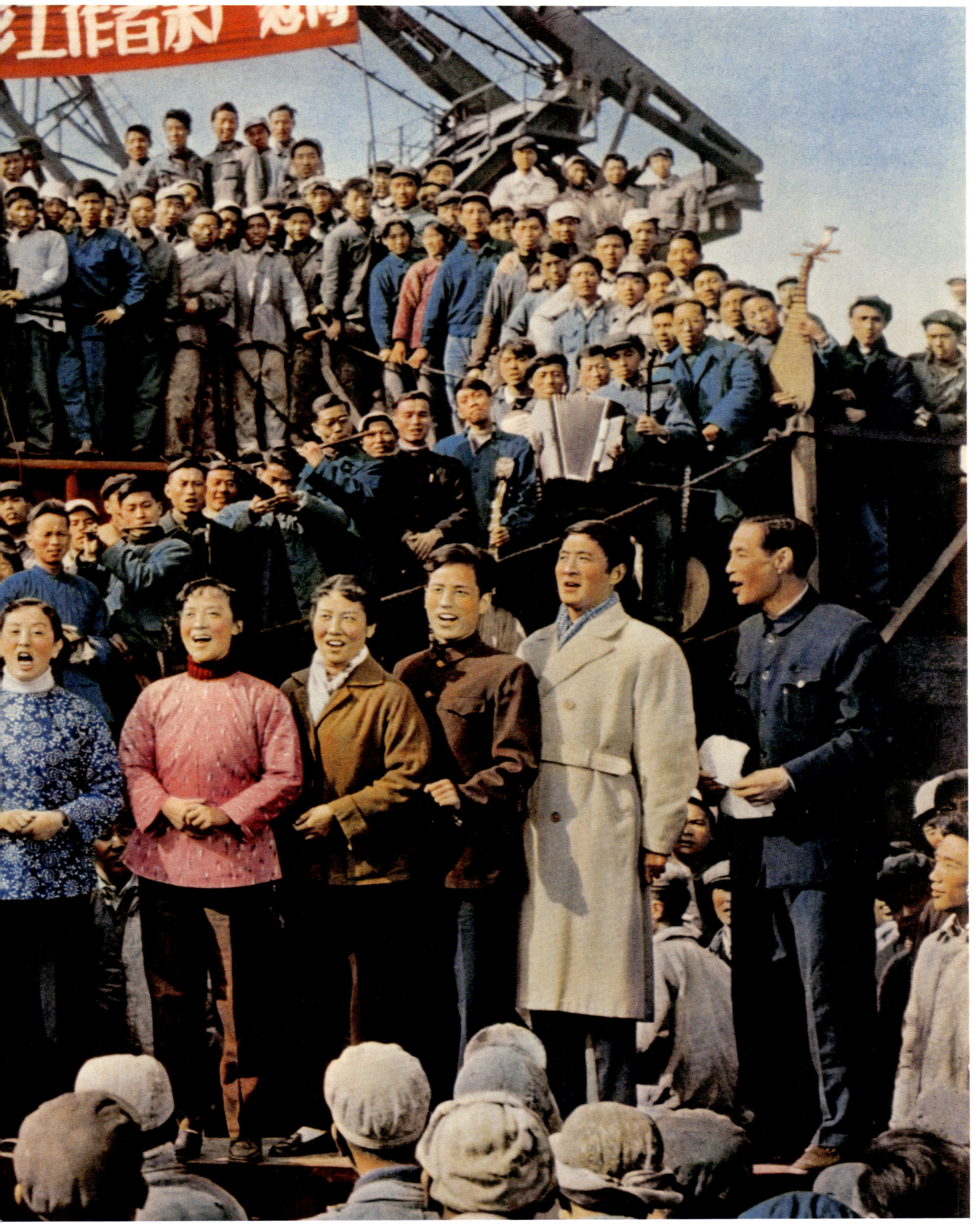

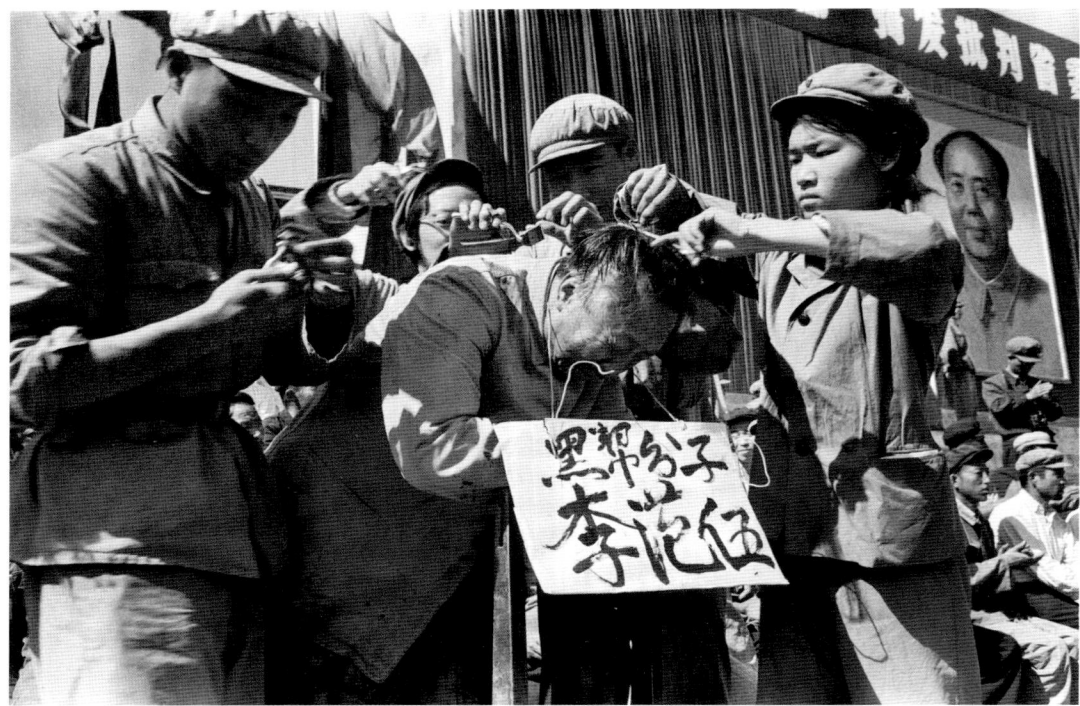

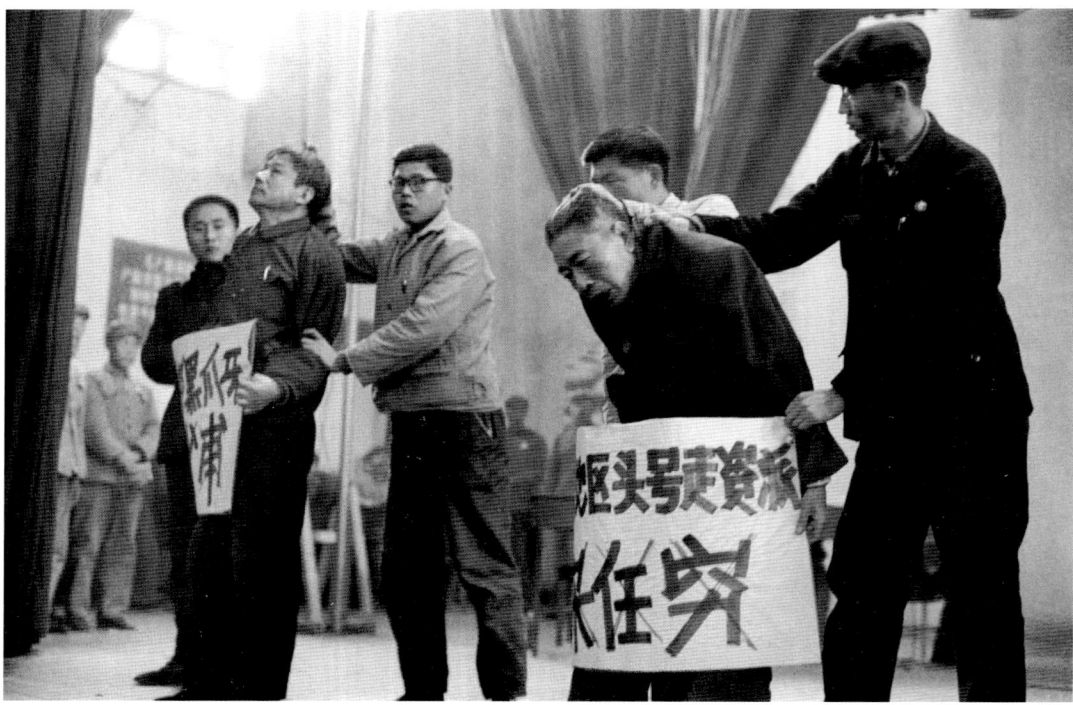

←
Li Zhensheng, 1966

*Li Fanwu, a senior Heilongjiang Party offi-
cial, accused of being a counterrevolutionary,
is publicly "half" shaved and humiliated at
a mass rally in Harbin. The sign hanging
from his neck reads "Black Element Li
Fanwu." Li Fanwu was once a student of
Beiping Law College. He joined the Chinese
Communist Party in 1932, and went to the
USSR to study in 1936. In 1945, he became
leader of the Communist Party in northeastern China. He was governor of Heilongjiang province when the Cultural Revolution
broke out. He was finally rehabilitated in
1979. He died in Beijing in 1986.*

*Li Fanwu, leitender Parteifunktionär in
Heilongjiang, wird als Konterrevolutionär
angeklagt und bei einer Massenversammlung
in Harbin öffentlich „halb" geschoren und
gedemütigt. Auf dem Schild auf seiner Brust
steht zu lesen „Schwarzes Element Li Fanwu". Li Fanwu war einst Student an der
juristischen Hochschule in Peking. Er trat
1932 in die Kommunistische Partei ein und
ging 1936 zum Studium in die UdSSR. 1945
wurde er Führer der Kommunistischen Partei
Nordostchinas. Bei Ausbruch der Kulturrevolution war er Gouverneur der Provinz
Heilongjiang. 1979 wurde er schließlich
rehabilitiert und starb 1986 in Peking.*

*Li Fanwu, haut responsable du Parti du
Heilongjiang, accusé d'être un contre-révolu-
tionnaire, est publiquement «demi-rasé» et
humilié lors d'un rassemblement de masse à
Harbin. Le panneau qu'il porte dit « Élément
noir Li Fanwu ». Ancien étudiant de la faculté
de droit de Pékin, il avait rejoint le Parti
communiste en 1932 et était parti étudier en
URSS en 1936. En 1945, il fut responsable
du Parti pour le nord-est de la Chine, puis
gouverneur de la province du Heilongjiang
lorsqu'éclata la Révolution culturelle. Il fut
finalement réhabilité en 1979 et mourut à
Pékin en 1986.*

↑
Jiang Shaowu, 1966

*Senior party leaders Song Renqiong (right)
and Xu Shaofu (left) of Liaoning province are
humiliated in a public denunciation rally.*

*Die leitenden Parteifunktionäre Song
Renqiong (rechts) und Xu Shaofu (links)
aus der Provinz Liaoning werden in einer
öffentlichen Denunziationsversammlung
gedemütigt.*

*De hauts responsables du Parti de la province
du Liaoning, Song Renqiong (à droite) et
Xu Shaofu (à gauche) sont humiliés lors d'un
rassemblement de dénonciation.*

→
Li Zhensheng, 1966

*Senior Heilongjiang Party official Ren
Zhongyi bows his head in humiliation at
a mass rally in Harbin. In the 1980s, Ren
was appointed Party secretary of Guangdong
province, to steer forward the economic reform policy implemented by Deng Xiaoping.*

*Ren Zhongyi, hochrangiger Parteifunktionär
der Provinz Heilongjiang, senkt bei einer
Massenkundgebung in Harbin gedemütigt
den Kopf. In den 1980er-Jahren war Ren
zum Parteisekretär der Provinz Guangdong
ernannt worden, um die von Deng Xiaoping
eingeführte Wirtschaftsreform voranzutreiben.*

*Haut responsable du Parti pour le Heilongji-
ang, Ren Zonghi, courbe la tête en signe
d'humiliation, lors d'un rassemblement de
masse à Harbin. Dans les années 1980, il fut
nommé Secrétaire du Parti du Guangdong,
pour accélérer les réformes économiques
mises en œuvre par Deng Xiaoping.*

*[On seeing his father targeted by Red Guards] "I didn't even think
of trying to reason with them or protest, or to shout or fight. Would it
have been any worse if I had? I just stood there dumbly… as if I were
watching somebody else's dream."*

*[Beim Anblick seines Vaters in der Gewalt der Roten Garden] „Ich
kam gar nicht auf den Gedanken, mit ihnen vernünftig zu reden oder
zu protestieren oder zu schreien oder zu kämpfen. Wäre es schlimmer
gewesen, wenn ich das getan hätte? Ich habe nur stumm dagestanden
… so, als betrachtete ich den Traum eines anderen."*

*[Voyant son père persécuté par des Gardes rouges] «Je ne pensais
même pas essayer de les raisonner ou de protester, de crier ou de me
battre. Est-ce que ça aurait été pire si je l'avais fait ? Je restais juste là,
muet … comme si je regardais le rêve de quelqu'un d'autre. »*

CHEN KAIGE (1952–), filmmaker, 2001

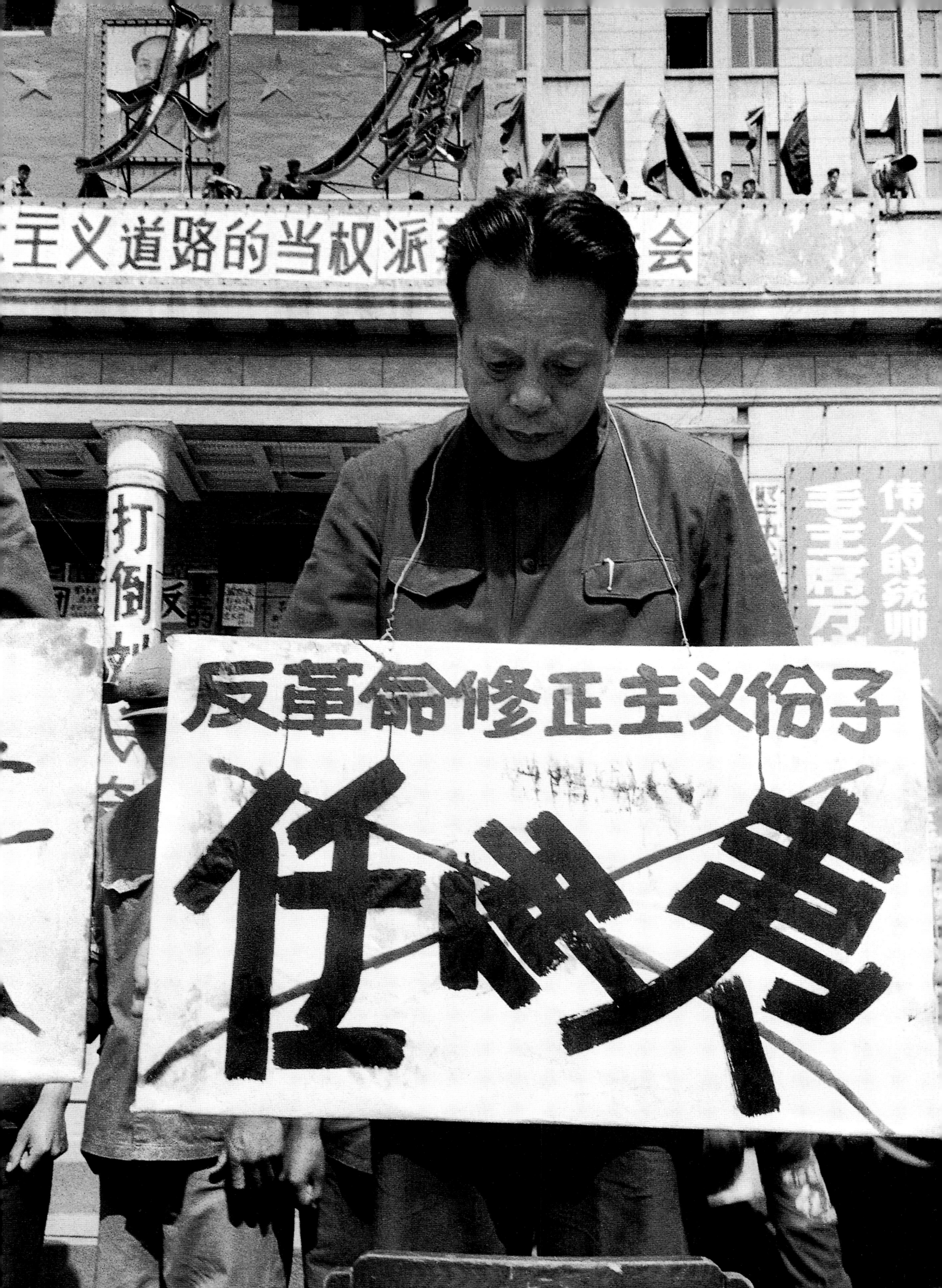

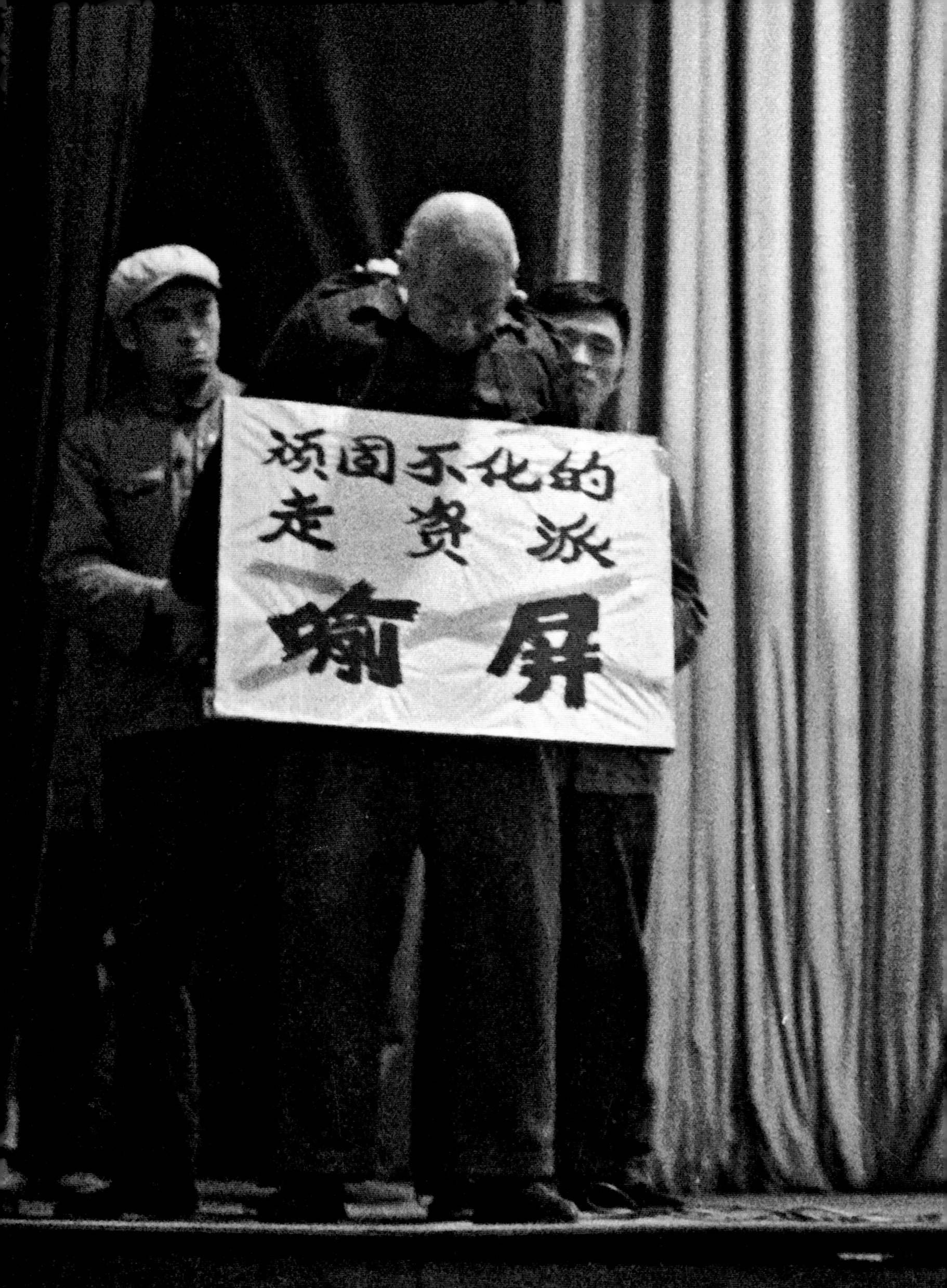

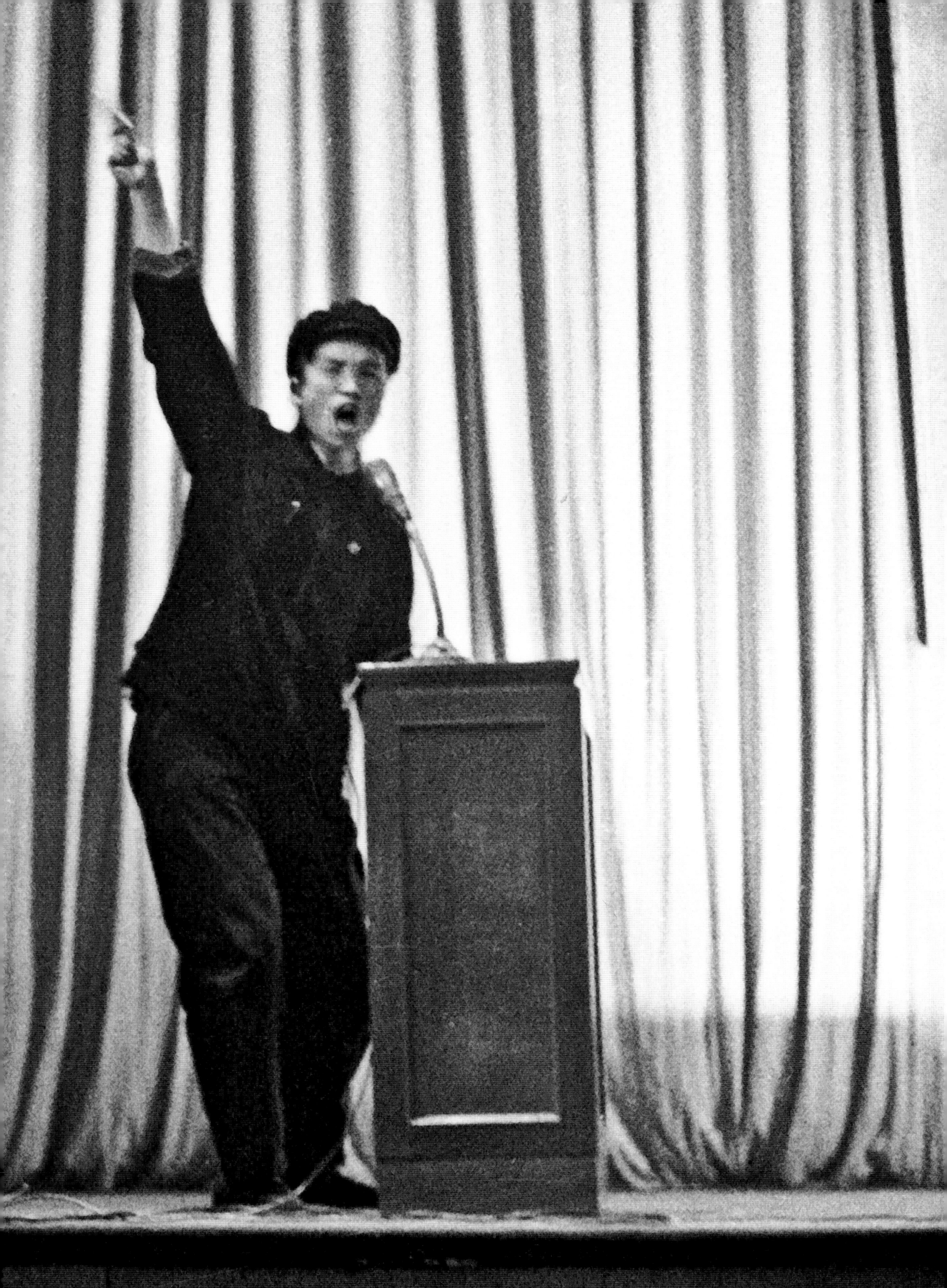

*"Better to be a dog in times of peace
than a man in times of turmoil."*

*„Es ist besser, in Friedenszeiten ein Hund zu sein,
als ein Mensch in Zeiten des Aufruhrs."*

*« Il vaut mieux être un chien en temps de paix
qu'un homme en temps de troubles. »*

PROVERB/SPRICHWORT/PROVERBE

pp. 174/175
Jiang Shaowu, 1966

*Senior leader Yu Ping being denounced by
a fanatical worker at a denunciation session
in Liaoning to humiliate officials ousted
by factions loyal to Mao. Yu Ping, one-time
secretary of Liaoning Provincial Committee
of the Chinese Communist Party, was ousted
at the beginning of the Cultural Revolution,
and then denounced in 100 denunciation
sessions. The sign hanging round his neck
reads: "Yu Ping, diehard capitalist-roader."
He survived the Cultural Revolution, and
may have had some satisfaction from being
appointed a member of the jury in the trial
of the Gang of Four. He died in 1995.*

*Der hochrangige Funktionär Yu Ping wird
von einem fanatischen Arbeiter in einer
Kampfsitzung in Liaoning angeprangert, um
Amtspersonen zu demütigen, die von mao-
loyalen Gruppierungen gestürzt worden
waren. Yu Ping, ehemaliger Sekretär des Provinzialkomitees der KPCh in der Provinz
Liaoning, wurde zu Beginn der Kulturrevolution aus seinem Amt entfernt und sodann
in 100 Kampfsitzungen angeprangert. Auf
dem Schild um seinen Hals steht „Yu Ping,
unbelehrbarer Kapitalistenknecht". Er über-
lebte die Kulturrevolution und mag ein wenig
Genugtuung erfahren haben, als er zum
Mitglied der Jury im Verfahren gegen die
Viererbande berufen wurde. Er starb 1995.*

*Le vieux leader Yu Ping est dénoncé par un
ouvrier fanatisé au cours d'un meeting de
lutte dans le Liaoning, organisé pour humilier
les officiels renversés par les factions loyales
à Mao. Yu Ping, jadis secrétaire du comité
du Parti communiste de la province du Liaoning, fut chassé au début de la Révolution
culturelle et dénoncé dans 100 meetings de
lutte. Le panneau accroché autour de son
cou dit : « Yu Ping, compagnon de route des
réactionnaires capitalistes ». Il survécut à cette
révolution et eut la satisfaction d'être nommé
membre du jury lors du procès de la Bande
des quatre. Il mourut en 1995.*

→
Li Zhensheng, 1966

*At Harbin Workers' Club, Party secretary
Chen Lei (left), Li Fanwu, governor of
Heilongjiang province (center), and Wang
Yilun, vice governor of Heilongjiang (right)
are humiliated by being forced to wear dunce
hats and placards denouncing themselves.*

*Im Arbeiterclub von Harbin werden Partei-
sekretär Chen Lei (links), Li Fanwu, Gouverneur der Provinz Heilongjiang (Mitte),
und Wang Yilun, Vizegouverneur von
Heilongjiang, gedemütigt, indem man
sie zwingt, Narrenkappen und Schilder zu
tragen, auf denen sie sich selbst verurteilen.*

*Au cercle des travailleurs de Harbin, le
secrétaire du Parti Chen Lei (à gauche), le
gouverneur de la province du Heilongjiang
Li Fanwu (centre) et le vice-gouverneur de
la province Wang Yilun sont humiliés en
public par le port de chapeaux ridicules et
de panneaux d'autocritique.*

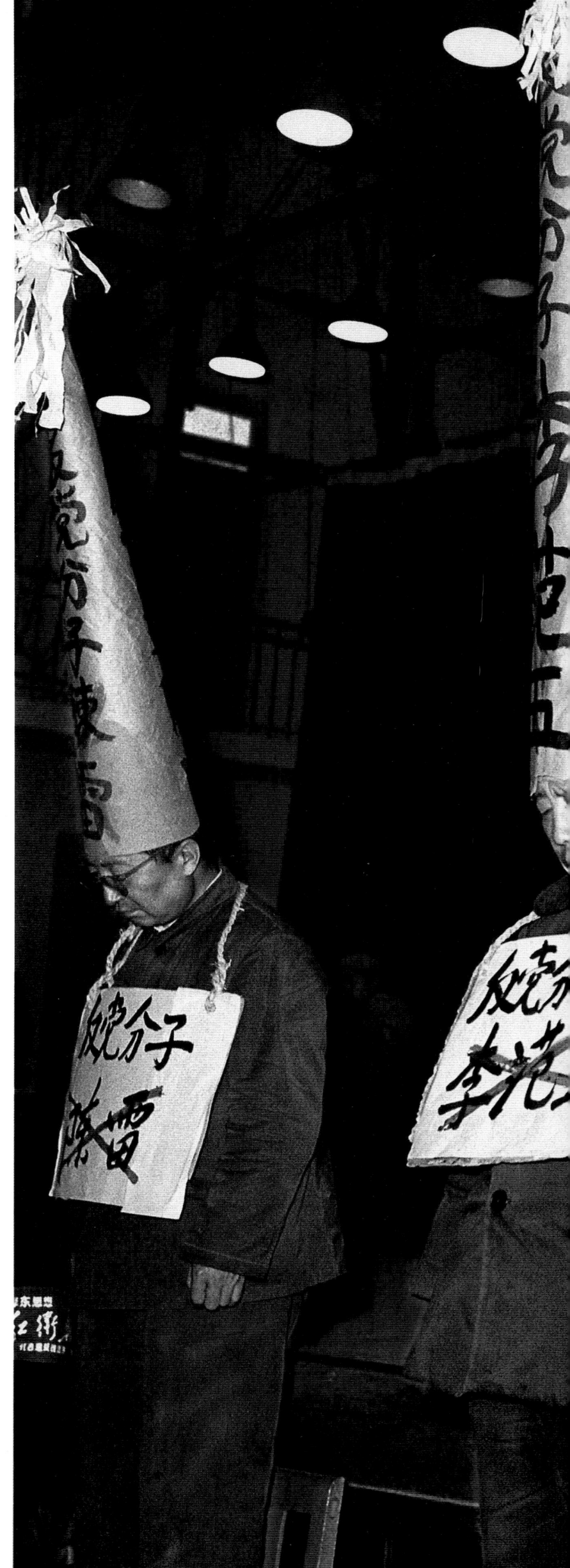

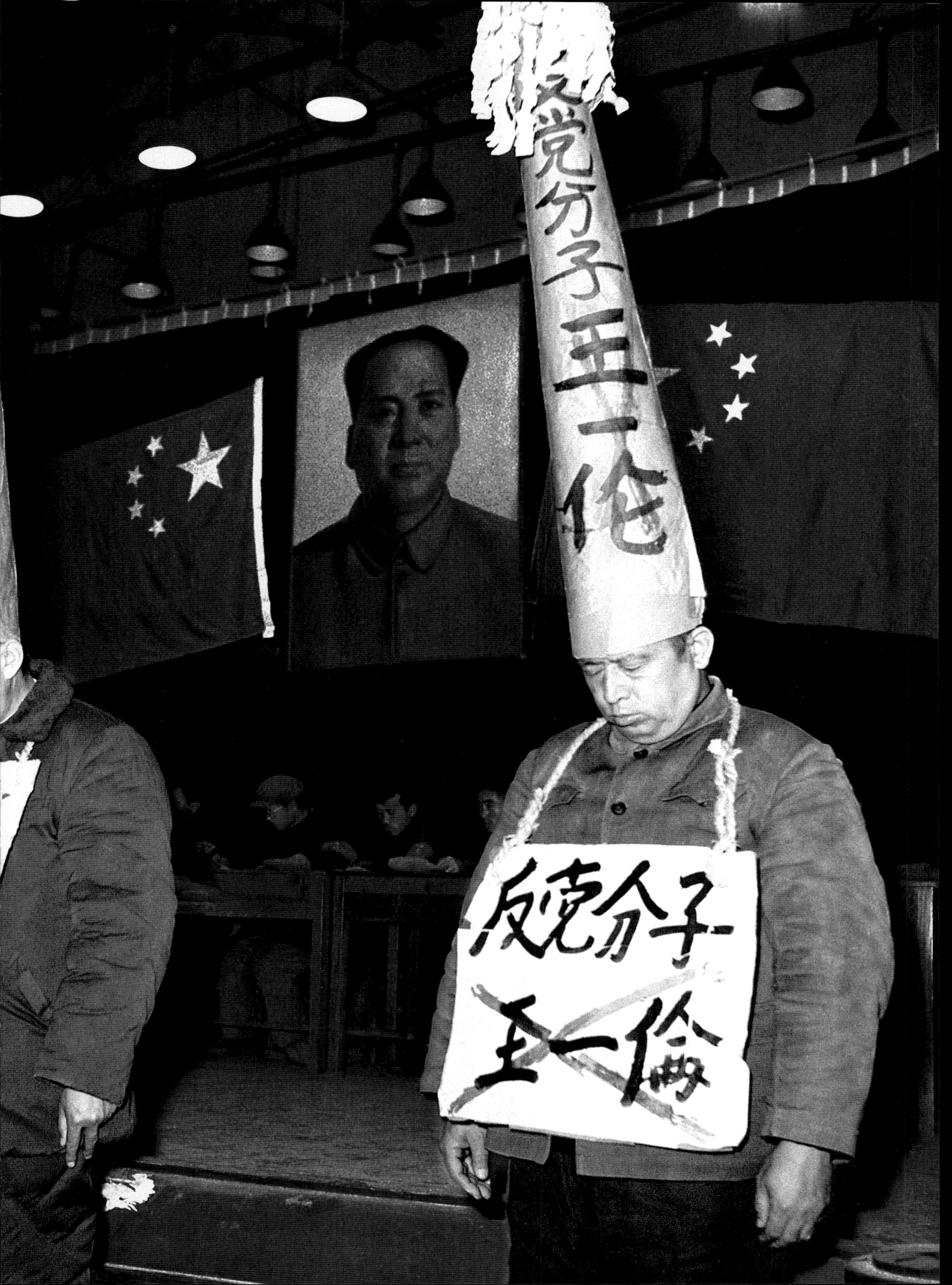

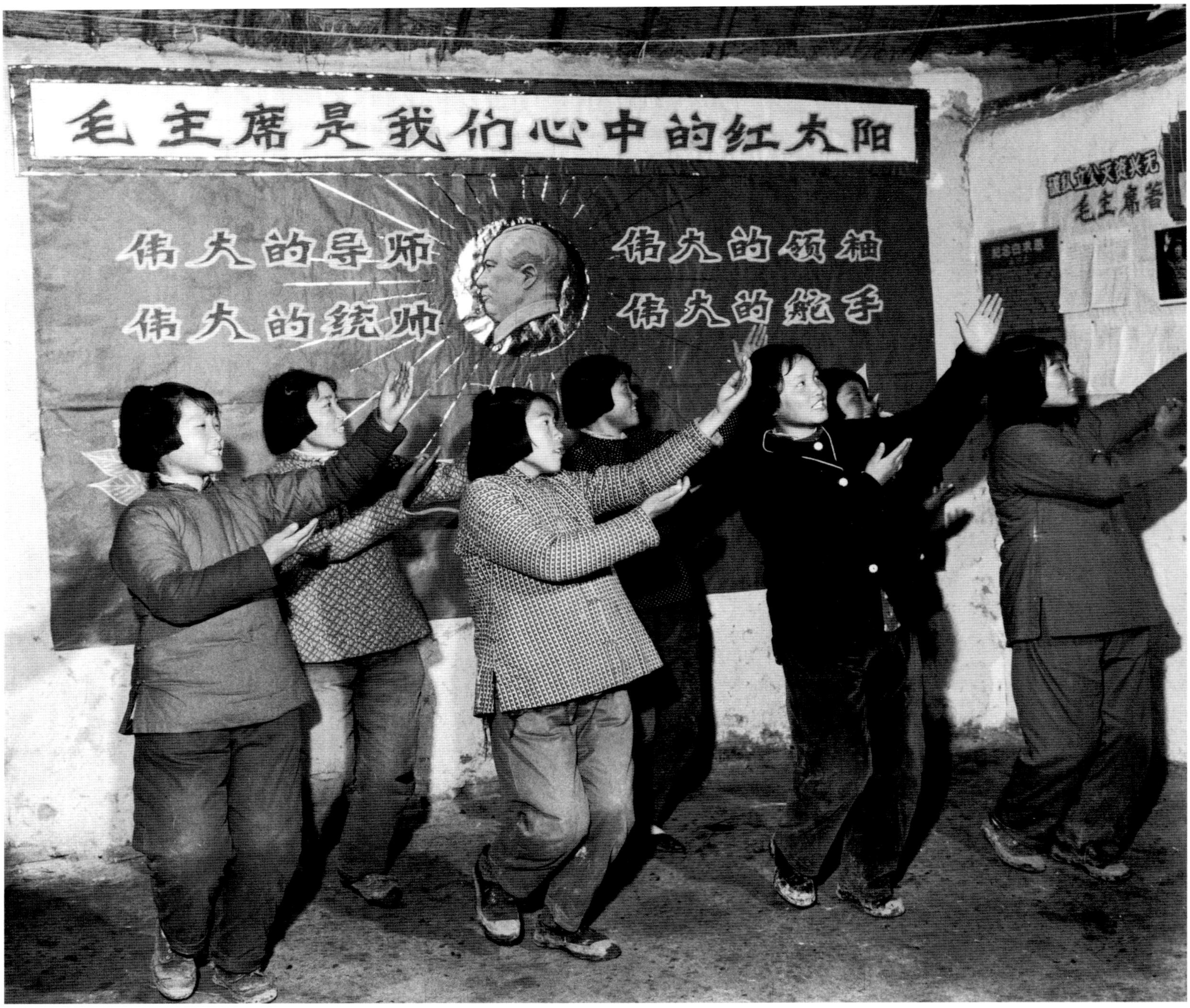

↑↘
Xiao Zhuang, 1966

Women workers at a factory in Nanjing perform the "loyalty dance" in honor of Chairman Mao. Every morning, the people were expected to announce the goals they set for the day, a ritual that was accompanied by a "loyalty dance," performed to the accompaniment of the song "Beloved Chairman Mao."

In einer Fabrik in Nanjing führen Arbeiterinnen zu Ehren des Vorsitzenden Mao den „Loyalitätstanz" auf. Jeden Morgen mussten die Menschen die Ziele verkünden, die sie sich für den Tag gesetzt hatten, ein Ritual, das von einem „Loyalitätstanz" zur Musik des Liedes „Geliebter Vorsitzender Mao" begleitet wurde.

Des ouvrières d'une usine de Nankin exécutent la « danse de la loyauté » en honneur du Président Mao. Chaque matin, les gens devaient annoncer les objectifs qu'ils s'étaient fixés pour la journée, rituel accompagné par cette danse interprétée sur le chant de « Bien aimé Président Mao. »

→
Li Zhensheng, 1968

A group of PLA soldiers in a military hospital salute Mao with copies of Quotations from Chairman Mao Zedong. *During the Cultural Revolution this was a "duty" that had to be carried out first thing every morning.*

Eine Gruppe von Soldaten der Volksbefreiungsarmee grüßt Mao mit Exemplaren von Die Worte des Vorsitzenden Mao Zedong. *Während der Kulturrevolution war dies eine tägliche Pflicht, der die Menschen allmorgendlich als Erstes nachkamen.*

Un groupe de soldats dans un hôpital militaire salue le portrait de Mao, chacun brandissant son exemplaire des Citations du Président Mao Zedong. *Pendant la Révolution culturelle, c'était un « devoir » que l'on devait accomplir chaque matin.*

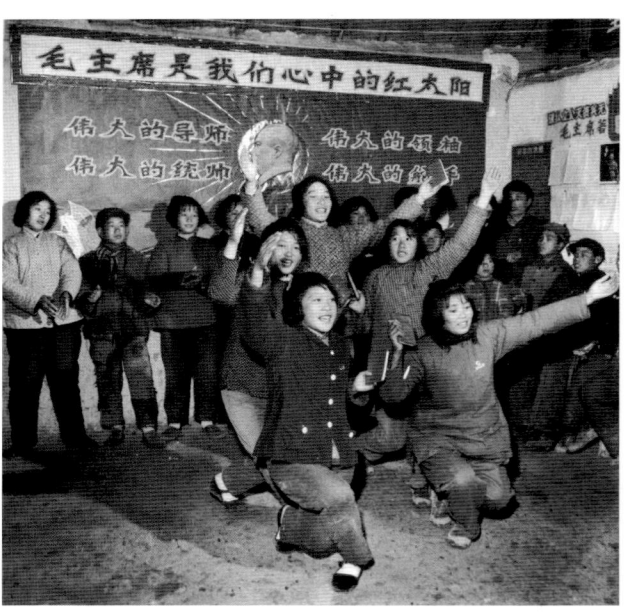

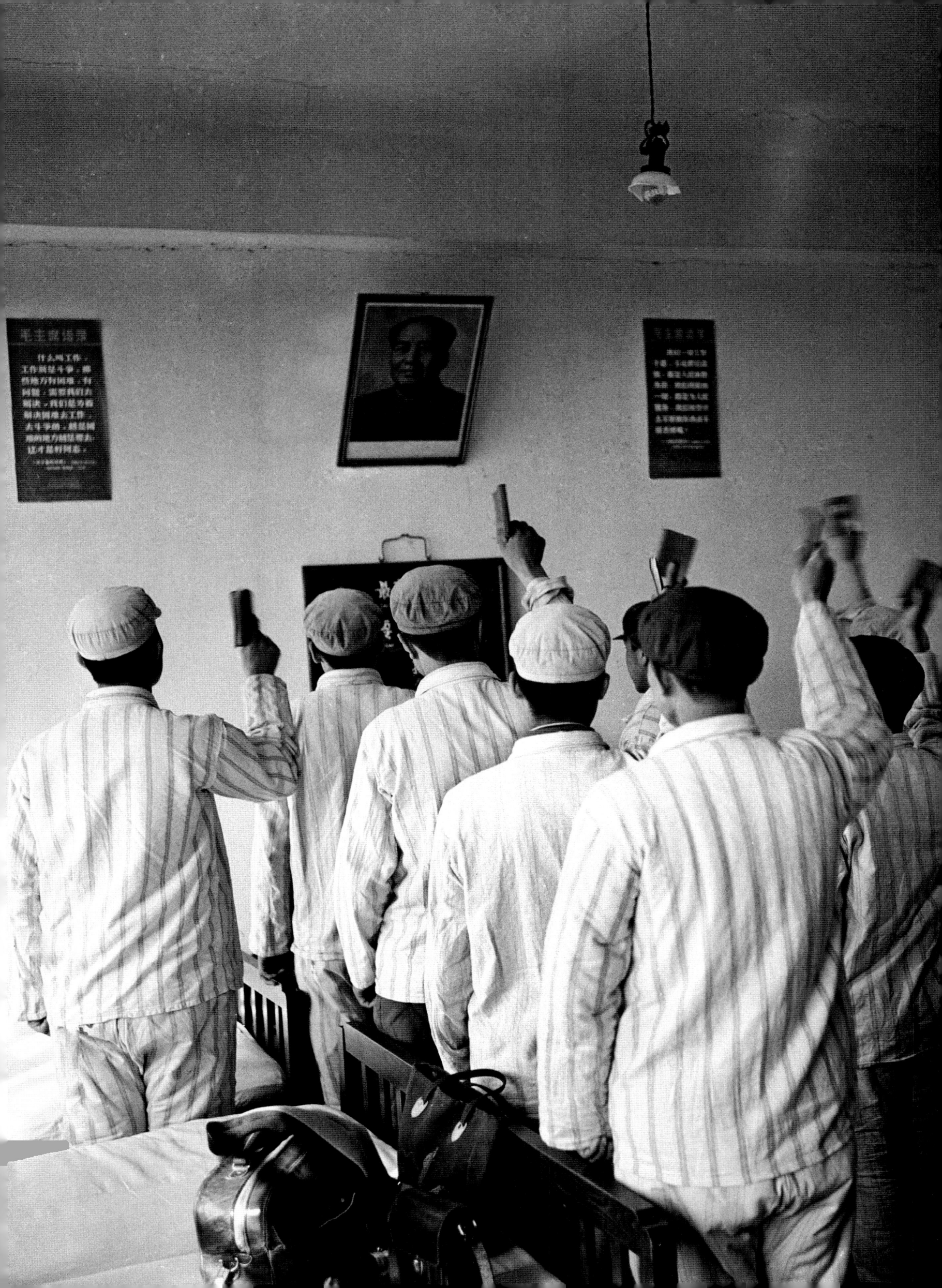

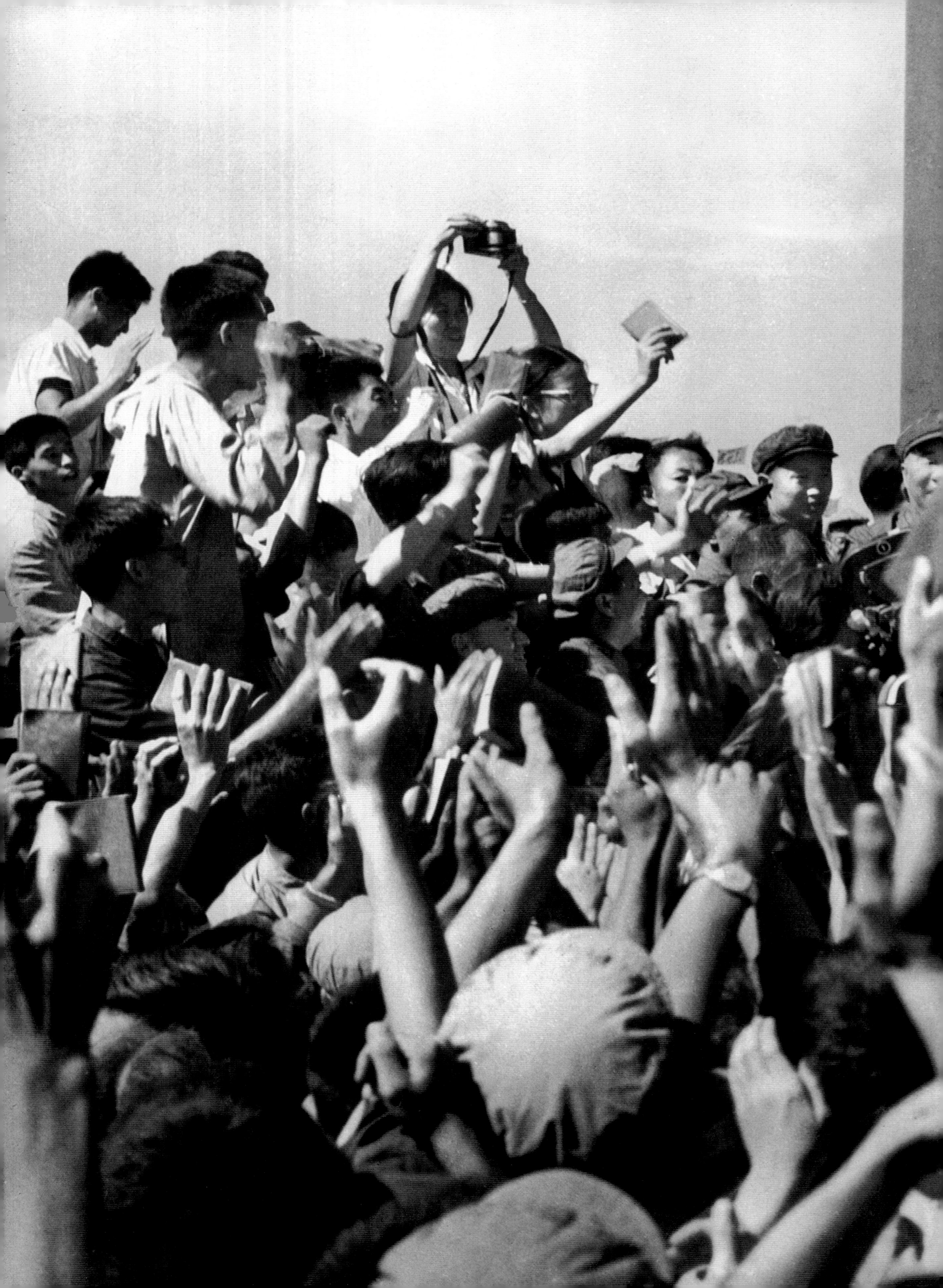

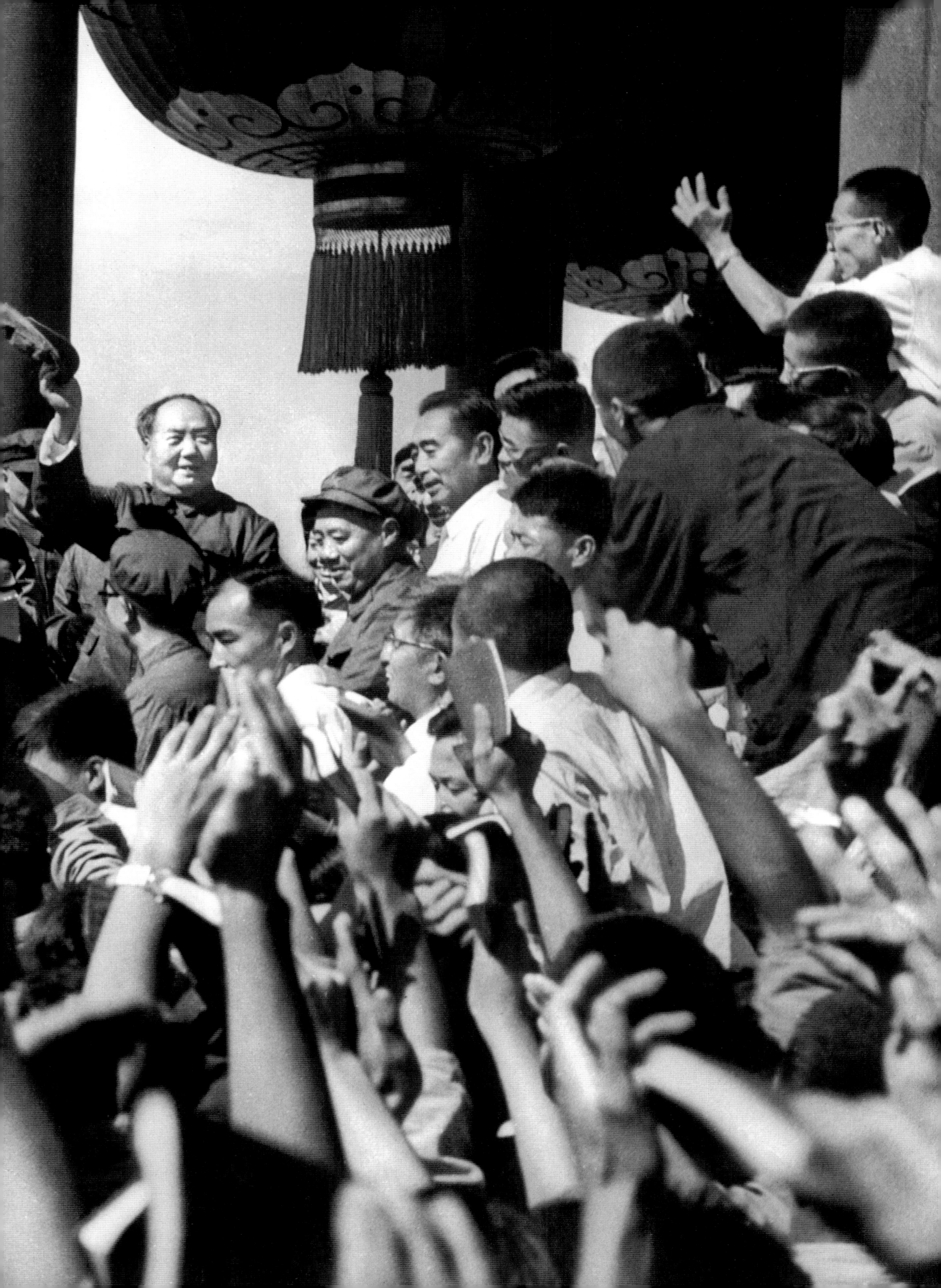

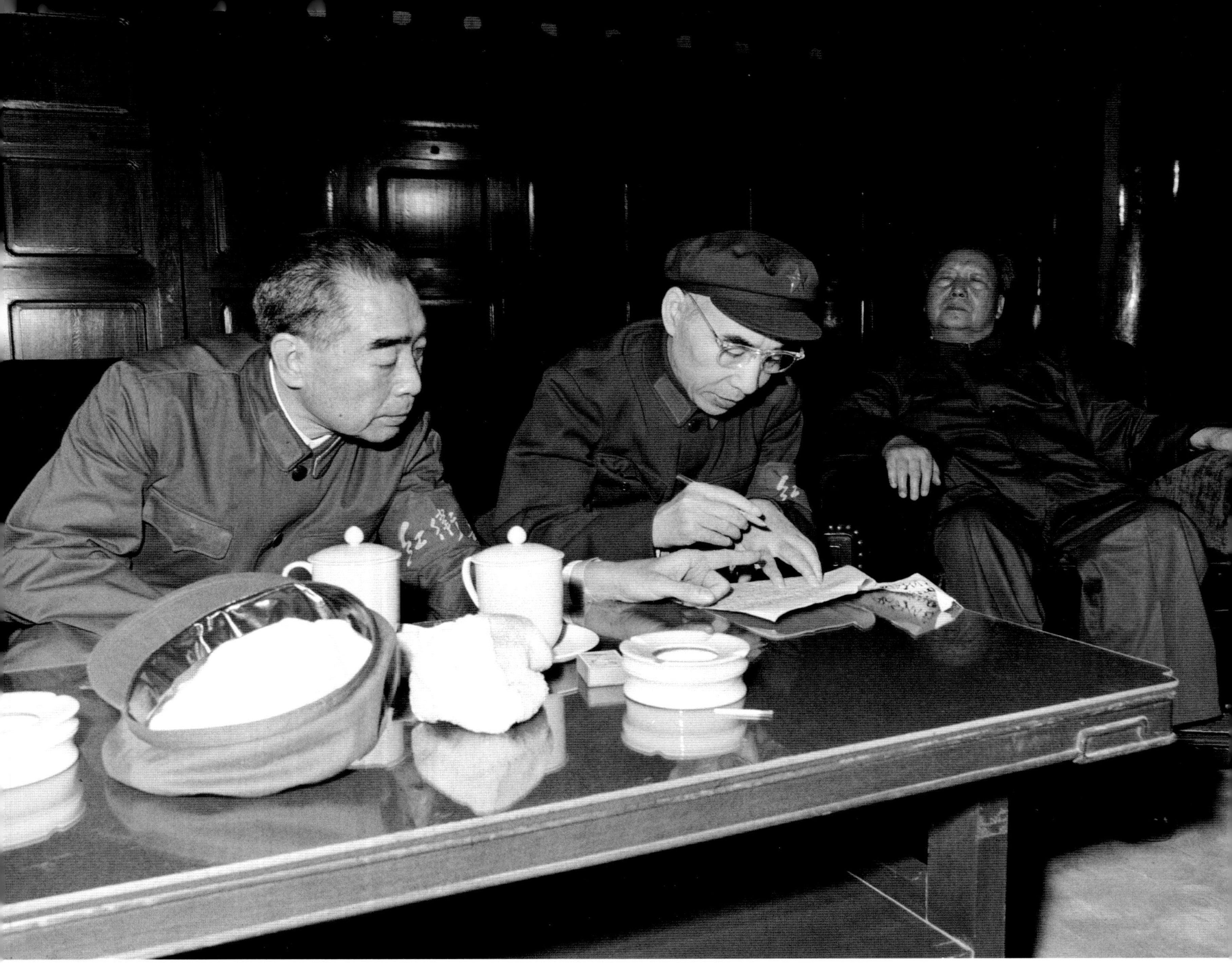

Meng Zhaorui, 1966

Mao watches as Premier Zhou Enlai and Marshal Lin Biao make last-minute changes to the speech to be delivered that day, September 15, 1966, by Lin Biao to the mass rally of Red Guards in Tiananmen Square. How portentous that expression appears with hindsight.

Mao sieht zu, wie Ministerpräsident Zhou Enlai und Marschall Lin Biao letzte Änderungen an der Rede vornehmen, die an diesem Tag, dem 15. September 1966, von Lin Biao vor der Masse der Roten Garden auf dem Tiananmen-Platz gehalten werden soll. Wie unheilvoll dieser Blick im Nachhinein wirkt.

Mao observe Zhou Enlai et le maréchal Lin Biao qui apportent des modifications de dernière minute à un discours qui doit être fait ce même 15 septembre 1966 par Lin Biao à la foule des Gardes rouges rassemblés sur la place Tian'anmen. Rétrospectivement, l'expression de Mao semble de mauvais augure.

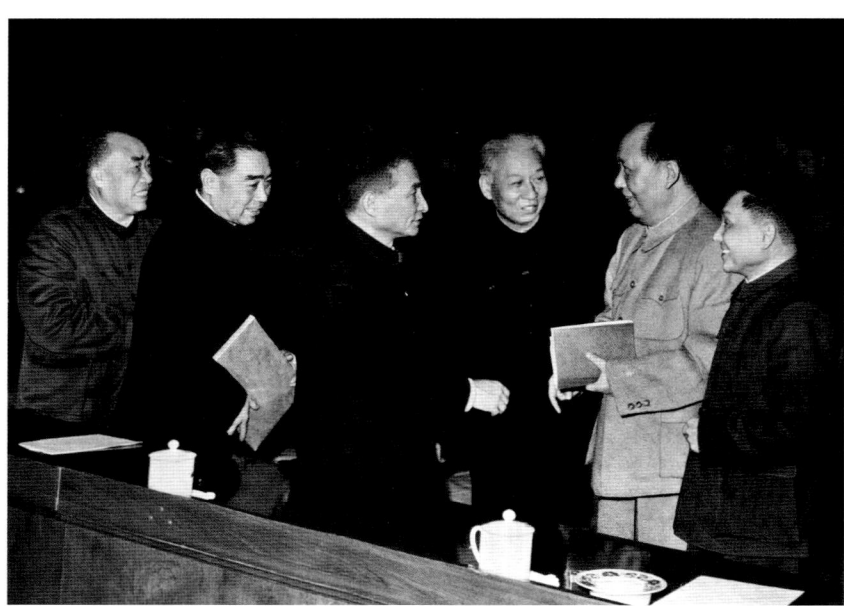

Du Xiuxian, 1962

Mao surrounded by the country's most senior leaders (left to right): Zhu De, Zhou Enlai, Chen Yun, Liu Shaoqi, and Deng Xiaoping.

Mao, umgeben von seinen ranghöchsten Funktionären (v. links n. rechts): Zhu De, Zhou Enlai, Chen Yun, Liu Shaoqi und Deng Xiaoping.

Mao entouré des plus hauts responsables du moment (de gauche à droite) : Zhu De, Zhou Enlai, Chen Yun, Liu Shaoqi et Deng Xiaoping.

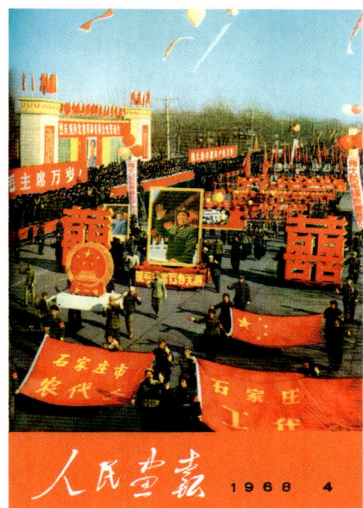

China Pictorial, April 1968

A parade in Shijiachuang, provincial capital of Hebei province

"When it came to the point where you could choose freely, you didn't know what to do. I felt like someone who'd been tied up and stuck in a pot; after a few years the pot was smashed and I was set free. It was like they said, you can go now, but I couldn't go because my body was still stuck in the shape of the pot."

„Als der Zeitpunkt kam, wo man frei wählen konnte, wusste man nicht, was man tun sollte. Ich fühlte mich wie jemand, den man gefesselt und in einen Topf gesteckt hatte; nach einigen Jahren war der Topf zertrümmert, und ich war frei. Es war, als hätten sie gesagt, du kannst jetzt gehen, aber ich konnte nicht gehen, weil mein Körper immer noch die Form des Topfes hatte."

« Lorsqu'arriva le moment de pouvoir choisir librement, on ne savait plus quoi faire. J'avais l'impression d'avoir été enchaîné et enfermé dans une jarre. Au bout de quelques années, la jarre avait été cassée, et j'étais libre. C'était comme s'ils disaient : 'Tu peux t'en aller maintenant', mais je ne pouvais pas partir parce que mon corps avait conservé la forme du pot. »

LI YANG (1959–), filmmaker, 2007

pp. 180/181
Qian Sijie, 1966

Chairman Mao and Premier Zhou Enlai (in the white shirt to the right of Mac) greet the surging crowd of Red Guards who had gathered in Tiananmen Square in August of 1966, to celebrate the launch of the Cultural Revolution.

Vorsitzender Mao und Premierminister Zhou Enlai (rechts neben Mao im weißen Hemd) grüßen die herandrängende Masse von Roten Garden, die sich im August 1966 auf dem Tiananmen-Platz versammelt haben, um den Beginn der Kulturrevolution zu feiern.

Le Président Mao et le premier ministre Zhou Enlai (en chemise blanche à droite de Mao) saluent la foule des Gardes rouges réunie sur la place Tian'anmen en août 1966, pour célébrer le lancement de la Révolution culturelle.

→
Meng Zhaorui, 1966

In a rare color image from the 1960s, Chairman Mao is seen surveying the Red Guards from an open-top jeep on a cold day in November in Beijing. This was his last inspection of the Red Guards. To the right, waving a copy of Quotations from Chairman Mao Zedong, *is Marshal Ye Jianying. Ye would later spearhead the arrest of the Gang of Four following their attempted coup after Mao's death in 1976.*

Auf einem der seltenen Farbbilder aus den 1960er-Jahren ist der Vorsitzende Mao zu sehen, wie er trotz des kühlen Novemberwetters in Peking im offenen Jeep die Roten Garden inspiziert. Dies war das letzte Mal, dass er eine Parade der Roten Garden abnahm. Zu seiner Rechten, mit einer Ausgabe der Mao-Bibel winkend, ist Marschall Ye Jianying zu sehen. Ye sollte später die Verhaftung der Viererbande leiten, nachdem diese nach Maos Tod einen Staatsstreich versucht hatte.

Dans une rare photo en couleur des années 1960, Mao passe en revue les Gardes rouges en Jeep par une froide matinée de novembre à Pékin, d'où son grand manteau. Ce fut la dernière revue des gardes. À sa droite, agitant une copie des Citations du Président Mao, *se trouve le maréchal Ye Jianying, qui dirigera par la suite l'arrestation de la « Bande des quatre » après leur tentative de coup d'État, à la mort de Mao en 1976.*

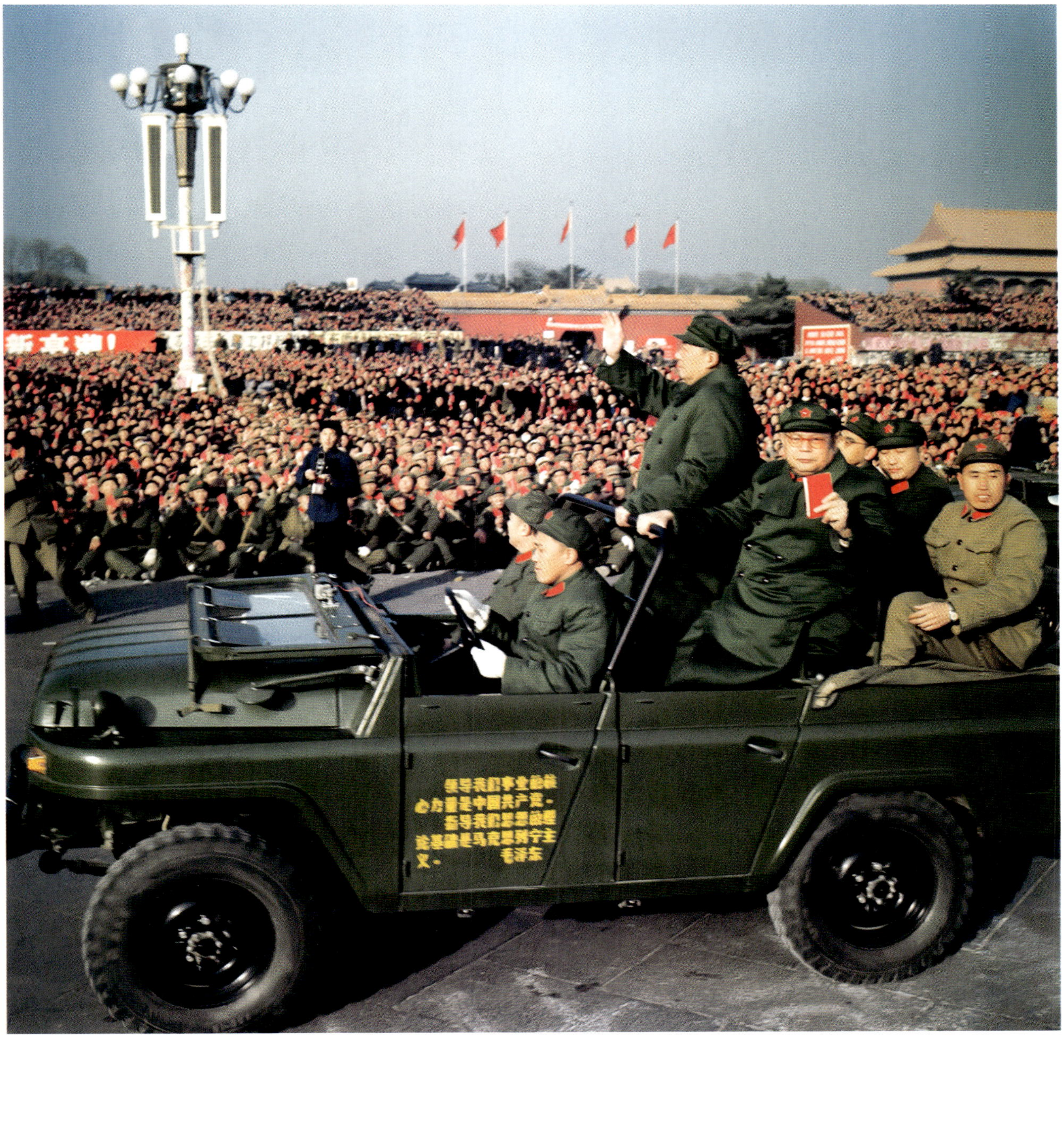

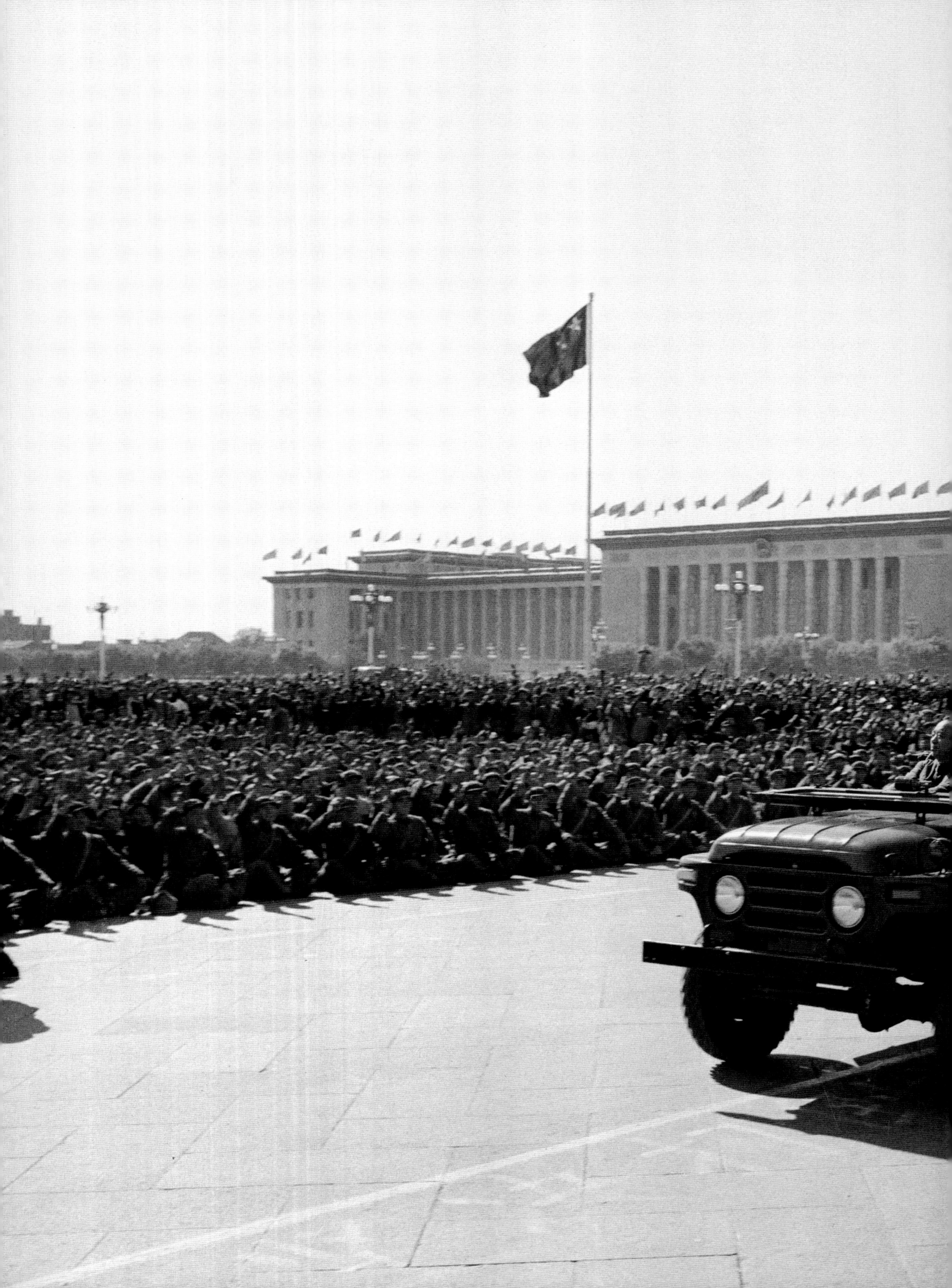

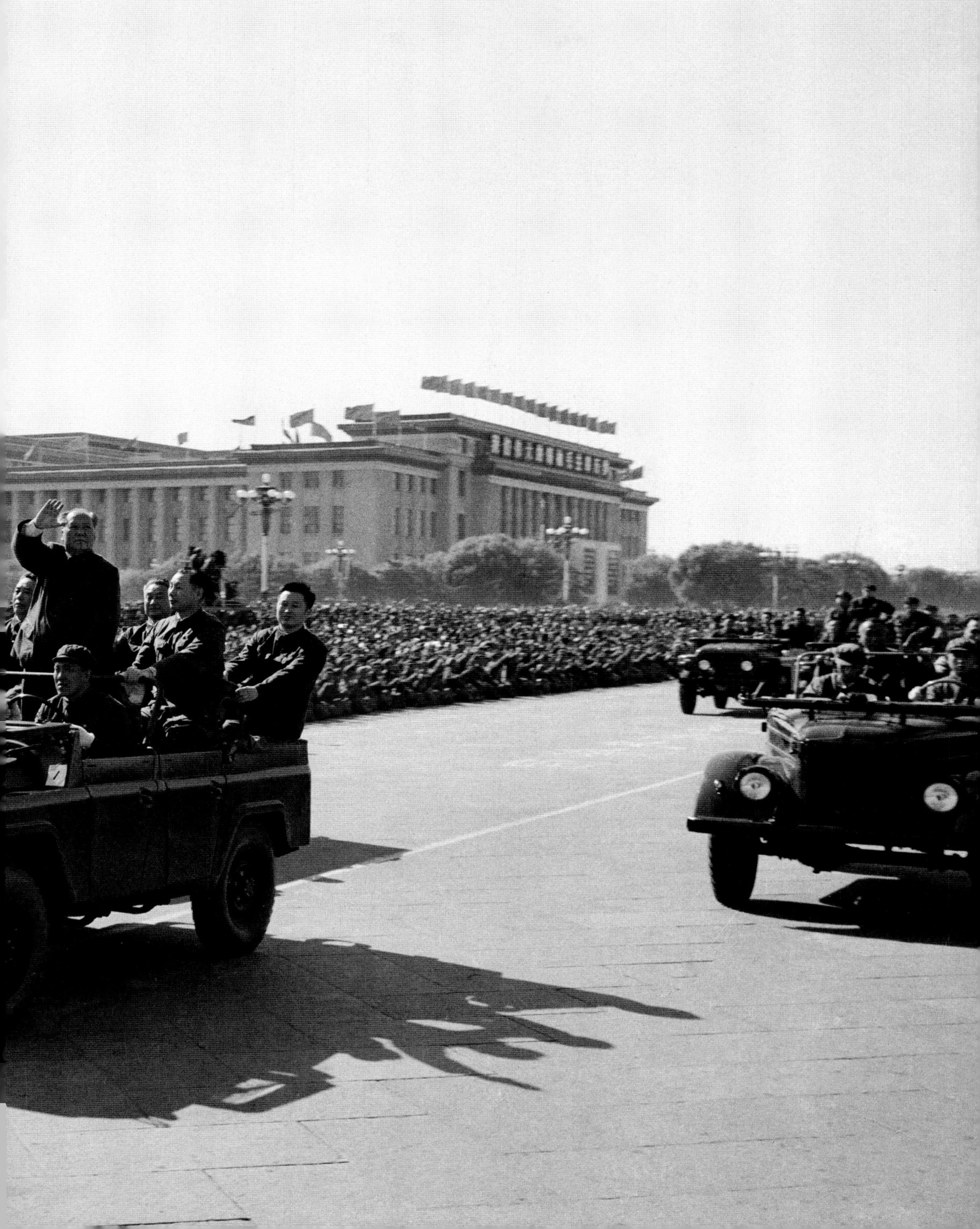

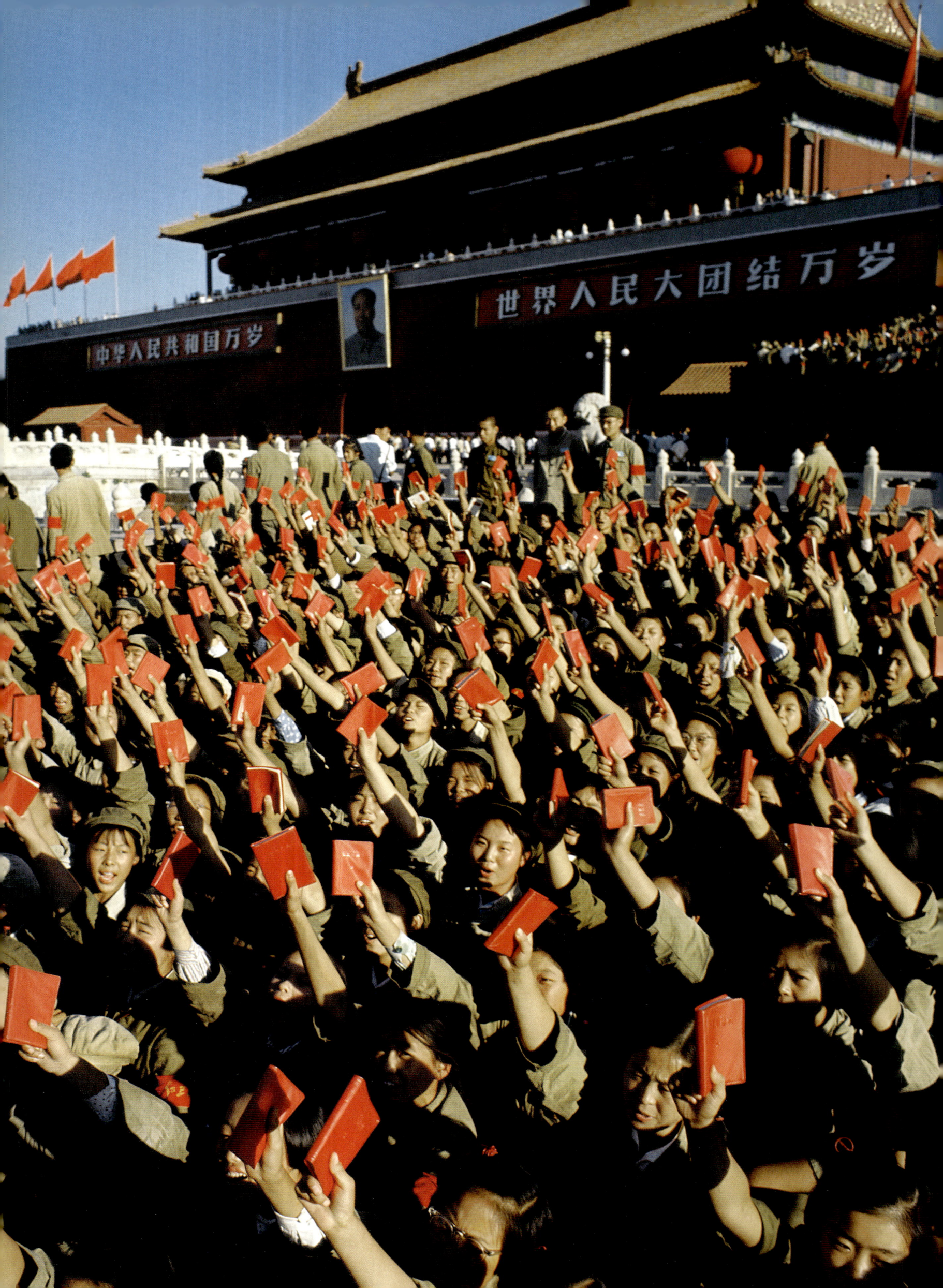

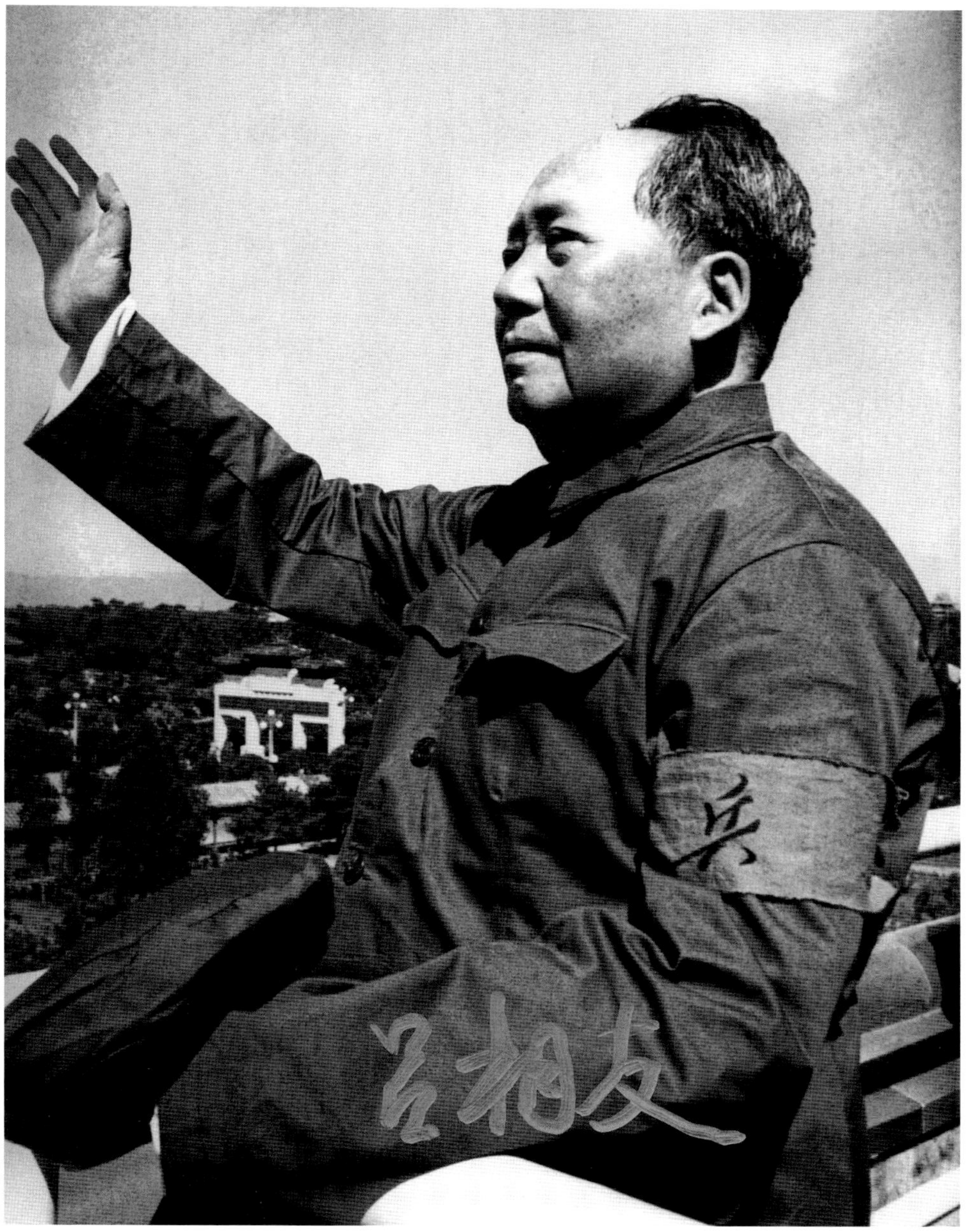

"Never before in Chinese history had any book been read by hundreds of millions of ordinary people, as was Mao's Quotations *during the Cultural Revolution. Even as one laments the book as an intellectual straitjacket, one salutes it as a unifying force."*

„Niemals zuvor in der chinesischen Geschichte hatten Hunderte von Millionen einfacher Menschen ein Buch gelesen, wie es während der Kulturrevolution mit Maos Worten *geschah. Selbst wenn man das Buch als intellektuelle Zwangsjacke beklagt, verneigt man sich vor seiner einenden Kraft."*

« Jamais auparavant dans l'histoire chinoise un livre n'avait été lu par des centaines de millions d'individus ordinaires comme les Citations du Président Mao *pendant la Révolution culturelle. Même si l'on juge que l'ouvrage est une camisole de force intellectuelle, on doit saluer sa puissance de rassemblement. »*

ROSS TERRILL, sinologist and research associate at Harvard East Asian Research Center, 1999

←
Weng Naiqiang, 1966

A total of 13 million Red Guards streamed into Tiananmen Square to be inspected by Chairman Mao and his chosen successor, Marshal Lin Biao, on ten separate occasions. Here they can be seen waving the colored Quotations from Chairman Mao Zedong. *A total of 1.2 billion copies of the Little Red Book were printed.*

Insgesamt zehn Mal strömten 13 Millionen Rotgardisten auf den Tiananmen-Platz, um vom Vorsitzenden Mao und seinem erwählten Nachfolger Marschall Lin Biao inspiziert zu werden. Hier sieht man sie mit dem farbigen Buch der Worte des Vorsitzenden Mao Zedong *winken. Insgesamt wurden 1,2 Milliarden Exemplare des Kleinen Roten Buches in China gedruckt.*

13 millions de Gardes rouges affluèrent sur la place Tian'anmen pour être passés en revue par le Président Mao et le successeur qu'il s'était choisi, le maréchal Lin Biao, à dix occasions. Ici, ils agitent le petit livre des Citations du Président Mao, *qui fut édité à 1,2 milliard d'exemplaires.*

pp. 184/185
Meng Zhaorui, 1966

Chairman Mao rides in an open military jeep to witness the first major gathering of Red Guards in Tiananmen Square, in August 1966. Having paid homage to the leader, the Red Guards dispersed across the country, overthrowing any cadre suspected of dissent.

Der Vorsitzende Mao nimmt im August 1966 im offenen Militärjeep die erste große Versammlung Roter Garden auf dem Tiananmen-Platz ab. Nachdem sie dem Führer ihre Reverenz erwiesen hatten, verteilten sich die Roten Garden im ganzen Land und stürzten sämtliche abweichlerischer Gesinnung verdächtigen Kader.

Le Président Mao passe en revue en Jeep le premier grand rassemblement de Gardes rouges sur la place Tian'anmen en août 1966. Après avoir rendu hommage à leur chef, ils se dispersèrent dans le pays pour chasser les cadres suspects de dissidence.

↑
Lü Xiangyou, 1966

Wearing the Red Guard armband, Mao waves to a cheering throng of Red Guards hundreds of thousands strong, below him in Tiananmen Square, in August of 1966. Red Guards traveled from all over China to demonstrate their allegiance to the Great Helmsman and to the Revolution.

Mao, der die Armbinde der Roten Garden trägt, winkt der jubelnden Masse von Hunderttausenden Roter Garden zu, die sich im August 1966 zu seinen Füßen auf dem Tiananmen-Platz versammelt haben. Sie reisten aus ganz China an, um ihre Treue zum großen Steuermann zu bekunden und ihre revolutionäre Gesinnung unter Beweis zu stellen.

Mao, qui porte le brassard des Gardes rouges, salue un rassemblement de milliers de gardes sur la place de Tian'anmen en août 1966. Ils vinrent de toute la Chine pour assurer le Grand Timonier de leur allégeance et de leur engagement au service de la Révolution.

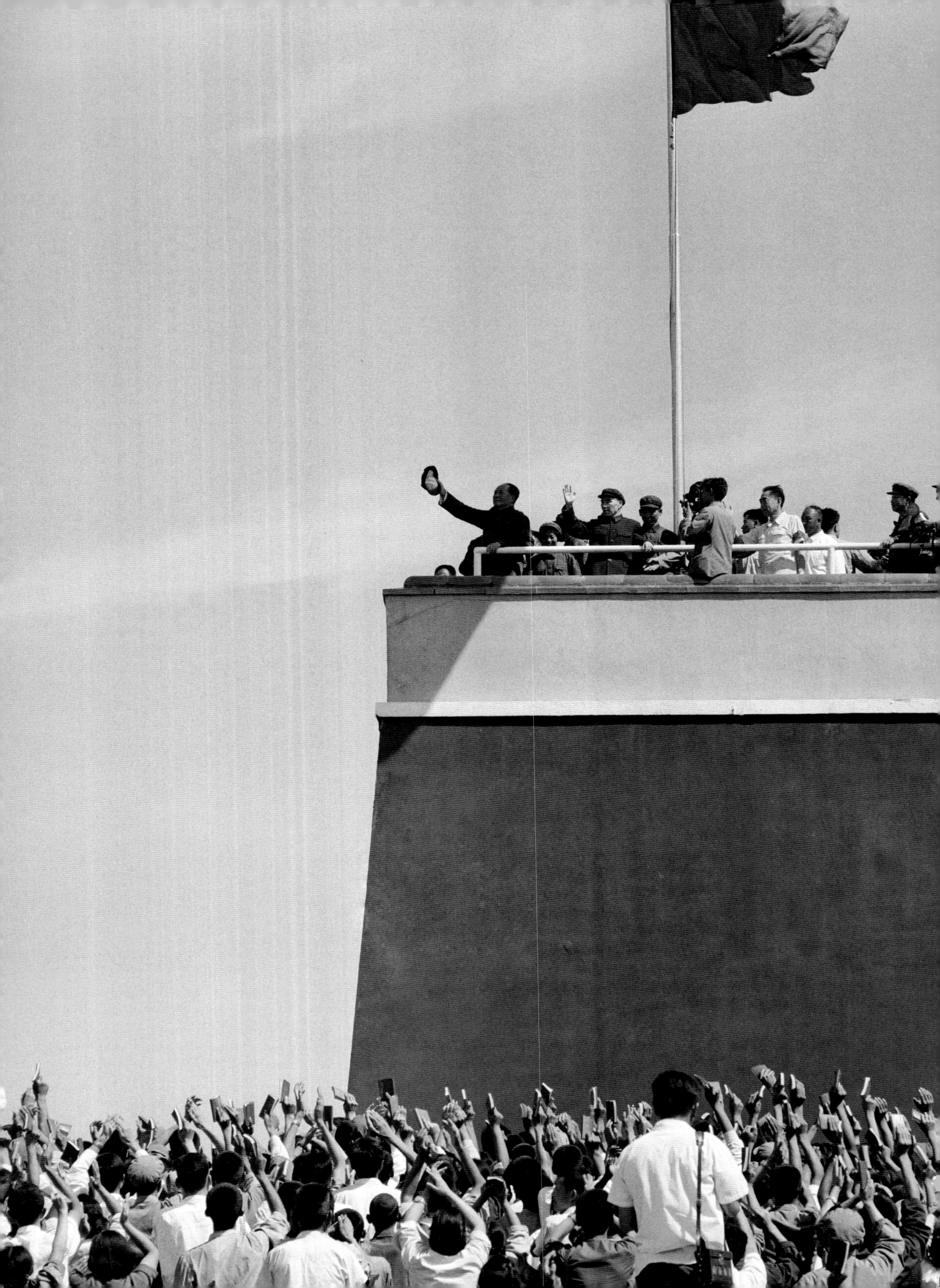

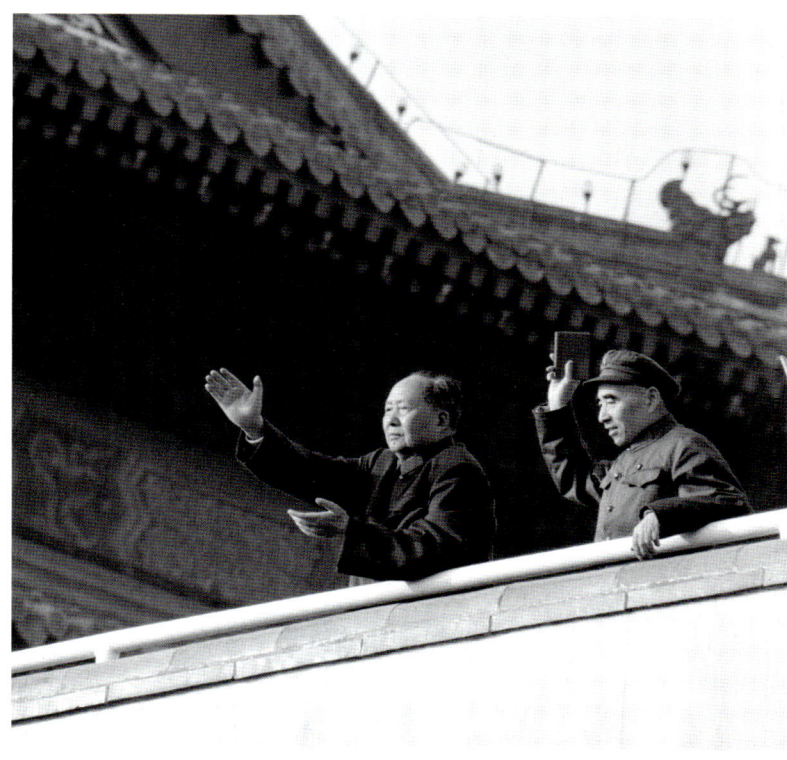

"A revolution is not the same as inviting people to dinner, or writing an essay, or painting a picture, or doing fancy needlework; it cannot be anything so restrained and magnanimous. A revolution is an uprising, an act of violence whereby one class overthrows another."

„Eine Revolution ist nicht das Gleiche wie Leute zum Abendessen einzuladen oder einen Aufsatz zu schreiben oder ein Bild zu malen oder eine feine Handarbeit anzufertigen; sie kann nicht etwas so Maßvolles, Edelmütiges sein. Eine Revolution ist ein Aufstand, ein Akt der Gewalt, mit der eine Klasse eine andere stürzt."

« Une révolution, ce n'est pas inviter des gens à dîner ou écrire un essai, ou peindre un tableau, ou faire du travail d'aiguille. Ce ne peut être quelque chose d'aussi limité et banal. Une révolution est un soulèvement, un acte de violence par lequel une classe en renverse une autre. »

MAO ZEDONG (1893–1976), first Chairman of the People's Republic of China, 1927

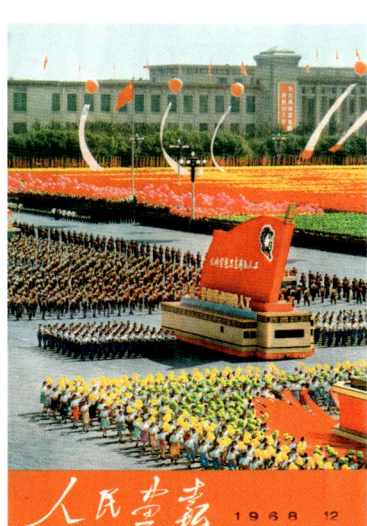

China Pictorial, December 1968

A parade on Tiananmen square, Beijing

←↗
Meng Zhaorui, 1966

Mao and Lin Biao surveying the Red Guards from the gate overlooking Tiananmen Square. Five years later, Lin Biao would die in a PLA Trident jet, shot down by a Chinese missile on the orders of Zhou Enlai, according to one version, whilst allegedly fleeing to the USSR. He was posthumously accused of plotting a coup against Mao. The charge that Lin Biao's crime was an attempted military coup provided the convenient pretext for purging Lin's military associates. The details of the crash have never been revealed.

Mao und Lin Biao nehmen die Parade der Roten Garden auf den Tiananmen-Platz vom Tor über dem Platz aus ab. Fünf Jahre später starb Lin Biao in einem Trident-Jet der Volksbefreiungsarmee, der – nach einem Befehl Zhou Enlais – von einer chinesischen Rakete abgeschossen wurde, während er offenbar auf der Flucht in die UdSSR war. Lin Biao wurde nach seinem Tod beschuldigt, einen Staatsstreich gegen Mao geplant zu haben. Die Anschuldigung, Lin Biao habe einen Militärputsch versucht, bot einen willkommenen Vorwand zur Brandmarkung von Lins militärischen Gefolgsleuten. Einzelheiten des Absturzes wurden nie veröffentlicht.

De la porte donnant sur la place Tian'anmen, Mao et Lin Biao passent en revue les Gardes rouges. Cinq ans plus tard, Lin Biao allait disparaître dans un avion Trident de l'armée, touché par un missile tiré sur les ordres de Zhou Enlaï selon une version, alors qu'il fuyait apparemment vers l'URSS. Il fut accusé après sa mort d'avoir comploté un coup d'État contre Mao. Les charges selon lesquelles le crime de Lin Biao était bien une tentative de coup militaire offraient un prétexte pratique pour se débarrasser de ses alliés. Les détails de la chute de l'avion n'ont jamais été révélés.

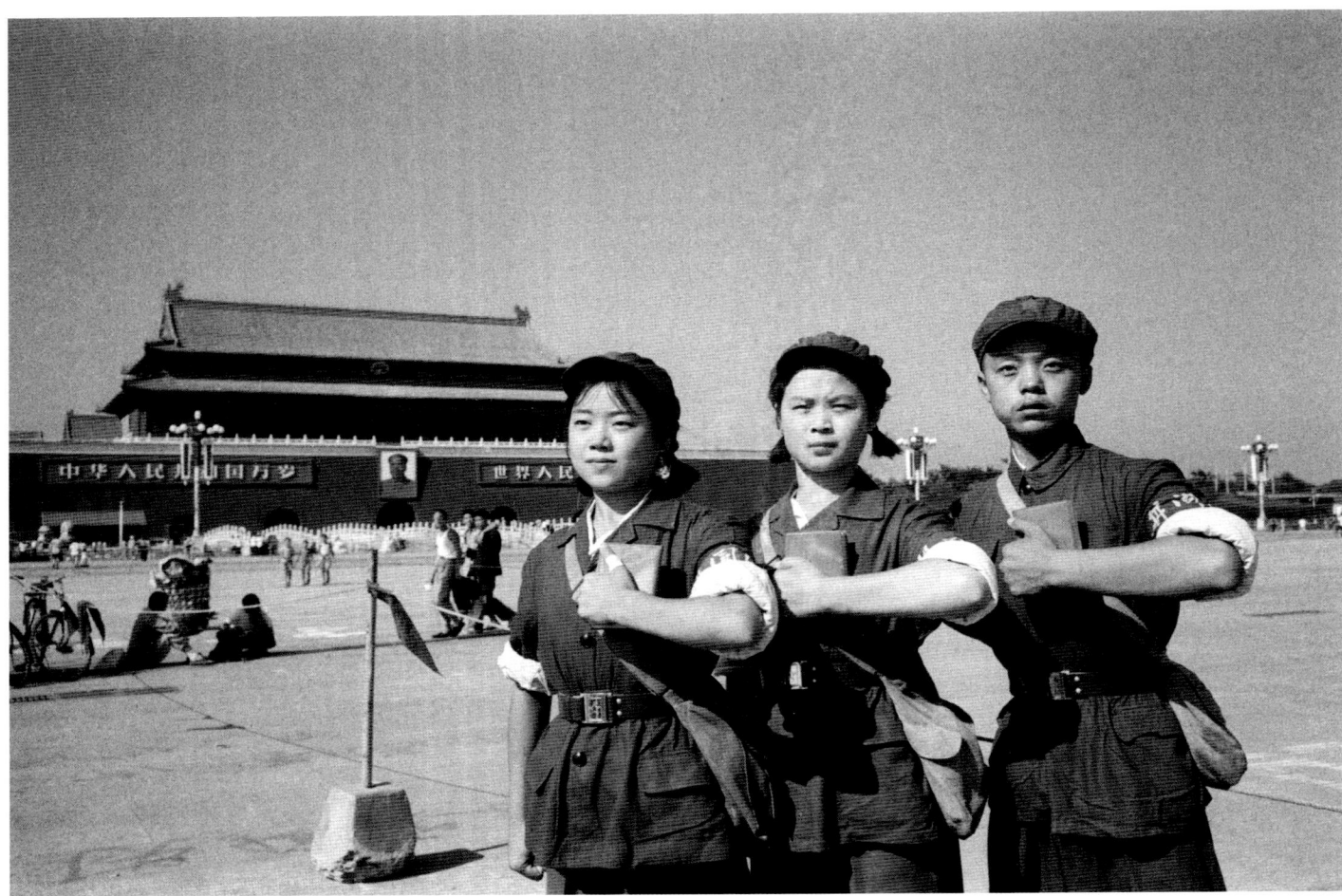

↑
Jiang Shaowu, 1966

Three Red Guards pose in Tiananmen Square, each clutching a copy of Quotations from Chairman Mao Zedong. *When Mao signaled his approval for China's youth to "rebel," and to leave the classroom and revolt, students were permitted to travel on trains and buses.*

Drei Rotgardisten nehmen Haltung auf dem Tiananmen-Platz an, jede mit einem Exemplar der Worte des Vorsitzenden Mao Zedong *in der Hand. Als Mao erkennen ließ, dass er es guthieß, wenn Chinas Jugend rebellierte und die Klassenzimmer verließ, um Revolution zu machen, war es den Schülern und Studenten erlaubt, kostenlos mit Zügen und Bussen zu reisen.*

Trois Gardes rouges posent sur la place Tian'anmen. Chacune porte son exemplaire des Citations du Président Mao. *Lorsque Mao fit savoir qu'il approuvait la «rébellion» de la jeunesse chinoise, sa décision d'abandonner l'école et de faire la révolution, les jeunes purent voyager librement en train et en bus.*

→
Xiao Zhuang, 1967

Children from a Nanjing Primary School clutch copies of Quotations from Chairman Mao Zedong, *as they sing revolutionary songs.*

Kinder einer Grundschule in Nanjing halten Exemplare der Worte des Vorsitzenden Mao Zedong *in der Hand, während sie Revolutionslieder singen.*

Des enfants d'une école primaire de Nankin chantent des chants révolutionnaires en tenant les Citations du Président Mao.

"Even in chaos there are always small moments of stillness: one time during the Cultural Revolution, amidst the exchange of fire between rival Red Guard factions… a few of us were holed up talking about our first loves, when a stray bullet hit the iron window frame, and then buried itself in my friend's head. It was so sudden that my friend was still talking even as he hit the ground. We were just kids with peachfuzz on our chins."

„Auch im größten Chaos gab es immer Augenblicke der Ruhe: Einmal, während der Kulturrevolution, inmitten eines Schusswechsels rivalisierender Roter Garden … hatten sich ein paar von uns verkrochen und sprachen über unsere ersten Liebesbeziehungen, als eine verirrte Kugel den eisernen Fensterrahmen traf und sich dann in den Kopf meines Freundes bohrte. Es geschah so plötzlich, dass mein Freund noch redete, als er auf den Boden fiel. Wir waren bloß Kinder mit Flaum am Kinn."

«Dans tout grande période de chaos se produisent toujours de petits moments d'accalmie : un jour, durant la Révolution culturelle, en plein échange de feu entre des factions rivales de Gardes rouges… quelques-uns d'entre nous s'étaient terrés dans un coin et nous parlions de nos premières amours, lorsqu'une balle vint rebondir sur le châssis métallique de la fenêtre et frapper mon ami en pleine tête. C'était si soudain, qu'il parlait encore en s'effondrant. Nous n'étions encore que des enfants, avec du lait dans les oreilles. »

AH CHENG (Zhong Acheng, 1949–), writer and painter, 1998

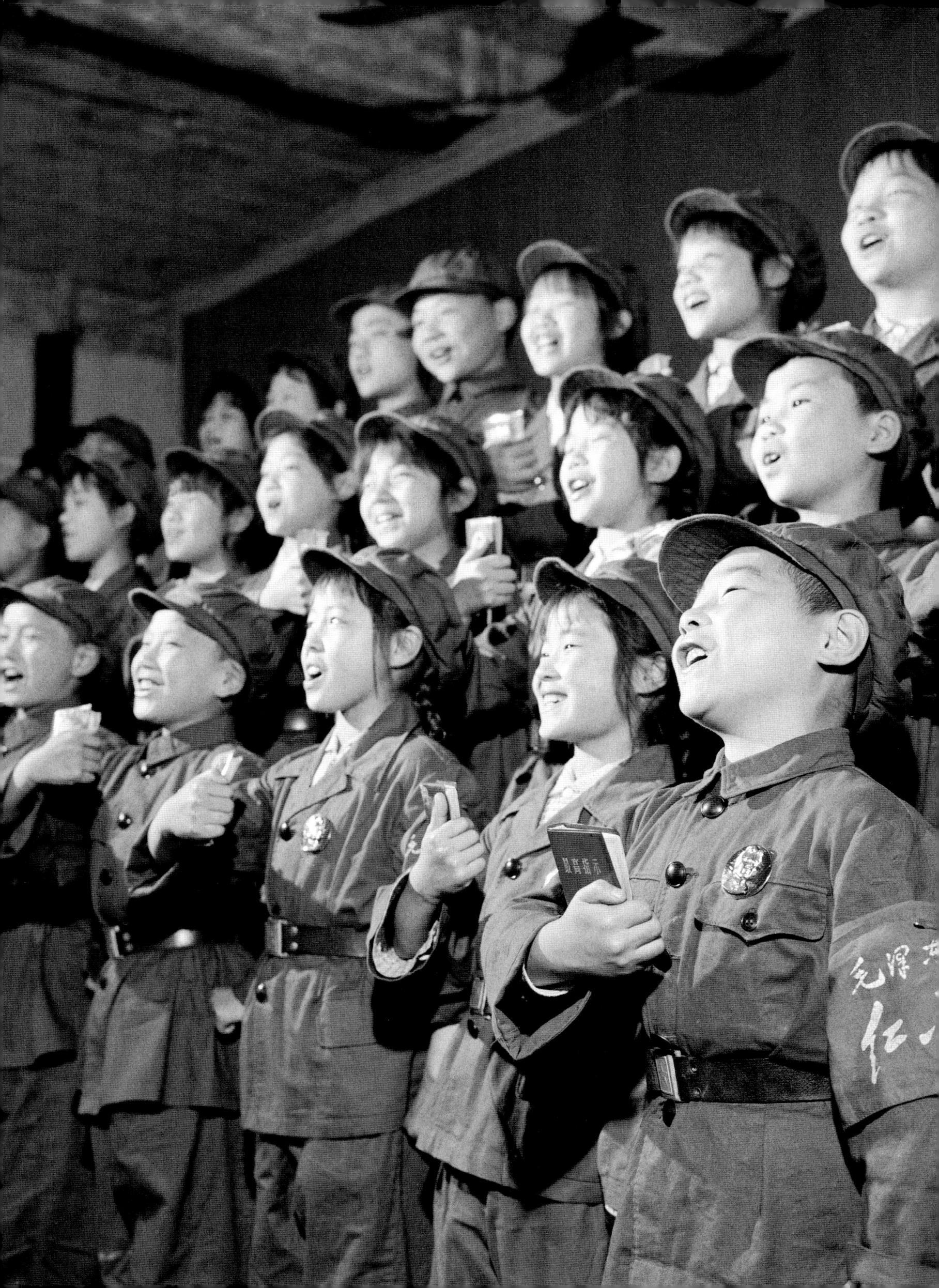

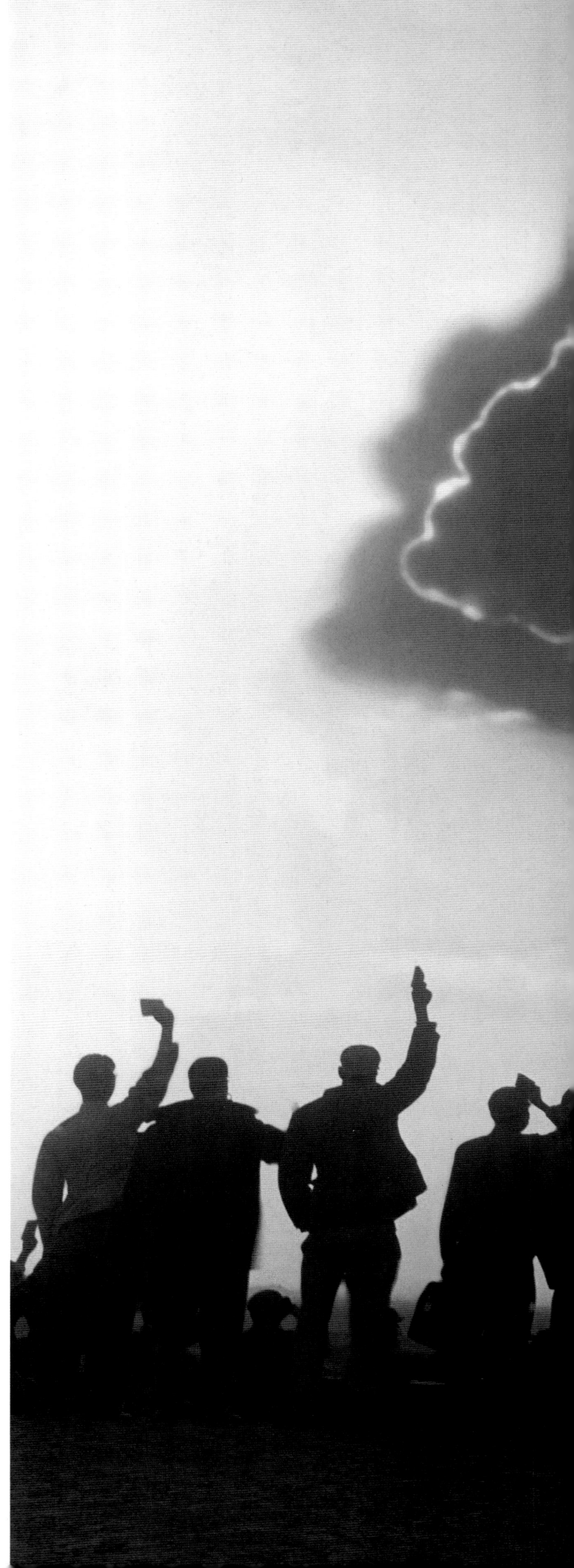

192

"The discovery of how to use saltpetre led both to the making of fireworks and crackers, and of gunpowder and explosives. It was the Chinese who made the first experiments in what we call pyrotechnics, but they only used the explosive qualities of the mixture for harmless though gorgeous displays of fireworks, whereas the western nations turned the discovery into the channel of making ammunition for purposes of warfare."

„Die Entdeckung der Verwendungsmöglichkeiten von Salpeter führte zur Herstellung von Feuerwerk und Knallfröschen, von Schießpulver und Sprengstoff. Die Chinesen waren die Ersten, die mit Pyrotechnik experimentierten, aber sie nutzten die explosiven Eigenschaften der Mixtur nur für harmlose, wenngleich prächtige Feuerwerksspektakel, während die westlichen Nationen die Entdeckung für die Herstellung von Munition für kriegerische Zwecke nutzten."

« La découverte de l'utilisation du salpêtre conduisit à la fabrication de feux d'artifice, de la poudre noire et des explosifs. Ce furent les Chinois qui réalisèrent les premières expériences dans le domaine de ce que nous appelons la pyrotechnique, mais ils ne se servirent des qualités explosives du mélange découvert que pour le spectacle inoffensif et splendide des feux d'artifice, alors que les nations occidentales les utilisèrent pour faire des munitions et pour la guerre. »

MILDRED CABLE (1878–1952), British Protestant missionary, 1946

→

Meng Zhaorui, 1967

On June 17, 1967, PLA soldiers cheer as the mushroom cloud from the successful explosion of China's first hydrogen bomb billows before them in the distance. Following the breakdown of relations with the USSR, Mao stepped up the development in military defense. The first recorded nuclear test took place in 1964, and by 1969, ten such devices had been tested.

Am 17. Juli 1967 jubeln Soldaten der Volksbefreiungsarmee, während sich im Hintergrund die Wolke von Chinas erster erfolgreicher Zündung einer Wasserstoffbombe erhebt. Nach dem Zusammenbruch der Beziehungen zur UdSSR verstärkte Mao die Entwicklung der militärischen Abwehr. Der erste bekannte Nukleartest fand 1964 statt, und 1969 hatte man bereits zehn solcher Sprengsätze getestet.

Le 17 juin 1967, des soldats saluent le champignon de la première explosion de la bombe à hydrogène chinoise. À la suite de la rupture des relations avec l'URSS, Mao accéléra le développement de la défense nationale. Les premiers essais nucléaires se déroulèrent en 1964. En 1969, dix essais avaient déjà été menés.

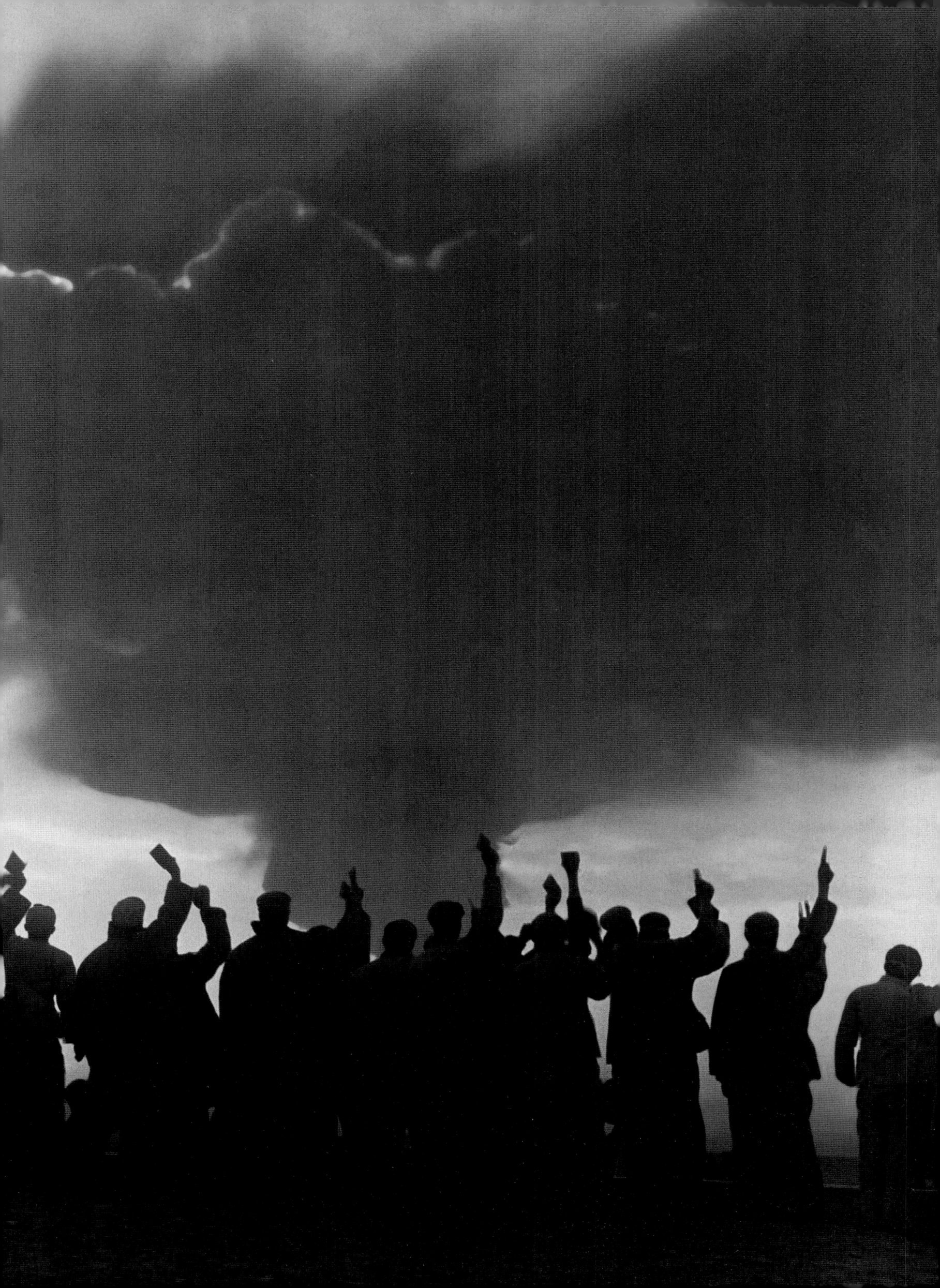

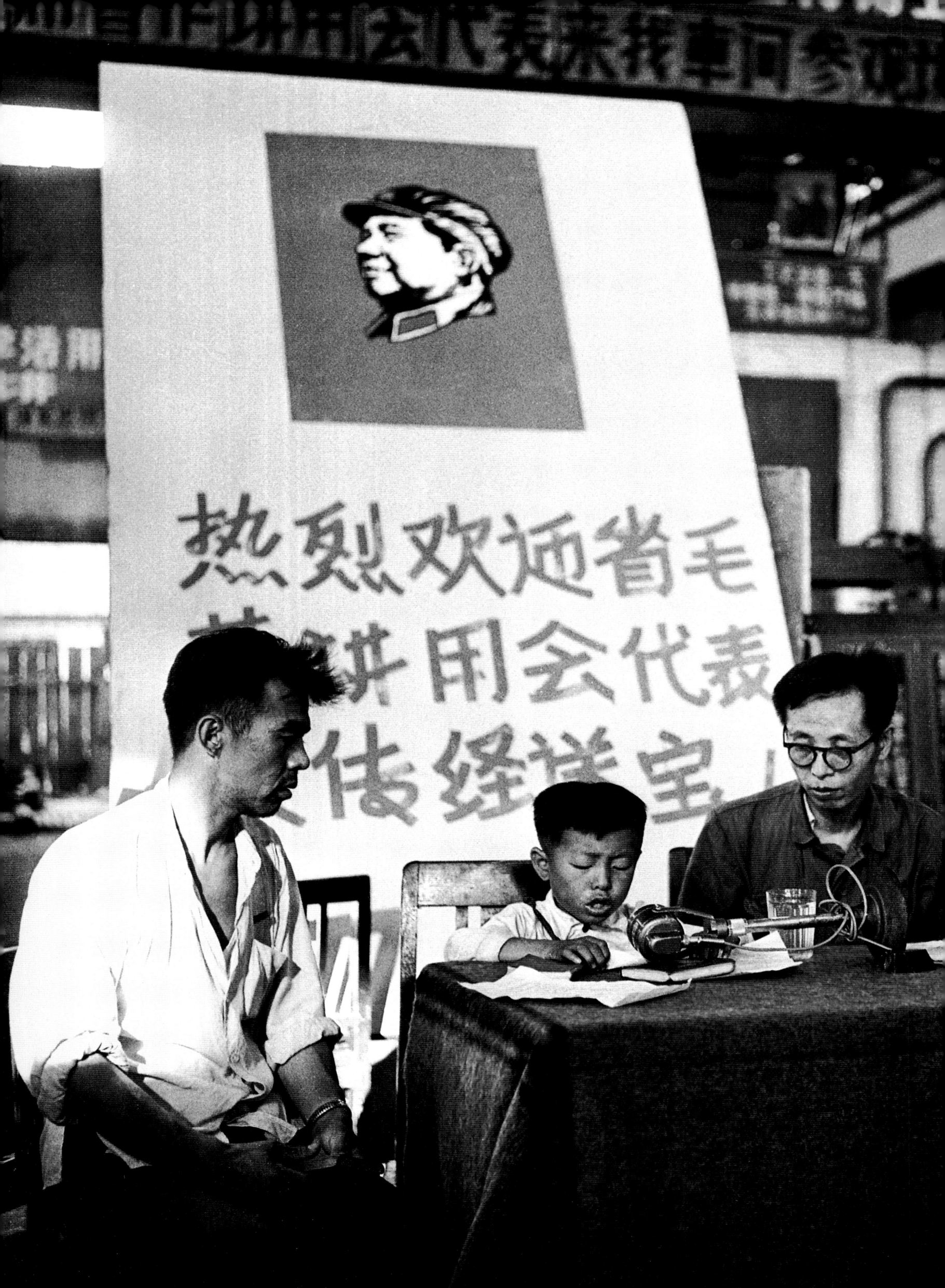

←
Li Zhensheng, 1967

At Harbin Power Equipment Factory in Harbin, Heilongjiang province, a child explains the merits of Mao's theories. Mao considered children to be more ideologically pure, and less corruptible than adults.

In einer Generatorenfabrik in Harbin, Provinz Heilongjiang, erklärt ein Kind die Vorzüge von Maos Theorien. Mao hielt Kinder für ideologisch unverfälschter und weniger korrumpierbar als Erwachsene.

Dans une usine d'appareils électriques de Harbin, province du Heilongjiang, un enfant explique les mérites des théories de Mao. Celui-ci pensait que les enfants étaient idéologiquement plus purs et moins facilement corruptibles que les adultes.

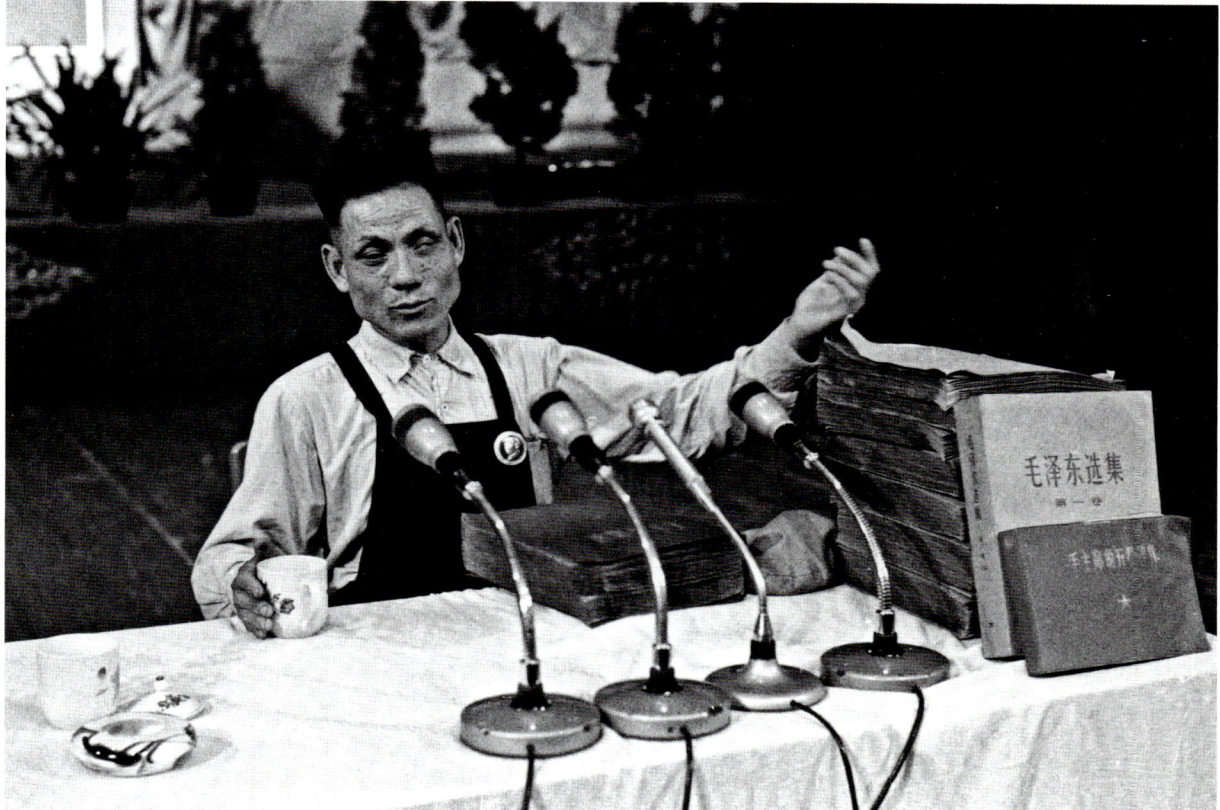

"Society can exist only on the basis that there is some amount of polished lying and that no one says exactly what he thinks."

„Die Gesellschaft kann nur auf der Basis bestehen, dass es ein gewisses Maß an Schönfärberei gibt und dass keiner genau das sagt, was er denkt."

« La société ne peut exister que sur la base d'un certain mensonge poli et que si personne ne dit exactement ce qu'il pense. »

LIN YUTANG (1895–1976), writer, philosopher, and inventor of the Chinese typewriter

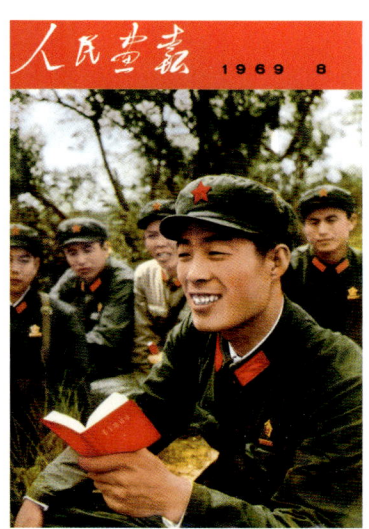

China Pictorial, August 1969

PLA solders studying Quotations from Chairman Mao Zedong

↑
Jiang Shaowu, 1967

During the Cultural Revolution, it was common for people to talk in public about their experience of studying Mao Thought. A blind worker is photographed giving a lecture to fellow factory workers in Shenyang, Liaoning province, about the rewards of studying Mao Thought.

Während der Kulturrevolution erfreute es sich bei den Chinesen einiger Beliebtheit, öffentlich über ihre Erfahrungen beim Studium von Maos Ideen zu sprechen. Ein Blinder wird dabei fotografiert, wie er seinen Kollegen in einer Fabrik in Shenyang in der Provinz Liaoning einen Vortrag darüber hält, wie lohnend die Beschäftigung mit Maos Gedanken ist.

Pendant la Révolution culturelle, les gens prirent goût à exprimer en public leur expérience de l'étude de la pensée de Mao. Un ouvrier aveugle donne ici une conférence à ses collègues d'usine à Shenyang, province du Liaoning, sur les gratifications qu'apporte la lecture de Mao Zedong.

pp. 196/197
Li Zhensheng, 1968

Buddhist monks who were rounded up and forced to hold a banner proclaiming, "Fuck Buddhist scriptures, they are nothing but dog farts."

Buddhistische Mönche werden zur Selbstkritik zusammengetrieben und gezwungen, Transparente mit der Aufschrift „Verflucht seien buddhistische Schriften. Sie sind nichts als Hundefürze" zu halten.

Des moines bouddhistes sont rassemblés pour faire leur autocritique. Ils sont forcés à tenir une bannière proclamant : « À bas les textes bouddhistes, ce ne sont que des pets de lapin. »

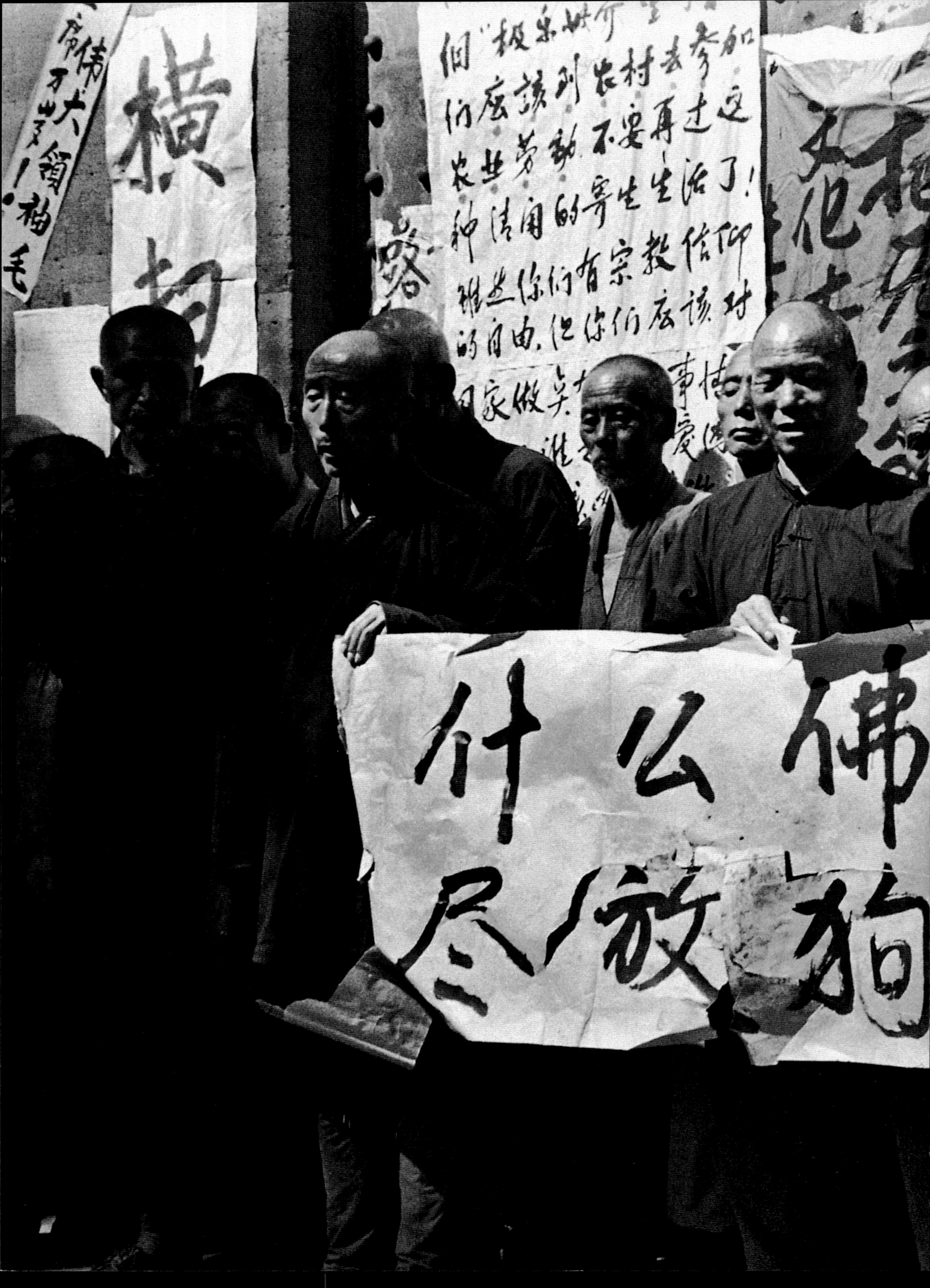

们应该到农村去参加
农业劳动，不要再过这
种清闲的寄生活了！
虽然你们有宗教信仰
的自由，但你们应该对
什么佛

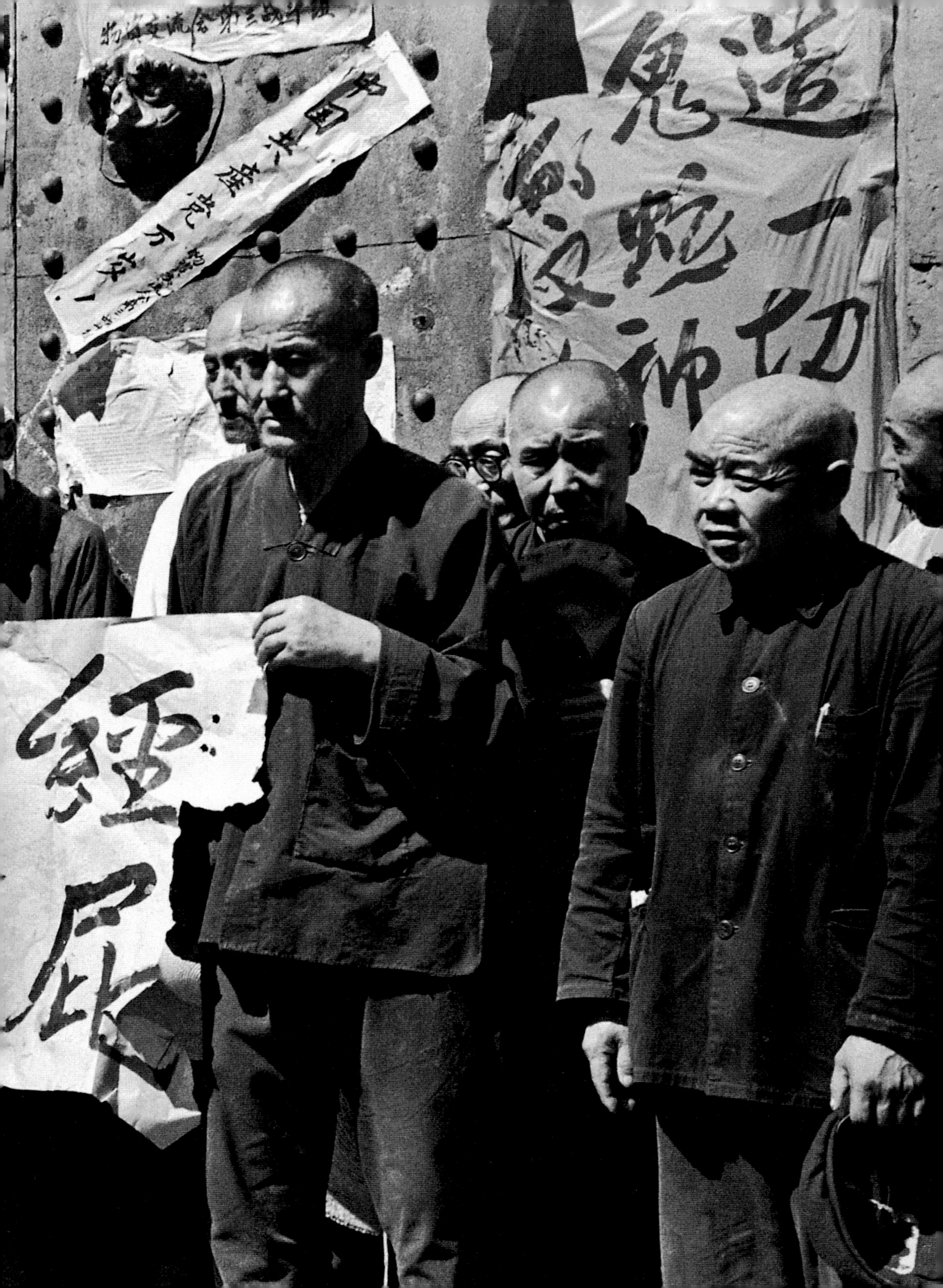

↙
Li Zhensheng, 1968

Eight criminals and counterrevolutionaries are executed on the outskirts of Harbin, Heilongjiang province.

Acht Kriminelle und Konterrevolutionäre werden am Stadtrand von Harbin, in der Provinz Heilongjiang, exekutiert.

Huit criminels et contre-révolutionnaires sont exécutés dans la banlieue de Harbin, province du Heilongjiang.

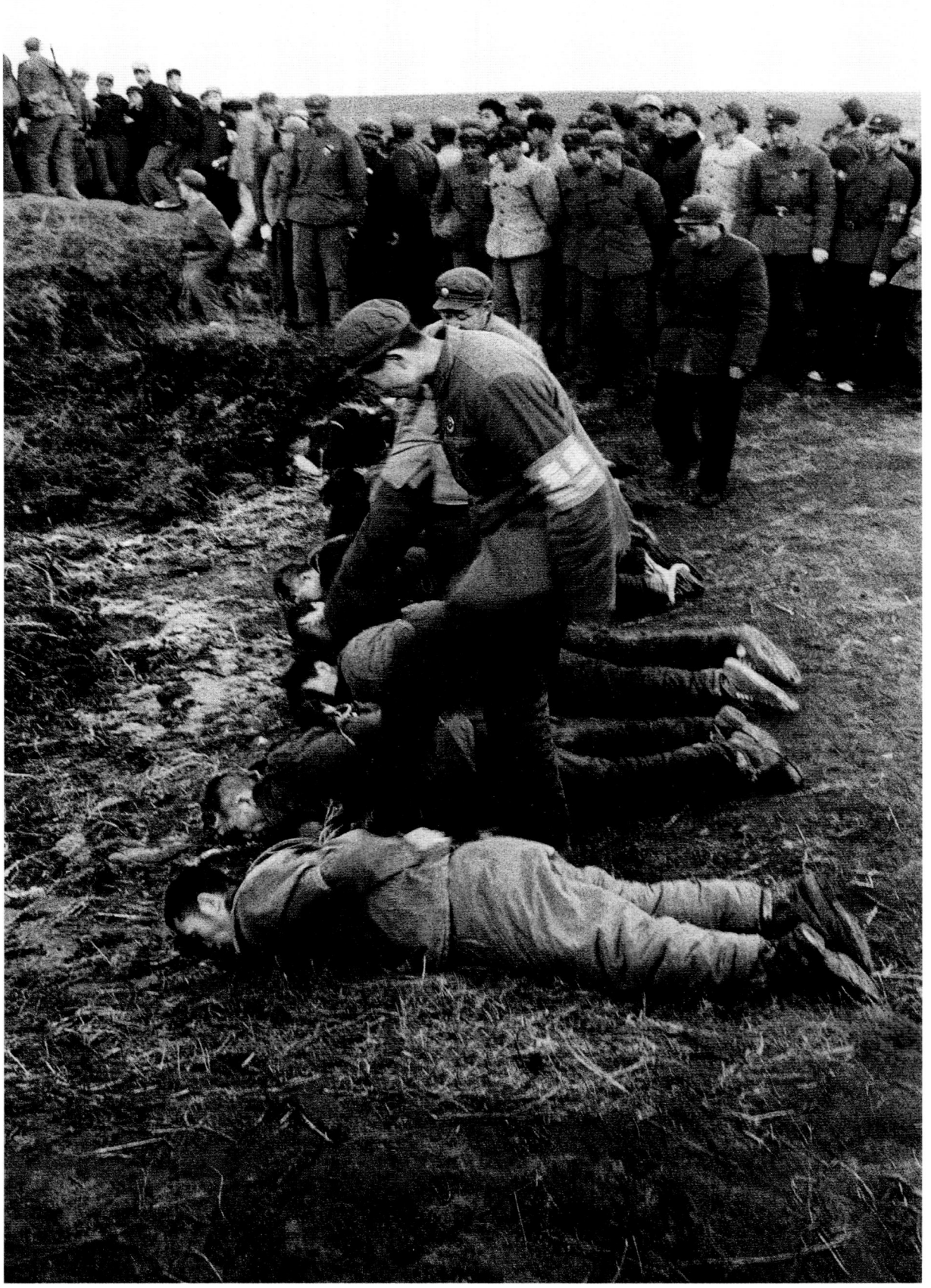

"Persons who... have to be executed to assuage the people's anger must be put to death for this purpose."

„Personen, die ... exekutiert werden müssen, um den Zorn des Volkes zu besänftigen, müssen zu diesem Zweck getötet werden."

« Les personnes qui... doivent être exécutées pour assouvir la colère du peuple sont à mettre à mort dans ce but. »

MAO ZEDONG (1893–1976), first Chairman of the People's Republic of China, 1951

→
Jiang Shaowu, 1968

Two Chinese officials are told to kneel in a "jet-plane" position during a rally in Shenyang, Liaoning province. One official was quoted in 1990 as saying "4.6 million class enemies are still alive," which leaves to conjecture the total number of people affected by the relentless political campaigns during the Cultural Revolution.

Zwei chinesischen Funktionären wird bei einer Kundgebung in Shenyang in der Provinz Liaoning befohlen, sich in der „Flugzeughaltung" hinzuknien. Ein Funktionär wurde 1990 mit dem Satz zitiert: „4,6 Millionen Klassenfeinde sind noch am Leben", was über die Gesamtzahl der Menschen, die von der gnadenlosen Durchführung politischer Kampagnen während der Kulturrevolution betroffen waren, nur Vermutungen zulässt.

Deux officiels sont contraints à prendre la « position de l'avion » lors d'un rassemblement à Shenyang, province du Liaoning. Un responsable cité en 1990 aurait dit : « 4,6 millions d'ennemis de classe sont encore vivants », ce qui laisse deviner le nombre de gens affectés par les campagnes d'action impitoyables de la Révolution culturelle.

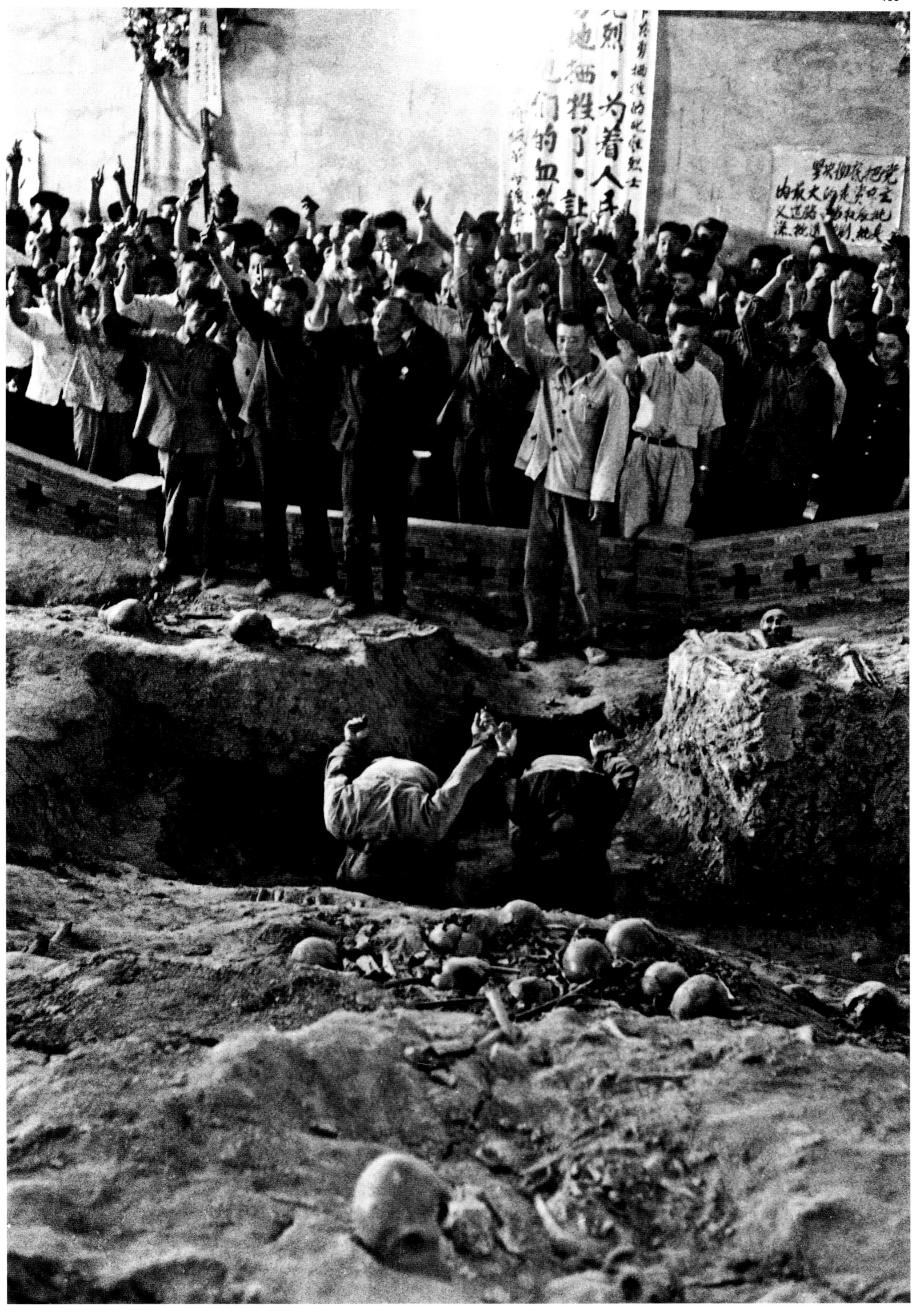

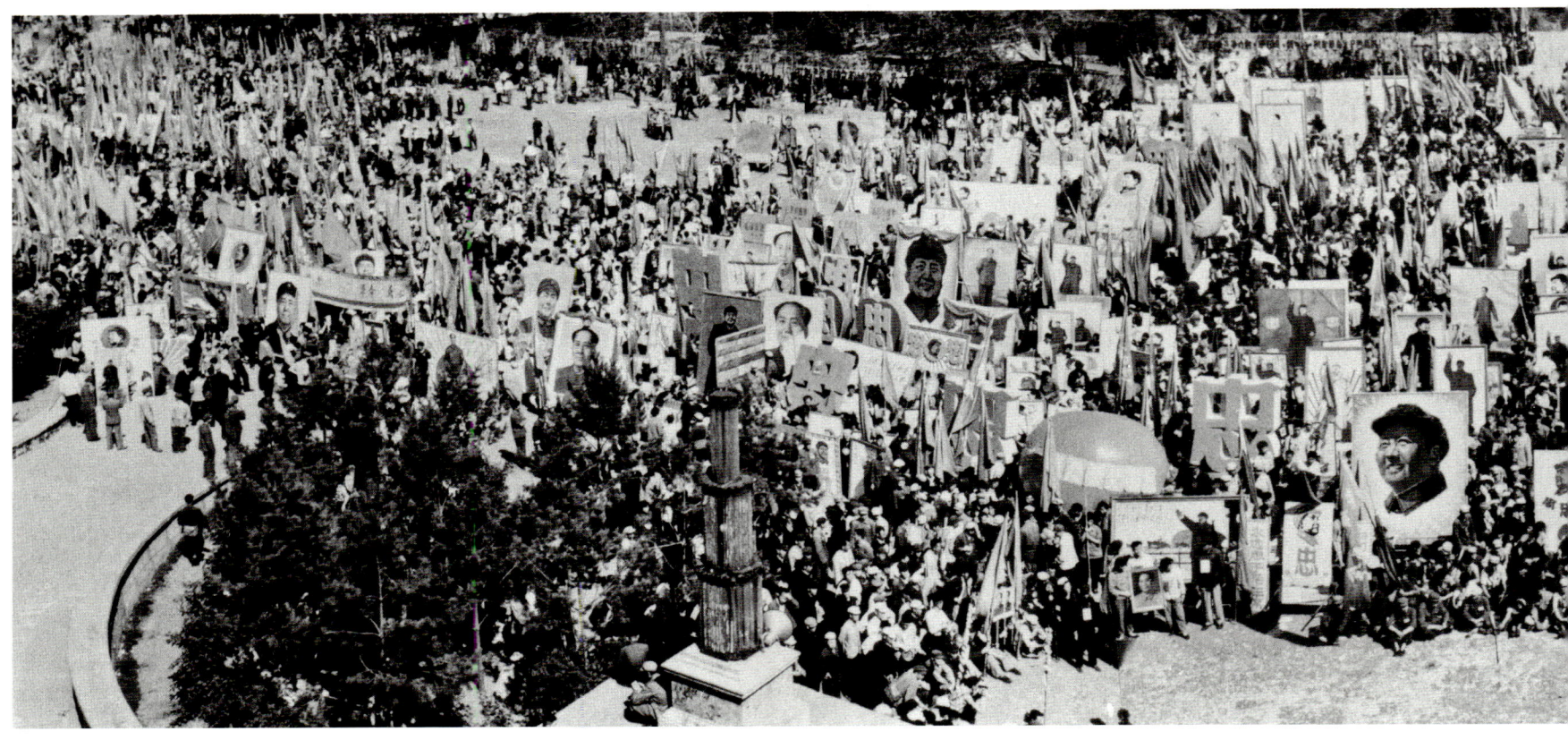

↑
Li Zhensheng, 1968

Hundreds of thousands of Red Guards and workers attend a mass rally in Shenyang, holding up banners displaying portraits of Mao to show their loyalty and support.

Hunderttausende von Rotgardisten und Arbeitern tragen auf einer Massenversammlung in Shenyang selbst gemachte Banner mit Porträts von Mao, um ihre Loyalität und Unterstützung zu demonstrieren.

Des centaines de milliers de Gardes rouges et de travailleurs participent à une manifestation de masse à Shenyang. Ils brandissent les bannières à l'effigie de Mao qu'ils ont fabriquées pour montrer leur loyauté et leur soutien.

↓
Xiao Zhuang, 1968

Nanjing steel workers in pristine work clothes march at a rally during the Cultural Revolution.

Stahlarbeiter aus Nanjing marschieren in makelloser Arbeitskleidung bei einer Kundgebung während der Kulturrevolution auf.

Ouvriers d'une aciérie de Nankin en tenue de travail impeccable lors d'un rassemblement pendant la Révolution culturelle.

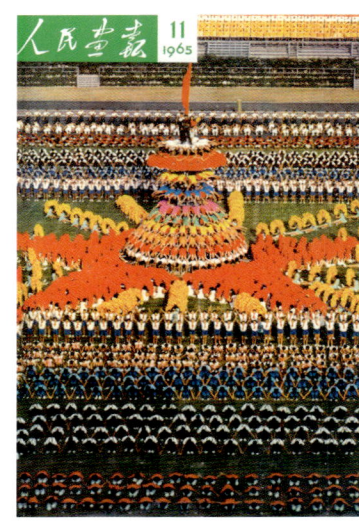

China Pictorial, December 1968

Opening ceremony of national athletic games

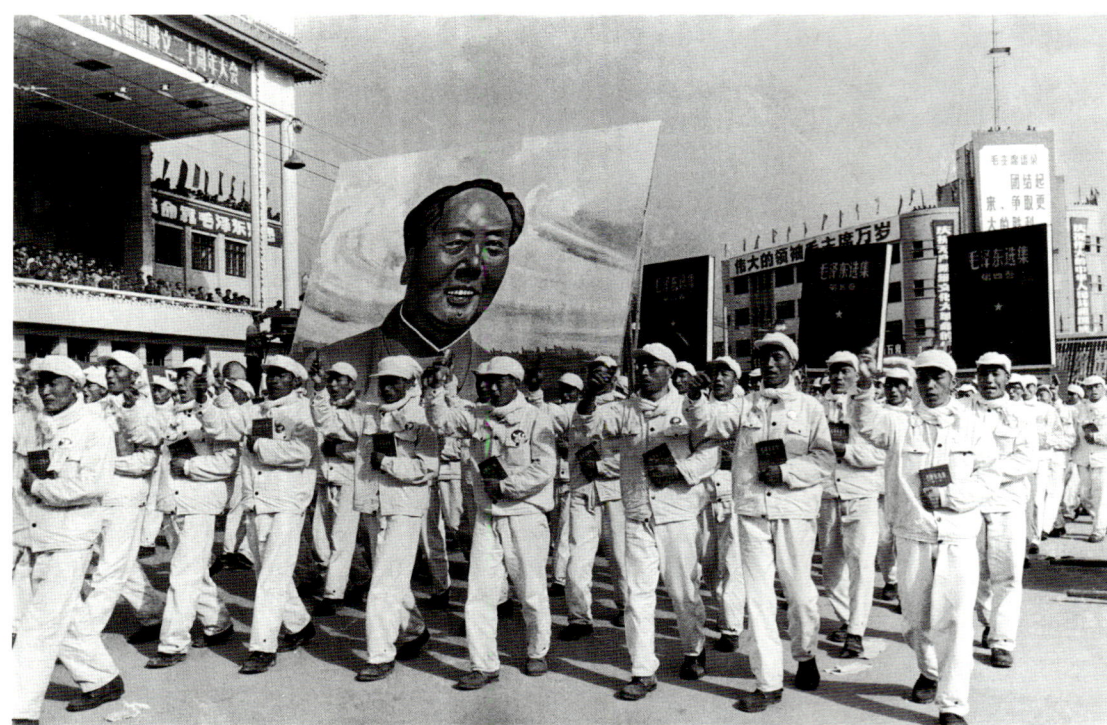

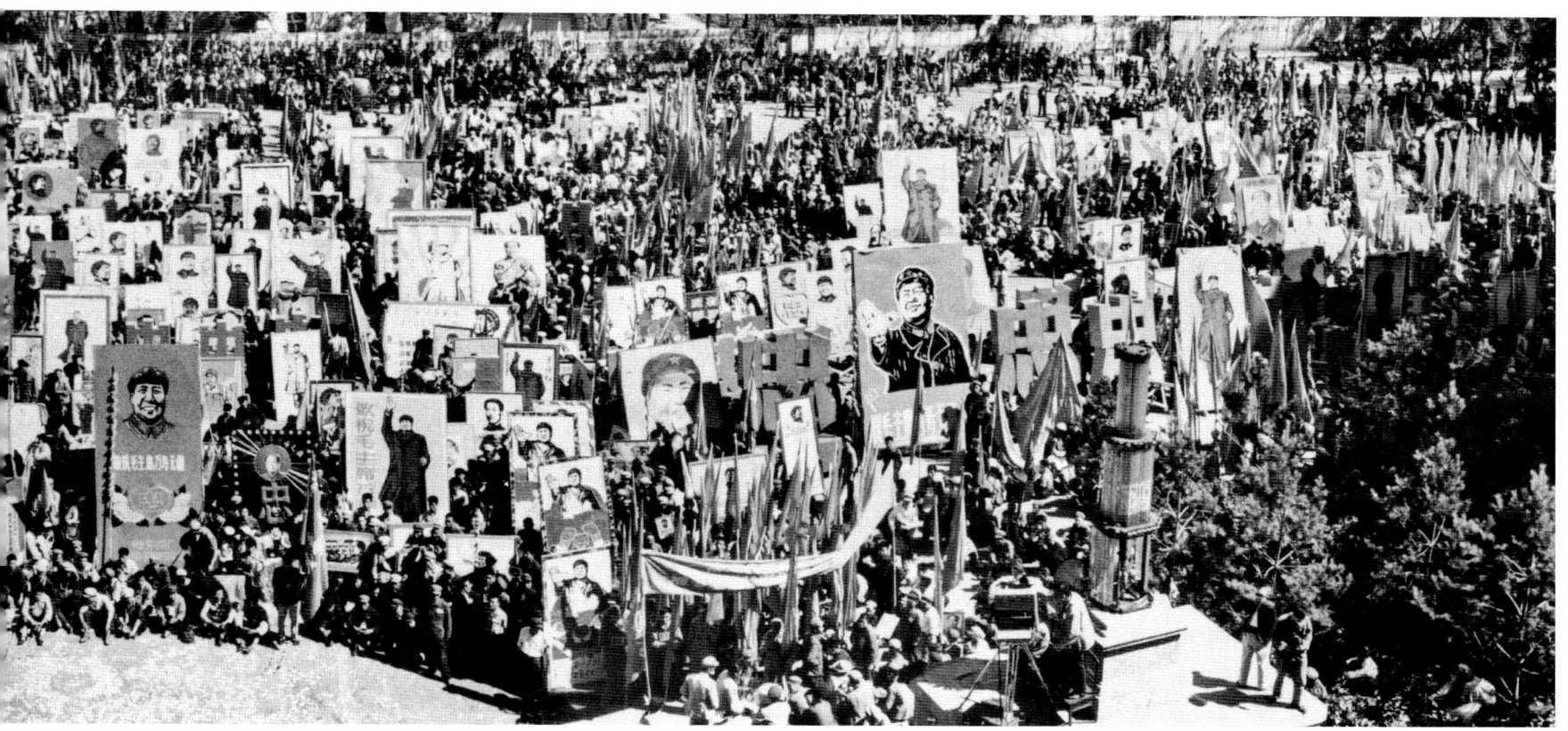

"*The dictatorship of the proletariat is ravenous, more fearsome than the dictatorship of the bourgeoisie. In a bourgeois society, one can run when one violates the law, but when society is so tightly organized, where can one run to? There is no place to vent one's grief and no place to submit an appeal… In our society, there is indeed the phenomenon that men are not treated as men.*"

"*Die Diktatur des Proletariats ist gierig, noch furchterregender als die Diktatur der Bourgeoisie. In einer bürgerlichen Gesellschaft kann man fliehen, wenn man das Gesetz übertreten hat, aber wenn die Gesellschaft derart straff organisiert ist, wohin könnte man da fliehen? Es gibt keinen Ort, an dem man seiner Trauer freien Lauf lassen könnte, keinen Ort, Einspruch zu erheben … In unserer Gesellschaft gibt es tatsächlich das Phänomen, dass Menschen nicht wie Menschen behandelt werden.*"

"*La dictature du prolétariat est dévorante, plus redoutable que la dictature de la bourgeoisie. Dans une société bourgeoise, on peut s'enfuir quand on viole la loi, mais lorsque la société est si étroitement organisée, où s'enfuir ? Il n'y a plus le moindre endroit où se plaindre, plus de possibilité d'appel… Dans notre société, les hommes ne sont pas traités comme des hommes.*"

ZHOU YANG (1908–1989), Chinese literary critic and theorist who introduced Marxist theories of literature to China, 1966

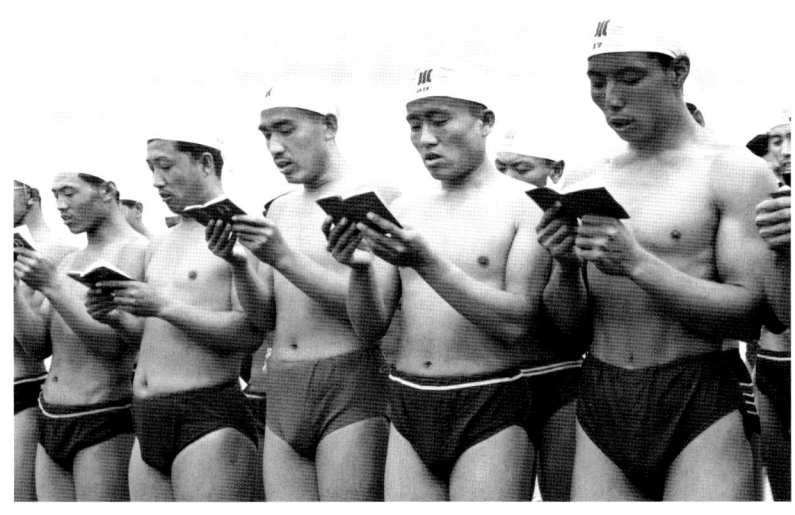

↑
Li Zhensheng, 1967

Swimmers read from Quotations from Chairman Mao Zedong *before plunging into the Songhua river in Harbin to commemorate the first anniversary of Mao's last swim in the Yangtze river, aged 73, on July 16, 1966. The fever pitch of the personality cult surrounding Mao saw the PLA publish a waterproof version of the* Quotations from Chairman Mao Zedong.

Schwimmer lesen die Worte des Vorsitzenden Mao, *ehe sie in den Fluss Songhua in Harbin springen, um damit an den ersten Jahrestag von Maos letztem Bad im Jangtse zu erinnern, das er am 16. Juli 1966 im Alter von 73 Jahren nahm. Der mit fieberhafter Erregung betriebene Personenkult um Mao führte zu Absurditäten wie einer wasserfesten Ausgabe der* Worte des Vorsitzenden Mao.

Des nageurs lisent les Citations du Président Mao *avant de plonger dans les eaux du fleuve Songhua à Harbin pour commémorer le premier anniversaire du dernier bain de Mao dans le Yang-Tsé le 16 juillet 1966 à l'âge de 73 ans. Le culte fiévreux de la personnalité du président vit même l'armée publier une version des* Citations *résistant à l'eau.*

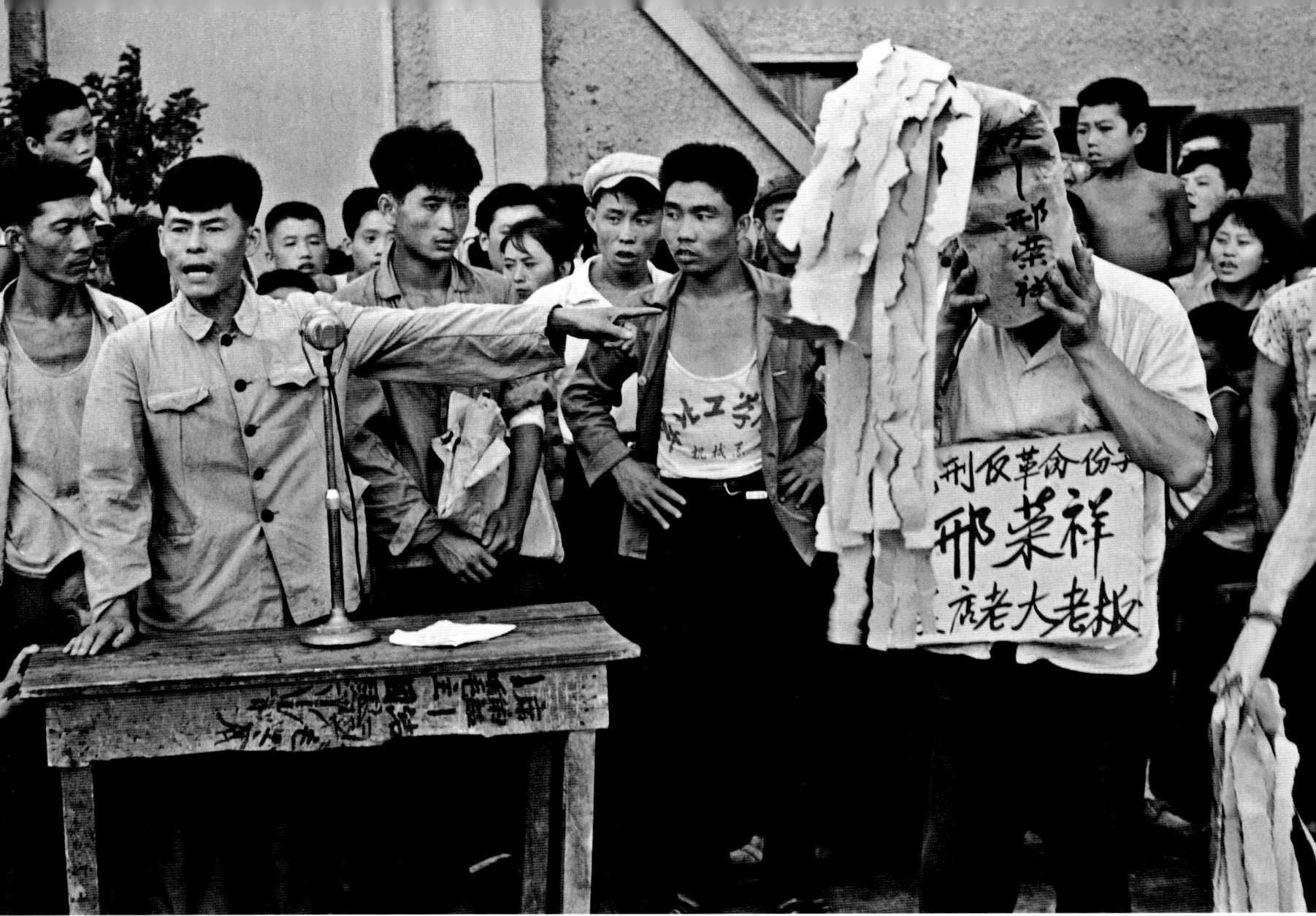

pp. 204/205

↑
Jiang Shaowu, 1967

A catch phrase during the Cultural Revolution was "foster proletarianism and eradicate capitalism." Capitalist economic activities were to be eliminated too, so here, "shopowner Xing Rongxiang" is humiliated at a mass rally in Shenyang.

Eine Parole während der Kulturrevolution lautete: „Das Proletariat fördern, den Kapitalismus ausrotten." Kapitalistische Wirtschaftsaktivitäten galt es ebenfalls zu eliminieren, und so wird hier bei einer Massenkundgebung in Shenyang der „Ladenbesitzer Xing Rongxiang" gedemütigt.

Un des grands slogans de la Révolution culturelle fut « développer le prolétariat et éradiquer le capitalisme ». Les activités économiques capitalistes devaient également être éliminées. Ici, le propriétaire d'un magasin, Xing Rongxiang, est humilié lors d'un rassemblement de masse à Shenyang.

Jiang Shaowu, 1968

Students in Shenyang, Liaoning province, carry placards bearing portraits of Mao during a rally to celebrate being sent to the countryside to do manual labor with peasants. For a time, students were encouraged to travel on foot, spreading news of revolution as they went. This was part of a process termed the "big link-up," which fostered a nationwide network of Red Guard activities.

Studenten in Shenyang in der Provinz Liaoning tragen bei einer Kundgebung zur Feier der Landverschickung, wo sie mit Bauern körperlich arbeiten sollten, Plakate mit Mao-Porträts. Eine Zeitlang wurden Studenten aufgefordert, zu Fuß zu reisen, um unterwegs revolutionäre Neuigkeiten zu verbreiten. Dies war Teil eines als „große Verkettung" bezeichneten Prozesses, der eine landesweite Vernetzung der Aktivitäten der Roten Garden förderte.

Des étudiants de Shenyang, dans la province de Liaoning, arborent des portraits de Mao pendant une manifestation organisée en l'honneur de leur « expédition » à la campagne pour effectuer des travaux manuels auprès des paysans. Pendant un temps, les étudiants furent encouragés à voyager à pied pour diffuser au passage les nouvelles de la Révolution. Tout ceci faisait partie d'un processus appelé « échanges des expériences révolutionnaires » qui alimentaient le réseau national d'activité des Gardes rouges.

"The Struggle... is a peculiarly Chinese invention, combining intimidation, humiliation, and sheer exhaustion. Briefly described, it is an intellectual gangbeating of one man by many, sometimes even thousands, in which the victim has no defense, not even the truth."

„Der Kampf ... ist eine eigentümlich chinesische Erfindung, bei der Einschüchterung, Demütigung und pure Erschöpfung zusammenkommen. Kurz beschrieben, handelt es sich um das geistige Verprügeln eines Mannes durch viele, bisweilen Tausende, bei der das Opfer kein Mittel der Gegenwehr hat, noch nicht einmal die Wahrheit."

« La Lutte ... est une invention très chinoise, combinant intimidation, humiliation et épuisement total. En bref, c'est l'acharnement intellectuel contre un homme déployé par beaucoup d'autres, parfois même des milliers, dans lequel la victime ne dispose d'aucune défense, pas même celle de la vérité. »

BAO RUOWANG (Jean Pasqualini, 1926–1997), French-Chinese writer imprisoned for seven years during the Anti-Rightist Movement, 1973

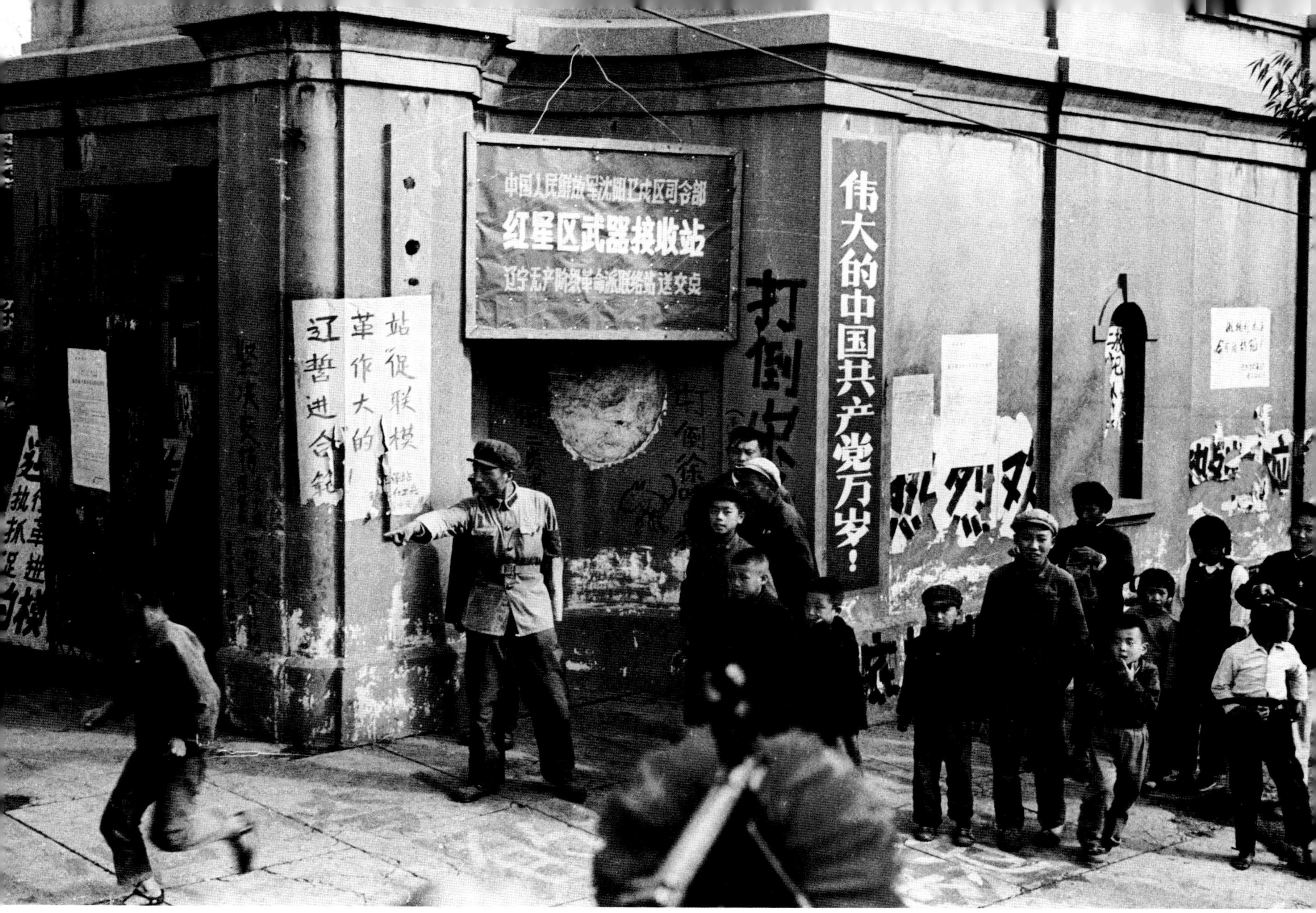

Jiang Shaowu, 1968

During the Cultural Revolution, public buildings were covered with slogans. A soldier scolds children who have gathered outside a government building in Shenyang, Liaoning province.

Während der Kulturrevolution wurden öffentliche Gebäude mit Parolen beschrieben und beklebt. Ein Soldat schimpft mit Kindern, die sich vor einem Regierungsgebäude in Shenyang in der Provinz Liaoning aufhalten.

Pendant la Révolution culturelle, les bâtiments publics étaient couverts de slogans. Ici, à Shenyang, province du Liaoning, un soldat gronde des enfants rassemblés devant un bâtiment gouvernemental.

Li Zhensheng, 1966

Red Guards perform "It is right to rebel" in Harbin, Heilongjiang province. This was the slogan with which Mao manipulated the Red Guards into overthrowing any leader who was deemed "reactionary."

Rote Garden führen in Harbin, Provinz Heilongjiang, „Es ist richtig, zu rebellieren" auf. Dies war der Wahlspruch, mit dem Mao die Roten Garden dazu brachte, jeden Führer, der als reaktionär galt, zu bekämpfen und zu stürzen.

Des Gardes rouges jouent « Il est juste d'être un rebelle » à Harbin, province du Heilong-jiang. C'était un des slogans utilisés par Mao pour manipuler les Gardes et les inciter à renverser les responsables accusés d'être « réactionnaires ».

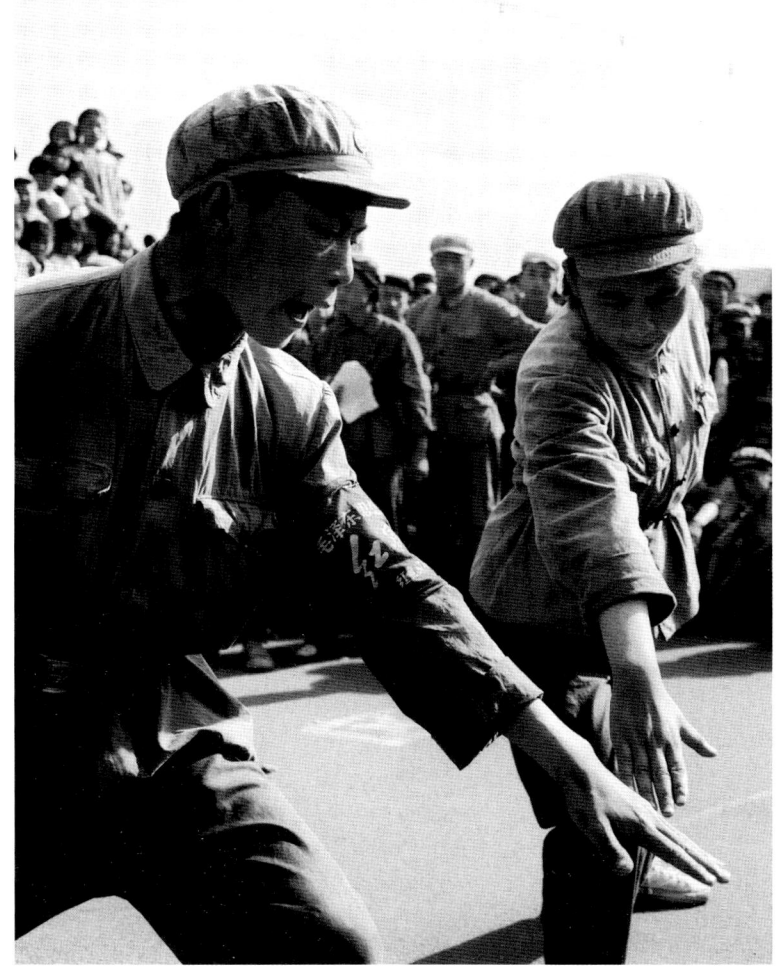

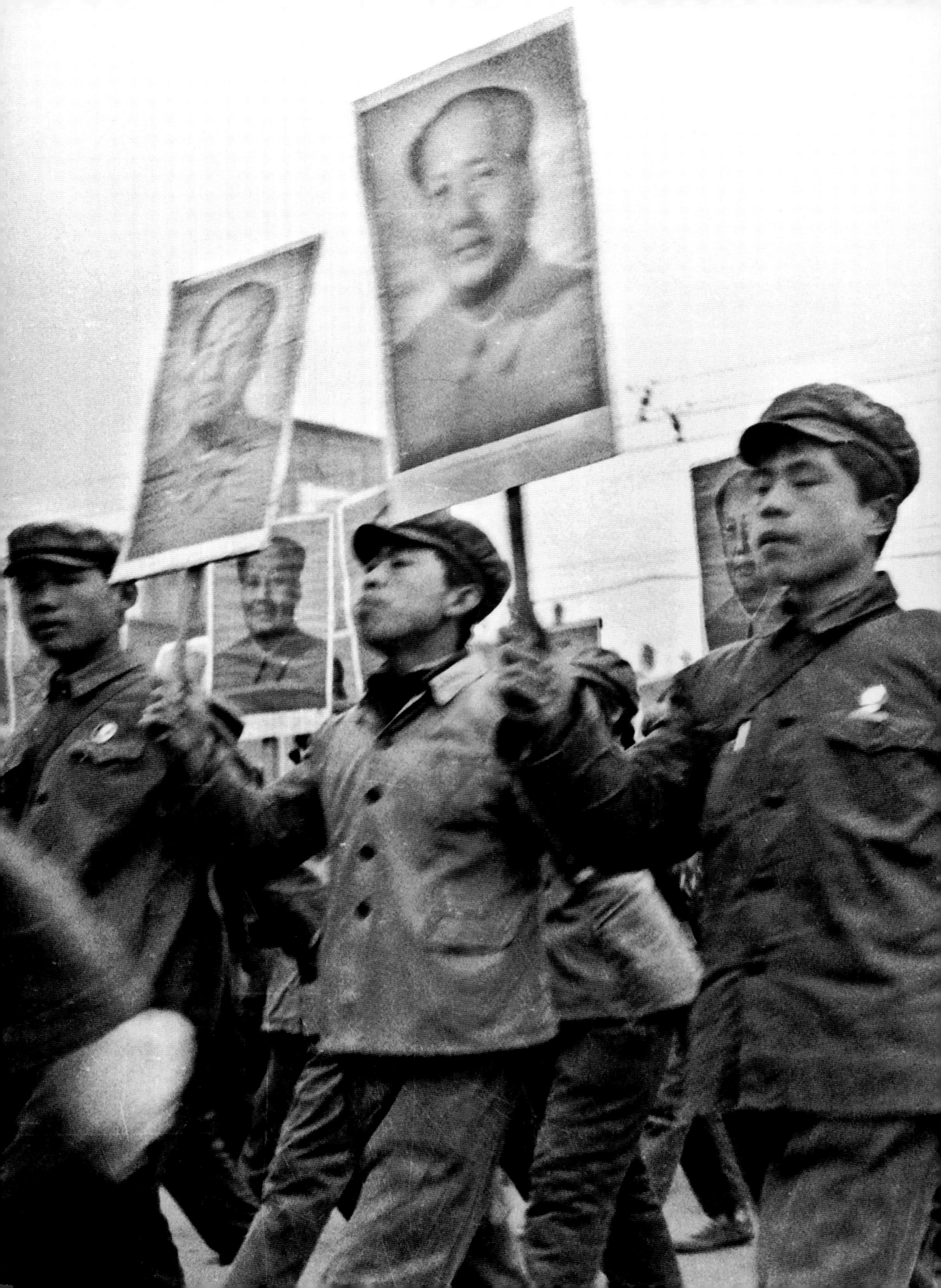

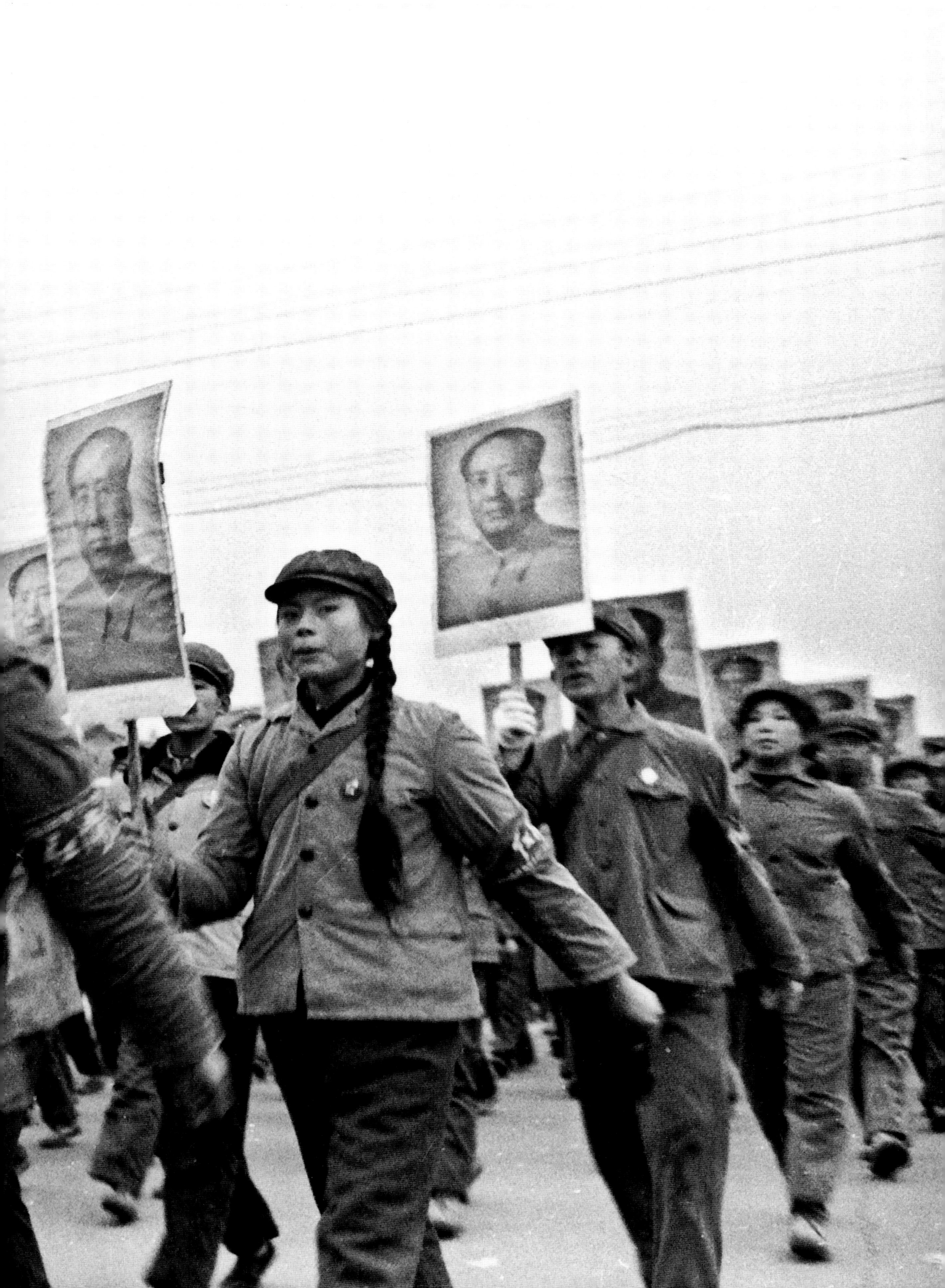

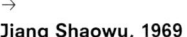
Jiang Shaowu, 1969

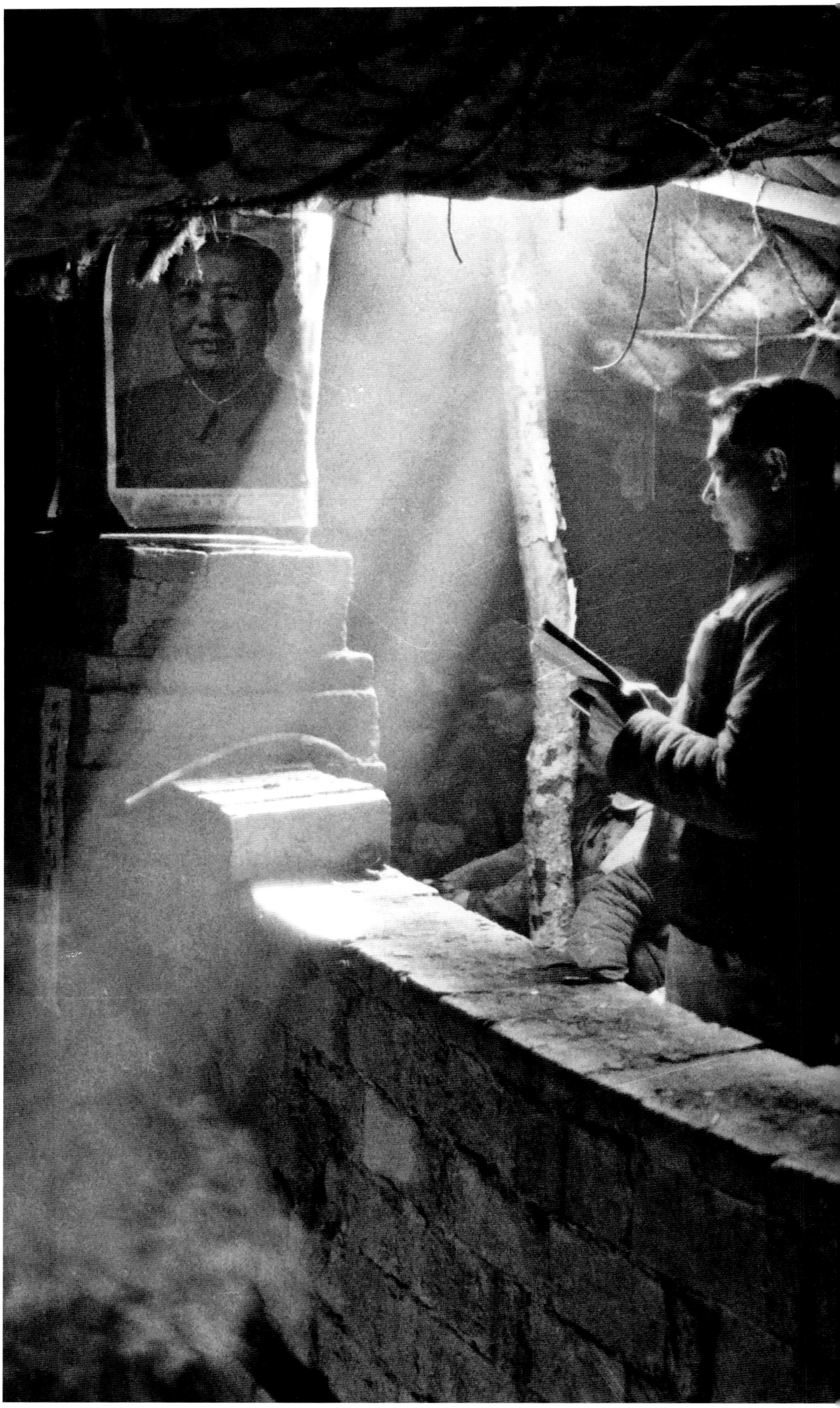

*During the Cultural Revolution, the term
"ox-demons and snake-spirits" (niu gui
she shen) referred to scholars, state officials,
former owners of private businesses, and other
people condemned as counterrevolutionaries,
revisionists, or reactionary authorities in
academic studies. Since they were "ox-demons
and snake-spirits," their detention house was
called the "ox-shed." Thousands of such
people were detained in "ox-sheds," where
they were subjected to forced labor and
study. Here, a group of disgraced intellectuals
in Shenyang are thrown into the "ox-shed"
to study Mao Thought to rectify their thinking
and attitudes towards revolution.*

*Während der Kulturrevolution bezeichnete
man in wissenschaftlicjen Studien mit den
Begriffen „Ochsendämonen" und „Schlangengeister" (niu gui she shen) Gelehrte, Amtspersonen, ehemalige Besitzer von Privatge-
schäften und andere als Konterrevolutionäre,
Revisionisten oder reaktionäre Autoritäten.
Da sie Ochsendämonen und Schlangengeister
waren, nannte man ihre Haftanstalt den
Ochsenschuppen. Tausende dieser Personen
wurden in Ochsenschuppen zu Zwangsarbeit
und Umschulung festgehalten. Hier wurde
eine Gruppe in Ungnade gefallener Intellektueller in Shenyang im Ochsenschuppen
inhaftiert, um Maos Werk zu studieren und
die eigene Denkweise und Einstellung zur
Revolution zu korrigieren.*

*Au cours de la Révolution culturelle, le
qualificatif de « démon de bœuf et esprit
de serpent » (niu gui she shen) s'appliquait
aux universitaires, hauts responsables,
anciens propriétaires d'entreprises privées
et à d'autres personnes condamnées comme
contre-révolutionnaires, révisionnistes ou
réactionnaires dans les travaux universitaires.
Leur lieu de détention était surnommé
« l'étable ». Des milliers de gens furent ainsi
détenus dans ces « étables » pour accomplir
des travaux forcés et étudier. Ici, un groupe
d'intellectuels disgraciés de Shenyang sont
jetés dans une « étable » pour étudier les
écrits de Mao et rectifier leurs attitudes et
leur pensée envers la Révolution.*

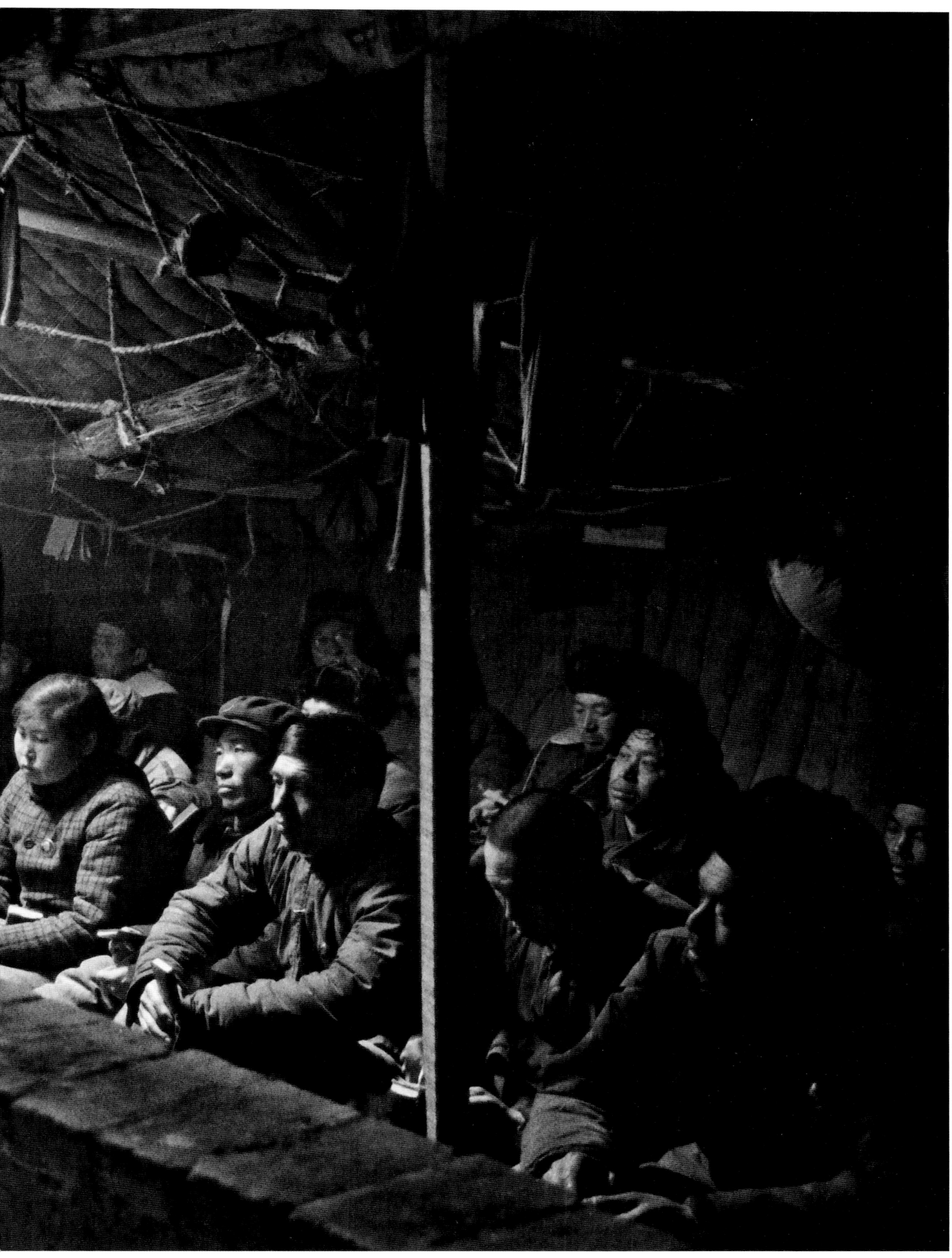

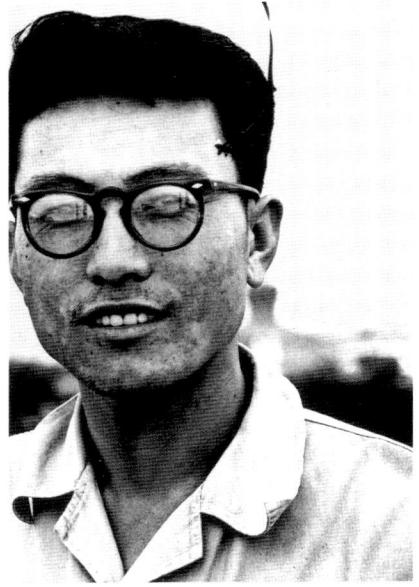 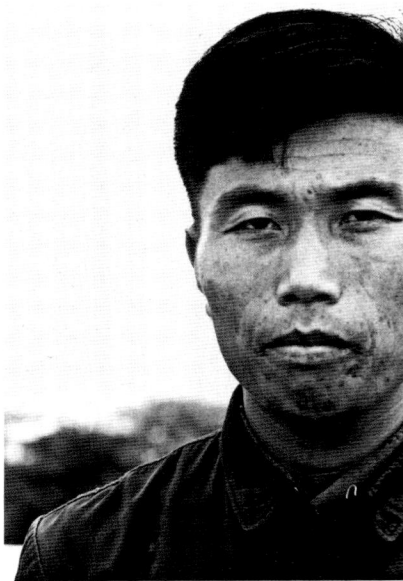 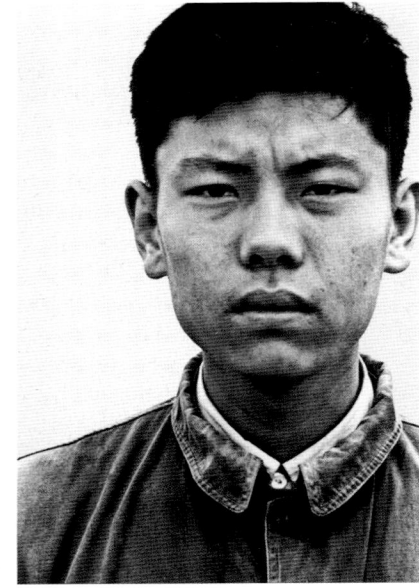 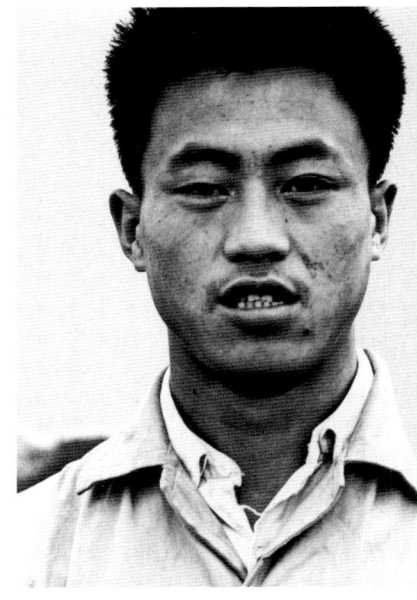

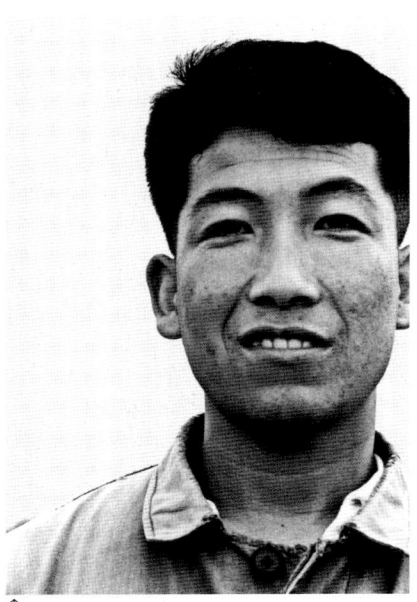 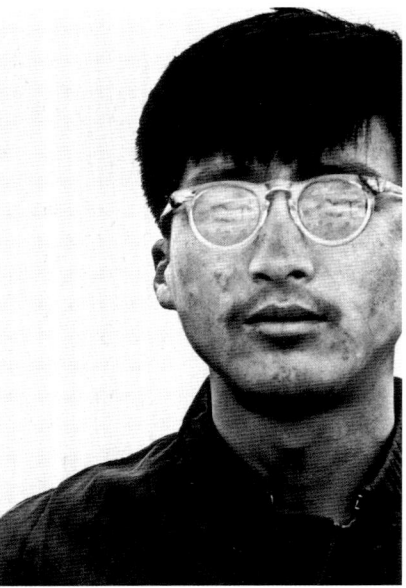 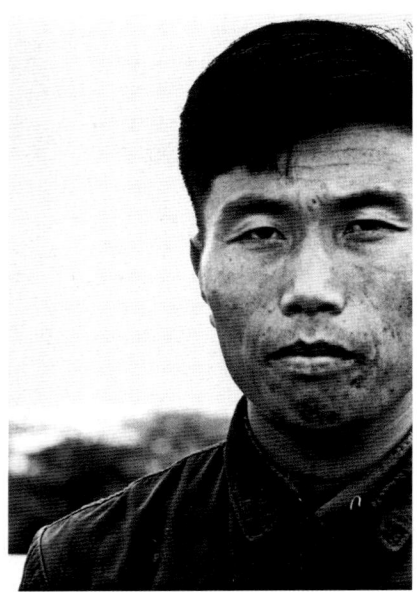 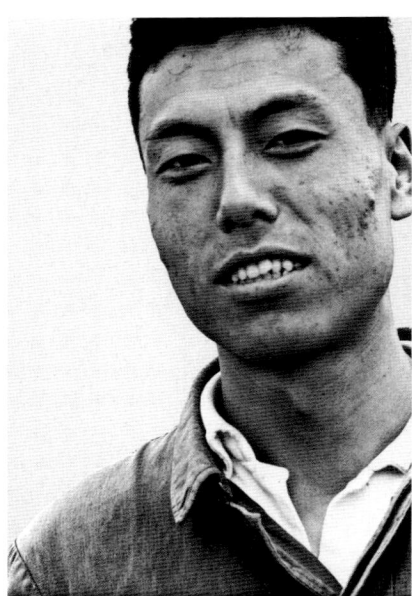

↑
Jiang Shaowu, 1968

Typical faces of young men from China's northeast region during the Great Proletarian Cultural Revolution.

Typische Gesichter junger Männer aus dem Nordosten Chinas während der Großen Proletarischen Kulturrevolution.

Visages typiques de jeunes hommes du nord-est de la Chine pendant la Grande révolution culturelle prolétarienne.

→
Xiao Zhuang, 1969

Workers at a rally in Nanjing, where thousands of official cadres were sent to the countryside to be "reeducated" by the peasants. It is estimated that a total of 20 million people migrated to the countryside during the Cultural Revolution. Many were effectively banished to rural areas for decades, although from the early 1980s, those who had not yet reached retirement age were able to return to their former positions.

Arbeiter bei einer Kundgebung in Nanjing, bei der Tausende von leitenden Funktionären aufs Land geschickt wurden, um von den Bauern umerzogen zu werden. Schätzungsweise 20 Millionen Menschen wurden während der Kulturrevolution zwangsweise umgesiedelt. Viele wurden für Jahrzehnte in ländliche Regionen verbannt, obwohl diejenigen, die noch nicht das Rentenalter erreicht hatten, ab den frühen 1980er-Jahren an ihre alten Positionen zurückkehren konnten.

Ouvriers lors d'un rassemblement à Nankin où des milliers de cadres de l'administration sont envoyés à la campagne pour être rééduqués par les paysans. On estime à 20 millions le nombre de personnes exilées à la campagne pendant la Révolution culturelle. Beaucoup furent bannies pendant des décennies bien que, à partir du début des années 1980, ceux qui n'avaient pas encore atteint l'âge de la retraite aient pu récupérer leurs anciens postes.

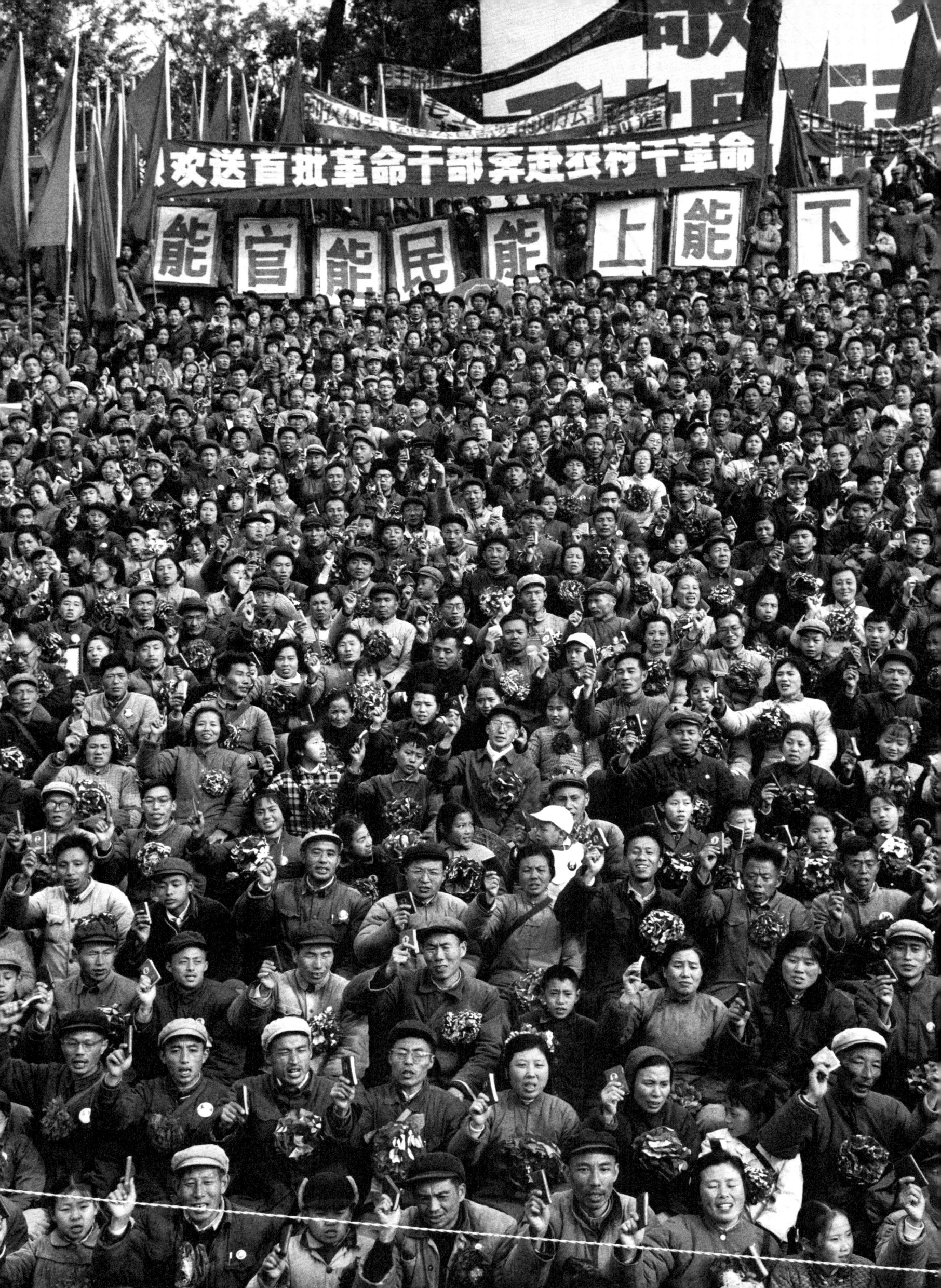

#3

1970–1979 *Suspicion, Subversion, and Continued Madness*

In the twilight of Mao's incredible political life, it was clear to both Mao and Zhou Enlai that they needed to choose a successor, especially since Mao's earlier choice of Marshal Lin Biao had ended disastrously in perceived betrayal. It was now that Deng Xiaoping emerged as the man who would steer China away from the decade of madness towards economic reform. Given his failing health, Mao knew that the days of his paramount authority and prestige were numbered. Thus he began actively to seek a diplomatic engagement with the United States in order to counter the threat that now loomed from across the northern border in the form of a newly estranged, and somewhat frustrated, Soviet Union.

When Mao launched the Cultural Revolution in June of 1966, his long-estranged wife, Jiang Qing, began to emerge as a political force in her own right. Pleading the support of Mao and his Cultural Revolution in public, she forged an alliance with three cadres based in the industrial and economic powerhouse of Shanghai. This clique was to go down in history as the "Gang of Four." During the early 1970s, it would persistently push the ultra-leftist agenda in order to shift power away from the pragmatists. A year before Mao died in September 1976, Deng was again removed from the leadership. Jiang Qing also claimed the role of cultural commissar, taking charge of determining the production of entertainment for the masses. This became the era of the model operas, a series of eight stories of revolutionary heroism, commitment, and self-sacrifice in the name of building socialism. As the power of the Red Guards grew, films were made based on students like Zhang Tieshen, who was celebrated as a national hero for opposing traditional education (by handing in a blank exam paper), and rejecting defunct aspects of the pre-Communist system.

In 1972 came the surprise announcement of the death of Lin Biao, killed in a plane crash on September 13, 1971, whilst allegedly fleeing China in the wake of a failed coup against Mao. The precise circumstances surrounding the crash, and Lin Biao's possible motives for leading such a coup, were never revealed. With Lin Biao and his family out of the picture, Mao rehabilitated Deng Xiaoping as an interim measure, so that, once again, economic order could be restored.

The war in Vietnam and the Cold War provided Mao with an important opportunity: despite a diplomatic channel that ran through Warsaw led by Chinese diplomat Wang Bingnan, China and the U.S. continued their standoff until 1972 with the official visit of U.S. President Richard Nixon to China. A flurry of diplomatic activities had begun the preceding year with an initiative that would become known as "Ping Pong diplomacy"—Zhou Enlai extended an invitation to U.S. table-tennis players to participate in a series of friendly games in China. This led to a secret visit by Nixon's national security advisor Henry Kissinger. As a result, the U.S. and China took this opportunity to sign the landmark Shanghai Communiqué. In light of this communiqué, the two countries established full diplomatic relations on January 1, 1979.

Goodbye Chairman Mao, Down with the Gang of Four, Hello Deng Xiaoping

In 1978, following the arrest of the Gang of Four on October 6, 1976, the thrice disgraced Deng Xiaoping finally succeeded in persuading the Chinese leadership to adopt a pro-economic reform agenda. Deng's plan pivoted on the introduction of "Four Modernizations." To outmaneuver his political rivals, Deng initially sanctioned a degree of free speech, centered on the "Democracy Wall" in Xidan, a bus depot on the west side of Chang'an boulevard. As a result, thousands of aggrieved petitioners streamed into Beijing from all over China to seek a redress of personal grievances resulting from the Cultural Revolution. However, when "dissidents" began demanding a "fifth modernization," something akin to Western-style democracy, there was a swift government crackdown.

"Historically the Chinese have always preferred a single, unambiguous authority."

LUCIAN W. PYE (1921–), Professor of Political Science, Massachussetts Institute of Technology, 1972

#3

1970–1979
Misstrauen, Verrat und andauernder Wahnsinn

Gegen Ende seiner unglaublichen politischen Laufbahn musste Mao, ebenso wie auch Zhou Enlai, einen Nachfolger wählen, vor allem weil Maos früherer Kandidat, Marschall Lin Biao, unter dem Verdacht des Verrats ein böses Ende genommen hatte. Jetzt entpuppte sich Deng Xiaoping als derjenige, der China aus einem Jahrzehnt des Irrsinns zu wirtschaftlichen Reformen führen sollte. Angesichts seiner schwindenden Gesundheit war Mao klar, dass die Tage seiner unangefochtenen Autorität und Herrschaft gezählt waren. Er bemühte sich um diplomatische Beziehungen zu den Vereinigten Staaten, um der Bedrohung an der nördlichen Grenze in Gestalt einer neu erstarkten und einigermaßen ernüchterten Sowjetunion etwas entgegensetzen zu können.

Als Mao im Juni 1966 die Kulturrevolution entfesselte, begann der Aufstieg seiner seit langem von ihm getrennt lebenden Ehefrau Jiang Qing zu einer eigenständigen politischen Größe. Öffentlich gelobte sie, Mao und seine Kulturrevolution zu unterstützen, schmiedete jedoch gleichzeitig mit drei im industriellen und ökonomischen Machtzentrum Shanghai ansässigen Kadern eine Allianz. Diese Clique ging als „Viererbande" in die Geschichte ein. Sie propagierte zu Beginn der 1970er-Jahre hartnäckig ein ultralinkes Parteiprogramm, um die Pragmatiker von der Macht abzudrängen. Ein Jahr bevor Mao im September 1976 starb wurde Deng erneut von der Führung entbunden (1975). Jiang Qing beanspruchte nun auch die Rolle der Kulturkommissarin und war damit zuständig für die Produktion von Unterhaltung für die Massen. Die Zeit der Modellopern begann, einer Serie von acht Geschichten, die von revolutionärem Heldentum, Verpflichtung und Aufopferung im Namen des Sozialismus handelten. Als die Macht der Roten Garden zunahm, entstanden Filme über Studenten wie Zhang Tieshen, der bei der Prüfung ein leeres Blatt abgab und als Nationalheld gefeiert wurde, weil er mit dieser Geste gegen die traditionelle Bildung und überholte Aspekte des vorkommunistischen Systems opponierte.

1972 ging die überraschende Nachricht vom Tod Lin Biaos um die Welt, der bei einem Flugzeugabsturz am 13. September 1971 starb, als er offenbar nach einem gescheiterten Putsch gegen Mao aus China fliehen wollte. Die genauen Umstände des Absturzes und Lin Biaos mögliche Motive für seinen Coup kamen nie ans Licht. In dieser Situation rehabilitierte Mao als Zwischenlösung Deng Xiaoping, damit dieser erneut für geordnete wirtschaftliche Verhältnisse sorgen konnte.

Der Krieg in Vietnam und der Kalte Krieg in Europa eröffneten Mao eine wichtige Chance: Trotz der diplomatischen Verbindung, die unter Leitung des chinesischen Diplomaten Wang Bingnan über Warschau bestand, blieb die reservierte Haltung Chinas gegenüber den USA bis 1972 bestehen, als der amerikanische Präsident Richard Nixon China einen offiziellen Besuch abstattete. Im Jahr zuvor hatten hektische diplomatische Aktivitäten eingesetzt, die später als „Pingpong-Diplomatie" bekannt wurden. Zhou Enlai leitete eine Einladung amerikanischer Tischtennisspieler in die Wege, die an einer Reihe von Freundschaftsspielen in China teilnahmen. Dies führte zu einem geheimen Besuch von Nixons Sicherheitsberater Dr. Henry Kissinger, in dessen Folge die Vereinigten Staaten und China das grundlegende Kommuniqué von Shanghai unterzeichneten. Im Anschluss daran nahmen die beiden Länder am 1. Januar 1979 uneingeschränkte diplomatische Beziehungen auf.

Adieu Vorsitzender Mao, Nieder mit der Viererbande, Willkommen Deng Xiaoping

Nach der Verhaftung der Viererbande am 6. Oktober 1976 gelang es dem dreimal in Ungnade gefallenen Deng Xiaoping 1978 endlich, die chinesische Führung von einem wirtschaftsfreundlichen Reformprogramm zu überzeugen. Dreh- und Angelpunkt von Dengs Plan war die Umsetzung der „Vier Modernisierungen". Um seine politischen Gegner auszuschalten, duldete Deng zunächst ein gewisses Maß an Meinungsfreiheit, die sich ein Forum an der Mauer der Demokratie in Xidan, einem Busbahnhof an der Westseite des Chang'an Boulevards, schuf. In der Folge strömten Tausende aufgebrachter Bittsteller aus ganz China nach Peking, um Wiedergutmachung für infolge der Kulturrevolution erlittenes persönliches Unrecht zu beantragen. Als jedoch Dissidenten anfingen, eine „fünfte Modernisierung" im Sinne einer Demokratie westlichen Stils zu fordern, griff die Regierung ohne Zögern hart durch.

„Historisch gesehen haben die Chinesen immer eine einzige, unmißverständliche Autorität bevorzugt."

LUCIAN W. PYE (1921–), Professor für Politikwissenschaft, Massachussetts Institute of Technology, 1972

#3

1970–1979
Suspicions, subversion et folie

Au crépuscule de l'incroyable vie politique de Mao, il devenait évident que lui et Zhou Enlai devaient choisir un successeur. Le choix initial du maréchal Lin Biao s'était achevé par un désastre perçu comme une trahison. C'est à ce moment que Deng Xiaoping apparut comme le seul homme capable de sauver le pays d'une décennie de folie et de le conduire sur la voie de la réforme économique. De santé déclinante, Mao savait que les jours de son autorité absolue et de son prestige étaient comptés. Il commença alors à rechercher activement un rapprochement diplomatique avec les États-Unis pour contrer la menace qui pesait sur la frontière nord, sous la forme d'une Union soviétique qui s'était éloignée et manifestait certaines frustrations.

Lorsque Mao lança la Révolution culturelle en juin 1966, son épouse Jiang Qing, dont il était depuis longtemps séparé, devint une force politique montante. Se réclamant en public du soutien du Président et de sa nouvelle révolution, elle constitua une alliance avec trois cadres du Parti de la puissante cité industrielle et commerciale de Shanghai. Cette clique allait prendre pour l'histoire le nom de « Bande des quatre ». Au début des années 1970, elle soutenait les objectifs de l'extrême gauche pour enlever le pouvoir aux pragmatistes (Deng perdit alors ses fonctions en 1975). Jiang Qing réclama le rôle de commissaire culturel et prit en charge la production de divertissements pour les masses. Ce fut la grande période des opéras modèles, un ensemble de sept narrations sur les thèmes de l'héroïsme, de l'engagement et du sacrifice révolutionnaire au service de la construction du socialisme. Le pouvoir des Gardes rouges s'affirmant, des étudiants comme Zhang Tieshen, qui rendit copie blanche dans un examen, devinrent des héros de la nation pour s'être opposés à l'éducation traditionnelle et aux défunts aspects du système pré-communiste.

Le début de 1972 vit l'annonce-surprise de la mort de Lin Biao dans un accident d'avion le 13 septembre 1971 alors qu'il s'enfuyait, apparemment après un coup d'État manqué contre Mao. Les circonstances précises de son décès et la possibilité qu'il ait monté un tel coup ne furent jamais éclaircies. Le maréchal et sa famille éliminés, Mao réhabilita provisoirement Deng Xiaoping, chargé une fois de plus de restaurer l'ordre économique.

La guerre au Vietnam et la Guerre froide en Europe offrirent à Mao une opportunité intéressante : grâce à des contacts diplomatiques à Varsovie, pilotés par le diplomate chinois Wang Bingnan, la Chine et les États-Unis renouèrent des liens au travers de la visite officielle du président américain, Richard Nixon, en Chine. Le flux des échanges diplomatiques avait commencé l'année précédente par une initiative appelée « la diplomatie du ping-pong », c'est-à-dire l'invitation lancée par Zhou Enlai aux champions de tennis de table américains à participer à des matches amicaux en Chine. Ceci permit la visite secrète du conseiller national pour la sécurité Henry Kissinger. Les États-Unis et la Chine signèrent alors le communiqué historique de Shanghai par lequel les deux pays ouvraient des relations diplomatiques complètes le 1er janvier 1979.

Au revoir Mao. À bas la Bande des quatre. Salut Deng Xiaoping

En 1978, à la suite de l'arrestation de la Bande des quatre le 6 octobre 1976, Deng Xiaoping, qui avait été disgracié à trois reprises, réussit à convaincre le pouvoir chinois d'adopter ses réformes économiques. Son plan reposait sur l'introduction de « Quatre modernisations ». Pour contourner ses rivaux politiques, il accepta un certain degré de liberté d'expression sur le Mur de la démocratie à Xidan, dépôt de bus du boulevard Chang'an à Pékin. Des milliers de pétitionnaires affluèrent de toute la Chine vers la capitale pour réclamer que les torts dont ils avaient été victimes pendant la Révolution culturelle soient réparés. Néanmoins, lorsque des dissidents commencèrent à demander une « cinquième modernisation », synonyme de démocratie à l'occidentale, le gouvernement réagit rapidement.

« Historiquement, les Chinois ont toujours préféré avoir affaire à une autorité unique, sans ambiguïté. »

**LUCIAN W. PYE (1921–), Professeur de science politique,
Massachussetts Institute of Technology, 1972**

"Imagine—eight model operas in ten years, and only one author! Art had reached this level of simplicity. Everyone watched the model operas, and their heads became filled with 'heroic imagery.' How could it fail to produce a great revolution? But people were not simply watching opera; they were watching people—watching the people who wielded the power. Over those ten years, people's way of thinking gradually grew more sophisticated."

„Man stelle sich vor – acht Modellopern in acht Jahren und nur ein Autor! Die Kunst hatte diesen Grad der Einfachheit erreicht. Alle sahen sich die Modellopern an, und ihre Hirne füllten sich mit ‚heroischen Bildern'. Was konnte schief gehen beim Anzetteln einer Revolution? Aber die Leute schauten sich nicht nur Opern an; sie schauten Menschen zu – den Menschen, die die Macht ausübten. Im Laufe dieser zehn Jahre wurde die Denkweise der Menschen allmählich komplizierter."

« Imaginez : huit opéras modèles en dix ans et un seul auteur ! L'art avait atteint ce niveau de simplicité. Tout le monde regardait ces opéras et avait la tête remplie de leur 'imagerie héroïque'. Comment aurait-il pu ne pas se produire une grande révolution ? Mais les gens ne se contentaient pas seulement de regarder l'opéra, ils observaient les autres – ceux qui détenaient le pouvoir. Au cours de ces dix années, la manière de penser des gens se compliqua de plus en plus. »

BA JIN (Li Feikan, 1904–2005), novelist

pp. 218/219
Zhang Yaxin, 1971

A scene from Taking Tiger Mountain by Strategy.

Eine Szene aus Mit taktischem Geschick den Tigerberg erobern.

Scène de l'opéra La prise de la montagne du tigre.

→
Zhang Yaxin, 1974

A scene from The Red Lantern.

Eine Szene aus Die rote Signallaterne.

Scène de l'opéra La Lanterne rouge.

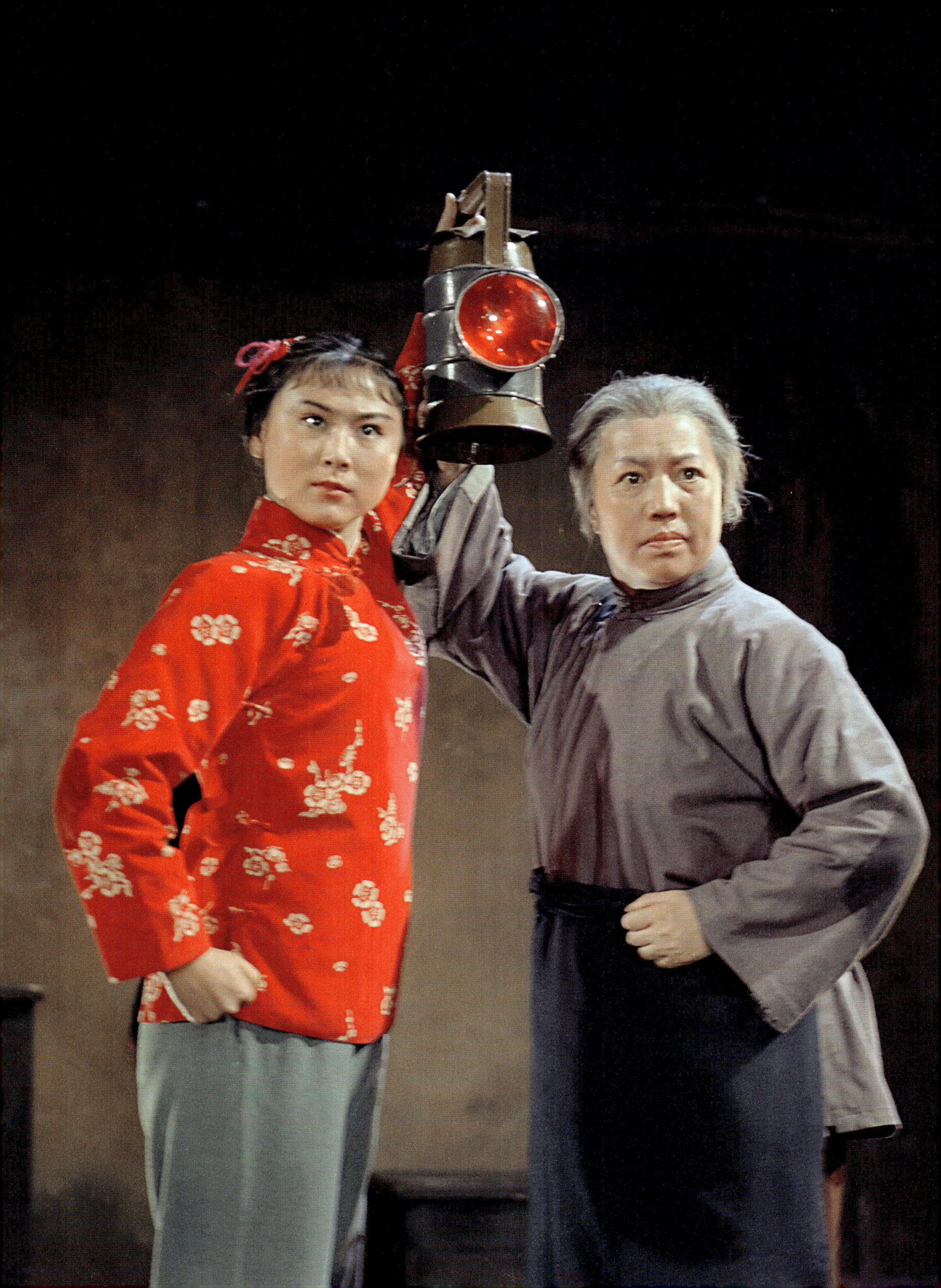

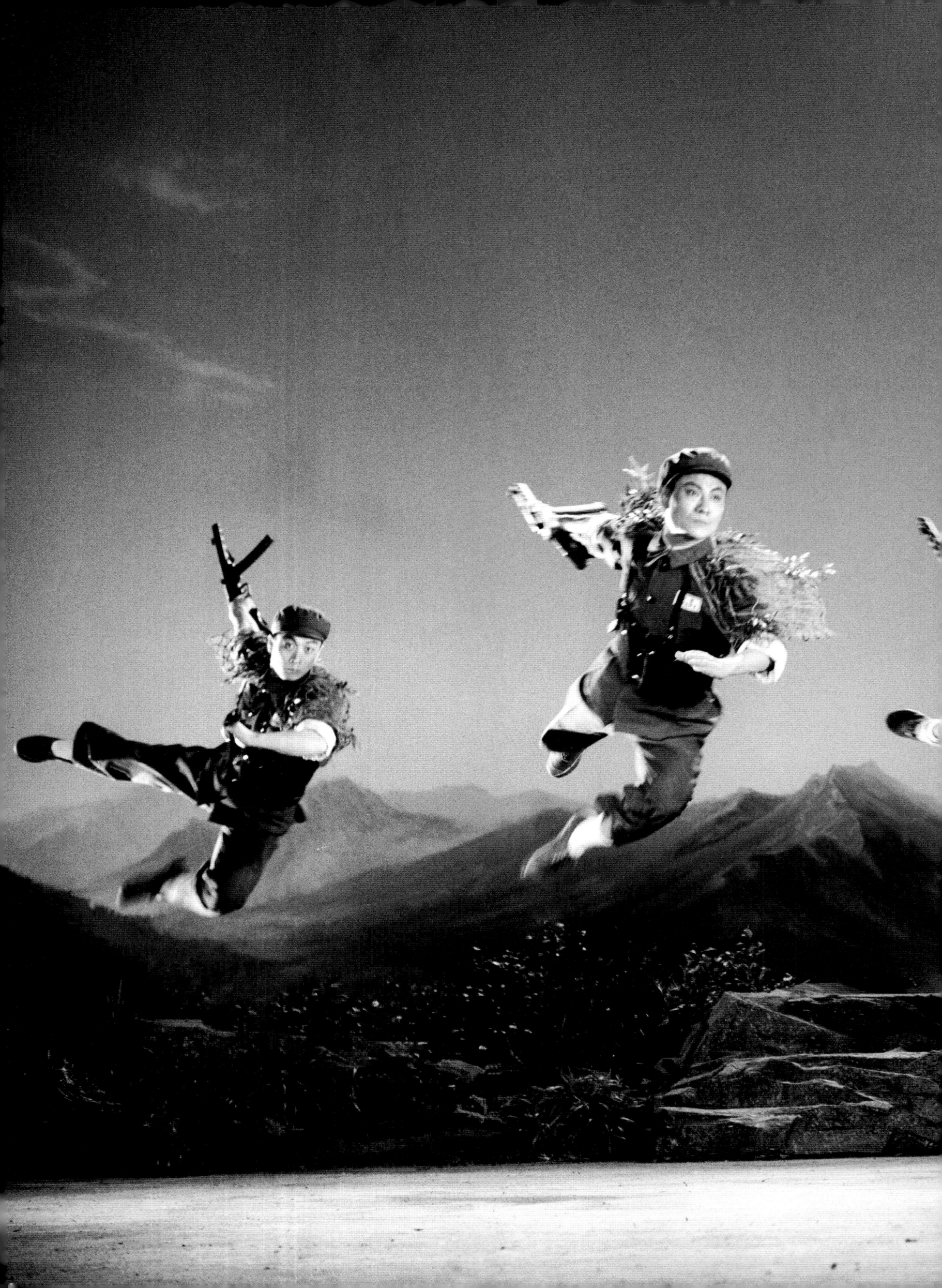

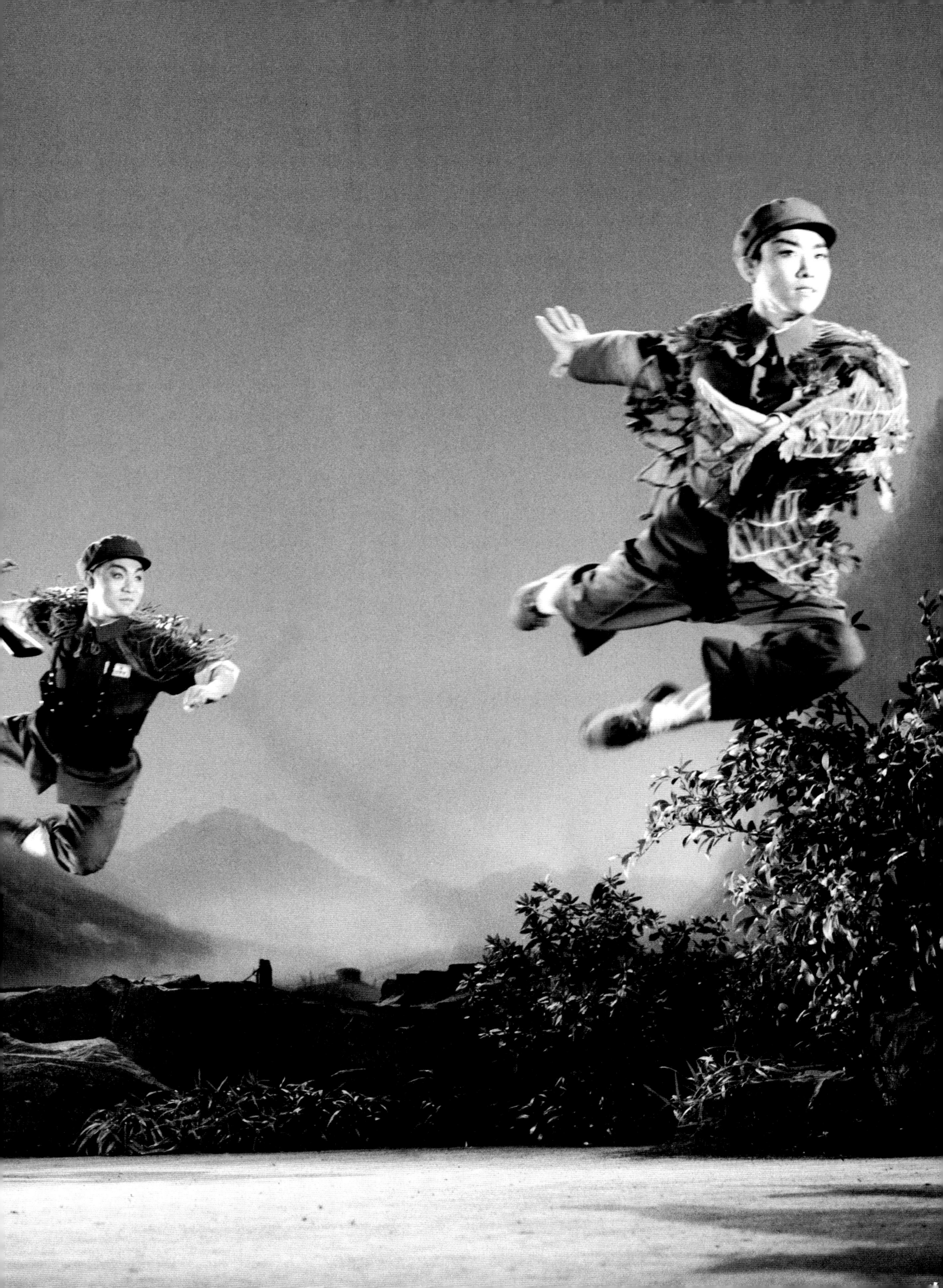

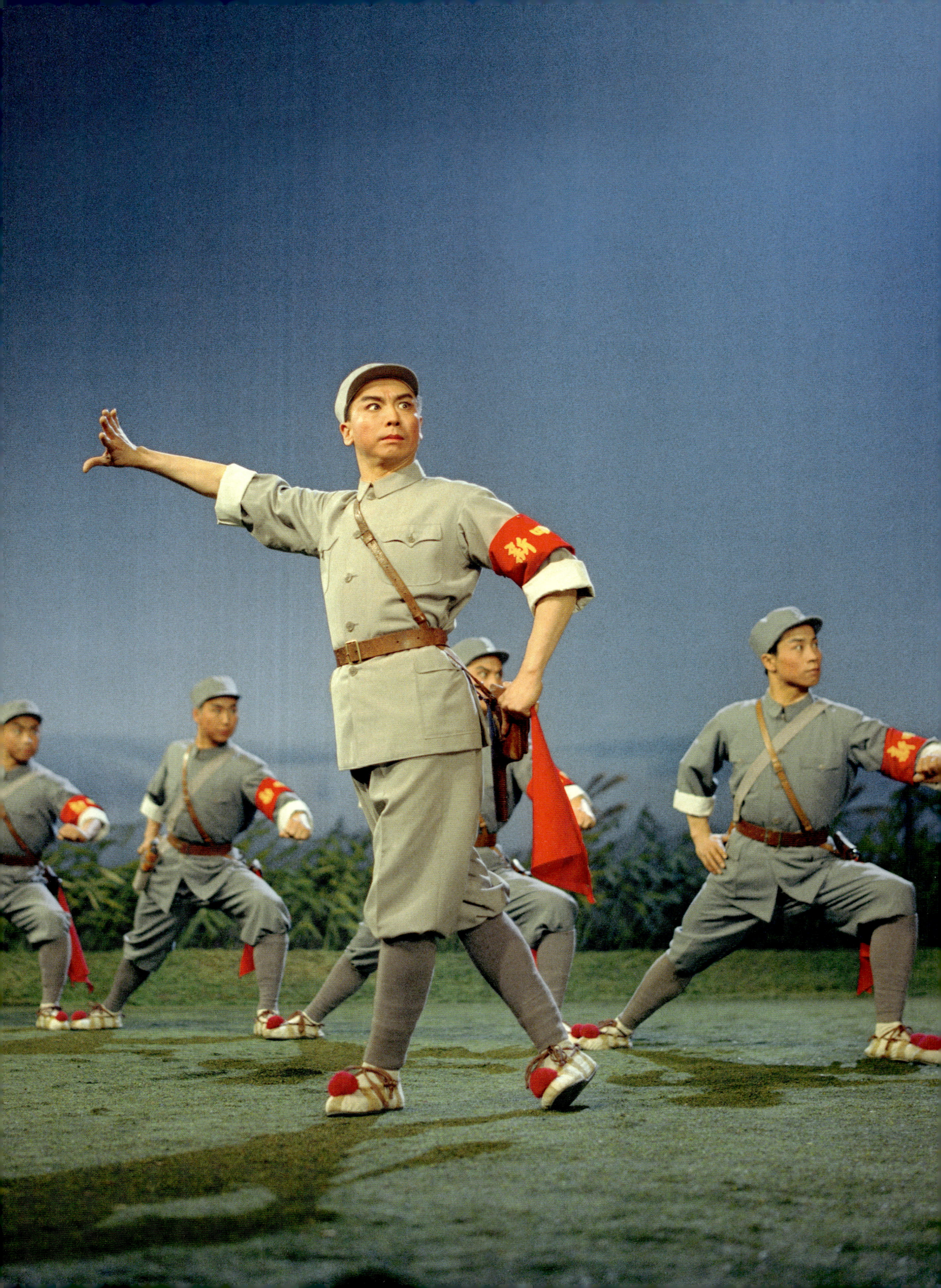

"In the world today all culture, all literature and art belong to definite classes and are geared to definite political lines. There is in fact no such thing as art for art's sake; art that stands above classes, art that is detached from or independent of politics. Proletarian literature and art are part of the whole proletarian revolutionary cause; they are, as Lenin said, cogs and wheels in the whole revolutionary machine."

„In der heutigen Welt gehört die ganze Kultur, Literatur und Kunst bestimmten Klassen und ist auf bestimmte politische Richtungen abgestimmt. Es gibt tatsächlich keine Kunst um der Kunst willen, Kunst die über den Klassen steht, Kunst die von Politik gelöst oder unabhängig ist. Proletarische Literatur und Kunst sind Teil der ganzen proletarisch-revolutionären Sache; sie sind, wie Lenin sagte, Zapfen und Rädchen im revolutionären Getriebe."

« Dans le monde d'aujourd'hui, toute culture, toute littérature et tout art appartient à une classe bien définie et est orienté selon des lignes politiques précises. Il n'existe en fait rien de tel qu'un art pour l'art, un art au-dessus des classes, un art détaché ou indépendant de la politique. La littérature et l'art prolétariens font partie de la cause prolétarienne révolutionnaire toute entière. Elles sont, comme Lénine l'a dit, les roues et les rouages de la machine révolutionnaire. »

MAO ZEDONG (1893–1976), first Chairman of the People's Republic of China, 1942

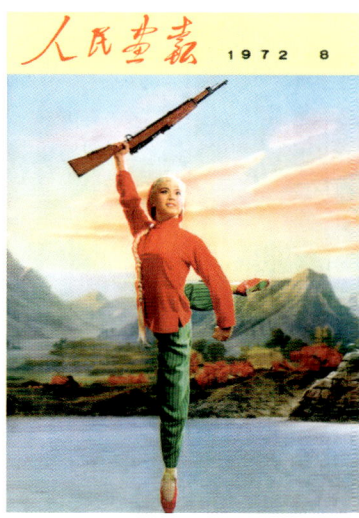

China Pictorial, August 1972

Revolutionary model opera
The White Haired Girl

←
Zhang Yaxin, 1971

A scene from Shajiabang. When Mao launched the Cultural Revolution, his wife, Jiang Qing, a former actress, assumed the role of cultural czar. She banned all but five Beijing operas, and had those reworked as "model operas" (yangban xi). Two revolutionary modern ballets and one symphony were also chosen to join this select group of revolutionary performance pieces. All eight were later made into films, which allowed them to be widely distributed, and provided the entire Chinese population with its only officially sanctioned entertainment.

Eine Szene aus Shajiabang. Als Mao die Kulturrevolution ausrief, übernahm seine Frau Jiang Qing, eine ehemalige Schauspielerin, die Rolle der Kulturzarin. Sie verbot sämtliche Pekingopern bis auf fünf und ließ diese in „Modellopern" (yangban xi) umarbeiten. Außerdem wurden zwei moderne Revolutionsballettstücke und eine Symphonie dieser speziellen Gruppe von Revolutionsaufführungen zugeordnet. Alle acht wurden später verfilmt, was ihre Verbreitung erleichterte und der ganzen chinesischen Bevölkerung Zugang zur einzig offiziell erlaubten Form der Unterhaltung verschaffte.

Scène de Shajiabang. Lorsque Mao lança la Révolution culturelle, son épouse Jiang Qing, ancienne actrice, devint une véritable tsarine de la culture. Elle interdit tous les opéras sauf cinq et les fit réécrire en « opéras modèles » (yangban xi). Deux ballets révolutionnaires modernes et une symphonie furent également sélectionnés. Les huit œuvres furent par la suite adaptées pour le cinéma, ce qui leur permit d'être très largement diffusées et d'offrir à la population un divertissement officiellement approuvé.

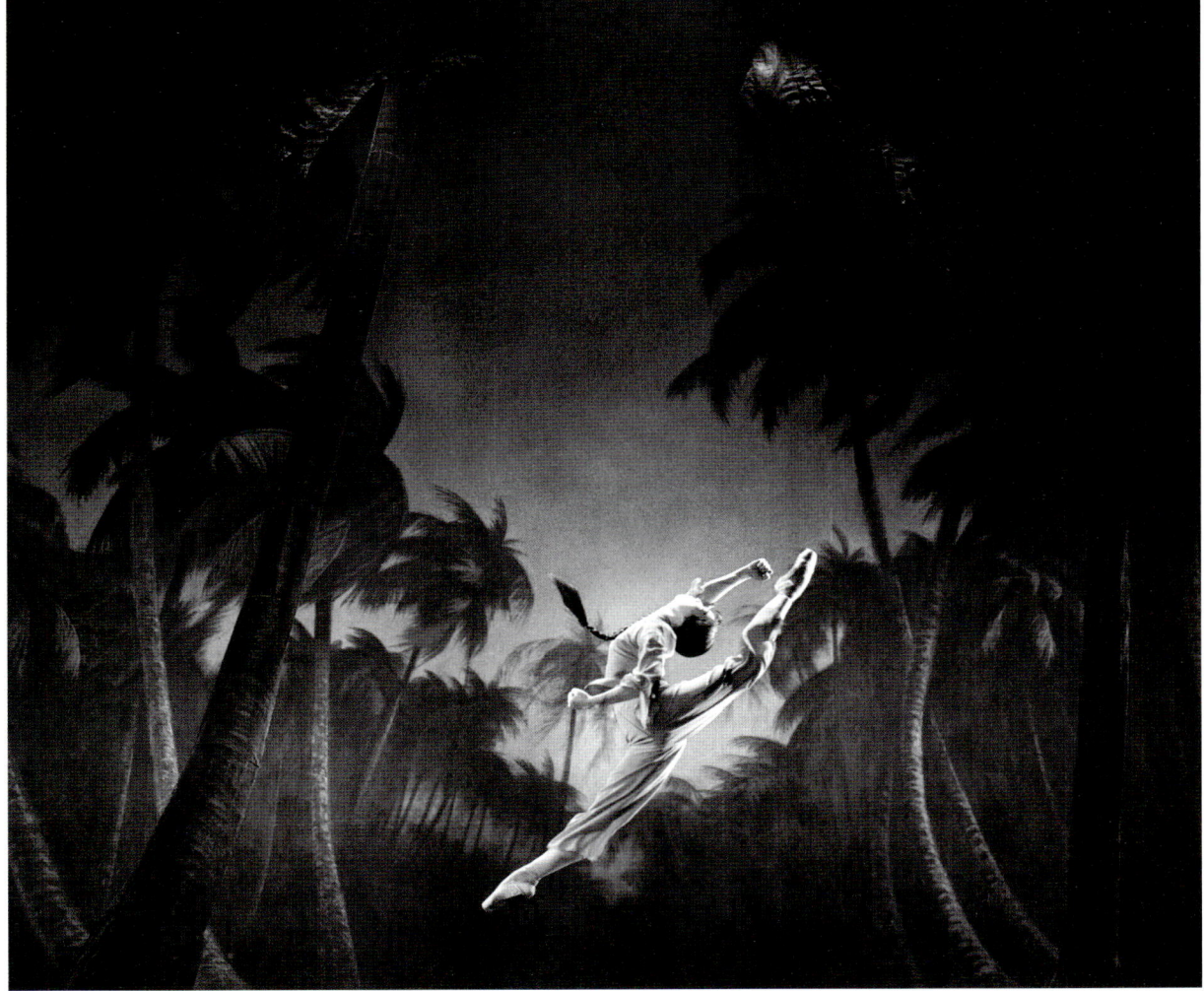

←
Zhang Yaxin, 1974

A Chinese ballet dancer performs the lead role in The White Haired Girl, one of the most enduring revolutionary model operas created by Jiang Qing.

Eine chinesische Tänzerin spielt die Hauptrolle in Das weißhaarige Mädchen, eine der revolutionären Modellopern, die Jiang Qing geschaffen hatte.

Une danseuse chinoise joue La Fille aux cheveux blancs, un opéra-modèle révolutionnaire créé par Jiang Qing.

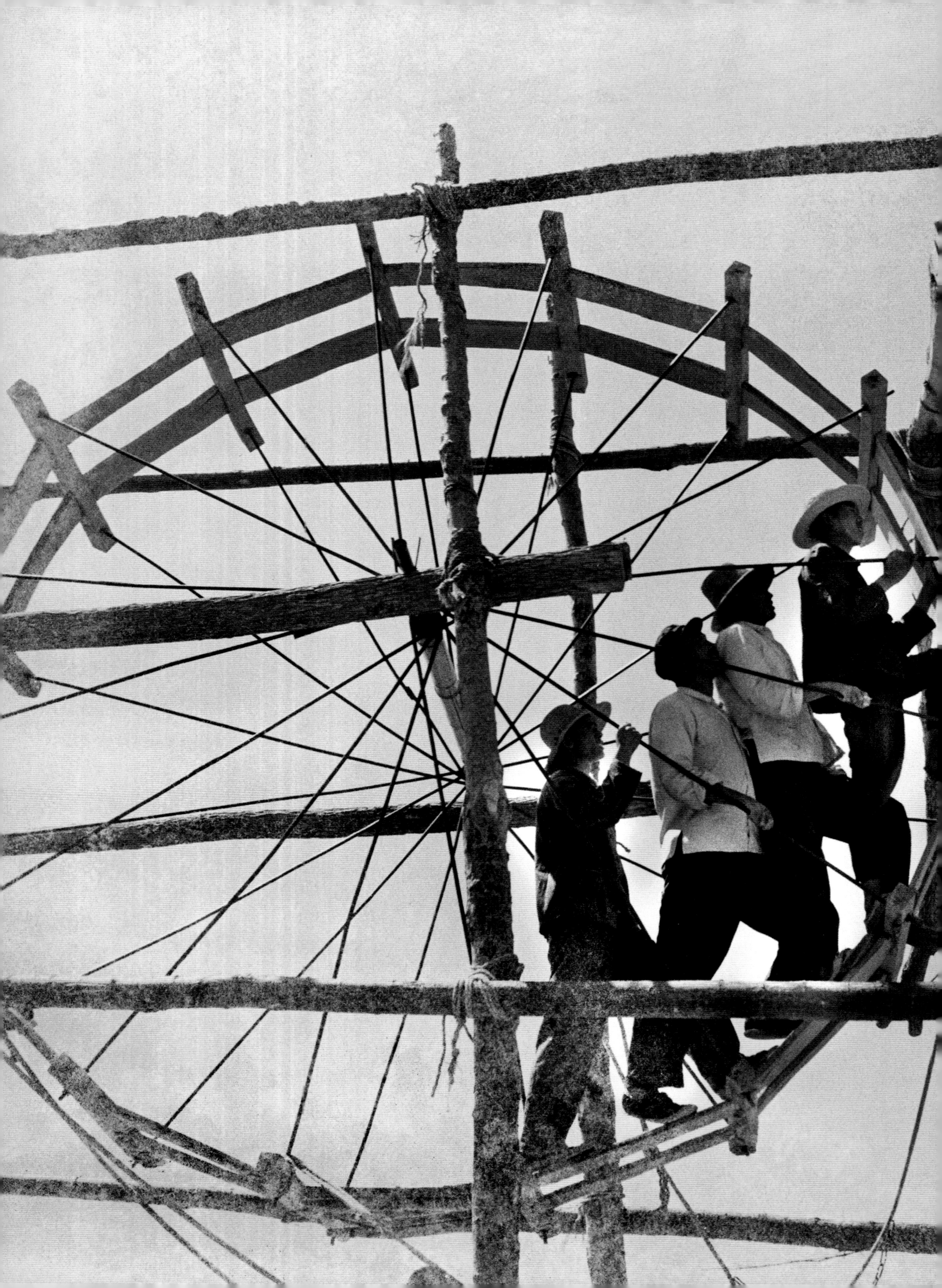

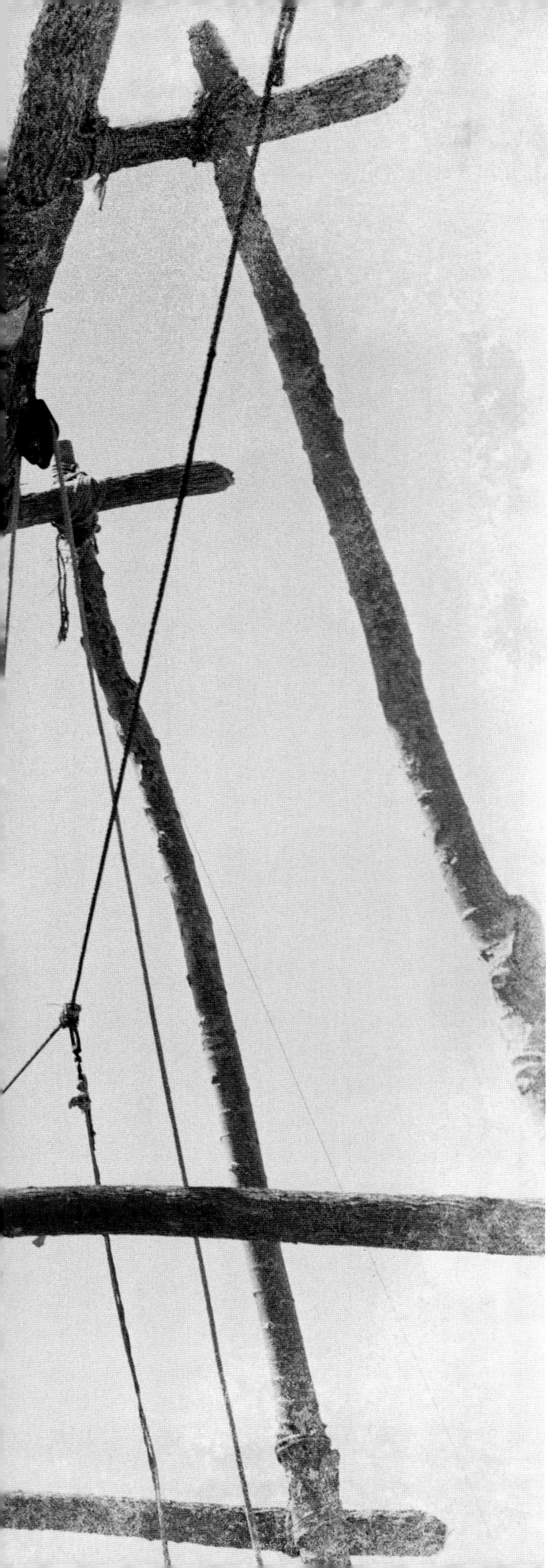

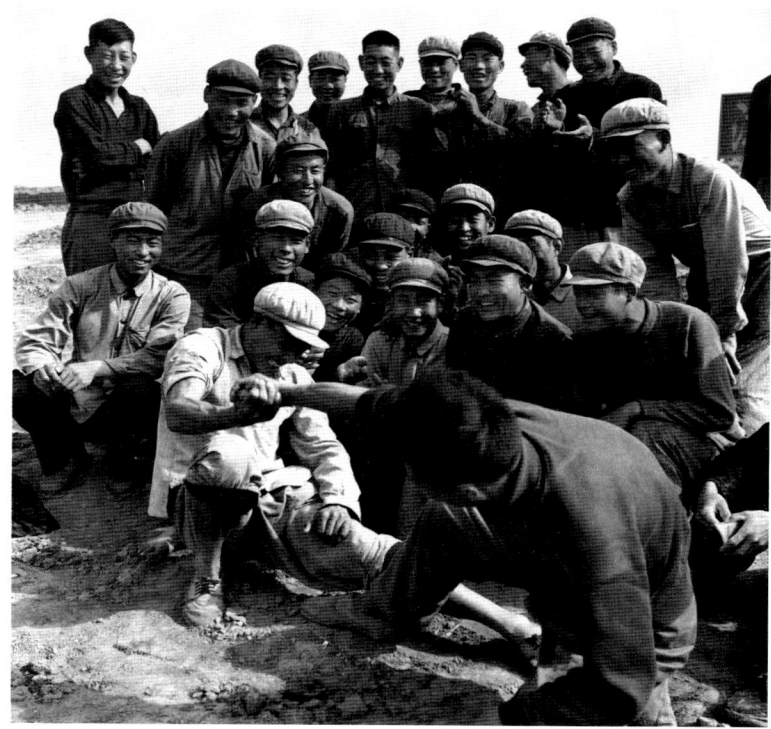

↑
Zhao Qunying, 1970

In 1970, in a rural area of Hebei province, peasants pit their strength against each other.

1970 messen Bauern auf dem Land in der Provinz Hebei ihre Kräfte.

En 1970, dans la province du Hebei, des paysans testent leur force.

"Mountain trees plunder themselves for timber; the grease in a pan fries itself. Cinnamon may be eaten, thus it is chopped; lacquer may be used, thus it is stripped. All men know the use of usefulness, but none knows the use of uselessness."

„Bäume in den Bergen werden gefällt, um damit zu zimmern; Fett in der Pfanne brät von ganz alleine. Zimt ist essbar, deshalb wird er gehackt; Lack kann man nutzen, deshalb wird er geschliffen. Alle Menschen kennen den Nutzen von Nützlichkeit, aber keiner kennt den Nutzen von Nutzlosigkeit."

« Les arbres de la montagne se dénudent de leurs feuilles pour être coupés. La graisse dans la poêle frit toute seule. La cannelle peut être mangée, et donc on la hache menu. On peut utiliser le laque, donc il est débité. Tous les hommes connaissent l'usage de l'utilité, mais aucun ne connaît l'usage de l'inutilité. »

ZHUANGZI (c. 4th century BC), Chinese philosopher

←
Zhao Qunying, 1970

In rural Hebei province outside Beijing, peasants power a manual water pump.

In der ländlichen Provinz Hebei, außerhalb von Peking, treiben Bauern eine mechanische Wasserpumpe mit eigener Kraft an.

Dans la province rurale du Hebei, non loin de Pékin, des paysans font fonctionner une pompe à eau à traction humaine.

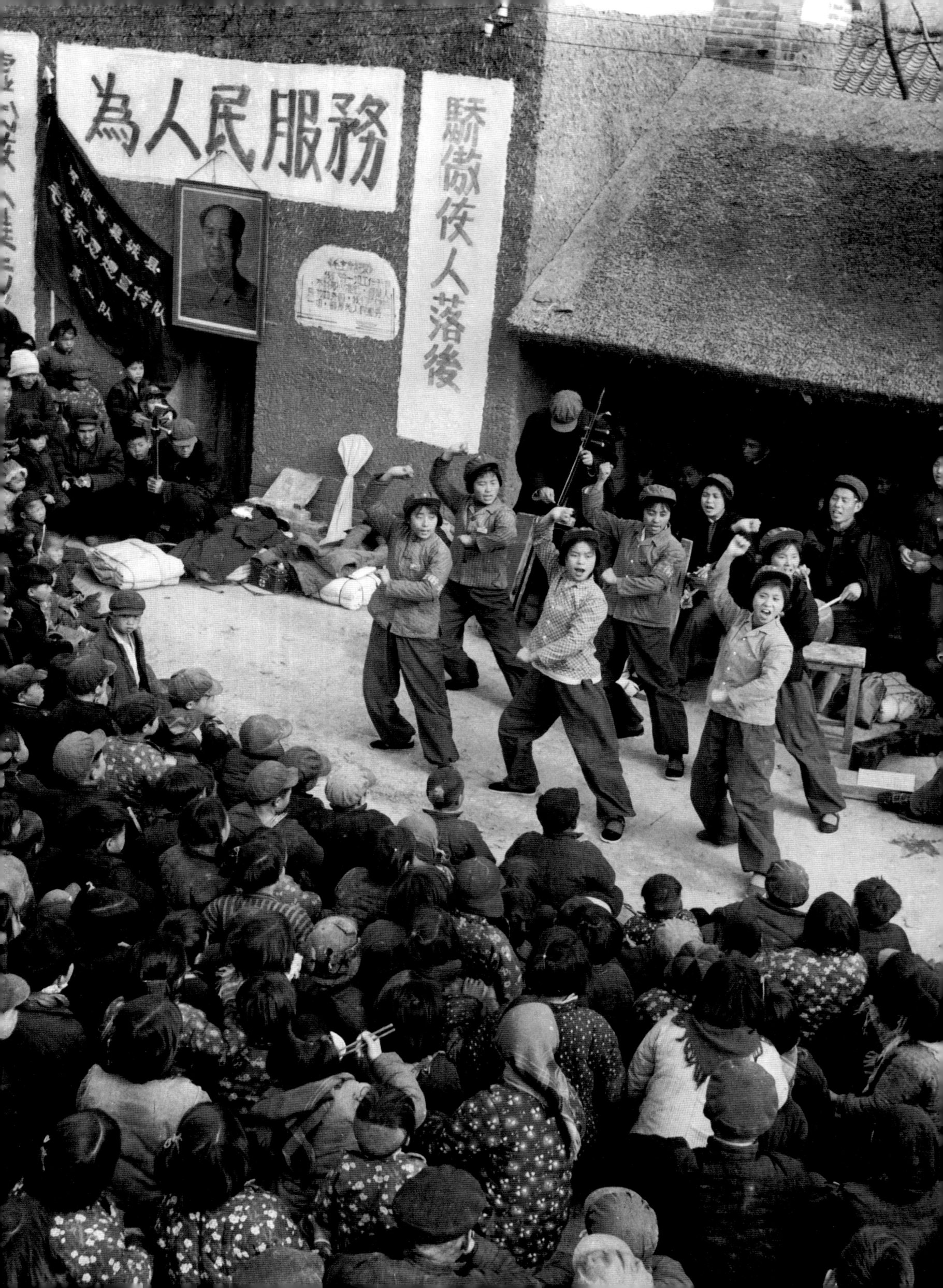

"In many of the families around us, I saw wrecks of the Cultural Revolution. There were children who had denounced parents, wives who had divorced husbands, husbands who had reported on wives. Now that passions had ebbed, they were lost and adrift, their human ties severed."

„In vielen der Familien um uns herum sah ich Opfer der Kulturrevolution. Da waren Kinder, die ihre Eltern denunziert hatten, Ehefrauen, die sich von ihren Männern hatten scheiden lassen, Ehemänner, die ihre Frauen angezeigt hatten. Jetzt, da die hitzigen Gefühle abgeflaut waren, fühlten sie sich verloren und haltlos, ihre menschlichen Bindungen waren gekappt."

« Dans beaucoup de familles voisines, j'ai remarqué des épaves de la Révolution culturelle : des enfants qui avaient dénoncé leurs parents, des épouses qui avaient divorcé de leur mari, des maris qui avaient fait des rapports sur leurs épouses. Maintenant que les passions s'étaient calmées, ils étaient perdus, à la dérive, leurs liens sociaux rompus. »

SIDNEY RITTENBERG (1921–), American interpreter and scholar who spent a total of 16 years in solitary confinement in China, 2001

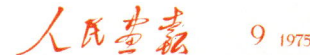
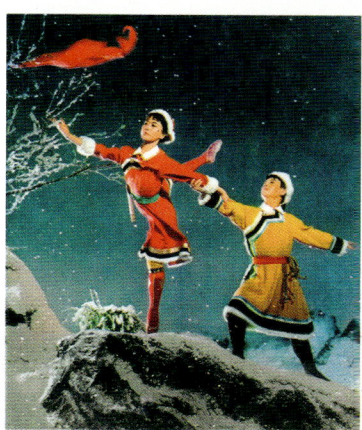

China Pictorial, September 1975

Performers dressed in ethnic Korean costumes, depicting glorious Chinese socialism

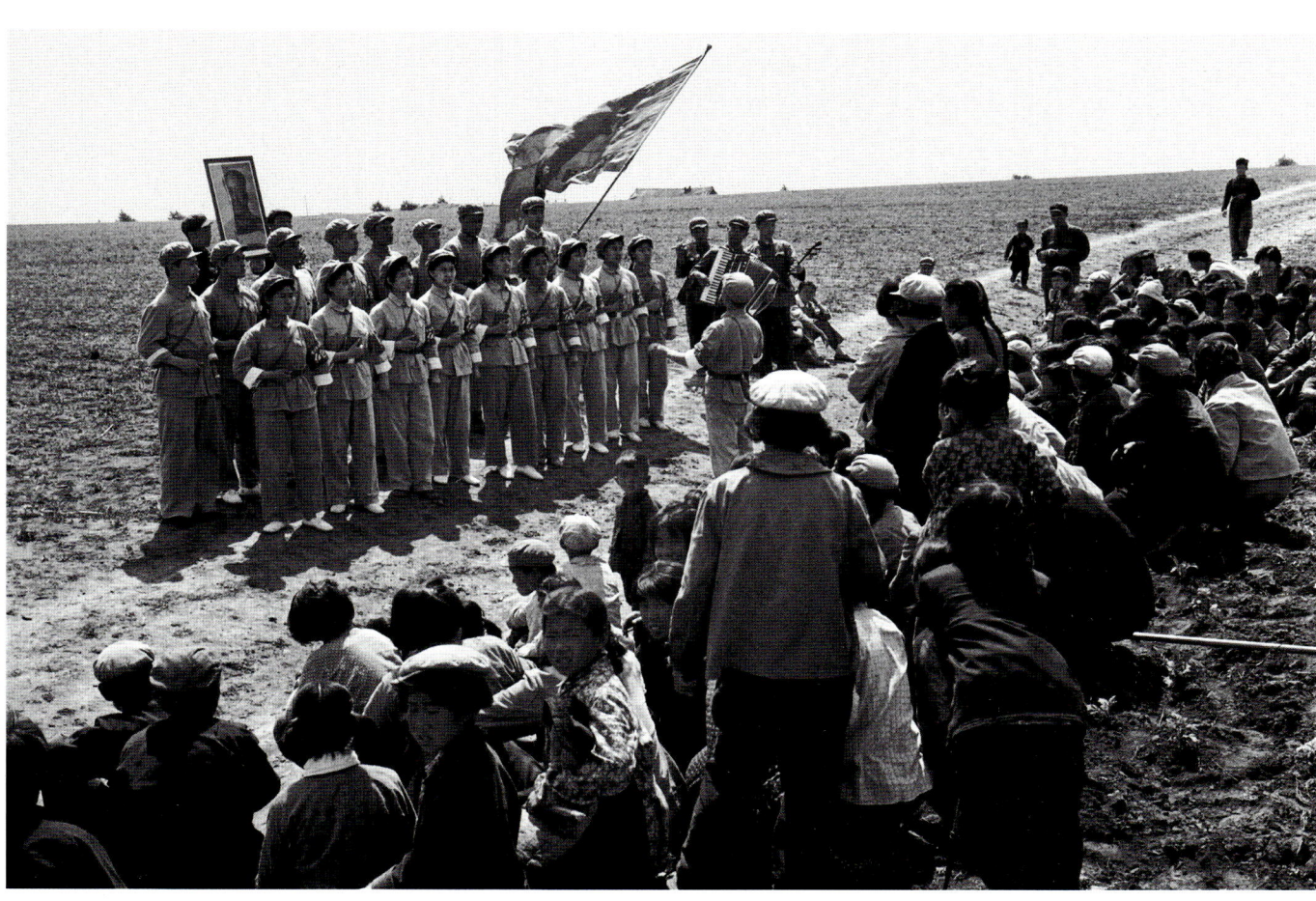

←

Wang Shilong, 1972

Workers in Henan province perform a propaganda dance to show their loyalty to Chairman Mao. Such performances were widespread during the Cultural Revolution.

Arbeiter in der Provinz Henan führen einen Propagandatanz auf, um ihre Loyalität zum Vorsitzenden Mao zu bekunden. Vorführungen dieser Art waren während der Kulturrevolution weit verbreitet.

Des travailleurs de la province du Hénan exécutent un ballet de propagande pour témoigner de leur loyauté au Président Mao. Ce genre de spectacle était très répandu pendant la Révolution culturelle.

↑

Li Zhensheng, 1973

A propaganda team performs for peasants in the countryside.

Eine Propagandatruppe tritt vor Bauern auf dem Land auf.

Une équipe de propagande exhorte des paysans.

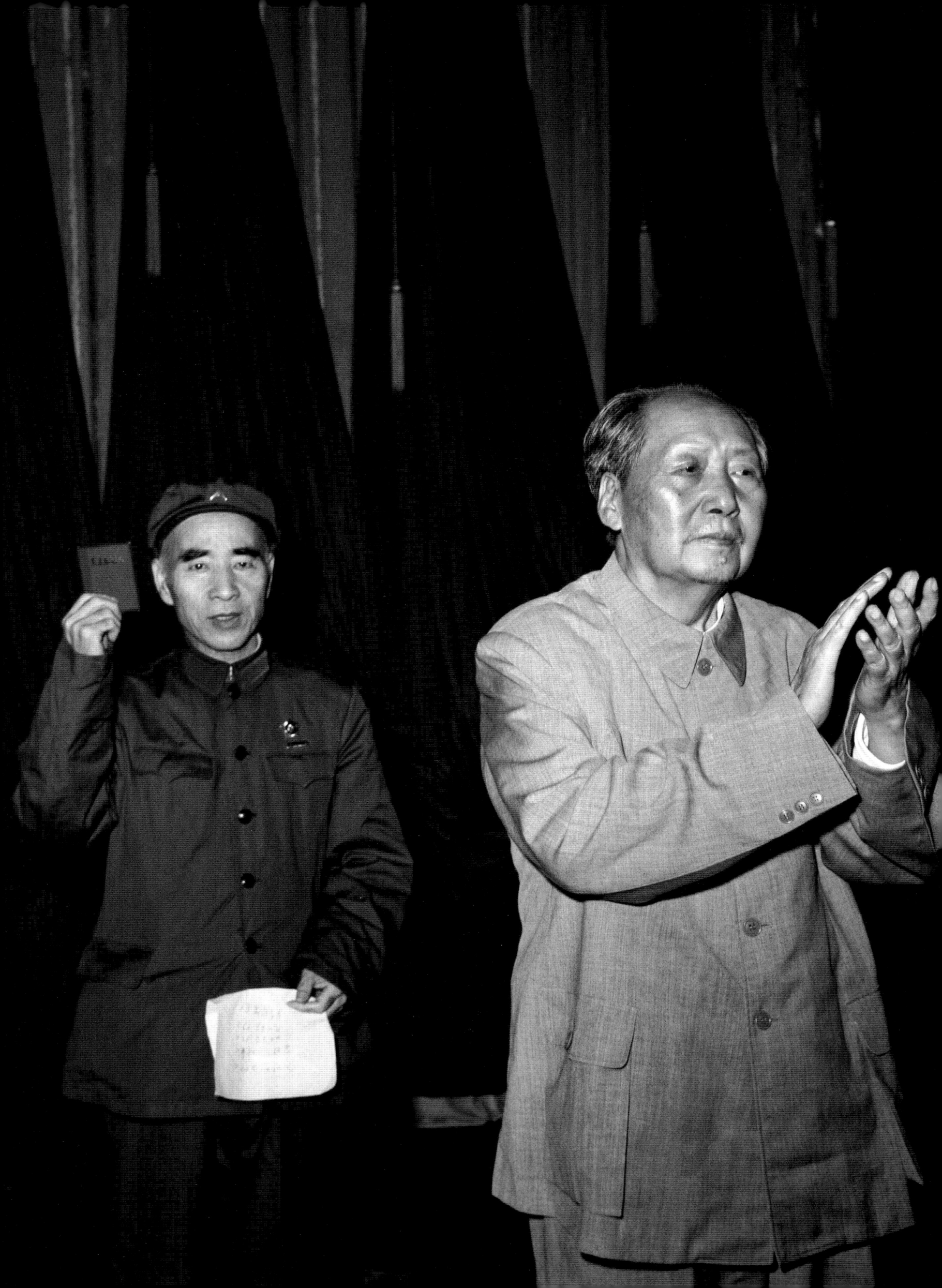

"Tough times make for tough people."

„Harte Zeiten schaffen harte Menschen.“

« Les temps durs font des gens durs. »

ZHOU ENLAI (1898–1976), first Premier of the People's Republic of China, 1950

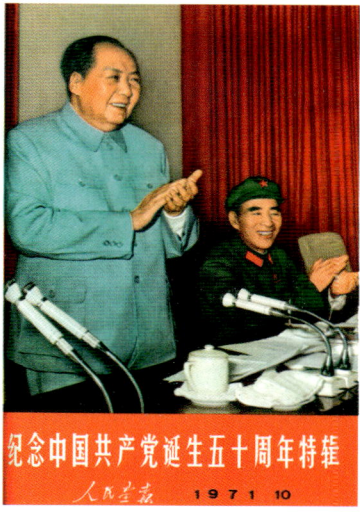

China Pictorial, October 1971

50th Anniversary of the founding of the Chinese Communist Party. Mao with Defence Minister Lin Biao

←

Du Xiuxian, 1970

Chairman Mao appears at the Lushan Conference in 1970, behind whom stands Marshal Lin Biao, who holds up a copy of Quotations from Chairman Mao Zedong. *Lin had already fallen out of favor with Mao. A few months after the conference, Lin Biao was allegedly fleeing to the USSR when his jet was believed to be shot down by the PLA on the orders of Zhou Enlai. The official version claims Lin was attempting a coup to overthrow Mao.*

Der Vorsitzende Mao 1970 bei der Konferenz in Lushan, gefolgt von Marschall Lin Biao, der eine Ausgabe der Worte des Vorsitzenden Mao Zedong *in die Höhe hält. Mao hatte sich schon von Lin distanziert. Wenige Monate nach der Konferenz war Lin Biao angeblich auf der Flucht in die UdSSR, als sein Flugzeug vermutlich auf Befehl Zhou Enlais von der Volksbefreiungsarmee abgeschossen wurde. Die offizielle Fassung lautete, Lin habe einen Putsch gegen Mao geplant.*

Le Président Mao apparaît à la conférence de Lushan en 1970, suivi du maréchal Lin Biao qui tient un exemplaire des Citations du Président Mao Zedong. *Mao était déjà déçu par Lin. Quelques mois plus tard, Lin Biao qui fuyait, dit-on, vers l'URSS en avion fut abattu par un missile de l'Armée de libération sur les ordres de Zhou Enlai. La version officielle prétendit que Lin avait tenté un coup d'État pour renverser Mao.*

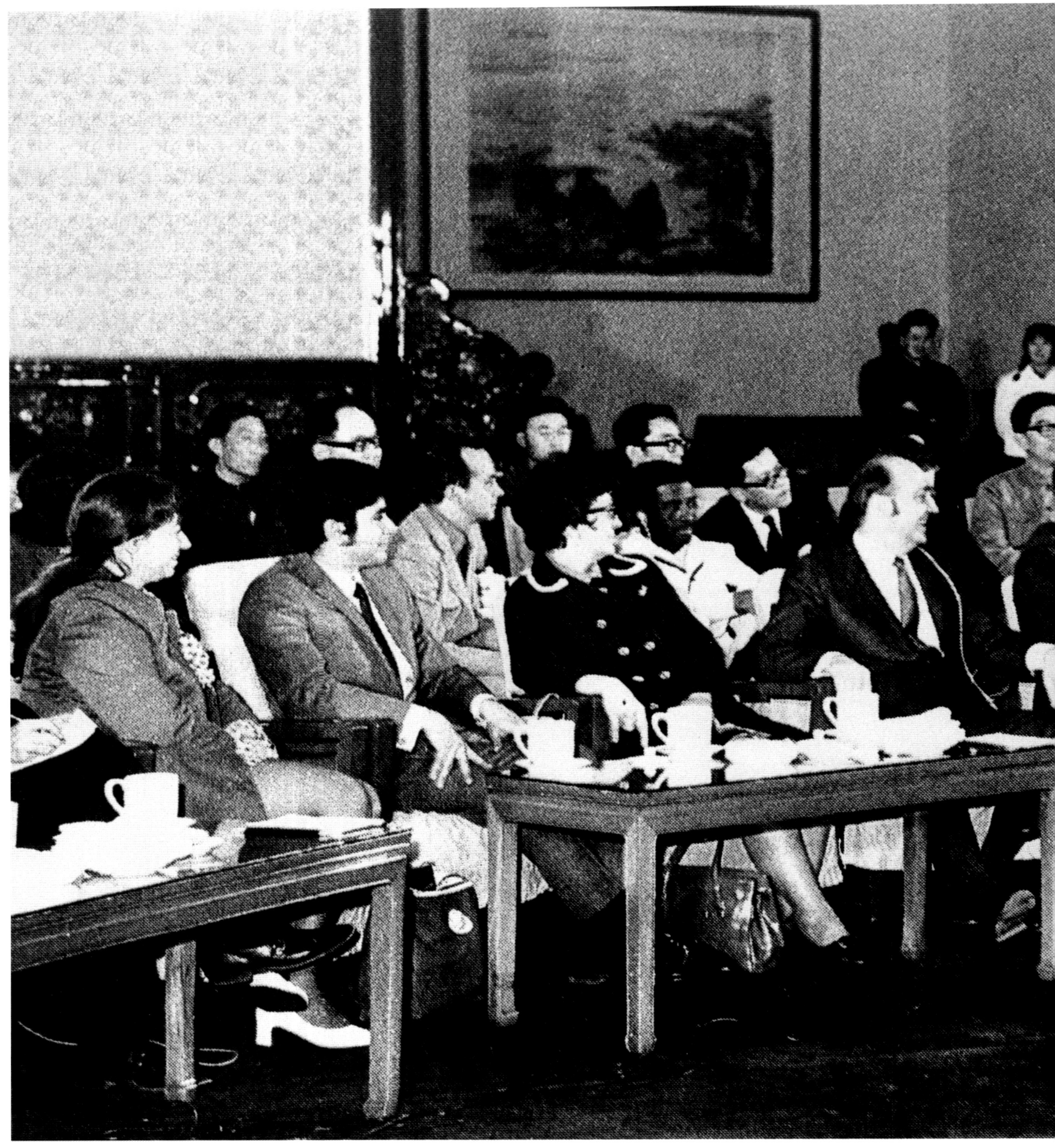

↑

Du Xiuxian, 1971

"Ping-Pong diplomacy": Premier Zhou Enlai meets with representatives from the American Table Tennis delegation invited to hold a friendly match with Chinese players: an invitation approved by Mao.

„Pingpong-Diplomatie": Premier Zhou Enlai trifft Repräsentanten der amerikanischen Tischtennis-Delegation, die zu einem Freundschaftsturnier mit chinesischen Spielern eingeladen waren; eine von Mao gebilligte Einladung.

La « diplomatie du ping-pong. » Le premier ministre Zhou Enlai rencontre une délégation de l'American Table Tennis Association invitée à jouer un match amical contre les champions chinois, avec l'approbation de Mao.

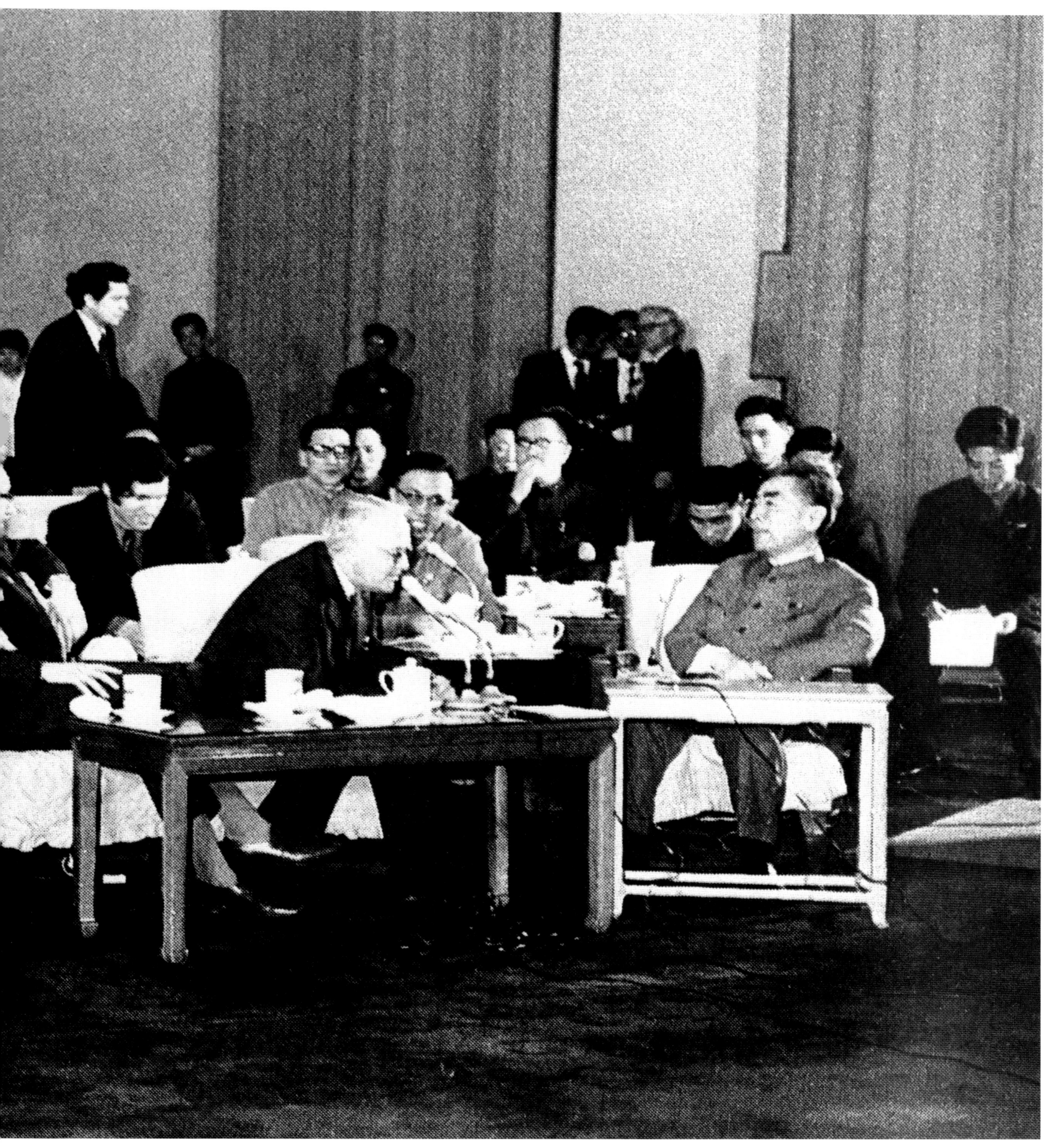

"…all I've ever known is ping-pong—I just hit the ball from this side of the table to that side of the table, and even when it came to that I was always out of bounds or under the net. Hitting the ball from this side of the world to that side of the world—only Mao Zedong and Nixon could do that!"

„…alles was ich kann, ist Tischtennis spielen – ich schlage einfach den Ball von dieser Seite des Tischs auf die andere, und selbst dabei passiert es mir, dass er im Aus oder unter dem Netz landet. Den Ball von dieser Seite der Welt auf die andere zu spielen – nur Mao Zedong und Nixon konnte das gelingen!"

« … Je n'ai jamais connu que le pingpong. Frapper la balle d'un côté de la table à l'autre, et malgré ça, il m'arrivait d'être hors limites ou sous le filet. Frapper la balle d'un côté du monde à l'autre, seuls Mao et Nixon pouvaient le faire ! »

ZHUANG ZEDONG (1942–), three-times world table tennis champion, 2006

*"Simply by shaking hands at Peking Airport, Zhou Enlai and Richard Nixon had
fundamentally altered the contours of global geopolitics. From a strategic perspective,
it was indeed, as Nixon would later claim, 'the week that changed the world'."*

*"Nur durch einen Händedruck am Flughafen von Peking sorgten Zhou Enlai und
Richard Nixon für eine grundlegende Veränderung der Konturen der globalen Geopolitik.
Aus strategischer Sicht sollte Nixon mit seiner späteren Behauptung, dies sei eine
‚Woche, die die Welt veränderte' gewesen, in der Tat Recht behalten."*

*« Par le simple geste de se serrer la main à l'aéroport de Pékin, Zhou Enlai et Richard Nixon
ont fondamentalement changé les contours de la politique mondiale. D'une perspective
stratégique, cet événement fut bien, comme Nixon l'affirma par la suite, 'la semaine qui
changea le monde'. »*

HARRY HARDING (1946–), China specialist and advisor to several US presidential administrations on China, 1992

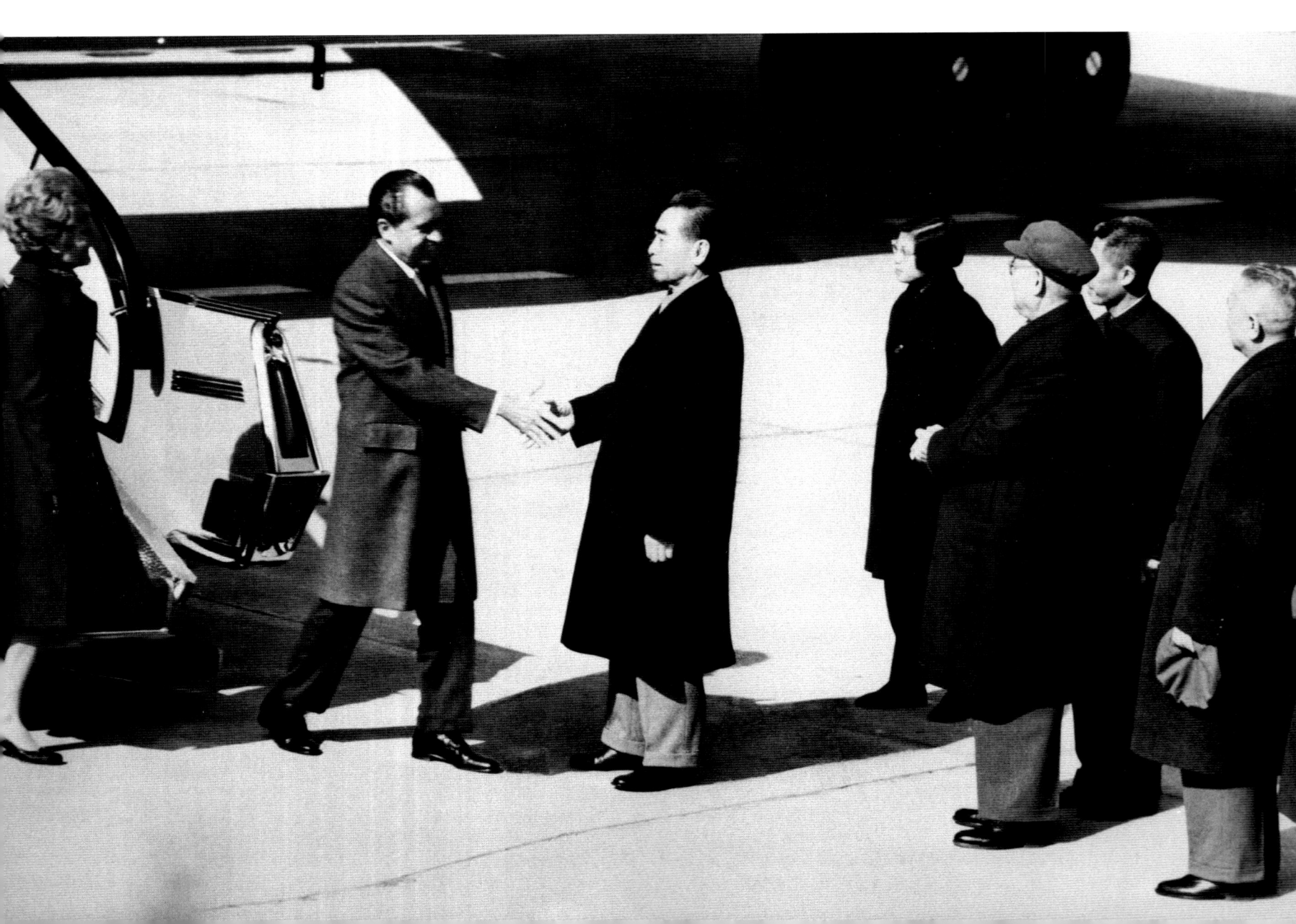

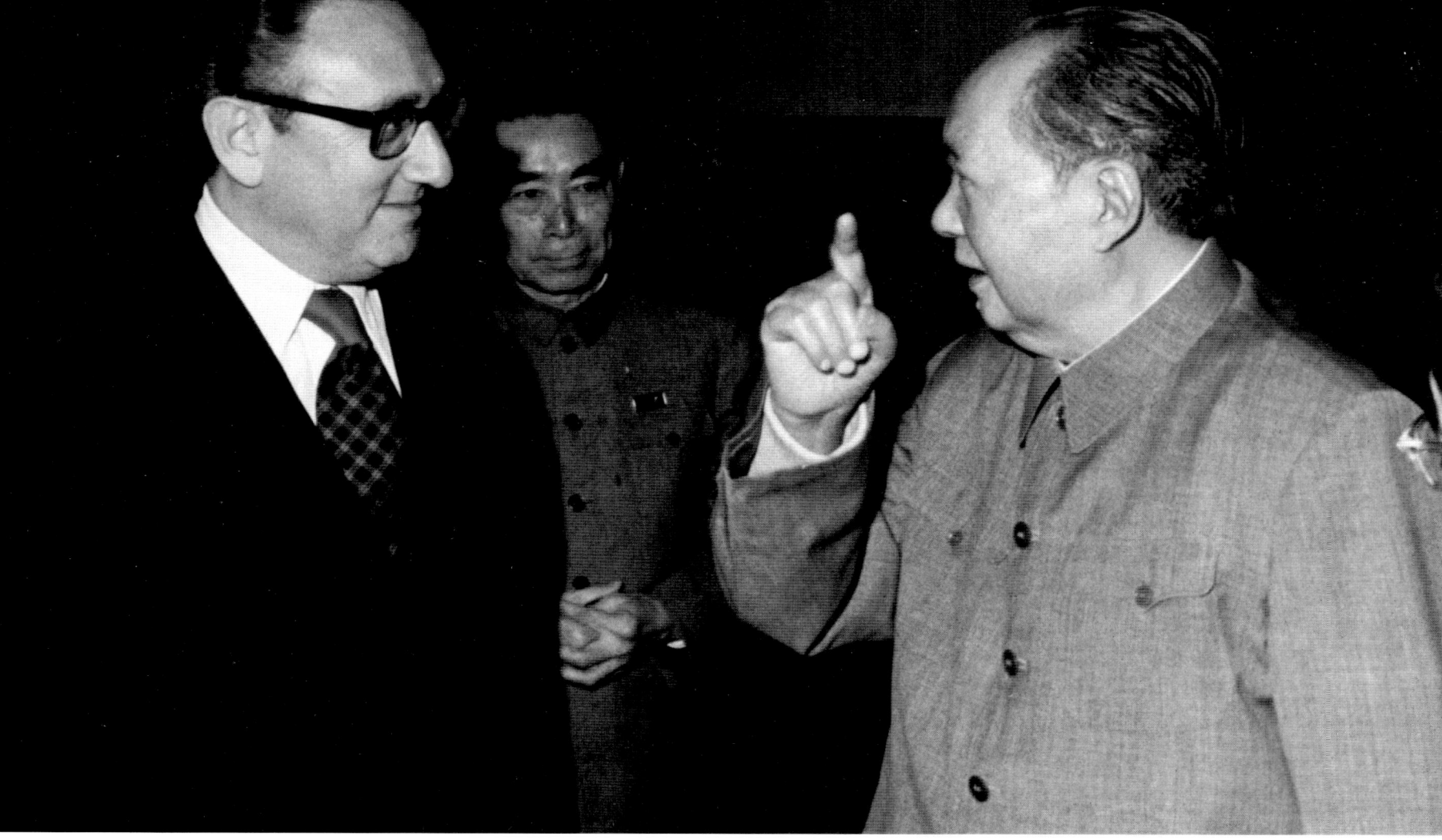

↑

Du Xiuxian, 1972

Mao gestures to Henry Kissinger, Nixon's national security advisor and envoy, who paved the way for the state visit by Richard Nixon.

Mao gestikuliert vor Henry Kissinger, Nixons Sicherheitsberater und Missionschef, der den Weg für Richard Nixons Staatsbesuch ebnete.

Mao s'adresse à Henry Kissinger, conseiller pour la sécurité de Nixon, de passage pour préparer la visite d'État du président américain.

pp. 232/233
Du Xiuxian, 1972

Mao meets Richard Nixon in Beijing during the latter's first state visit to China.

Mao trifft Richard Nixon bei dessen erstem Staatsbesuch in China.

Mao rencontre Richard Nixon au cours de la première visite officielle de celui-ci en Chine.

←

Du Xiuxian, 1972

U.S. President Richard Nixon arrives for an official state visit to the People's Republic of China and is greeted at the airport by Premier Zhou Enlai. Roger Ailes, director of communications at the White House under Nixon, later revealed that he ordered all American journalists and cameramen to remain on board the aircraft to achieve an unimpeded view of Nixon shaking Zhou's hand. This was contrived to make amends for the insult Zhou suffered at the hands of the late U.S. Secretary of State John Foster Dulles during the Geneva Conference in 1954: Zhou extended his hand, and Dulles walked straight by him.

US-Präsident Richard Nixon trifft zu einem offiziellen Staatsbesuch in der Volksrepublik China ein und wird am Flughafen von Premier Zhou Enlai begrüßt. Roger Ailes, unter Nixon im Weißen Haus für die Presse zuständig, verriet später, dass er amerikanische Journalisten und Kameraleute gebeten hatte, im Flugzeug zu bleiben, damit der Blick auf den Handschlag zwischen Nixon und Zhou ungestört bliebe. Dies wurde eingefädelt, um den Affront wieder gutzumachen, den der frühere amerikanische Außenministers John Foster Dulles während der Indochinakonferenz in Genf 1954 gegenüber Zhou begangen hatte: Zhou streckte seine Hand aus und Dulles ging geradewegs an ihm vorbei.

Le président américain Richard Nixon arrive à Pékin pour une visite d'état. Il est salué à l'aéroport par le premier ministre Zhou Enlai. Roger Ailes, directeur de la communication à la Maison blanche sous Nixon, révéla plus tard qu'il avait ordonné à tous les journalistes et cameramen américains de rester à bord de l'avion pour disposer d'une image forte de Nixon serrant la main de Zhou. C'était une façon de se faire pardonner l'insulte faite à celui-ci par l'ancien secrétaire d'État américain, John Foster Dulles, à la conférence de Genève en 1954, où il avait fait semblant de ne pas voir la main tendue du premier ministre.

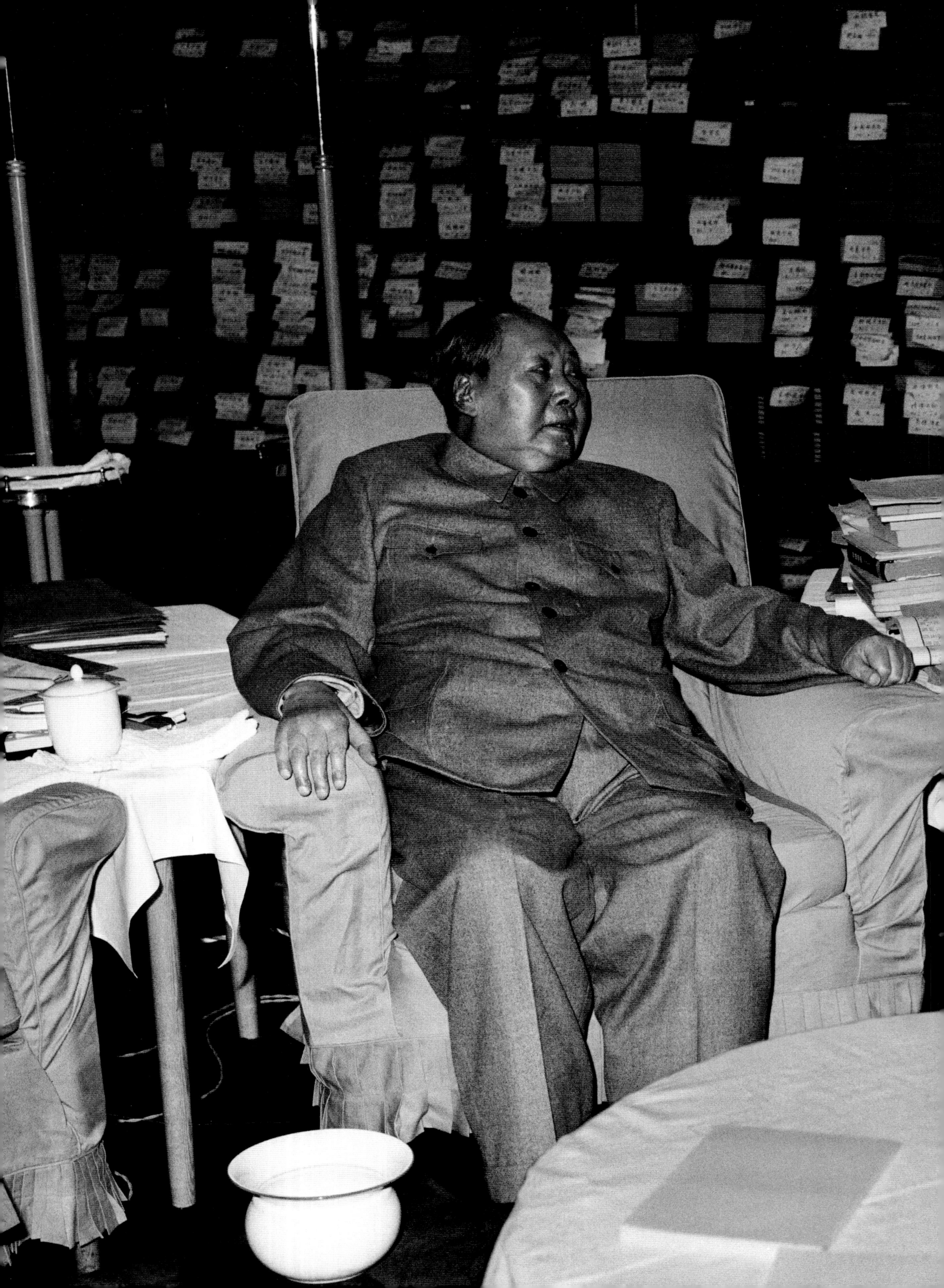

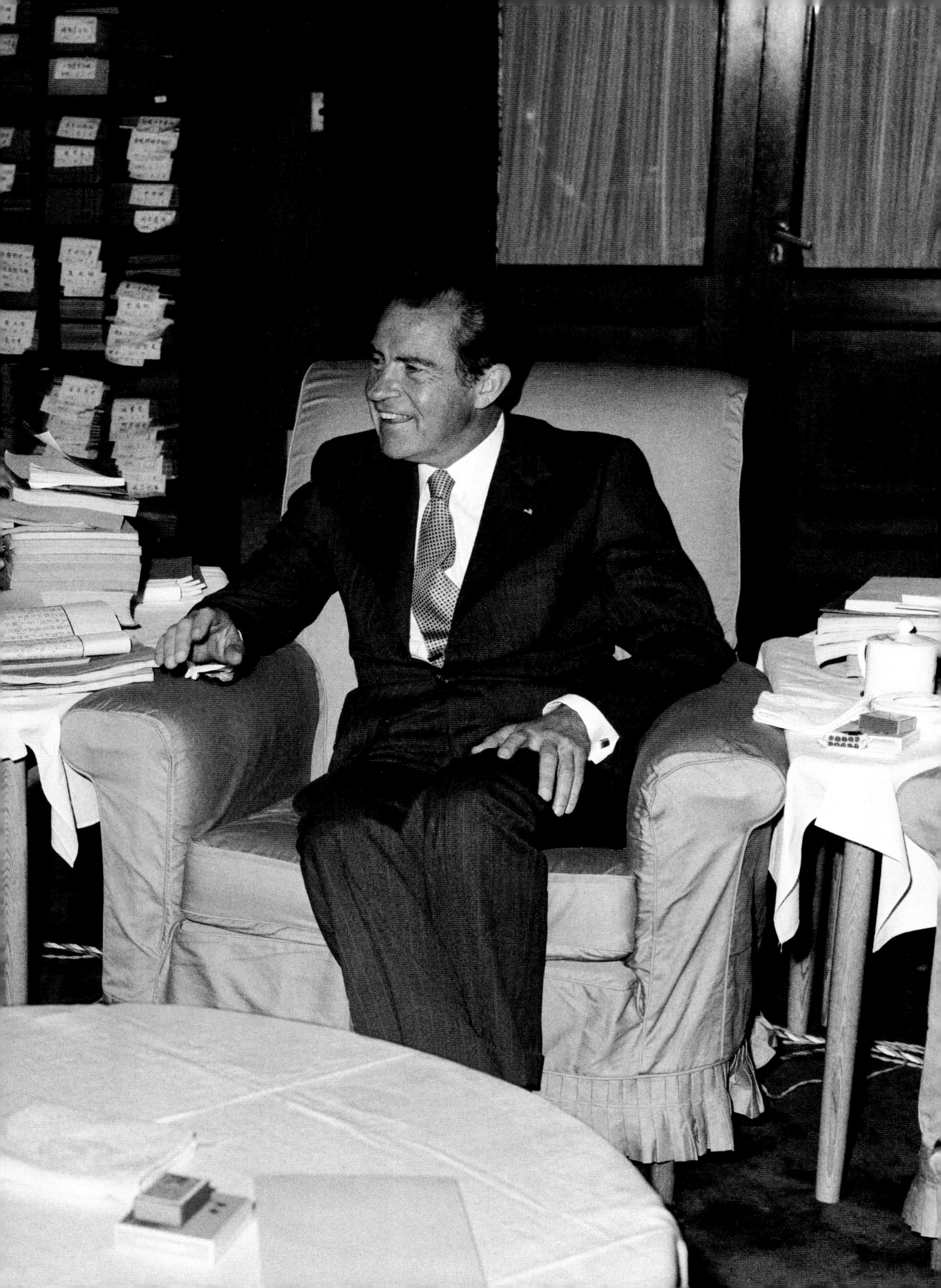

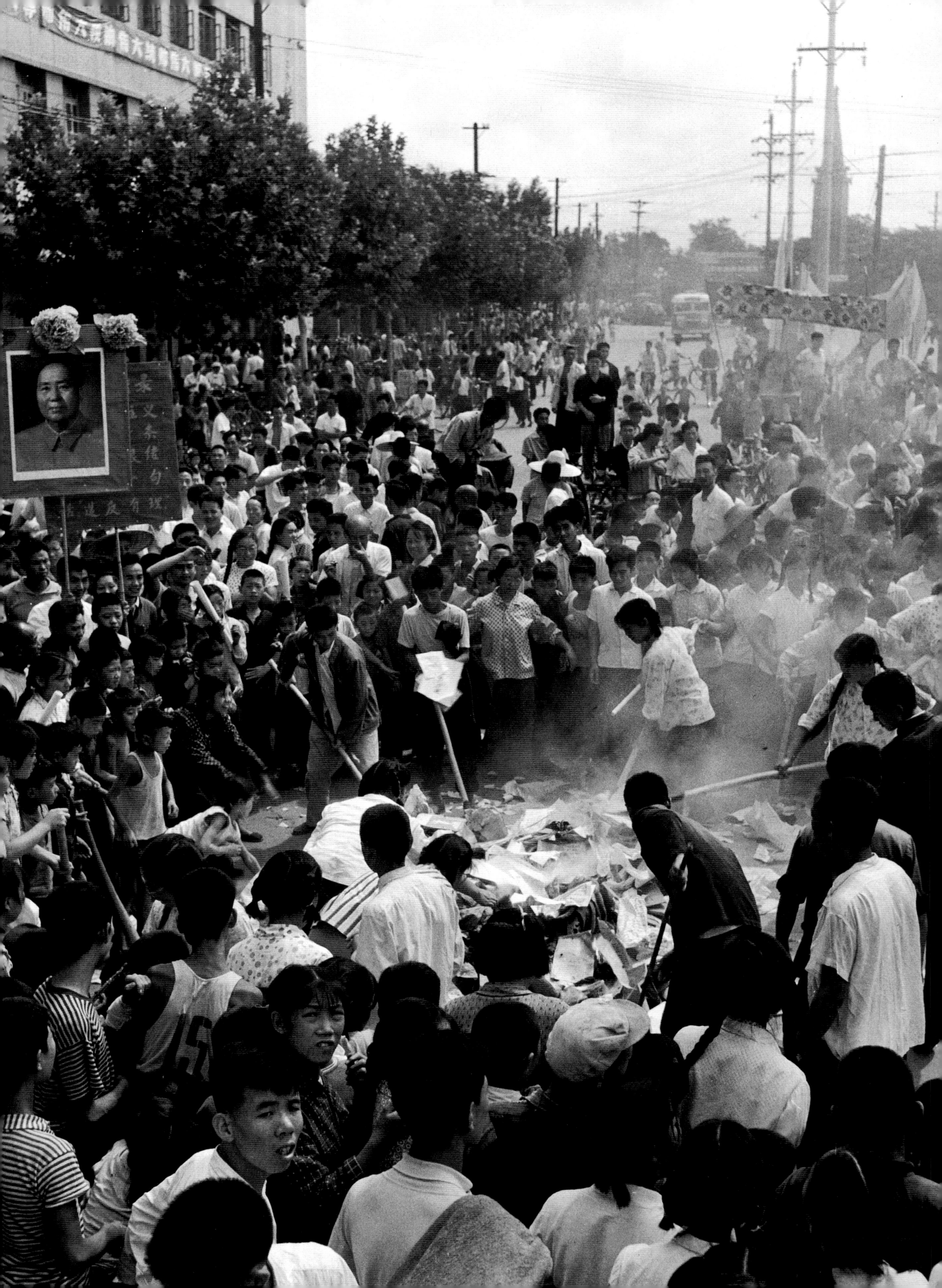

235

←
Wang Shilong, 1972

The devastating sight of destruction during a mass rally in Henan province organized to destroy antiques, books, and other bourgeois objects. In fact, it was the disgraced Lin Biao who was the real target of the campaign.

Das verheerende Bild der Zerstörung während einer Massenkundgebung in der Provinz Henan, bei der Antiquitäten, Bücher und anderen ‚bourgeoise' Objekte zerstört wurden. Tatsächlich war der in Ungnade gefallene Lin Biao das wahre Ziel der Kampagne.

Images de destructions pendant un rassemblement de masse dans la province du Hénan, organisé pour détruire des antiquités, des livres, des œuvres d'arts et autres objets bourgeois. En fait, la cible de cette campagne était Lin Biao, déjà disgracié.

→
Xiao Zhuang, 1976

A People's Liberation Army rally in Nanjing, Jiangsu province, to denounce "Wang, Zhang, Jiang, Yao", the Gang of Four.

Kundgebung der Volksbefreiungsarmee in Nanjing, Provinz Jiangsu, bei der „Wang, Zhang, Jiang, Yao", die Viererbande, gebrandmarkt werden sollte.

L'armée populaire de libération au cours d'un rassemblement à Nankin, province du Jiangsu, organisé pour dénoncer «Wang, Zhang, Jiang, Yao », la Bande des quatre.

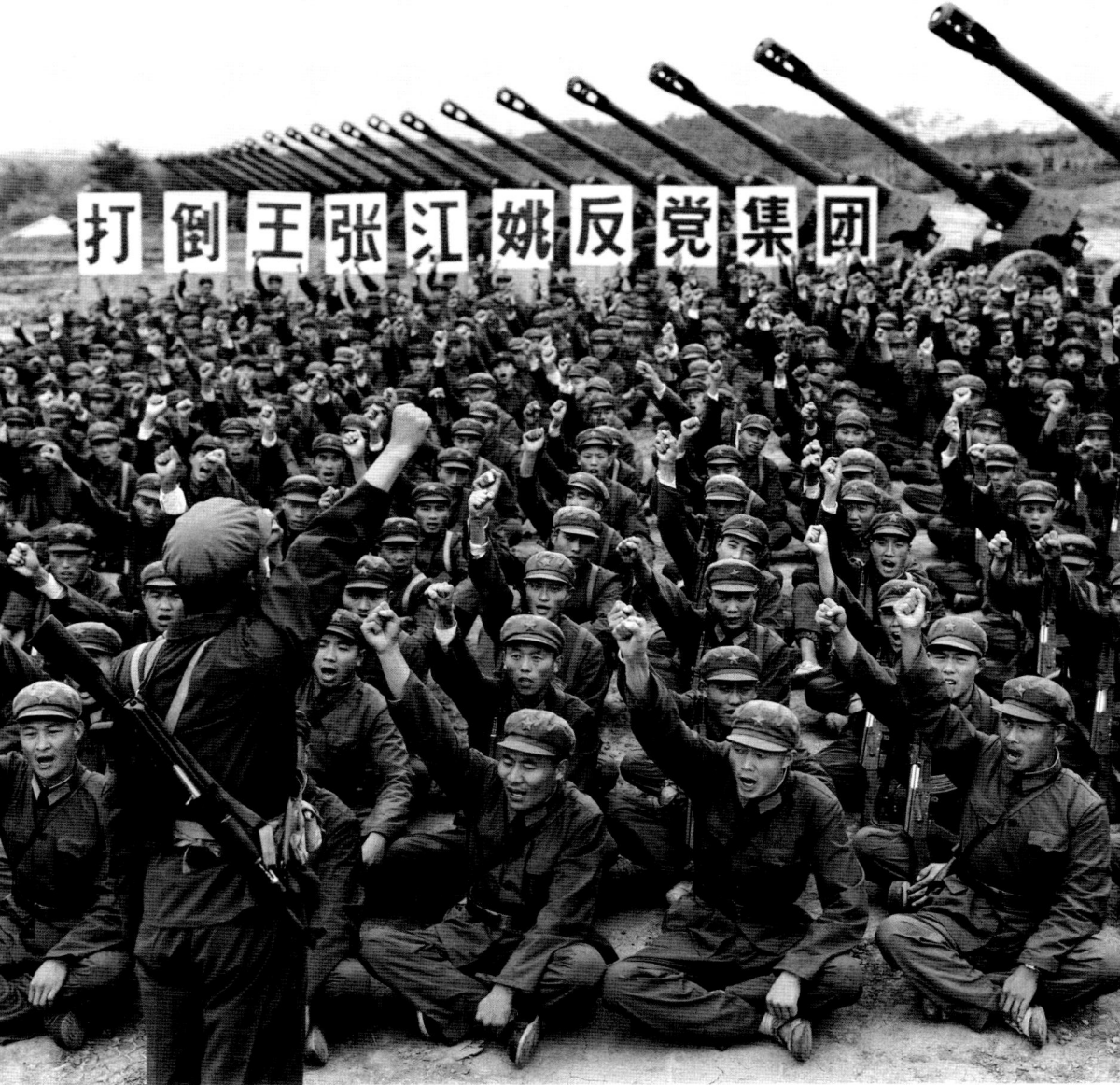

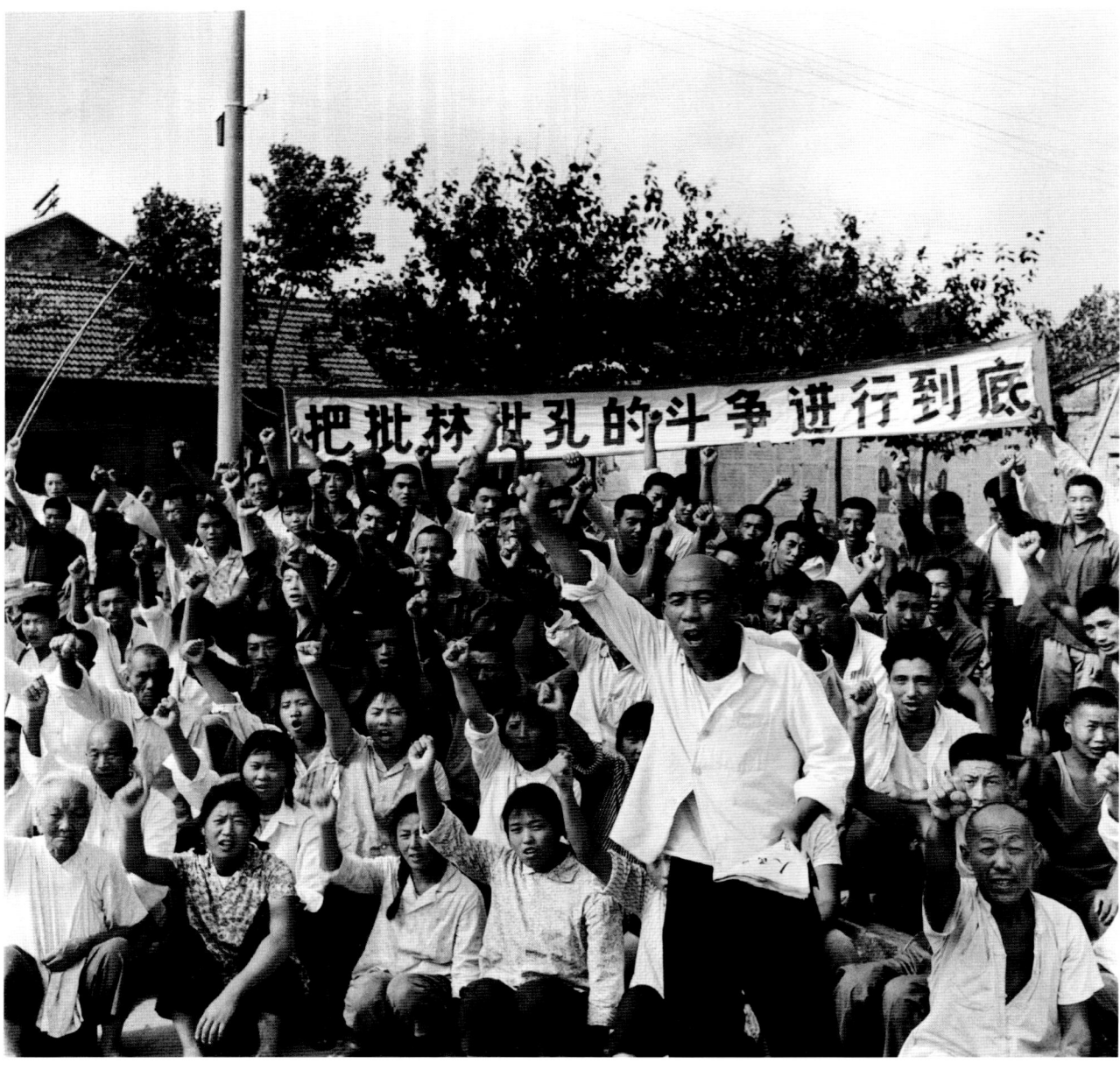

→
Du Xiuxian, 1974

Jiang Qing (left) together with Zhang Yufeng, Mao's mistress and nurse, who wears a dress designed by Jiang Qing, at Diaoyutai State Guest House. Zhang was a train attendant who took care of Mao when he traveled throughout China. Towards the end of his life, he relied on Zhang to read his lips and convey his instructions to the other leaders. The frock became known as the "Jiang Qing dress"; a look to which fashion-conscious Chinese women aspired.

Jiang Qing (links) mit Zhang Yufeng, Maos Geliebte und Pflegerin, die am staatlichen Gästehaus Diaoyutai ein von Jiang Qing entworfenes Kleid trägt. Zhang war als Zugbegleiterin tätig und kümmerte sich um Mao auf seinen Reisen durch China. Gegen Ende seines Lebens war es Zhang, die seine „Lippen" las und seine Anordnungen an die übrigen Führer weiterleitete. Das Gewand wurde als Jiang-Qing-Kleid bekannt, ein Look, dem modebewusste Chinesinnen nacheiferten.

Jiang Qing (à gauche) accompagnée de Zhang Yufeng, maîtresse et infirmière de Mao, portant une robe dessinée par Jiang Qing dans la résidence des hôtes d'État de Diaoyutai. Zhang était une employée de train qui suivait le Président quand il voyageait en Chine. Vers la fin de sa vie, il lui confiait la tâche de lire sur ses lèvres et de transmettre ses instructions aux autres responsables. La robe fut appelée «robe Jiang Qing», style auquel les Chinoises sensibles à la mode aspiraient.

↑
Xiao Zhuang, 1974

A peasant leads the crowd chanting slogans to denounce Confucius and Lin Biao at a rally in Nanjing. The campaign against Lin Biao began when his death was made public in 1972. In 1974, the campaign extended to China's ancient sage, Confucius.

Bei einer Versammlung in Nanjing führt ein Bauer die Massen und stimmt Parolen an, die Konfuzius und Lin Biao verunglimpfen. Die Kampagne gegen Lin Biao begann, als sein Tod 1972 öffentlich bekannt wurde. 1974 griff sie auf Chinas alten Weisen Konfuzius über.

Un paysan dirige la foule qui chante des slogans de dénonciation de Confucius et de Lin Biao lors d'un rassemblement à Nankin. La campagne contre Lin Biao commença lorsque sa mort fut rendue publique en 1972. En 1974, elle s'étendit au vieux sage Confucius.

"The Chinese habit of saying nothing frontally about momentous occurrences gives the impression of a 'deaf and blind history'."

„Die Gewohnheit der Chinesen, über folgenschwere Geschehnisse nichts direkt zu sagen, vermittelt den Eindruck einer ‚tauben und blinden Geschichte'."

«L'habitude chinoise de ne rien dire de direct sur les événements qui se produisent donne l'impression d'une ' histoire muette et aveugle'.»

ROSS TERRILL, sinologist and research associate at Harvard East Asian Research Center, 1999

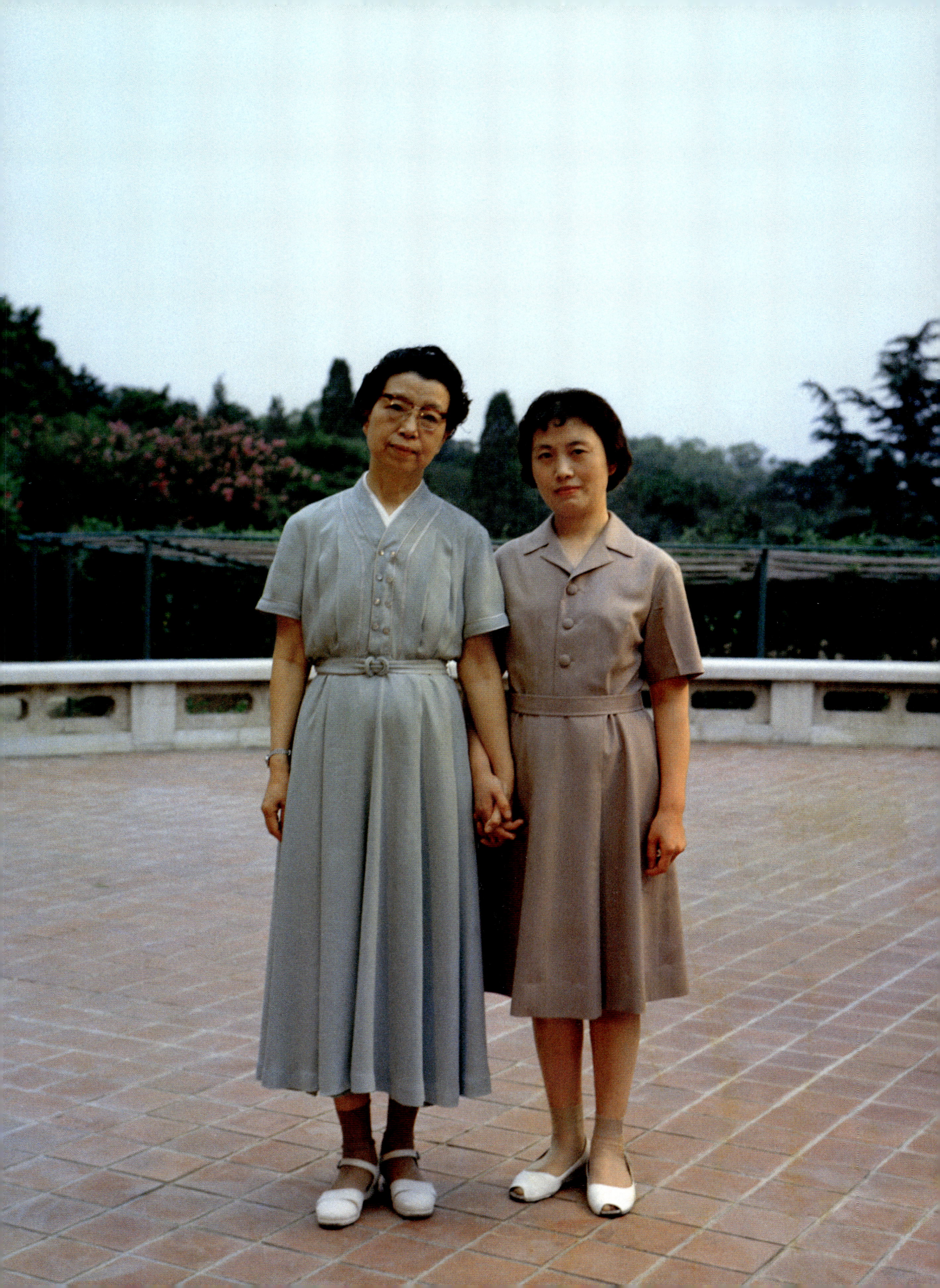

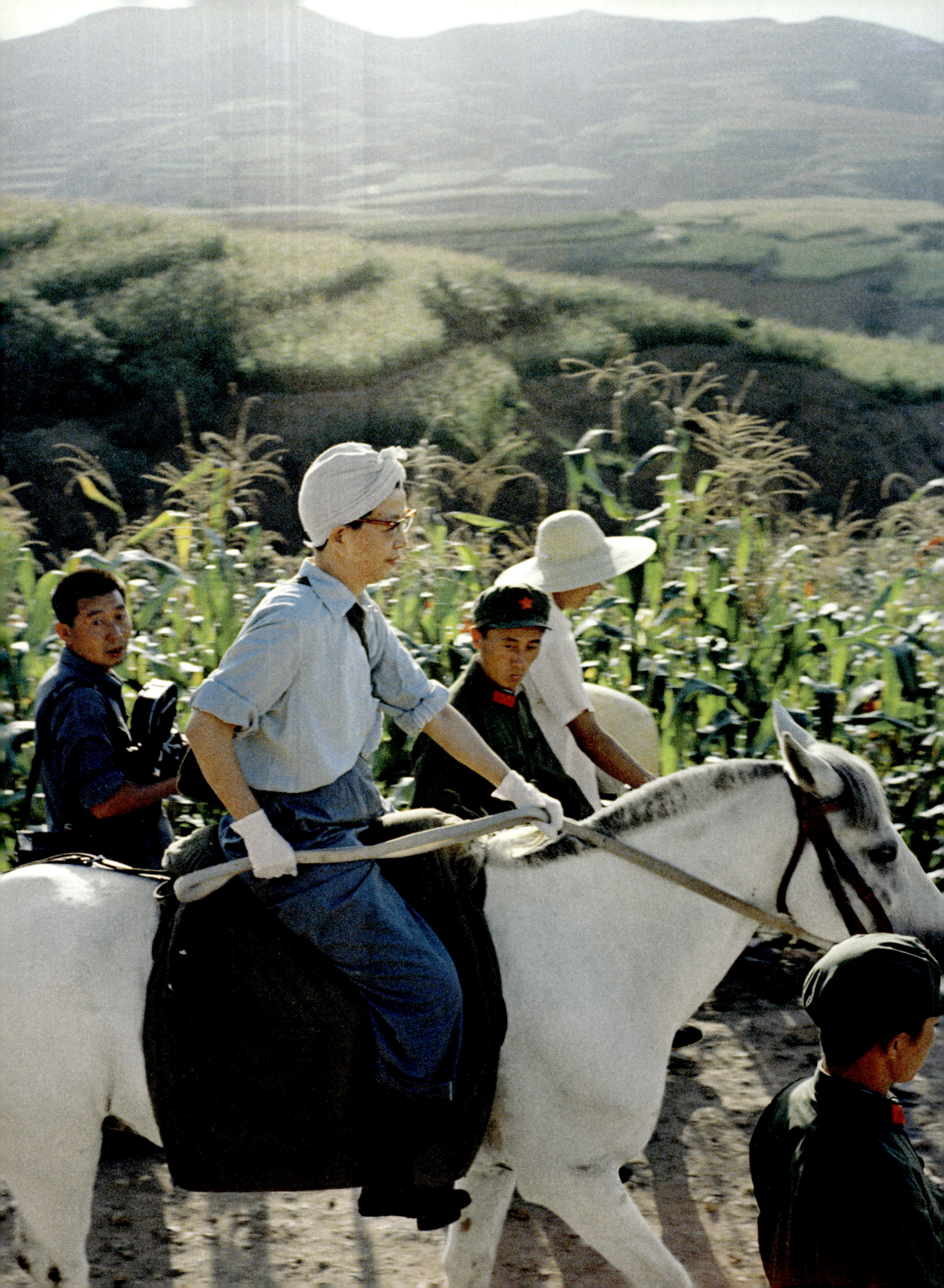

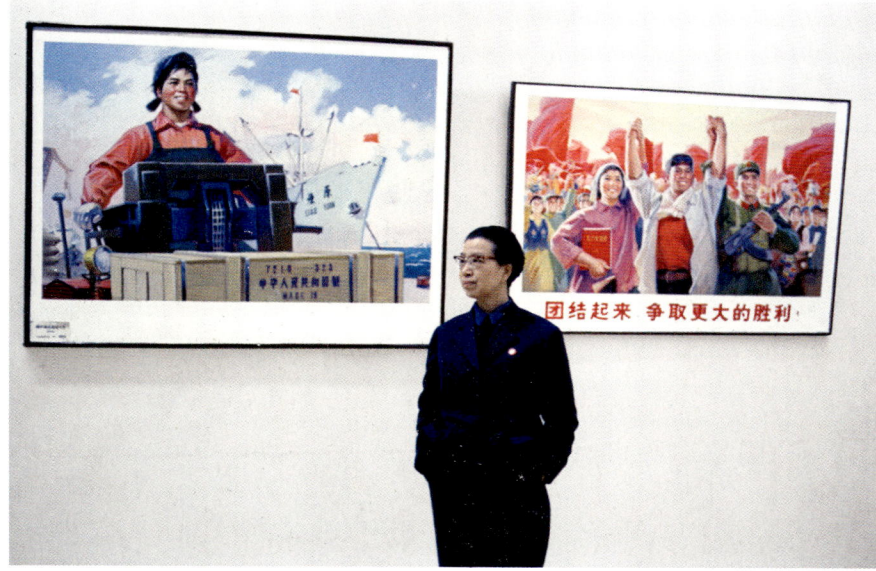

↑
Du Xiuxian, 1975

Jiang Qing, who assumed charge of culture and the arts in Mao's wake, is pictured at an exhibition in Dazhai commune.

Jiang Qing, die unter Mao die Kontrolle über Kultur und Künste übernahm, bei einer Ausstellung in der Kommune Dazhai.

Jiang Qing, chargée de la culture et des arts sous Mao, prise en photo lors d'une exposition dans la commune de Dazhai.

"While it might seem strange that the Communist Party leadership could continue to hail Mao during the 1980's while excoriating and imprisoning his widow, the two were not close by the time Ms. Jiang achieved power. By the 1970's they lived apart, and a Chinese book published last year asserted that Jiang Qing had to request permission from the party Central Committee's Work Office to see her husband."

„Es mag seltsam erscheinen, dass die Führung der Kommunistischen Partei während der 1980er-Jahre dabei blieb, Mao zu bejubeln, während seine Witwe heftig angegriffen und inhaftiert wurde, aber die beiden standen sich zu dem Zeitpunkt, als Jiang Qing an die Macht kam, nicht mehr nahe. Schon in den 1970er-Jahren hatten sie getrennt gelebt, und in einem im letzten Jahr erschienenen chinesischen Buch wird behauptet, sie habe im Arbeitsbüro des Zentralkomitees um Erlaubnis nachsuchen müssen, wenn sie ihren Mann treffen wollte."

« Alors qu'il peut sembler étrange de voir que les responsables du Parti communiste continuent à saluer la mémoire de Mao pendant les années 1980 tout en persécutant et emprisonnant sa veuve, il faut savoir que ce couple n'en était plus un lorsque Jiang Qing accéda au pouvoir. Dès les années 1970, ils vivaient séparément et un livre publié l'an passé en Chine assurait qu'elle devait demander l'autorisation d'un bureau du Comité central du Parti pour voir son mari. »

NICHOLAS KRISTOF (1959–), Pulitzer Prize-winning journalist and author, 1991

←
Du Xiuxian, 1975

Jiang Qing takes to the saddle to inspect crops at Dazhai commune, which served as a model of agricultural success for Mao, and an obligatory model for others to follow.

Jiang Qing steigt in den Sattel, um in der Kommune Dazhai, die für Mao als Modell landwirtschaftlichen Erfolges und als beispielgebend für andere galt, das Getreide auf dem Halm zu inspizieren.

Jiang Qing inspecte à cheval les moissons dans la commune de Dazhai, modèle de réussite agricole pour Mao, que devaient suivre les autres communes.

→
Du Xiuxian, 1976

Jiang Qing sits amidst her personal staff for a group photograph at her residence in Diaoyutai, Beijing.

Jiang Qing sitzt für ein Gruppenfoto vor ihrem Wohnhaus in Diaoyutai, Peking, inmitten ihres persönlichen Mitarbeiterstabs.

Jiang Qing assise au milieu de son équipe personnelle pour une photographie de groupe prise dans sa résidence de Diaoyutai.

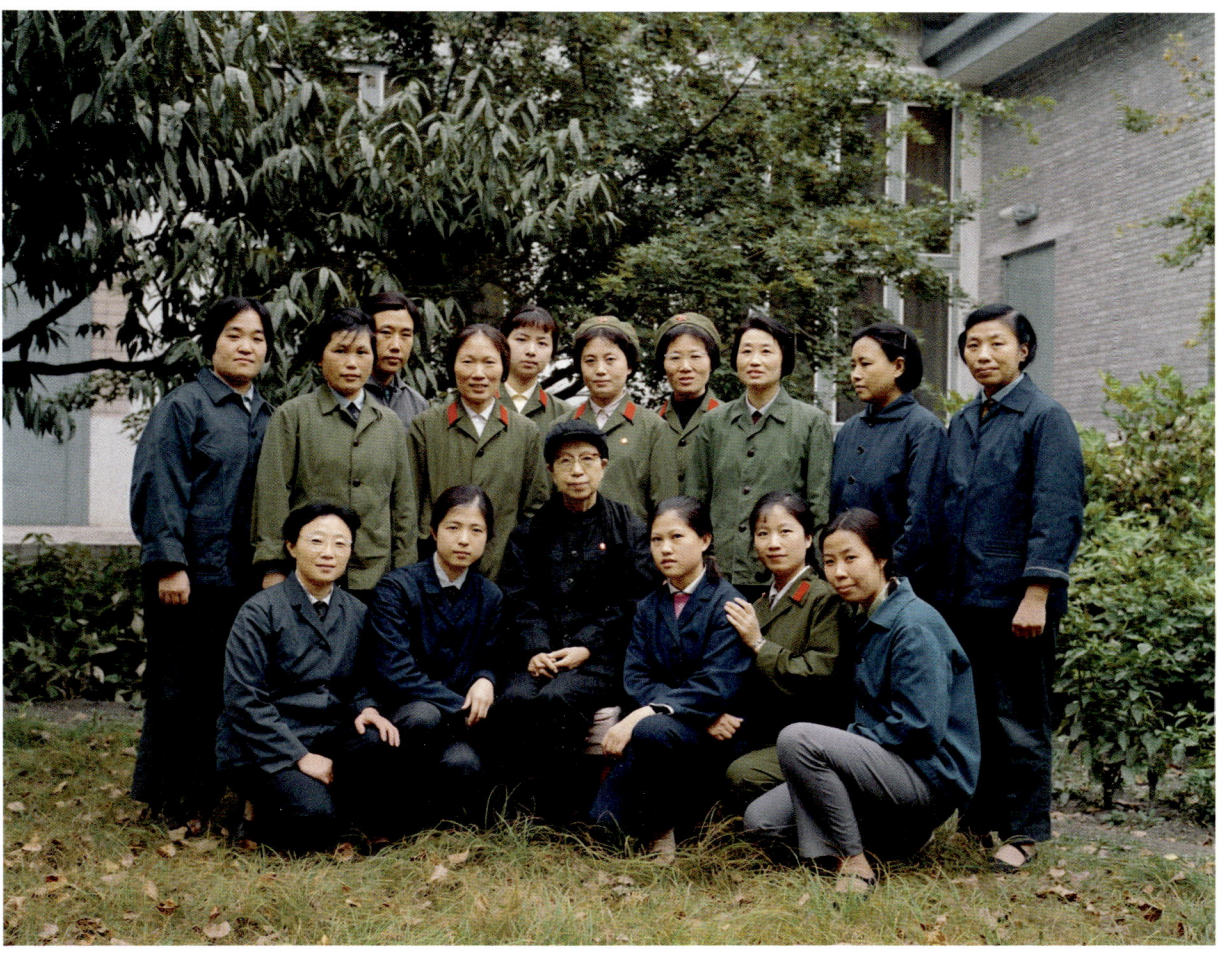

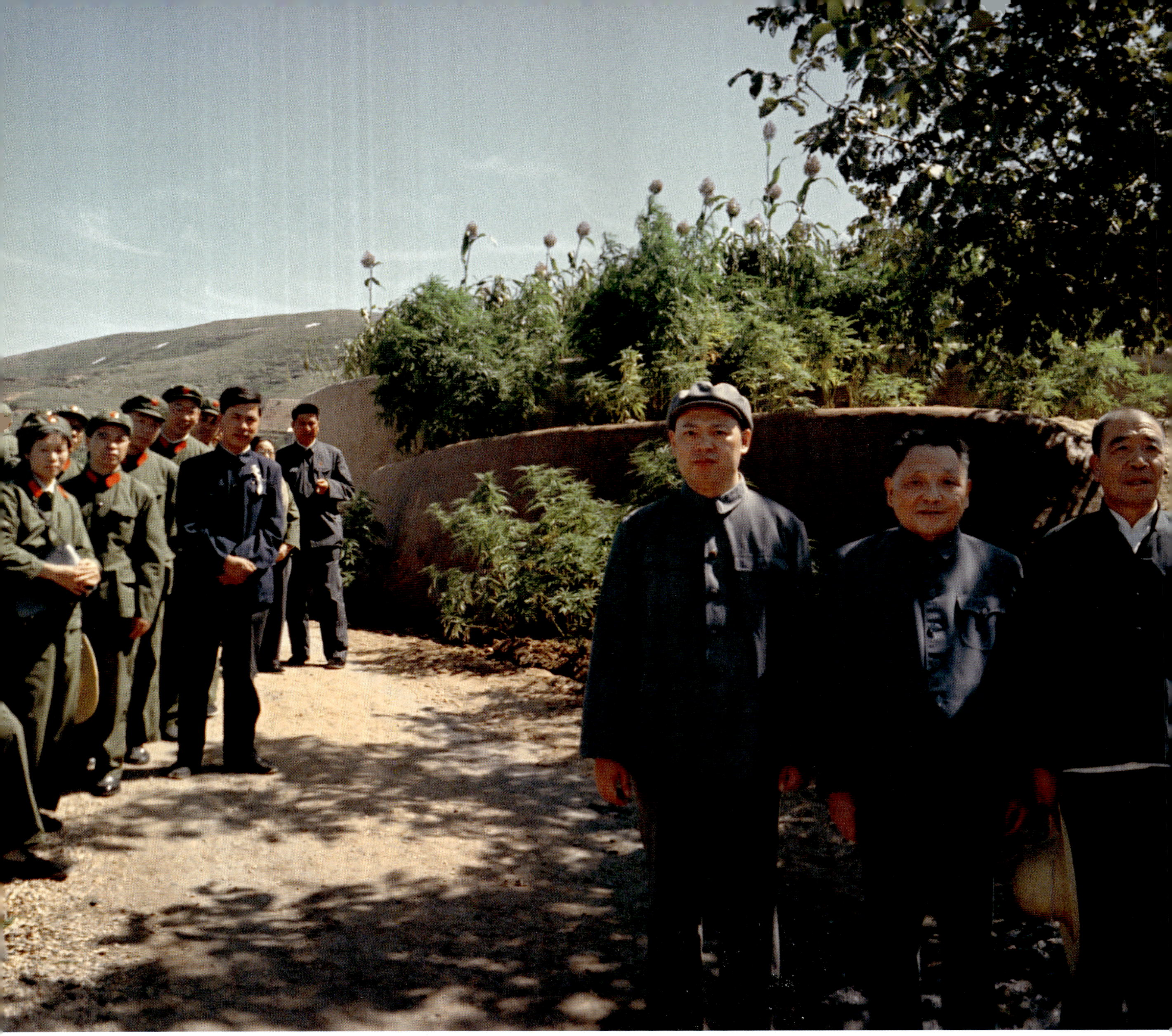

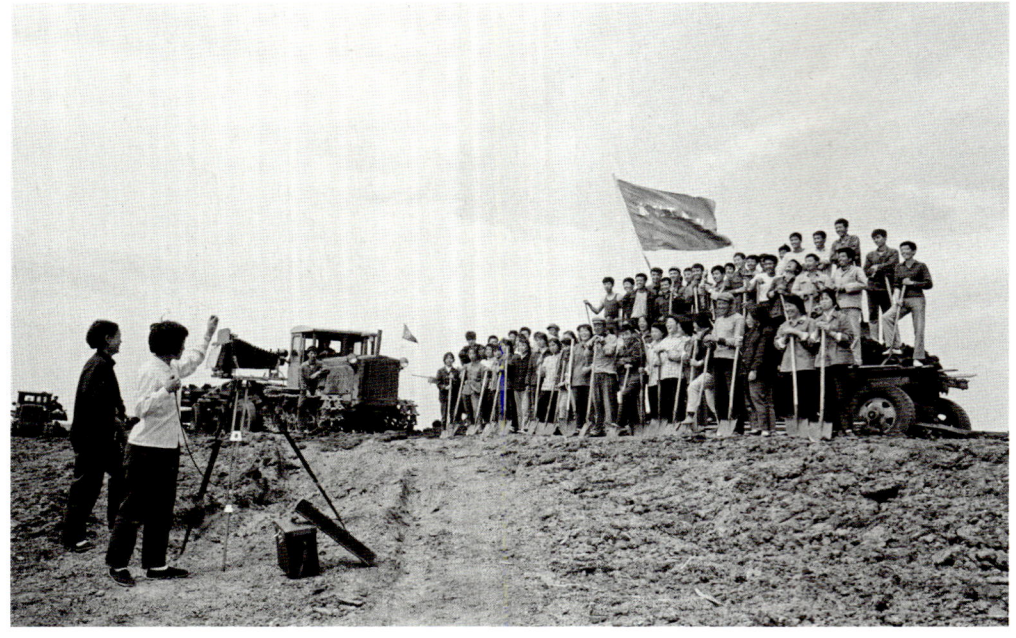

←

Li Zhensheng, 1976

A group of high-school graduates, sent to the countryside in Heilongjiang province, gather for a group portrait.

Eine Gruppe von Oberschülern, die aufs Land in die Provinz Heilongjiang verschickt worden ist, versammelt sich für ein Gruppenfoto.

Des lycéens, envoyés à la campagne dans la province du Heilongjiang, sont réunis pour un portrait de groupe.

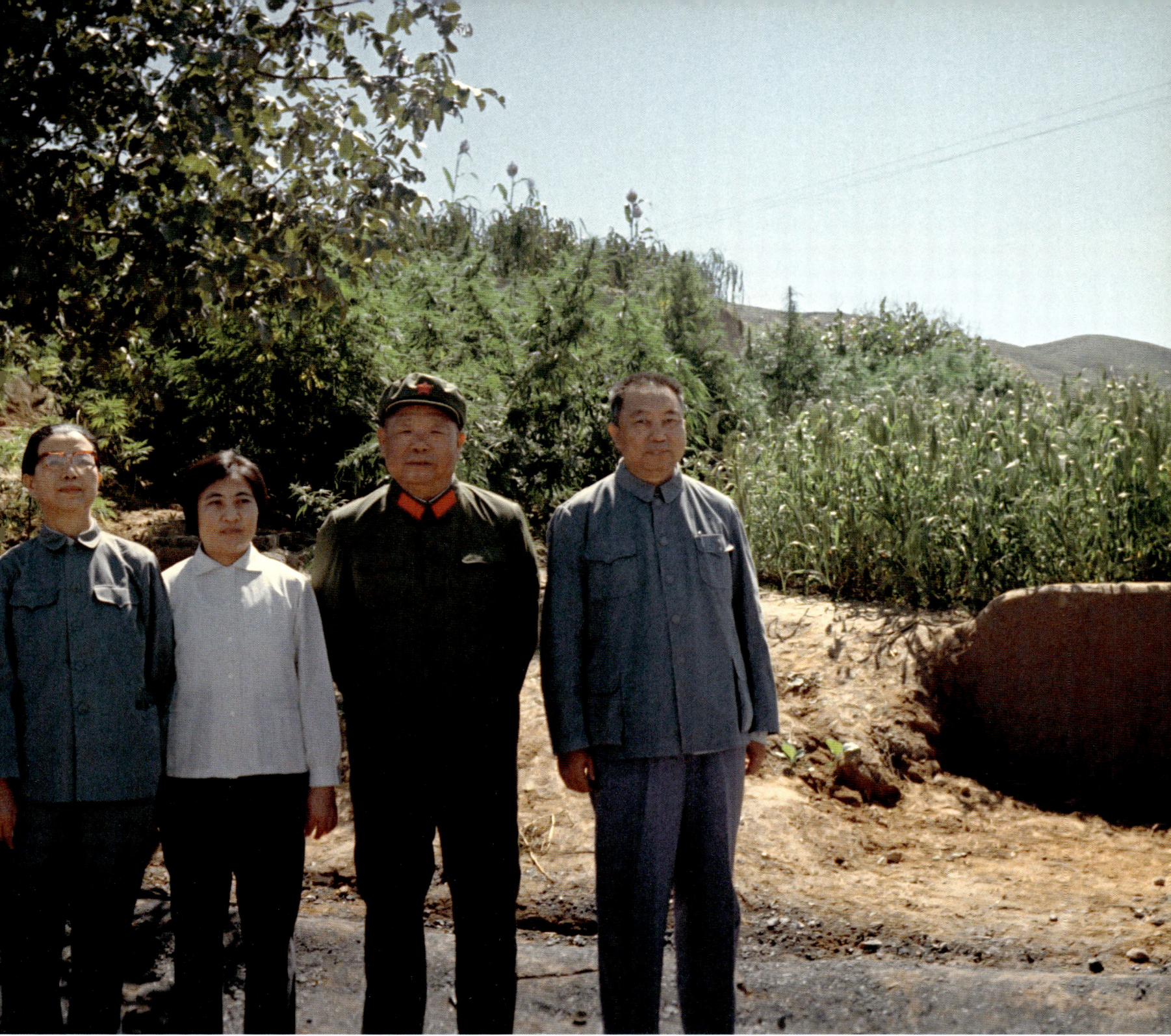

↑
Du Xiuxian, 1975

*Deng Xiaoping (second left) stands with
Jiang Qing and Hua Guofeng (first right) for
a group photograph at Dazhai commune.
During the visit, Deng and Jiang clashed as
Deng made no secret of his objections to
blindly copying the Dazhai commune model
nationwide. Left to right: Yao Wenyuan,
Deng Xiaoping, Chen Yonggui, Jiang Qing,
Wu Guixian, General Chen Xilian, and Hua
Guofeng.*

*Deng Xiaoping (2. von links) posiert mit
Jiang Qing und Hua Guofeng (1. von rechts)
für eine Gruppe von Fotografen in der Kommune Dazhai. Während des Besuchs geraten
Deng und Jiang Qing aneinander, als Deng
offen seinen Widerspruch gegen die landesweite blinde Übernahme des Modells der
Volkskommune Dazhai anmeldet. Von links
nach rechts: Yao Wenyuan, Deng Xiaoping,
Chen Yonggui, Jiang Qing, Wu Guixian,
General Chen Xilian und Hua Guofeng.*

*Deng Xiaoping (second à gauche) avec Jiang
Qing et Hua Guofeng (premier à droite)
dans une photographie de groupe prise à
Dazhai. Au cours de cette visite, Deng et
Jiang s'opposèrent car Deng ne cachait pas
son refus de faire copier aveuglément dans
tout le pays le modèle de la commune de
Dazhai. De gauche à droite : Yao Wenyuan,
Deng Xiaoping, Chen Yonggui, Jiang Qing,
Wu Guixian, le général Chen Xilian et Hua
Guofeng.*

pp. 242/243
Gu Shoukang, 1973

*A sky burial in Tibet. Tibetan people believe
that the spirit departs the body to follow its
next reincarnation. Being of no further use to
the spirit, the body is fed to the local wildlife,
thus playing a vital role in the cycle of life.*

*Eine Himmelsbeerdigung in Tibet. Die Tibeter
glauben, dass der Geist den Körper verlässt,
um seiner nächsten Reinkarnation zu folgen.
Da der Körper dem Geist künftig nicht mehr
von Nutzen ist, wird er den Tieren zum Fraß
überlassen und spielt so im Kreislauf des
Lebens eine wichtige Rolle.*

*Funérailles au Tibet. Les Tibétains croient que
l'esprit s'échappe du corps pour se préparer à
sa future réincarnation. Sans utilité, le corps est
abandonné aux animaux sauvages et joue
ainsi un rôle dans le cycle de la vie*

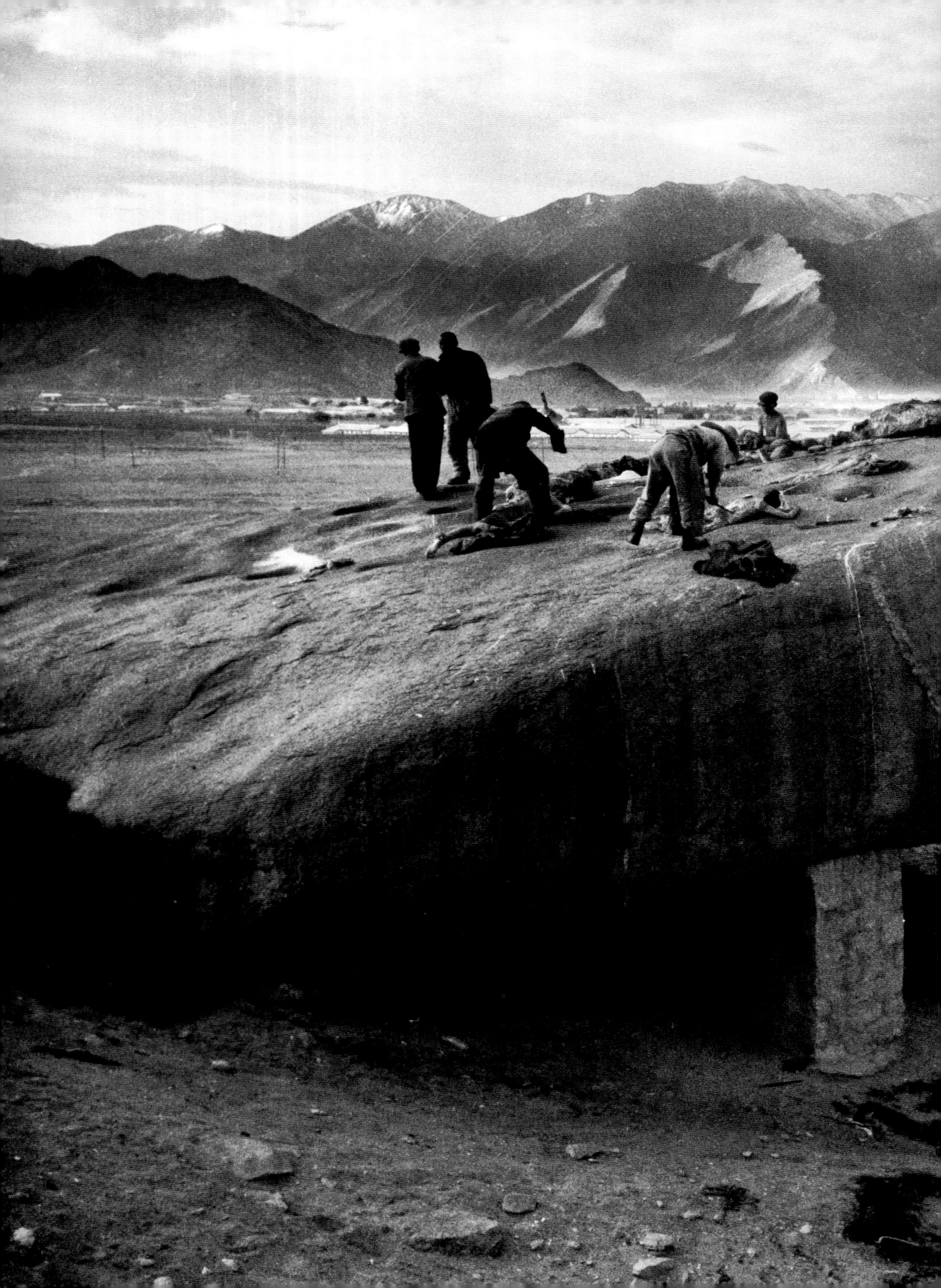

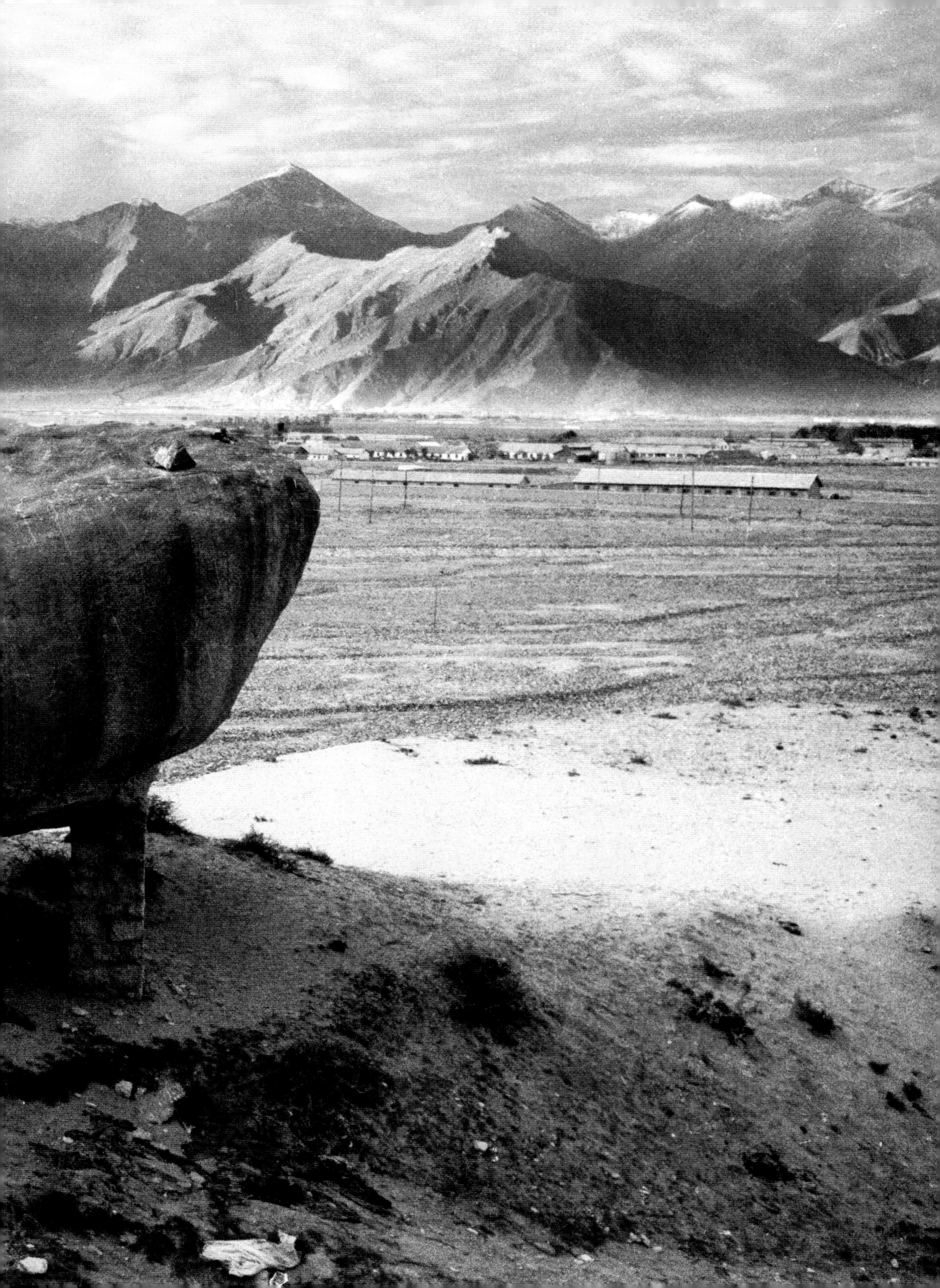

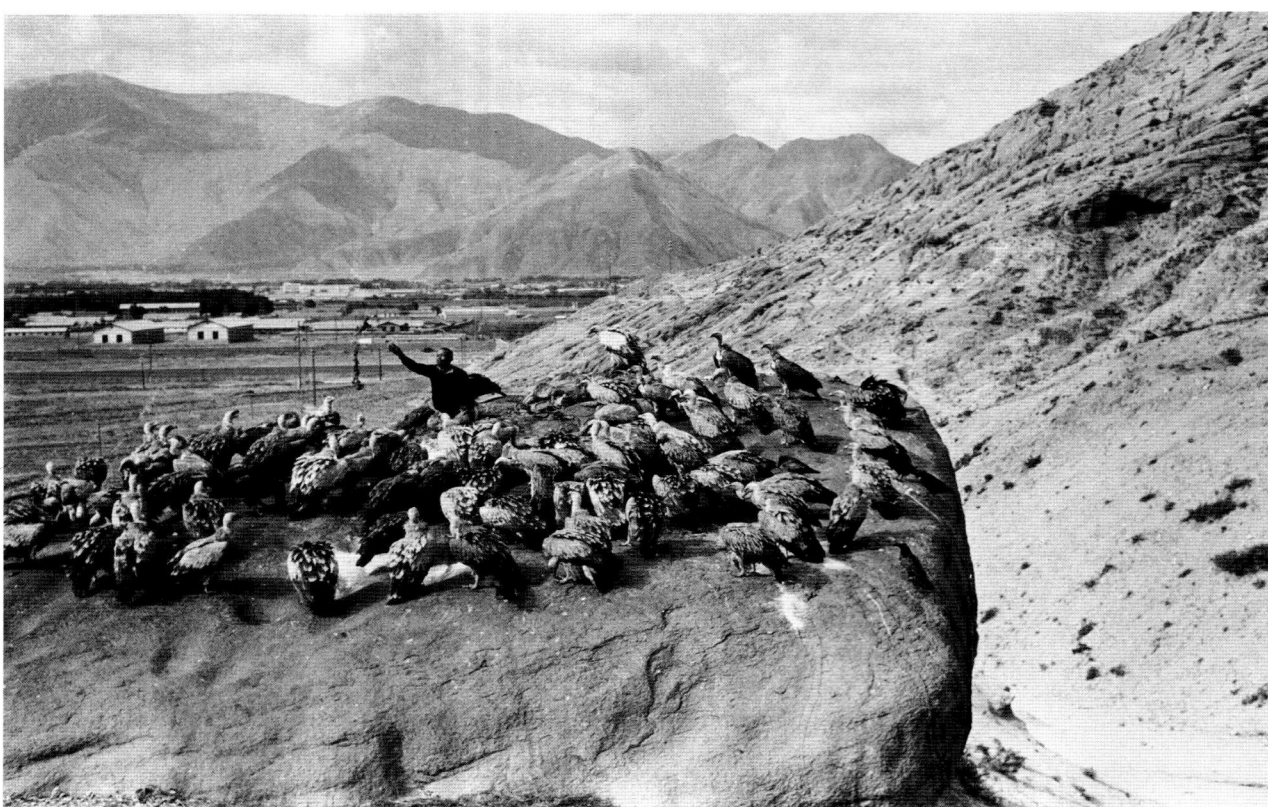

←
Gu Shoukang, 1973

A Tibetan Akha priest throws portions of a corpse to the huge flock of vultures that has gathered to feed. Tibetans practice this type of "sky burial," to return the deceased to the great cycle of life.

Ein tibetischer Akha-Priester wirft einem Schwarm von Geiern Teile eines Leichnams vor. Die Tibeter praktizieren diesen Brauch der ‚Himmelsbestattung', um so den Verstorbenen dem großen Kreislauf des Lebens zurückzugeben.

Un prêtre Akha tibétain jette des morceaux de cadavre humain à des vautours qui affluent pour se nourrir. Les Tibétains croient que cette pratique de « l'enterrement céleste » permet au décédé de réintégrer le grand cycle de la vie.

→
Ji Lianbo, 1974

Chen Yonggui was born in Dazhai village, Shanxi province, in northern China. In the early 1960s, he became leader of the Dazhai Production Brigade (a production brigade was a unit under a People's Commune; usually a village). Dazhai was an extraordinary success. In 1964, Mao called on the nation to learn from Dazhai in agriculture. Following the failings of the Great Leap Forward, Dazhai emerged as a much-needed success story, and the commune was upheld as a national model. At first, Chen Yonggui was simply a model farmer, but later he began to wage war against "class enemies" that did not exist in his poverty-stricken mountain village. In the mid-1960s, Dazhai became the seat of Dazhai People's Commune and Chen Yonggui became commune head. During the Cultural Revolution, he took up a position in local government, and in 1975, was appointed vice premier in charge of agriculture. In 1980, he was forced out of office by Deng Xiaoping. He died in March 1986.

Chen Yonggui wurde im Dorf Dazhai in der Provinz Shanxi in Nordchina geboren. Anfang der 1960er-Jahre wurde er Anführer der Dazhai-Produktionsbrigade (eine Produktionsbrigade war eine Einheit innerhalb einer Volkskommune, in der Regel ein Dorf). Dazhai erwies sich als außerordentlich erfolgreich. 1964 rief Mao die Nation dazu auf, von Dazhai in puncto Landwirtschaft zu lernen. Nach den Misserfolgen des Großen Sprungs nach vorn wurde Dazhai dringend als Erfolgsmodell benötigt und die Kommune wurde als nationales Beispiel hochgehalten. Zu Anfang war Chen Yonggui nur ein Modellbauer, aber später begann er, in seinem verarmten Bergdorf nicht vorhandene „Klassenfeinde" zu bekämpfen. Mitte der 1960er-Jahre wurde Dazhai Sitz der Volkskommune Dazhai und Chen Yonggui Leiter der Kommune. Während der Kulturrevolution nahm er eine Stelle in der Lokalregierung ein, 1975 wurde er zum stellvertretenden Ministerpräsident, zuständig für Landwirtschaft, berufen. 1980 entfernte Deng Xiaoping ihn aus dem Amt, er starb im März 1986.

Chen Yonggui était né dans le village de Dazhai, province du Shanxi, dans le nord de la Chine. Au début des années 1960, il devint chef de brigade de production (unité de travail d'une commune populaire, généralement un village). Dazhai fut un extraordinaire succès. En 1964, Mao incita le pays à s'inspirer de ses pratiques agricoles. Après l'échec du Grand bond en avant, Dazhai se révéla un exemple très utile et la commune devint un modèle national. Au début, Chen Yonggui n'était qu'un fermier modèle, mais il devint plus tard le meneur du combat contre les « ennemis de classe » pourtant totalement absents de ce pauvre village de montagne. Au milieu des années 1960, le village devint le siège de la commune populaire de Dazhai dont Cheng fut nommé responsable. Pendant la Révolution culturelle, il occupa une position dans le gouvernement local et, en 1975, fut nommé vice-premier ministre en charge de l'agriculture. En 1980, il fut renvoyé par Deng Xiaoping et mourut en 1986.

→
Ji Lianbo, 1974

Chen Yonggui (right) addressing fellow peasants at Dazhai commune, Shanxi province. Mao later elevated Chen to the position of vice premier.

Chen Yonggui, rechts, spricht zu seinen bäuerlichen Kollegen in der Kommune Dazhai, Provinz Shanxi. Chen wurde später von Mao zum Vize-Ministerpräsidenten befördert.

Chen Yonggui (à droite) s'adresse aux paysans de la commune de Dazhai, dans la province du Shanxi. Par la suite, Mao fit de lui un vice-premier ministre.

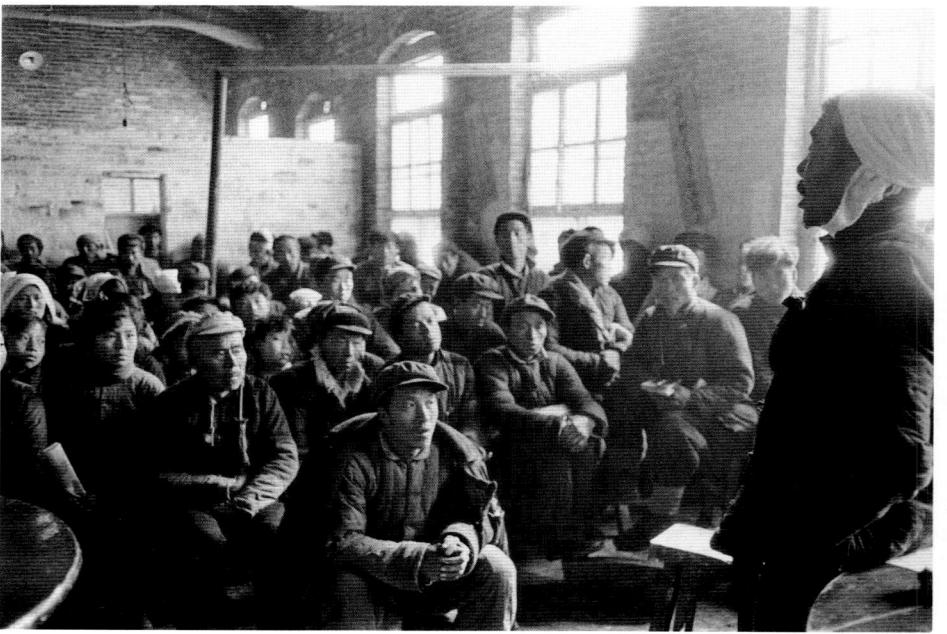

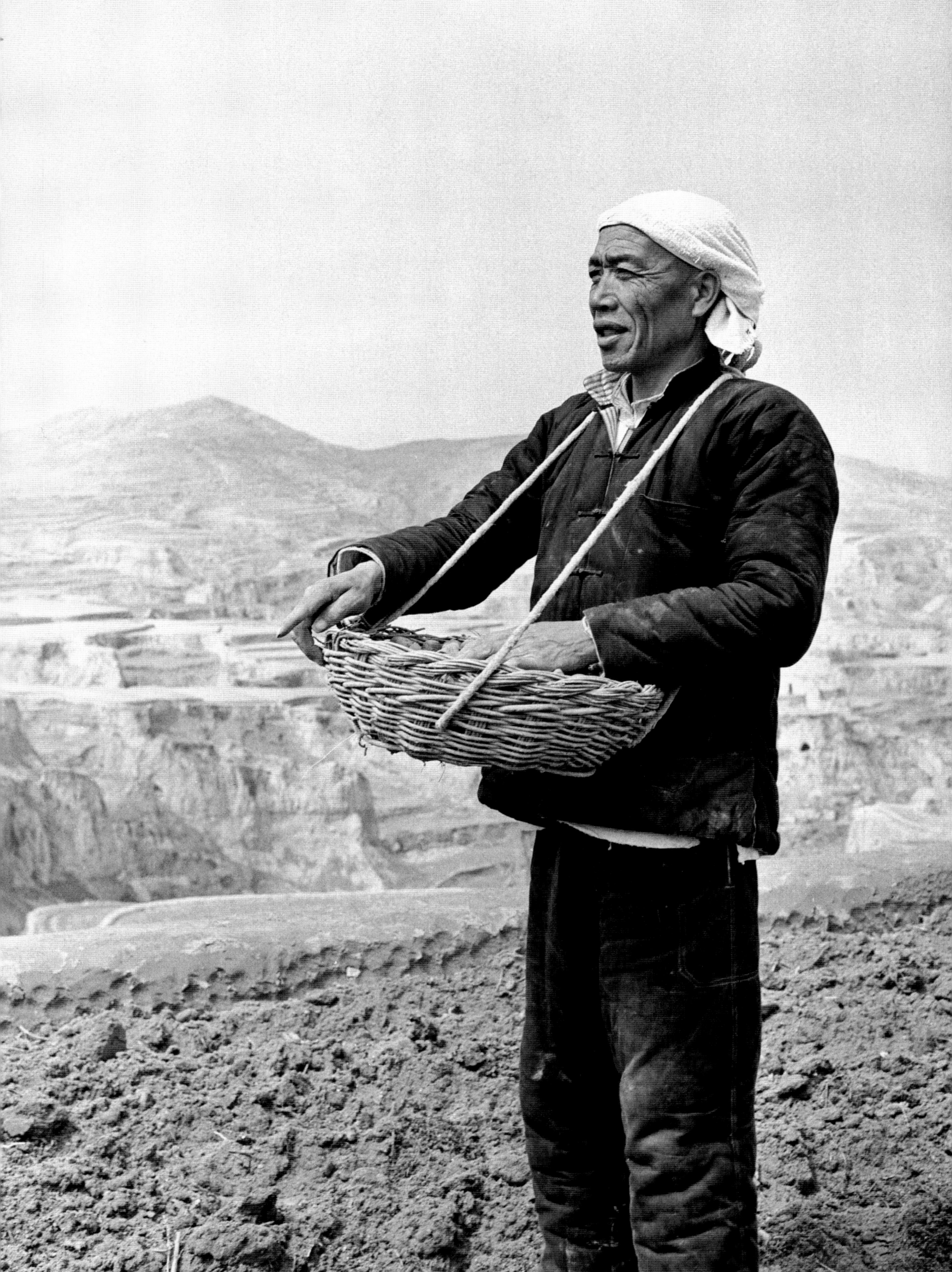

→
Wang Shilong, 1974

In one of three famous tracts, in 1945, Mao invoked the story of the "Old man who moved the mountain," to encourage the masses to "overthrow the two great mountains"— imperialism and feudalism—"oppressing the Chinese people." This article, together with "Serve the People" and "In Memory of Norman Bethune," was repeatedly cited during the Cultural Revolution. This photograph shows thousands of peasants following the example of peasants from Linxian county who dug a massive irrigation project that would become known as the great Red Flag Canal. Work began in 1960, and was not completed until 1969. In between, the people built a waterway 1,500 kilometers long that plowed through 1,250 hills, with 134 tunnels and 6.5 kilometers of aqueduct. The determination of the people of Linxian was an example to all.

In einem seiner drei berühmten Traktate beruft sich Mao 1945 auf die Geschichte vom „Alten Mann, der den Berg bewegte," um die Massen zum „Umsturz der beiden großen Berge" – Imperialismus und Feudalismus –, „die das chinesische Volk unterdrücken" zu ermutigen. Neben „Dem Volke dienen" und „Zum Gedächtnis an Norman Bethune" wurde diese Geschichte während der Kulturrevolution wiederholt zitiert. Dieses Bild zeigt Tausende von Bauern, die dem Beispiel von Bauern aus dem Kreis Linxian folgen, die ein weit verzweigtes Bewässerungssystem schufen, das als großer Rote-Fahne-Kanal bekannt wurde. Die Arbeit daran begann 1960 und war erst 1969 abgeschlossen. In dieser Zeit bauten die Menschen eine 1500 km lange Wasserstraße, die durch 1250 Hügel führte, 134 Tunnel und 6,5 km Aquädukte benötigte. Die Entschlossenheit der Menschen von Linxian galt allen als Vorbild.

Dans l'un des trois célèbres tracts politiques, Mao invoqua l'histoire du « Vieil homme qui déplaça la montagne », en 1945, pour encourager les masses à « renverser les deux grandes montagnes » de l'impérialisme et du féodalisme oppressant le peuple chinois. Ce texte et ceux intitulés « Servir le peuple » et « En mémoire du Norman Bethune » furent sans cesse cités pendant la Révolution culturelle. Cette photographie montre des milliers de paysans suivant l'exemple de ceux de la région du Linxian qui avait creusé un énorme ouvrage d'irrigation, le Canal du drapeau rouge. Les travaux entamés en 1960 ne furent achevés qu'en 1969. C'est un peuple tout entier qui creusa un canal de 1500 km franchissant 1250 collines, 134 tunnels et 6,5 km d'aqueducs. La détermination des habitants du Linxian fut un exemple pour tous.

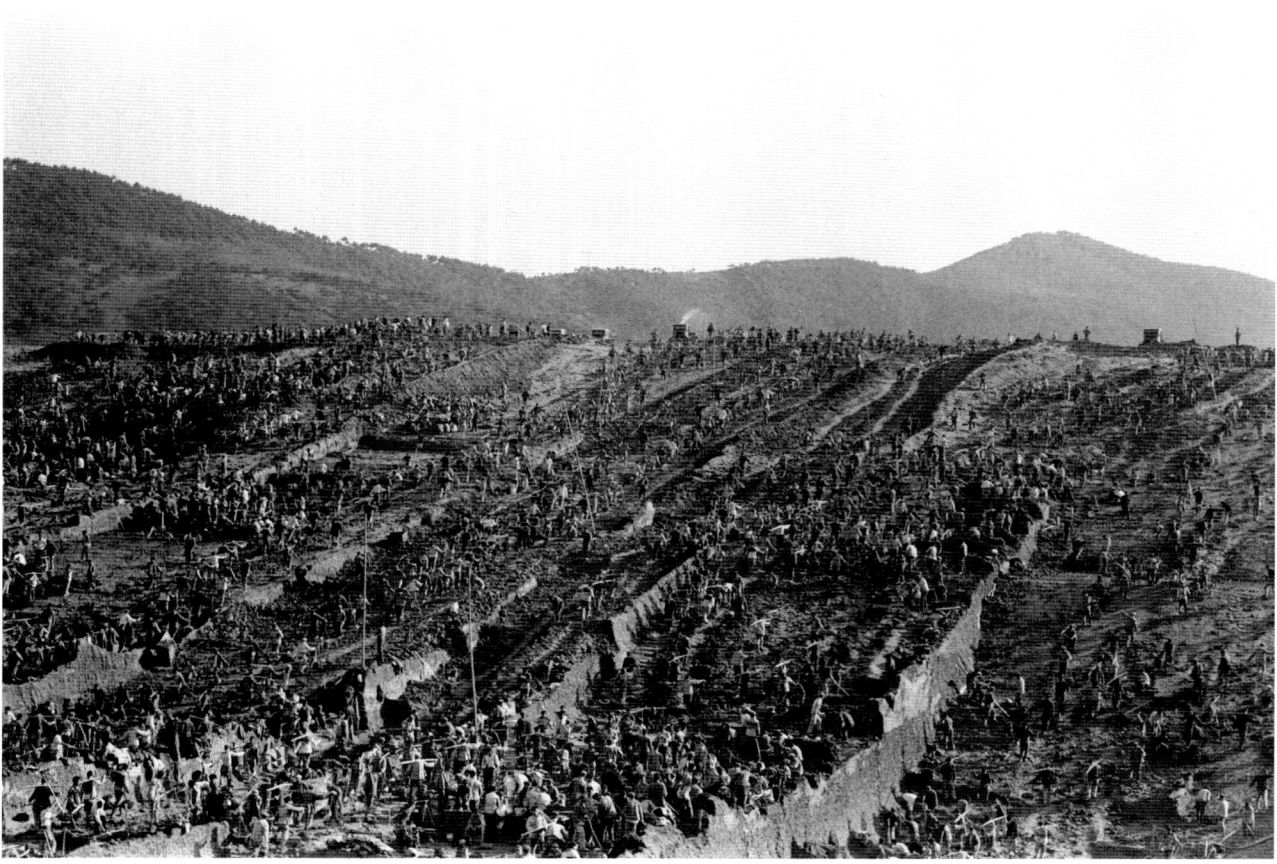

"It is by this severe moderation in everything that the Chinese Empire has sustained itself for thousands of years and will endure hereafter."

„Eben durch diese strenge Mäßigung in allem hat sich denn auch das chinesische Reich seit Jahrtausenden erhalten und wird dadurch ferner bestehen."

« C'est par une stricte modération en toute chose que l'empire chinois s'est maintenu pendant des milliers d'années et perdurera. »

JOHANN WOLFGANG VON GOETHE
(1749–1832), German poet and novelist, 1827

↑
Tang Desheng, 1972

Thousands of peasants are deployed to work on the expansion project for the Grand Canal in Jiangsu province. The Grand Canal is the world's oldest and longest canal, begun in 486 BC, and extended through to AD 610. It links the "garden city" of Hangzhou in the south to Beijing in the north, a distance of almost 2,000 kilometers.

Tausende von Bauern werden zu Erweiterungsarbeiten am Großen Kanal in der Provinz Jiangsu abkommandiert. Beim Großen Kanal handelt es sich um den ältesten und längsten Kanal der Welt, der 486 v. Chr. begonnen und an dem bis 610 n. Chr. weitergearbeitet wurde. Er verbindet über eine Distanz von 2000 Kilometern die „Gartenstadt" Hangzhou im Süden mit Peking im Norden.

Des milliers de paysans sont déployés sur le terrain pour participer au projet d'extension du Grand canal dans la province du Jiangsu. Ce canal est le plus long et le plus ancien du monde, creusé de 486 av. J.-C. à 610. Il relie la « ville-jardin » méridionale de Hangzhou à Pékin, à 2 000 km plus au nord.

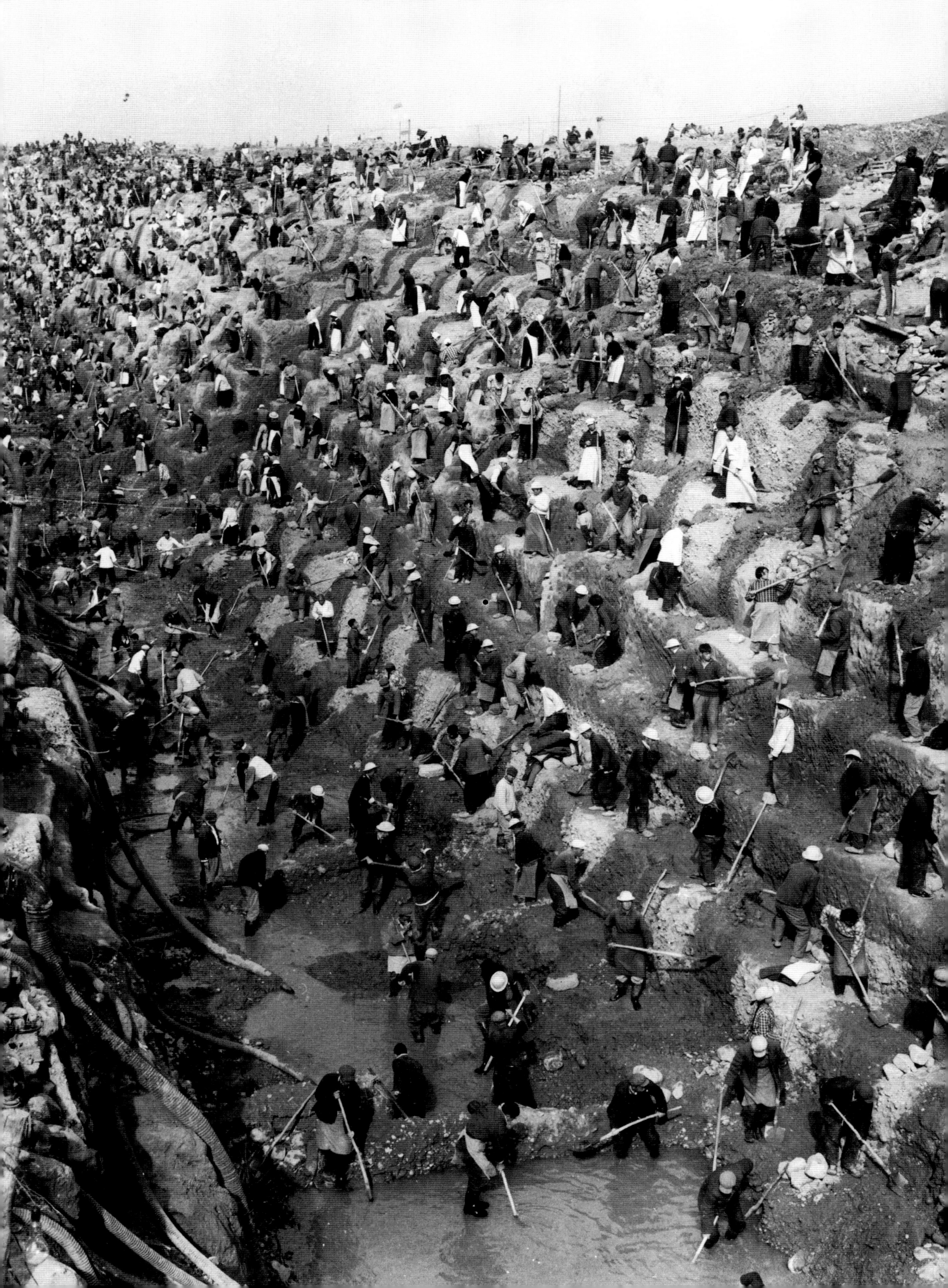

↓
Tang Desheng, 1976

A rally organized to denounce the Gang of Four shortly after the four members were arrested in Beijing in October of 1976, and which followed in the wake of Mao's death in early September.

Eine Versammlung zur Verurteilung der Viererbande. Sie war kurz nach der Verhaftung der vier Beteiligten im Oktober 1976 in Peking organisiert worden, wenige Wochen nach Maos Tod Anfang September.

Rassemblement destiné à fustiger la bande des quatre, peu après leur arrestation à Pékin en octobre 1976, survenue dans la foulée de la mort de Mao, début septembre.

→
Tang Desheng, 1975

Workers join a hillside rally organized to denounce China's disgraced former Defense Minister, Marshal Lin Biao, and to criticize Confucius as the symbol of feudalism.

Arbeiter versammeln sich auf einem Hügel, um den in Ungnade gefallenen früheren Verteidigungsministers Lin Biao zu verurteilen und Kritik an Konfuzius als Symbol des Feudalismus zu üben.

Rassemblement de travailleurs sur une colline, organisé pour fustiger l'ancien ministre de la Défense tombé en disgrâce, Lin Biao, et dénoncer Confucius en tant que symbole du féodalisme.

"Collective amnesia is so pervasive in China that the national memory has difficulty recalling even the decade of the Cultural Revolution (1966–76), let alone the disaster of the Great Leap Forward (1958) or the brutality of the Anti-Rightist campaign (1957)."

„Die kollektive Amnesie ist in China derart verbreitet, dass man sich kaum mehr an das Jahrzehnt der Kulturrevolution (1966–1976) erinnern kann, ganz zu schweigen vom katastrophalen Großen Sprung nach vorn (1958) oder der Brutalität der Kampagne gegen rechts (1957)."

« L'amnésie collective est si étendue en Chine, que la mémoire nationale remonte même difficilement jusqu'à la décennie de la Révolution culturelle (1966–1976), sans parler du désastre du Grand bond en avant (1958) ou de la brutalité de la campagne anti-droitière (1957). »

TU WEI-MING, Professor of History and Philosophy, and Director of the Harvard Yenching Institute, 1991

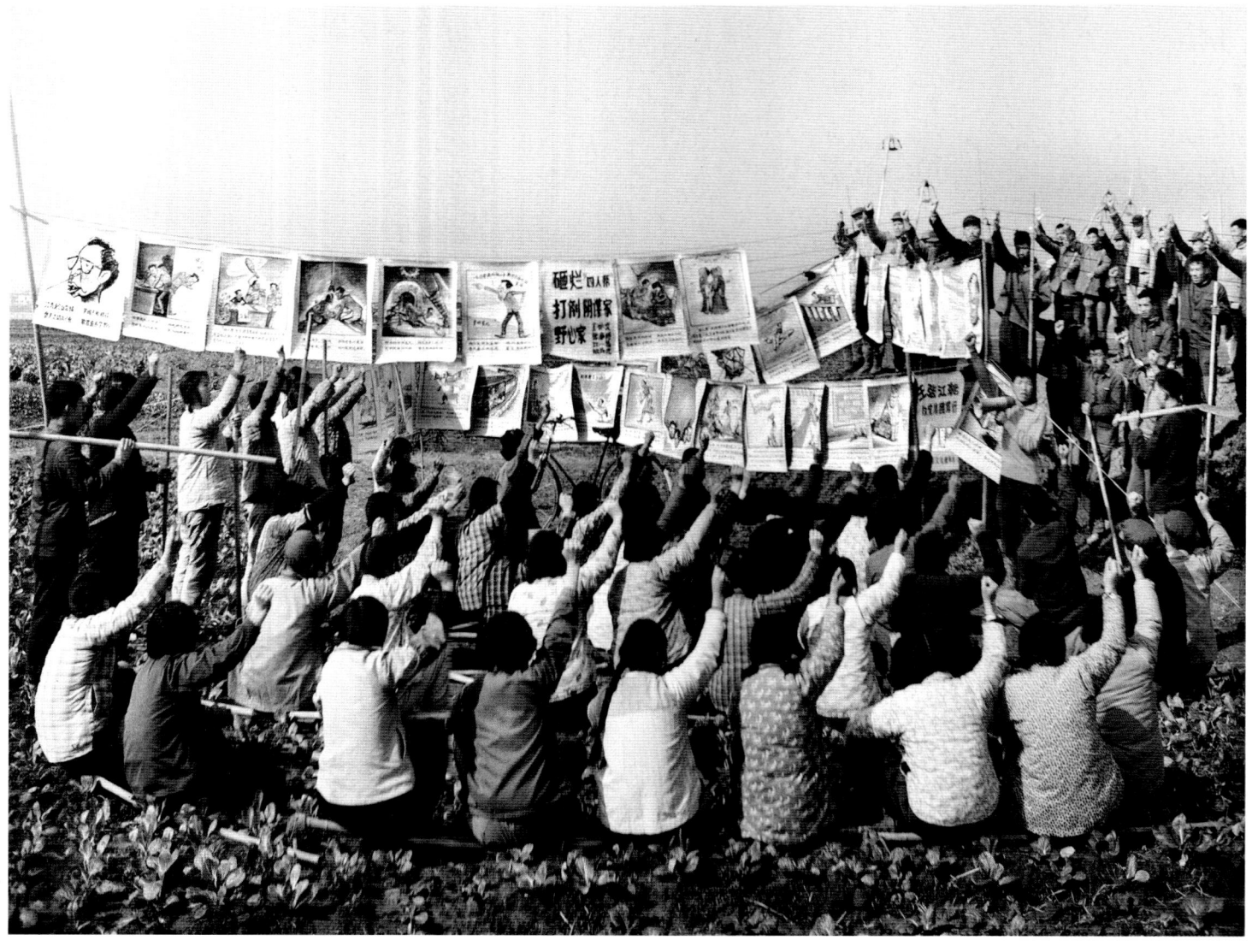

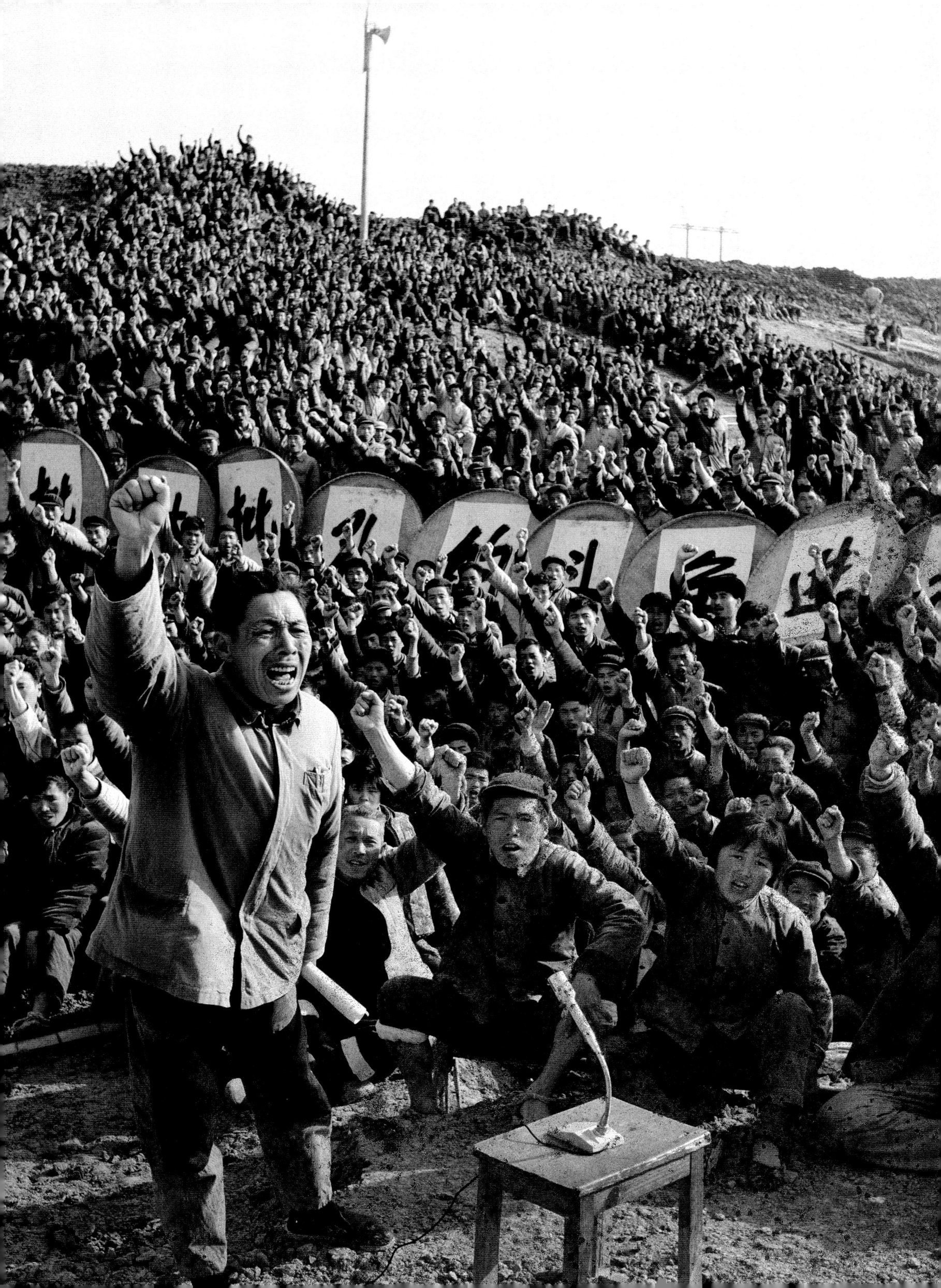

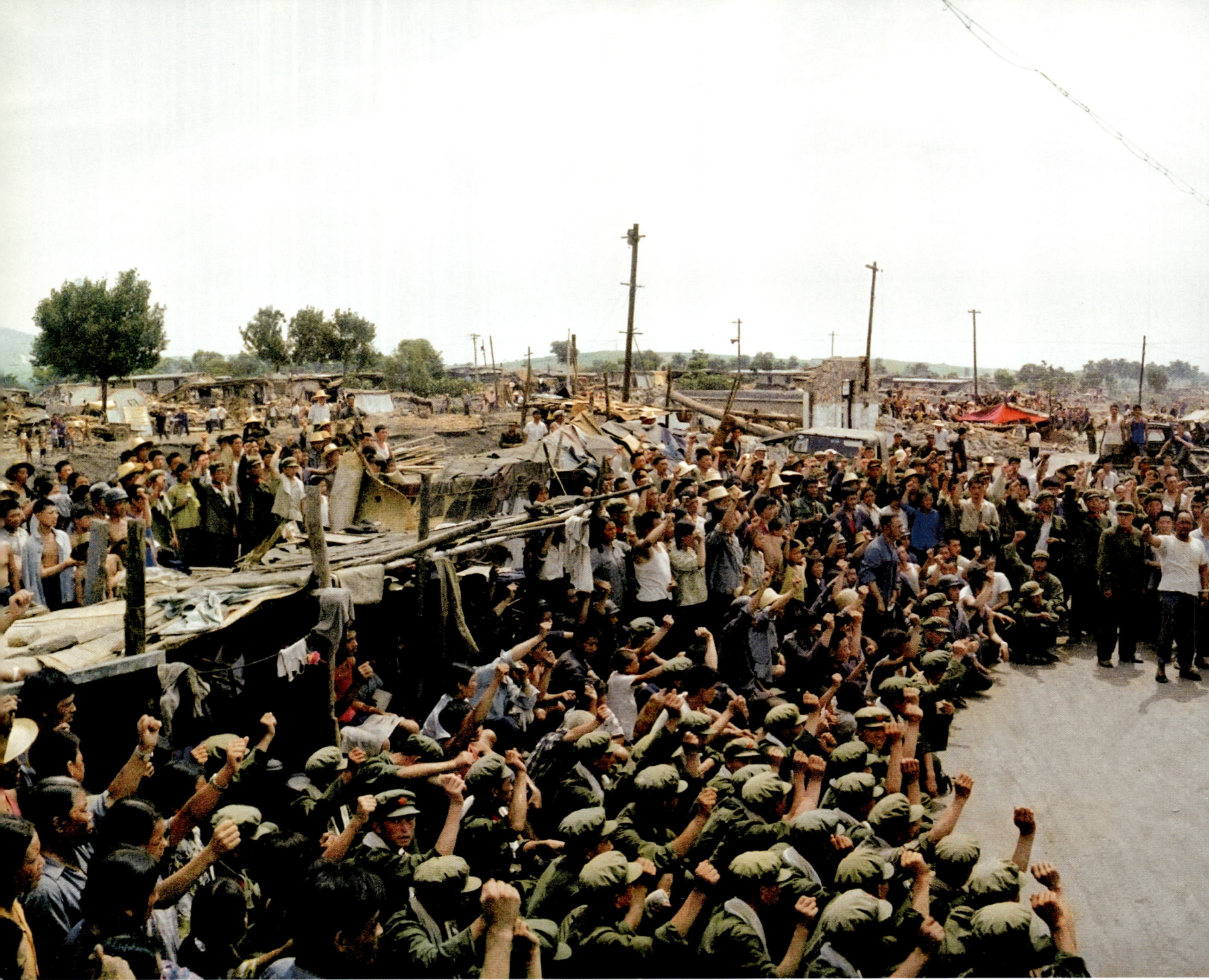

↑

Du Xiuxian, 1976

Government officials inspect the vast area in Tangshan hit by an earthquake, causing the death of 242,000 people, with more than 164,000 severely wounded. The superstitious segment of the Chinese masses interpreted the earthquake as portending a change in the Mandate of Heaven. Chinese leaders Chairman Mao, Premier Zhou Enlai, and Marshal Zhu De all died that year.

Regierungsfunktionäre inspizieren das große, von einem Erdbeben heimgesuchte Gebiet in Tangshan, bei dem 242.000 Menschen starben und mehr als 164.000 schwer verletzt wurden. Der abergläubische Teil der chinesischen Massen deutete das Erdbeben als Hinweis auf einen Wechsel im Himmlischen Mandat. Der Vorsitzende Mao, Premier Zhou Enlai und Marschall Zhu De starben in diesem Jahr.

Des responsables gouvernementaux inspectent la vaste zone frappée par le tremblement de terre de Tangshan qui fit 242000 morts et plus de 164 000 blessés graves. Les éléments superstitieux des masses chinoises interprétèrent cette catastrophe comme l'annonce d'un changement dans le Mandat du Ciel. Mao, Zhou Enlai et le maréchal Zhu De moururent cette même année.

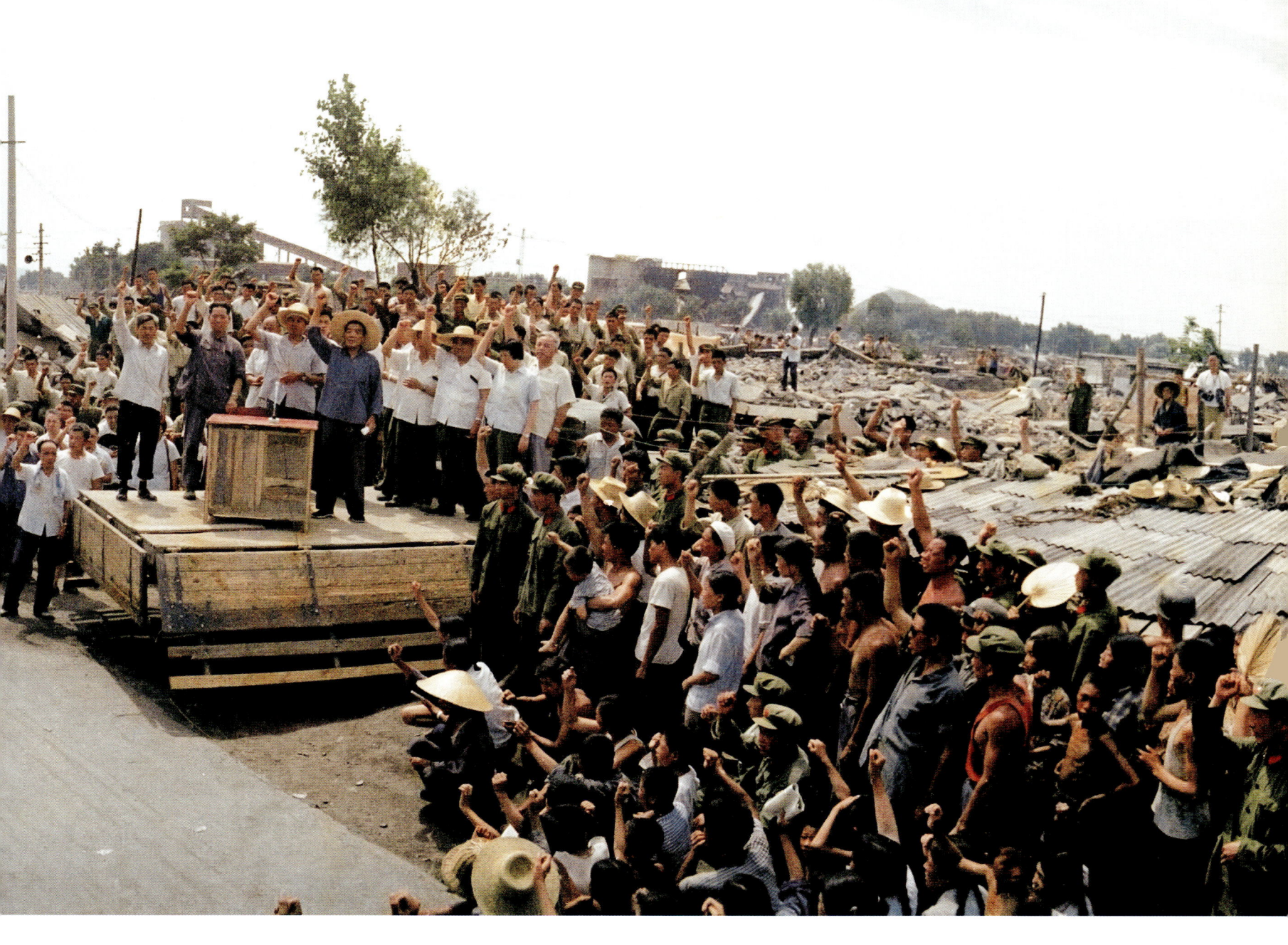

"When a devastating earthquake obliterated the industrial city of Tangshan in north China in 1976 and severely shook Peking…the press gave no details. Only more than two years later, in a small box at the bottom of page four, did the People's Daily disclose that the quake had killed 242,000 people and seriously injured another 164,000."

„Als 1976 ein verheerendes Erdbeben die Industriestadt Tangshan dem Erdboden gleichmachte und Peking schwer erschütterte … meldete die Presse keine Einzelheiten. Mehr als zwei Jahre später berichtete People's Daily in einem kleinen Kasten unten auf Seite vier, dass das Beben über 242.000 Menschen getötet und weitere 164.000 verletzt hatte."

« Lorsqu'un terrible séisme ravagea la ville industrielle de Tangshan dans le nord de la Chine, en 1976, et frappa durement Pékin…la presse ne donna aucun détail. Ce n'est que plus de deux ans plus tard, dans un petit cartouche en bas de la page 4, que People's Daily révéla que la catastrophe avait fait 242 000 morts et 164 000 blessés graves. »

FOX BUTTERFIELD (1939–), former head of The New York Times Beijing bureau, 1982

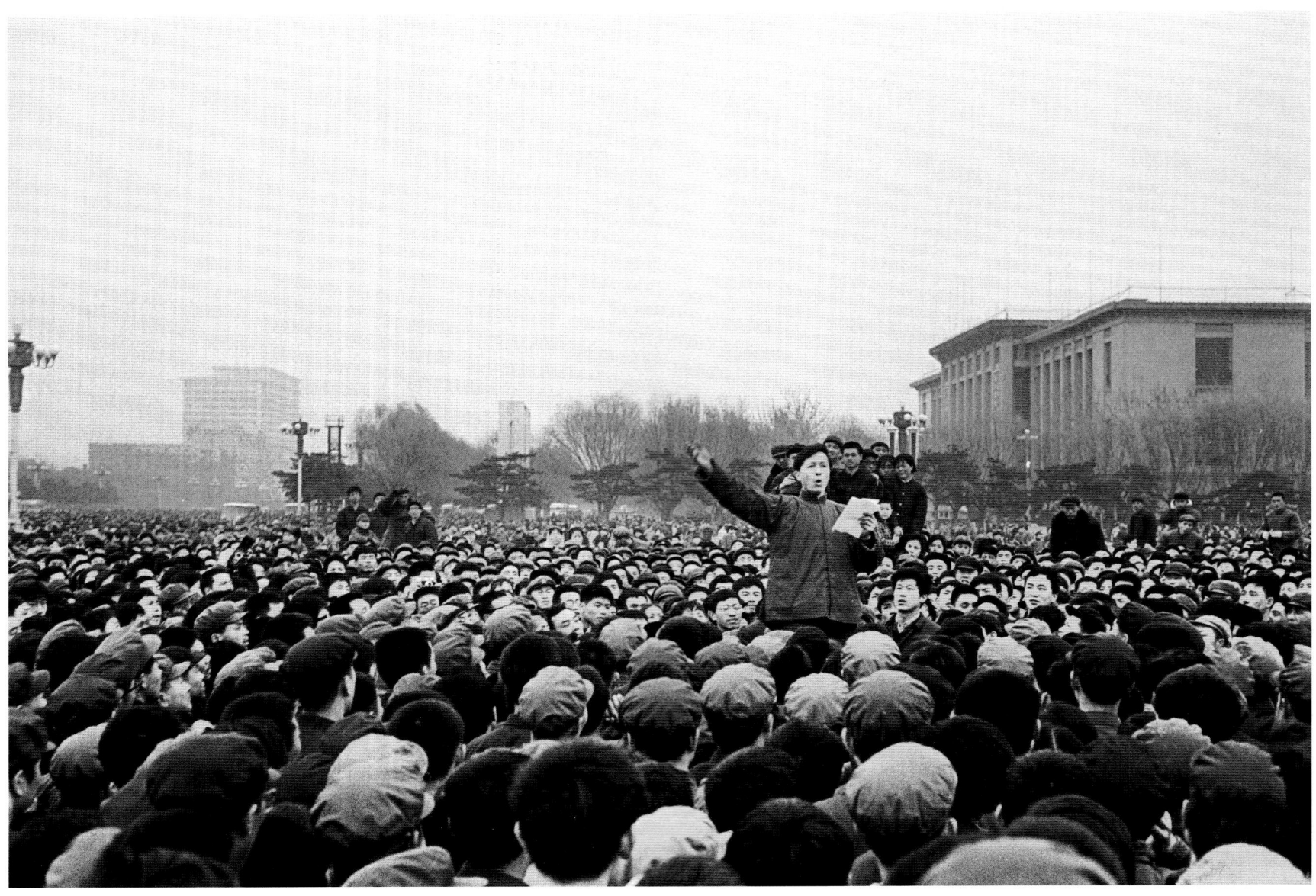

↑
Luo Xiaoyun, 1976

*In April 1976, three months after the death of
Premier Zhou Enlai, hundreds of thousands
of people gathered in Tiananmen Square to
mourn him. Here, one mourner stands above
the crowd to recite a poem commemorating
Zhou. The mass gathering was later denounced
by Mao's widow Jiang Qing as counterrevolutionary.*

*Im April 1976 versammeln sich Tausende
von Menschen auf dem Tiananmen-Platz,
um Premier Zhou Enlai drei Monate nach
seinem Tod zu betrauern. Hier erhebt sich
ein Trauernder über die Menge und rezitiert
im Gedenken an Zhou ein Gedicht. Die
Massenversammlung wurde später von Maos
Witwe Jiang Qing als konterrevolutionäre
Aktivität verurteilt.*

*En avril 1976, trois mois après la mort de
Zhou Enlai, des centaines de milliers de personnes se réunirent sur la place Tian'anmen
pour le pleurer. Ici, un participant porté par
la foule récite un poème à sa mémoire. Les
rassemblements de masse furent dénoncés
comme autant d'activités contre-révolutionnaires par la veuve de Mao, Jiang Qing.*

→
Zhang Yaxin, 1976

*In Shanghai, Red Guards perform propaganda
skits in the People's Square.*

*In Shanghai führen Rote Garden auf dem
Volksplatz propagandistische Sketche auf.*

*Gardes rouges interprétant des scénettes de
propagande sur la place du Peuple à Shanghai.*

"We have killed the 'soul,' but we have created for ourselves a thousand-odd social and political
slogans (revolutionary, counter revolutionary, bourgeois, capitalist-imperialist, escapist), which
tyrannize our thoughts, and have created similar beings like the 'class,' the 'destiny,' and the 'state',
and we proceed logically to transform the state into a monster to swallow up the individual."

„Wir haben die ‚Seele' getötet, aber wir haben uns ungefähr 1000 soziale und politische Parolen
ausgedacht (revolutionär, konterrevolutionär, bourgeois, kapitalistisch-imperialistisch, eskapistisch),
die unsere Gedanken tyrannisieren und Wesen schufen wie ‚Klasse', ‚Schicksal' und ‚Staat', und
wir fahren logischerweise damit fort, den Staat in ein Monster zu verwandeln, der das Individuum
verschlingt."

« Nous avons tué ‚l'âme', mais nous nous sommes créé des milliers de termes politiques et
sociaux (révolutionnaires, contre-révolutionnaires, bourgeois, capitalistes-impérialistes) qui
tyrannisent nos pensées et nous avons créé des êtres comme la ‚classe', le ‚destin' et l'État'.
Nous procédons logiquement pour transformer l'État en un monstre qui avalera l'individu. »

LIN YUTANG (1895–1976), Chinese writer and inventor, 1937

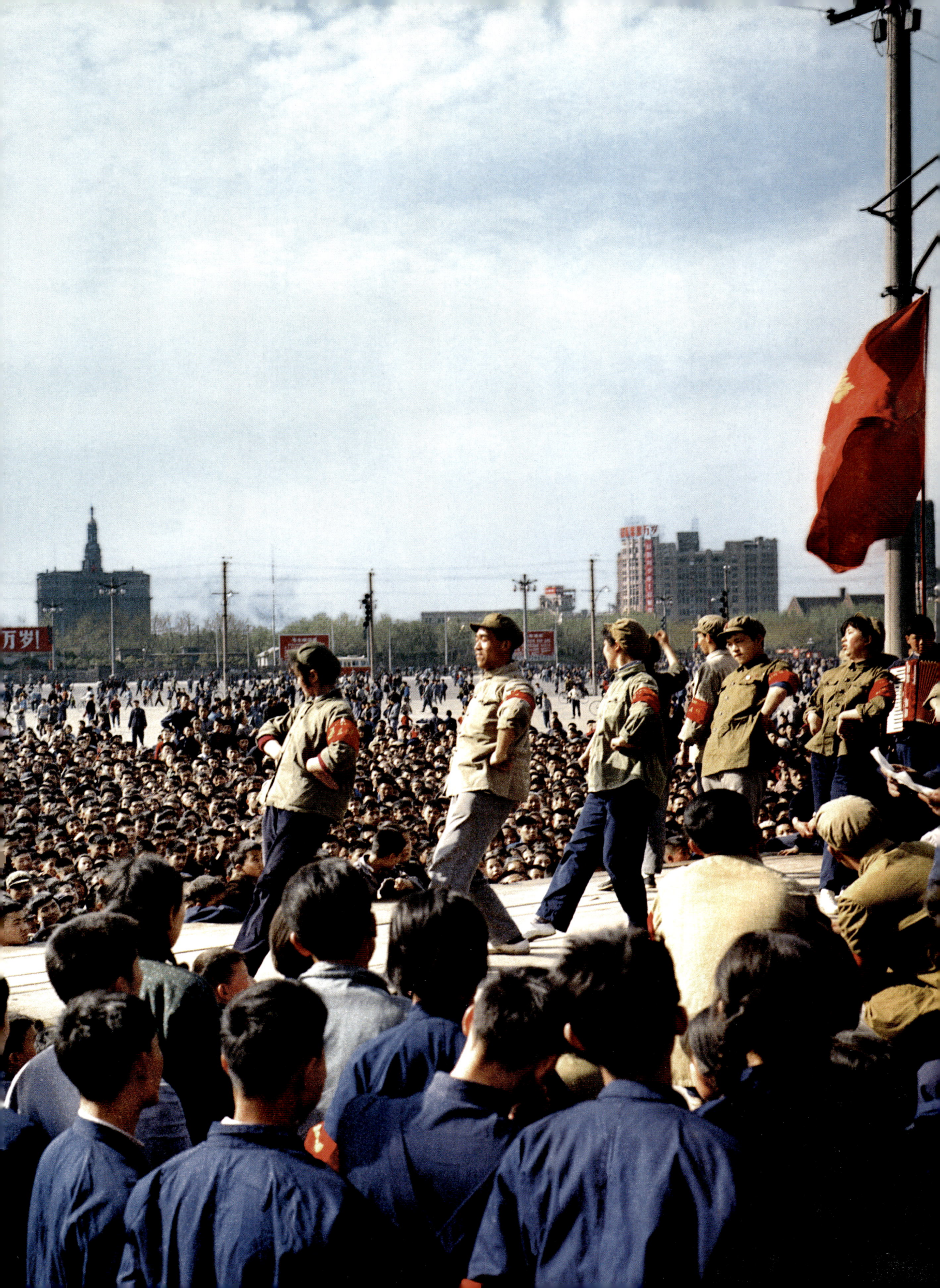

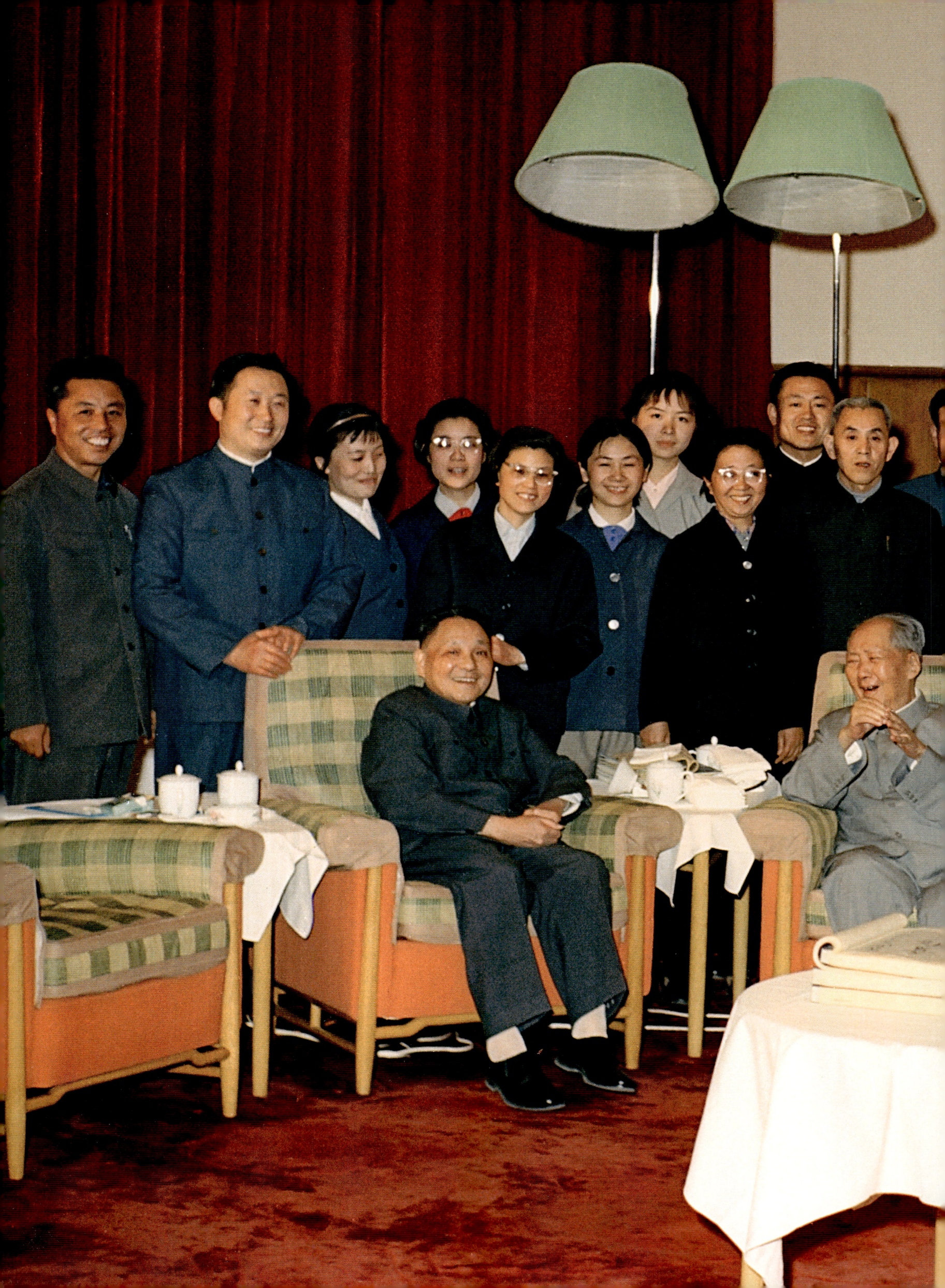

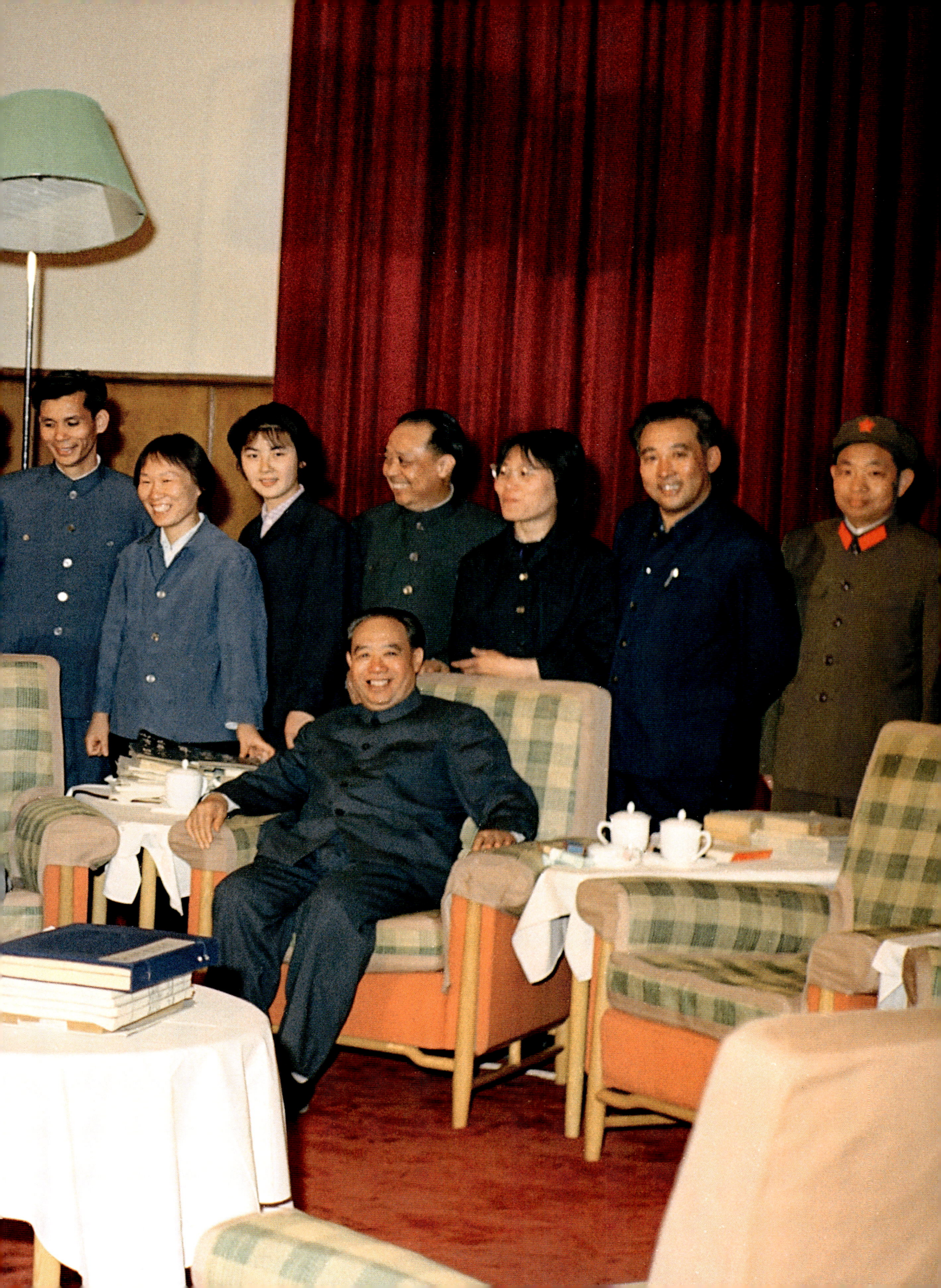

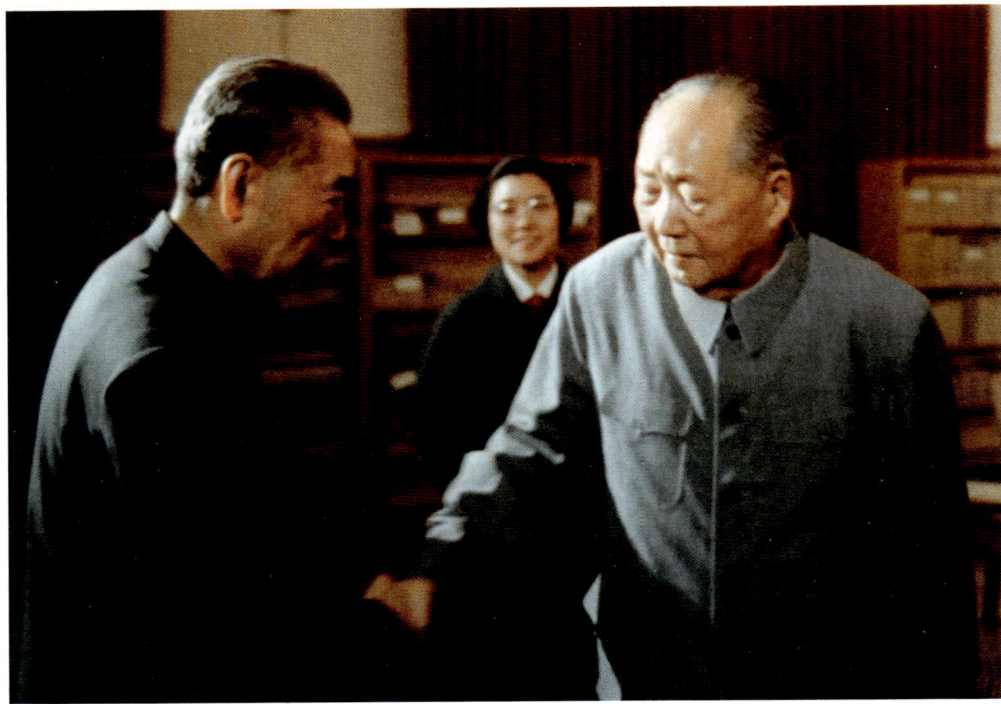

pp. 254/255
Du Xiuxian, 1975

Deng Xiaoping, who had just been reinstated
as vice premier, sits to the right of Mao, in
Mao's study in Zhongnanhai. On Mao's left
is his chief body guard, Huang Dongxing, and
behind the group stands Mao's personal staff.

Der soeben als Vizepremier wieder eingesetzte
Deng Xiaoping sitzt zur Rechten Maos in
dessen Arbeitszimmer in Zhongnanhai. Links
von Mao sitzt sein oberster Leibwächter
Huang Dongxing, hinter der Gruppe stehen
Maos persönliche Mitarbeiter.

Deng Xiaoping, qui vient de reprendre sa
place de vice premier ministre, est assis à
droite de Mao à Zhongnanhai. À la gauche
du Président se trouve le responsable de ses
gardes du corps, Huang Dongxing, et derrière,
les membres de son cabinet personnel.

↑
Du Xiuxian, 1974

Mao greeting Zhou Enlai, who was
terminally ill with cancer. It was to be
their last meeting in Zhongnanhai.

Mao begrüßt den schwer krebskranken Zhou
Enlai. Hier in Zhongranhai trafen sie sich
zum letzten Mal.

Mao salue Zhou Enlai qui souffrait d'un
cancer en phase terminale. Ce fut leur dernière
rencontre à Zhongnanhai.

"It is not often that one can recapture as an adult the quality that in one's youth made
times seem to stand still; that gave every event the mystery of novelty; that enabled each
experience to be relished because of its singularity. As we grow older … only some truly
extraordinary event, both novel and mooring, both unusual and overwhelming, restores
the innocence of the years when each day was a precious adventure in defining the meaning of life. This is how it was for me as the aircraft crossed the snow-capped Himalayas,
thrusting towards the heavens in the roseate glow of a rising sun."

„Es geschieht nicht häufig, dass man als Erwachsener das Gefühl wiedergewinnt, das
einem in der Jugend zu dem Eindruck verhalf, die Zeit bliebe stehen; es verlieh jedem
Ereignis das Mysterium des Neuen; jede Erfahrung konnte als einzigartig genossen
werden. Wenn wir älter werden … kann nur ein wahrhaft außerordentliches Ereignis,
so neuartig wie fesselnd, so ungewöhnlich wie überwältigend, die Unschuld jener Jahre
wiederherstellen, als jeder Tag ein kostbares Abenteuer bedeutete, mit dem man den Sinn
des Lebens zu erklären suchte. So erging es mir, als das Flugzeug die schneebedeckten
Gipfel des Himalaja überquerte und sich im rosigen Schimmer der aufgehenden Sonne
dem Himmel näherte."

« Il n'est pas fréquent de retrouver une fois adulte ce sentiment de sa jeunesse qui donnait
l'impression que le temps ne passait pas, qui conférait à chaque évènement le mystère de
la nouveauté, ou permettait d'apprécier chaque expérience pour sa singularité. En vieillis-
sant …, seul quelque événement vraiment extraordinaire, à la fois nouveau et signifiant,
inhabituel et enthousiasmant, ravive l'innocence de ces années où chaque journée était
une précieuse aventure qui donnait un sens à la vie. C'est ce à quoi je pensais dans l'avion
qui survolait les sommets enneigés de l'Himalaya, se frayant son chemin à travers les
cieux dans l'éclat rose du soleil levant. »

HENRY KISSINGER (1923–), politician and Nobel Peace Prize laureate, 1979

→

Du Xiuxian, 1976

Nixon introduces Mao to his wife, Patricia, during the now disgraced U.S. president's second visit to China. Mao had by this time becoming terminally ill. He died in September 1976.

Der inzwischen zurückgetretene US-Präsident Nixon stellt bei seinen zweiten Besuch in China Mao seiner Frau Patricia vor. Mao war damals schon schwer krank; er starb im September 1976.

Nixon présente à Mao son épouse Patricia pendant la seconde visite en Chine du président déchu, alors que le leader chinois était gravement malade. Il mourut en Septembre 1976.

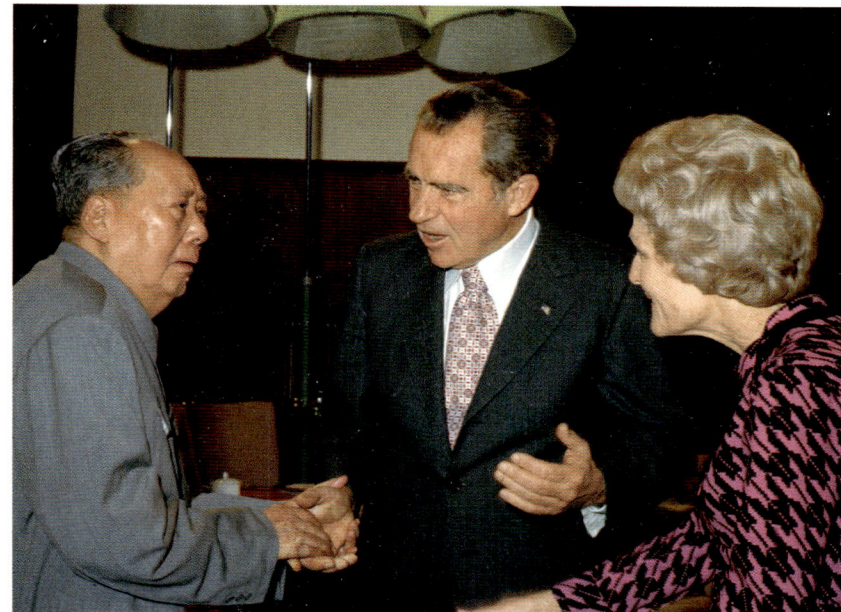

↓

Du Xiuxian, 1976

Taking tea in Mao's private study, former U.S. President Richard Nixon and Chairman Mao Zedong are seen toasting to better relations. In an effort to counter Soviet influence in eastern Europe and in Vietnam, where U.S. troops were entrenched, Nixon's gesture marked a ground-breaking diplomatic overture, and a willingness to rebuild Sino-U.S. relations. He came in February 1976 to bid farewell to Mao, who was by then visibly in decline.

Beim Tee in Maos privatem Arbeitszimmer stoßen der frühere US-Präsident Richard Nixon und der Vorsitzende Mao Zedong auf bessere Beziehungen an. In dem Bemühen, dem sowjetischen Einfluss in Osteuropa und Vietnam, wo die US-Truppen sich verschanzt hatten, entgegenzuwirken, markiert Nixons Geste eine bahnbrechende diplomatische Annäherung und die Bereitschaft, die chinesisch-amerikanischen Beziehungen wieder aufzunehmen. Nixon kehrte im Februar 1976 zurück, um von Mao Abschied zu nehmen, der schon sichtbar schwer krank war.

Prenant le thé dans le bureau privé du président chinois, Richard Nixon et Mao portent un toast à de meilleures relations. Dans une tentative de contrer l'influence soviétique en Europe de l'Est et au Vietnam, où les troupes américaines étaient embourbées, le geste de Nixon marquait une ouverture diplomatique sans précédent et la volonté de reconstruire les relations sino-américaines. Il revint dire adieu à Mao, alors très malade, en février 1976.

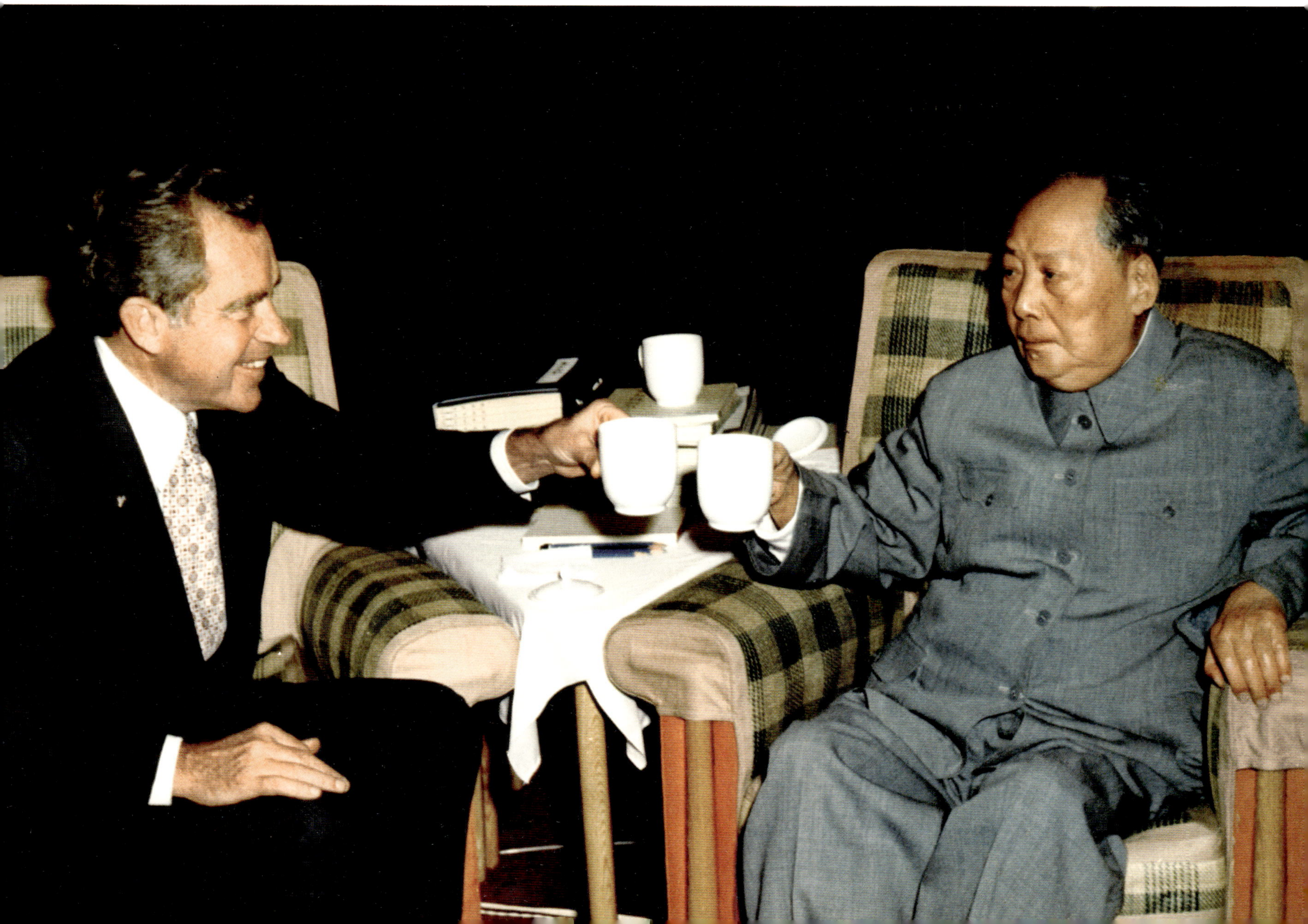

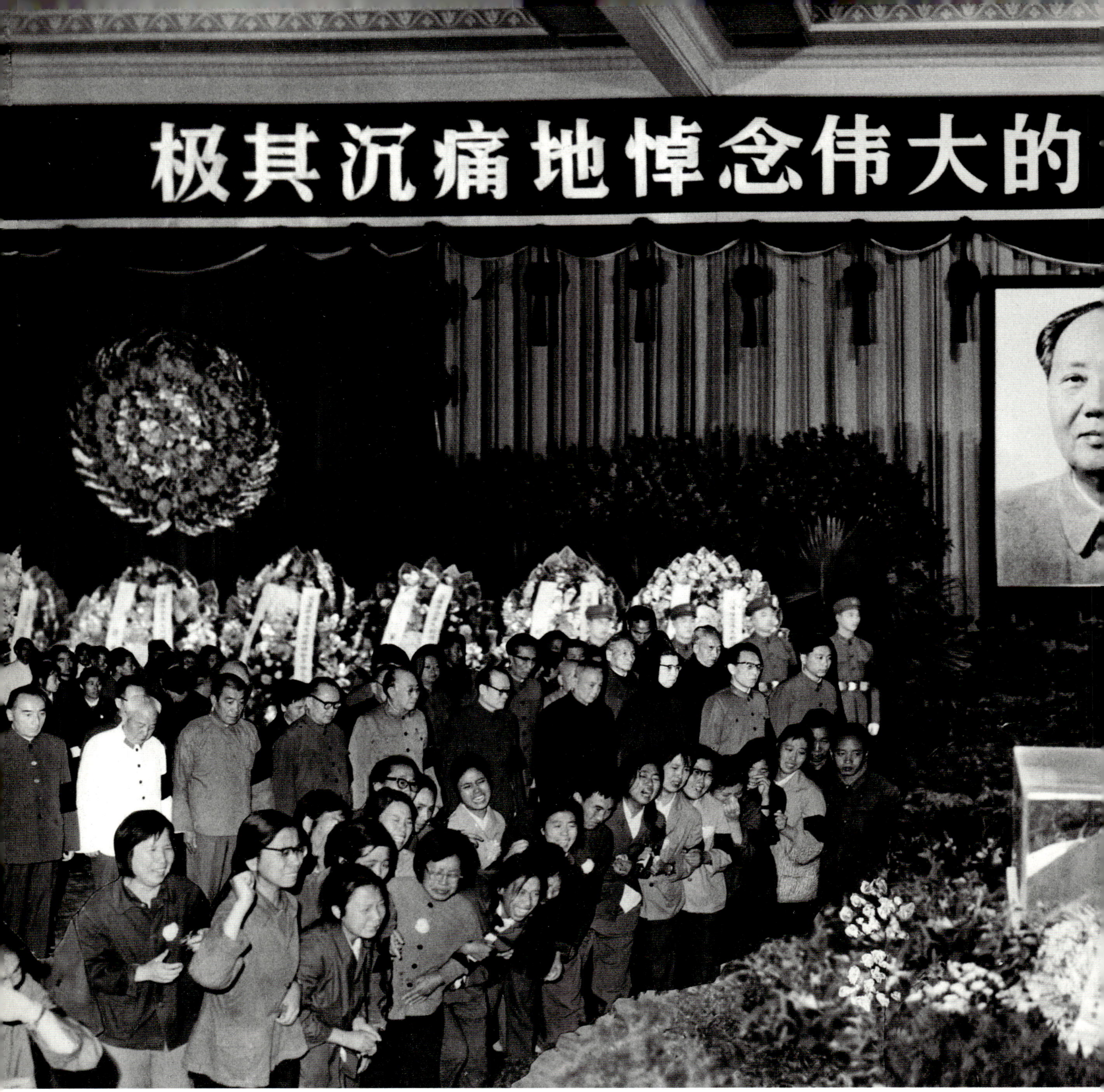

极其沉痛地悼念伟大的

"The citizens of China had not been told their leader was ill. They had traced Mao's physical decline only through occasional photographs of his rare visits with foreign dignitaries. The last of them was the photograph of Mao meeting with Laotian leader Kaysone Phomvihane in May 1976. The press continued to say [Mao] was healthy, but the photograph with Phomvihane proved that their leader had grown shockingly old."

„Man hatte den Chinesen nicht gesagt, dass ihr Führer krank war. Sie hatten den körperlichen Verfall Maos nur anhand gelegentlicher Fotografien bei seinen seltenen Zusammenkünften mit ausländischen Würdenträgern verfolgen können. Die letzte dieser Art war die Aufnahme von Mao beim Treffen mit dem laotischen Führer Kaysone Phomvihane im Mai 1976. In der Presse hieß es weiterhin, Mao sei gesund, aber das Foto mit Phomvihane bewies, dass ihr Führer erschreckend gealtert war."

« On n'avait pas dit aux citoyens chinois que leur chef était malade. Ils n'avaient perçu le déclin physique de Mao que sur quelques photographies prises lors des rares visites de dignitaires étrangers. La dernière d'entre elles fut une photographie de Mao rencontrant le responsable laotien Kaysone Phomvihane en mai 1976. La presse continuait à dire qu'il était en bonne santé, mais la photo avec Phomvihane prouvait que le grand leader avait terriblement vieilli. »

LI ZHISUI (1919–1995), former private doctor to Mao Zedong

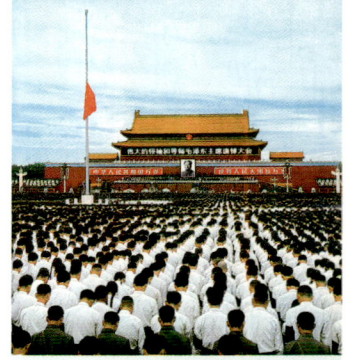

伟大的领袖和导师毛泽东主席永垂不朽!

人民画报 1976 11

China Pictorial, November 1976

Memorial issue, for Chairman Mao

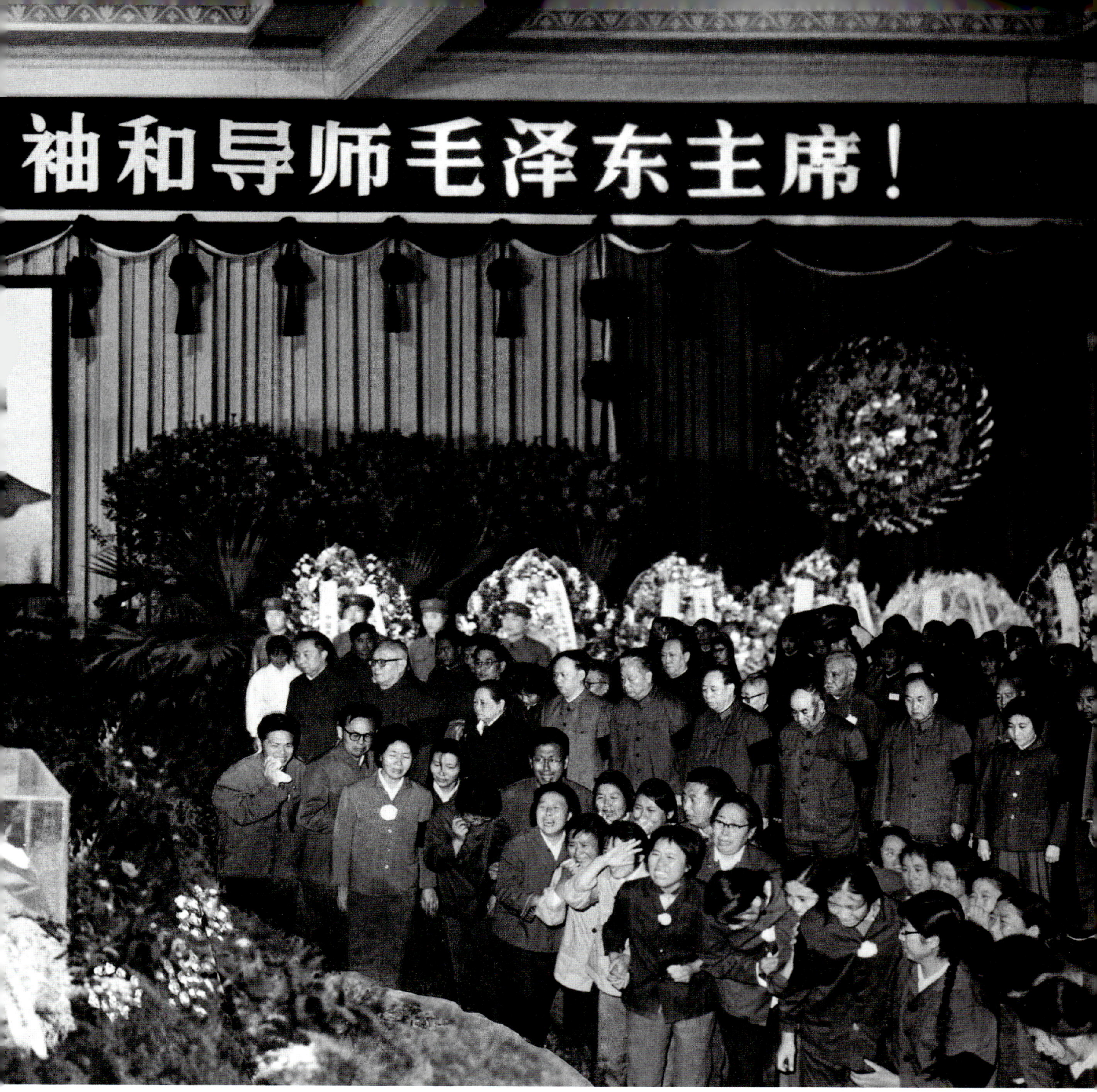

袖和导师毛泽东主席！

↑ →
Du Xiuxian, 1976

Mao died on September 9, 1976, which plunged the PRC into mourning. His funeral was attended by thousands.

Mao stirbt am 9. September 1976 und stürzt die Volksrepublik in tiefe Trauer. Seiner Beisetzung wohnten Tausende bei.

Mao meurt le 9 septembre 1976, ce qui plonge le Parti communiste dans le deuil. Ses funérailles sont suivies par des milliers de personnes.

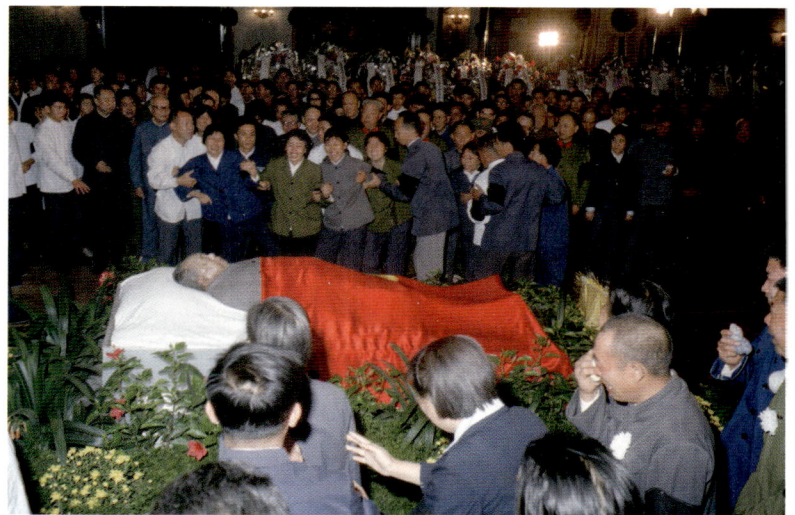

260

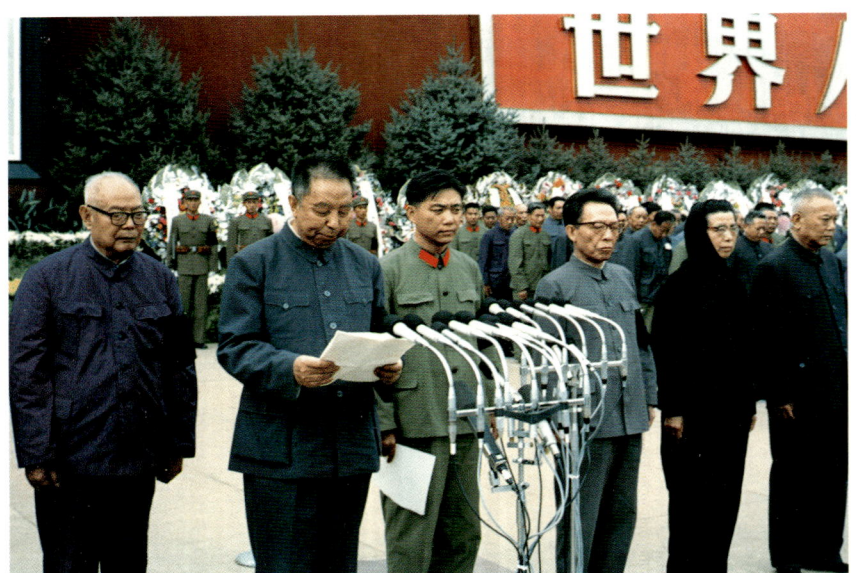

←

Du Xiuxian, 1976

At the state funeral for Chairman Mao, his designated successor, Hua Guofeng (second from left) reads a eulogy in honor of the deceased. To the left is Marshal Ye Jianying, who would shortly after lead the arrest of the Gang of Four. Three of the four stand on the right: Wang Hongwen, Zhang Chunqiao, and Jiang Qing. To the right of Jiang Qing is Li Xiannian, who aided Marshal Ye in the arrest.

Beim Staatsbegräbnis für den Vorsitzenden Mao verliest sein designierter Nachfolger Hua Guofeng (zweiter von links) eine Laudatio für den Verstorbenen. Zu seiner Linken steht Marschall Ye Jianying, der wenig später die Verhaftung der Viererbande leiten sollte. Drei der vier stehen rechts von ihm: Wang Hongwen, Zhang Chunqiao und Jiang Qing. Rechts von ihr steht Li Xiannian, der Marschall Ye bei der Verhaftung unterstützte.

Aux funérailles officielles de Mao, son successeur désigné, Hua Guofeng (second à gauche), lit un hommage au défunt. À sa gauche figure le maréchal Ye Jianying qui, peu après, fera arrêter la Bande des quatre. Trois d'entre eux sont à sa droite : Wang Hongwen, Zhang Chunqiao et Jiang Qing. À sa droite, Li Xiannian qui collaborera avec le maréchal Ye dans la mise au point de l'arrestation.

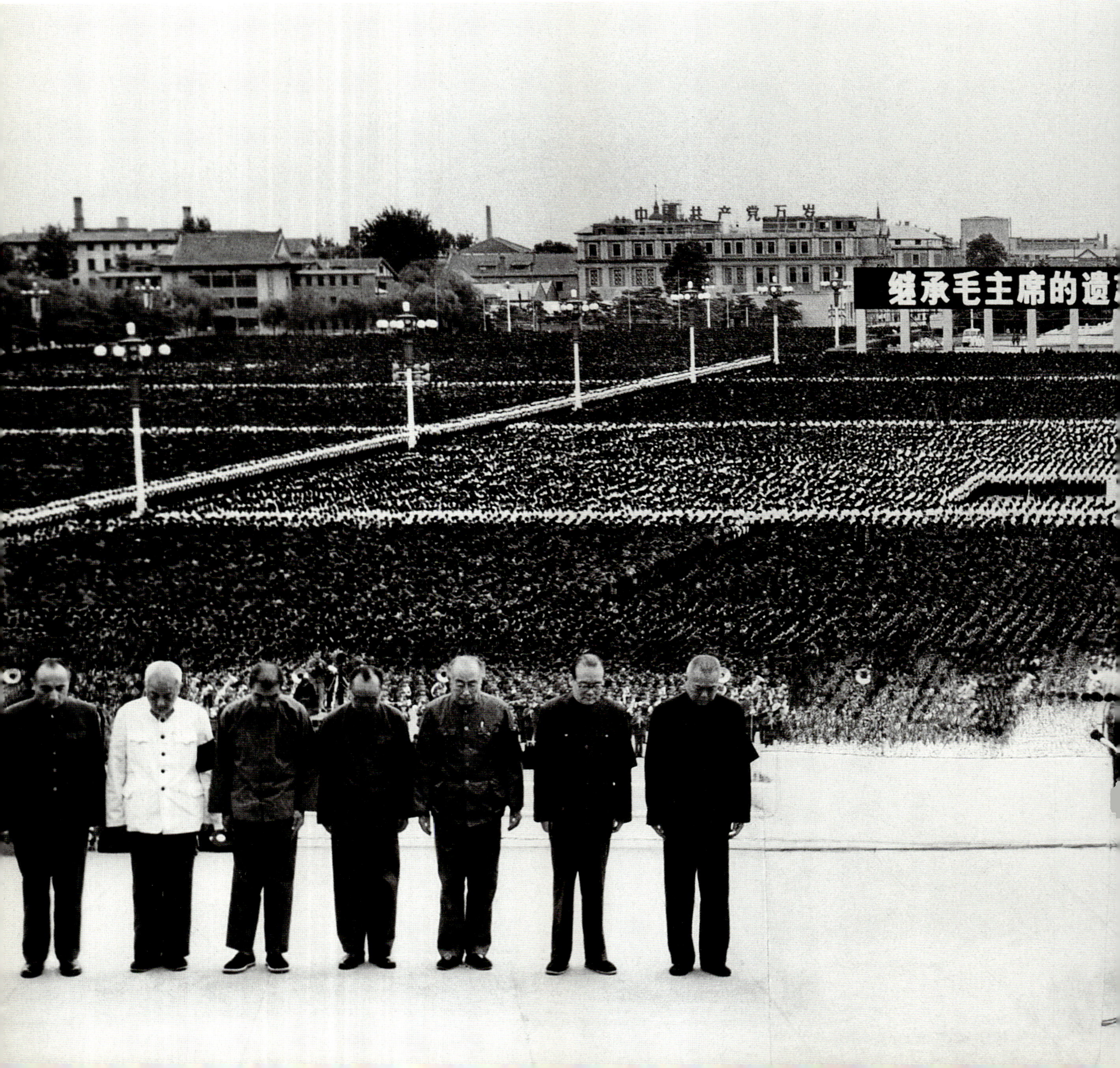

Xinhua News Agency, 1976

Chinese leaders headed by Hua Guofeng (center, behind the microphones) conduct the funeral service for Chairman Mao. Behind the leaders, a million people stand in mourning in Tiananmen Square. The state-owned news agency has airbrushed out the members of the Gang of Four from this group photo (see opposite page).

Die chinesischen Führer unter Leitung von Hua Guofeng (in der Mitte hinter den Mikrofonen) leiten die Beisetzungsfeierlichkeiten des Vorsitzenden Mao. Hinter ihnen stehen eine Million Trauernde auf dem Tiananmen-Platz. Die staatliche Nachrichtenagentur hat die Mitglieder der Viererbande aus diesem Gruppenfoto herausretuschiert (vgl. Abb. auf der gegenüberliegenden Seite).

Les responsables chinois sous l'autorité de Hua Guofeng (au centre, derrière le micro) conduisent les funérailles officielles de Mao. Derrière, un million de personnes est réuni place Tian'anmen. L'agence de presse gouvernementale a retouché cette photo de groupe pour en effacer les membres de la Bande des quatre (voir page ci-contre).

"We must carry on Chairman Mao's legacy and consolidate the great unity of the people of all nationalities under the leadership of the working class and based on the worker-peasant alliance, deepen the criticism of Deng Xiaoping, continue the struggle to repulse the Right deviationist attempt at reversing correct verdicts, consolidate and develop the victories of the Great Proletarian Cultural Revolution, enthusiastically support the socialist new things, restrict the bourgeois right and further consolidate the dictatorship of the proletariat in our country."

„Wir müssen die Sache, die der Vorsitzenden Mao uns hinterlassen hat, weiterführen und die große Einigkeit der Menschen aller Nationalitäten unter der Führung der Arbeiterklasse und der Allianz von Bauern und Arbeitern festigen, die Kritik an Deng Xiaoping verstärken, den Kampf gegen die rechten abweichlerischen Versuche, gerechte Urteile umzukehren, vorantreiben, die Siege der Großen Kulturrevolution stärken und weiterentwickeln, mit Eifer die neuen sozialistischen Dinge unterstützen, die bürgerlichen Rechte einschränken und die Diktatur des Proletariats in unserem Land weiter stärken."

« Nous devons poursuivre sur la voie du Président Mao et consolider la grande unité de toutes les nationalités qui constituent notre peuple sous le leadership de la classe ouvrière et en nous appuyant sur l'alliance de l'ouvrier et du paysan, approfondir la critique de Deng Xiaoping, poursuivre le combat pour repousser les tentatives déviationnistes de droite d'inverser des décisions correctes, consolider et développer les victoires de la Grande Révolution culturelle prolétarienne, soutenir avec enthousiasme les nouveaux apports du socialisme, restreindre les droits bourgeois et consolider davantage encore la dictature du prolétariat dans notre pays. »

XINHUA NEWS AGENCY, Chinese State news agency, 1976

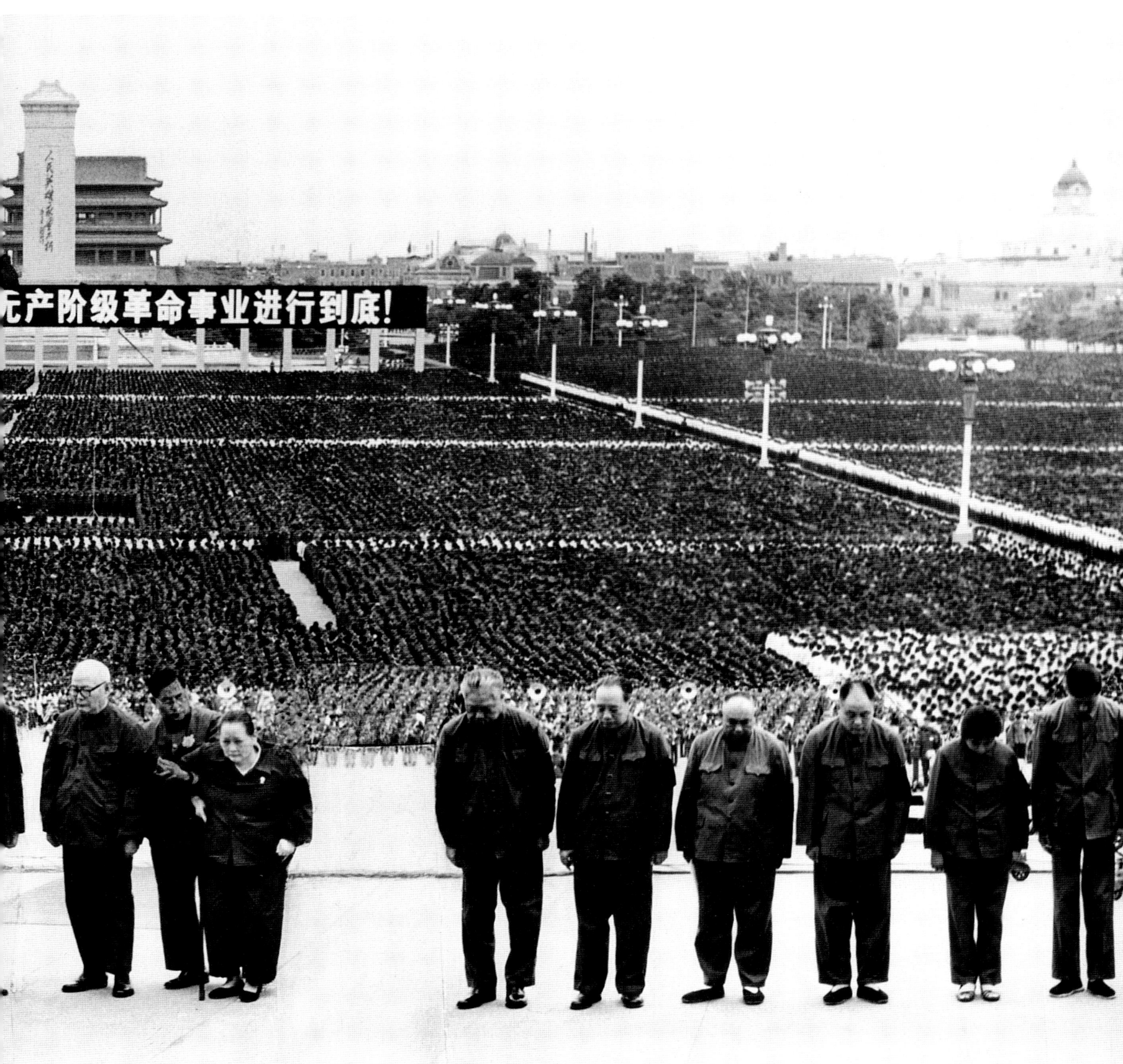

"The Chinese seemed to be mourning Mao in a heartfelt fashion. But I wondered how many of their tears were genuine. People had practiced acting to such a degree that they confused it with their true feelings. Weeping for Mao was perhaps just another programmed act in their programmed lives."

„Die Chinesen schienen um Mao aufrichtig zu trauern. Aber ich fragte mich, wie viele ihrer Tränen echt waren. Die Menschen hatten in einem solchen Maß gelernt, sich zu verstellen, dass sie das Schauspielern mit ihren wahren Gefühlen verwechselten. Weinen um Mao war vielleicht nur eine weitere programmierte Nummer in ihrem programmierten Leben."

« Les Chinois semblaient pleurer Mao du fond de leur cœur. Mais je me demandais si ces larmes étaient vraiment authentiques. Les gens avaient appris à jouer à un point tel qu'ils confondaient ce jeu avec leurs vrais sentiments. Pleurer Mao n'était peut-être qu'un autre de ces innombrables actes programmés dans leurs vies programmées. »

JUNG CHANG (1952–), author, 1992

→
Jiang Shaowu, 1976
Red Guards in Shenyang, Liaoning province, mourning the death of Chairman Mao.

Rote Garden in Shenyang in der Provinz Liaoning betrauern den Tod des Vorsitzenden Mao.

Des Gardes rouges de Shenyang, province du Liaoning, pleurent la mort du Président Mao.

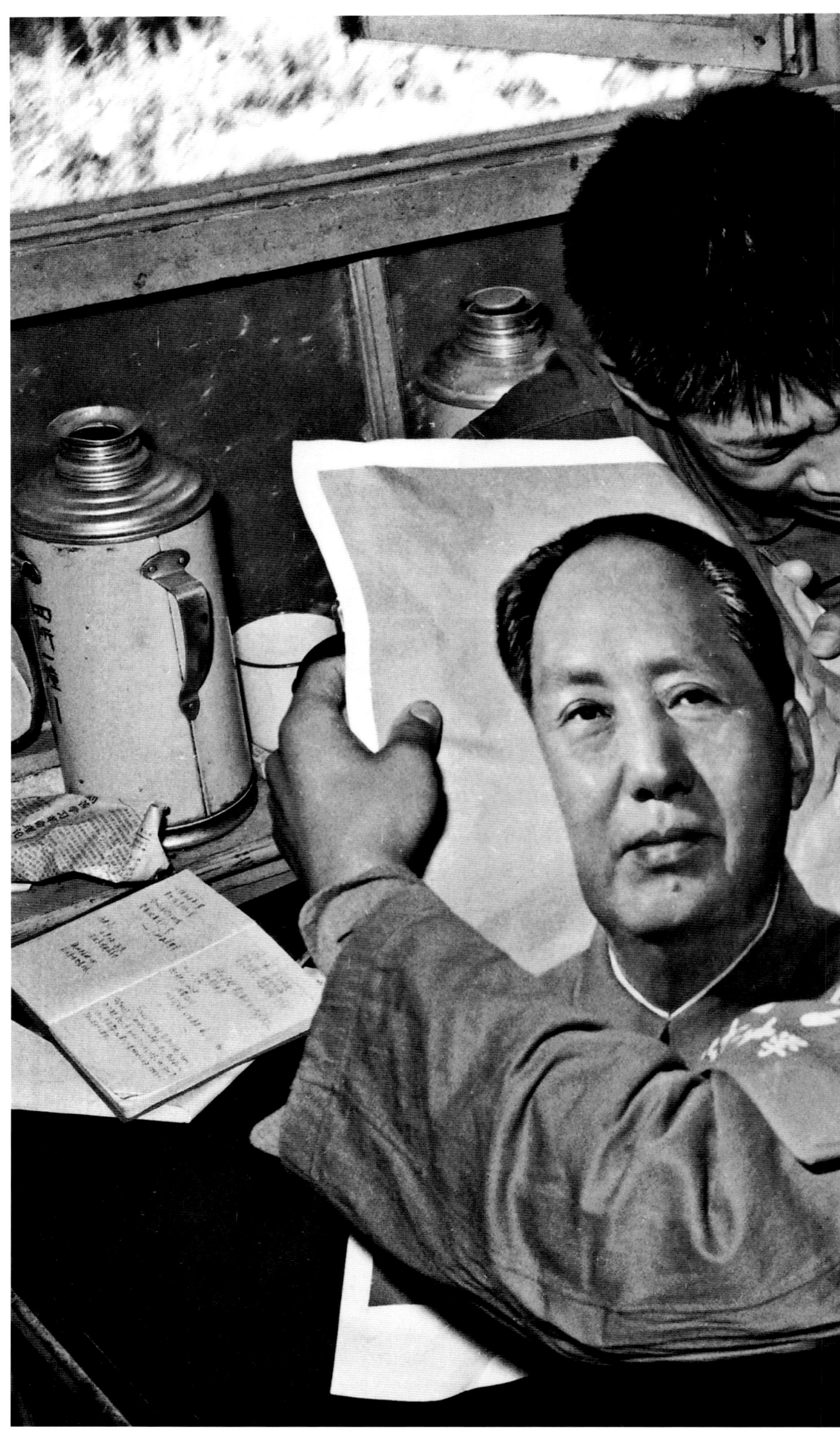

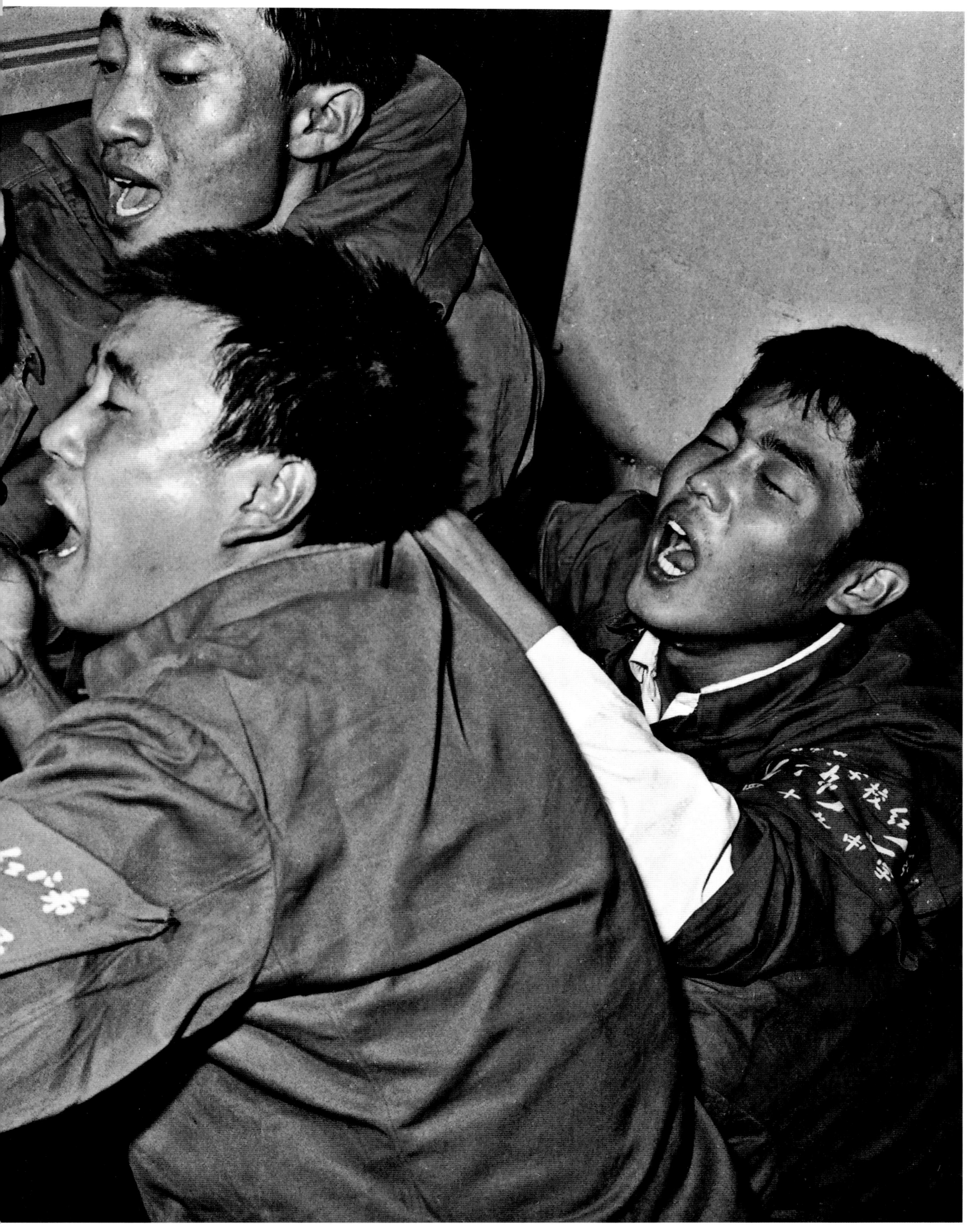

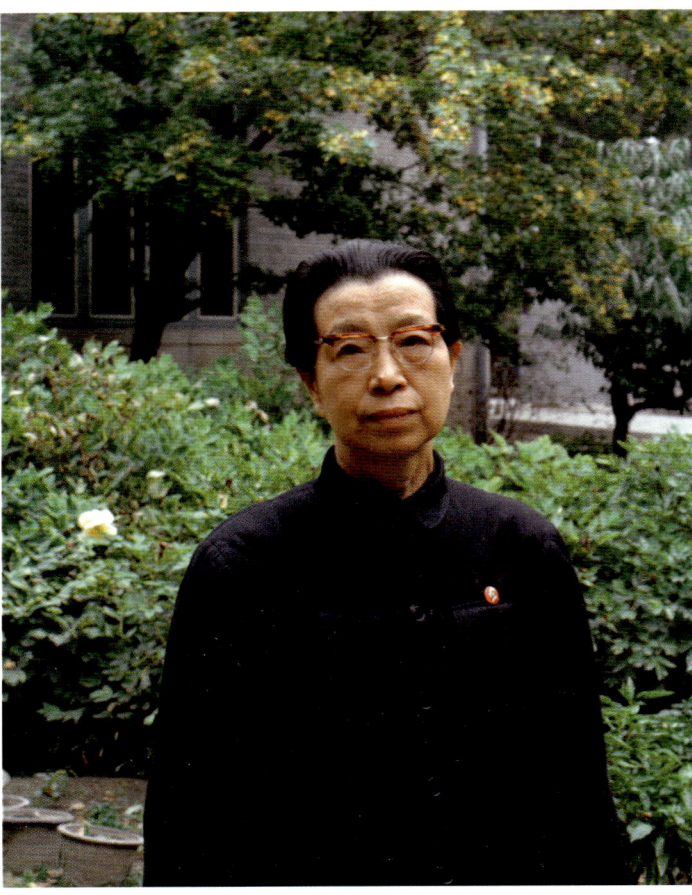

↑
Du Xiuxian, 1976

*Jiang Qing, seen here in the black dress of
mourning for Mao, is captured in the last
known portrait of her as a free woman.
She was arrested on the same day this
photograph was taken, and remained a
prisoner until she died, in 1991.*

*Dies ist das letzte bekannte Porträt Jiang
Qings in Freiheit, die hier in schwarzer
Trauerkleidung für Mao zu sehen ist. Sie
wurde kurz nachdem diese Aufnahme
gemacht wurde verhaftet und blieb bis
zu ihrem Tod 1991 in Haft.*

*Dernier portrait de Jiang Qing libre, en tenue
de deuil après la mort de Mao. Elle fut arrêtée
le jour même de cette prise de vue et resta
prisonnière jusqu'à sa mort en 1991.*

→
Du Xiuxian, 1976

*Members of the elite Politburo of the CCP,
headed by Chairman Hua Guofeng (third
from left) and Jiang Qing (far left) at a
meeting in early October, following Mao's
death. Two members of the Gang of Four
did not attend this meeting. Two days later,
members of the Gang of Four were called
to meet with the Politburo again, and were
arrested one by one as they arrived at the
appointed meeting. This officially brought
the Mao era to an end.*

*Mitglieder des elitären Politbüros der KPCh
unter Führung des Vorsitzenden Hua Guofeng
(Dritter von links) und Jiang Qing (Erste
von links) treffen sich Anfang Oktober nach
Maos Tod. Zwei Mitglieder der Viererbande
nahmen nicht an diesem Treffen teil. Zwei
Tage später wurden die Mitglieder der
Viererbande erneut zu einem Treffen mit
dem Politbüro einberufen und verhaftet, als
sie einer nach dem anderen zu dem verein-
barten Treffen kamen. Dies bedeutete das
offizielle Ende der Mao-Ära.*

*Des membres de l'élite du Bureau politique
présidé par Hua Guofeng (troisième à partir
de la gauche) et Jiang Qing (première à partir
de la gauche) sont réunis début octobre après
la mort de Mao. Deux de la Bande des quatre
n'assistent pas à la réunion. Deux jours plus
tard, la Bande est convoquée au Bureau et
chacun de ses membres est arrêté à son arrivée,
ce qui marque officiellement la fin de l'ère
de Mao.*

"To serve me is to serve the people."

„Mir zu dienen, heißt dem Volk zu dienen."

« Me servir, c'est servir le peuple. »

**JIANG QING (1914–1991), last wife of Chairman Mao
and leader of the Gang of Four**

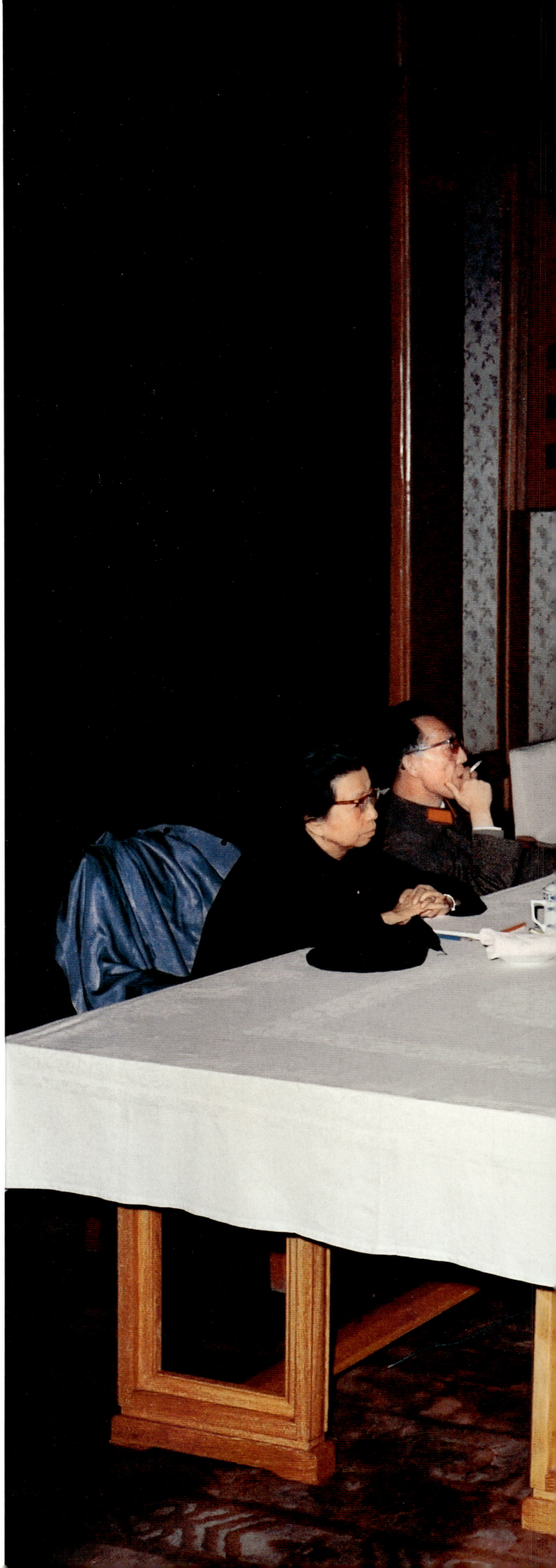

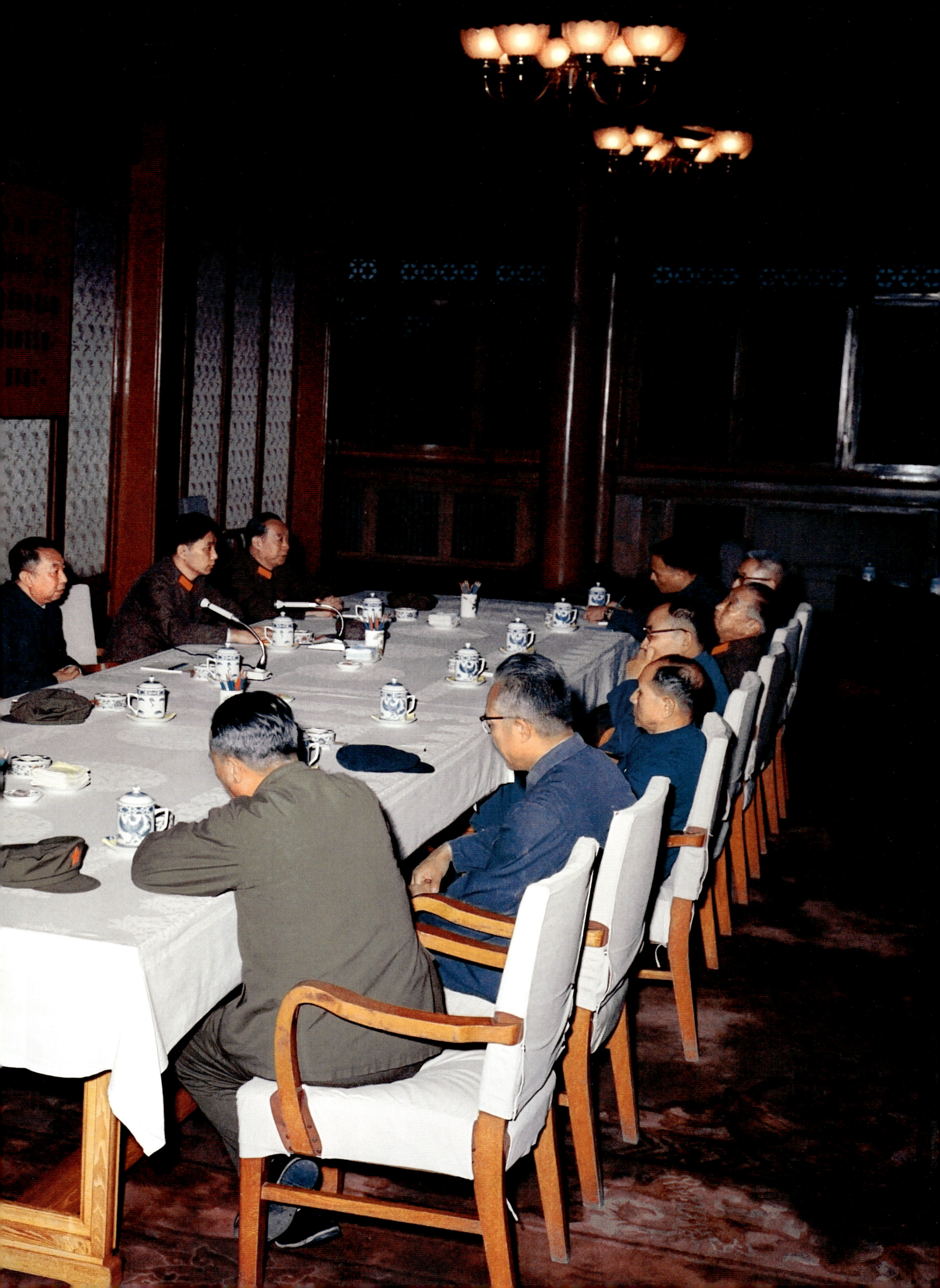

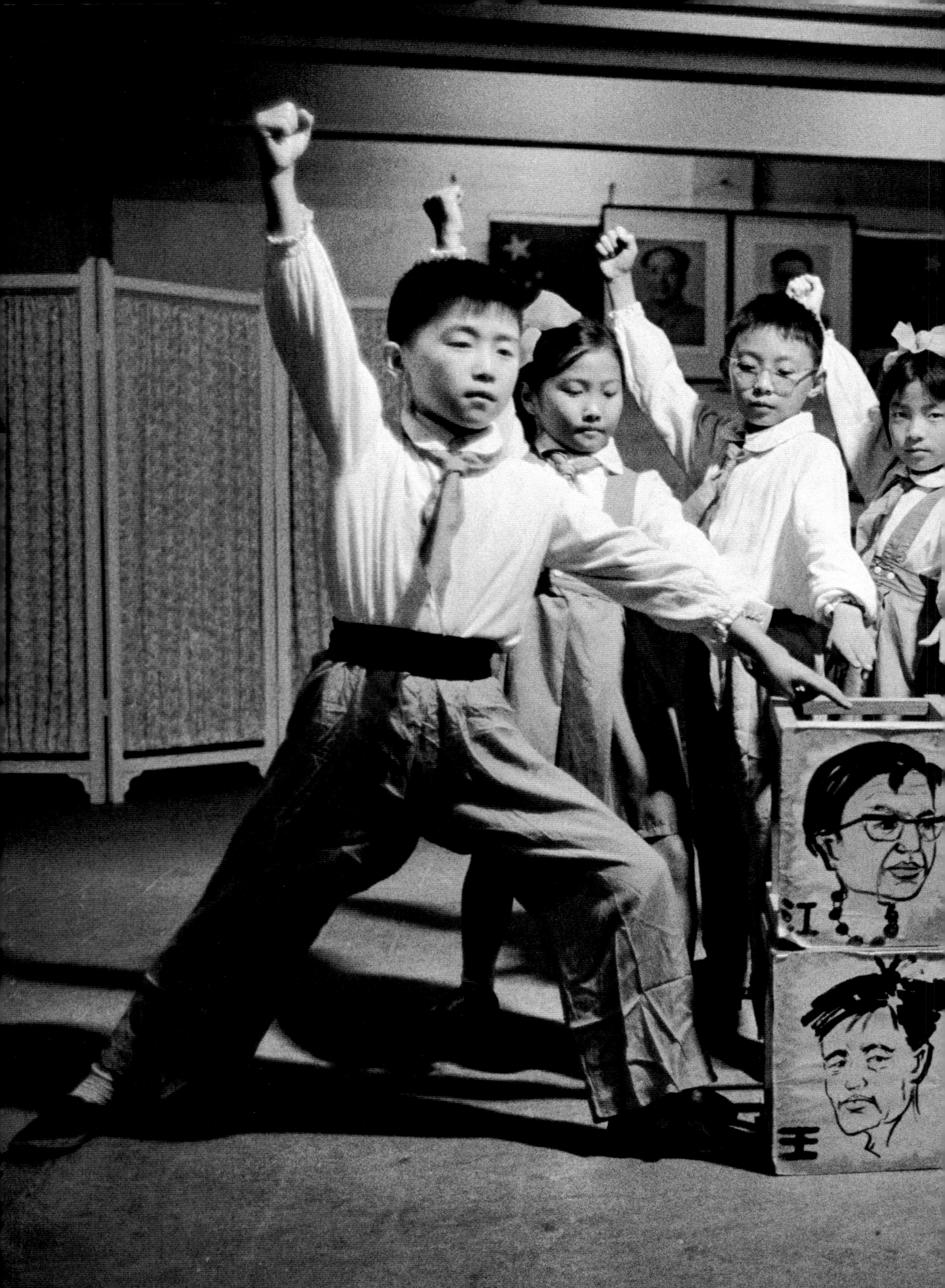

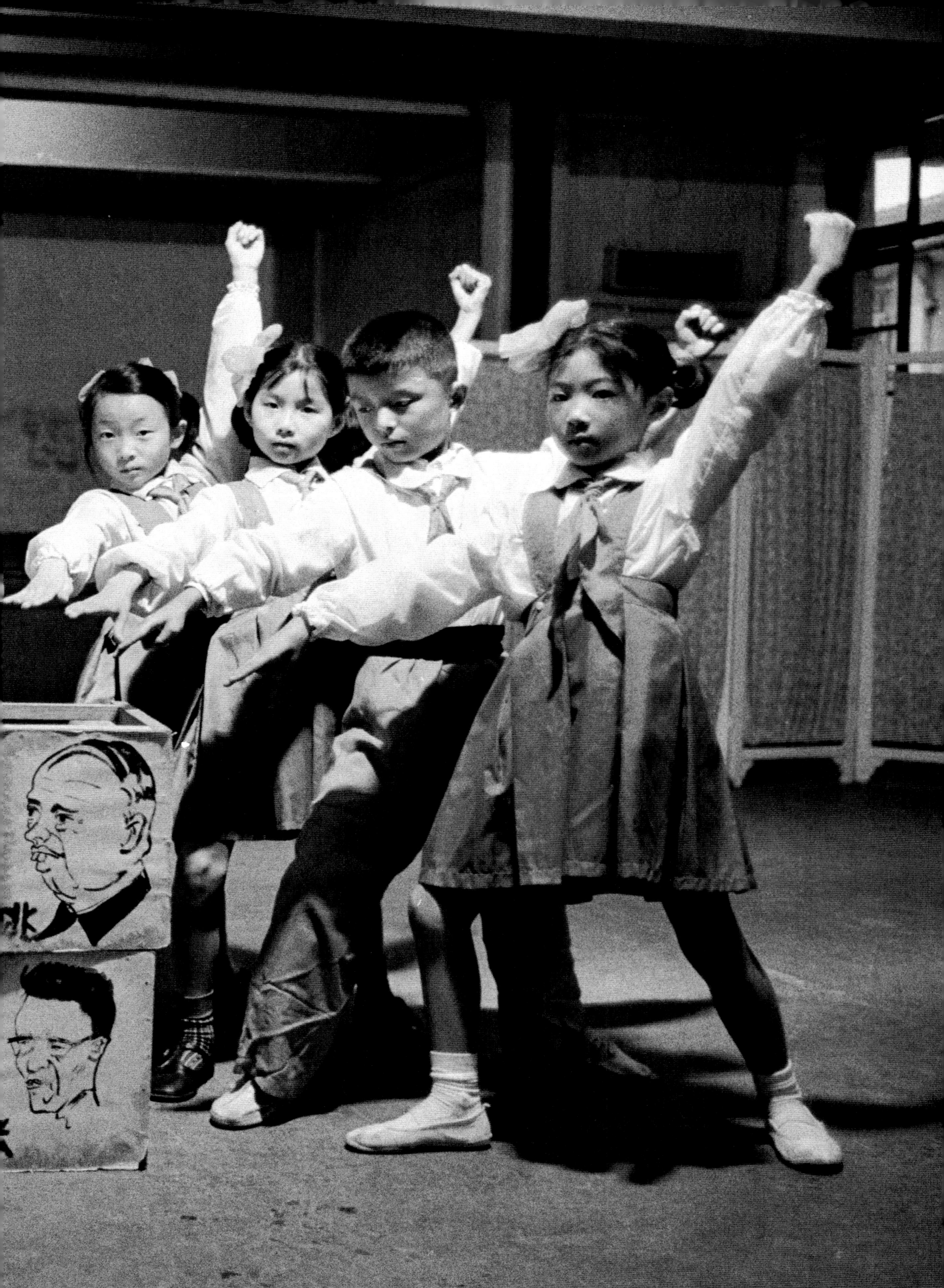

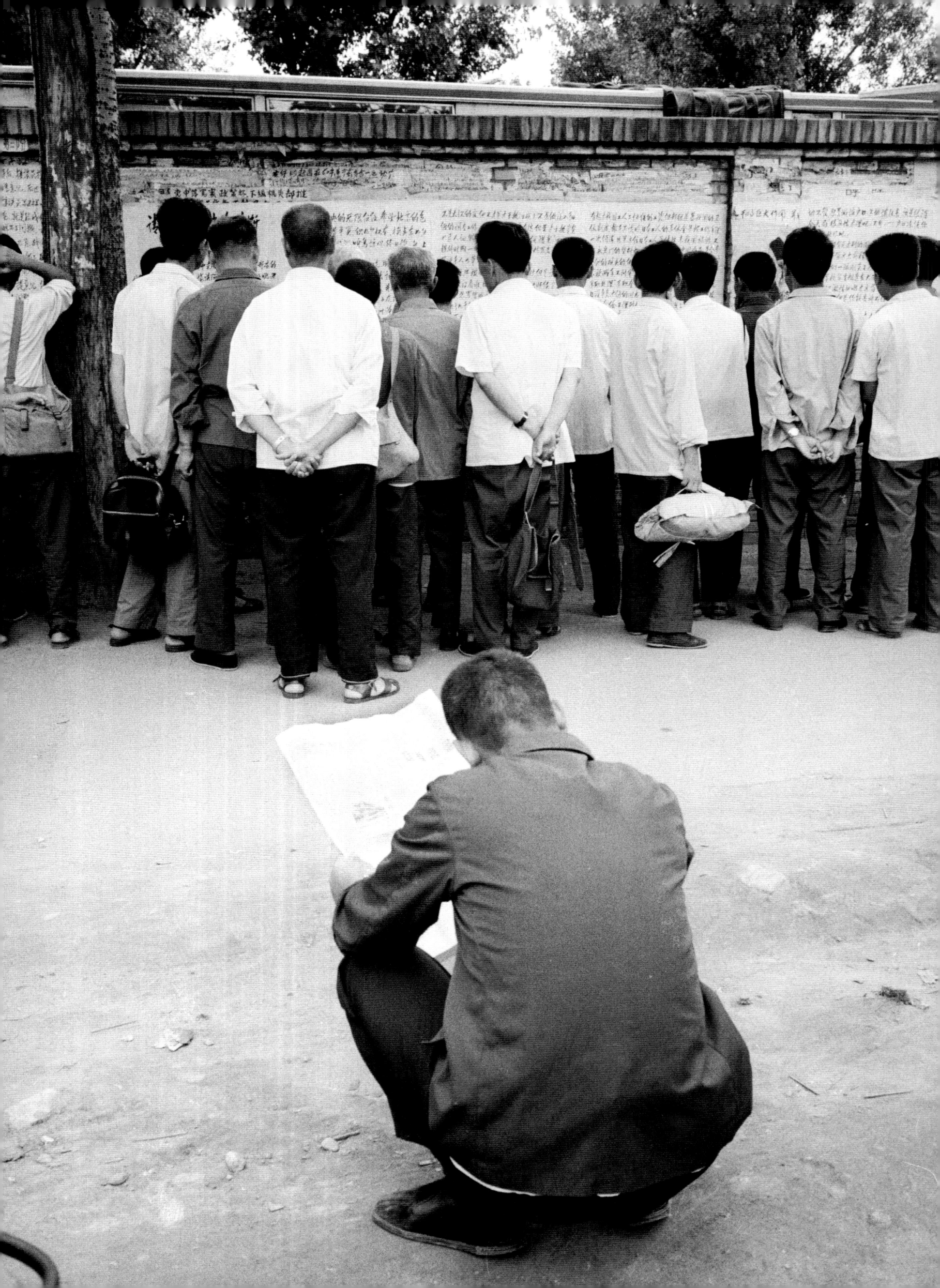

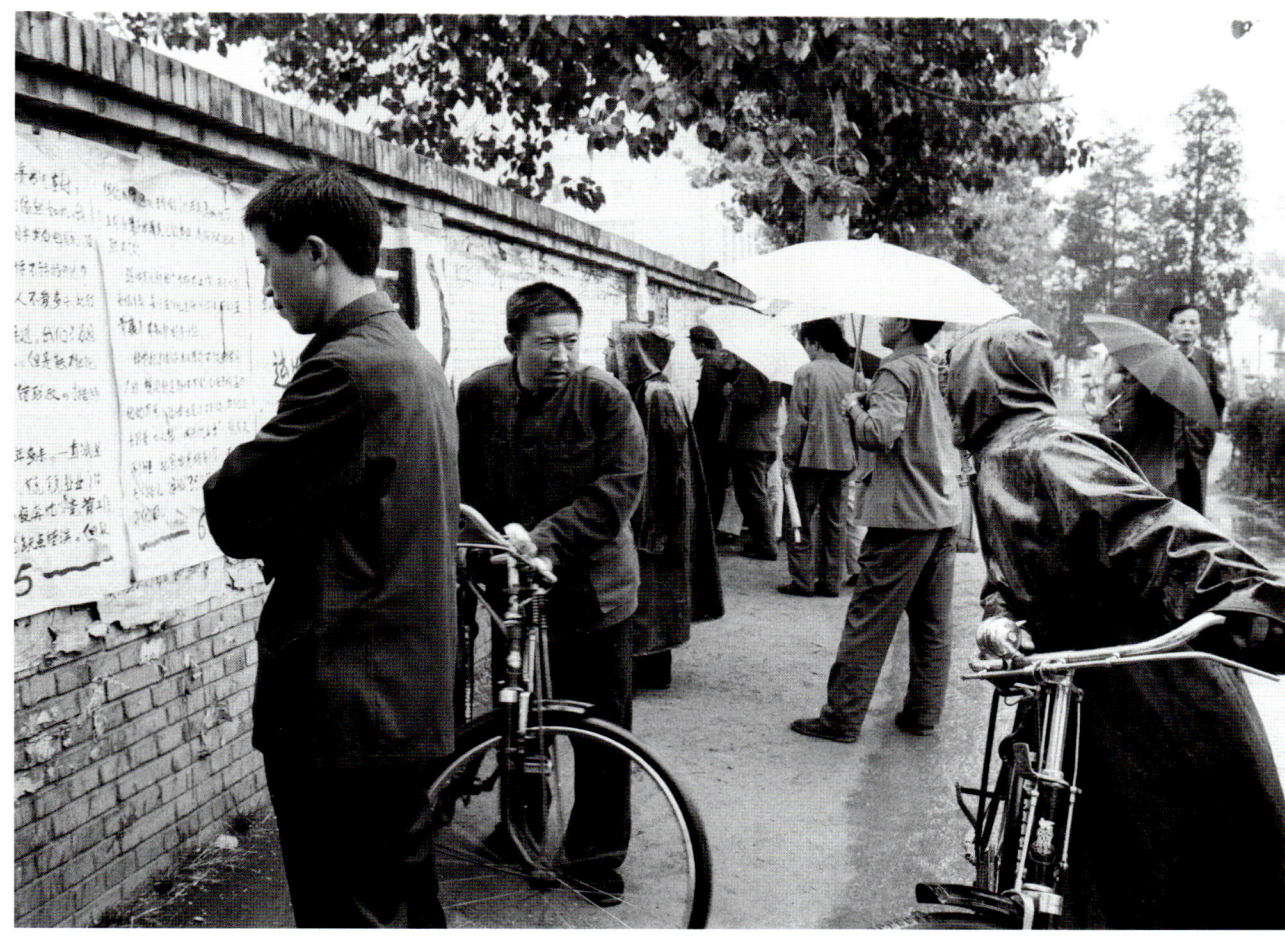

pp. 266/267
Liu Heung Shing, 1977

Young pioneers in Shanghai perform a skit denouncing the disgraced Gang of Four led by Mao's widow, Jiang Qing. The Gang of Four was arrested by Marshal Ye Jianying in October 1976. Jiang Qing is portrayed in the caricature (top left), with the other members: the literary critic Yao Wenyuan (top right), Wang Hongwen (bottom left), and the Communist Party theorist Zhang Chunqiao (bottom right).

Junge Pioniere in Shanghai führen einen Sketch auf, der die in Ungnade gefallene Viererbande anprangert. Sie wurde im Oktober 1976 von Marschall Ye Jianying verhaftet. Jiang Qing ist auf der Karikatur oben links neben den übrigen Mitgliedern dargestellt, dem Literaturkritiker Yao Wenyuan (oben rechts), Wang Hongwen (unten links) und dem Theoretiker der kommunistischen Partei Zhang Chunqiao (unten rechts).

De jeunes pionniers de Shanghai jouent un sketch dénonçant la Bande des quatre animée par la veuve de Mao et arrêtée par le maréchal Ye Jianying en octobre 1976. Jiang Qing est représentée en haut à gauche avec les autres membres, le critique littéraire Yao Wenyuan (en haut à droite), Wang Hongwen (en bas à gauche) et le théoricien communiste Zhang Chunqiao (en bas à droite).

← ↑
Liu Heung Shing, 1979

In the spring of 1979, a bus depot on the west side of Beijing was the focus of attention as local residents flocked to read the growing number of hand-written "big character" posters on its walls, which criticized the government and aired personal grievances. It was dubbed China's "Democracy Wall," and was largely tolerated by Deng Xiaoping's reformist government—itself busy implementing the Four Modernizations—until one young "dissident" used his poster to urge the government to adopt democracy as the fifth modernization. He was arrested and sentenced to 15 years' imprisonment. The man squatting in the foreground keeps his focus on the official newspaper, the People's Daily.

Im Frühjahr 1979 wird ein Busdepot im Westen von Peking zum Zentrum der Aufmerksamkeit, da die Anwohner herbeiströmen, um die wachsende Zahl handgeschriebener Plakate mit großen Schriftzeichen an seinen Mauern zu lesen, auf denen die Regierung kritisiert und persönliche Unbill geschildert wird. Sie wird Chinas Mauer der Demokratie genannt und von Deng Xiaopings reformistischer Regierung – selbst damit beschäftigt, die Vier Modernisierungen einzuführen – weitgehend toleriert, bis ein junger Dissident auf seinem Poster die Regierung auffordert, Demokratie als Fünfte Modernisierung zu übernehmen. Er wird festgenommen und zu 15 Jahren Gefängnis verurteilt. Der im Vordergrund hockende Mann konzentriert sich auf die offizielle Zeitung, die People's Daily.

Au printemps 1979, un dépôt de bus des quartiers ouest de Pékin devint le centre de tous les regards lorsque les habitants commencèrent à s'intéresser au nombre grandissant d'affichettes en « grands caractères » collées sur les murs, qui critiquaient le gouvernement et exprimaient des doléances personnelles. L'endroit fut surnommé le Mur de la démocratie chinoise et fut longtemps toléré par le gouvernement réformiste de Deng Xiaoping – lui-même très occupé par la mise en place des Quatre modernisations – jusqu'à ce qu'un jeune dissident demande au gouvernement d'adopter la démocratie, la cinquième modernisation. Il fut arrêté et condamné à 15 ans de prison. L'homme au premier plan se concentre sur la lecture du journal gouvernemental, le People's Daily.

→
Liu Heung Shing, 1979

Artists and intellectuals who call themselves the "Stars Painting Group" march towards City Hall in Beijing to demand "freedom for art."

Künstler und Intellektuelle, die sich die „Stars Painting Group" nennen, marschieren zum Rathaus von Peking, um „Freiheit für die Kunst" zu fordern.

Des artistes et des intellectuels qui s'appellent eux-mêmes « Stars Painting Group » défile vers l'hôtel de ville pour demander la « liberté pour l'art. »

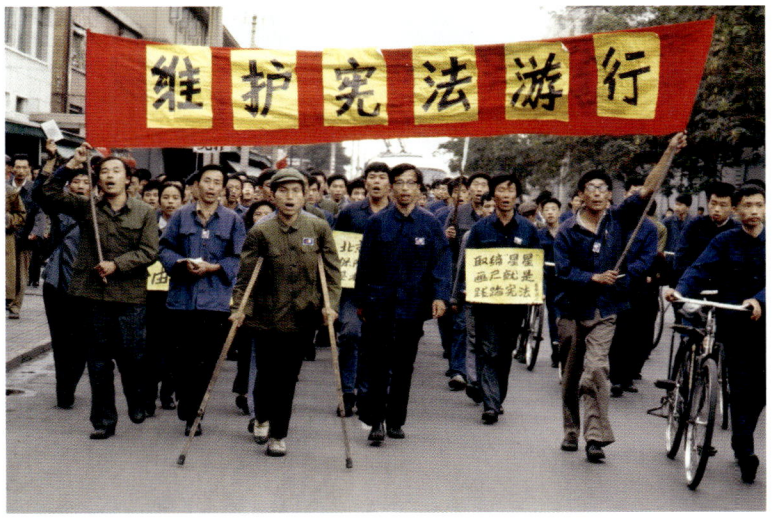

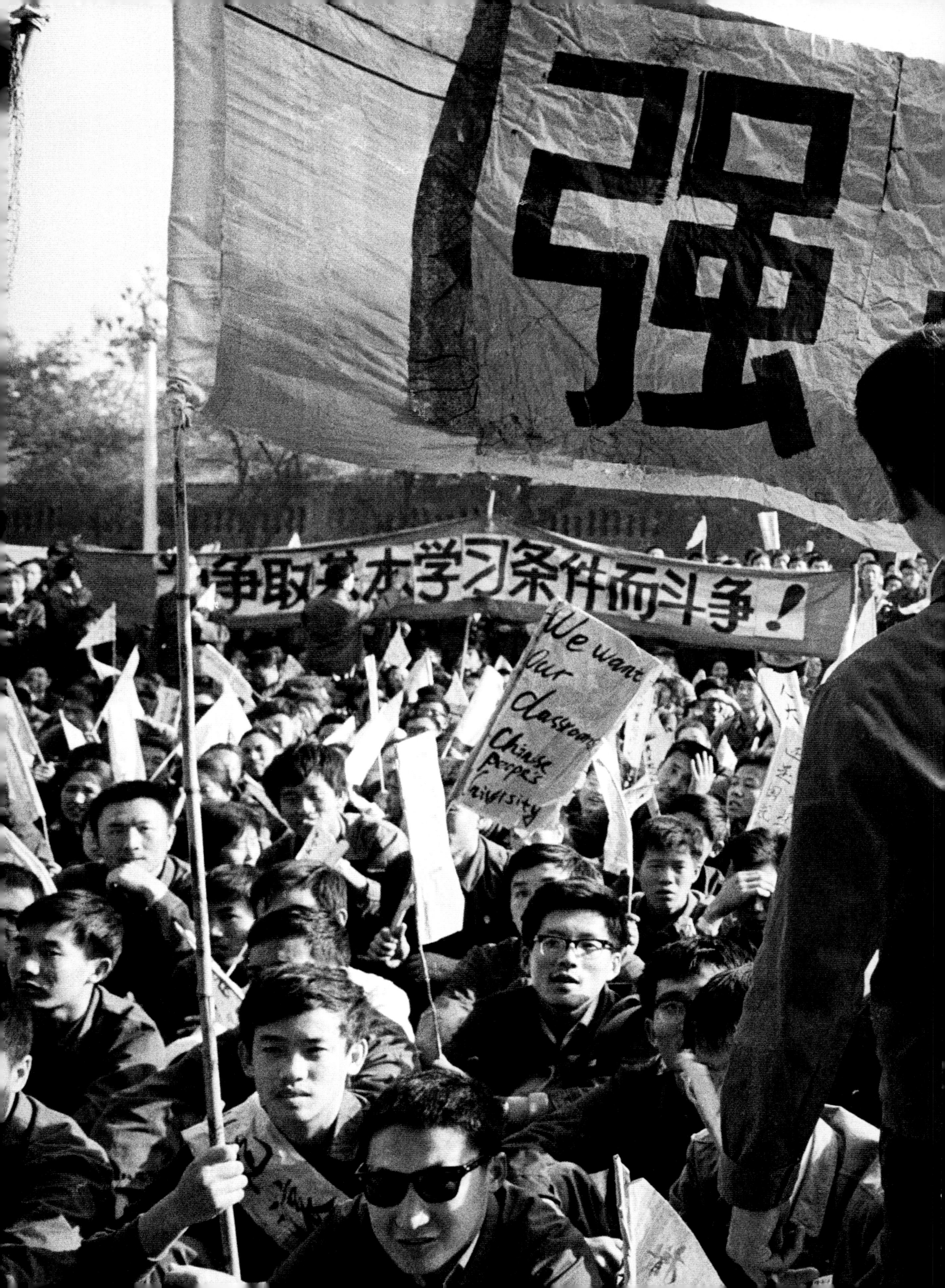

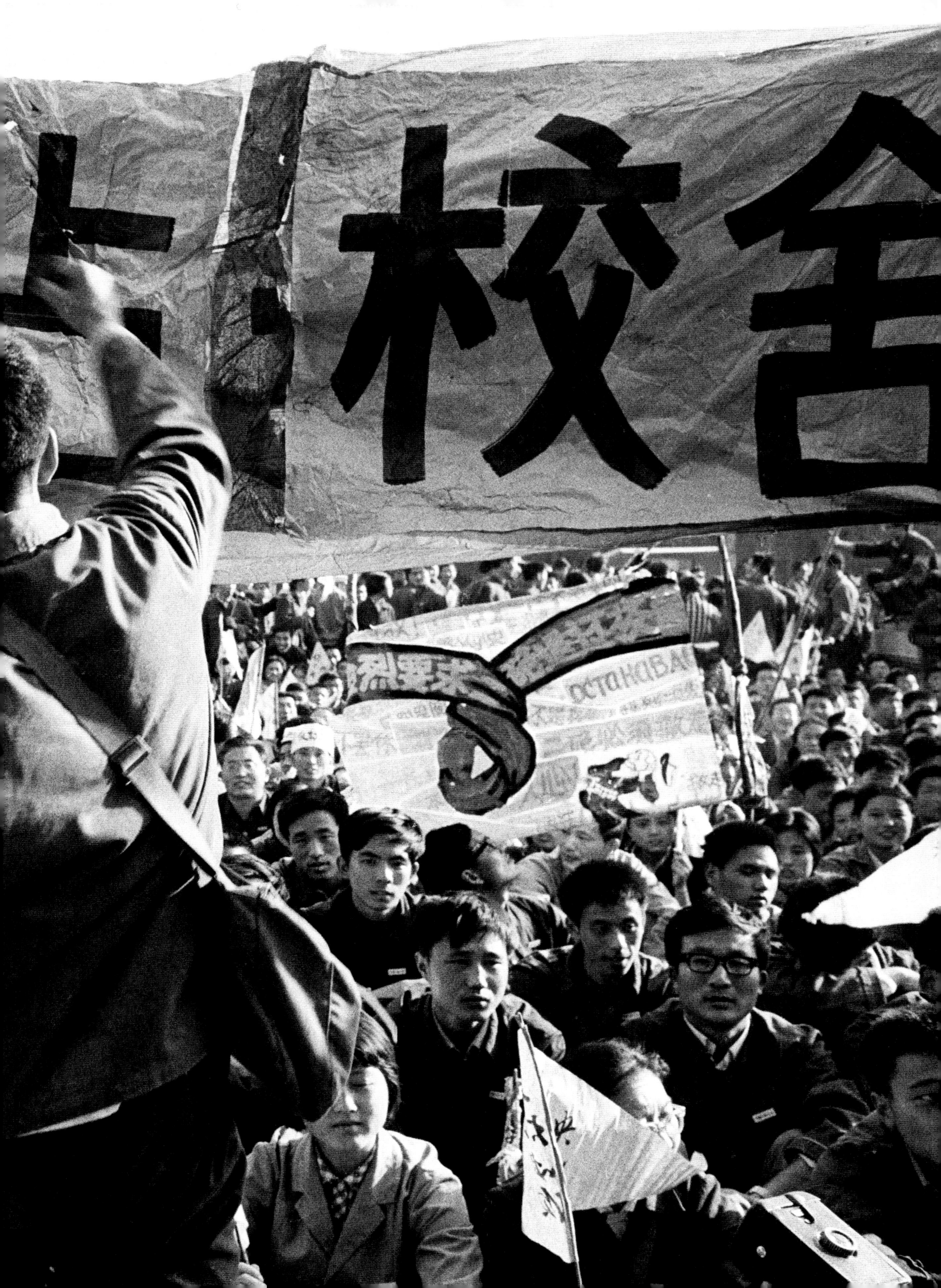

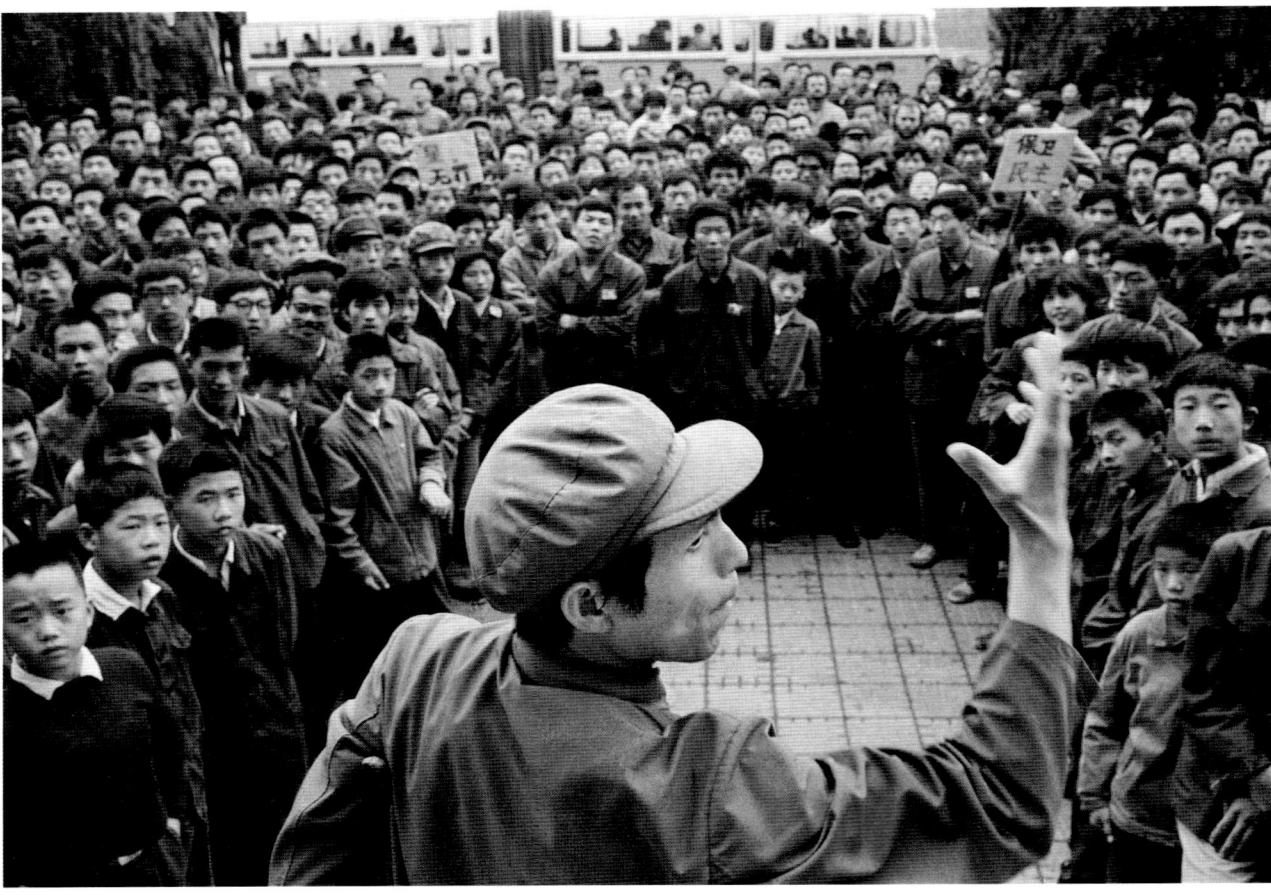

↑
Liu Heung Shing, 1979

Chinese artist, and leader of the "Stars Paint-ing Group," Ma Desheng, speaks on the steps of the municipal government offices in Beijing to demand freedom for art. He subsequently found "artistic freedom" in France, where he lives today.

Ma Desheng, chinesischer Künstler und Anführer der „Stars Painting Group", spricht auf den Stufen des Rathauses und fordert Freiheit für die Kunst. Er fand später in Frankreich ‚künstlerische Freiheit", wo er noch immer lebt.

Ma Desheng, artiste chinois et leader du « Stars Painting Group », prend la parole sur les marches de l'hôtel de ville de Pékin pour réclamer la liberté artistique. Il trouva finalement cette liberté en France où il vit actuellement.

"Over the last ten years, the more intellectuals have fought for the reforms launched by Deng, the more they have been attacked for breaching the Four Cardinal Principles, including the violation of Marxist-Leninist Mao Zedong Thought. Since the reforms are totally opposed to the economic ideas of Mao, the officials launching reforms have found it necessary to proclaim their unanimous loyalty to the Four Cardinal Principles. In fact, these principles, which have been put into a constitution that guarantees freedom of thought and expression, do not belong there. I suppose these weird juxtapositions can only happen in China."

„Im Lauf der letzten zehn Jahre galt, je mehr die Intellektuellen für die von Deng angestoßenen Reformen kämpften, desto mehr wurden sie des Verstoßes gegen die Vier Grundprinzipien beschuldigt, darunter die Verlet-zung des marxistisch-leninistisch-maoistischen Denkens. Da die Reformen der Wirtschaftspolitik Maos Vorstellungen diametral entgegengesetzt sind, erschien es den Funktionären, die die Reformen in Gang setzen, nötig, einstimmig ihre Treue zu den Vier Grundprinzipien zu erklären. Tatsächlich gehören diese Prinzipien, die Eingang in eine Verfassung fanden, in der Freiheit des Denkens und Redens garantiert wird, nicht hierher. Ich nehme an, dieses eigenartige Nebeneinander kann es nur in China geben."

« Au cours des dix dernières années, plus les intellectuels se sont battus pour les réformes lancées par Deng, plus ils ont été accusés de porter atteinte aux Quatre principes cardinaux, parmi lesquels figure la violation de la pensée marxiste-léniniste de Mao Zedong. Bien que ces réformes aient été totale-ment à l'opposé des idées économiques de Mao, les responsables qui les ont lancées proclamaient leur fidélité à ces Quatre principes cardinaux. En fait, ces principes, qui ont été inclus dans une constitution qui garantit la liberté de pensée et d'expression, n'ont rien à y faire. Je suppose que des juxtapositions aussi bizarres ne peuvent se produire qu'en Chine. »

LIU BINYAN (1925–2005), author, journalist, and dissident, 1989

pp. 270/271
Liu Heung Shing, 1979

Students from the People's University in Tiananmen Square protesting against the Second Artillery Battalion of the PLA, which had occupied sections of the campus during the Cultural Revolution. Students demanded the army relinquish these areas and vacate the campus.

Studenten der Volksuniversität protestieren auf dem Tiananmen-Platz gegen das Zweite Artilleriebataillon der Volksbefreiungsarmee, das während der Kulturrevolution Teile des Campus besetzt hatte. Die Studenten fordern die Freigabe des Geländes und den Abzug der Soldaten.

Des étudiants de l'Université du peuple sur la place de Tian'anmen protestent contre le Second bataillon d'artillerie, qui a occupé des parties du campus pendant la Révolution culturelle. Ils demandent à l'armée de quitter le campus.

→
Liu Heung Shing, 1979

Artist Wang Keping holds up a sign demanding "Freedom for Art" at the head of a demonstration in Beijing. Wang was a member of the "Stars Painting Group," the first non-official collective of artists to emerge in the post-Mao era.

Der Künstler Wang Keping hält an der Spitze eines Demonstrationszuges ein Schild mit der Forderung „Freiheit für die Kunst" hoch. Wang gehörte der „Stars Painting Group" an, dem ersten nicht staatlichen Künstlerkollektiv der Zeit nach Mao.

L'artiste Wang Keping brandit un panneau réclamant la «liberté pour l'art», à la tête d'une manifestation à Pékin. Wang était membre du « Stars Painting Group », premier collectif non officiel d'artistes à apparaître après la fin de la période de Mao.

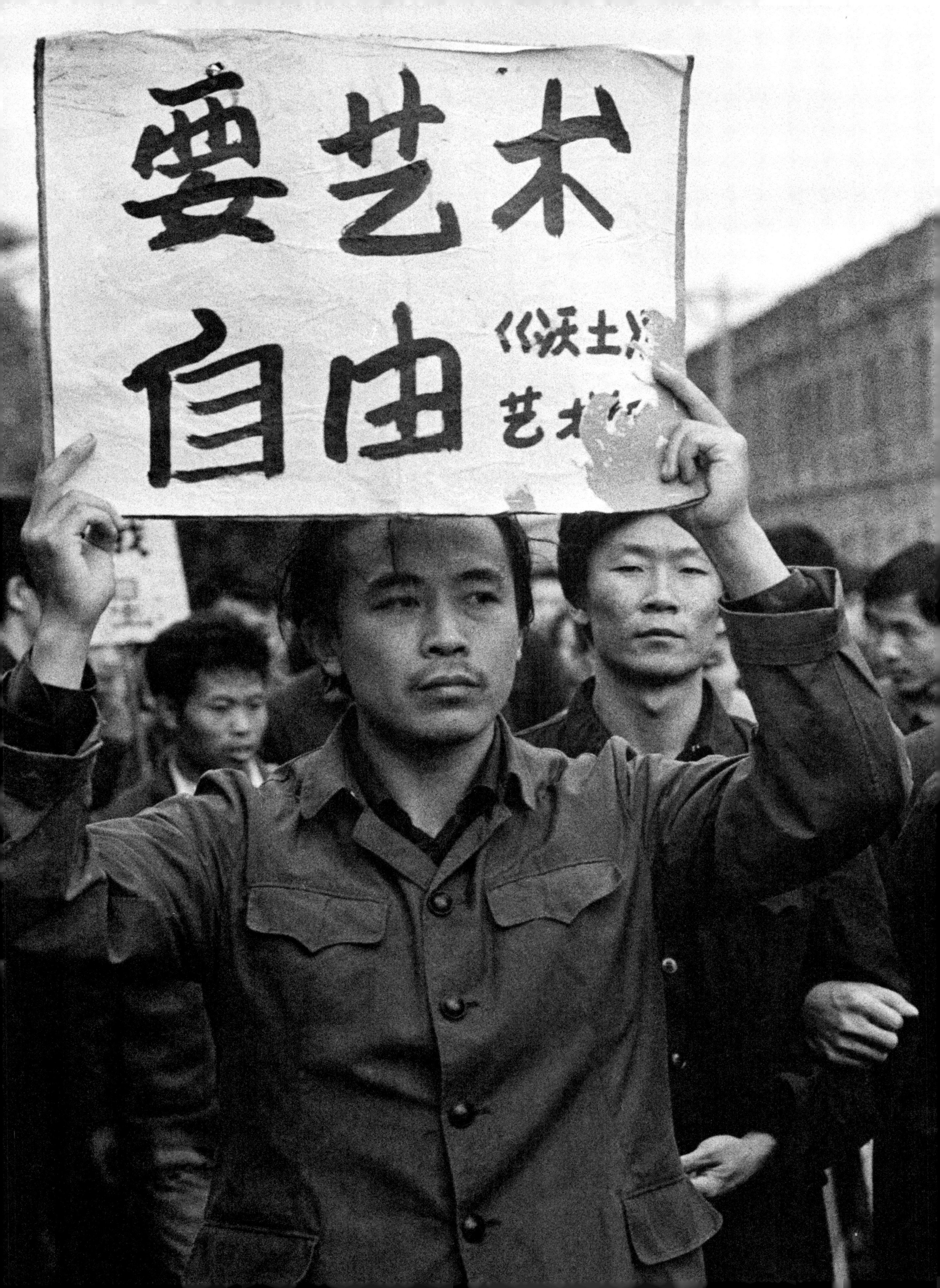
要艺术
自由

#4

1980–1989
Rock 'n' Roll and Modernization

"It doesn't matter whether the cat is black or white, so long as it catches mice, it is a good cat." With this saying, Deng Xiaoping articulated and effected a paradigm shift in the Chinese economy as well as a new Chinese mindset.

Deng Xiaoping, the architect of China's economic reform, wasted little time in putting the Gang of Four on trial and, simultaneously, the followers of Marshal Lin Biao. It was a deliberately public affair, televised across China. In 1981, the CCP also publicly announced an official assessment of Mao's policies: the Cultural Revolution was described as a disastrous holocaust for the people. Deng sent his trusted aide, Wan Li, former mayor of Beijing, to Anhui province, which had been hardest hit during the Great Leap Forward, to begin the experiment of the agrarian "Responsibility System." This allowed the peasants to work to a crop quota set by the State, allowing them to plant additional crops and trade surpluses on the free market.

Taking a cue from the robust economies of the "Four Asian Tigers" of South Korea, Taiwan, Singapore, and Hong Kong, Deng established a succession of Special Economic Zones (SEZ) in four cities along China's eastern coast. These were Shenzhen, Zhuhai, Shantou, Xiamen, and on the island Hainan. He also began to reverse the policy of confiscating private property during the land reform movement of the 1950s, promising to return all property, especially that belonging to the Chinese living overseas, and from neighboring Hong Kong, who contributed to the first direct foreign investment in China.

During the 1980s, the return of Hong Kong to China became an urgent political issue requiring negotiations between Britain and China. The formidable Margaret Thatcher, known as the Iron Lady, met her match in her Chinese counterpart Deng Xiaoping. Eventually, with the promise of "one country, two systems," which guaranteed the capitalist system in Hong Kong would remain unchanged for 50 years, Deng and Thatcher at last came to an agreement, which led to the signing of the return protocol in 1987.

Deng furthermore pursued a policy of "openning up to the outside world," a way of importing advanced Western technologies. Hu Yaobang, one of Deng's chosen successors, was given the task of rehabilitating Chinese intellectuals who had been wrongfully branded as "rightists" during the late 1950s. Many of those who had been wrongly persecuted during the Cultural Revolution were re-assigned to their former jobs. In his haste to reinstate many senior bureaucrats, and for his criticism of entrenched Party conservatives, Hu would soon find himself sidelined by conservatives, who complained to Deng that he was moving too fast.

"Standing at a Crossroads that No One Comprehends"

Deng's other successor in the 1980s was Zhao Ziyang. Zhao steered the economy through the 1980s, and maintained an average of nine percent GDP growth throughout the decade. He would soon find himself unable to quell the rising demands made by student protestors and people frustrated by rising inflation and official corruption as the decade approached its close. In 1989, Zhao was shown on national television visiting the students camped out in Tiananmen Square, shedding tears, and pleading with student leaders and hunger strikers to go home. He was quoted as saying "I have come too late." Indeed, on June 4, PLA troops and tanks rolled onto the avenue of Eternal Peace, sending shock waves across China.

"The pitiable thing about the 80s was that we didn't know how bad we had it—we talked about a new Renaissance! It was like a paralytic being hoisted around by a nurse thinking he was dancing!"

CHEN DANQING (1953–), Chinese artist, 2006

#4

1980–1989
Rock 'n' Roll und Modernisierung

„Es ist gleichgültig, ob die Katze schwarz oder weiß ist, solange sie Mäuse fängt, ist sie eine gute Katze." Mit diesem Sprichwort trat Deng Xiaoping erfolgreich für eine paradigmatische Umkehr in der chinesischen Wirtschaftspolitik und für eine neue chinesische Denkweise ein.

Deng Xiaoping, der Architekt von Chinas Wirtschaftsreform, hielt sich mit dem Prozess gegen die Viererbande und gegen die Anhänger von Marschall Lin Biao nicht lange auf. Die gezielt öffentliche Verhandlung wurde in ganz China im Fernsehen übertragen. 1981 ließ die Partei darüber hinaus eine offizielle Bewertung von Maos Programm verkünden: Die Kulturrevolution wurde als verheerender Holocaust für das Volk bezeichnet. Deng schickte seinen Vertrauten Wan Li, den früheren Bürgermeister von Peking, in die Provinz Anhui, die vom „Großen Sprung nach vorn" am härtesten betroffen war, um dort mit der Umsetzung des landwirtschaftlichen Systems der „Haushaltsverantwortlichkeit" zu beginnen. Danach konnten die Bauern ein vom Staat festgesetztes Ertragskontingent erarbeiten und darüber hinaus erzeugte Produkte auf dem freien Markt anbieten.

Nach dem Vorbild der stabilen Ökonomien in den vier asiatischen „Tigerstaaten" Südkorea, Taiwan, Singapur und Hongkong richtete Deng in vier Städten entlang der Ostküste Chinas Sonderwirtschaftszonen ein, und zwar in Shenzhen, Zhuhai, Shantou, Xiamen und auf der Insel Hainan. Außerdem begann er, die während der Landreform der 1950er-Jahre gängige Praxis der Einziehung von Privateigentum zu revidieren, indem er zusagte, sämtliches Eigentum, insbesondere das von im Ausland oder im benachbarten Hongkong lebenden Chinesen, zurückzuerstatten, zumal die Hongkong-Chinesen als Erste zum Zufluss ausländischer Investitionen nach China beigetragen hatten.

Während der 1980er-Jahre wurde die Rückgabe von Hongkong an China zu einer dringenden politischen Frage, die Verhandlungen zwischen Großbritannien und China erforderte. Die als Eiserne Lady bekannte, un-

erschrockene Margaret Thatcher traf in ihrem chinesischen Verhandlungspartner Deng Xiaoping auf einen ebenbürtigen Gegner. Mit der Devise „ein Land, zwei Systeme", die den Fortbestand des kapitalistischen Systems in Hongkong für die nächsten 50 Jahre garantierte, einigten sich Deng und Thatcher schließlich und unterzeichneten 1987 den Rückgabevertrag.

Mit der Politik der Öffnung zur Außenwelt, einer Strategie, um hoch entwickelte Technologie aus dem Westen zu importieren, trug Deng zusätzlich zur Stärkung Chinas bei. Hu Yaobang, einer von Dengs möglichen Nachfolgern, wurde mit der Aufgabe betraut, chinesische Intellektuelle zu rehabilitieren, die man zu Ende der 1950er-Jahre fälschlich als „Rechtsabweichler" verurteilt hatte. Viele, die man während der Kulturrevolution zu Unrecht verfolgt hatte, kehrten in ihre alten Positionen zurück. In seinem Bemühen, viele der älteren Bürokraten rasch wieder einzusetzen, und aufgrund seiner Kritik an etablierten konservativen Parteigenossen fand Hu sich bald selbst von Konservativen ausmanövriert, die sich bei Deng darüber beklagten, dass er übereilt vorginge.

„Ein Wendepunkt, den niemand versteht"

Zhao Ziyang galt in den 1980er-Jahren als ein weiterer potenzieller Nachfolger Dengs. Er steuerte die Wirtschaft durch dieses Jahrzehnt und konnte während dieser Zeit eine durchschnittliche Steigerungsrate des Bruttosozialprodukts von neun Prozent erzielen. Als gegen Ende des Jahrzehnts die Menschen von steigender Inflation und amtlicher Korruption frustriert waren, sah er sich außerstande, die wachsenden Forderungen protestierender Studenten zu unterdrücken. Als 1989 Studenten auf dem Tiananmen-Platz kampierten, konnte man im Fernsehen Zhao sehen, wie er unter Tränen Studentenführer und Hungerstreikende inständig bat, nach Hause zu gehen. Es hieß, er habe gesagt: „Ich bin zu spät gekommen." Tatsächlich marschierten am 4. Juni Truppen der Volksbefreiungsarmee und rollten Panzer über die Straße des Himmlischen Friedens und erschütterten das Land.

„Das Bedauerliche an den 1980er-Jahren war die Tatsache, dass wir nicht wussten, wie schlecht es uns ging – wir sprachen von einer neuen Renaissance! Es war, als dächte ein Lahmer, den eine Pflegerin herumhievt, er würde tanzen!"

CHEN DANQING (1953–), chinesischer Künstler, 2006

#4

1980–1989
Rock 'n' roll et modernisation

« Que le chat soit noir ou blanc n'a pas d'importance. Tant qu'il attrape des souris, c'est un bon chat. » Par ce dicton, Deng Xiaoping fournissait un argumentaire efficace en faveur d'une nouvelle orientation de l'économie chinoise et créait un nouvel état d'esprit.

Deng Xiaoping, le grand architecte des réformes économiques, ne perdit guère de temps à éliminer la Bande des quatre et, simultanément, les partisans du maréchal Lin Biao. Il en fit délibérément une affaire publique, télévisée dans toute la Chine. En 1989, le Parti communiste annonça par ailleurs une remise en perspective de la politique de Mao : la Révolution culturelle était maintenant présentée comme une catastrophe humanitaire. Deng envoya son collaborateur de confiance et ancien maire de Pékin, Wan Li, dans la province d'Anhui qui avait été le plus durement frappée par le Grand bond en avant, pour expérimenter le nouveau « Système de responsabilité ». Il permettait aux paysans de travailler pour les quotas de production fixés par l'état, tout en ayant la possibilité de cultiver davantage et de commercialiser le surplus sur des marchés libres.

S'inspirant des économies florissantes des « Quatre tigres asiatiques » – Corée du Sud, Taiwan, Singapour et Hong Kong –, il créa des Zones économiques spéciales (ZES) dans quatre villes de la côte orientale : Shenzhen, Zhuhai, Shantou, Xiamen et sur l'île Hainan. Il commença également à inverser la politique de confiscation de la propriété privée qui avait débuté avec la réforme agraire des années 1950, et promit de rendre les biens saisis, en particulier ceux qui appartenaient aux Chinois de l'étranger et de Hong Kong. Ceux-ci furent les premiers à contribuer à l'injection d'investissements étrangers en Chine.

Pendant les années 1980, le retour de Hong Kong à la Chine devint un enjeu politique urgent nécessitant des négociations entre le Royaume-Uni et la Chine. La formidable Margaret Thatcher, surnommée la « Dame de fer », trouva à qui parler en Deng Xiaoping. Finalement, sur la promesse de « un pays, deux systèmes » qui garantissait la préservation du système capitaliste dans l'ancienne colonie pendant 50 ans, Deng et Thatcher parvinrent à un accord qui conduisit à la signature du protocole de retour en 1987.

Deng imposa la politique de « l'ouverture au monde extérieur », qui permettait d'importer les technologies occidentales les plus récentes. Hu Yaobang, l'un de ses successeurs désignés, fut chargé de réhabiliter les intellectuels accusés à tort d'être des « droitistes » à la fin des années 1950. Beaucoup de ceux qui avaient été persécutés pendant la Révolution culturelle retrouvèrent leur ancien travail. Trop pressé de remettre en place beaucoup de hauts fonctionnaires et trop critique à l'égard des conservateurs figés du Parti, Hu allait être bientôt lui-même écarté par ceux-ci qui se plaignirent auprès de Deng qu'il allait trop vite.

« Un carrefour sans panneaux d'orientation »

Un autre successeur de Deng désigné pendant les années 1980 fut Zhao Ziyang, qui pilota l'économie tout au long de cette période et réussit à maintenir un taux de croissance annuelle moyen de 9 % tout au long de la décennie. Il ne fut bientôt plus en mesure de répondre aux demandes pressantes des protestataires étudiants et du peuple frustré par l'inflation croissante et la corruption de l'administration. En 1989, on le vit rendre visite aux étudiants campant sur la place Tian'anmen, pleurant et suppliant leurs responsables et les grévistes de la faim de rentrer chez eux. Il aurait dit « Je suis venu trop tard. » Le 4 juin, l'armée et ses tanks arrivèrent par l'avenue de la Paix éternelle et leur intervention provoqua une vague de choc dans toute la Chine.

« Dans les années 1980, le plus pitoyable était que nous ne savions pas à quel point nous allions mal, alors que nous parlions d'une nouvelle Renaissance ! C'était comme un paralytique relevé par une infirmière et qui pense qu'il va danser ! »

CHAN DANQING (1953–), artiste chinois, 2006

"Mao is painting on sand. When he passes from the scene, the rains will come and wash away what he has painted, and there will still be China, always China."

„Mao zeichnet in den Sand. Wenn er die Szene verlässt, wird der Regen kommen und seine Zeichnungen wegwaschen, und es wird immer noch China geben, immer China."

« Mao peint sur le sable. Lorsqu'il disparaîtra, la pluie viendra qui effacera ce qu'il a peint, mais il restera la Chine, toujours la Chine. »

LEE KUAN YEW (1923–), first prime minister of Singapore, 1994

→

Liu Heung Shing, 1981

A student at the Dalian Institute of Technology skates past a statue of Chairman Mao, a monumont found in virtually every large university campus and State-owned enterprise in China.

Ein Student am Technischen Institut von Dalian fährt auf Rollschuhen an einer Statue des Vorsitzenden Mao vorbei, wie man sie auf nahezu jedem großen Universitätscampus und dem Gelände jedes staatlichen Unternehmens in China findet.

Un étudiant de l'Institut de technologie de Dalian passe en patins à roulettes devant une de ces statues de Mao que l'on trouve dans pratiquement tous les campus universitaires et les grandes entreprises de Chine.

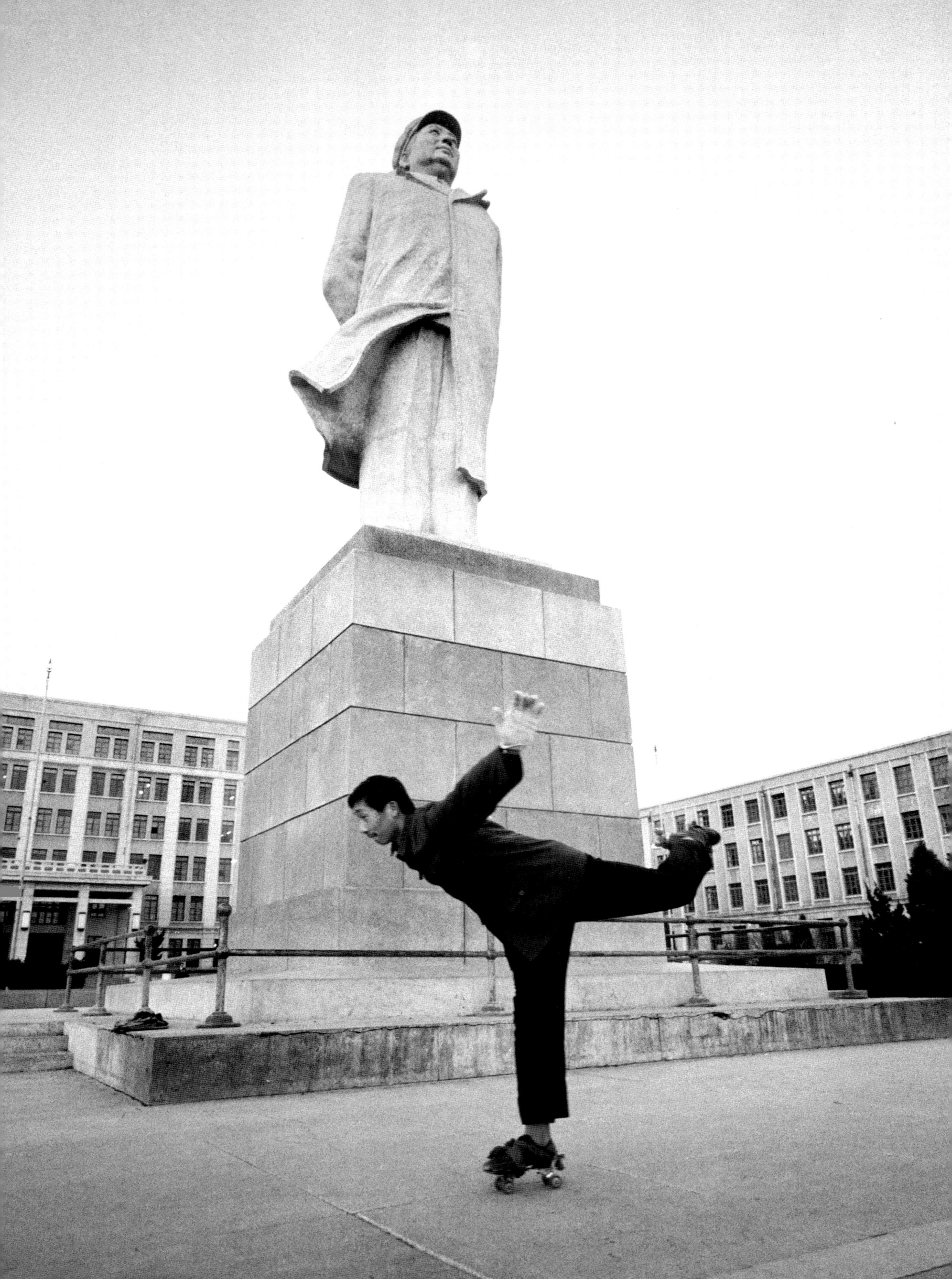

*"When it comes to political survival,
I think I would be qualified for an
Olympic Gold Medal."*

*„Wenn es ums politische Überleben
geht, hätte ich meiner Meinung nach
Anspruch auf eine olympische
Goldmedaille."*

*« Pour ce qui est de la survie politique,
je crois que je suis qualifié pour la
médaille d'or olympique. »*

**DENG XIAOPING (1904–1997),
early member of the Chinese Communist
Party and de facto leader of the People's
Republic of China from 1976 to 1997, 1979**

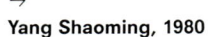

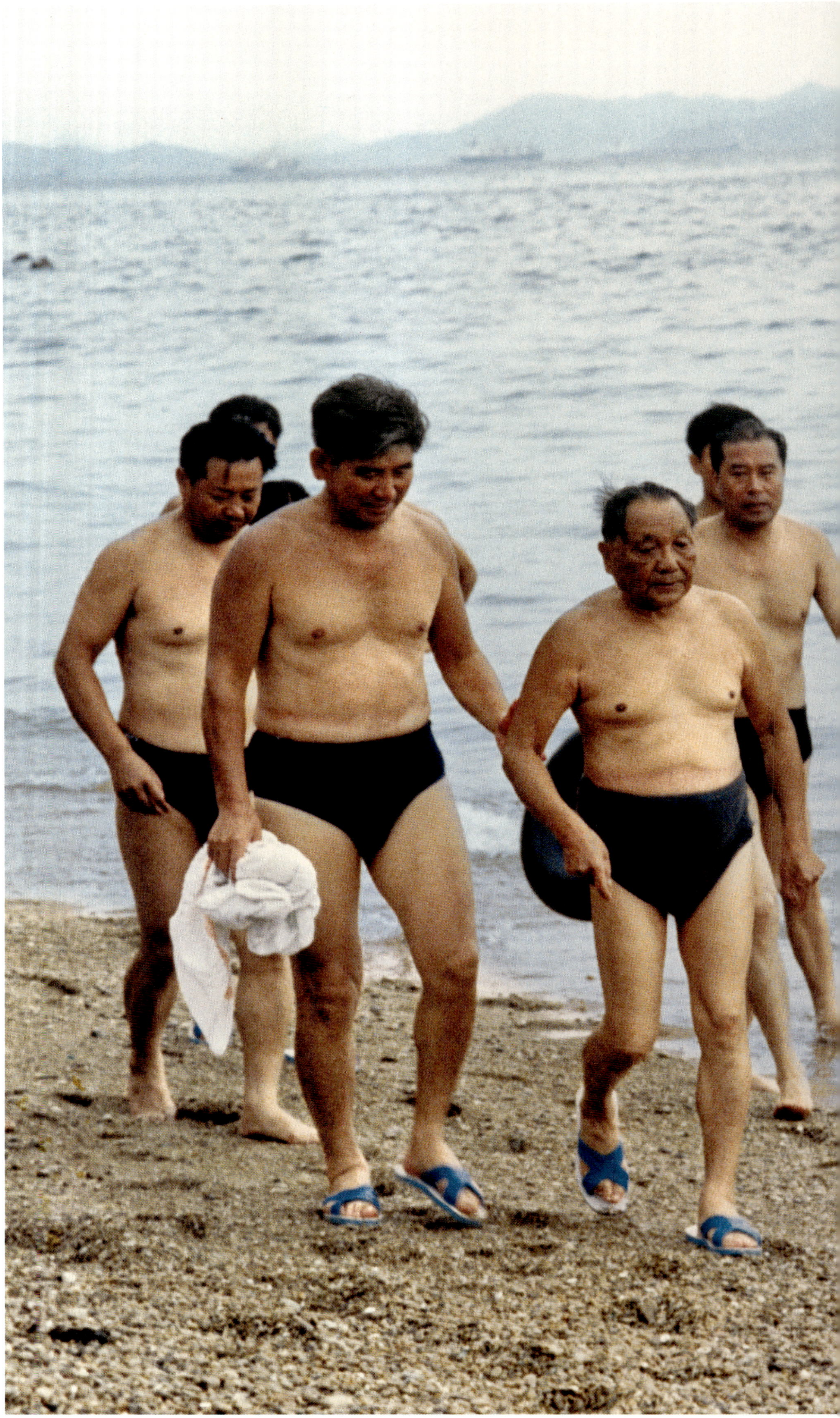

Yang Shaoming, 1980

*Chinese leader Deng Xiaoping, surrounded
by security guards, strolls along the beach at
Beidaihe, a summer resort in Hebei province,
favored by the Chinese leaders.*
"Deng will go down in history either as
a sage for his understanding that what
authoritarian China required to be rescued
from socialist oblivion and chaos was
economic reform alone, or as a transitional
autocrat who failed to appreciate the crucial
role political reform also plays in maintain-
ing stability." Orville Schell

*Der von Sicherheitskräften umringte chine-
sische Führer Deng Xiaoping geht am Strand
von Beidaihe, einem bei hochrangigen
chinesischen Politikern beliebten Badeort
in der Provinz Hebei, spazieren.*
„Deng wird entweder als Weiser in die
Geschichte eingehen, weil er begriff, dass
das autoritäre China einzig Wirtschaftsreformen brauchte, um aus dem sozialistischen Chaos gerettet zu werden, oder
als Übergangsautokrat, der nicht erkannte,
welch entscheidende Rolle auch politische
Reformen beim Erhalt der Stabilität
spielen." Orville Schell

*Deng Xiaoping entouré de gardes du corps
se promène sur la plage de Beidaihe, station
estivale de la province du Hebei fréquentée
par les hauts responsables chinois.*
« Deng restera dans l'histoire soit comme
un sage, parce qu'il comprit que ce dont la
Chine autoritariste avait besoin pour être
sauvée du chaos socialiste était la réforme
économique, soit comme un autocrate
de transition qui échoua à apprécier le rôle
crucial que la réforme politique pouvait
jouer dans le maintien de la stabilité ».
Orville Schell

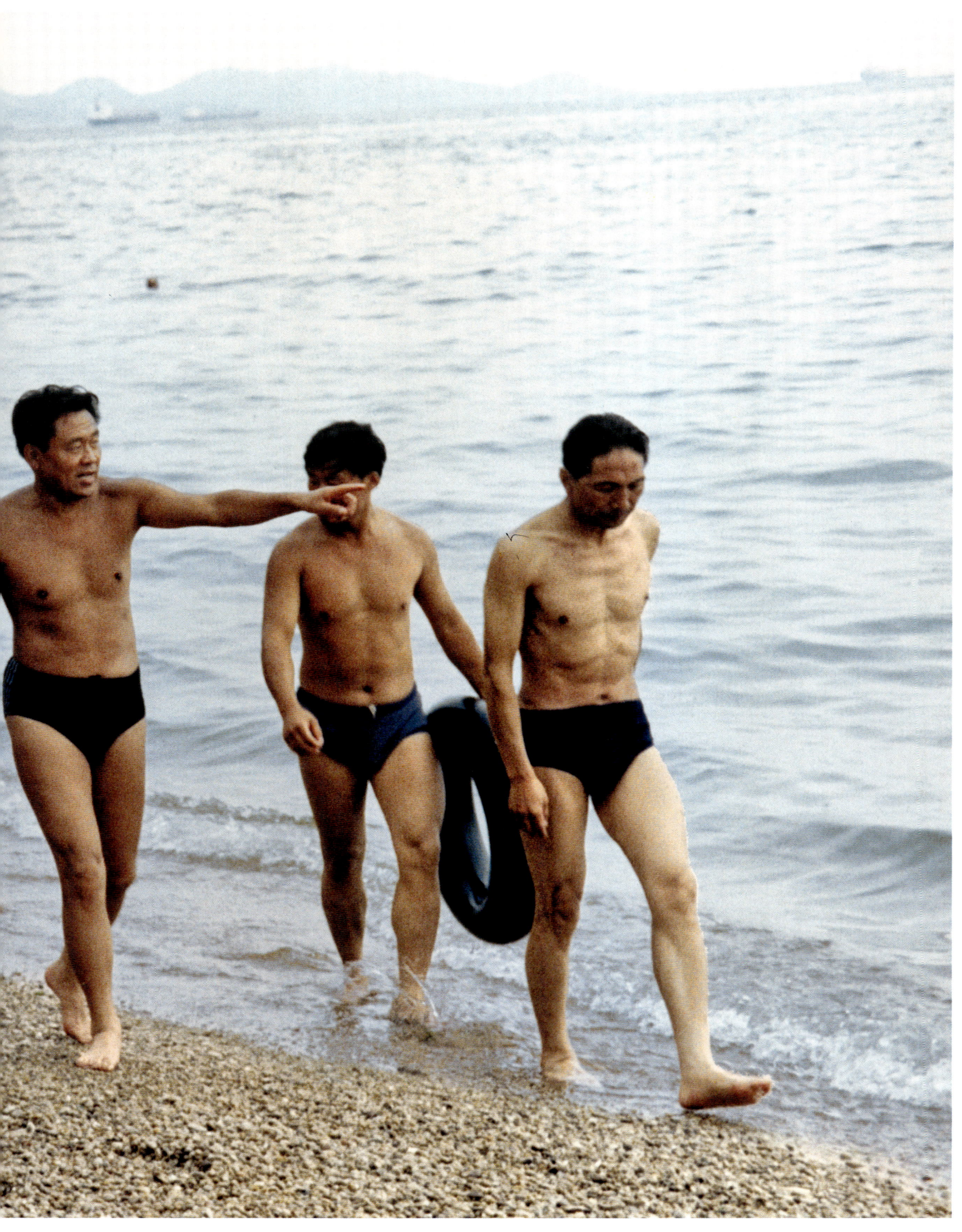

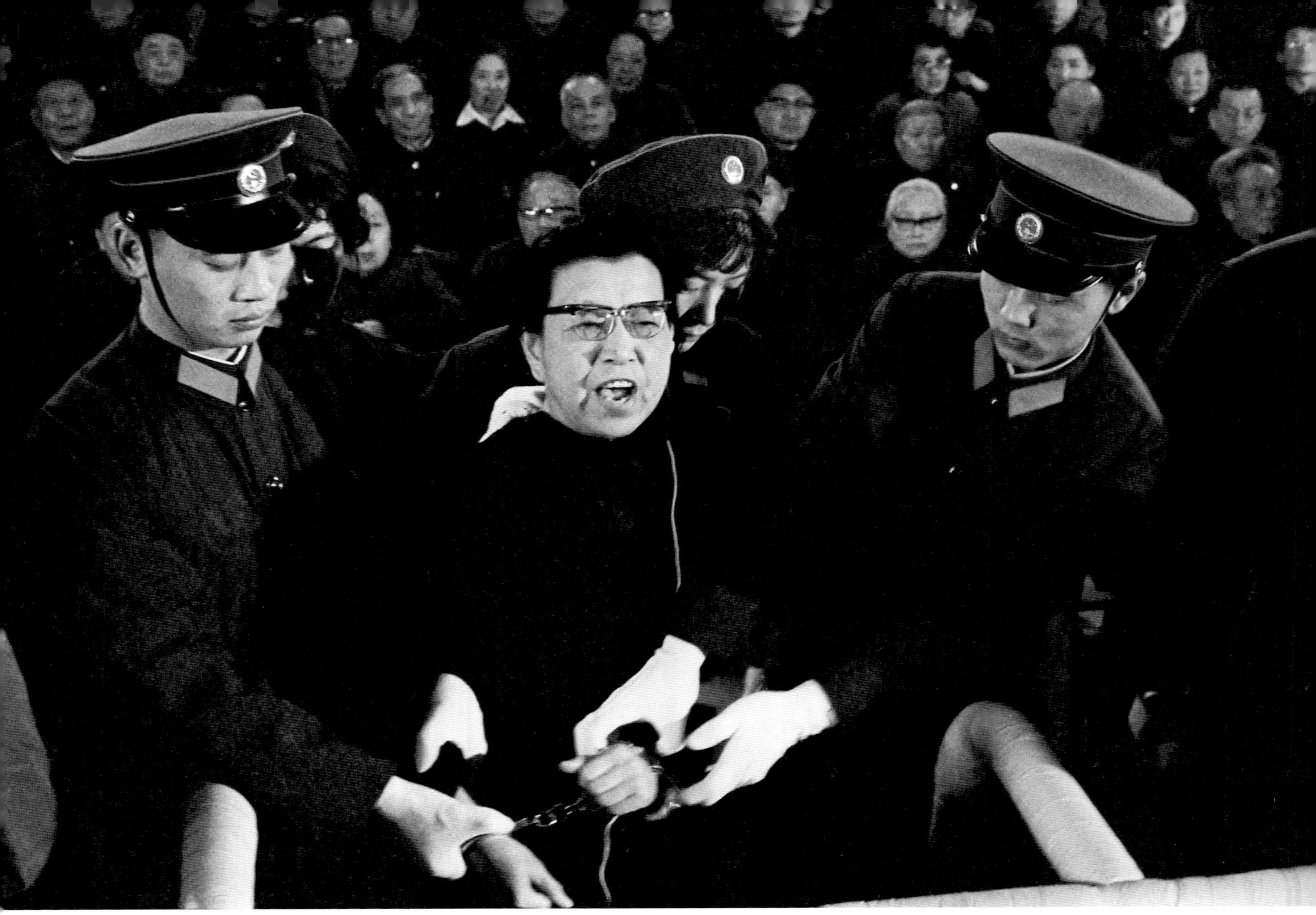

Anon., c. 1981 (China News Agency)

Mao's widow, Jiang Qing, is handcuffed during her trial to control her persistent denunciation of the jury and all present. She repeatedly claimed to have been Chairman Mao's "dog": "…whoever he told me to bite, I bit." Jiang Qing received a death penalty with a two-year reprieve. She died in 1991.

Maos Witwe Jiang Qing werden während ihrer Gerichtsverhandlung Handschellen angelegt, um ihren ständigen Beschimpfungen der Jury und aller Anwesenden Einhalt zu gebieten. Sie behauptete wiederholt, sie sei der „Hund" des Vorsitzenden Mao gewesen und habe jeden angegriffen, auf den Mao sie hetzte. Jiang Qing wurde zum Tode verurteilt, zwei Jahre später wurde das Urteil in lebenslängliche Haft umgewandelt. Sie starb 1991.

La veuve de Mao, Jiang Qing, est menottée pendant son procès en réaction à ses dénonciations constantes du jury et de toutes les personnes présentes. Elle répétait avoir été « la chienne de Mao, quand il me disait de mordre, je mordais. » Elle fut condamnée à mort, sentence commuée en prison à vie. Elle mourut en 1991.

Meng Zhaorui, 1981

The Gang of Four on trial in the auditorium of the Public Security Ministry in Beijing. At the conclusion of the trial, the Central Committee of the Communist Party of China issued a resolution defining the Cultural Revolution as a holocaust for the Chinese people. Mao's policies were described as being 70 percent correct, and 30 percent at fault. Of the 6,843 monuments that were recorded as still standing in 1958, by 1976, only 1,921 remained. The number of human casualties was similarly devastating: in Beijing alone, 33,695 homes were raided, and 1,772 people had been tortured, or beaten to death.

Die Viererbande vor Gericht im Auditorium des Ministeriums für Öffentliche Sicherheit in Peking. Zum Abschluss der Verhandlung gab das Zentralkomitee der KPCh eine Resolution heraus, in der die Kulturrevolution als Holocaust für das chinesische Volk bezeichnet wurde. Maos Vorgehen wurde zu 70 Prozent als richtig und zu 30 Prozent als fehlerhaft bezeichnet. Von den 1958 als vorhanden registrierten 6843 kulturhistorischen Monumenten waren 1976 nur noch 1921 übrig. Auch die Zahl der kriminellen Übergriffe war verheerend: Allein in Peking wurden 33.695 Wohnhäuser geplündert, und 1772 Menschen waren gefoltert oder erschlagen worden.

Procès de la Bande des quatre dans l'auditorium du ministère de la sécurité publique à Pékin. À son issue, le Comité central du Parti communiste vota une résolution définissant la Révolution culturelle comme une persécution du peuple chinois. La politique de Mao fut présentée comme correcte à 70 % et donc mauvaise à 30 %. Des 6 843 monuments répertoriés en 1958, seuls 1 921 subsistaient en 1976. Le nombre des crimes fut tout aussi élevé : rien qu'à Pékin, 33 695 logements furent pillés, 1 772 personnes torturées ou battues à mort.

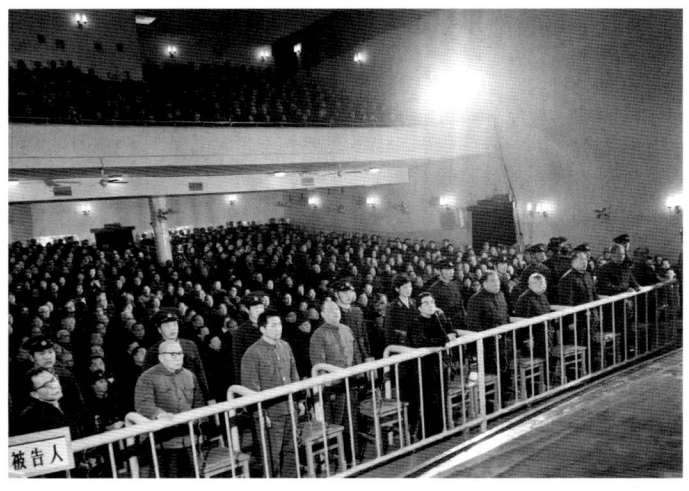

"I was Chairman Mao's dog. Whoever he told me to bite, I bit."

„Ich war der Hund des Vorsitzenden Mao. Ich biss jeden, den er mir zu beißen befahl."

« J'étais la chienne du Président Mao, quand il me disait de mordre, je mordais. »

JIANG QING (1914–1991), last wife of Chairman Mao and leader of the Gang of Four

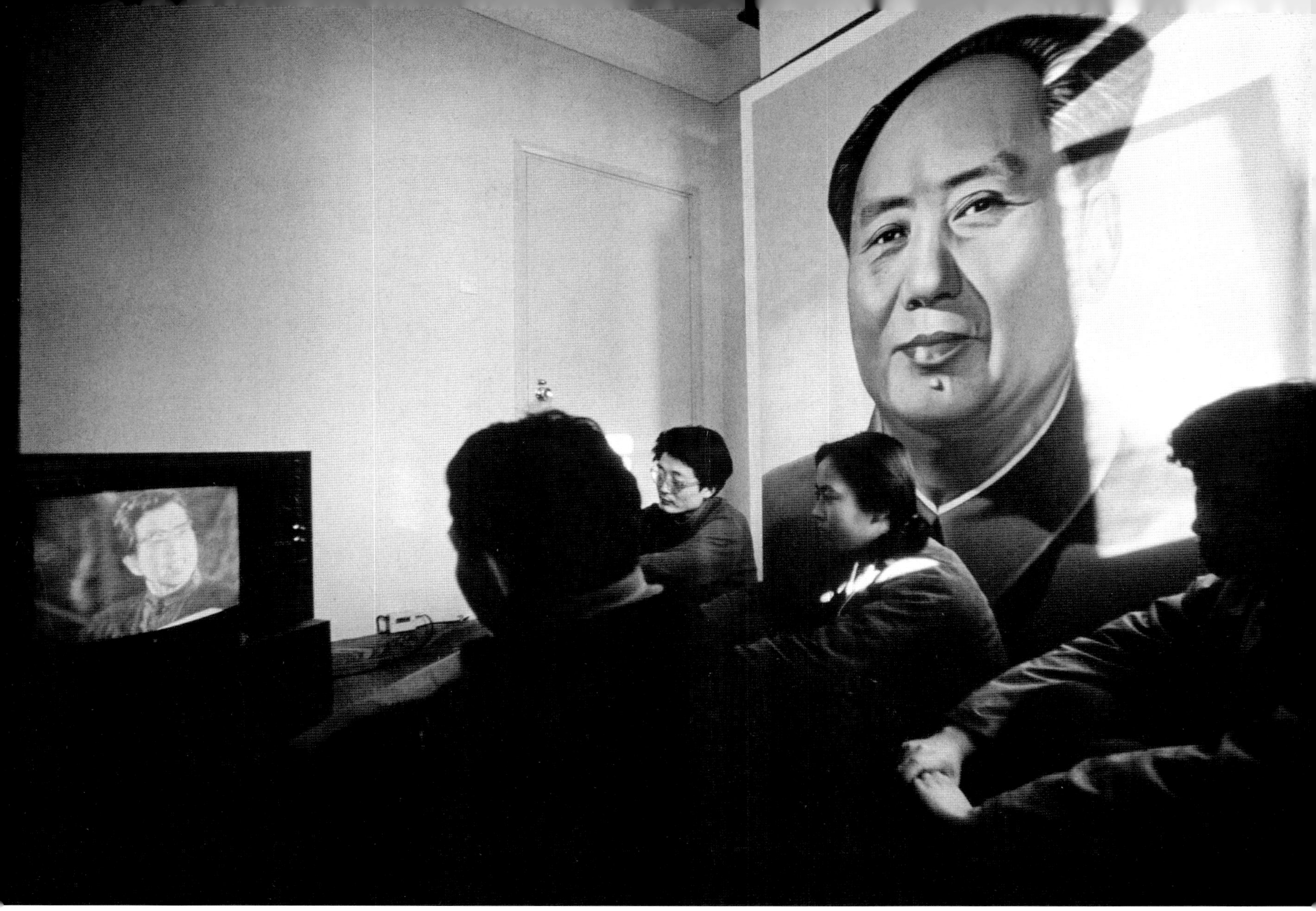

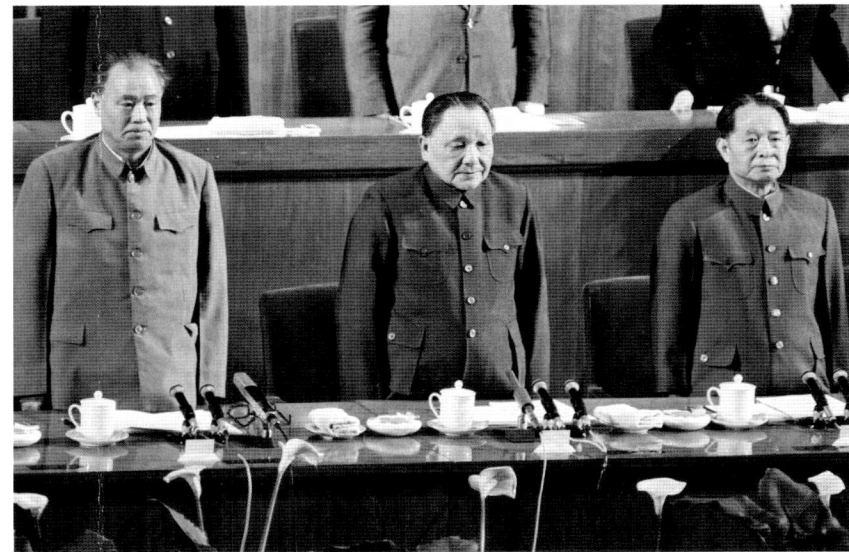

Liu Heung Shing, 1981

A group of young men and women in Beijing watch the trial of the Gang of Four on national television.

Eine Gruppe junger Männer und Frauen verfolgt die Gerichtsverhandlung gegen die Viererbande im chinesischen Fernsehen.

Un groupe de jeunes pékinois suit le procès de la Bande des quatre à la télévision.

Liu Heung Shing, 1983

Chinese leader Deng Xiaoping, flanked by Zhao Ziyang (left) and Hu Yaobang (right), stand for the national anthem to mark the centenary of the death of Karl Marx. Both Zhao and Hu were successors of Deng Xiaoping. But Hu Yaobang was accused of not being firm enough in suppressing "bourgeois liberalization" as the door opened to the outside world, and was removed from his post in 1987. It was his death in 1989 that sparked the student protest movement. Zhao Ziyang showed sympathy towards the students, and was removed from office in 1989, and placed under house arrest until his death in 2005.

Die Führungselite Chinas, Deng Xiaoping zwischen Zhao Ziyang (links) und Hu Yaobang (rechts), hat sich für die National-hymne erhoben, die zum hundertsten Jahres-tag des Todes von Karl Marx erklingt. Zhao und Hu waren beide als Nachfolger Deng Xiaopings vorgesehen. Hu Yaobang wurde beschuldigt, nicht hart genug gegen eine „bourgeoise Liberalisierung" vorgegangen zu sein, als sich China zur Außenwelt öffnete, und wurde 1987 abgesetzt. Sein Tod 1989 löste die Studentenproteste aus. Zhao Ziyang zeigte sich den Studenten gegenüber nach-giebig, wurde 1989 abgesetzt und bis zu seinem Tod 2005 unter Hausarrest gestellt.

Les hauts responsables chinois, Deng Xiao-ping, Zhao Ziyang (à gauche) et Hu Yaobang (à droite) se lèvent pour l'hymne national joué lors des cérémonies du centenaire de la mort de Karl Marx. Zhao et Hu étaient cités comme des successeurs possibles de Deng. Hu Yaobang fut accusé de ne pas avoir été assez ferme dans l'élimination de la « libérali-sation bourgeoise » consécutive à l'ouverture sur le monde extérieur et fut écarté de son poste en 1987. En 1989, sa mort déclencha le mouvement de contestation des étudiants. Zhao Ziyang, qui avait montré de la sym-pathie envers les protestataires, perdit son poste en 1988 et fut placé en résidence sur-veillée jusqu'à sa mort en 2005.

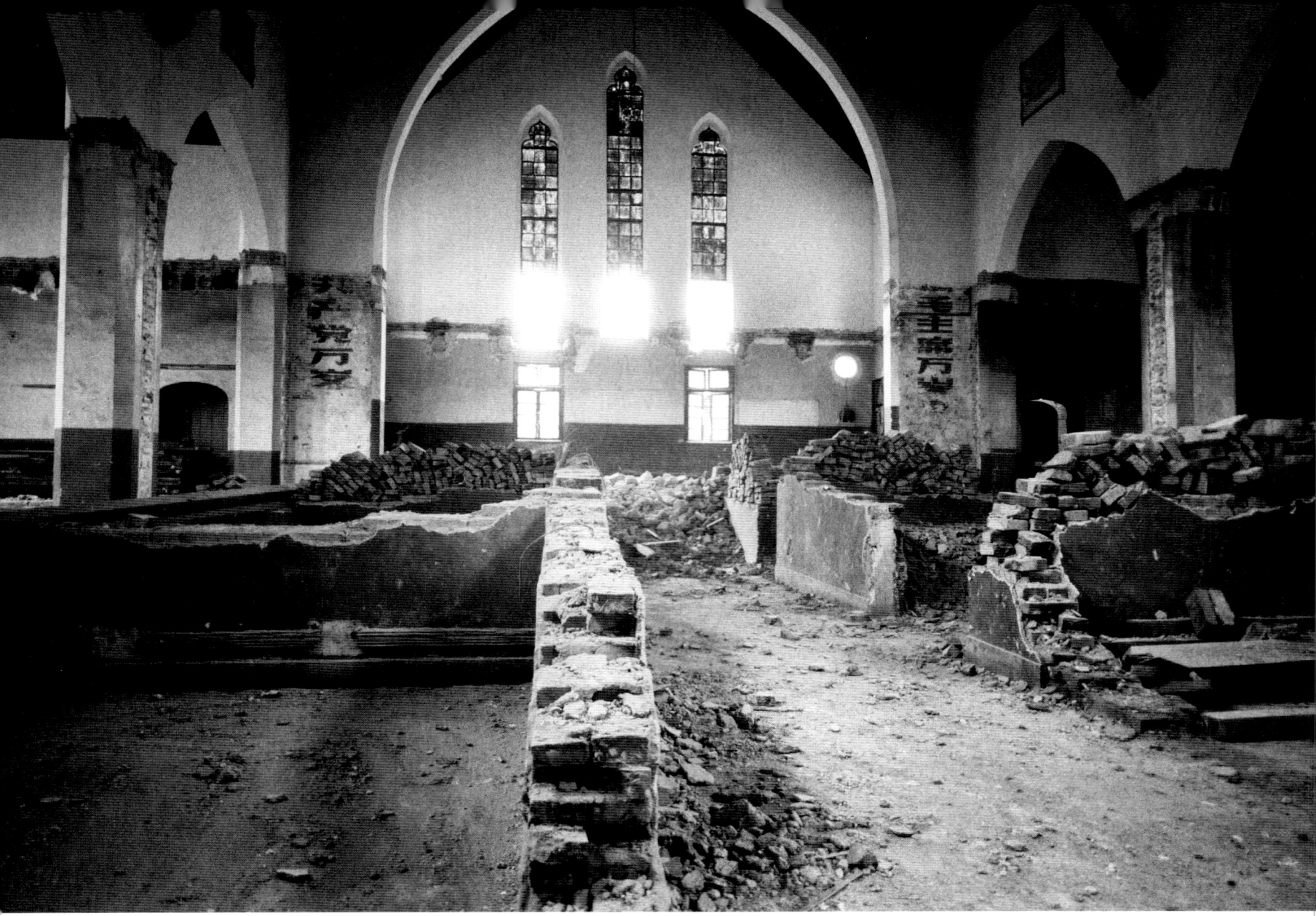

↑

Liu Heung Shing, 1981

A Protestant church in Nanjing, destroyed by the Red Guards during the Cultural Revolution, is later turned into a warehouse.

Eine während der Kulturrevolution von den Roten Garden zerstörte protestantische Kirche in Nanjing wurde später in ein Lagerhaus umgewandelt.

Ce temple protestant de Nankin détruit par les Gardes rouges pendant la Révolution culturelle, avait été transformé en entrepôt.

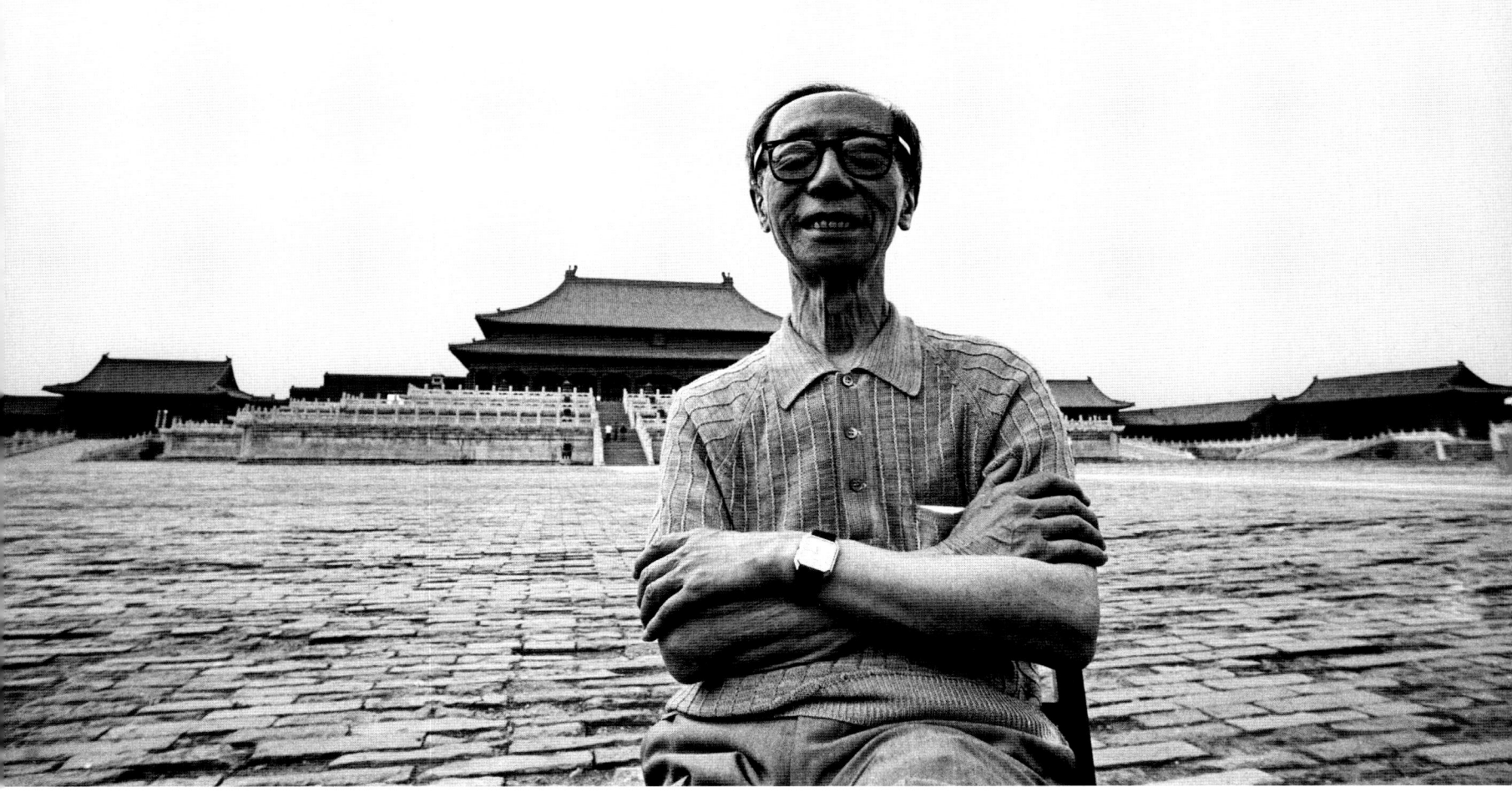

↑
Liu Heung Shing, 1980

Pu Jie, younger brother of the last Qing emperor, Pu Yi, sits for a portrait at his former residence, the Forbidden City, Beijing. There, he and his brother learned English from their Scottish tutor Reginald Fleming Johnston, (author of Twilight in the Forbidden City, *published in 1934, and used as the source of Bertolucci's famous film* The Last Emperor*), and how to ride a bicycle in the imperial courtyards.*

Pu Jie, der jüngere Bruder des letzten Qing-Kaisers Pu Yi, lässt sich vor seinem ehemaligen Wohnsitz in der Verbotenen Stadt fotografieren. Hier lernten er und sein Bruder bei ihrem schottischen Lehrer Reginald Fleming Johnston (dem Autor des 1934 erschienenen Buches Twilight in the Forbidden City, *das als Quelle für Bertoluccis berühmten Film* Der letzte Kaiser *diente) Englisch und wie man in den kaiserlichen Hofanlagen Fahrrad fährt.*

Pu Jie, frère cadet du dernier empereur Qing, pose devant son ancienne résidence, la Cité interdite à Pékin. C'est ici qu'en compagnie de son frère, il avait appris l'anglais de leur tuteur écossais Reginald Fleming Johnston (auteur de Twilight in the Forbidden City, *publié en 1934 et source du film de Bertolucci* Le Dernier empereur*), et aussi comment rouler en vélo dans les cours du palais.*

"In China one does not have to learn to become a realist: here one is born a realist."

„In China muss man nicht lernen, ein Realist zu werden: Hier wird man als Realist geboren."

« En Chine, on n'apprend pas à devenir réaliste : on naît réaliste. »

LIN YUTANG (1895–1976), writer, philosopher, and inventor of the Chinese typewriter, 1935

pp. 288/289
Liu Heung Shing, 1980

High-school students studying for university entrance exams under the street lights in Tiananmen Square. Public housing was cramped, leading students to prefer to study in peace outside the home. After a hiatus in education of more than a decade, the revival of high-school entrance examinations assumed tremendous importance.

Oberschüler lernen für eine Zulasssungs-prüfung zur Universität unter den Laternen auf dem Tiananmen-Platz. Bei den beengten Verhältnissen im staatlichen Wohnungsbau zogen es die Schüler vor, in Ruhe im Freien zu lernen. Nach einer Zwangspause des Er-ziehungssytems von über zehn Jahren gewann die wieder aufgenommene Zulasssungsprü-fung zur Oberschule enorme Bedeutung.

Des élèves d'un collège préparent leurs examens d'entrée à l'université sous les lampadaires de la place Tian'anmen. Les logements surpeuplés poussaient les étudiants à aller travailler au calme hors de leur foyer. Après une interruption du système éducatif de plus de dix ans, les examens d'entrée prirent une importance considérable.

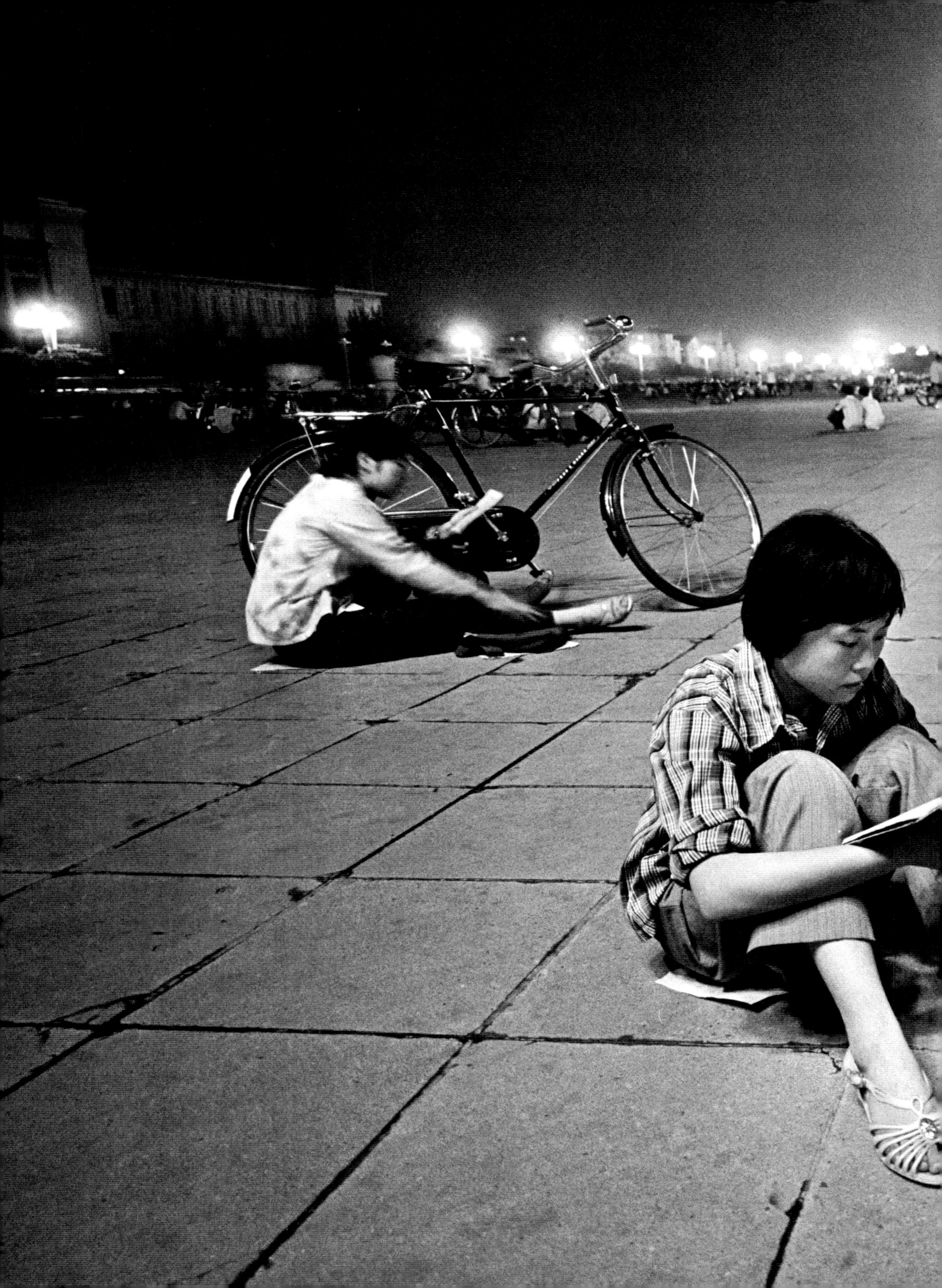

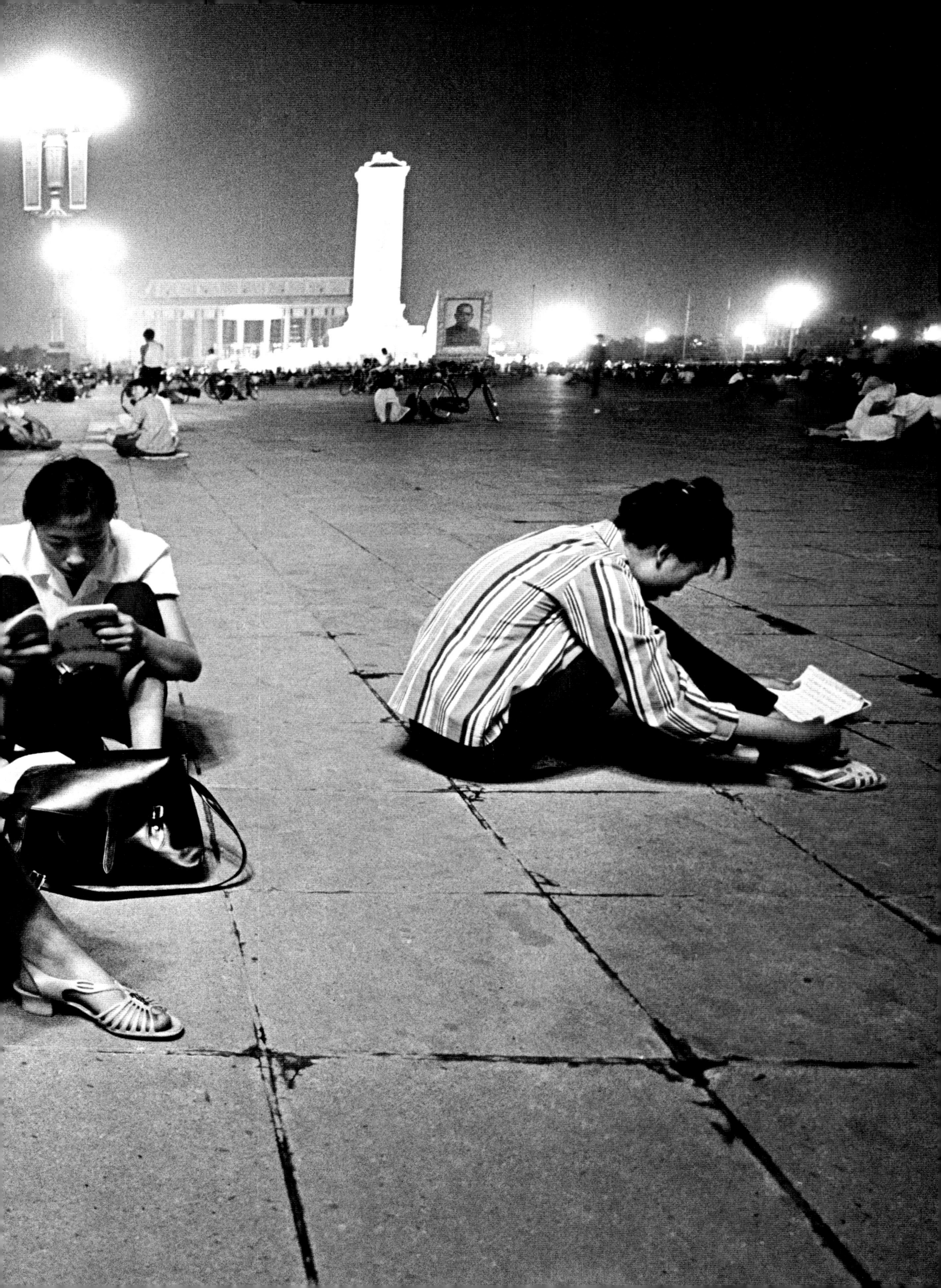

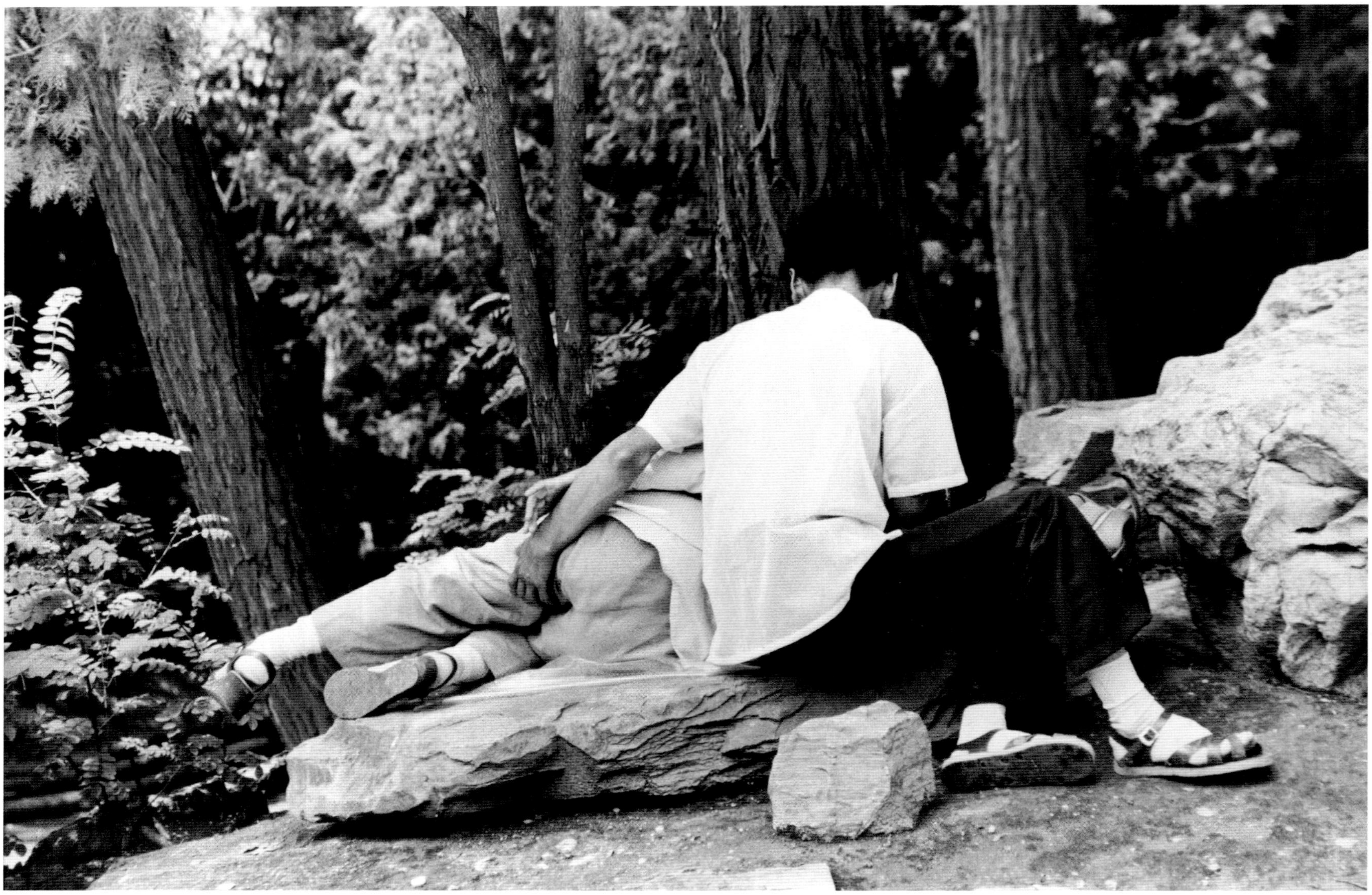

↑

Liu Heung Shing, 1980

Chinese lovers in Beijing zoo. Cramped housing conditions, where parents, children, and grandparents all lived in one room, allowed for neither privacy nor intimacy. In post-Mao China, as the people began to return to normal life, they also began to allow personal emotions to be revived.

Ein chinesisches Liebespaar im Zoo von Peking. Beengte Wohnverhältnisse, bei denen Eltern, Kinder und Großeltern alle in einem Raum lebten, ließen weder Privatsphäre noch Intimität zu. Als die Menschen in der Zeit nach Mao allmählich zu einem normalen Leben zurückkehrten, gestatteten sie sich auch wieder persönliche Gefühle.

Amoureux chinois au zoo de Pékin. Les logements surpeuplés où parents, enfants et grands-parents cohabitaient dans une seule pièce n'autorisaient aucune intimité. Après Mao et avec le retour à une vie normale, les gens commencèrent à exprimer leurs émotions.

→

Liu Heung Shing, 1980

A young Shanghai couple has their wedding photograph taken in a photo studio. Due to the cost involved, the couple rents only the upper part of the wedding gown for the photo.

Ein junges Paar in Shanghai lässt sein Hochzeitsfoto in einem Fotostudio aufnehmen. Wegen der damit verbundenen Kosten, mietet das Paar für das Foto nur das Oberteil des Hochzeitskleides.

Un couple de jeunes mariés de Shanghai se fait prendre en photo dans un studio. Pour des raisons d'économie, la jeune femme ne porte que la partie supérieure de la robe de mariée, seule visible sur le cliché.

pp. 292/293
Liu Heung Shing, 1981

A giant portrait of Mao is removed from the Museum of Chinese History on the east side of Tiananmen Square, signaling an official end to the personality cult of Mao, and the start of de-Maoification of China.

Ein riesiges Mao-Porträt wird vom Museum für Geschichte an der Ostseite des Tiananmen-Platzes entfernt, Anzeichen für das offizielle Ende des Personenkultes um Mao und der Beginn der Entmaoisierung Chinas.

Un portrait géant de Mao est descendu du mur du Musée de l'histoire chinoise sur le côté est de la place Tian'anmen, début de la fin officielle du culte de la personnalité de Mao et la démaoïsation de la Chine.

→

Liu Heung Shing, 1981

Lovers chat in a park in Beijing.

Plauderndes Liebespaar in einem Park in Peking.

Conversation d'amoureux dans un parc à Pékin.

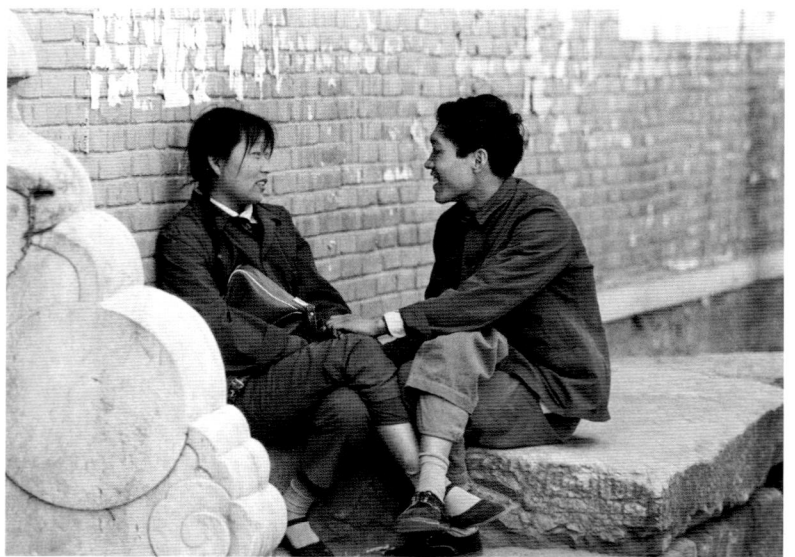

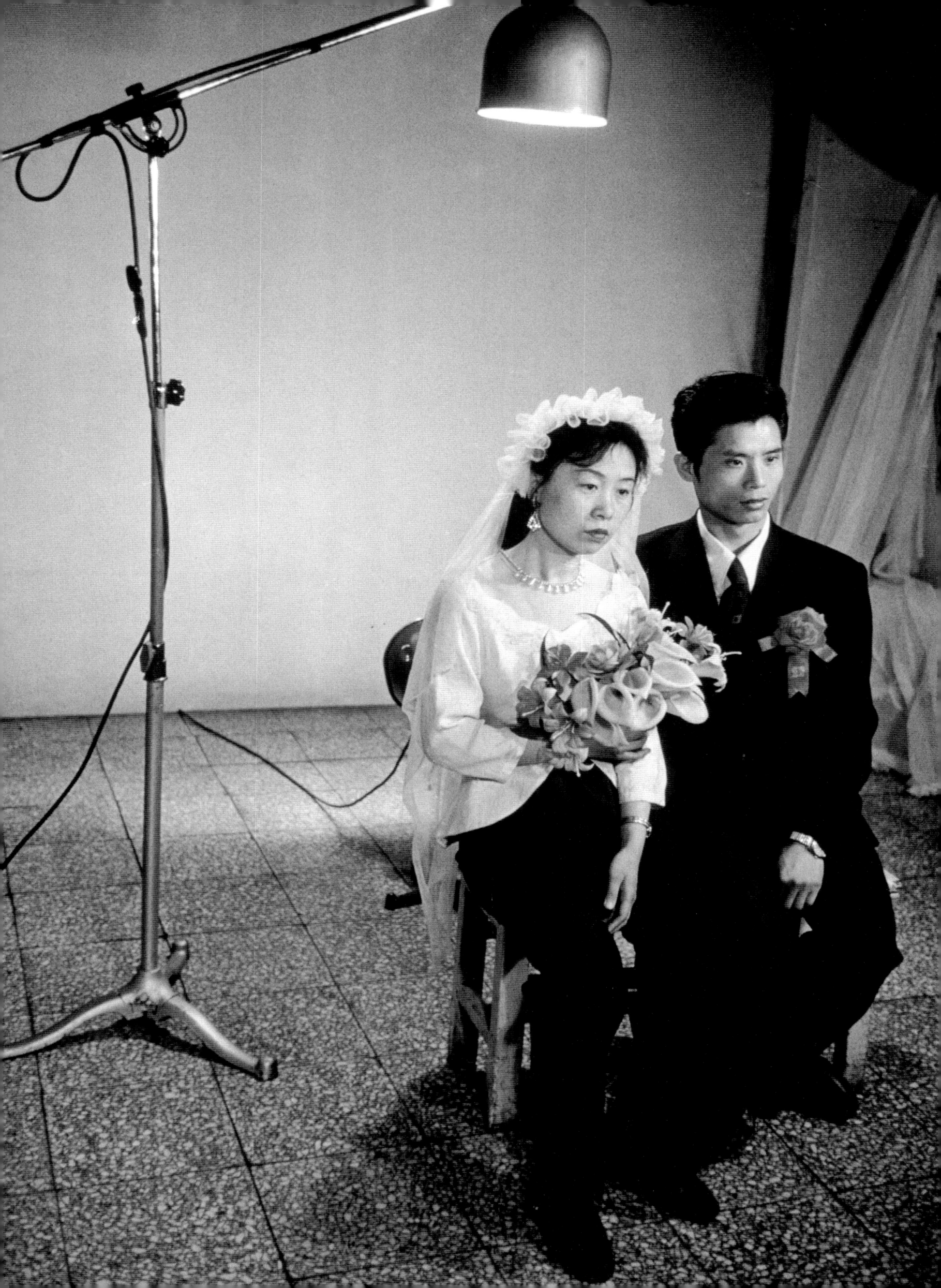

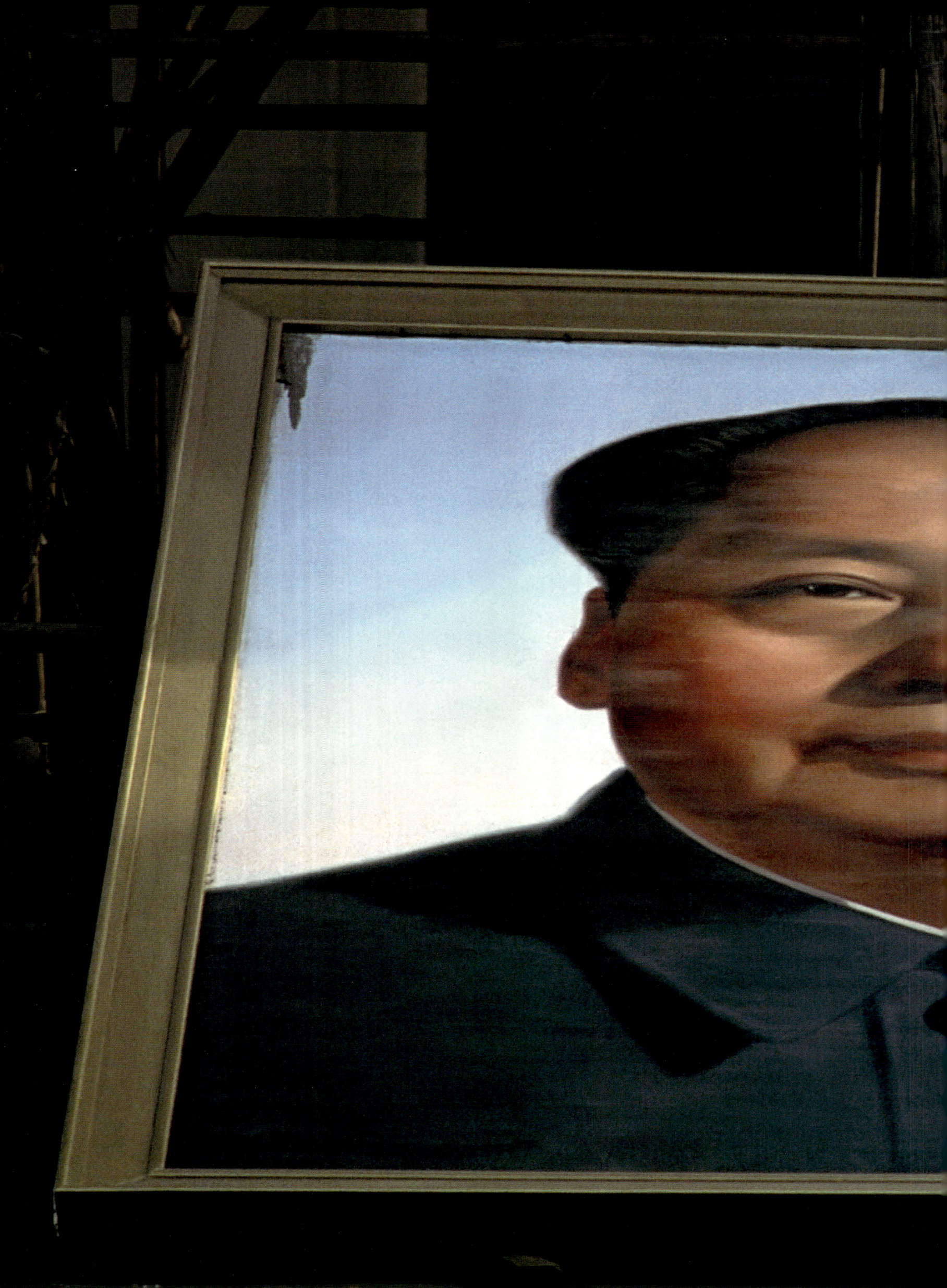

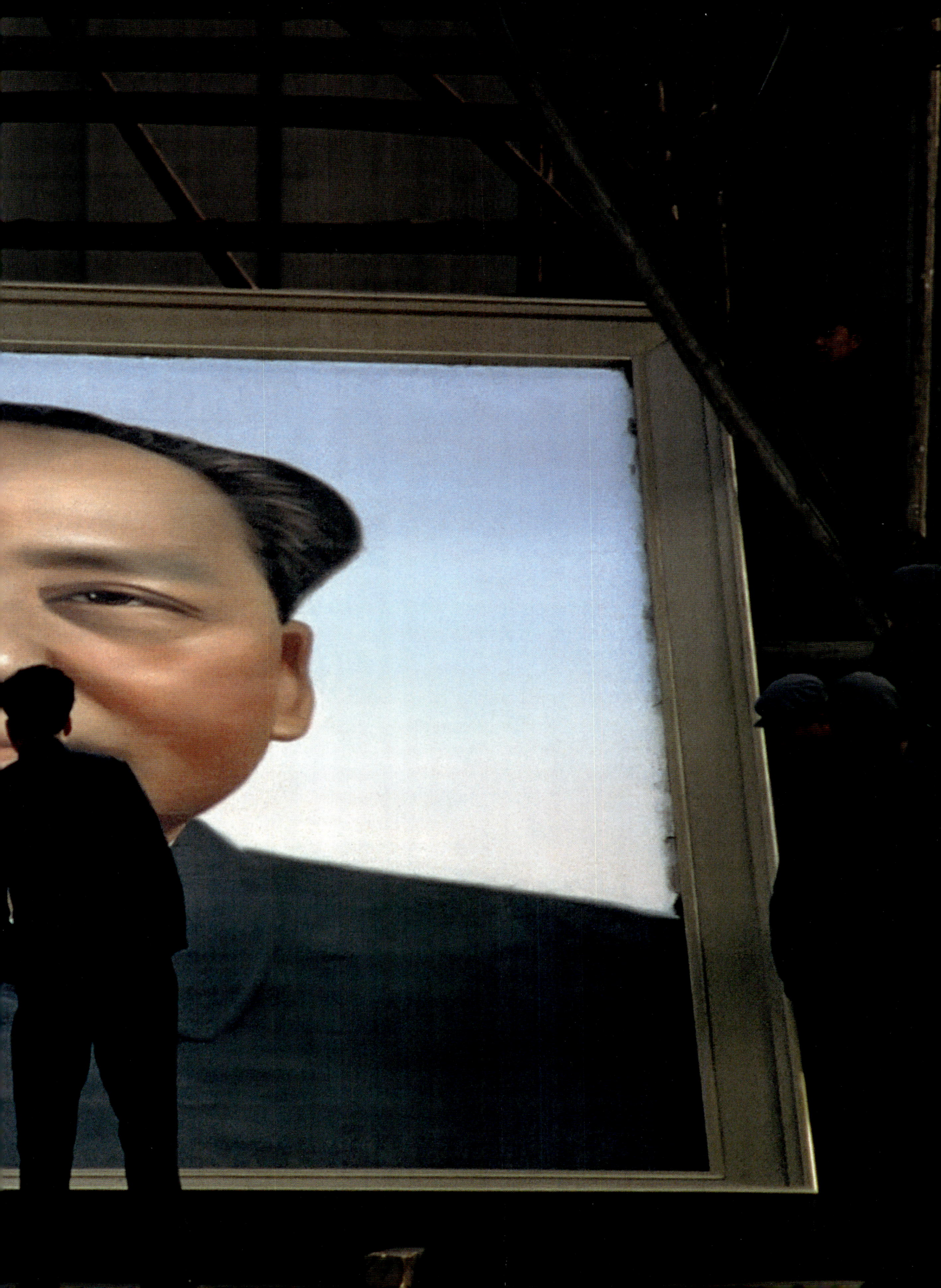

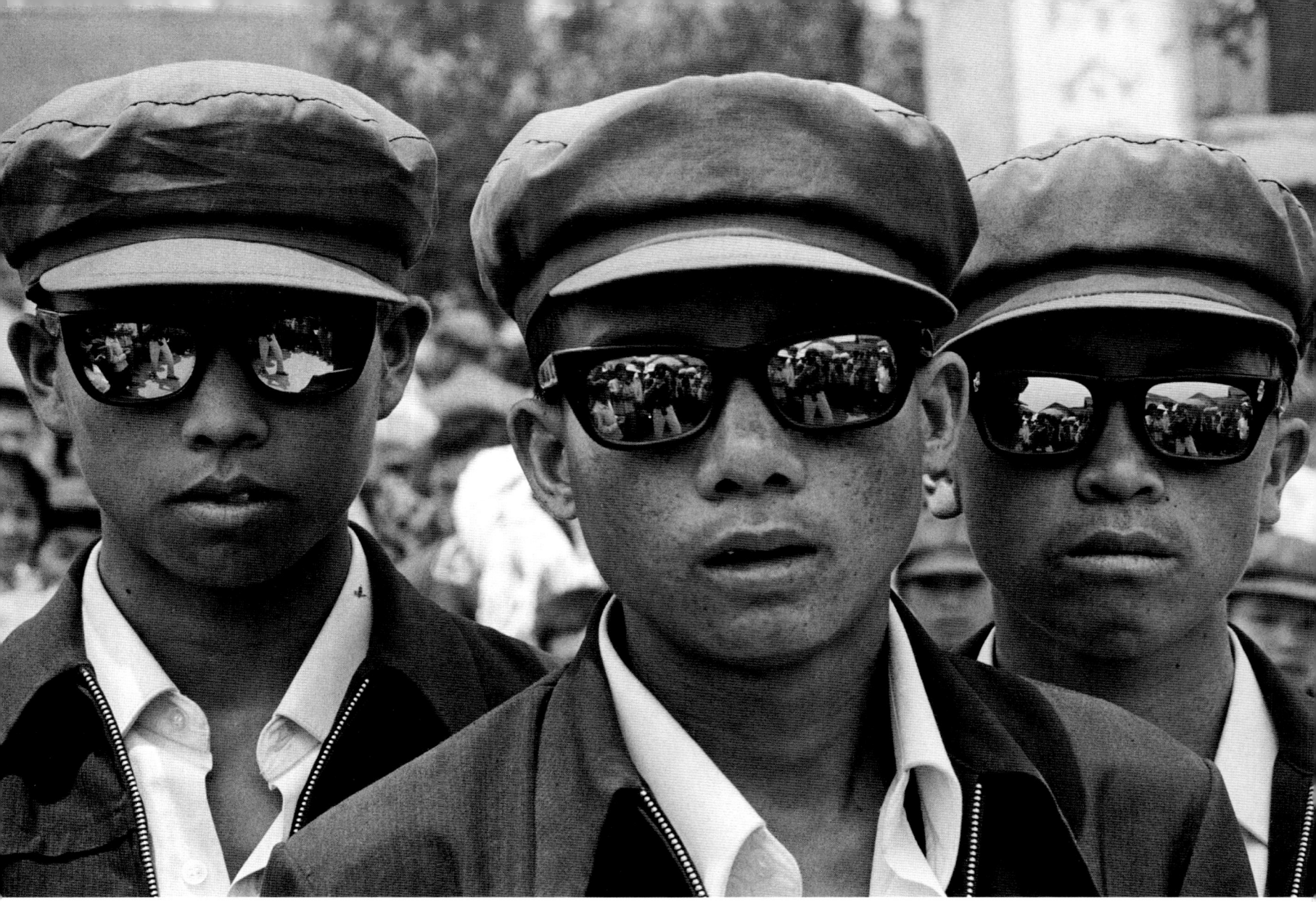

↑
Liu Heung Shing, 1980

For decades under Mao, the entire population dressed only in clothes fashioned from blue serge and practical green army uniforms. In the post-Mao era, and as a result of Deng's "open-door" policy, modern fashions began to influence China's youth. Here, we are shown the "cool" Yunnan style, as three hip young men demonstrate the trend of the moment: mirror sunglasses and military-style clothing.

Unter Mao trug die gesamte Bevölkerung jahrzehntelang ausschließlich Kleidung, die aus blauem Serge geschneidert war, oder praktische grüne Armeeuniformen. In der Zeit nach Mao und als Folge von Dengs Politik der offenen Tür geriet Chinas Jugend unter den Einfluss der Mode. Hier führen drei modebewusste junge Männer den „coolen" Yunnan-Stil als Trend der Zeit vor: verspiegelte Sonnenbrillen und Kleidung im Militärlook.

Pendant des décennies, sous Mao, la population n'avait le droit qu'à des tenues taillées dans de la serge bleue ou à des uniformes kaki. Grâce à la politique des « portes ouvertes » de Deng Xiaoping, la mode commença à intéresser la jeunesse. Ici, exemple du style « cool » du Yunnan : des jeunes gens portent des lunettes de soleil à verres réfléchissants et des vêtements de coupe militaire.

→
Liu Heung Shing, 1981

Following the announcement of Deng Xiaoping's reform policy, China embarked on the road to economic development, inviting investment from foreign enterprises. Coca-Cola set up its first plant in Beijing in 1980. Here, a youth is seen waving a bottle of Coca-Cola in the Forbidden City.

Nach der Verkündung von Deng Xiaopings Reformpolitik schlug China den Weg zum wirtschaftlichen Aufschwung ein und forderte ausländische Firmen zu Investitionen auf. Coca-Cola eröffnete 1980 in Peking seine erste Fabrik. Hier sieht man einen Jugendlichen, wie er in der Verbotenen Stadt eine Flasche Coca-Cola schwenkt.

Après l'annonce de la politique de réformes par Deng Xiaoping, la Chine s'engage sur la voie du développement économique et encourage les investissements étrangers. Coca-Cola implante sa première usine à Pékin en 1980. Ici, un jeune homme agite une bouteille de Coke à l'intérieur de la Cité interdite.

"Coke is no stranger to China. It was sold from 1928 to 1949 and bottled in Shanghai, Qingdao and Tianjin. Coca-Cola returned to China in January 1979 after China and the United States normalized relations. It was one of the first United States products to be advertised on Chinese billboards since the Communist revolution.

Chinese can purchase Coke with foreign exchange certificates and sometimes their own currency – if they are willing to pay the equivalent of about 50 cents for a bottle or $1 for a can, the cost of an average worker's lunch in Peking. So far, there has been no rush to buy the beverage."

„Cola-Cola ist in China wohlbekannt. Es wurde von 1928 bis 1949 verkauft und in Shanghai, Qingdao und Tianjin abgefüllt. Nachdem China und die Vereinigten Staaten ihre Beziehungen normalisiert hatten, kehrte Coca-Cola 1979 nach China zurück. Es war eines der ersten amerikanischen Produkte, für das seit der kommunistischen Revolution auf chinesischen Reklametafeln geworben wurde.

Die Chinesen können Coca-Cola mit Devisencoupons und bisweilen mit ihrer eigenen Währung kaufen – wenn sie denn gewillt sind, etwa 50 Cents für eine Flasche und $ 1 für eine Dose auszugeben, den durchschnittlichen Preis für das Mittagessen eines Arbeiters in Peking. Bisher gab es keinen Ansturm auf das Getränk."

« La Chine connaît bien le Coca-Cola. Il était déjà vendu de 1928 à 1949 et conditionné à Shanghai, Qingdao et Tianjin. La marque revint en Chine en janvier 1979 après la normalisation des relations sino-américaines. Ce fut l'un des premiers produits américains vantés sur les panneaux d'affichage depuis la révolution communiste.

Les Chinois peuvent acheter du Coca-Cola avec des bons d'échange et parfois dans leur propre monnaie, s'ils veulent bien payer l'équivalent d'un demi-dollar pour une bouteille ou 1 $ pour une boîte, soit le coût moyen d'un déjeuner d'ouvrier à Pékin. Jusqu'à présent, on ne s'est pas précipité pour l'acheter. »

ASSOCIATED PRESS, 1981

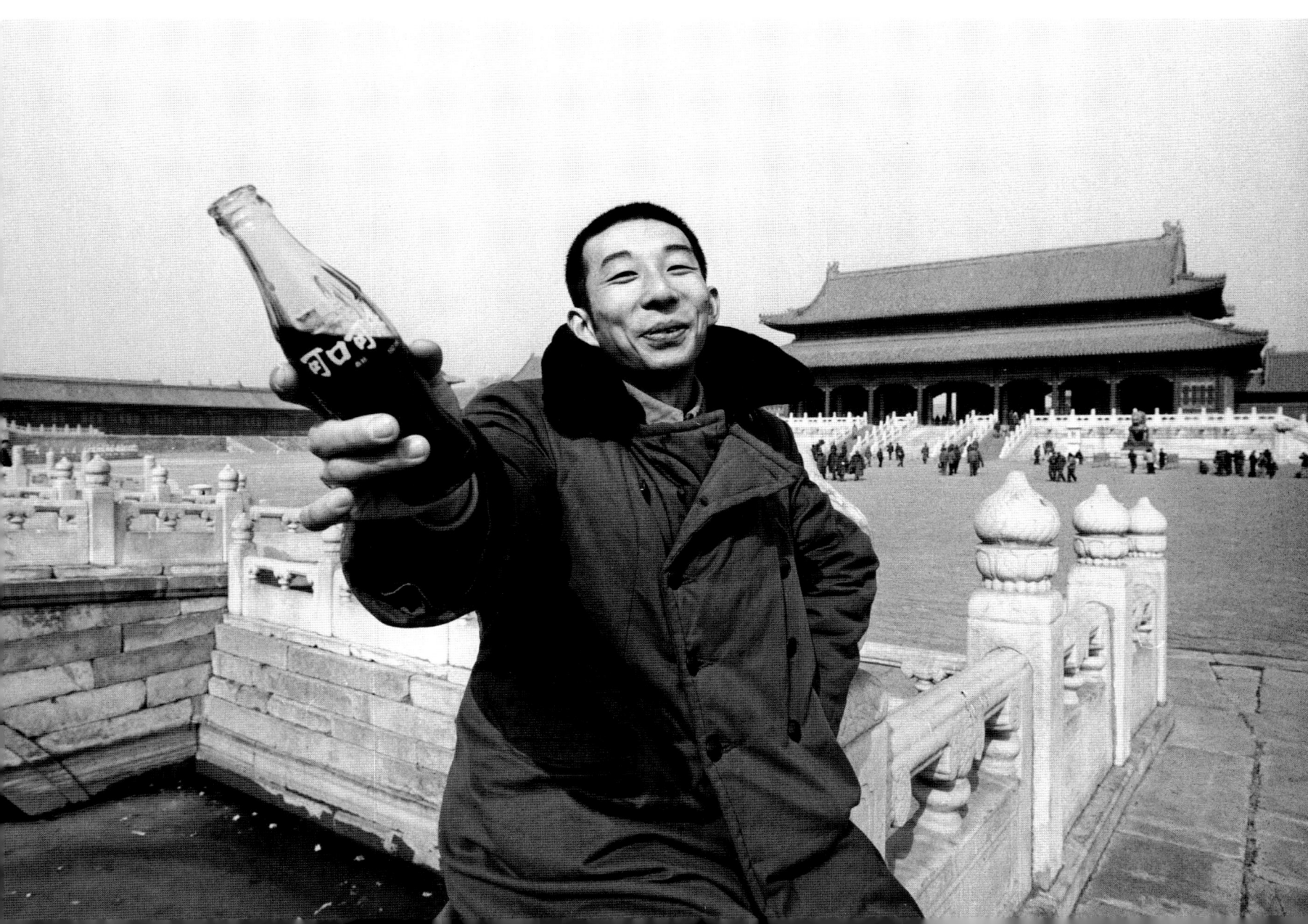

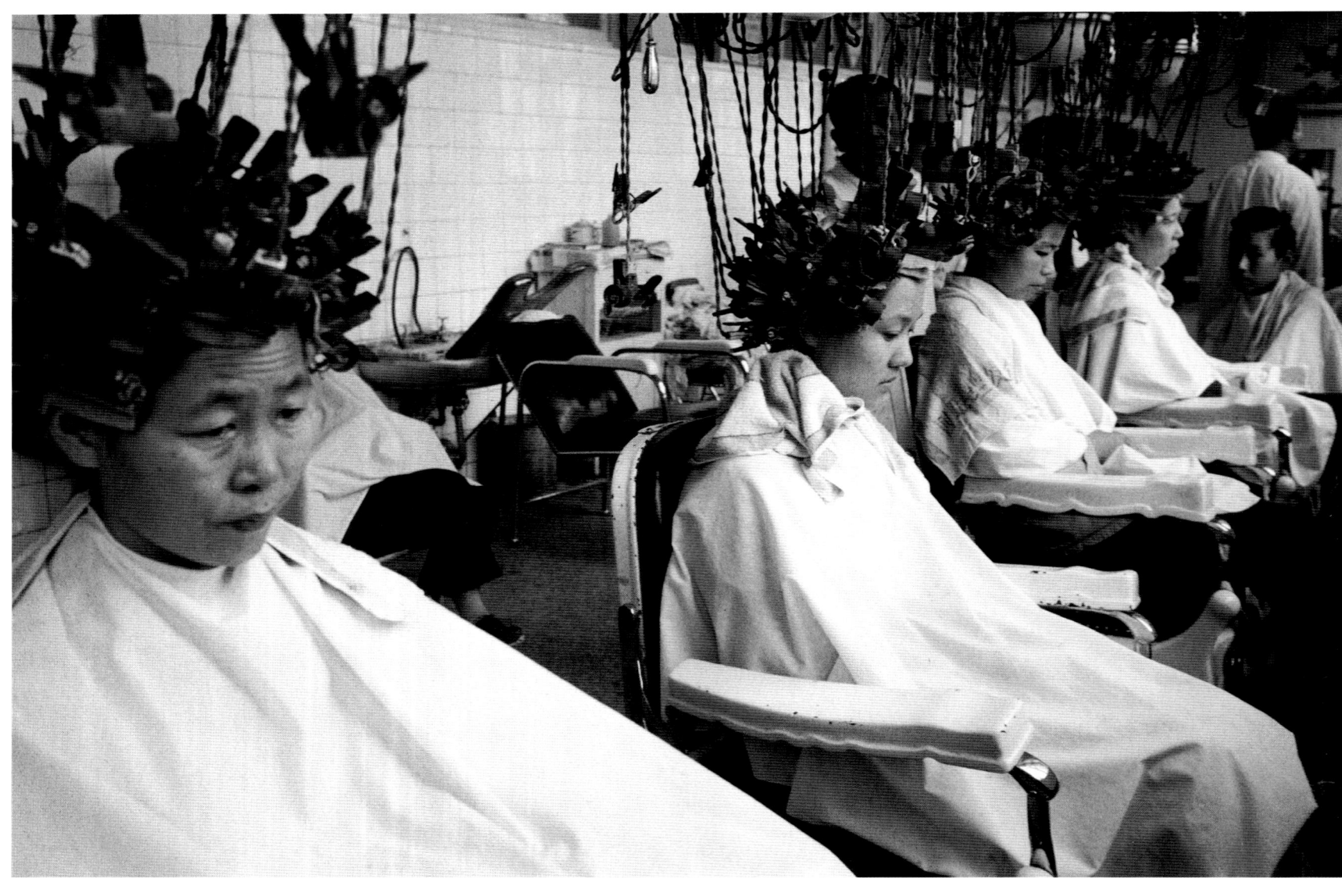

↑
Liu Heung Shing, 1981

*Beijing women get their hair permed at
a new salon.*

*Frauen in Peking lassen sich in einem neuen
Friseursalon eine Dauerwelle legen.*

*Pékinoises se faisant faire une permanente
dans un nouveau salon de coiffure.*

*"Young couples and teenagers from all social strata are regulars of McDonald's and KFC
outlets because the dining environment is considered romantic and comfortable. The
restaurants are brightly lit, clean, and feature light Western music, and except during busy
periods they are relatively quiet, making them ideal for courtship."*

*„Junge Paare und Teenager aus allen sozialen Schichten sind regelmäßige Besucher von
McDonalds und KFC, weil ihre Gasträume als romantisch und komfortabel empfunden
werden. Die Restaurants sind hell, sauber und spielen leichte westliche Musik, und abgesehen
von Stoßzeiten sind sie relativ ruhig und von daher ideal geeignet zum Kennenlernen und
Flirten."*

*« De jeunes couples et des adolescents de toutes les couches sociales sont des clients réguliers
de McDonald's et de KFC car leur cadre est considéré comme romantique et confortable.
Les restaurants sont très éclairés, propres, diffusent de la musique de variété occidentale
et sont relativement tranquilles, sauf pendant les heures d'affluence, ce qui en fait un lieu idéal
pour flirter. »*

**JAMES L. WATSON, Fairbank Professor of Chinese Society and Professor of Anthropology,
Harvard University, 1997**

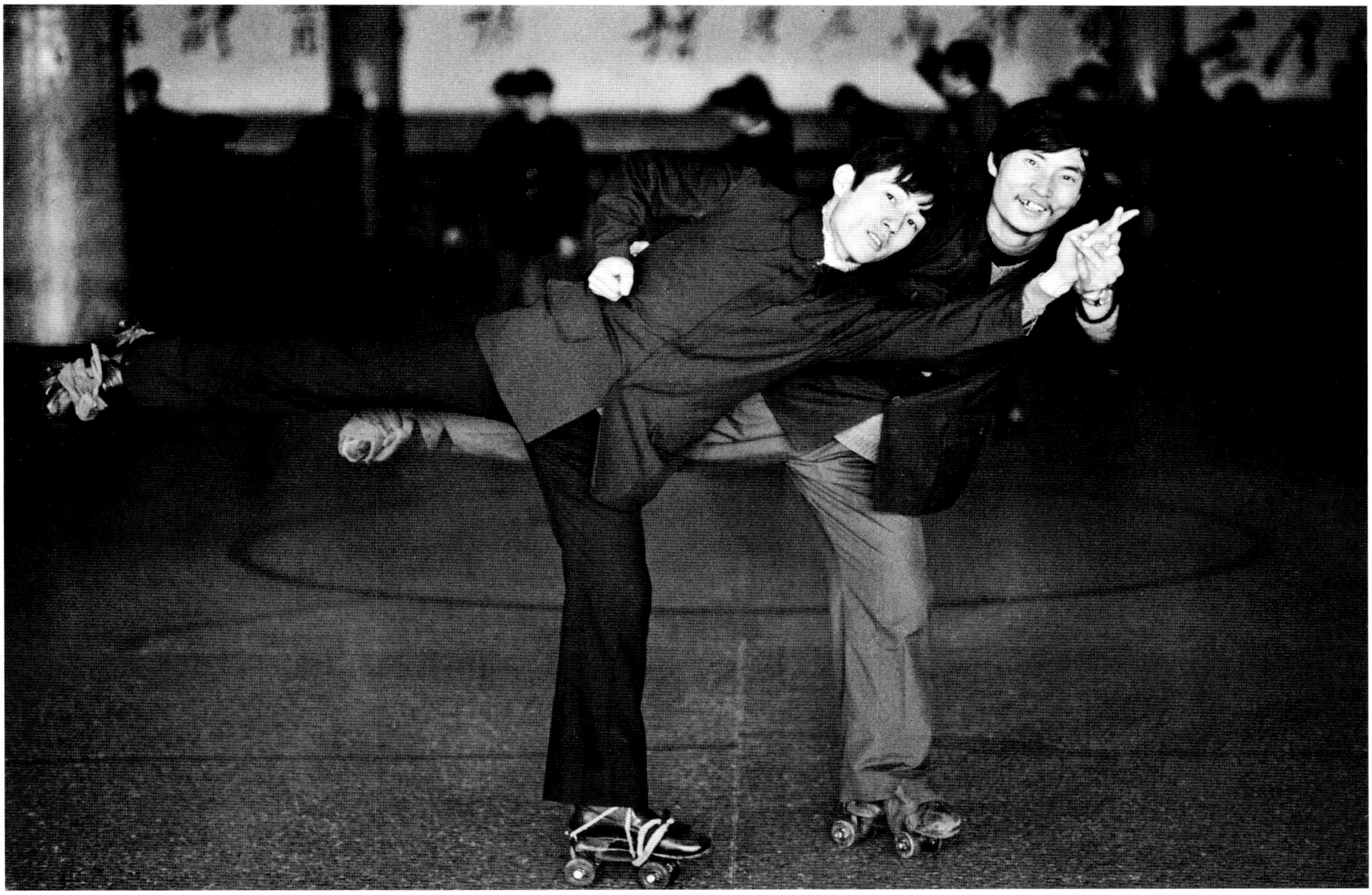

Liu Heung Shing, 1980

Young men roller skate at a recreational club in Shanghai: a simple pleasure that was unimaginable during the Cultural Revolution.

Junge Männer beim Rollschuhlaufen in einem Freizeitklub in Shanghai: ein schlichtes Vergnügen, das während der Kulturrevolution unvorstellbar war.

Des jeunes gens en planche à roulettes dans un club de loisirs de Shanghai : un plaisir simple mais inimaginable pendant la Révolution culturelle.

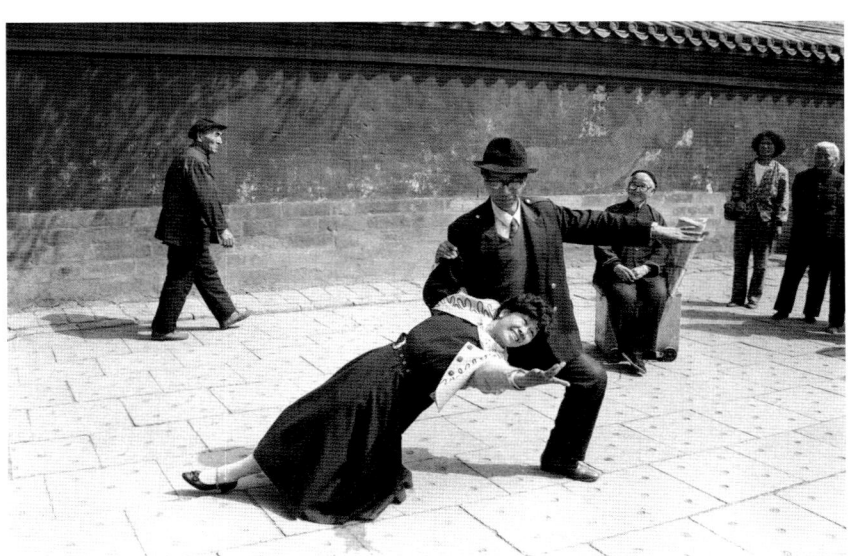

Yang Shizhong, 1985

Beijing's main parks are a huge draw for local residents, who amuse themselves dancing, singing, or engaging in a multitude of exercise programs.

Pekings große Parkanlagen ziehen die Einwohner in Scharen an, die sich dort mit Tanzen, Singen oder einer Vielzahl von Bewegungsübungen die Zeit vertreiben.

Les principaux parcs de Pékin attirent les habitants qui s'y distraient en dansant, chantant ou en pratiquant divers exercices physiques.

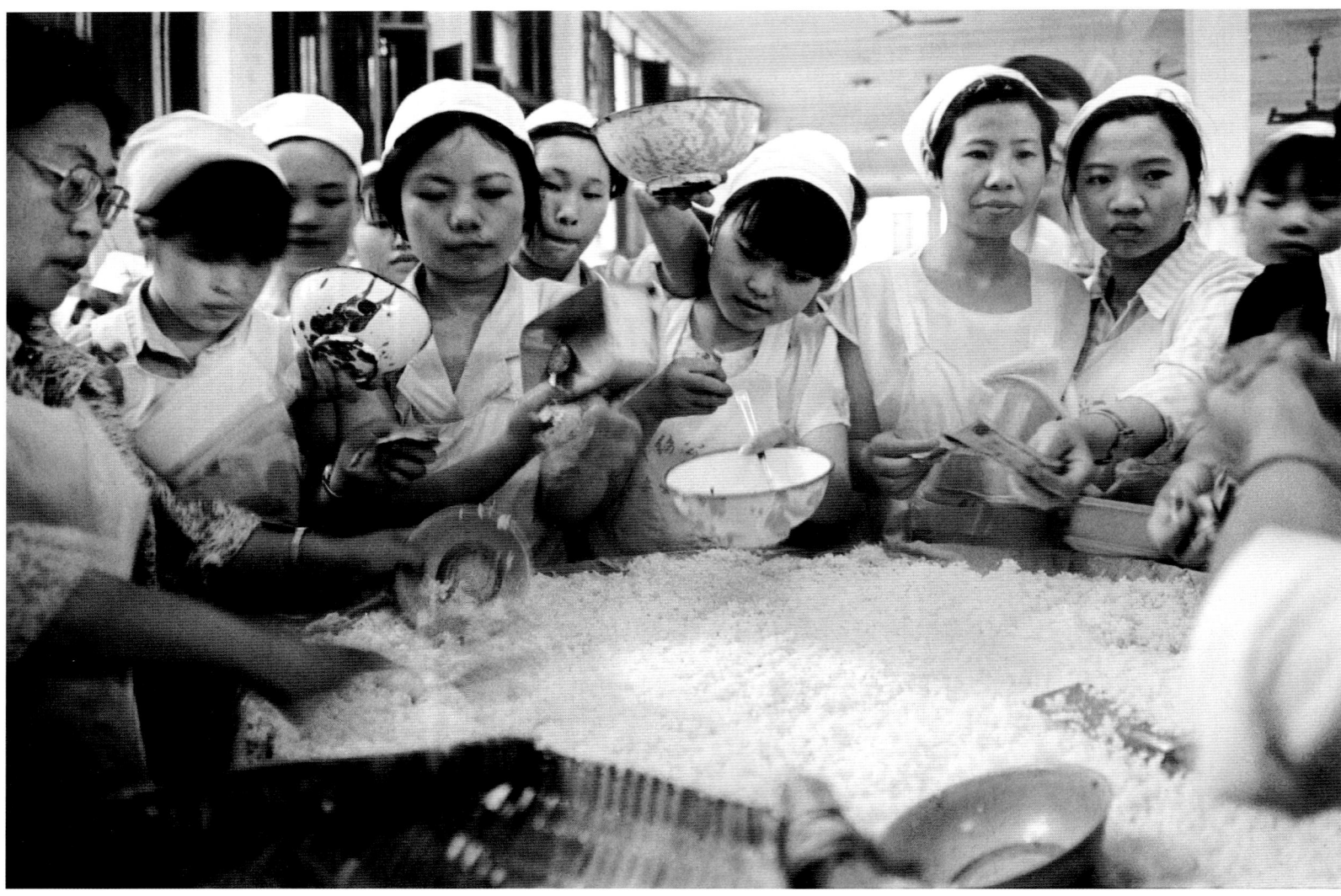

↑
Xiao Quan, 1989

Textile workers take lunch from an "iron rice bowl" in a factory in Sichuan province. State-owned enterprises and collectives were once known as "iron-rice bowls" for providing those in their employ with all that they needed to live—especially their food rations. Today, large factories, which have sprung up across China in line with economic growth, fulfill this role.

Textilarbeiterinnen in einer Fabrik in der Provinz Sichuan bedienen sich mittags aus einer „eisernen Reisschüssel". Staatseigene Betriebe und Kollektive wurden früher als „eiserne Reisschüsseln" bezeichnet, da sie ihre Beschäftigten mit allem Lebensnotwendigen, insbesondere mit Mahlzeiten, versorgten. Heutzutage übernehmen große Fabriken, die im Zuge der Wirtschaftsreform überall in China entstanden sind, diese Rolle.

Des ouvriers du textile se servent pour leur déjeuner dans un « bol de riz en fer » dans une usine de la province du Sichuan. Les entreprises et les collectivités étatiques étaient jadis surnommées de « bol de riz en fer » parce qu'elles offraient à leurs employés tout ce dont ils avaient besoin pour vivre, en particulier des rations de nourriture. Aujourd'hui, ce sont les grandes entreprises, qui se sont multipliées avec la croissance économique, qui remplissent ce rôle.

"Mao Zedong gave us an empty rice bowl, but Deng Xiaoping put a big piece of meat in it. He changed the fate of so many people."

„Mao Zedong gab uns eine leere Reisschüssel, aber Deng Xiaoping legte ein großes Stück Fleisch hinein. Er änderte das Schicksal so vieler Menschen."

« Mao Zedong nous a donné un bol de riz vide, mais Deng Xiaoping y a mis un gros morceau de viande. Il a changé le destin de tant de gens. »

HUANG SIGAO, self-made man, 2007

→
Hu Wugong, 1989

A father in rural Shanxi province attends to a child while a second, wrapped in a traditional quilted winter cape and velvet hat, looks on.

Ein Vater in der ländlichen Provinz Shanxi kümmert sich um ein Kind, während ein zweites, eingemummt in ein traditionelles, wattiertes Wintercape und Samtmütze, zuschaut.

Un père de la province rurale du Shanxi corrige la tenue d'un enfant sous les yeux d'un second, habillé de la traditionnelle cape d'hiver et d'un bonnet de velours.

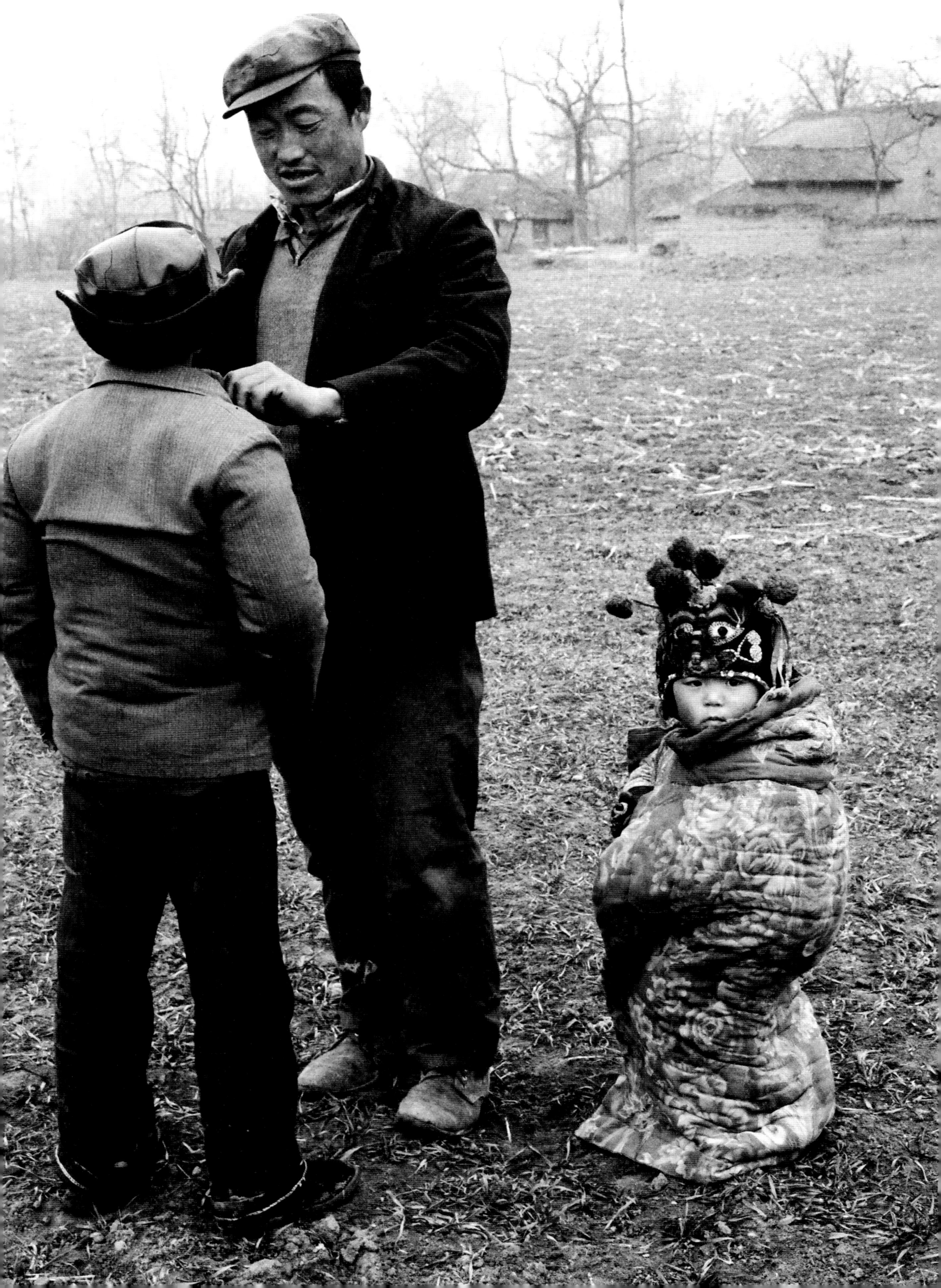

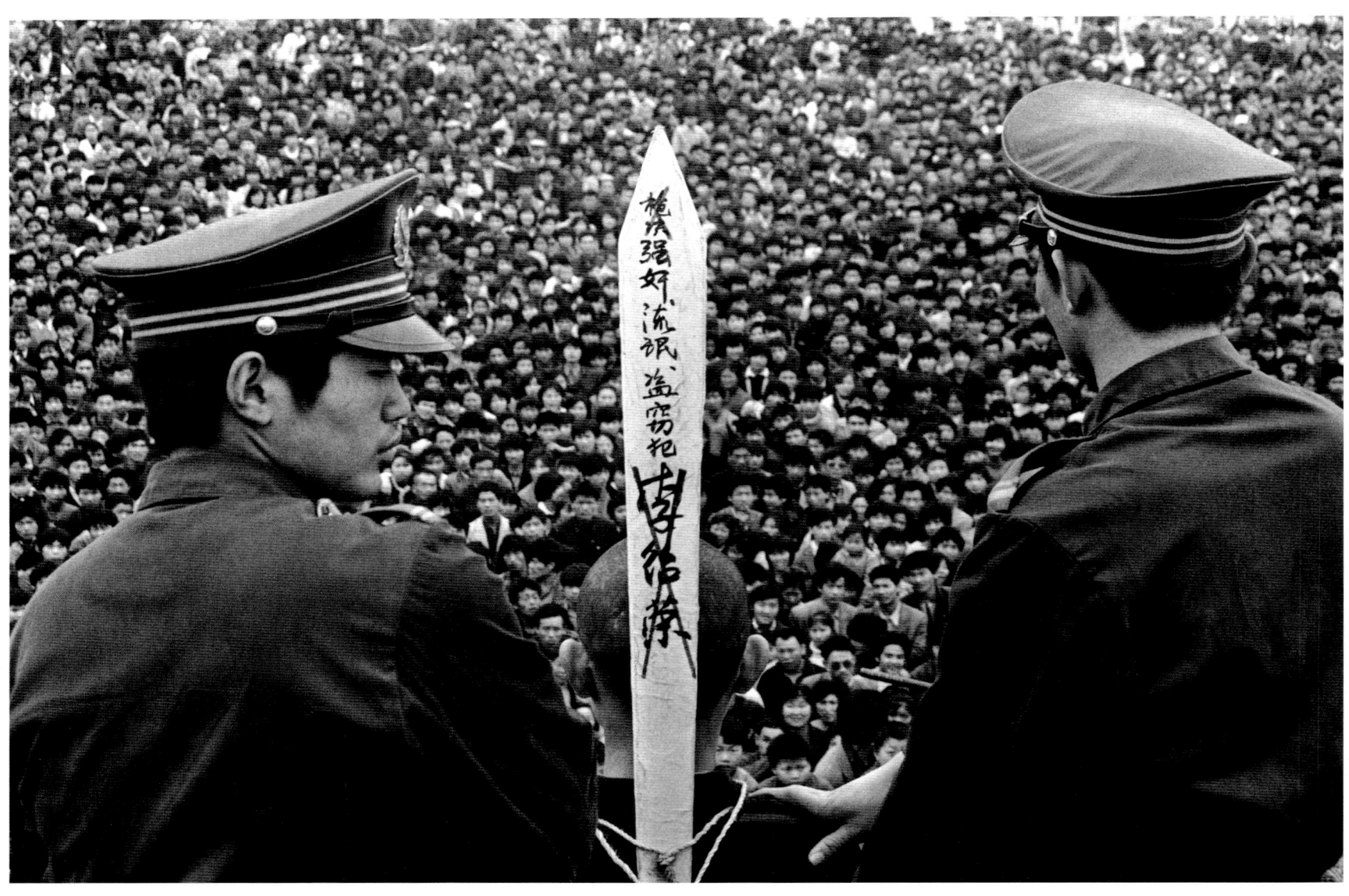

↑
Qiu Yan, 1989

A public execution in Hubei province. Chinese authorities keep the number of executions a secret, but estimates put the figure at about 15,000 a year, many carried out in sports stadiums. The death penalty is resorted to in cases of serious crimes having been committed against a person, armed robbery, drug trafficking, corruption, and political violence. The year 2003 saw the introduction of mobile execution vans, in a shift away from the bullet to the head in favor of lethal injection.

Öffentliche Hinrichtung in der Provinz Hubei. Die chinesischen Behörden geben keine Auskunft über die Zahl der Hinrichtungen, aber sie wird auf etwa 15.000 pro Jahr geschätzt, von denen viele in Sportstadien vollzogen werden. Die Todesstrafe wird für schwere Verbrecher gegen Menschen, bewaffneten Raub, Drogenhandel sowie schwerwiegende Fälle von Korruption und politischer Gewalt verhängt. 2003 wurden mobile Hinrichtungstransporter eingeführt und der vorher übliche Kopfschuss durch eine tödliche Spritze ersetzt.

Exécution publique dans la province du Hubei. Les autorités chinoises ont gardé secret le nombre d'exécutions mais des estimations les chiffrent à 15 000 par an environ, dont beaucoup organisées dans des stades. La peine de mort est prononcée dans les cas de crimes sérieux contre une personnes le vol à main armée, le trafic de drogue, les cas importants de corruption et la violence politique. 2003 vit l'introduction de camions d'exécution mobiles où la balle dans la nuque était remplacée par une injection mortelle.

"Lies written in ink cannot conceal facts written in blood."

„Lügen, mit Tinte geschrieben, können keine Fakten verbergen, die mit Blut geschrieben sind."

« Les mensonges écrits à l'encre ne peuvent cacher les faits écrits dans le sang. »

LU XUN (Zhou Shuren, 1881–1936), short-story writer, essayist, poet, the "father of modern Chinese literature," 1926

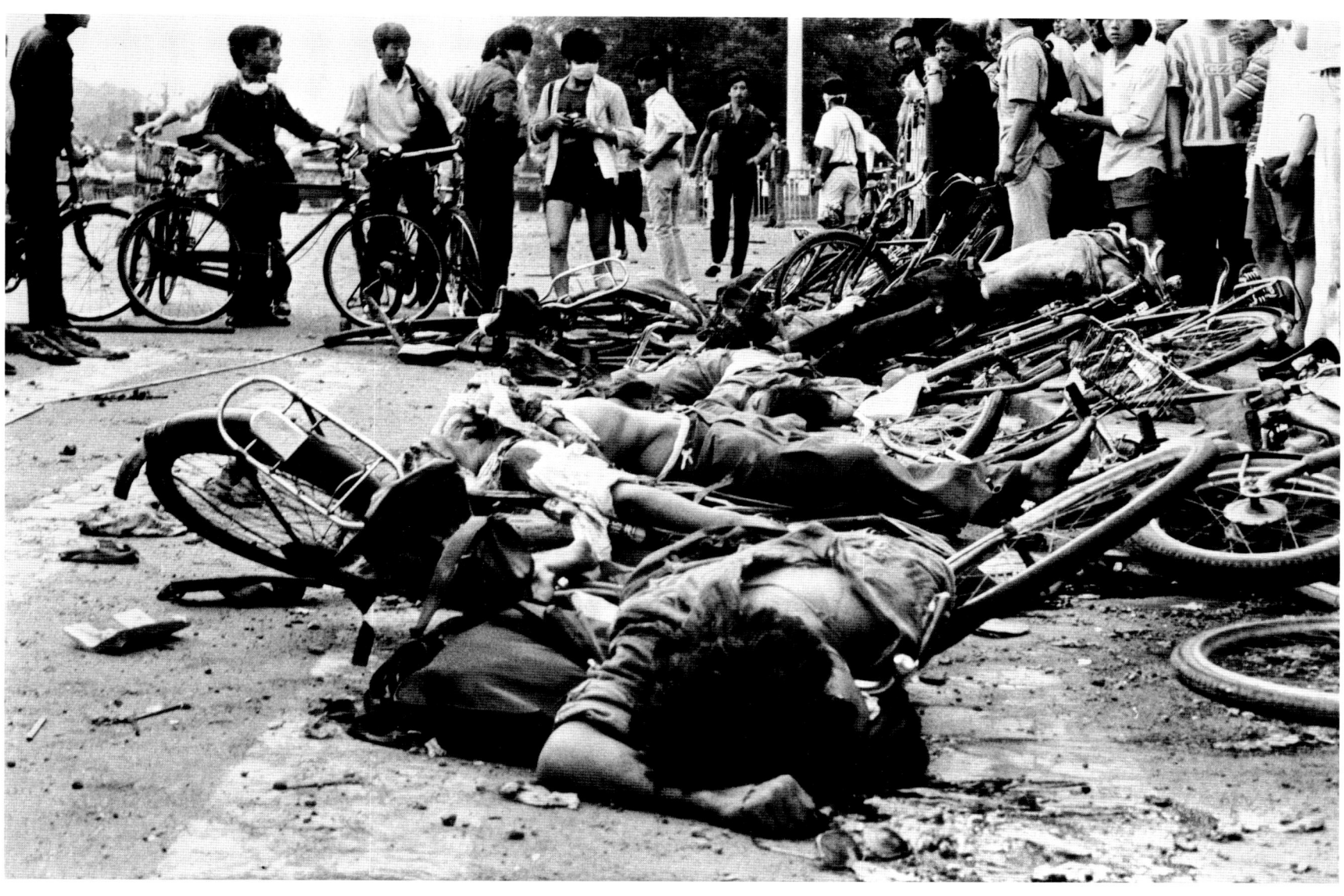

↑
Anon., 1989

Victims lie beside crushed bicycles in Tiananmen Square following government reprisals against the student protesters camped out there. Unconfirmed reports put the death toll at anywhere from several hundred to a thousand.

Nach den Vergeltungsmaßnahmen der Regierung gegen die protestierenden Studenten liegen Opfer neben zermalmten Fahrrädern auf dem Tiananmen-Platz. Unbestätigten Berichten zufolge kamen damals mehrere Hundert bis 1000 Menschen zu Tode.

Des victimes au milieu de bicyclettes écrasées sur la place Tian'anmen après la répression gouvernementale contre les étudiants qui s'y étaient installés. Selon des sources non confirmées, le nombre des morts s'est élevé de plusieurs centaines à un millier.

pp. 302/303
Liu Heung Shing, 1989

An exhausted Chinese student sleeps amidst abandoned banners by the Monument to the People's Heroes in Tiananmen Square after a month-long hunger strike by the student demonstrators.

Ein erschöpfter chinesischer Student schläft am Mahnmal für die Helden des Volkes auf dem Tiananmen-Platz inmitten zurückgelassener Spruchbänder, nachdem studentische Demonstranten dort in einen einmonatigen Hungerstreik getreten waren.

Après un mois de grève de la faim, un étudiant épuisé dort parmi des bannières abandonnées près du monument aux héros du peuple sur la place Tian'anmen.

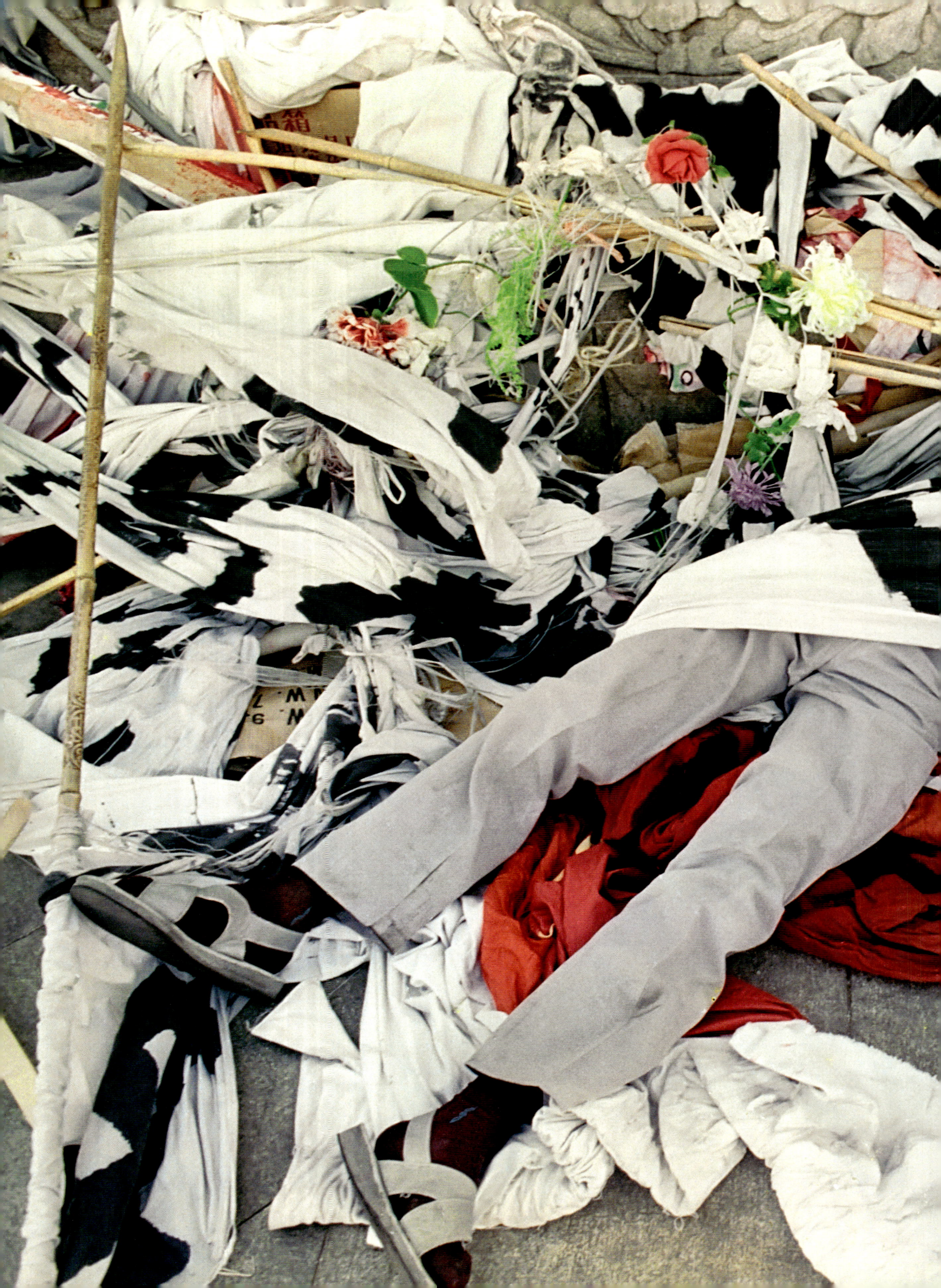

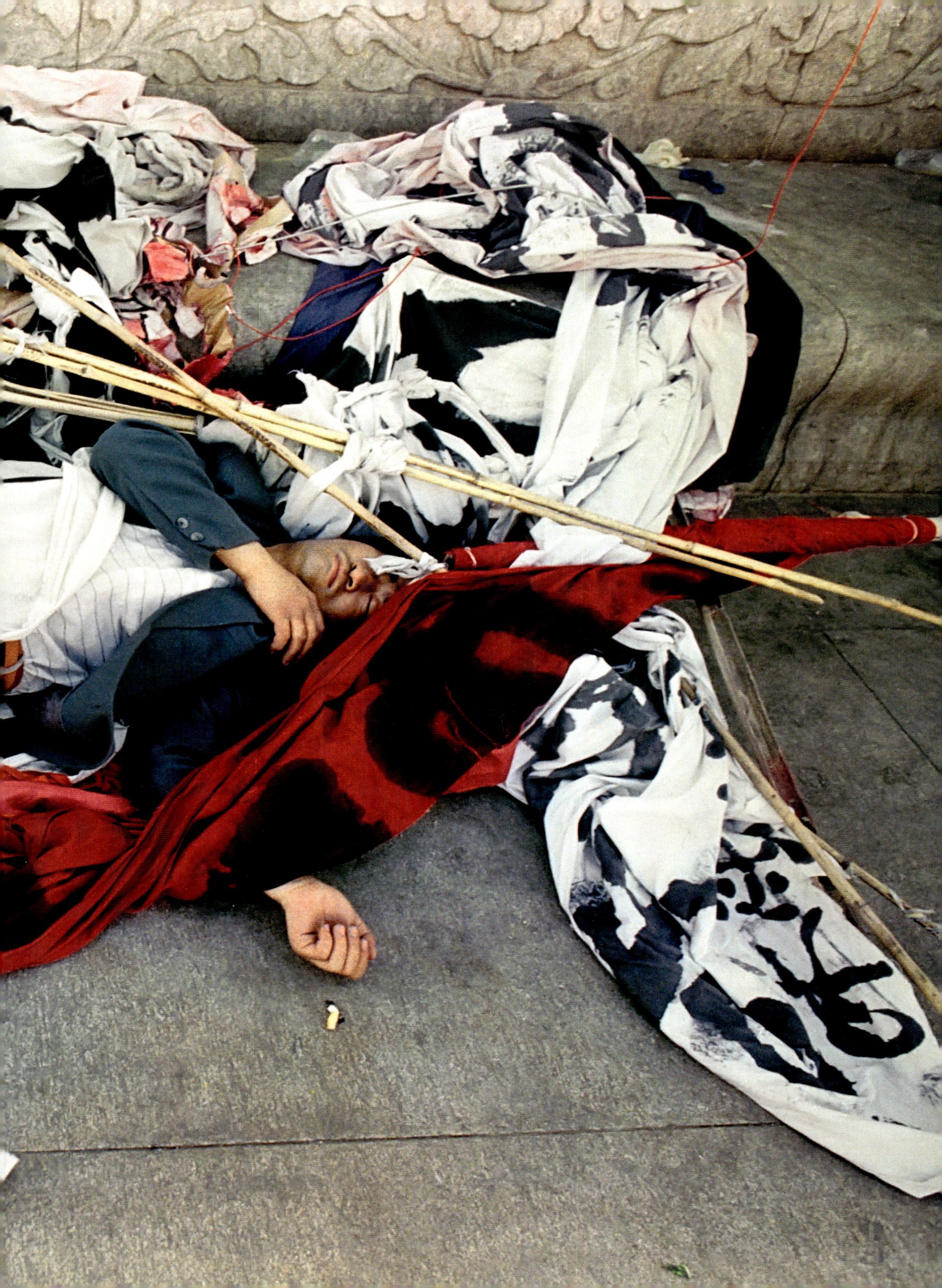

→

Liu Heung Shing, 1989

On June 5, 1989, a young couple waits beneath Jianguomenwai bridge on the fringes of Beijing's diplomatic quarter, as PLA tanks roll above them. Martial law had been in place since the end of May.

Am 5. Juni 1989 wartet ein junges Paar unter der Jianguomenwai-Brücke am Rand von Pekings Diplomatenviertel, während Panzer der Volksbefreiungsarmee über sie hinwegrollen. Seit Ende Mai hatte Kriegsrecht geherrscht.

Le 5 juin 1989, un jeune couple s'abrite sous le pont de Jianguomenwai à la limite du quartier des ambassades de Pékin, tandis que des tanks passent au-dessus de lui. La loi martiale était en vigueur depuis la fin du mois de mai.

"In this May of glowing sunshine, we are starting our hunger strike… We do not want to die; we would like to live good lives, because we are at the best moment of our lives. We do not want to die; we want to go on studying, because our Motherland is still so impoverished. It seems that we are leaving our Motherland behind…and yet we do not want to die. But if the death of one person or a group of people can permit more people to live happily and allow our nation to prosper and flourish, then we do not have the right to go on living an ignoble existence."

DECLARATION OF THE STUDENT HUNGER STRIKERS, May 13, 1989

„In diesem strahlend sonnigen Mai beginnen wir unseren Hungerstreik… Wir wollen nicht sterben, wir wollen ein gutes Leben haben, weil wir uns im besten Abschnitt unseres Lebens befinden. Wir wollen nicht sterben; wir wollen weiter studieren, weil unser Mutterland immer noch so verarmt ist. Es scheint, als verließen wir unser Mutterland…und doch wollen wir nicht sterben. Wenn aber der Tod einer Person oder einer Gruppe von Personen es mehr Menschen möglich macht, glücklich zu leben, und es unserer Nation erlaubt, zu wachsen und zu gedeihen, dann haben wir nicht das Recht, unsere unwürdige Existenz weiterzuführen."

DEKLARATION DER STUDENTEN IM HUNGERSTREIK, 13. Mai 1989

« Dans ce radieux mois de mai, nous entamons notre grève de la faim… Nous ne voulons pas mourir, nous aimerions avoir une belle vie, parce que nous sommes au meilleur moment de notre existence. Nous ne voulons pas mourir. Nous voulons étudier, parce que notre mère-patrie est encore si pauvre. C'est comme si nous abandonnions notre mère-patrie, et pourtant nous ne voulons pas mourir. Mais si la mort d'une seule personne ou d'un groupe de personnes peut permettre à davantage de gens de vivre bien et à notre nation de prospérer, alors nous n'avons pas le droit de continuer à vivre cette existence ignoble. »

DÉCLARATION DES ÉTUDIANTS EN GRÈVE DE LA FAIM, le 13 Mai 1989

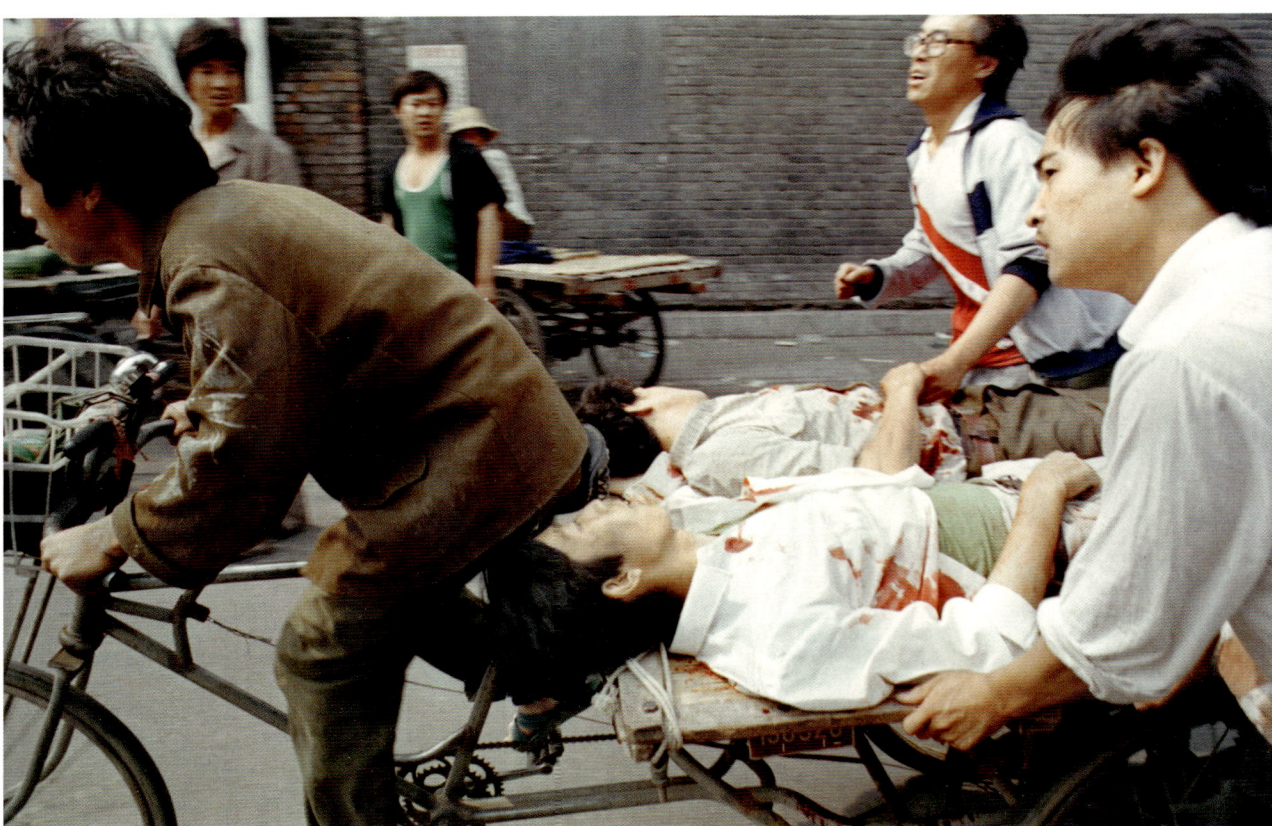

↑

Liu Heung Shing, 1989

Chinese rickshaw drivers and local residents rush two people wounded during the government crackdown on the students in Tiananmen Square to the hospital.

Chinesische Rikschafahrer und Anwohner bringen zwei Männer, die beim brutalen Vorgehen der Regierung gegen die Studenten auf dem Tiananmen-Platz verwundet wurden, auf dem schnellsten Weg ins Krankenhaus.

Des conducteurs de pousse-pousse et des habitants du quartier emmènent à l'hôpital deux personnes blessées pendant la répression des étudiants sur la place Tian'anmen.

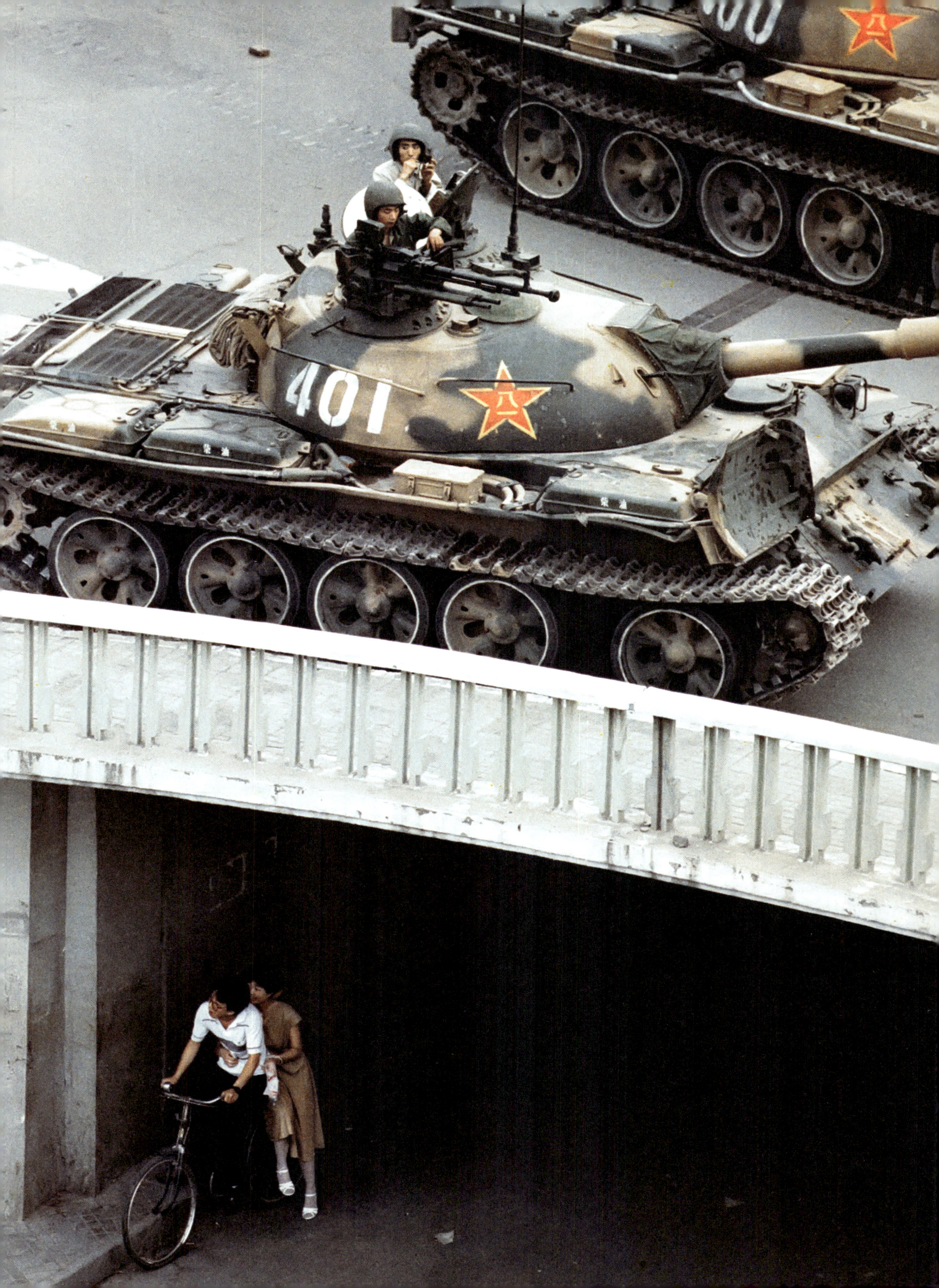

#5

1990–1999
Actions Speaking Louder than Words

Following the stunned silence that marked the national and world response to the 1989 Tiananmen Incident, and in the face of imposed international sanctions, Deng Xiaoping cast his eye around for a competent successor to take over the reins in his wake. His choice was Jiang Zemin, who followed Deng's lead, hastening economic reform, in tandem with a 13-year negotiation prior to China's accession to the World Trade Organization in 2001. Meanwhile, reform was changing China at a grassroots level in ways that were entirely unimaginable prior to 1989.

In 1989, in the wake of reprisals against the student demonstrations, Deng Xiaoping sought strength in the support of trusted colleagues. He turned to Jiang Zemin, who was Shanghai Party Secretary, and elevated him to the post of General Secretary of the Chinese Communist Party. An unknown quantity at the time of his appointment, Jiang would oversee 14 years of unimpeded economic growth and continue the reform initiated by Deng.

Some CCP conservatives were beginning to have their doubts about the policy of "opening up to the outside world" and questioned the role of increasing foreign joint ventures and how it may affect Chinese socialism. Impatient with the situation, in 1992, Deng made his landmark Southern Tour to Shanghai, Shenzhen, and Zhuhai, urging the nation instead to speed up reforms and "open up to the outside world."

In an internal speech, Deng warned his wavering reformer colleagues that China must not "act like women with bound feet." He also insisted that China should adhere to the basic line of economic reform for a hundred years without vacillation. He warned the Chinese senior party officials that without economic reform, China might not have survived the universal condemnation after June 4. He repeatedly told CCP party members that "practice is the sole criterion for testing truth."

Deng also told his colleagues to push ahead along the road to Chinese-style socialism. He said: "Capitalism has been developing for several hundred years. How long have we been building socialism? Besides, we wasted 20 years (1958–78)."

Between 1992 and 1993, with an annual GDP growth approaching 13 per cent, it was felt that China's red hot economy had to be reined in. Even so, it would continue to grow at an average of ten per cent in the remaining years of the decade. At the same time, and with the exception of the U.S., China attracted more direct foreign investment than any other country. The construction boom in Shanghai in particular reportedly concentrated two-fifths of the world's construction cranes and lifts in the city, which worked around the clock.

Hand-overs, Handshakes, and Headaches

When the Asian financial crisis began in Thailand in 1997, quickly spreading to the economies of Southeast Asia, China alone remained unscathed.

Even throughout the negotiation period over the return of Hong Kong, Deng never set foot there: and he died before he could see Hong Kong returned to Chinese sovereignty on July 1, 1997. It was followed in 1999 by the return of Macao from Portugal. The legacy of Deng Xiaoping's Theories was adopted by the next CCP congress and enshrined in the Party constitution.

"Let some people get rich first."

DENG XIAOPING (1904–1997), de facto leader of the People's Republic of China (1976–1997), 1992

#5

1990–1999
Taten sprechen lauter als Worte

Nachdem auf nationaler und auch auf internationaler Ebene das blutige Ereignis auf dem Tiananmen-Platz mit lähmendem Schweigen beantwortet worden war und angesichts der Verhängung internationaler Sanktionen, schaute sich Deng Xiaoping nach einem Nachfolger um, der fähig wäre, nach ihm die Führung zu übernehmen. Seine Wahl fiel auf Jiang Zemin, der Dengs Vorbild folgte, die Wirtschaftsreform beschleunigte und gleichzeitig 13 Jahre lang über die Aufnahme Chinas in die Welthandels-organisation verhandelte, ehe sie 2001 stattfand. Unterdessen veränderten Reformen auf unterster Ebene China in einer Weise, die vor 1989 voll-kommen unvorstellbar gewesen wäre.

Infolge der Repressalien wegen der Studentendemonstrationen suchte Deng Xiaoping 1989 Stärke in der Unterstützung bewährter Mitstreiter. Er wandte sich an Jiang Zemin, der Parteisekretär von Shanghai war, und beförderte ihn auf den Posten des Generalsekretärs der Kommunistischen Partei. Zum Zeitpunkt seiner Ernennung konnte Jiang nicht ahnen, dass er 14 Jahre ungehinderten Wirtschaftswachstums erleben und die von Deng initiierten Reformen fortsetzen würde.

Einige Parteikonservative hegten verstärkt Zweifel hinsichtlich der „Öffnung nach außen" und hinterfragten die Rolle vermehrter Joint Ventures mit ausländischen Firmen und ihre möglichen Auswirkungen auf den chinesischen Sozialismus. Unzufrieden mit der Lage, unternahm Deng 1992 seine richtungweisende Reise in den Süden nach Shanghai, Shenzhen und Zhuhai und mahnte die Nation, die Reformen zu beschleu-nigen und sich „der Welt zu öffnen".

In einer internen Rede warnte Deng seine zaudernden Mitreformer, China dürfe sich nicht „wie Frauen mit gebundenen Füßen benehmen". Darüber hinaus bestand er darauf, China solle 100 Jahre lang ohne zu schwanken an den wesentlichen Prinzipien der Wirtschaftsreform fest-halten. Überdies wies er die altgedienten Parteikader warnend darauf hin, dass China ohne Wirtschaftsreform möglicherweise die nach dem 4. Juni einsetzende allgemeine Verurteilung nicht überstanden hätte. Wiederholt schärfte er den Parteimitgliedern ein, dass „Praxis das einzige Kriterium zur Prüfung der Wahrheit" ist.

Deng forderte seine Kollegen außerdem auf, den Weg zum Sozialismus chinesischer Art energisch zu verfolgen. Er sagte: „Der Kapitalismus entwickelt sich schon seit mehreren hundert Jahren. Wie lange arbeiten wir schon am Sozialismus? Außerdem haben wir 20 Jahre vergeudet (1958–1978)."

Als sich zwischen 1992 und 1993 das jährliche Wachstum des Bruttoinlandsprodukts der Marke von 13 Prozent näherte, war man der Meinung, Chinas boomender Wirtschaft müssten Zügel angelegt werden. Immerhin wuchs sie in den verbleibenden Jahren der Dekade um durchschnittlich zehn Prozent. Gleichzeitig lockte China, mit Ausnahme der USA, mehr ausländisches Kapital an als jedes andere Land. Es heißt, der Bauboom, insbesondere in Shanghai, habe zwei Fünftel der auf der Welt verfügbaren Baukräne und Hubplattformen dort versammelt, wo sie rund um die Uhr im Einsatz waren.

Übergaben, Händeschütteln und Probleme

Als 1997 in Thailand die asiatische Finanzkrise begann und sich rasch auf die Volkswirtschaften Südostasiens ausbreitete, blieb einzig China davon unberührt.

Deng Xiaoping erlebte die Übergabe Hongkongs an China am 1. Juli 1997 nicht mehr. Er selbst hatte auch während der Verhand-lungen über die Rückgabe des Territoriums den Boden der Stadt nie betreten. 1999 folgte die Rückgabe Macaos durch Portugal. Das Ver-mächtnis von Deng Xiaopings Thesen wurde von den folgenden Partei-kongressen der KP Chinas übernommen und fand Eingang in die Satzung der Partei.

„Lasst einige Leute zuerst reich werden."

**DENG XIAOPING (1904–1997), de facto Vorsitzender
der Volksrepublik China (1976–1997), 1992**

#5

1990–1999
Des actes plus forts que des mots

À la suite du silence atterré qui suivit les événements de la place Tian'anmen en 1989 et face aux sanctions internationales, Deng Xiaoping commença à se chercher un successeur pour reprendre les rênes du pouvoir. Son choix se porta sur Jiang Zemin, qui suivit la voie ouverte par Deng, accéléra les réformes économiques aidées par l'entrée du pays à l'Organisation mondiale du commerce en 2001, après treize années de négociations. D'une façon inimaginable avant 1989, les réformes survenues modifiaient de fond en comble le pays.

En 1989, à la suite de la répression des manifestations d'étudiants, Deng Xiaoping rechercha l'appui de fidèles. Il se tourna vers Jiang Zemin, Secrétaire du Parti à Shanghai, qu'il éleva au poste de Secrétaire général du Parti communiste chinois. Pratiquement inconnu au moment de sa nomination, Jiang allait animer 14 ans de croissance économique ininterrompue et poursuivre l'œuvre de réformes initiée par Deng.

Certains conservateurs du Parti commencèrent à émettre des doutes et proposèrent de ralentir les réformes économiques. Deng, que cette situation impatientait, accomplit un voyage historique dans le sud du pays à Shanghai, Shenzhen et Zhuhai, pressant le pays d'accélérer au contraire la réforme et de « s'ouvrir au monde extérieur ».

Dans un discours destiné au Parti, Deng avertit les hésitants que la Chine ne devait pas agir « comme des femmes aux pieds bandés ». Il insista pour que le pays adhère sans la moindre hésitation aux principes de base de la réforme économique pour un siècle. Il avertit les responsables du Parti les plus anciens que sans ces réformes, le pays n'aurait pas survécu à la condamnation universelle des événements du 4 juin. Il expliqua sans relâche que « la pratique est le seul critère qui permette de tester la vérité ».

Il annonça également qu'il fallait avancer sur la route d'un socialisme à la chinoise : « Le capitalisme s'est développé pendant plusieurs centaines d'années. Depuis combien de temps construisons-nous le socialisme ? Et en plus, nous avons perdu 20 ans (1958–78). »

La croissance du produit national brut ayant atteint 13 % entre 1992 et 1993, on comprit que cette surchauffe devait être calmée. Malgré les mesures prises, l'économie continua de progresser de 10 % en moyenne jusqu'à la fin de la décennie. Au même moment, et à l'exception des États-Unis, la Chine attirait davantage d'investissements étrangers que n'importe quel autre pays dans le monde. Le boom de la construction à Shanghaï en particulier, concentrait disait-on les deux cinquièmes des grues utilisées dans le monde, qui travaillaient vingt-quatre heures sur vingt-quatre.

Poignées de main et maux de tête

La Chine fut épargnée par la crise financière asiatique qui s'annonça en 1997 en Thaïlande d'abord avant de se répandre dans tout le Sud-Est asiatique.

Deng ne se rendit jamais à Hong Kong et mourut avant de voir ce territoire restitué à la souveraineté chinoise le 1er juillet 1997. En 1999, Macao fut rendue par le Portugal. L'héritage de Deng Xiaoping et de ses « théories » fut entériné par le Parti lors des congrès successifs du PCC.

« Que certains deviennent riches avant les autres. »

DENG XIAOPING (1904–1997), leader de facto de la
République populaire de Chine (1976–1997), 1992

"Whether peasants cultivated their land or not, they were liable for capitation taxes, ground-rent for housing, and fees for private allotments…[they] were still asked to pay no less than 600 yuan ($73) for a child to go to elementary school, or 1,200 yuan ($145) for junior high school each year. Even if you were in your eighties… or if you were born yesterday, certain charges remained the same. I often met elderly people who would hold my hands, weeping and praying for an early death, and little children kneeling down to appeal for a chance to go to school."

„Ob die Bauern ihr Land bestellten oder nicht, sie unterlagen der Kopfsteuer, der Grundsteuer fürs Wohnen sowie Gebühren für private Erträge … darüber hinaus erwartete man von ihnen, dass sie nicht weniger als 600 Yuan [$73] für ein Jahr Unterricht in der Grundschule, oder 1200 Yuan [$145] für ein Jahr Unterricht in der Oberschule zahlten. Egal ob man über achtzig Jahre alt … oder gestern auf die Welt gekommen war, manche finanziellen Belastungen blieben gleich. Ich habe häufig ältere Leute getroffen, die weinend meine Hand hielten und für einen frühen Tod beteten, und kleine Kinder, die auf Knien um die Chance zum Schulbesuch bettelten."

« Qu'ils cultivent leur terre ou pas, les paysans devaient acquitter des taxes de capitation, un loyer pour leur logement et des droits pour des concessions… on leur réclamait encore chaque année pas moins de 600 yuan [73 $] pour envoyer un enfant à l'école élémentaire ou 1200 yuan [145 $] pour un élève au collège. Que vous ayez quatre-vingt ans… ou soyez né la veille, certaines charges restaient les mêmes. J'ai souvent rencontré des personnes âgées qui me prenaient les mains et priaient pour une mort rapide ou des petits enfants qui se mettaient à genoux pour supplier d'aller à l'école. »

LI CHANGPING (1963–), former Party secretary for Qipan township, Hubei, 2000

→
Liu Heung Shing, 1996

A child in a village school of Liupanshui, considered the poorest place in China in the mid-1990s. He walks 20 kilometers through mountain roads to reach school each day. Since 1978, 400 million people have been lifted out of poverty in China although against the World Bank poverty standard, almost 17 percent of the Chinese population lives on less than the UN standard of one U.S. dollar per day; nearly 47 percent live on less than two dollars per day. Getting children like this to school has not become any easier.

Ein Kind in einer Dorfschule von Liupanshui, das Mitte der 1990er-Jahre als der ärmste Ort Chinas gilt. Es läuft jeden Tag 20 km über Gebirgsstraßen zur Schule. Seit 1978 konnten in China 400 Millionen Menschen aus der schlimmsten Armut befreit werden, wenngleich gemessen am Armutsstandard der Weltbank fast 17 Prozent der chinesischen Bevölkerung von weniger als dem UN-Standard von 1 US-Dollar pro Tag leben und fast 47 Prozent von weniger als 2 US-Dollar pro Tag. Ein Kind wie dieses in die Schule zu schicken, ist keineswegs einfacher geworden.

Enfant d'une école de village de Liupanshui, l'endroit le plus pauvre de Chine au milieu des années 1990. Il doit parcourir chaque jour 20 km de chemins de montagne pour se rendre en classe. Depuis 1978, 400 millions de personnes ont pu dépasser le niveau de la pauvreté en Chine bien que, par rapport aux critères de la Banque mondiale, près de 17 % de la population vivent avec moins d'un dollar US par jour et et près de 47 % avec moins de 2 $. Il est toujours aussi difficile pour des enfants comme celui-ci de se rendre à l'école.

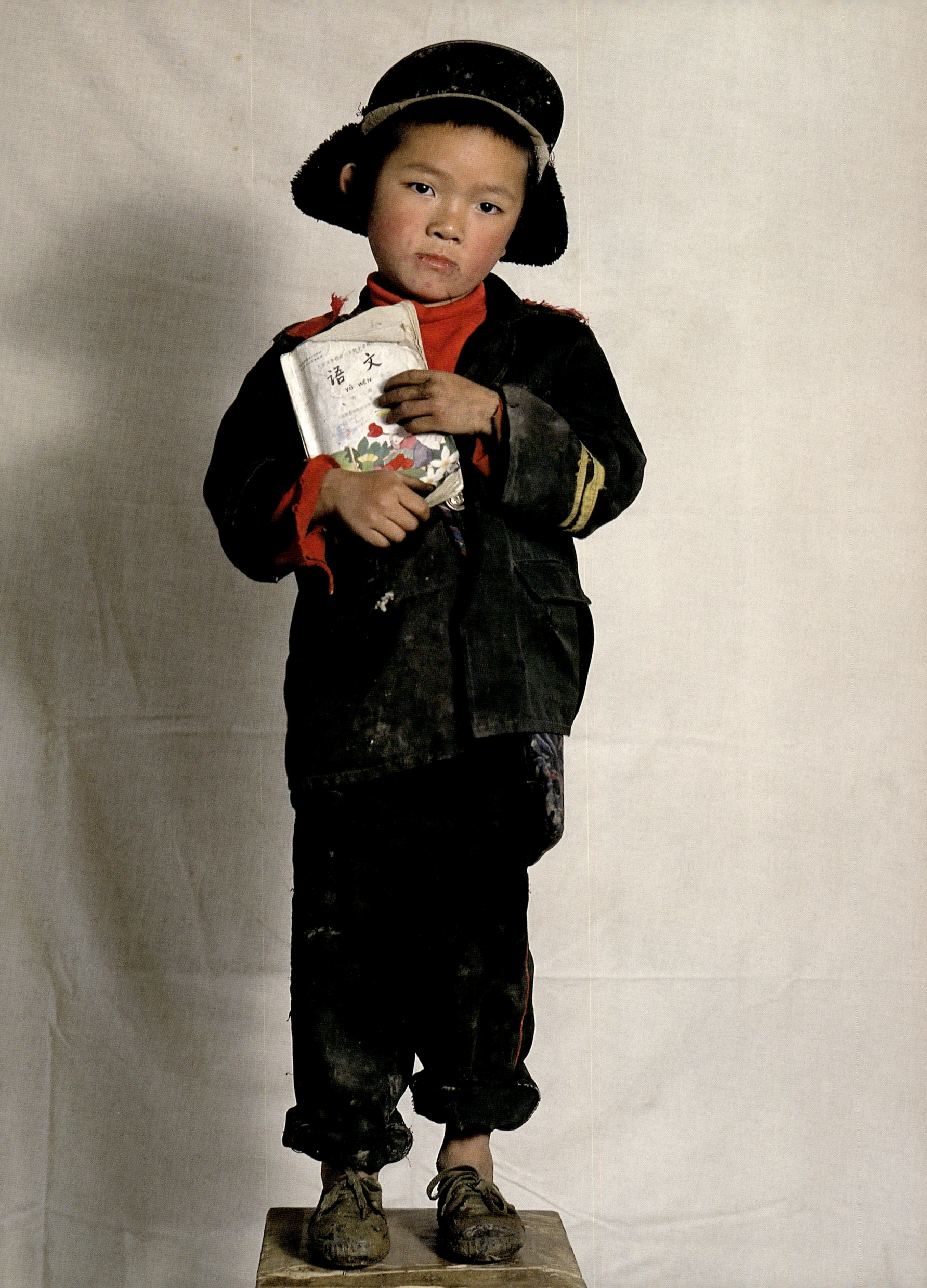

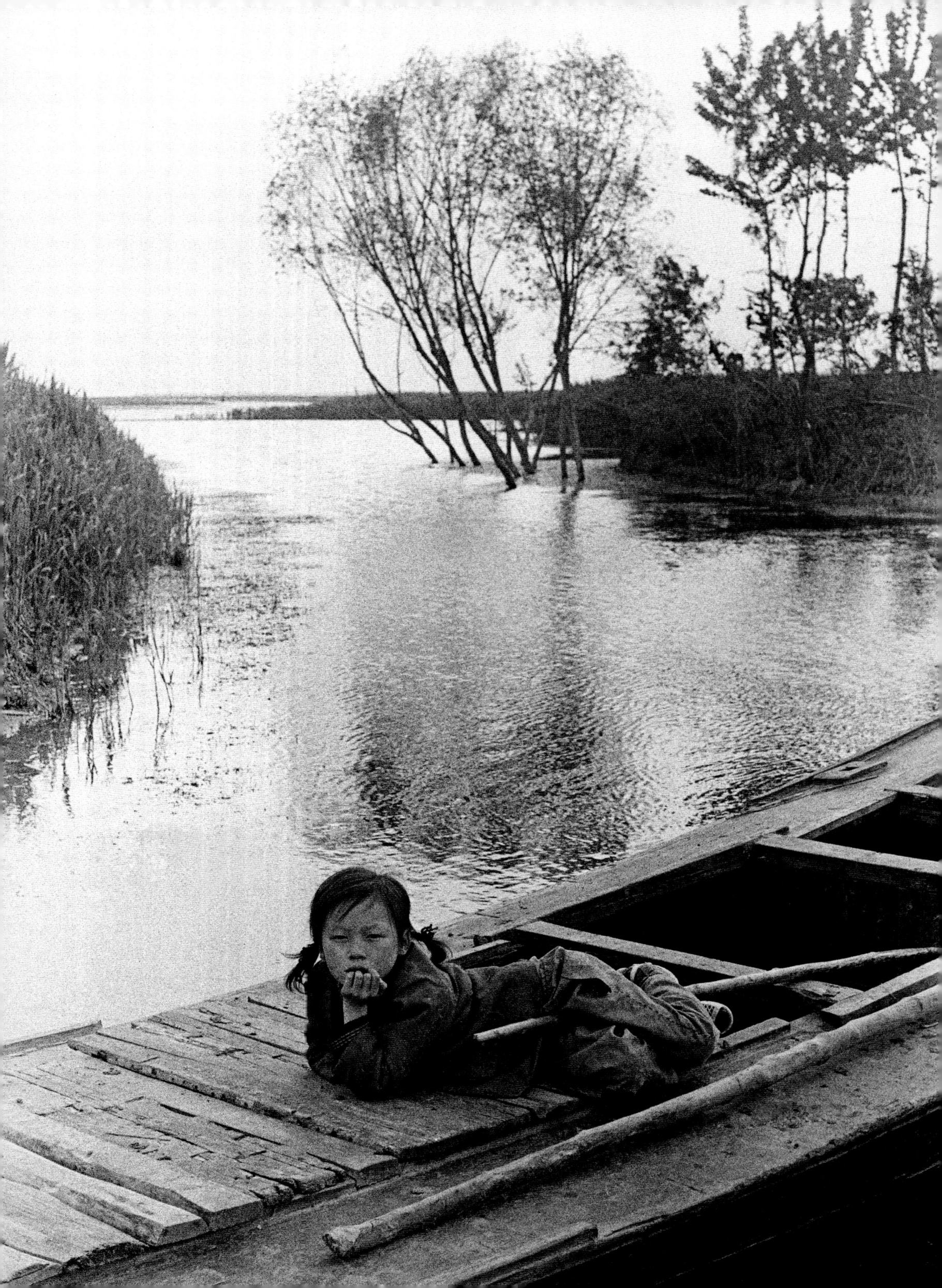

→

Li Nan, 1993

Although "missed" by Marco Polo, the phenomenon of "bound-foot" women in China is one mind-boggling fact of Chinese cultural history known to most foreigners: a curious myth of an exotic past that is accounted for in terms of sexual allure. The Republican government made the first move to ban the practice of foot binding in 1912, liberating women from a tradition that had been practiced for almost 1000 years (since the Song dynasty 960–1279), but which became widespread through the Ming and Qing dynasties. The practice would begin around age seven, the body affected ever after. Here, one of the few remaining bound-foot ladies braids.

Wenngleich von Marco Polo „übersehen", ist das Phänomen der Frauen mit gebundenen Füßen ein den meisten Ausländern bekanntes und sehr befremdliches Phänomen der chinesischen Kulturgeschichte: der seltsame, mit sexueller Verlockung begründete Mythos einer exotischen Vergangenheit. Die republikanische Regierung unternahm 1912 erste Versuche, die Praxis des Füßebindens zu verbieten und die Frauen damit von einer nahezu 1000 Jahre alten Tradition zu befreien (seit der Song-Dynastie 960–1279, Ausbreitung in der Ming- und Qing-Dynastie). Die Prozedur begann im Alter von sieben Jahren und beeinträchtigte das körperliche Wohlbefinden bis zum Lebensende. Hier eine der wenigen noch lebenden Frauen mit gebundenen Füßen.

Bien que « manqué » par Marco Polo, le phénomène des femmes aux « pieds bandés » est un des faits culturels les plus troublants de l'histoire chinoise aux yeux des étrangers : mythe étrange tiré d'un passé exotique et traduit en termes de séduction sexuelle. Le gouvernement républicain avait tenté une première fois en 1912 d'interdire cette pratique pour libérer les femmes de cette tradition pratiquée depuis près de 1000 ans (depuis la dynastie Song, 960–1279) mais qui s'était répandue sous les dynasties Ming et Qing. La pratique commençait vers l'âge de sept ans, et le corps en restait marqué à jamais. Ici l'une des rares femmes aux pieds bandés encore en vie.

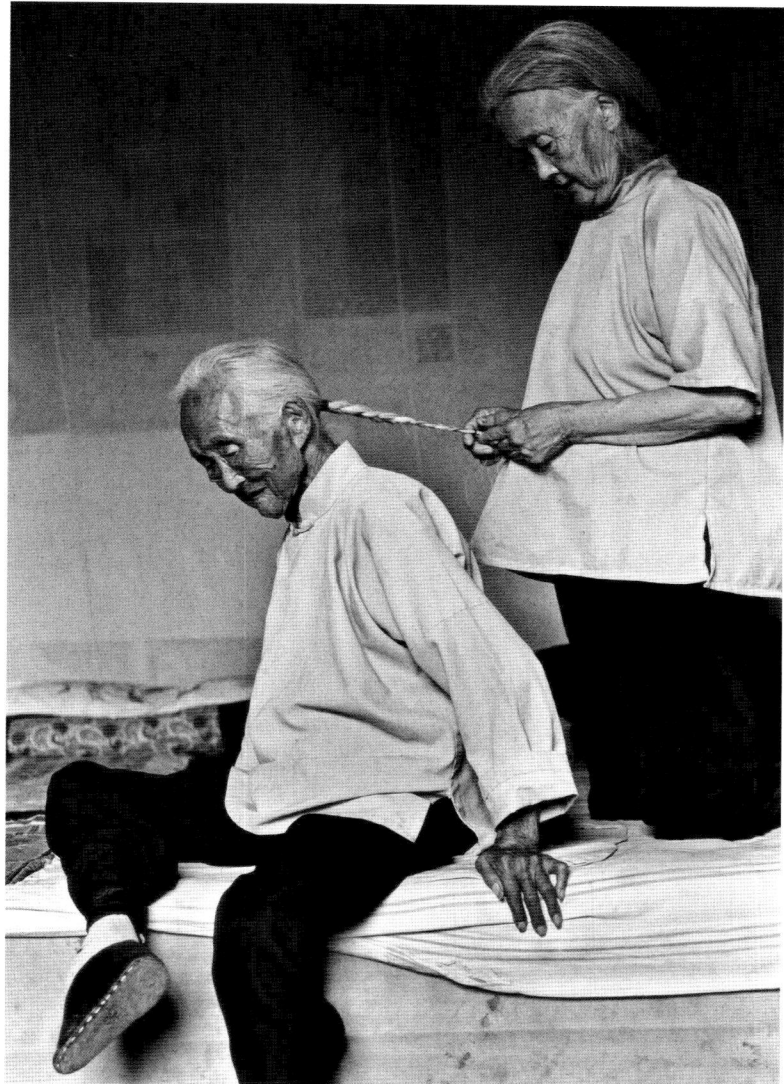

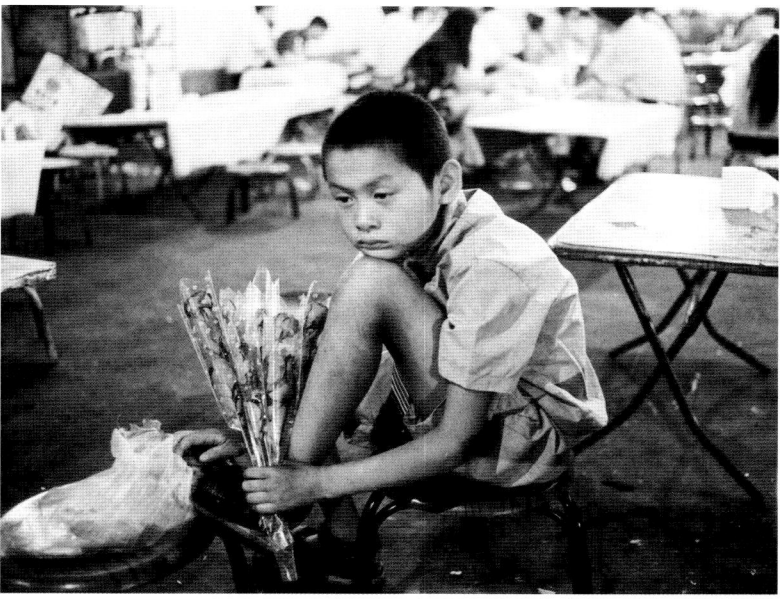

←
Peng Xiangjie, 1998

A child selling flowers at midnight in Xi'an. In urban areas, this is the thin end of a much larger wedge of child labor in China.

Ein Kind verkauft um Mitternacht Blumen in Xian. In städtischen Regionen stellt dies eine weniger dramatische Ausprägung des andernorts sehr viel größeren Problems der Kinderarbeit in China dar.

Un enfant vend des fleurs à minuit à Xian. Il ne s'agit là que d'une manifestation urbaine anecdotique du grave problème du travail des enfants en Chine.

← ←
Wei Dong, 1990

A child relaxes on a boat in an idyllic village setting in Hebei province.

In einer idyllischen Dorfszenerie in der Provinz Hebei ruht ein Kind auf einem Boot.

Un enfant se repose sur un bateau dans un village idyllique de la province du Hebei.

→

Xie Hailong, 1992

Children study by a grain mill in a remote rural area of Shanxi province. The school comprises one teacher and three students. This is one of several iconic images produced to promote Project Hope, which was launched to fund schools in China's poorest areas. As a developing country, China's rural population faces a shortage of education funds, especially in poverty-stricken areas, where there are more than 30 million children between the ages of 5 and 14, largely due to limited government spending and because allocated funds frequently get diverted to other projects. Many children are forced to drop out of school because their parents can't afford the tuition fees.

Kinder lernen auf einer Getreidemühle in einem abgelegenen ländlichen Gebiet der Provinz Shanxi. Die Schule besteht aus einem Lehrer und drei Schülern. Dies ist eine von mehreren symbolträchtigen Aufnahmen, die entstanden, um das Projekt Hoffnung zu befördern, das angestoßen wurde, um Schulen in den ärmsten Regionen Chinas zu finanzieren. Als Entwicklungsland muss Chinas Landbevölkerung mit knappen Mitteln für Bildung auskommen, besonders in den verarmten Landesteilen, wo es über 30 Millionen Kinder im Alter zwischen 6 und 14 Jahren gibt. Ursächlich hierfür sind Ausgabenbegrenzungen seitens der Regierung und die Tatsache, dass zugeteilte Gelder häufig für andere Projekte abgezweigt werden. Viele Kinder sind gezwungen, ihre Ausbildung abzubrechen, weil ihre Eltern das Schulgeld nicht mehr bezahlen können.

Des enfants étudient sur une meule à grain dans un village reculé de la province du Shanxi. L'école compte un instituteur et trois élèves. Cette image fait partie d'un projet photographique « Espoir » lancé pour financer des écoles dans les régions les plus pauvres de la Chine. Pays en voie de développement, elle manque d'argent pour financer les écoles, en particulier dans les régions pauvres où vivent plus de 30 millions d'enfants âgés de 6 à 14 ans. Les fonds sont souvent détournés pour d'autres projets. De nombreux enfants sont forcés de quitter l'école parce que leurs parents ne peuvent payer les contributions demandées.

"At the nearby village of Yang Shang, 10-year-old Liang Yuqin does not join the boys who leave for school each day. 'I really want to go and I might go next semester if my family has the money,' she said hopefully. Teacher Hu, as he is called in a sign of respect, even offered to pay the girl's tuition, $6.10 a semester. But the father demurred because he is planning to move his family to Guangxi Province to rent a fertile piece of land and raise livestock."

„Im nahe gelegenen Dorf Yang Shang begleitet die 10-jährige Liang Yuqin die Buben nicht, wenn sie jeden Morgen zur Schule gehen. ‚Ich möchte wirklich gern hingehen, und vielleicht gehe ich im nächsten Jahr, wenn meine Familie das Geld hat', sagt sie hoffnungsvoll. Lehrer Hu, wie er respektvoll genannt wird, hat sogar angeboten, das Schulgeld in Höhe von $ 5,10 für sie zu übernehmen, aber der Vater lehnte ab, weil er plant, mit seiner Familie in die Provinz Guangxi umzuziehen, wo er ein fruchtbares Stück Land pachten und Vieh züchten will."

« Dans le village voisin de Yang Shang, la petite Liang Yuqin, 10 ans, n'accompagne pas les garçons qui partent pour l'école chaque matin. « Je veux y aller et j'irai peut-être le semestre prochain, si ma famille trouve de l'argent, » dit-elle pleine d'espoir. Le Professeur Hu, comme on l'appelle ici en signe de respect, avait même offert de payer les frais d'éducation de la petite fille, 6,10 $ par semestre, mais le père a refusé car il prévoit de déménager vers la province voisine du Guangxi pour louer une terre plus fertile et élever du bétail. »

PATRICK TYLER, journalist and former Beijing bureau chief for The New York Times, 1995

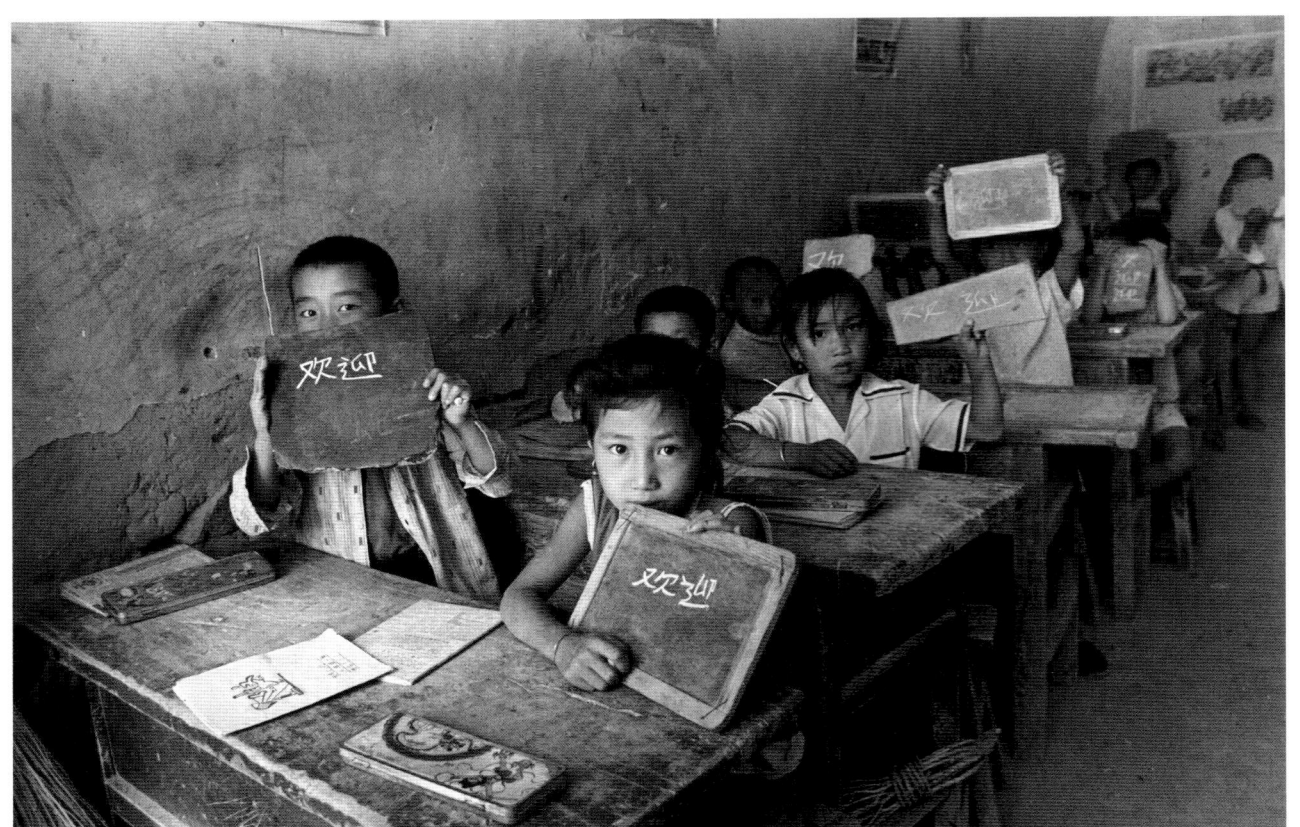

←

Xie Hailong, 1992

Schoolchildren in a makeshift classroom in a mountainous region of Shanxi province. Xie Hailong's name is synonymous with this series of images produced to publicize Project Hope, which helps keep China's rural children in school.

Grundschüler in einem provisorischen Klassenzimmer in einer gebirgigen Gegend der Provinz Shanxi. Der Name Xie Hailongs ist gleichbedeutend mit dieser Bilderserie, die entstand, um für das Projekt Hoffnung zu werben, das den Kindern auf dem Land den Besuch einer Schule ermöglichen soll.

Des écoliers dans une salle de classe reconstituée dans une zone montagneuse de la province du Shanxi. Le nom du photographe Xie Hailong est lié à cette série d'images réalisée pour promouvoir le programme « Espoir » qui aide à envoyer les enfants des zones agricoles à l'école.

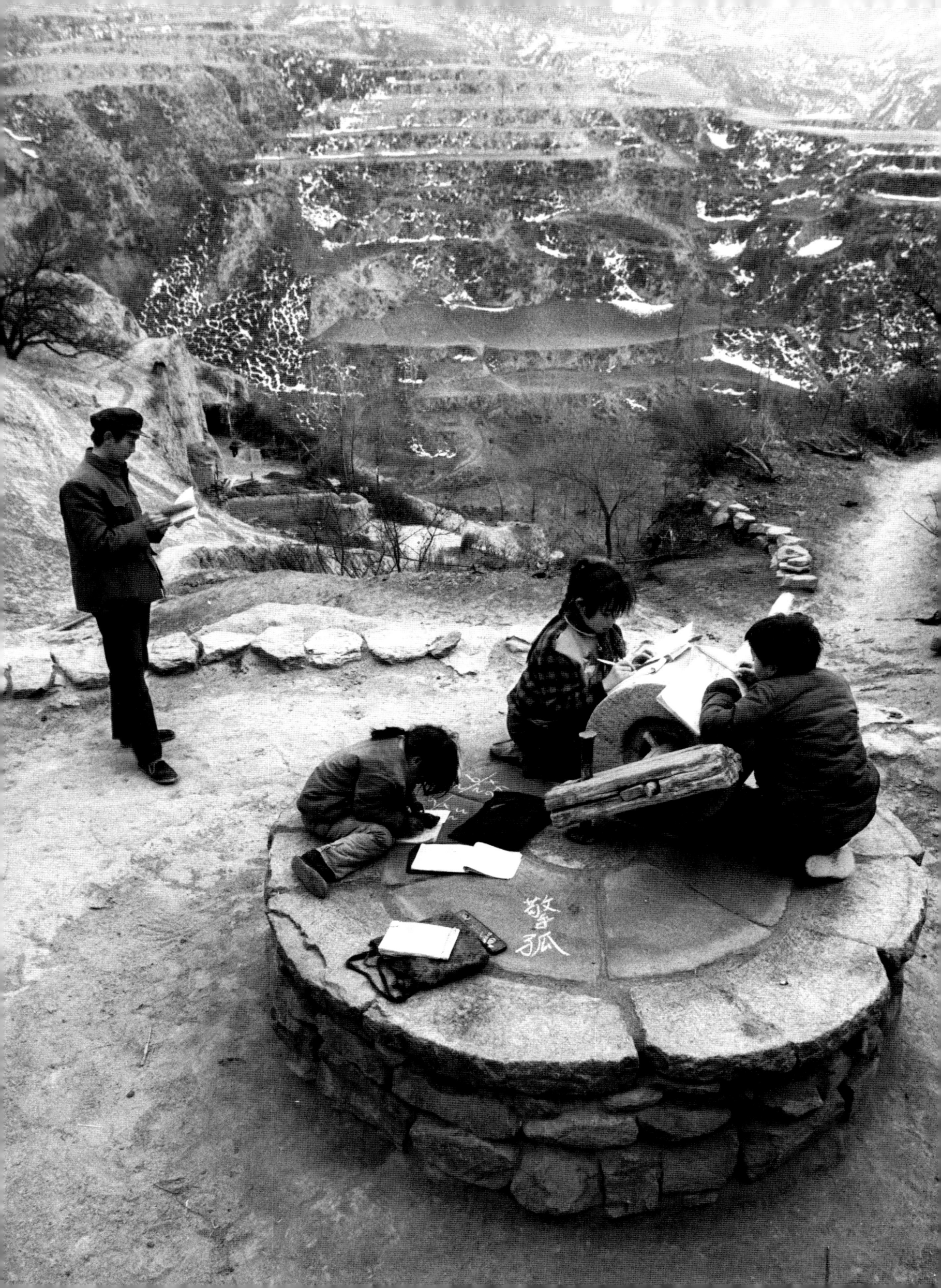

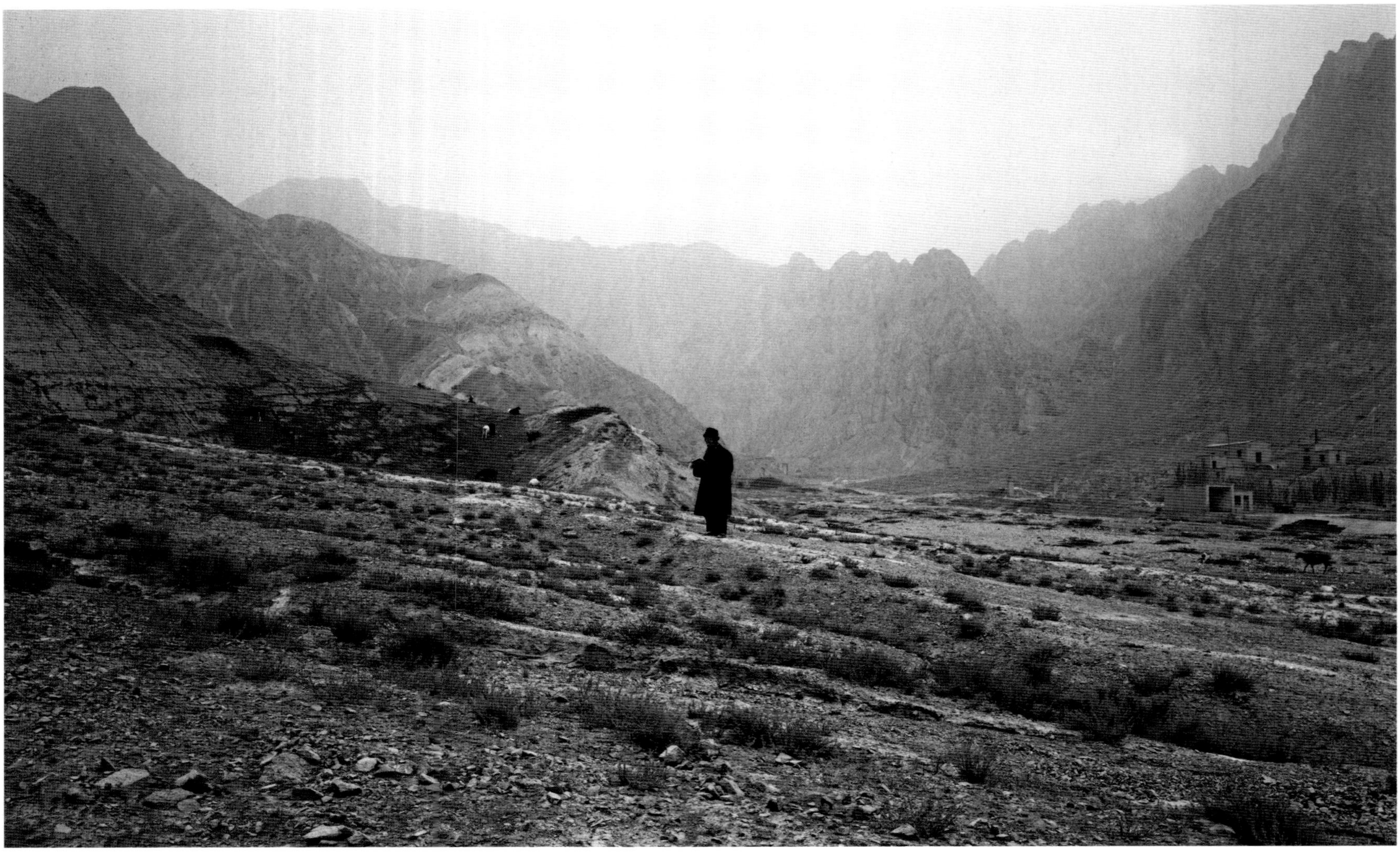

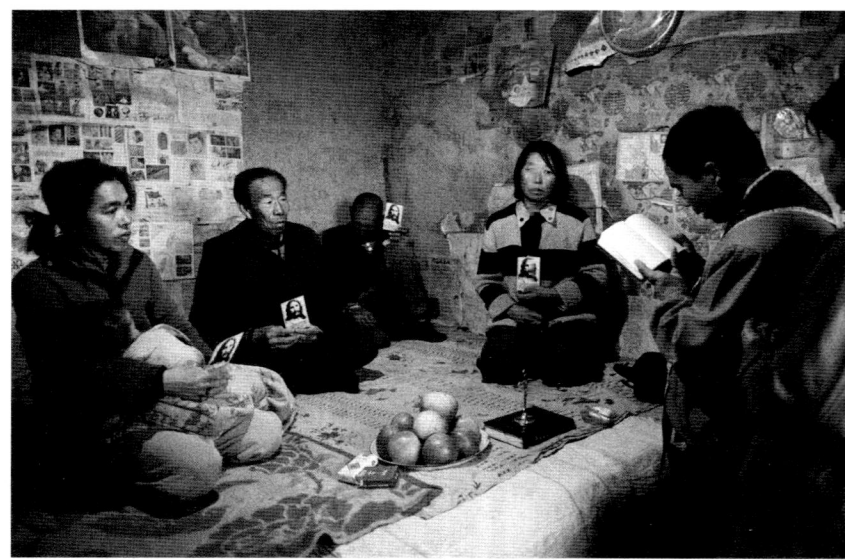

↑
Feng Jianguo, 1996

An Uyghur Muslim herdsman prays on a remote pass in Xinjiang, an autonomous region in the far west of China. There are approximately 20 million Muslims in China.

Ein muslimischer uigurischer Hirte betet an einem Pass in Xinjiang, einer autonomen Region im fernen Westen Chinas. Es gibt in China etwa 20 Millionen Muslime.

Un berger ouïgour musulman prie dans un col du Xinjiang, région autonome de l'extrême ouest de la Chine. On compte environ 20 millions de musulmans en Chine.

↓
Yang Yankang, 1997

Peasants of Catholic faith hold images of Christ as they kneel on their kang *bed for a mass with a priest in Shaanxi province. Catholics in China make up approximately one per cent of the population. It has two aspects: the State-controlled portion with its affiliation with the Chinese Catholic Patriotic Association, and the unofficial community that accepts only the authority of the Pope, and Rome. The activities of these communities continue to be quashed when discovered. China's diplomatic ties with the Vatican were severed in 1951 during the purge of anti-communist foreigners.*

Katholische Bauern halten Christusbilder, während sie bei einer Messe mit einem Priester in der Provinz Shaanxi auf ihrem Kang-Bett knien. Ungefähr ein Prozent der Bevölkerung Chinas ist katholischen Glaubens. Sie teilen sich in zwei Gruppen: den staatlichen kontrollierten Teil, der mit der Gesellschaft chinesisch-katholischer Patrioten verbunden ist, und die inoffizielle Gemeinde, die nur die Autorität des Papstes und Roms anerkennt. Werden die Aktivitäten dieser Gemeinden entdeckt, werden sie auch weiterhin unterdrückt. Chinas diplomatische Beziehungen zum Vatikan wurden 1951 während der Verfolgung anti-kommunistischer Ausländer abgebrochen.

Des paysans catholiques agenouillés sur leur lit kang *tiennent des images du Christ lors d'une messe organisée par un prêtre dans la province du Shaanxi. Les catholiques chinois représentent environ 1 % de la population. Une partie est affiliée à l'Association patriotique catholique chinoise, organisme officiel, l'autre n'accepte que l'autorité du pape et de Rome. Les activités de ces communautés sont encore réprimées lorsqu'elles sont découvertes. Les liens diplomatiques de la Chine et du Vatican ont été interrompus en 1951 pendant la purge des étrangers anticommunistes.*

→
Lü Nan, 1993

Catholics in a rural area of Yunnan province gather for a funeral service.

In einer ländlichen Region der Provinz Yunnan versammeln sich Katholiken zu einer Trauerfeier.

Catholiques assistant à des funérailles dans une zone rurale de la province du Yunnan.

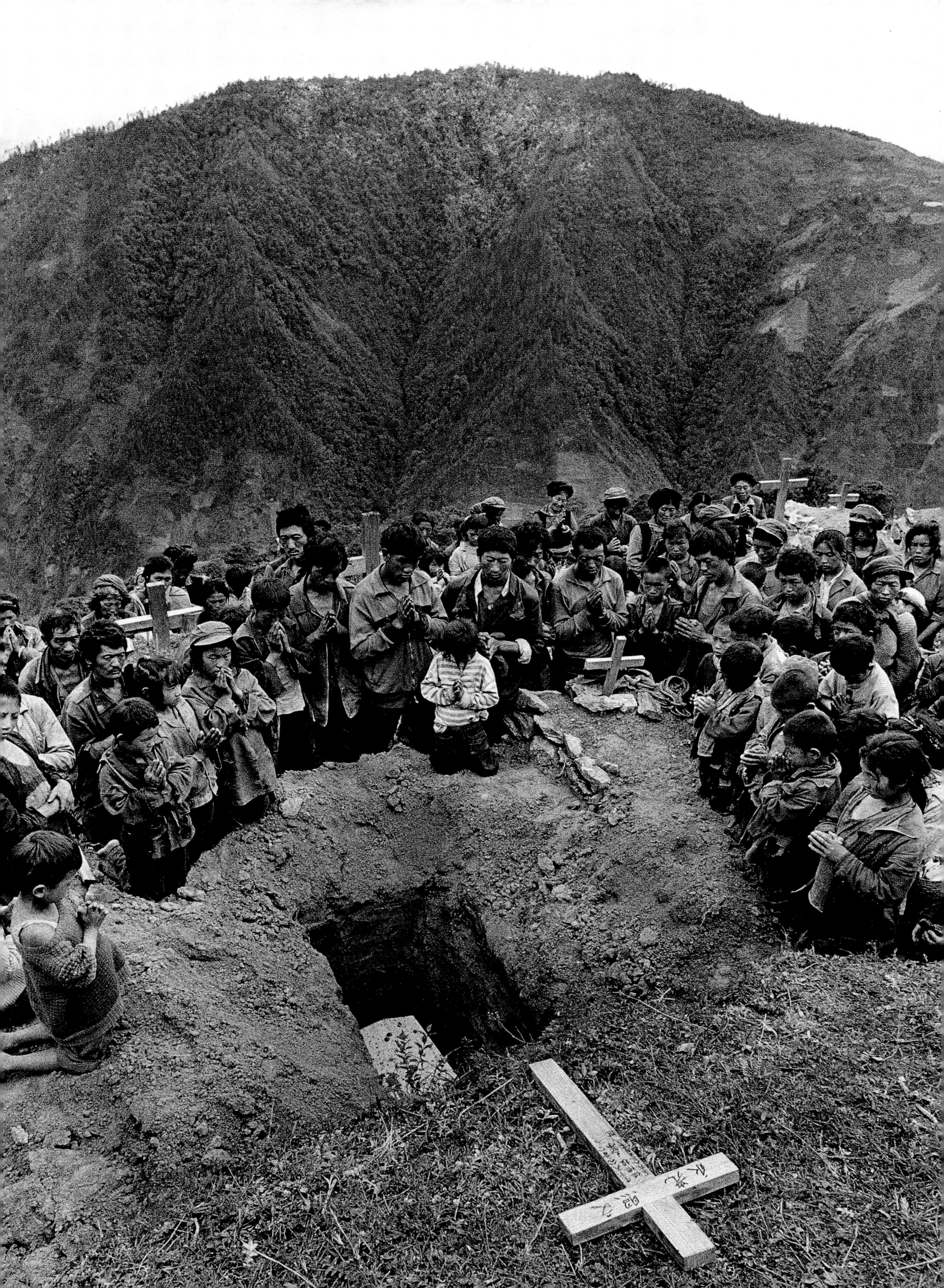

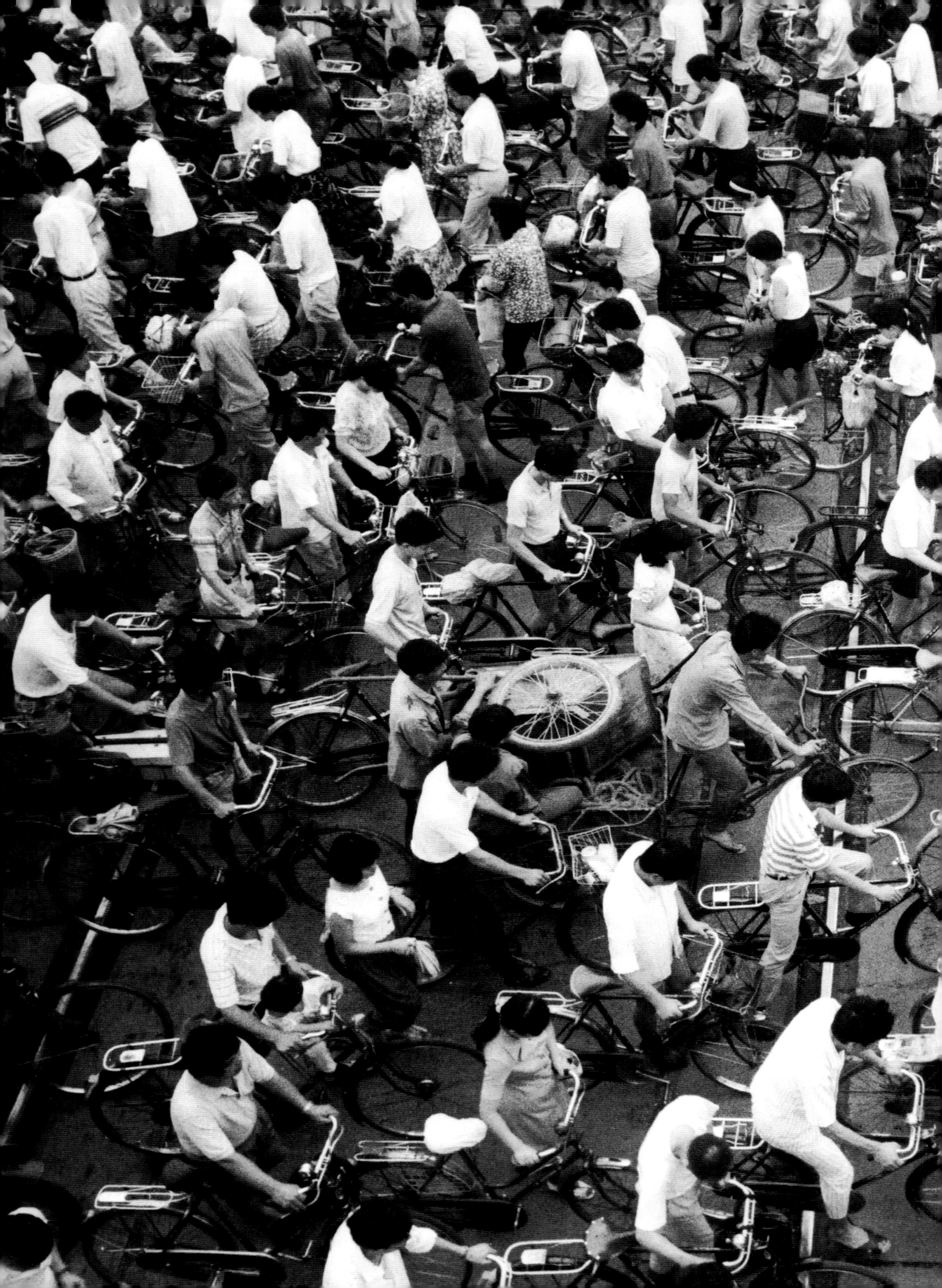

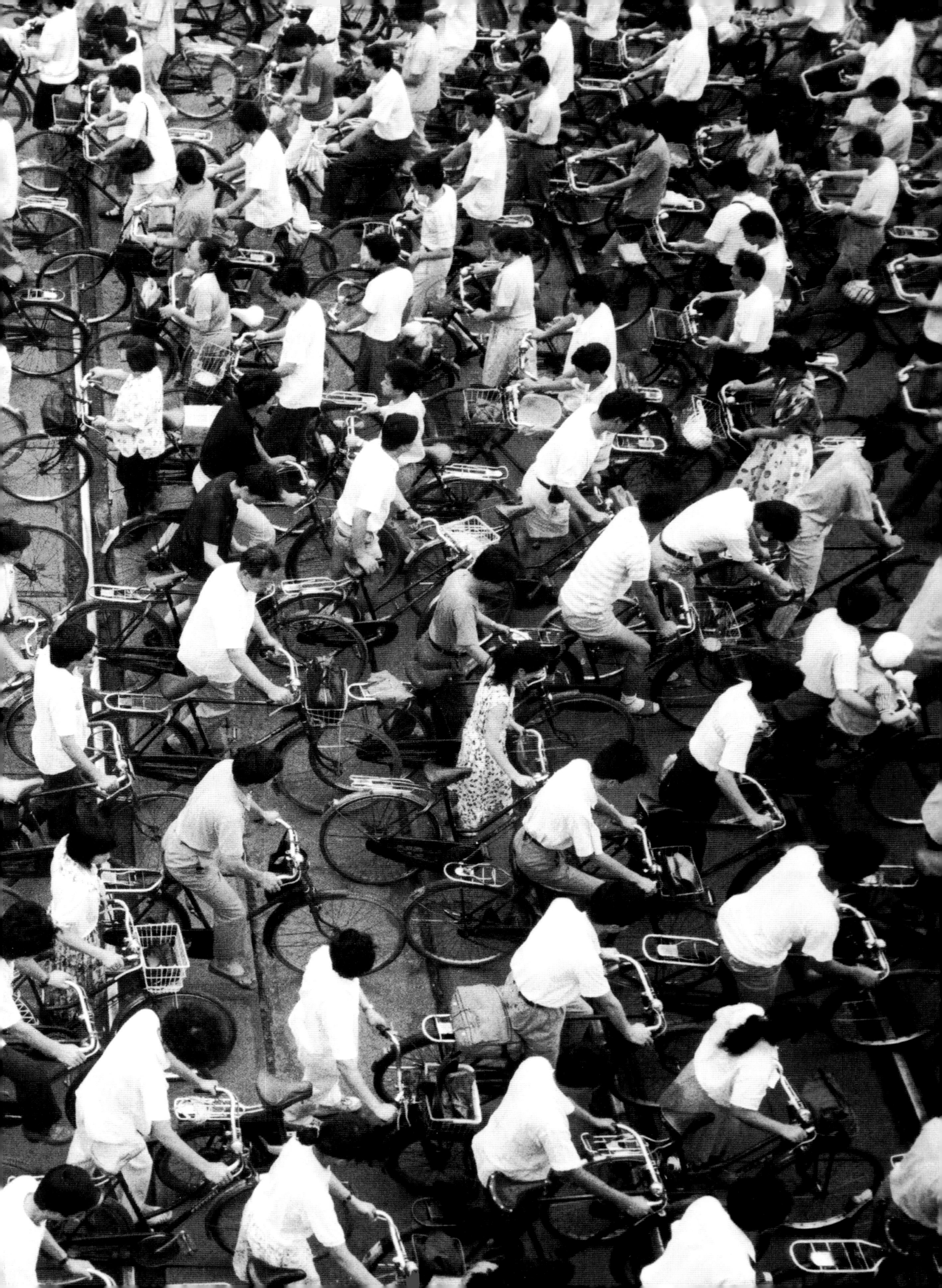

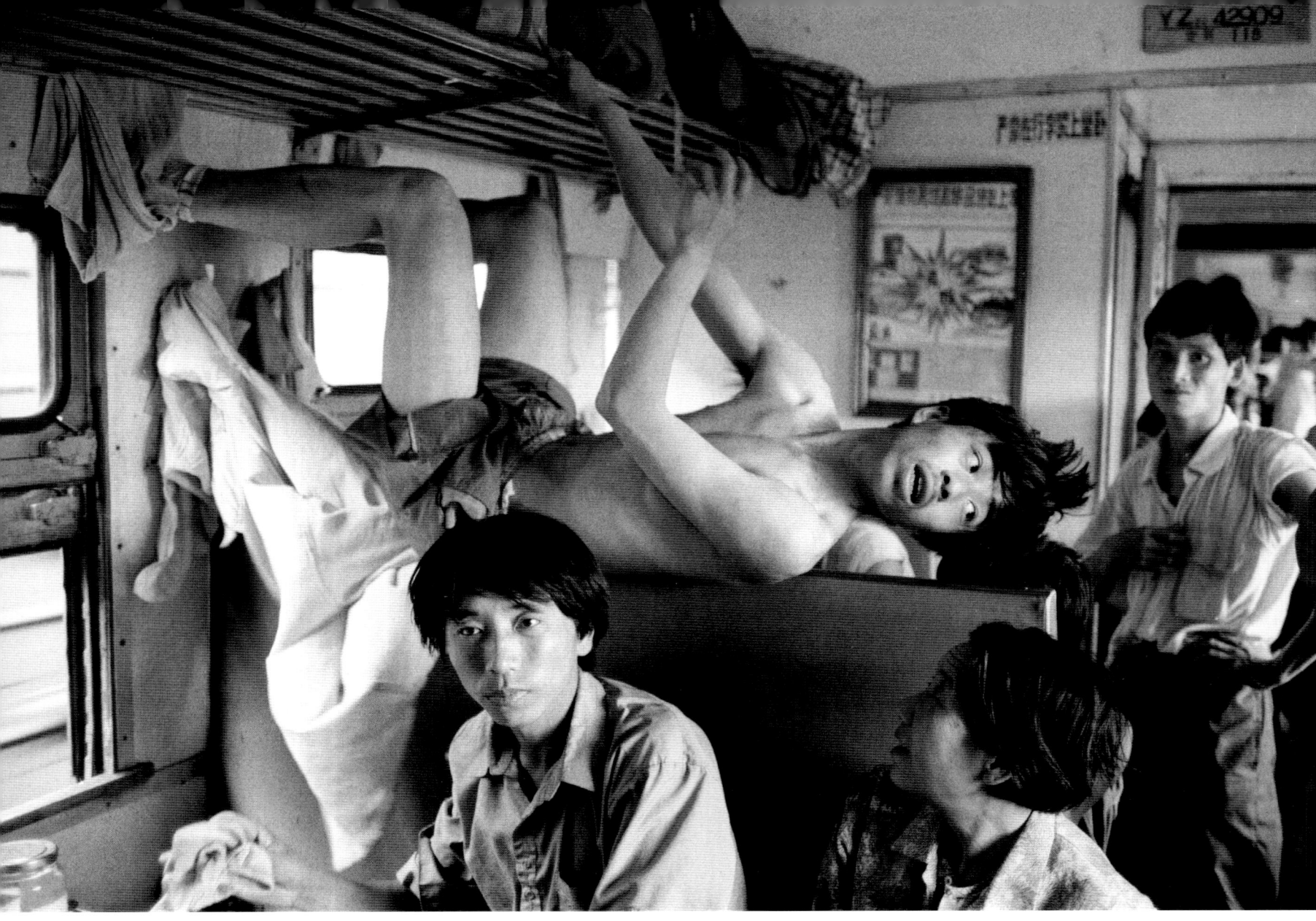

↑

Wang Fuchun, 1995

Passengers on a crowded train leaving
Wuhan bound for Changsha. China's vast
train network carries almost 1.2 billion
passengers annually, with predictions of
train travel reaching 1.9 billion by 2010.

Passagiere in einem überfüllten Zug, der aus
Wuhan in Richtung Changsha fährt. Chinas
weit verzweigtes Eisenbahnnetz befördert
fast 1,2 Milliarden Passagiere pro Jahr; im
Jahr 2010 wird mit bis zu 1,9 Milliarden
gerechnet.

Les passagers d'un train bondé quittant le
Wuhan pour Changsha. Le réseau ferré
chinois transporte annuellement près de
1,2 milliard de voyageurs, un chiffre qui
devrait atteindre 1,9 milliard en 2010.

p. 323 ↑

Zhang Xinmin, 1992

On August 7, 1992, 1.5 million people went
to Shenzhen to buy bond application forms.
Many people stood in line for two days and
nights but were unsuccessful in their bid.
When it transpired that officials in the financial organizations had distributed most of the
forms amongst themselves, the public was
enraged. On August 10, they rushed the city
hall, bringing traffic to a standstill. This
became known as the "August 10 Incident."
The photo shows a young man from Jiangxi
province distraught about the underhand
dealings of the financial institutions involved.

Am 7. August 1992 kamen 1,5 Millionen
Menschen nach Shenzhen, um Antragsformu-
lare für Schuldverschreibungen zu erwerben.
Viele Leute standen zwei Tage und Nächte
lang Schlange, ohne mit ihrem Gebot zum
Zuge zu kommen. Als durchsickerte, Funktionäre der Finanzgesellschaften hätten die
meisten Anträge unter sich aufgeteilt, war die
Menge aufgebracht. Am 10. August stürmte
sie das Rathaus und brachte den Verkehr zum
Erliegen. Dies wurde als „Zwischenfall vom
10. August" bekannt. Das Foto zeigt einen
jungen Mann aus der Provinz Jiangxi, dem
der Ärger über die illegalen Machenschaften
der beteiligten Institutionen ins Gesicht geschrieben steht.

Le 7 août 1992, 1,5 million de personnes
affluèrent à Shenzhen pour acheter des bons
de souscription d'obligations. Beaucoup
d'entre elles firent la queue pendant deux
jours et deux nuits mais ne purent obtenir
ce qu'elles voulaient. Lorsque l'on apprit
que des responsables d'organismes financiers
avaient détourné la plupart de ces titres pour
eux, la foule se mit en colère. Le 10 août,
elle envahit l'hôtel de ville et bloqua la
circulation : ce fut « l'incident du 10 août ».
La photo montre un jeune homme de la
province du Jiangxi ulcéré d'apprendre le
comportement des institutions financières
impliquées.

pp. 320/321

Wang Wenlan, 1991

The bicycle kingdom: Shanghai's urban
residents ride their bicycles on their way to
work. Although the car is now an increasingly popular mode of transport, there are
still more than 500 million bicycles in use
in China.

Königreich des Fahrrads: Die Bewohner von
Shanghai fahren mit dem Rad zur Arbeit.
Obgleich sich das Auto als Transportmittel
zunehmender Beliebtheit erfreut, sind in
China immer noch über 500 Millionen
Fahrräder in Gebrauch.

Le royaume de la bicyclette : des habitants
de Shanghai se rendent au travail à vélo.
Bien que la voiture soit un mode de transport
de plus en plus populaire, on compte encore
plus de 500 millions de bicyclettes en Chine.

"They are a voiceless class of people. In this bustling metropolis with all its millions, they are many and they work the filthiest and most exhausting jobs and are repaid with contempt and malice. They never raise their voices, nor can they give voice to what they would say. Nobody knows what they think, what they suffer, what they celebrate, what they fear or what they rejoice in."

„Sie sind eine Kategorie von Menschen ohne Stimme. In dieser geschäftigen Metropole mit ihren Millionen von Einwohnern sind sie zahlreich, und sie leisten die schmutzigsten und anstrengendsten Arbeiten und werden dafür mit Verachtung und Bosheit gestraft. Weder erheben sie je ihre Stimme noch können sie das, was sie sagen würden, in Worte fassen. Niemand weiß, was sie denken, was sie erleiden, was sie feiern, was sie fürchten oder was sie erfreut."

« C'est une classe sans voix. Dans cette métropole qui bourdonne de millions d'habitants, ils sont nombreux à exécuter les tâches les plus sales et les plus épuisantes et à être payés de mépris et de tromperies. Ils n'élèvent jamais la voix, ni ne peuvent exprimer ce qu'ils voudraient dire. Personne ne sait ce qu'ils pensent, ce qu'ils souffrent, ce qu'ils célèbrent, ce qu'ils craignent ou de quoi ils se réjouissent. »

YU JIE, writer, activist, and Christian convert, 2003

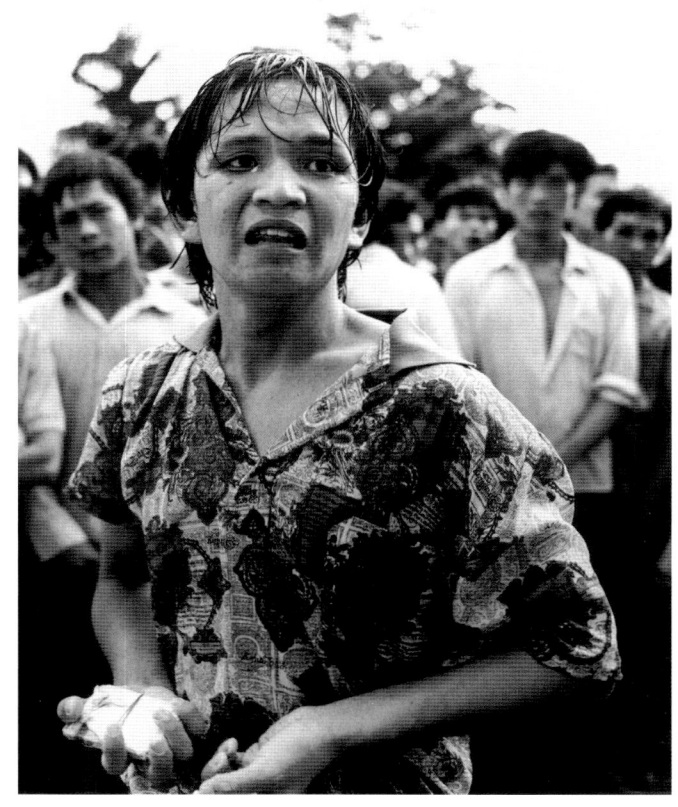

↓
Yu Deshui, 1994

Unemployed rural workers heading to other cities in search of work, wait at a train station in Shaanxi province. At present about 200 million former farmers work in cities.

Arbeitslose Landarbeiter, auf der Suche nach Beschäftigung unterwegs in andere Städte, warten an einem Bahnhof in der Provinz Shaanxi. Gegenwärtig arbeiten etwa 200 Millionen ehemalige Bauern in Städten.

Ces travailleurs agricoles sans emploi qui attendent dans une gare du Shaanxi partent vers les villes en quête de travail. Environ 200 millions d'ex-paysans travaillent aujourd'hui dans les zones urbaines.

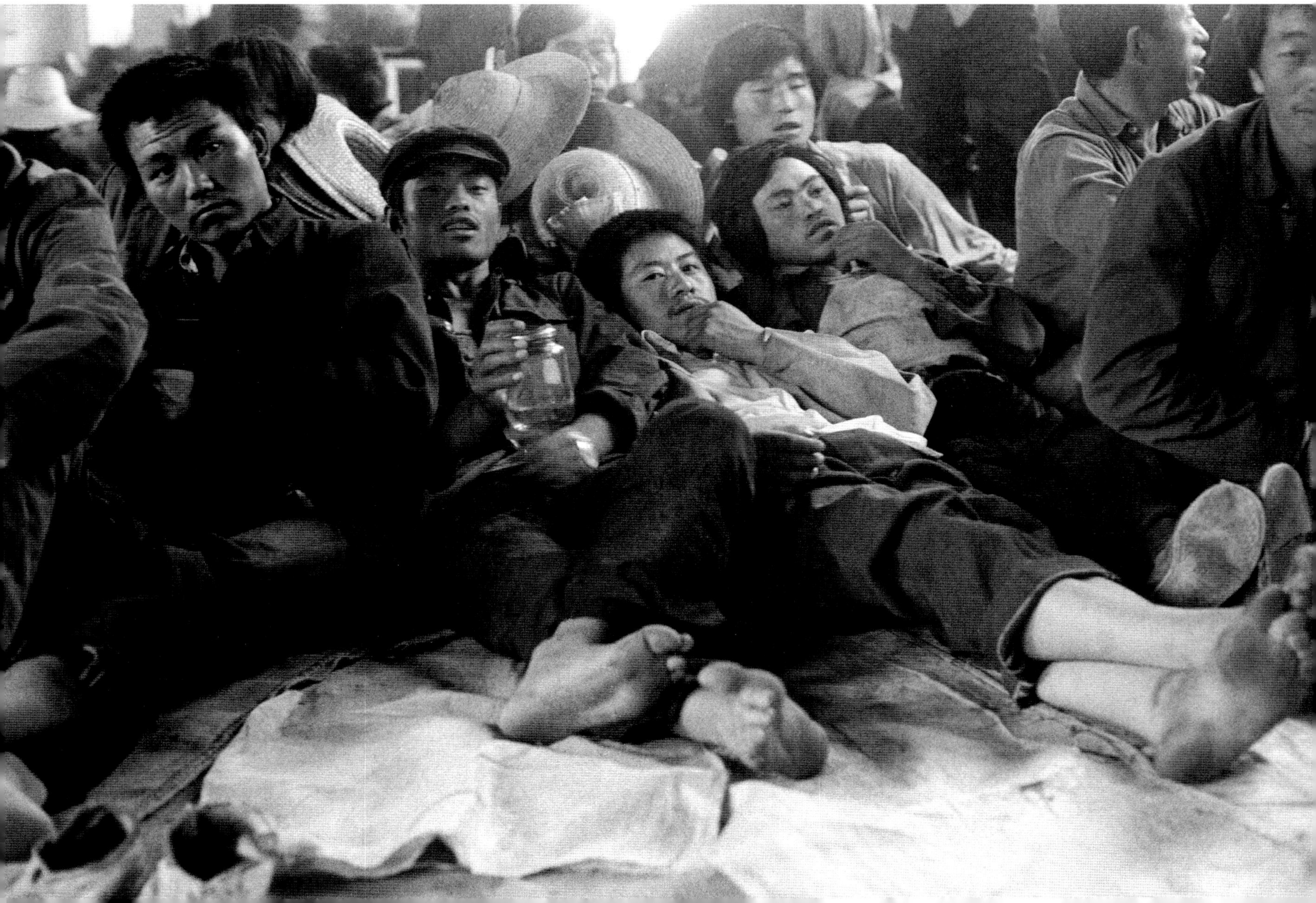

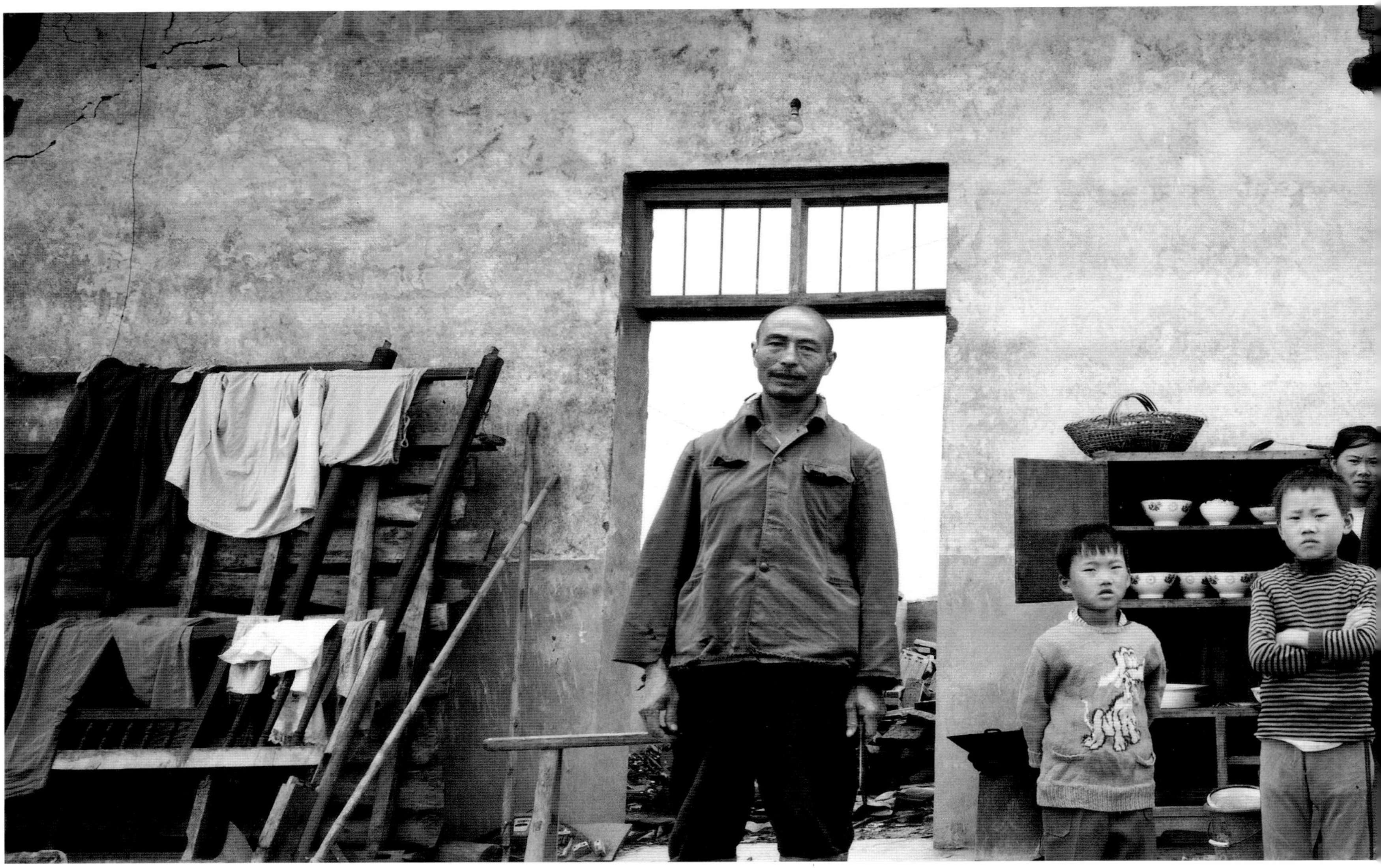

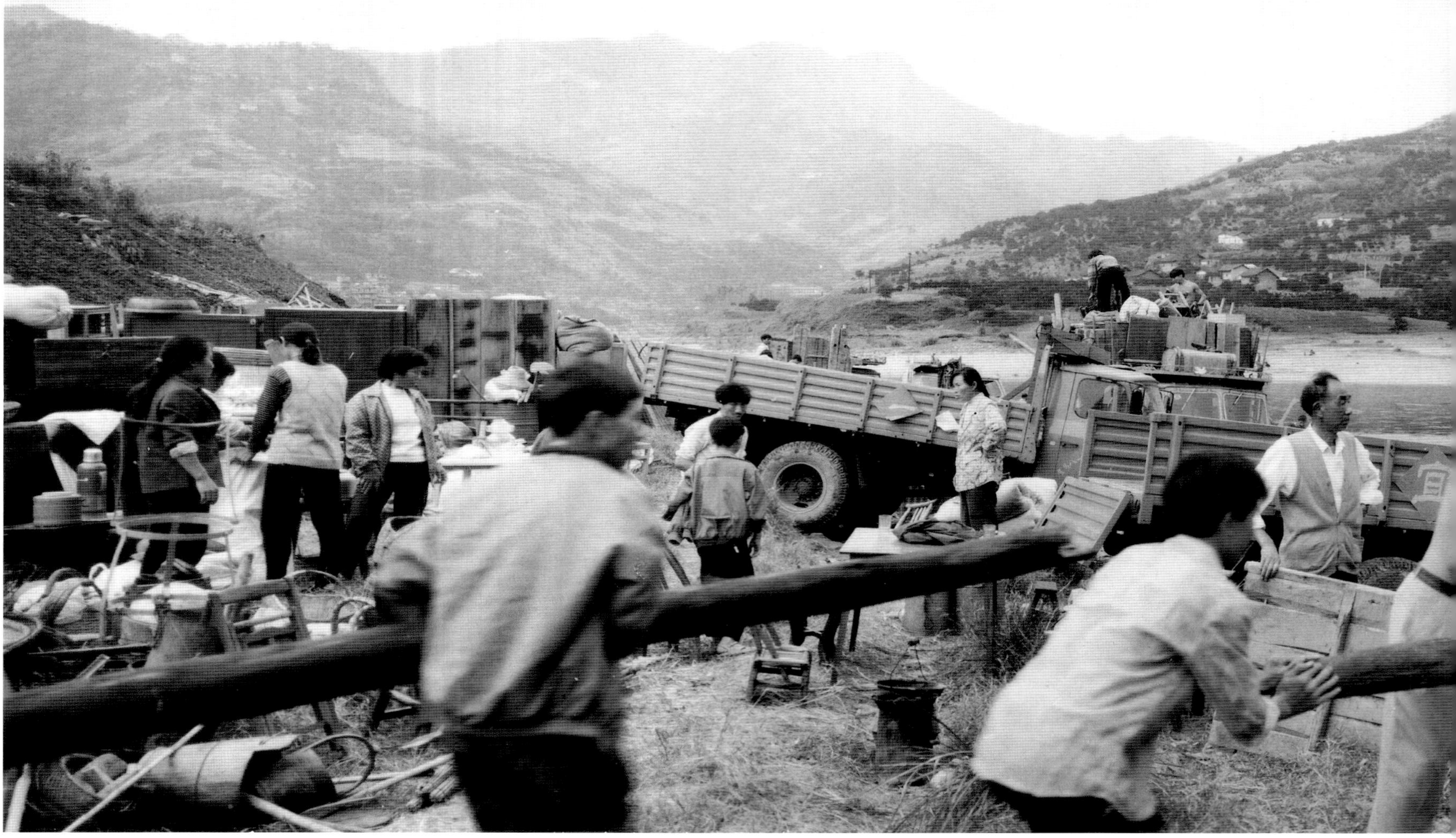

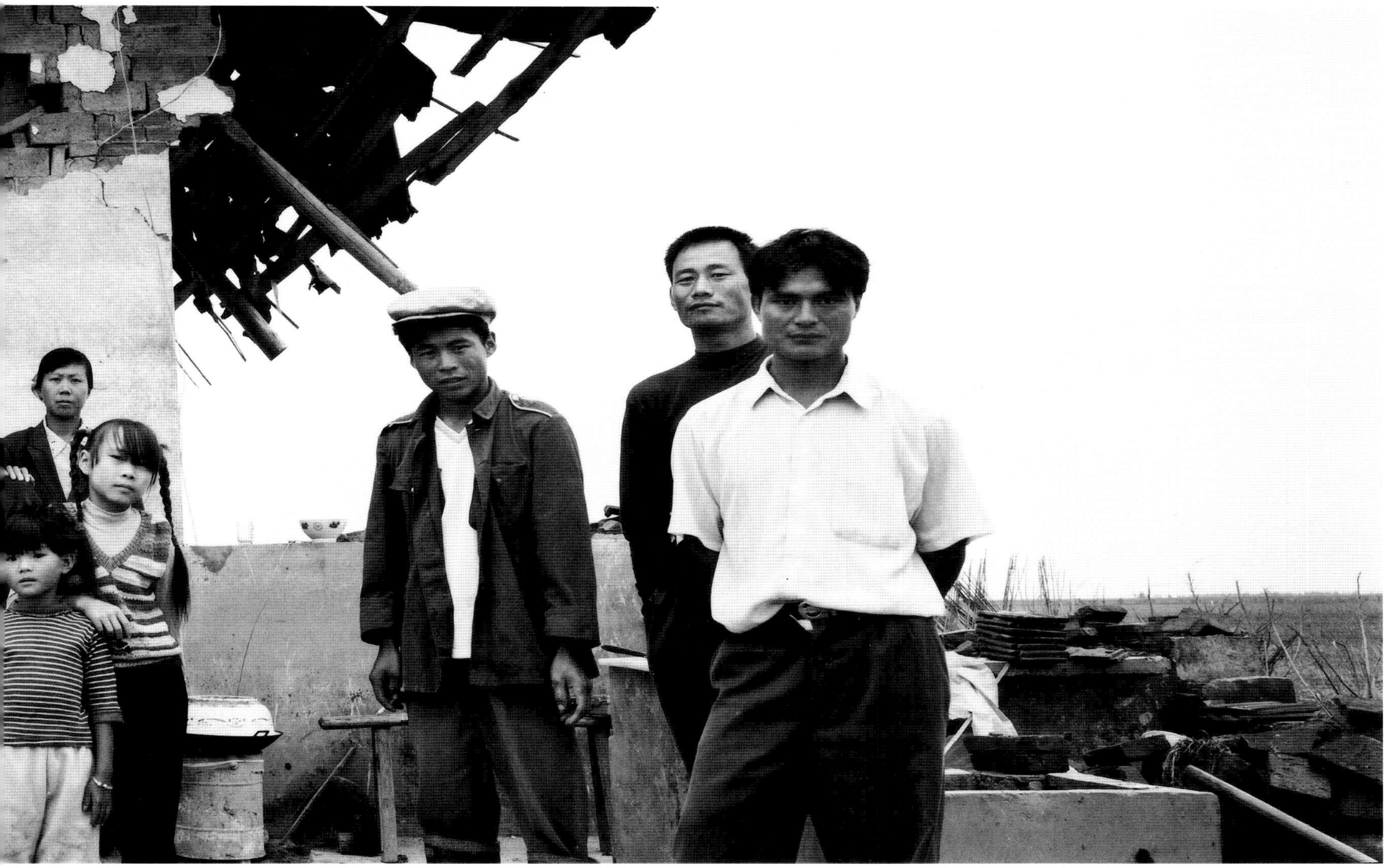

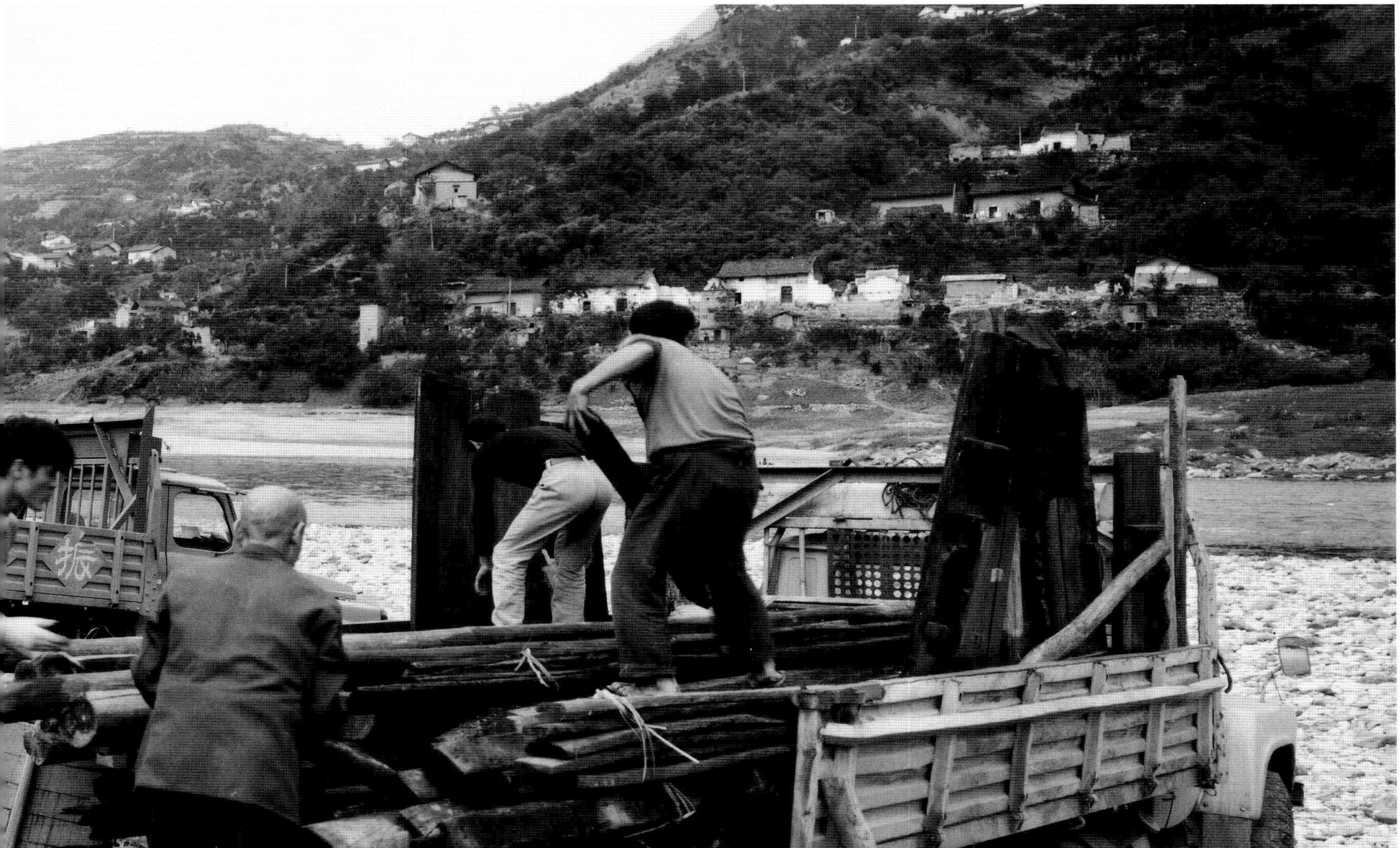
振

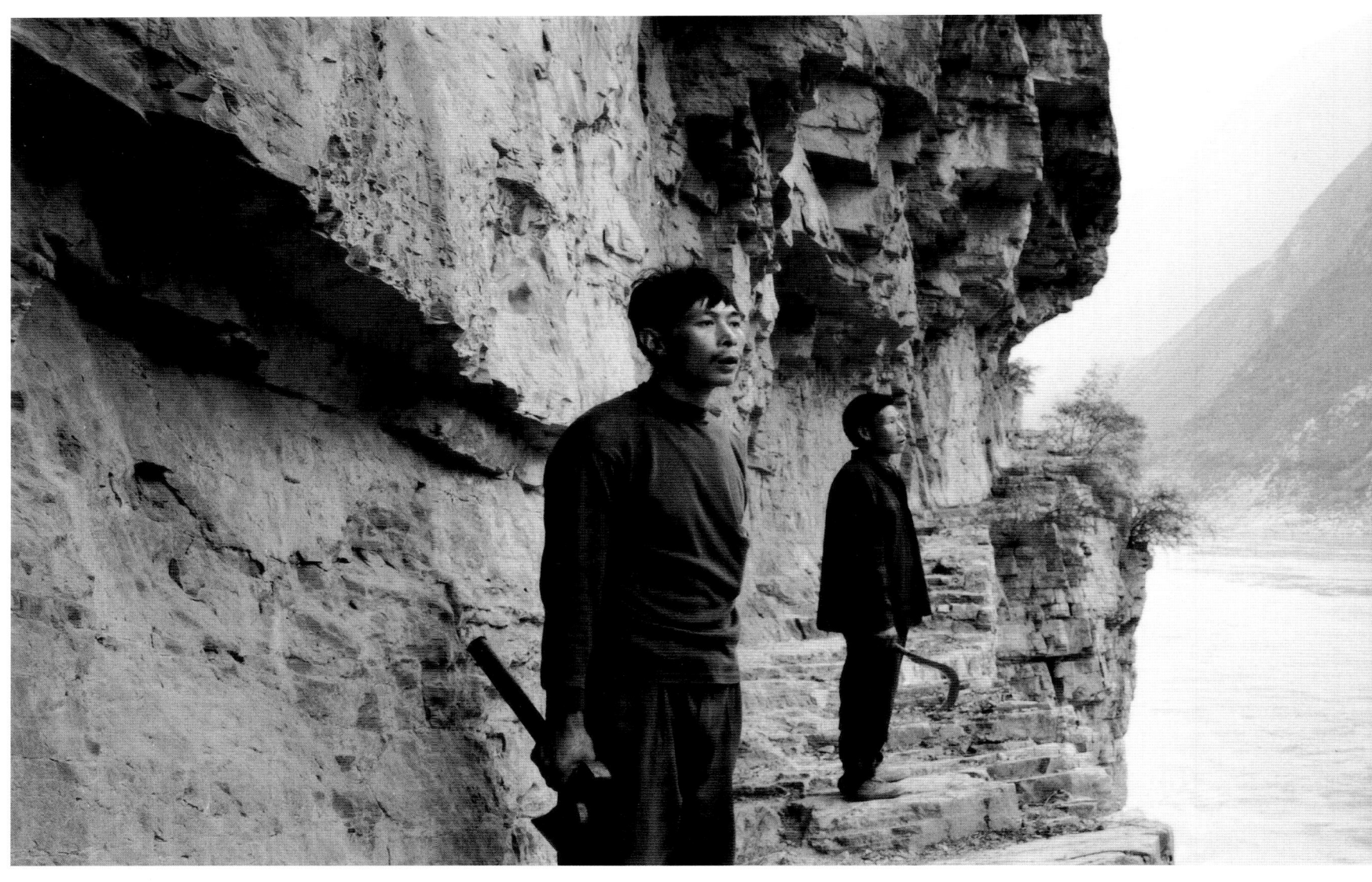

pp. 324/325 ↑
Zeng Nian, 1996

Local residents stand outside homes soon
to be demolished to make way for the Three
Gorges dam. The dam was a monumental
project to create a reservoir of water nearly
400 miles long between the municipality
of Chongqing (formerly part of Sichuan
province) and Hubei province. It has been
termed the largest construction project in
China since the Great Wall. A hydroelectric
dam was first proposed for this site in 1919,
a plan that was reviewed by Mao Zedong in
the 1950s, following extensive flooding along
the Yangtze river. Environmentalists and
critics describe it as "environmentally and
socially destructive." Archeologists estimate
that nearly 1,300 important sites are lost
under the waters. It also required the resettlement of almost 1.5 million people. Chinese
officials say the dam will make a significant
contribution to the nation's electrical power
production.

Bewohner stehen vor ihren Häusern, die wegen
des Drei-Schluchten-Damms bald abgerissen
werden. Der Damm ist ein riesiges Projekt,
bei dem zwischen der Gemeinde Chongqing
(früher Teil der Provinz Sichuan) und der
Provinz Hubei ein fast 650 Kilometer langes
Wasserreservoir entstehen soll. Es wird
als größtes Bauvorhaben Chinas seit der
Chinesischen Mauer bezeichnet. Schon 1919
war von einem Wasserkraftwerk für dieses
Gebiet die Rede, ein Plan, der von Mao nach
ausgedehnten Überflutungen am Jangtse in
den 1950er-Jahren aufgriffen wurde. Von
Umweltschützern und Kritikern wird das
Projekt als „umweltfeindlich und sozial des-
truktiv" bezeichnet. Archäologen gehen davon
aus, dass fast 1300 bedeutende Fundstätten
unter dem Wasser verloren gehen werden.
Darüber hinaus mussten fast 1,5 Millionen
Menschen umgesiedelt werden. Chinesischen
Funktionären zufolge wird der Damm einen
wesentlichen Beitrag zur Energiegewinnung
des Landes leisten.

Des gens devant leur maison qui sera bientôt
démolie pour la construction du barrage des
Trois Gorges, projet monumental de création
d'un réservoir d'eau de près de 650 km de
long entre les villes de Chongqing (faisant an-
ciennement partie de la province du Sichuan)
et la province du Hubei. Il a été qualifié de
plus vaste projet de construction chinois depuis la Grande muraille. Un premier barrage
avait été proposé sur ce site dès 1919, plan repris dans les années 1950 par Mao Zedong
à la suite d'inondations importantes dans la
vallée du Yang-Tsé. Les écologistes et les
critiques parlent d'un projet « environnemen-
talement et socialement destructeur ». Les
archéologues estiment que près de 1300 sites
importants disparaîtront sous les eaux. 1,5
million de personnes devront être déplacées
et relogées. Les responsables chinois affirment
que le barrage apportera une contribution
significative à la production électrique du
pays.

pp. 324/325 ↓
Zeng Nian, 1996

Local residents of the Three Gorges area of
the Yangtze river are relocated in preparation
for the building of the monumental hydraulic
dam, the largest of its kind on earth. A controversial project from the outset, the dam
required that the Three Gorges be flooded,
placing huge areas under water.

Bewohner der Drei-Schluchten-Region des
Jangtse werden wegen der bevorstehenden
Errichtung des weltweit größten hydrauli-
schen Damms umgesiedelt. Das von Anfang
an umstrittene Projekt erfordert die Über-
flutung der Drei Schluchten, wodurch große
Teile dieses Gebietes unter Wasser gesetzt
werden.

Habitants de la région des Trois Gorges qui
ont été déplacés avant la construction de ce
monumental ouvrage hydraulique, le plus
grand du monde. Projet controversé dès le
départ, il a entraîné la disparition sous les
eaux d'immenses territoires.

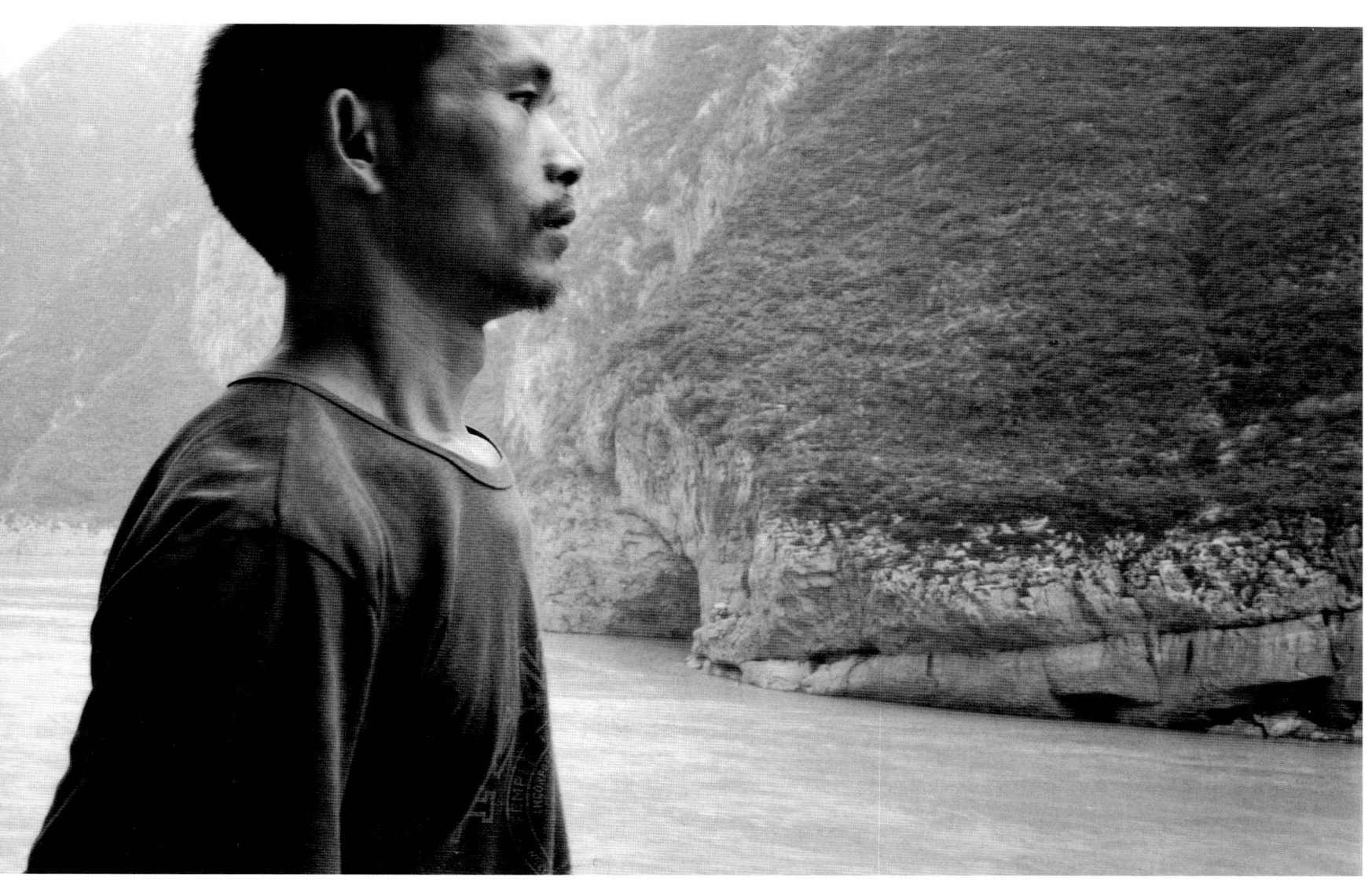

↑
Zeng Nian, 1996

Local farmers gaze across the Three Gorges, soon to be submerged as part of the dam project.

Einheimische Bauern schauen über die Drei Schluchten, die als Teil des Damm-projektes bald überflutet sein werden.

Des fermiers regardent la gorge qui sera bientôt submergée.

"Whatever lies ahead, be it a field of landmines or an unfathomable abyss, I will exert all my efforts and contribute all my best to the country till the last minute of my life."

„Was auch immer vor uns liegt, sei es ein Minenfeld oder ein bodenloser Abgrund, ich werde solange ich lebe für das Land all meine Kraft aufwenden und mein Bestes geben."

« Quel que soit l'avenir, que ce soit un champ de mines ou un abysse sans fond, je consacrerai tous mes efforts et contribuerai de mon mieux à l'histoire de ce pays jusqu'à la dernière seconde de ma vie. »

ZHU RONGJI (1928–), Premier of the People's Republic of China (1998–2003), 1998

pp. 328/329
Wang Jinsong, 1996

One school, 200 one-child families, and myriad expressions of contemporary existence and attitudes amongst urban Chinese. The one-child policy was adopted in 1980, as a desperate means of limiting a population growth that threatened to expand exponentially.

Eine Schule, 200 Ein-Kind-Familien und zahllose Physiognomien, die von Leben und Denken chinesischer Stadtbewohner künden. Die Ein-Kind-Regelung wurde 1980 als verzweifelte Maßnahme zur Begrenzung eines Bevölkerungswachstums eingeführt, das drohte, exponenziell anzusteigen.

Une école, 200 familles à enfant unique, et des myriades d'expressions de l'existence actuelle de Chinois des villes. La politique de l'enfant unique a été adoptée en 1980, mesure désespérée pour limiter les menaces de la croissance exponentielle de la population.

pp. 330/331
Zhang Xinmin, 1997

Chinese migrant workers share dormitory space, accepting cramped, often unsavory conditions as a small price to pay for a regular wage.

Chinesische Wanderarbeiter teilen sich den Platz in einem Schlafraum und nehmen die beengten, häufig unhygienischen Zustände hin als kleinen Preis für sichere Löhne.

Travailleurs migrants chinois partageant un dortoir. Ils acceptent de vivre dans la promis-cuité, une des conditions pour recevoir un vrai salaire.

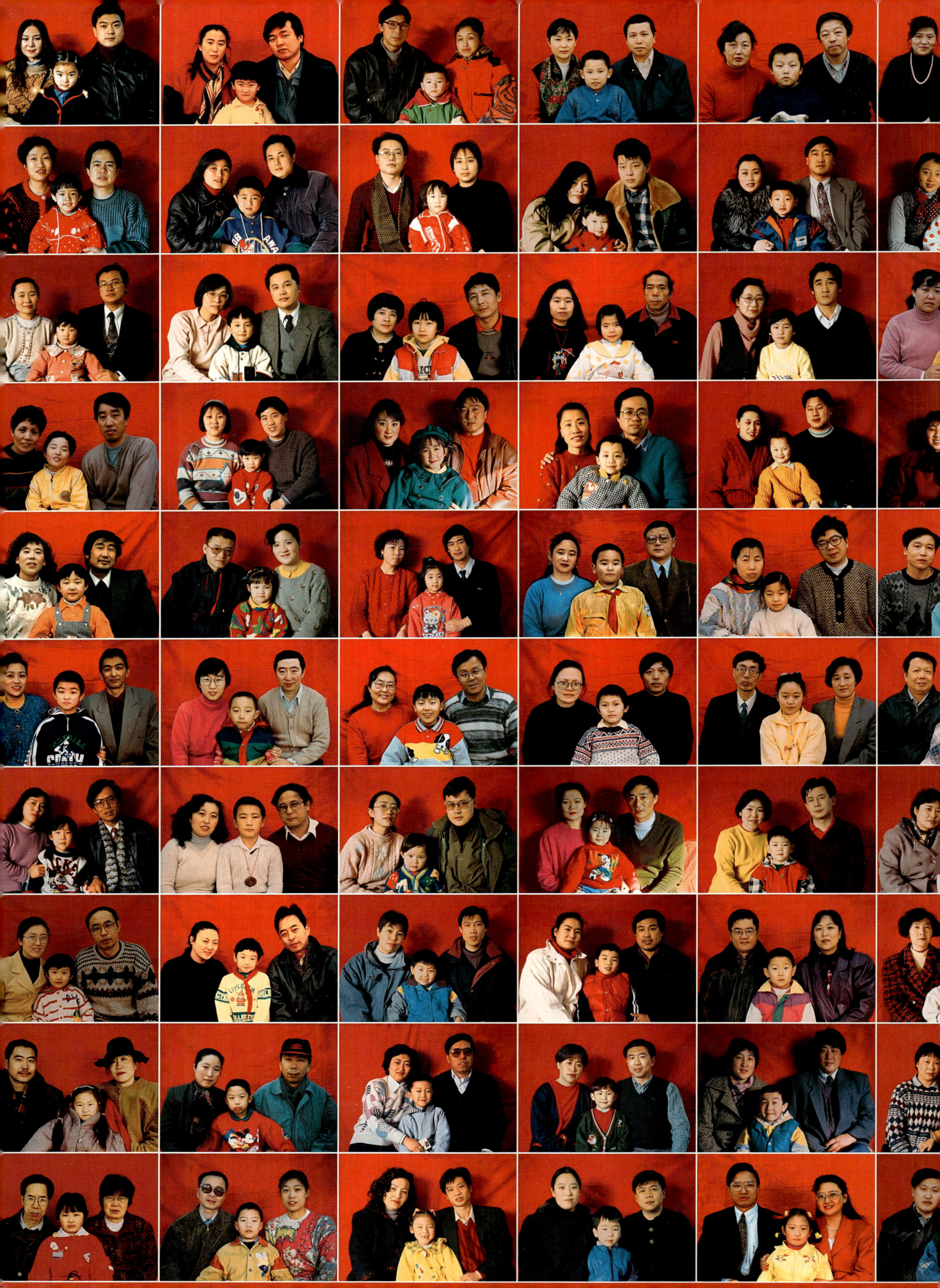

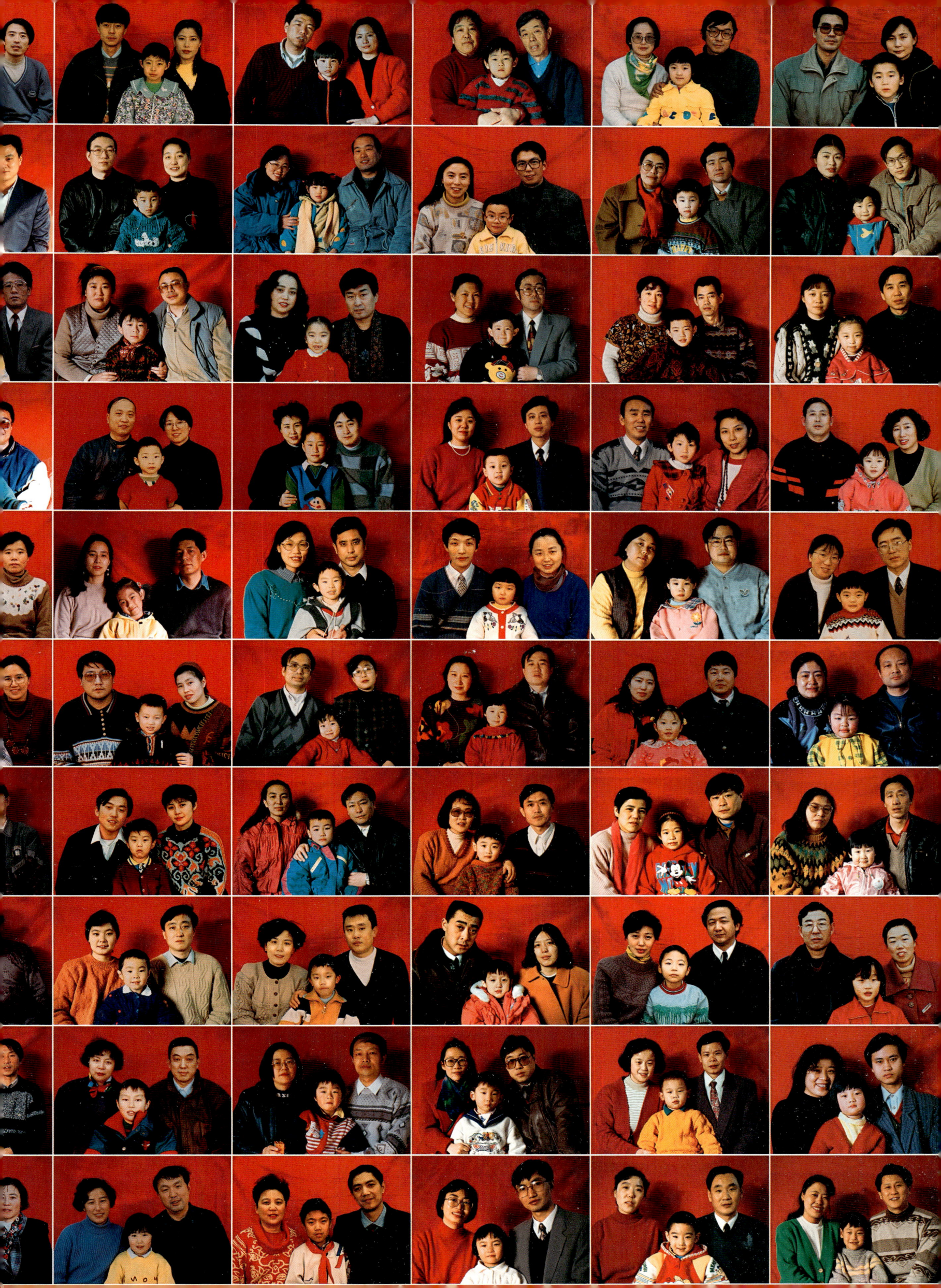

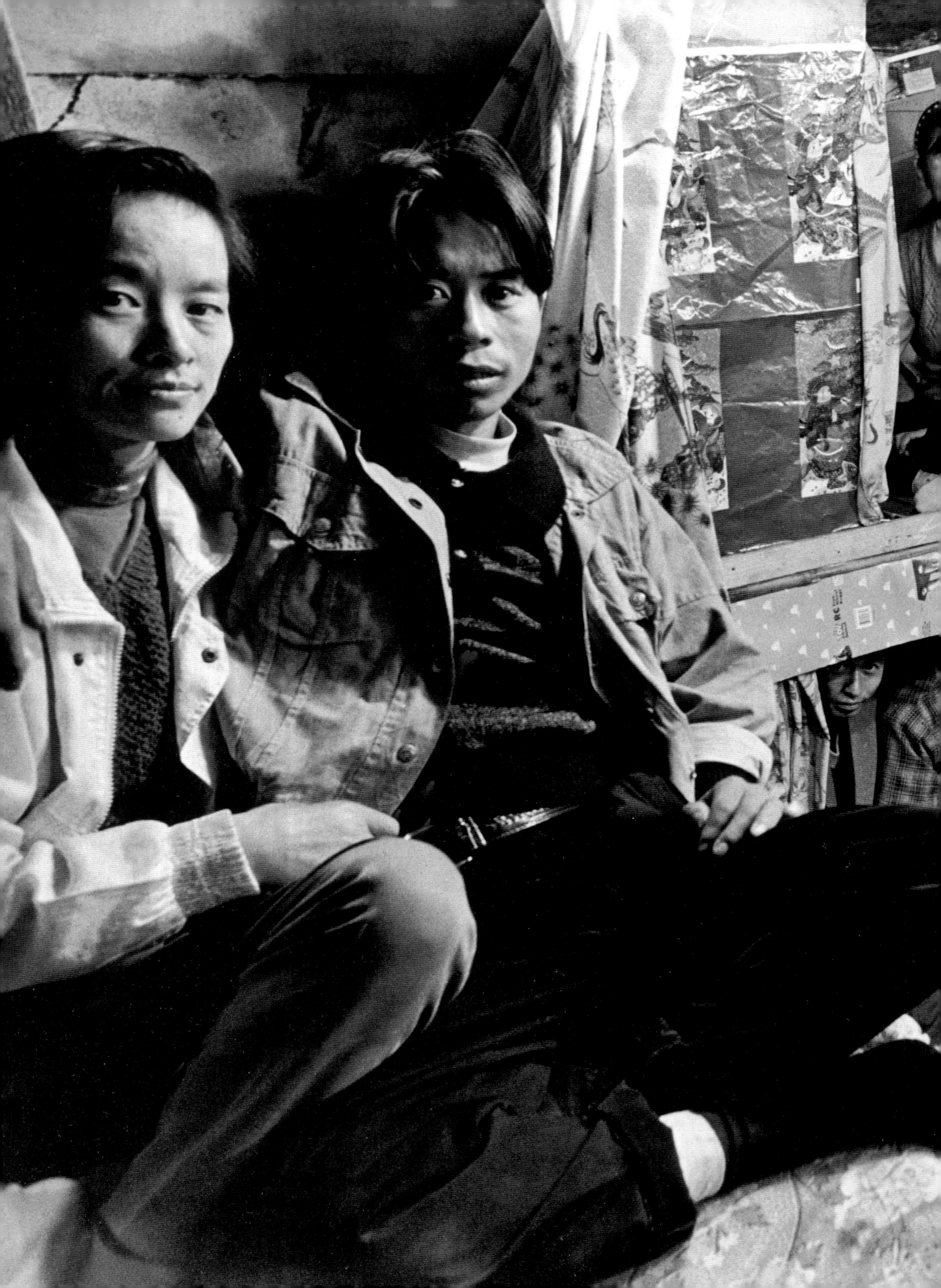

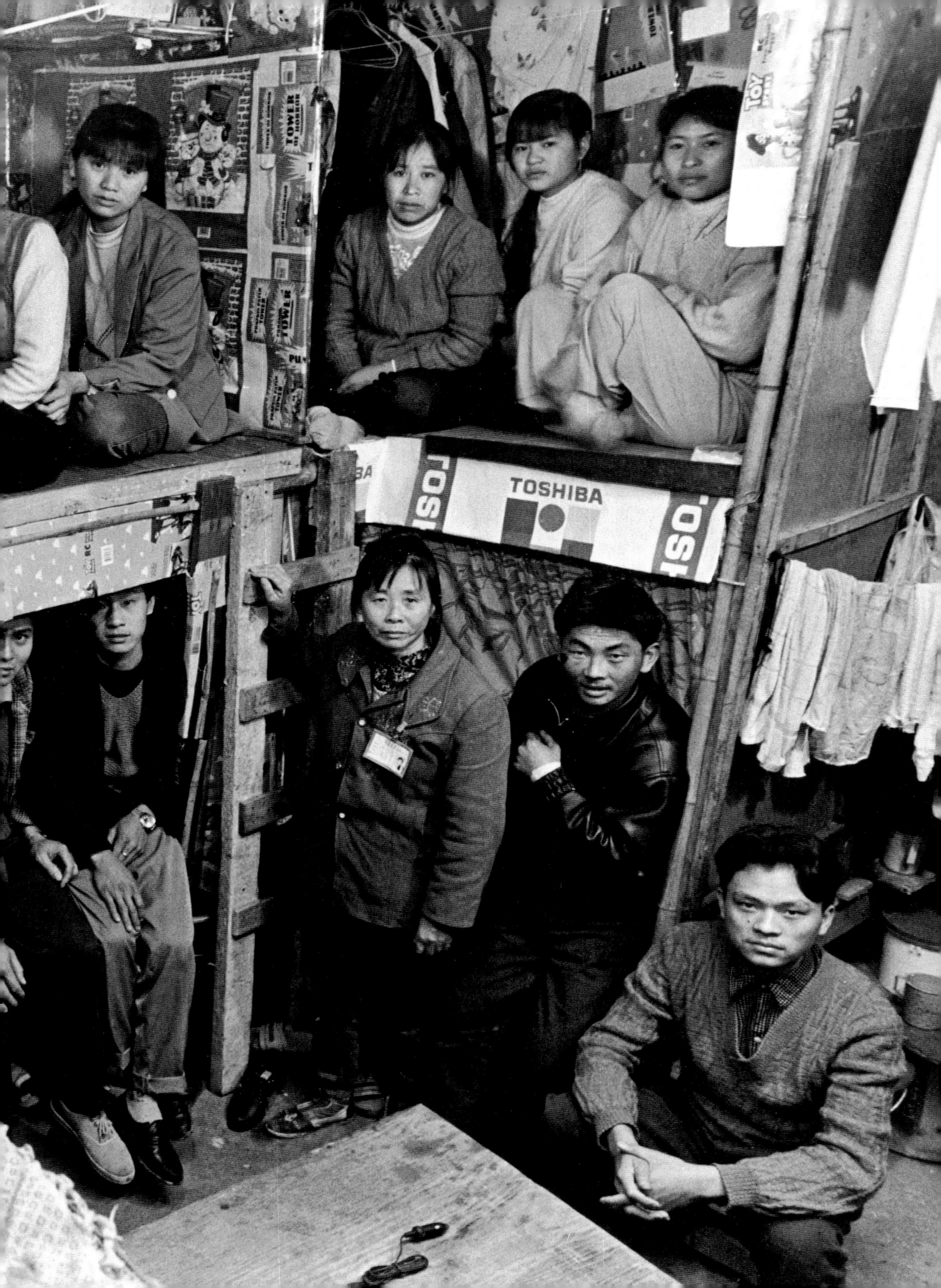

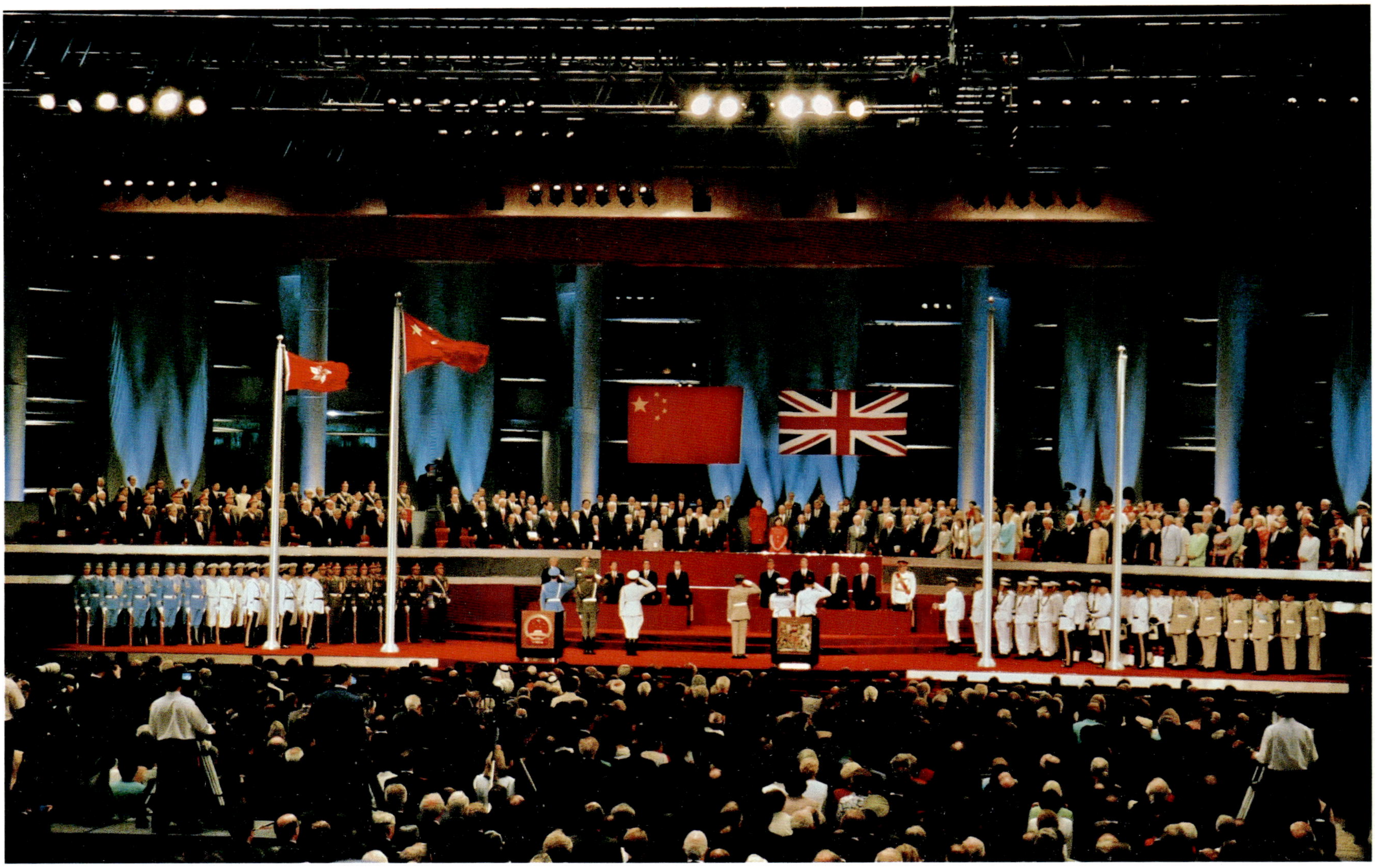

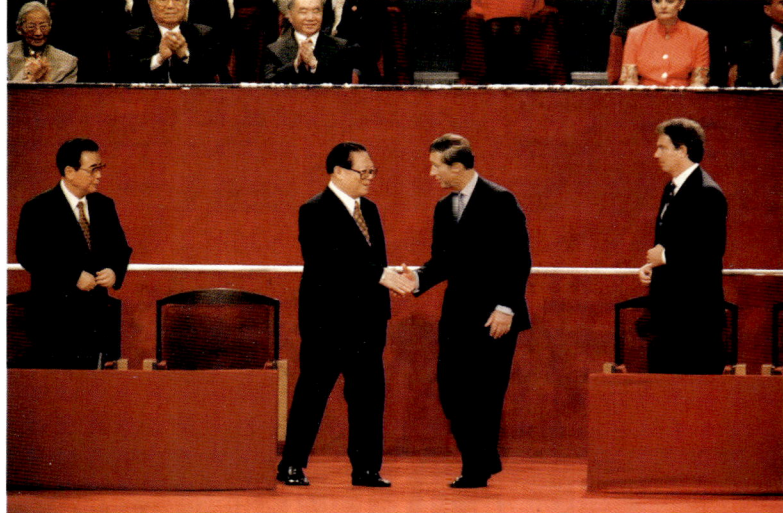

Li Zhensheng, 1997

The ceremony to mark the handover of Hong
Kong to the People's Republic of China on
June 30, 1997.

Die Zeremonie zur Übergabe Hongkongs an
die Volksrepublik China am 30. Juni 1997.

Cérémonie organisée pour saluer la remise
de Hong Kong à la République populaire de
Chine le 30 juin 1997.

Xie Guanghui, 1997

At the Hong Kong handover ceremony
China's President Jiang Zemin shakes hands
with Britain's Prince Charles to mark the
handover of administrative rule to China on
July 1, 1997, 150 years after Hong Kong
was ceded to Britain in the aftermath of the
Opium War in 1847.

Bei der Übergabezeremonie reicht Chinas
Präsident Jiang Zemin dem britischen Prinzen
Charles die Hand, um die Übergabe der
Verwaltungshoheit an China am 1. Juli 1997
zu bekräftigen, 150 Jahre nachdem man
Hongkong in den Nachwehen des Opium-
krieges 1847 an Großbritannien abgetreten
hatte.

Lors de la cérémonie de remise de Hong Kong
à la Chine, le président Jiang Zemin serre
la main du prince Charles le 1er juillet 1997,
150 ans après que le territoire a été cédé à
la Grande-Bretagne à la suite de la guerre de
l'opium en 1847.

"It is risky to make predictions about China. To paraphrase
Lord Curzon, Great Britain's Viceroy in India one hundred years
ago, China is like a great university from which the scholar
never gets a degree."

„Es ist riskant, Vorhersagen über China abzugeben. Lord Curzon,
vor hundert Jahren Großbritanniens Vizekönig in Indien, sagte
sinngemäß dazu: ‚China ist wie eine große Universität, von der die
Studenten nie ein Abschlusszeugnis erhalten.'"

« Il est risqué de faire des prédictions sur la Chine. Pour paraphraser Lord Curzon, le vice-roi des Indes britannique d'il y a
cent ans, la Chine est comme une grande université dont les
étudiants ne reçoivent jamais de diplôme. »

**RICHARD NIXON (1913–1994), former US president who started
the process of normalization between the U.S.A. and the People's Republic of
China, 1994**

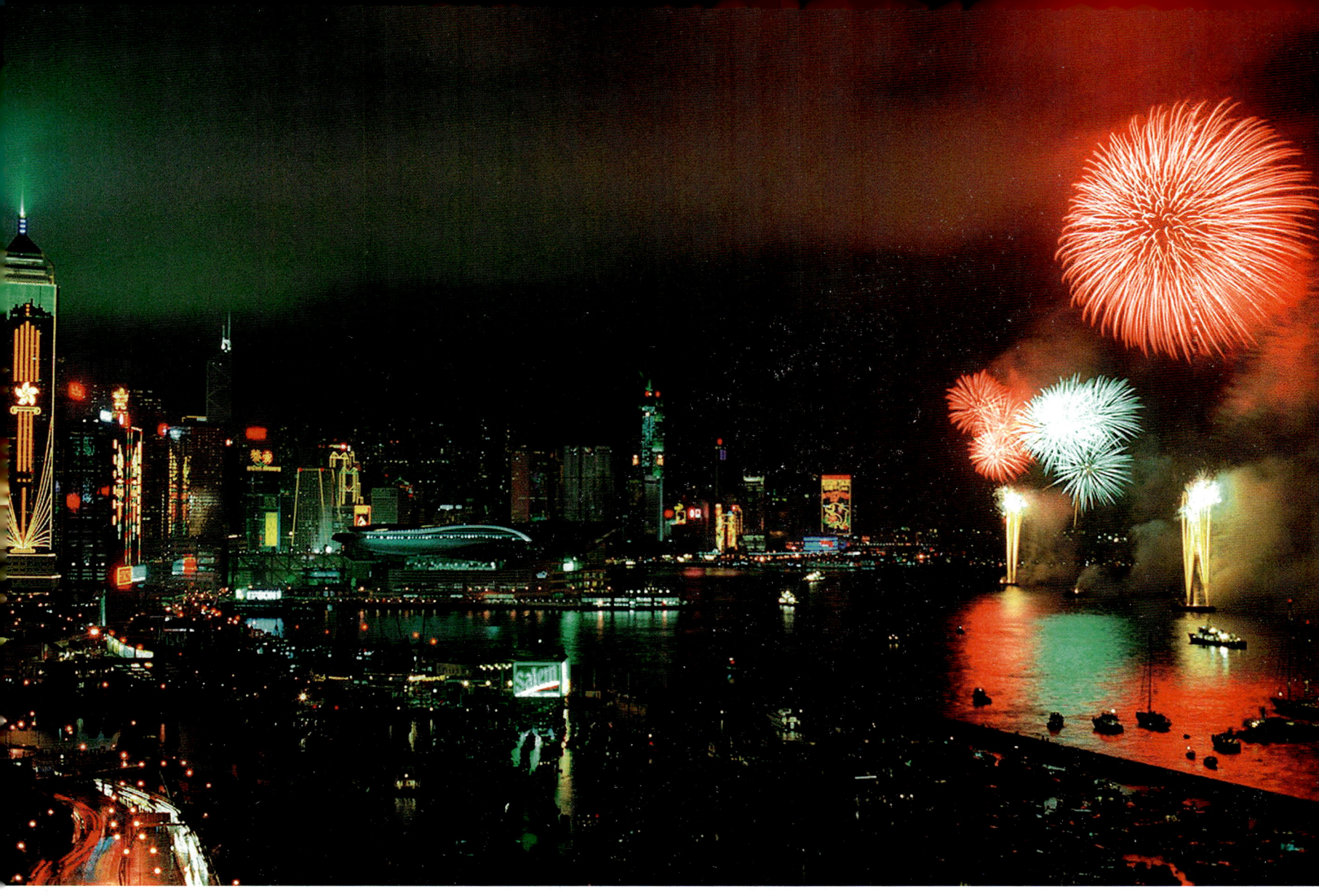

↑

Ricky Chung, 1997

The brooding drizzle that hung over Hong Kong on July 31st, 1997 may have put a damper on the spectators' spirits, but it didn't diminish the spectacle of the magnificent firework display that filled the sky above the Territory. Below, on the rain-soaked streets, many wondered what was to become of them as the 150-year British lease on Hong Kong reached the end of its term. Much of the worry proved groundless: Hong Kong remains a commercial and economic beacon that can rival most any firework. The Basic Law, the mini constitution of Hong Kong which was negotiated between the paramount leader Deng Xiaoping and the British Prime Minister Margaret Thatcher, ensures that the capitalist system and the rule of law in Hong Kong will remain unchanged for 50 years.

Der Nieselregen, der am 31. Juli 1997 über Hongkong hing, mag die Stimmung der Betrachter getrübt haben, aber er minderte nicht das Spektakel des prächtigen Feuerwerks, das den Himmel über der Stadt erfüllte. Unten auf den regennassen Straßen fragten sich viele, was aus ihnen werden sollte, jetzt, da die britische Hoheit über Hongkong nach 150 Jahren zu Ende ging. Viele der Sorgen erwiesen sich als unbegründet: Hongkong ist in punkto Handel und Wirtschaft nach wie vor ein Fanal, das es mit jedem Feuerwerk aufnehmen kann. Dem Grundrecht oder der Mini-Verfassung zufolge, die zwischen dem obersten Führer Deng Xiaoping und der britischen Premierministerin Margaret Thatcher ausgehandelt wurde, bleiben das kapitalistische System und die Rechtsstaatlichkeit in Hongkong in den kommenden 50 Jahren unverändert bestehen.

La triste bruine qui tombait sur Hong Kong le 31 juillet 1997 aurait pu décourager la bonne humeur des spectateurs, mais ne réussit pas à faire pâlir le spectacle du magnifique feu d'artifice qui remplit le ciel du Territoire. Dans les rues détrempées de pluie, beaucoup se demandaient ce qu'ils allaient devenir après la fin de la présence britannique qui avait duré 150 ans. Une grande partie des inquiétudes s'est révélée sans raison : Hong Kong est resté une puissance commerciale et économique qui peut éclipser bien des feux d'artifice. Avec la « Basic Law », la mini-constitution négociée entre Deng Xiaoping et le Premier ministre britannique Margaret Thatcher, le système capitaliste et la règle de droit resteront inchangés pendant 50 ans.

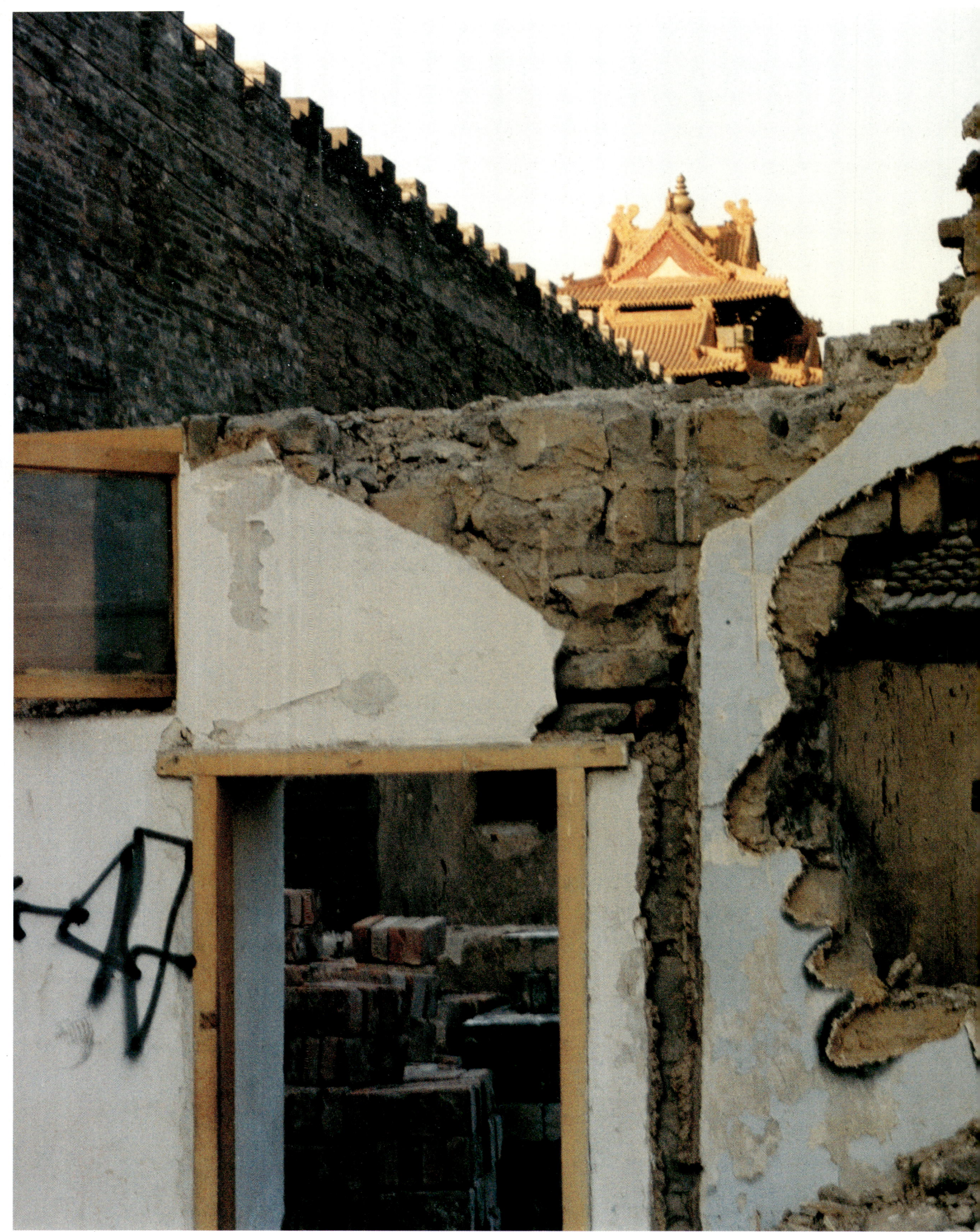

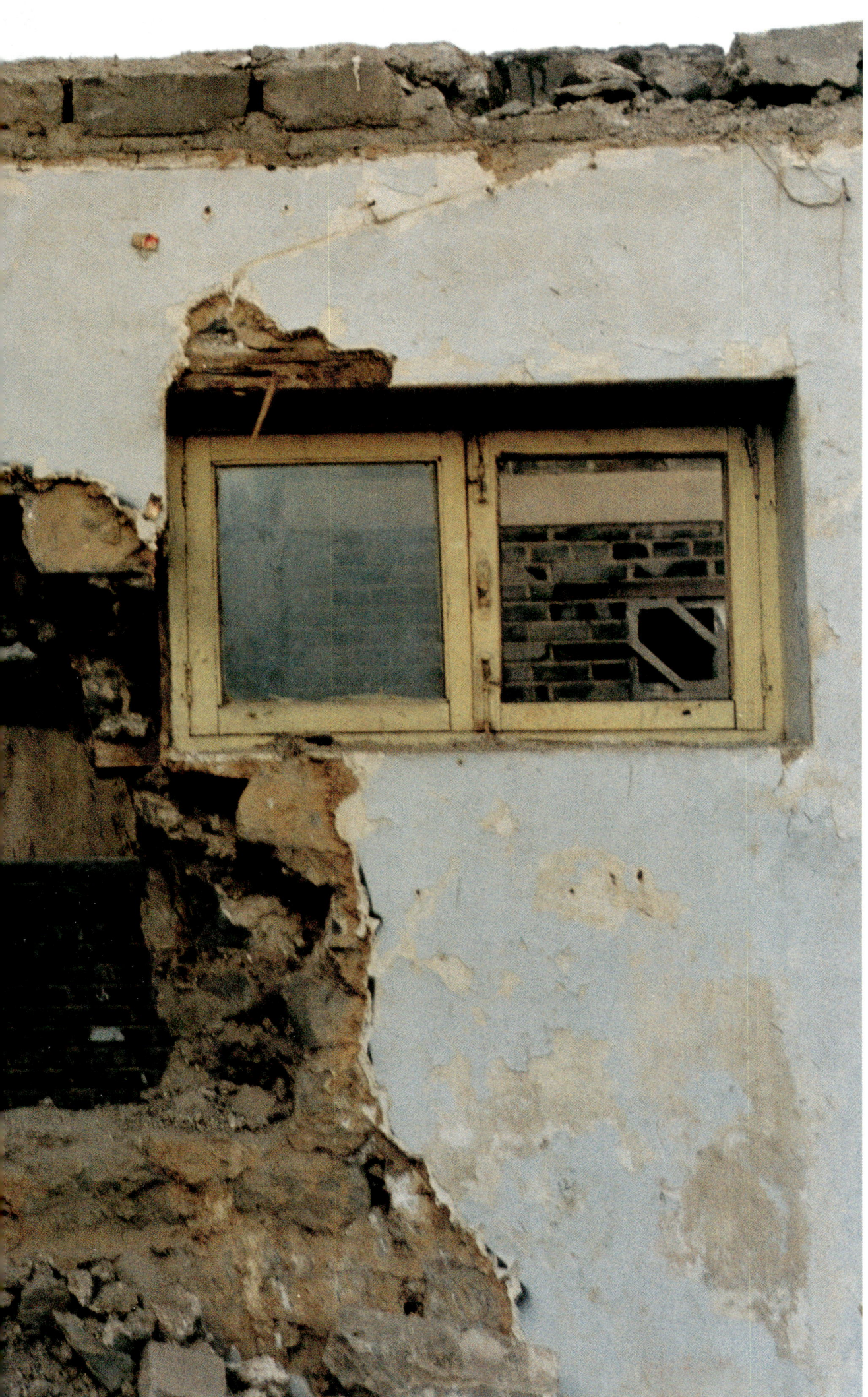

←

Zhang Dali, 1998

The roof of a pavilion on the east side of the Forbidden City peeps out behind the rubble of buildings that once lined the moat. In the late 1990s, Beijing succumbed to a demolition frenzy to make way for modern developments. Little information about the scale of the inner city redevelopment was made public during those few intense years of destruction at the end of the 1990s, but by the early 2000s, the municipal government had confirmed that a number of hutong areas in the old city center would be protected. The city center had been shifting east since the 1990s, and was now cemented in the Central Business District on the southeast corner of the capital. The pace of change has made some areas of the city unrecognizable.

Das Dach eines Pavillons auf der Ostseite der Verbotenen Stadt lugt hinter den Ruinen der Gebäude hervor, die einst den Wassergraben säumten. Ende der 1990er-Jahre verfiel man in Peking in eine fieberhafte Zerstörungswut, um Platz zu schaffen für moderne Bauprojekte. Während der wenigen Jahre intensiver Abrisstätigkeit in den späten 1990er-Jahren, gelangten nur wenig Informationen über das Ausmaß der Bautätigkeit in der Innenstadt in die Öffentlichkeit. Bereits in den ersten Jahren des neuen Jahrtausends wurden von der Stadtregierung im alten Stadtzentrum einige Hutong-Bezirke ausgewiesen, die geschützt werden sollten. Seit den 1990er-Jahren hatte sich das Stadtzentrum nach Osten verschoben und wurde jetzt als zentraler Geschäftsbezirk an der südöstlichen Ecke der Hauptstadt im wahrsten Sinn des Wortes zementiert. Durch das Tempo des Wandels sind einige Stadtviertel nicht mehr wiederzuerkennen.

Le toit d'un pavillon du côté est de la Cité interdite pointe derrière les ruines des bâtiments qui bordaient jadis les douves. À la fin des années 1990, Pékin fut victime d'une frénésie de démolitions pour faire place à des constructions modernes. Peu d'informations furent données sur l'échelle de ces opérations en centre-ville mais au début de 2005, la municipalité a confirmé qu'un certain nombre de zones de hutong de la vieille cité seraient protégées. Le centre s'est déplacé vers l'est depuis les années 1990 et a maintenant rejoint le Quartier d'affaires central dans le sud-est de la capitale. Le rythme du changement a rendu certains quartiers méconnaissables.

336

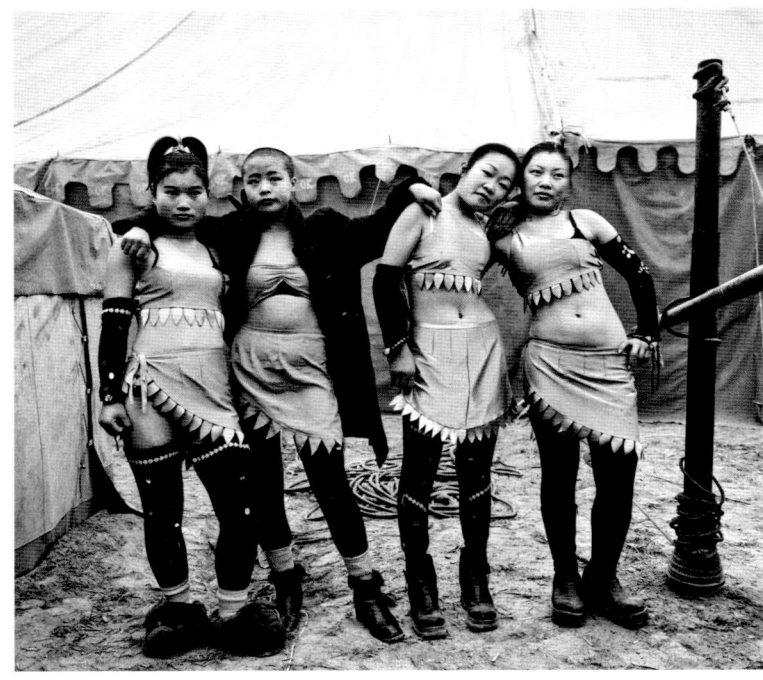

Li Nan, 2001

Four women dancers pose outside a circus
in a tent in rural Shandong. Acrobats and
dancers were recruited to give performances
to attract people to the nearby trade fair.

Vier Tänzerinnen posieren vor einem Zirkus-
zelt im ländlichen Shandong. Akrobaten
und Tänzer wurden für Auftritte rekrutiert,
um die Menschen zum Besuch einer nahe
gelegenen Handelsmesse zu locken.

Quatre danseuses devant une tente dans
le Shandong. Des acrobates et des danseuses
ont été recrutées pour attirer des visiteurs
dans la foire qui se déroule à proximité.

Peng Xiangjie, 1999

Young women in a small town in Shaanxi
province perform on stage dressed only in
bathing suits. For a society that continues to
view public displays of flesh as taboo—in
spite of the modern fads amongst China's
youth to wear mini skirts and hot pants like
their peers in London, New York, or Paris—
saucy performances in the public realm have
increased steadily since the mid-1990s.

Junge Frauen treten in einer Kleinstadt in
Shaanxi nur mit einem Badeanzug bekleidet
auf einer Bühne auf. Für eine Gesellschaft,
die mehrheitlich die öffentliche Zurschau-
stellung nackten Fleisches immer noch als
Tabu betrachtet – ungeachtet der Tatsache,
dass die chinesische Jugend genau wie ihre
Altersgenossen in London, New York oder
Paris Modeerscheinungen wie Miniröcke
und Hotpants schätzt –, haben seit Mitte
der 1990er-Jahre gewagte Aufführungen
im öffentlichen Bereich zugenommen.

Dans une petite ville du Shaanxi, des jeunes
femmes dansent sur scène seulement vêtues
d'un maillot de bain. Pour une société où
l'exposition du corps humain dénudé est
encore un tabou – et malgré la mode chez
les jeunes chinoises des mini-jupes et des
pantalons moulants comme à Londres,
New York ou Paris –, les spectacles osés se
sont multipliés depuis le milieu des années
1990.

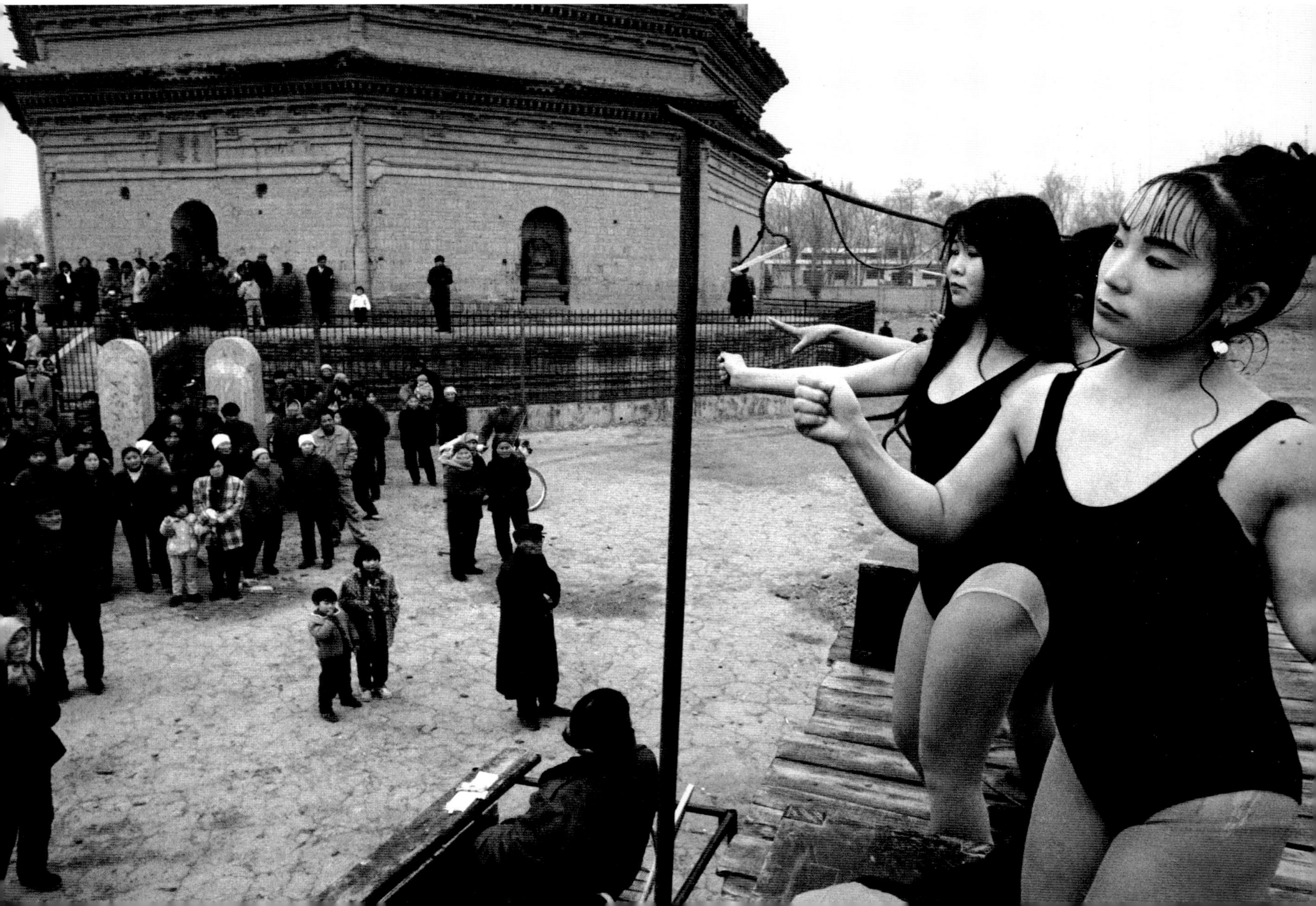

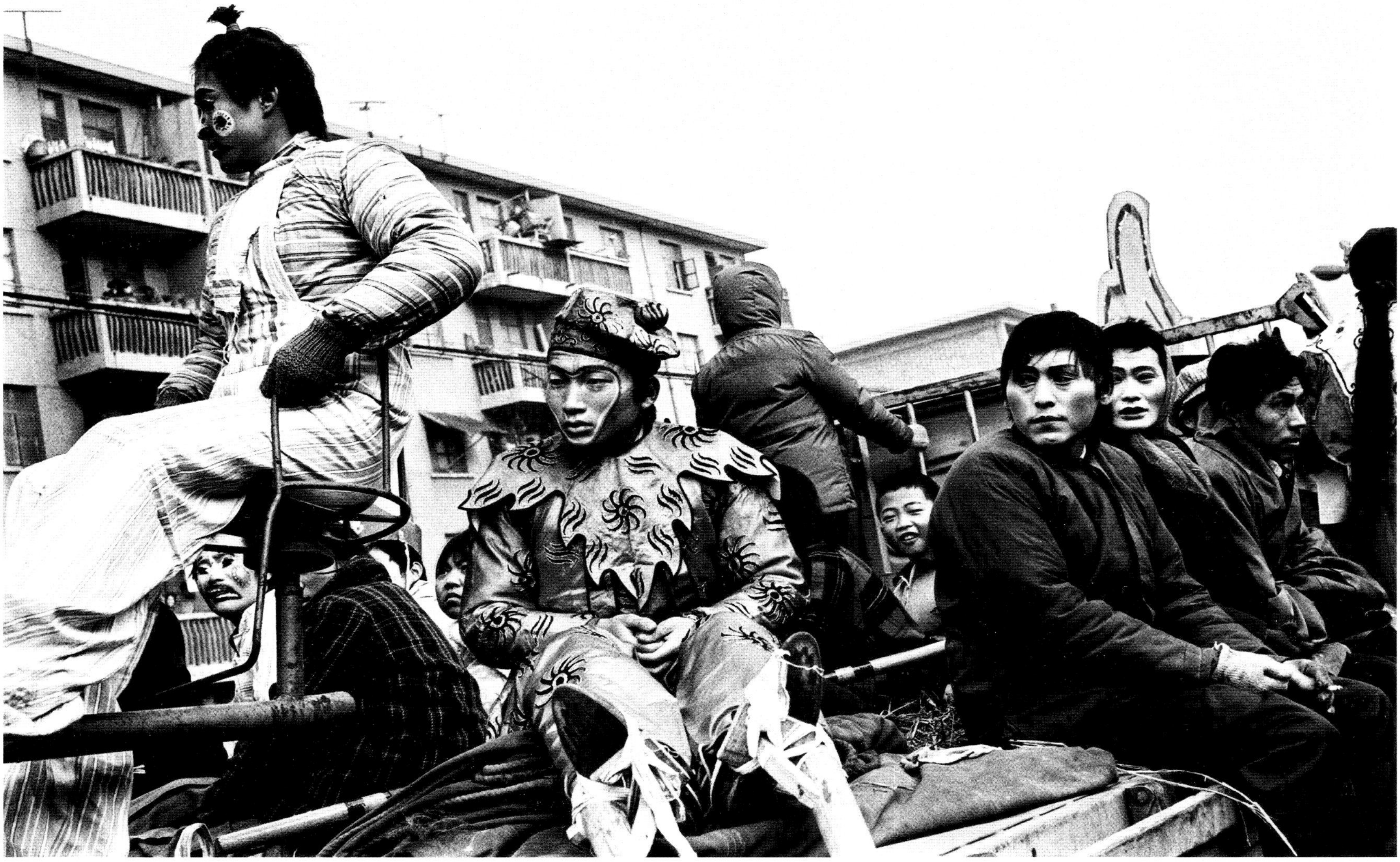

Han Lei, 1999

A circus performer dressed as Sun Wukong, the Monkey King, a hero from Journey to the West, rides on the back of a wagon en route to a performance.

Ein als Sun Wukong, der Affenkönig, einer der Heroen aus Die Reise nach Westen, verkleideter Zirkusartist fährt hinten auf einem Wagen sitzend zu einer Aufführung.

Un artiste de cirque habillé en Sun Wukong, le roi-singe héro du Pèlerinage vers l'Ouest, est assis à l'arrière d'un chariot pour se rendre sur le lieu du spectacle.

→

Liu Zheng, 1999

A man plies a trade with an opera costume and a donkey in Shanxi province, allowing people to pay for the use of both to take a photograph.

Ein Mann in der Provinz Shanxi treibt Handel mit einem Opernkostüm und einem Esel; beides kann gegen eine Gebühr für Fotos gemietet werden.

Un homme fait un petit commerce de la location d'un costume d'opéra et d'un âne qu'il loue pour des prises de vue (province du Shanxi).

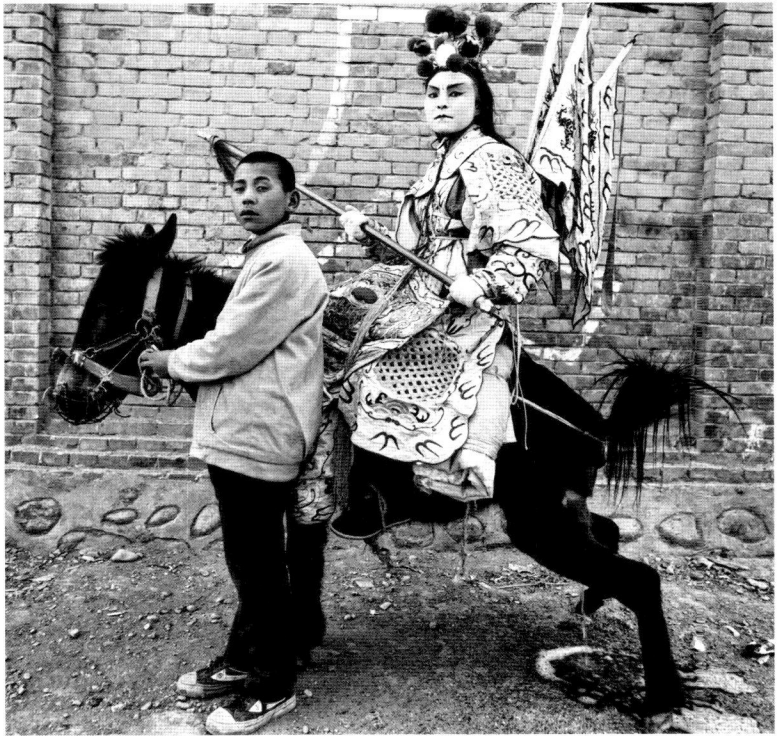

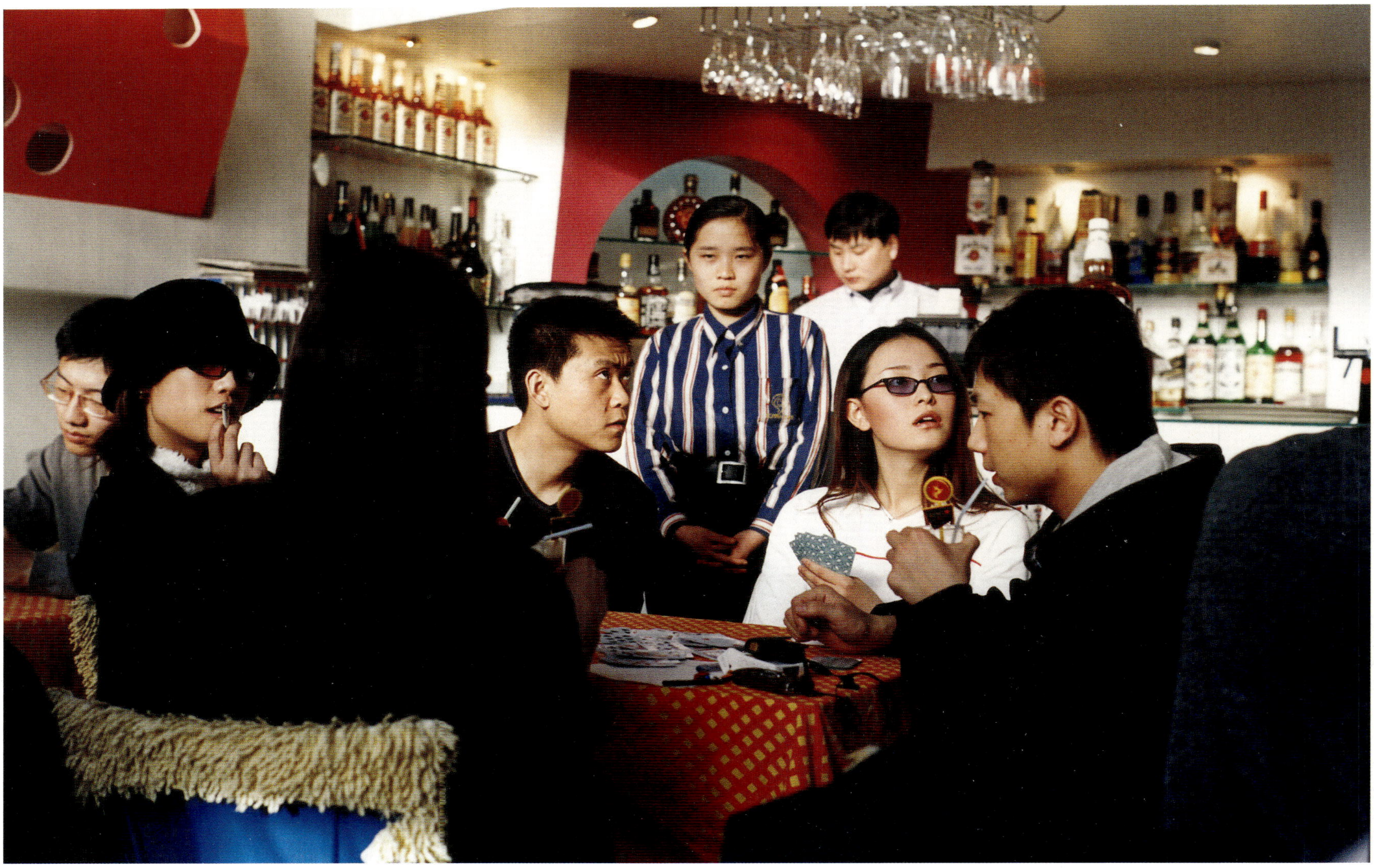

↑

Zhou Yue, 1997

*Chinese yuppies gather at a watering hole
in the infamous Beijing bar street known as
Sanlitun. In 1994, there was just one bar,
but six months later the street already divided
into the northern section and the southern.
The area was given a makeover, with a
monumental new shopping center, the Village
at Sanlitun, begun in 2007 and completed
in 2008. The huge project comprises 19
buildings and a boutique hotel, not least an
eight-screen cinema and a huge selection
of restaurants and bars.*

*Chinesische Yuppies treffen sich in einer Bar
an der als Sanlitun bekannten berüchtigten
Barmeile in Peking. 1994 gab es dort nur
eine Bar, aber sechs Monate später war die
Straße bereits in einen nördlichen und einen
südlichen Bezeich unterteilt. Mit einem 2007
begonnenen und 2008 fertiggestellten imposanten Einkaufszentrum, dem Village von
Sanlitun, wurde die Gegend völlig verändert.
Das gewaltige Bauprojekt umfasst 19 Gebäude
und ein Boutique-Hotel, ein Kino mit acht
Vorführsälen sowie eine große Auswahl von
Restaurants und Bars.*

*Yuppies chinois dans un bar d'une rue mal
famée de Pékin appelée Sanlitun. En 1994,
un seul bar existait, mais six mois plus tard la
rue était déjà divisée en section sud et section
nord. Le quartier fut rénové et doté d'un
centre commercial monumental, le « Village
de Sanlitun », commencé en 2007 et achevé
en 2008. L'énorme projet comprend 19 bâtiments et un boutique hôtel, un complexe de
18 salles de cinéma et quantité de restaurants
et de bars.*

→

Zhou Yue, 1999

*China's youth now has its own culture:
two young women hang out at one of
Beijing's proliferating new clubs.*

*Chinas Jugend hat jetzt eine eigene Kultur:
zwei junge Frauen in einem der sich ständig
vermehrenden Clubs von Peking.*

*La jeunesse chinoise possède aujourd'hui sa
propre culture : deux jeunes femmes dans un
des nouveaux clubs qui prolifèrent à Pékin.*

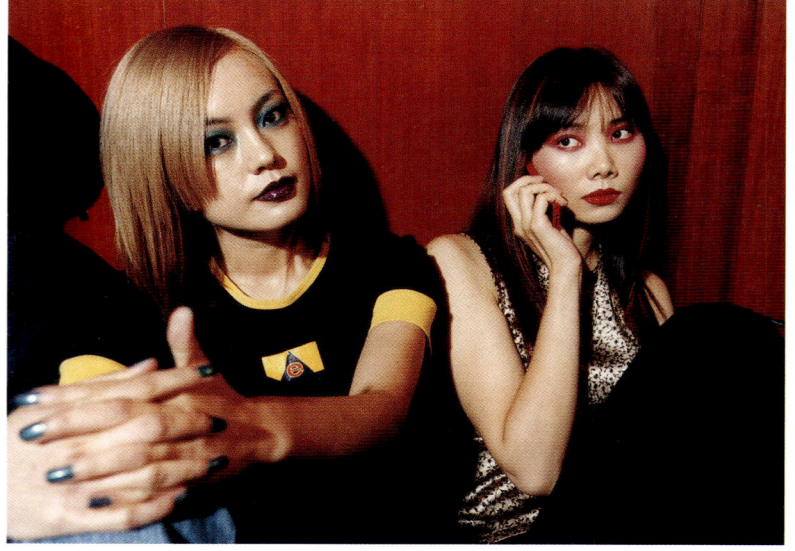

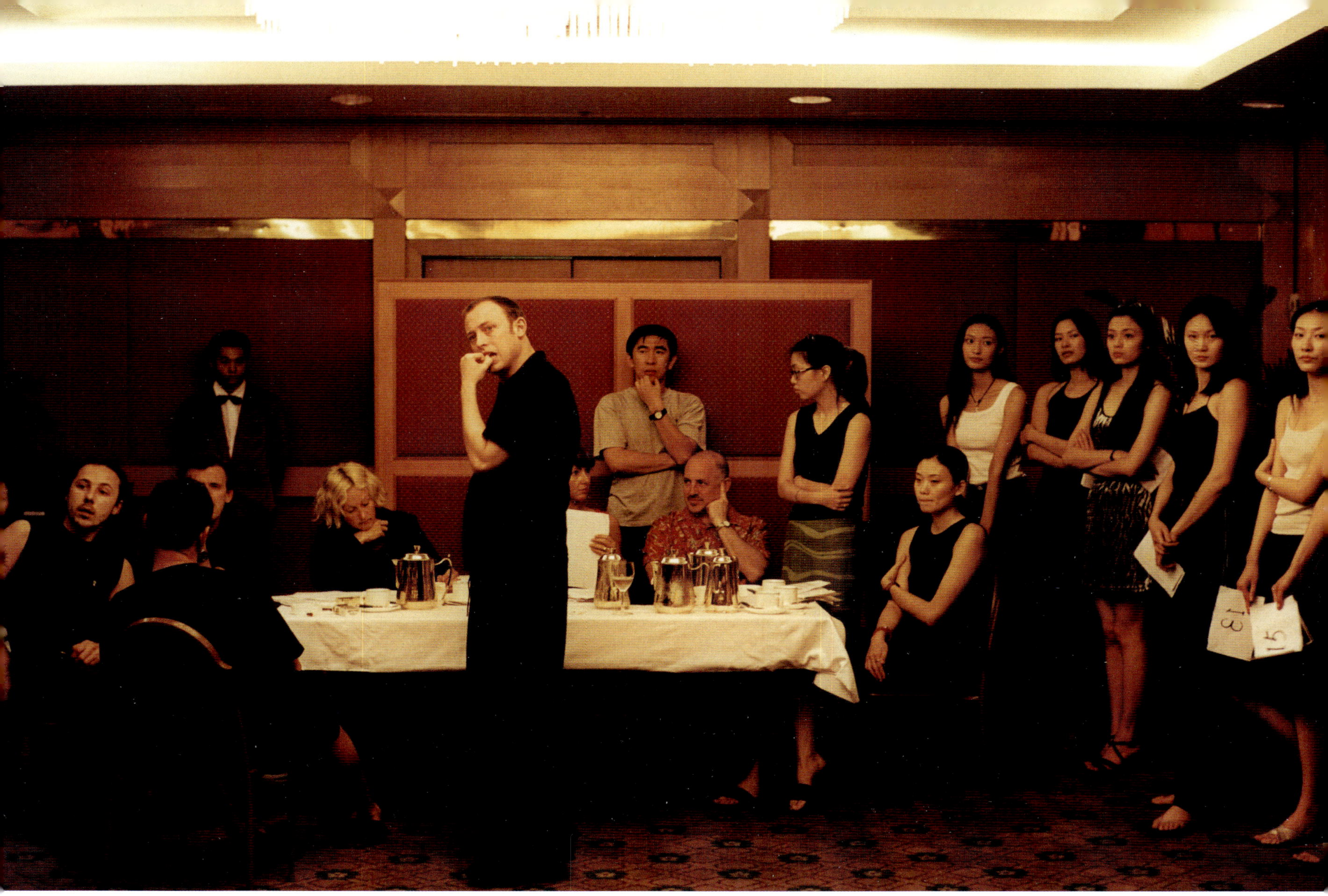

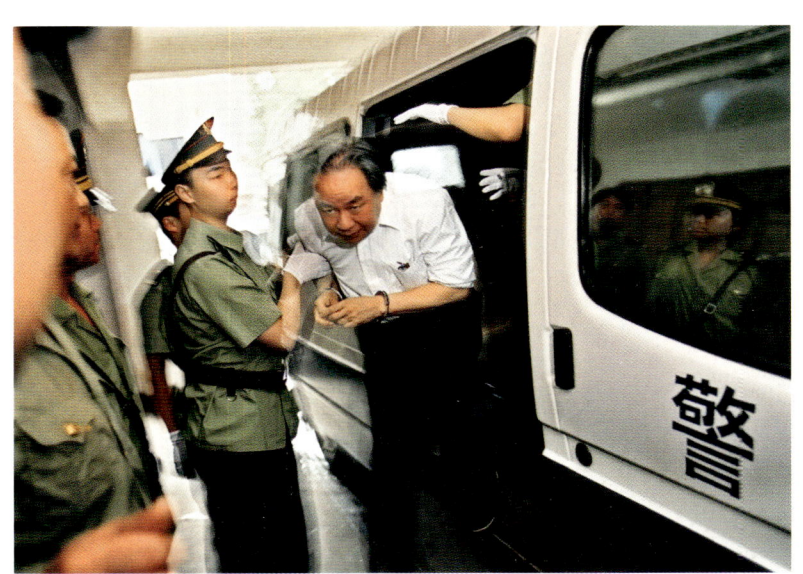

Zhou Yue, 1999

↑

Chinese models put their best foot forward at a casting for a fashion show to be held in Beijing for a foreign designer.

Chinesische Models bei einem Casting für eine Modenschau, die in Peking im Auftrag eines ausländischen Kunden stattfinden sollte.

Des mannequins se préparent à un casting pour le défilé de mode d'un créateur étranger.

Qiu Yan, 1999

↘

In 1992, when interviewed by The New York Times, private entrepreneur Mu Qizhong was described in a headline as "Product of Old China, Leading the New." Already a millionaire in 1994, his name made it onto the Forbes Rich List, ranking fourth for the Chinese mainland. Five years later, he was arrested on fraud charges involving 75 million dollars, and brought before a court of law in Wuhan, Hubei province. He was sentenced to life, a term commuted to 18 years.

Als der Privatunternehmer Mu Qizhong 1992 von der New York Times interviewt wurde, bezeichnete man ihn in einer Überschrift als „Produkt des Alten China, führend im Neuen". Der Name des bereits 1994 millionenschweren Mu wurde in die Forbes-Liste der Reichen aufgenommen und rangierte für das chinesische Festland auf Platz vier. Fünf Jahre später wurde er wegen Unterschlagung von 75 Millionen Dollar verhaftet und vor einem Gericht in Wuhan, Provinz Hubei, angeklagt. Das Urteil lautete auf lebenslange Haft, die später in 18 Jahre umgewandelt wurde.

En 1992, interrogé par le New York Times, l'homme d'affaires Mu Qizhong était présenté en titre de l'article comme « Un produit de la Chine ancienne, en route vers la nouvelle ». Déjà millionnaire en 1994, son nom figurait en quatrième place sur la liste Forbes des grandes fortunes chinoises. Cinq ans plus tard, il fut arrêté pour des fraudes portant sur 75 millions de US $ et poursuivi devant un tribunal de Wuhan, province du Hubei. Il fut condamné à la prison à vie, sentence commuée par la suite en 18 années.

"The problem now is how to spur young people on, and get them to use their right to speak out … in China we've never given young people the right to speak out! It's an Eastern thing: we always look to older people, and no matter how wrong they are, we always listen."

„Das Problem ist jetzt, wie man junge Leute dazu anspornen kann, ihr Recht auf freie Meinungsäußerung zu nutzen … In China hatten junge Leute nie das Recht, sich zu äußern! Es ist ein Problem des Ostens: Wir wenden uns immer an ältere Leute, und ganz gleich, wie sehr sie im Unrecht sind, wir hören immer auf sie."

« Le problème aujourd'hui est : comment stimuler les jeunes et les amener à se servir de leur droit à s'exprimer … en Chine nous n'avons jamais donné aux jeunes le droit de parler ! C'est quelque chose d'oriental : nous nous tournons toujours vers les vieux, et même s'ils ont complètement tort, nous les écoutons toujours. »

CUI JIAN (1961–), the "Father of Chinese rock," 2006

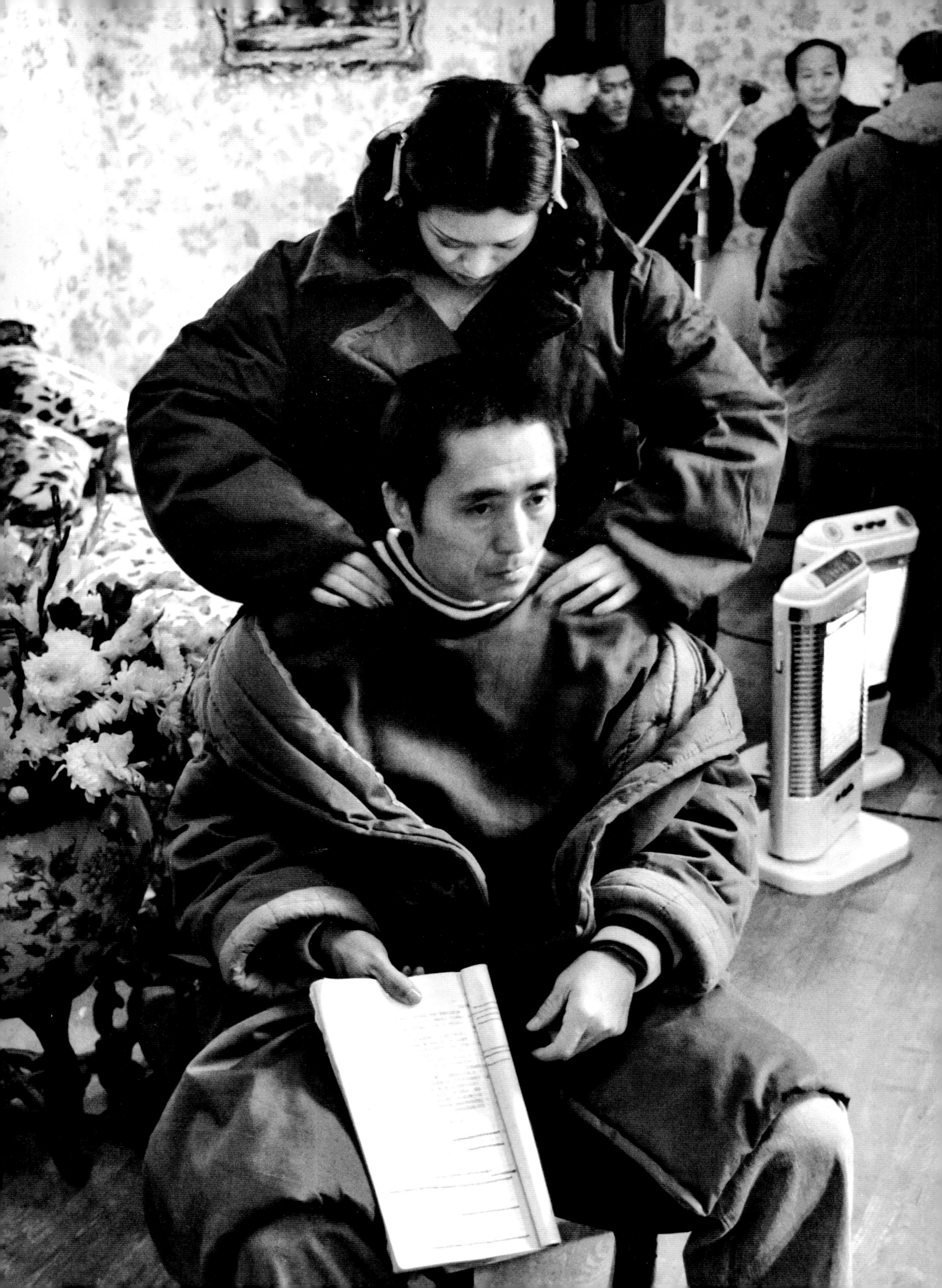

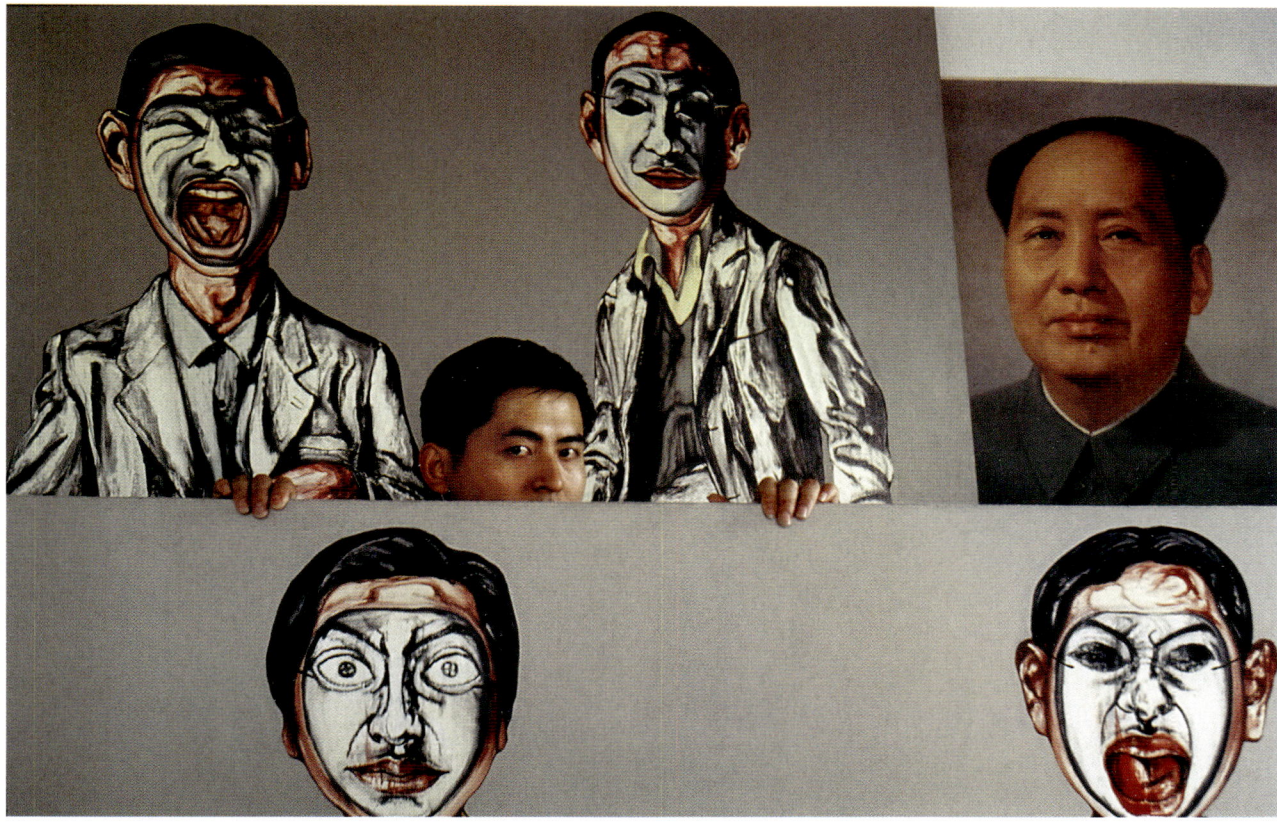

↑
Xing Danwen, 1998

Painter Zeng Fanzhi surrounded by iconic works from the Mask *paintings that made him a contemporary art star. At the time this photograph was taken, the works fetched around 5,000 US-dollars. In 2007, Zeng Fanzhi topped the list of record-breaking auction prices for works by China's contemporary artists, second only to master Zhang Xiaogang. Several works sold for more than one million US-dollars.*

Der Maler Zeng Fanzhi, umgeben von seinen Maskenbildern, die ihn zu einem Star der zeitgenössischen Kunstszene machten. Als dieses Foto entstand, verkauften sich seine Bilder für etwa 5000 US-Dollar. 2007 stand Zeng Fanzhi an der Spitze der Liste der Rekordauktionspreise für Werke zeitgenössischer chinesischer Künstler, nur noch übertroffen vom Meister Zhang Xiaogang. Mehrere seiner Werke brachten über eine Million US-Dollar ein.

Le peintre Zeng Fanzhi entouré d'exemples de ses peintures de masques iconiques qui ont fait de lui une vedette de l'art contemporain. Au moment où cette photographie a été prise, ses œuvres valaient environ 5 000 US $. En 2007, elles étaient les plus cotées des ventes aux enchères d'art contemporain chinoises, juste derrière Zhang Xiaogang. Plusieurs pièces se sont vendues à plus d'un million de US $.

←
Xiao Quan, 1995

Famous actress Gong Li gives film director Zhang Yimou a massage on the set in Shanghai, at the time the two were an item: their professional and personal relationship shaped Chinese cinema for the next decade, and made Gong Li an international household name. Her last film with Zhang Yimou was Shanghai Triad. *Following their break up around that time, she married Singaporean tycoon Ooi Hoe Soeng.*

Die bekannte Schauspielerin Gong Li massiert Filmregisseur Zhang Yimou am Set in Shanghai. Damals verband die beiden ein Liebesverhältnis. Ihre professionelle und private Beziehung prägte das chinesische Kino während des folgenden Jahrzehnts und machte Gong Li zu einer internationalen Berühmtheit. Ihr letzter Film mit Zhang Yimou war Shanghai Serenade. *Um diese Zeit trennten sich die beiden, und Gong Li heiratete den aus Singapur stammenden Tycoon Ooi Hoe Soeng.*

Sur un tournage à Shanghai, la célèbre actrice Gong Li masse le dos du metteur en scène de cinéma Zhang Yimou. Tous deux étaient très liés et leur relation professionnelle et personnelle joua un grand rôle dans le cinéma chinois de la décennie suivante qui fit de Gong Li une star internationale. Son dernier film avec Zhang Yimou fut Shanghai Triad. *Après leur rupture, elle a épousé le grand homme d'affaires de Singapour, Ooi Hoe Soeng.*

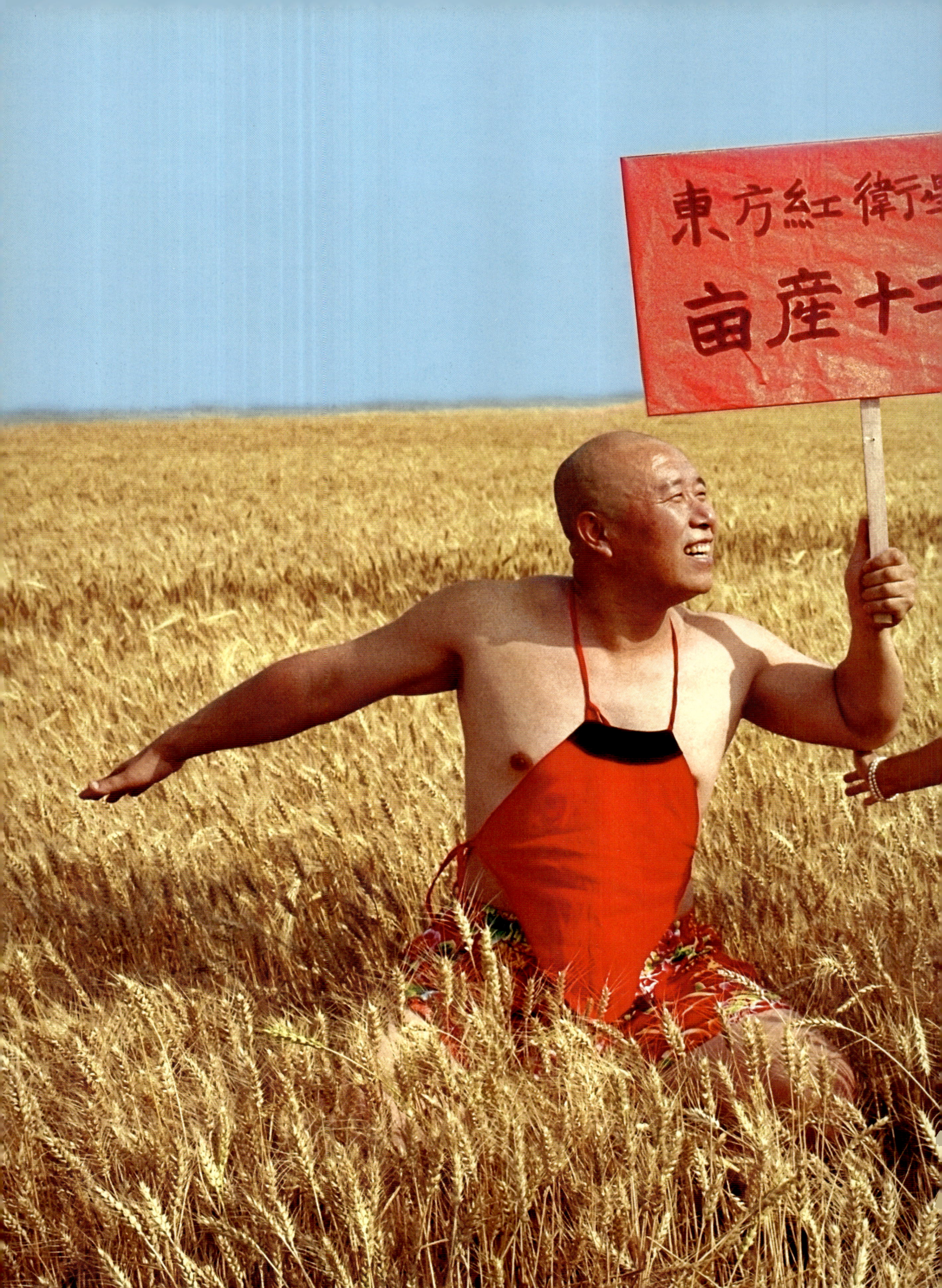

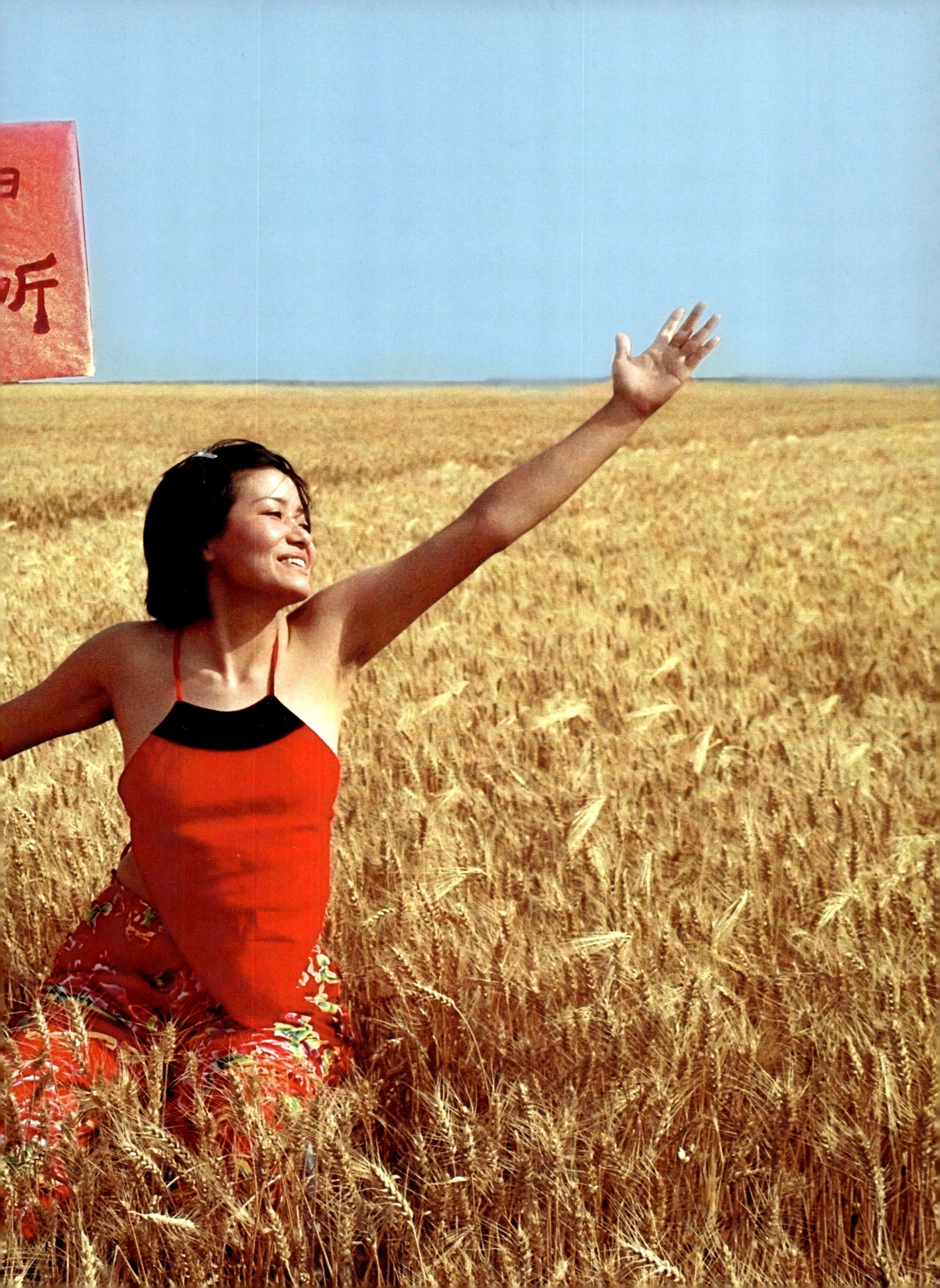

pp. 342/343
Guo Gai, 1999

In 1958, the Red Banner People's Commune in the west of China reported a record-making per-acre yield of 397 tons of rice. This was acclaimed by local newspapers as the very model of a "shooting satellite"—the term "satellite" was a popular metaphor used to articulate the goals of socialism in simple but exciting terms—to express the miraculous increase in agricultural (and later industrial) production. This encouraged other communes to follow suit, contributing to food shortages and the famine of 1960–62. Wheat Harvest lampoons the exaggerated production targets that were set and "met" during the Great Leap Forward, which ultimately served only to ingratiate commune leaders with political officials. Photographer Guo Gai and his wife, Sun Yiwai, are both former newspaper reporters who object to the news media being used as a propaganda tool.

1958 meldete die Volkskommune Rotes Banner den rekordverdächtigen Ertrag von 980 Tonnen Reis pro Hektar. Dies wurde von den Lokalzeitungen als das wahre Modell eines „aufsteigenden Satelliten" bezeichnet – der Begriff Satellit war eine populäre Metapher, um die Ziele des Sozialismus in einfache, aber treffende Worte zu fassen –, und verlieh dem unglaublichen Anstieg der landwirtschaftlichen (und später der industriellen) Produktion Ausdruck zu verleihen. Dies ermunterte andere Kommunen dazu, gleiches zu tun, was zu Knappheit von Nahrungsmitteln und der Hungersnot von 1960 bis 1962 führte. Die Weizenernte verspottet die übertrieben hoch angesetzten und auch erreichten Erträge während des Großen Sprungs nach vorn, die letztlich nur den Führern der Kommunen dazu dienten, sich bei den politischen Funktionären einzuschmeicheln. Fotograf Guo Gai und seine Frau Sun Yiwai waren beide früher als Zeitungsreporter tätig und lehnen die Verwendung der Medien als Propagandawerkzeuge ab.

En 1958, la commune populaire du Drapeau rouge dans l'ouest de la Chine annonça une récolte record de 980 tonnes de riz par hectare. Ce résultat fut applaudi par la presse locale qui en fit le modèle même de « l'objectif satellite » (« satellite » étant alors une métaphore utilisée pour exprimer les objectifs du socialisme en termes simples mais parlants) de l'accroissement miraculeux de la production agricole, puis industrielle. Ce record encourageait les autres communes à faire de même, contribuant aux disettes et à la famine de 1960–62. Le groupe Récolte de blé se moque des objectifs de production exagérés qui étaient prescrits et « atteints » pendant le Grand bond en avant et qui servaient aux responsables des communes à s'attirer les faveurs des responsables politiques. Le photographe Guo Gai et son épouse, Sun Yiwai, sont tous deux d'anciens reporters photographes qui s'opposent à l'utilisation des médias comme outils de propagande.

→
Xing Danwen, 1996

Beijing-based conceptual artist Wang Jin "marries a mule." No one is quite sure why, but it made for a great frame.

Der in Peking lebende Konzeptkünstler Wang Jin „heiratet ein Maultier". Keiner weiß so recht, warum, aber es sorgte für einige Berühmtheit.

L'artiste conceptuel pékinois Wang Jin « épouse une mule ». Sans que l'on sache bien pourquoi, cela lui valut un grand succès.

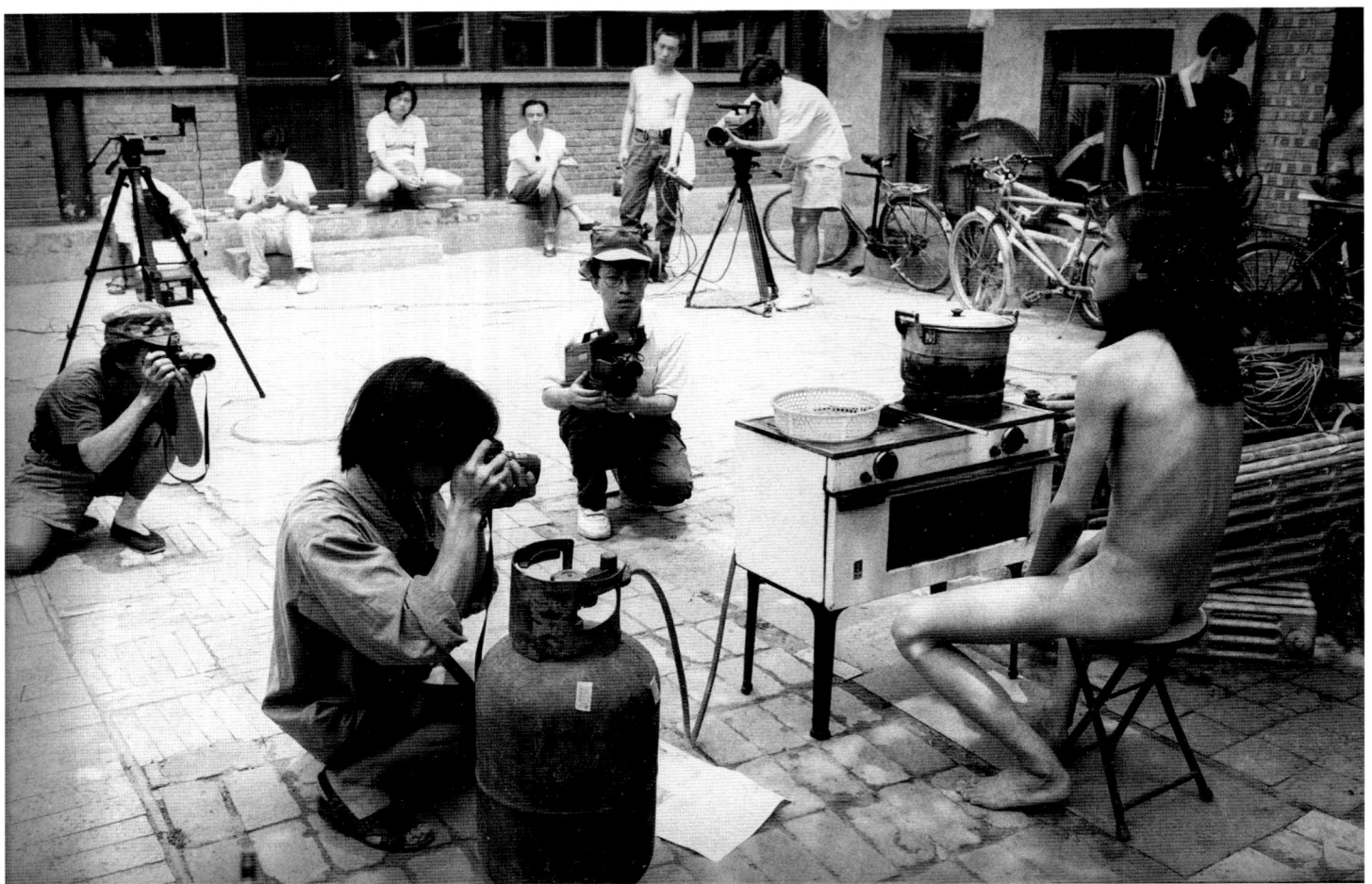

↑
Xing Danwen, 1994

East Village performance artist Ma Liuming "cooks lunch." He was arrested an hour later, and held for two months on charges of public indecency.

Der Performancekünstler Ma Liuming aus dem Pekinger East Village „bereitet das Mittagessen zu". Eine Stunde später wurde er verhaftet und unter der Anklage, öffentliches Ärgernis erregt zu haben, zwei Monate festgehalten.

L'artiste de performance de l'East Village pékinois, Ma Liuming « prépare le repas ». Il fut arrêté une heure plus tard et détenu pendant deux mois pour conduite publique indécente.

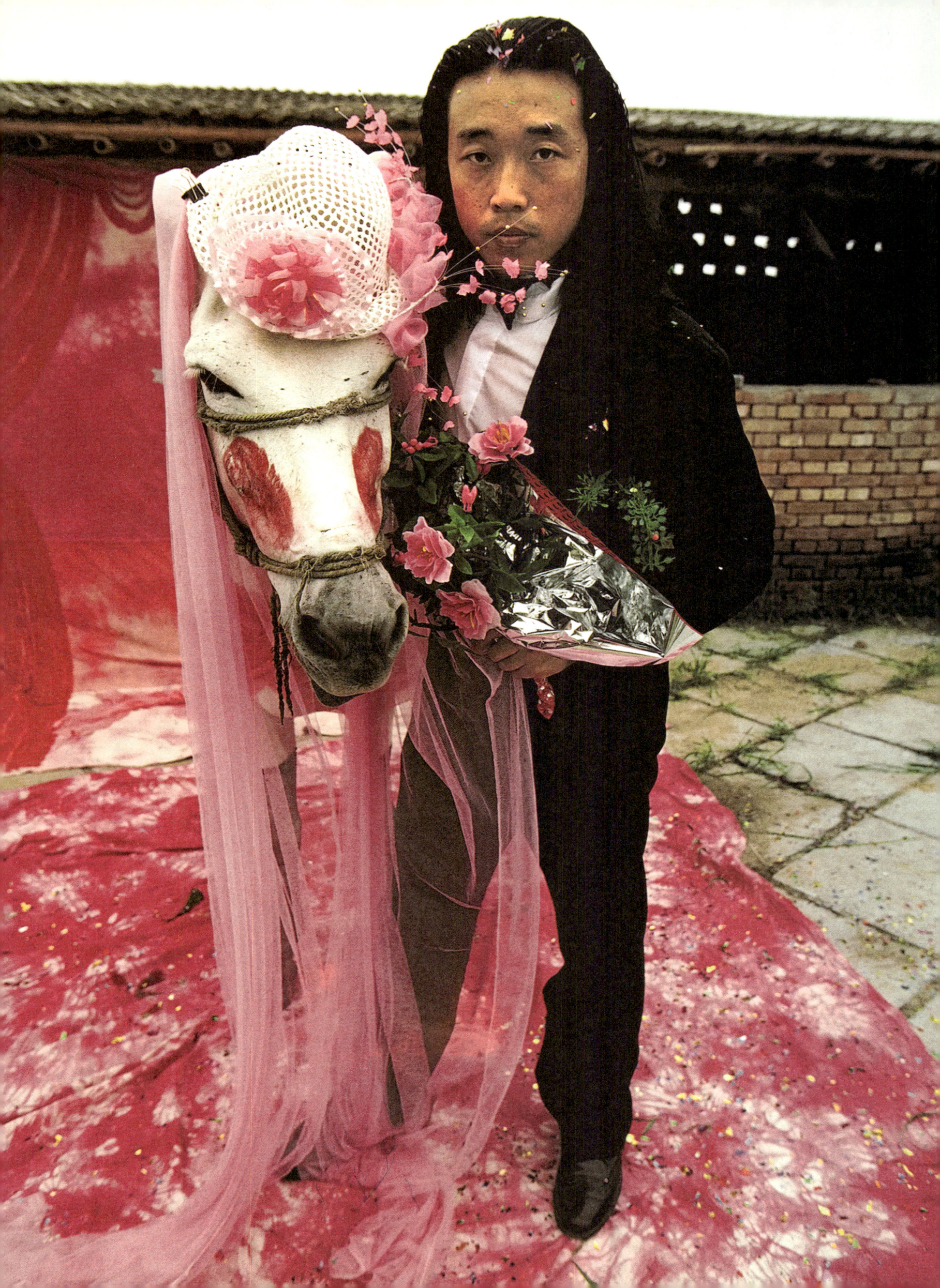

#6

2000–today
China Joins the World

"China is experiencing the paradox of globalization—economic indicators may rise, but an increase in poverty, loss of jobs, and social inequities, accompany the financial indicators of 'success'. With the mounting rural crises, workers abuses, ecological degradation, income gap … China is standing at the crossroads."

DALE WEN, International Forum on Globalization, 2006

Even after Tibet became effectively linked to the outside world by train with the opening of the Beijing-Lhasa railway in July 2007, Tibetan nomads continued to tend their yaks on the plateaus romantically known as the "roof of the world". In spite of economic advances, the northwest of China, in particular the region close by the Gobi desert, faced severe water shortages that parched the land across northern China almost to the east coast.

Against extraordinary odds, China nonetheless managed to build an economy that would become tagged the "manufacturing center of the world." In light of China's succession to the World Trade Organization, of ongoing reforms and opening up to the world, in 2001 Beijing was awarded the 2008 Olympic Games. Simultaneously, China unwittingly opened itself up to the toughest international scrutiny it had had to contend with in known history.

Heated Economics

Just under three decades after Deng Xiaoping launched reforms in 1978, by 2006 (when the most recent official State statistics were available), China's economy had grown almost 57.85 times, to an annual GDP of US $ 2.8 billion. By early 2007, China's foreign reserves amounted to US $ 1.2 trillion dollars. China also claimed 370 million landline telephone subscribers, and 460 million mobile-phone users. The statistics are overwhelming: 210 million Internet users, 100 million homes with a television set, 230 million privately owned vehicles, 14 million university students, and 40 million high-school students. Since the founding of the People's Republic, China has built 45,000 kilometers of new roads. Four hundred million people have been lifted above the official poverty line in the last 30 years, which represents 75 per cent of the world's poor people (living on an annual income of 2,822.6 Yuan or US $ 400). Just over 60 per cent of the population, 745 million people, continue to live in the rural areas, although the drift towards the urban centers is still gathering momentum.

Brave New World

The Chinese capital, Beijing, is just one example of the urban renaissance in planning, redevelopment, and architecture that is sweeping China. Recent years have brought massive construction projects, such as the Grand Opera House, the Olympic Stadium, the CCTV Tower—an ultra-modern skewed arch, which could accommodate a small plane between the two main towers—and the expansive Central Business District. Criss-crossing the city, beneath the crowded streets, are kilometers of new subway lines. Brand-new highways have been cut across the city proper, and carry the huge volume of traffic to the burgeoning new suburbs. Hundreds of mid-sized cities are springing up nationwide. In the Three Gorges area of the Yangtze river, a massive dam that is capable of generating 39 billion KWH of electricity was completed in 2007. The damage to the environment remains unknown, but the desperate shortage of water across northern China is, for the time being, alleviated.

American economist Lawrence Summers stated that during the Industrial Revolution the average European's living standards rose about 50 per cent over the course of his lifetime (then about 40 years). In Asia, principally China, he calculated, the average person's living standards will rise by 10,000 percent in one lifetime! In two decades, China has experienced the same degree of industrialization, urbanization, and social transformation as Europe did in two centuries.[1]

The record-breaking pace of industrialization is rapidly depleting China's natural resources, and increasingly the world's. What will be the cost of the relentless pursuit of economic growth? The State has moved aggressively to forgive debts in areas of rural development, waiving land and crop taxes for the peasants. Efforts are being made to address the widening gap between the rich and the poor, the cities and the countryside, especially with regard to education.

Rules of Engagement for Playing a New Game

In 2007, the new collective leadership of the 17th CCP Party Congress pledged a harmonious and scientifically sound development within China and peaceful relations in its foreign policy. Many observers believe that China's future will largely depend on achieving a sustainable economic development, in tandem with gradual political reform of the 70 million-member strong one-party system. In seeking to establish a position vis-à-vis the developed world, Chinese people are mindful of the horrific history of the first three decades of misguided policy. Though the youth of China today is not keenly aware of recent history, this Internet generation is hungry for greater and faster change. Yet, one suspects that it will be one of the Chinese people's greatest virtues, their peerless pragmatism coupled with an ingrained idealism, that will guide the nation through any future crisis, as well as precipitating a long-overdue rebirth of Chinese culture.

1. Fareed Zakaria, "The Rise of a Fierce Yet fragile Superpower", *Newsweek*, January 7, 2008.

#6

2000–heute
China tritt der Welt bei

„China erlebt das Paradoxon der Globalisierung – ökonomische Indikatoren mögen steigen, aber die steigende Armut, der Verlust von Arbeitsplätzen und soziale Ungleichheiten begleiten die finanziellen Anzeichen des ‚Erfolgs‘. Mit der sich verschärfenden Krise in der Landwirtschaft, der Ausbeutung von Arbeitern, zunehmenden Umweltschäden, der Einkommensschere … steht China am Scheideweg.“

DALE WEN, International Forum on Globalization, 2006

Auch nachdem Tibet mit der Eröffnung der Bahnstrecke von Peking nach Lhasa im Juli 2007 faktisch mit der Außenwelt verbunden war, hüteten die tibetischen Nomaden weiterhin ihre Yaks auf den Hochplateaus, die romantisch als „Dach der Welt“ bezeichnet werden. Ungeachtet des ökonomischen Fortschritts leidet der Nordwesten Chinas, insbesondere das Land um die Wüste Gobi, unter bedrohlicher Wasserknappheit, die das Land fast bis zur Ostküste Chinas austrocknen ließ.

Trotz außerordentlich schlechter Voraussetzungen ist es China gelungen, in rasantem Tempo eine Wirtschaft aufzubauen, die zur „zentralen Produktionsstätte der Welt“ wurde. Angesichts von Chinas Aufnahme in die Welthandelsorganisation im Jahre 2001, laufender Reformen und seiner Öffnung zur Welt wurden Peking 2001 die Olympischen Spiele 2008 zugesprochen. Damit setzte sich China ungewollt der strengsten internationalen Überwachung aus, mit der es je konfrontiert war.

Schwungvolle Ökonomie

In nur knapp drei Jahrzehnten, seit Deng Xiaoping 1978 die Reformpolitik einleitete, wuchs Chinas Wirtschaft bis 2006 (als die letzten offiziellen Statistiken erstellt wurden) um nahezu das 57,85-Fache auf das jährliche Bruttoinlandsprodukt von 2,8 Milliarden US-Dollar. Anfang 2007 belief sich Chinas Devisenbestand auf 1,2 Billionen US-Dollar. Außerdem zählte China 370 Millionen Telefonanschlüsse im Festnetz sowie 460 Millionen Nutzer von Mobiltelefonen. Die Statistiken sind überwältigend: 210 Millionen Internetnutzer, 100 Millionen Haushalte mit Fernsehgeräten, 230 Millionen Privatfahrzeuge, 14 Millionen Universitätsstudenten sowie 40 Millionen Schüler in weiterführenden Schulen. Seit Gründung der Volksrepublik hat China 45.000 Kilometer neue Straßen gebaut. Innerhalb der letzten 30 Jahre gelang 400 Millionen Menschen der Sprung über die Armutsgrenze, was weltweit 75 Prozent der Armen entspricht, die von einem Jahreseinkommen von 2822,6 Yuan oder 400 US-Dollar leben. Etwas mehr als 60 Prozent der Bevölkerung, entsprechend 745 Millionen Menschen, leben weiterhin in ländlichen Gebieten, obgleich der Zustrom in die Großstädte noch immer wächst.

Schöne neue Welt

Chinas Hauptstadt Peking ist nur ein Beispiel dafür, wie Städte durch Planung, Neugestaltung und Architektur wiedererstehen können. In jüngster Zeit wurden riesige Bauprojekte realisiert, etwa das Opernhaus, das Olympiastadion, die CCTV-Zentrale, ein ultramoderner, assymetrischer Bogen, zwischen dessen beiden Haupttürmen ein kleines Flugzeug Platz fände, sowie das ausgedehnte zentrale Geschäftsviertel. Unterhalb der stark befahrenen Straßen durchqueren endlose Kilometer neuer U-Bahnlinien die Stadt. Nagelneue mehrspurige Straßen durchschneiden die Innenstadt und befördern das riesige Verkehrsaufkommen in die expandierenden neuen Vorstädte. Im ganzen Land schießen mittelgroße Städte aus dem Boden. In der Drei-Schluchten-Region des Jangtse wurde 2007 eine riesige Talsperre fertiggestellt, die 39 Milliarden Kilowattstunden Elektrizität produzieren kann. Das Ausmaß der hierdurch zu erwartenden Umweltschäden ist noch nicht abzusehen, aber die extreme Wasserknappheit im Norden Chinas ist fürs Erste beseitigt.

Der amerikanische Wirtschaftswissenschaftler Lawrence Summers konstatiert, dass während der industriellen Revolution der Lebensstandard eines durchschnittlichen Europäers im Laufe seines damals etwa 40 Jahre währenden Lebens um etwa 50 Prozent stieg. Seinen Berechnungen zufolge steigt der Lebensstandard eines Durchschnittsbewohners Asiens, in erster Linie Chinas, in einer Generation um 10.000 Prozent! In zwei Jahrzehnten erlebte China eine Industrialisierung, Urbanisierung und einen gesellschaftlichen Wandel wie Europa in zwei Jahrhunderten.[1]

Die alle Rekorde brechende Geschwindigkeit der Industrialisierung dezimiert schnell die natürlichen Ressourcen Chinas und zunehmend auch die der Welt. Was wird der Preis des gnadenlos vorangetriebenen Wirtschaftswachstums sein? Der Staat bemüht sich, insbesondere im Bildungsbereich, die wachsende Kluft zwischen Besitzenden und Besitzlosen, Reichen und Armen, Stadt und Land zu schließen.

Verhaltensmaßregeln für ein neues Spiel

Im Jahr 2007 verpflichtete sich das Führungskollektiv auf dem 17. Parteikongress, in China eine harmonische, wissenschaftlich fundierte Entwicklung anzustreben und in seiner internationalen Diplomatie auf eine nach allen Seiten offene, friedliche Koexistenz hinzuarbeiten. Viele Beobachter glauben, Chinas Zukunft hänge weitgehend vom Gelingen einer nachhaltigen Wirtschaftsentwicklung und einer allmählichen politischen Reform des 70 Millionen Mitglieder starken Einparteiensystems ab. Im Bemühen, gegenüber der Ersten Welt eine Position aufzubauen, würden die Chinesen die grausame Geschichte der ersten drei Jahrzehnte verfehlter Politik überdenken. Obwohl sich die heutige chinesische Jugend der jüngsten Geschichte kaum bewusst ist, wartet diese Internet-Generation ungeduldig auf größere und schnellere Veränderungen. Man kann jedoch davon ausgehen, dass eine der größten Tugenden der Chinesen, ihr beispielloser Pragmatismus, das Land wohl durch jede künftige Krise führen und darüber hinaus eine seit Langem überfällige Renaissance der chinesischen Kultur beschleunigen wird.

1 Fareed Zakaria, „The Rise of a Fierce Yet fragile Superpower“, *Newsweek*, 7. Januar 2008.

#6

2000 – aujourd'hui
Quand la Chine s'ouvre au monde

« *La Chine fait l'expérience du paradoxe de la globalisation. Les indicateurs économiques peuvent progresser, mais l'augmentation de la pauvreté, la diminution du nombre des emplois et les inégalités sociales accompagnent aussi ces indicateurs financiers de 'succès'. Avec la crise rurale qui augmente, l'exploitation des travailleurs, la dégradation écologique, les différences de revenus… la Chine est à un carrefour.* »

DALE WEN, International Forum on Globalization, 2006

Même si le Tibet est aujourd'hui relié au monde extérieur par l'ouverture de la ligne de chemin de fer Pékin–Lhassa en juillet 2007, les nomades tibétains continuent à faire paître leurs yaks sur les immenses plateaux romantiquement appelés « le toit du monde ». Malgré de réels progrès économiques, le nord-ouest de la Chine, en particulier la région proche du désert de Gobi a connu une succession de sévères sécheresses qui ont dessèché les terres du nord du pays, pratiquement jusqu'à la côte est.

Contre toute attente, la Chine a cependant réussi à édifier une économie surnommée « l'atelier du monde ». Après son entrée à l'OMC, les réformes économiques et la politique d'ouverture au monde extérieur, Pékin s'est vue confier en 2001 l'organisation des Jeux olympiques 2008. Simultanément, elle découvre qu'elle est maintenant soumise à une surveillance internationale qu'elle n'avait jamais connue dans sa longue histoire.

Une économie surchauffée

En moins de trois décennies depuis le lancement de la politique réformatrice de Deng Xiaoping en 1978, l'économie chinoise a pratiquement multiplié son produit national brut par six, lequel s'élevait en 2006 (plus récentes statistiques disponibles), à près de 2,8 milliards de $. Début 2007, les réserves de change étaient de 1,2 trillions de $. La Chine annonçait également 370 millions d'abonnés à une ligne de téléphone fixe et 460 millions de téléphones mobiles en service. Les statistiques sont impressionnantes : 210 millions d'utilisateurs d'Internet, 100 millions de foyers équipés d'une télévision, 230 millions de véhicules privés, 14 millions d'étudiants à l'université et 40 millions dans les collèges. Fin 2006, la Chine avait construit 45 000 km de routes nouvelles. 400 millions de personnes ont dépassé le niveau de pauvreté officiel au cours des trente dernières années ce qui représente 75 % des populations pauvres du monde (vivant avec un revenu annuel de 400 $). 745 millions de personnes, un peu plus de 60 % de la population, vivent encore à la campagne, bien que l'exode vers les centres urbains ne cesse de croître.

Le meilleur des mondes

La capitale chinoise, Pékin, est un des multiples exemples de la renaissance urbaine. L'urbanisme et l'architecture sont en plein essor. Au cours des récentes années, ont été lancés d'énormes projets de construction comme l'Opéra de Pékin, le stade olympique, la tour de la CCTV – sorte d'arc cubiste entre les piliers duquel pourrait passer un petit avion – et l'immense Quartier d'affaires central. Des kilomètres de nouvelles lignes de métro filent sous les rues encombrées. De nouvelles autoroutes traversent la ville, et facilitent une circulation gigantesque vers les banlieues. Des centaines de villes nouvelles de la seconde ou troisième couronne émergent dans tout le pays. Dans la vallée des Trois Gorges sur le Yang-Tsé, un énorme barrage, le plus grand du monde, capable de produire 39 milliards de kW/h a été achevé en 2007. Le coût sur l'environnement reste inconnu, mais la pénurie d'eau qui sévit dans le nord de la Chine, est en partie compensé.

L'économiste américain Lawrence Summers fait remarquer que pendant la Révolution industrielle, les standards de vie moyens des Européens s'étaient améliorés de 50 % au cours de la durée d'une vie (40 ans à l'époque). En Asie et principalement en Chine, il a calculé que l'augmentation des mêmes standards s'élèvera de 10 000 % pendant la même durée ! En deux décennies, la Chine a connu le même degré d'industrialisation, d'urbanisation et de transformation sociale que l'Europe en deux siècles. [1]

Le rythme effréné de l'industrialisation épuise à grande vitesse les ressources naturelles du pays et, de plus en plus, celles du monde. Quel sera le coût final de cette quête sans répit de croissance économique ? L'État a pris des mesures drastiques d'allégement des dettes dans les zones de développement rural et a renoncé à des impôts sur les récoltes et sur les terres. Des efforts ont également été déployés pour combler l'écart toujours plus grand entre les possédants et ceux qui n'ont rien, les riches et les pauvres, les villes et les campagnes en particulier dans le domaine de l'éducation.

De nouvelles règles du jeu

En 2007, le nouveau pouvoir collectif mis en place lors du XVIIe congrès du Parti communiste a plaidé pour la recherche d'un développement harmonieux et scientifique et pour l'adoption d'une coexistence pacifique multipolaire dans ses relations internationales. De nombreux observateurs pensent que l'avenir de la Chine dépendra largement de sa capacité à adopter un développement économique durable, allié à une réforme progressive du système du parti unique. En cherchant à se positionner par rapport au monde développé, le peuple chinois doit garder en tête la terrible histoire des trois premières décennies de politiques aventureuses de la république populaire. Bien que la jeunesse actuelle ne soit pas vraiment informée sur l'histoire récente, cette génération d'Internet attend avec impatience des plus grands changements. On peut penser que l'une des plus grandes vertus de ce peuple, son pragmatisme unique, guidera le pays à travers les crises qui peuvent encore surgir et accélérera la renaissance longtemps attendue de la culture chinoise.

1. Fareed Zakaria, « The Rise of a Fierce Yet fragile Superpower », *Newsweek*, 7 janvier 2008.

"There are 20 million children who can play the piano in China, and that number is growing every day. I believe that in another 10 years, the Chinese will account for half the field of classical music, and the era of classical music will be upon us."

„Es gibt in China 20 Millionen Kinder, die Klavier spielen, und diese Zahl nimmt täglich zu. Ich glaube, dass in zehn Jahren Chinesen die Hälfte der auf dem Gebiet der klassischen Musik Aktiven ausmachen werden, und wir werden das Zeitalter der Klassik erreicht haben."

« On compte en Chine 20 millions d'enfants qui jouent au piano, et ce nombre s'accroît chaque jour. Je crois que dans dix ans, les Chinois représenteront la moitié du potentiel de la musique classique et que la nouvelle ère de la musique classique passera par nous. »

LANG LANG (1982–), virtuoso pianist

→
Ge Xin, 2006

Young revelers dance in a disco in Shanghai.

Junge Nachtschwärmer in einer Disco in Shanghai.

Jeunes fêtards dans une discothèque de Shanghai.

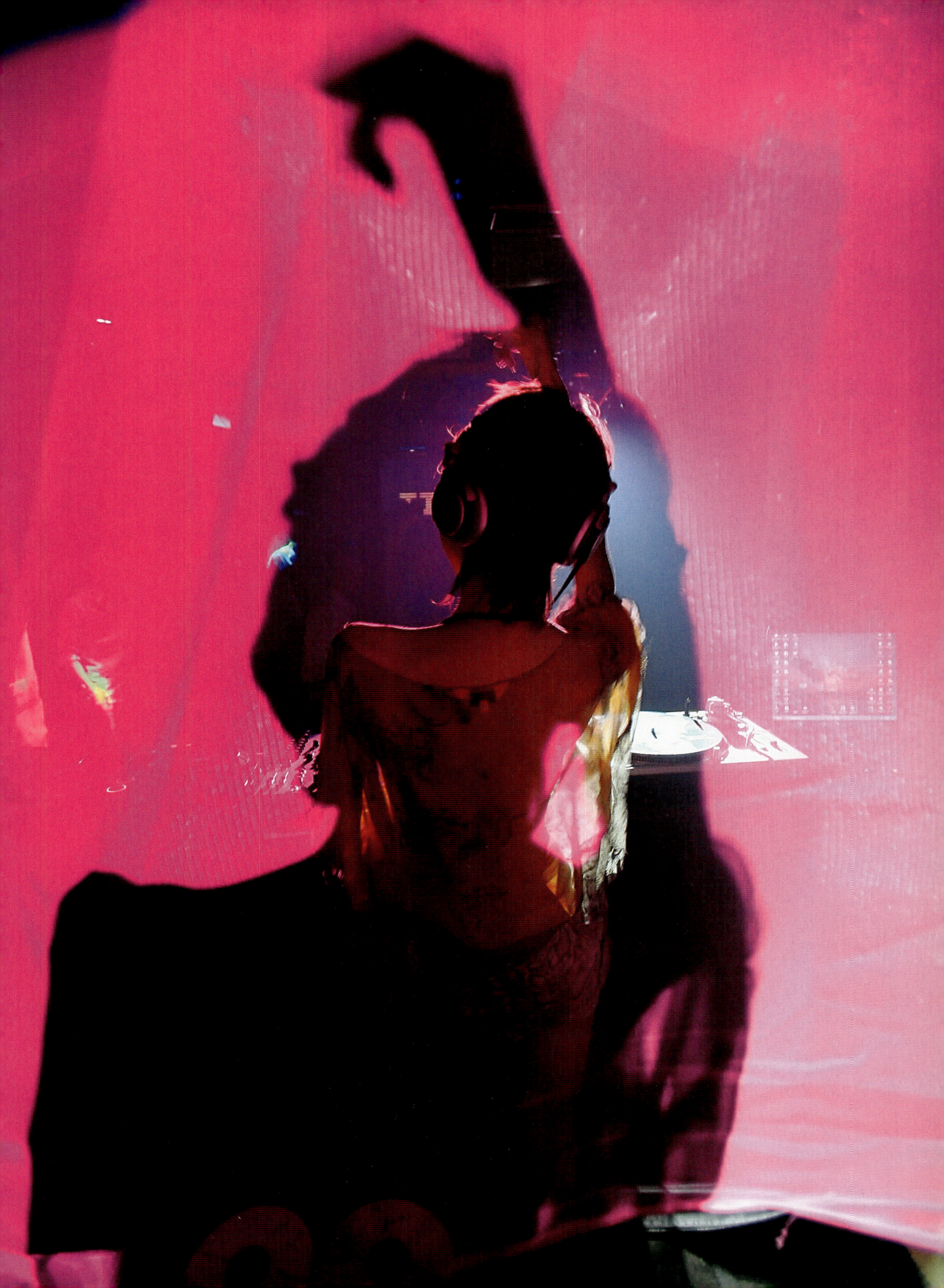

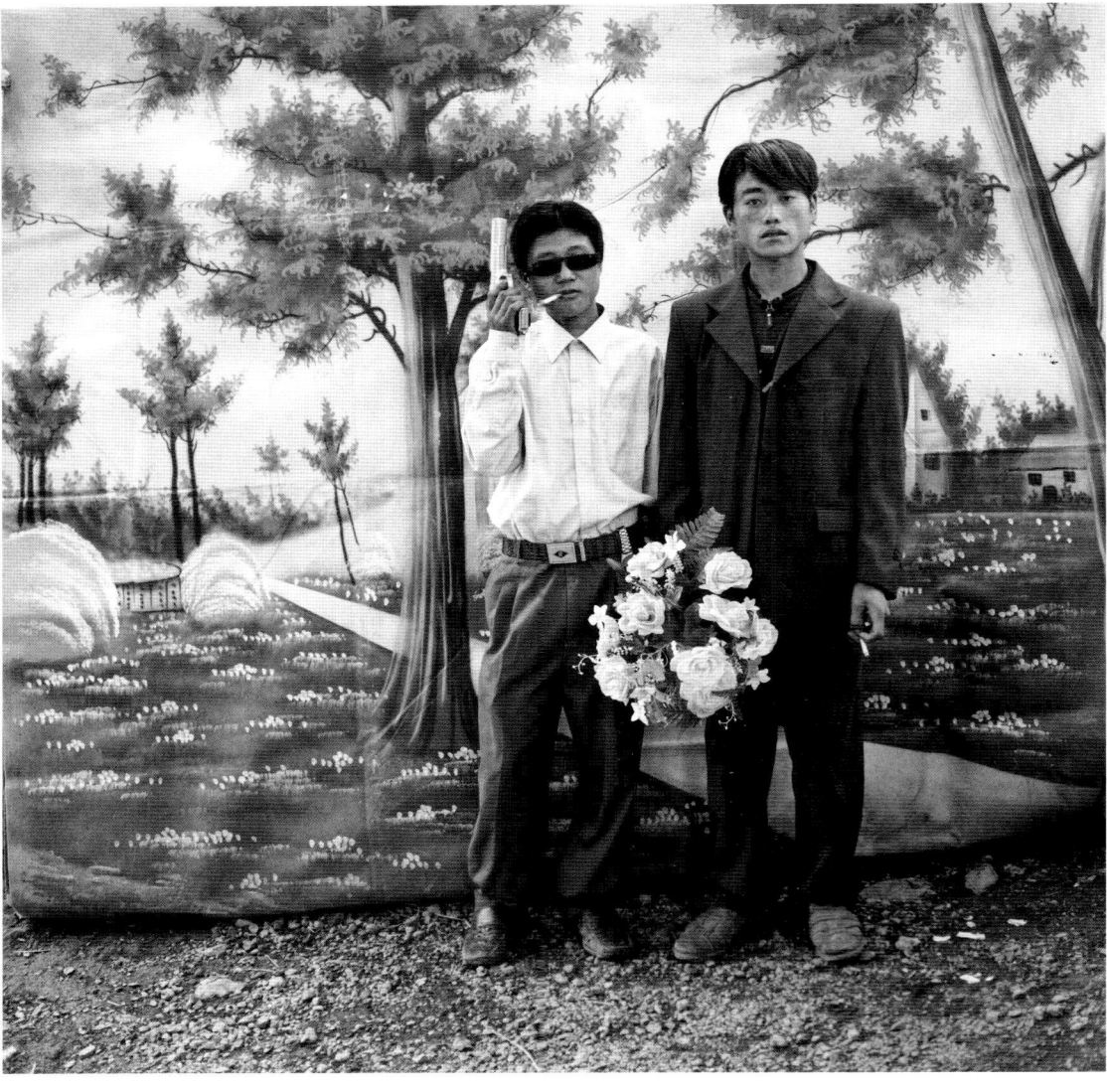

→

Rong Rong & inri, 2000

Performance artist Rong Rong is photographed lying precariously on a rock at the start of the Great Wall in Jiayuguan, Gansu province, in the western part of China. Beneath him the Yellow river flows past. At one time this marked the boundary of the "known" Chinese world. Beyond lay only the unknown and nomadic barbarian tribes. Not far from here was also the start of the Silk Road.

Foto des Performancekünstlers Rong Rong in prekärer Lage auf einem Felsen am Anfang der Chinesischen Mauer in Jiayuguan in der Provinz Gansu im Westen Chinas. Unten fließt der Gelbe Fluss. Einst war dies die Grenze zwischen der „bekannten" chinesischen Welt und den jenseits davon lebenden unbekannten barbarischen Nomadenstämmen. Unweit von hier nahm auch die Seidenstraße ihren Anfang.

L'artiste de performance Rong Rong photographié en position précaire sur un rocher au point de départ de la Grande muraille à Jiayuguan, province du Gansu, en Chine occidentale, au dessus du Fleuve jaune. A une certaine période, elle marquait la limite du monde chinois «connu» derrière lequel vivaient des tribus nomades barbares. La route de la soie débute également non loin de là.

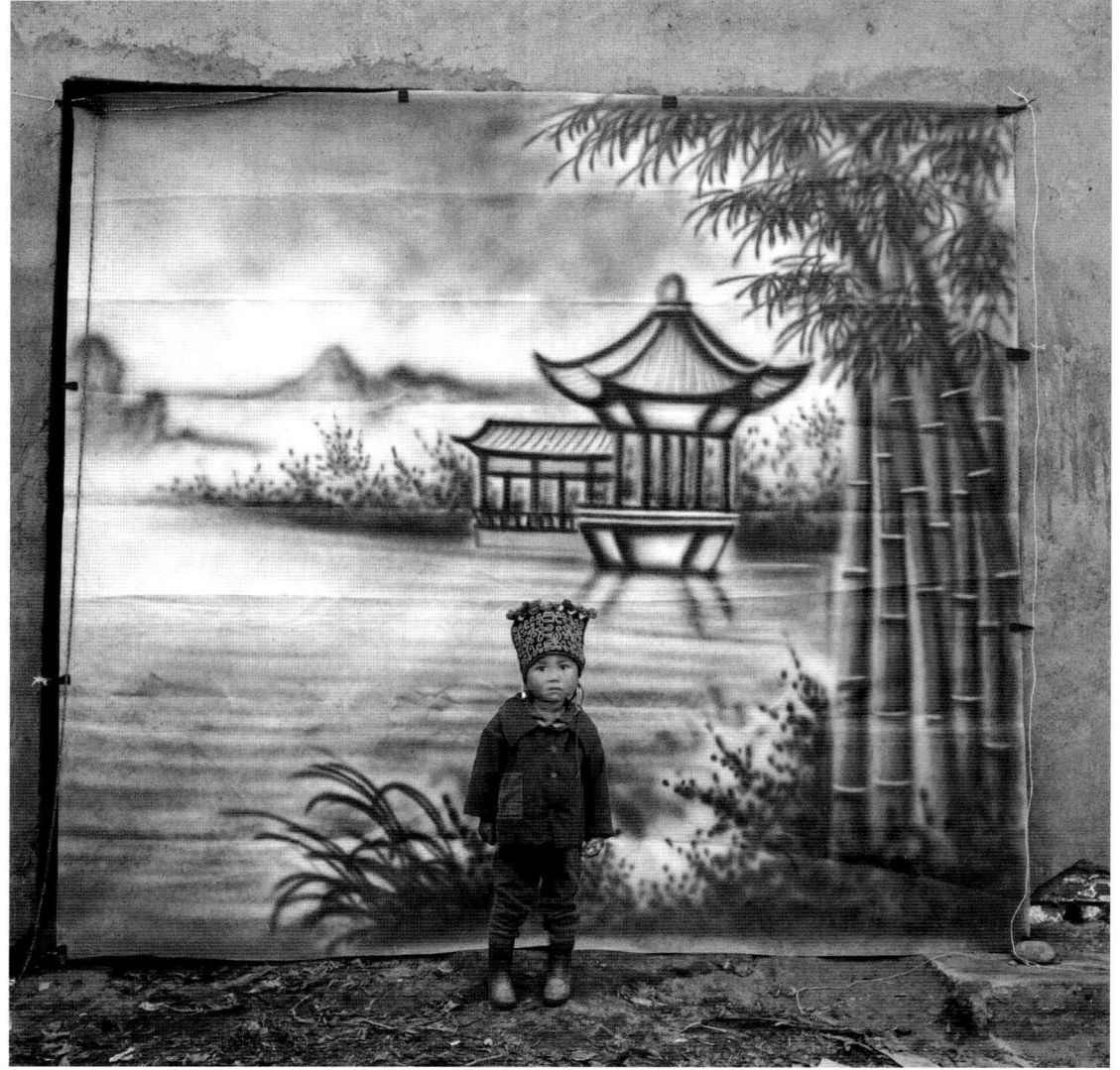

↖

Li Lang, 2000

Studio portrait of two young men from the Yi minority in Sichuan province. The Yi are one of China's 56 ethnic minorities, with a population of 6.5 million.

Studioporträt von zwei jungen Männern aus dem Volk der Yi in der Provinz Sichuan. Die Yi sind eine der 56 ethnischen Minderheiten in China und zählen 6,5 Millionen Menschen.

Portrait de studio de deux jeunes hommes de la minorité Yi dans la province du Sichuan. Les Yi sont l'une des 56 minorités ethniques chinoises, avec 6,5 millions de membres.

←

Li Lang, 2000

Studio portrait of a child of the Yi minority in Sichuan province.

Studioporträt eines Kindes aus dem Volk der Yi in der Provinz Sichuan.

Portrait de studio d'un enfant de la minorité Yi dans la province du Sichuan.

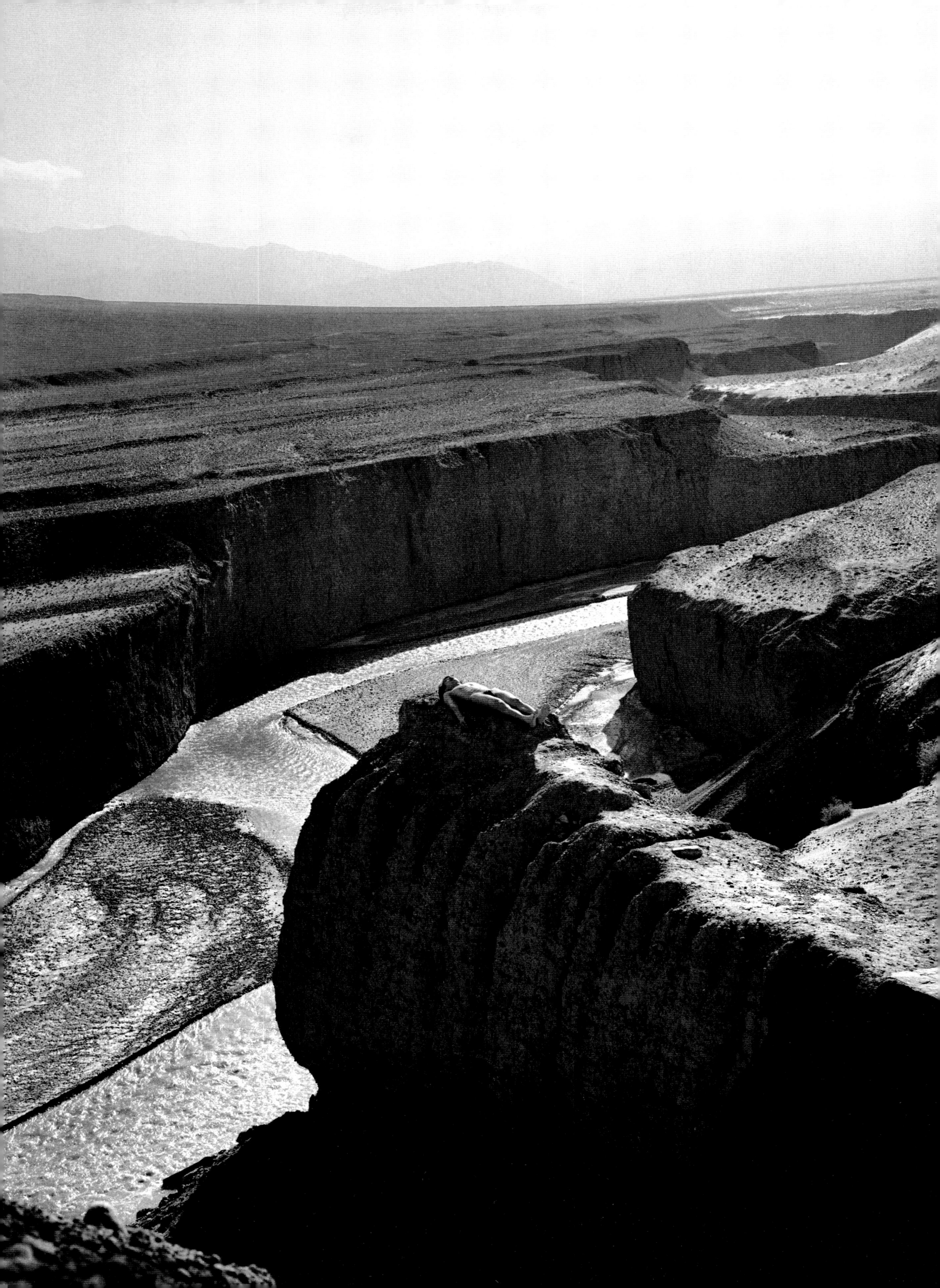

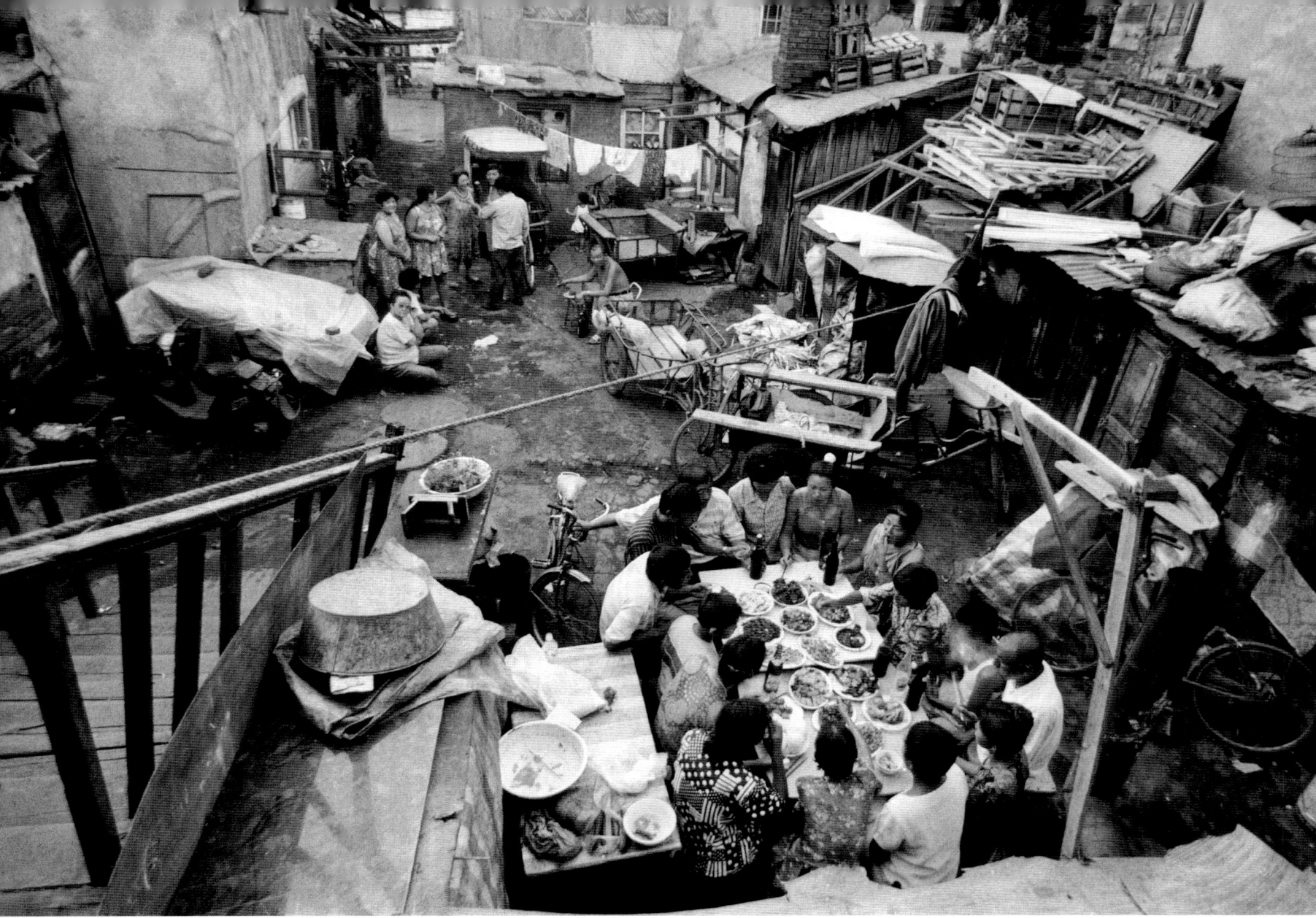

↑

Chen Ling, 2001

*Three generations of a Chinese family gather
for lunch in a dilapidated housing compound
in Harbin, Heilongjiang province.*

*Drei Generationen einer chinesischen
Familie treffen sich zum Mittagessen in einer
baufälligen Behausung in Harbin, Provinz
Heilongjiang.*

*Trois générations d'une même famille sont
réunies pour le déjeuner dans un logement
délabré de Harbin, province du Heilongjiang.*

"On the basis of economic growth, efforts should be made to increase
income for urban and rural residents, to constantly improve their living
conditions, including food, clothing, housing, transport and daily necessi-
ties, improve the social security system, and medical and health facilities,
with a view to bettering their life."

„Auf der Basis wirtschaftlichen Wachstums müssen Anstrengungen
unternommen werden, die Einkommen von Stadt- und Landbewohnern
zu steigern, ihre Lebensbedingungen beständig zu verbessern – darunter
Ernährung, Kleidung, Wohnen, Transport und Grundbedürfnisse –, das
soziale Sicherungssystem sowie medizinische Einrichtungen zu reformieren,
im Hinblick auf bessere Lebensverhältnisse der Menschen."

« Sur la base de la croissance économique, des efforts devraient être faits
pour accroître les revenus des habitants des villes et des campagnes, pour
améliorer leurs conditions de vie y compris la nourriture, l'habillement,
le logement, les transports et les nécessités de la vie quotidienne et pour
perfectionner le système de sécurité sociale ainsi que les services médicaux
et de santé, ceci afin de leur assurer une vie meilleure. »

JIANG ZEMIN (1926–), President of the People's Republic of China (1993–2003), 2001

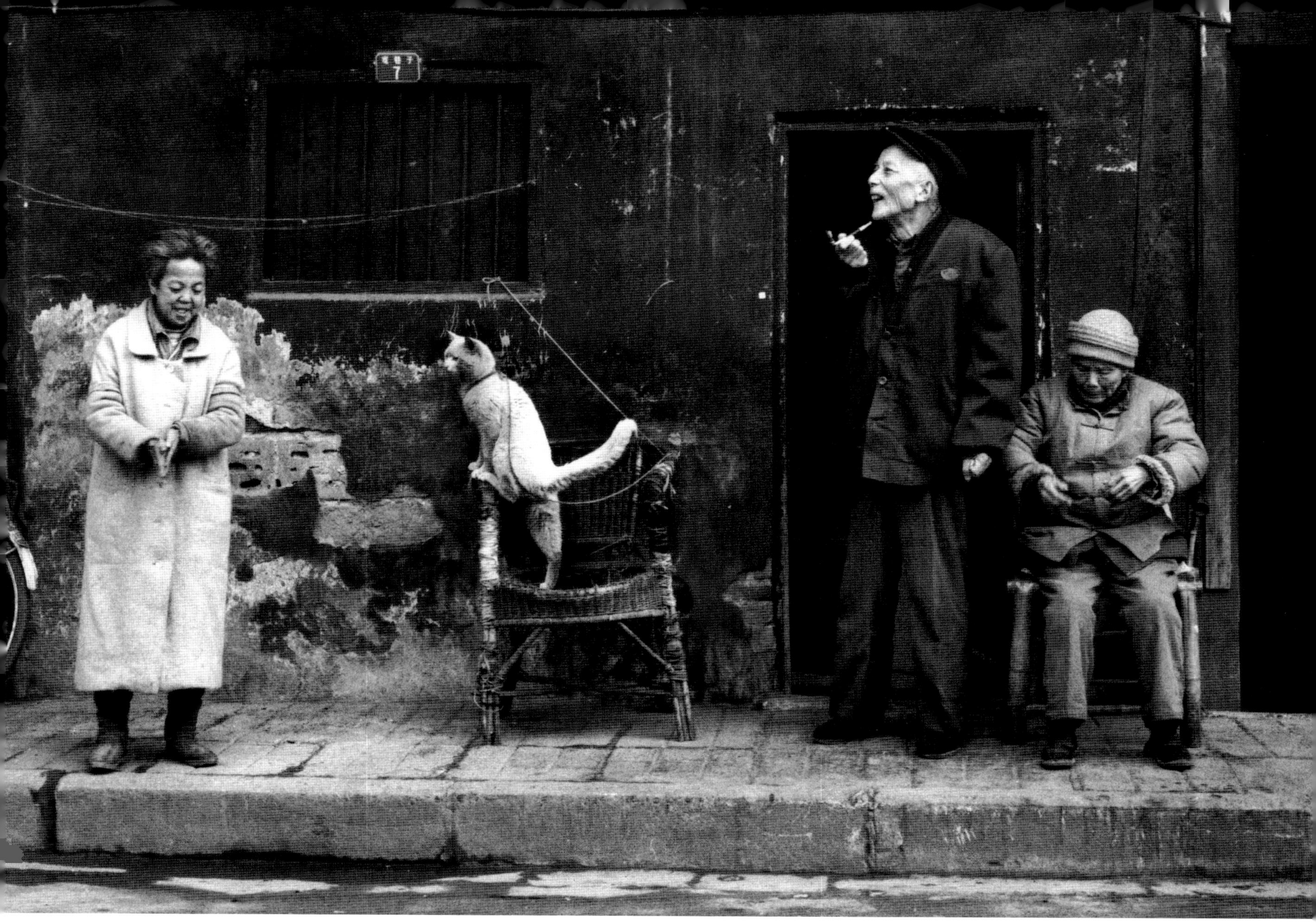

Wu Jialin, 1999

A street scene that captures the daily life of ordinary people in Chengdu, a major city in Sichuan, China's most populous province.

Die Straßenszene zeigt den Alltag einfacher Menschen in Chengdu, einer größeren Stadt in Chinas bevölkerungsreichster Provinz Sichuan.

Scène de rue de la vie quotidienne à Chengdu, une grande ville du Sichuan, la plus peuplée des provinces chinoises.

pp. 358/359
Li Nan, 2001

Four old ladies with bound feet visit the Forbidden City. It is a tradition that dates back to the Song dynasty when Chinese women were encouraged to bind their feet from early childhood. It is a painful process that prevents a child's feet from growing. Chinese men considered ladies with bound feet as more erotic.

Vier alte Frauen mit gebundenen Füßen besuchen die Verbotene Stadt. Einer alten Tradition zufolge, die ihren Ursprung in der Song Dynastie hat, sollen chinesische Frauen von frühester Kindheit an ihre Füße binden. Diese schmerzhafte Prozedur verhindert ein normales Wachstum der kindlichen Füße. Chinesische Männer fanden Frauen mit gebundenen Füßen erotischer.

Quatre vieilles dames aux pieds bardés visitent la Cité interdite. Cette tradition remonte à la dynastie Song où l'on bandait les pieds des filles dès le plus jeune âge. Ce procédé qui empêchait les pieds de grandir était très douloureux, mais la petite taille du pied était jugée érotique par les hommes.

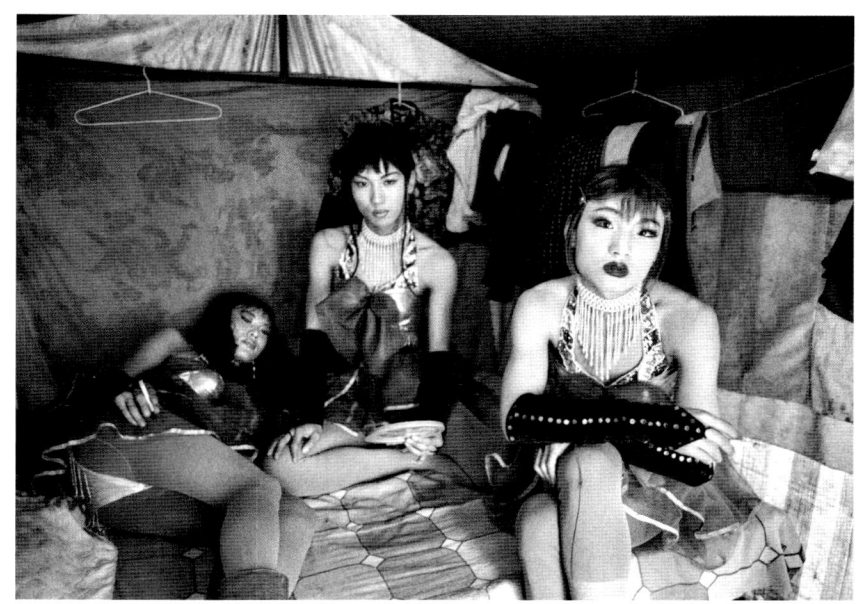

Peng Xiangjie, 2000

Three Chinese transvestites rest in their tent between performances in Shanxi province.

Drei chinesische Transvestiten ruhen sich zwischen ihren Auftritten in der Provinz Shanxi in ihrem Zelt aus.

Trois travestis chinois se reposent sous leur tente avant un spectacle (province du Shanxi).

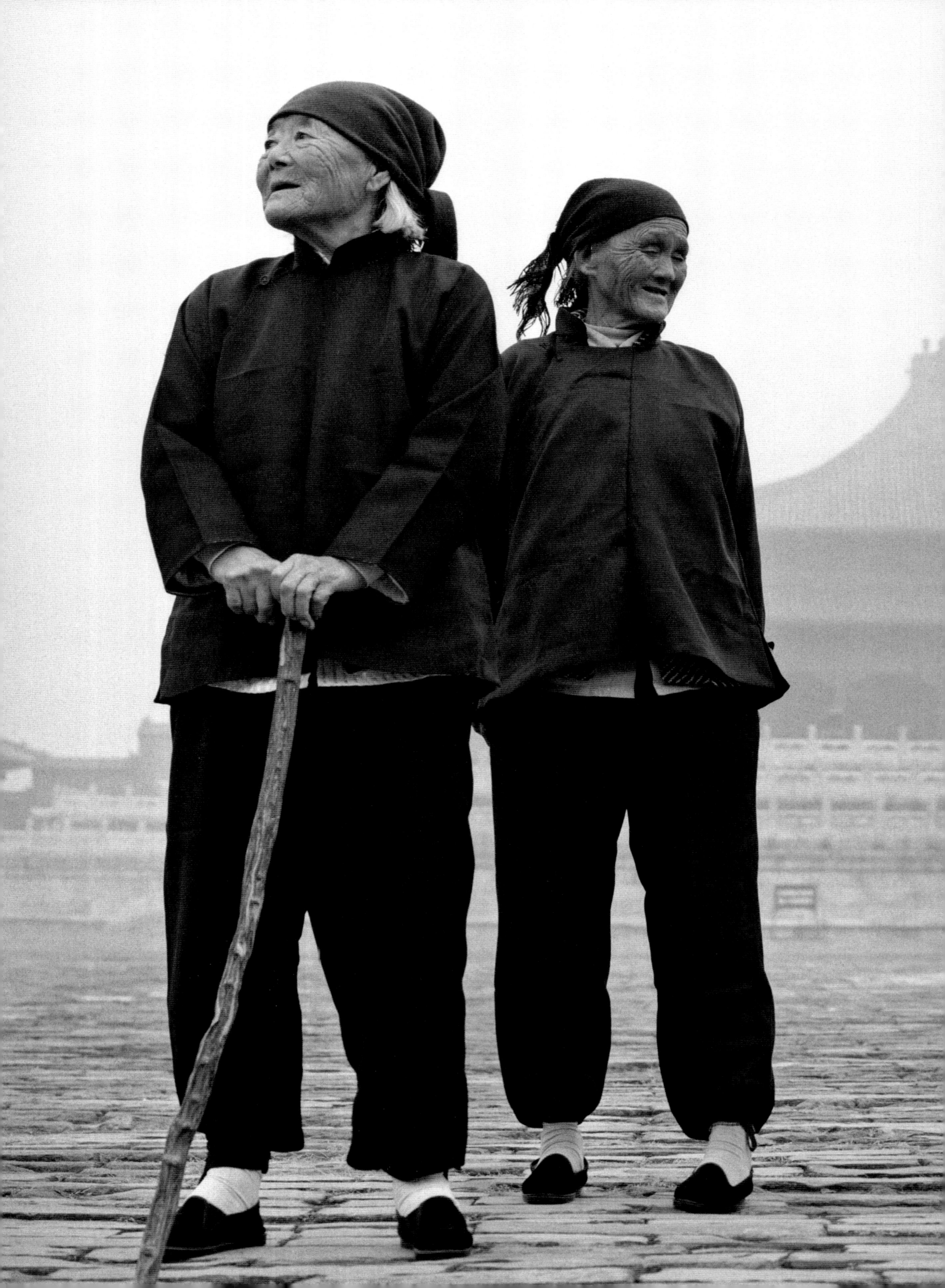

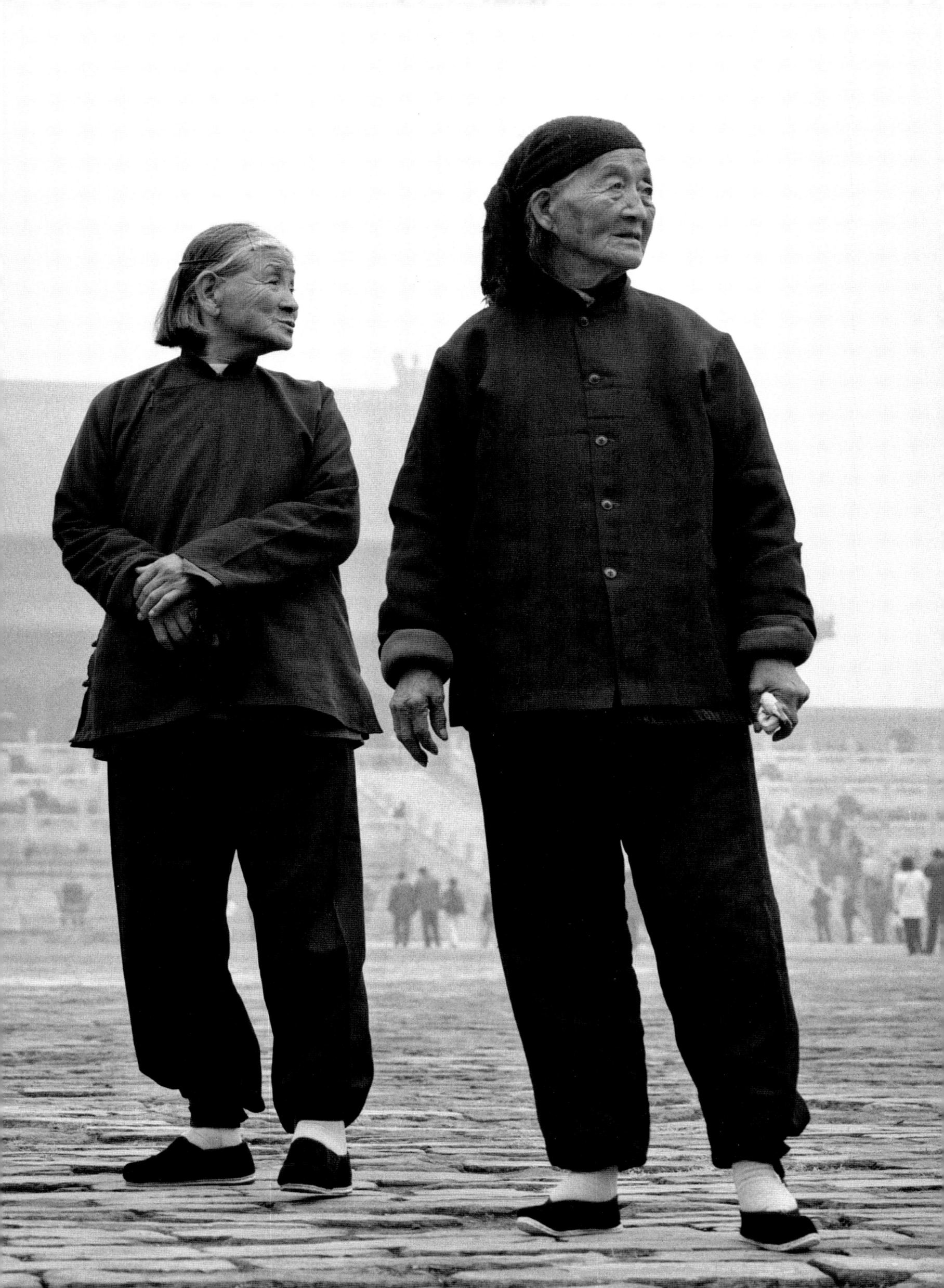

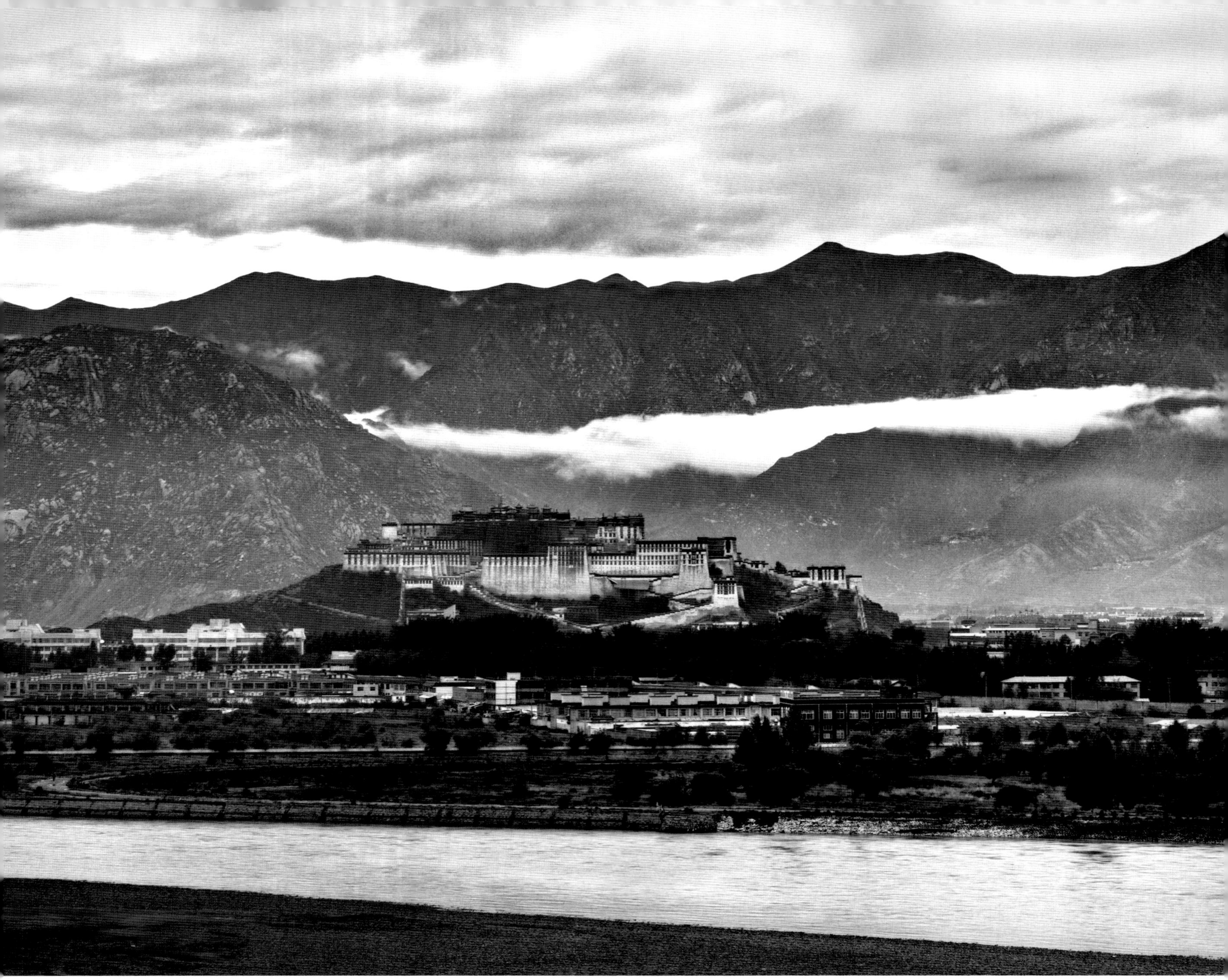

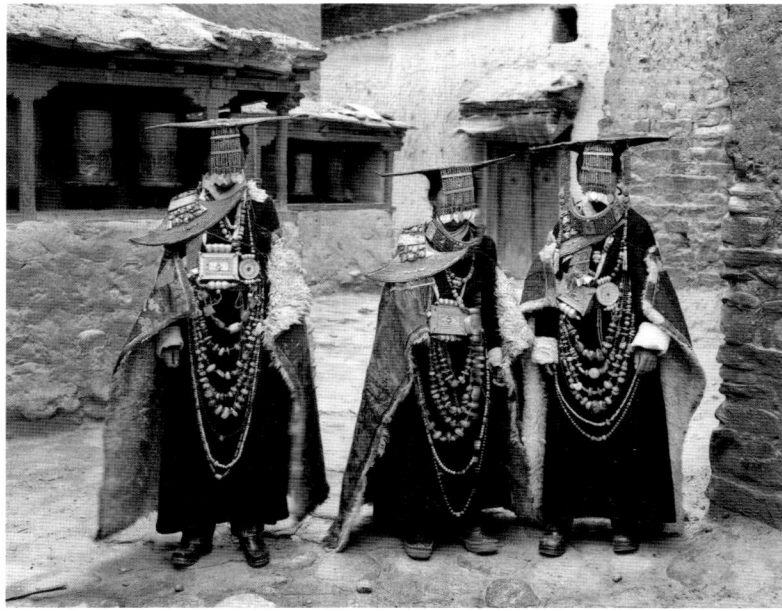

↑
Feng Jianguo, 2003

Potala Palace in Lhasa, Tibet, the seat of Tibetan Lamaism and formerly the home of its spiritual leader.

Der Potala-Palast in Lhasa, Tibet, Sitz des tibetischen Lamaismus und ehemals Wohnstatt seines geistigen Führers.

Le palais du Potala à Lhassa au Tibet, siège du lamaisme tibétain et ancien siège de son chef spirituel.

"We can never obtain peace in the outer world until we make peace with ourselves."

„Wir werden mit der uns umgebenden Welt nie Frieden schließen können, solange wir mit uns selbst nicht im Reinen sind."

« Nous ne pourrons jamais accéder à la paix dans le monde qui nous est extérieur si nous ne sommes pas d'abord en paix avec nous-mêmes. »

14th DALAI LAMA (1935–), winner of 1989 Nobel Peace Prize

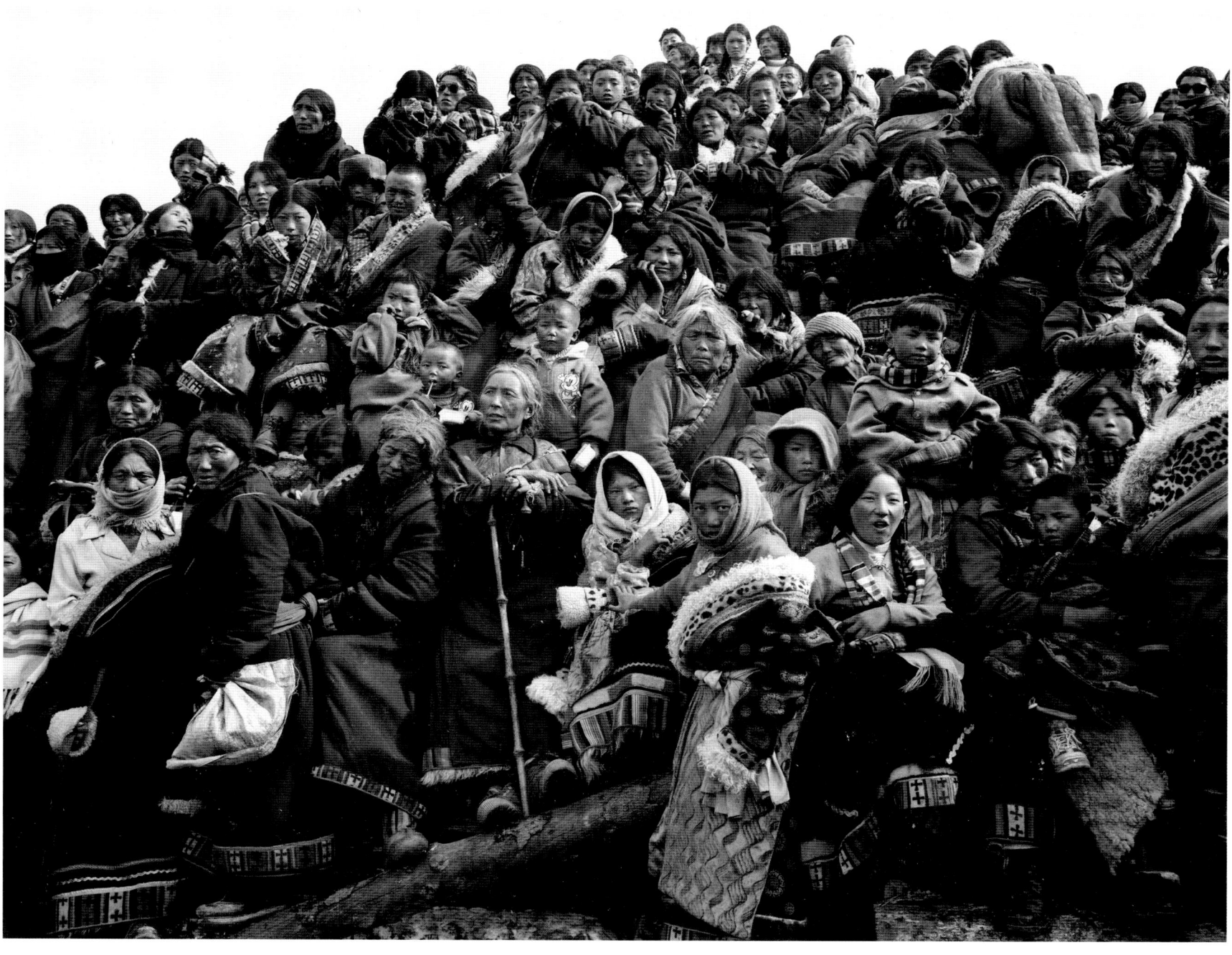

↑
Feng Jianguo, 2002

Tibetan pilgrims outside Labrang monastery in southern Gansu province. Every year thousands of pilgrims make their way to this 300-year-old temple, home to more than 1,000 monks and the largest school of Lamaism outside of Lhasa.

Tibetische Pilger vor dem Kloster Labrang im Süden der Provinz Gansu. Jedes Jahr machen sich Tausende von Pilgern auf den Weg zu dieser 300 Jahre alten Tempelanlage, in der über 1000 Mönchen leben und in der die größte Schule für Lamaismus außerhalb von Lhasa untergebracht ist.

Des pèlerins tibétains devant le monastère de Labrang au sud de la province Gansu. Chaque année, des milliers d'entre eux se rendent dans ce temple vieux de 300 ans, qui abrite plus de 1 000 moines. C'est la plus grande école du lamaïsme en dehors de Lhassa.

←
Feng Jianguo, 2003

Three Tibetan women wearing the traditional costume of ancient Tibetan aristocrats. Only four complete costumes exist in Tibet.

Drei Tibeterinnen im traditionellen Gewand alter tibetischer Aristokraten. Nur vier vollständige Gewänder dieser Art blieben in Tibet erhalten.

Trois Tibétaines vêtues du costume traditionnel des anciens nobles. Seuls quatre costumes complets de ce type existent encore au Tibet.

"The Dalai Lama should have closed down the Hollywood strategy a decade ago and focused on back-channel diplomacy with Beijing. He should have publicly renounced the claim to a so-called Greater Tibet, which demands territory that was never under the control of the Lhasa government. Sending his envoys to talk with the Chinese while simultaneously encouraging the global pro-Tibet lobby has achieved nothing."

„Der Dalai Lama hätte vor einem Jahrzehnt seine theatralische Strategie beenden und sich auf stille Diplomatie mit Peking konzentrieren sollen. Er hätte öffentlich den Anspruch auf das sogenannte Groß-Tibet aufgeben sollen, der Gebiete einfordert, die nie zum Hoheitsgebiet der Regierung in Lhasa gehörten. Seine Abgesandten zu den Chinesen zu schicken, um dort Gespräche zu führen, und gleichzeitig die globale pro-tibetische Lobby zu bestärken, hat nichts gebracht."

« Le Dalaï-Lama aurait dû mettre fin à sa stratégie hollywoodienne depuis dix ans et se concentrer sur une diplomatie discrète avec Pékin. Il aurait dû publiquement renoncer au soi-disant Grand Tibet, comprenant des territoires qui n'ont jamais été sous le contrôle du gouvernement de Lhassa. Envoyer des représentants pour parler avec les Chinois tout en encourageant simultanément le lobby international pro-Tibet n'a abouti à rien. »

PATRICK FRENCH, writer, The New York Times 2008

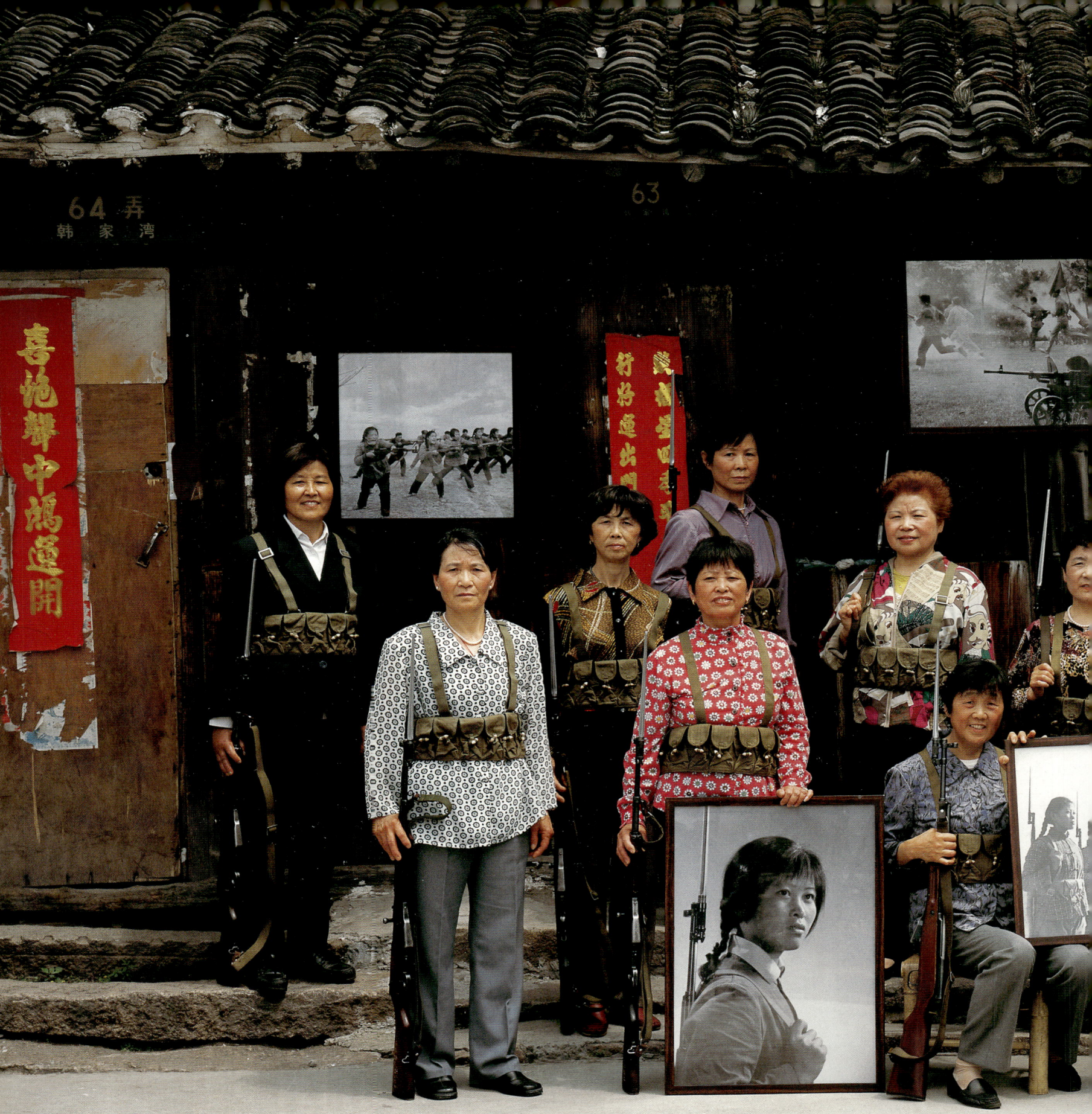

↑
Kou Shanqin, 2003

Former members of a women's militia group during the Cultural Revolution pose for a photograph at a reunion gathering in Jiangsu province.

Ehemalige Mitglieder einer während der Kulturrevolution aktiven Frauen-Miliz posieren für ein Foto bei einem Ehemaligentreffen in der Provinz Jiangsu.

D'anciens membres d'une milice féminine de l'époque de la Révolution culturelle posent lors d'une rencontre dans la province du Jiangsu.

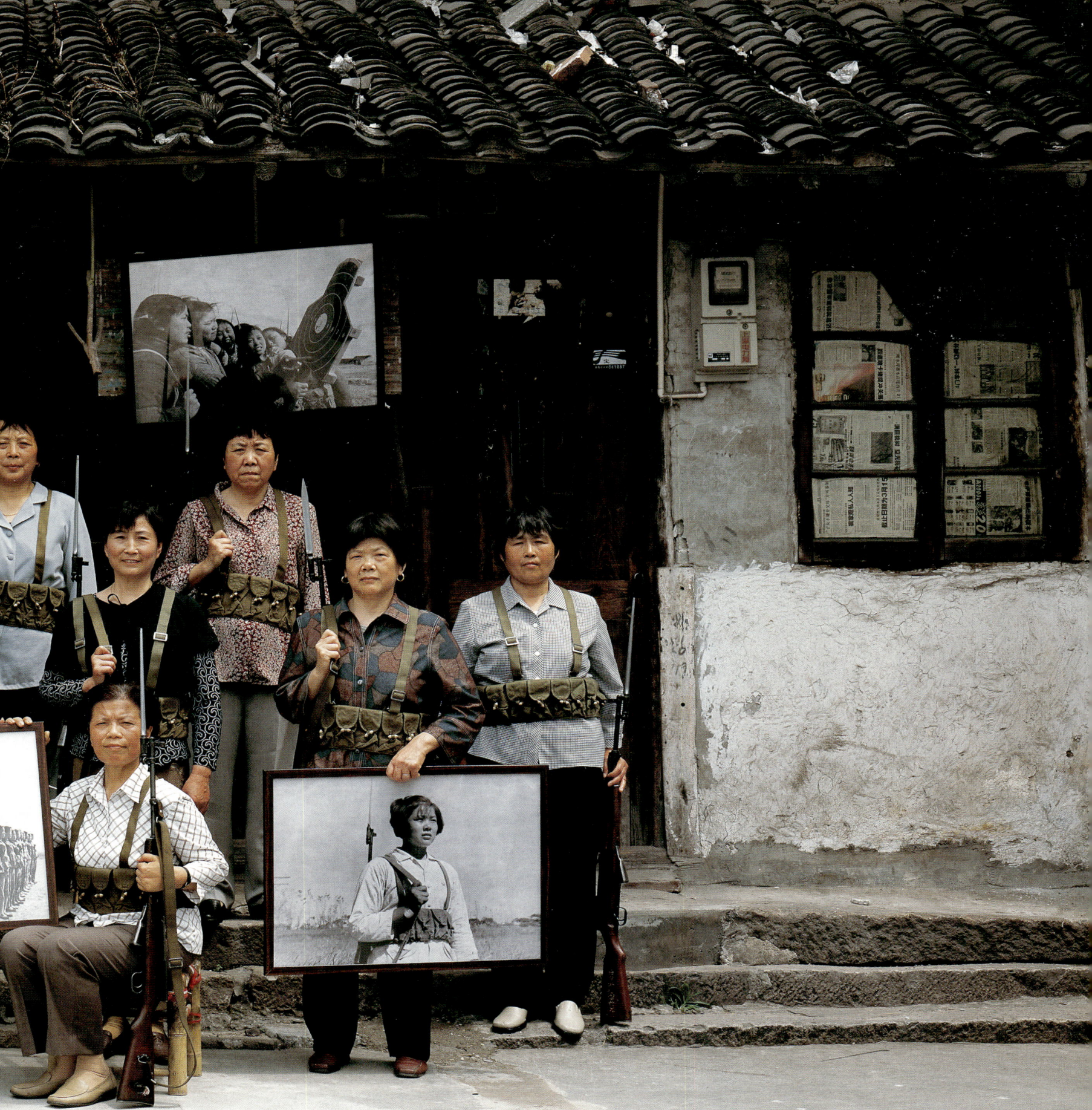

"I don't think China is a communist country in the sense of Soviet communism. It has institutions that we consider different and in many ways incompatible with our notions of domestic institutions. But it is also clear, that the China 10 years from now, after the huge changes which it has already undergone will be far different from the China of today."

„Ich glaube nicht, dass China ein kommunistisches Land im Sinne des sowjetischen Kommunismus ist. Es verfügt über Institutionen, die wir für anders und in vieler Hinsicht mit unserer Vorstellung einheimischer Institutionen für unvereinbar halten. Ebenso klar ist aber auch, dass China nach den riesigen Umwälzungen, die es bereits hinter sich hat, in zehn Jahren ganz anders als das heutige China sein wird."

« Je ne pense pas que la Chine soit un pays communiste au sens du communisme soviétique. Elle possède des institutions que nous jugeons différentes et qui sont à de nombreux égards incompatibles avec nos propres conceptions. Mais il est également clair que dans dix ans, la Chine, après les énormes changements qu'elle connaît déjà, sera très différente de celle d'aujourd'hui. »

HENRY KISSINGER (1923–), politician and Nobel Peace Prize laureate, 2002

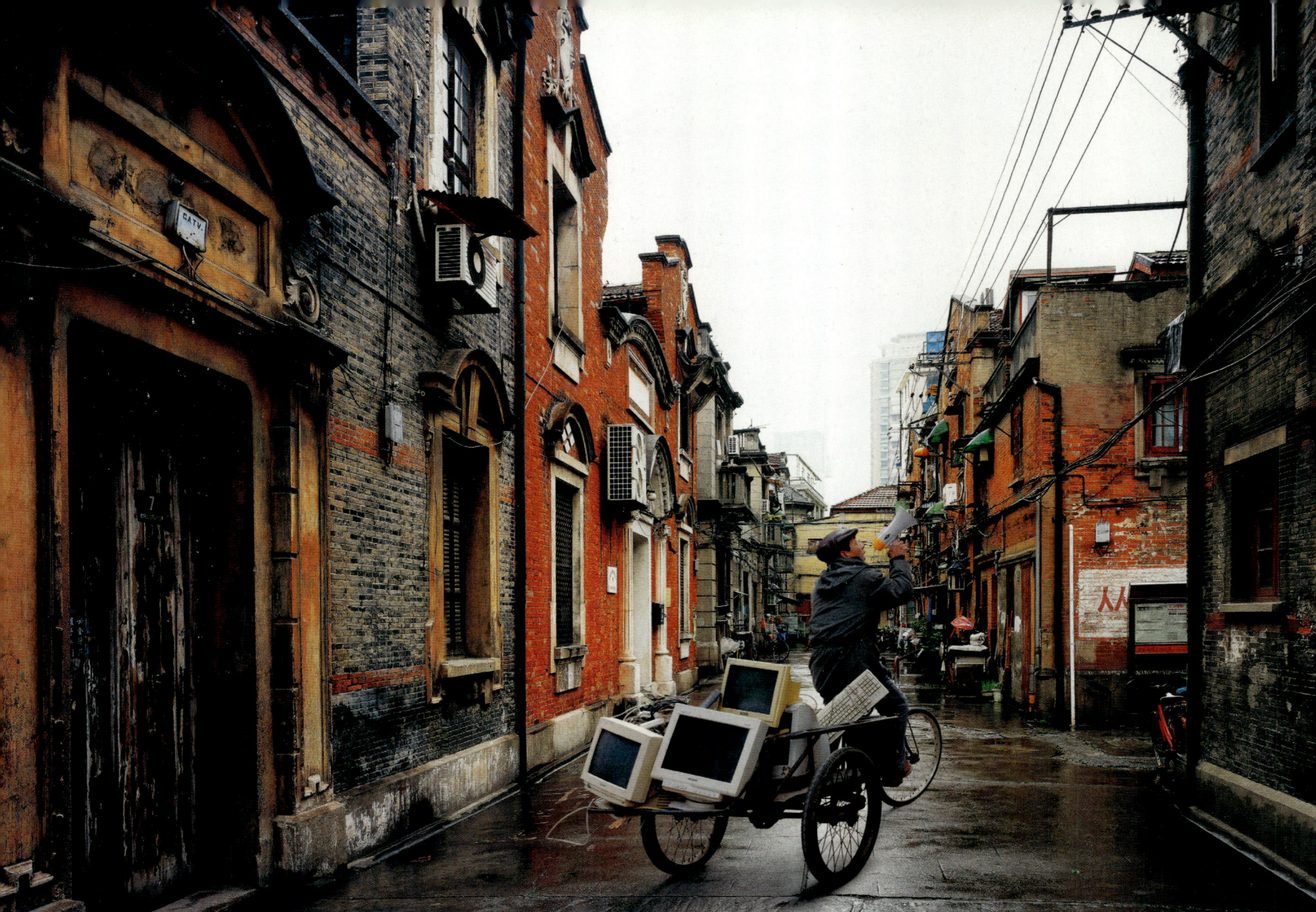

↑
Cui Xinhua, 2003

A worker collects used computer monitors from residents in a Shanghai neighborhood.

Ein Arbeiter sammelt bei Anwohnern in einem Viertel in Shanghai gebrauchte Computerbildschirme ein.

Un ouvrier collecte de vieux écrans d'ordinateur dans un quartier de Shanghai.

"After a state dinner hosted by Jiang Zemin and his wife, Wang Yeping, he and I took turns conducting the People's Liberation Army Band … The more time I spent with Jiang, the more I liked him. He was intriguing, funny, and fiercely proud, but always willing to listen to different points of view. Even though I didn't always agree with him, I became convinced that he believed he was changing China as fast as he could, and in the right direction."

„Nach einem von Jiang Zemin und seiner Frau Wang Yeping ausgerichteten Staatsbankett dirigierten er und ich abwechselnd das Orchester der Volksbefreiungsarmee … Je mehr Zeit ich mit Jiang verbrachte, desto sympathischer wurde er mir. Er war faszinierend, witzig und glühend stolz, aber stets willens, sich andere Ansichten anzuhören. Obwohl ich mit ihm nicht immer einer Meinung war, überzeugte er mich davon, dass er glaubte, China so schnell er konnte und in die richtige Richtung zu verändern."

«Après un dîner officiel donné par Jiang Zemin et son épouse, Wang Yeping, lui et moi avons dirigé tout à tour l'orchestre de l'Armée de libération du peuple … Plus je passais de temps avec Jiang, plus je l'appréciais. Il était curieux, drôle, furieusement fier, mais toujours prêt à écouter les différents points de vue. Même si je n'étais pas toujours d'accord avec lui, je suis convaincu qu'il croyait faire changer la Chine aussi vite qu'il le pouvait, et dans la bonne direction.»

BILL CLINTON (1946–), 42nd U.S. president, 2004

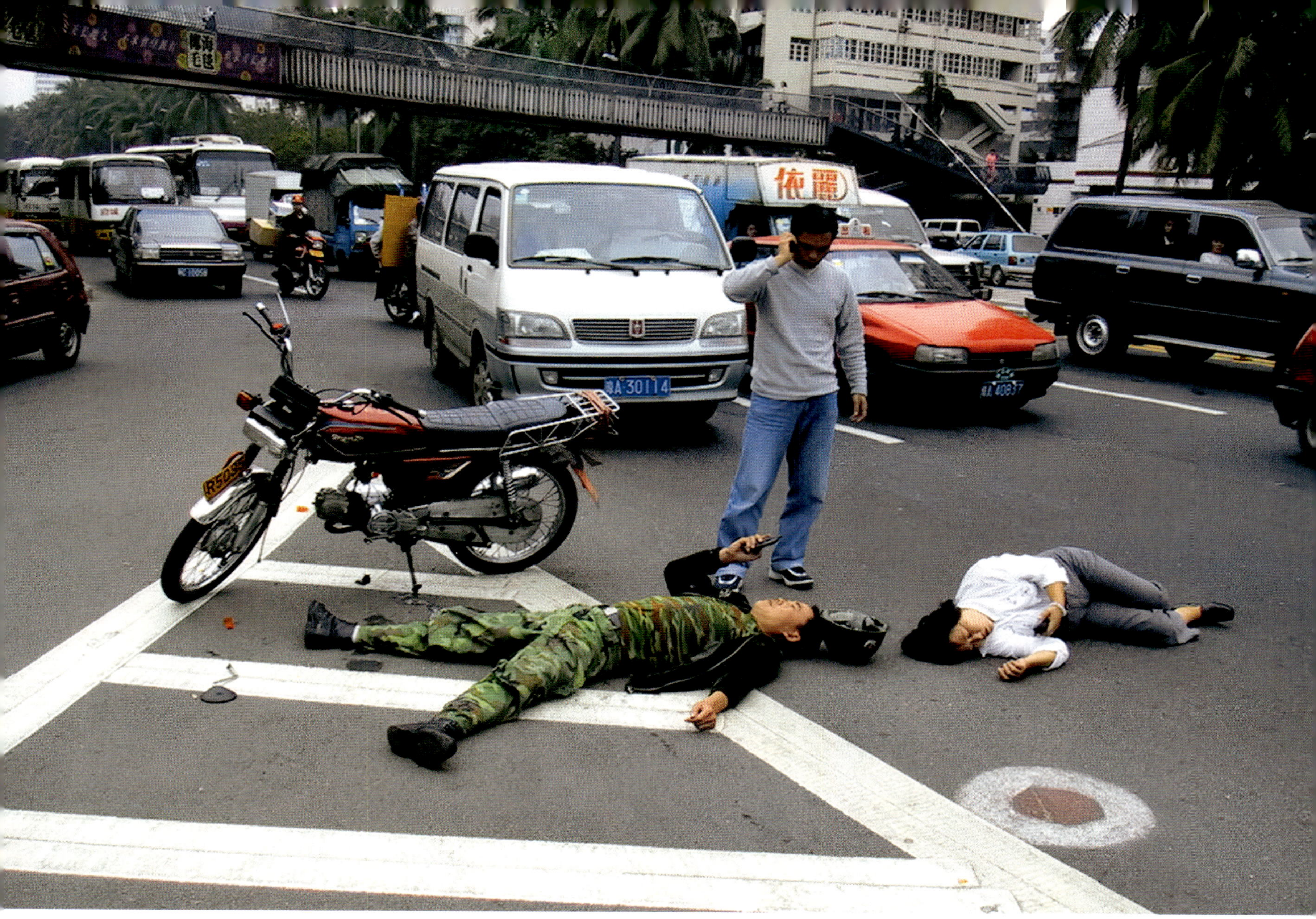

Huang Yimin, 2005

Victims of a traffic accident reach for their mobile phones to report the incident. Traffic accidents are increasingly commonplace as motorbikes, bicycles, and cars compete for right of way, their owners paying little heed to traffic laws.

Opfer eines Verkehrsunfalls greifen nach ihren Mobiltelefonen, um den Zwischenfall zu melden. Die Zahl der Verkehrsunfälle steigt ständig, da Motorräder, Fahrräder und Autos um die Vorfahrt streiten und die jeweiligen Fahrer den Verkehrsregeln wenig Beachtung schenken.

Des victimes d'un accident de la circulation téléphonent pour le rapporter. Avec la multi-plication des vélos, motos et voitures et le manque de respect du code de la route, les accidents sont de plus en plus fréquents.

Qiu Yan, 2003

A male nurse attends to a SARS patient in Wuhan, Hubei province. SARS, or severe acute respiratory syndrome, is a viral respiratory illness that was recognized as a global threat in March 2003, after first appearing in southern China in November 2002. The official death toll in China was fewer than 100 people, although the number of confirmed cases was more than 1,000.

Ein Pfleger kümmert sich um einen SARS-Patienten in Wuhan, Provinz Hubei. SARS, eine schwere Virusinfektion der Atemwege, wurde im März 2003 als weltweite Bedro-hung erkannt, nachdem es im November 2002 in Südchina zum ersten Mal aufgetreten war. Nach offiziellen Angaben belief sich die Zahl der bestätigten Fälle in China auf 1000, es starben weniger als 100 Menschen.

Un infirmer s'occupe d'un malade au SRAS à Wuhan, province du Hubei. Le SRAS, ou syndrome respiratoire aigu sévère, est une maladie virale identifiée comme une menace mondiale en 2003 après son apparition en Chine méridionale en 2002. Les autorités ont annoncé moins de 100 morts bien que le nombre de cas confirmés se soit élevé à plus de 1000.

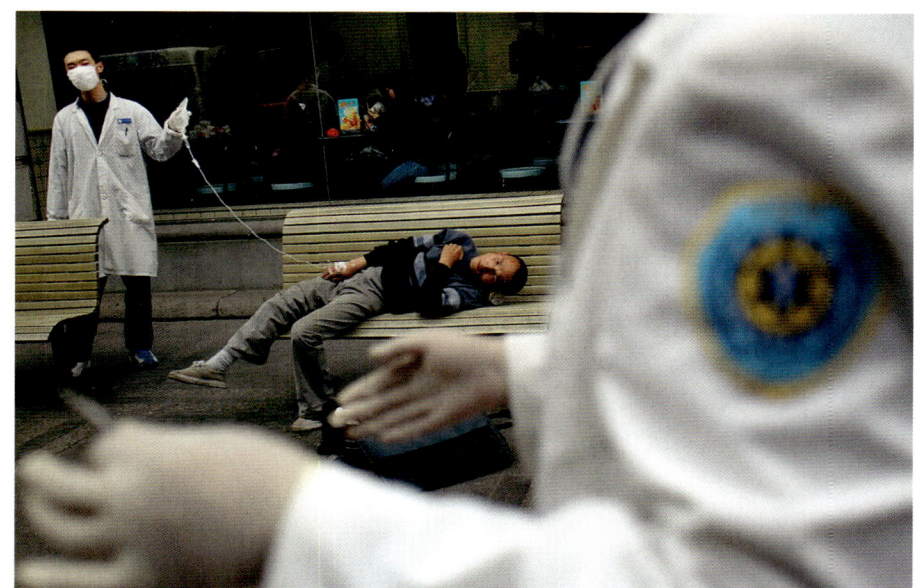

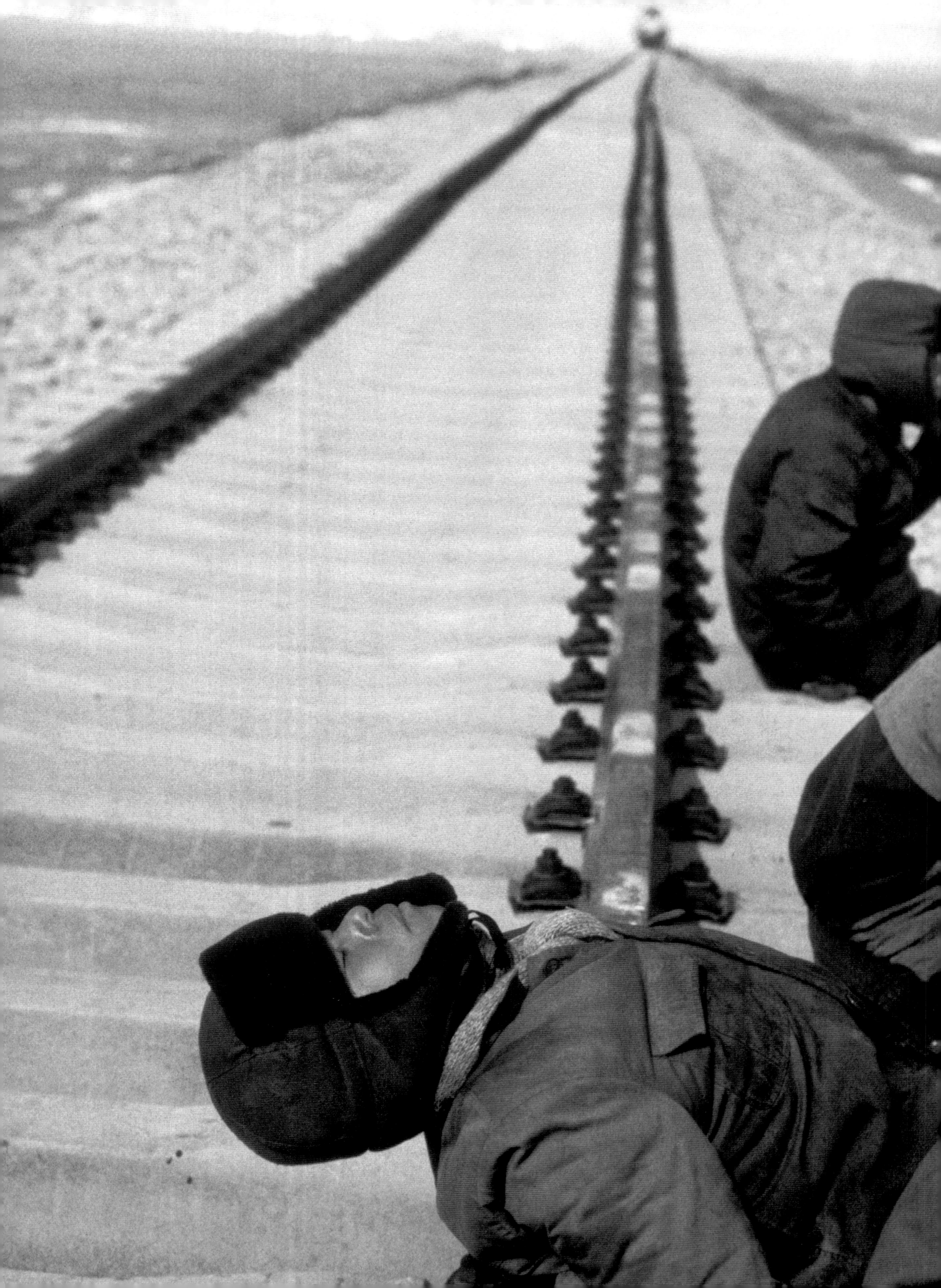

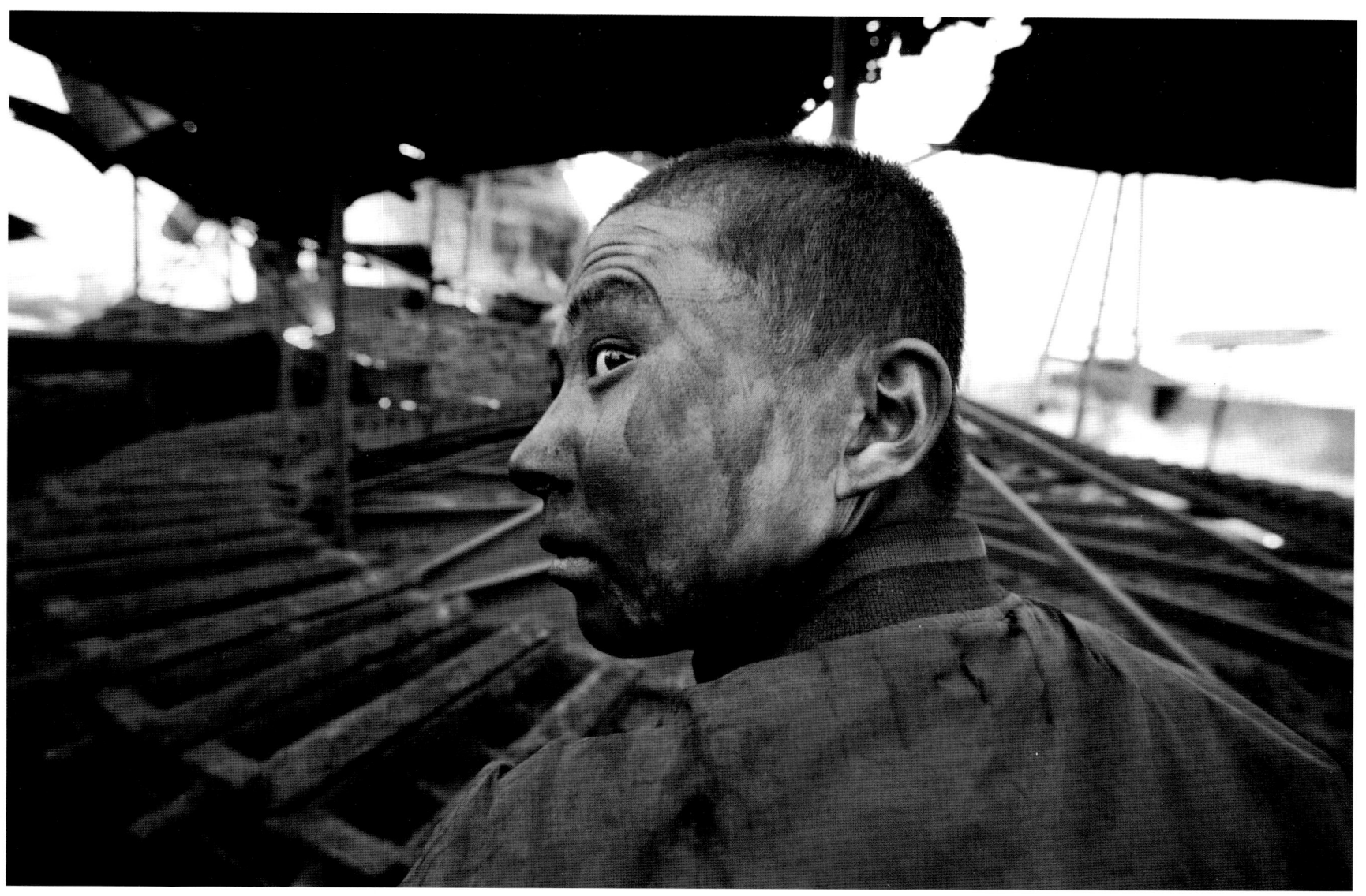

↑
Lu Guang, 2004

A worker at a coal refinery in Inner Mongolia. Even China's official news agency, Xinhua, describes mining as the "deadliest job" in China, done in what are termed "killer mines." Recent years have produced an average of 7,000 deaths a year in private mines: "the fatality rate for China's coal mine accidents is 100 times that of the U.S. and 30 times that of South Africa" (Michael Zhao, China Digital Times, December 22, 2007).

Ein Arbeiter in einer Kohleveredelungsanlage in der Inneren Mongolei. Selbst die offizielle chinesische Nachrichtenagentur Xinhua beschreibt den Kohleabbau als „tödlichsten Job" in China, der in so genannten Killer-minen geleistet wird. In jüngster Zeit waren in privaten Minen jährlich im Durchschnitt 7000 Tote zu beklagen: „Die Sterblichkeitsrate liegt bei Unfällen in chinesischen Kohleminen 100-mal höher als in den USA und 30-mal über der in Südafrika." (Michael Zhao, China Digital Times, 22. Dezember 2007)

Un ouvrier d'une mine de charbon de Mongolie intérieure. Même l'agence de presse officielle Xinhua décrit la mine comme « le plus dangereux des emplois » en Chine. On parle même de « mines tueuses ». Ces dernières années plus de 7000 personnes sont mortes chaque année dans ces exploitations privées. « Le taux d'accidents mortels dans l'industrie minière chinoise est 100 fois plus élevé qu'aux États-Unis et 30 fois plus qu'en Afrique du Sud. » (Michael Zhao, China Digital Times, 22 décembre 2007).

←
Lu Guang, 2004

A worker dozes against the railway track at Nagqu, in Tibet. This stretch of railroad is the last section of the track that now runs all the way from Beijing to Lhasa. The Qing-Zang (Qinghai-Tibet) Railway is the highest and longest railway in the world running across a plateau, reaching an altitude of more than 5,000 meters above sea level. One of its bridges spans 12 kilometers.

Ein Arbeiter döst auf einer Bahnschiene in Nagqu, in Tibet. Diese Bahnstrecke ist der letzte Abschnitt des Schienenstrangs, der heute Peking mit Lhasa verbindet. Die Linie Qing-Zang (Qinghai-Tibet) ist die weltweit längste und am höchsten gelegene Bahnstrecke auf einem Plateau, die eine Höhe von über 5000 Meter über dem Meeresspiegel erreicht. Eine der Brücken ist 12 Kilometer lang.

Un ouvrier se repose contre un rail de chemin de fer à Nagqu, au Tibet. Cette section est la dernière de la ligne Pékin-Lhassa. La ligne Qing-Zang (Qinghai-Tibet) est la plus haute jamais construite au monde. Elle monte à plus de 5 000 mètres. L'un de ses ponts mesure 12 km de long.

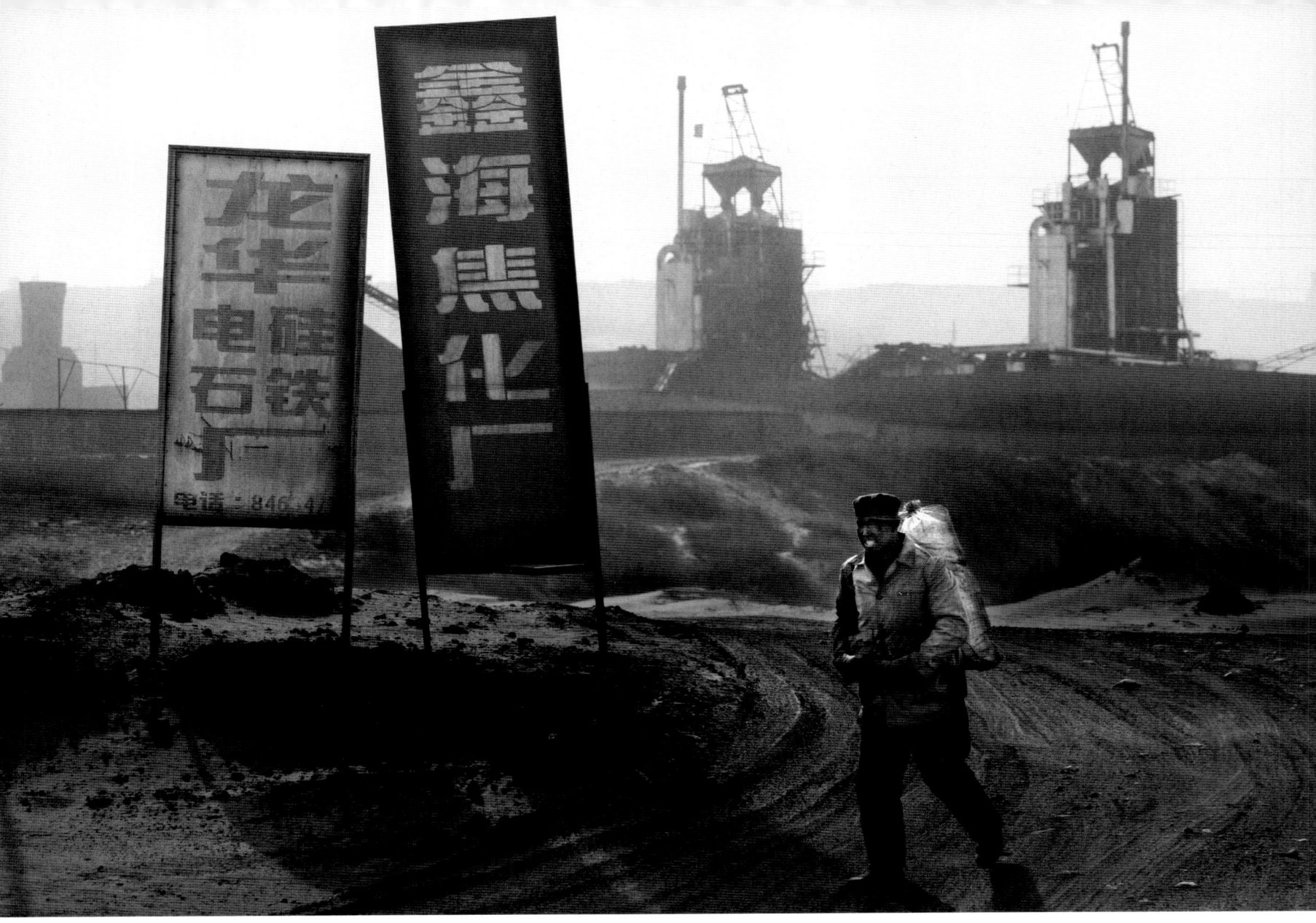

↑

Lu Guang, 2005

A worker transports drilling equipment at a coal refinery site on the border of Shaanxi province and Inner Mongolia.

Ein Arbeiter transportiert Bohrgerät auf dem Gelände einer Anlage zur Veredelung von Kohle an der Grenze zwischen der Provinz Shaanxi und der Inneren Mongolei.

Un ouvrier porte du matériel sur un site minier à la frontière de la province du Shaanxi et de la Mongolie intérieure.

"I have lived for three-fourths of the last century, and I can tell you with certainty: should China embrace the parliamentary democracy of the Western world, the only result would be that 1.3 billion Chinese people would not have enough food to eat. The result would be great chaos, and if that were to happen, it would not be conducive to world peace and stability."

„Ich habe Dreiviertel des vergangenen Jahrhunderts erlebt, und ich kann ihnen mit Gewissheit sagen: Wenn China die parlamentarische Demokratie der westlichen Welt übernähme, wäre das einzige Ergebnis, dass 1,3 Milliarden Chinesen nicht genug zu essen hätten. Die Folge davon wäre ein riesiges Chaos, das Frieden und Stabilität in der Welt nicht zuträglich wäre."

« J'ai vécu les trois quarts du siècle dernier et je peux vous le dire avec certitude : si la Chine appliquait la démocratie parlementaire occidentale, le seul résultat serait que 1,3 milliard de Chinois n'auraient pas assez à manger. Ce serait un immense chaos, et si cela devrait arriver, le monde ne s'orienterait certainement pas vers la paix et à la stabilité. »

JIANG ZEMIN (1926–), President of the People's Republic of China (1993–2003), 2001

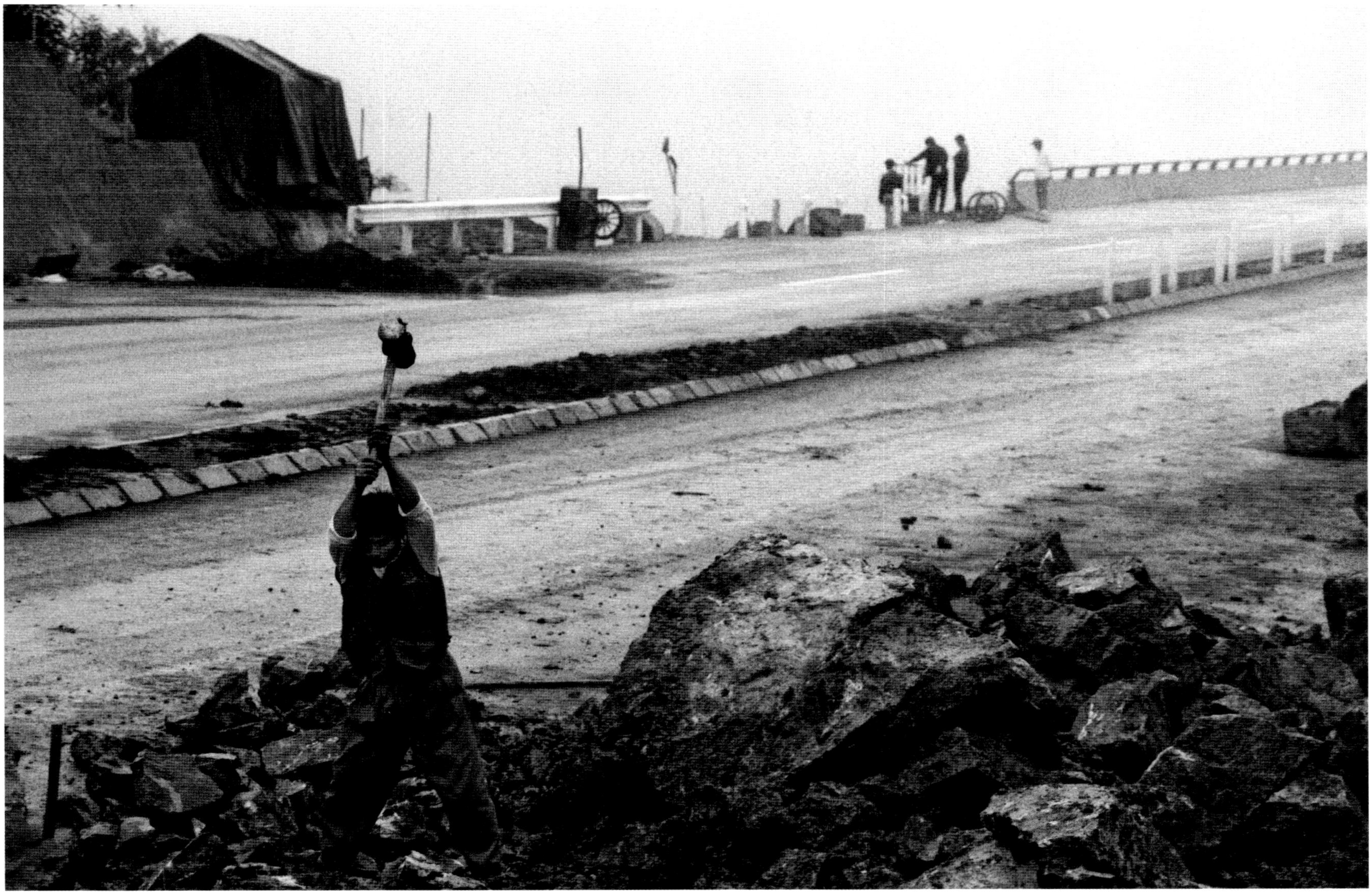

He Yanguang, 2005

A worker labors at the construction of a new highway linking Taiyuan in Shanxi province to Jiuquan in Gansu province. Between 2002 and 2007, China built a total of 200,000 kilometers of new roads nationwide.

Ein Arbeiter schuftet beim Bau einer neuen Verbindungsstraße zwischen Taiyuan in der Provinz Shanxi und Jiuquan in der Provinz Gansu. Zwischen 2002 und 2007 entstanden in China insgesamt 200.000 Kilometer neuer Straße.

Un ouvrier sur le chantier de construction d'une nouvelle autoroute entre Taiyuan dans la province du Shanxi, et Jiuquan, dans la province du Gansu. La Chine a construit plus de 200 000 kilomètres de routes entre 2002 et 2007.

pp. 370/371
Wang Fuchun, 2005

Five men from Heilongjiang province, near the border with Russia in the far northeast of China, emerge from icy waters after a traditional New Year's swim.

Fünf Männer aus der Provinz Heilongjiang nahe der russischen Grenze im fernen Nordosten Chinas sind nach dem traditionellen Neujahrsschwimmen dem eisigen Wasser entstiegen.

Cinq habitants de la province du Heilongjiang, près de la frontière russe dans le nord-est de la Chine, sortent de l'eau glacée après le traditionnel bain du Nouvel an.

→

Lu Guang, 2005

"Please don't pollute, we want to live": villagers in Inner Mongolia protest against the severe pollution caused by coal mining in the area around their village.

„Bitte verschmutzt die Umwelt nicht, wir wollen leben": Dorfbewohner in der Inneren Mongolei protestieren gegen die vom Kohleabbau in der Umgebung ihres Dorfes verursachte schwere Verschmutzung.

« S'il-vous-plaît, ne polluez pas, nous voulons vivre »: des villageois de Mongolie intérieure protestent contre l'importante pollution provoquée par les mines de charbon qui entourent le village.

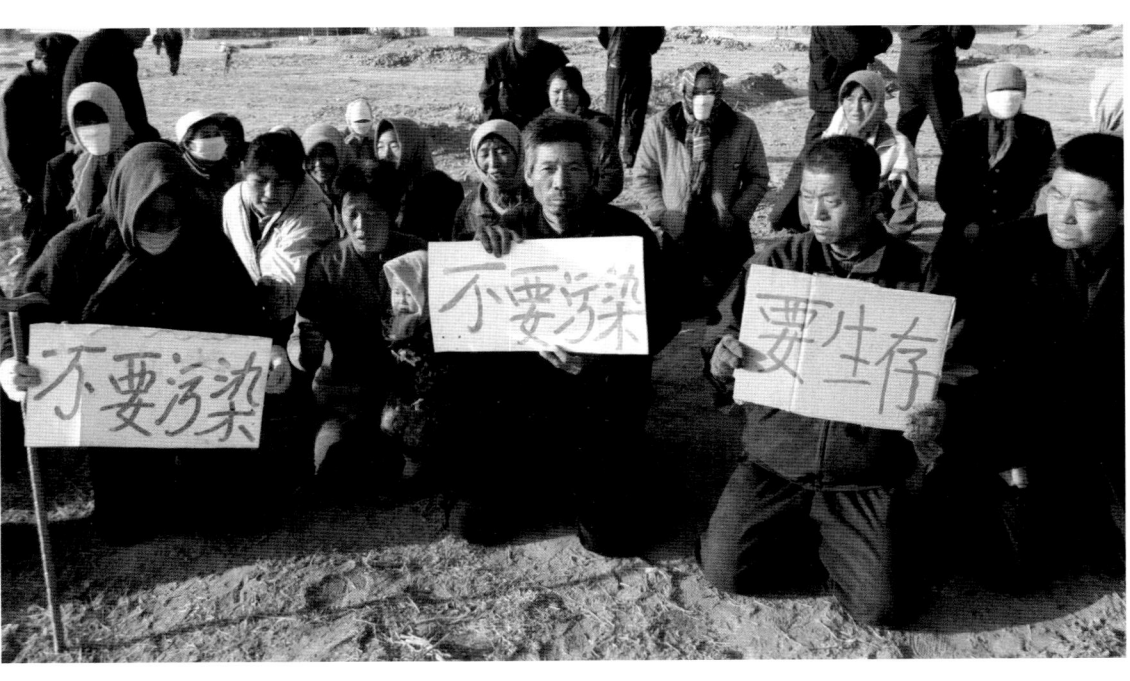

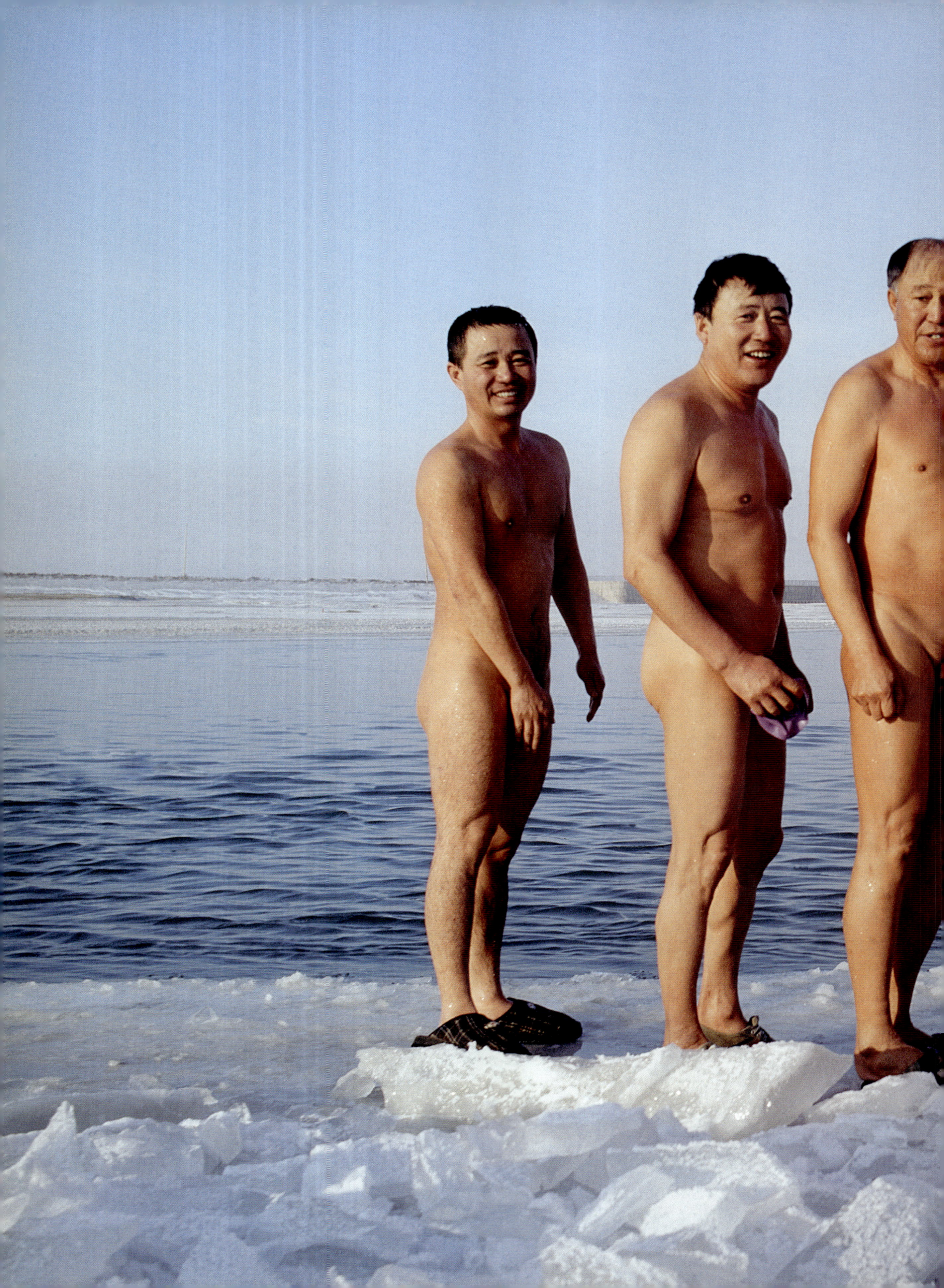

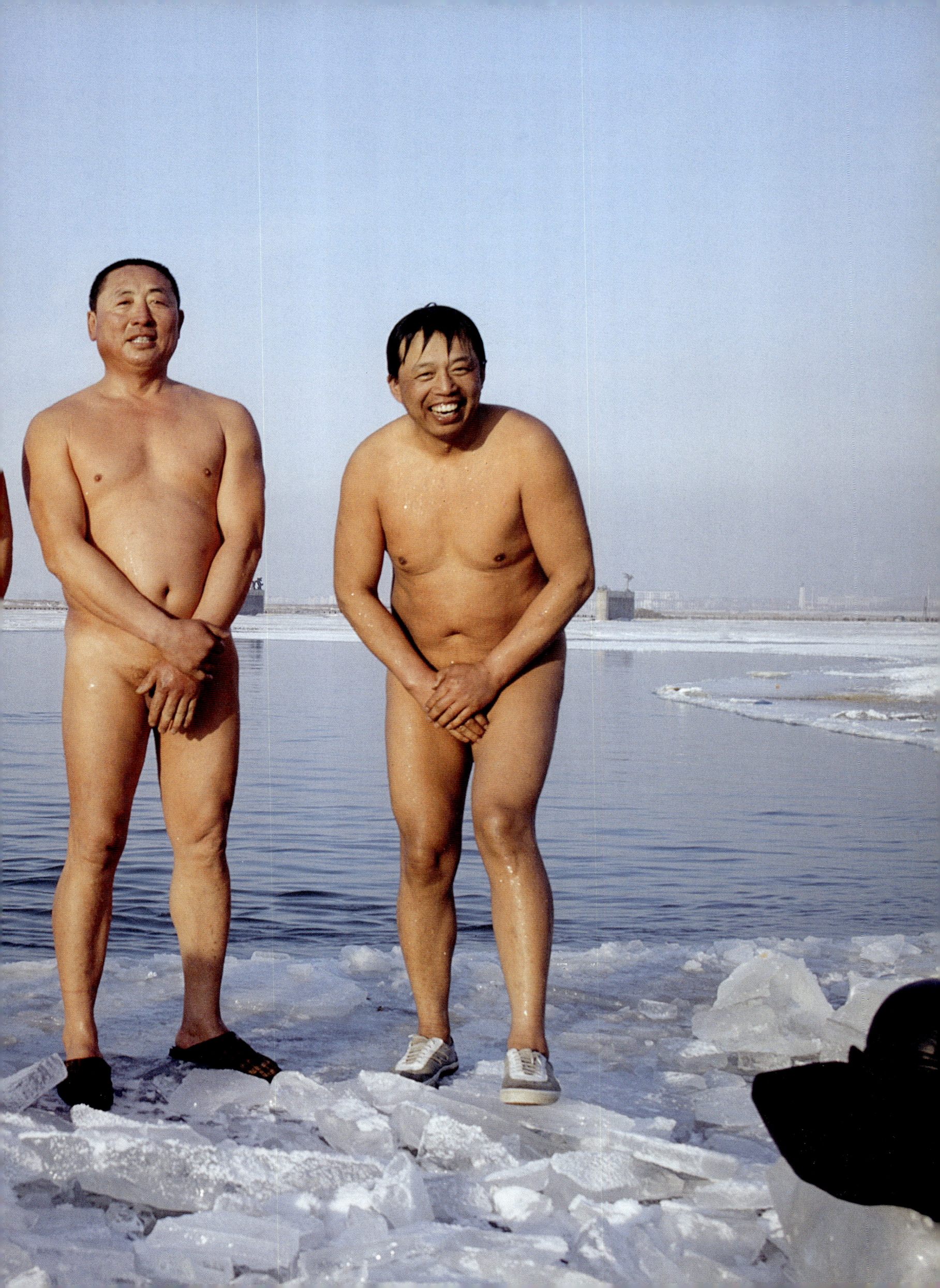

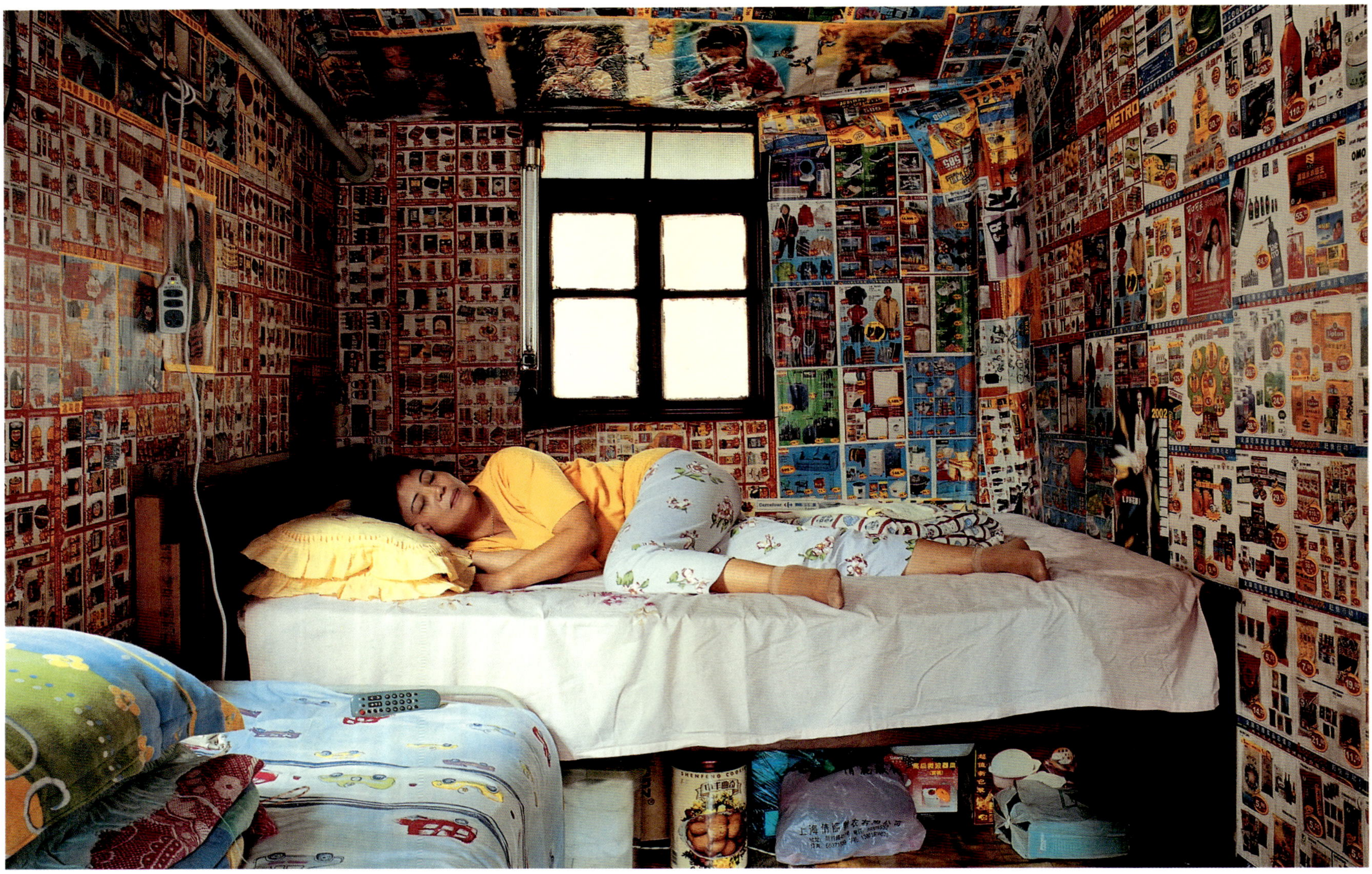
METRO

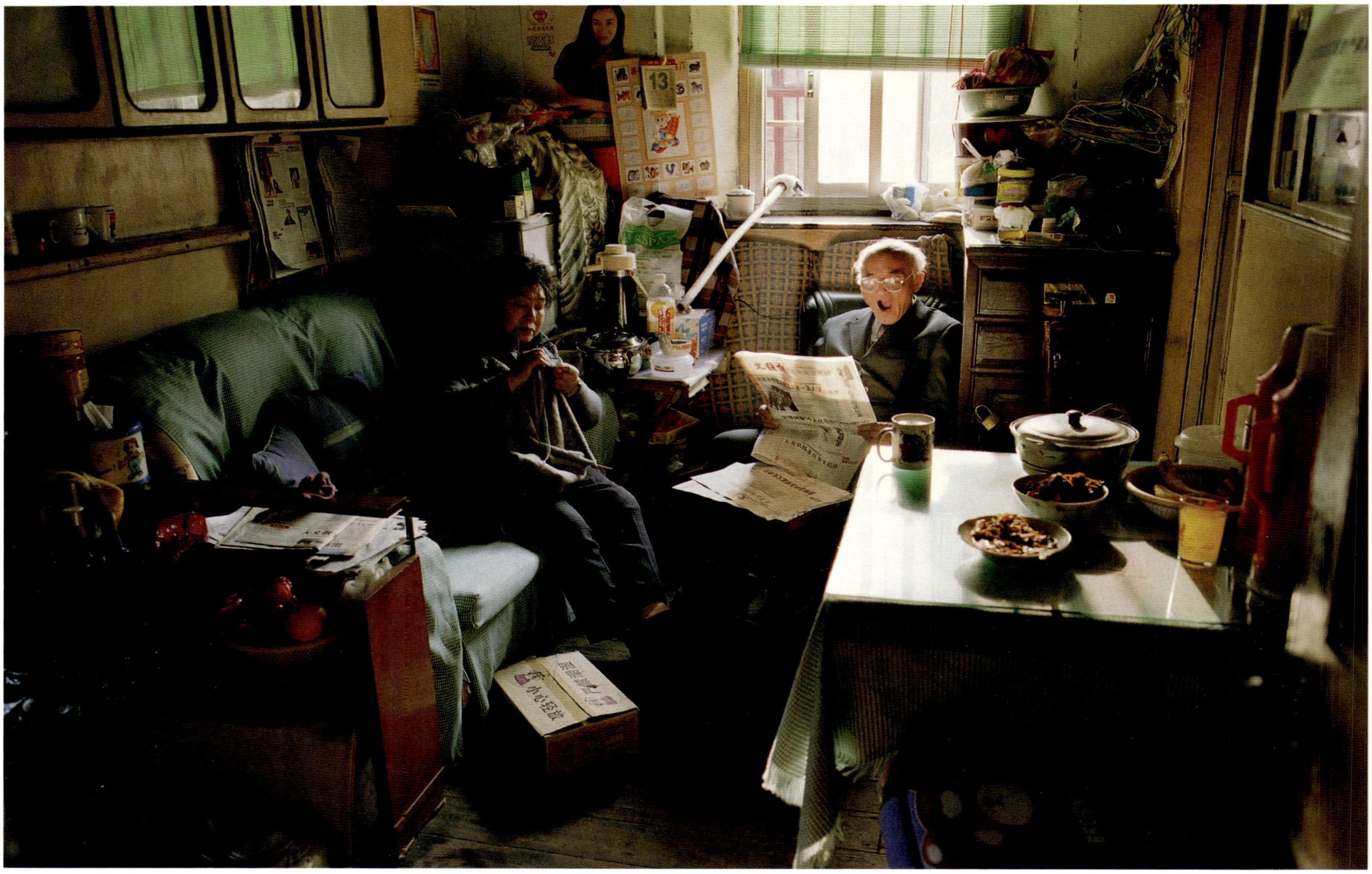

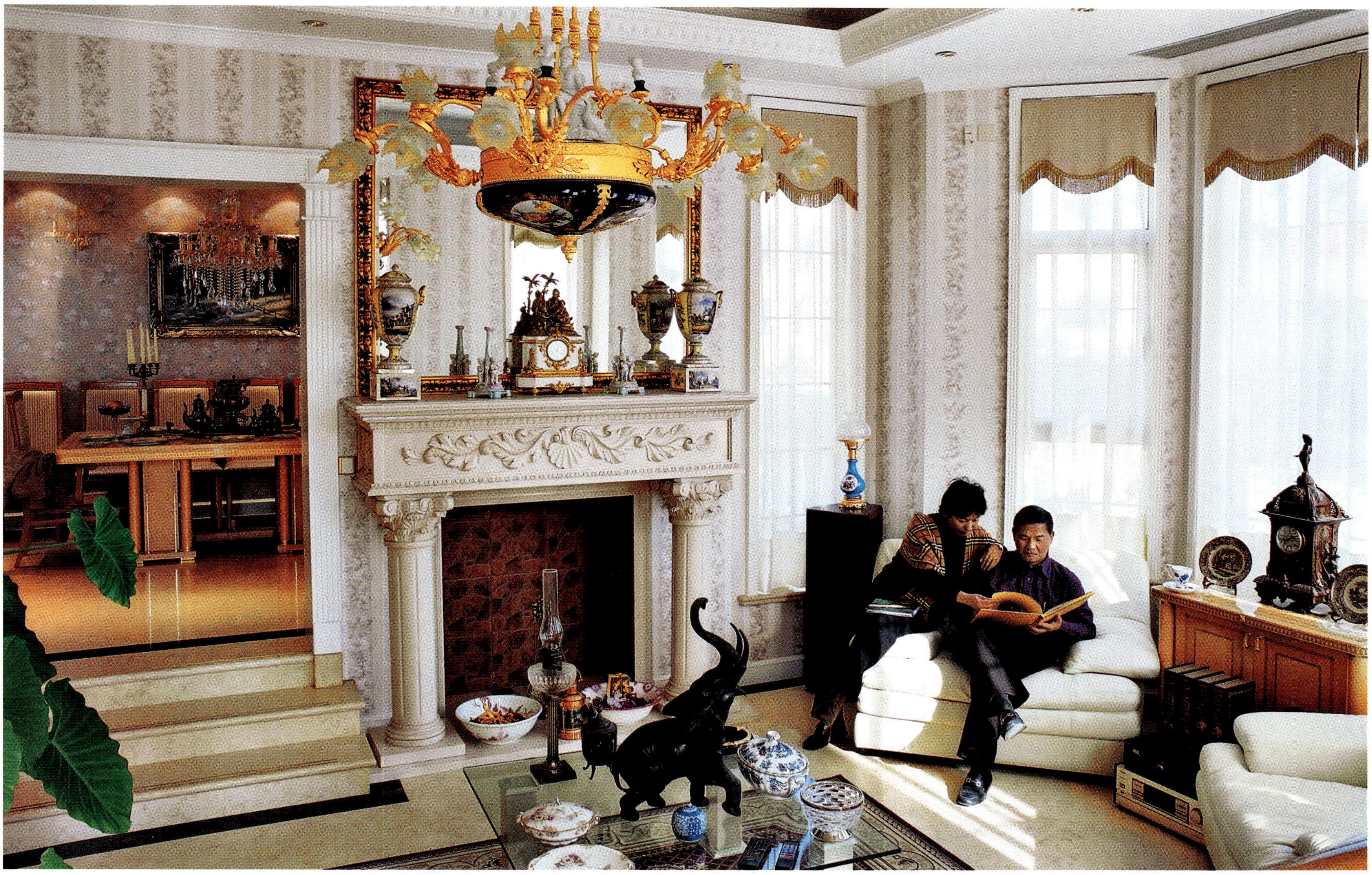

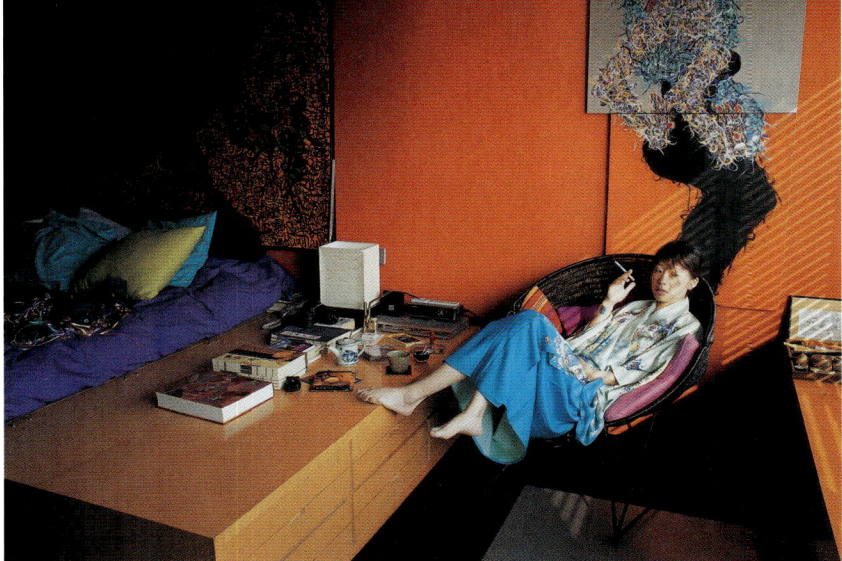

↑

Hu Yang, 2005

An affluent Chinese couple at their "bourgeois" Shanghai home.

Wohlhabendes chinesisches Paar in seinem "bourgeoisen" Heim in Shanghai.

Couple de riches Chinois dans leur résidence de Shanghai.

↖

Hu Yang, 2005

A Chinese woman rests in her tiny one-room dwelling, the walls and ceiling plastered with newsprint.

Eine Chinesin ruht sich in ihrer winzigen Einzimmerwohnung aus, deren Wände und Decke mit Zeitschriftenpapier tapeziert sind.

Une Chinoise se repose dans son petit studio dont les murs et le plafond sont tapissés de journaux.

←

Hu Yang, 2005

Older couple at home in Shanghai.

Älteres Ehepaar zu Hause in Shanghai.

Couple âgé chez lui à Shanghai.

→

Hu Yang, 2005

A Chinese woman yuppie working in advertising relaxes at her home in Shanghai.

Ein in der Werbung tätiger weiblicher Yuppie entspannt sich in seiner Wohnung in Shanghai.

Une yuppie chinoise qui travaille dans la publicité se détend chez elle.

"China is more prosperous than before. The people have better lives but they are not happy and confident because the scars are still there."

„China ist wohlhabender als zuvor. Die Menschen haben ein besseres Leben, aber sie sind nicht glücklich und zuversichtlich, weil die Narben noch schmerzen."

« La Chine est plus prospère qu'auparavant. Le peuple vit mieux mais n'est ni heureux ni confiant parce que les cicatrices sont encore visibles. »

JUNG CHANG (1952–), author of "Wild Swans"

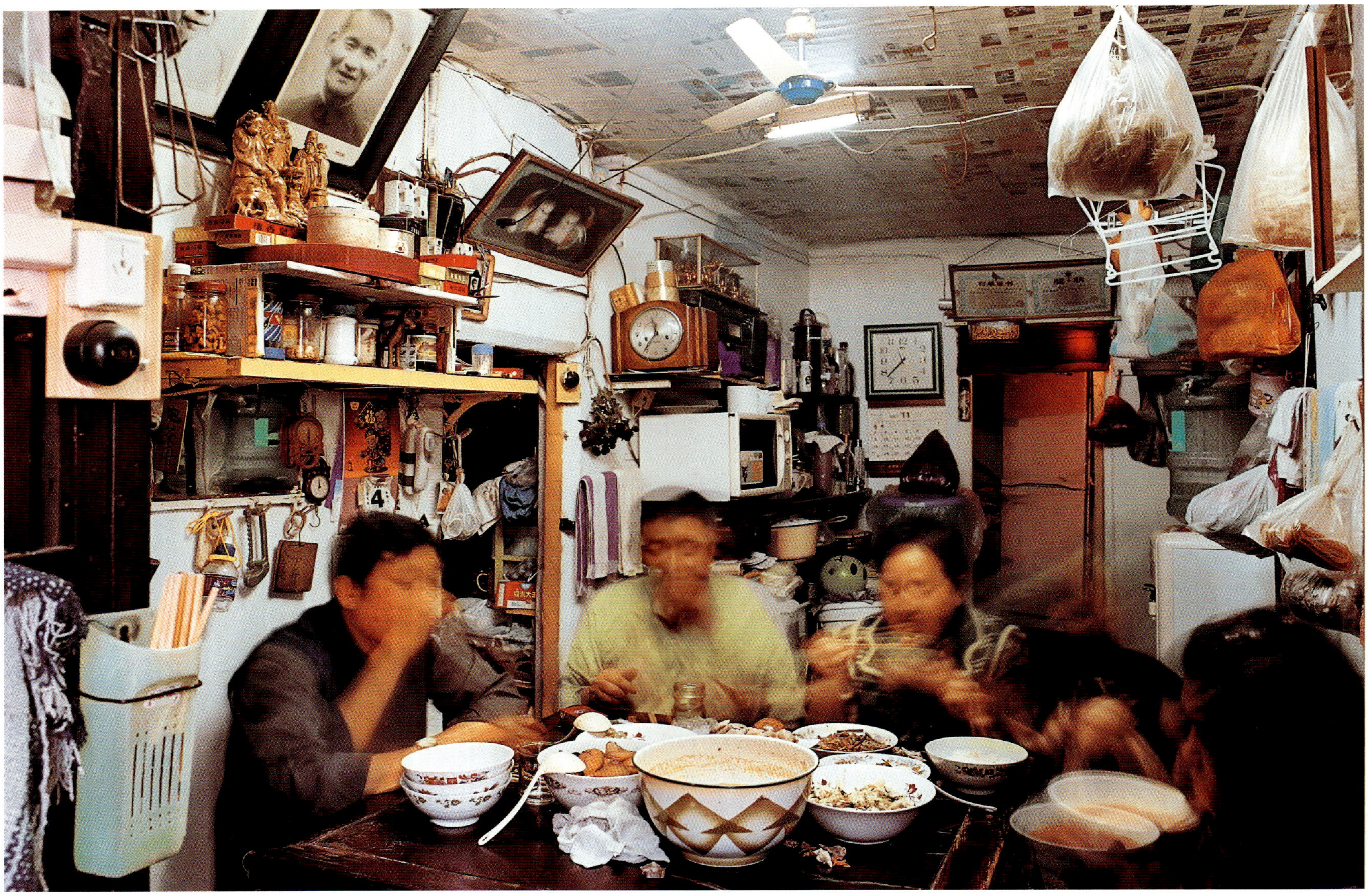

↑↓↘
Hu Yang, 2005

From the Shanghai Family *Series.*

Shanghai-based photographer Hu Yang takes an intimate look at a cross section of local families that range from workers to Chinese Yuppies.

Aus der Serie Familien in Shanghai

Der in Shanghai lebende Fotograf Hu Yang nimmt einen Querschnitt ortsansässiger Familien unter die Lupe, der von Arbeitern bis zu chinesischen Yuppies reicht.

De la Série Familles de Shanghai

Le photographe de Shanghai, Hu Yang a réalisé à travers cette série un portrait intime de diverses familles de la ville, des ouvriers aux yuppies chinois.

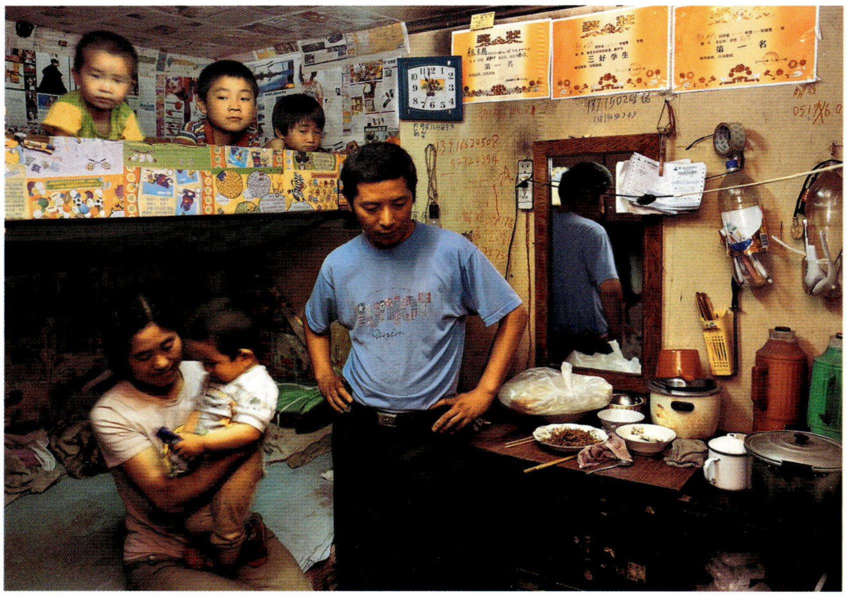

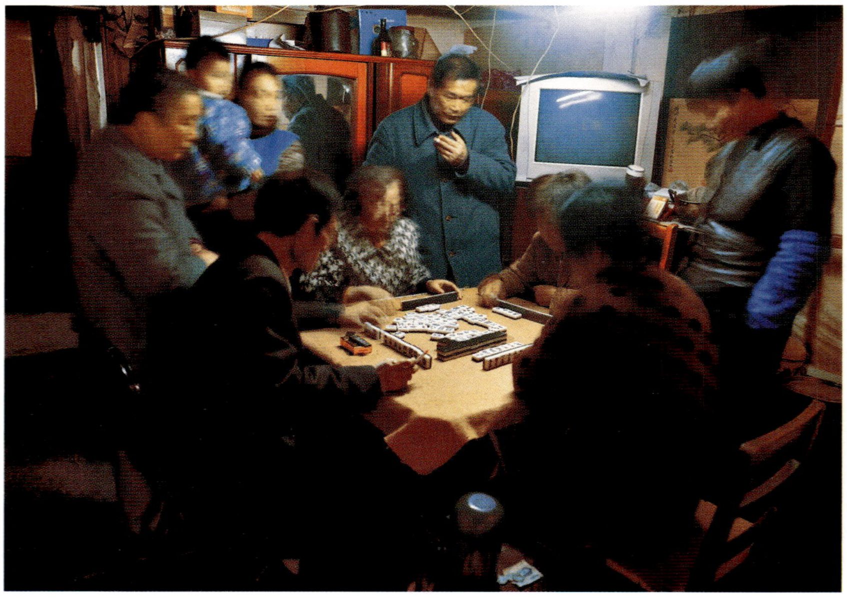

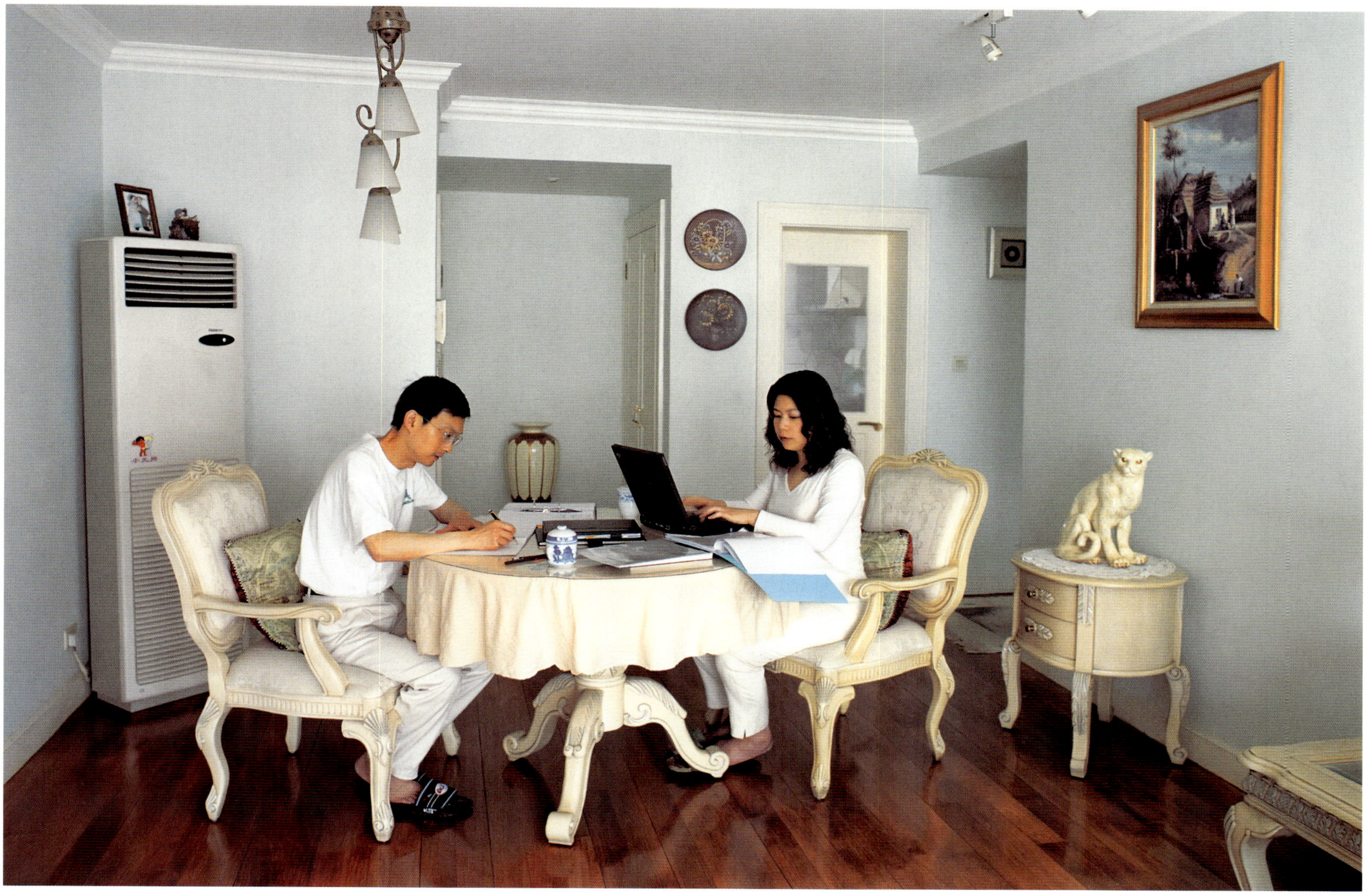

Hu Yang, 2005

*A Chinese white-collar couple at their
Shanghai home.*

*Chinesisches Ehepaar aus der Angestellten-
schicht in seinem Heim in Shanghai.*

*Un couple d'employés de bureaux chez lui,
à Shanghai.*

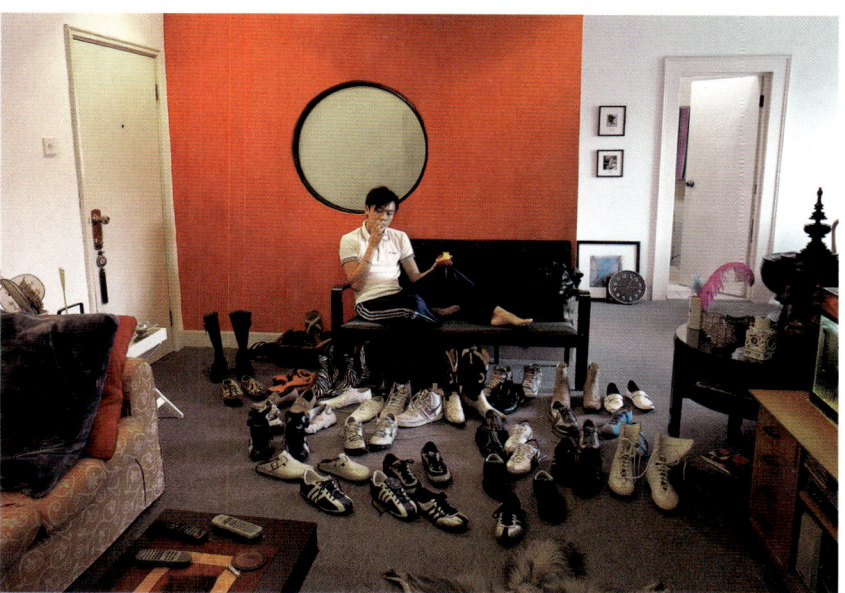

↑
Hu Yang, 2005

*A young man in Shanghai with his shoe
collection.*

*Ein junger Mann in Shanghai mit seiner
Schuhsammlung.*

*Un jeune homme à Shanghai avec sa
collection de chaussures.*

pp. 376/377
Zhu Yan, 2005

*Reflecting the overspill of urban centers into
the rural suburbs, Zhu Yan captures a man
staring at the city looming in the distance.*

*Als Symbol für die in die ländlichen Vororte
ausufernden urbanen Zentren fotografiert
Zhu Yan einen Mann, der auf die sich in der
Ferne bedrohlich auftürmende Stadt schaut.*

*Image du développement urbain qui repousse
les banlieues rurales : un homme regarde la
ville dans le lointain.*

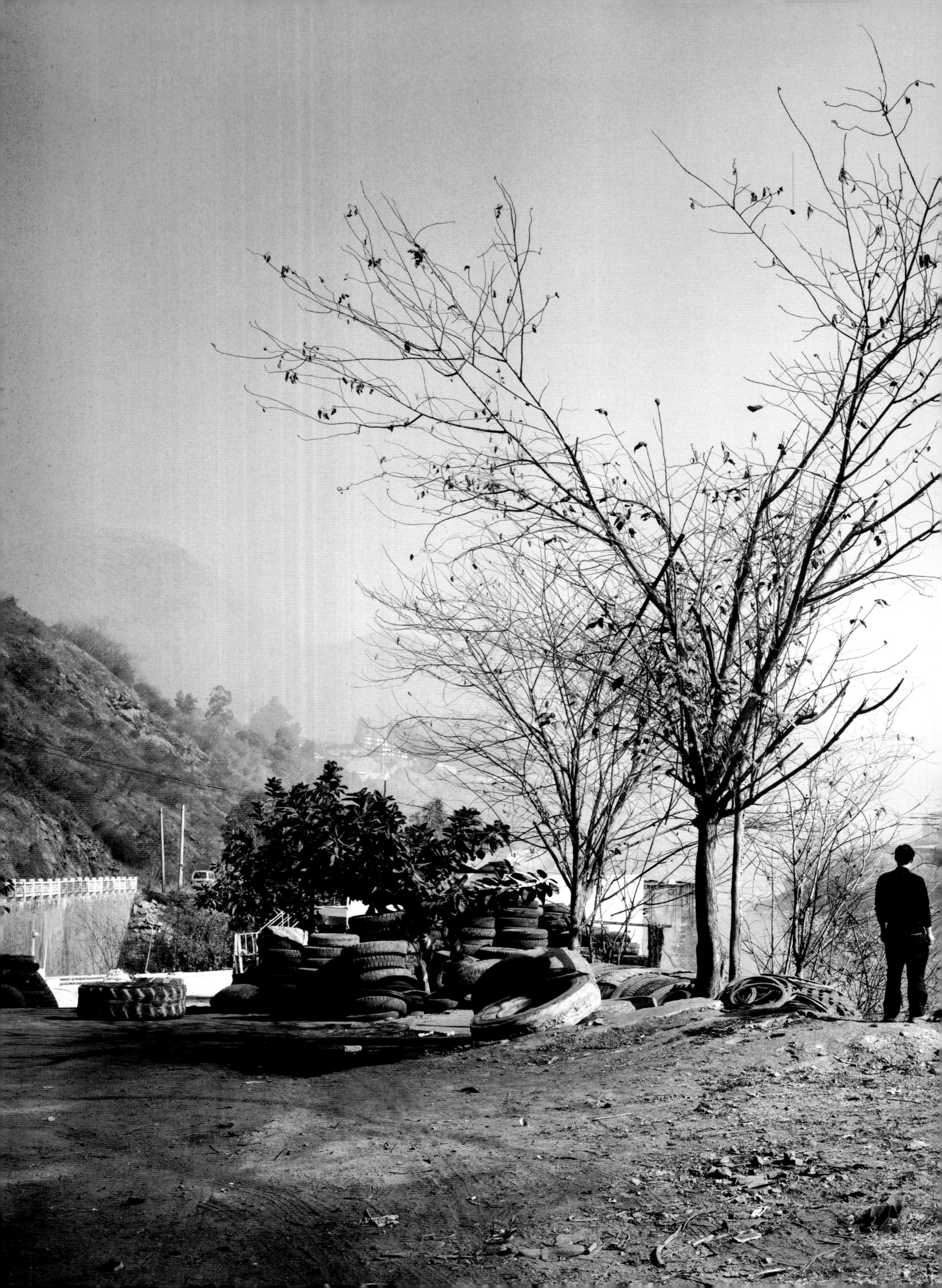

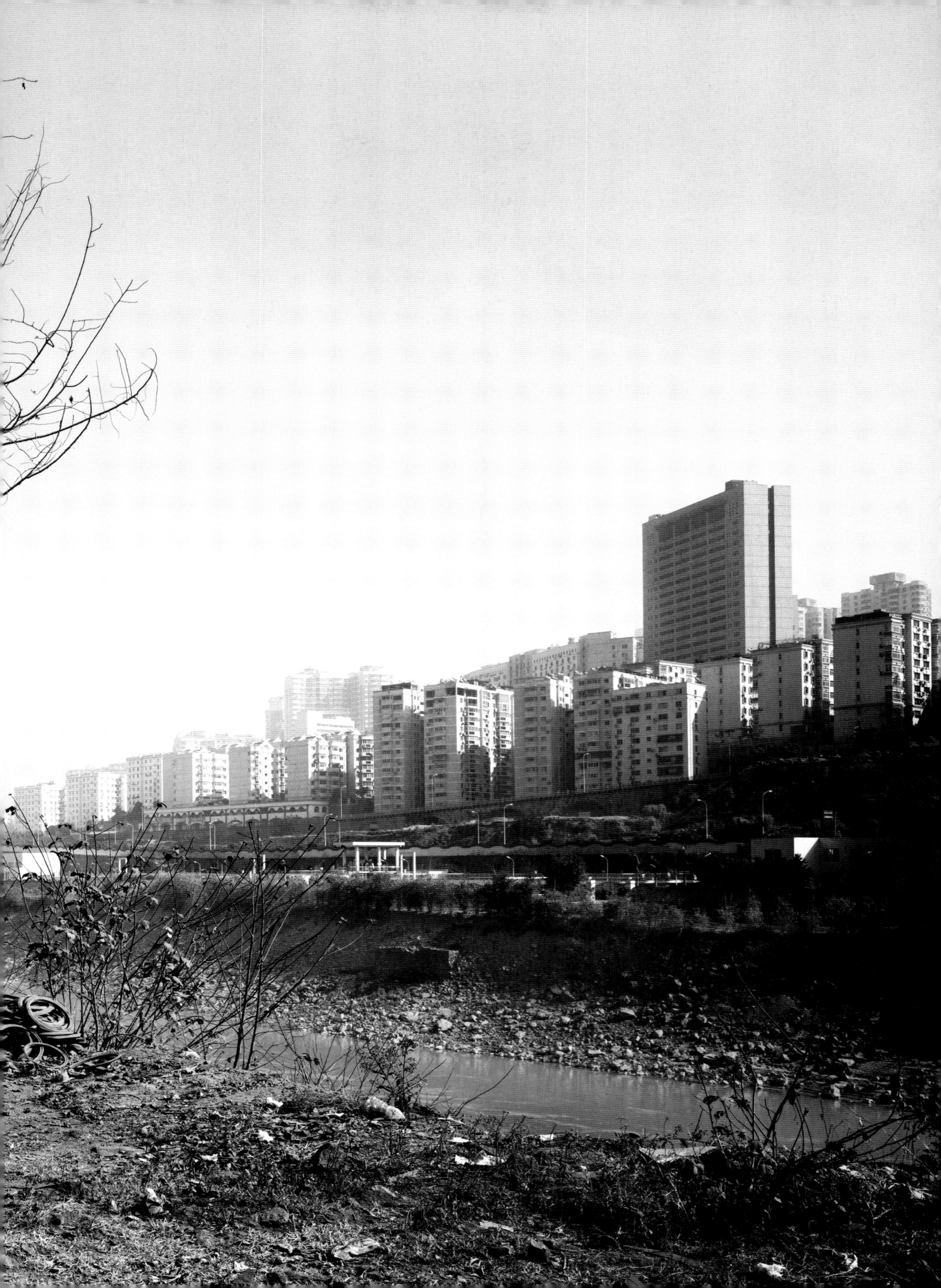

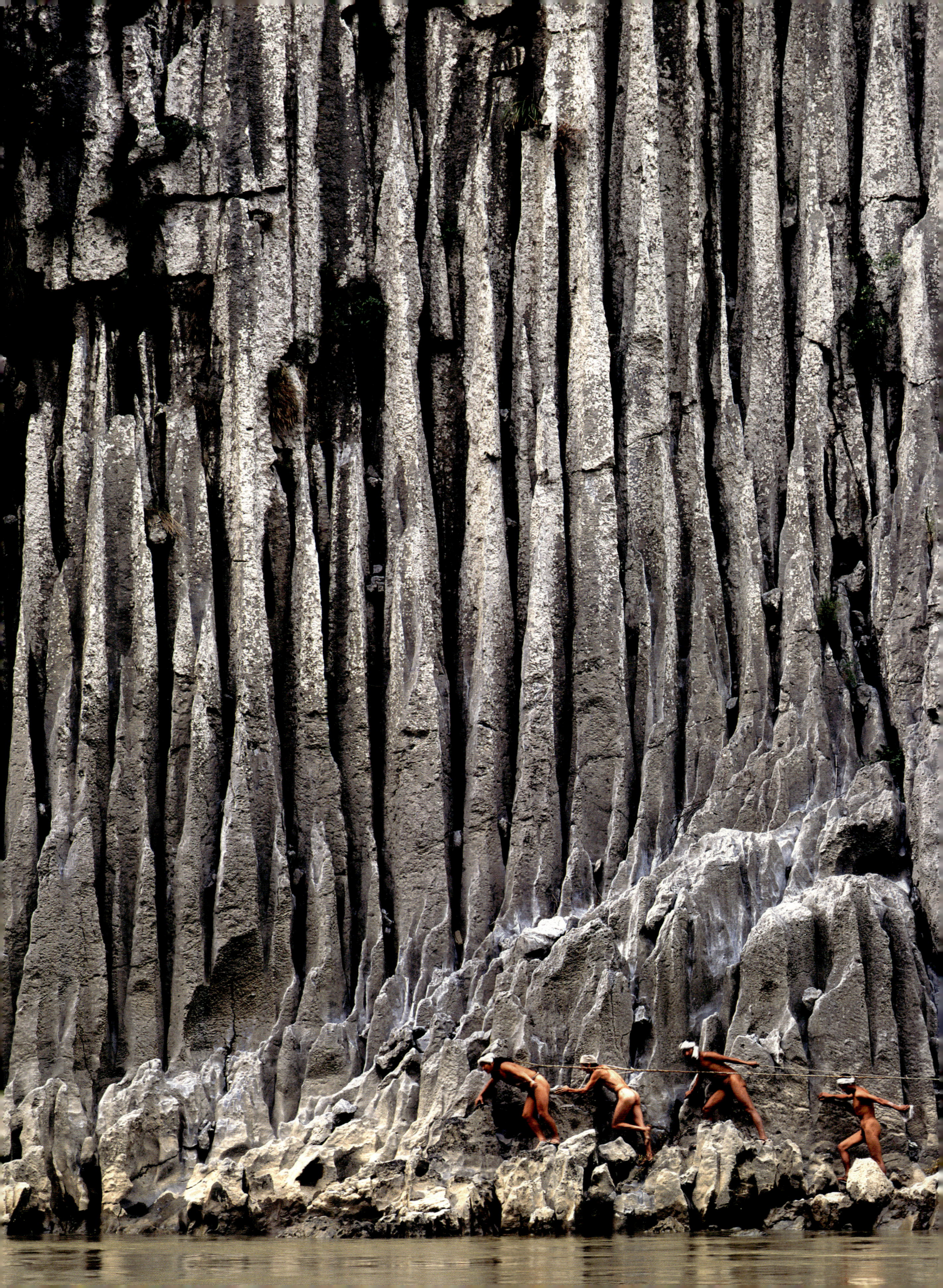

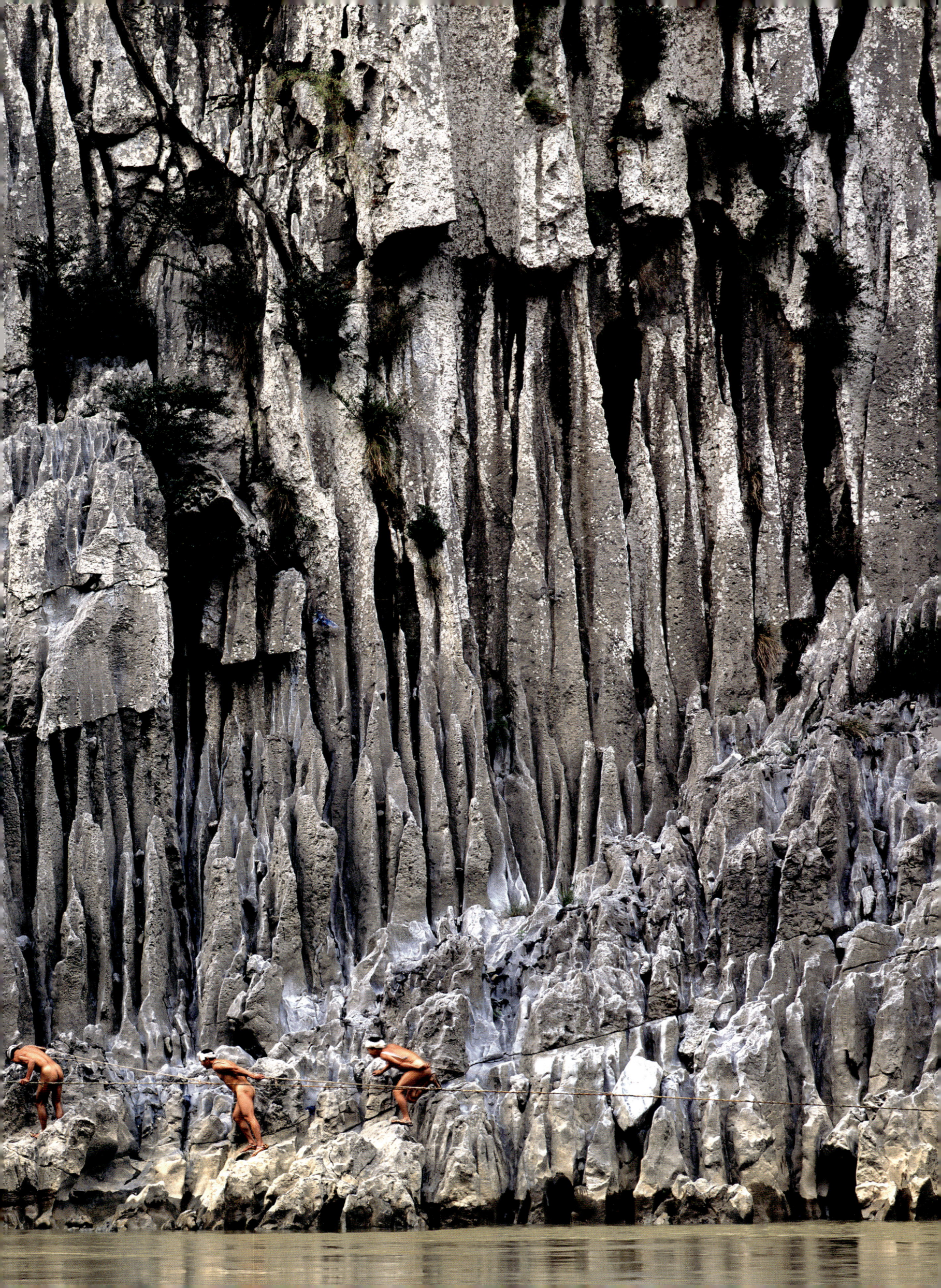

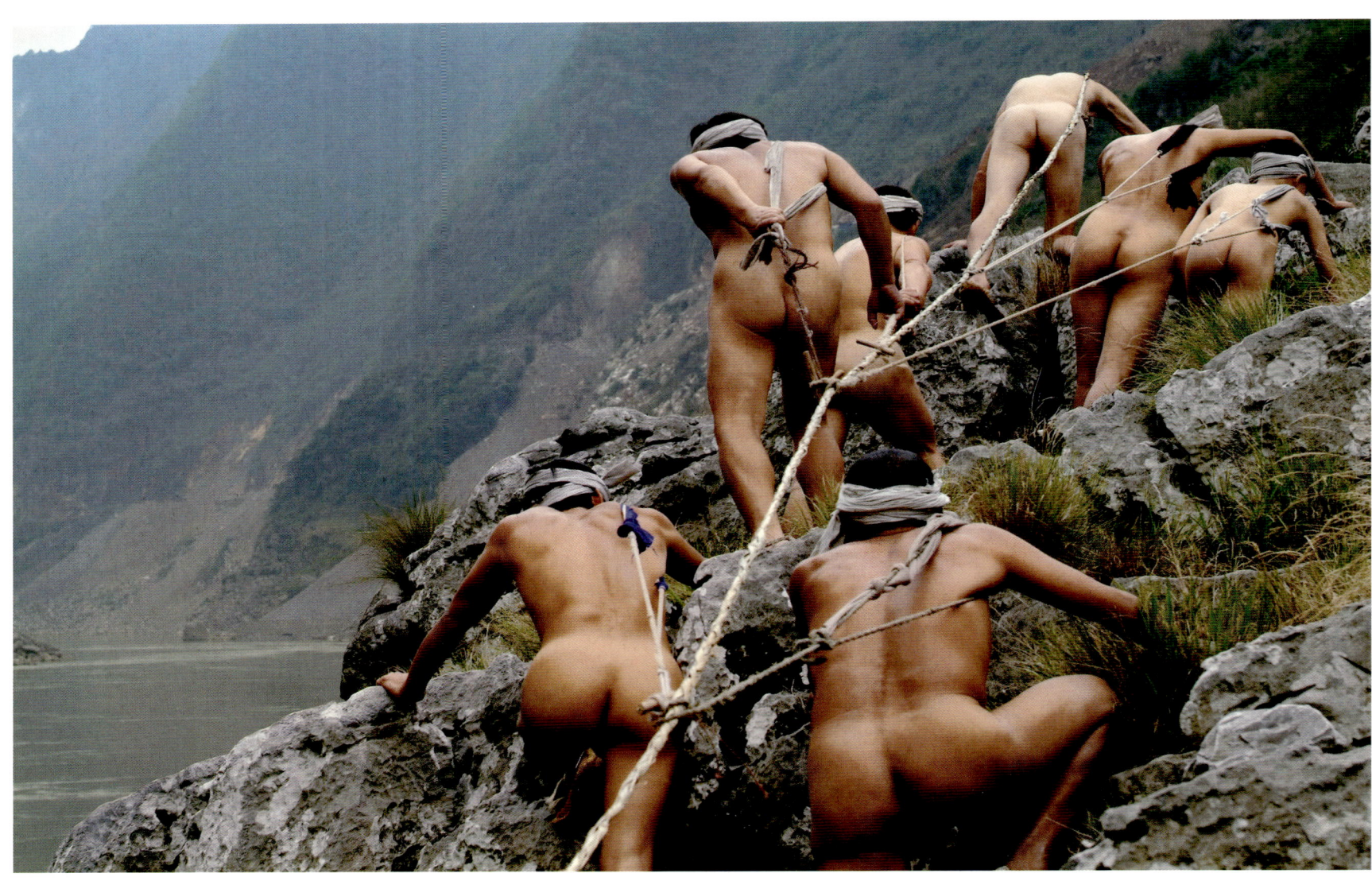

↑ *and pp. 378/379*
Qin Wen, 2005

*Chinese workers ply their trade on the
upper reaches of the Yangtze river. Here
pulling a boat upstream; they work naked
to protect the few clothes they possess.*

*Chinesische Arbeiter bei ihrer Tätigkeit am
Oberlauf des Jangtse. Hier ziehen sie ein
Boot flussaufwärts, was sie zur Schonung ihrer
wenigen Kleidungsstücke nackt erledigen.*

*Travailleurs chinois en pleine action sur
le cours supérieur du Yang-Tsé. Ils halent un
bateau à contre-courant, nus pour ne pas
user les rares vêtements qu'ils possèdent.*

pp. 382/383
He Yanguang, 2005

*A landmark handshake between visiting
KMT Chairman Lien Chan and CCP
General Secretary Hu Jintao, representing
the two rival parties that have kept Taiwan
separated from the Chinese mainland since
1949. The historic normalization of relations
between the two parties took place when
Lien led the first high level KMT delegation
to Beijing since the rift emerged in 1949.*

*Der bedeutsame Händedruck des zu Besuch
weilenden KMT-Vorsitzenden Lien Chan und
des Generalsekretärs der KPCh Hu Jintao,
Repräsentanten der beiden gegnerischen Lager,
die seit 1949 Taiwan vom chinesischen Festland getrennt halten. Die historische Norma-
lisierung der Beziehungen zwischen den beiden
Kontrahenten ergab sich, als Lien die erste
hochrangige KMT-Abordnung seit dem Beginn
der Spaltung 1949 nach Peking begleitete.*

*Poignée de main historique entre le Président
du Kuomintang en visite, Lien Chan, et le
Secrétaire général du PCC, Hu Jintao, les
deux représentants des partis rivaux qui ont
maintenu la séparation entre Taïwan et la
Chine continentale depuis 1949. La normalisation des relations a débuté avec cette
première visite d'une délégation de haut
niveau du Kuomintang à Pékin depuis la
rupture de 1949.*

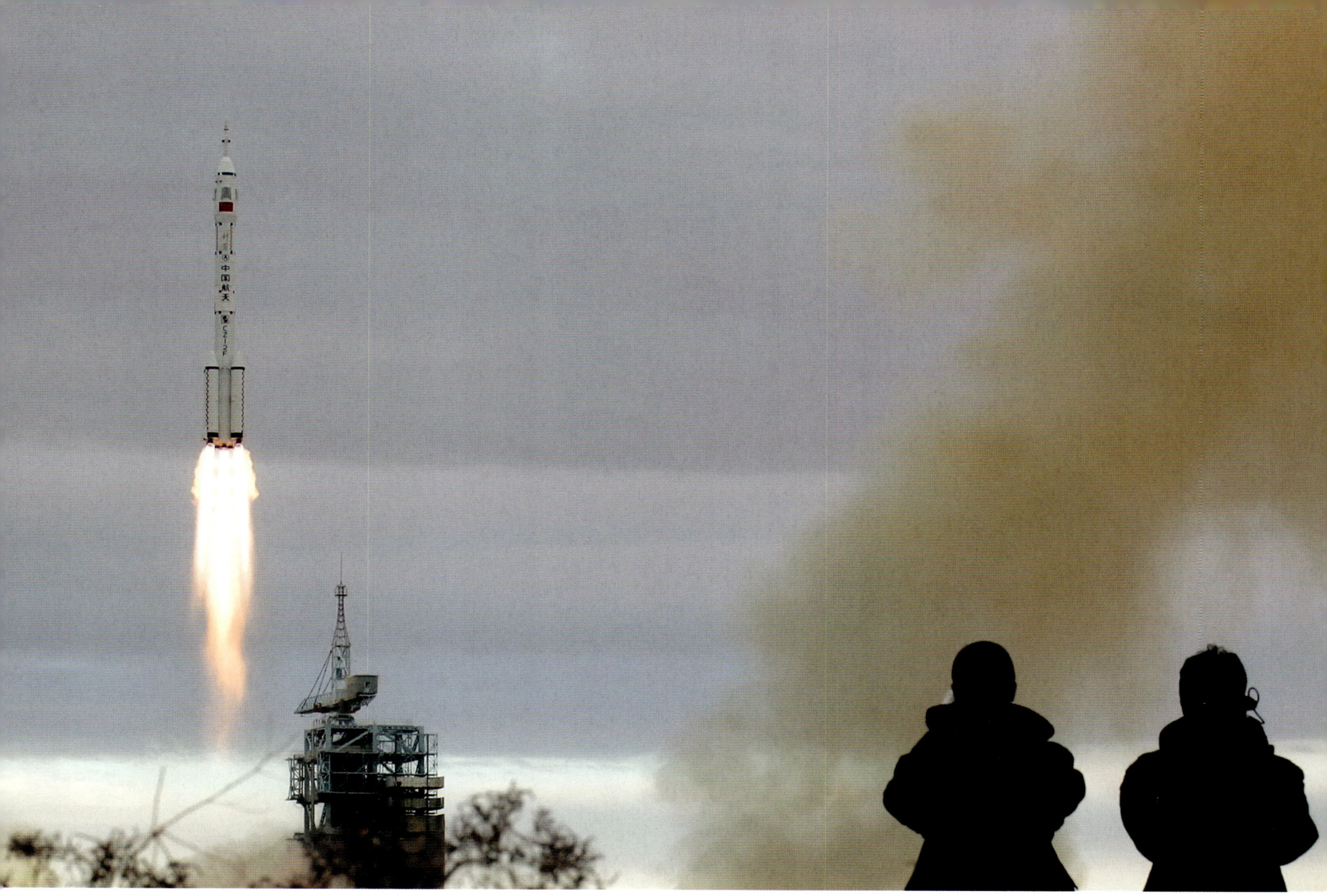

↑

Zheng Pingping, 2005

China launches the Shenzhou 6, its first spacecraft, from Jiuquan Space Center in the Gobi desert.

China schießt Shenzhou 6, sein erstes Raumschiff, vom Jiuquan-Raumfahrt-zentrum in der Wüste Gobi ins All.

La Chine lance Shenzhou 6, son premier vaisseau spatial, à partir du Centre spatial de Jiuquan dans le désert de Gobi.

"Events like this [the Shenzhou 5 launch] bring pride and satisfaction not just to people here but also to Overseas Chinese around the world … Now they will realize that we don't only make clothes and shoes."

„Ereignisse wie dieses [der Start von Shenzou 5] erfüllen nicht nur die Menschen hier-zulande mit Stolz und Genugtuung, sondern auch die Auslandschinesen in aller Welt … Jetzt werden sie begreifen, dass wir nicht nur Kleidung und Schuhe herstellen."

« Des événements comme celui-ci [le lancement de Shenzhou 5] provoquent fierté et satisfaction non seulement chez les gens d'ici mais aussi dans toute la communauté chinoise d'outre-mer … Maintenant, ils comprennent que nous ne fabriquons pas seulement des vêtements et des chaussures. »

YAN XUETONG, Director of the Institute of International Studies, Tsinghua University, Beijing, 2003

→

Zheng Pingping, 2005

At 5 o'clock on October 12, 2005, the two astronauts Fei Junlong (left) and Nie Haisheng (right) boarded the spacecraft Shenzhou 6 at Jiuquan Space Center. The spacecraft remained in orbit for five days before touching down, on October 17.

Am 12. Oktober 2005 um 5 Uhr besteigen die beiden Astronauten Fei Junlong (links) und Nie Haisheng (rechts) das Raumschiff Shenzhou 6 an der Raumstation Jiuquan. Das Raumschiff blieb fünf Tage in der Umlauf-bahn, ehe es am 17. Oktober wieder landete.

Le 12 octobre 2005 à 5 heures du matin, les deux astronautes Fei Junlong (à gauche) et Nie Haisheng (à droite) s'embarquent à bord du vaisseau spatial Shenzhou 6 lancé de la station spatiale de Jiuquan. Il restera en orbite cinq jours avant de redescendre sur terre le 17 octobre.

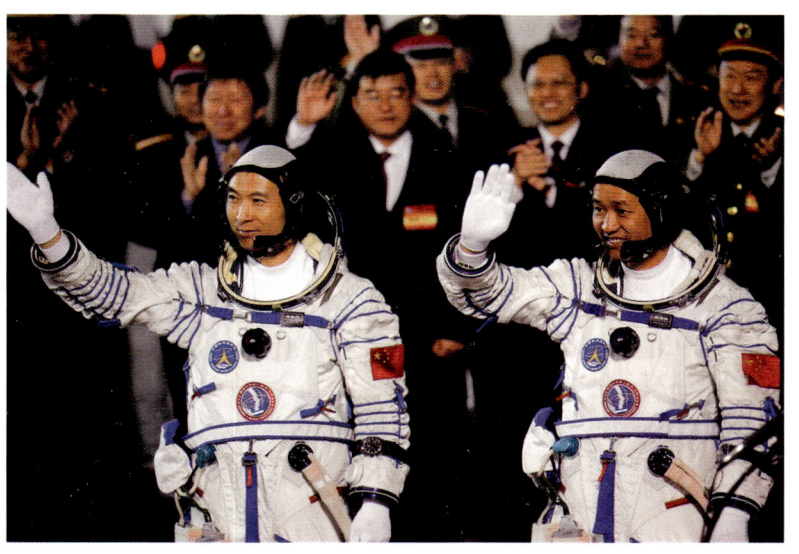

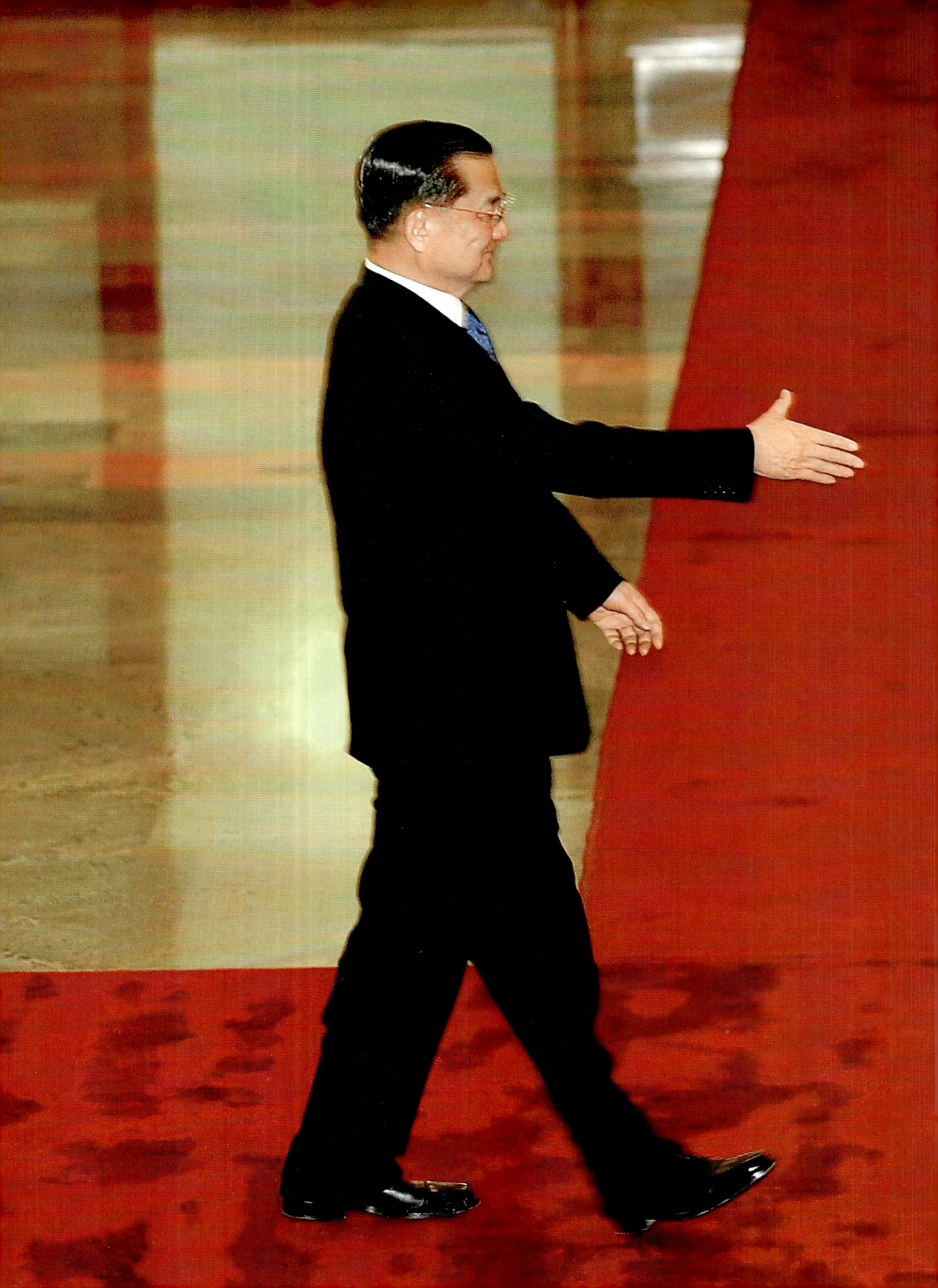

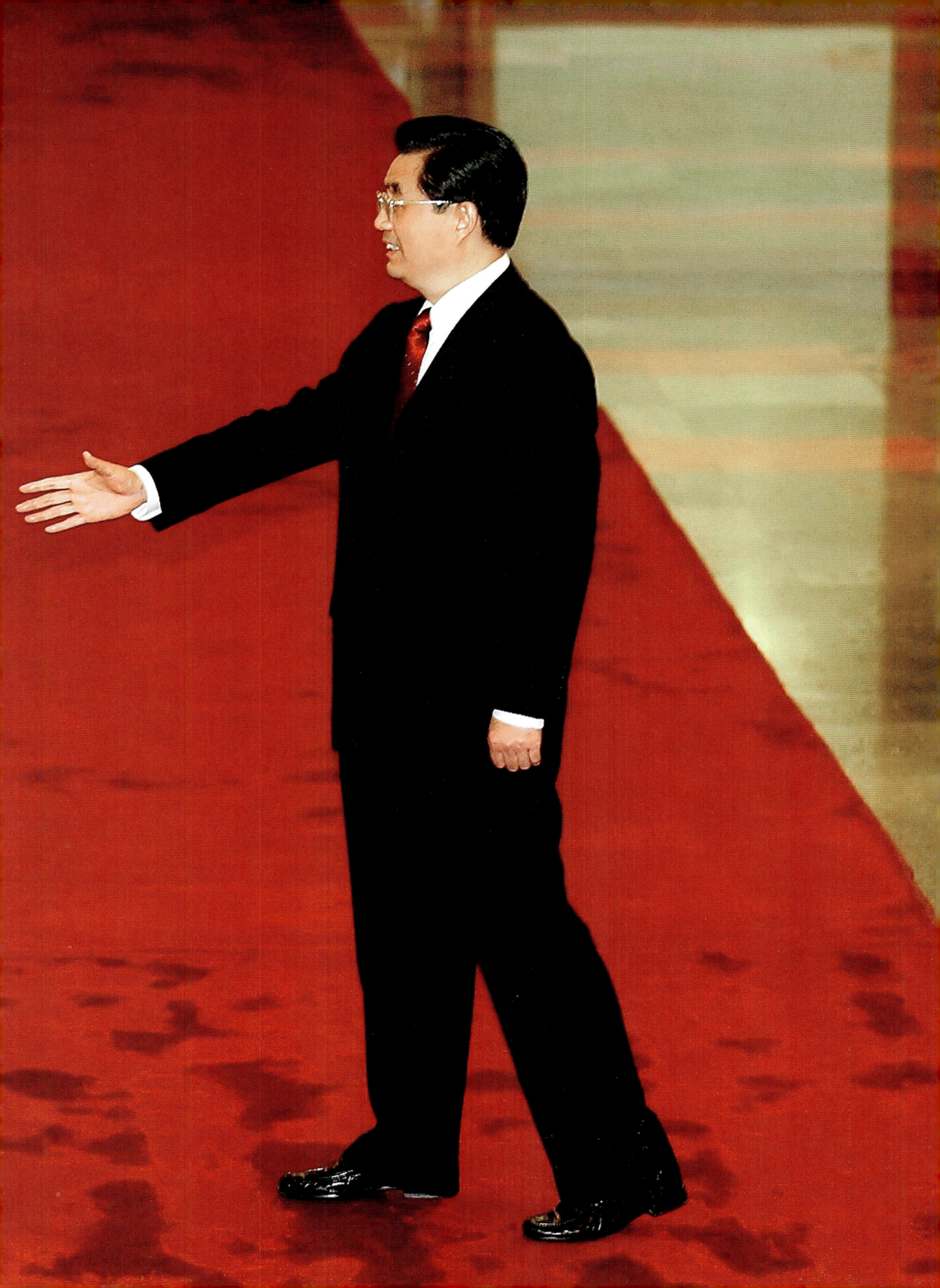

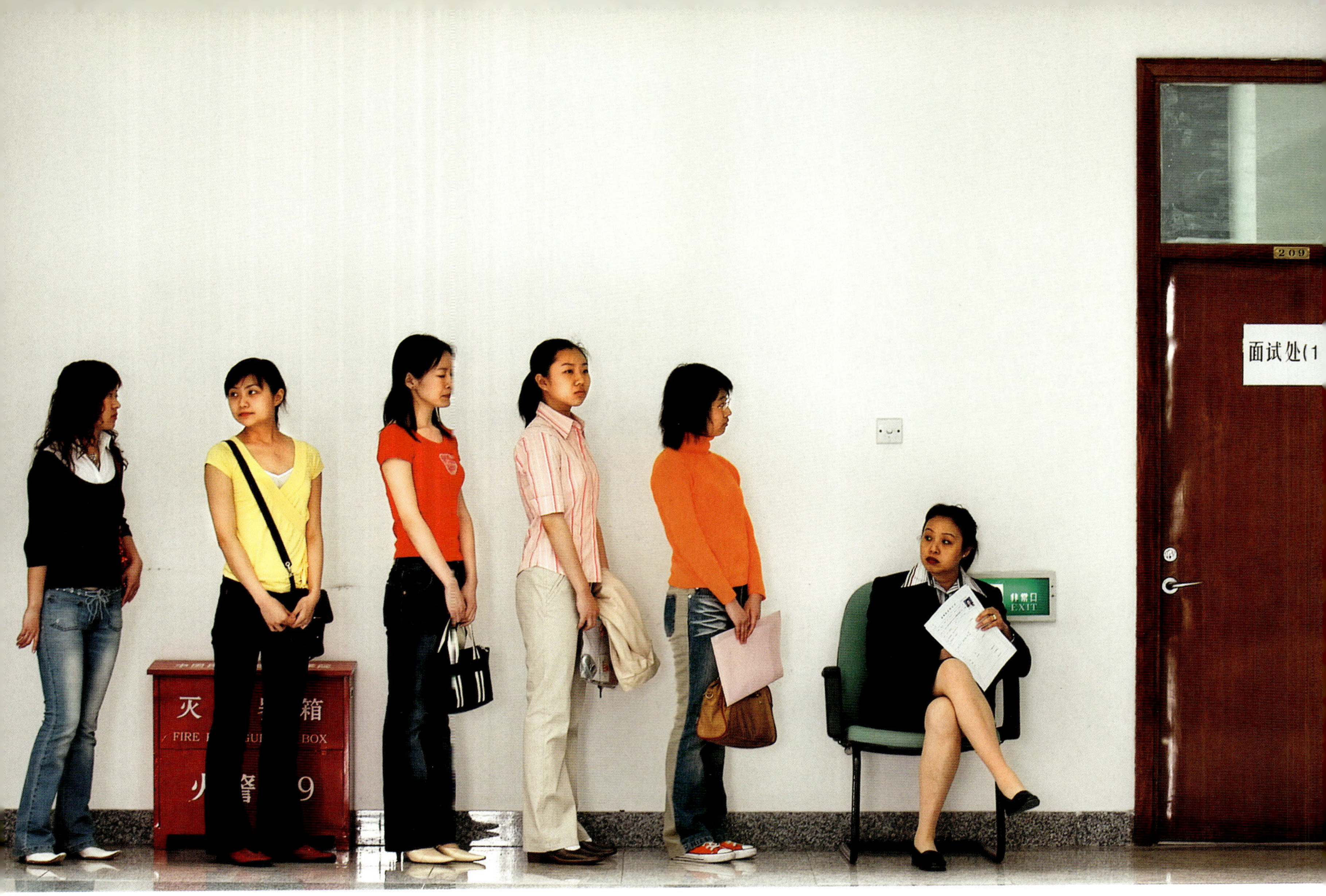

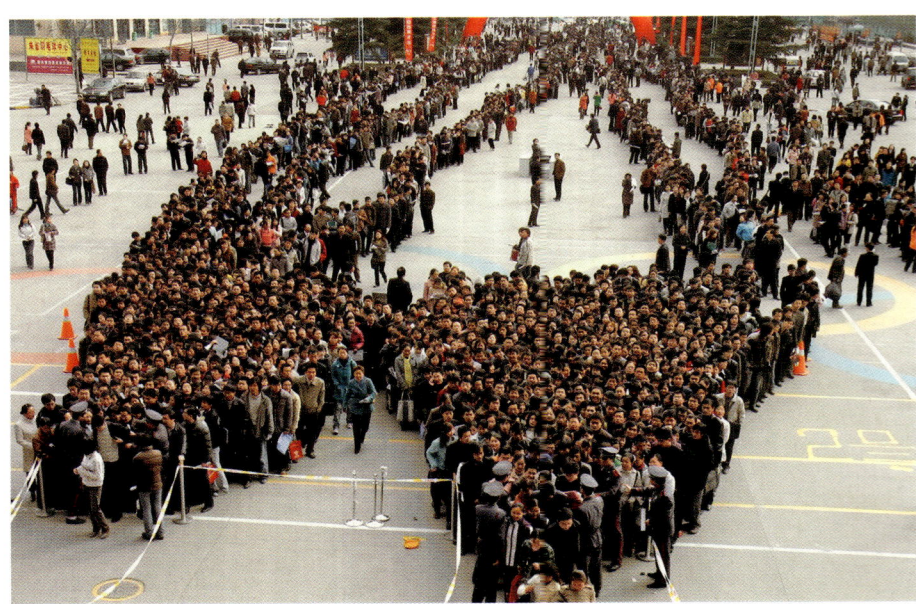

↑

Pu Feng, 2006

Female job seekers in line for an interview with a potential employer.

Weibliche Arbeitsuchende stehen bei einem potenziellen Arbeitgeber für ein Vorstellungsgespräch an.

Des femmes à la recherche d'un travail font la queue pour un entretien avec un employeur potentiel.

↓

Wang Jing, 2005

Queues outside of an employment office in Xi'an. University graduates are increasingly faced with the unfamiliar challenge of seeking employment. In 2006, the Ministry of Education estimated that just under five million students would graduate from university in 2007, also just under a million more than in 2006. Almost to the end of the 1990s, graduates were assigned work by the State. Today, they can attend the burgeoning number of job fairs springing up around the country.

Vor einer Arbeitsvermittlung in Xi'an bilden sich lange Schlangen. Universitätsabsolventen sehen sich zunehmend mit der ungewohnten Situation der Arbeitssuche konfrontiert. 2006 schätzte das Erziehungsministerium, dass 2007 etwa 5 Millionen Studenten ihr Studium beenden würden, knapp eine Million mehr als 2006. Fast bis Ende der 1990er Jahre wurde den Absolventen vom Staat Arbeit zugewiesen. Heute können sie die wachsende Zahl der Jobmärkte besuchen, die überall im Land entstehen.

De longues queues se forment devant un bureau du travail à Xi'an. Les diplômés de l'université sont de plus en plus confrontés au nouveau défi de trouver un emploi. En 2006, le Ministère de l'éducation estimait que près de cinq millions d'étudiants seraient diplômés en 2007, soit près d'un million de plus qu'en 2006. Presque jusqu'à la fin des années 1990, l'État offrait des postes à ces étudiants. Aujourd'hui ils assistent aux nombreux salons de l'emploi qui se multiplient dans l'ensemble du pays.

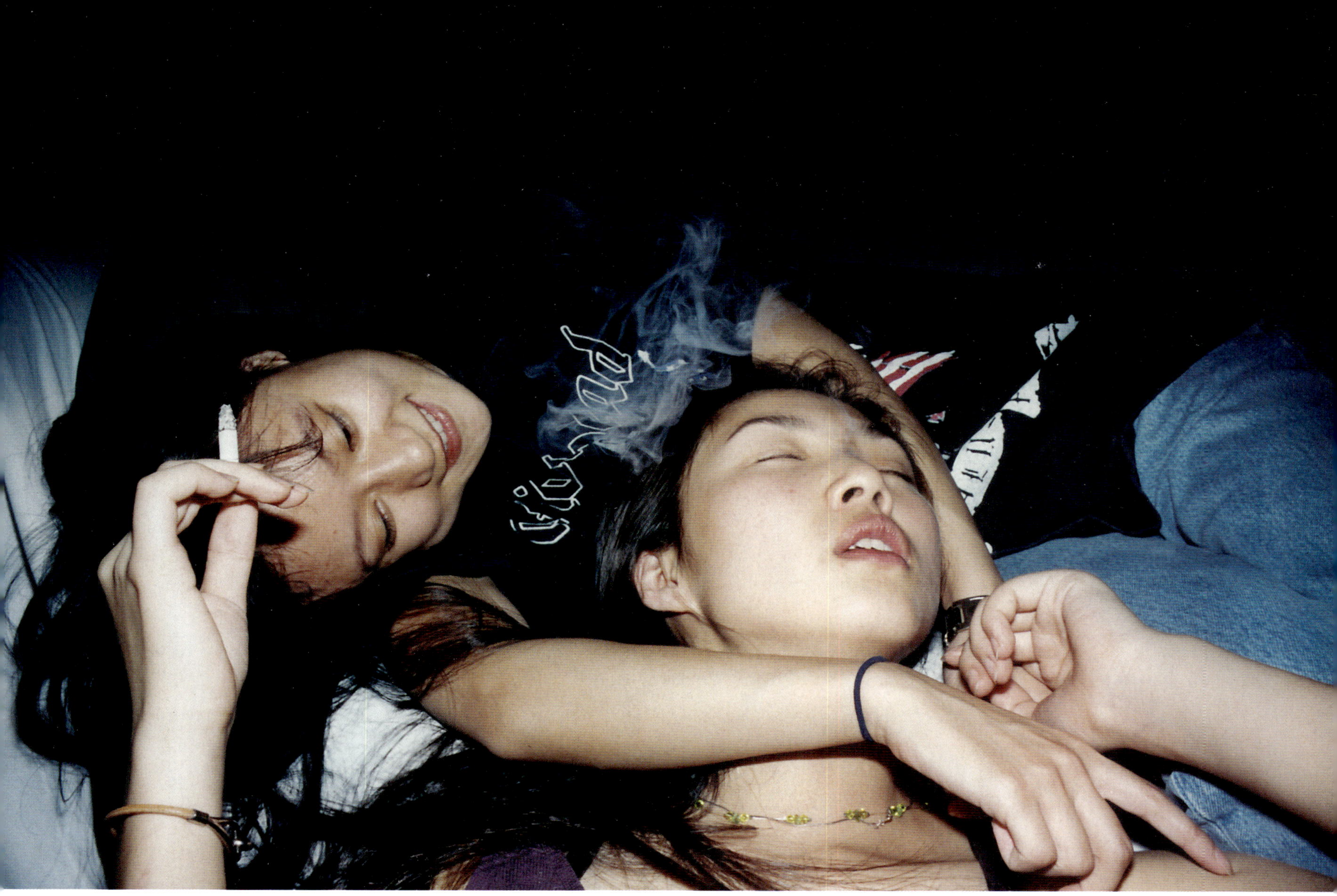

↑
Zhou Yue, 2000

In the small hours of the morning, two very laid back Chinese friends hang out in a Beijing nightclub.

In den frühen Morgenstunden hängen zwei sehr ,entspannte' chinesische Freundinnen in einem Nachtclub in Peking ab.

Aux petites heures du matin, deux amis chinois très décontractés traînent dans un night-club de Pékin.

→
Yong He, 2003

Two Chinese women dancing in a Shanghai nightclub. This type of "head shaking" was a common sight from the late 1990s, as China's youth followed its counterparts in other, developed countries and began to explore the influx of happy drugs, like ecstasy.

Zwei Chinesinnen tanzen in einem Nachtclub in Shanghai. Das „Kopfschwenken" kam Ende der 1990er-Jahre in Mode, als Chinas Jugend dem Vorbild ihrer Altersgenossen in anderen Industrieländern folgte und begann, die Wirkung von Partydrogen wie Ecstasy zu erproben.

Deux jeunes Chinoises dansent dans une boîte de nuit de Shanghai. Cette façon d'agiter la tête était très répandue à la fin des années 1990 lorsque la jeunesse chinoise suivait les modes des pays développés et commençait à explorer l'effet des drogues dites du bonheur, comme l'ecstasy.

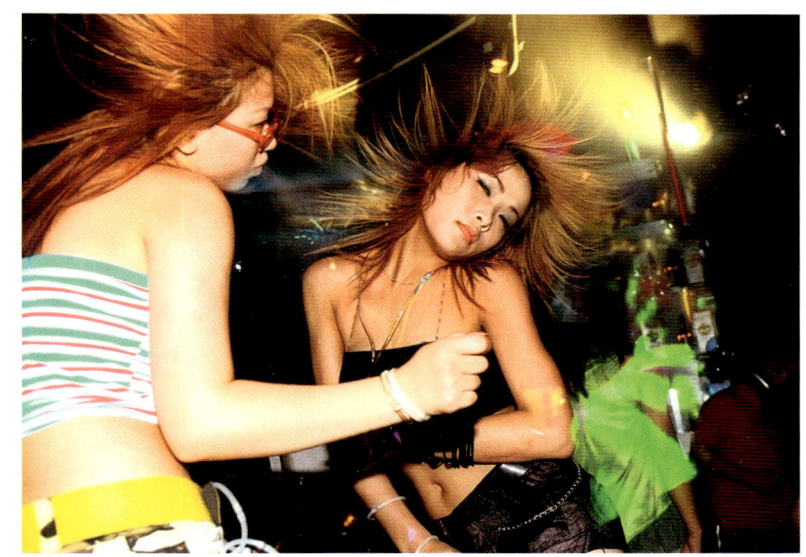

pp. 386/387
Xu Haifeng, 2006

Shanghai's famed Xiangyang market, prior to its closure in June 2006 to make way for new development amidst soaring property prices across China, but especially in Shanghai.

Shanghais berühmter Xiangyang-Markt vor seiner Schließung im Juni 2006. Bei den rapide steigenden Grundstückspreisen in ganz China, insbesondere aber in Shanghai, sollte Platz für neue Bebauung geschaffen werden.

Le fameux marché de Xiangyang à Shanghai avant sa clôture en juin 2006 pour laisser place à une opération immobilière. Les prix des terrains ont connu une très forte hausse, en particulier à Shanghai.

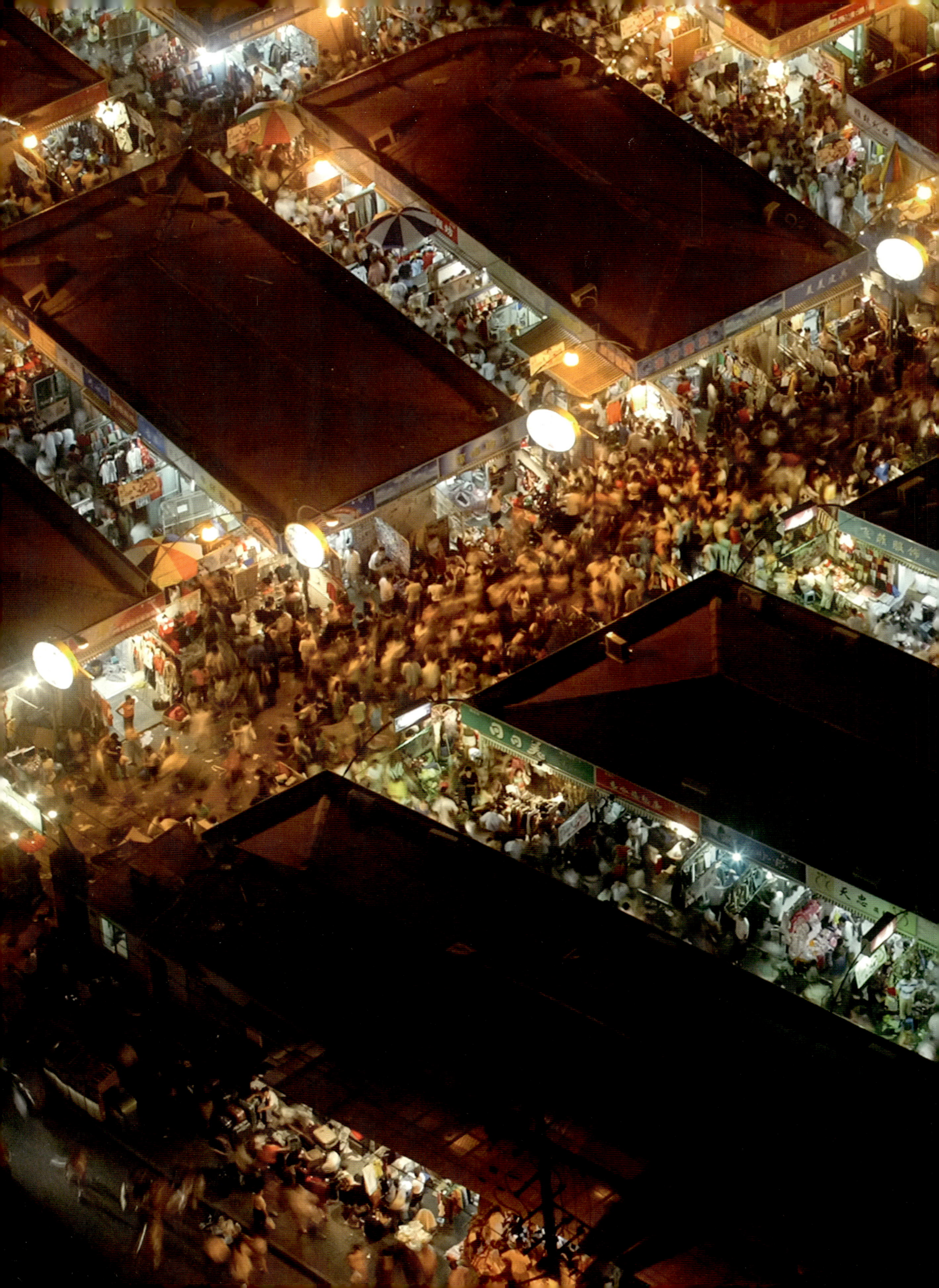

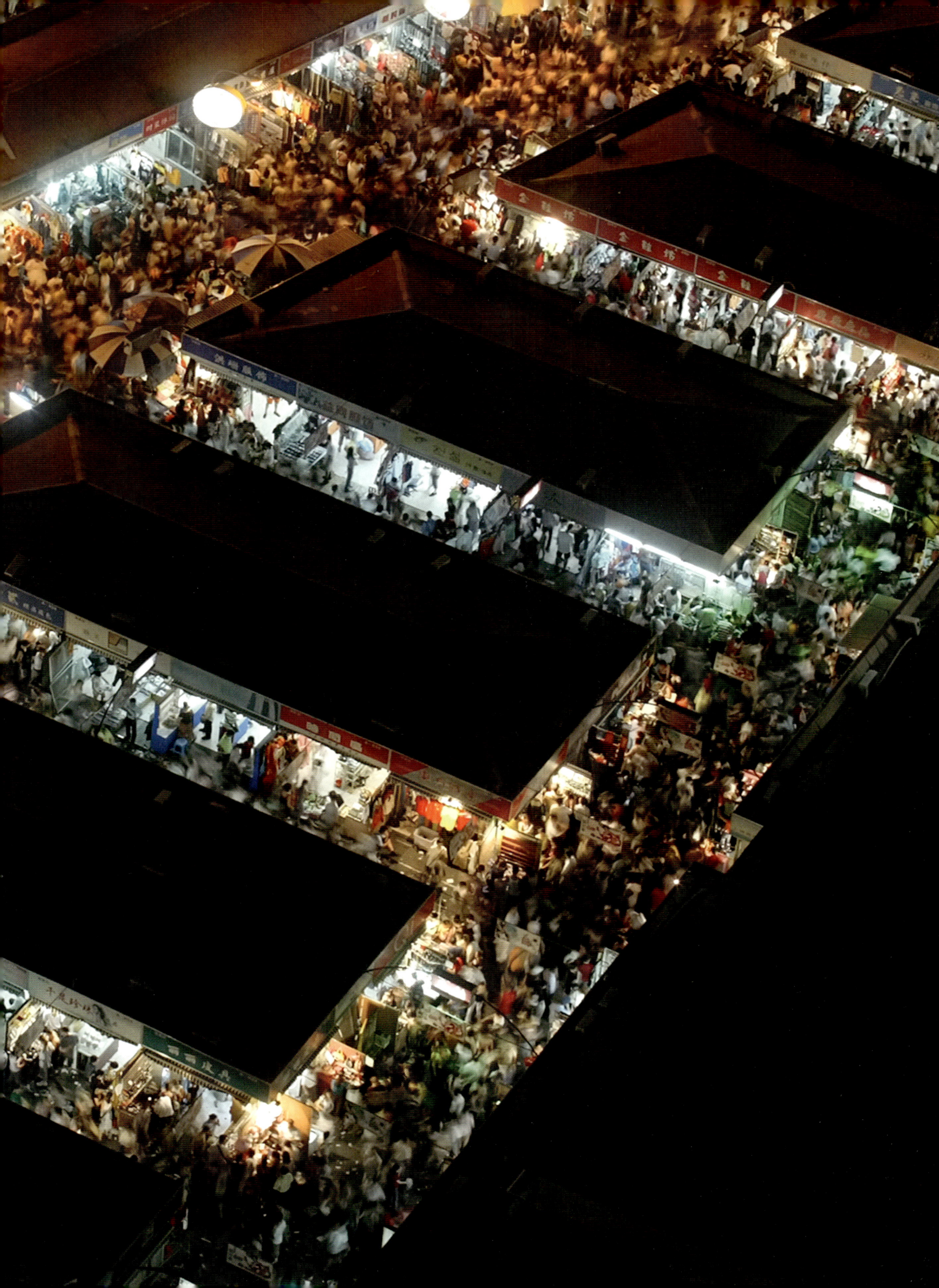

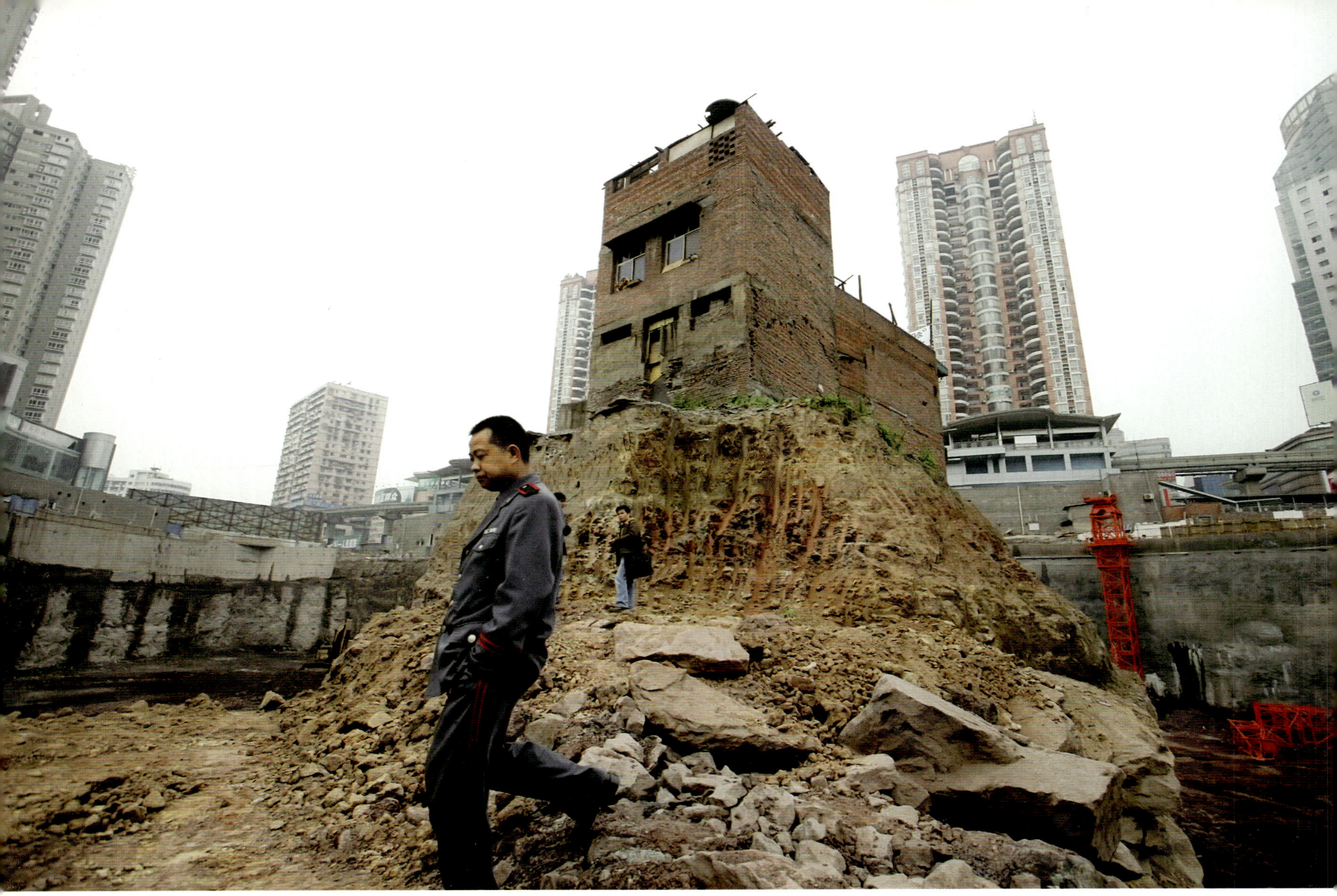

Ren Wen 2007

One lone house in Chongqing, and its owner who refused to vacate it, becomes an island in a monstrous pit dug to lay the foundations of a massive new construction. The story made headlines around the world. The National People's Congress in 2007 at last approved the constitutional rights of private property for the first time in the history of the new People's Republic. The owner of the house that remains standing, received a large compensation from the developer. The house was demolished to make way for a shopping mall .

Ein einsames Haus in Chongqing und seine Besitzerin, die sich weigert auszuziehen, wird zu einer Insel in einer riesigen Baugrube, die für die Fundamente eines großen Neubauprojekts ausgehoben wurde. Die Geschichte sorgte überall auf der Welt für Schlagzeilen. Schließlich billigte der Nationale Volkskongress 2007 zum ersten Mal in der Geschichte der neuen Volksrepublik die verfassungsmäßigen Rechte auf Privatbesitz. Die Besitzerin des stehen gebliebenen Hauses wurde vom Bauträger mit einem großzügigen Geldbetrag entschädigt. Das Haus wurde abgerissen, um Platz für den Bau eines Einkaufszentrums zu machen.

Une maison de Chongqing que sa propriétaire refuse d'évacuer s'est transformée en îlot au centre d'une monstrueuse excavation creusée pour les fondations d'un grand programme immobilier. L'histoire a fait les titres des journaux du monde entier. En 2007 enfin, le Congrés national populaire a approuvé des droits à la propriété privée pour la première fois dans l'histoire de la République. La propriétaire de la maison a fini par recevoir une forte somme du promoteur pour accepter la démolition de sa maison et faire place nette à la construction d'un centre commercial.

Lu Guang, 2006

Soil erosion in the Yellow river region of Inner Mongolia is so severe that sands threaten to cover this village.

Die Bodenerosion am Gelben Fluss in der Inneren Mongolei ist so gravierend, dass der Sand droht, dieses Dorf unter sich zu begraben.

L'érosion des sols dans la région du Fleuve jaune en Mongolie intérieure est si sévère que le sable menace ce village.

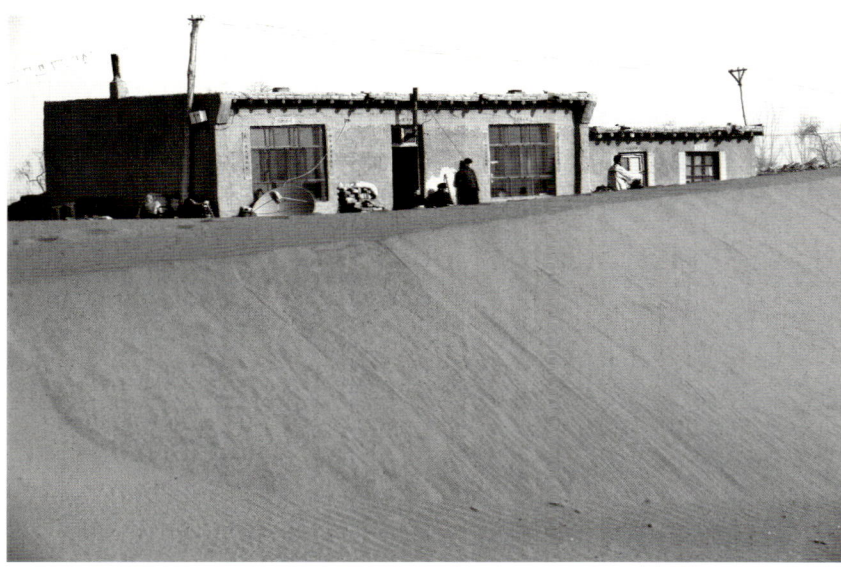

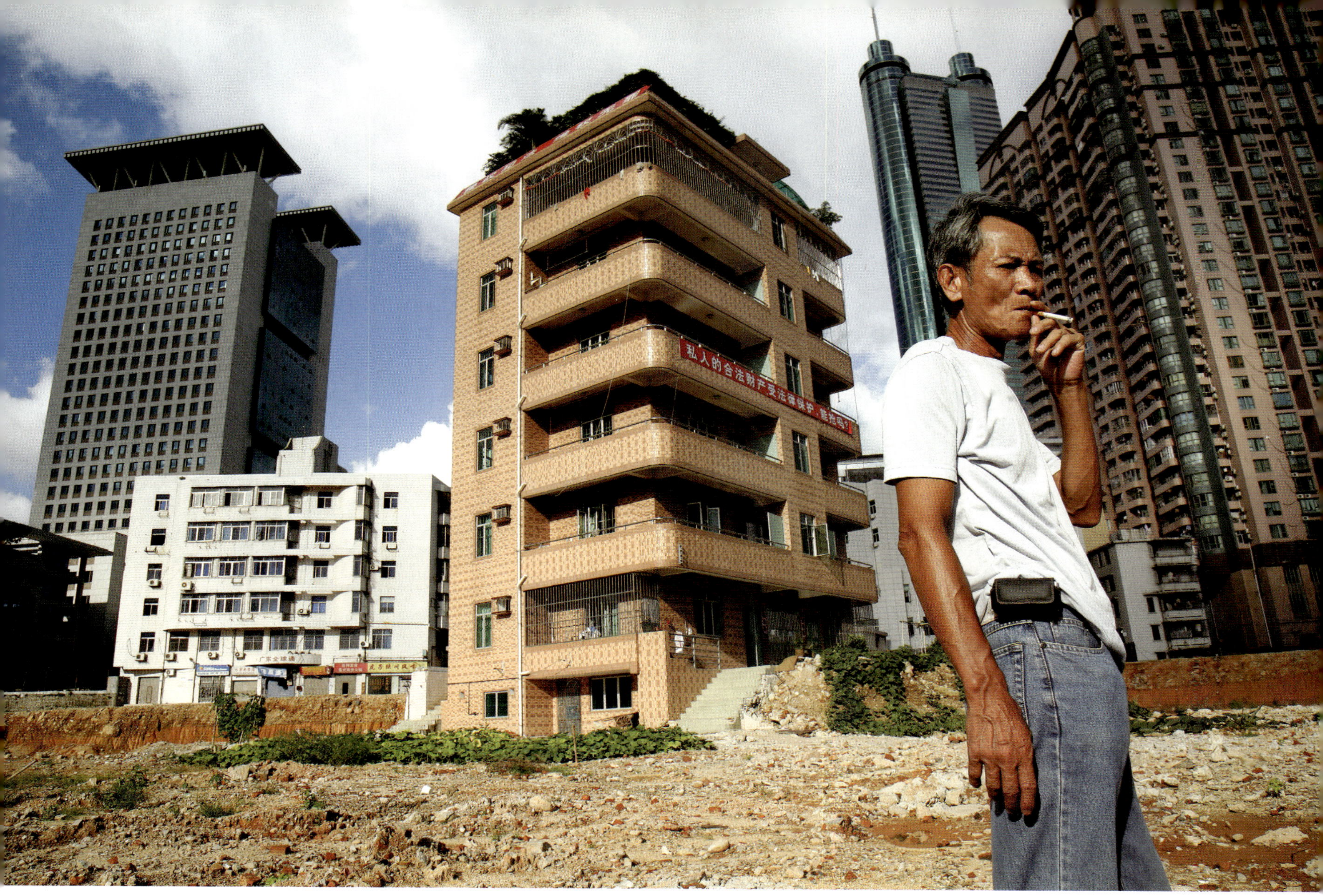

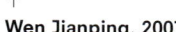

↑

Wen Jianping, 2007

Shenzhen resident Cai Zhuxiang owns one floor of the building that stands behind him. Although the building is due for demolition, Cai refuses to move. In 2004, a revision of the Constitution described the protection of private property for the first time in China's history. But prior to governmental approval for a new property law in 2002, local governments and developers repeatedly forced people to vacate their land and buildings to make way for the new projects. It is hoped that the new property law will better protect private property.

Cai Zhuxiang, Einwohner von Shenzhen, ist Eigentümer eines Geschosses in dem hinter ihm aufragenden Gebäude. Obgleich das Gebäude abgerissen werden soll, weigert sich Cai auszuziehen. Aufgrund einer 2004 erfolgten Revision der Verfassung ist in Chinas Geschichte zum ersten Mal vom Schutz des Privateigentums die Rede. Ehe aber vonseiten der Regierung ein neues Eigentumsrecht anerkannt wurde, das über den Besitz von Liegenschaften weitere Klarheit schuf, zwangen noch 2002 Kommunalverwaltungen und Bauträger wiederholt Menschen, ihr Land und ihre Häuser zu räumen, um Platz für neue Projekte zu schaffen. Man hofft, dass das neue Vermögensrecht zum Schutz des Privateigentums Rechtssicherheit schaffen wird.

Résident de Shenzhen, Cai Zhuxiang possède un étage de l'immeuble situé derrière lui. Bien qu'il soit voué à la démolition, il refuse de partir. En 2004, une révision de la constitution a abordé la protection de la propriété privée pour la première fois dans l'histoire chinoise. Mais avant que le gouvernement ne fasse voter un nouveau loi clarifiant le statut de la propriété, en 2002, des administrations locales et des promoteurs ont fréquemment forcé des gens à quitter leur terre et leurs logements pour laisser la place à de nouveaux projets. On espère que la nouvelle loi précisera davantage la protection de la propriété privée.

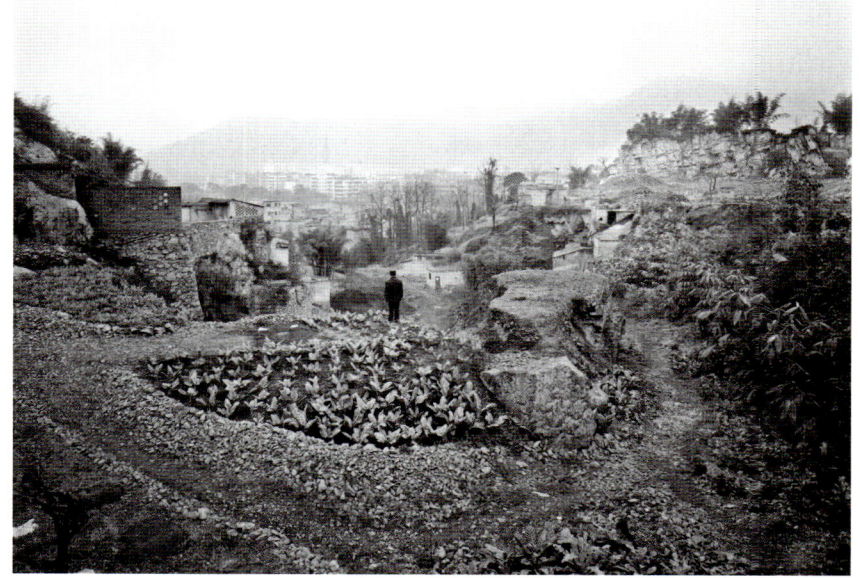

↑

Zhu Yan, 2006

Reflecting the overspill of urban centers into the rural suburbs, Zhu Yan juxtaposes a typical vegetable plot with a city looming in the distance.

Indem Zhu Yan neben einem typischen Gemüsegarten eine in der Ferne aufragende Stadt fotografiert, thematisiert er das Vordringen der Stadtzentren in die ländlichen Vororte.

Image du débordement des centres urbains sur les faubourgs ruraux. Le photographe a juxtaposé un champ de légumes et la menace de la grande ville qui s'élève dans le lointain.

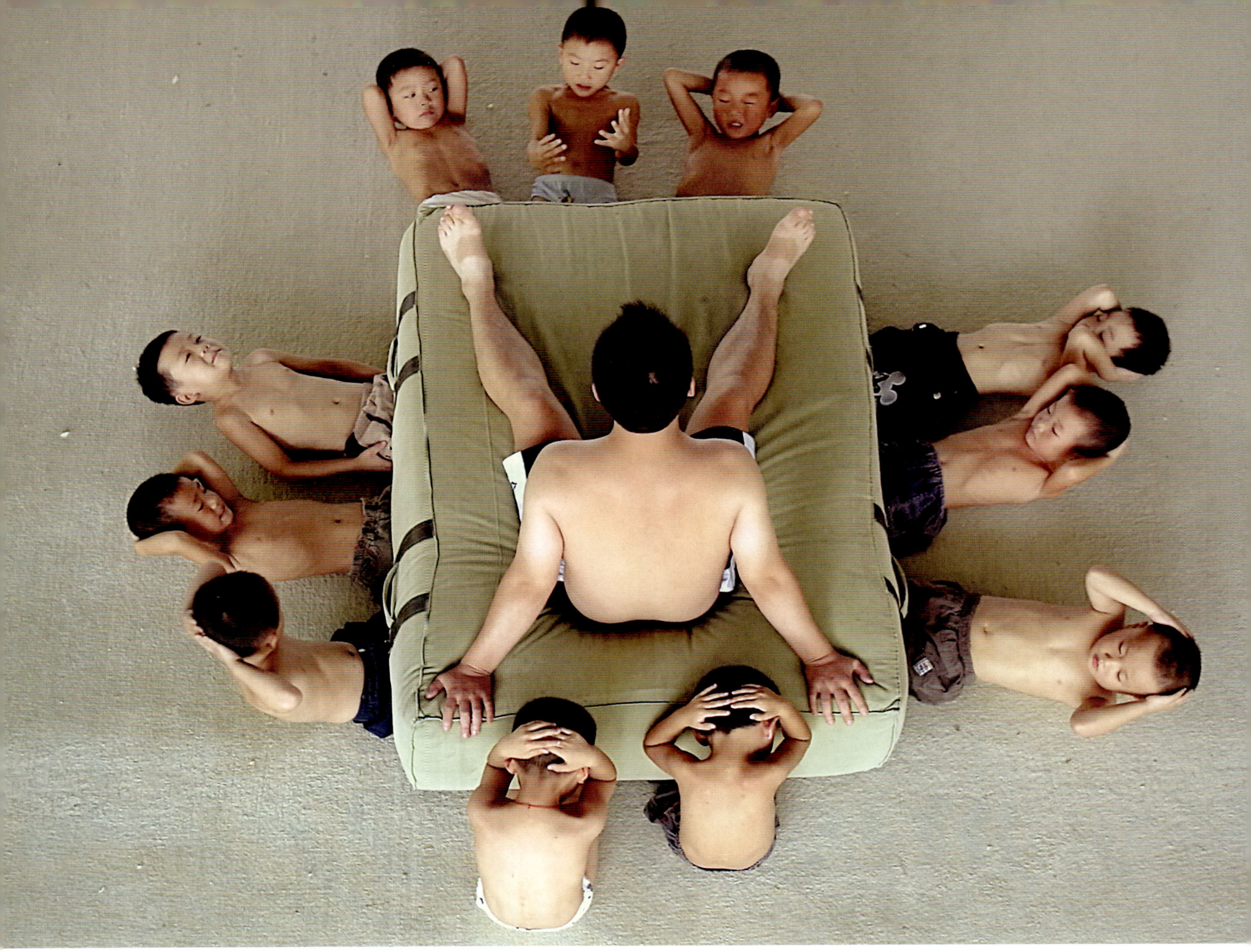

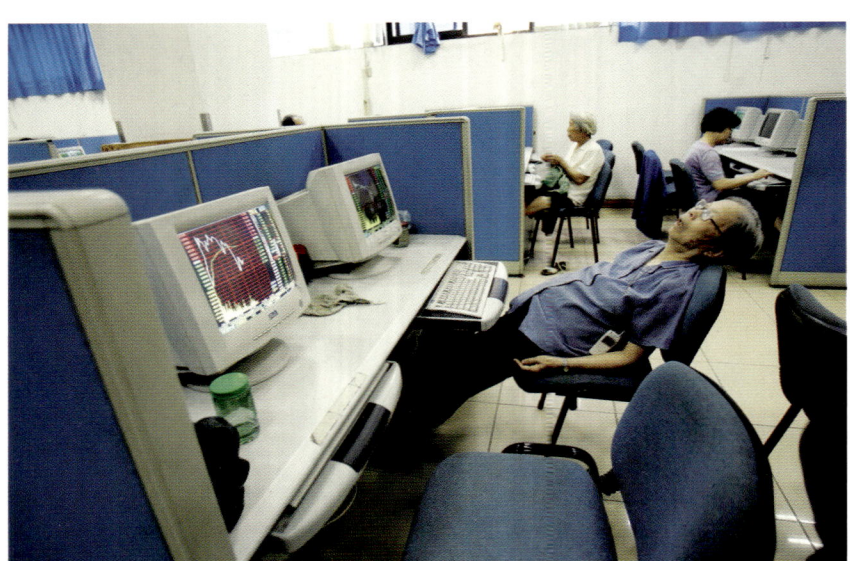

↑

Qiu Yan, 2004

Children practising gymnastics at a special school for athletes in Hubei province.

Kinder bei Turnübungen an einer speziellen Sportschule in der Provinz Hubei.

Des enfants à l'entraînement de gymnastique dans une école d'athlétisme de la province du Hubei.

←

Lei Yu, 2007

An elderly lady in the southwestern municipality of Chongqing takes a break from the hectic pace of her day-trading activities in a community computer center.

Eine ältere Frau in der im Südwesten gelegenen Stadtprovinz Chongqing legt bei ihrer hektischen Arbeit als Tagesspekulantin in einem gemeindeeigenen Computerzentrum eine Pause ein.

Une vieille dame de la ville méridionale de Chongqing se repose des rudes heures passées à boursicoter devant un ordinateur dans un centre local d'informatique.

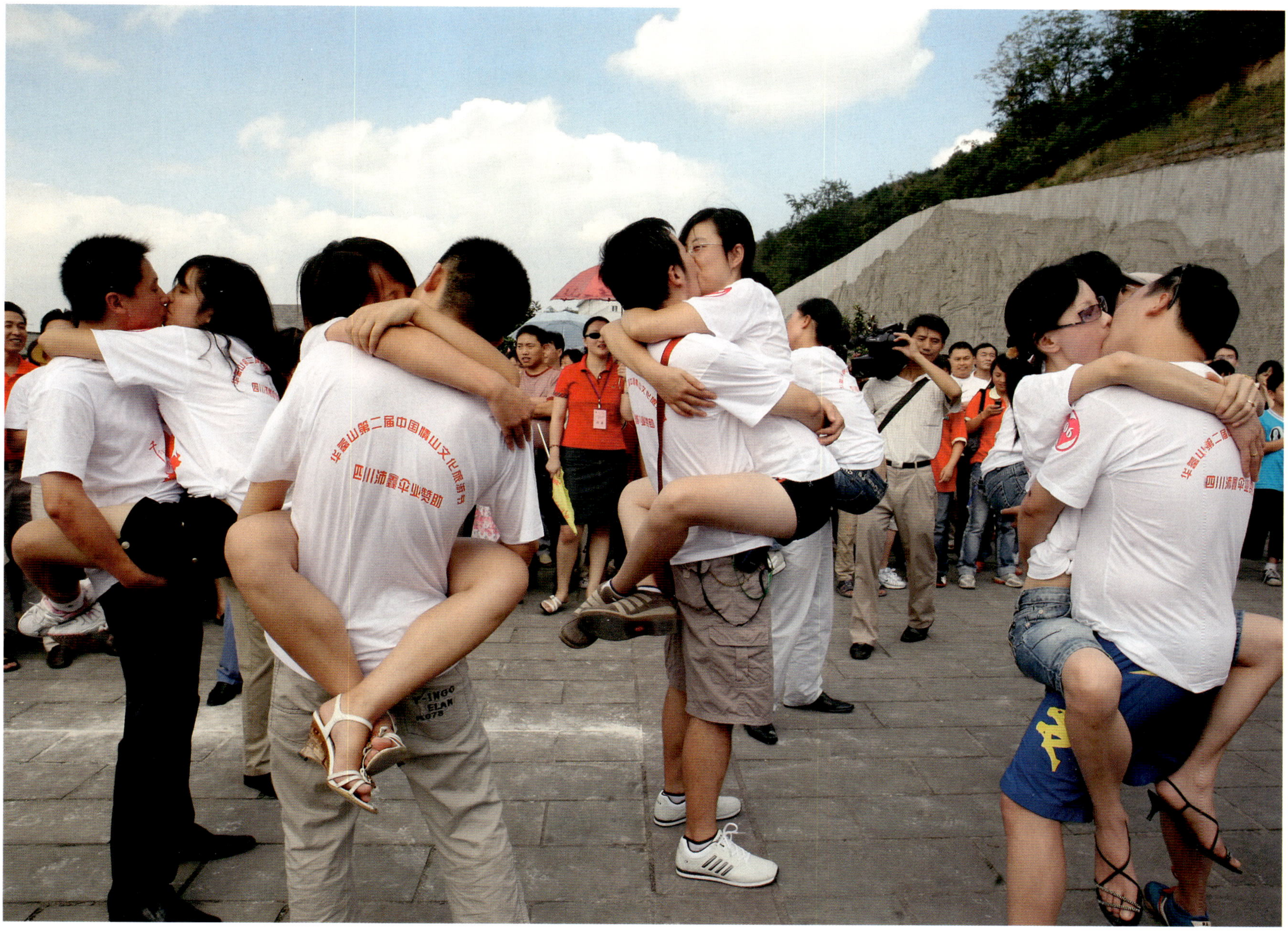

Miao Jiaxin, 2004

A Shanghai bride has her picture taken in the full splendor of an imported wedding gown. Nowadays, weddings are huge productions. In the northeast region, a news report described that one wedding motorcade consisted of 34 SUVs and eight Landcruisers, which caused a traffic jam stretching for many kilometers. The same wedding banquet had one hundred tables, each costing 1,900 Yuan (US $ 250).

Eine Braut in Shanghai lässt sich in der ganzen Pracht eines importierten Hochzeitskleides fotografieren. Heutzutage werden Hochzeiten aufwendig inszeniert. Im Nordosten des Landes berichtete ein Nachrichtenbeitrag anlässlich einer Hochzeit, von einer aus 34 SUVs und acht Landcruisers bestehenden Autokolonne, die einen kilometerlangen Stau verursachte. Bei dieser Hochzeit wurde das Festessen an einhundert Tischen serviert, von denen jeder über 1.900 Yuan (200 Euro) kostete.

Une jeune mariée de Shanghai habillée d'une splendide robe importée se fait prendre en photo. Aujourd'hui, les mariages sont l'occasion de grandes mises en scène. Dans le nordest, un journal a parlé d'un défilé de mariage de plus de 34 SUV et huit Landcruisers, qui provoquèrent un embouteillage sur plusieurs kilomètres. Point d'orgue de la cérémonie : un banquet de 100 tables, chacune coûtant 1900 Yuan (200 Euro).

Qiu Haiying, 2007

A sign of the changing times: young couples take part in a daring kissing contest in Sichuan province.

Zeichen der sich ändernden Zeiten: Junge Paare nehmen an einem gewagten Kusswettbewerb in der Provinz Sichuan teil.

Signe des temps qui changent : de jeunes couples participent à un concours de baisers dans la province du Sichuan.

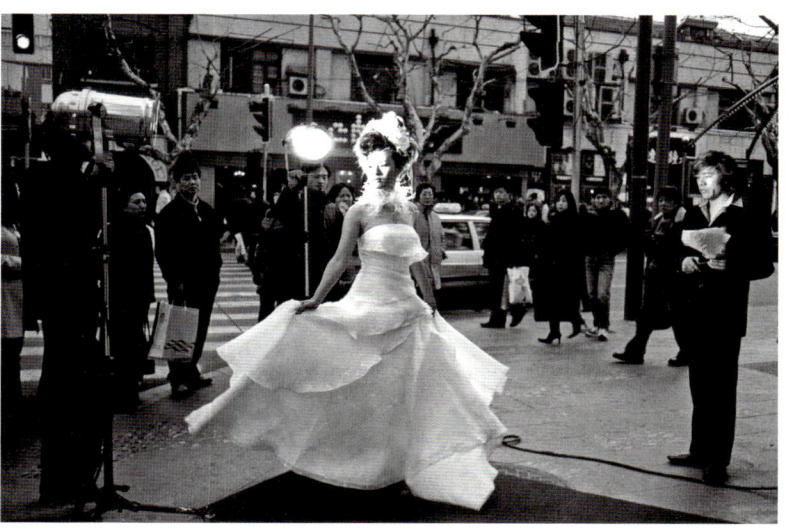

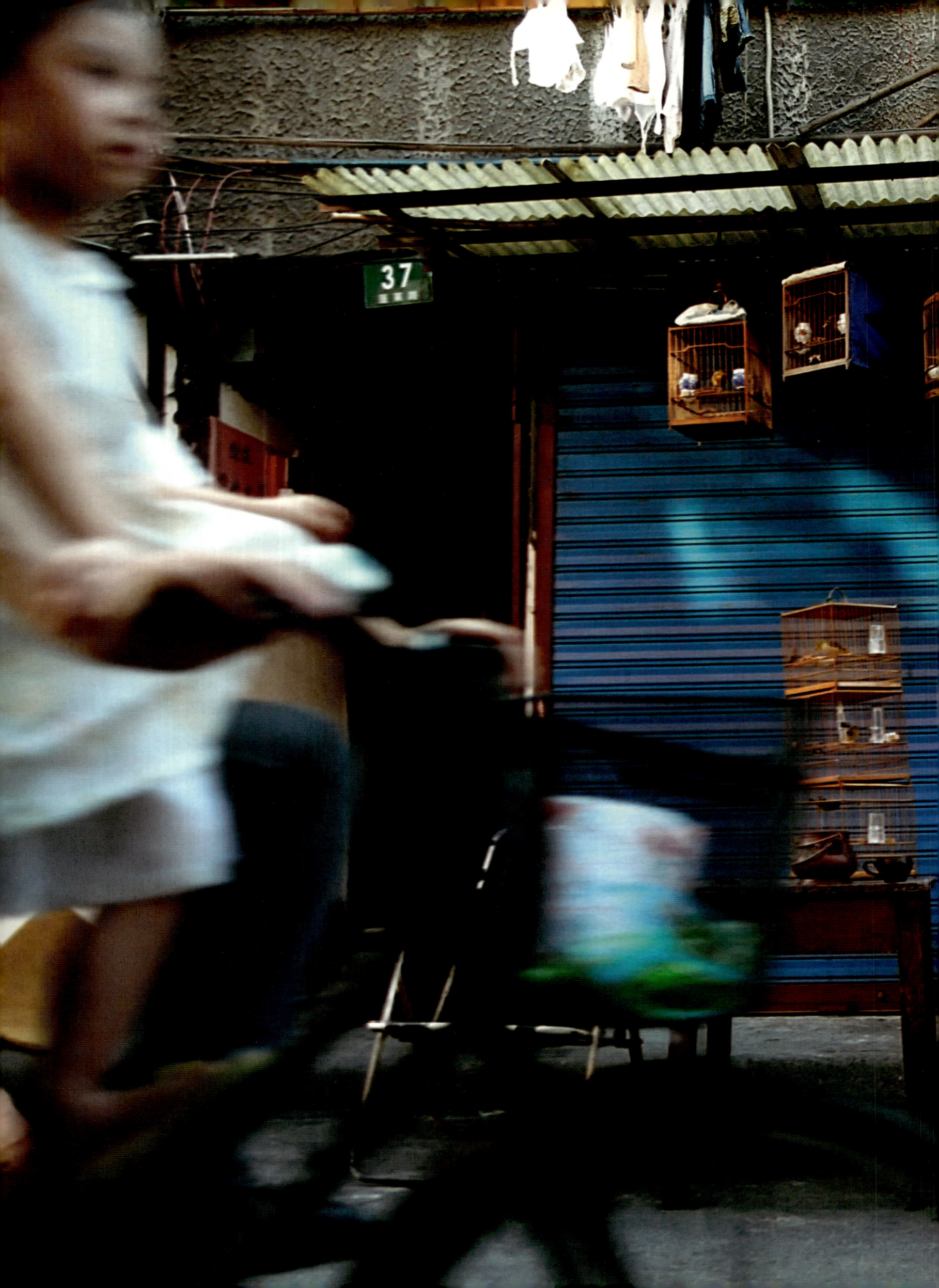

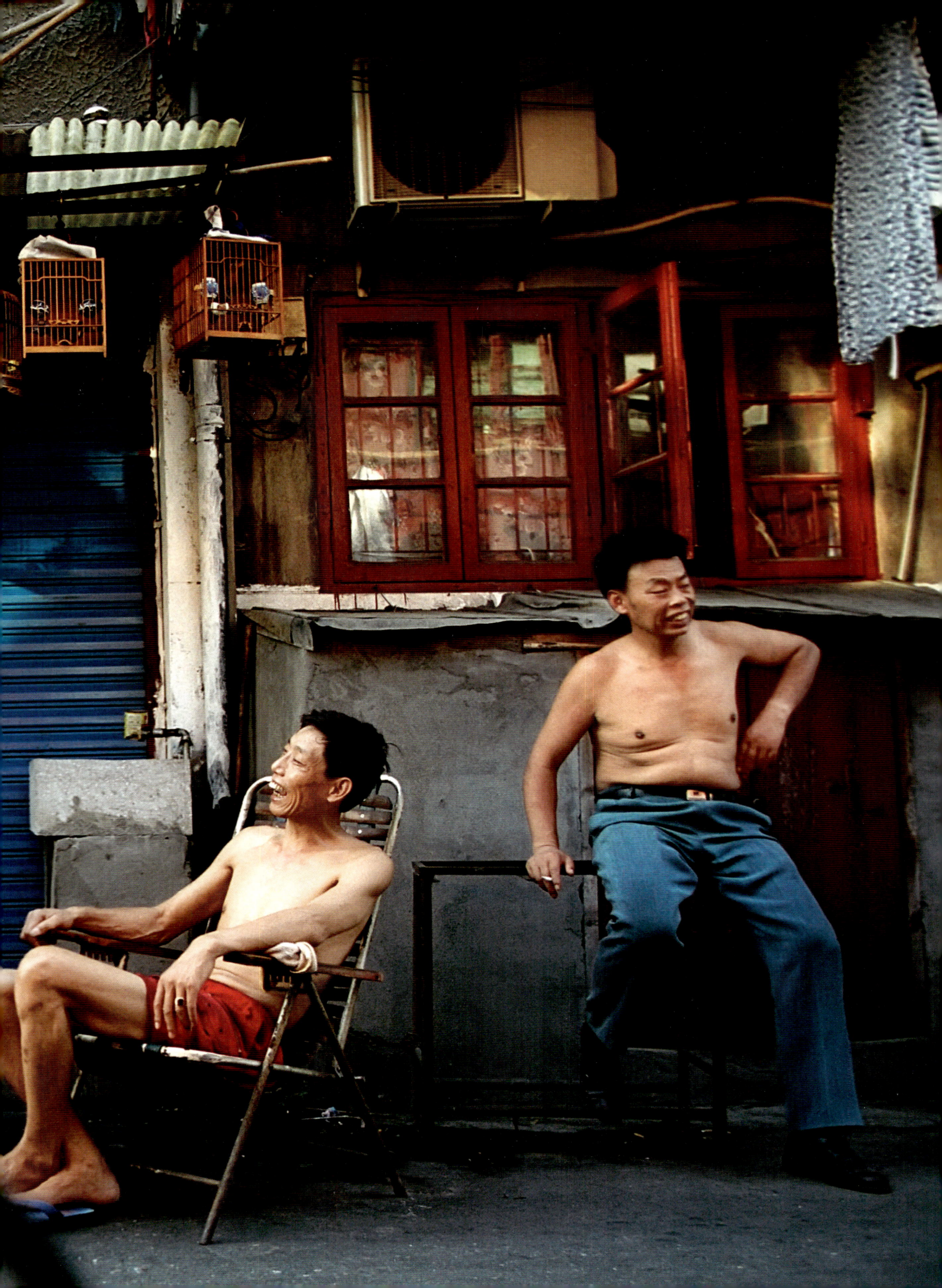

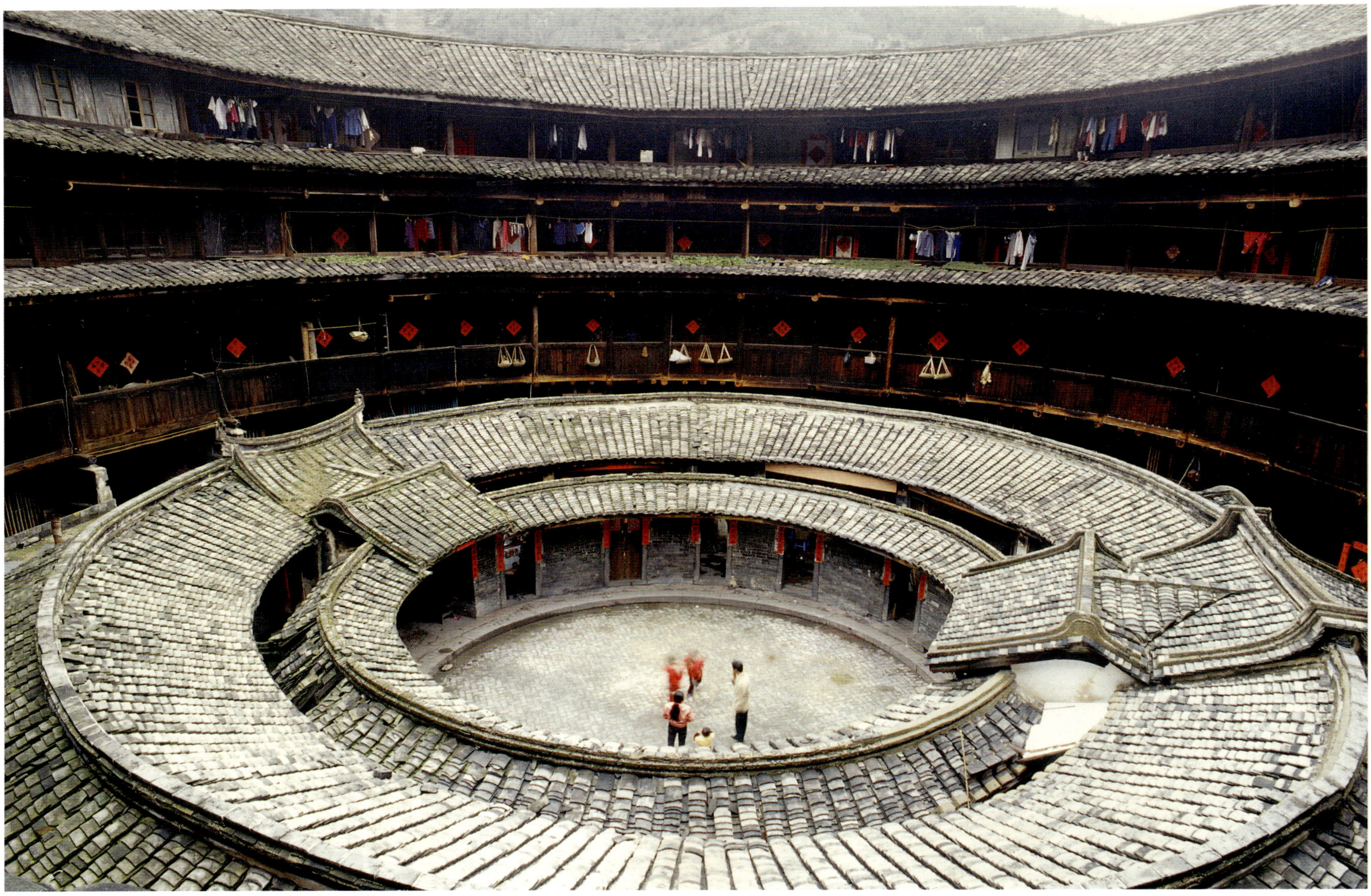

↑↓
Wei Ruoxun, 2007

Chinese earth houses in Yongding county, Fujian province. Chinese people from the northern plains (present-day provinces of Henan and Hebei) migrated south during the Song dynasty. The ancestral migrants are today known as the Hakka people whose descendants, about 30 families, still live in the houses and plant the rice fields in the area. The site is now under state protection, and has been designated a World Heritage Site by the United Nations.

Chinesische Erdhäuser im Kreis Yongding, Provinz Fujian. Während der Song Dynastie wanderten Chinesen aus den nördlichen Ebenen (den heutigen Provinzen Henan und Hebei) nach Süden. Die Nachfahren der Migranten werden heute Hakka-Leute genannt, deren Nachkommen, etwa dreißig Familien, noch immer in den Häusern wohnen und die Reisfelder in der Gegend bebauen. Die Stätte unterliegt jetzt dem staatlichen Schutz und wurde von den Vereinten Nationen zum Weltkulturerbe bestimmt.

Maisons en terre du canton de Yongding, province du Fujian. Des Chinois des plaines septentrionales (actuelles provinces du Hénan et du Hebei) émigrèrent vers le sud sous les dynasties Song. Les descendants – une trentaine de familles – de ces anciens migrants appelés aujourd'hui les Hakka, vivent toujours dans les mêmes maisons de terre et cultivent le riz. Le site est maintenant protégé et fait partie du Patrimoine de l'humanité de l'UNESCO.

pp. 392/393
Yong He, 2007

For those lucky enough to remain in the older communities of low-rise buildings in the center of Shanghai, the street is the focus of daily life. Here, residents gather to chat and give their birds some fresh air.

Für jene Glücklichen, die in den alten Vierteln mit niedriger Bebauung im Zentrum von Shanghai bleiben können, spielt sich das Alltagsleben auf der Straße ab. Hier treffen sich Bewohner zu einem Schwatz und gönnen ihren Vögeln etwas Frischluft.

Pour ceux qui ont la chance d'habiter dans les logements anciens des petits immeubles du centre de Shanghai, la rue est le centre de la vie quotidienne. Ici des résidents bavardent ou font prendre de l'air à leurs oiseaux.

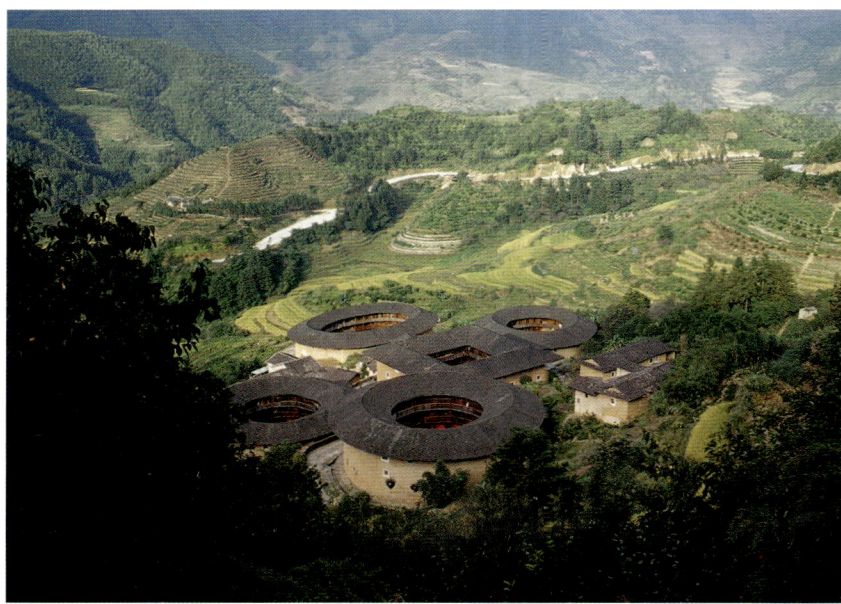

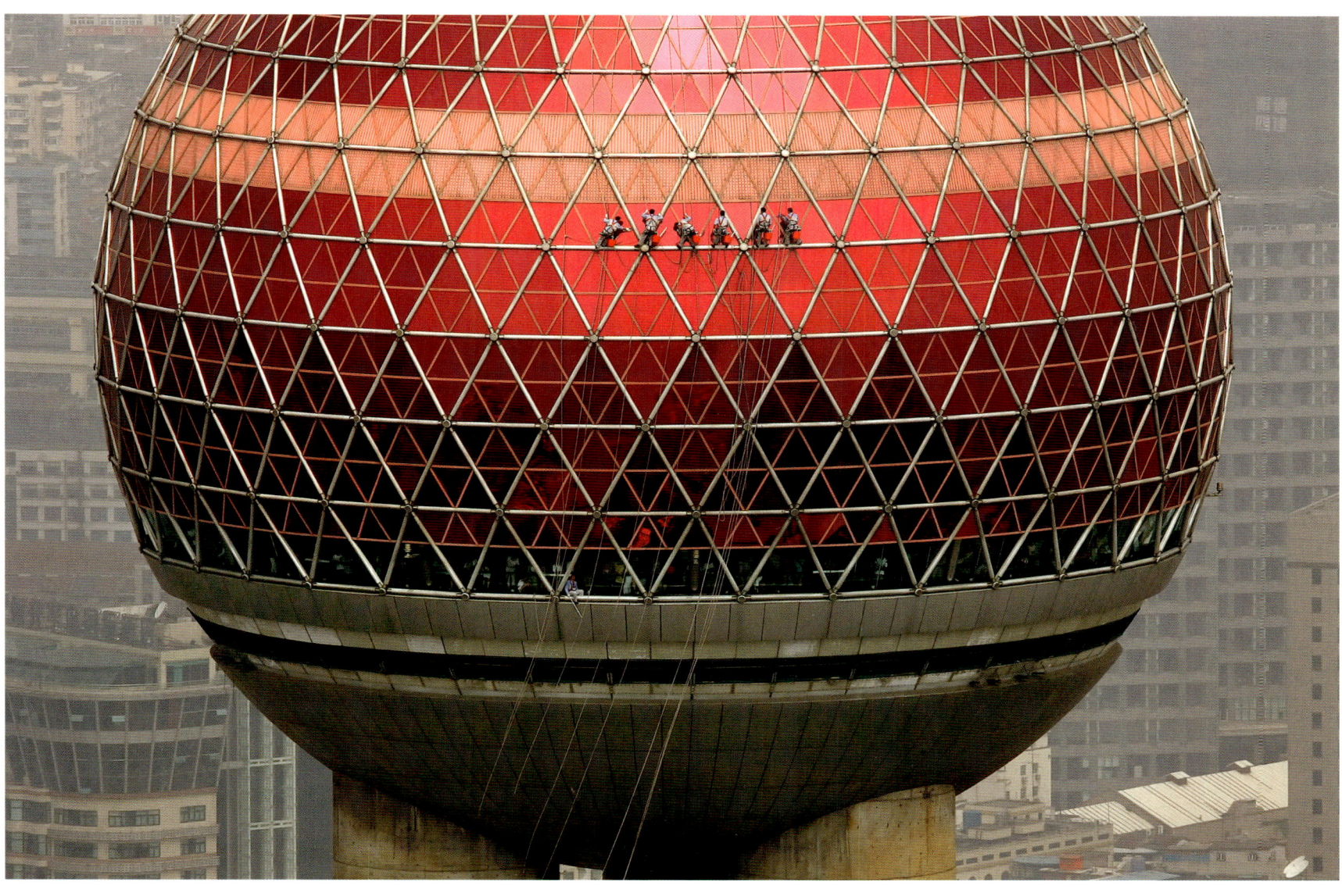

↑
Wang Jie, 2006

Window cleaners in Shanghai, dubbed "spidermen" for the routine feat they perform in cleaning the façade of the "pearl of Shanghai," the city's landmark television tower on the Pudong side of the famous Bund.

Fensterputzer in Shanghai werden „Spidermen" genannt, wegen der routinemäßigen Heldentat, die sie vollbringen, wenn sie die Fassade der „Perle von Shanghai" säubern, des imposanten Fernsehturms der Stadt auf der Pudong-Seite des berühmten Bund.

Des laveurs de vitres de Shanghai surnommés « Spidermen » nettoient la façade de la « Perle de Shanghai », la monumentale tour de télévision qui domine Pudong.

pp. 396/397
Chen Changfen, 2007

Snaking across northern China is the country's most famous landmark, the Great Wall. The Great Wall was conceived in the Spring and Autumn periods, when the work was begun, continuing through the Warring States Periods, the goal being to defend the three states of Yan, Zhao, and Qin. The separate walls created for the different states did not become a "great" wall until the Qin dynasty, when Emperor Qin Shihuang succeeded in joining the walls to fend off the Huns in the north. United, the Wall stretches almost 6,700 kilometers (4,200 miles) from east to west. Today, 2,000 years later, some sections of the Great Wall have fallen into ruin or others disappeared entirely, but efforts at conservation are beginning to be made.

Chinas berühmtestes Wahrzeichen, die Große Mauer, windet sich wie ein endlose Schlange durch den Norden des Landes. Erste Planungen für eine Große Mauer gehen auf die „Frühlings- und Herbstperiode" zurück. In jener Epoche begannen auch die Bauarbeiten, die während der „Zeit der Streitenden Reiche" fortgesetzt wurden. Ursprünglich waren die Befestigungen als Verteidigungswälle für die drei Staaten Yan, Zhao und Qin gedacht. Die für diese unterschiedlichen Reiche konzipierten Wälle wuchsen erst während der Qin-Dynastie zu einer „Großen Mauer" zusammen, nachdem es Kaiser Qin Shihuang gelungen war, die einzelnen Abschnitte zum Schutz gegen Einfälle der Hunnen miteinander zu verbinden. Der so zusammengefügte Wall schlängelt sich fast 6700 Kilometer weit von Osten nach Westen. Heute, 2000 Jahre später, sind manche Abschnitte der Großen Mauer nur noch Ruine, manche vollständig verfallen, doch die Bemühungen um einen Erhalt des Bauwerks zeigen erste Erfolge.

Serpentant à travers le nord du pays, la Grande muraille est le monument le plus célèbre de Chine. Sa réalisation débuta lors de la période des Printemps et Automnes et se prolongea lors de la période des Royaumes Combattants. L'objectif était alors de défendre les trois États de Yan, Zhao et Qi. Il fallut attendre la dynastie Qin pour que les trois murailles créées par chaque état n'en deviennent plus qu'une, lorsque l'Empereur Qin Shi Huangdi entreprit avec succès de les relier afin de repousser les Huns attaquant au nord. La muraille s'étend sur plus de 6 700 kilomètres d'est en ouest. Aujourd'hui, 2 000 ans plus tard, certaines parties tombent en ruine, quand elles n'ont pas complètement disparues, mais des efforts visant à sa conservation commencent à prendre effet.

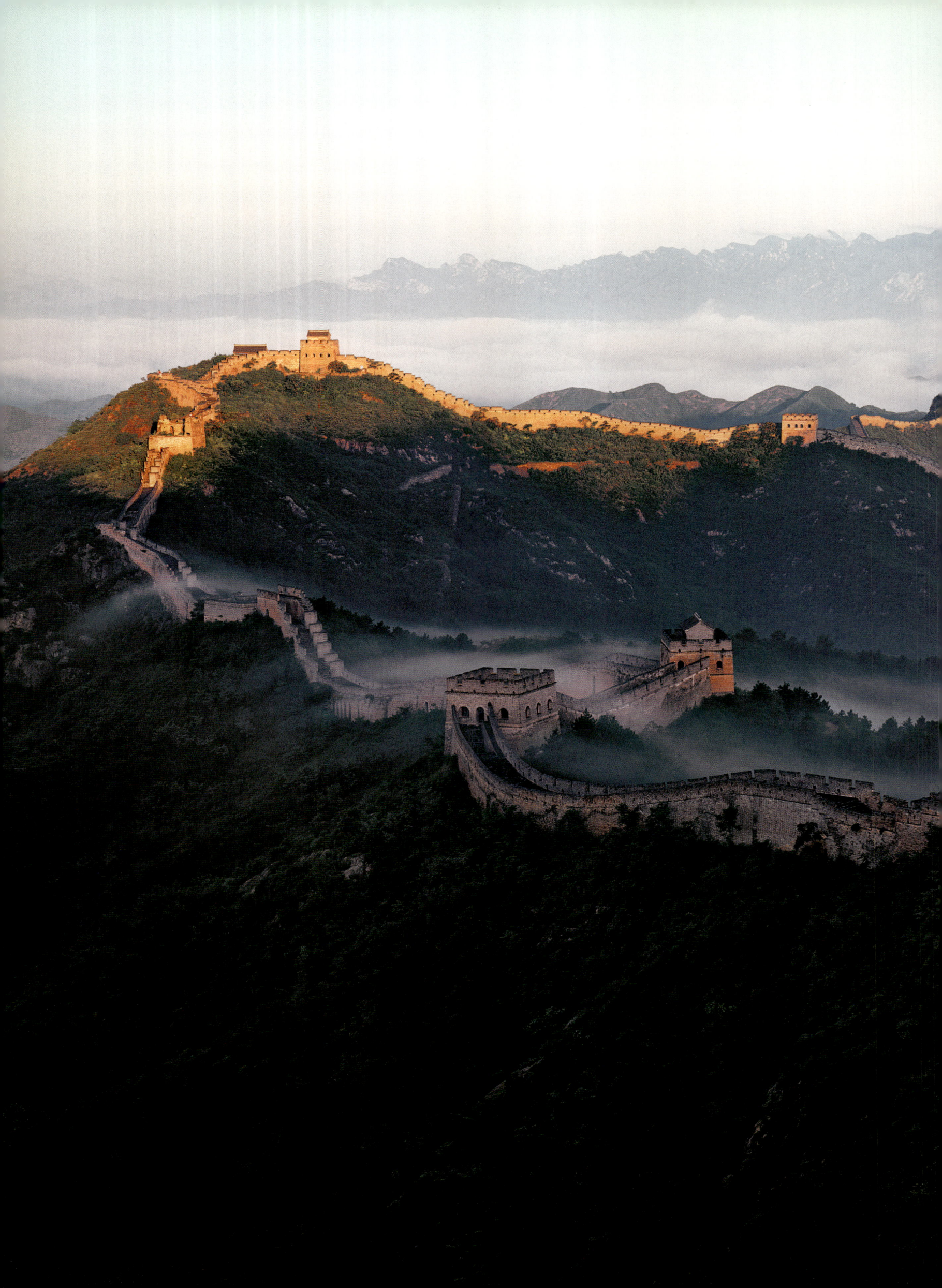

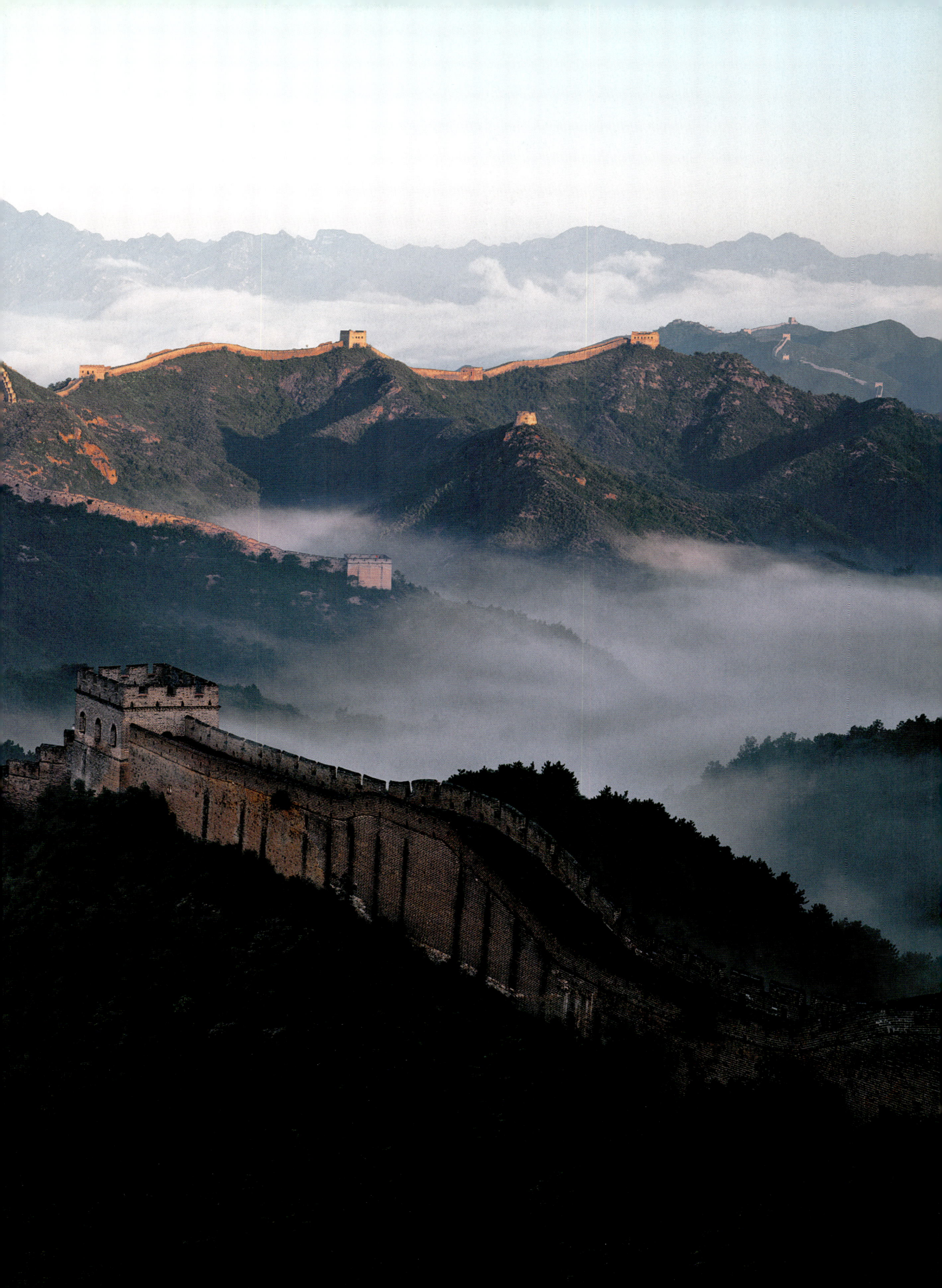

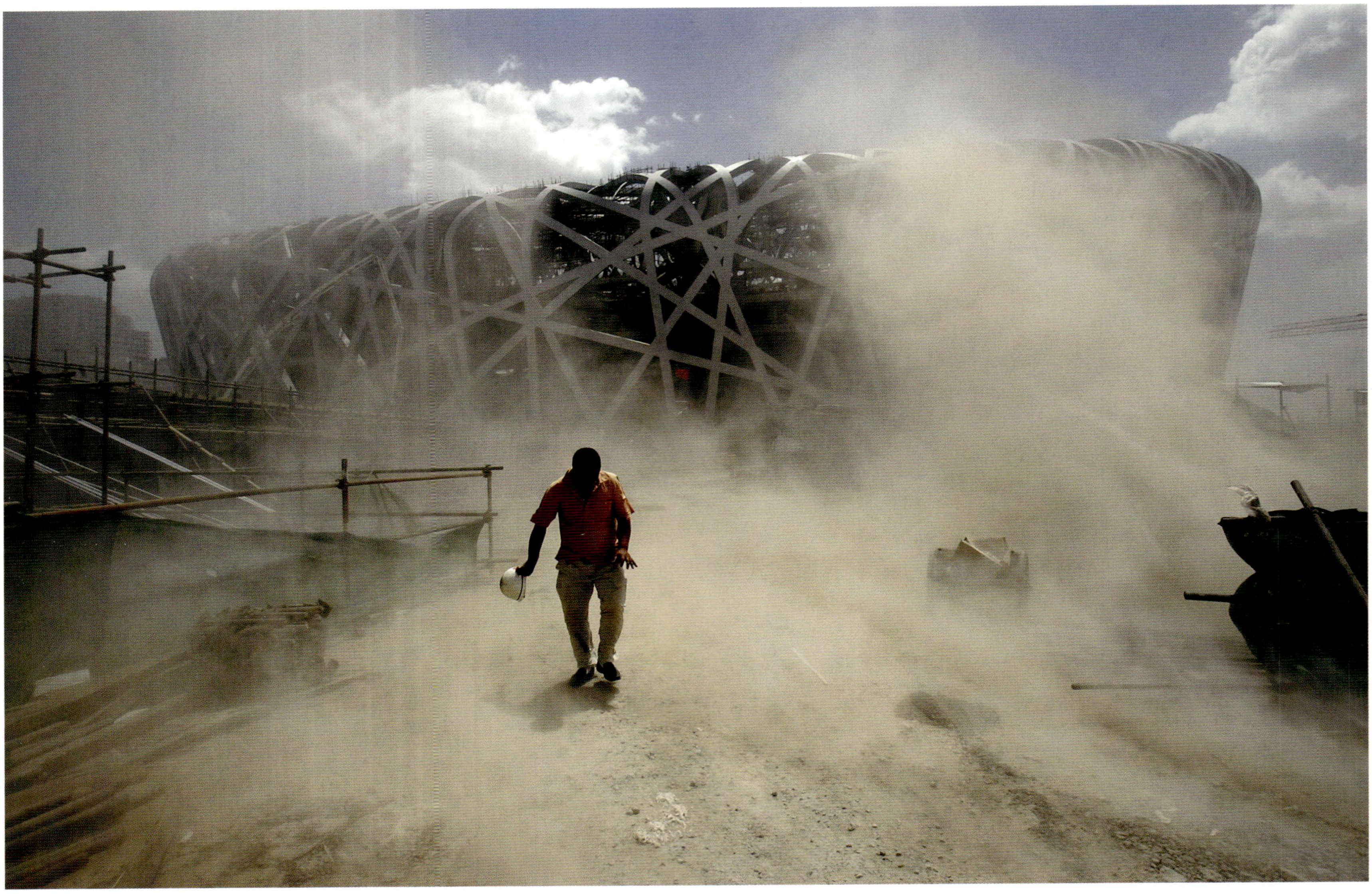

↑

Jin Cheng, 2007

A worker emerges from a dust cloud enveloping the futuristic national sports stadium, affectionately known as the "bird's nest," designed by leading international architects Herzog & de Meuron for the 2008 Beijing Olympics. As a landmark of modern engineering and design, the project was controversial from the outset. High costs and technical problems made the headlines, but the sheer feat of creating this unusual building justifies its monumental presence as a valuable addition to 21st-century architecture.

Ein Arbeiter taucht aus einer Staubwolke auf, die das futuristische – liebevoll Vogelnest genannte – nationale Sportstadion einhüllt, das von den zur internationalen Elite der Architektenschaft zählenden Schweizern Herzog & de Meuron für die Olympiade 2008 in Peking entworfen wurde. Dass dieses als Meilenstein moderner Technik und aktuellen Designs konzipierte Projekt umstritten sein würde, wusste man von Anfang an. Hohe Kosten und technische Probleme machten Schlagzeilen, aber schon der Entwurf dieses höchst ungewöhnlichen Gebäudes allein rechtfertigt seine monumentale Präsenz als wertvollen Beitrag zur Architektur des 21. Jahrhunderts.

Un ouvrier émerge du nuage de poussière qui enveloppe le futuriste stade national surnommé le «nid d'oiseau», conçu par les grands architectes suisses Herzog et de Meuron pour les Jeux olympiques de 2008. Monument d'ingénierie et de conception, le projet a été controversé dès l'origine. Son coût élevé et de multiples problèmes techniques ont fait les gros titres de la presse, mais la satisfaction de créer une construction aussi novatrice justifie cette présence impressionnante, apport remarqué à l'architecture du XXIe siècle.

→

Jason Lee, 2007

The waterlogged public area in front of the Grand National Theater in Beijing during a waterproof test. Construction of the theater was completed in October 2007, opening its doors to the public in December with performances by the China National Symphony Orchestra.

Der überschwemmte Platz vor dem Großen Nationaltheater in Peking während eines Tests auf Wasserdichtigkeit. Der Bau des Theaters wurde im Oktober 2007 fertig gestellt, und im Dezember öffnete es seine Pforten mit einem Konzert des Nationalen Chinesischen Symphonieorchesters.

La place publique devant le Grand théâtre national de Pékin pendant un test d'étanchéité. La construction de cette salle s'est achevée en octobre 2007. L'inauguration en décembre a été marquée par des concerts de l'Orchestre philharmonique national de Chine.

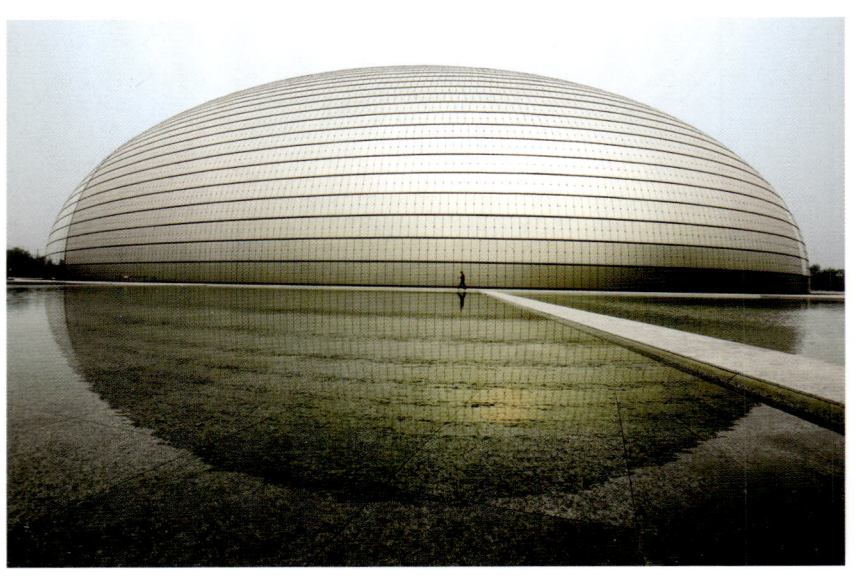

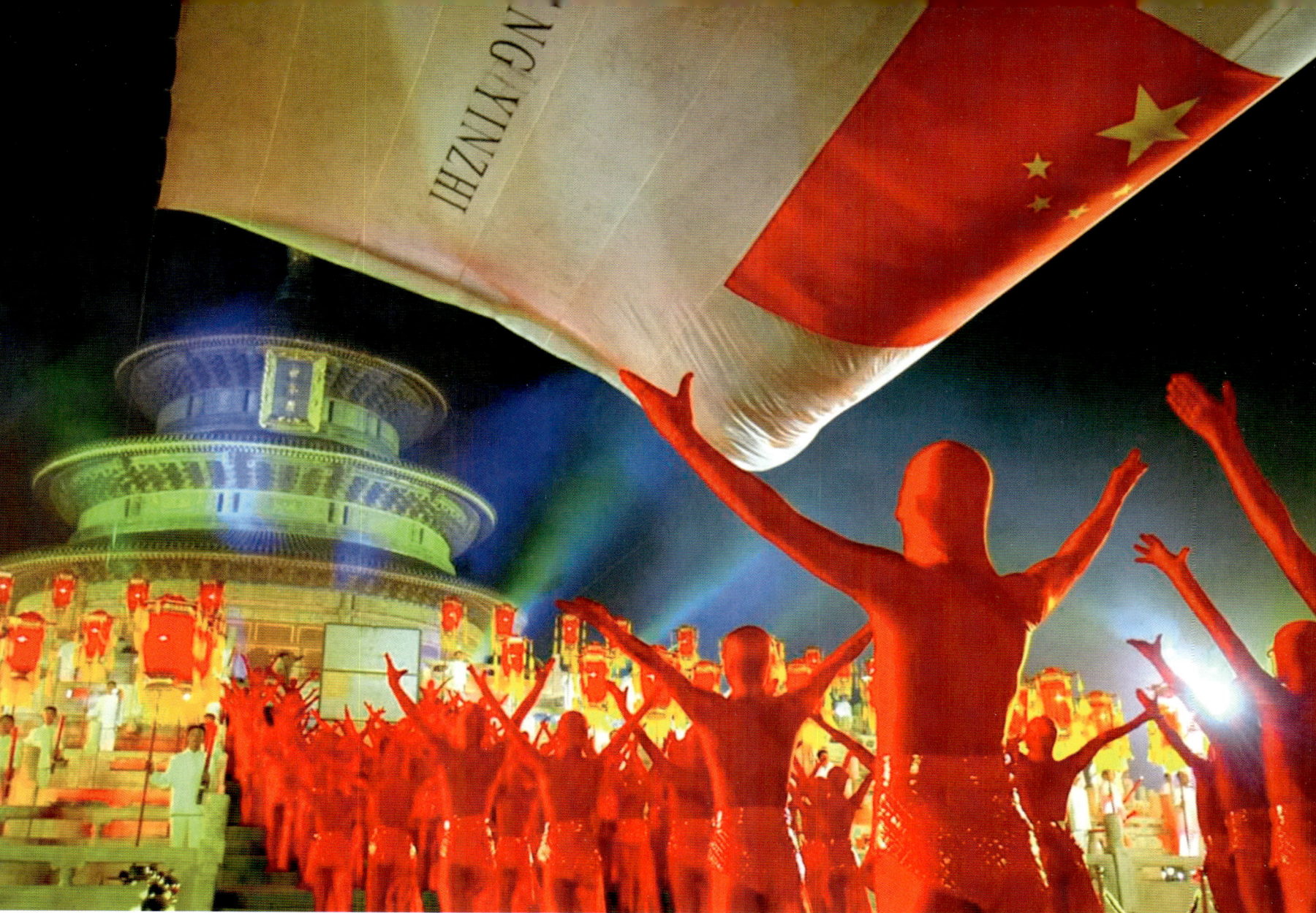

↑
Lu Beifeng, 2003

Performers at the Temple of Heaven take part in the opening ceremony for the official logo of the Beijing Olympics.

Tänzer am Himmelstempel nehmen teil an der Feier zur Präsentation des offiziellen Logos der Olympischen Spiele in Peking.

Devant le Temple du ciel, des acteurs participent à la cérémonie de lancement du logo officiel des Jeux olympiques de Pékin.

"Some people say, because of serious human rights issues, 'Let's close the door and say no.' The other way is to bet on openness. Bet on the fact that in the coming seven years, openness, progress and development in many areas will be such that the situation will be improved. We bet that seven years from now we will see many changes."

„Wegen schwerwiegenden Fragen der Menschenrechte sagen einige: ‚Wir schließen die Tür und sagen nein.' Der andere Weg ist es, auf Öffnung zu setzen. Auf die Tatsache setzen, dass in den kommenden sieben Jahren Öffnung, Fortschritt und Entwicklung in vielen Bereichen so sein werden, dass sich die Lage bessern wird. Wir setzen darauf, dass wir in sieben Jahren viele Änderungen sehen werden."

« Du fait de sérieux problèmes avec les droits de l'Homme, certains disent : 'Fermons la porte et disons non.' L'autre voie est de parier sur l'ouverture. Parier sur le fait qu'au cours des sept années à venir, l'ouverture, le progrès et le développement dans de nombreux domaines seront tels que la situation se sera améliorée. Nous relevons le pari que dans sept ans nous aurons constaté de nombreux changements. »

FRANÇOIS CARRARD (1938–), executive director of the IOC, on awarding the 2008 Summer Olympics to Beijing, 2001

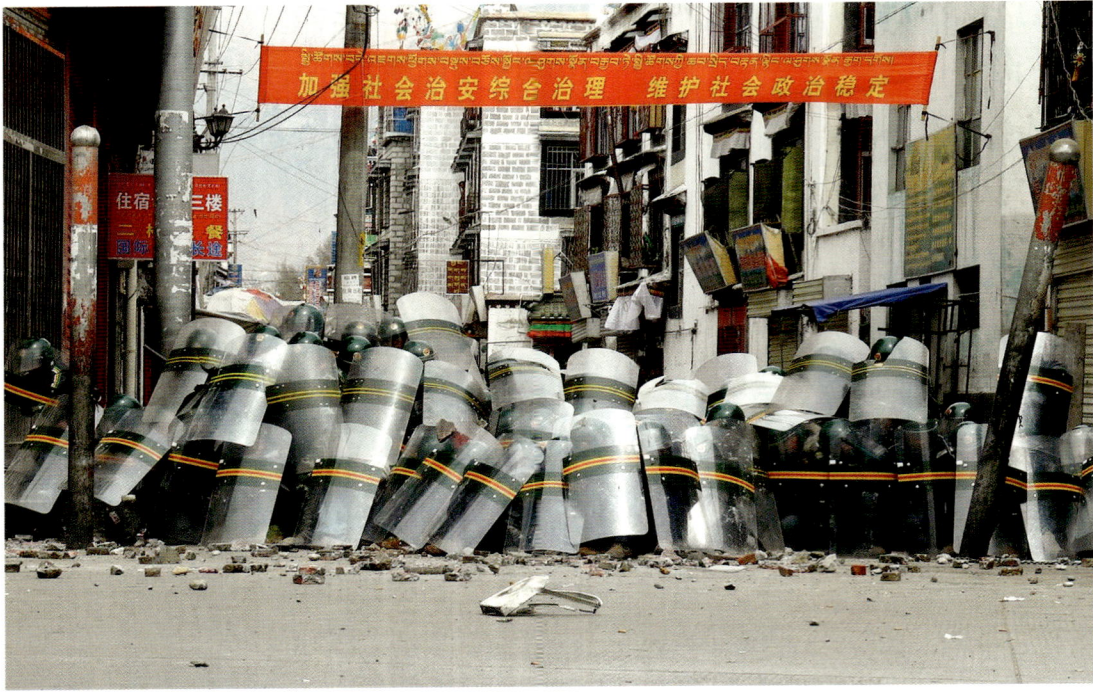

→
Anon., 2008 (image provided by Beijing Organizing Committee for the Games of the XXIX Olympiad (BOCOG))

Chinese mountain climbers carried the Olympic flame to the summit of Mount Everest in the Himalaya as part of the torch relay for the 2008 Summer Olympic in Beijing. This photo was shot by one of the climbers with his mobile phone camera.

Chinesische Bergsteiger bringen die olympische Flamme auf den Gipfel des Mount Everest im Himalaja im Rahmen als Station des Fackellaufs der Olympischen Sommerspiele in Peking 2008. Dieses Foto hat einer der Kletterer mit seiner Handy-Kamera aufgenommen.

Des alpinistes chinois ont porté la torche olympique jusqu'au sommet de l'Everest dans l'Himalaya dans le cadre du relais de la flamme pour les Jeux olympiques d'été 2008 à Pékin. Cette photo a été prise avec son mobile appareil photo par un des alpinistes.

↑
Anon., 2008

Chinese riot police form a wall with shields to protect against rock-throwing in Lhasa. In mid-March 2008, predominantly ethnic Tibetan protesters riot in Lhasa and the neighboring Tibetan speaking area of Sichuan province to protest against perceived religious and cultural interference of the government. After weeks of acrimonious charges and counter charges between the Chinese government and Dalai Lama, both sides resume talks in the southern city of Shenzhen.

Mitte März 2008 bildet die chinesische Bereitschaftspolizei mit ihren Schutzschilden eine Mauer, um sich vor Steinewerfern in Lhasa zu schützen. Überwiegend Volkstibeter beteiligen sich an einem Aufruhr in Lhasa und dem benachbarten, tibetischsprachigen Gebiet der Provinz Sichuan, um gegen die empfundene Einmischung der Regierung in religiöse und kulturelle Angelegenheiten zu protestieren. Nachdem die chinesische Regierung und der Dalai Lama wochenlang erbittert gegenseitige Schuldzuweisungen ausgetauscht hatten, nehmen beide Seiten die Gespräche in der südchinesischen Stadt Shenzhen wieder auf.

La police chinoise anti-émeutes forme un mur de boucliers pour se protéger contre les jets de pierre de manifestants à Lhassa. À la mi-mars 2008, des émeutes de protestataires d'ethnie tibétaine se sont déroulées à Lhassa et dans les régions voisines tibetophones de la province du Sichuan pour protester contre ce qu'ils jugent être ingérences culturelles et religieuses du gouvernement chinois. Après des semaines d'accusations et de contre-accusations entre le pouvoir chinois et le Dalaï-Lama, des pourparlers ont repris entre les deux parties dans la ville méridionale de Shenzhen.

→
Guo Tieliu, 2008

26-year-old Chen Jian is crushed by the collapsed concrete blocks in Beichuan of Sichuan province. A powerful earthquake of 7.9 on the Richter scale struck Sichuan on May 12th, 2008. Chen Jian is rescued after 70 hours beneath the rubbles and he dies shortly afterwards. As of May 23 the Chinese government announced that the quake has killed 55,740 people and leave 24,960 people still missing.

Der 26jährige Chen Jian ist unter zusammengestürzten Betonblöcken in Beichuan in der Provinz Sichuan verschüttet. Ein starkes Erdbeben der Stärke 7,9 auf der Richter-Skala erschütterte Sichuan am 12. Mai 2008. Chen Jian wird nach 70 Stunden aus den Trümmern gerettet und stirbt kurz danach. Am 23. Mai veröffentlichte die chinesische Regierung, dass das Erdbeben 55 470 Tote verursacht hat und 24 960 Menschen noch immer vermisst werden.

A Beichuan dans la province de Sichuan, Chen Jian, âgé de 26 ans, est enseveli sous les blocs de béton qui se sont écroulés. Le 12 mai 2008, un violent tremblement de terre de force 7,9 sur l'échelle de Richter a secoué Sichouan. Chen Lian est tiré des ruines au bout de 70 heures et meurt peu après. Le 23 mai, le gouvernement chinois a annoncé que le séisme avait fait 55 470 morts et que 24 960 personnes sont encore portées disparues.

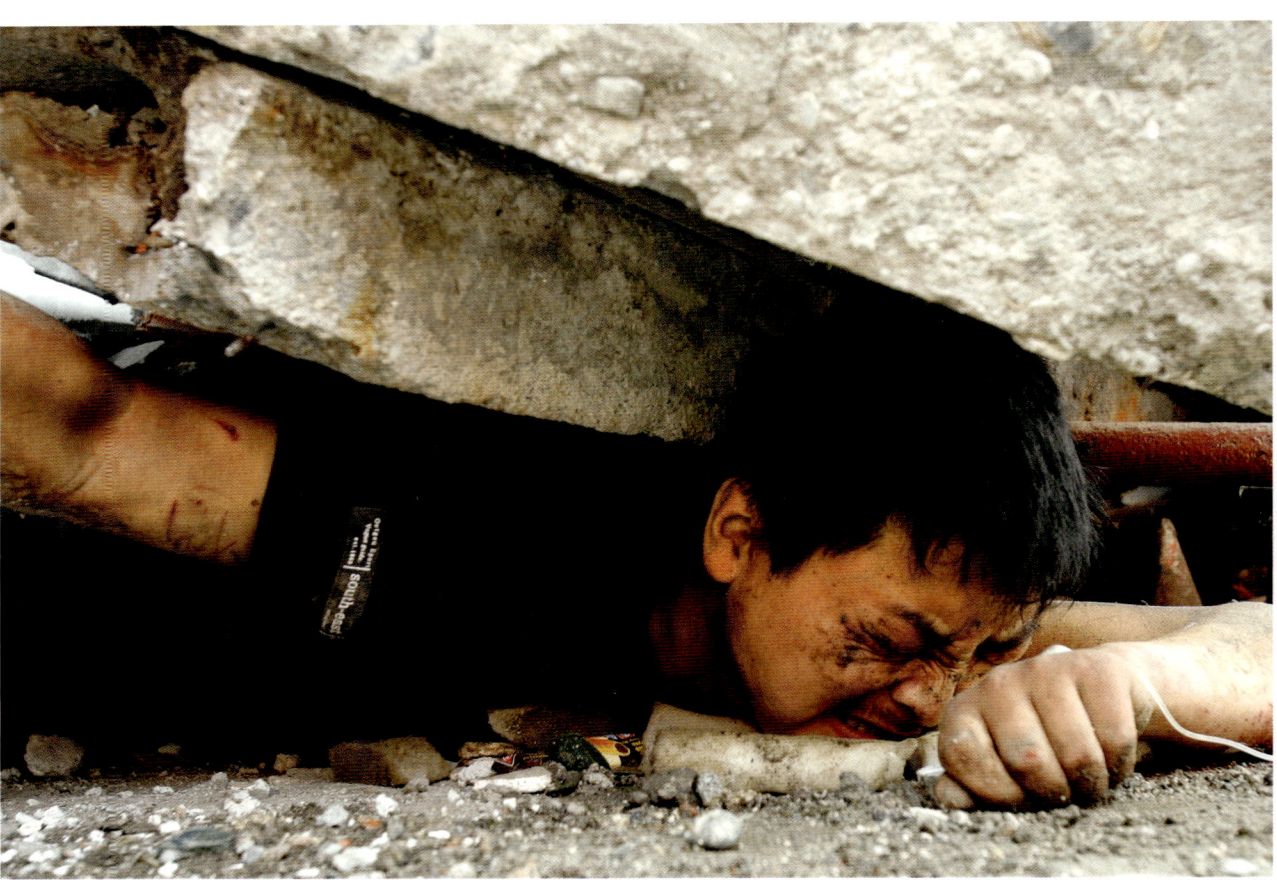

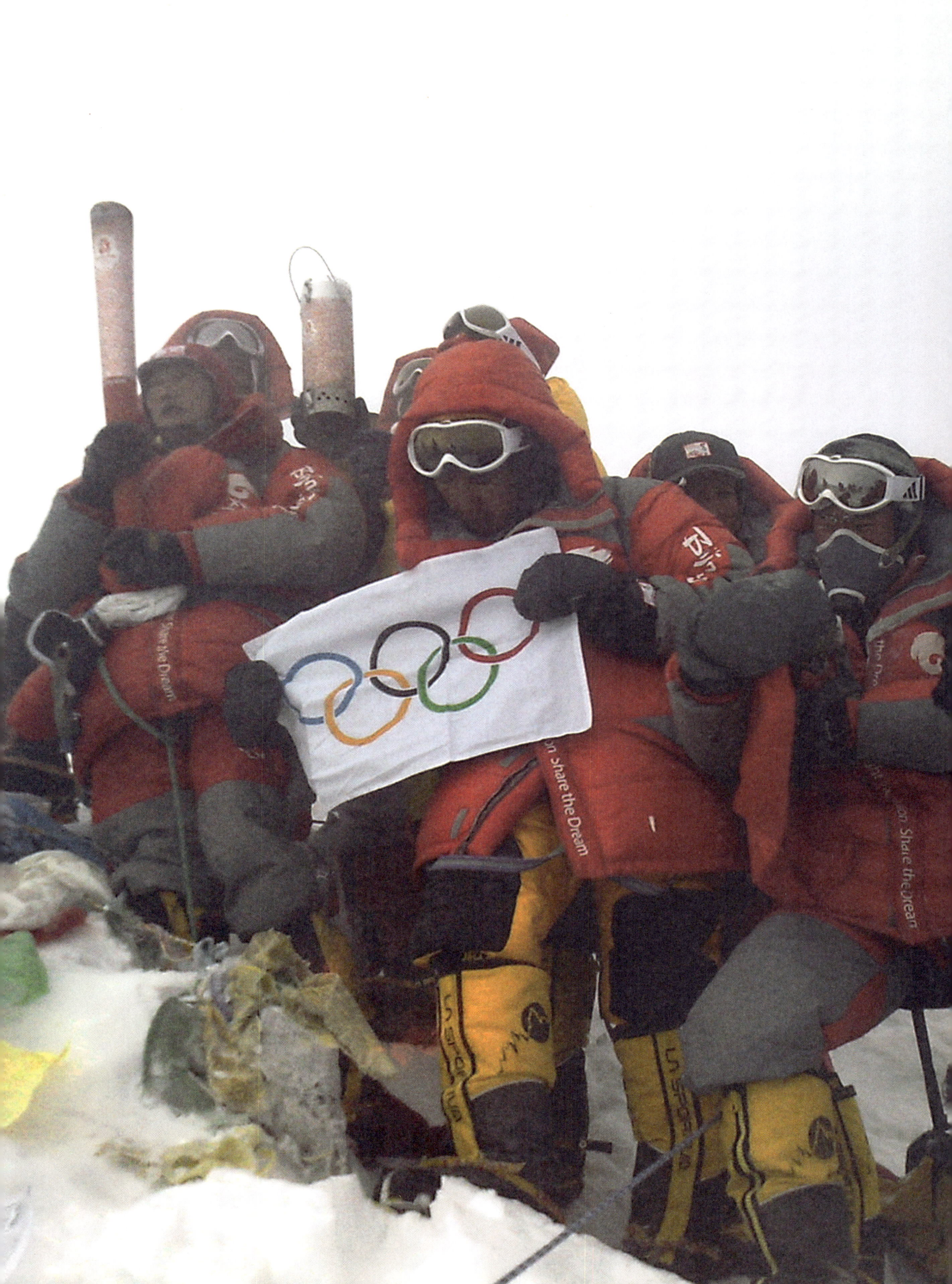

Appendix
Anhang
Annexe

China
Empire – Republic – People's Republic

Empire

1644–1911 Qing (Manchu) dynasty. Largest territorial expansion of the empire. Internal weakness favors the invasion of foreign powers from 1800.

1796–1804 Rebellion of the "White Lotus" sect.

1839–1842 "Opium War." China cedes Hong Kong to Great Britain and subsequently surrenders numerous ports and city districts to foreign powers, which open "concessions" there. Exterritorial areas on Chinese soil.

1850–1864 "Taiping Rebellion," regarded as the most destructive civil war in history: 17 provinces devastated, and an estimated death toll of 20 million.

1884–1885 Sino-French War. China loses prerogatives in South-East Asia.

1894–1895 Sino-Japanese War. China cedes Taiwan to Japan.

1897–1898 Taking advantage of China's weakness, foreign powers secure further privileges and leasehold territories; Germany leases Qingdao (Tsingtao).

1900 "Boxer Rebellion," a xenophobic, nationalist movement, which is put down by foreign military intervention. China is forced to pay large sums in compensation.

1911 On October 10, local military rebellion against the empire, which spreads rapidly and in February 1912 leads to the abdication of the last emperor.

Republic

1912 Proclamation of the Republic of China.

1919 "May Fourth Movement": intellectual and social reformation movement.

1921 Founding of the Communist Party of China.

1931 Japan invades northeastern China; establishment in 1934 of the puppet state of Manzhuguo, with Pu Yi, the last emperor of China, as the emperor of this new state.

1934–1935 Communist units and sympathizers undertake, in a "Long March" attended by huge loss of life, a retreat to safe areas in the region around Yan'an. The "Long March" becomes the heroic epic of the Communist Party of China.

1935 Mao Zedong is elected Chairman of the Central Committee and Politburo of the Communist Party of China, an office that he will hold until his death in 1976.

1937–1945 Sino-Japanese War.

1945 End of the war on August 14 and formal capitulation of Japan on September 2. Taiwan is returned to China.

1946–1949 Civil war again.

People's Republic

1949 On October 1, proclamation of the People's Republic of China by Mao Zedong in Beijing.

1949–1952 Political and economic reorganization by violent mass campaigns.

1950 In October, Tibet is seized by Chinese troops; in 1951, Tibet is incorporated into the People's Republic as an autonomous region.

1950–1953 Korean War; from 1950, intervention by Chinese units.

1951 "Three-antis Campaign" against corruption, waste, and bureaucracy.

1952 "Five-antis Campaign" against bribery, tax evasion, theft of state property, fraud, and betrayal of state secrets.

1953 Adoption of the first Five-Year Plan, following the Soviet model.

1955 Participation of the People's Republic of China in the conference of non-aligned countries in Bandung (Indonesia). Advocation of "peaceful co-existence."

1957 Originally conceived as an opportunity to speak out, the "Hundred Flowers Movement" results in massive criticism, is abandoned, and re-launched as an "Anti-Rightist Campaign."

1958 Start of the "Great Leap Forward." Mass campaigns like the creation of People's Communes and the steel campaign (backyard furnaces) are intended to achieve Mao's aim of "overtaking Great Britain and catching up with America."

1959 Measures taken in the "Great Leap Forward" aggravate conflicts in Tibet. Unrest, armed insurrection and flight of the Dalai Lama to India.

1959–1961 Failure of the "Great Leap Forward." Natural catastrophes make the situation worse. The "Great Leap Forward" is estimated to have caused over 30 million deaths.

1960 Nuclear support from the Soviet Union is revoked and the Soviets withdraw their advisors.

1960–1963 The "three bitter years."

1961 The Central Committee of the Chinese Communist Party announces the failure of the "Great Leap Forward." Emergency measures are introduced, land is returned to private ownership by the peasants.

1962 Border war between China and India.

1963 The split between China and the Soviet Union is made public.

1964 China explodes its first atom bomb.

1966 All universities and schools are closed. Liu Shaoqi, Deng Xiaoping, and other high-ranking party leaders are removed from office.

1966–1976 "Great Proletarian Cultural Revolution." Factional dispute with civil-war similarities, which Mao tries to win by mobilizing the young Red Guards.

1968 Mao calls for young people "to learn from the masses." Some 15 million young people are sent to the countryside for several years.

1969 Fighting on the border between China and the Soviet Union (along the Ussuri river and in Xinjiang).

1970 Successful launch of China's first space satellite. Qinghua University in Beijing is the first university in the country to open again.

1971 In October, the People's Republic is awarded the Chinese seat in the United Nations. Death of Lin Biao.

1972 In February, President Nixon visits China and meets Mao. Numerous Western countries and Japan enter into diplomatic relations with the People's Republic.

1973 Rehabilitation of Deng Xiaoping.

1974 Lin Biao and Confucius are denounced by the masses.

1976 Death of Zhou Enlai. Mao Zedong dies on September 9 at the age of 82. Hua Guofeng becomes the new party chairman. Shortly afterwards, arrest of the Gang of Four.

1978 On the initiative of Deng Xiaoping, rehabilitation of intellectuals and "rightists" begins. Start of openness and reform in the People's Republic of China. "Democracy Wall" in Beijing with critical wall newspaper.

1979 The USA and the People's Republic of China enter into full diplomatic relations. Deng Xiaoping visits the USA. Special economic zones are established. Military intervention of China in North Vietnam. In March, Deng criticizes the "Democracy Wall." Those who demand democracy are sentenced and the democratic movement is quashed.

1980 Rehabilitation of Liu Shaoqi. In September, Zhao Ziyang replaces Hua Guofeng as Prime Minister. Except in areas of national minorities, a one-child policy is to be enforced.

1981 Conviction of the Gang of Four and six other high-ranking former party and military leaders. In June, Hua Guofeng loses his party offices. The party agrees on a document about its own history, in which the politics of Mao Zedong are judged to have been 70 percent good and 30 percent bad.

1982 The XIIth party congress abolishes the office of party chairman and elects Hu Yaobang as general secretary. British Prime Minister Margaret Thatcher travels to Beijing to conduct talks on the future of Hong Kong.

1983 Resumption of diplomatic relations between India and China, which were broken off in 1968.

1984 Joint declaration by the British and Chinese governments on the future of Hong Kong, whose economic and social system is to remain unchanged for 50 years after the hand-over in July 1997. The "Resolution on reforming the economic system" sanctions the expansion of elements of a market economy.

1986 Student demonstrations in numerous big cities, which Hu Yaobang, in the eyes of his detractors, fails to deal with decisively enough.

1987 Hu Yaobang is removed from office in January and replaced by Zhao Ziyang. China and Portugal reach agreement on the hand-over of Macao in 1999 on the model of Hong Kong.

1989 Military strike on Tibet because of unrest. The death of Hu Yaobang in April is followed by spontaneous professions of sympathy, which turn into demands for more democracy. Hunger strikes and escalating demonstrations interfere with the visit of the Soviet president Michael Gorbachev. In the night of June 3 to 4, demonstrators are dispersed by the military in the Square of Heavenly Peace (Tiananmen Square); estimates say several hundred were killed. At the end of June, Zhao Ziyang is deposed as general secretary of the party because of his sympathy with the students. He is succeeded by Jiang Zemin.

1992 Deng Xiaoping sets out on a "Southern Tour," on which he emphatically advocates a stepping up of economic reforms.

1995 Work starts on the "Three Gorges Dam."

1997 Deng Xiaoping dies in February at the age of 92. On July 1, hand-over of Hong Kong, which becomes a "Special Administrative Region."

1998 Start of persecution of the Falungong sect.

2002 Hu Jintao takes over the office of party leader and head of state from Jiang Zemin. The Communist Party opens up to new social groups: in other words, entrepreneurs can also become members.

2007 Hu Jintao is confirmed in office and advocates the development of China into a harmonious society based on scientific tenets.

2008 Summer Olympic Games in Beijing.

China
Kaiserreich – Republik – Volksrepublik

Kaiserreich

1644–1911 Qing (Mandschu) Dynastie, größte Flächenausdehnung des Kaiserreiches. Innere Schwäche begünstigt ab 1800 das Vordringen ausländischer Mächte.

1796–1804 Aufstand der „Weißer Lotus"-Sekte.

1839–1842 „Opiumkrieg", China muss Hongkong an Großbritannien abtreten und in der Folge zahlreiche Häfen sowie Stadtteile ausländischen Mächten überlassen, die dort „Konzessionen" eröffnen, exterritoriale Gebiete auf chinesischem Boden.

1850–1864 „Taiping"-Aufstand, gilt als größter Bürgerkrieg der Geschichte; 17 zerstörte Provinzen, 20 Millionen Tote.

1884–1885 Chinesisch-französischer Krieg; China verliert Vorrechte in Südostasien.

1894–1895 Chinesisch-japanischer Krieg; China muss Taiwan an Japan abtreten.

1897–1898 Chinas Schwäche ausnutzend, verschaffen sich ausländische Mächte weitere Vorrechte und Pachtgebiete; Deutschland pachtet Qingdao (Tsingtao).

1900 „Boxeraufstand", eine fremdenfeindliche, nationalistische Bewegung, die durch ausländische Militärintervention niedergeschlagen wird. China wird zu hohen Entschädigungszahlungen gezwungen.

1911 Am 10. Oktober lokale Militärrevolte gegen das Kaiserreich, die sich schnell ausbreitet und im Februar 1912 zur Abdankung des letzten Kaisers führt.

Republik

1912 Proklamation der Republik China.

1919 „Bewegung des 4. Mai"; intellektuelle und gesellschaftliche Erneuerungsbewegung.

1921 Gründung der Kommunistischen Partei Chinas

1931 Vordringen Japans im Nordosten Chinas; 1934 Errichtung des Marionettenstaates Manzhuguo, mit Pu Yi, dem letzten Kaiser Chinas, als Kaiser dieses neuen Staates.

1934–1935 Kommunistische Verbände und Sympathisanten ziehen sich durch den äußerst verlustreichen „Langen Marsch" in sichere Gebiete der Gegend von Yan'an zurück. Der „Lange Marsch" wird zum Heldenepos der KP Chinas.

1935 Mao Zedong wird zum Vorsitzenden des Zentralkomitees und Politbüros der KP Chinas gewählt, ein Amt, das er bis zu seinem Tod (1976) innehat.

1937–1945 Japanisch-chinesischer Krieg.

1945 Kriegsende am 14. August und formelle Kapitulation Japans am 2. September, Rückgabe Taiwans an China.

1946–1949 Erneuter Bürgerkrieg.

Volksrepublik

1949 Am 1. Oktober in Peking Proklamation der Volksrepublik China durch Mao Zedong.

1949–1952 Massenkampagnen zur politischen und wirtschaftlichen Umgestaltung.

1950 Im Oktober Einnahme Tibets durch chinesische Truppen; Tibet wird 1951 der Volksrepublik als autonome Region eingegliedert.

1950–1953 Koreakrieg; ab November 1950 Eingreifen chinesischer Verbände.

1951 „Drei-Anti-Kampagne" gegen Korruption, Verschwendung und Bürokratismus.

1952 „Fünf-Anti-Kampagne" gegen Bestechung, Steuerhinterziehung, Veruntreuung von Staatseigentum, Betrug und Verrat von Staatsgeheimnissen.

1953 Verabschiedung des ersten Fünfjahresplans (1953–1957) in Anlehnung an das sowjetische Modell.

1955 Teilnahme der VR China an der Konferenz der „Blockfreien" in Bandung (Indonesien). Propagierung der „Friedlichen Koexistenz".

1957 Die ursprünglich als große Aussprache konzipierte „Hundert-Blumen-Bewegung" bewirkt massive Kritik, wird abgebrochen und zur „Anti-Rechtsabweichler-Kampagne" umfunktioniert.

1958 Beginn des „Großen Sprungs nach vorn". Durch Massenkampagnen wie die Schaffung von Volkskommunen und die Stahlkampagne (Minihochöfen) soll Maos Ziel erreicht werden, „Großbritannien zu überholen und zu Amerika aufzuschließen".

1959 Maßnahmen des „Großen Sprungs" verschärfen Konflikte in Tibet; Unruhen, bewaffneter Aufstand und Flucht des Dalai Lama nach Indien.

1959–1961 Scheitern des „Großen Sprungs". Naturkatastrophen verschlimmern die Lage; der „Große Sprung" soll über 30 Millionen Tote verursacht haben.

1960 Aufkündigung der nuklearen Unterstützung durch die Sowjetunion und Abzug sowjetischer Berater.

1960–1963 Die „Drei Bitteren Jahre".

1961 Das Zentralkomitee der KP Chinas gibt das Scheitern des „Großen Sprungs" bekannt. Durchführung von Notstandsmaßnahmen, Rückgabe von Privatparzellen an Bauern.

1962 Grenzkrieg zwischen China und Indien.

1963 Öffentliche Bekanntgabe des Bruchs zwischen China und der Sowjetunion.

1964 Zündung der ersten chinesischen Atombombe.

1966–1976 „Große Proletarische Kulturrevolution". Teilweise bürgerkriegsähnlicher Richtungskampf, den Mao u. a. durch Massenmobilisierung von jugendlichen „Roten Garden" zu gewinnen versucht.

1966 Schließung aller Universitäten und Schulen. Entmachtung von Liu Shaoqi, Deng Xiaoping und anderen hohen Parteiführern.

1968 Aufforderung Maos, Jugendliche „müssen von den Massen lernen"; etwa 15 Millionen Jugendliche werden für mehrere Jahre in Dörfer geschickt.

1969 Kämpfe an der Grenze zwischen China und der Sowjetunion (am Ussuri Fluss und in Xinjiang).

1970 China startet erfolgreich seinen ersten Weltraumsatelliten. Die Qinghua-Universität in Peking nimmt als erste Hochschule des Landes den Lehrbetrieb wieder auf.

1971 Im Oktober wird der Volksrepublik der chinesische Sitz in den Vereinten Nationen zugesprochen. Tod von Lin Biao.

1972 Im Februar besucht Präsident Nixon China, Treffen mit Mao. Zahlreiche westliche Staaten und Japan nehmen diplomatische Beziehungen zur Volksrepublik auf.

1973 Rehabilitierung von Deng Xiaoping.

1974 Kritikkampagne gegen Lin Biao und Konfuzius.

1976 Tod von Zhou Enlai. Mao Zedong stirbt am 9. September im Alter von 82 Jahren. Hua Guofeng wird neuer Parteivorsitzender. Kurze Zeit später Verhaftung der Viererbande.

1978 Auf Initiative von Deng Xiaoping Beginn der Rehabilitierung von Intellektuellen und „Rechtsabweichlern". Beginn der Öffnung und Reform der Volksrepublik China. „Mauer der Demokratie" mit kritischen Wandzeitungen in Peking.

1979 Aufnahme voller diplomatischer Beziehungen zwischen den USA und der VR China. Besuch von Deng Xiaoping in den USA. Einrichtung von Sonderwirtschaftszonen. Militärische Intervention Chinas im Norden Vietnams. Deng kritisiert im März die „Mauer der Demokratie". Prozesse gegen Oppositionelle und Zerschlagung der Demokratiebewegung.

1980 Rehabilitierung von Liu Shaoqi. Im September löst Zhao Ziyang Hua Guofeng als Ministerpräsident ab. Außer in Gebieten nationaler Minderheiten soll eine Ein-Kind-Politik durchgesetzt werden.

1981 Verurteilung der Viererbande und sechs anderer hoher ehemaliger Partei- und Militärführer. Im Juni verliert Hua Guofeng seine Parteiämter. Die Partei verabschiedet ein Dokument über ihre Geschichte, in der die Politik von Mao Zedong als zu 70 Prozent gut und zu 30 Prozent schlecht beurteilt wird.

1982 Der XII. Parteitag schafft das Amt des Parteivorsitzenden ab und wählt Hu Yaobang zum Generalsekretär. Die britische Premierministerin Margaret Thatcher kommt zu Gesprächen über die Zukunft Hongkongs nach Peking.

1983 Wiederaufnahme diplomatischer Beziehungen zwischen Indien und China, die 1968 abgebrochen wurden.

1984 „Gemeinsame Erklärung" der britischen und chinesischen Regierung über die Zukunft Hongkongs. Dessen wirtschaftliche und soziale Ordnung soll nach der Übergabe im Juli 1997 für fünfzig Jahre unverändert bleiben. Im „Beschluss über die Reform des Wirtschaftssystems" wird die Ausdehnung marktwirtschaftlicher Elemente gebilligt.

1986 Studentendemonstrationen in zahlreichen Großstädten, denen Hu Yaobang nach Meinung seiner Kritiker nicht entschlossen genug entgegentritt.

1987 Hu Yaobang wird im Januar seines Amtes enthoben, das Zhao Ziyang übernimmt. China und Portugal einigen sich auf die Übergabe von Macao im Jahre 1999 nach dem Modell von Hongkong.

1989 Militäreinsatz in Tibet wegen Unruhen. Dem Tod von Hu Yaobang im April folgen spontane Sympathiebekundungen, die zu Forderungen nach mehr Demokratie führen. Hungerstreiks und sich ausweitende Demonstrationen behindern auch den Besuch des sowjetischen Präsidenten Michael Gorbatschow. In der Nacht vom 3. zum 4. Juni werden die Demonstrierenden durch Militär von Platz des Himmlischen Friedens (Tiananmen) vertrieben; Schätzungen nennen mehrere Hundert Tote. Wegen seiner Sympathie den Studenten gegenüber verliert Zhao Ziyang Ende Juni das Amt des Generalsekretärs der Partei, Nachfolger wird Jiang Zemin.

1992 Deng Xiaoping unternimmt eine „Reise in den Süden", auf der er sich nachdrücklich für eine Intensivierung wirtschaftlicher Reformen einsetzt.

1995 Beginn der Bauarbeiten für den „Drei-Schluchten-Staudamm".

1997 Deng Xiaoping stirbt im Februar im Alter von 92 Jahren. Am 1. Juli Übergabe von Hongkong, das eine „Sonderverwaltungsregion" wird.

1998 Beginn der Verfolgung der Falungong-Sekte.

2002 Hu Jintao übernimmt die Ämter des Partei- und Staatschefs von Jiang Zemin. Die Kommunistische Partei öffnet sich neuen Gesellschaftsgruppen, d. h. auch Unternehmer können Mitglied werden.

2007 Hu Jintao wird in seinen Ämtern bestätigt und propagiert die Entwicklung Chinas im Rahmen einer harmonischen, auf Wissenschaft gegründeten Gesellschaft.

2008 Olympische Sommerspiele in Peking.

Chine
Empire – République – République populaire

Empire

1644–1911 Dynastie Qing (mandchoue) ; plus grande extension territoriale de l'Empire. À partir de 1800, la faiblesse intérieure favorise l'avancée de puissances étrangères.

1796–1804 Soulèvement de la secte du « Lotus blanc ».

1839–1842 « Guerre de l'opium » ; la Chine doit céder Hong Kong à la Grande-Bretagne et abandonner par la suite de nombreux ports et des quartiers urbains à des puissances étrangères, qui y ouvrent des « concessions », zones extra-territoriales sur le sol chinois.

1850–1864 « Révolte des Taiping » ; considérée comme la plus grande guerre civile de l'histoire – 17 provinces dévastées, probablement 20 millions de morts.

1884–1885 Guerre franco-chinoise ; la Chine perd des prérogatives en Asie du Sud-Est.

1894–1895 Guerre sino-japonaise ; la Chine doit céder Taiwan au Japon.

1897–1898 Exploitant la faiblesse de la Chine, des puissances étrangères s'attribuent de nouvelles prérogatives et des territoires à bail ; l'Allemagne se fait céder Qingdao (Tsingtao).

1900 « Révolte des Boxeurs », mouvement nationaliste, hostile aux étrangers, qui sera réprimé par une intervention militaire étrangère. La Chine est contrainte à payer de forts dédommagements.

1911 Le 10 octobre, révolte militaire locale contre l'Empire, qui se répand rapidement et qui conduit à l'abdication du dernier empereur en février 1912.

République

1912 Proclamation de la République chinoise.

1919 « Mouvement du 4 mai » ; mouvement de renouveau intellectuel et social.

1921 Fondation du Parti communiste chinois.

1931 Avancée du Japon au nord-est de la Chine ; en 1934, création de l'État fantoche Manzhuguo, dont Puyi, dernier empereur de Chine, est l'empereur.

1934–1935 Des associations et des sympathisants communistes se retirent dans des territoires sûrs de la région de Yan'an après la « Longue Marche », qui leur vaudra des pertes considérables. La « Longue Marche » devient l'épopée du Parti communiste chinois.

1935 Mao Zedong est élu président du comité central et du bureau politique du Parti communiste chinois, poste qu'il occupera jusqu'à sa mort en 1976.

1937–1945 Guerre sino-japonaise.

1945 Fin de la guerre le 14 août et capitulation formelle du Japon le 2 septembre ; rétrocession de Taiwan à la Chine.

1946–1949 Nouvelle guerre civile.

République populaire

1949 Le 1er octobre à Pékin, Mao Zedong proclame la république populaire de Chine.

1949–1952 Restructuration politique et économique par des campagnes massives violentes.

1950 En octobre, occupation du Tibet par des troupes chinoises.

1950–1953 Guerre de Corée ; à partir de novembre 1950, intervention d'unités chinoises, dont les pertes sont estimées à environ un demi million de morts.

1951 Campagne contre les « trois anti » – corruption, gaspillage, bureaucratisme.

1952 Campagne contre les « cinq anti » – pots-de-vin, fraude fiscale, détournement des biens de l'État, malversation, trahison de secrets d'État.

1953 Adoption du premier plan quinquennal (1953–1957) inspiré du modèle soviétique.

1955 Participation de la Chine à la conférence des « non-alignés » à Bandung (Indonésie). Propagation de la « co-existence pacifique ».

1957 La « campagne des Cent Fleurs », initialement conçue comme un grand débat, déclenche des critiques massives, est interrompue et refondue en « campagne anti-droitière ».

1958 Début du « Grand Bond en avant ». Des campagnes de masse comme la création de communes populaires et la campagne sidérurgique (petits hauts fourneaux) doivent permettre d'atteindre l'objectif de Mao : « dépasser la Grande-Bretagne et rejoindre l'Amérique ».

1959 Les mesures du « Grand Bond » aiguisent les conflits au Tibet ; troubles, soulèvement armé et fuite du Dalaï-Lama en Inde.

1959–1961 Échec du « Grand Bond ». Des catastrophes naturelles aggravent la situation ; le « Grand Bond » aurait causé la mort de plus de 30 millions de personnes.

1960 Résiliation de l'aide nucléaire de l'Union soviétique et départ des conseillers soviétiques.

1960–1963 Les « trois années amères ».

1961 Le Comité central du Parti communiste chinois reconnaît l'échec du « Grand Bond ». Instauration de mesures d'urgence, restitution de parcelles privées à des paysans.

1962 Guerre frontalière entre la Chine et l'Inde.

1963 Proclamation officielle de la rupture sino-soviétique.

1964 Premier essai nucléaire de la Chine.

1966–1976 « Grande révolution culturelle prolétarienne ». Lutte apparentée en partie à une guerre civile que Mao tente de gagner notamment par la mobilisation massive de jeunes « Gardes rouges ».

1966 Fermeture de toutes les écoles et universités. Liu Shaoqi, Deng Xiaoping et d'autres hauts dirigeants du Parti sont démis de leurs fonctions.

1968 Mao déclare que les jeunes doivent « apprendre des masses » ; quelque 15 millions de jeunes sont envoyés pour plusieurs années dans des villages.

1969 Incidents frontaliers entre la Chine et l'Union soviétique (sur l'Oussouri et dans le Xinjiang).

1970 La Chine lance avec succès son premier satellite artificiel. À Pékin, l'université Qinghua est la première du pays à reprendre les cours.

1971 En octobre, la République populaire de Chine se voit attribuer un siège aux Nations unies. Mort de Lin Biao.

1972 En février, le président Nixon visite la Chine ; rencontre avec Mao. De nombreux États occidentaux et le Japon établissent des relations diplomatiques avec la République populaire de Chine.

1973 Réhabilitation de Deng Xiaoping.

1974 Campagne de critiques contre Lin Biao et Confucius.

1976 Mort de Zhou Enlai. Mao Zedong meurt le 9 septembre à l'âge de 82 ans. Hua Guofeng devient le nouveau président du Parti. Peu après, arrestation de la bande des Quatre.

1978 À l'initiative de Deng Xiaoping, début de la réhabilitation d'intellectuels et de « droitiers ». Début de l'ouverture et de la réforme de la République populaire de Chine. « Mur de la démocratie » avec des journaux muraux critiques à Pékin.

1979 Normalisation complète des relations entre les États-Unis et la République populaire de Chine avec l'établissement de relations diplomatiques. Visite de Deng Xiaoping aux États-Unis. Création de Zones économiques spéciales. Intervention militaire de la Chine au Nord-Vietnam. En mars, Deng critique le « mur de la démocratie ». Procès d'opposants et répression du mouvement démocratique

1980 Réhabilitation de Liu Shaoqi. En septembre, Hua Guofeng est remplacé par Zhao Ziyang au poste de Premier ministre. À l'exception des régions à minorités nationales, une politique de l'enfant unique doit être imposée.

1981 Condamnation de la bande des Quatre et de six autres anciens hauts dirigeants du Parti et chefs militaires. En juin, Hua Guofeng est démis de ses fonctions au Parti. Le Parti approuve un document sur son histoire dans lequel la politique de Mao Zedong est jugée bonne à 70 pour cent et mauvaise à 30 pour cent.

1982 Le XIIème Congrès du Parti supprime le poste de président du Parti et élit Hu Yaobang au poste de secrétaire général. Le Premier ministre britannique Margaret Thatcher se rend à Pékin pour des entretiens sur l'avenir de Hong Kong.

1983 Reprise des relations diplomatiques entre l'Inde et la Chine, rompues depuis 1968.

1984 « Déclaration commune » des gouvernements britannique et chinois sur l'avenir de Hong Kong, dont l'ordre économique et social devra rester inchangé pendant cinquante ans après la rétrocession de juillet 1997. L'intégration accrue d'éléments d'économie de marché est approuvée dans la « Résolution sur la réforme du système économique ».

1986 Manifestations d'étudiants dans de nombreuses grandes villes ; de l'avis des critiques, Hu Yaobang n'y répond pas avec assez de fermeté.

1987 En janvier, Hu Yaobang est démis de son poste que reprend Zhao Ziyang. La Chine et le Portugal signent un accord sur la rétrocession de Macao en 1999 sur le modèle de Hong Kong.

1989 Intervention militaire au Tibet suite à des troubles. La mort de Hu Yaobang en avril entraîne des mouvements de sympathie spontanés qui se transforment en revendications pour plus de démocratie. Les grèves de la faim et les manifestations prennent de l'ampleur, empêchant notamment la visite du président de l'Union soviétique Mikhaïl Gorbatchev. Dans la nuit du 3 au 4 juin, les manifestants sont chassés de la place Tian'anmen par l'armée ; le nombre de morts est estimé à plusieurs centaines. Fin juin, du fait de la sympathie qu'il suscite chez les étudiants, Zhao Ziyang perd son poste de secrétaire général du Parti ; Jiang Zemin lui succède.

1992 Deng Xiaoping entreprend un « voyage dans le Sud », lors duquel il s'engage énergiquement en faveur d'une intensification des réformes économiques.

1995 Début des travaux de construction du « barrage des Trois Gorges ».

1997 Deng Xiaoping meurt en février à l'âge de 92 ans. Le 1er juillet, rétrocession de Hong Kong, qui devient une « région d'administration spéciale ».

1998 Début des persécutions de la secte Falungong.

2002 Hu Jintao succède à Jiang Zemin aux postes de chef du Parti et de l'État. Le Parti communiste s'ouvre à de nouveaux groupes sociaux : des entrepreneurs peuvent désormais en devenir membres.

2007 Hu Jintao est confirmé dans ses fonctions et propage le développement de la Chine dans le cadre d'une société harmonieuse fondée sur la science.

2008 Jeux olympiques d'été à Pékin.

pp. 406/407
Map of the People's Republic of China, 2008

© *Chinese National Institute of Geography, Beijing, China 2008*
Cartographer: Chen Yun

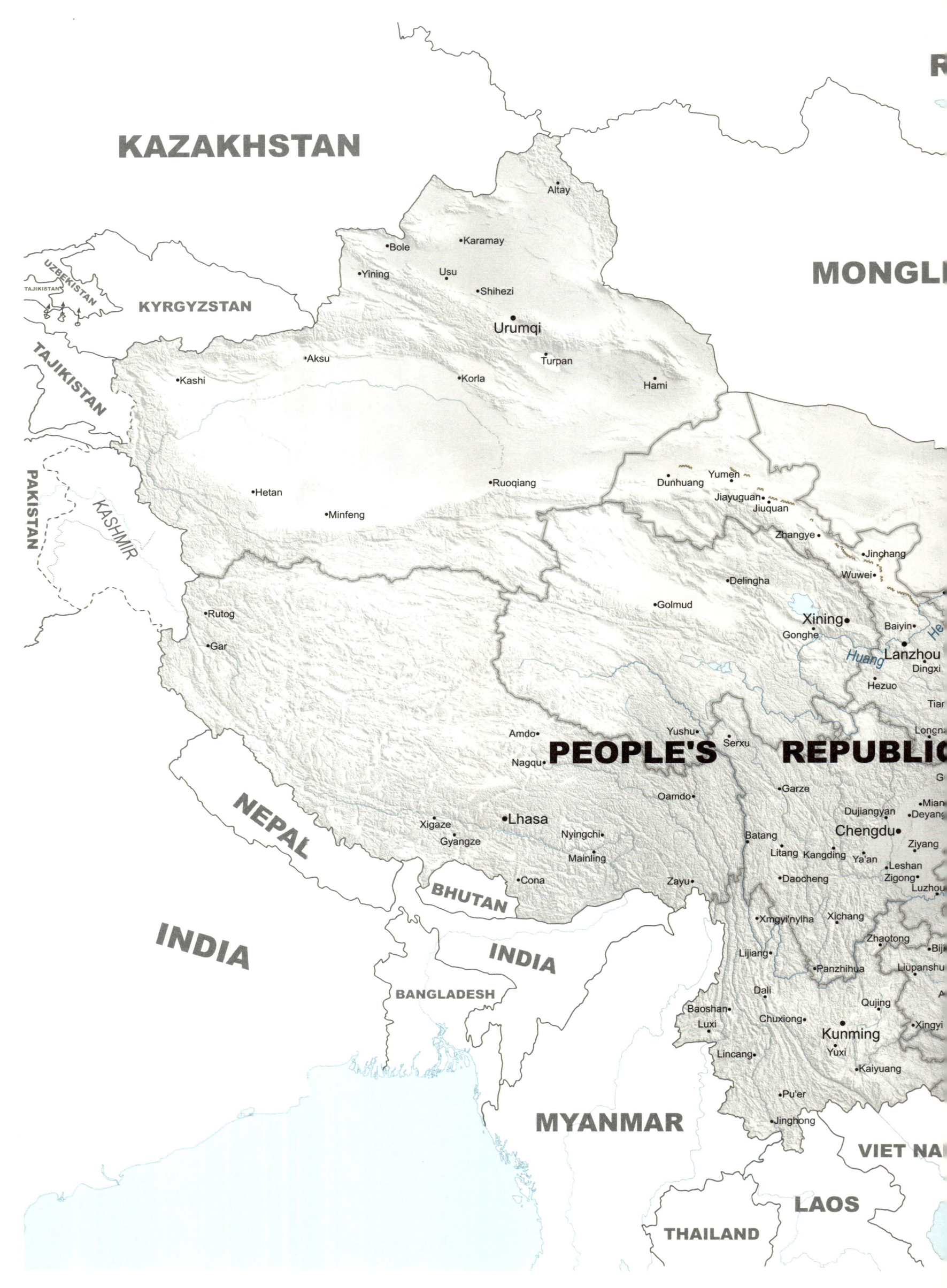

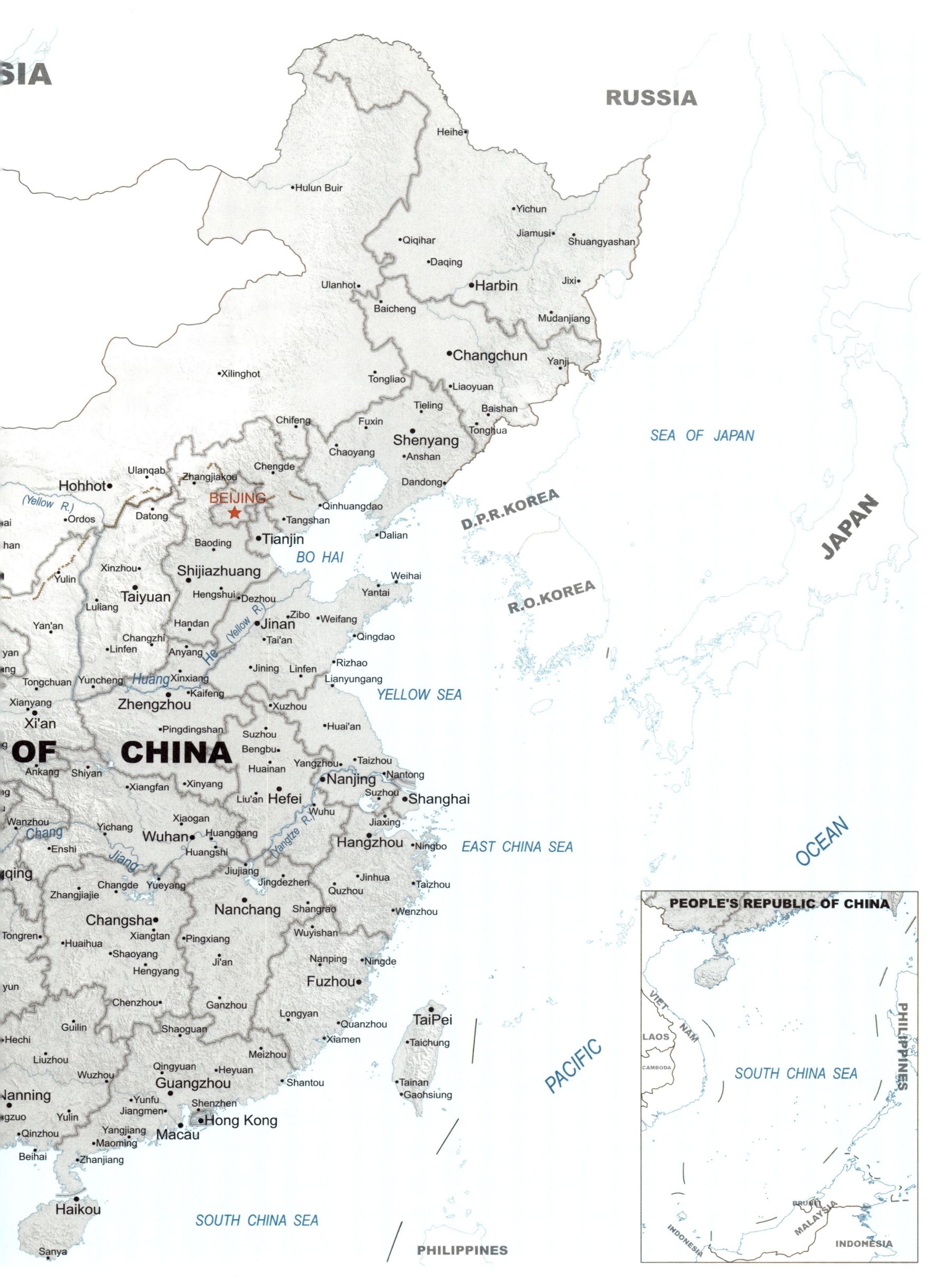

Short Biographies of the Photographers
Kurzbiografien der Fotografen
Courtes biographies des photographes

It was not possible to obtain information on photographers who do not appear in this listing.
Daten zu den hier nicht genannten Fotografen konnten nicht eruiert werden.
Le coordonnées des photographes non cités ci-dessous n'ont pu être obtenues.

CAI Shangxiong *(born 1919, Zhongshan, Guangdong province)*
After joining the Chinese Communist Party in 1939, Cai graduated from the Northwest University in Xi'an in 1942. In 1950, he enrolled as a staff photographer with the 4th Field Army of the People's Liberation Army. From 1950 to his retirement in 1987 Cai worked at *China Pictorial* magazine.

Cai, der 1939 der Kommunistischen Partei Chinas beitritt, absolviert 1942 sein Studium an der Nordwest-Universität in Xi'an. 1950 schließt er sich als Redaktionsfotograf der 4. Feldarmee der Volksbefreiungsarmee an. Von 1950 bis zu seiner Pensionierung 1987 arbeitet er für die Illustrierte *China Pictorial*.

Membre du Parti communiste chinois depuis 1939, Cai obtient son diplôme de l'Université du Nord-Ouest à Xi'an en 1942. En 1950, il s'engage comme photographe dans le 4ᵉ corps de l'Armée populaire de libération. De 1950 à sa retraite en 1987, il travaille pour la revue *China Pictorial*.
→ p. 134

CHEN Changfen *(born 1941, Hunan province)*
Chen began freelancing in 1959, settling into a full-time position in 1980 as deputy editor-in-chief of Air China's in-flight magazine. In 1999, he contributed to *Fifty Years Inside the People's Republic*, produced by the Aperture Foundation, New York. In 2007, a collection of his images was published as *The Great Wall of China*, by Yale University Press.

Chen beginnt 1959 mit freiberuflicher Arbeit, ehe er 1980 eine Ganztagsstelle als stellvertretender Chefredakteur bei der Bordzeitschrift von Air China übernimmt. 1999 beteiligt er sich an dem Buch *Fifty Years Inside the People's Republic*, das bei Aperture, New York, verlegt wird. 2007 erscheint eine Auswahl seiner Bilder in dem von der Yale University Press herausgegebenen Band *The Great Wall of China*.

Chen a débuté son activité de photographe indépendant en 1959, puis est devenu rédacteur-en-chef délégué du magazine d'Air China. En 1999, il a participé à Fifty Years Inside the People's Republic, produit par Aperture à New York. En 2007, un ensemble de ses images a été publié sous le titre de The Great Wall of China par Yale University Press.
→ pp. 396/397

CHEN Ling *(born 1954, Harbin, Heilongjiang province)*
Since graduating from university, Chen has been working as a freelance photographer. His works have been included in numerous group exhibitions in China. Chen currently lives and works as a freelance photographer in Harbin.

Chen ist seit seinem Universitätsabschluss als freier Fotograf tätig. Seine Arbeiten waren in mehreren Gruppenausstellungen in China zu sehen. Chen lebt und arbeitet gegenwärtig als freier Fotograf in Harbin.

Après ses études universitaires, Chen s'est établi comme photographe indépendant. Ses œuvres ont figuré dans plusieurs expositions de groupe en Chine. Chen vit et travaille actuellement à Harbin comme photographe indépendant.
→ p. 356

CHUNG, Ricky *(born 1969, Hong Kong)*
Having taught himself photography, in 1994 Chung was given the job of staff photographer at the *South China Morning Post*. Since then, Chung has received a string of awards, including Spot News in Focus at the Front Line, 1997; "Feature" section and Photograph of the Year Award, Hong Kong, and Best Photographs of the Year Award, 1998; and Excellence in News Photography, SOPA Award, 2007.

Nachdem er selbst Fotografie gelehrt hat, erhält Chung 1994 eine Stelle als Redaktionsfotograf bei der *South China Morning Post*. Seither wurde Chung mit einer Reihe von Preisen ausgezeichnet, darunter 1997 Spot News in Focus at the Front Line; Gewinner der „Feature'-Gruppe und Auszeichnung für das Foto des Jahres, 1998; Preis für beste Fotografien des Jahres in Hongkong, Excellence in News Photography, SOPA-Award, 2007.

Autodidacte de formation, Chung devient photographe permanent au South China Morning Post en 1994. Depuis, il a reçu de nombreuses distinctions dont Spot News in Focus à Front Line en 1997, Photographe de l'année et gagnant de la section «Exclusivité» au Prix des meilleurs photographes de l'année à Hong Kong en 1998 et le prix SOPA «Excellence in Photography» en 2007.
→ p. 333

DU Xiuxian *(born 1926, Mizhi, Shaanxi province)*
In 1940, Du joined Mao's revolutionary base in Yan'an. In 1944, he studied photography in the People's Liberation Army's Art Troupe headed by photographer Wu Yinhan. In 1954, he joined the Xinhua News Agency, where in 1960 he was appointed chief photographer of the team that covered Zhongnanhai, the headquarters of the Chinese leaders. Du retired in 1986. His works have been widely published in China, among others in the anthology *Red Lenses* edited by the Chinese Communist Party Publishing House in 2006.

1940 schließt sich Du Maos revolutionärer Basis in Yan'an an. In der Kunsttruppe der Volksbefreiungsarmee wird er 1944 unter der Leitung von Wu Yinhan zum Fotografen ausgebildet. Ab 1954 arbeitet er für die Nachrichtenagentur Xinhua, wo er 1960 zum leitenden Fotografen des Teams aufsteigt, das aus Zhongnanhai berichtet, der Zentrale der chinesischen Führungselite. Du tritt 1986 in den Ruhestand. Seine Arbeiten sind in zahlreichen chinesischen Publikationen erschienen, so etwa im 2006 vom Verlag der Kommunistischen Partei Chinas herausgegebenen Sammelband *Rote Objektive*.

En 1940, Du rejoint la base révolutionnaire de Mao à Yan'an. En 1944, il étudie la photographie au sein de la troupe d'art de l'Armée populaire de libération, dirigée par le photographe Wu Yinhan. Il entre à l'agence de presse Xinhua en 1954, où il est nommé photographe en chef de l'équipe qui couvre les événements à Zhongnanhai, siège du gouvernement central chinois. Du prend sa retraite en 1986. Ses photographies ont fait l'objet de nombreuses publications en Chine, dont l'anthologie *Objectifs rouges*, parue en 2006 aux Éditions du Parti communiste chinois.
→ pp. 31, 150, 151, 161, 182, 226, 228/228, 230, 231, 232/233, 237, 238, 239, 240, 241, 250/251, 254/255, 256, 257, 258/259, 259, 260, 264, 265

FENG Jianguo *(born 1962, Hainan island)*
After graduating from Guangdong Provincial Broadcasting and Television University in 1983, Feng began working for Guangdong Television as an editor and assistant director. In 1988, he started studying advertising photography in Japan, graduating in 1996. In 2000, he joined the faculty of the Beijing Film Academy to teach photography. Feng's photographic documentation retracing the ancient Chinese Silk Road through Qinghai and Tibet, which took him almost ten years to complete, was published by the China Photographic Press under the title *A Western Journey on the Silk Road*.

Im Anschluss an sein Studium an der Universität für Rundfunk und Fernsehen der Provinz Guangdong wird Feng 1983 als Redakteur und stellvertretender Direktor des Fernsehsenders Guangdong verpflichtet. 1988 beginnt er das Studium der Werbefotografie in Japan, das er 1996 abschließt. Seit 2000 unterrichtet er Fotografie an der Filmakademie Peking. Sein Fotoband über Chinas Seidenstraße, die einst durch Qinghai und Tibet führte, erscheint 2007 bei China Photography Press unter dem Titel *Westwärts: Auf den Spuren der Seidenstraße*. Er ist das Ergebnis einer fast zehnjährigen Recherche.

Diplômé de l'Université de radiodiffusion et de télévision de la province du Guangdong, Feng débute en 1983 comme rédacteur et directeur assistant à la télévision du Guangdong. En 1988, il entame des études de photographie publicitaire au Japon, où il obtient son diplôme en 1996. Depuis 2000, il enseigne la photographie à l'Académie de cinéma de Pékin. Fruit d'un travail de près de dix ans, sa documentation photographique retraçant l'ancienne route de la soie chinoise à travers la province du Qinghai et le Tibet a été publiée par China Photography Press sous le titre de *Voyage à l'Ouest sur la route de la soie*.
→ pp. 318, 360, 361

GU Shoukang *(born 1933, Zhejiang province)*
Gu worked as a photo retoucher from 1954 to 1956. Between 1977 and 1982, he was the Xinhua News Agency's chief photographer in Lhasa, Tibet. In 1982, he moved on to become a deputy editor for *Photography World* magazine. In 1988, he was hired as a staff photographer by the Xinhua News Agency in Beijing, where he worked until his retirement in 1993.

Von 1954 bis 1956 arbeitet Gu als Fotoretoucheur. Zwischen 1977 und 1982 ist er als leitender Fotograf für die Nachrichtenagentur Xinhua in Lhasa, Tibet, tätig. 1982 übernimmt er den Posten des stellvertretenden Herausgebers der Zeitschrift *Photography World*. Von 1988 bis zu seiner Pensionierung im Jahr 1993 ist er als Redaktionsfotograf der Nachrichtenagentur Xinhua in Peking tätig.

Entre 1954 et 1956, Gu travaille en tant que retoucheur photographique. De 1977 à 1982, il est le photographe en chef du bureau de Lhassa, au Tibet, de l'agence de presse Xinhua. Entré à la revue *Photography World* en 1982 en tant que rédacteur en chef délégué, il est engagé en 1988 comme photographe par l'agence Xinhua à Pékin, où il travaille jusqu'à sa retraite en 1993.
→ p. 244

GUO Gai *(born 1957, Beijing)*
In 1975, Guo attended Beijing's No. 110 Middle School. In 1976, he was assigned to labor duty on a farm. From 1979 to 1994, he worked as a stonemason in the Beijing Stone Scripture Factory. Between 1995 and 2000, he was a journalist with the weekly newspaper *Music & Life*. Guo currently works as a freelance photographer and sculptor.

1975 besucht Guo die Mittelschule Nr. 110 in Peking. 1976 wird er zum Arbeitsdienst auf einem Bauernhof beordert. Von 1979 bis 1994 arbeitet er als Steinmetz in der Pekinger Werkstatt für Steinbeschriftung. Zwischen 1995 und 2000 ist er als Journalist für die Wochenzeitung *Music & Life* tätig. Derzeit arbeitet Guo als freischaffender Fotograf und Bildhauer.

Élève au collège n°110 à Pékin en 1975, Guo est envoyé à la campagne en 1976 dans le cadre du service du travail obligatoire. De 1979 à 1994, il est tailleur de pierres à la Manufacture de gravure sur pierre de Pékin. En 1995, il entre en tant que journaliste à l'hebdomadaire *Music & Life*, qu'il quitte en 2000. Guo travaille actuellement en tant que photographe indépendant et sculpteur.
→ pp. 342/343

HAN Lei *(born 1967, Kaifeng, Henan province)*
Han graduated from Beijing's Central Institute of Arts and Design in 1989. Han's practice is closely linked to his nomadic lifestyle. Inspired by Cartier-Bresson's concept of the "decisive moment," his travel photographs document his interest in life in small towns and social outcasts. Han belongs to the first generation of independent Chinese photographers to emerge in the late 1980s whose work has had significant influence on the use of photography in art and various approaches to image-making by the subsequent generation.

Han schließt sein Studium am Central Institute of Arts and Design in Peking 1989 ab. Hans künstlerische Praxis leitet sich unmittelbar aus seinem nomadenhaften Leben ab. Seine Reisefotografien zeugen von einem besonderen Interesse am Alltag in der Kleinstadt und an gesellschaftlichen Außenseitern, wobei er sich stets am Cartier-Bressons Prinzip des „entscheidenden Augenblicks" orientiert. Han gehört der ersten Generation freischaffender chinesischer Fotografen an, deren Arbeiten gegen Ende der 1980er-

Jahre wegen der Verwendung von Fotografie in der Kunst und unterschiedlichen Bildgestaltungstechniken einen entscheidenden Einfluss auf die nachfolgende Generation ausüben.

Han a obtenu son diplôme du Central Institute of Arts and Design à Pékin en 1998. La pratique artistique de Han est le fruit d'une vie de nomade. Inspirées de la notion de l'« instant décisif » chère à Cartier-Bresson, ses photographies de voyage témoignent de son intérêt pour le quotidien dans les petites villes et les parias de la société. Han appartient à la première génération de photographes chinois indépendants, qui émerge à la fin des années 1980 et dont le travail exerce une influence décisive sur l'utilisation de la photographie dans l'art et dans différents procédés de fabrication d'images par les générations suivantes. → p. 337

HE Yanguang (born 1951, Wuyuan county, Inner Mongolia)
From 1968 to 1973, He was assigned to an army camp in Heilongjiang province. Between 1973 and 1979, he worked in a factory and studied photography on his own. In 1980, he joined the China Youth Daily as a staff photographer and subsequently became its director of photography, a post he still occupies. He won the China Newspaper Picture of the Year Award in 2003 and 2005.

Von 1968 bis 1973 verrichtet He seinen Arbeitsdienst auf einem Armeebauernhof in der Provinz Heilongjiang. Zwischen 1973 und 1979 arbeitet er in einer Fabrik und erlernt als Autodidakt das Handwerk des Fotografen. 1980 wird er zum Redaktionsfotograf der Jugendzeitung China Youth Daily berufen, wo er schließlich zum Bildchefredakteur avanciert, ein Posten, den er bis heute inne hat. 2003 und 2005 wird He von der chinesischen Tagespresse für das Bild des Jahres ausgezeichnet.

De 1968 à 1973, He fait son service du travail obligatoire dans une ferme de l'armée dans la province du Heilongjiang. Entre 1973 et 1979, il travaille dans une usine, tout en étudiant la photographie en autodidacte. Il entre au quotidien China Youth Daily comme photographe avant de devenir son directeur de la photo, poste qu'il occupe jusqu'à ce jour. En 2003 et 2005, il est récompensé du Prix de l'image de l'année par la presse chinoise.
→ pp. 369, 382/383

HONG Ke (Liu Hongkai, 1929–1993)
Hong was a staff photographer with the Shandong Daily News before joining the China Youth Daily, where he worked as chief photographer.

Hong ist als Redaktionsfotograf der Tageszeitung Shandong Daily News tätig, ehe er als leitender Fotograf zum China Youth Daily wechselt.

Hong a travaillé en tant que photographe au quotidien Shandong Daily News avant de rejoindre le China Youth Daily comme photographe en chef. → p. 144

HOU Bo (born 1924, Xiaxian county, Shanxi province)
Hou joined the Chinese Communist Party in 1938. From 1939 to 1944, she studied at Yanbian Middle School and Yan'an Women's University (Mao's revolutionary base). In 1949, she was appointed director of the Department of Photography at the Public Security Bureau of the Central Committee of the Communist Party of China. As such, she was the official photographer of the founding ceremony of the People's Republic of China the same year. As Mao's personal photographer until 1961, she followed the Chairman on his trips across China and was present at his meetings with foreign heads of state or visiting delegations from friendly nations. In 1986, she exhibited together with Xu Xiaobing in China, Japan, and France. Her work has been published widely, such as in Palace of Eternal Happiness, Oral Autobiography, and Road.

Hou tritt 1938 der Kommunistischen Partei Chinas bei. Von 1939 bis 1944 besucht sie die Yanbian Mittelschule und die Frauenuniversität in Yan'an (Maos revolutionäre Basis). 1949 wird Hou zur Direktorin der Fotografieabteilung des Staatlichen Sicherheitsbüros des Zentralkomitees der Kom-

munistischen Partei Chinas berufen. In dieser Funktion darf sie die im gleichen Jahr stattfindende Gründungszeremonie der Volksrepublik China als offizielle Fotografin im Bild festhalten. Als Maos persönliche Fotografin bis 1961 begleitet sie den Großen Vorsitzenden auf seinen Reisen durch China und wohnt seinen Treffen mit auswärtigen Staatsoberhäuptern und Delegationen aus befreundeten Ländern bei. 1986 stellt sie zusammen mit Xu Xiaobing in China, Japan und Frankreich aus. Ihre Bilder sind in zahlreichen Publikationen erschienen, darunter Palace of Eternal Happiness, Oral Autobiography und Road.

Hou adhère au Parti communiste chinois en 1938. Entre 1939 et 1944, elle étudie au collège de Yanbian, puis à l'Université pour femmes de Yan'an (siège des troupes révolutionnaires de Mao). Nommée directrice du département photographique du Bureau de la sécurité publique du Comité central du Parti communiste chinois en 1949, elle couvre la cérémonie marquant la fondation de la République populaire de Chine en tant que photographe officielle. Photographe personnelle de Mao jusqu'en 1961, elle suit le Grand Timonier lors de ses déplacements en Chine et assiste à ses rencontres avec des chefs d'États étrangers ou des délégations de pays amis. En 1986, elle expose avec Xu Xiaobing en Chine, au Japon et en France. Ses photographies ont fait l'objet de nombreuses publications, dont Palace of Eternal Happiness, Oral Autobiography et Road.
→ pp. 13, 113, 116, 117, 138, 140/141, 142/143, 145, 153

HU Wugong (born 1949 in Xi'an, Shaanxi province)
Hu began working as a photographer in the army in 1969. In 1975, he joined Shanjin Metropolitan News as a staff photographer and is now its director of photography. He is currently the president of Shaanxi Photographers Association. He was awarded the China's Distinguished Journalist Prize for his 1983 coverage of the flood in Ankang. He has edited several books on Chinese photography, including China Humanism in 2003, published by Guangdong Fine Arts Museum.

Hu beginnt 1969 in der Armee als Fotograf zu arbeiten. 1975 geht er als Redaktionsfotograf zur Shanjin Metropolitan News und ist heute dort fotografischer Direktor. Zur Zeit steht er dem Fotografenverband von Shaanxi als Präsident vor. Für seine Berichterstattung von der Überschwemmung in Ankang 1983 wurde er mit dem China Distinguished Journalist Prize ausgezeichnet. Er hat mehrere Bücher über chinesische Fotografie herausgegeben, darunter den vom Kunstmuseum Guangdong publizierten Band China Humanism.

Hu débute comme photographe militaire en 1969. En 1975, il entre au Shanjin Metropolitan News dont il est aujourd'hui directeur de la photographie. Il est président de l'Association des photographes du Shaanxi et a reçu le Prix du meilleur photographe de Chine pour son reportage de 1983 sur les inondations d'Ankang. Il a dirigé l'édition de plusieurs livres sur la photographie chinoise dont China Humanism, publié par le Musée des Beaux-Arts du Guangdong en 2003. → p. 299

HU Yang (born 1959, Shanghai)
Hu started teaching himself photography in 1986. In 2004, a selection of his works was published under the title Shanghai Families. In 2005, his photographs were exhibited in Shanghai and abroad. Hu currently works as a freelance photographer.

Hu erlernt das Fotografieren als Autodidakt ab 1986. Eine Auswahl seiner Arbeiten wird 2004 unter dem Titel Shanghai Families publiziert. 2005 sind seine Fotos in mehreren Ausstellungen in Shanghai und im Ausland zu sehen. Hu arbeitet gegenwärtig als freischaffender Fotograf.

Hu apprend la photographie en autodidacte à partir de 1986. Une sélection de ses photographies paraît en 2004 sous le titre de Shanghai Families. En 2005, son travail a fait l'objet de plusieurs expositions à Shanghai et à l'étranger. Hu travaille actuellement en tant que photographe indépendant.
→ pp. 372, 373, 374, 375

HUANG Yimin (born 1960, Hainan island)
Huang started teaching himself photography in 1981. He graduated from the Department of Journalism at Ningnan University in Guangdong province in 1988. Huang is currently based in Hainan province and works as a staff photographer at China Daily.

Huang erlernt das Fotografieren als Autodidakt ab 1981. 1988 schließt er sein Studium an der Abteilung für Journalismus der Universität Ningnan in der Provinz Guangdong ab. Huang lebt zurzeit in der Provinz Hainan und arbeitet als Redaktionsfotograf für die China Daily.

Huang apprend la photographie en autodidacte à partir de 1981. En 1988, il obtient son diplôme du département de journalisme de l'Université de Ningnan, dans la province du Guangdong. Huang vit actuellement dans la province du Hainan et travaille comme photographe au China Daily.
→ p. 365

JI Lianbo (born 1921, Yuancheng, Hubei province)
In 1937, Ji joined the 8th Route Army of the Chinese Communist Forces. In 1940, he started working as a photographer for the Northern China Pictorial and the People's Liberation Army Pictorial. In 1956, he was hired by the state-owned Xinhua News Agency as a staff photographer and became its African correspondent in 1958. He returned to Beijing after his assignment and resumed work at the agency until his retirement in 1982.

Ji schließt sich 1937 der 8. Feldarmee der Kommunistischen Streitkräfte Chinas an. Ab 1940 arbeitet er als Fotograf für die Illustrierten Northern China Pictorial und People's Liberation Army Pictorial. 1956 wird er der staatlichen Nachrichtenagentur Xinhua als Redaktionsfotograf zugewiesen, für die er ab 1958 als Afrikakorrespondent tätig ist. Nach seiner Rückkehr arbeitet er bis zu seiner Pensionierung 1982 im Pekinger Büro der Agentur.

En 1937, Ji s'engage dans la 8e Armée des Forces armées communistes chinoises. En 1940, il débute en tant que photographe aux revues Northern China Pictorial et People's Liberation Army Pictorial. En 1956, il entre à l'agence de presse étatique Xinhua, dont il devient le correspondant en Afrique à partir de 1958. À son retour, il réintègre le bureau de l'agence à Pékin jusqu'à sa retraite en 1982.
→ pp. 244, 245

JIANG Jian (born 1953, Kaifeng, Henan province)
From 1969 to 1978, Jiang was assigned to the countryside in the northeast in Liaoning province, where he worked as an electrician and played the violin in the factory's orchestra. Jiang started his photographic career in 1984.

Zwischen 1969 und 1978 verrichtet Jiang seinen Arbeitsdienst im Nordosten der Provinz Liaoning, wo er als Elektriker arbeitet und die Violine im Orchester der Fabrik spielt. 1984 beginnt er eine Laufbahn als Fotograf.

Entre 1969 et 1978, dans le cadre de son service du travail obligatoire dans le nord-est de la province du Liaoning, Jiang travaille comme électricien et joue du violon dans l'orchestre de l'usine. Il entame une carrière de photographe en 1984. → p. 92

JIANG Shaowu (born 1932, Shenyang, Liaoning province)
In 1947, Jiang, aged 15, joined the Communist resistance force in China's northeastern Jiaodong region. From 1954 to 1985, he was assigned to the Liaoning Daily News as a staff photographer. A loyal communist, he describes his work as "using my hands, which exchanged the spear (used in the War of Resistance against Japan) for a camera." Jiang's photographic coverage of the turmoil caused by the Cultural Revolution in his native province of Liaoning is considered unprecedented. His photographs have seldom been shown or published abroad as they might cause embarrassment to his country. Jiang retired in 1995, but gives occasional lectures.

Im Jahr 1947, im Alter von 15 Jahren, schließt sich Jiang den kommunistischen Widerstandskämpfern in der Gegend von Jiaodong im Nordosten Chinas an. Von 1954 bis 1985 arbeitet er als Redaktionsfotograf für die *Liaoning Daily News*. Der loyale Kommunist sagt von sich selbst, er habe „den Speer in seiner Hand (aus dem Widerstandskrieg gegen Japan) gegen den Fotoapparat eingetauscht". Jiangs fotografische Berichterstattung vom Chaos der Kulturrevolution in seiner Heimatprovinz Liaoning gilt als einzigartig. Jiangs Arbeiten sind selten im Ausland publiziert oder ausgestellt worden, da sie sein geliebtes Heimatland in Verlegenheit bringen könnten. Jiang, seit 1995 im Ruhestand, hält gelegentlich Vorträge.

En 1947, Jiang, âgé de 15 ans, rejoint les forces de résistance communistes dans la région de Jiaodong dans le nord-est de la Chine. De 1954 à 1985, il est employé comme photographe au *Liaoning Daily News*. Communiste loyal, il dit avoir « troqué l'épée dans sa main (de la Guerre de résistance contre le Japon) contre l'appareil photo ». Sa couverture des bouleversements causés par la Révolution culturelle dans sa province natale du Liaoning est sans égale. Les photographies de Jiang ont rarement été publiées ou exposées à l'étranger, étant donné qu'elles sont susceptibles d'embarrasser son pays tant aimé. Ayant pris sa retraite en 1995, Jiang donne parfois des conférences.
→ *pp. 18, 52/53, 172, 174/175, 190, 195, 199, 202, 203, 204/205, 206/207, 208*

JIN Cheng (*born 1982, Wuhan, Hubei Province*)
Jin was appointed UNICEF Children's Ambassador of China in 2001. In 2004, he joined the Reuters News Agency as staff photographer. In 2005, his work was awarded First Prize in the photo contest "Beijing—An Olympic City in View." He was promoted to photographic editor at Reuters' Beijing bureau in 2006. In 2007, Jin received the Picture of the Year Award from Reuters Pictures and graduated with a Master's Degree from the Department of Journalism and Communication at Tsinghua University.

Im Jahr 2001 wird Jin zum UNICEF-Kinderbotschafter in China berufen. 2004 wird er von der Nachrichtenagentur Reuters als Redaktionsfotograf verpflichtet. 2005 gewinnt er den Ersten Preis im Fotowettbewerb *Beijing – An Olympic City in View*. 2006 wird er zum Fotoredakteur des Pekinger Büros von Reuters befördert. 2007 wird Jin von Reuters Pictures für das Foto des Jahres ausgezeichnet und schließt sein Studium des Journalismus und der Kommunikation an der Tsinghua Universität mit einem Master ab.

Nommé Ambassadeur des enfants pour la Chine par l'UNICEF en 2001, Jin entre comme photographe à l'agence de presse Reuters en 2004. En 2005, il gagne le Premier prix du concours photographique *Beijing – An Olympic City in View*. En 2006, il est promu rédacteur photographique du bureau pékinois de l'agence Reuters. En 2007, il est récompensé du Prix de l'image de l'année décerné par Reuters Pictures et obtient un mastère en journalisme et communication de l'Université Tsinghua. → *p. 398*

LEI Yu (*born 1970, Tazhou, Sichuan province*)
Lei graduated from the Department of Journalism at Lanzhou University in Gansu province in 1994. In 1996, he began work as a staff photographer for the *Chengdu Business Daily News*, where he covers the Chinese stock market.

Lei schließt 1994 sein Journalismusstudium an der Universität Lanzhou in der Provinz Gansu ab. 1996 beginnt er seine Tätigkeit als Redaktionsfotograf der Wirtschaftszeitung *Chengdu Business Daily News*, für die er von der chinesischen Börse berichtet.

En 1994, Lei obtient son diplôme du département de journalisme de l'Université de Lanzhou dans la province du Gansu. En 1996, il entre au quotidien économique *Chengdu Business Daily News*, pour le compte duquel il couvre la bourse chinoise. → *p. 390*

LI Lang (*born 1972, Chengdu, Sichuan province*)
Li graduated from the Shanxi University of Finance and Economics in 1970. In 1999, he was awarded the Medal of Excellence by the Mother Jones International Fund for Documentary Photography. In 2005, his works were shown

in several exhibitions, including the Rome International Photography Festival, "Shifting Views: Chinese Urban Documentary Photography," at the Institute for the Humanities, University of Michigan, and the Guangzhou Triennial at the Guangdong Museum of Art in Guangzhou. In 2006, he participated in "Ran: China Contemporary Art" at the Jendela Visual Art Space in Singapore. In 2007, his work was shown in "Vision of China: Contemporary Photography" at the Trevi Cultural Centre and "The Yi: Photographs by Li Lang" at the Shanghai Art Museum. Li currently lives in Guangzhou, where he works as a freelance photographer.

Li erhält seinen Abschluss 1970 an der Shanxi Universität für Finanzen und Ökonomie. 1999 wird er vom Mother Jones International Fund for Documentary Photography mit der Medaille für Exzellenz ausgezeichnet. 2005 sind seine Arbeiten in zahlreichen Ausstellungen zu sehen, darunter das Internationale Fotofestival in Rom, *Shifting Views: Chinese Urban Documentary Photography* am Institut für Humanwissenschaften der Universität von Michigan und die Triennale von Guangzhou im Kunstmuseum der Provinz Guangdong in Guangzhou. 2006 nimmt er an der Ausstellung *Ran: China Contemporary Art* im Jendela Visual Art Space in Singapur teil. 2007 sind seine Arbeiten in den Ausstellungen *Vision of China: Contemporary Photography* im Kulturzentrum Trevi und *The Yi: Photographs by Li Lang* im Kunstmuseum Shanghai zu sehen. Li lebt und arbeitet als freier Fotograf in Guangzhou.

Li obtient son diplôme de l'Université de l'économie et des finances de Shanxi en 1970. En 1999, il est distingué par la Médaille de l'Excellence du Mother Jones International Fund for Documentary Photography. En 2005, son travail figure dans plusieurs expositions, dont le Festival international de la photographie à Rome, *Shifting Views: Chinese Urban Documentary Photography* à l'Institut des sciences humaines de l'Université du Michigan et la Triennale de Guangzhou au Musée d'art du Guangdong à Guangzhou. En 2006, il a participé à *Ran: China Contemporary Art* au Jendela Visual Art Space à Singapour. En 2007, son travail est exposé dans *Vision of China: Contemporary Photography* au Centre culturel de Trevi et *The Yi: Photographs by Li Lang* au Musée d'art de Shanghai. Li vit et travaille en tant que photographe indépendant à Guangzhou. → *p. 354*

LI Nan (*born 1961, Jinan, Shandong province*)
Li graduated from the Shandong Art Institute in 1989. In 1993, she began working in news photography as a staff photographer with *Shandong Pictorial*, before joining the *Dazhong Daily*. In 1996, she won First Prize in the "Art Photography" category of the World Press Photo Contest. In 1998, China Photography Press published Li Nan's collected works. Since 1998, Li has participated regularly in international photography exhibitions.

Li schließt ihr Studium am Kunstinstitut von Shandong 1989 ab. 1993 beginnt sie als Redaktionsfotografin der Zeitschrift *Shandong Pictorial* im Bereich des Fotojournalismus zu arbeiten, bevor sie zum *Dazhong Daily* wechselt. 1996 gewinnt sie den Ersten Preis in der Kategorie „Kunstfotografie" des World Press Photo-Wettbewerbs. 1998 werden ihre gesammelten Werke vom Verlag China Photography Press veröffentlicht. Li nimmt seit 1998 regelmäßig an internationalen Fotoausstellungen teil.

Li obtient son diplôme de l'Institut d'art du Shandong en 1989. En 1993, elle entame une carrière de journaliste photo à la revue *Shandong Pictorial*, avant de rejoindre le *Dazhong Daily*. En 1996, elle remporte le Premier prix du concours World Press Photo dans la catégorie « Photographie d'art ». En 1998, l'éditeur China Photography Press publie une anthologie de ses travaux. Depuis 1998, Li participe régulièrement à des expositions photographiques internationales. → *pp. 315, 336, 358/359*

LI Zhensheng (*born 1940, Dalian, Shandong province*)
Li graduated from the Department of Photography at the Changchun Film Institute in 1963. From 1963 to 1983, he worked as a staff photographer for the *Heilongjiang Daily*

News. Between 1983 and 1998, he taught news photography at China's Police Academy. Li's documentation of the Cultural Revolution in Heilongjiang province, published as *Red Colour News Soldier: A Chinese Photographer's Odyssey through the Cultural Revolution*, was awarded the 2003 Oliver Rebbot Award for best photographic reporting from abroad by the Overseas Press Club of America.

Li schließt 1963 sein Studium an der Abteilung für Fotografie am Filminstitut von Changchun ab. Von 1963 bis 1983 arbeitet er als Pressefotograf für die *Heilongjiang Daily News*. Zwischen 1983 und 1998 unterrichtet er Pressefotografie an Chinas Polizeiakademie. Lis Dokumentation der Kulturrevolution in der Provinz Heilongjiang, *Red Colour News Soldier: A Chinese Photographer's Odyssey Through the Cultural Revolution*, wird 2003 vom Overseas Press Club of America mit dem Oliver-Rebbot-Preis für die beste ausländische Fotoreportage ausgezeichnet.

Li obtient son diplôme du département de photographie de l'Institut du cinéma de Changchun en 1963. De 1963 à 1983, il travaille comme photographe au *Heilongjiang Daily News*. De 1983 à 1998, il enseigne la photographie de presse à l'Académie de police chinoise. Publié sous le titre de *Red-Color News Soldier: A Chinese Photographer's Odyssey Through the Cultural Revolution*, son travail documentaire sur la Révolution culturelle dans la province du Heilongjiang reçoit le Prix Oliver Rebbot du Overseas Press Club of America pour le meilleur reportage photo étranger en 2003.
→ *pp. 25, 26/27, 165, 169, 172, 173, 177, 179, 194, 196/197, 198, 200, 201, 203, 225, 240, 332*

LIU Heung Shing (*born 1951, Hong Kong*)
In 1954, Liu attended primary school in Fuzhou in Fujian province. He returned to Hong Kong in 1960, when the People's Republic of China was mired in economic problems following the Great Leap Forward. From 1971 to 1975, Liu studied Political Science and graduated from Hunter College, City University of New York. An apprentice with Gjon Mili at *Life* magazine, Liu became *Time* magazine's first accredited photographer in China, in 1978. In 1981, he joined the Associated Press as a staff photographer based in Beijing. From 1984 to 1994, he worked as a staff photographer for the Associated Press in Los Angeles, New Delhi, Seoul, and Moscow, covering major events in the last decades of the 20th century.

1954 besucht Liu die Grundschule in Fuzhou in der Provinz Fujian. 1960 kehrt er nach Hongkong zurück, nachdem die Volksrepublik China in der Folge des Großen Sprungs nach vorn in eine wirtschaftliche Notlage geraten ist. Von 1971 bis 1975 studiert er Politikwissenschaft am Hunter College der City University of New York. Im Anschluss an seine Ausbildung bei der Zeitschrift *Life* unter der Leitung von Gjon Mili wird Liu 1978 als erster akkreditierter Fotograf von *Time Magazine* in China verpflichtet. 1981 wechselt er als Redaktionsfotograf zu Associated Press in Peking. Von 1984 bis 1994 ist er als Redaktionsfotograf für Associated Press in Los Angeles, Neu Delhi, Seoul und Moskau tätig und berichtet von bedeutenden Ereignissen des ausgehenden 20. Jahrhunderts.

Liu termine ses études primaires à Fuzhou, dans la province du Fujian, en 1954. En 1960, il repart à Hong Kong, fuyant les difficultés économiques à la république populaire de Chine à la suite du Grand bond en avant. À partir de 1971, il est étudiant en sciences politiques au Hunter College de la City University of New York, où il obtient son diplôme en 1975. Après un apprentissage auprès de Gjon Mili à la revue *Life*, il devient le premier photographe chinois accrédité de *Time Magazine*. Il rallie *Associated Press* à Pékin en 1981. De 1984 à 1994, il travaille en tant que photographe pour *Associated Press* à Los Angeles, New Delhi, Séoul et Moscou et couvre les événements majeurs de la fin du XXᵉ siècle.
→ *pp. 2, 4, 58, 67, 74, 266/267, 268, 269, 270/271, 272, 273, 281, 285, 286, 287, 288/289, 290, 291, 292/293, 294, 295, 296, 297, 302/303, 304, 305, 313, 424*

LIU Zheng (born 1969, Wugiang county, Hebei province)
Liu graduated from the Institute of Optics at Beijing Poly-technic University in 1989. In 1990, he started teaching himself photography. In 1991, he joined *The Worker's Daily* in Beijing as a staff photographer. Liu was a co-founder with Rong Rong of the short-lived independent magazine *New Photo*. Although to the Western eye, many of Liu's photographs from the best-known series *The Chinese* bear a resemblence to the works of Richard Avedon or August Sander, they focus on subjects that were considered taboo at the time to reveal the heterogeneity of Chinese society.

Nach seinem Abschluss am Institut für Optik der Polytechnischen Universität Peking 1989 erlernt Liu ab 1990 das Fotografieren als Autodidakt. 1991 schließt er sich der Tageszeitung *The Worker's Daily* in Peking als Redaktions-fotograf an. Zusammen mit Rong Rong gründet er die kurz-lebige unabhängige Fotozeitschrift *New Photo*. Wenngleich für westliche Augen viele der Bilder in *The Chinese*, seiner bekanntesten Fotoserie, eine gewisse Ähnlichkeit mit den Arbeiten Richard Avedons oder August Sanders aufweisen, behandeln sie Themen, die zur Zeit ihrer Entstehung als Tabus galten, da sie die Heterogenität der chinesischen Ge-sellschaft offenlegen.

Diplômé de l'Institut d'optique de l'Université polytech-nique de Pékin en 1989, Liu apprend la photographie en autodidacte à partir de 1990. En 1991, il rejoint l'équipe du quotidien *The Worker's Daily* à Pékin comme photographe. Il est cofondateur avec Rong Rong de l'éphémère revue photographique indépendante *New Photo*. Bien qu'aux yeux de l'Occident, les images de sa série la plus connue, *The Chinese*, rappellent les travaux de Richard Avedon ou d'August Sander, elles traitent de sujets considérés tabous à l'époque, qui révèlent l'hétérogénéité de la société chinoise.
→ *p. 337*

LU Beifeng (born 1960, Beijing)
Lu started teaching himself photography in 1988. In 1992, he joined the *Beijing Youth Daily* as a staff photographer. Lu is currently director of photography at the *Beijing Youth Weekly Magazine*.

Lu erlernt das Fotografieren als Autodidakt ab 1988. 1992 beginnt er als Fotograf bei der Jugendzeitung *Beijing Youth Daily*. Lu arbeitet gegenwärtig als leitender Fotograf für die Wochenzeitschrift *Beijing Youth Weekly Magazine*.

En 1988, Lu apprend la photographie en autodidacte. En 1992, il entre au quotidien *Beijing Youth Daily* comme photographe. Lu est actuellement directeur de la photo-graphie de l'hebdomadaire *Beijing Youth Weekly Magazine*.
→ *p. 399*

LU Guang (born 1961, Yongkang, Zhejiang province)
Lu began working in a factory in 1980. In 1987, he joined the Workers Cultural Workshop as a commercial photog-rapher. In 1993, he enrolled at the Central Institute of Art and Design in Beijing to study photography. Since 1994, Lu has been working as a freelance photographer, traveling extensively across China to document social issues that are deemed controversial. His topics include the gold and coal mining industries, women drug addicts, AIDS victims, and the construction of the Qinghai-Tibet railway.

Lu arbeitet ab 1980 in einer Fabrik. 1987 tritt er der Kulturwerkstatt der Arbeiter als Werbefotograf bei. 1993 schreibt er sich am Zentralen Institut für Kunst und Design in Peking ein, wo er Fotografie studiert. Seit 1994 unter-nimmt er als freiberuflicher Fotograf ausgedehnte Reisen durch China, bei denen er kontroverse soziale Probleme aufgreift wie die Gold- und Kohleindustrie, drogenabhän-gige Frauen, AIDS oder den Bau der Eisenbahnverbindung Qinghai-Tibet.

Lu gagne sa vie en tant qu'ouvrier dans une usine à par-tir de 1980. En 1987, il entre à l'Atelier culturel des ouvriers comme photographe commercial. En 1993, il s'inscrit à l'Institut central d'art et de design à Pékin, où il étudie la photographie. Depuis 1994, il sillonne la Chine en tant que photographe indépendant, documentant des sujets jugés

controversés, comme l'industrie de l'extraction d'or et de charbon, les femmes droguées, le sida ou encore la construc-tion de la voie ferrée Qinghai-Tibet.
→ *p. 85, 366, 367, 368, 369, 388*

LÜ Nan (born 1962, Beijing)
In the course of his long-standing practice in the field of docu-mentary photography, Lü has addressed a number of social subjects ranging from Chinese Catholicism and the situation in the Golden Triangle to the fate of the Tibetan people and life in mental institutions. Lü's series on Tibet, entitled *Four Seasons: Daily Life of Tibetan Peasants*, was published in 2007. Lü is a member of the Magnum Photos agency.

In seiner langjährigen Arbeit als Dokumentarfotograf hat Lü unzählige soziale Themen aufgegriffen, von der katholischen Kirche Chinas und der Situation im Goldenen Dreieck bis hin zum Alltag der Tibeter und dem Leben in der Psychiatrie. Seine Arbeit über den Tibet erscheint 2007 unter dem Titel *Four Seasons: Daily Life of Tibetan Peasants*. Lü ist Mitglied der Agentur Magnum Photos.

Au cours de sa longue carrière de photographe docu-mentaire, Lü s'est intéressé à un large éventail de problémati-ques sociales allant de l'Église catholique chinoise à la situation dans le Triangle d'Or en passant par le quotidien des Tibétains et la vie dans les institutions psychiatriques. Son travail sur le Tibet a paru en 2007 sous le titre de *Four Seasons: Daily Life of Tibetan Peasants*. Lü est membre de l'agence Magnum Photos.   → *p. 319*

LÜ Xiangyou (1928–2007)
Lü enrolled in the People's Liberation Army in 1947 and started working in photography in 1948. After joining the Chinese Communist Party in 1950, he accompanied the People's Army when it crossed the Yalu river into North Korea to fight U.S. troops. He was subsequently decorated by the army for his coverage of the Korean War. In 1957, he joined the *People's Daily*, for which he photographed Chinese leaders, including Mao Zedong and Deng Xiaoping, in their daily activities. In 1979, he joined the China News Agency.

Lü tritt 1947 der Volksbefreiungsarmee bei und beginnt 1948 als Fotograf zu arbeiten. 1950 wird er Mitglied der Kommunistischen Partei Chinas und überquert den Fluss Yalu im Gefolge der Armee, die in Nordkorea gegen US-Truppen kämpft. Für seine Berichterstattung über den Koreakrieg wird ihm eine Auszeichnung der Armee zuteil. 1957 dokumentiert er für die Tageszeitung *People's Daily* den Alltag der chinesischen Führungselite, darunter Mao Zedong und Deng Xiaoping. Ab 1979 arbeitet er für die Presseagentur China News Agency.

En 1947, Lü s'engage dans l'Armée populaire de libéra-tion. Il commence à travailler avec la photographie en 1948. Après avoir adhéré au Parti communiste chinois en 1950, il franchit le fleuve Yalu dans le sillage de l'armée, qui part combattre les troupes américaines en Corée du Nord. Sa couverture de la guerre de Corée lui vaudra d'être décoré par l'armée. En 1957, il entre au *People's Daily*, pour le compte duquel il documente le quotidien des responsables chinois, dont Mao Zedong et Deng Xiaoping. En 1979, il entre à l'agence de presse China News Agency.   → *p. 187*

LUO Xiaoyun (born 1953, Beijing)
Luo graduated from the Department of Photography at Beijing's People's University in 1985. Before she returned to university, Luo worked as a staff photographer for the China News Agency. In 1987, she launched her own agency, which catered to the Taiwan-based *Great Earth Geographic Magazine*. In 2007, her works documenting the 1976 pro-tests in Tiananmen Square were published under the title *Unforgettable 1976*.

Luo schließt ihr Studium an der Fotografieabteilung der Volksuniversität Peking 1985 ab. Bevor sie zur Univer-sität zurückkehrt, arbeitet sie als Redaktionsfotografin in der Agentur China News Agency. 1987 gründet sie ihre eigene Agentur mit Vertrieb an das in Taiwan erscheinende *Great*

Earth Geographic Magazine. 2007 werden ihre Fotografien des Protests auf dem Tiananmen-Platz 1976 unter dem Ti-tel *Unvergessliches 1976* veröffentlicht.

Luo obtient son diplôme du département de photo-graphie de l'Université du peuple à Pékin en 1985. Avant de retourner à l'université, elle travaille en tant que photo-graphe à l'agence de presse China News Agency. En 1987, elle lance sa propre agence, qui alimente le magazine taïwa-nais *Great Earth Geographic Magazine*. En 2007, son travail documentaire sur les manifestations de la place Tian'anmen en 1976 est publié sous le titre de *Unforgettable 1976*.
→ *p. 252*

MENG Zhaorui (born 1930, Tangshan, Hebei province)
Meng joined the Chinese Communist Party in 1946. In 1948, he began his career as staff photographer for China's first illustrated magazine, the *Northwest Pictorial*. Among others, he recorded the battle of Beiping-Tianjin during the Civil War. Meng then joined the *PLA Pictorial* as a staff photographer. In 1949, his work took him to Beijing as part of the army's liberating forces. Between 1950 and 1952, he covered the Korean War. In 1967, he photographed China's first hydrogen bomb test and in 1981 he documented the trial of the "Gang of Four."

1946 tritt Meng der Kommunistischen Partei Chinas bei. 1948 beginnt er seine Laufbahn als Redaktionsfotograf der ersten Illustrierten Chinas, der *Northwest Pictorial*. Un-ter anderem fotografiert er die Schlacht von Peking-Tianjin im Bürgerkrieg. Anschließend arbeitet er als Redaktions-fotograf für die Illustrierte *PLA Pictorial*. 1949 führt ihn seine Arbeit im Gefolge der kommunistischen Befreiungs-streitkräfte nach Peking. Zwischen 1950 und 1952 berichtet er vom Koreakrieg. 1967 fotografiert er den ersten Wasser-stoffbombentest Chinas. 1981 dokumentiert er den Prozess gegen die Viererbande.

Meng entre au Parti communiste chinois en 1946. En 1948, il entame une carrière de photographe au sein du premier magazine illustré de Chine, le *Northwest Pictorial*. Entre autres, il documente la bataille de Pékin-Tianjin lors de la Guerre civile. Il rejoint ensuite le magazine illustré *PLA Pictorial* comme photographe. En 1949, son travail le mène à Pékin dans le sillage des troupes de libération communistes. Entre 1950 et 1952, il couvre la guerre de Corée. En 1967, il photographie le premier essai de bombe à hydrogène chinois. En 1981, il couvre le procès de la Bande des quatre.
→ *pp. 118, 119, 182, 183, 184/185, 188, 189, 193, 284*

MIAO Jiaxin (born in 1976, Shanghai)
Miao graduated from Shanghai Teachers' University and is currently studying photography in New York. His works have been exhibited in a group show at the Pingyao Pho-tography Festival in Shaanxi province, 2005.

Nach einem Abschluss an der Pädagogischen Hoch-schule von Shanghai studiert Miao jetzt Fotografie in New York. Seine Arbeiten wurden 2005 in einer Gruppenausstel-lung beim Pingyao Photography Festival in der Provinz Shaanxi gezeigt.

Diplômé de l'École normale supérieure de Shanghai, il étudie actuellement la photographie à New York. Ses travaux ont été présentés dans des expositions de groupe au Festival de photographie de Pingyao, province du Shaanxi, en 2005.   → *p. 391*

PENG Xiangjie (born 1961, Xi'an, Shaanxi province)
Peng worked as a photographer for the China Xi'an Aeronautic Engineering Company from 2002 to 2005. His works have been exhibited in South Korea, France, the USA, and Germany.

Peng war von 2002 bis 2005 als Fotograf für die China Xi'an Aeronautic Engineering Company tätig. Seine Arbeiten werden in Südkorea, Frankreich, den USA und Deutschland ausgestellt.

De 2002 à 2005, Peng a travaillé comme photographe pour la compagnie d'ingénierie aéronautique China Xi'an.

Ses travaux ont été exposés en Corée du Sud, en France, aux États-Unis et en Allemagne.　→ p. 315, 336, 357

PU Feng *(born 1977, Nanjing, Jiangsu province)*
Pu graduated in 2000 from Nanjing Industrial University, where he studied Business Management. In 2003, he moved to Beijing and taught himself photography before he joined the *Xinjing Daily News*.

Pu schließt 2000 an der Nanjing Industrial University ein Wirtschaftsstudium ab. 2003 zieht er nach Peking und versucht sich autodidaktisch als Fotograf, ehe er zu *Xinjing Daily News* geht.

Pu est diplômé de l'Université des techniques industrielles de Nanjing (2000) où il a étudié la gestion des affaires. En 2003, il s'installe à Pékin et apprend par lui-même la photographie avant d'entrer au *Xinjing Daily News*.
→ p. 384

QIAN Sijie *(born 1929, Haihe county, Heilongjiang province)*
Qian joined the Chinese Liberation Army without having finished high school. He was made an army photographer after learning photography at *Northeast Illustrated* magazine. Qian was assigned to the news bureau of the central government following the establishment of the People's Republic. He covered the Korea War, 1951–1953. He was sent to photograph African countries between 1959 and 1964. When he returned to Beijing he was sent to cover Mao in 1964. Qian accompanied Deng Xiaoping on his visit to the United States in 1979. He also worked in Tokyo for Xinhua News Agency from 1983 to 1988. He has retired and lives in Beijing.

Ohne die Schule zu beenden, schließt sich Qian der chinesischen Befreiungsarmee an und wird der Armee als Fotograf zugewiesen, nachdem er beim *Northeast Illustrated Magazine* das Fotografieren erlernt hat. Von 1951 bis 1953 berichtet er vom Koreakrieg. Zwischen 1959 und 1964 hat er den Auftrag, in afrikanischen Ländern zu fotografieren. Nach seiner Rückkehr nach Peking erhält er 1964 die Anweisung, über Mao zu berichten, 1979 begleitet er Deng Xiaoping bei seinem Besuch in den USA. Von 1983 bis 1988 ist er in Tokio für die Nachrichtenagentur Xinhua tätig. Heute hat er sich zur Ruhe gesetzt und lebt in Peking.

Qian s'engage dans l'Armée de libération chinoise avant de terminer ses études au collège. Il est photographe pour l'armée après avoir appris les rudiments du métier au *Northeast Illustrated Magazine*. Après la fondation de la république, il est nommé au bureau de l'information du gouvernement central. Il couvre la guerre de Corée en 1951–53, puis travaille en Afrique de 1959 à 1964. À son retour à Pékin, il est nommé auprès de Mao Zedong en 1964. Il accompagne Deng Xiaoping lors de sa visite aux États-Unis en 1979. Il travaille également à Tokyo pour l'agence de presse Xinhua de 1983 à 198. Retraité, il vit à Pékin.
→ pp. 180/181

QIN Wen *(born 1954, Chongqing, Sichuan province)*
From 1972 to 1988, Qin taught at Chongqing's Middle School No. 83. Between 1985 and 1988, he studied photography at the Chongqing Teachers' College. His best-known body of work is a comprehensive photographic documentation on the Three Gorges area of the Yangtze river. His photographs have been exhibited at the annual Pingyao Photography Festival in Shanxi province, among other venues. Qin lives and works as a freelance photographer in Chongqing, where he runs his own business.

Von 1972 bis 1988 unterrichtet Qin an der Mittelschule Nr. 83 in Chongqing. Zwischen 1985 und 1988 studiert er Fotografie am Pädagogischen Kolleg von Chongqing. Seine bekannteste Arbeit ist eine umfassende Fotodokumentation der Drei-Schluchten-Region des Jangtse. Sie war unter anderem im Rahmen des jährlichen Fotofestivals von Pingyao in der Provinz Shanxi zu sehen. Qin lebt und arbeitet als freier Fotograf in Chongqing, wo er eine eigene Agentur betreibt.

De 1972 à 1988, Qin enseigne au collège n°83 à Chongqing. Entre 1985 et 1988, il étudie la photographie au Collège pédagogique de Chongqing. Son œuvre majeure est une vaste documentation photographique de la région des Trois Gorges sur le Yang-Tsé. Elle a notamment été exposée au Festival annuel de la photographie de Pingyao dans la province du Shanxi. Qin vit et travaille comme photographe indépendant à Chongqing, où il a sa propre agence.
→ pp. 378/379, 380

QIU Haiying *(born 1964, Yilong county, Sichuan province)*
Qiu joined the Chinese Communist Party and received university education. He worked as a clerk and teacher before joining the *Guang'an Daily* in 1994 as a staff photographer. His work has been widely published in the *People's Daily* and distributed by the Xinhua News Agency.

Qiu tritt der Kommunistischen Partei Chinas bei und absolviert eine Universitätsausbildung. Er arbeitet zunächst als Büroangestellter und Lehrer, bevor er 1994 als Redaktionsfotograf zur *Guang'an Daily* geht. Seine Arbeiten werden regelmäßig in der Tageszeitung *People's Daily* abgedruckt und von der Nachrichtenagentur Xinhua verbreitet.

Qiu devient membre du Parti communiste chinois et fait des études universitaires. Il a d'abord été employé de bureau et enseignant avant d'entrer en tant que photographe au quotidien *Guang'an Daily* en 1994. Ses travaux sont régulièrement publiés par le *People's Daily* et diffusés par l'agence de presse Xinhua.　→ p. 391

QIU Yan *(born 1961, Gongan county, Hubei province)*
In 1970, Qiu was sent to the countryside to be "reeducated" by the peasants. In 1987, he graduated from the Central China Technical College in Wuhan and studied journalism. Between 1994 and 2006, he worked as a staff photographer at the *Wuhan Evening News*. In 1998, he was voted one of China's Ten Best Photographers by *China Youth Daily*. In 2004 and 2005, his work was distinguished in the "Daily Life" and "Sports" categories of the World Press Photo Contest. In 2007, he joined the *Yangtze River Daily* as a staff photographer.

1970 wird Qiu zur Umerziehung durch Bauern aufs Land geschickt. 1987 schließt er sein Studium an der Technischen Hochschule Zentralchinas in Wuhan ab und studiert Journalismus. Von 1994 bis 2006 arbeitet er als Redaktionsfotograf bei der Abendzeitung *Wuhan Evening News*. 1998 wird er von *China Youth Daily* zu einem der Zehn Besten Fotografen Chinas gewählt. 2004 und 2005 wird seine Arbeit in den Kategorien „Alltagsleben" und „Sport" beim World Press Photo-Wettbewerb ausgezeichnet. 2007 wechselt er als Redaktionsfotograf zur Tageszeitung *Yangtze River Daily*.

En 1970, Qiu est envoyé à la campagne pour être rééduqué par les paysans. En 1987, il obtient son diplôme de l'École supérieure technique de Chine centrale à Wuhan et étudie le journalisme. De 1994 à 2006, il travaille comme photographe au quotidien du soir *Wuhan Evening News*. En 1998, il est élu l'un des Dix meilleurs photographes de Chine par le *China Youth Daily*. En 2004 et 2005, son travail est distingué dans les catégories « Vie quotidienne » et « Sports » du concours World Press Photo. Depuis 2007, Qiu est photographe au *Yangtze River Daily*.
→ pp. 300, 339, 365, 391

REN Wen *(born 1973, Chongqing, Sichuan province)*
Ren graduated from the Military Mechanical Engineering College in 1995. He worked as a photographer in the army for more than ten years before becoming a staff photographer with the *Chongqing Evening News*.

Ren erhält 1995 seinen Abschluss an der Hochschule für Militärtechnik. Er arbeitet über zehn Jahre lang als Fotograf in der Armee, bevor er als Redaktionsfotograf zur Abendzeitung *Chongqing Evening News* wechselt.

Ren obtient son diplôme du Collège d'ingénierie mécanique de l'armée en 1995. Pendant plus de dix ans, il travaille en tant que photographe pour l'armée avant d'entrer au quotidien du soir *Chongqing Evening News*.　→ p. 388

Rong Rong & inri
Rong Rong (born 1968, Zhangzhou, Fujian province) and inri (born 1973, Yokohama, Japan)
From 1993 to 1995, Rong Rong studied at the Central Institute of Art and Design in Beijing. He currently lives and works as an independent photographer in Beijing, where he is the co-founder and co-director of the Three Shadows Photography Art Center. Inri moved to Beijing in 1999. She currently lives and works as an independent photographer in Beijing, where she is the co-founder and co-director of the Three Shadows Photography Art Center. In the late 1980s, Rong Rong wanted to be an oil painter. After three failed attempts to enter art school, he rented a medium-format Seagull camera (a Shanghai brand) and decided to start a career in photography. He moved to Beijing in 1992 and began part-time photography studies at the Central Institute of Art and Design. Like Xing Danwen, his first major subject was Shanghai's performance-art community. More recently, he has been producing his own performance works, which he implements and photographs in collaboration with his wife, inri. Their works explore the body in landscape and the essence of human civilization.

Rong Rong studiert von 1993 bis 1995 am Zentralen Institut für Kunst und Design in Peking. Rong ist Mitbegründer und Kodirektor des Three Shadows Photography Art Center in Peking, wo er zurzeit lebt und als freischaffender Fotograf arbeitet. Inri zieht 1999 nach Peking. Inri ist Mitbegründerin und Kodirektorin des Three Shadows Photography Art Center in Peking, wo sie zurzeit lebt und als freischaffende Fotografin arbeitet. Ende der 1980er-Jahre will Rong Rong Maler werden. Nach drei gescheiterten Versuchen, zum Studium an der Kunstakademie zugelassen zu werden, mietet er eine Seagull-Mittelformatkamera (ein Shanghaier Fabrikat) und beschließt, eine Laufbahn in der Fotografie einzuschlagen. 1992 zieht er nach Peking und nimmt ein Teilzeitstudium in Fotografie am Zentralen Institut für Kunst und Design auf. Wie Xing Danwen widmet er seine ersten Arbeiten der Performance-Szene Shanghais. Seit geraumer Zeit veranstaltet er selbst Performances, die er gemeinsam mit seiner Frau inri ausführt und fotografiert. Sie loten dabei den Körper in der Landschaft und das Wesen der menschlichen Zivilisation aus.

De 1993 à 1995, Rong a étudié à l'Institut central d'art et de design à Pékin. Rong est co-fondateur et co-directeur du Three Shadows Photography Art Center à Pékin, où il vit et travaille comme photographe indépendant. Inri s'est installée à Pékin en 1999. Inri est co-fondatrice et co-directrice du Three Shadows Photography Art Center à Pékin, où elle vit et travaille comme photographe indépendante. À la fin des années 1980, Rong Rong veut devenir peintre. Après avoir essuyé trois refus d'admission à l'école d'art, il loue un appareil photo moyen format de marque Seagull (une fabrication de Shanghai) et décide de poursuivre une carrière de photographe. Il s'installe à Pékin en 1992 et entame des études à temps partiel à l'Institut central d'art et de design. À l'instar de Xing Danwen, il commence par photographier des performances d'artistes à Shanghai. Depuis quelques années, il produit ses propres performances, qu'il exécute et photographie en collaboration avec son épouse inri. Leurs performances explorent le corps dans le paysage et l'essence de la civilisation humaine.　→ p. 355

RU Suichu *(born 1932, Nanjing, Jiangsu province)*
In 1949, Ru worked as a staff photographer in the publicity department of the Chinese Communist Party's Northwestern Administrative Bureau. He was subsequently assigned to the Xinhua News Agency, where he worked as a staff photographer. In 1954, he became a staff photographer at *China Pictorial*. Throughout his career, he has edited numerous geographic books on China, including *Out of China's Earth*, published in New York in 1981.

Ru arbeitet 1949 als Fotograf in der Abteilung für Öffentlichkeitsarbeit der Verwaltungsabteilung der Kommunistischen Partei Chinas für den Nordwesten. Anschließend wird er der Nachrichtenagentur Xinhua als Redaktionsfotograf zugewiesen. 1954 wird er Redaktionsfotograf bei *China Pictorial*. Im Lauf seiner Karriere publiziert er zahlreiche Bücher zur Geografie Chinas, darunter *Out of China's Earth*, das 1981 in New York erscheint.

En 1949, Ru travaille comme photographe au département de propagande du Bureau administratif pour le Nord-ouest du Parti communiste chinois. En 1954, il est assigné à l'agence de presse Xinhua. En 1954, il rejoint le *China Pictorial* en tant que photographe. Au cours de sa carrière, il a publié de nombreux livres sur la géographie chinoise, dont *Out of China's Earth*, paru à New York en 1981.
→ *pp. 120, 124, 125*

SHI Xunfeng *(born 1976, Wenzhou, Zhejiang province)*
In 1998, Shi joined the staff of the *Wenzhou Evening News*. In 2002, he moved on to become a photo editor with the *Hangzhou Metro News*, before becoming a staff photographer at the *Shanghai Oriental Daily* in 2003.

1988 wird Shi von den *Wenzhou Evening News* verpflichtet. 2002 wird er Fotoredakteur der *Hangzhou Metro News*, bevor er 2003 als angestellter Fotograf zur Tageszeitung *Shanghai Oriental Daily* wechselt.

En 1998, Shi entre au quotidien du soir *Wenzhou Evening News*. En 2002, il est recruté comme rédacteur photographique par le *Hangzhou Metro News* avant de rejoindre le *Shanghai Oriental Daily* en tant que photographe en 2003. → *pp. 96/97*

TANG Desheng *(born 1948, Wujing county, Jiangsu province)*
From 1965 to 1970, Tang was a photographer with the People's Liberation Army. In 1971, like millions of Chinese intellectuals, Tang was sent to the countryside to be "reeducated" by the peasants. In 1989, Tang's works were published by the Chinese Photography Press. His works have been widely published in China and shown in a range of exhibitions in China and abroad.

Von 1965 bis 1970 dient Tang als Fotograf in der Volksbefreiungsarmee. 1971 wird er wie Millionen andere chinesische Intellektuelle zur Umerziehung durch Bauern aufs Land geschickt. Seine Arbeiten werden 1989 von dem Verlag Chinese Photography Press veröffentlicht. Sie werden häufig in China publiziert und waren in mehreren Ausstellungen in China und im Ausland zu sehen.

De 1965 à 1970, Tang est photographe dans l'Armée populaire de libération. En 1971, comme des millions d'intellectuels chinois, il est envoyé à la campagne pour être rééduqué par des paysans. En 1989, ses œuvres ont été publiées par les éditions Chinese Photography Press. Elles ont été abondamment diffusées en Chine et ont fait l'objet de plusieurs expositions en Chine et à l'étranger.
→ *pp. 341, 246, 248, 249*

WANG Fuchun *(born 1943, Harbin, Heilongjiang province)*
From 1970 to 1998, Wang worked as a staff photographer for the Harbin Railway Institute, which enabled him to travel for free on the national rail system. His best-known works coincide with these travels. In 1991, he studied in the Department of Photography at Harbin Teachers' College. In 2004, his work received several distinctions at the Pingyao Photography Festival. In 2001, Wang published *Chinese on the Train*.

Von 1970 bis 1998 arbeitet Wang als Fotograf für das Harbiner Eisenbahninstitut, was es ihm erlaubt, auf dem nationalen Schienennetz kostenlos zu reisen. Seine bekanntesten Arbeiten sind diesen Reisen zuzuordnen. 1991 studiert er an der Abteilung für Fotografie des Pädagogischen Kollegs von Harbin. 2004 wird seine Arbeit anlässlich des Fotofestivals von Pingyao mehrfach ausgezeichnet. 2001 veröffentlicht Wang *Chinese on the Train*.

De 1970 à 1998, Wang travaille en tant que photographe à l'Institut ferroviaire de Harbin, ce qui lui permet de voyager gratuitement sur l'ensemble du réseau national. Ses œuvres les plus connues documentent ces voyages. En 1991, il s'inscrit au département de photographie du Collège pédagogique de Harbin. En 2004, son travail reçoit plusieurs distinctions au Festival de la photographie de Pingyao. En 2001, Wang publie *Chinese on the Train*.
→ *pp. 322, 370/371*

WANG Jie *(born 1960, Shanghai)*
Wang graduated from Shanghai's Northeast Educational University in 1976. He was subsequently sent to the countryside to be "reeducated" by peasants for a period of three years. In 1979, he joined the People's Liberation Army. In 1982, Wang returned to Shanghai to work as a photographer for various local newspapers before joining the Liberation Daily Group's *Morning Daily News*. In 2003, his works were published in *Photography's Mission*. Wang is currently the chief staff photographer of the Shanghai-based *Liberation Daily*.

Nach seinem Studium an der Shanghaier Pädagogischen Universität des Nordostens wird Wang 1976 für drei Jahre zur Umerziehung durch Bauern aufs Land geschickt. 1979 tritt er in die Volksbefreiungsarmee ein. 1982 kehrt er nach Shanghai zurück, wo er als Fotograf für verschiedene Lokalzeitungen arbeitet, bevor er zur *Morning Daily News* der Liberation Daily Group wechselt. 2003 werden seine Arbeiten in *Photography's Mission* veröffentlicht. Wang ist zurzeit leitender Redaktionsfotograf der in Shanghai erscheinenden *Liberation Daily*.

Après avoir obtenu son diplôme de l'Université pédagogique du Nord-Est à Shanghai en 1976, Wang est assigné pendant trois ans à la rééducation par les paysans. En 1979, il s'engage dans l'Armée populaire de libération. En 1982, il retourne à Shanghai, où il travaille en tant que photographe pour divers journaux locaux avant d'entrer au quotidien *Morning Daily News* du Liberation Daily Group. En 2003, ses œuvres ont été publiées dans *Photography's Mission*. Wang est actuellement directeur de la photographie du *Liberation Daily* à Shanghai. → *p. 395*

WANG Jing *(born 1975, Xi'an City, Shaanxi Province.)*
Wang graduated from Hebei Science and Technology University in 1997, where he studied Economic Law. He worked in the mining industry for two months before he joined the staff of *China Economic Daily* based in Xian in 2000.

Er schließt 1997 sein Studium des Unternehmensrechts an der Wissenschafts- und Technikuniversität von Hebei ab. Ehe er sich 2000 der Redaktion der in Xi'an erscheinenden *China Economic Daily* anschließt, arbeitete er zwei Monate lang in einem Bergwerk.

Diplômé en droit économique de l'Université des Sciences et technologies en 1997, il travaille ensuite dans une mine puis entre au *China Economic Daily* à Xi'an en 2000.
→ *p. 384*

WANG Jinsong *(born 1963, Shuilin county, Heilongjiang province)*
Wang graduated in 1987 from the Department of Chinese Painting at the Zhejiang Academy of Fine Arts in Hangzhou. He is currently a teacher in the Department of Art at the Beijing Institute of Education. Wang's practice ranges from Chinese ink paintings to performance and installation art. His main topics are ordinary people and culture in the context of social change in modern China.

Wang schließt 1987 sein Studium an der Abteilung für Chinesische Malerei der Zhejiang Kunstakademie in Hangzhou ab. Er unterrichtet zurzeit Kunst am Pädagogischen Institut Peking. Wangs künstlerische Praxis reicht von chinesischer Tuschemalerei bis hin zu Performance- und Installationskunst. Seine bevorzugten Themen sind Menschen und Kultur im Kontext des gesellschaftlichen Wandels im modernen China.

Wang obtient son diplôme du département de peinture chinoise à l'Académie des beaux-arts du Zhejiang à Hangzhou en 1987. Il est enseignant au département d'art de l'Institut pédagogique de Pékin. Sa pratique artistique revêt des formes diverses allant de la peinture traditionnelle à l'encre aux performances et aux installations. Son travail s'intéresse aux individus et à la culture dans le contexte du changement social qui caractérise la Chine moderne.
→ *pp. 328/329*

WANG Shilong *(born 1930, Ru'nan county, Henan province)*
Wang went to high school before he joined the army as a photographer in 1948. He followed the People's Liberation Army into Tibet, where he was wounded. In 1951, he was demobilized and started to work for various newspapers in Henan province until he joined the *Henan Daily* as a staff photographer in 1956. In 1958, he recorded the Great Leap Forward, and went on to document the systematic development of communes and agriculture in rural China in the 1960s. In 1960, he was named Model Cultural Worker. In 1976, he served as Honorary Chairman of the Henan Photographers Association. Wang retired in 1992 and lives in his native city of Zhengzhou in Henan province.

Nach dem Besuch der Hauptschule schließt sich Wang 1948 als Fotograf der Armee an. Er folgt der Volksbefreiungsarmee nach Tibet, wo er verwundet wird. Nach seiner Freistellung 1951 arbeitet er für verschiedene Zeitungen in der Provinz Henan, bevor er 1956 als Redaktionsfotograf für die *Henan Daily* tätig wird. 1958 dokumentiert er den Großen Sprung nach vorn, anschließend den systematischen Ausbau von Kommunen und Landwirtschaft im ländlichen China der 1960er-Jahre. 1960 wird er als Kulturmodellarbeiter ausgezeichnet. 1976 amtiert er als Ehrenvorsitzender der Fotografenvereinigung von Henan. Wang setzt sich 1992 zur Ruhe und lebt seitdem in seiner Heimatstadt Zhengzhou in der Provinz Henan.

Après des études au collège, Wang rejoint l'armée en 1948 en tant que photographe. Il suit l'Armée populaire de libération au Tibet, où il est blessé. Au lendemain de sa démobilisation en 1951, il travaille pour divers journaux du Hénan avant d'entrer au quotidien *Henan Daily* en 1956. En 1958, il documente le Grand bond en avant, puis documente le développement systématique des communes populaires et de l'agriculture en Chine durant les années 1960. En 1960, il est nommé travailleur modèle de la culture. En 1976, il est élu président honoraire de l'Association des photographes du Hénan. Wang prend sa retraite en 1992 et vit depuis dans sa ville natale de Zhengzhou, dans la province du Hénan.
→ *pp. 127, 128, 136/137, 166/167, 224, 234, 247*

WANG Wenlan *(born 1953, Beijing)*
Wang's primary and secondary-school education was interrupted from 1960 to 1968 by the Cultural Revolution. Wang was sent to the countryside to be "reeducated" by peasants for a period of 12 years, after which time he joined the People's Liberation Army. Following his demobilization in 1980, he started working for the newly founded *China Daily*. From 1980 to 2008, he covered a wide range of events, including the 1976 Tangshan earthquake, the 1984 Olympics in Los Angeles, and the 1988 Olympics in Seoul. Wang is currently a chief photographer with *China Daily* and vice president of the China Photographers Association.

Wangs Studium an der Grund- und Hauptschule wird von 1960 bis 1968 durch die Kulturrevolution unterbrochen. Wang wird für zwölf Jahre zur Umerziehung durch Bauern aufs Land geschickt und tritt anschließend der Volksbefreiungsarmee bei. Nach seiner Freistellung 1980 arbeitet er für die neu gegründete *China Daily*. Zwischen 1980 und 2008 berichtet er von zahlreichen Ereignissen, darunter dem Erdbeben in Tangshan 1976, den Olympischen Spielen von Los Angeles 1984 und den Olympischen Spielen von Seoul 1988. Wang ist zurzeit leitender Fotograf der *China Daily* und Vizepräsident der Fotografenvereinigung Chinas.

Les études primaires et secondaires de Wang sont interrompues de 1960 à 1968 par la Révolution culturelle. Wang est assigné pendant douze ans à la rééducation par les paysans, puis s'engage dans l'Armée populaire de libération. Après sa démobilisation en 1980, il rejoint le quotidien nouvellement fondé *China Daily*. Entre 1980 et 2008, il couvre de nombreux événements, dont le séisme de Tangshan en 1976, les Jeux olympiques de Los Angeles en 1984 et les Jeux olympiques de Séoul en 1988. Wang est actuellement photographe en chef du *China Daily* et vice-président de l'Association des photographes de Chine.
→ pp. 320/321

WEI Dezhong (born 1934, Xincai county, Henan province)
In 1949, Wei joined the People's Liberation Army. In 1957, he started working as a staff photographer at *Henan Daily*. Between 1957 and 1960, Wei documented the various stages of China's modernization process, including the People's Communes and the Great Leap Forward. He received an Honorable Mention in the 14th World Press Photo Contest. Wei is currently a guest lecturer at Zhengzhou University in Henan province. His works have been widely published in China.

1949 tritt Wei in die Volksbefreiungsarmee ein. 1957 kommt er als Redaktionsfotograf zur Tageszeitung *Henan Daily*. Zwischen 1957 und 1960 dokumentiert er die verschiedenen Etappen des chinesischen Modernisierungsprozesses, darunter die Volkskommunen und den Großen Sprung nach vorn. Seine Arbeit erhält eine lobende Erwähnung beim 14. World Photo-Wettbewerb. Wei ist Gastdozent an der Universität Zhengzhou in der Provinz Henan. Seine Arbeiten werden regelmäßig in China publiziert.

Wei s'engage dans l'Armée populaire de libération en 1949. En 1957, il entre comme photographe au quotidien *Henan Daily*. Entre 1957 et 1960, il documente les phases successives du processus de modernisation en Chine, dont les communes populaires et le Grand bond en avant. Son travail reçoit une mention honorable lors du 14ᵉ concours World Press Photo. Wei est professeur invité à l'Université de Zhengzhou dans la province du Hénan. Ses travaux ont fait l'objet de nombreuses publications en Chine.
→ pp. 162/163

WEI Dong (born 1965, Anxin county, Hebei province)
Wei entered Hebei Fine Arts Academy in 1985, and since 1989 has worked as a photographer for the cultural development department of the city of Shijiazhuang. In 2005, Wei moved to Beijing, where he lives and works as a freelance artist and photographer.

Wei beginnt 1985 eine Ausbildung an der Kunstakademie in Hebei und arbeitet seit 1989 als Fotograf bei der Kulturförderungsstelle der Stadt Shijiazhuang. 2005 zog Wei nach Peking, wo er als freiberuflicher Künstler und Fotograf lebt und arbeitet.

Après s'être formé à l'Académie des Beaux-Arts du Hebei en 1985, Wei est depuis 1989 photographe au département du développement culturel de la ville de Shijiazhuang. En 2005, il s'est installé à Pékin où il vit et travaille comme artiste et photographe.
→ p. 314

WEI Ruoxun (born 1961, Guangzhou, Guangdong province)
In 1963, Wei's family moved to Ningxia province. In 1983, Wei graduated from the Department of Mathematics at Ningxia University. She has since been teaching at a high school in Shenzhen. Wei taught herself photography. Her works were exhibited at the 2000 Pingyao Photography Festival in Shanxi province.

1963 zieht Weis Familie in die Provinz Ningxia. 1983 schließt Wei ihr Studium an der Abteilung für Mathematik der Universität Ningxia ab. Sie arbeitet seitdem als Lehrerin in Shenzhen. Wei erlernt das Fotografieren als Autodidaktin. Ihre Arbeiten werden 2000 im Rahmen des Fotofestivals in Pingyao in der Provinz Shanxi ausgestellt.

En 1963, la famille de Wei s'installe dans la province du Ningxia. Wei obtient son diplôme du département de

mathématiques de l'Université du Ningxia. Elle enseigne depuis dans un lycée à Shenzhen. Wei a appris la photographie en autodidacte. Son travail a été exposé en 2000 au Festival de la photographie de Pingyao dans la province du Shanxi.
→ p. 394

WENG Naiqiang (born 1936, Indonesia)
In 1951, Weng returned from Indonesia to China. In 1963, he graduated from the Central Academy of Fine Arts in Beijing, after which he was assigned to *China Pictorial* as a staff photographer. In 1990, he returned to the faculty of the Central Academy, where he teaches ink painting.

1951 kehrt Weng aus Indonesien nach China zurück. 1963 schließt er sein Studium an der Zentralen Kunstakademie in Peking ab und wird anschließend der Illustrierten *China Pictorial* als Redaktionsfotograf zugeteilt. 1990 kehrt er an die Kunstakademie zurück, wo er Tuschemalerei lehrt.

En 1951, Weng quitte l'Indonésie pour retourner en Chine. Il obtient son diplôme de l'Académie centrale des beaux-arts à Pékin en 1963 avant d'être assigné au journal illustré *China Pictorial* en tant que photographe. En 1990, il retourne à l'Académie centrale, où il enseigne la peinture à l'encre.
→ p. 186

WU Jialin (born 1942, Shaotong county, Yunnan province)
Wu first worked as a farmer in Yunnan province before teaching himself photography. Between 1989 and 2007, his works were published widely and shown in domestic and international photography exhibitions. In 2004, a solo exhibition in Moscow retraced his career.

Wu arbeitet zunächst als Bauer in der Provinz Yunnan, bevor er sich autodidaktisch zum Fotografen ausbildet. Zwischen 1989 und 2007 werden seine Arbeiten in zahlreichen Publikationen veröffentlicht und in chinesischen und internationalen Fotoausstellungen gezeigt. 2004 wird seine Arbeit in einer Einzelausstellung in Moskau gewürdigt.

Wu travaille d'abord comme paysan dans la province du Yunnan avant d'apprendre la photographie en autodidacte. Entre 1989 et 2007, ses travaux ont fait l'objet de nombreuses publications et expositions en Chine et à l'étranger. En 2004, une exposition personnelle à Moscou a retracé son œuvre.
→ p. 357

XIAO Quan (born 1959, Chengdu, Sichuan province)
Xiao graduated from China's Communication University in 1988. In 1976, he enrolled in the navy for a period of six years. In 1996, he joined the staff of *Modern Photography* before co-founding a magazine in Shenzhen called *Avenue*. His works were published in 1994 in a series of albums called *My Generation*.

1988 schließt Xiao sein Studium an der Chinesischen Universität für Kommunikation ab. 1976 verpflichtet er sich für sechs Jahre bei der Marine. 1996 arbeitet er bei *Modern Photography*, bevor er die in Shenzhen publizierte Zeitschrift *Avenue* mitbegründet. Seine eigenen Arbeiten erscheinen 1994 in einer Serie von Alben unter dem Titel *My Generation*.

Xiao obtient son diplôme de l'Université chinoise de communication en 1988. En 1976, il s'engage dans la marine pour six ans. En 1996, il rejoint la revue *Modern Photography* avant de co-fonder le magazine *Avenue* à Shenzhen. Ses travaux personnels ont été publiés en 1994 sous forme d'une série d'albums intitulée *My Generation*.
→ pp. 298, 340

XIAO Ye (born 1930, Shashi, Hubei province)
Xiao graduated from the Hubei Teachers' College in 1949. He subsequently enrolled in the People's Liberation Army, where he worked as a photographer. In 1958, he joined the State-owned Xinhua News Agency as a staff photographer. He retired in 1990 and today lives in Shenyang, in Liaoning province.

1949 schließt Xiao sein Studium am Pädagogischen Kolleg Hubei ab. Er tritt anschließend in die Volksbefrei-

ungsarmee ein, wo er als Fotograf tätig ist. 1958 wechselt er als Redaktionsfotograf zur staatlichen Nachrichtenagentur Xinhua. 1990 setzte er sich zur Ruhe und lebt seitdem in Shenyang in der Provinz Liaoning.

Xiao obtient son diplôme du Collège pédagogique de Hubei en 1949. Il s'engage alors dans l'Armée de libération, où il travaille comme photographe. En 1958, il entre comme photographe à l'agence de presse étatique Xinhua. Il prend sa retraite en 1990 et vit depuis à Shenyang dans la province du Liaoning.
→ p. 149

XIAO Zhuang (born 1933, Fenghua, Zhejiang province)
In 1949, Xiao joined the Chinese Communist guerrilla force to fight the Kuomintang. In 1950, she enlisted with the 22nd Chinese Liberation Army and studied photography. She joined the *Xinhua Daily News* as a staff photographer in 1951. In 1970, she was banished to the rural area of Nantong county in Jiangsu province, where she continued to work as a photographer for the local administration. After her political rehabilitation in 1980, she worked for the Jiangsu Province People's Publishing House as an editor and later a chief editor. Though she retired in 1994, she still photographs for her own pleasure. Her works have been widely exhibited and published in China.

1949 stößt Xiao zur Guerillatruppe der chinesischen Kommunisten, die gegen die Armee der Kuomintang kämpft. 1950 kommt sie zur 22. Chinesischen Befreiungsarmee und erlernt das Fotografieren. Ab 1951 arbeitet sie als Redaktionsfotografin bei der Tageszeitung *Xinhua Daily News*. 1970 wird sie in die ländliche Region des Kreises Nantong in der Provinz Jiangsu verbannt, wo sie weiterhin als Fotografin für die Bezirksverwaltung tätig ist. Nach ihrer politischen Rehabilitierung 1980 arbeitet sie zunächst als Redakteurin, dann als Chefredakteurin des Verlags Jiangsu Province People's Publishing House. Obwohl sie sich 1994 zur Ruhe setzt, fotografiert sie weiterhin zu ihrem eigenen Vergnügen. Ihre Arbeiten werden häufig in China ausgestellt und publiziert.

En 1949, Xiao s'engage dans la guérilla communiste contre l'armée du Kuomintang. En 1950, elle rejoint la 22ᵉ Armée chinoise de libération et apprend la photographie. En 1951, elle entre comme photographe au quotidien *Xinhua Daily News*. En 1970, elle est bannie à la campagne dans le canton de Nantong, dans la province du Jiangsu, où elle continue à travailler comme photographe pour l'administration locale. Après sa réhabilitation politique en 1980, elle entre à la maison d'édition Jiangsu Province People's Publishing House, dont elle est successivement l'éditrice et l'éditrice en chef. Ayant pris sa retraite en 1994, elle continue de photographier pour le plaisir. Son œuvre a été largement exposée et publiée en Chine.
→ pp. 35, 48, 126, 129, 131, 135, 146, 148, 164, 168, 178, 191, 200, 209, 235, 236

XIE Guanghui (born 1959, Hangzhou, Zhejiang province)
From 1978 to 1980, Xie was "reeducated" by the peasants in rural Fuyang. In 1982, he taught himself photography and took long-distance courses in Communication with the People's University in Beijing. In 1988, he joined the *Zhejiang Pictorial* as a staff photographer, where he worked until 1992. In 2008, his work was shown in a solo exhibition in Lyon. Xie is currently a staff photographer at the China National Tourist Office.

Von 1978 bis 1980 wird Xie zur Umerziehung durch Bauern ins ländliche Fuyang geschickt. 1982 erlernt er das Fotografieren als Autodidakt und belegt einen Fernkurs in Kommunikation an der Volksuniversität in Peking. Zwischen 1988 und 1992 arbeitet er als Redaktionsfotograf des Magazins *Zhejiang Pictorial*. 2008 werden seine Arbeiten in einer Einzelausstellung in Lyon gewürdigt. Xie ist gegenwärtig Redaktionsfotograf der Nationalen Chinesischen Tourismusagentur.

De 1978 à 1980, Xie est assigné à la rééducation par les paysans de la campagne de Fuyang. En 1982, il apprend la photographie en autodidacte et suit des cours à distance en communication de l'Université du peuple de Pékin. De 1988 à 1992, il est photographe à la revue *Zhejiang Pictorial*. En 2008, son travail fait l'objet d'une exposition individuelle à Lyon. Xie travaille en tant que photographe pour l'Agence nationale chinoise du tourisme. → *p. 332*

XIE Hailong (*born 1968, Jing county, Hebei province*)
Xie enlisted with the People's Liberation Army in 1991. After his dismissal from the army, he worked in a factory. In 1992, he joined the staff of the *China Youth Daily* as a photographer. Xie is best known for his documentation of socially disadvantaged children in rural areas. His photographs have had a significant impact in creating social awareness and raising charity funds. In 2002, Xie joined the government-supported China Photographers Association. He currently serves as the association's Secretary General.

1991 tritt Xie in die Marine der Volksbefreiungsarmee ein. Nach seiner Freistellung arbeitet er in einer Fabrik. 1992 schließt er sich als Redaktionsfotograf der Tageszeitung *China Youth Daily* an. Xie ist vor allem für seine Dokumentation des Alltags sozial schwacher Kinder in ländlichen Gebieten bekannt. Seine Bilder tragen zur öffentlichen Wahrnehmung dieser Problematik und der Beschaffung von Spendengeldern bei. 2002 wird Xie Mitglied der regierungsnahen Fotografenvereinigung Chinas, als deren Generalsekretär er zurzeit fungiert.

En 1991, Xie s'engage dans la marine de l'Armée populaire de libération. À sa sortie de l'armée, il devient ouvrier dans une usine. En 1992, il rejoint l'équipe du *China Youth Daily* comme photographe. Xie est surtout connu pour sa documentation de la vie d'enfants pauvres en zone rurale. Ses photographies contribuent à sensibiliser l'opinion publique et à collecter des dons. En 2002, il adhère à l'Association des photographes de Chine, organisme financé par l'État et dont il est actuellement le Secrétaire général. → *pp. 316, 317*

XING Danwen (*born 1967, Xi'an, Shanxi province*)
Xing studied at the Central Academy of Fine Arts in Beijing from 1988 to 1992. In 2001, she graduated from the School of Visual Arts in New York. Xing was born into a family of engineers in the ancient capital of Xi'an. She is a self-taught photographer with experience as a photojournalist, but most of her photographic work focuses on China's burgeoning avant-garde art scene. Her interests converge in a series of documentary images of artists who were representative of the emerging Chinese art scene from the early to the mid-1990s. Xing is also one of the few active women artists whose work has had a significant influence on China's contemporary art scene. She currently lives and works as an independent photographer in Beijing.

Xing stammt aus der einstigen Hauptstadt Xi'an aus einer Familie von Ingenieuren. Sie studiert von 1988 bis 1992 an der Zentralen Kunstakademie in Peking. 2001 schließt sie ihr Studium an der School of Visual Arts in New York ab. Sie lernt das Fotografieren als Autodidaktin und sammelt Erfahrung im Fotojournalismus, doch der größte Teil ihrer Arbeiten entsteht im Umfeld von Chinas junger avantgardistischer Kunstszene. Ihre Interessen bündeln sich in einer Serie von dokumentarischen Porträts von Repräsentanten der aufkeimenden chinesischen Kunstszene von Anfang bis Mitte der 1990er-Jahre. Xing ist darüber hinaus eine der wenigen aktiven Künstlerinnen, deren Arbeit einen Einfluss auf die zeitgenössische Kunstszene Chinas ausübt. Xing lebt und arbeitet zurzeit als freischaffende Fotografin in Peking.

Xing a étudié de 1988 à 1992 à l'Académie centrale des beaux-arts à Pékin. En 2001, elle obtient son diplôme de la School of Visual Arts à New York. Xing est issue d'une famille d'ingénieurs de l'ancienne capitale de Xi'an. Photographe autodidacte avec une expérience du photojournalisme, elle a élaboré l'essentiel de son œuvre dans le contexte de la jeune avant-garde artistique chinoise. Ses intérêts convergent dans une série d'images documentaires

sur les artistes représentatifs de la scène artistique du début au milieu des années 1990. Xing est également une des rares artistes femmes en activité, dont le travail a un impact sur la scène artistique chinoise. Elle vit et travaille actuellement comme photographe indépendante à Pékin. → *pp. 341, 344, 345*

XU Xiaobing (*born 1916, Tongxiang county, Zhejiang province*)
From 1921 to 1931, Xu attended private school. In 1930, he worked as a photographic assistant on feature films such as *The Graduate's Fate, Angel in the Street, God of Freedom, Sons and Daughters of the Times*, and *City Sights*. He also participated in left-wing theater activities in Shanghai. In 1937, he worked as a photographer in the Publicity Division of the Political Department of the People's Liberation Army. From 1949, he carried out photographic assignments for which he followed senior leaders. In 1951, he took part in the coverage of the Korean War. In 1986, he edited the anthologies *Road* and *Yangtze River*, and published with his wife Hou Bo *Oral Autobiography*. His work has been shown in numerous exhibitions in China, Japan, and France.

Von 1921 bis 1931 besucht Xu eine Privatschule. 1930 arbeitet er als Fotoassistent bei Spielfilmen wie *The Graduate's Fate, Angel in the Street, God of Freedom, Sons and Daughters of the Times* und *City Sights*. Er beteiligt sich zudem an linksgerichteten Theaterveranstaltungen in Shanghai. 1937 arbeitet er als Fotograf in der Öffentlichkeitsdivision der Politischen Abteilung der Volksbefreiungsarmee. Ab 1949 entstehen Fotoserien über Führungspersonen. 1951 berichtet er vom Koreakrieg. 1986 stellt er die Sammelbände *Road* und *Yangtze River* zusammen und veröffentlicht gemeinsam mit seiner Frau Hou Bo *Oral Autobiography*. Xus Arbeit war in mehreren Fotoausstellungen in China, Japan und Frankreich zu sehen.

De 1921 à 1931, Xu est inscrit dans une école privée. En 1930, il travaille comme assistant photographe sur des longs métrages dont *The Graduate's Fate, Angel in the Street, God of Freedom, Sons and Daughters of the Times* et *City Sights*. Il participe également à des activités théâtrales gauchistes à Shanghai. En 1937, il devient photographe à la division de la propagande du département politique de l'Armée populaire de libération. À partir de 1949, il a pour mission de photographier les responsables politiques chinois. En 1951, il couvre la guerre de Corée. En 1986, il coordonne l'édition des anthologies *Road* et *Yangtze River* et publie avec sa femme Hou Bo *Oral Autobiography*. Son travail a été exposé en Chine, au Japon et en France. → *pp. 114/115*

YANG Shaoming (*born 1942, Yan'an, Shaanxi province*)
In 1978, Yang graduated from the Department of History at Beijing University. As the child of the prominent Chinese army general Yang Shangkun, he was persecuted during the Cultural Revolution and sent to the countryside to be "reeducated" by peasants in 1969. From 1979 to 1987, he worked at the State-owned Xinhua News Agency. Because of his father's close relationship with Deng Xiaoping, Yang had access to China's top leader. His photograph of the diminutive leader was awarded Second Prize in the "Feature" category of the World Press Photo Contest in 1988. Yang is currently Vice-Chairman of China's Contemporary Photography Society and of the Song Qingling Charity Foundation.

Yang schließt 1978 sein Studium an der Abteilung für Geschichte der Universität Peking ab. Als Sohn des prominenten chinesischen Armeegenerals Yang Shangkun wird er während der Kulturrevolution verfolgt und 1969 zur Umerziehung aufs Land geschickt. Von 1979 bis 1987 arbeitet er bei der staatlichen Nachrichtenagentur Xinhua. Dank der Beziehung seines Vaters zu Deng Xiaoping gelingt es Yang, den chinesischen Führer zu fotografieren. Sein Foto des kleingewachsenen Führers wird in der Kategorie „Presse" des World Press Photo-Wettbewerbs mit dem Zweiten Preis ausgezeichnet. Derzeit ist Yang Vizevorsitzen-

der von Chinas Gesellschaft für zeitgenössische Fotografie und der Song Qingling Wohltätigkeitsstiftung.

Yang obtient son diplôme du département d'histoire de l'Université de Pékin en 1978. Fils du général connu Yang Shangkun, il est persécuté pendant la Révolution culturelle et envoyé à la campagne pour être rééduqué en 1969. De 1979 à 1987, il travaille à l'agence de presse officielle Xinhua. Grâce aux relations de son père avec Deng Xiaoping, il a accès à ce dernier. Sa photographie du petit homme d'État lui vaut le Second prix dans la catégorie « Presse » du concours World Press Photo en 1988. Yang est actuellement vice-président de la Société chinoise de photographie contemporaine et de la Fondation caritative Song Qingling. → *pp. 282/283*

YANG Shizhong (*born 1962, Beijing*)
Yang started teaching himself photography in 1984. In 1988, he joined *China Daily* as a staff photographer. In 2002, he was voted one of the Ten Best Photographers in China by the China Photographers Association and received various other prizes in domestic photography contests.

Yang erlernt das Fotografieren als Autodidakt ab 1984. 1988 wird er Redaktionsfotograf bei der Tageszeitung *China Daily*. 2002 wird er vom Fotografenverband zu einem der Zehn Besten Fotografen Chinas gewählt und mit mehreren Preisen bei nationalen Fotowettbewerben ausgezeichnet.

Yang apprend la photographie en autodidacte à partir de 1984. En 1988, il rejoint le quotidien *China Daily* comme photographe. En 2002, il est élu l'un des Dix meilleurs photographes de Chine par l'Association des photographes chinois et reçoit plusieurs prix lors de concours de photographie nationaux. → *pp. 257*

YANG Yankang (*born 1954, Guizhou province*)
In 1984, Yang joined the magazine *Modern Photography* in Shenzhen. Since 1992, he has been documenting Catholic communities across China. Since 2001, he has participated in various group and solo exhibitions in China and Europe. In 2005, Yang was awarded the Henri Nannen Prize by *Geo* magazine. Yang currently works as a freelance photographer with Agence VU in Paris.

1984 arbeitet Yang bei der in Shenzhen ansässigen Zeitschrift *Modern Photography*. Seit 1992 dokumentiert er katholische Gemeinschaften in ganz China. Seit 2001 nimmt er an mehreren Gruppen- und Einzelausstellungen in China und Europa teil. 2005 wird Yang von der Zeitschrift *Geo* mit dem Henri-Nannen-Preis ausgezeichnet. Yang arbeitet zurzeit als freischaffender Fotograf für die Agentur VU in Paris.

En 1984, Yang entre à la revue *Modern Photography* à Shenzuen. Depuis 1992, il photographie les communautés catholiques dans toute la Chine. Depuis 2001, il a participé à différentes expositions personnelles et collectives en Chine et en Europe. En 2005, il a reçu le Prix Henri Nannen du magazine *Geo*. Yang travaille actuellement comme photographe indépendant pour le compte de l'agence VU à Paris. → *pp. 80, 318*

YIN Fukan (*born 1927, Nanjing, Jiangsu province*)
In 1949, Yin joined the *Northeastern Pictorial* as a staff photographer. In 1950, he was assigned to the Shanghai People's Fine Arts Press as an editor of photography-related publications. Yin retired in 1979 and currently serves as Vice-President of the Shanghai Photographers Association.

1949 geht Yin als Fotograf zur Illustrierten *Northeastern Pictorial*. 1950 wird ihm bei der Shanghaier People's Fine Arts Press eine Stelle als Redakteur für Fotopublikationen zugewiesen. Er setzt sich 1979 zur Ruhe. Yin ist gegenwärtig Vizepräsident des Shanghaier Fotografenverbandes.

En 1949, Yin entre comme photographe au magazine illustré *Northeastern Pictorial*. En 1950, il est nommé éditeur en charge des publications photographiques de la maison d'édition Shanghai People's Fine Arts Press. Il prend sa retraite en 1979. Yin est actuellement vice-président de l'Association des photographes de Shanghai. → *pp. 170/171*

YONG He (born 1956, Shanghai)

In 1973, Yong was sent to the countryside and worked on a farm. He started teaching himself photography in 1981. From 1985 to 1992, he worked as a staff photographer for China City News. In 1992, he was appointed chief photographer of Shanghai Youth Daily News, where he stayed until 1998. From 1998 to 2003, he was photography director at Xinmin Weekly. Yong is currently Associate Executive Member of the China Photographers Association.

1973 wird Yong aufs Land geschickt, wo er auf einem Bauernhof arbeitet. Ab 1981 erlernt er das Fotografieren als Autodidakt. Von 1985 bis 1992 ist er als Redaktionsfotograf der China City Newspaper tätig. Ab 1992 ist er leitender Fotograf der Jugendzeitung Shanghai Youth Daily Newspaper, wo er bis 1998 arbeitet. Von 1998 bis 2003 ist Yong fotografischer Direktor des Wochenblatts Xinmin Weekly. Yong ist gegenwärtig Mitglied des Vorstands der Fotografenvereinigung Chinas.

En 1973, Yong est envoyé à la campagne, où il travaille dans une ferme. À partir de 1981, il apprend la photographie en autodidacte. De 1985 à 1992, il est photographe auprès du China City Newspaper. En 1992, il est nommé responsable de la photo du quotidien de jeunesse Shanghai Youth Daily Newspaper, fonction qu'il occupe jusqu'en 1998. De 1998 à 2003, il est directeur de la photo de l'hebdomadaire Xinmin Weekly. Yong est membre associé de l Association des photographes de Chine.
→ pp. 86/87, 392/393

YU Deshui (born 1953, Henan province)

Yu started his career as a photographer in Henan province in 1978. In 1994 he received the First Prize for Feature Photography in the China News Photography contest. His works documenting the lives of northern Chinese villages have been widely published in China.

Yu beginnt seine Laufbahn als Fotograf 1978 in der Provinz Henan. 1994 erhält er den Ersten Preis für Feature-Fotografie im China News Photography-Wettbewerb. Seine Fotografien über den Alltag in nordchinesischen Dörfern sind in China häufig publiziert worden.

Yu débute sa carrière de photographe en 1978 dans la province du Hénan. En 1994, il reçoit le Premier prix de la photo de presse au concours China News Photography. Ses travaux sur la vie dans les villages en Chine du Nord ont été abondamment publiés en Chine.
→ p. 323

YU Haibo (born 1962, Yongcheng, Henan province)

In 1989, Yu graduated from the Department of Photography at Wuhan University. In 1987 and 2001, he was distinguished as one of China's Ten Best Photographers. In 1989, his works were included in a touring exhibition in France, Italy, and Germany. In 2006, his work received First Prize in the "Art Photography" category of China's International Photography Contest.

Yu schließt 1989 sein Studium an der Abteilung für Fotografie der Universität Wuhan ab. 1987 und 2001 wird er als einer der Zehn Besten Fotografen Chinas ausgezeichnet. 1989 sind seine Arbeiten Teil einer Wanderausstellung in Frankreich, Italien und Deutschland. 2006 erhält Yus Werk den Ersten Preis in der Kategorie „Kunstfotografie" des Internationalen Fotowettbewerbs Chinas.

Yu obtient son diplôme du département de photographie de l'Université de Wuhan en 1989. En 1987 et 2001, il est élu comme l'un des Dix meilleurs photographes de Chine. En 1989, ses travaux font partie d'une exposition de groupe itinérante montrée en France, en Italie et en Allemagne. En 2006, il remporte le Premier prix dans la catégorie « Photographie d'art » du Concours international de photographie en Chine.
→ pp. 68/69

YUAN Kezhong (1921–2008)

Yuan joined the Eighth Route Army of the Chinese Communists in 1938 and photographed the ensuing battles in the civil war with Kuomingtang and the Japanese invading army. He was decoratded army photographer for his photographic coverage of the wars. Yuan followed the Chinese army into Tibet in 1950. The journey on mule and yak took 60 days to reach Lhasa. He also photographed the Sino-India border war in 1962. Yuan died in February of 2008.

Yuan schließt sich 1938 der 8. Feldarmee der chinesischen Kommunisten an und fotografiert die anschließenden Kämpfe im Bürgerkrieg gegen die Kuomintang und gegen die japanische Besatzungsmacht. Für seine Berichterstattung von diesen Kriegen wurde er als Armeefotograf ausgezeichnet. Yuan folgte der chinesischen Armee 1950 nach Tibet. Auf den Rücken von Maultieren und Yaks dauerte der Zug nach Lhasa 60 Tage. Außerdem fotografiert er 1962 im chinesisch-indischen Grenzkrieg. Yuan verstarb im Februar 2008.

Yuan s'engage dans l'Armée de la huitième route des communistes chinois en 1938 et photographie des batailles de la guerre civile avec le Kuomintang ou contre les armées d'invasion japonaises. Pour cette couverture de la guerre, il est décoré. Il accompagne ensuite l'armée au Tibet en 1950, et met 60 jours pour atteindre Lhassa à dos de yak ou de mule. Il a également photographié le conflit de frontière sino-indien en 1962. Yuan est décédé en février 2008.
→ p. 139

ZENG Nian (born 1954, Wuxi, Jiangsu province)

Zeng's studies were interrupted by the start of the Cultural Revolution in 1966. In 1984, he started teaching himself photography and drawing. From 1970 to 1982, he worked as a sailor on the Yangtze river. In 1996, he won Second Prize in the "Arts Photography" category of the World Press Photo Contest. He has since been working with Contact Press Images and Gamma Photo Agency in Paris. His works have been published in the New York Times, Geo, and various other publications.

Zengs Studium wird 1966 durch den Beginn der Kulturrevolution unterbrochen. Ab 1984 erlernt er das Fotografieren und Zeichnen als Autodidakt. Von 1970 bis 1982 arbeitet er als Matrose auf dem Jangtse. 1996 erhält er den Zweiten Preis in der Kategorie „Kunstfotografie" des World Press Photo-Wettbewerbs. Zeng arbeitet seitdem für Contact Press Images und Gamma Photo Agency in Paris. Seine Arbeiten erscheinen in der New York Times, Geo und zahlreichen anderen Publikationen.

En 1966, les études de Zeng sont interrompues par le début de la Révolution culturelle. À partir de 1984, il apprend la photographie et le dessin en autodidacte. De 1970 à 1982, il travaille comme marin sur le Yang-Tsé. En 1996, il remporte le Deuxième prix dans la catégorie « Photographie d'art » du concours World Press Photo. Zeng travaille depuis pour les agences Contact Press Images et Gamma Photo à Paris. Ses travaux ont paru dans le New York Times, Geo et de nombreuses autres publications.
→ pp. 324/325, 326/327

ZHANG Dali (born 1963, Harbin, Heilongjiang province)

Zhang graduated from the Central Institute of Art and Design in Beijing in 1987. Zhang lives and works as an independent artist in Beijing. He is known as the capital's phantom graffiti artist. His signature tag, a bald head, became a familiar sight on surfaces throughout the city in the late 1990s. Most of these tags were sprayed on buildings marked for demolition, producing a dynamic contrast between the old and the new Beijing. In 1998, Zhang took his work a step further when he employed construction workers to cut out the heads along their outlines. Houses and walls marked for demolition thus featured holes in the shape of bald heads. Sadly none of these works has been preserved.

Zhang schließt 1987 sein Studium am Zentralen Institut für Kunst und Design in Peking ab. Zhang lebt und arbeitet als freischaffender Künstler in Peking. Er ist als Phantom-Graffitikünstler der Hauptstadt bekannt. Sein Tag, ein kahler Kopf, wurde Ende der 1990er Jahre zum vertrauten Anblick auf Oberflächen in der ganzen Stadt. Die Tags erschienen meist auf Gebäuden, die zum Abriss freigegeben waren, was einen dynamischen Kontrast zwischen dem alten und dem neuen Peking bewirkt. 1998 führt Zhang seine Aktionen einen Schritt weiter und lässt Bauarbeiter die Köpfe entlang der Linien ausschneiden. Die zum Abriss bestimmten Häuser und Wände weisen nun Öffnungen in Form kahler Köpfe auf, von denen leider keine erhalten sind.

Zhang obtient son diplôme de l'Institut central d'art et de design à Pékin en 1987. Il vit et travaille comme artiste indépendant à Pékin. Zhang est connu pour être le graffitiste-fantôme de la capitale. Son tag, une tête chauve, s'est retrouvé sur d'innombrables murs et surfaces de la ville à la fin des années 1990. La plupart de ces têtes étaient peintes au pistolet sur des bâtiments voués à la démolition, d'où un contraste dynamique entre le vieux et le nouveau Pékin. En 1998, Zhang a développé son travail en demandant à des ouvriers du bâtiment de découper les têtes qu'il avait dessinées. Les maisons et les murs arboraient ainsi des ouvertures en forme de têtes chauves, dont aucune malheureusement n'a été conservée.
→ pp. 334/335

ZHANG Peng (born 1981, Zhibo county, Shandong province)

Zhang graduated from the Department of Oil Painting at the Central Fine Arts Academy in Beijing in 2002. His works have been exhibited in China, Singapore, Thailand, and Germany. Zhang currently lives and works as an art photographer in Beijing.

Zhang schließt 2002 sein Studium an der Abteilung für Ölmalerei der Zentralen Kunstakademie in Peking ab. Seine Arbeiten werden in China, Singapur, Thailand und Deutschland ausgestellt. Zhang lebt und arbeitet zurzeit als Kunstfotograf in Peking.

Zhang obtient son diplôme du département de peinture à l'huile de l'Académie centrale des beaux-arts de Pékin en 2002. Ses œuvres ont été exposées en Chine, à Singapour, en Thaïlande et en Allemagne. Zhang vit et travaille comme photographe d'art à Pékin.
→ p. 101

ZHANG Yaxin (born 1933, Haishan county, Liaoning province)

Zhang graduated from the Changchun Film Institute in 1963. He then joined the State-owned Xinhua News Agency as a staff photographer. From 1969 to 1976, he photographed Jiang Qing's eight Revolutionary Operas. In 1978, he joined the staff of People's Daily, the official newspaper of the Central Committee of the CCP.

Zhang schließt 1963 sein Studium am Filminstitut in Changchun ab und beginnt, als Redaktionsfotograf für die staatliche Nachrichtenagentur Xinhua zu arbeiten. Zwischen 1969 und 1976 fotografiert er die acht Revolutionsopern von Jiang Qing. 1978 wird Zhang Mitarbeiter von People's Daily, dem offiziellen Organ des Zentralkomitees der Kommunistischen Partei Chinas.

Zhang obtient son diplôme de l'Institut du cinéma de Changchun en 1963. Il entre ensuite comme photographe permanent à l'agence de presse officielle Xinhua. Entre 1969 et 1976, il photographie les huit opéras révolutionnaires de Jiang Qing, l'épouse de Mao. En 1978, Zhang entre au People's Daily, organe de presse officiel du Comité central du Parti communiste chinois.
→ p. 217, 218/219, 220, 221, 253

ZHAO Qunying (1925–2002)

Zhao began his work as a cadre in the local Anxin county museum, organizing art and photography exhibitions. He as a self-taught photographer and artist, documenting daily life. He retired in 1995 and died in 2002.

Zhao beginnt seine Arbeit als Kader im Kreismuseum von Anxin, wo er Kunst- und Fotoausstellungen organisiert. Er ist als Fotograf und Künstler Autodidakt und dokumentiert das Alltagsleben im heimischen Kreis. Bis zu seiner Pensionierung 1995 bleibt er auf diesem Posten und verstirbt 2002.

Zhao entame sa carrière à une poste de responsabilité dans le musée local d'Anxin où il organise des expositions d'art et de photographie. Il est un artiste et un photographe autodidacte qui travaille sur des sujets de la vie quotidienne dans sa région. Il reste en poste jusqu'à sa retraite en 1995 et décède en 2002.   → pp. 222, 223

ZHENG Pingping *(born 1978, Hefei, Anhui province)*
Zheng graduated from Nanjing University. In 2000, she was hired as a staff photographer by the China News Agency. She participated in the World Press Photo Masterclass held in China in 2003. In 2004, she won First Prize in the "Art Photography" category of China's International Photography Contest. In 2005, she joined *China Youth Daily* as a staff photographer.

Zheng schließt ihr Studium an der Universität von Nanjing ab. 2000 wird sie als Redaktionsfotografin von der Nachrichtenagentur China News Agency verpflichtet. 2003 nimmt sie an der World Press Photo Masterclass in China teil. 2004 gewinnt sie den Ersten Preis in der Kategorie „Kunstfotografie" des Internationalen Fotowettbewerbs Chinas. Seit 2005 arbeitet sie als Redaktionsfotografin der *China Youth Daily.*

Zheng obtient son diplôme de l'Université de Nankin. En 2000, elle entre comme photographe à l'agence China News Agency. En 2003, elle participe à la Masterclass de World Press Photo en Chine. En 2004, elle remporte le Premier prix dans la catégorie « Photographie d'art » du Concours international de la photographie en Chine.
→ p. 381

ZHOU Chao *(born 1980, Wuhan, Hubei province)*
In 2004, Zhou graduated from the Huazhong Teachers' College in Wuhan. In 2005, he joined *Changjiang Daily News* as a staff photographer. In 2006, he received the Golden Lenses Award in the "Daily Life" category of the China News Photography Contest.

Zhou schließt 2004 sein Studium am Pädagogischen Kolleg Huazhong in Wuhan ab. 2005 geht er als Redaktionsfotograf zur Tageszeitung *Changjiang Daily News.* 2006 wird er mit der Goldenen Linse in der Kategorie „Alltagsleben" des China News Photography-Wettbewerbs ausgezeichnet.

Zhou obtient son diplôme du Collège pédagogique de Huazhong à Wuhan en 2004. En 2005, il entre comme photographe salarié au quotidien *Changjiang Daily News.* En 2006, il reçoit la Lentille d'Or dans la catégorie « Vie quotidienne » du concours China News Photography.
→ pp. 104/105

ZHOU Yue *(born 1964 Liaoyang, Liaoning province)*
Zhou studied Oil Painting in the Department of Fine Arts at Central Nationalities University in Beijing from 1981 to 1984. He has since worked as a freelance photographer.

Zhou studiert von 1981 bis 1984 Ölmalerei an der Abteilung für Kunst der Zentralen Universität der nationalen Minderheiten in Peking. Er arbeitet seitdem als freischaffender Fotograf.

Zhou étudie la peinture à l'huile au département des beaux-arts de l'Université centrale des minorités nationales à Pékin de 1981 à 1984. Il travaille depuis comme photographe indépendant.   → pp. 338, 339, 385

ZHU Yan *(born 1965, Beijing)*
Zhu graduated from the Wuhan Institute of Technology in 1986. He currently works as a freelance art photographer. He prefers working with large-format cameras. His photographs have been shown in various exhibitions, including the Pingyao Photography Festival in China.

Zhu erhält seinen Abschluss am Technischen Institut von Wuhan 1986. Er arbeitet zurzeit als freischaffender Kunstfotograf. Er bevorzugt die Arbeit mit der Großformatkamera. Seine Arbeiten waren in verschiedenen Ausstellungen zu sehen, so etwa im Rahmen des Pingyao Fotofestivals in China.

Zhu a obtenu son diplôme de l'Institut de technologie du Wuhan en 1986. Il travaille comme photographe d'art

indépendant. Il préfère travailler avec des appareils grand format. Son œuvre a fait l'objet de nombreuses expositions, dont le Festival de la photographie de Pingyao en Chine.
→ pp. 376/377

ZUO Jiazhong *(born 1929, Shanghai)*
After graduating from Shanghai Finance University in 1952, Zuo joined the Shanghai Generator Machinery Factory as a staff photographer. In 1962, he began serving as a board member of the Shanghai Photographers Association. Since his retirement in 1993, he has lived in Shanghai.

Nachdem er 1952 seinen Abschluss an der Finance University in Shanghai erreicht hat, geht Zuo als angestellter Fotograf an eine Generatoren- und Maschinenfabrik in Shanghai. Seit 1962 gehört er dem Vorstand des Shanghaier Fotografenverbandes an. Auch nach dem Eintritt in den Ruhestand im Jahre 1993 lebt er in Shanghai.

Diplômé de l'Université des Finances de Shanghai en 1952, Zuo entre à l'usine de générateurs et de machines de Shanghai comme photographe. En 1962, il devient membre du bureau de l'Association des photographes de Shanghai. Il y vit après avoir pris sa retraite en 1993.   → p. 132

Bibliography
Bibliografie
Bibliographie

An Ge, Hu Wugong, and Wang Huangsheng, *Humanism in China,* Guangdong Art Museum/Lingnan Fine Arts Press, Guangdong, 2003

Bao Kun, *Photographing China,* China Photographic Press, Beijing, 2006

Changing Asia, exh. cat., Asia Press Photo Contest, *China Daily,* Beijing, 2006

Days We Have Shared: The 50th Anniversary of the Chinese Photographers Association, issued by the Chinese Photographers Association, China Photographic Publishing House, Beijing, 2006

Feng Jianguo, *Vision of the West,* China Photographic Publishing House, Beijing, 2007

Forbidden City International Photography Exhibition, exh. cat., Forbidden City Museum, Beijing, 2004

Gu Baozi, *Red Lenses of the Republic,* Liaoning Publishing House, Shenyang, 2007

Han Lei, *Alienation,* self-published, Beijing, 1995

Ho, Oscar, *Contemporary Photography—Mainland China, Hong Kong and Taiwan,* Hong Kong Arts Centre, Hong Kong, 1994

Hou Bo and Xu Xiaobing, *Road,* Zhejiang Fine Arts Press, Hangzhou, 1995

Hu Wugong, *Image Revolution in China,* China Literary Association Press, Beijing, 2005

Hu Wugong, Hou Dengke, and Qiu Xiaoming, *A Square City,* Shaanxi People's Fine Arts Press, Xi'an, 1996

Hu Yang, *Shanghai Living,* Shanghai People's Fine Arts Press, Shanghai, 2006

Huang Yimin, *Shadow of the Era,* No. 6, Lingnan Fine Arts Press, Guangdong, 2002

Hutchings, Graham, *Modern China: A Guide to a Century of Change,* Harvard University Press, Cambridge, MA, 2001

Jiang Jian, *Storytellers from Majian: Photographs by Jiang Jian,* China Photographic Press, Beijing 2003

Jiang Shaowu, *Written in a Moment,* Liaoning Fine Arts Publishing, Shenyang, 1993

Li Mei and Yuan Yizhong, *Zheng Nong,* Chinese Photographers Series, China Workers Publishing Press, Beijing, 2004

Li Zhensheng, *Red Colour News Soldier: A Chinese Photographer's Odyssey through the Cultural Revolution,* Phaidon Press Ltd., London, 2003

Lieberthal, Kenneth, *Governing China: From Revolution through Reform,* Norton & Company, New York, 2004

Liu Heung Shing, *China after Mao: Seek Truth from Facts,* Penguin, New York, 1983

Liu Yang, *My Fellow Villagers in Northern Sichuan: An Album by Yang Hui,* China Book Press Limited, 2003

Liu Zheng, *The Chinese,* Dragon Work Chinese Photo, Beijing, 2004

Lü Nan, *The Four Seasons: Everyday Life of Tibet Peasants,* Sichuan Fine Arts Publishing House, Chengdu, 2006

Lu Yuanmin, *Shanghainese 1990–2000,* Shanghai Literature and Art Publishing House, Shanghai, 2003

Luetgens, Annelie, and Karen Smith, *Die Chinesen—Fotografie und Video aus China/The Chinese: Photography and Video from China,* Kunstmuseum Wolfsburg, Wolfsburg, 2004

Ren Xihai, *Experiencing Photography,* China Photographic Press, Beijing, 2002

Rong Rong, Karen Smith, et al., *New Photo Ten Years,* Three Shadows Art Photography Centre Press, Beijing, 2007

Saich, Anthony, *Governance and Politics of China,* Palgrave Macmillan, New York, 2004

Schmid, Andreas, and Xu Xiaoyu, *Zeitgenössische Fotokunst aus der Volksrepublik China,* Edition Braus, Heidelberg, 1997

Sontag, Susan, *On Photography,* Picador, New York, 1977

Spada, Clayton, *Hsin: A Visible Spirit—Contemporary Photography from the People's Republic of China,* Cypress College, Cypress, CA, 1999

Spence, Jonathan D., and Ping Annping, *The Chinese Century,* HarpersCollins UK, London, 1996

Wang Fuchun, *Chinese on the Train,* Heilongjiang Fine Arts Publishing House, Harbin, 2001

Wang Fuchun, *The Story of Chinese People,* self-published, Beijing, 2003

Wang Tong, *Shadow of the Era* No.12, Lingnan Fine Arts Press, Guangdong, 2003

Wang Wenlan and Ni Ping, *Life with Bicycles,* China Literary Association Press, Beijing, 2004

Wu Hung, *Rong Rong & Inri: Tui-Transformation,* Timezone 8, Beijing, 2004

Wu Hung, *Zhang Dali: A Secret History,* Warsh Gallery, Chicago, 2006

Wu Hung and Christopher Philips, *Between Past and Future: New Photography and Video from China,* Smart Museum of Art, Chicago/Steidl, Göttingen/International Center for Photography, New York, 2004

Xiao Yan, *2006 Works Annals of Beijing Kingart,* Kingart Visual Culture Communications Company, Beijing, 2006

Xiao Zhuang, *Recollection of Moments,* Jiangsu People's Press, Nanjing, 2003

Xiao Zhuang, *The Irrational Times,* Zhonghua Publishing House, China, 2004

Xie Hailong, *China Hope Project Document,* self-published together with China Hope Project, 2006

Xie Shusen, *Footprints of History,* Haiyan Publishing House, 1995

Xing Danwen, *With Chinese Eyes,* China National Economic Press, 1994

Xu Xiaoyu, *Talking is the Road,* Hunan Fine Arts Press, 1999

Yang, Rae, *China: Fifty Years Inside the People's Republic,* Aperture Foundation, New York, 1999

Zeng Nian, *Peking: Photographs by Zeng Nian,* Studio Publications, Hong Kong, 1990

Zhang Dali, *Zhang Dali Monograph,* Courtyard Gallery, Beijing, 1999

Quotation Sources
Zitatnachweis
Source des citations

9, 15, 21 Henry Kissinger, *Does America Need a Foreign Policy?*, Simon & Schuster, New York, 2001, p. 136

33, 39, 47 Mo Yan, preface to the English translation of the anthology *Shifu, You'll Do Anything for a Laugh!*, translated by Howard Goldblatt, Arcade Publishing, New York, 2003, pp. VII–VIII

61, 77, 95 Mao Zedong, speech delivered at the Moscow Meeting of the Communist and Workers' Parties, November 18, 1957, quoted after: *Selected Works of Mao Zedong*, Vol. 7, People's Publishing House, Beijing, 1999, p. 321

107, 109, 111 The slogan's origin comes from the Warring States (475 BC to 221 BC) when Confucianism and Taoism are the dominant thought among hundreds of other schools of thought.

112 Mao Zedong, "The Chinese People have Stood up!," opening address by Mao Zedong, Chairman of the Chinese Communist Party, at the First Plenary Session of the Chinese People's Political Consultative Conference, September 21, 1949, in: *Selected Works of Mao Tsetung*, Vol. IV, Foreign Languages Press, Beijing, English edition, 1961

117 Mao Zedong, "Introducing a Co-operative" (April 15, 1958), quoted after: *Quotations from Mao Zedong*, chapter 3 "Socialism and Communism," Foreign Languages Press, Beijing, first published 1966

118 Lu Xun, *The Burning Forest*, translated by Simon Leys, Paladin Books, Colorado, 1998, p. 223

121 Huang Kejian (ed.), Wang Xin, *Collected Works of Liang Sumin*, Qunyan Press, Beijing, 1993, p. 338

124 Gu Cheng, *I've Walked Eleven Thousand Miles*, translated by Cindy Carter, quoted after: http://paper-republic.org/index.php?/blogentry/some-poetry-by-gu-cheng

126 Lucian W. Pye, *China: An Introduction*, Little, Brown, New York, 1972, p. 342

135 Paul Theroux, *Riding the Iron Rooster*, Ivy Books, East Sussex, 1989, p. 2

139 Matteo Ricci, *The Diary of Matteo Ricci*, translated by Louis Gallagher, first published by Random House, 1942, as excerpted in Mark A. Kishlansky, *Sources of World History*, vol. 1, HarperCollins, New York, 1995, p. 269–273

144 Laozi, *Daode Jing*, Chinese original text available on www.guoxue.com, translated by Brendan O'Kane

148 Sima Qian, *Records of the Grand Historian*, c.91 BC, "Letter to Ren An," written in either 91 or 93 BCE, though the standard citation appears to be 91 BCE. Chinese original text available on www.guoxue.com, translated by Brendan O'Kane

150 Zhao Qizhen, press conference responding to a question comparing the degree of political reform in the two nations, ahead of Gorbachev's imminent State visit, March 27, 1989

155, 157, 159 Mao Zedong, calling on the Communist Party to take him to task over his failures in the Great Leap Forward, but also asked his own party members to look at themselves and their performance, 1959. Quoted after: Stuart Schram (ed.) *Chairman Mao Talks to the People*, Pantheon Books, New York, 1974, p. 146

160 Jonathan Spence & Annping Chin, *The Chinese Century*, HarperCollins, London, 1996, p. 183

172 Chen Kaige, *The Young Kaige*, People's Literature Publishing House, Beijing, 2001, p. 41

176 Chinese Proverb

183 Zhang Lixian, *Li Yang before Blind Mountain*, Duku Magazine, issue 0703, Beijing, June 2007

187 Ross Terrill, *Mao: A Biography*, Stanford University Press, Stanford, 1999, p. 462

189 Mao Zedong, *A Report on the Investigation of the Hunan Peasant Movement*, 1927, in: *Selected Works of Mao Tse-tung*, vol. I, 3rd ed., Foreign Languages Press, Beijing, 1975, pp. 23–29

190 Ah Cheng, *Venice Diaries*, Writers' Publishing House, 1998, p. 2

192 Mildred Cable, *China–Her Life and Her People*, University of London Press Ltd, London, 1946

195 Lin Yutang, quoted after www.quotegarden.com/honesty

198 Mao Zedong, directive in 1951, quoted after: Mao, *A Life, Philip Short*, Henry Holt & Co., New York, 2000, p. 436

201 Zhou Yang, 1966, quoted in: Fox Butterfield, *China: Alive in the Bitter Sea*, New York Times Books, New York, 1982, p. 319

202 Bao Ruowang, quoted in: Bao Ruowang and Rudolph Chelminski: *Prisoner of Mao: An Eyewitness Account of China's Forced Labor Camp System*, Coward, McCann & Geoghegan, New York, 1973, p. 58

211, 213, 215 Lucian W. Pye, *China: An Introduction*, Little, Brown, New York, 1972, p. 344

216 Ba Jin, *Random Thoughts*, China Writers' Publishing House, Beijing, 2005, p. 113

221 Mao Zedong, "Talks at the Yan'an Forum on Literature and Art," 1942, quoted after: *Selected Works of Mao Zedong*, vol. 3, Foreign Languages Press, Beijing, 1967, p. 86

223 Zhuangzi, *Inner Chapters*, "Worldly Ways," Chinese original text available on www.guoxue.com, translated by Brendan O'Kane

225 Sidney Rittenberg, *The Man Who Stayed Behind*, Duke University Press, Durham, 2001, p. 441

227 Zhou Enlai, *On the Question of Achieving a Basic Turnaround in State Finance and Economy*, Beijing, September 14, 1950

228 Zhuang Zedong, quoted after: Sina Sports: "Zhuang Zedong: I Changed Mao Zedong's Mind–Ping-Pong Diplomacy Was My Greatest Achievement," www.sina.com.cn

228 Harry Harding, *A Fragile Relationship: The United States and China Since 1972*, Brookings Institution, Washington, 1992, p. 3

236 Ross Terrill, *Madame Mao: The White-Boned Demon*, Stanford University Press, Stanford, 1999, p. 13

239 Nicholas Kristof, "Suicide of Jiang Qing, Mao's Widow, Is Reported," *The New York Times*, New York, June 5, 1991

240 Lucian W. Pye, *China: An Introduction*, Little, Brown, New York, 1972, p. 355

246 Johann Wolfgang von Goethe, 1827, quoted in: Johann Peter Eckermann: *Gespräche mit Goethe in den letzten Jahren seines Lebens*, Insel Verlag, Frankfurt am Main, 1981, p. 288

248 Tu Wei-Ming, "Cultural China: The Periphery as the Center," *Daedalus*, Spring 1991, Academic Research Library, p. 25

251 Fox Butterfield, *China: Alive in the Bitter Sea*, New York Times Books, New York, 1982, p. 393

252 Lin Yutang, *The Importance of Living*, Reynal & Hitchcock, New York, 1937, p. 401

256 Henry Kissinger, *White House Years*, Little, Brown, New York, 1979, p. 742

258 Li Zhisui, *The Private Life of Chairman Mao*, Random House, New York, 1996, p. 3

261 Xinhua News Agency, *Obituary of Mao Zedong*, October 1976

262 Jung Chang, *Wild Swans: Three Daughters of China*, Touchstone, New York, 1992, p. 633

264 Jiang Qing, frequent comment to staff, cited by Jung Chang and Jon Halliday, *Mao: The Unknown Story*, Anchor Books/Doubleday, New York, 2006, p. 731

272 Liu Binyan, "The Price China Has Paid," Nathan Gardels, *New York Review of Books*, New York, Vol. 35, no. 21 & 22, January 19, 1989

275, 277, 279 Chen Danqing, quoted in: Zha Jianying, *The 80s*, Sanlian Book Publishing, Beijing, 2006, p. 102

280 Lee Kuan Yew, quoted in: Richard Nixon, *Beyond Peace*, Random House, New York, 1994, p. 123

282 Deng Xiaoping, 1979, quoted in: Peng Cun (Ed.), *Chinese Leaders Remarks during Foreign Travel*, Hunan People's Publishing House, Hunan, 2001, p. 116

284 Jiang Qing, quoted in: Philip Short, *Mao: A Life*, Henry Holt & Co., New York, 2000, p. 521

287 Lin Yutang, *My Country and My People*, Reynal & Hitchcock, New York, 1935, p. 53

295 Associated Press, "Coke Bottled in China Plant," April 14, 1981

296 James L. Watson (Ed.), *Golden Arches East: McDonald's in East Asia*, Stanford University Press, Stanford, 1997, p. 50

298 Huang Sigao, quoted in: "Ten years after his death, Deng's impact is as profound as ever," by Dan Martin, AFP, Feb. 14, 2007

300 Lu Xun, *In Memory of Miss Liu Hezhen*, 1926, in: *Selected Works of Lu Hsun Volume II*, Foreign Languages Press, Beijing, 1980, pp. 267–272

304 Declaration of the student hunger strikers, May 13, 1989, quoted after: Pei-Kai Cheng and Michael Lestz, with Jonathan D. Spence, *The Search for Modern China: A Documentary Collection*, W. W. Norton & Company, London, 1999, pp. 495–496

307, 309, 311 Deng Xiaoping, *Southern Tour*, 1992

312 Li Changping, "The Crisis in the Countryside," quoted in: Chaohua Wang (Ed.), *One China, Many Paths*, W.W. Norton & Company, London, 2003, pp. 198–199

316 Patrick Tyler, "For China's Girls, Rural Schools Fail," *The New York Times*, New York, December 31, 1995

323 Yu Jie, *The Soul Monologues: Collected Essays*, Hainan Publishing House, Hainan, 2003, p. 34

327 Zhu Rongji, speaking at the press conference for the First Session of the Ninth National People's Congress, Beijing, March 19, 1998

332 Richard Nixon, *Beyond Peace*, Random House, New York, 1994, p. 128

339 Cui Jian, quoted in: Zha Jianying, The 80s, Sanlian Book Publishing, Beijing, 2006, p. 161

347, 349, 351 Dale Wen, "China Copes with Globalization," The International Forum on Globalization, report, 2006-2007, p. 10

356 Jiang Zemin, speech on the eightieth anniversary of the Chinese Communist Party, July 1, 2001, translated by Jon Gittings, 2006

360 Dalai Lama, quoted after www.thinkexist.com

361 Patrick French, quoted in the opinion and editorial page of *The New York Times*, March 22, 2008

363 Henry Kissinger, quoted in: Jim Burns, "Kissinger Says China Not a Communist Country," CNSNews.com, March 5, 2002

364 Bill Clinton, *My Life*, Random House, New York, 2004, pp. 1274–1275

368 Jiang Zemin, "About Relations With the U.S.," *The New York Times*, August 10, 2001

373 Interview with Jung Chang, author of *Wild Swans*, published by HarperCollins, www.readinggroups.co.uk

381 Yan Xuetong, "Mixed emotions for Chinese public," *BBC News*, October 15, 2003

399 Ai Weiwei, quoted after: *The Guardian, August 9, 2007*

400 François Carrard, quoted in: Jere Longman, "Olympics: Beijing Wins Bid for 2008 Olympic Games," *The New York Times*, July 14, 2001

424 Voltaire, *Dictionnaire philosophique*, quoted after: The works of Voltaire, vol. 4, Dingwall-Rock, New York, 1927, p. 94

Index

Acknowledgments
Dank
Remerciements

This project could not have been completed without the help of many people. I would like to thank the following individuals for their generous support and unfailing faith in the project: Karen Smith for her introductory essay and research on the captions; James Kynge for his insight into China, expressed in his introduction; Gao Lei for his tireless efforts in scanning and toning so many of these images despite the many demands on his time, and for always putting me at ease with a freshly brewed cup of coffee whenever I visited him with the precious negatives.

I also wish to thank the individual photographers Xiao Zhuang, He Yanguang, and Xu Jingxin for their patience with me in expanding my contacts with new photographers. Thanks also go to Wang Baoguo of *Chinese Photography Magazine*, Chen Xiaobo of Xinhua News Agency, Andrew Wong of Getty Images, and Alfred Jin of Reuters, who all lent their insight and generous support. Xiao Yan of the Qiya Gallery was also extremely helpful concerning the photographs of Jiang Shaowu.

Last but not least are the people who made the publication of this book possible: Jo Lusby (Penguin China), and my book agent Marysia Juszczakiewicz, for their perseverance; publisher Benedikt Taschen for his insight and his suggestion to take the book beyond the conventional coffee-table book. To editor Simone Philippi for her guidance and careful editing. To Andy Disl for his clear and beautiful design of the book. I also want to thank research assistant Brendan O'Kane and Lei Huang for their assistance with the quotes, and to Chen Yun of China's Geographical Society for preparing a new map of China. Chen Yi'er was extremely helpful in creating the all-important photographic archives. I alone bear the responsibility for omitting any important photographs or for making any errors of judgment.

I would also like to thank Arnold Drapkin of *Time* magazine and Lou Boccardi, Hal Buell, and Vin Alabiso of the Associated Press for first sending me to China, and on subsequent journalistic postings to India, South Korea, and the former USSR. Without having lived and worked in other countries and cultures, I would have reached a quite different, and perhaps rather less nuanced, perspective of China.

Ein Projekt wie dieses kann nur mithilfe vieler Menschen zustande kommen. Den Folgenden möchte ich für ihre großzügige Unterstützung und ihren unerschütterlichen Glauben an das Projekt danken: Karen Smith für ihren einführenden Text und die Recherche der Bildunterschriften; James Kynge für das in seiner Einführung spürbare Verständnis für China; Gao Lei für seine unermüdliche Arbeit beim Scannen und Bearbeiten der Bilder, trotz seiner großen zeitlichen Belastung. Wann immer ich ihn mit einem neuen Satz kostbarer Negative aufsuchte, konnte er mich mit einer Tasse frisch gebrühten Kaffees beruhigen. Außerdem möchte ich den Fotografen Xiao Zhuang, He Yanguang und Xu Jingxin für ihre Geduld mit mir danken und dafür, dass sie Kontakte zu neuen Fotografen herstellten; Wang Baoguo vom *Chinese Photography Magazine*, Chen Xiabo von der Xinhua News Agency, Andrew Wong von Getty Images und Alfred Jin von Reuters für ihre großzügige zeitliche und moralische Unterstützung. Die Galerie Qiya leistete bei den Fotografien Jiang Shaowus wertvollen Beistand.

Schließlich sind diejenigen an der Reihe, die das Erscheinen dieses Buches ermöglichten: Mein Dank gilt Jo Lusby (Penguin China) und meiner Agentin Marysia Juszczakiewicz für ihre Ausdauer und Langmut, Verleger Benedikt Taschen für seine Erfahrung im Verlagswesen und seinen Vorschlag, das Buch zu etwas ganz Besonderem jenseits eines normalen Bildbandes zu machen. Lektorin Simone Philippi für ihre Anleitung und ihr Lektorat, Andy Disl für seine klare und schöne Gestaltung des Buches. Außerdem möchte ich dem wissenschaftlichen Assistenten Brendan O'Kane sowie Lei Huang für ihre Hilfe bei der Recherche der Zitate danken. Ebenso gilt mein Dank Chen Yun von Chinas Geografischer Gesellschaft, der die Karte von China aufbereitet hat. Chen Yi'er war bei den digitalen Fotoarchiven und den dort laufenden Bestellungen hilfreich. Selbstverständlich trage ich die Verantwortung für eventuell übersehene wichtige Fotografien und falsche Beurteilungen.

Ich möchte auch Arnold Drapkin von der Zeitschrift *Time* danken, ebenso Lou Boccardi, Hal Buell und Vin Alabiso von Associated Press, dafür dass Sie mich damals zuerst nach China und danach zu weiteren journalistischen Stationen in Indien, Südkorea und in der früheren UdSSR geschickt haben. Ohne das Leben und Arbeiten in Ländern und Kulturen außerhalb von China hätte ich heute einen anderen, wahrscheinlich weniger nuancierten Blick auf China.

Un tel ouvrage n'aurait pu être mené à bien sans de multiples collaborations. Je voudrais remercier tous ceux qui ont apporté leur généreux soutien et leur confiance sans faille à ce projet : Karen Smith pour son article d'introduction et ses recherches sur les légendes, James Kynge pour la vision de la Chine qu'il exprime dans son introduction, Gao Lei pour ses efforts intensifs dans la pré-production des images, malgré les multiples pressions exercées sur son agenda. Il a toujours su me mettre à l'aise, même lorsque je venais lui apporter un nouvelle pile de précieux négatifs.

Je souhaite également remercier les photographes Xiao Zhuang, He Yanguang et Xu Jingxin pour leur patience à mon égard et pour m'avoir procuré des contacts avec de nouveaux photographes ainsi que les éditeurs-photo chinois Wang Baoguo de *Chinese Photography Magazine*, Chen Xiaobo de Xinhua News Agency, Andrew Wong de Getty Images et Alfred Jin de Reuters pour m'avoir accordé leur temps avec générosité et leur soutien moral. La galerie Qiya a été d'une aide particulièrement utile dans la recherche des photographies de Jiang Shaowu.

Enfin, je dois saluer tous ceux et celles qui ont permis la publication de cet ouvrage : Jo Lusby (Penguin China) et mon agente chargée de mes livres, Marysia Juszczakiewicz, pour leur persévérance ; l'éditeur Benedikt Taschen pour sa vision et sa suggestion de faire de cet ouvrage bien davantge qu'un « beau livre » ; l'éditrice Simone Philippi pour son travail approfondi et ses conseils et Andy Disl pour la clarté et la beauté de sa maquette. Je souhaite remercier l'assistant de recherches Brendan O'Kane et Lei Huang pour leur assistance sur les citations ainsi que Chen Yun de la Société géographique de Chine, qui a mis au point la carte de la Chine. Chen Yi'er a été d'une aide précieuse dans le traitement numérique des photographies. Naturellement, j'assume la responsabilité de toute omission de travaux et d'erreurs de jugement éventuelles.

Je tiens aussi à remercier Arnold Drapkin du magazine *Time* et Lou Boccardi, Hal Buell et Vin Alabiso d'Associated Press pour m'avoir envoyé rejoindre la Chine et mes autres postes de correspondant en Inde, en Corée du Sud et dans l'ancienne URSS. Si je n'avais vécu et travaillé dans d'autres pays et au sein de cultures extérieures à celle de la Chine, ma perspective aurait sans doute été assez différente et peut-être moins nuancée.

Imprint
Impressum
Mention d'impression

To stay informed about upcoming TASCHEN titles,
please request our magazine at www.taschen.com/
magazine or write to TASCHEN, Hohenzollernring 53,
D-50672 Cologne, Germany, contact@taschen.com,
Fax +49-221-254919. We will be happy to send you
a free copy of our magazine which is filled with
information about all of our books.

© 2008 TASCHEN GmbH
Hohenzollernring 53, D-50672 Köln
www.taschen.com

Design: Sense/Net, Andy Disl and Birgit Reber, Cologne
Editorial coordination: Dr. Simone Philippi, Cologne
Chronology and scientific advice: Dr. Werner Pfennig, Berlin
Production coordination: Stefan Klatte, Cologne
German translation: Christiane Court, Frankfurt am Main
French translation: Jacques Bosser, Paris; Wolf Fruhtrunk, Asnières-sur-Seine (Chronology)
English translation: Hilary Heltay, Hereford (Chronology)

Printed in Spain
ISBN 978-3-8365-0569-7

p. 424

Liu Heung Shing, 1981

*In Chengdu, an unseen figure walks along
a street carrying a newly painted portrait of
the late Chairman Mao.*

*Ein unsichtbarer Zeitgenosse schleppt in
Chengdu ein frisch gemaltes Portrait des
verstorbenen Vorsitzenden Mao durch die
Straßen.*

*À Chengdu, une personne passe dans la rue,
cachée derrière le portrait fraîchement réalisé
du président Mao décédé.*

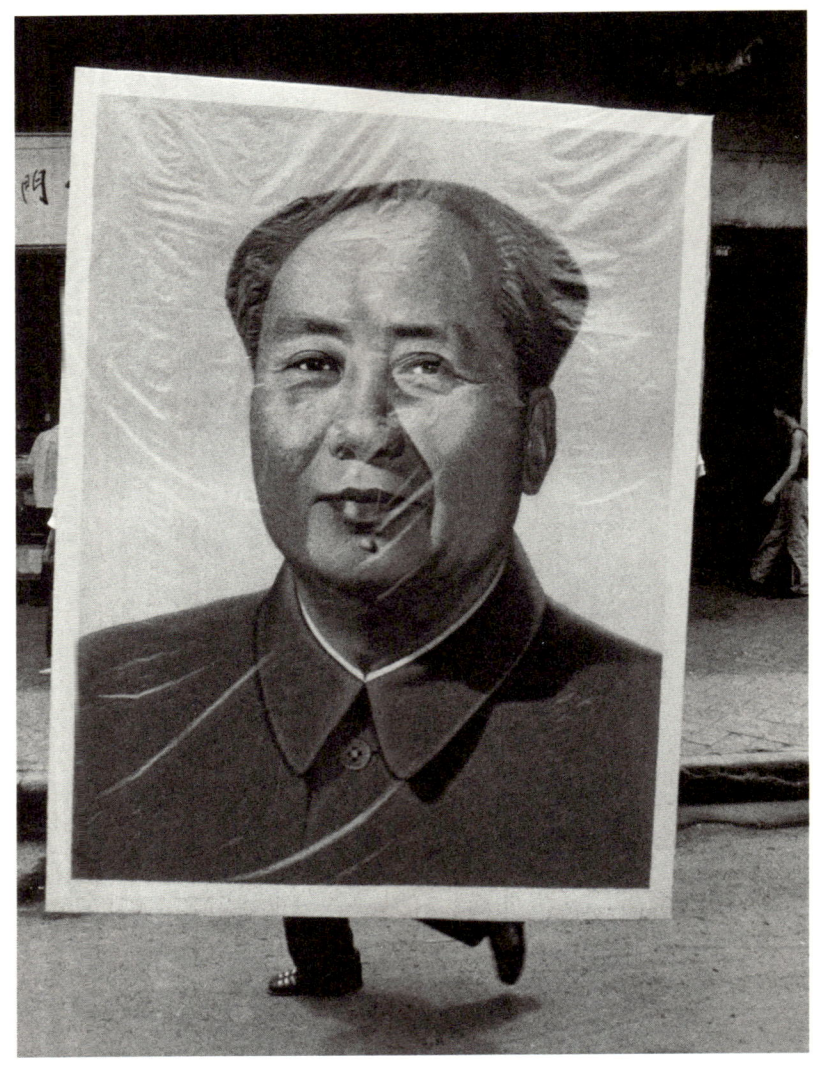

"The Chinese, for four thousand years, when we were unable even to read, knew everything essentially useful of which we boast at the present day."

„Die Chinesen kennen seit viertausend Jahren, als wir noch nicht einmal lesen konnten, im Prinzip alles Nützliche, dessen wir uns heutzutage rühmen."

« …mais tout cela n'empêche pas que les Chinois, il y a quatre mille ans, lorsque nous ne savions pas lire, ne sussent toutes les choses essentiellement utiles dont nous nous vantons aujourd'hui. »

VOLTAIRE (1694–1778), French writer and philosopher